The Encyclopedia of Religion

The Encyclopedia of Religion

Mircea Eliade

EDITOR IN CHIEF

Volume 11

MACMILLAN PUBLISHING COMPANY
New York

Collier Macmillan Publishers
London

MACMILLAN PUBLISHING COMPANY
866 Third Avenue, New York, NY 10022

Collier Macmillan Canada, Inc.

Library of Congress Catalog Card Number: 86-5432

PRINTED IN THE UNITED STATES OF AMERICA

printing number
1 2 3 4 5 6 7 8 9 10

Library of Congress Cataloging-in-Publication Data

The Encyclopedia of religion.

Includes bibliographies and index.
1. Religion—Dictionaries. I. Eliade, Mircea, 1907–1986. II. Adams, Charles J.
BL31.#46 1986 200'.3'21 86-5432
ISBN 0-02-909480-1 (set)
ISBN 0-02-909820-3 (v. 11)

Acknowledgments of sources, copyrights, and permissions to use previously published materials are gratefully made in a special listing in volume 16.

Abbreviations and Symbols Used in This Work

abbr. abbreviated; abbreviation
abr. abridged; abridgment
AD *anno Domini,* in the year of the (our) Lord
Afrik. Afrikaans
AH *anno Hegirae,* in the year of the Hijrah
Akk. Akkadian
Ala. Alabama
Alb. Albanian
Am. *Amos*
AM *ante meridiem,* before noon
amend. amended; amendment
annot. annotated; annotation
Ap. *Apocalypse*
Apn. *Apocryphon*
app. appendix
Arab. Arabic
ʿArakh. *ʿArakhin*
Aram. Aramaic
Ariz. Arizona
Ark. Arkansas
Arm. Armenian
art. article (pl., arts.)
AS Anglo-Saxon
Asm. Mos. *Assumption of Moses*
Assyr. Assyrian
A.S.S.R. Autonomous Soviet Socialist Republic
Av. Avestan
ʿA.Z. *ʿAvodah zarah*
b. born
Bab. Babylonian
Ban. Bantu
1 Bar. *1 Baruch*
2 Bar. *2 Baruch*
3 Bar. *3 Baruch*
4 Bar. *4 Baruch*
B.B. *Bava' batra'*
BBC British Broadcasting Corporation
BC before Christ
BCE before the common era
B.D. Bachelor of Divinity
Beits. *Beitsah*
Bekh. *Bekhorot*
Beng. Bengali
Ber. *Berakhot*
Berb. Berber
Bik. *Bikkurim*
bk. book (pl., bks.)
B.M. *Bava' metsiʿa'*
BP before the present
B.Q. *Bava' qamma'*
Brāh. *Brāhmaṇa*
Bret. Breton
B.T. Babylonian Talmud
Bulg. Bulgarian
Burm. Burmese
c. *circa,* about, approximately
Calif. California
Can. Canaanite
Catal. Catalan
CE of the common era
Celt. Celtic
cf. *confer,* compare
Chald. Chaldean
chap. chapter (pl., chaps.)
Chin. Chinese
C.H.M. Community of the Holy Myrrhbearers
1 Chr. *1 Chronicles*
2 Chr. *2 Chronicles*
Ch. Slav. Church Slavic
cm centimeters
col. column (pl., cols.)
Col. *Colossians*
Colo. Colorado
comp. compiler (pl., comps.)
Conn. Connecticut
cont. continued
Copt. Coptic
1 Cor. *1 Corinthians*
2 Cor. *2 Corinthians*
corr. corrected
C.S.P. Congregatio Sancti Pauli, Congregation of Saint Paul (Paulists)
d. died
D Deuteronomic (source of the Pentateuch)
Dan. Danish
D.B. Divinitatis Baccalaureus, Bachelor of Divinity
D.C. District of Columbia
D.D. Divinitatis Doctor, Doctor of Divinity
Del. Delaware
Dem. *Demaʾi*
dim. diminutive
diss. dissertation
Dn. *Daniel*
D.Phil. Doctor of Philosophy
Dt. *Deuteronomy*
Du. Dutch
E Elohist (source of the Pentateuch)
Eccl. *Ecclesiastes*
ed. editor (pl., eds.); edition; edited by
ʿEduy. *ʿEduyyot*
e.g. *exempli gratia,* for example
Egyp. Egyptian
1 En. *1 Enoch*
2 En. *2 Enoch*
3 En. *3 Enoch*
Eng. English
enl. enlarged
Eph. *Ephesians*
ʿEruv. *ʿEruvin*
1 Esd. *1 Esdras*
2 Esd. *2 Esdras*
3 Esd. *3 Esdras*
4 Esd. *4 Esdras*
esp. especially
Est. Estonian
Est. *Esther*
et al. *et alii,* and others
etc. *et cetera,* and so forth
Eth. Ethiopic
EV English version
Ex. *Exodus*
exp. expanded
Ez. *Ezekiel*
Ezr. *Ezra*
2 Ezr. *2 Ezra*
4 Ezr. *4 Ezra*
f. feminine; and following (pl., ff.)
fasc. fascicle (pl., fascs.)
fig. figure (pl., figs.)
Finn. Finnish
fl. *floruit,* flourished
Fla. Florida
Fr. French
frag. fragment
ft. feet
Ga. Georgia
Gal. *Galatians*
Gaul. Gaulish
Ger. German
Giṭ. *Giṭṭin*
Gn. *Genesis*
Gr. Greek
Ḥag. *Ḥagigah*
Ḥal. *Ḥallah*
Hau. Hausa
Hb. *Habakkuk*
Heb. Hebrew
Heb. *Hebrews*
Hg. *Haggai*
Hitt. Hittite
Hor. *Horayot*
Hos. *Hosea*
Ḥul. *Ḥullin*
Hung. Hungarian
ibid. *ibidem,* in the same place (as the one immediately preceding)
Icel. Icelandic
i.e. *id est,* that is
IE Indo-European
Ill. Illinois
Ind. Indiana
intro. introduction
Ir. Gael. Irish Gaelic
Iran. Iranian
Is. *Isaiah*
Ital. Italian
J Yahvist (source of the Pentateuch)
Jas. *James*
Jav. Javanese
Jb. *Job*
Jdt. *Judith*
Jer. *Jeremiah*
Jgs. *Judges*
Jl. *Joel*
Jn. *John*
1 Jn. *1 John*
2 Jn. *2 John*
3 Jn. *3 John*
Jon. *Jonah*
Jos. *Joshua*
Jpn. Japanese
JPS Jewish Publication Society translation (1985) of the Hebrew Bible
J.T. Jerusalem Talmud
Jub. *Jubilees*
Kans. Kansas
Kel. *Kelim*

Ker. *Keritot*
Ket. *Ketubbot*
1 Kgs. *1 Kings*
2 Kgs. *2 Kings*
Khois. Khoisan
Kil. *Kil'ayim*
km kilometers
Kor. Korean
Ky. Kentucky
l. line (pl., ll.)
La. Louisiana
Lam. *Lamentations*
Lat. Latin
Latv. Latvian
L. en Th. Licencié en Théologie, Licentiate in Theology
L. ès L. Licencié ès Lettres, Licentiate in Literature
Let. Jer. *Letter of Jeremiah*
lit. literally
Lith. Lithuanian
Lk. *Luke*
LL Late Latin
LL.D. Legum Doctor, Doctor of Laws
Lv. *Leviticus*
m meters
m. masculine
M.A. Master of Arts
Ma'as. *Ma'aserot*
Ma'as. Sh. *Ma'aser sheni*
Mak. *Makkot*
Makh. *Makhshirin*
Mal. *Malachi*
Mar. Marathi
Mass. Massachusetts
1 Mc. *1 Maccabees*
2 Mc. *2 Maccabees*
3 Mc. *3 Maccabees*
4 Mc. *4 Maccabees*
Md. Maryland
M.D. Medicinae Doctor, Doctor of Medicine
ME Middle English
Meg. *Megillah*
Me'il. *Me'ilah*
Men. *Menaḥot*
MHG Middle High German
mi. miles
Mi. *Micah*
Mich. Michigan
Mid. *Middot*
Minn. Minnesota
Miq. *Miqva'ot*
MIran. Middle Iranian
Miss. Mississippi
Mk. *Mark*
Mo. Missouri
Mo'ed Q. *Mo'ed qaṭan*
Mont. Montana
MPers. Middle Persian
MS. *manuscriptum*, manuscript (pl., MSS)
Mt. *Matthew*
MT Masoretic text
n. note
Na. *Nahum*
Nah. Nahuatl
Naz. *Nazir*
N.B. *nota bene*, take careful note
N.C. North Carolina
n.d. no date
N.Dak. North Dakota
NEB New English Bible
Nebr. Nebraska
Ned. *Nedarim*
Neg. *Nega'im*
Neh. *Nehemiah*
Nev. Nevada
N.H. New Hampshire
Nid. *Niddah*
N.J. New Jersey
Nm. *Numbers*
N.Mex. New Mexico
no. number (pl., nos.)
Nor. Norwegian
n.p. no place
n.s. new series
N.Y. New York
Ob. *Obadiah*
O.Cist. Ordo Cisterciencium, Order of Cîteaux (Cistercians)
OCS Old Church Slavonic
OE Old English
O.F.M. Ordo Fratrum Minorum, Order of Friars Minor (Franciscans)
OFr. Old French
Ohal. *Ohalot*
OHG Old High German
OIr. Old Irish
OIran. Old Iranian
Okla. Oklahoma
ON Old Norse
O.P. Ordo Praedicatorum, Order of Preachers (Dominicans)
OPers. Old Persian
op. cit. *opere citato*, in the work cited
OPrus. Old Prussian
Oreg. Oregon
'Orl. *'Orlah*
O.S.B. Ordo Sancti Benedicti, Order of Saint Benedict (Benedictines)
p. page (pl., pp.)
P Priestly (source of the Pentateuch)
Pa. Pennsylvania
Pahl. Pahlavi
Par. *Parah*
para. paragraph (pl., paras.)
Pers. Persian
Pes. *Pesaḥim*
Ph.D. Philosophiae Doctor, Doctor of Philosophy
Phil. *Philippians*
Phlm. *Philemon*
Phoen. Phoenician
pl. plural; plate (pl., pls.)
PM *post meridiem*, after noon
Pol. Polish
pop. population
Port. Portuguese
Prv. *Proverbs*
Ps. *Psalms*
Ps. 151 *Psalm 151*
Ps. Sol. *Psalms of Solomon*
pt. part (pl., pts.)
1 Pt. *1 Peter*
2 Pt. *2 Peter*
Pth. Parthian
Q hypothetical source of the synoptic Gospels
Qid. *Qiddushin*
Qin. *Qinnim*
r. reigned; ruled
Rab. *Rabbah*
rev. revised
R. ha-Sh. *Ro'sh ha-shanah*
R.I. Rhode Island
Rom. Romanian
Rom. *Romans*
R.S.C.J. Societas Sacratissimi Cordis Jesu, Religious of the Sacred Heart
RSV Revised Standard Version of the Bible
Ru. *Ruth*
Rus. Russian
Rv. *Revelation*
Rv. Ezr. *Revelation of Ezra*
San. *Sanhedrin*
S.C. South Carolina
Scot. Gael. Scottish Gaelic
S.Dak. South Dakota
sec. section (pl., secs.)
Sem. Semitic
ser. series
sg. singular
Sg. *Song of Songs*
Sg. of 3 *Prayer of Azariah and the Song of the Three Young Men*
Shab. *Shabbat*
Shav. *Shavu'ot*
Sheq. *Sheqalim*
Sib. Or. *Sibylline Oracles*
Sind. Sindhi
Sinh. Sinhala
Sir. *Ben Sira*
S.J. Societas Jesu, Society of Jesus (Jesuits)
Skt. Sanskrit
1 Sm. *1 Samuel*
2 Sm. *2 Samuel*
Sogd. Sogdian
Soṭ *Soṭah*
sp. species (pl., spp.)
Span. Spanish
sq. square
S.S.R. Soviet Socialist Republic
st. stanza (pl., ss.)
S.T.M. Sacrae Theologiae Magister, Master of Sacred Theology
Suk. *Sukkah*
Sum. Sumerian
supp. supplement; supplementary
Sus. *Susanna*
s.v. *sub verbo*, under the word (pl., s.v.v.)
Swed. Swedish
Syr. Syriac
Syr. Men. *Syriac Menander*
Ta'an. *Ta'anit*
Tam. Tamil
Tam. *Tamid*
Tb. *Tobit*
T.D. *Taishō shinshū daizōkyō*, edited by Takakusu Junjirō et al. (Tokyo, 1922–1934)
Tem. *Temurah*
Tenn. Tennessee
Ter. *Terumot*
Ṭev. Y. *Ṭevul yom*
Tex. Texas
Th.D. Theologicae Doctor, Doctor of Theology
1 Thes. *1 Thessalonians*
2 Thes. *2 Thessalonians*
Thrac. Thracian
Ti. *Titus*
Tib. Tibetan
1 Tm. *1 Timothy*
2 Tm. *2 Timothy*
T. of 12 *Testaments of the Twelve Patriarchs*
Ṭoh. *Ṭohorot*
Tong. Tongan
trans. translator, translators; translated by; translation
Turk. Turkish
Ukr. Ukrainian
Upan. *Upaniṣad*
U.S. United States
U.S.S.R. Union of Soviet Socialist Republics
Uqts. *Uqtsin*
v. verse (pl., vv.)
Va. Virginia
var. variant; variation
Viet. Vietnamese
viz. *videlicet*, namely
vol. volume (pl., vols.)
Vt. Vermont
Wash. Washington
Wel. Welsh
Wis. Wisconsin
Wis. *Wisdom of Solomon*
W.Va. West Virginia
Wyo. Wyoming
Yad. *Yadayim*
Yev. *Yevamot*
Yi. Yiddish
Yor. Yoruba
Zav. *Zavim*
Zec. *Zechariah*
Zep. *Zephaniah*
Zev. *Zevaḥim*

* hypothetical
? uncertain; possibly; perhaps
° degrees
+ plus
− minus
= equals; is equivalent to
× by; multiplied by
→ yields

N

(CONTINUED)

NUBŪWAH. Communicating with supernatural beings or realms is a major element in religious life. It is usually accomplished by persons acting as direct or indirect intermediaries, be they human, divine, or part human and part divine. Shamans, mystics, and oracles are examples of direct intermediaries. Unlike them, indirect intermediaries do not communicate with the divine directly but rather rely on interpreting a "text," natural or supernatural, so as to uncover the sacred message presumed to be embedded within. Someone who "reads" entrails, casts horoscopes, or performs charismatic exegesis is an indirect intermediary. An individual can be both a direct and indirect intermediary or specialize, and he or she can intermediate regularly or only occasionally.

A very important sort of direct intermediary is referred to in English by such terms as *prophet* and *apostle,* in Greek by *prophētēs* and *promantis,* in Hebrew by *navi',* in Arabic by *nabī* or *rasūl,* in Persian and Turkish by *payghambar* or *peygamber,* and so forth. Since each of these labels has connotations associated with the religious life of a particular culture, generic terms are needed for comparative discussions. All of these terms refer to some kind of "commissioned communicator": a human being who feels called upon to speak on behalf of a force perceived to be beyond his or her control. Within monotheistic communities, commissioned communication took on the form of messengership, since it came to involve delivery to other human beings of intelligible messages that evaluated or challenged the status quo.

This minimal definition would seem to distinguish messengers from such commissioned communicators as shamans, whose primary function is not to deliver intelligible messages. It would also seem to exclude another phenomenon sometimes called prophecy, one in which the "messages" take the unintelligible form of speaking in tongues. However, there have been prophets, such as Isaiah Shembe, who delivered intelligible and unintelligible messages alternately, while the "mystery letters" that begin certain chapters in the Qur'ān have remained unintelligible. Perhaps one should say that messengers must deliver intelligible messages as a primary task but may also deliver unintelligible ones.

Within these parameters, significant variability obtains. Some commissioned communicators "publish" their messages in response to the request of other human beings; others, only in response to an inner urging interpreted as having a supernatural source. Biblical prophets did both; the human channels for the Greek oracles, only the former; Muḥammad, only the latter. Although the sense of being called usually keeps such figures from social and political passivity, the degree of their activism and leadership varies greatly. Sometimes their messages are random and disorganized, or of only localized significance. At other times they are canonized into a book with decisive and universal moral applicability.

Beyond functional similarities, there are historical reasons to argue that messengers can be grouped for purposes of cross-cultural study; in fact, few roles provide so good a case for comparative study, and few have such strong historical commonalities. Monotheistic messengership grew out of an ancient tradition of direct intermediation prevalent throughout the Mediterranean and the Near East. After it emerged, first in Judaism, then in Christianity, Zoroastrianism, and Islam, the role was conveyed to various societies not only through scriptures but also through a shared folklore. These common symbols, figures, and stories have continued to supply, to the present day, standards against which claimants to the role can be evaluated. Although near-contemporary messenger figures such as Tenskwatawa, Joseph Smith, Bahā' Allāh, and Isaiah Shembe may have been culturally disparate in many respects, this shared inheritance ties them together. However, despite the extensiveness and cohesiveness of messengership as a religious phenomenon, scholarly generalizations have accounted for only a fraction of the relevant data and have tended to use Old Testament prophethood as their norm. Ironically, they have paid little attention to Islam, a religious tradition in which messengers and messengership are central.

The Qur'anic Messenger Figure. The Qur'ān, the first "text" of Islam, uses two Arabic nouns for messenger figures: *nabī* and *rasūl.* The latter frequently appears in the phrase *rasūl Allāh* ("messenger of God"), which became the preferred term for Muḥammad and a key element in the *shahādah,* or profession of faith. A common Persian equivalent, *payghambar,* literally means "messenger," as does *rasūl.* The noun for the role or office of *nabī* is *nubūwah; risālah* is sometimes used for the mission or message of a *rasūl.*

Much has been made of the Qur'ān's use of two terms for such figures and naturally Muslim and non-Muslim scholars alike have made efforts to clarify the presumed distinctions between the two. Some have concluded that the words are interchangeable; others have identified *nabī* as a word for figures who are "called," or given revelation, and reserved *rasūl* for those sent on a mission to a particular community, or *nabī* with ordinary messengers and *rasūl* with the few greatest (for example, Adam, Noah, Abraham, Moses, David, Jesus, and Muḥammad). A less common interpretation links *nabī* with messengers from the descendants of Abraham, who were specially gifted with *nubūwah,* while associating *rasūl* with a messenger sent to bring his own community to God.

Even if the full significance of this etymological problem remains uncertain, its existence calls attention to the fact that in the Qur'ān *nubūwah* is a rich, complex, and central topic. *Nubūwah* has been God's primary means of communicating with humankind, involving a long and continuous chain of revelation-bearers who were related both functionally and genetically. They were sent to help God communicate to humankind his desire for their surrender (*islām*) to his will; therefore, they were all given the same message, except that certain ones were sent to achieve very specific leadership missions within their own communities. The chain stretched from the first human, Adam, to the deliverer of the Qur'ān, Muḥammad, and included figures considered prophets by Jews and Christians (Abraham, Jacob, Moses), others familiar to them but not classed by them as prophets (Jesus, David, Joseph), and yet others entirely unfamiliar (Hūd, Ṣāliḥ, Shu'ayb). Moses and Abraham would appear to be the most important prophetic models in the Qur'ān, although Joseph is the subject of the longest Qur'anic narrative (surah 12).

Furthermore, these divine messengers were drawn largely from the same "family," whose patriarch was Abraham (Ibrāhīm) and whose lineages, for the Israelites and the Arabs respectively, stemmed from Isaac (Isḥāq) and Ishmael (Ismā'īl). In "doing" *islām,* in surrendering to God's utter authority and in putting themselves in the only right relationship with him, the Arabs of Muḥammad's time, whose forefathers included divine messengers, were returning to their "original" religion, indeed, the original religion of humankind. Mecca was not only spiritually close to *nubūwah;* it was physically close as well: it was the site of Abraham's house of God.

Therefore, the Qur'anic Muḥammad, as *rasūl Allāh,* messenger of God, is naturally a composite of the messengers who preceded him—a radical monotheist like Abraham, a lawgiver and warrior like Moses, a friend of God like Jesus. He is the recipient of a perfect form of the revealed truth God has sent through every messenger since the beginning of the world. He is said to be like his predecessors in other ways as well:

- He is chosen by God from among his own people, neither seeking to be chosen nor showing enthusiasm for the task; he is guided by God, whose guidance is parceled out as needed; he is distinct from the angels, who are neither human nor divine. These qualities call attention to his mortality, just as his humanity emphasizes God's power; in the terminology of the modern religionist, he is an instrumental messenger.
- He polarizes his audience: he is believed by some and opposed by many, including Satan, partly because he rejects polytheistic ancestral custom in favor of *tawḥīd* (declaring God's oneness). Those who oppose him call him a liar and may even harm or expel him; their belying is semantically associated with their *kufr* (unfaithful ingratitude to God).
- He has two major functions related to the day of judgment: to bring good tidings of the possibility of salvation and to warn of punishment for wrongdoers. These he fulfills by bringing a book that comprises God's messages to humankind.
- He possesses a constellation of exemplary personal characteristics: patience, unswerving devotion, compassion, trust in God, and a pure faith that is the absolute opposite of *shirk* (letting anything share in God's power).
- Obeying him is not separate from the need to obey God and believe in God's book, the angels, and the last day; the obedience of those who accept him as God's messenger enables him to establish an *ummah,* a community based on God's revelation, and to transmit to it the rules necessary for its survival and salvation.

The special significance of *nabī/rasūl* is further underscored by the Qur'ān's insistence on distinguishing this from other roles that presumed to intermediation in seventh-century Arabia, specifically *kāhin* (diviner, shaman, seer) and *shā'ir* (poet). Similarly, the biblical *nevi'im* had to distinguish themselves from figures who claimed direct intermediation but not the same historical and moral significance.

Notably absent from the Qur'ān's picture of *nubūwah* is the degree of futurism—prophecy as prediction—that dominates many Christian understandings of Old Testament prophetic action. Although many of Muḥammad's messages are future-oriented in an apocalyptic sense, prediction of specific historical events is virtually absent, as are miraculous acts; also missing is any implication that either is necessary to validate a messenger. As for the arrival of what he foretells—the day of judgment—it is not debatable; it is knowable from clear signs.

The Sealing of Prophecy. Shortly after Muḥammad's death, the core of his supporters articulated and enforced a particular understanding of a Qur'anic reference to Muḥammad as *khatm al-anbiyā'*, or "seal of the *nabī*s": Muḥammad was the culmination and finale of that long process of direct revelation that God had begun with Adam. The decision to view Muḥammad in this way was necessitated by competing claims to revelation of other Arab tribal leaders. Although it invalidated them and made Muḥammad unique, it did not demote previous messengers. However, accepting the finality of Muḥammad's messengership did become a *sine qua non* of being a Muslim. Although the decision did not entirely prevent later Muslims from using the labels *nabī* and *rasūl* or even claiming to bring a new Qur'ān, it did restrict such activity severely, privileging implicit over explicit claims to being "like" Muḥammad.

It is difficult to overestimate the historical impact of the concept of *nubūwah* as exemplified in Muḥammad's life and clarified after his death. It expanded previous Near Eastern notions of prophetic action to their limits, directed the course of leadership patterns within Islamic societies, and affected subsequent non-Muslim conceptualizations.

Literary developments. Muslims enlarged previous notions of *nubūwah* simply by putting all messengers into a class that ended with Muḥammad. Just as Muḥammad had to be shown to be like them, they had to be shown to be like Muḥammad. This "leveling" is particularly evident in three literary genres, *ḥadīth, sīrah,* and *qiṣaṣ al-anbiyā'*.

The *ḥadīth* comprise an enormous corpus of reports that convey Muḥammad's *sunnah*—his exemplary words, deeds, and silent approval. Through them, the *nabī* became a personal exemplar in an unprecedented manner; the wide circulation of *ḥadīth* about other *nabī*s, including Moses, Joseph, Abraham, and Jesus, made them exemplary as well. Later Muslim scholars explored the possibility of extrascriptural revelation to prophets, both in interpretations of the distinction between *nabī* and *rasūl* and in a subclass of *ḥadīth* known as *ḥadīth qudsī,* which quote direct speech from God to Muḥammad that does not appear in Qur'ān.

Because the chain of Muslim messengers grew so large (numbering 124,000 by some counts) and included figures not considered prophets by non-Muslims, the concept of messengership expanded even further. For example, Muslims viewed Jesus as a major *rasūl,* a completely human emissary whom God saved from dying by substituting another on the cross. Thus they preserved, in reworked form, an early Judeo-Christian view of Jesus that had fallen into disuse with the rise of gentile Christianity.

Using the *ḥadīth* as an important source, a genre known as *sīrah* presented the life of Muḥammad specifically as the life of a messenger of God. Most early *sīrah*s were written in the intercommunal environment of the empire's central cities; some, such as the *Sīrat Rasūl Allāh* of Ibn Isḥāq (d. 767?), were produced by converts to Islam. Consequently they sought to establish Muḥammad's legitimacy with regard to previous messengers and, by extension, the right of Muslims to rule over Jewish and Christian subjects. Naturally, they viewed Muḥammad's particular blend of social, military, and political leadership, as well as his spiritual guidance, lawgiving, and scripture-bringing, as a standard against which others could be measured. For the first time in the history of Near Eastern concepts of prophetic leadership, its latent social and political activism was institutionalized and idealized, for Muḥammad not only brought a book but through it constructed a lasting, divinely guided community. Gradually, a Muslim vision of world history crystalized: Muḥammad's creation of a divinely guided community was the culmination of world history and the permanently present past ideal for leading the good Muslim life. He was preeminent among messengers, although a small number of others were major messengers also. Jews and Christians had been sent "Muslim" messengers but had not remained strictly true to their messages. As a consequence, they could either become Muslim "again" or remain protected minorities (*dhimmī*s).

The *sīrah* of Ibn Isḥāq also established a paradigm for the career of the messenger of God that many Muslim leaders were to emulate, in part or in sum, even when they were not claiming *nubūwah* for themselves. It described a birth and infancy filled with propitious occurrences and omens; a youth of involvement with conventional religious practices accompanied by spiritual searching and confusion; a sudden call at age forty, resisted three times; acceptance by a few and rejection by most; emigration *(hijrah);* consolidation of power in an adopted home and a triumphal return to the original home. Gradually legists and theologians elaborated other *dalā'il al-nubūwah* ("signs of prophethood"), such as a mark between the shoulders, innocence of youth, and paranormal experiences. They went on to develop, by the thirteenth century, the doctrine of *'iṣmah* (protectedness from sin and error), which was applied broadly to Muḥammad and selectively to previous messengers. Thereafter, insulting Muḥammad became a serious misdeed, and Mecca and Medina were closed to non-Muslims. Eventually the scholars added an eschatological role: Muḥammad would lead his community into Paradise, there to intercede for those whom God had excluded.

The comparability of Muḥammad with all previous messengers, and vice versa, came to be demonstrated in another literary form, *qiṣaṣ al-anbiyā'* ("tales of the *nabīs*"). By the time al-Kisā'ī (fl. 1200) composed one of its most famous works, the genre had become comprehensive, dramatic, and influential. Because its authors believed in prophetic continuity, they could rework non-Muslim tales about the prophets into an Islamic vision of the religious history of the world. When the predictive, miracle-working facets of Jewish and Christian prophecy resurfaced here, they did so in "islamized" fashion. The preempting of pre-Islamic messengers and the exalting of Muḥammad assumed architectural form in the Dome of the Rock in Jerusalem, a late seventh-century monument that came to be associated with the Prophet's night journey (Mi'rāj) to the seventh heaven.

Sufism and philosophy. Another kind of reinterpretation, consolidation, and expansion of the concept of *nubūwah* occurred when Ṣūfī thinkers gave these stories an esoteric, interiorized meaning. Messengers became prototypes for individual spiritual development, illustrating the ability of human beings to receive divine inspiration. In well-known early modern examples of the genre, the *Ta'wīl al-aḥādīth* and the *Fuṣūṣ* of the Indian Ṣūfī theologian Shāh Walī Allāh (1703–1762), numerous messengers exhibit one or more aspects of the Ṣūfī search for truth and of humanity's complete dependence on God. They are quintessential servants and friends of God who serve as instruments in God's plan as they strive for human perfection in their devotion, self-control, and discipline. For example, Adam is a microcosm of all the realities of the universe, physical and spiritual. His fall was designed by God to ensure his becoming an earthly delegate: the prohibitions against eating from the tree were revealed in a dream; the violation of the prohibitions were brought about by satanic action. Noah is the first messenger to lead a community forcibly to God's will, bringing law in order to subordinate animal to spiritual impulses. Abraham exemplifies utter devotion to God and the unstinting pursuit of the true religion. Joseph triumphs over affliction by his constancy. For many Ṣūfīs, Muḥammad is the *insān al-kāmil,* the perfect or universal human being who epitomizes union with God.

Muslim philosophers found it more difficult to appreciate the messenger's mission. At the least, they distinguished prophetic truth, which is communicated in easily comprehensible everyday language and expressed in stories and analogies that appeal to the common people in particular communities, from philosophical truth, which is universal, esoteric, abstract, and rational. Some, such as al-Kindī (d. after 870), saw prophetic and philosophical truth as two sides of the same coin, the former a parable for the latter. Others, however, might publicly state that the two truths should not contradict each other but privately think of revelation as a vulgar form of higher truth. For example, al-Fārābī (c. 870–950) implied that prophetic knowledge was inferior to philosophical knowledge by demonstrating that the true knower, the philosopher-king, had to do what the prophets had done, and more. According to Ibn Ṭufayl (d. 1185), ultimate truth could be gained—without recourse to divine revelation—by reflective, reasoning human beings like the island-dwelling protagonist of his philosophical story *Ḥayy ibn Yaqẓān* (Living, Son of the Wakeful). Despite such condescension, many philosophers did value Muḥammad's lawgiving role because it fostered the ordering of society that they too cherished and pursued.

Leadership and legitimacy. In the Islamic faith, as in other religious traditions, the death of the final messenger and the cessation of new revelation tended to enhance the importance of other forms of leadership based on divine guidance and inspiration. Simultaneously, the maintenance of the stability grounded in revelation had to coexist, as in other traditions, with the pursuit of the spontaneity that had characterized the faith in its origins. The growth of a multivalent conception of *nubūwah* provided numerous ways in which its legitimacy could be emulated without being imitated, in stability and spontaneity alike.

When *nubūwah* was sealed, its authority had to flow into other leadership roles if the *ummah* was to survive. However, because none of them could duplicate the legitimacy of *nubūwah,* each had to establish a particular identity that could never compete successfully with *nubūwah.* Out of this paradox was born one of the great problems of Islamic civilization—the inimitability of the ideal leader.

Among Sunnī Muslims, the ending of *nubūwah* eventuated in a relationship of mutual dependence between the *khalīfah*s (caliphs), whose temporal authority protected and defended the unity of the *ummah*, and the *'ulamā'* (religious scholars), whose acquisition of authentic religious knowledge enabled them to define the proper Muslim life. These men, like rabbis, acted as indirect intermediaries, teasing out the legal and moral implications of God's direct revelations and shaping them into a system of rules: the *sharī'ah*. Thus were preserved the spiritual guidance and earthly power of the prophetic experience, if not its immediacy. Although neither *'ulamā'* nor *khalīfah*s could claim Muḥammad's full authority, both derived their legitimacy from him, and jointly they possessed the two powers he had combined.

The leadership model preferred by Shīʿī Muslims, *imāmah*, overcame this bifurcation with paradoxical consequences: it both greatly extended and radically contained charismatic authority; its successful combination of spiritual and temporal power was bought at the price of never exercising the latter; by virtue of its having to remain distinct from *nubūwah, imāmah* eventually became the superior of the two. The imams of the mainstream Shīʿah (the Imāmīyah or "Twelvers") were twelve descendants of Muḥammad believed to have inherited not only his blood and his weapons but also his charismatic ability to interpret the meaning of revealed truth without altering it. They were conceived in God's mind as the principle of absolute good, which was transmitted in the loins of the *nabī*s and wombs of holy women as entities of light and made concrete after Muḥammad's death. Together with the messengers, they are the proofs of God, but while the earth is sometimes without a messenger, it is never without an imam. So the imams are the "speaking Qur'ān," keeping the true meaning common of the "silent Qur'ān" alive and fresh.

In one Shīʿī view, these special qualities and esoteric knowledge, or *wilāyat Allāh*, that empowered Muḥammad's family to rule were entrusted to the angel Gabriel, who gave them to all the prophets and finally to Muḥammad, who passed them on to his cousin and son-in-law ʿAlī, who in turn passed them on to Muḥammad's grandsons and through them to the rest of the imams. Thus the imams became the only individuals capable of bringing divine guidance to the world after Muḥammad sealed *nubūwah*. Though they were therefore the only rightful spiritual and temporal authorities after Muḥammad, a series of erroneous decisions by the Muslim majority postponed their actual exercise of temporal power until the return of their last member, the Mahdi (messiah).

Despite the obvious temptation, all but extremist Shīʿah refused to call the imams *nabī*, insisting on one fundamental distinction: the imams, unlike Muḥammad, did not bring new revelation or new law. However, since they possessed all the other qualities of the messenger as well as the distinct, inimitable, and infallible characteristics of the imam, it was easy for their devoted followers to view them as preeminent. Ironically, the absence of new revelation further enhanced the significance of their error-free *(maʿṣūm)* abilities in charismatic exegesis.

In Shīʿī popular devotion all the messengers of God came to be thought of as having participated in the suffering of the holy family (ʿAlī, his wife and Muḥammad's daughter, Fāṭimah, and their sons Ḥasan and Ḥusayn) by being forewarned of it and by themselves tasting a little of it through their own persecution. Shīʿī devotional poetry expanded the tales of the prophets in new ways by likening them to the experiences of the holy family and the imams; at the same time, it raised the imams above all these figures except Muḥammad. Thus did *imāmah* "complete" *nubūwah* in such an absolutely essential way that the latter came to be, in the eyes of many of the Shīʿah, merely a precursor to the former.

Among both Sunnīs and the Shīʿah, other roles reflected the impact of the sealing of *nubūwah*. The Ṣūfī *shaykh* identified with the spiritual, if not genealogical, legacy of the *nabī* because he could receive individual divine inspiration and achieve intimacy with God. In so doing, such figures reclaimed the immediacy of the *nabī*'s experience; sometimes they also emulated his political and social activism, as did Sayyid Idrīs (1890–1983), the Libyan nationalist leader of the Sanūsīyah.

Perhaps even more important are the myriad apocalyptic, millenarian, and reformist figures, Sunnī and Shīʿī alike, who have adopted labels such as *mujaddid* ("centennial renewer"), *mahdī* ("divinely guided one," messiah), or *mujāhid/jihādī* (leader of a *jihād*). Often these figures have emerged in circumstances perceived to be like those of Muḥammad, for example, in an area where Islam was imperfectly established or not established at all. Although a few, such as the Almohad *mahdī* Ibn Tūmart (c. 1082–1130), may have claimed to bring new revelation, most managed to emulate Muḥammad's activist, reformist leadership without making dangerously explicit claims to his most distinguishing characteristic. By reintroducing Muḥammad's spiritual spontaneity and social renewal, and by emulating aspects of his *sunnah* and *sīrah*, they have evoked *nubūwah* without claiming it.

Exchanges with non-Muslims. The impact of the concept of *nubūwah* extended beyond the Muslim community, too. While developing it, Muslims were beginning to interact with their empire's subject population of Jews, Christians, and Zoroastrians. In the course of the ensuing polemic, each group had to adjust its understanding of the history of messengership so as to remain distinct from the others. Post-Islamic Zoroastrian biographies of Zarathushtra viewed him as an Islamic-type *payghambar,* a messenger sent with a book to a particular community. Some went on to exalt him above all other messengers, just as Muslims exalted Muḥammad. Arab Christian reactions were diametrically opposite: they defined genuine prophets as everything they argued Muḥammad was not—devoid of earthly motives, nonmaterialistic, nonmilitant, and miracle working. This familiar picture of prophethood, somewhat awkward from the point of view of the Old Testament, eventually found its way into Western Christian medieval polemic as well. Muslims accommodated themselves to Christian polemic by clarifying the doctrine of *i'jāz al-Qur'ān* (the "miracle of the Qur'ān"): the inimitability of the Qur'ān, combined with Muḥammad's illiteracy, constituted his God-given miracle.

Miracle working also found other routes into Islamic views of Muḥammad. In popular literature, as well as in genres like *qiṣaṣ al-anbiyā',* the mountain began to come to him as his life story filled with a plethora of extracanonical prodigies. Such glorification appears, for example, in one of the most lastingly popular poems used to celebrate Muḥammad's birthday, or *mawlid,* the *Burdah* or *Mantle Ode* of al-Būṣīrī (d. 1296), composed in Egypt during the Crusades, when it might have served polemical as well as devotional purposes. In popular practice, Muḥammad's tomb became a place to seek his earthly intercession.

Modern Muslim thinkers have continued to enlarge the concept of *nubūwah* by emphasizing particular dimensions of Muḥammad's *sunnah;* because the *ḥadīth* document the *sunnah,* they have become more important than ever. In modernist thought, the Messenger's mission is often likened to that of the modern social reformer; his ability to serve as a moral exemplar and rehabilitator in a time of decay is stressed. According to such interpretations, Muḥammad's teachings demonstrated the primacy of the social in humankind's goals and encouraged the use of consultation and cooperation, indeed flexibility. His ability to relate eternal truth to his own special circumstances was a model of and justification for applying Islamic principles according to circumstances.

Despite such updating, one aspect of *nubūwah,* its having come to an end with Muḥammad, remains nonnegotiable. When, in the last century, a group of former Shī'ī Muslims accepted the possibility of new revelation and new messengers, the explicit claims of their messenger, Bahā' Allāh (1817–1892), led inevitably to the founding of a separate religious tradition, just as it did for the Mormon followers of his American near-contemporary Joseph Smith (1805–1844). Clearly *nubūwah* remains as critical an issue now as it was at Islam's inception.

[*See also* Imamate; Prophecy; Walāyah; *and the biographies of the prophetic figures mentioned herein.*]

BIBLIOGRAPHY

There is no single comprehensive study of *nubūwah,* but the issue has been addressed within a number of broader investigations. Tor Andrae's classic work, *Die person Muhammeds in lehre und glauben seiner gemeinde* (Stockholm, 1918), offers valuable insights into the process by which the figure of Muḥammad and his mission as Messenger of God expanded and deepened through centuries of devotion. A thorough survey and synthesis of previous views on the Qur'anic distinction between *nabī* and *rasūl* can be found in Willem A. Bijlefeld's "A Prophet and More Than a Prophet?" *Muslim World* 59 (January 1969): 1–28, which also suggests a new and less dichotomous interpretation.

William A. Graham's *Divine Word and Prophetic Word in Early Islam* (Paris, 1977), especially part 1, "Revelation in Early Islam," provides an imaginative description of how two separate sacred messages, scripture and prophetic example, crystallized out of the unitary prophetic experience; the bibliography includes many major European works on Muḥammad. On the Shī'ī tradition in particular, Mahmoud M. Ayoub's *Redemptive Suffering in Islam: A Study of the Devotional Aspects of 'Ashurā' in Twelver Shī'ism* (The Hague, 1978) presents extensive materials on the history of the prophets as it was incorporated into the history of Shī'ī martyrdom, while Abdulaziz Abdulhussein Sachedina's *Islamic Messianism: The Idea of Mahdi in Twelver Sh'ism* (Albany, 1981) offers a clear and effective historical account that includes an examination of the relationship between *imām* and *nabī* in Shī'ī thought.

Several specific case studies also shed valuable light on *nubūwah.* One unusual effort to explain the appearance and displacement of Muḥammad's competitors in the claim to divine messengership is Dale F. Eickelman's "Musaylima: An Approach to the Social Anthropology of Seventh Century Arabia," *Journal of the Social and Economic History of the Orient* 10 (1967): 17–52. The impact of early Muslim-Christian polemic on evolving notions of revelation and prophetic mission in both communities, a topic that has not gained the attention it deserves, receives enlightening treatment in two articles by Sidney H. Griffith, "Comparative Religion in the Apologetics of the First Christian Arabian Theologians," in *Proceedings of the PMR Conference* (annual publication of the Patristic, Mediaeval and Renaissance Conference) 4 (1979), pp. 63–87, and "The Prophet Muḥammad: His Scripture and His Message According to the Christian Apologies in Arabic and Syriac from the First Abbasid Century," in *La vie du prophète Mahomet: Colloque de Strasbourg, 1980* (Paris, 1983), pp. 99–146.

Another unusual perspective can be gleaned from Sven S. Hartman's "Secrets for Muslims in Parsi Scriptures," in *Islam and Its Cultural Divergence,* edited by Girdhari L. Tikku (Urbana, Ill., 1971), pp. 67–75, which traces the impact of *nubūwah* on post-Islamic Zoroastrian conceptualizations of Zarathushtra. For a look at the impact of Muḥammad's biographical representation on the careers of nineteenth-century West African Muslim reformers and the complementary effect of the reformers' own lives on their representations of Muḥammad's career, see my article "The Popular Appeal of the Prophetic Paradigm in West Africa," *Contributions to Asian Studies* 17 (1982): 110–114. In the twentieth-century context, an Egyptian study of the Prophet's life is analyzed by Antoine Wessels in *A Modern Arabic Biography of Muḥammad: A Critical Study of Muḥammad Ḥusayn Haykal's Ḥayāt Muḥammad* (Leiden, 1972).

In addition to these critical studies, a number of primary sources, reflecting various genres and time periods, are available in English translation. *The Life of Muḥammad: A Translation of* [*Ibn*] *Isḥāq's Sīrat Rasūl Allāh,* translated by Alfred Guillaume (1955; reprint, Lahore, 1967), is the well-known eighth-century biography that sought to establish the Prophet's legitimacy vis-à-vis Judeo-Christian messenger figures. A tenth-century example of a philosophical middle position on the relationship between philosophical and revealed truth, and between the philosopher-king and the messenger of God, can be found in *Alfarabi's Philosophy of Plato and Aristotle,* translated by Muhsin Mahdi (New York, 1962), part 1, "The Attainment of Happiness." *The Tales of the Prophets of al-Kisā'ī,* translated by Wheeler M. Thackston, Jr. (Boston, 1978), reflects the important genre of *qiṣaṣ al-anbiyā'* in which extracanonical Jewish and Christian tales are reborn in an Islamic context. "The Mantle Poem of al-Buṣīrī," in *A Reader on Islam,* edited by Arthur Jeffery (The Hague, 1962), pp. 605–620, presents another form of popular literature, the devotional poem that commemorates the Prophet's birthday and stresses the miraculous dimension of his life. Finally, *A Mystical Interpretation of Prophetic Tales by an Indian Muslim, Shāh Wālī Allāh's Ta'wīl al-Aḥādīth,"* translated by J. M. S. Baljon (Leiden, 1973), although the translation is not entirely satisfactory, offers an example of Ṣūfī esoteric interpretation by a major eighteenth-century Indian mystic and theologian.

Marilyn Robinson Waldman

NUDITY is of widespread ritual significance. Various types of ritual nudity will be set forth here in an effort to comprehend the relation of particular instances to the broader religious context.

Initiation Rituals. Rituals of initiation often involve nudity. Christian baptism originally involved nudity, as did conversion to Judaism. Among the primitive societies of Australia and Africa there exists "a well-developed scenario, comprising several moments: consecration to death; initiatory torture; [and] death itself, symbolized by segregation in the bush and ritual nudity" (Eliade, 1958, p. 32). Although in the above passage Mircea Eliade associates ritual nudity with the symbolism of death, elsewhere he also suggests that "even the quite widespread custom of ritual nudity during the period of segregation in the bush can be interpreted as symbolizing the novice's asexuality." The implication here seems to be that asexuality as such refers to the totality of being that enhances the novice's chance of "attaining a particular mode of being" (that is, becoming a man or a woman), for in "mythical thought, a particular mode of being is necessarily preceded by a *total* mode of being" (ibid., p. 26).

However, ritual nudity in initiatory rites is most consistently explained as symbolic association with death or the beginning of a new life. For while John the Baptist saw the significance of baptism in terms of repentance preparatory to entering the kingdom of God, Paul saw in the ritual of baptism a replication of the death and resurrection of Jesus Christ. The neophytes were baptized naked, which symbolized the death of their former selves and their rebirth. It should be noted, however, that not all forms of baptism use the symbolism of death.

The Judaic explanation for nudity during baptism was that it "was essential that water reach every part of the proselyte's body" although Jonathan Z. Smith suggests that deeper symbolic reasons may be involved (Smith, 1966, p. 228). The Hindu ritual by which one becomes "twice-born" does not involve nudity. It seems possible to suggest that the role of ritual nudity varies depending on sex; for men it could be associated primarily with being reborn into a new state (symbolized by nakedness) while for women ritual nudity could be associated with the idea of fertility and productivity in addition to being led into a new state. However, the comparative secrecy of rules of initiation for girls makes it difficult to assess the role played by ritual nudity in their case.

Magic. Ritual nudity has often been associated with magic. A folk tale illustrates this point:

> Rise up in the last watch of the night, and with dishevelled hair and naked, and without rinsing your mouth, take two handfuls of rice as large as you can grasp with your two hands, and, muttering the form of words, go to a place where four roads meet, and there place the two handfuls of rice, and return in silence without looking behind you. Do so until the Piśācha (cannibal demon) appears.
>
> (Crooke, 1910, p. 447)

Another example is found in Abbé Dubois's clear statement that "the magician must be stark naked while he offers up these sacrifices to Laksmi, the wife of Vishnu," although he must "be decorously clad when such sacrifices are offered to Rama" (Dubois, 1906, p. 388).

It is of course well known that witches are said to perform their rites in the nude. It has been suggested that the real motivation for this might be mere unconventionality, though a "typical piece of rationalization [may be] observed here, for witches frequently say that they work naked so as not to impede the release of magical force which their ceremonies generate in their bodies" (Cavendish, 1970, p. 2019).

Among the numerous and rigorous conditions associated with the practice of Greco-Roman magic, "the most important is the observance of nudity or its ceremonial equivalent" (Smith, 1915, p. 283). Robert Hans van Gulik cites instances from China indicative of an even more general link between nudity and magic in Chinese culture. In an account of circa 350 CE, a Buddhist nun "famous for her magical arts" is described as performing her arts naked, and in the seventeenth century a warlord "exposed the nude bodies of slain women outside the wall of a town he was attacking in order to produce a magical effect and prevent the defenders' cannon from firing" (Gulik, 1961, pp. 113, 230). There is also evidence to suggest that erotic pictures were used as amulets.

Why the successful working of magic and charms should be associated with nudity is not entirely clear. It has been variously suggested that (1) this represents abject submission to the spirit power; that (2) clothes used in such rites become taboo and cannot be used again; and that (3) clothing may be seen as preventing the innate magical potency from being manifested to its fullest. Nudity could also indicate some form of compact with the devil, especially in the case of witches. However, this does not exhaust the range of possible explanations if we consider the variety of magical uses of nudity. In Bohemia, for instance, naked girls dance round flax fields to make the flax grow higher. Southern Slavs are said to have exorcised disease-spirits by exposing themselves, which led E. Louis Backman (1952) to suggest that nakedness was believed to possess healing properties. This is supported by Pliny's statement that "a remedy of abcess, compounded of seven ingredients, was given to the naked patient by a naked virgin." It is therefore quite plausible that, at various times and in various climes, nudity was believed to be magically preventive. There is more recent evidence from Russia to support this view: in July 1905 peasant girls "clothed only in their shifts, warded off cholera from their village by dragging a plough round it at midnight."

The belief in the magically protective quality of nudity does not seem to have been confined to diseases. Pliny writes of the notion that the course of storms could be altered by women baring themselves, and one of the many explanations offered for the depiction of copulation (probably ritual in nature) on Hindu temples is the belief that these protect the temples from being struck by lightning. This may well have something to do with a belief in the apotropaic properties of sexual organs, or even sex itself.

Fertility. The association of ritual nudity with fertility, both human and agricultural, may now be considered. The heroine of the famous Hindu epic the *Rāmāyaṇa* is named Sītā because she is said to have sprung fully formed from the furrow made by King Janaka while he plowed the ground in preparation for sacrifice. Some accounts of the event hint at ritual nudity, which has been associated with reproductive processes both human and agricultural. Women in Manipur, India, for instance, strip themselves naked and plough at night as a last-resort effort to end drought. The connection between seasonal festivals and nudity would seem to constitute another link between fertility and nudity. This link, hitherto analogical, is more directly seen in the case of sterility. India provides examples of women stripping naked and embracing the image of Hanuman, the monkey-god, or of walking naked 108 times (an auspicious number) around a fig tree, to obtain progeny. Though one cannot be certain if the Venus of Willendorf and similar figurines were used ritually, much less whether such use was in the context of ritual nudity, such evidence does suggest that the connection between nudity and fertility reaches into Paleolithic times.

Rain. The association of ritual nudity with rain is remarkable for its recurrence, particularly in the Indian context. Nakedness does not figure prominently in Vedic ritual, but its potency in the case of rain spells is recognized (Keith, [1925] 1971, p. 388). The early Tamil account of what was to become the celebrated episode of the stealing of the clothes of the *gopīs* by Kṛṣṇa involves the rain god Indra. The Rajbansi tribe in Cooch Behar performs the rain dance in the nude, while similar rites among the Kapu tribe in Madras involve girls exposing themselves. In these cases the explanation of ritual nudity can be connected with agricultural fertility, in which rain is a key factor. Attempts might even be made to move the rain god to pity. This is supposed to explain the reports that "high caste women or girls in times of drought are in the habit of divesting themselves of clothing at night and dragging a plough through the fields" (Cavendish, 1970, pp. 2017–2018). But when it rains excessively, ritual nudity is again brought into play as a force controlling the operation of nature, either by shocking the rain god into restraint or by invoking pity. Thus it was reported from Tiruchchirappalli in 1912 that "when the tanks and rivers threaten to breach their banks, men stand naked on the embankment and beat their drums; and if too much rain falls, naked men point firebrands at the sky. Their nudity is supposed to shock the powers that bring rain, and arrest their further progress" (Cavendish, 1970, p. 2017).

It may be a matter of significance that while female nudity is utilized to induce rain, as in the village of Ploska where naked women and girls pour water at the boundary of the village by night to put an end to drought, male nudity is invoked to put an end to excessive rain, as in the case cited from Tiruchchirappalli. It is possible that in cultures in which the female represents nature, fertility, and abundance, and the male represents control and restraint, the different roles of ritual nudity could be symbolically correlated, but any such generalization needs further corroboration. An exception is provided by Kabui men who go on the roof at night and strip naked to make rain. There may also be a parallel between urination and the falling of rain. The association of human fertility and the fertility of the soil with rain could have mythic connections. Certain groups in Africa, for instance, "think that the Earth is the wife of the Sky, and that their marriage takes place in the rainy season, when the rain causes the seeds to sprout and bear fruit" (Frazer, 1911–1915, vol. 5, p. 282). It is also worth noting that rain charms often involve the use of obscene language. This "link between ribaldery and rain is not obvious to the European mind" (ibid., vol. 1, p. 284 n.). But, as A. E. Crawley explains, if the idea underlying the connection between nudity and rainmaking is that "a violent change in the course of Nature may be assisted by a violent change of habit on the part of those concerned", and if "obscene language, like nudity" constitutes such a change, then the connection is clearly discernible (Crawley, 1912, p. 60).

Liturgy. Liturgical nudity as a form of ritual nudity is quite ancient. S. G. F. Brandon points out that "Sumerian priests ministered completely naked: the reason is not clear, but physical deformity disqualified from priesthood, thus suggesting gods enjoyed sight of perfect human bodies" (Brandon, 1970, p. 475). Aelianus, a Greek author of the second century CE, attests that a naked virgin ministered as priestess of Apollo at Epirus. The association of both Apollo and nudity with medicine and healing may provide a connection here. Some Christian sects, such as the Adamites of Russia, observed liturgical nudity to rid themselves of modesty, a relic of the Fall, but some sects have also used the concept of pre-Adamic innocence to justify sexual license. In the same vein, nuns have been ordered to attend Mass naked "as a sign of humility and poverty," the explanation being that nakedness is a symbol of humiliation and shame (*Is.* 20:4).

Church pilgrimages have sometimes been undertaken in the nude, and the explanation for this is not entirely clear. In some contexts the association of healing and nudity seems to provide an explanation; a more general psychological explanation has been offered by Father Zoepfl in terms of self-humiliation. This is questioned by Backman, who links a therapeutic and a theological rationale in his attempt to explain nudity.

> The role of nakedness elsewhere in the world of antiquity, in the account of Saul and in popular medicine, all seems to show that nakedness originally had its own magical significance in healing processions and pilgrimages. Ultimately this nakedness is the same thing as the possession of Saul by a divine spirit and can only be interpreted according to Genesis 1:27, "And God created man in his own image." Because naked man is God's image the devils flee from him and avoid his body. For this reason nakedness is a powerful force in expelling the demons which plague and torture man.
>
> (Backman, 1952, p. 287)

The ritual nudity associated with the practices of Tantric Hinduism seems to possess a very different religious significance. In the rites of Kumārī *pūjā*, a nude maiden is worshiped as an embodiment of Devī, the divine as a feminine principle. For the *tāntrika* it is not "the woman who personifies the Goddess, but the Goddess who appears in the woman" (Rawson, 1973, p. 17).

Funeral rites also sometimes involve nudity. William Crooke surmises that the original act of mourning in ancient Israel involved ritual nudity as suggested by the *Book of Micah* 1:8, "I will go stripped and naked," especially if this passage is taken in conjunction with the phrase "in nakedness and shame" of *Micah* 1:11. A possible justification is also suggested by Crooke, that the mourner might "have desired not to appear at a greater advantage than the mourned dead," and he regards the subsequent adoption of sackcloth as a concession to decency (Crooke, 1910, p. 447). In Hindu mortuary ritual, the mourner removes his upper garments, and if it be accepted that "the idea of nakedness is often satisfied by the removal of upper garments only" (Crawley, 1912, p. 61), then the parallel is obvious, as with ancient Egyptian women baring their breasts. Engravings of nudes on tombs found in medieval Europe may also be mentioned here. Their exact significance seems hard to determine, but they could be connected with the idea of resurrection.

In ritual, the connection between nudity and expiation may reflect a belief that nudity "brings man back to his primitive dress" (Keith, [1925] 1971, p. 388, n. 3), and in these cases nakedness may well signify sinfulness (Smith, 1966, p. 220). One may also note that some religious sects associate ritual nudity with a moral regimen (the Jains and Ājīvikas), and with some individuals the observance of nudity paradoxically indicates the overcoming of ritual restrictions. Mahādevī of Karṇāṭaka and Lallā of Kashmir in India are prime examples here, as perhaps also the case of Saul prophesying naked.

It is clear from the foregoing discussion that no single explanation of ritual nudity is likely to suffice. The suggestion that a sartorial adaptation to a change in the course of nature or events may, however, explain a great deal. Thus it is related in the *Book of Genesis* how Adam and Eve became aware of their nudity after eating the forbidden fruit, and so they tried to conceal their nakedness. Later, Yahveh provides them with garments. A sense of shame is often closely associated with nudity; in fact, the argument given by the Jain sect, which opts for total nudity for its monks, is that no one can be fully emancipated so long as he retains such a sense of shame. In the *Epic of Gilgamesh,* the origin of clothing is connected with a climactic event of human history: the passage from barbarism to a civilized existence. Enkidu learns to wear clothes upon becoming civilized. Thus, paradoxically, both nudity and being clothed can mark the transition from one state to another.

In terms of human ritual rather than human destiny, nudity is best associated with the phase of liminality or transition, as expressed in van Gennep's celebrated division of rites of passage into three phases: separation, transition, and incorporation. During the phase of transition, "liminal entities such as neophytes" may "be disguised as monsters, wear only a strip of clothing, or even go naked" (Turner, 1969, p. 95). The nakedness or near-nakedness in such a context is suggestive of "both a grave and a womb," typical liminal symbols. The same holds true of other rites of passage, as illustrated earlier by mortuary rituals. Associated with, on the one hand, the intermediate stage between the emergence and the end of humanity and, on the other, the rituals marking the stages of an individual's life cycle, nudity figures in rituals by which human societies try to achieve prosperity and avert calamity.

In conclusion, the role of nudity in the context of secularization may also be examined. Apart from the suggestion that modern beauty pageants replace the liturgical role of nudity, the association of ritual (and indeed of religion) with the nonrational dimension of human existence should be noted. Some consider the rise of the cult of nudism in modern times as symptomatic of modern man's loss of confidence in rationality. Furthermore, nudism is said to be democratic in that it removes all distinctions of secular rank. This is reminiscent of the comradeship and egalitarianism that characterizes initiates. Thus the role of nudity in the ritual process may not be irrelevant even in a modern, secular context.

[*See also* Human Body.]

BIBLIOGRAPHY

Backman, E. Louis. *Religious Dances in the Christian Church and in Popular Medicine.* Translated by Ernest Classen. London, 1952.

Brandon, S. G. F., ed. *A Dictionary of Comparative Religion.* London, 1970.

Cavendish, Richard, ed. *Man, Myth and Magic: An Illustrated Encyclopedia of the Supernatural.* 24 vols. New York, 1970.

Crawley, A. E. "Dress." In *Encyclopaedia of Religion and Ethics,* edited by James Hastings, vol. 5. Edinburgh, 1912.

Crooke, William. "Charms and Amulets (Indian)." In *Encyclopedia of Religion and Ethics,* edited by James Hastings, vol. 3. Edinburgh, 1910.

Dubois, Jean Antoine. *Hindu Manners, Customs and Ceremonies.* 3d ed. Translated by Henry K. Beauchamp. Oxford, 1906.

Eliade, Mircea. *Birth and Rebirth: The Religious Meanings of Initiation in Human Culture.* London, 1958.

Frazer, James G. *The Golden Bough.* 12 vols. 3d ed., rev. & enl. London, 1911–1915.

Gulik, Robert Hans van. *Sexual Life in Ancient China.* Leiden, 1961.

Keith, Arthur Berriedale. *The Religion and Philosophy of the Veda and the Upanishads* (1925). 2 vols. 2d ed. Westport, Conn., 1971.

Lévi-Strauss, Claude. *The Naked Man.* Translated by John and Doreen Weightman. New York, 1981.

Margoliouth, George. "Ancestor Worship and Cult of the Dead (Hebrew)." In *Encyclopaedia of Religion and Ethics,* edited by James Hastings, vol. 1. Edinburgh, 1908.

Rawson, Philip. *Tantra: The Indian Cult of Ecstasy.* London, 1973.

Smith, Jonathan Z. "The Garments of Shame." *History of Religions* 5 (Winter 1966): 217–238.

Smith, Kirby F. "Magic (Greek and Roman)." In *Encyclopaedia of Religion and Ethics,* edited by James Hastings, vol. 8. Edinburgh, 1915.

Turner, Victor. *The Ritual Process: Structure and Anti-Structure.* Chicago, 1969.

ARVIND SHARMA

NUER AND DINKA RELIGION. The Nuer and Dinka peoples belong to the Nilotic group of the Nilo-Saharan language family and inhabit the savanna and sudd region of the upper Nile in the southern part of the Republic of the Sudan. The Nuer number some 300,000 and the Dinka about 1 million; the figures are approximate, partly because some sections of each group have intermingled. It has been argued that they should be considered a single people, but cultural and political differences are marked enough to distinguish them, and each considers itself to be distinct from the other. Their religious systems should also be differentiated, although perhaps as variants of a common system.

Both Nuer and Dinka are cattle herders on the vast savannas of the region. The Nuer are fully transhumant; the Dinka less so as their environment is less harsh and better watered, consisting of orchard savanna rather than the treeless plains of Nuerland. Relations between local groups based on patrilineal clans and lineages take place largely through exchanges of cattle at marriages and, in times of hostility, through cattle raiding; cattle also have a central religious importance, with a strong sense of spiritual identification between humans and cattle. The Nuer lack any form of traditional political authority other than the rudimentary (and essentially religious) authority of Leopard-skin priests and prophetic leaders. The Dinka leaders, the Masters of the Fishing Spear, exercise more consistent authority over more clearly defined groupings. Today the traditional patterns have changed considerably due to colonial rule and, in recent years, to political independence. Both peoples are characterized by their fierce sense of independence, seeing themselves alone in a world that is hostile to them both environmentally and politically. Observers have all stressed the importance of religion to them in their everyday affairs.

Divinities and Spirits. In both religions the world is said to have been created by a high god. The Nuer refer to this God as Kwoth (a word that also means "spirit" or "breath"), or as Kwoth Nhial; among the Dinka the supreme being is known as Nhialic, which might be translated as "sky." Even though the two concepts may not be identical it is convenient to use the term *Deity* here for both. The source both of life and of its paradoxes, the Deity is omnipotent, ubiquitous, everlasting, and beyond the comprehension and the control of ordinary living people. Although now remote from human beings (in both religions there are myths of the separation of people from the sky), the Deity remains ultimately concerned with the world and liable to interfere in its everyday affairs at any time. Prayers and offerings are made continually and informally to the Deity, never far from the thoughts of the living.

In terms of everyday behavior the mystical or spiritual forces that are in most constant watch over people and in communication with them are the many kinds of spirits, or lesser deities, that are nearer to the mundane world. The natures, identities, and motives of these lesser deities are many. They represent, on a mystical plane, the countless and always changing aspects of the human experience of the world, of the acts of the Deity, and of themselves; any attempted classification of them except in general terms can only be uncertain and ever shifting. In both religions a somewhat similar pattern is discernible, but similarities should not be pushed too far.

The Nuer divide the lesser deities into spirits of the air (or of the above) and spirits of the below. The former are more powerful, more wide ranging, and more dangerous. Most are thought of as alien, originating from the Dinka. They are distinct from the Deity, even though both they and the Deity are known as *kwoth*. There is only one Deity, and it is original to the Nuer; the spirits of the above are many and may come from other peoples (although the *colwic*, spirits of people killed by lightning, appear to be older and not of alien origin). The Deity is seen as a benevolent father and friend, whereas the spirits are less benevolent and more immediately demanding. They possess people by sickness to signal that the latter have committed sins, and the relationship thus established between spirit and person may be inherited. Sacrifice is made to remove the sin from the possessed person, who is thereby cured, and the spirit is sent back to its proper place in the outside world. And it is the spirits of the above who possess certain people who thereby become prophets.

The spirits of the below are nearer to people. They include totemic spirits, attached to local groups; totemistic spirits, attached to individuals; and various nature and other spirits. They are all of less importance than the spirits of the above and not held in great esteem. But being more closely attached to individuals they may partake of ordinary human spite and hatred and so be demanding and unpleasant.

The Dinka distinguish what they call the sky divinities or free divinities, the more important, from the clan divinities that are attached to local groups, lesser divinities, and ancestors. The main distinction in everyday life is that a clan divinity, associated with an animal species or a class of objects, is the concern of all the members of a particular clan, whereas the sky divinities force themselves upon the living by possession and so create a permanent relationship with them individually and irrespective of clan affiliation. They are more difficult to understand and predict and thus more powerful and more dangerous. A divinity that possesses an individual is identified by divination so it can be separated from the possessed person by sacrifice. Sky divinities are regarded as external realities that represent inner psychological states and so are linked with situations of social and moral ambiguity, confusion, and sin.

Priests and Sacrifice. Each society has ritual experts who are thought to cope with the spiritual powers and to protect ordinary people from them. Among the Nuer they are the Leopard-skin priests, members of particular lineages who possess powers, the principal of which is to purify those who have been placed, through their own or others' deeds, in a state of pollution and spiritual danger. Among the Dinka they are known as Masters of the Fishing Spear, the heads of priestly lineages. They are said to be "the lamps of the Dinka" as they "carry life" and guide their people through the darkened ways of the everyday world. They have a life-giving power given to them by the divinity Ring ("flesh"). Oral traditions state that the first Master of the Fishing Spear was Aiwel Longar, whose prayers were powerful and truthful enough to maintain the fertility of people, livestock, and land. Longar's spears were accurate and deadly when used to kill sacrificial oxen, and so are those of the present-day masters; the spiritual power resides in the spears, used for sacrificial killing and thereby also to preserve life. The invocation and the immolation of the victim is a repetition of Longar's original ritual action. The sacrificial animal is symbolically identified with the person on whose behalf the rite is performed. Guilt and sickness are placed "on the back" of the sacrificial victim and carried away at its death: its death expels sin and sickness from the group and releases the individual concerned from them.

Masters of the Fishing Spear bring and retain the "life" of their people. They may not die a normal death and so are buried alive at their own request. Since the master's life is not lost (it remains among the living to strengthen them), the people do not mourn him and feel only joy.

Prophets. The Nuer and Dinka have long had to face the radical (and seemingly both destructive and irrational) effects of outside interference and to make some satisfying response to them. Besides such natural disasters as famines and epidemics, the most serious cases in recent centuries have been Arab slavers, British colonial rule and "pacification," and then overrule under the Republic of the Sudan.

We know little about their earliest responses, but during the late nineteenth and early twentieth centuries both the Nuer and Dinka produced religious movements led by prophets. Nuer prophets organized large groups of people to raid the Dinka, introduced new rites to stop new epidemics, and led the resistance against slavers. Toward the end of the last century there appeared a prophet called Ngundeng, a member of a Leopard-skin priest lineage and perhaps of foreign (Dinka) origin. He acquired a reputation for healing, announced that his powers came from a Dinka sky divinity called Deng and went into ritual seclusion and fasting, which marked his acquisition of a new and prophetic role. He had a wide following, and his supporters spent two years building a pyramid of earth and ashes, a "house of spirit" in honor of his sky divinity. After his death in 1906 his powers passed to his son Gwek. A deformed and ugly man known for his healing powers, Gwek appeared regularly at the top of the pyramid in a state of extreme possession, uttering prophecies. Like his father, he periodically fasted in solitude and wore long and unkempt hair, signs of being imbued with divine power. He headed the resistance to the British administration and was killed by government forces. Many other Nuer prophets have had generally similar attributes.

Dinka prophets were also important and numerous. The most famous was Arianhdit, who was at his height during World War I and lived until 1948. Dinka prophets were Masters of the Fishing Spear who, by acquiring additional powers directly from the Deity, also became Men of Divinity. They were thus more directly involved with traditional authority and social organization than were the Nuer prophets. They led many risings and movements of political significance in the early years of this century.

Christian missionaries have been active among both peoples. They have had little success among the Nuer and rather more among the Dinka, perhaps because the Dinka, as the largest group in the southern Sudan, give greater importance to Western forms of education and to their political ambitions in the modern world.

[*See also* Kwoth *and* Nhialic.]

BIBLIOGRAPHY

The principal sources for the religions of the Nuer and Dinka are E. E. Evans-Pritchard's *Nuer Religion* (Oxford, 1956) and Godfrey Lienhardt's *Divinity and Experience: The Religion of the Dinka* (Oxford, 1961). Both are based on meticulous and rich ethnographic research and on intensive understanding of the theoretical and comparative problems in studies of alien religious beliefs and rites. Both are outstanding studies of highly complex matters. Evans-Pritchard also published scores of articles on various aspects of Nuer religion, which are listed in *A Bibliography of the Writings of E. E. Evans-Pritchard*, compiled by himself and edited by T. O. Beidelman (London, 1974). Other works include J. Pasquale Crazzolara's *Zur Gesellschaft und Religion des Nueer* (Mödling bei Wien, 1933), by a Catholic missionary with long experience of the Sudan, and F. M. Deng's *The Dinka of the Sudan* (New York, 1972), by a distinguished Dinka scholar.

JOHN MIDDLETON

NUM is the highest god of the Nentsy, a Samoyed people of western Siberia. He is the creator of the world but remains relatively remote from humans, both during life and after death (when humans descend to the underworld). Contact with Num is established only exceptionally, through spirits and through shamans and their assistant spirits. In the Nenets religion Num is the father of Nga, the god of evil and of death, and is therefore his antipode. (Among the Selkup, Nom is the highest god but does not participate in a polar opposition;

in Selkup *nga* means simply "god.") The sacrifices offered to Num on specified occasions are in the form of animals, food, clothing, and money. In the terminology of syncretic Samoyed Christianity, "Num bread" refers to the eucharistic wafer, the Host.

Literally, *num* means not only "the highest god who resides in the heavens" but also "sky, firmament." The term is found in all Samoyed languages and can be reconstructed for proto-Samoyed religion with the meanings "heaven above" and "highest god." However, since the obviously cognate forms *nu-* and *num* with the meanings "up, above, top" and "sky" are also found in Khanty and Mansi (two Finno-Ugric languages related to Samoyed and spoken to the west and south of the Samoyed area), it is likely that *num* is a cultic word that in the course of time has migrated over western Siberia. Attempts to connect *num* with the root *jum(a)* found in the Finnish word for "god," *jumala* (*-la* is a local suffix), must be rejected on phonological grounds in favor of the assumption that *jumala* and related terms in some other Finno-Ugric languages are borrowed from Indic (cf. the Sanskrit *dyumān*, "bright, shining," which refers to an attribute of Indra).

BIBLIOGRAPHY

There are no works specifically devoted to Num. The interested reader may, however, profitably consult *The Samoyed Peoples and Languages* (Bloomington, Ind., 1963) by Péter Hajdú and *The Mythology of All Races*, vol. 4, *Finno-Ugric, Siberian* (Boston, 1927) by Uno Holmberg.

ROBERT AUSTERLITZ

NUMBERS. [*This entry consists of two articles. The first presents a general overview of the religious valorization and symbolism of numbers; the second is a discussion of the particular symbolism of binary numbers.*]

An Overview

Numbers, in which the power and sanctity of both time and space are experienced in visible form, have fascinated mankind since early days, although methods of counting and systems of expressing numerals have differed considerably from culture to culture. The highest achievements in this field are the Maya system and the "Arabic" (originally Indian) numbers that were introduced in the West in the twelfth century. The presence of zero in them facilitated mathematical operations.

The Mathematical Spirit. Augustine found numbers in the scriptures to be both sacred and mysterious, and modern man still reacts positively or negatively to numbers like seven and thirteen, for the mathematical spirit is innate in man and manifests itself wherever human beings live, beginning with simple geometrical ornaments. Observation of the rhythm of days and nights and the phases of the moon seem to have led to man's early occupation with numbers, and the Sumerian-Babylonian astral system lies behind much of the later development. Numbers have sometimes been given divine qualities: in India, the number is called "of the kind of Brahmā," and the name of Sāṃkhya philosophy alludes to the system's reliance on numbers, for it literally means "count."

But the first religio-philosophical interest in numbers appeared in Greece with the Pythagoreans, who regarded numbers as metaphysical potencies and the cosmos as isomorphic with pure mathematics (Bell, 1933, p. 140). They defined geometrical theorems, tried to develop objective standards of beauty (the Golden Section), and found the relations between numbers and music. (In the sixteenth century, Kepler's work was still permeated by the idea of the *harmonia mundi.*) Pythagorean thought remained basic for later numerology and arithmology, all of which lays particular stress on the first ten integers, in which, as it were, the fullness of the world is contained. The classification of odd numbers as masculine and lucky and even numbers as feminine and unlucky stems from the Pythagorean system. "Lucky" odd numbers have therefore been preferred for use in magic spells, in religious repetitive formulas, and in rites of healing.

Speculations on the properties of numbers were continued in the works of Iamblichus and Philo Judaeus, and arithmology as the philosophy of the powers and virtues of particular integers was further elaborated by Nikomachos of Gerasa, Capella, Boethius, and others. It played an important role in Augustine's hermeneutics, offering him and numerous medieval Christian authors (among them particularly Hugh of Saint-Victor) a clue to biblical allegories. In the early seventeenth century, Peter Bongo (Bungus), in *De numerorum mysteria* (1618), was still trying to prove that numerology alone enables us to understand the world.

Similar numerical allegory is found, in its most developed form, in Jewish Qabbalah; it is also incorporated into Islamic mystical thought, as in the philosophy of the Ikhwān al-Ṣafā' and the Ḥurūfī tradition. In both Jewish and Islamic works (as in ancient Greek) the interchangeability of letters and numerals was central for the mystico-magical interpretation of texts (i.e., in *gematriah* and *jafr*). The qualities of numbers as they appear in the biblical tradition became significant for the Christian liturgy and visible in Christian architecture; they permeate the structure and imagery of medieval and Renaissance literature. Proverbial and folkloristic usage of certain numbers, such as three or seven, reveals the general feeling toward these integers, and both religious and popular literature use the device of ascending numbers, or descending numbers (as in the *Aṅguttara Nikāya*), for counting purposes. The widespread use of magic squares is only one example of the faith in certain numbers.

Interpretation of Numbers. Although the numbers have been interpreted in various ways, it can be seen that these are generally rather similar.

1. One, according to the Pythagoreans, is both odd and even. Not a number in the normal meaning of the word, it points to the all-embracing unity that incorporates the possibility of multiplicity. "God is an odd number and loves odd numbers," says a Muslim tradition derived from classical antiquity (see Vergil's *Numero deus impare gaudet).* Geometrically, one is represented by the dot, out of which forms and figures are developed.

2. Unity breaks up into duality. Two is the number of duality, of contrast and tension: the German *zwei* ("two") in *Zwietracht* ("discord") expresses this relation, as do compounds formed with the prefix *dis.* Two signifies the tension between the positive and negative current, between systole and diastole, inhaling and exhaling, between male and female; in short, it signifies the tension that generates the continuous flow of life, for the world is composed of pairs of opposites.

"Whatever comes from the tree of knowledge has duality," says a qabbalistic text. This principle is well expressed in the Chinese figuration of *yang* and *yin.* Zoroastrian religion postulates the constant strife between the principle of darkness and that of light, which in gnostic religions develops into the strife between material evil and spiritual good. Islam sees the manifestation in time and space of the peerless, numinous One in two aspects: *jamāl* ("beauty") and *jalāl* ("majesty"). Two is further valorized in the creative word *kun* ("Be!"), which consists of the two letters *k* and *n*, and in the letter *b* (whose numerical value is two) of the Basmalah ("In the name of God . . .") at the beginning of the Qur'ān, similar to the *b* at the beginning of the Torah. In the biblical tradition, the two stone tablets of Old Testament law, like the two testaments themselves, the Old and the New, are complementary, as are the two types of life, the active and the contemplative, personified in Leah and Rachel and in Martha and Mary. Geometrically, two corresponds to the line. The presence of the dual in many languages shows how the I and Thou are juxtaposed against the multiplicity of beings. [*See also* Dualism.]

3. Three "heals what two has split." As the first number that has a beginning, a middle, and an end, it is the first real number, "the eldest of odds, God's number properly," as Joshua Sylvester (after Du Barlas) calls it. It is the first and basic synthesis, represented in the first geometrical figure, the triangle, and in the triadic rhythm of thesis, antithesis, and synthesis. As the first number beyond I and Thou, it is the first to mean "multitude" and therefore implies the superlative.

Numerous are the divine triads that can be named, from the Sumerian An, Enlil, and Enki and the Babylonian Shamash, Sin, and Ishtar to the Hindu triad of Viṣṇu, Śiva, and Brahmā and to the Christian Trinity. Concerning the last-named group, it has been pointed out that

> the paramount doctrinal weakness of Christianity, as the Arian heresy testifies, was the duality of the Godhead (Father and Son). . . . That the Father and Son were one was questionable on numerical as well as philosophical ground. But Father, Son and Holy Spirit were unquestionably One by very virtue of being Three. (Hopper, 1938, p. 73)

Lesser divine or semidivine beings also appear in groups of three: the Greek Moira, the Nordic Norns, and the Roman Maters, and tricephalic deities are found in many traditions, from the Celtic to the Hindu. Even Islamic monotheism knows groupings of three, such as, among the Shī'ah, Allāh, Muḥammad, and 'Alī.

"All good things come in threes," it is said, and everything seems to fall in tripartite units: heaven-earth-water or, as in China, heaven-earth-man, hence the concept of three worlds. The *Ṛgveda* knows Viṣṇu's three strides (connected with the position of the sun during the day), and three is the number of the twice-born social classes in Vedic religious anthropology. Three is also an important liturgical number, as the tripartition of places of public worship shows. Threefold invocation of the deity is common to most traditions, be it the Trisagion of Christian liturgy, the threefold repetition of *śāntiḥ* ("peace") at the end of recitation of Hindu scriptures, or the threefold blowing of the shofar on Jewish holy days.

Metaphysical concepts often occur in groups of three: *sat-cit-ānanda* ("being, knowledge, bliss") is a common triad in Indian thought; wisdom, reason, and gnosis were manifested, according to the *Zohar*, in Abraham, Isaac, and Jacob. Buddhism conceives of *triloka* ("three worlds") and of *trikāya* ("three bodies" of the Buddha), and Islam distinguishes between *islām* ("surrender"), *īmān* ("faith"), and *iḥsān* (acting perfectly beautifully). The spiritual path is usually divided into three, as, for example, *via purgativa, via illuminativa,* and *via unitiva* or as *sharī'ah* ("law"), *ṭarīqah* ("the path"), and *ḥaqīqah* ("truth"). Three plays a role in anthropological concepts, too: the spiritual powers can be divided into intellect, will, and mind or, in Islam, into *nafs ammārah* ("inciting to evil"), *lawwāmah* ("blaming") and *muṭma'innah* ("at peace"). In Indian thought, one finds the *triguṇa*, the "three strands" of matter: *tamas* ("heaviness, dullness"), *rajas* ("activity, change") and *sattva* ("brilliance, perfect equanimity").

Time is commonly periodicized in three, as past, present, and future, and the Christian church knows the kingdom of the Father, the Son, and the Holy Spirit. The latter concept is important in millenarian prophecies such as that preached in the thirteenth century by Joachim of Fiore. In our time, with the Third Reich (which was, historically speaking, at least the fourth German state) myth overcame history.

Three is cumulative; whatever happens thrice is law. It often simply denotes the plural, or "everything." Therefore it is used in folk tales and legends as a statistical number: Joseph was three days in the well, Jonah three days in the belly of the whale. The three Magi are as well known as groups of three brothers or sisters; three roses, three ravens, three wishes, and three guesses are frequent in folk songs, fairytales, and legends. One also finds the action triangle in practice *(ménage à trois)* and in drama, and the number of titles of fiction and nonfiction works that group persons or events into three is legion. [*See also* Triads.]

4. Four "brings order into the chaos." It is a material and cosmic number. The four phases of the moon and the four cardinal points of the earth (pre-formed in the name *Adam*) offer such ordering; so do the four elements and the four humors, and on the mythical plane, in Islam, the four rivers in Paradise and, in the Vedic tradition, the four milk streams that flow from the udder of the heavenly cow. The Pythagoreans considered four the number of justice, and their geometry discovered the four perfect solids. The term *square* still points to right, orderly, and ordering structure. As a number of cosmic order, four often divides the time: the four seasons, Hesiod's four ages of man, the Hindu concept of four world epochs *(yugas)*, and the Zoroastrian idea of four periods. Chinese religion and Islam know four sacred scriptures, as Christianity accepts only four gospels as authoritative. For the Christian, the cross, with its four right angles, is "the rightest figure of all," extending over the four corners of the world, while the Jewish tradition emphasizes the mystery of the tetragrammaton, *YHVH*. Quaternity as an ancient symbol of perfection was reevaluated by C. G. Jung as an antidote to the unstructured, "Wotanic" spirit of his time. [*See also* Quaternity.]

5. Five is the number of natural man, the first number mixed of even and odd. It does not constitute an ordering number in crystals, but it occurs frequently in botanical forms, in petals and leaves (see Sir Thomas Browne's *Garden of Cyrus,* 1658), and it has therefore been considered by some as a "revolutionary" number. In antiquity, five was the number of Ishtar and Venus and is thus connected with sexual life and marriage, as in the parable of the five foolish virgins and the five wise virgins in *Matthew* 25. The pentagram, which can be derived from the zodiacal stations of Venus, is endowed with apotropaic and magic powers, while in alchemy the *quinta essentia* contains the rejuvenating force of life.

In China, five has traditionally been a lucky number; in the Western tradition one usually thinks of the five senses. Manichaeism knows five archons and the five corresponding aeons of darkness, while Islam, it is said, is "founded on five," for there are no more than five unconnected letters at the beginning of any Qur'anic surah, and there are five Pillars of Faith, five daily prayers, and five lawgiving prophets. In Shī'ī Islam the *panjtan* (Muḥammad, Fāṭimah, 'Alī, Ḥasan, and Ḥusayn) appears as a protective unit, popularly connected with the "hand of Fāṭimah." The human hand with its five fingers is a basis of some numeral systems, and its image has been frequently used in magic. The number of philosophical pentads ranges from the five Platonic bodies to Islamic Neoplatonic formulations.

6. Six is the macrocosmic number: the hexagon, consisting of two triangles, expresses the combination of the spiritual and the material world, hence the idea that "what is there is here." Six is a perfect number, formed from both the sum and the product of one, two, and three ($1 + 2 + 3$ and $1 \times 2 \times 3$). Therefore, according to both Philo and Augustine, the world had to be created in six days. In Islam, six is used to symbolize the phenomenal world, which appears like a six-sided solid, that is, a cube.

7. Seven is a sacred number in many traditions. Because it is, according to Hippocrates of Chios, related to the lunar phases, seven influences all sublunar things. It appears in the periodicity of chemical elements and of music, and it has generally been connected with the phases of human development to a Grand Climacterium of sixty-three (7×9). Seven is the first prime number of symbolic meaning; it is "virgin," since it does not generate by multiplication any number under ten, and it is the only integer of the first decade that is not a divisor of 360. Consisting of the spiritual ternary and the practical quarternary ($3 + 4$), seven embraces everything created.

Whether the sanctitude of seven was derived by the Sumerians from the seven planets (the five visible planets plus sun and moon) or whether, conversely, they looked for seven planets to match their idea of the perfect number is a matter of dispute. The number of planets in turn determined the number of days in a week. (Niẓāmī's Persian epic *Haft paikar* expresses this belief poetically.) In Babylon every seventh day was considered dangerous, and it was thought that nothing should be undertaken; the seventh day was then sanctified in Judaism as Sabbath, the day on which God rested after creation.

The demonic qualities of seven are preserved in heptads of devils, witches, magic knots, and so on, but its sacred qualities are perhaps more numerous. Some traditions speak of seven worlds, or, in accordance with the "planets," seven spheres; therefore, the ascension of the soul usually leads through seven gates, steps, valleys, or veils (thus from the Mithraic mysteries to ʿAṭṭār, Ruusbroec, and Teresa of Ávila). In extension, Islam knows seventy thousand veils between the soul and God. Seven appears also in connection with deities of other religions; it is Apollo's number, and, in India, it is especially prominent in connection with Agni. In Iran, the heptad of the Amesha Spentas consists of six plus the all-embracing Ahura Mazdā.

But the number seven gained its greatest importance in the Judaic tradition, whence it extends into Christianity and Islam. From the seven days of creation to the seven pillars of wisdom, the Hebrew scriptures contain "unnumbered heptads." The *menorah* with its seven candles points to some of the secrets of seven. Numerous biblical stories use seven as a statistical number (Pharaoh's dream of seven fat cows and seven thin cows; Jacob's seven years of service, and then seven more). Blood should be avenged seven times, or seventy-seven times (*Gn.* 4:24), but seventy times seven should be the times of forgiving (*Mt.* 18:22). The *Book of Revelation* is filled with heptads, too, leading John of Salisbury in the twelfth century to write his treatise *De septem septenis*. Both the Lord's Prayer and the Qur'anic Fātiḥa consist of seven sentences. Catholic churches speak of seven major sins and seven virtues, seven sacraments, and seven gifts of the Holy Spirit, and the Mass consists of seven parts.

The sevenfold repetition of religious acts is common in Islam; thus the sevenfold run between Ṣafah and Marwah and the three times seven stones cast at the devil during the pilgrimage. Sufism knows seven *laṭā'if*, subtle centers of the body, connected in meditation with the seven essential attributes of God and the seven great prophets. A *ḥadīth* speaks of seven layers of Qur'anic interpretation, which has been practiced especially by the Ismā'īlīyah, whose basis is the seventh imam of the Shīʿah. They know seven cyclical periods with seven imams; the seven great prophets correspond to the seven spheres, the imams to the seven earths.

In folk tales and legends, seven is a round number: to do anything seven times is especially effective. Christian and Islamic legends know groups of seven feminine or masculine saints, most prominently the Seven Sleepers. The continuing preference for the number seven is reflected today even in the designation of airplanes as Boeing 707, 747, and so on.

8. Eight, the double four, is associated with good fortune. In Judaism the eighth day is singled out for circumcision. Christian tradition sees in the eighth day (the day after Sabbath) the resurrection of Christ; hence eight points to eternity. The eight paradises in Islam and the eight pillars of heaven in Chinese religion belong to the same concept; the eight blessings in the Sermon on the Mount as well as the Eightfold Path of the Buddha are equally connected with eternal bliss. Therefore, the traditional shape of a Christian baptistery is octagonal.

9. Nine, as three times three, is the number of completion. Only rarely in Christian theology is it considered incomplete, as ten minus one. Christianity speaks of the nine orders of angels, and Dante thus saw Beatrice as the embodiment of nine. But the number is more widely connected with Germanic, Celtic, and Inner Asian peoples. The traditions about King Arthur as well as the songs of the Nordic *Vǫluspá* show an abundance of nines, from the nine days that Óðinn (Odin) was hanging on the tree to the number of Valkyries, from ninefold sacrifices to rituals in which nine or a ninefold number of men had to participate. This predilection for nine has been attributed to the nine months of winter in the northern areas of Eurasia, although nine occurs frequently in the more southerly lore of the ancient Greeks as well.

Such expressions as "to the nines," meaning "perfect," and "to be on cloud nine" show the old Germanic esteem for nine. The number frequently appears in Germanic popular tales, although it has often been replaced by seven under Christian influence. Its role in folklore among Germanic peoples is important, and it often occurs in connection with witchcraft (a cat, which has nine lives, can turn into a witch at the age of nine). Among the Chinese and Turco-Mongolian peoples, everything valuable has traditionally had to be ninefold: a prince has owned nine yak-tail standards; ninefold prostration has been required; and gifts have been offered in groups of nine, so that the word *tōqūz* ("nine") often means simply "present." In China a nine-storied pagoda represents the nine spheres, which are also known in the eastern Islamic tradition. The eight roads that lead to the central palace in Peking reflect the ninefold structure of the universe.

10. Ten, the number of human fingers, and thus a basis of the decimal system, is connected with completion. In the decade, multiplicity returns again to unity, and the system is closed. The Pythagoreans regarded ten as the perfect number, since it is the sum of the first four integers (1 + 2 + 3 + 4) and is represented in the perfect triangle:

Both the Hebrew and the Buddhist scriptures teach a decalogue, and sets of ten principles are known for the Ṣūfī novice. Likewise, Aristotle's ten categories show "completeness." In early Christianity, the three persons of the Trinity and the seven elements of created beings were thought to be represented by ten; but already the Torah had provided the ten words of creation that became the basis of "practical" (i.e., magical) Qabbalah, with its concept of ten *sefirot* ("numbers"). These ten *sefirot,* along with the twenty-two letters of the Hebrew alphabet, point to the thirty-two ways of salvation. Ten were the best companions of Muḥammad, and of several Ṣūfī masters, while the Ismāʿīlī system knows the ten higher orders of the *ḥudūd,* consisting of groups of three and seven.

11. Eleven is normally explained as a number of transgression, being beyond the perfect ten, or as incomplete, being beneath the equally perfect twelve; it is therefore an unfortunate, "mute" number.

12. Twelve (3 × 4; 5 + 7) is the great cosmic number. From Sumer and ancient China onward, it is the number of the signs of the zodiac and the basis of the sexagesimal system. In many cultures, day and night were divided into twelve hours, the year into twelve months, and gnostic religions speak of twelve aeons. The "great period" in Babylon was twelve times twelve thousand days, and multiples of twelve appear frequently in later mythology. The meaning of completion is as evident in the twelve tribes of Israel as in the twelve disciples of Christ and the twelve gates of the heavenly Jerusalem, where twelve times twelve blessed will adore the Lamb of God. The minor prophets of Israel, the Greek sibyls, and the imams of the Twelver Shīʿah number twelve. For medieval Christian exegetes, twelve meant faith in the Trinity that had to be diffused to the four corners of the earth. In popular traditions and sayings, it is, again, a round number, manifest in periods of twelve days or years, in twelve endangered heroes, and so forth.

13. Thirteen (12 + 1) disrupts the perfection of the duodecimal system and, being connected with the intercalary month, was considered unlucky in Babylon, a superstition that continues to our day. In fairytale, Death becomes the godfather of a thirteenth child. But one can see thirteen also as a combination of one leader and twelve followers, of twelve members of a jury and a judge, of twelve open rooms and a closed one, of a father and twelve sons, and so on. Thirteen therefore sometimes alternates with twelve. In ancient Israel, thirteen was sacred, for thirteen items were necessary for the tabernacle. It also corresponds to the numerical value of *aḥad* ("one"); thus, thirteen rivers of balsam await the believer in paradise. The superstition that thirteen people should not sit at one table (based on the Last Supper) is comparatively recent.

14. Fourteen (2 × 7) is a lucky number, manifested in the fourteen helping saints *(Nothelfer)* of Christianity and the fourteen innocent martyrs of Shīʿah Islam. It is the number of the full moon and is, therefore, the ideal age of the moonlike beloved of which Persian poets sing. In Islam, it is further connected with the so-called sun- and moon-letters and with the unconnected letters at the beginning of certain surahs, both of which sum up to fourteen, half of the twenty-eight letters of the Arabic alphabet. The Ḥurūfīyah emphasize that the Arabic words *yad* ("hand") and *wajh* ("face") both have the numerical value of fourteen, twice the sacred seven.

15. Fifteen is the key number in the Taoist liturgical dance known as the Pace of Yü; the nine stations, or "gates," of the dance follow the sequence of a magic square whose rows, columns, and diagonals all add to fifteen.

16. Sixteen (4 × 4), in the Indian tradition, expresses completeness, in ornaments, features, meters, and poetry.

17. Seventeen, nowadays barely popular, appears in antique music and poetry (9:8 = simple interval) and in the seventeen consonants of the Greek alphabet. In Christianity it signifies the Ten Commandments plus the seven gifts of the Holy Spirit, and it figures in calculations of the number of the fishes mentioned in *John* 21:11 (9 × 17 = 153; 1 + ⋯ + 17 = 153). Seventeen appears in Islamic alchemy (e.g., in the writings of Jābir ibn Ḥayyān), in the Shīʿah tradition, and in Turkish epics. There are seventeen *rakʿah*s (sequences of prostration) in the ritual prayers of one day, and God's Greatest Name is thought to consist of seventeen letters.

18. Eighteen (2 × 9; 3 × 6) is sacred in Qabbalah, as it is the numerical value of the Hebrew word *ḥay* ("living"). In Islam, it is the number of the letters of the Basmalah, and it is highly respected among the Mevlevi order of dervishes, inasmuch as the introductory verses of Rūmī's *Mathnavī* number eighteen. By extension, the number of the worlds is eighteen thousand. The perfection of eighteen can also be understood from the fact that the Buddha had eighteen principal *arhats*.

19. Nineteen, with the numerical value of *wāḥid* ("one"), is the sacred number of the Bahā'īs, who count a year of nineteen months with nineteen days each.

20–29. Among the lower twenties, twenty-two is the number of letters of the Hebrew alphabet and the number of the great arcana of Tarot. Augustine divided *De civitate Dei* into twenty-two chapters, ten (2 × 5) devoted to refutation (ten negative commandments) and twelve (3 × 4) to positive teachings. Twenty-four can be numerically interpreted in several religiously significant ways (3 × 8; 4 × 6; 12 × 2), and medieval Christian interpreters used whichever combination fit with what they sought to prove. Among the higher twenties, twenty-five is the Jubilee number, and twenty-eight is the lunar number, central to the whole heptadic system.

30–39. Among the thirties, thirty-three means perfection, as a multiple of three, and as the years of Christ's earthly life. For Muslims as for Christians, it is also the age of the blessed in Paradise. Thirty-six, four times the perfect number nine, was in early China the number of the provinces and the foreign peoples beyond the borders.

40. The most important higher number is forty. As the number of days that the Pleiades disappeared (i.e., were not visible), in Babylon forty came to signify a fateful period, connected with expectation and patience. Human pregnancy lasts seven times forty days. Purifications and rites connected with death were measured according to forty in ancient Israel, as they are in Islam. The times of affliction of Israel were counted by forty: the Flood lasted forty days, the wandering in the desert forty years. Moses, Elijah, and Jesus each spent forty days in the wilderness, and Jesus remained forty hours in the grave. Forty is the span of days between the resurrection and ascension of Jesus, and it is the time of preparation for the dervish, who spends forty days in retirement *(chilla),* poetically interpreted in 'Aṭṭār's *Muṣībatnāma.* At forty years man becomes wise; the Prophet of Islam was called to preach at this age. In the Pythagorean system, forty is the perfected tetractys (4 × 10).

Forty often appears in Islamic lore as a coterminus with "very many," such as Ali Baba's forty thieves; groups of forty dervishes, forty saints, or forty Christian martyrs; and the customary selection of forty *ḥadīth,* representing the fullness of the tradition. In the Persian and Turkish tradition, women miraculously give birth to forty children. As forty in the Old Testament means "one generation," it is a temporal measure. In Turkey, where the number forty is extremely popular, great events and feasts last forty days and forty nights; to see someone "once in forty years" means "rarely." In many areas, weather predictions are made for forty days.

50. Fifty (7 × 7 + 1) is the number of the *jobel* year, a year of peace, the divine eternal rest. In connection with Psalm 50, it can point to repentance and forgiveness. A predilection for 50 and 150 is apparent in Irish folk tales.

60. Among the higher numbers, many are endowed with qualities similar to those of the bases in the first decade. Sixty is especially important as the basis for the Babylonian sexagesimal system, in which it forms the higher unit after ten; from these units, sixty and ten, result the multiples that are associated with cosmic time. According to Plato, the "cosmic day" and the "cosmic year" are reckoned by sixties. Because sixty can be easily divided, it still rules our temporal system. The Chinese, who reckon time in cycles of sixty years, have traditionally considered that number as the full complement of a person's life. The Talmud knows fragments of sixtieths: dream is one-sixtieth of prophecy, fire one-sixtieth of hell, and so on.

70–79. Seventy participates in the qualities of seven, and the numbers seventy to seventy-three are often interchanged in the Semitic tradition. Among them, seventy-two is most important; it is one-fifth of the circumference of the circle as well as the product of eight and nine. It usually designates great diversity: from the seventy-two disciples of Christ who were sent into the world to the seventy-two martyrs of Karbala and the seventy-two sects of Islam. Abulafia speaks of the seventy-two letters of the name of the Lord.

Higher numbers. Ninety-nine, the heightened angelic perfection of nine, is the number of the Most Beautiful Names of God in Islam, while one hundred as the new basis of the decimal system, is another complete number. Higher than that is 108 (12 × 9), the number of beads in the Buddhist rosary, the number of books of the Tibetan Kanjur, and the number of beautiful *gopīs* who danced with Lord Kṛṣṇa. Higher still are 360 and 365, which are connected with the annual cycle, and 666, the "number of the beast" (*Rv.* 13), which has been interpreted ever since antiquity as the name of a man particularly detested at various times, be it Nero, Pope Leo X, Luther, Napoleon, or some other. Symbolically, one thousand and ten thousand are both endless; 1,001 thus transgresses the largest imaginable number, while ten thousand means immortality in the Chinese tradition. The enormous numbers of Hindu and Buddhist cosmology form a theme in themselves.

Concluding Remark. The interest in numbers and their specifications continues in spite of the modern scientific worldview, especially among those who seek for a meaningful structure of the world. As Le Corbusier once wrote: "Behind the wall, the gods play; they play with numbers, of which the universe is made up."

BIBLIOGRAPHY

The literature on numbers cannot be numbered; many highly specialized works have been written, especially in German, and a vast literature on modern numerology exists in German, French, and English. As a basic source, the article "Numbers" in the *Encyclopaedia of Religion and Ethics*, vol. 9, edited by James Hastings (Edinburgh, 1917), is still useful. On the development of counting systems, see Karl Menninger's *Number Words and Number Symbols*, translated by Paul Broneer (Cambridge, Mass., 1969). *Numerology* (Baltimore, 1933), a study by Eric T. Bell and others, sharply criticizes numerology from the vantage point of a mathematician. A good survey by Franz C. Endres, *Mystik und Magie der Zahlen*, 3d ed. (Zurich, 1951), has now been updated by my enlarged version of his work, *Das Mysterium der Zahl: Zahlensymbolik im Kultur-Vergleich* (Cologne, 1984). *Number Symbolism* (London, 1970) by Christopher Butler is a useful introduction. Vincent Foster Hopper's *Medieval Number Symbolism* (1938; reprint, Ann Arbor, 1966), an excellent introductory study, has in a certain way been continued by Heinz Meyer's *Die Zahlenallegorese im Mittelalter* (Munich, 1975). For a Jungian approach, see Ludwig Paneth's *Zahlensymbolik im Unbewussten* (Zurich, 1952).

Numerous studies have been devoted to single numbers, primarily three, seven, nine, and thirteen; among them, Desmond Varley's *Seven: The Number of Creation* (London, 1976) stands out not only for its quantity of information but also for its daring hypotheses. Articles on Germanic lore by Karl Weinhold and on classical antiquity by W. H. Roscher, both of whom wrote at the turn of the century, are still fundamental. On the number forty in the Islamic-Turkic tradition, see Abdul Kadir Karahan's "Aperçu général sur les 'Quarante Hadiths' dans la littérature islamique," *Studia Islamica* 4 (1955): 39–55.

ANNEMARIE SCHIMMEL

Binary Symbolism

Binary numbers are a system of counting and computing using two digits, 1 and 0. This system is known today as the principle of the digital computer that represents numbers through the presence (1) and absence (0) of electrical current. The first electronic digital circuit was created in 1919. As early as 1932 binary numeration was used in electronic counting circuits. However, the first binary calculator was designed in 1679 by the great German mathematician and philosopher Gottfried Wilhelm Leibniz (1646–1716), who invented the binary number system. His plan called for using moving balls to represent binary digits. The first completed statement of the number system and its operations was made eighteen years later in a New Year's greeting Leibniz sent to Duke Rudolph Augustus of Brunswick on 2 January 1697. The letter provided a detailed description of a design that Leibniz hoped the duke would strike in the form of a silver medallion. The image reproduced here (see figure 1) was created in 1734 by Rudolph August Nolte following Leibniz's instructions.

The symbol contains three of the chief number systems the Roman, the decimal (base 10), and the binary (base 2). Roman numerals provide the date (1697) of the greeting to the duke, no doubt to "copyright" the system for Leibniz. In the table in the center are the binary numbers up to 10001 and their decimal analogs up to 17. At the sides of the table are examples of binary addition and multiplication. The system was an *imago creationis* ("image of creation"), as Leibniz explained to the duke, because it showed how God, the almighty one, created the world out of nothing, the zero. Thus the caption over the design reads: "2, 3, 4, 5, etc. / For everything to be drawn out of nothing, the one suffices." Leibniz claimed that the binary system practically proved the Christian doctrine of creation *ex nihilo* (the creation of the universe out of nothing, through God's omnipotence) by showing the origin of numbers through the use of one and zero. He decorated the symbol with imagery from the creation myth that appears at the beginning of the *Book of Genesis*. The rays at the top of the design represent the breath of God, the "almighty one," hovering over the waters, the "nothingness and void," in the moment before creation begins. The system also demonstrated the goodness of creation alluded to several times in *Genesis*. Binary numbers revealed the innate order of numerical relations hidden by decimal numbers. For example, the relation between 2, 4, 8, 16, (2, 2^2, 2^3, 2^4), is obviously the same as that between 10, 100, 1000, 10000; hence the asterisks.

Leibniz's cosmogonic symbol documents the great

FIGURE 1. *Leibniz's Symbol*

themes of science and religion in the seventeenth century and their secularizing and syncretistic aspects. The conviction that the universe was a mathematical artifact was almost unanimous among seventeenth-century scientists and philosophers. But this notion did not have a traditional source; scripture provides scant references to God creating with numbers. Instead, it represents the legacy of the Pythagoreans (sixth century BCE), which haunted the Western philosophic tradition for millennia. According to Pythagoras, numbers were the origins of things, proceeding from the relation of the one (limit) and the void (unlimited). The mathematical structure of physical phenomena had been so well realized in the seventeenth century that Leibniz took the equation of numbers and the universe for granted. It was the religious doctrine of creation *ex nihilo* that needed justification. In the letter Leibniz states that the doctrine was one of the main points of Christianity "which have met with the least acceptance on the part of the worldly wise and are not easily imparted to the heathen," making a distinction Paul reserved for the doctrine of the son of God crucified (*1 Cor.* 1:24–25). But in the seventeenth century the Incarnation was no longer the primary manifestation of God. Instead men read of God's activities in the sacred book of nature. Science provided a means to read nature—mathematics—and with it demonstrated the power and wisdom of God in his creation. Leibniz was so convinced of his system's success in making God's creative act transparent that he sent his invention to the Jesuit mathematical tribunal in China. He wrote Duke Rudolph that the emperor of China might now see for himself the mystery of creation and the excellency of the Christian faith. It seems clear that mystery here means a logical conundrum and excellency, rationality. The secularizing of the tradition is confirmed by Leibniz's remark in the letter that he added the imagery from *Genesis*, the breath of God over the waters, "so that something more pleasing than number be on the design." The mythical imagery only ornamented the now reasonable doctrine of creation out of nothing.

Leibniz's symbol is more than a brilliant reflection of seventeenth-century science and religion. It also documents a historical process made possible by the nature of symbolism itself. By making relations between different realms of meaning and experience specific, transparent, and concrete, symbols can remain of continuing relevance beyond their original cultural manifestations, as the rich histories of the one and the zero demonstrate.

Leibniz's ease in combining the Pythagorean doctrine and the Jewish and Christian teaching on creation was made possible by the sacrality of the one. The paradigmatic command of the religion of Israel demanded: "Hear, O Israel: the Lord our God, the Lord is one" (*Dt.* 6:4). In the Hebrew and Arabic languages counting began with two, one being reserved for God alone. Likewise the Pythagoreans did not consider one a number because it generated all numbers—a consideration held by Aristotle and repeated up through the Middle Ages. Leibniz was certainly aware of some of these aspects of the symbolism of the one, but there is no evidence he was aware of the religious associations in the history of the zero. However, Leibniz's appropriation of the zero from the decimal system in his binary number system was just one development in a long process of religious and mathematical creativity.

Place value notation is often hailed as one of mankind's great inventions. In numerical place value the position a number symbol occupies determines its value. As a result a minimum of symbols can convey a maximum of numbers. The success of this mode of numbering depends upon the zero, the symbol of the empty place in a number that preserves the value of the position. As the uncounted counter it makes rapid calculation possible. Though possibly invented independently in several civilizations, the Babylonian and Indian inventions of place value notation were the ones that influenced Leibniz's system.

By 1600 BCE the Babylonian sexagesimal number system (base 60) employed a marker for the empty place. A functional place value symbol was employed in astronomical observations recorded in sexagesimal numbers by 300 BCE. These observations became available to the Greeks, who then used an empty circle for the place value. The sexagesimal number system is still employed in astronomy and in calculations involving circles (degrees, minutes, seconds). The earliest Indian translations of Greek astronomical texts (c. 150 CE) use the Sanskrit words *kha* ("sky") and *bindu* ("dot") for the sexagesimal place value. At the same time, the Indian decimal system was so well developed and widely known that a Buddhist text used place value, the marker of the empty position, to explain how *dharmas* ("elements") exist in time. This was at the time when Nāgārjuna, the founder of Mādhyamika Buddhism, described the reality of *dharmas* by *śūnyatā* ("emptiness"). *Śūnya*, from the Sanskrit root *śvi* (to "swell" and hence "hollow out"), had been used since Vedic times (c. 1000 BCE) as a synonym for words describing the sky or celestial vault, for example, *kha* and *ākāśa* ("ether"). But these words along with *bindu*, were used to name the place value symbol. The subsequent evidence suggests a gradual process of syncretic symbolization. By the third century CE the *bindu* had been used as the decimal place value notation in an Indian astronomical text. In the sixth century *śūnyabindu* was used to name the zero in a metaphor about the stars being ciphers scattered in the sky. *Śūnya* is thereafter found with increasing frequency as the name for the zero. The *bindu* (the dot) was incorporated into the typical Buddhist shrine, the *stūpa.* As the summit it symbolized the point where *śūnyatā* and *dharmadhātu* (the realm of element), were unified as *ākāśa,* the all-pervading ether. Emptiness and plenum were one. It was the realization of the idea of enlightenment.

It remains difficult to specify the exact relation between the religious symbolism of emptiness and the mathematical zero. The mathematical symbol of an emptiness that bears a value seemed an obvious representation of the Buddhist insight into phenomenal and conceptual reality. Interestingly enough, Leibniz's use of the zero in his binary number design gives to it a meaning not altogether different from the Buddhist value and thus helps to clarify what is centrally important. The place value suggested how conditioned or created being was absolutely distinguished from what is ultimately real, yet inseparable from it.

Leibniz took the zero from the decimal system brought to the West from India by the Muslims in the twelfth century. *Zero* and *cipher* both come from Latin transliterations of the Arabic *ṣifr* ("empty"), a straightforward translation of *śūnya.* Its symbols were the dot and the empty circle. Dots are still used today in the ellipsis, to indicate omission.

Knowingly or not, Leibniz drew upon ancient religious and mathematical expressions, the achievements of the cultures of Babylon, Greece, Israel, Arabia, and India, to fashion a number system of unforeseen usefulness. The history of the system manifests the processes of secularization, syncretism, and symbolization, as well as the processes of mathematical invention and discovery. It is a useful reminder of the global nature of the relations of the religions and the sciences. Few today may see the image of creation in their video display terminals, but the changes wrought by the technology employing the binary number system testify to the cosmogonic effectiveness of Leibniz's system.

BIBLIOGRAPHY

The complete text of Leibniz's letter describing his invention is found in his *Deutsche Schriften,* edited by G. E. Guhrauer, vol. 1 (Berlin, 1838), pp. 394–407. An English translation of part of the letter is provided in Florian Cajori's "Leibniz's 'Image of Creation,'" *The Monist* 26 (October 1916): 557–565. It is accompanied by a patronizing discussion of its religious significance. He mentions how Leibniz's system caused the Jesuits in China to interpret the figures of the *I ching* as a binary number system and thus the invention of the zero and binary numbers was attributed to the Chinese. A great part of Leibniz's letter is translated in Anton Glaser's *History of Binary and Other Nondecimal Numeration,* rev. ed. (Los Angeles, 1981), pp. 31–35, but he refrains from including two paragraphs where the references to *Genesis* are quite explicit. He also discusses the history of the *I ching* as a binary system. The book includes a chapter on seventeenth-century experimentation with number systems and an account of the application of binary numbers to electronic computation. The best introduction to the problems inherent in discussing the origin of the zero is Carl B. Boyer's "Zero: The Symbol, the Concept, the Number," *National Mathematics Magazine* 18 (May 1944): 323–330. For a summation of the controversy over the Indian origin of the zero with bibliographic references, see Walter Eugene Clark's "Hindu-Arabic Numerals," in *Indian Studies in Honor of Charles Rockwell Lanman* (Cambridge, Mass., 1929), pp. 217–236. David S. Reugg's "Mathematical and Linguistic Models in Indian Thought: The Case of the Zero and *Śūnyatā*," *Wiener Zeitschrift für die Kunde Südasiens und Archiv für Indische Philosophie* 22 (1978): 171–181, examines new information concerning the history of place value in India and its connection to Buddhism, though he declines to specify any relationship between the mathematical zero and Buddhist doctrines of "emptiness." The symbolism of *bindu* in Buddhist architecture is discussed in Lama Anagarika Govinda's *Psycho-cosmic Symbolism of the Buddhist Stūpa* (Emeryville, Calif., 1976), esp. pp. 92–98.

MICHAEL A. KERZE

NUMEN. The word *numen* is a neuter form ending in *-men* and derived from **nuere* (found in the composite verbs *adnuere,* "agree with a nod of the head," and *abnuere,* "refuse with a nod of the head"). The formation is Latin, even though it is based on an Indo-European root, **neu-,* which produced a parallel word of the same meaning in Greek, *neuma. Numen* is semantically related to *nutus* ("nod of the head"), as correctly pointed out by Varro: "numen . . . dictum ab nutu" (*De lingua Latina* 7.85). It signifies the manifestation, will, or power of a divinity. Since this is its characteristic meaning until the end of the republic (including Cicero), *numen* never appears unless accompanied by the genitive form of the divinity's name. The most ancient example is in a text of Accius cited by Varro: "Alia hic sanctitudo est aliud nomen et numen Iouis" ("Here, the holiness of Jupiter is one thing, the name and power of Jupiter another"; *De lingua Latina* 7.85).

This usage is also reflected in the balanced definition of Festus: "The numen is, as it were, the nod or power of a god" (Festus, ed. Lindsay, 1913, p. 178 L.). Even when the poets of the Augustan period began to substitute at times *numina* for *dei,* by way of simplication and, often, metric accommodation, the ancient usage still made itself felt. Theodor Birt has shown that Vergil was able to maintain the original sense of the word in a phrase from the opening verses of the *Aeneid* (1.8), "quo numine laeso," which here refers to the queen of the gods and can only mean "in consequence of the violation of her [Juno's] will."

Certain scholars, in search of "primitive culture," have tried to give a completely different orientation to the Latin term by identifying *numen* with a Melanesian word, *mana.* In his book *The Melanesians,* R. H. Codrington in 1891 advanced the latter term, as meaning an "autonomous, impersonal force." This assimilation of *numen* to "an impersonal active power" led Hendrik Wagenvoort to pass over the constant usage of the republican period and to postulate a pre-deist world that in Rome would have preceded the advent of personal divinities. He reached the point of questioning the antiquity of the expression *di novensiles.* He preferred to shorten it simply to *novensiles.* Interpreted in his own way, novensiles would mean, with reference to *numen (*nou-men),* "filled with motive power." This etymological lucubration would be no more than a venial fault if at the same time it did not betray a serious error of perspective. Indeed, the attempt to abolish every individual and personal divinity at the origins of Rome results in misunderstanding the universality of an Indo-European fact: the presence of the term **deiwos* for the idea of divinity, represented at the eastern and western extremes of the Indo-European domain. *Numen,* from the ancient times until Vergil, only expresses the manifestation of a **deiwos* become *deus* in Latin.

BIBLIOGRAPHY

Dumézil, Georges. *Archaic Roman Religion.* 2 vols. Translated by Philip Krapp. Chicago, 1970.

Meillet, Antoine. "La religion indo-européenne." In *Linguistique historique et linguistique générale.* Paris, 1948. See pages 323–334 and, above all, page 326 on **deiwos.*

Pfister, Friedrich. "Numen." In *Paulys Real-encyclopädie,* vol. 17. Stuttgart, 1937. See especially pages 1273–1274, a fact list of the republican epoch.

Rose, H. J. *Primitive Culture in Italy.* 1926.

Wagenvoort, Hendrick. *Roman Dynamism.* Oxford, 1947. See pages 73–103 and, in particular, pages 75 and 83–85, which provide an exegesis of *novensilis.*

ROBERT SCHILLING

Translated from French by Paul C. Duggan

NUMINOUS, THE. *See* Numen; Sacred and the Profane, The; Holy, Idea of the; *and the biography of Rudolf Otto.*

NUM-TŪREM. The Khanty (Ostiaks) and the Mansi (Voguls) live in an area in northwestern Siberia bordered on the west by the Ural Mountains. For the most part, they are settled on the banks of the rivers there, with the Ob River flowing through the middle of their territory. As speakers of Ugric languages, they are thus known as the Ob-Ugrians. Fishing and hunting are their most important means of subsistence, although some of these peoples tend reindeer and others, especially in the southern part of the area, farm and keep livestock. Their widely differing languages belong to the Finno-Ugric family. Similar living conditions and a neighborly relationship have produced similarities in both material and spiritual culture, but the obvious variations that are nonetheless found lead scholars to distinguish between different cultural areas. The boundaries between these are fluid, however, so that certain phenomena—in this case the god of the heavens—may be treated as common to all of them.

The Ob-Ugrians, like other peoples of northern Siberia, consider that the universe consists of several worlds: earth, an upper world, and a netherworld. Popular tradition divides the upper world into a number of spheres—certain stories speak of three, others of seven—and each world is ruled by its own deity.

Prayers and the stereotyped formulas that accompany sacrificial rites address a god of the heavens as Num-Tūrem (Khanty) or Numi-Tārem (Mansi). *Tūrem* or *tārem* is interpreted as "up there" or "the high god." *Num* or *numi* denotes the visible sky, while *tūrem* or *tārem* expresses "weather, air, sky, heavens, world," "higher being, lord of the heavens," and "lord of the universe"; it may therefore be a general expression for "god." According to K. F. Karjalainen, the word also means "time" or "period of time"—for instance, "lifetime"—as well as "situation" or "state"—"state of dreaming," for example. There are different theories as to its etymology. Attempts have been made to link it to the Saami (Lapp) *Tiermes,* the name of a god of the air and heavens, or to the Turco-Tatar *tengri,* meaning "heavens." [*See* Tengri.]

However, the sky god has many other names in which the adjectival epithet indicates its nature; he is "great," "radiant," "bright," "lustrous as gold," and "white" as well as "Lord" and "Father." These epithets are important; some of them have become detached from their head-words to serve as proper names. Thus the name of the Khanty god of the heavens is Sängke-Tūrem, "the radiant or bright Tūrem," or quite simply Sängke ("light"), which indicates the god's connection with the sun or the sky in daylight.

Num-Tūrem is a powerful being in folk poetry; he takes part in the creation of both the world and man, and as such he is also a god of fate worshiped in various ways by the two peoples. He is never portrayed in pictures, however, although in mythical accounts he is personified. In the Khanty myths he is enthroned as an anthropomorphic (male) deity in one of the upper worlds, where he lives with his family and a large retinue (like that of a prince). From there he supervises the entire creation: his ears "great as the Ob" hear everything, his eyes "large as lakes" see all, and he is all-powerful. Since nothing is hidden from him, he is also regarded as the guard of morals and justice. Many scholars, however, hold that this omnipotence bears traces of foreign influence from Islam, Orthodox Christianity, and Turco-Tatar myths concerning their major deities. We know from historical sources that the Mansi heard Christian sermons as early as the fifteenth century and that the Tatars acquired a certain influence in the Khanty area, thus spreading both their own popular beliefs and Muslim doctrine.

Although Num-Tūrem is the Ob-Ugric god about whom the most numerous and most detailed stories have been told, he nevertheless does not seem to be worshiped by all the different groups with a special cult dedicated to him alone, nor does he have a specific field of activity. He is revered and asked to bring good health, prosperity, and good hunting, the same favors that are requested of other divinities such as the god of the forest, the Old Man of the Urals, the Great Goddess of Kazym, called Vut-imi, and Jalpus, the guardian spirit of the Khanty. Compared with other deities Num-Tūrem is more of an abstraction.

Although the narrative tradition centering on Num-Tūrem is richer among the Mansi, it is the Khanty of the southeast who perform the most elaborate sacrifices to him. These offerings, in which a white horse is the most important sacrificial animal, are addressed directly to him. This southeastern group of Khanty are small-scale farmers, and it is believed that they may have acquired these horse sacrifices from the nomadic Tatar horsemen and more generally from the large-scale stock breeders of Central Asia, since the horse does not belong to the biotope of this northern area. Extensive sacrifices to different deities were still being performed as recently as the 1930s. Similarly, the fact that the god of the heavens is ranked as the supreme being and father is ascribed to Muslim and Christian influence. In other areas, among the other Ob-Ugric hunters and reindeer breeders, sacrifices are much less prominent in the worship of the god, although he is the focus of an elaborate myth.

According to K. F. Karjalainen and others, the Ob-Ugric god of the heavens was regarded originally as a personal being "in the upper world nearest the earth," that is, in the visible sky. He was a *deus otiosus*, high above and far away from man's everyday life, mostly responsible for such atmospheric phenomena as storms, the wind, thunder, rain, and so on. He was Num-Tūrem, the "god on high," but Islamic and Christian influences brought him nearer to man and the old sacrificial custom was invested with a new conceptual framework.

Judging from the fragments at our disposal, the god of thunder known by the eastern Saami as Diermes or Tiermes also has uranian features. The etymology of the word is unknown, but *Tiermes* and *Tūrem* probably have a common origin. The name occurs very rarely in source materials, however. This and the fact that his function is only vaguely indicated make him a very elusive being.

[*See also* Khanty and Mansi Religion *and* Sky, *article on* The Heavens as Hierophany.]

BIBLIOGRAPHY

Russian chroniclers mention Ob-Ugric religion as early as the twelfth century. K. F. Karjalainen has compiled available information in the first part of a detailed survey, *Die Religion der Jugra-Völker*, 3 vols., "Folklore Fellow Communications," nos. 41, 44, and 63 (Helsinki, 1921, 1922, 1927). Much earlier, in *Die Weltgottheiten der wogulischen Mythologie*, vol. 3, "Keleti Szemle," no. 9 (Budapest, 1908), Bernhard Munkàcsi wrote about the Mansi supreme deity, giving him thoroughly Christian features. Munckàcsi's very worthwhile work contains both prayers and mythological narratives. An important treatment of mythology is Artturi Kannisto's *Materialien zur Mythologie der Wogulen*, edited by E. A. Virtanen and Matti Liimola (Helsinki, 1958). Other valuable information can be found in A. F. Anisimov's "Cosmological Concepts of the Peoples of the North," in *Studies in Siberian Shamanism*, edited by Henry N. Michael (Toronto, 1963), pp. 157–229; this work is number 4 in the series "Anthropology of the North: Translations from Russian Sources," issued by the Arctic Institute of North America. The Russian ethnographer Zoia Sokolova is an expert on the Ob-Ugrians and has described the people and their traditions in *Das Land Jugorien* (Moscow and Leipzig, 1982), where she notes that their tenacious religious beliefs and superstitions live on in their contemporary religious practices.

LOUISE BÄCKMAN

NUNS. *See* Monasticism *and* Religious Communities.

NŪR MUḤAMMAD ("light of Muḥammad") or *nūr Muḥammadī* ("Muhammadan light") is a term central to later Ṣūfī and Shīʿī speculation. Although the Qurʾān repeatedly states that Muḥammad is only human, a messenger entrusted with the guidance of the people (see surahs 6:50, 25:8, 25:22), later currents in Islam transformed him increasingly into a spiritual, luminous being. The historical Muḥammad was thus metamorphosed into a transcendent light, like the sun, around which everything created revolves. This idea has colored later mystical Islam on both the elite and folk levels.

The basis for such speculations, however, was found in the Qur'ān, where Muḥammad is called "a shining lamp" (*sirāj munīr,* 33:45) and where it is said, "There came to you from God a light and a clear book" (5:15). Ḥassān ibn Thābit, the Medinese poet who eulogized Muḥammad, reflects these ideas in his verse; he is the first in a long series of writers to compare the face of the Prophet to the full moon at night, a comparison that plays on the words *badr* ("full moon") and *Badr,* the name of the site of the Muslims' first victorious battle in 624.

Such poetical expressions, however, still lacked a theological basis. It was left to the theologian Muqātil (d. 767?) to interpret the famous "light verse" of the Qur'ān (24:35) as a reference to the Prophet:

> God is the light of the heavens and the earth; the likeness of his light is as a niche wherein there is a lamp, the lamp in a glass, the glass as it were a glittering star, kindled from a blessed tree, an olive tree neither of the East nor of the West, whose oil wellnigh would shine, even if no fire touched it. Light upon light. God guides to his light whom he will. And God strikes similitudes for man, and God has knowledge of everything.

It is the lamp, *miṣbāḥ,* that Muqātil sees as a fitting symbol for Muḥammad; through him the divine light shines upon the world, and through him humanity is guided to the origin of this light. The formula "neither of the East nor of the West" could then be taken as a reference to Muḥammad's comprehensive nature, which is not restricted to one specific people or race and which transcends the boundaries of time and space.

Up to the present day one of the most common epithets used for the Prophet is *nūr al-hudā* ("the light of right guidance"), and allusions to his luminous nature are found even in the titles of *ḥadith* collections, such as *Mashāriq al-anwār* (The Rising Points of Lights), *Maṣābīḥ al-sunnah* (The Lamps of the *Sunnah*), or *Mishkāt al-maṣābīḥ* (The Niche for Lamps). Likewise, through the centuries one of the most famous prayers attributed to Muḥammad is the prayer for light:

> O God, place light in my heart, light in my soul, light upon my tongue, light in my eyes, and light in my ears; place light at my right, light at my left, light behind me, and light before me, light above me, and light beneath me. Place light in my nerves, and light in my flesh, light in my blood, light in my hair and light in my skin. Give me light, increase my light, make me light.

Theories about Muḥammad's luminous nature began to develop, on the basis of Muqātil's exegesis, in the second half of the ninth century. The Iraqi Ṣūfī Sahl al-Tustarī (d. 896) was the first to express the whole *Heilsgeschichte* in the terminology of the light of Muḥammad as suggested in the light verse. The inaccessible divine mystery of light articulates itself in the pre-eternal manifestation of "the likeness of his light." The origin of the *nūr Muḥammad* in pre-eternity is depicted as "a luminous mass of primordial adoration in the presence of God, which takes the shape of a transparent column of divine light and constitutes Muḥammad as the primal creation of God" (Böwering, 1980). When this light reached "the veil of majesty," it prostrated itself before God, and from its prostration God formed a mighty column, one both outwardly and inwardly translucent. Sahl even interpreted surah 53:13, "And he saw [God] still another time," as pertaining to the beginning of time, when this luminous column was standing before God in worship "with the disposition of faith, and [to him] was unveiled the mystery of the mystery itself 'at the Lote-tree of the Boundary.'" Then, when the actual creation began, God created Adam, and finally all else that exists, from the light of Muḥammad. The light is thus seen as the primordial material out of which everything is formed; it becomes the ultimate source of existence, and through Muḥammad, the historical form of this light, beings become illuminated, thus participating in the divine light as embodied in the actual Prophet.

Sahl's high-soaring speculations were elaborated more poetically by his disciple al-Ḥallāj (d. 922), who devoted the first chapter of his *Kitāb al-ṭawāsīn* to Muḥammad, calling it *Ṭāsīn al-sirāj* (The *Ṭāsīn* of the Lamp, alluding to the Arabic letters *ṭā* and *sīn* found at the head of surah 27):

> He was a lamp from the light of the invisible . . . a moon radiating among the moons, whose mansion is in the sphere of mysteries . . . . The lights of prophethood—from his light did they spring forth, and their lights appeared from his light, and there is no light among the lights more luminous and more visible and previous to preexistence than the light of this noble one.

As preceding preexistence, Muḥammad is seen as absolutely eternal, mentioned "before the Before and after the After."

Al-Ḥallāj's rhyming prose was written less than three centuries after Muḥammad's death. During those years there appeared several *ḥadīth* pointing to the mystery of the *nūr Muḥammad:* "The first thing God created was my light," says the Prophet, and his remark, "My companions are like stars," fits well with his role as the central sun or the full moon of the world.

The Ṣūfīs lovingly interpreted this idea. Al-Thaʿlabī (d. 1038), in his *ʿArāʾis al-bayān,* written shortly after the year 1000, cites a colorful myth in which the light appears as a radiant pearl. Najm Dāyā Rāzī, in the early thirteenth century, offers an elaborate story of creation using similar imagery; the pearling drops of sweat that emerge from the primordial *nūr Muḥammad* are the substance out of which the 124,000 prophets sent before Muḥammad were created. ʿAbd al-Karīm al-Jīlī (d. 1408?) elaborates on this idea by comparing the *nūr Muḥammad*—also interpreted as the *ḥaqīqah muḥammadīyah*, the archetypal "Muhammadan reality"—to a luminous pearl, or a white chrysolith, which grows embarrassed when God looks at it lovingly and thus begins to perspire, finally dissolving into waves and other watery substances out of which the created world emerges.

This image has inspired hundreds of poets in the Islamic world. In the sixteenth century, for example, a Turkish poet, Khāqānī, speaks in his *ḥilyah* (the poetical description of the Prophet's noble features and qualities) of this event: "God loved this light and said 'My beloved friend!' and became enamored of this light." Overwhelmed by this divine love, the primordial Muhammadan light produced drops of perspiration from bashfulness, and from them the world emerged in descending degrees. The same idea is found in Bengali mystical folk poetry of the fifteenth and sixteenth centuries, especially in the work of Shaykh Chānd.

Sahl's ideas of the column of light seem to have been quite well known in mystical circles even before their systematization by Ibn al-ʿArabī (d. 1240) in the first half of the thirteenth century. Few passages in medieval Persian poetry prior to Ibn al-ʿArabī reflect this idea more eloquently than those of Farīd al-Dīn ʿAṭṭār (d. 1220). In the introduction of his epic *Manṭiq al-ṭayr* (The Conversation of the Birds), ʿAṭṭār speaks of how, from this Muhammadan light, the divine Throne, Footstool, Pen, and Tablet appeared, and how the great light then prostrated itself before the Lord and remained for ages in prostration, genuflection, and standing, thus prefiguring the movements of Muslim ritual prayer. The Turkish mystical poet Yunus Emre (d. 1321) puts in God's mouth the words.

> I created him from my own light
> And I love him yesterday and today.
> What would I do with the world without him?
> My Muḥammad, my Aḥmad of light!

In the same period, a Ṣūfī in India claimed that the light of Muḥammad became embodied in the Prophet's person "just as the light of the moon is taken from the sun." For the faithful, the participation in the light of Muḥammad is the goal of life, for whosoever is surrounded by this uncreated light will not be touched by the created fire of Hell.

That the idea of the Muhammadan light was popular even before Ibn al-ʿArabī is clear from the very title of al-Ghazālī's (d. 1111) booklet *Mishkāt al-anwār* (The Niche for Lights), which contains his prophetology, in which Muḥammad appears as the *muṭāʿ* ("one who is obeyed"). This attribution also occurs quite frequently in poetry at later periods; there, however, it does not assume the mysterious role as a kind of demiurge, a being between the undifferentiated One and the phenomenal world, as described by al-Ghazālī. For him, this primordial "light of lights" illuminates the darkness, and, even more, it brings all things into manifestation out of "not-being."

These theories on the *nūr Muḥammad* were, like so many early trends in Sufism, elaborated and systematized by Ibn al-ʿArabī, who states in his probably spurious profession of faith that "the first light appears out of the veil of the Unseen and from knowledge to concrete existence and is the light of our prophet Muḥammad." He then goes on to compare Muḥammad, the *sirāj munīr*, to the sun and infers that the heavenly intelligences, the spirits, the intuitions, and the essences are nourished by the luminous essence of (Muḥammad) Muṣṭafā the Elect, "who is the sun of existence." In philosophical terms, with Muḥammad, the first self-determination of the Absolute, the Divine begins to manifest itself gradually to the world, and the primordial light, which has permeated all prophets from the beginning, reaches its full development in the Perfect Man, the historical prophet Muḥammad.

As such, Muḥammad is praised in ever new images. It is no accident that the literature dealing with his miraculous birth always points to the light that shone from his father's forehead and was carried in Amīnah's womb; following the Prophet's birth, this light illuminated the world to the castles of Bostra in Syria. Muḥammad is the *shamʿ-i maḥfil*, the "candle of the assembly," which illuminates the night of this world as medieval Persian poets wrote; and it is "the light of his name" by which the Muslims should bring light into the darkness of our time, as Muhammad Iqbal (d. 1938), the Indo-Pakistani modernist poet, says in his Urdu poem *Answer to [Man's] Complaint* (1912). The mystics and poets were happy to interpret the beginning of surah 93 ("By the morning light!") as pertaining to Muḥammad's radiant face, which represents at the same time the radiance of faith—an image probably coined by Sanāʾī of Ghaznah (d. 1131?) and lovingly repeated through the centuries by poets in all parts of the Muslim world.

One can say without exaggeration that, in eulogies composed for Muḥammad, his luminous character is among those features most frequently noted. One finds, for example, mention of the Prophet as "the light of all lights" and the beliefs that he did not cast a shadow and that his light was visible in the dark night. Following these ideas, calligraphers writing in Arabic found it logical that none of the Prophet's original names—Muḥammad, Aḥmad, Ḥāmid, and Maḥmūd—nor his epithet—*rasūl Allāh* ("messenger of God")—was written with diacritical marks. One even finds attempts to write eulogies for him in which all diacritical marks are left out as a way of stressing his luminous purity.

The origin and early development of the theory of the light of Muḥammad are difficult to trace. One source of this mysticism of light might have been Hellenistic gnostic speculations. Shīʿī theories about the light of the imams also may have strongly contributed to the development of these ideas. Ibn al-ʿArabī associated this concept with the tradition *(ḥadīth qudsī)* in which God says, "I was a hidden treasure and wanted to be known; therefore I created the world." Following Ibn al-ʿArabī's lead, Jāmī (d. 1492) addressed the Prophet in this manner:

> From "I was a treasure" your true nature has become clear:
> Your person is the mirror of the unqualified light.

According to Ibn al-ʿArabī and his followers, the *nūr Muḥammad* appears in all prophets, each of them bearing a certain particle of this light, as well as those mystics who tried to reach union with the *ḥaqīqah muḥammadīyah.* These individuals sometimes claimed that they were in the heights with the light of Muḥammad long before Adam was created. The historical Muḥammad is thus endowed with the "totalizing nature" comprising all the divine names and forming the principle in which the divine light can reflect its glory in order to be known and loved. His relation to the inaccessible essence of light is like that of the sunlight in relation to the sun.

On the basis of these ideas later writers compared Muḥammad to the dawn that appears at the border between night and day, between human contingent existence and divine reality. The *nūr Muḥammad* thus becomes a central concept that appears in varied expressions in the Islamic world, and although the emphasis in prophetology has tended to shift from the mythical Muḥammad to the historical man Muḥammad, the "light of guidance" is still admired and praised in the verses of mystically minded poets.

BIBLIOGRAPHY

For more on the *nūr Muḥammad,* see William H. T. Gairdner's translation, *Al-Ghazzālī's Mishkāt al-anwār ("The Niche for Lights")* (1924; reprint, Lahore, 1952). A better translation of the *Mishkāt* is Roger Deladrière's *Le tabernacle des Lumières* (Paris, 1981). Indispensable for the study of the *nūr Muḥammad* is Tor Andrae's important work *Die person Muhammeds in lehre und glauben seiner gemeinde* (Stockholm, 1918). Andrae deals especially with the transformation of the image of Muḥammad as reflected in Islamic mysticism and theology. My own *And Muhammad Is His Messenger* (Chapel Hill, 1985) is a survey of the veneration of Muḥammad in mystical and popular traditions. See also Louis Massignon's classic study *The Passion of al-Hallaj: Mystic and Martyr of Islam,* 4 vols., translated by Herbert Mason (Princeton, 1982), and Gerhard Böwering's *The Mystical Vision of Existence in Classical Islam: The Qur'ānic Hermeneutics of the Ṣūfī Sahl al-Tustarī (d. 283/896)* (Berlin and New York, 1980). Robert C. Zaehner's *Hindu and Muslim Mysticism* (New York, 1969) is an original work that compares Sufism and Hindu mysticism and contains some interesting observations on the *nūr Muḥammad.*

ANNEMARIE SCHIMMEL

NUṢAYRĪYAH. *See* ʿAlawīyūn.

NYAKYUSA RELIGION. The traditional religion of the Nyakyusa-speaking people and of the neighboring Ngonde (who speak a dialect of the same language) was closely observed from 1934 to 1938 and again in 1955. The Nyakyusa occupied the fertile Rungwe Valley of what is now Tanzania, 9° south longitude, 34° east latitude; the Ngonde occupied the adjoining plain in what is now Malawi. Together they numbered perhaps half a million. They were settled cultivators and herdsmen, rotating crops and sustaining banana groves with manure from the byres. Groups of thirty to fifty age mates, with their wives and young children, lived together in villages. The religion of this distinctive people was expressed in two cycles of rituals, one concerning families, the other chiefdoms and groups of chiefdoms. Celebration of these rituals involved acting out dramas that expressed the proper relationships among humans and between humanity and divinity; in essence, they were intended to both regulate human behavior and to mediate between human and divine realms.

There was little elaboration of dogma, though the family rituals were shaped by a conviction that kinsmen, living and dead, were inextricably bound together, by the definition of kinship and by marriage law. Communal rituals were shaped by a mythological charter concerning the coming of certain chiefly lineages which had brought fire, iron, and cattle to a people who had no chiefs, no iron, and no cattle, and who ate their food raw. Theological speculation was expressed through a general awareness of symbolism—a "common symbolic language" of which poets speak. Fire was recognized as representing "lordship" and authority; "eating food raw" was the mark both of a witch and of a person without culture. A detailed interpretation of symbolism was provided by specialists—priests and doctors (both men and women) and by elderly people in general. The associations given here are not the product of guesswork, but rest on the statements given by participants in the rituals. In a rapidly changing and diverse society much of ancient symbolism may become a forgotten language.

The occasions for celebration of family rituals were death and birth, especially abnormal birth; maturity and marriage; and misfortune. The essence of each ritual was a purification, the participants washing and shaving with medicines; a "speaking out," for any individuals who came to the ritual with "anger in the heart" must admit that anger openly and cease to nurse any grudge against those with whom they celebrated; and a communion feast in which living and dead kin shared beer, the staple foods (which varied with altitude), and, at a funeral, beef. Each ritual implied a change in status for the chief participants: spouse, parent, sibling, and child, at a funeral; parents if twins were born, or the mother alone at an ordinary birth; a girl at first menstruation; and her groom as she moved from the confinement at puberty to marriage. But kinsmen also celebrated and were obliged to do so, the range being further in the father's than in the mother's line and varying with the type of ritual. The explicit reason given for celebrating was that the chief mourners, parents of twins, or nubile girl would go mad should the ritual be neglected, and indeed the "actions of a madman" were mimed in the death ritual—mimed and rejected—for the ritual was directed at ensuring acceptance of a new life, a new place in society for a distraught widow, a girl who had grown up, a young mother, or a man bereaved, married, or fearful as the father of twins. In every ritual the chief participants symbolically died and were reborn, and while in the world of the dead they were "brooded over" by the shades. This was something terrible, for the shades, though kinsmen, were numinous, and the awfulness of divinity oppressed humans, who sought to separate themselves from it.

Celebrations for a chiefdom were of various sorts. The first was the coronation ritual during which two heirs (for a chiefdom should split each generation) were secluded with the commoners chosen by the older generation to be their village headmen, instructed in their future duties, and treated with medicines to make them respected—men of authority. At a given signal the young men burst out of the seclusion hut and rushed out to the pasturage, where each chief and his senior headman made fire by friction. All fires throughout the country had been extinguished, and each new fire had to be lit from that of the chief. Each of the heirs established authority in one half of the country and planted two trees and a stone commemorating his coronation and royal marriage. Land in the chiefdom was reallocated, with the older generation moving aside to make way for the younger. The old chief was expected to "die soon," for fertility in men, land, and cattle was believed to be dependent upon the vitality of the chief, and an old, ailing chief was unacceptable. He was smothered and buried beside the trees planted at his coronation.

The second sort of celebration for a chiefdom involved the slaughter of a cow and prayers offered to a former ruler in the sacred grove that had sprung up around his burial place. There no one might chop wood or cultivate, and, as a result, the vegetation in such a sacred place would eventually grow into a forest.

Third, a general purification was held at the break of the rains after the dry season or in national emergency. All the old ashes from homestead fires were thrown out, and grudges between people were openly admitted.

Regional celebrations concerning a group of chiefdoms were directed to a founding hero in his grove. Prayers for rain, fertility, and health for the whole region were then offered. The two greatest of the heroes, Lwembe and Kyungu, had living representatives who were thought to exercise power over rain and fertility, and they too were honored. Lwembe's grove contained a great python (a creature held to represent the hero) that was believed to lick Lwembe's priest, who spent a night alone in the grove, protected by a wicker cage.

The name of one founding hero, Kyala, to whom offerings were made in a cave, was used not only for the hero but also in the sense of "the lord," and it was used by the first missionaries (in 1891) to translate the Christian conception of God. As traditional Nyakyusa religion interacted with Christianity, the idea of a god wholly distinct from the heroes became more and more clear: in 1934 old men still spoke of Kyala "beneath" with the shades, but to most young men—traditional as well as Christian—he was "above" *(kumwanya)*, and "above" implied then "in the sky" rather than "on earth" (as opposed to beneath the earth).

The celebrations for Lwembe crossed language as well as political boundaries. Priests brought iron hoes and salt, commodities from the mountains to the east, as gifts to the shrine. People in the rich Rungwe Valley traded grain, pulses, and bananas for these commodities. Kyungu was sent iron hoes and ivory from the mountains surrounding the Ngonde Plain, and unlike Lwembe, he gradually developed secular power and became a chief with subordinate chiefs under him.

Besides celebrations for the shades of a family, chiefdom, or region, Nyakyusa speakers had a lively belief in witchcraft, a mystical power thought to be exercised by certain persons (for selfish purposes) to injure others. Witches were spoken of as greedy, envious, and as consumed with jealousy and anger against their neighbors. They killed men and cattle and caused grain to diminish and cows to dry up by reason of a "python in the belly" that worked evil. So real was this python in imagination that it was sought in autopsies, which were performed both to discover the mystical cause of death and to prove whether the dead person had been a witch.

Witchcraft was wholly evil, but a power akin to it was thought to be properly exercised by village headmen and others to protect a village against the attacks of witches. People known as *abamanga* ("the strong ones") were said to fight witches in dreams. Commoners—the ordinary people—were thought to punish an inhospitable chief or one who had given an unjust judgment in court, or any member of their village who was mean, inhospitable, too conspicuously successful, or who committed some breach of customary obligation such as neglecting a ward or insulting a father. The "breath of men"—murmurs of outraged public opinion—was believed to fall on the miscreant and cause him or her to fall ill of a fever, pine away, or become paralyzed.

There were also "medicines" *(imiti)*, chiefly vegetable substances thought to be used for both good and evil ends: to kill or cure, to destroy or promote crops, to murder or to maintain constituted authority.

The moral aspect of religion was constantly stressed: a man who was good was protected by his shades, and his family, stock, and crops increased; a chief who loved and cherished his men and ancestors attracted followers; if the founding hero and his living representative were duly honored, the region would be blessed with gentle rain. The good man gave no cause for offense and hoped never to arouse the anger of a neighbor who was a witch or sorcerer. Evil was personified in witchcraft, but any sort of power might be misused. A father who cursed his son or daughter so that the child became sterile should forgive and bless the child when he or she begged pardon with an appropriate gift, even if the anger was justified. The angered father might say, "I forgive you now" and spit on the ground, and all the anger that was in him would come out like spit. Rituals had to be celebrated, correct in every detail, but if participants nursed anger in the heart no ritual could be efficacious. Anger was the root of misfortune.

Like other societies, Nyakyusa society has never been static. The coronation rituals and offerings on behalf of chiefs and regions explicitly celebrated a change that had once occurred: the coming of heroes who brought fire, iron, cattle, and the institution of chieftainship. This was pictured as a single event that had occurred ten generations back. Archaeologists are now tracing the spread of iron and of cattle in Africa, and the first hearths are being sought. Chieftainship, including the secular power of the Kyungu, is known to have spread within historical times. The myths therefore recall real events, but they telescope time. Events such as the domestication of fire and first forging of iron, separated perhaps by a million years, are fused with the coming of cattle and the institution of chieftainship as symbols of the beginning of civilized life.

From 1891 onward, with the coming of Christian missions, trade, and colonial rule, the pace of change accelerated greatly. By 1938, 16 percent of the population in the Rungwe Valley and more on the Ngonde Plain were professing Christians and had largely abandoned traditional rituals; by 1955 even those who did not profess Christianity had curtailed or abandoned some of the rituals, notably that on the birth of twins; and after the independence of Tanganyika in 1961 the institution of chieftainship was abolished in Rungwe Valley and coronation rituals lapsed.

Two trends are clear: first, a growing importance to most people of the idea of God (Kyala) distinct from shades and heroes, and of prayer and worship directed to him; second, a lessening of fear of contamination in death and birth. A sense of the awfulness of divinity and of biological processes in which divinity was manifest have decreased.

Celebration of rituals may be observed and accounts of dogma and myth recorded, but evidence of religious experience is difficult to document. Many people spoke of a sense of presence of the shades in dreams and waking moments, and if a wife or child were ill a man might go to his banana grove with his calabash cup at dusk and blow out water, expressing himself in love and charity with all, living and dead, and calling upon his shades for blessing; but repeated dreams of the dead were feared as an omen of death, and the period of seclusion during a ritual, when the participant dwelt with the shades was felt to be deeply distasteful. Christian converts, familiar with the traditional patterns, asserted that they valued a sense of presence and communion with God in a different manner from any traditional communion with divinity. All were aware of the destructive power of evil within men and sought to purge themselves and others of it.

BIBLIOGRAPHY

Park, George K. "Kinga Priests: The Politics of Pestilence." In *Political Anthropology*, edited by Marc J. Swartz, Victor Turner, and Arthur Tuden, pp. 229–237. Chicago, 1966. Compares Kinga with Nyakyusa priesthood.

Wilson, Monica. *Good Company: A Study of Nyakyusa Age-Villages*. London, 1951. An account of Nyakyusa and Ngonde people, particularly of age-villages and accusations of witchcraft.

Wilson, Monica. *Rituals of Kinship among the Nyakyusa.* London, 1957.

Wilson, Monica. *Communal Rituals of the Nyakyusa.* London, 1959. Descriptions of rituals and interpretations of their symbolism based on associations made by participants.

Wilson, Monica. *For Men and Elders.* London, 1977. Change among the Nyakyusa and Ngonde from 1875 to 1971, with particular reference to marriage and relationships between generations.

MONICA WILSON

NYAME is the supreme god among the Akan peoples of present-day Ghana and the Ivory Coast, including the Twi and Ashanti. Nyame has a variety of other names, including Onyame and Onyankopon. The origin of the name is disputed: some have claimed that it is derived from the Akan word *nyam* ("glory, shining, bright, sky"); others claim it comes from the Akan word *nyan* ("to wake, to arise," i.e., "the awakener"). The origin of the name may even be more prosaic, however, since it is similar to the Bambara *nyama*, which simply means "force" or "spirit of nature."

Nyame is held in high regard by the Akan peoples and is given many praise names, such as Twereduampon ("lean on a tree do not fall"), Odomankama ("he who gives in abundance"), and Abommubuwafre ("the one on whom we call in distress"). As the supreme being, Nyame is believed to be the creator, carving the world into existence. He is also depicted as a spider who weaves the creation into existence as he, Nyame, sits at the center (J. B. Danquah states that Nyame is sometimes identified as Ananse, "the spider"). Furthermore, Nyame is not only the giver but also the sustainer of life; he is believed to be all-seeing and all-powerful.

According to Akan mythology, divinity and humanity were originally much closer together than they are today. In fact, they were so close that humans could literally reach up and touch the deity. One day, a woman pounded *fufu* (mashed yams or plantains) in a mortar and hit the deity repeatedly with her pestle, so angering the deity that he withdrew from the earth. Ever since then, there has been a separation between Nyame, who now dwells in the sky, and mankind. As in many other West African religions, most immediate problems are mediated by lesser deities or ancestors.

Among the Ashanti people R. S. Rattray reports that there is a cult of Nyame. This cult consists of priests, temples, and limited public observances; in fact, almost every Ashanti house had a small shrine dedicated to Nyame. The shrines that Rattray saw most frequently consisted of a three-forked stick set in the ground with a pot containing water placed in the center. Neolithic celts ("God's axes," according to the Ashanti) are placed in the water, and other offerings are left at the shrine. This association of cult objects commonly found in the cult of deities of lightning, such as Ṣango among the Yoruba, leads one to speculate about a possible historical connection or diffusion of this cult, but lack of historical data leaves it a mere speculation.

In the cult of Nyame among the Ashanti, the priests wear special insignia (two gold crescents with depictions of the sun, the moon, and the stars) and shave their heads in a particular manner. At the annual ceremony, sacrifices are made to Nyame for eight days in succession, after which two white fowl are killed in his honor.

Lastly, it should be pointed out that while Nyame is an extremely powerful figure, from whom all life and spiritual power ultimately derive, most Ashanti rituals, like those of other Akan peoples who acknowledge Nyame as supreme in their pantheon, deal with lesser deities (*obosom*, in Ashanti). These lesser deities, like the Yoruba *oriṣa*, are the spiritual figures who oversee and regulate the day-to-day lives of the people and are consulted and implored for aid in times of illness or need.

The relation between Nyame and the various *obosom* is complex. In one sense the *obosom* are seen as Nyame's children and spokesmen who mediate between Nyame and the earth. In another sense—and this can be seen in much of the Ashanti folklore—the status and activities of the *obosom* stand apart from, and even in opposition to, Nyame. Asase Yaa, a female deity closely associated with Nyame, is neither his creation nor his consort but stands in relation to him as the Ashanti queen mother stands to the king. Many tales relate that Ananse, the trickster figure, connives and acts against Nyame, sometimes successfully.

BIBLIOGRAPHY

Danquah, J. B. *The Akan Doctrine of God.* 2d ed. London, 1968. A good, but eccentric, discussion of the subject, in which Danquah tries to trace Akan names, concepts, doctrines, and so on to an origin in the Middle East.

Rattray, R. S. *Ashanti.* Oxford, 1923. A thorough and definitive work.

JAMES S. THAYER

NYĀYA. The Nyāya school of Indian philosophy was founded by Gotama (sixth century BCE?) and has existed without any real discontinuity from pre-Christian times to the present. While the Vaiśeṣika, its sister philosophical school, concentrated more on issues and problems of ontology, philosophers of the Nyāya school took greater interest in questions and themes of epistemology. The Nyāya accepts four distinct sources of knowledge: *pratyakṣa* (perception), *anumāna* (inference), *upamāna* (analogy), and *śabda* (testimony). Perception is knowledge arising from contact between a sense organ and an object and must be certain and nonerroneous. It is of two kinds, relational and nonrelational. From a different point of view perception is classified into two other kinds, perceptions that arise from ordinary contact between a sense organ and an object and those that arise from a nonordinary contact. The latter includes perceptions by a yogin of all things past, present, and future.

Inference is of more than one kind, but the most common kind is typified by the case where the knowledge that the probandum *(sādhya)* belongs to the subject *(pakṣa)* arises from the knowledge that the connector *(hetu)* belongs to the subject and that the connector is pervaded *(vyāpta)* by the probandum. Analogy is identification of the denotation *(vāchya)* of a word whose denotation is not already known, based on information received that the thing denoted is similar to another known thing. Testimony is an authoritative statement. Here knowledge *(pramā)* is characterized by truth *(yāthārthya)* and is a species of ascertainment *(nischaya)*. An ascertainment that something *s* is qualified by something *p* is said to be true if *p* actually belongs to *s*. This account of truth is due to Gaṅgeśa (twelfth century CE), reputedly the founder of Navya Nyāya (New Nyāya), who introduced and sharpened a number of concepts and techniques for logical, linguistic, and semantic studies.

Unlike many other schools of Indian philosophy, the Nyāya has accepted and sought to prove the existence of Īśvara (God), who is regarded as a soul having eternal knowledge encompassing everything (and also eternal desire and motive). Although Īśvara is not a creator of the universe (which is beginningless and includes many other eternal entities besides him), he nevertheless functions as an efficient cause in the production of any effect. Every living being, human or nonhuman, has a soul that is eternal and ubiquitous. The ultimate goal of life is liberation *(mokṣa)* of the soul from worldly bondage. In keeping with the general Indian tradition, the Nyāya upholds the theory of *karman,* maintaining that one's actions influence later events in one's history and that one must reap the consequences of one's actions, either in the present life or in a subsequent life. Liberation is not regarded as a state of bliss, but is conceived negatively as a state of absolute cessation of all suffering. Knowledge of truth (which is held to be embodied in the Nyāya philosophy) is an indispensable means for attainment of liberation. Such knowledge dispels false beliefs, such as the belief that the soul is identical with the body, and eventually through successive stages this knowledge leads to the arrest of the beginningless cycle of birth and rebirth and thus to the ultimate state of unending freedom from all suffering.

[*See also* Vaiśeṣika. *Nyāya theories of cognition receive further attention in* Indian Philosophies.]

BIBLIOGRAPHY

The best book on Nyāya-Vaiśeṣika philosophy is Gopinath Bhattacharya's edition and translation of the *Tarkasaṃgrahadīpikā* (Calcutta, 1976). For readers who are less technically minded, but still want a comprehensive and precise account, the best book is *Indian Metaphysics and Epistemology: The Tradition of the Nyāya-Vaiśeṣika up to Gaṅgeśa,* edited by Karl H. Potter (Princeton, 1977), volume 2 of *The Encyclopedia of Indian Philosophies.* The general reader may profitably consult Mysore Hiriyanna's *Essentials of Indian Philosophy* (London, 1949).

KISOR K. CHAKRABARTI

NYBERG, H. S. (1889–1974), Swedish Orientalist and historian of religions. Born in Söderbärke in Dalecarlia, Henrik Samuel Nyberg received his early education at home and at the senior high school in Västerås. In 1908 he entered the university at Uppsala, and there he stayed, working in various positions, for the rest of his life. He earned his Ph.D. in 1919 and was professor of Semitic languages from 1931 to 1956. Concentrating from the beginning on comparative Semitic philology, Arabic, Hebrew, Aramaic, and Ethiopic, Nyberg became an inspiring teacher and one of the most brilliant representatives of the humanities Sweden has ever had, exerting a great influence on the cultural life of his country. His doctoral thesis, "Kleinere Schriften des Ibn al-ʿArabī," already showed the admirable scope that was to characterize his later studies. It is an edition of three minor writings of the great mystic, with an introduction that investigates the origin of Islamic mysticism and attempts to understand the system of Ibn al-ʿArabī as a phenomenon of syncretism.

In 1924–1925 Nyberg sojourned in Egypt for practical studies of Arabic. The most remarkable result of the trip was his discovery of the manuscript of *Kitāb al-Intiṣār* by the Muʿtazilī al-Khayyāṭ (ninth century). Nyberg published the text in Cairo in 1925 with an important commentary in Arabic: *Le livre du triomphe et de la réfutation d'Ibn er-Rawendi/Ibn Mohammed/l'hérétique par Abou l-Hosein Abderrahim/Ibn Mohammed ibn Osman el-Khayyat.* His deep penetration into the earlier polemic literature of Islam later enabled him to write his famous article, "Mu'tazila," for *The Encyclopaedia of Islam* (1934).

Nyberg's interest in the dialectology of Aramaic led him to the investigation of some documents from Avroman in Kurdistan. The Aramaic script of the documents appeared to contain a Middle Iranian dialect, and in 1923 he published his pioneering study "The Pahlavi Documents from Avromān" (*Monde oriental* 17). Thenceforth he was to devote much of his time to the study of Pahlavi; he eventually created the first scientific handbook of this language and was responsible for introducing Iranian studies as an academic discipline in Uppsala.

Influenced by Nathan Söderblom (1866–1931) and by his friend Tor Andrae (1885–1946), Nyberg now began his investigations of the Avesta, especially the *Gāthās*. In this field he made his most important contribution to the study of Iranian religious history, collected in the monumental book *Irans forntida religioner* (1937). One of the most remarkable traits of this work is the revaluation of the historical impact of Zarathushtra (Zoroaster), considered by Nyberg as a conservative champion of the religion of his own tribe. The consciousness of Zarathushtra's vocation was, according to Nyberg, conditioned by a type of Central Asian shamanism. Highly contested on many points, Nyberg's view in this work has nevertheless exerted a strong influence on scientific discussion in this field.

Familiar with the world of the Bible, Nyberg also worked from time to time in Hebrew. In his much debated *Studien zum Hoseabuche* (1935), he strongly emphasizes the importance of the oral tradition for the historical understanding of the textual form of the Hebrew scriptures, deliberately practicing a conservative textual criticism and eschewing the predilection for emendations common among many Old Testament scholars.

BIBLIOGRAPHY

Nyberg's monumental study *Irans forntida religioner* (Stockholm, 1937) was translated into German as *Die Religionen des alten Iran* (Leipzig, 1938) by H. H. Schaeder. It was reprinted in 1966 with a *Begleitwort* by Nyberg. Obituary notices and a complete bibliography of Nyberg's works can be found in the *Monumentum H. S. Nyberg*, 4 vols., "Acta Iranica," vols. 1–4 (Leiden, 1975).

Frithiof Rundgren

O

OATHS. *See* Vows and Oaths.

OBEDIENCE consists in the act of voluntary submission to an authority. Religious obedience, the subject of this article, is therefore the voluntary submission to a specifically religious authority, and its different forms correspond to differences in the types and levels of such authority. [*See* Authority.] In many world religions, authority rests with a single principle, being, or god, and religious obedience is accordingly due to an all-embracing law or to the divine will. But even in these cases, where there is clearly a single and absolute source of authority, the obligation of obedience may be expressed on a variety of levels. Thus in Hinduism, for instance, obedience to the *Laws of Manu* is enjoined upon all, but at the individual level a disciple's obedience to his *guru,* or, at a corporate level, to the rules of his sect, religious establishment, or *maṭha* may be equally or even more important.

Obedience in Christianity can similarly be seen as extending from the general principles of the Decalogue, through the observance of the rules of the church or monastery, to the individual's obedience of his own immediate ecclesiastical superior. In Islam, obedience may extend from the observance of the *sharīʿah,* to the rules of one's *ṭarīqah,* and finally to obeying one's spiritual mentor or *pir.* Likewise in Buddhism, apart from the moral precepts, the corporate rules of the *saṃgha* are to be observed by the monks and nuns, and even though Buddhism generally places less emphasis on the unique master-disciple relationship common in Hinduism, even here each novitiate is assigned initially to an individual elder.

Differences in the forms of religious association will also result in different forms of obedience. In religions that continue to be organized along the lines of natural kinship groups, religious obedience will often be a simple extension of one's normal obligations to one's family. Thus in Confucianism the filial relationship becomes paradigmatic for obedience of all kinds. But even when natural forms of association are left behind, obedience may continue to be understood metaphorically in terms of spiritual parentage. In the mystical traditions of several religions, including Christianity, the spiritual mentor is often compared to a father. Each individual, or even the religious community as a whole, may be visualized as undergoing a period of religious tutelage that requires the unquestioning obedience of a child. In many cases, the rite of religious initiation closely parallels that of birth and is often considered a kind of rebirth. Just as children are not supposed to disobey, so the neophytes undergoing initiation or puberty rites must behave humbly, obeying their instructors and accepting arbitrary punishment without complaint. Here one thinks of the obedience that Zen monks owe to their *rōshi.* [*See* Spiritual Guide.]

With the spiritual coming-of-age of an individual or a community, as in the biological parallel of growth during adolescence, obedience becomes more problematic, and at times even self-defeating. One encounters both the problem of disobedience and the more subtle problem of the conflict between the "spirit" and the "letter." The latter problem is illustrated by the Christian attitude toward Jewish law and by the Buddhist rejection of the cumbersome Hindu codes of conduct. More enlightened approaches emerge at the individual level in which disobedience becomes a higher form of obedience. Thus the Hindu religious leader Rāmānuja (eleventh century CE) disobeyed his master by making public formerly esoteric doctrines of salvation in order that all might be saved. Such "disobedient" transcendence of the conventional letter of the law is well illustrated by a Zen master's response to his disciple, who one evening questioned the propriety of his master's carrying a lady across a flooded rivulet that morning because it infringed the Vinaya rule against touching women: "I left her on the bank in the morning," he replied, "and you are still carrying her!" Similarly the Chinese sage Meng-tzu (Mencius) held that a man who would not pull his drowning sister-in-law out of a river, for fear of disobeying the rule that she not be touched, is no better than a wolf.

The appropriateness of obedience, or indeed the very question of what constitutes obedience in a given situation, cannot always be mechanically ascertained. Nevertheless, the consequences of disobedience cannot simply be dismissed. According to the Tibetan tradition, Mi-la-ras-pa had to suffer the consequences of disobeying his master's orders to the full, which were designed to wear out his *karman.* Thus although theoretically and retrospectively one may speak of enlightened disobedience, it presents difficulties in practical terms.

Another important issue in relation to obedience pertains to the conflict of different laws or values within a single tradition. This conflict was clearly recognized by the Hindu tradition, which sought to deal with it by relegating such conflicting norms to different historical epochs. The *dharma* appropriate to one age, it was held, may not be appropriate to another. But even without introducing this historical dimension, such conflict may be recognized as part of the essential tension present within a tradition at any given time, the tension, once again, between the "spirit" and the "letter." The recognition of this tension is exemplified by Confucius's remark to the duke, who had praised the rectitude of a son in testifying against his father in a case of theft: "The honest men of my country are different from this. The father covers up for his son, the son covers up for his father—and there is honesty in that too." The case is similar with Islam, which requires unquestioning obedience to the Qur'ān, but at the same time provides for *ijtihād.*

A closely related issue is that of law and freedom; how much freedom is to be allowed in the interpretation of the law? Is obedience to the law compatible with a relative freedom in its interpretation? Or does true obedience require a "rigorist" reading of the letter of the law, with the interpreter being allowed only the absolute minimum of freedom? This issue has been particularly important in the Christian tradition, where a broad range of positions has been defined. [*See also* Casuistry.]

The importance of obedience in religious life is undoubtedly due in part to its importance for the successful operation of family, society, and polity in general. However, obedience also functions as a specifically religious virtue. The triple vows of poverty, chastity, and cenobitic obedience in the context of Christian monasticism offer a possible example of such specifically religious obedience. However, all forms of cenobitic monasticism, as distinguished from the eremitic, involve rules necessary to the maintenance of a community and may therefore merely reflect the need for the maintenance of order. [*See* Monasticism.] No such reductionistic explanation is possible, however, in the practice of spiritual and ascetic disciplines. Here obedience has an exclusively religious goal, as an essential precondition of spiritual knowledge. Thus when a Greek king wished to learn the wisdom of India from the gymnosophists, the first thing required of him was obedience: "No one coming in the drapery of European clothes—cavalry cloak and broad-brimmed hat and top-boots, such as Macedonians wore—could learn their wisdom. To do that he must strip naked and learn to sit on the hot stones beside them." Obedience is the necessary prerequisite for entry upon the spiritual path. It is also in a sense the goal. This is particularly clear in the case of Islam, which literally means "surrender." Here man is viewed as having his final end outside himself, in the transcendence of the divine. True peace is accordingly to be found only in surrender, in true and total obedience to the divine will.

BIBLIOGRAPHY

Majumdar, R. C., ed. *The Age of Imperial Unity.* Bombay, 1951.

Schuon, Frithjof. *Islam and the Perennial Philosophy.* Translated by J. Peter Hobson. London, 1976.

Smith, Huston. *The Religions of Man.* New York, 1958.

Turner, Victor. *The Ritual Process: Structure and Anti-Structure.* Chicago, 1969.

Zaehner, R. C., ed. *The Concise Encyclopedia of Living Faiths.* 2d ed. New York, 1971.

ARVIND SHARMA

OB-UGRIANS. *See* Khanty and Mansi Religion; *see also* Finno-Ugric Religions.

OCCAM, WILLIAM OF. *See* William of Ockham.

OCCASIONALISM. [*This entry deals specifically with Islamic occasionalism. For notions of Christian occasionalism, see* Scholasticism *and the biography of* Descartes.]

The adjective *occasional,* as applied to causes or events, is used by medieval European theologians such as Thomas Aquinas to mean an "indirect cause which determines any disposition to any effect" (*Summa theologiae* 1.114.3, 2.1.88.3, 2.1.98.1–2, 2.1.113.7, *et passim*). In modern philosophy, the term *occasional* and its derivatives are used by Cartesians such as Malebranche (d. 1715), Guelincks (d. 1669), and Cordemoy (d. 1685) to refer to the relations between the modifications of mind and those of body, as well as to natural occurrences in general. Malebranche in particular denies any necessary connection between those two classes of modifications and refers all natural occurrences, human actions, and other events to God's direct intervention, of which the manifest or natural causes are nothing but the "occasions" (*Entretien sur la métaphysique* 7.11, 7.13).

In the history of Islamic theology *(kalām),* an "occasionalist" tendency is clearly discernible from the eighth century on. The earliest writers on theological questions, such as al-Ashʿarī and his followers, were overwhelmed with the Qur'anic concept of God "who is unlike anything else" (surah 42:11) and whose decrees are irreversible and inscrutable. Accordingly, they attempted to formulate a cosmological view that would justify the referral of all activity or development in the world to this God, whom they called the "Lord of the worlds" and the "Lord of the heavens and the earth."

By the eighth century the Muslim theologians *(mutakallimūn)* realized that Aristotelian physics, which presupposes a necessary connection between natural events or entities, is incompatible with the concept of God's lordship or sovereignty in the world. In its place they proposed a more theologically acceptable metaphysics of atoms and accidents in which every entity or event comes into being and passes away at the behest of God. According to this metaphysics, probably derived from Greek (Democritean) sources with certain Indian modifications, everything in the world is made up of substance and accident. The majority of the *mutakallimūn* define substance *(jawhar)* as that which bears the accidents, although some argue that this is the specific characteristic of body. Substance and accident, however, always exist in conjunction. Some accidents are more primary than others and include the "modes" or original properties of unity, motion, rest, composition, and location. A body can never be divested of these accidents, although it can be divested of the other "secondary" accidents, such as weight and shape. Most of the later *mutakallimūn* appear to have held that no substance can be divested of the accident of color, so that they define substance as "anything endowed with color."

The most characteristic feature of substance is its indivisibility; hence the majority of the *mutakallimūn* identify substance with the atom *(juz')* and dwell on its relation to the primary and secondary accidents. Thirty positive accidents, or their opposites, are said to inhere in each substance. When God wishes to create an entity, by "commanding" it to be (as the Qur'ān has put it), he first creates the atoms, then the accidents making up its physical or biological nature or character. But since accidents cannot endure for two moments of time, as a leading Ashʿarī theologian of the tenth century, al-Bāqillānī, put it, this entity will not continue to exist unless God constantly re-creates the atoms and accidents it is made of. This theory of "continuous re-creation" (Macdonald, 1927) constitutes the basis of Islamic cosmology and moral theology, especially in its Ashʿarī form. It presupposes, in addition to the duality of atom and accident, the atomic composition of time and that of the soul. Should God decide to put an end to the existence of a particular entity, the theory requires that he either cease to re-create the "accident of duration" in it (the Muʿtazilī view) or simply stop re-creating the stream of atoms and accidents making it up (the Ashʿarī view), whereupon the particular entity would cease to exist at all.

This theory had its critics in subsequent centuries, the most important and vocal of whom was probably the great Aristotelian commentator, Ibn Rushd (Averroës) of Cordova (d. 1198). In general it might be said that the theologians were sympathetic to the occasionalist view of the universe or some aspects of it, whereas the philosophers as a rule were either hostile or critical.

BIBLIOGRAPHY

One of the earlier studies of Islamic occasionalism and its theological implications is D. B. Macdonald's "Continuous Recreation and Atomic Time in Muslim Scholastic Theology," *Isis* 9 (1927): 326–344. The standard work on Islamic atomism continues to be Salomon Pines's *Beiträge zur Islamischen Atomenlehre* (Berlin, 1936). My *Islamic Occasionalism and Its Critique by Averroës and Aquinas* (London, 1958) deals in a preliminary way with the implications of occasionalism for the struggle between the theologians and the philosophers. Max Horten's *Die philosophischen Systeme der spekulativen Theologen im Islam* (Bonn, 1912) includes a discussion of Islamic occasionalism and atomic theory. Moses Maimonides' summary in the *Guide of the Perplexed,* translated by Salomon Pines (Chicago, 1963), should also be consulted for the major propositions of *kalām* and their occasionalist significance.

MAJID FAKHRY

OCCULTISM. The term *occultism* is properly used to refer to a large number of practices, ranging from astrology and alchemy to occult medicine and magic, that are based in one way or another on the homo-analogical principle, or doctrine of correspondences. According to this principle, things that are similar exert an influence on one another by virtue of the correspondences that unite all visible things to one another and to invisible realities as well. The practices based upon this essentially esoteric principle express a living and dynamic reality, a web of cosmic and divine analogies and homologies that become manifest through the operation of the active imagination.

Occultism, as a group of practices, is to be distinguished from esotericism, which is, roughly speaking, the theory that makes these practices possible. [*See* Esotericism.] We may therefore accept the following distinction proposed by the sociologist Edward A. Tiryakian:

> By "occult," I understand intentional practices, techniques, or procedures which (a) draw upon hidden and concealed forces in nature or the cosmos that cannot be measured or recognized by the instruments of modern science, and (b) which have as their desired or intended consequences empirical results, such as obtaining knowledge of the empirical course of events or altering them from what they would have been without this intervention. . . . By "esoteric" I refer to those religiophilosophic belief systems which underlie occult techniques and practices; that is, it refers to the more comprehensive cognitive mappings of nature and the cosmos, the epistomological and ontological reflections of ultimate reality, which mappings constitute a stock of knowledge that provides the ground for occult procedures. By way of analogy, esoteric knowledge is to occult practices as the corpus of theoretical physics is to engineering applications.
>
> (Tiryakian, 1972, pp. 498–499)

To this must be added, however, that such a distinction has only become conceptually possible since the second half of the nineteenth century, an age of trivial esotericism during which the need for a word like *occultism* was strongly felt. Furthermore, it must be recognized that esotericism itself also has a practical dimension. It is not pure speculation, since the active knowledge, enlightenment, and imagination that constitute it correspond to a form of praxis. Similarly, occultism, in the most precise sense of the word, necessarily includes a form of theory. The problem of terminology is complicated by the fact that *occultism* is sometimes used in the sense of *esotericism,* as can be seen, for example, in the very title of an otherwise excellent work, Robert Amadou's *L'occultisme: Esquisse d'un monde vivant* (Paris, 1950), which mainly deals with esotericism and theosophy.

Occultism before Occultism. The first instances of something that can be called occultism appear in the early centuries of the Christian era, combined with esoteric and theosophical teachings. Theurgy can be found in the teachings of the fourth-century *Chaldean Oracles;* in the Alexandrine Hermetism of the *Corpus Hermeticum,* from the second and third centuries; and in the third-century Neoplatonism of Porphyry, that of Iamblichus in the fourth century, and that of Proclus in the fifth. [*See* Theurgy.] Alchemy flourished at Alexandria until the seventh century. [*See* Alchemy.] Even Stoicism had an occult aspect, insofar as it emphasized the necessity of knowing the concrete universe by harmoniously combining science and technique, and adopted an open attitude toward popular religion, especially toward all kinds of divination.

During the Middle Ages there was considerable interest in occultism. Sylvester II, who became pope in 1000, was among other things an astrologer and alchemist. The medieval interest in the occult was due in large part to the influence of Arabic thought, which combined a rational empiricism with a strongly mythologized vision of a world dominated by subtle, spiritual forces. During this period the Arabs themselves developed an interest in the esotericism and occultism that had been dormant since the sixth century, emphasizing the study of astrology and alchemy. They provided the Christian West with works such as the *Book of Images* by Pseudo-Ptolemy, *Picatrix,* the *Turba philosophorum,* the *Emerald Tablet,* the *Book of the Moon,* and the *Flower of Gold,* all of which discuss astrology, alchemy, or theurgy. These, along with the older Alexandrine writings already mentioned, became the historical foundation of occult philosophy in the West. The magical and Hermetic teachings of the Arabs also contributed to the spread of medical theories and practices.

Medieval interest in occult philosophy was stimulated by the symbolic orientation of Christian theology. The symbolic cosmos of the Middle Ages, a predecessor of the esoteric cosmological representations that multiplied rapidly in the Renaissance, was expressed through the Romanesque style, as in the works of Alain de Lille, Hildegarde von Bingen, and Honorius. It promoted an interest in magic and the occult properties of natural things; hence the widespread taste for precious stones, their symbolism and their occult virtues, as in the *Liber lapidum seu gemmis* of Marbed. In astrology, the names of Roger of Hereford and John of Spain were prominent.

The year 1144 marked an important event: Robert of Chester's translation of the first important book of medieval alchemy, the *Liber de compositione alchemiae,* from Arabic into Latin. Other translations contributed to the spread of Proclus's influence, such as the *Liber de causis,* translated into Latin by Gerard of Cremona. There were also, in the twelfth century, numerous pseudo-Aristotelian writings, some of an alchemical, astrological, or pneumatological character, some concerning the occult virtues of stones and herbs, still others dealing with chiromancy and physiognomy. The most famous of these writings, the *Secreta secretorum,* a veritable handbook of occultism that placed a particular emphasis on astrology, was one of the most popular books of the Middle Ages.

Among twelfth-century works on magic, the Spanish and Latin translations of the *Picatrix,* compiled by the Arab Norbar, are important. Texts that attribute the origin of different occult traditions and treatises to Solomon also appear at this time; he is presented as a magician who received his occult knowledge through the revelation of an angel. These treatises were also believed to be dependent on the *ars notoria,* the art by which, it was thought, one could obtain knowledge of or communication with God through theurgical procedures such as the invocation of angels, the utilization of figures and designs, or the use of the appropriate prayers. To this category of writings belongs the *Liber secretus,* or *Liber juratus,* attributed to a certain Honorius, a book full of angels' names, theurgical prayers, and strange words derived from Hebrew and Chaldean.

In the thirteenth century, Albertus Magnus wrote a treatise on minerals and referred to both alchemy and magic. Thomas Aquinas himself believed in alchemy and attributed its efficacy to the occult forces of the heavenly bodies. Roger Bacon, too, took a close interest in the occult, since for him "experimental science" meant a secret and traditional science; that is, a concrete science, but one inseparable from holy scripture.

Astrology is best represented by the Scotsman Michael Scot, astrologer to Frederick II, a patron of seers and magi, and by Guido Bonatti, whose *Liber astronomicus* is undoubtedly the most important work of the period in this domain. Geomancy is represented by the great *Summa* of Bartholomew of Parma, published at Bologna. Iberian alchemy is best represented by the Catalan Arnau de Villanova, author of the *Rosarium philosophorum.* Indeed, the age's most beautiful work of literature, the *Roman de la rose,* begun by Guillaume de Lorris and continued by Jean de Meun, shows the influence of the science of Hermes.

The fourteenth century opens with the *Ars magna* of Ramón Lull, whose theosophical figures were intended for theological, medical, or astrological purposes. Lull's search for the absolute was carried out through these games played with number symbolism, which can be compared to the geometric schemes developed by Wronski at the beginning of the nineteenth century or to the famous "archaeometry" of Saint-Yves d'Alveydre. Alchemical literature progressed by leaps and bounds during the late Midde Ages and remained plentiful through the Enlightenment. Among its most powerful proponents were John Dastin, Petrus Bonus, Jean de Rupescissa, and Nicholas Flamel.

The occult philosophy of the Renaissance profited from this medieval legacy. It was also stimulated by the revival of Neoplatonism at the Florentine court that began in 1439 under the influence of George Gemistus Plethon and saw the translation of the *Corpus Hermeticum* by Marsilio Ficino (1463) and the christianization of the Qabbalah by Giovanni Pico della Mirandola. From then on there was a proliferation of magi and theosophists all over Italy, adhering to a truly philosophical esotericism and engaged in practices that prefigured the occultism of the nineteenth century.

Outside Italy, few people were as devoted to astrology and the occult arts as the monks. Astrology and medicine are directly connected in the work of the monk Jean Ganivet, whose *Amicus medicorum* (1431) went through many editions. Physiognomy was most notably represented by Michael Savonarola, the author of the *Speculum phisionomiae* and grandfather of the famous Florentine reformer. In this age, astrology and the Qabbalah held a larger place than alchemy. Trithemius (Johannes Heidenberg), for example, a father of Renaissance occult philosophy and the future teacher of Paracelsus, reserved only a modest place for alchemy. Nevertheless, alchemy could still be found in the new editions of older works written by George Ripley, Thomas Norton, and Bernhardus Trevisanus, and it was especially prominent in works of art.

In the Renaissance, we begin to hear of the "occult sciences," an expression that is common in the works of Blaise de Vigenère. Central to these sciences is the symbolic image of the two books: the "book of nature" and the "book of revelation," or, in other words, the universe and the Bible. The works of Paracelsus, who lived in the first half of the sixteenth century, best express the interest in the book of nature. Unlike the compilations of Heinrich Cornelius Agrippa or the abstract and laborious speculations of certain Christian qabbalists, Paracelsus showed a real interest in the concrete observation of nature. Like no one before him, he harmonized astrology and medicine in a philosophy of nature that is both typically Germanic and highly original, a philosophy that was to gain widespread acceptance. Plants, metals, minerals, relationships between the parts of the body and the planets—nothing escaped his observations. A powerful and genial wit, given to a rich and evocative use of language, Paracelsus transformed the medicine of his day by replacing the preconceived ideas of scholastic medicine with a genuine praxis. He was the great occultist of modern times, in the most elevated and noble sense of the word.

The concern for the book of nature found in magic, astrology, and alchemy was not as prominent in studies of the Qabbalah and Hermetism. Here again it can be helpful to distinguish between theosophy or esotericism proper and the occult sciences. In practice, however, things are often more complex. For example, Christian qabbalists like Pico della Mirandola and Franciscus Georgius Venetus made a rather forced effort to introduce astrology and alchemy into their qabbalistic works, in sharp contrast to the Jewish qabbalists, who paid little attention to alchemy. With the writings of Agrippa, however, an uninhibited syncretism appears, marking the beginning of modern occultism. In his influential work *De occulta philosophia libri tres* (1531), Agrippa combined magic, astrology, Qabbalah, theurgy, medicine, and the occult properties of plants, rocks, and metals. This work was an important factor in the spread of the idea of occult sciences. It should be noted, however, that Agrippa's work had been foreshadowed by a beautiful book by Ficino, his *De vita coelitus comparanda* (1489), and by the quite famous work of Giovanni della Porta, *Magia naturalis libri viginti* (1558).

It is only with some hesitation that one can classify the alchemy of this period as an occult science. In many ways it belongs more properly to esotericism. In spite of the inevitable presence of essentially practical alchemists, in the sixteenth and seventeenth centuries this "high science" increasingly became a technique of individual initiation, a spiritual activity involving a mystique of incarnation. Its rich iconography, particularly in the age of the German Baroque, was accompanied by texts laden with symbolism and philosophy. The metamorphoses of bodies and substances that these describe are given a metaphorical significance, and are intended to describe the procedure of the soul's transformation. For occultism in the strict sense, then, one must look not to alchemy but to astrology, which became dominant in Europe during the seventeenth and eighteenth centuries.

France in the seventeenth century in fact had an official astrologer, Morin de Villefranche, a professor of mathematics at the Collège de France, and the development of the printing press made possible the rapid diffusion of astrological literature. In 1666, however, astrology was banished from official teaching, when the Paris Academy of Science refused to recognize it. Nevertheless, this did not halt its popular expansion elsewhere. In 1791 the first monthly periodical devoted to astrology appeared in London. In its popular form, astrology was eventually reduced to a trivial occultism, devoid of a theology or even a consistent conception of the world. Originally, however, its foundations were esoteric.

The Illuminism of the eighteenth century, represented by thinkers such as Louis-Claude de Saint-Martin, Christoph Oetinger, and Jean-Philippe Dutoit-Membrini, was a spiritual current marked by a theosophy that often rose to a level worthy of its chief inspiration, Jakob Boehme. It too had its occultist side, which was sometimes exploited by entrepreneurs adept at profiting from human credulity. In addition to Illuminism, theurgy was also an object of sustained interest during this period, as can be seen from the works of Martínez Pasqualis.

Occultism and Modernity. The industrial revolution naturally gave rise to an increasingly marked interest in the "miracles" of science. It promoted the invasion of daily life by utilitarian and socioeconomic preoccupations of all kinds. Along with smoking factory chimneys came both the literature of the fantastic and the new phenomenon of spiritualism. These two possess a common characteristic: each takes the real world in its most concrete form as its point of departure, and then postulates the existence of another, supernatural world, separated from the first by a more or less impermeable partition. Fantasy literature then plays upon the effect of surprise that is provided by the irruption of the supernatural into the daily life, which it describes in a realistic fashion. Spiritualism, both as a belief and as a practice, follows the inverse procedure, teaching how to pass from this world of the living to the world of the dead, through séances of spirit rappings and table tippings, the table playing a role analogous to that of the traditional magic circle. It is interesting that occultism in its modern form—that of the nineteenth century—appeared at the same time as fantastic literature and spiritualism. The French term *occultisme* was perhaps first used by Eliphas Lévi (1810–1875), whose work is sometimes somewhat misleadingly identified with the beginnings of occultism itself. The English equivalent, *occultism,* was apparently first used by A. D. Sinnett in 1881. Like the fantastic and the quasi religion of spiritualism, nineteenth-century occultism showed a marked interest in supernatural phenomena, that is to say, in the diverse modes of passage from one world to the other.

Philosophically, occultism is founded on the theory of correspondences, and as such it of course comes under the heading of esotericism. In the nineteenth century, however, its representatives were generally more interested in various powers and phenomena than in salvational gnosis. Their works, which are often devoid of a sense of the sacred, generally lack theosophical range as well, or are characterized by a rather skeptical religious syncretism. The interest that they displayed in the science of their time, and their attempts to reconcile it with the supernatural, were often naive and awkward. It is regretable that the result of such praiseworthy efforts was not a philosophy of nature worthy of the name, comparable to that of the German Romantics.

Although occultism was an important movement in many different countries, its leading exponents were, for the most part, French. Nearly all were affected by the anticlericalism that raged in France at the time, and it is not surprising that some of them adopted the anti-Christian attitudes of the militant atheists. Occultism in France also came to be associated with the *fin de siècle* period of Symbolist and "decadent" literature, as can be seen in the work of Joris-Karl Huysmans (*Là-bas*, 1891), or in the painting of Gustave Moreau. In fact, however, the literary influence of occultism was exerted somewhat later, on surrealism, which is not surprising, given the experimental nature of the latter.

Of the great number of magi, thaumaturges, and experimenters who proliferated at the turn of the century, those for whom occultism was not only a practice but also a form of esotericism are of particular interest. Four Frenchmen who fit this description exercised a profound influence. Besides Eliphas Lévi, already cited, there were Saint-Yves d'Alveydre (1842–1909), the thaumaturge Philippe Vachot (known as "Maître Philippe"), and, most famous of all, Papus (Dr. Gérard Encausse, 1865–1916), who was with good reason called the "Balzac of occultism," and whose influence, in France as well as abroad, is still powerful. He was one of those who best succeeded in harmonizing magic and spirituality, occultism and theosophy, in works that were rich, sometimes chaotic, but always imposing and, as a whole, relatively traditional. He founded the very active Martinist order and contributed to making Saint-Martin better known. After a brief period of association with the Theosophical Society, he distanced himself from what he judged to be its "orientalizing" tendency. He shared with it, however, the fault of an often confused erudition. Besides Papus, other names stand out, interesting in their own right, such as Stanislas de Guaïta (1861–1897), Joséphin Péladan (1890–1915), Paul Sédir (1871–1926), Grillot de Givry (1874–1929), Albert Jounet (Dr. Emmanuel Lalande, 1868–1929), Charles Barlet (Albert Faucheux, 1838–1921), the editor-bookseller Chamuel, and the librarian Augustin Chaboseau. Victor-Émile Michelet, who knew most of these people, drew a lively portrait of them in his book, *Les compagnons de la hiérophanie*.

The sociologist Edward A. Tiryakian has noted that in our age there is a connection between the modernization of Western society and the interest in present-day occultism. We have already seen how the appearance of occultism in the nineteenth century was linked chronologically with the industrial revolution. To this may be added the following comment by Tiryakian: "The occult revival, at least in terms of the receptivity of witchcraft among segments of the middle-class, could . . . be seen as another step in the modernization of Western society, in this context as a secularization of the demonic. Such a perspective would be consonant with the secularization hypothesis concerning the relation of religion to modern society" (Tiryakian, 1972, p. 492).

The French esotericist René Guénon professed to be a severe critic of these occultists. His objectivity as a critic was compromised, however, by his own dependence upon an esotericism suffused with Orientalism, hardly relevant to an impartial study or appreciation of Western occult traditions. His own personal commitments led him to ignore Paracelsism, for instance, as well as other true philosophies of nature. Nevertheless, his criticisms remain eminently valuable, for no one did a better job of denouncing the confusion of values and of levels in an age in which surrealism had laid claim to occultism, the confusion of the psychic and the spiritual reigned, and the most dubious syncretisms flourished.

This situation has hardly changed since then. The confusion has even been aggravated by the proliferation of cults and sects, especially in the United States. There, even more than elsewhere, the media—film and television in particular—help to popularize a polymorphous occultism that sometimes openly declares itself to be satanic but that is nevertheless rendered harmless precisely by such publicity. The taste for magic in all its forms finds a psychological outlet in fantasy films (Roman Polansky's *Rosemary's Baby* is one example among hundreds). Occultist sects have proliferated as rapidly as the films, offering themselves as a similar sort of spectacle for the world at large. Such cults are in a sense the manifestations of the desire to explore the unknown.

Occultism, like esotericism in general, has been the object of a great number of scholarly works, especially in the last generation or two. If Eliphas Lévi, Papus, and others of their era made poor use of their erudition, they at least had the merit of calling attention to the historical density of esotericism and occultism. Arthur E. Waite, himself an "initiate," and Paul Vulliaud drew upon them for inspiration. Today, historians such as Alain Mercier, Guy Michaud, and Jean Richer are throwing new light on the relationships between occultism, literature, and philosophy. Similarly, the works of Eugenio Garin, Paul O. Kristeller, Wayne Shuhmaker, and Frances A. Yates give us a more accurate picture of the *philosophia occulta* of the Renaissance and post-Renaissance. Thus, like the popularization of occultism by the media, current erudition too contributes a new facet to the subject: its sociocultural dimension.

BIBLIOGRAPHY

A comprehensive survey of the history of occultism from antiquity to the seventeenth century is provided by Lynn Thorndike in *A History of Magic and Experimental Science*, 8 vols. (New York, 1923–1958). For the Renaissance and later periods, see the bibliographical notes for "Esotericism" and "Hermetism." See also Will-Erich Peuckert's *Gabalia: Ein Versuch zur Geschichte der Magia naturalis im 16. bis 18. Jahrhundert* (Berlin, 1967). A full account of recent writing on the Renaissance and a valuable summary of the major tendencies is found in Wayne Shuhmaker's study *The Occult Sciences in the Renaissance* (Berkeley, 1972). On modern occultism and literature, see Alain Mercier's *Les sources ésotériques et occultes de la poésie symboliste, 1870–1914*, 2 vols. (Paris, 1969–1974). On esotericism and occultism in general, see Robert Amadou's *L'occultisme: Esquisse d'un monde vivant* (Paris, 1950). An illuminating sociological account is provided by Edward A. Tiryakian in his article "Toward the Sociology of Esoteric Culture," *American Journal of Sociology* 78 (November 1972): 491–512. Valuable, insightful approaches to the study of the occult can be found in *The Occult in America: New Historical Perspectives*, edited by Howard Kerr and Charles L. Crow (Chicago, 1983), and in Mircea Eliade's *Occultism, Witchcraft, and Cultural Fashions: Essays in Comparative Religions* (Chicago, 1976).

ANTOINE FAIVRE
Translated from French by Kristine Anderson

OCEANIC RELIGIONS. [*This entry consists of three articles on the religious systems of Oceania:*

An Overview
Missionary Movements
History of Study

The introductory article discusses the general features of the religious traditions of the indigenous peoples of the Pacific islands. The second article details the impact of Christianity upon native Oceanic religious belief and practice, and the third article provides a history of the modern scholarly study of Oceanic religions. For more detailed treatment of the religious systems of the three regions into which Oceania has traditionally been divided, see Melanesian Religions; Micronesian Religions; *and* Polynesian Religions.]

An Overview

The Pacific islands are dispersed over the widest expanse of sea in our world. They comprise semicontinents (such as New Guinea), strings of large mountainous islands (along the curve of the Melanesian chain), and groups of more isolated larger and smaller islands further east, with many of those islets or islands arranged as atolls, or, more rarely, organized into whole archipelagoes such as the Tuamotus and the Carolines. The classic view is that one should distinguish between three large cultural areas: Micronesia in the northwest, Melanesia in the south, and Polynesia in the east. The reality is that while Micronesia is somewhat distinct in that its cultures display the influences of constant Asian contacts, Melanesia and Polynesia are artificial concepts created by Western powers. The Europeans settled and christianized Tahiti and eastern Polynesia, using the peoples of these islands to contact and control islands further west—as soldiers, Christian teachers, and petty civil servants who were accorded a status slightly higher than that of the so-called "cruel" Melanesian savages. In Polynesia the islanders resisted incursion settlement, and land transfers to Europeans were often obtained through marriages with the locals: these practices provided support for the queer conception that the islanders of the east were closer to their colonizers in terms of civilization, while those of the west were uncouth and dangerous.

The islands are in fact very similar. All the atolls are alike, with their peaceful lagoons ringed by white beaches crowned by endless rows of coconut trees, their dazzling sun, their fragility in time of hurricane, their lack of fresh water, and the many hardships of life and the precarious food conditions if no rain comes. Power and authority are held in trust, always with a streak of what is called "bigmanship," that is, the use of cajolery and intrigue, as well as good husbandry and economic sense, to further one's ambitions. Hereditary chieftainships exist, and chiefs are often surrounded by such formal behavior and etiquette that Westerners gave the title "king" to all such titular heads of social groups without checking to see if these "kings" in fact had kingdoms.

Across the range of social statuses, from hereditary chiefs who risk losing power and prestige by failure in war or in peace, to commoners who may gain the satisfaction of their ambitions and achieve greater "big man" prestige, most behavior can be explained in more or less equivalent terms. The words *tapu* (or *tabu*) and *mana* denote rank: but rank is something that fluctuates. One may see one's *mana* eroded through failure, with the result that one's *tapu* also diminishes. Success in intrigue and victory in war make one's *mana* grow, and then, correspondingly, one becomes the holder of a higher *tapu*. Wretched former princes who had lost their causes could be easily killed by the same commoner who would dread to touch an *aliki* ("chief") in

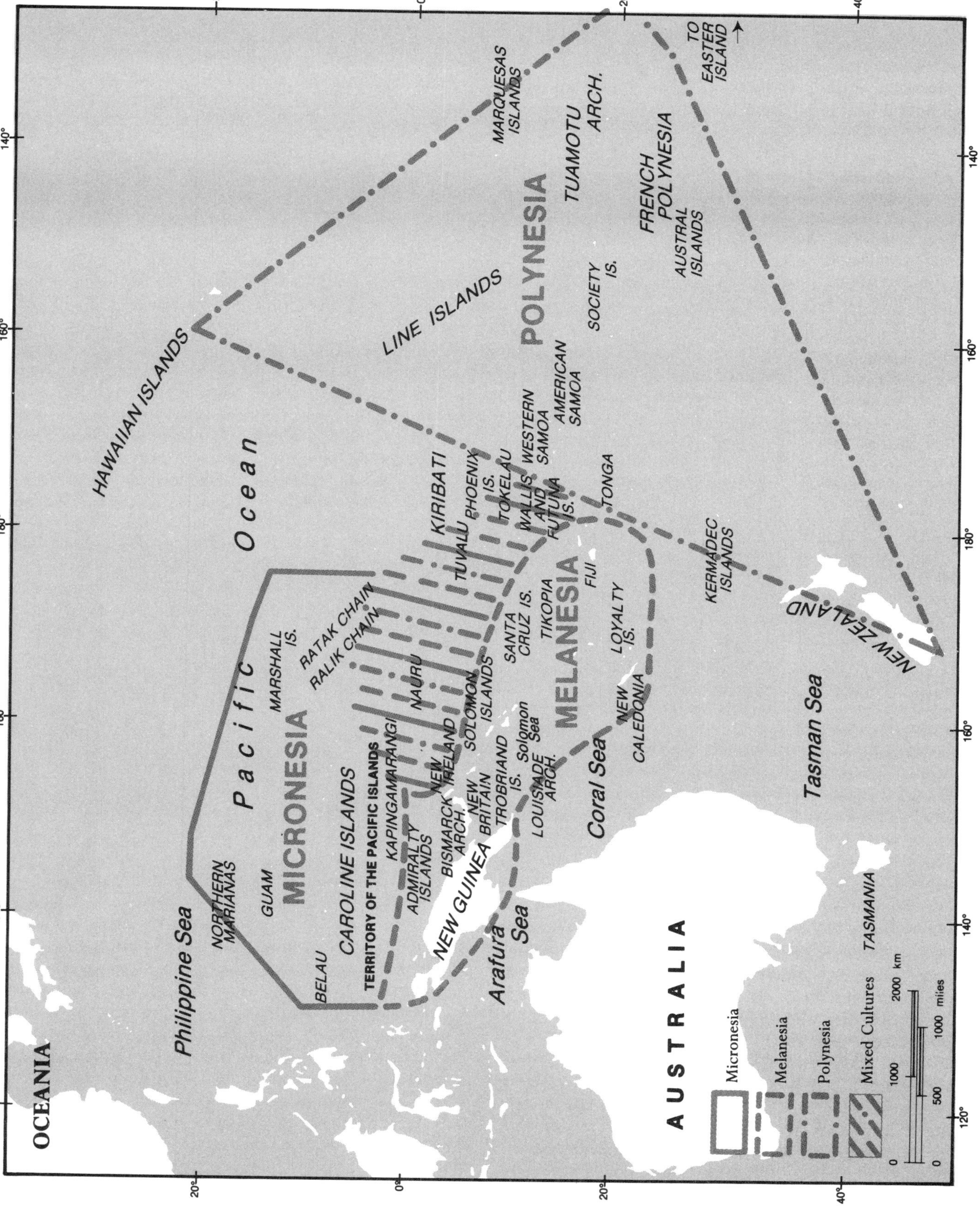
OCEANIA
Philippine Sea
Pacific Ocean
HAWAIIAN ISLANDS
LINE ISLANDS
MARQUESAS ISLANDS
TUAMOTU ARCH.
POLYNESIA
FRENCH POLYNESIA
SOCIETY IS.
AUSTRAL ISLANDS
TO EASTER ISLAND
AMERICAN SAMOA
WESTERN SAMOA
PHOENIX IS.
TOKELAU
KIRIBATI
TUVALU
WALLIS AND FUTUNA IS.
TONGA
FIJI
KERMADEC ISLANDS
NEW ZEALAND
MICRONESIA
NORTHERN MARIANAS
GUAM
MARSHALL IS.
RATAK CHAIN
RALIK CHAIN
CAROLINE ISLANDS
BELAU
TERRITORY OF THE PACIFIC ISLANDS
KAPINGAMARANGI
NAURU
ADMIRALTY ISLANDS
BISMARCK ARCH.
NEW IRELAND
NEW BRITAIN
SOLOMON ISLANDS
Solomon Sea
TROBRIAND IS.
LOUISIADE ARCH.
SANTA CRUZ IS.
TIKOPIA
MELANESIA
LOYALTY IS.
NEW CALEDONIA
NEW GUINEA
Arafura Sea
Coral Sea
Tasman Sea
AUSTRALIA
TASMANIA
Micronesia
Melanesia
Polynesia
Mixed Cultures
0 1000 2000 km
0 500 1000 miles
120° 140° 160° 180° 160° 140°
20° 0° 20° 40°

his splendor, and who would shiver even at the idea of looking in his face. [*For further treatment of these concepts, see* Power *and* Taboo.]

All things alive (social, biological, or material) are accounted for either by the actions of the dead (who hold, collectively or individually, enormous power), or by those of the so-called culture heroes of the cosmogonic or semicosmogonic myths. The origin of culture is often attributed to one of these heroes or to two who are brothers. In northern New Guinea, Madang district, these brothers are Kilibob, the inventor of all useful arts, and Manup, the brother responsible for love, magic, sorcery, and warfare. It is believed that they will both return: Kilibob will be announced by the arrival on the sea of a wooden plate carved in the Siasi Islands and Manup by the arrival of a canoe from the north. The so-called cargo cults have integrated this myth into their own system. Often, white explorers were taken at first for the dead coming back to give their riches to their descendants. What sometimes appears to be naïveté in those myths has been shown to have extraordinary mobilizing power through the messianic cults that have sprouted all over the Pacific, from the early Mamaia cult in Tahiti to the more recent cargo cults in New Guinea and Melanesia. [*See* Cargo Cults.] It appears today that such prophetic or messianic cults have existed in the area since ancient times: one case (the Roy Mata story, of central Vanuatu) has been archaeologically dated at 1300 BCE. However, religious concepts are usually a means of justifying the way in which a society and culture function, and thus support institutionalization and not change. Autochthonous Oceanic beliefs are responsible, even now, for stability in the societies of this area. Experience over recent decades has shown that aboriginal religious beliefs and concepts are far from dead in the Pacific islands, although the whole area is nominally Christian. Prayers are still offered to ancestors and to symbolic beings whose invisible presence is still felt.

In the nineteenth century, after research in Vanuatu (formerly New Hebrides) and the Solomon Islands, R. H. Codrington (1891) came to understand that there were two kinds of gods, those who had lived as human beings and those who had never been human. Maurice Leenhardt (1947) later confirmed that most of the so-called gods were believed to have once been human. The transformation from human to god began with their deaths. Their corpses, called *bao* (which is also the word for "human being," and is often translated as "spirit"), were from then on named in prayers.

Death and the Dead. The link between men and women and their dead is one of the keys for the understanding of Pacific islanders' religious behavior. The dead are believed to be living in another form of existence in some faraway place, under the sea or under the earth, where they have arrived after following a set path and after one of that group of gods who have never been human ordains their life in the afterworld. The path that the dead follow can be mapped: it may go from one island to another—so that the dead require, as in Vanuatu, the ghost of a canoe, which transports those from Malekula across to Ambrim—or it may follow, as between Lifou and Uvéa in the Loyalty Islands, some subterranean route where maiden temptresses will try to stop the dead person so as to devour him. When the path follows a known route to the sea or to the underworld, its protection is the responsibility of a given lineage, which will derive prestige and authority from such a privilege.

The geographical location of the dead is not always a precise one. Melanesian groups recognize different openings of the afterworld on each of the coasts of their principal islands, and these places are marked by names such as *Devil's Rock* or *Devil's Point*. Often there are believed to be secondary entryways, which one may discover, for example, by following the roots of banyan trees or of cordyline shrubs, or which may be found at rock outcrops or in caves. Using these avenues, men and women are said to have traveled to the subterranean village of the dead and to have brought back (such as on Tana, in Vanuatu) new technical knowledge, new songs and dances, and even ghostly wives or husbands endowed with magical powers. In the case of these last stories, the ghostly spouse usually returns home after a quarrel with its human husband or wife, taking away its power and sometimes killing the unhappy human adventurer.

Corpses receive all sorts of ritual treatment. They may be laid in a grave or buried fetuslike in the ground, with the head sticking out; the head might later be removed for use in special mortuary rites. In southern Malekula the corpse is put on a platform and a small fire kindled underneath so as to accelerate the putrefaction process. When this is accomplished, the villagers remove the head and place it in an ant's nest for thorough cleaning, after which the face is rebuilt with vegetable paste before being fixed to the top of a life-size puppet, the *rambaramb*, which bears marks indicating the dead man's rank. This puppet is present, six months after a man's death, at his last funerary ceremony and dance. After this the widow is allowed to remarry, usually with the dead man's junior brother, to whom she was in many cases forbidden to speak during her husband's lifetime. The skull is then everywhere put in a special place—in a rocky area, for example, or in a sacred grove, or on the flat stones at the back of the men's house—where it remains, and where it may be offered prayers. Mortuary techniques vary from place to place, and change according to fashion. For instance, the custom of eating parts of the dead body, particularly the brain, and of rubbing newborn children with the dead person's fat, was introduced into the Fore area of the New Guinea Highlands only four generations ago.

Very generally, a special rite often occurs ten days after death, during which the deceased person is reverentially asked to depart his lifelong place of residence and to go to join the other dead in their abode, where he now belongs. Each year, in Vanuatu and elsewhere, there is a display of food for the benefit of the dead, who are invited, often through calls on conch shells, to come and share the food. The next day, toward dusk, the dead are sent home by the same means. This does not prohibit the dead from being called for at any time in the year, as when the sickness of a close kinsman or one's own child warrants their help.

There are other special collective means of communicating with the dead. In Papua and in the Madang area of New Guinea a pole (or, in northern Malekula in central Vanuatu, a bundle of finely stripped coconut-frond stems) is carried upright on the shoulders of a group of young men; the dead are believed to hold the pole's other end. The people dance until frenzied, and then ask questions of the dead, who can only answer yes or no, which they indicate by causing the pole or bundle to sway to and fro. Thus one can learn the whereabouts of a wife who has run away, or of a lost pig, or of a witch.

Some of the dead are unwelcome at all times, since they can only be harmful; these include, for instance, the dead of another group, who should not be allowed to stray out of their own territory, and, especially, the ghosts of those who were left without normal burials, or of women who died in childbirth and who do not have their children—or carved representations of their babies—with them (New Caledonia). These members of the dead must not be allowed to enter either food or drink, and special precautions are taken to protect collective food preparation and kava brewing.

Throughout Oceania, the gods one most often meets with are those of the afterworld; for example, Teê Pijopac of northern New Caledonia (who is known farther south in the islands as Gomawe or Kaveureu, and who is often called "the great god"). His material aspect is a carved wooden mask, blackened, with a large and curvy nose, a dome, and a beard made of hair cut from the heads of men who have guarded the corpse of a chief (and who have been required to let their hair grow during that time). This mask is attached to a mantle made from a fishing net, the knots of which imprison a tuft of the black feathers of a forest pigeon, the *notu*. Questioners of the dead include the goddess Nyôwau of the west coast of New Caledonia and the god Marawa of northern Vanuatu. The Fijian tradition, as related by A. R. Brewster (1922), provides the longest description of the tribulations of the dead, who must evade being crushed, maimed, or eaten, and whose worst enemies are the goddesses who guard the paths along which the dead must travel.

When one looks at the texts of prayers, chants, or invocations (such as the Maori *karakia*), one always finds, directly or indirectly, the mention of the dead and their powers, or of superior beings. These beings often cannot be named because the *tapu* against saying their exact, or secret, name is too high for it to be uttered without great danger. The hints or roundabout ways that vernacular texts have of addressing the dead or superior beings are often incomprehensible even to those Europeans knowledgeable in Oceanic languages.

Status, Power, and Ancestry. Localization is the key to understanding how status and power systems function in the islands. Part of the status, independence, and prestige of each lineage involves its ownership, or mastery, of a portion of the universe. It is the function of each lineage to act in ways prescribed by the tradition so as to make the universe run smoothly and so that each group will benefit from the ritual actions of all of the others and will reciprocate through its own. Such mythical endowment, however, always includes both positive and negative powers. For instance, the capacity to fill one's own group's gardens with yams corresponds to the power to cause a bad crop in one's neighbor's gardens. The ability to protect one's irrigated taro patches from the worms that make holes in the banks of the terraces (letting the water out) has as its counterpart the ability to send this aggressor elsewhere to wreak havoc on other people's taro fields. To control mosquitoes in one's own domain (and hence to cure filariasis) means that one can send the insects—in droves—toward another tribe. One may have the power of making the sun shine: just enough for agricultural prosperity, or too much, causing the land to be scorched in revenge against, perhaps, a slight by one's own people. To be able to halt hurricanes implies that one is also able to bring them on. The word *master*, introduced by Maurice Leenhardt, is much better adapted to such a situation than the terms *magic* and *magicians*, used by so many authors.

Systems of relations also govern the gods who never were human, although there does not seem to be any general rule here. The Maori and the eastern Polynesians tend to build elaborate divine genealogies, always linked with human ones. Thus there are enough forms of the god Tane in the myths for a number of lineages to be able happily to claim him as forebear and thus express a claim for equality of status with other lineages. In the same way, any number of gods may serve as the ancestors of the human race, though a few do not. No Maoris claim descent from the Moon, for example, since she is thought to have been the ancestor of the white people.

Belief in a god of creation who is different from the culture heroes is common throughout Oceania. He seems to be a *deus otiosus*, however, who no longer deals with human problems. In New Caledonia, Gomawe, usually called "the great god" because his name should not be spoken, molded man and woman out of clay in one version of the cosmogonic myth. In another, the earth was at first covered by the sea, but then a rock emerged from the ocean. The Moon put one of its teeth on this rock; the tooth rotted, and worms got inside. Later these worms became lizards and eels, and the lizards took on human faces before the god Bume intervened, split their skins, and made men and women out of them. He then instituted marriage and organized the exchange between the two moieties, Bay and Dwi.

In Polynesian cosmogonical systems each lineage is accounted for in the cosmology. Political systems are based on linked lineages, so each political system must have its share of the local world of symbols. This means that each god must have an avatar for each of the competing social systems. The Maori cosmology, with all its brilliance and epic poetry, is only one of the possible applications of a general Pacific-islands rule: at the start, as well as at the end, the world of the gods is the same as the world of the dead; the gods and the dead intermingle constantly, emerging from and returning to the same perennial golden age, or dream-time. This mythical time is not far away, however, nor lost in this distant past. The world of myth is forever present, and the gods and the dead may enter the mundane world or be called for at any time. They lead an invisible, parallel existence. One might have to embark on a long voyage, with all its dangers, to get to the country where all power comes from (e.g., the Maori's Hawaiki), or it might appear before one at any moment, directly and unannounced. If a *tapu* is broken the retribution is swift, because nothing evades the gaze of the dead or the gods.

Initiation. One of the most imprecise terms used in accounts of Oceanic religions is *initiation.* It is well known that, throughout the Pacific islands, male teenagers are taken away from their mothers and kept in seclusion for a number of weeks. During this time they are given special food (without relish, and roasted instead of boiled). Their mettle is tested through painful experiences such as the incision of the foreskin—rarely complete circumcision—or scarification or tattooing. Older men teach the teenagers the traditional songs. The young men are taught the verse and the prose of their vernacular traditions, and are informed as to what can and cannot be said in the presence of women and children. They perform plays and dances dealing with the mythical beings associated with their local groups, and they learn to play musical instruments. Some Highland New Guinea youths start at this point to learn the technique of swallowing a rattan vine through the nose as a means of purifying the body of all bad influences. Generally youths are either beaten with stinging nettles or threatened with death if they talk to anybody about what they have been through.

These rites actually represent only a partial initiation, one that highlights the cohesion of allied groups and that teaches what can be told in front of a number of people of different lineages. Another important part of the traditional lore will be taught, over the years, by the mother, the father, the father's sister, the mother's brother, and the grandparents. The key to the lessons of this multiple process of tuition lies in the numerous place names that must be remembered. Each myth, each piece of oral lore is rooted somewhere, belonging not only to a specific social group but also to a specific point in space where—and only where—its story can be told. Another important aspect of this teaching deals with other lineages, close or far away, and so the father must take his wife and children from place to place: to where benefits from a privileged link that was his father's before him may be conferred on his son, to where his son can go to partake of a formal exchange, or to where the son can find a residence and a wife. The land is thus dotted, everywhere, with rocks, trees, caves, groves, waterholes, and springs, each of which is explained in both mythical and social (i.e., land tenure) terms. Some of the powers and ritual formulas might be kept by the father until his deathbed, because he has waited to transmit them until almost his last breath.

Divination and Witchcraft. Individuals pray directly to their own dead relatives for help, but on occasions when they are in need of greater help—to obtain the favors of a woman, for example, or to discover who has been sending sickness to a next of kin—they go to see a clairvoyant, who may be a man but is often a woman. The techniques of the seers vary from place to place. Divinatory dreams are quite common, as much today as during earlier times. In central New Caledonia, it was thought that these dreams could be induced by sleeping in a raised part of a round hut, on top of a carved plank on which was depicted a human face looking down (a *bödu*). Other divinatory methods included interpreting the decision of ants when they encounter an obstacle as to whether to go over or around it, or counting urine drops one by one, proposing and eliminating possible answers with each drop (until the last drop gives the correct answer). Other seers look into pools of dormant water; the seer stirs the pool, waiting to see what figures appear on its surface.

Witchcraft is used for retribution when full-scale war is not in order. However, many ideas about witchcraft as a negative institution are entirely wrong. The "sorcerer" is always an ambiguous person. He will heal as well as cause sickness or death, and he protects his own lineage against dangers. In his book *Malekula* (1934), A. B. Deacon has shown how, in southwestern Malekula, the prayers and sacrifices at the *nebrbrkon* (the sacred grove where all human bones are thrown in a heap) are meant for the good of the yam crop, but can also be used to kill or to make sick an enemy of the group.

First-Fruit Ceremonies. In Fiji, New Caledonia, and the Loyalty Islands, first-fruit ceremonies are a way of publicly showing the structure of the society as it actually works. This is accomplished through the chain of people eating the first-fruit fruits one after another—the priest, the chief, the men, and later the women and children—and through the ritualized exchange of young yams. In other words, the ceremony reveals who has authority over whom, who has an equal or unequal relation with whom, who has attained (or is striving for) an autonomous status, and who represents the senior lineage and the lineage most recently established. Where there are stone or wooden fences defining the space of a chief's court, or where there is an enclosed area *(marae)* dedicated to religious rites, the meaning of first-fruit ceremonies varies according to whether yam offerings may be brought inside the yard or must stay outside.

The day when the first yam is eaten is one of the most important of the year. By this act, the priest announces that sexual relations may begin again after their suspension during the time when the yam tubers were growing. On this day there is a general change of pandanus mats and of clothing, a cleaning of houses after the old fires have been killed, and the replacement of the old fires with new, which must never be allowed to die until the next year's first fruits.

Each chieftain's court does not always have its own first-fruits priest, though this seems to be the case in Fiji. In New Caledonia the "master of the yams" holds sway over a wide area containing several chieftainships. In a single day at the beginning of the yam season, the master initiates all of the technical agricultural procedures of the area at one small symbolic plot. At the end of the yam season he alone eats the very first yam of the crop, while praying at the same time. In between these ceremonies, the role of the chief dominates the agricultural cycle, each procedure of the yam cultivation being performed first in the chief's garden. This model is repeated throughout Polynesia and Melanesia, where the dual roles of chief and priest are everywhere manifest.

Material Aspects of Religion. Many of the objects used for religious purposes were made from perishable plant materials. Western museums have been entrusted with what navigators and missionaries brought or sent back home so as to justify their endeavors; thus, Westerners can view Hawaiian mantles and headdresses displaying vivid yellow and red parrot feathers. One or two Tahitian so-called priestly robes, with their elaborate shell ornamentation, have survived. However, much of the priestly costume was negative: the priest bared his body in the divine presence, wearing little more than a tapa loincloth or, better, nothing at all. In most instances, the contact between man and god was secretive, without any witness. Only in the cases of widely established institutions such as meetings between numerous interlocked lineages do we find large-scale public ceremonies, which had always as much a political as a religious meaning.

The Tahitian *marae,* or meeting ground, closely resembles the Fijian *nanga:* we know little of either except that, at least in the latter case, the symbolism of the rites enacted there had to do with ensuring bountiful crops. In recent centuries, some Tahitians added pyramidal structures at the end of these closed rectangular yards. The structures were built in the same fashion as the Tongan royal tombs, which in turn resemble the stone structures or raised pyramidal terraces found at some of the dancing squares *(nasara)* in some villages on the small islands of Vanuatu. (They resemble, too, some recently discovered Samoan architectural structures.) Most Tahitian local groups, however, kept their *marae* open; these cleared spaces served as the focus of the link between the living and the dead. The wooden towerlike structures of the Hawaiian *heiau* (ritual enclosure) were draped with tapa on ceremonial days only.

One important question regarding the material aspects of Oceanic religions involves the role of monumental stone or wooden carvings, or of the small carved pieces depicting the human figure and popularly called *tiki.* The first missionaries thought that these human carvings represented gods and were cult objects, dismissing them all as "heathen" idols. The only role of the monumental carvings was, however, architectural: they represented a way of conceiving space that took the sky into account. The smaller carved pieces were kept at home, carefully wrapped in rolls of tapa cloth and not taken out much more than once a year. The key to understanding these objects comes from Fiji, where small carvings of human figures, in wood or whale-tooth ivory, circulated in pre-European days; they were usually put inside a sennit representation of a *bure,* or chiefly house, as repositories for the divine presence when it was invoked. The well-known "abstract" sculpture called *uenuku,* from the Waikato Valley of New Zealand, is thought by the Maori to have been brought from the mythical land of Hawaiki in the Tainui canoe. This sculpture has a hole at the tip of what might be the symbol of the forehead; the god is meant to come and sit in this hole when he is called by deeply intoned chants.

A single principle is general throughout this area: a carved figure can be the repository of a godly presence, when it must, but the god has no obligation whatsoever to choose this particular abode. Gods can be incarnated at will in stones, trees, stone outcrops, whales, sharks, carefully wrapped sennit bundles (which have in Tahiti indications of facial features), or more deliberately constructed figures (which have an abundance of shell pendants). Or gods may take up residence in carved wooden human faces, called "heads of the shell money," which are linked in New Caledonia with Urupwe, one of the names of the god who reigns supreme over the land of the dead. Monumental carvings are rarely thought of as possible repositories for godly presences, with the exception of the Hawaiian wickerwork figures covered with parrot feathers that were carried to battle as representations of Kū-kā'ili-moku, the god of war.

BIBLIOGRAPHY

The earliest account of this area was William Ellis's *Polynesian Researches during a Residence of Nearly Eight Years in the Society and the Sandwich Islands,* 4 vols. (London, 1831), which gives us a view of what could be known at the time, translated into European words by an open-minded missionary. R. H. Codrington's *The Melanesians: Studies in Their Anthropology and Folklore* (1891; reprint, New Haven, 1957) provided a much better introduction to the Pacific, as he tried to analyze vernacular concepts. Codrington was followed on the English side by other brother missionaries such as Charles Elliot Fox, with *The Threshold of the Pacific: An Account of the Social Organization, Magic and Religion of the People of San Cristoval in the Solomon Islands* (London, 1924), and on the French side by Maurice Leenhardt, with *Do Kamo,* translated by B. M. Gulati (Chicago, 1979). Leenhardt was the first French author to publish a whole corpus of Oceanic vernacular texts. Following in his footsteps, I have studied Oceanic societies in Vanuatu and New Caledonia: *Un siècle et demi de contacts culturels à Tanna, Nouvelles-Hébrides* (Paris, 1956) shows a ni-Vanuatu society living with and talking to its dead; *Mythologie du masque en Nouvelle-Calédonie* (Paris, 1966) shows the way gods with local associations represented the different names of the lord of the land of the dead and were represented by the mask. Bronislaw Malinowski, in *Magic, Science and Religion* (New York, 1948), tried to express a functionalist, but balanced, view of Oceanic religions, but the best author remains Raymond Firth. Among Firth's numerous studies of Tikopia (a small Polynesian island far out off the eastern Solomon Islands, which remained entirely traditional until recently), two works are of particular importance: *The Work of the Gods in Tikopia,* 2d ed. (London, 1967), and *History and Traditions of Tikopia* (Wellington, 1961). Adolph Brewster's *The Hill Tribes of Fiji* (London, 1922) did bring to light interesting material, which still needs to be checked against vernacular corpora. Elsdon Best's *Maori Religion and Mythology, Being an Account of the Cosmogony, Anthropogeny, Religious Beliefs and Rites, Magic and Folk Lore of the Maori Folk of New Zealand* (Wellington, 1924) is still our best source on Maori religion. Two rival anthropologists whose fieldwork in New Guinea predates World War II have introduced us to the complex variations of the New Guinea systems, and their work should be cited here, although there are tens of other authors and titles left aside: Reo F. Fortune's *Manus Religion: An Ethnological Study of the Manus Natives of the Admiralty Islands* (1935; reprint, Lincoln, Nebr., 1965) and Gregory Bateson's *Naven: A Survey of the Problems Suggested by a Composite Picture of a New Guinea Tribe,* 2d ed. (Stanford, Calif., 1958). Nevertheless, the best recent book on Oceanic religion has been written by Maori authors and edited by Michael King: *Tihe mauri ora: Aspects of Maori Tanga* (Wellington, 1978) reanalyzes such Maori concepts as *mana, tapu,* and *mauri,* and for the first time puts them in the context of Maori society.

JEAN GUIART

Missionary Movements

While nearly all Pacific islanders today are Christians—except for the natives of inland New Guinea, where Christianity has made only partial inroads—one can still find here and there a village, family, or individual happily clinging to a "heathen" religion. Although Christianity is deeply entrenched in the Pacific, it is lived even now as only one of the several planes on which the islanders simultaneously exist without any sense of contradiction. Families still decide which son will be trained as a future chief, which will receive a European education in order to become a civil servant, Protestant pastor, or Catholic priest, and which will stay in the village to learn the traditional religious lore so that he can keep open the old paths to the invisible world.

The Christianity of the Pacific islanders has a predominantly mythical quality. Maurice Leenhardt captured the essence of the Pacific islanders' understanding of Christianity in his account of Melanesian soldiers passing through the Suez Canal in 1915 who were astonished to learn that they were near the lands of the Bible. They wrote home to express their surprise: they had never thought the places mentioned in the Bible had even existed. Even today, many islanders believe the biblical narrative is merely a story and that Jerusalem and other holy places have only a symbolic existence.

History of Christian Missions in the Pacific. Both Protestant and Catholic communities exist on most of the Pacific islands (with adherents of the Protestant churches usually being in the majority). The most recent missions have been those of the Seventh-day Adventists, Jehovah's Witnesses, Latter-Day Saints (Mormons), and Bahā'īs. Of these only the Seventh-day Adventists and the Mormons have had substantial success. In Hawaii, Tahiti, and the Tuamotus, Mormon missionary activity has even given rise to a breakaway church, the Kanito (or Sanito) movement.

In earlier times, Protestant churches carefully divided the Pacific area into regions in which the different missionary groups would carry out their activities. In 1795, the newly formed London Missionary Society chose Tahiti as its first field of endeavor. It later expanded its operations to the Austral Islands, the Cook Islands, the Loyalty Islands, western and eastern Papua (southeastern New Guinea), and the Torres Islands. The Wesleyan Missionary Society (founded in London in 1814) did its first work on Tonga, Fiji, and the Solomon Islands. The Anglican church, represented by the Melanesian Mission based in Auckland, New Zealand, was active in northern Vanuatu (formerly the New Hebrides) and the eastern Solomon Islands. The South Sea Evangelical Mission, based in Australia and theoretically nondenominational (though predominantly Baptist), worked in the central Solomons. The American Board of Commissioners for Foreign Missions, founded in Boston in 1820, was active in Hawaii and those parts of Micronesia that had not been converted to Catholicism at the time of Magellan. The Presbyterians converted southern and central Vanuatu. New Zealand was from the start shared among the Church Missionary Society (founded in London in 1799), the Wesleyan Mission, and the Anglican church. In New Guinea the authorities tried to organize mission work by allocating specific areas to different groups, but prior to 1914 the northern part of the country had been under the control of Germany, which allowed the Lutheran church and the Catholic orders freedom in missionary activities in that area.

Roman Catholic missions have rarely been the first to arrive in any area of Oceania, which explains why Catholics are in the minority in most places. The Marist Fathers (Société de Marie, founded in Lyons in 1818) missionized the Solomon Islands, Vanuatu, Fiji, Tonga, Samoa, New Zealand, Bougainville, the Wallis and Futuna Islands, and New Caledonia. Indeed, in the last three places, Catholics do make up a majority of the population. The Fathers of the Sacred Hearts of Jesus and Mary (based in Paris) have been active in Hawaii, Tahiti, and the Marquesas Islands. The Fathers of the Sacred Heart of Jesus (originally of Issoudun, France) worked first among the natives of Papua, and later in New Britain, the Admiralty Islands, the Gilbert Islands, and Nanu. Still other Catholic orders have been successful elsewhere in the area.

The history of christianization shows some regularities inasmuch as all of the missionary bodies, Protestant and Catholic, have used the same technique: mass conversions were precipitated through the conversion of members of the local aristocracy. Before direct colonial administration was instituted, native leaders often became Christians as a means of obtaining official recognition from European powers. Thereafter they often asked for and received firearms, which they then used to overcome local enemies. Rival chiefs adopted different faiths, and there have been full-fledged Christian religious wars in Samoa, Tonga, Wallis, Fiji, and the Loyalty Islands, especially between Catholic and Protestant converts. The Seventh-day Adventists, to the discomfort of the well-established churches, have thrived by converting groups whose politics do not agree with those of the majority church in any given area. The Assemblies of God, the Jehovah's Witnesses, and to a lesser extent the Mormons, have recently made gains in similar fashions.

Christian missions in the Pacific frequently became involved in local disputes over land and social status. Missionaries were often used by one party to thwart the ambitions of another. I have recorded examples of such cases from western Tana in Vanuatu, where the Presbyterian Mission was involved; similar cases on Wagap in New Caledonia, in which the Marist Fathers were used, have been documented by J.-C. Rivierre and Alban Bensa in their *Les chemins de l'alliance* (1982). There have been quite a number of other cases, the best documented having occurred on Samoa.

In order to consolidate the effects of sometimes hurried conversions, missionaries established programs to educate native youths as future leaders in the movement to spread the Christian faith. All of the missions set up institutions to which children were brought at an early age, where they were separated from their parents for many years, and taught by untrained, self-appointed teachers. When these children grew up, the missionaries arranged Christian marriages for them. It is therefore extraordinary that Pacific-island cultures have been able to maintain themselves despite such programs.

This system of conversion and indoctrination was first employed by the London Missionary Society, after initial difficulties in Tahiti, with a view toward using

Christian couples from one island to establish the society's influence on other islands. Henceforth, Europeans were introduced as evangelists only in areas where their safety was assured. Thus, except for the Reverend John Williams, killed on Eromanga in Vanuatu in 1839, and the Reverend G. N. Gordon, killed in the same place in 1861, most of the Christian martyrs in New Caledonia and Vanuatu were Polynesians. In fact martyrs as such were few. It was the Polynesian evangelists who began the public burning of wooden "idols," and in general these native missionaries used highly militant, even violent, tactics to gain converts. The best-documented cases of violent conversion occurred in Tahiti, the Cook Islands, Fiji, and southern Vanuatu. Nevertheless, it should be pointed out that such incidents occurred only because the missionaries who perpetrated them had wide popular support, since quick, mass conversion was seen either as a means of obtaining recognition from European powers or as a way of discouraging European encroachments, which might then be viewed as breaches of Christian ethics.

Impact of Christian Missions. Protestant missions tended to build village parishes around nuclei of adult communicant members, deacons, and native teachers (or, later, pastors). These teachers and their wives have been trained in centralized institutions, and they replaced the European evangelists who had performed the initial conversions. The London Missionary Society and the Anglican church added strong Bible-study groups and women's associations to this structure. Catholic missionaries were usually content with installing a catechist or two in each village to promote further conversions.

Missions eventually also became involved in promoting trade between Europe and the islands. The impetus for this trade came in part from the newly converted natives who from the outset wanted to obtain easy access to European money and goods. The London Missionary Society, the Anglicans, and the Church Missionary Society bought or leased ships in order to supply food to their widely dispersed converts, and they established chains of local trading stations. These well-organized local mission stations prospered and also acted as a means of bringing native produce to the European market. After some time, the missions also acquired plantations. At first the missionaries claimed that this acquisition was designed to prevent Europeans from staking claims to large tracts of land. Eventually, however, missions began to obtain lands merely for their own commercial profit, and the natives suffered economically. In some cases disputes concerning land acquired by the missions have not yet been resolved and the plantations have become a burning sore in the churches' flesh. Mission general stores were intended to provide native converts with access to European goods at a reasonable price. On islands that came under colonial rule, these stores attracted strong denunciations from European settlers, most of whom wanted to garner quick profits from trade with the natives and to establish themselves as agricultural barons. The resulting bad relations between the missions and local Europeans continued up to the time of independence.

Nuns and missionaries' wives trained women and girls in new ways of dressing, sewing, and cooking, and in new methods of child care and general hygiene. They also taught the women to read and write in their own languages, while their husbands were teaching the same skill to the native men. The acquisition of literacy was welcomed by the islanders and helped them to deal with the pressures introduced by the whites.

There were as many Catholic nuns involved in mission work as Catholic priests and brothers. The nuns attended to the daily needs of the priests, ran mission schools, and sometimes did medical work. Suborders, which recruited native women, were often founded in the islands; the Petites Sœurs de Marie in New Caledonia, for example, furnished servants for the European sisters.

It was, however, in the area of intellectual life that missionaries had their greatest impact on Pacific island societies. The London Missionary Society commissioned the German philologist F. Max Müller to design a system of writing for the Oceanic languages, and Protestant clergymen devoted much of their time to learning native vernaculars and translating the Bible into them. Newly literate islanders were proud to acquire Bibles and other publications, such as John Bunyan's *Pilgrim's Progress.* There was even a periodical for the natives, although it appeared only sporadically. Since the content of the Bible was familiar to all nineteenth-century Europeans, it could serve as common conceptual ground and as a medium of communication for natives and Europeans alike. The islanders adopted biblical patterns of speech and behavior to make themselves acceptable to Europeans. They also proposed the biblical kings David and Solomon as models of Christian statesmanship in an attempt to deter Europeans from establishing colonial control over the islands. However the Kingdom of Tonga (which managed to evade any sort of colonial system) and Western Samoa have maintained a carefully drawn line between European ideas and traditional patterns of political behavior.

The curricula of the missionary schools of the mid-nineteenth century were strikingly modern. In the lower grades, classes were taught exclusively in the vernacular. In the upper grades, instruction in the native language was supplemented by education in English or French for the most promising pupils. Eventually, parents demanded a thoroughly European education for their children. The Seventh-day Adventists were the first to open schools with curricula modeled on the European system and taught completely in European languages; other Christian groups quickly followed suit. Recently, however, these schools have gradually been returning to the original system of classes taught in native tongues, with English or French as a second language, as islanders have begun to desire the preservation of their own languages and cultures.

The medical work of the missions was difficult in the early years. Western medicine had few remedies for tropical diseases and was not much more successful at curing illnesses such as smallpox, measles, influenza, tuberculosis, and venereal diseases, all of which had been brought to the islands by Europeans. The natives died in droves while missionaries preached. Eventually, missionary organizations added trained doctors to their staffs and set up the first modern hospitals in the islands.

Much has been made of the connections between the French and British governments and their respective national missionary bodies. Admittedly, missionaries often called upon their nations' naval vessels to provide them with protection. On the other hand, the presence of these warships also proved to be an effective means of controlling the activities of unscrupulous traders, land hunters, and labor recruiters for Queensland, Australia, plantations. Conditions might have been worse for the natives without the French and British naval presence.

One aspect of nineteenth-century mission activity in this area that has received comparatively little attention is the churches' resistance to colonial annexation of the islands by European powers. Missionary organizations wanted their governments' sanction and protection—in part against the encroachments of rival missions—but they only slowly became reconciled to the establishment of direct colonial rule. In this way, missionaries actually protected the cultures of the island peoples. Overall, except in Hawaii and Tahiti, the early arrival of the missionaries helped to preserve indigenous ways of life from destruction at the hands of the settlers who arrived later. The independent nations of today owe much to the isolated and stubborn missionaries who refused to recognize any authority other than that of their God.

Today, in the 1980s, missions in the Pacific are a thing of the past, but the very recent past. The islanders' attachment to Christianity has remained strong. Ratu Sir Kamisese Mara, prime minister of Fiji, in the 1970s remarked to me: "We Pacific islanders are the only ones who still take seriously the Sermon on the Mount!" The islanders feel that Christianity, having been abandoned by the whites who brought it, now belongs to them.

[*See also* Christianity, *article on* Christianity in the Pacific Islands.]

BIBLIOGRAPHY

An early work, by Methodist missionaries Thomas Williams and James Calvert, is *Fiji and the Fijians, the Islands and Inhabitants: Mission History*, 2 vols., edited by G. S. Rowe (London, 1858). Another, by London Missionary Society missionary Archibald Wright Murray, is *Wonders of the Western Isles, Being a Narrative of the Commencement and Progress of Mission Work in Western Polynesia* (London, 1874). E. S. Armstrong's *The History of the Melanesian Mission* (London, 1900) tells the remarkable story of the Anglican Mission in northern Vanuatu and the Solomon Islands. Alexander Don's *Peter Milne, 1834–1924: Missionary to Nguna, New Hebrides, 1870 to 1924, from the Presbyterian Church of New Zealand* (Dunedin, 1927) describes the life of one of those very opinionated Presbyterian missionaries to Vanuatu. Eric Ramsden's *Marsden and the Missions, Prelude to Waitangi* (Sydney, 1936) describes the situation of the New Zealand missions prior to the British annexation of that country. A description of the French Protestant work in New Caledonia can be found in Maurice Leenhardt's *La grande terre: Mission de Nouvelle-Calédonie*, rev. & enl. ed. (Paris, 1922). James Clifford studied the brilliant figure of Maurice Leenhardt in his *Person and Myth: Maurice Leenhardt in the Melanesian World* (Berkeley, 1982).

The efforts of the Roman Catholic mission are best detailed in two little-known volumes: *Conférence sur la loi naturelle*, volume 5 of *Comptes-rendus des conférences ecclésiastiques du vicariat apostolique de la Nouvelle-Calédonie* (Saint-Louis, New Caledonia, 1905), and Victor Doucеré's *La mission catholique aux Nouvelles-Hébrides* (Lyons, 1934).

A more general analysis of the results of earlier efforts to convert the Pacific islanders to Christianity is given in my essay "The Millenarian Aspect of Conversion to Christianity in the South Pacific," in *Millennial Dreams in Action* (The Hague, 1962), pp. 122–138.

JEAN GUIART

History of Study

Oceania is conventionally defined in terms of the three major cultural divisions of the Pacific islanders: Polynesia, Micronesia, and Melanesia. The earliest European knowledge of Oceanic peoples is contained in the journals of Magellan's chronicler, Antonio Pigafetta, who in 1521 provides an account of the initial encounter with the inhabitants of an island that he called Los Ladrones, now identified as Guam. As with most contact narratives, the tale dwells upon visible details and practical difficulties, but it offers little insight into local life. And, as Andrew Sharp writes in his *The Discovery of the Pacific Islands* (2d ed., Oxford, 1962), much the same may be said of the journals of subsequent explorers such as Alvaro de Mendaña de Neira, Francis Drake, William Dampier, and Louis-Antoine de Bougainville. It is only toward the end of the eighteenth century that fuller accounts of Oceanic cultures become available with James Cook's journals on Tahiti and Hawaii, published as *The Journals of Captain James Cook on His Voyages of Discovery* (3 vols., Cambridge, 1957–1967) and with the narratives of castaways and beachcombers in, for example, George Keate's *An Account of the Pelew Islands* (London, 1788), *The Marquesan Journal of Edward Robarts, 1797–1824,* edited by Greg Dening (Honolulu, 1974), and *The Journal of William Lockerby,* edited by Everard Im Thurn and Leonard C. Wharton (London, 1925). The best nineteenth-century sources are largely the works of administrators and other long-term residents, such as Abraham Fornander's *An Account of the Polynesian Race* (1878–1885; reprint, Rutland, Vt., 1969) and George Grey's *Polynesian Mythology and Ancient Traditional History of the Maori as Told by Their Priests and Chiefs* (1855; reprint, New York, 1970).

Despite this growing wealth of information about Oceanic cultures, the systematic study of Oceanic religions remained largely undeveloped before the advent of anthropology in the latter part of the nineteenth century. Unlike the "high" religions such as Christianity, Islam, Buddhism, and so forth, the traditional religions of Oceania were not proselytizing creeds embodied in written texts but were instead embedded in the specifics of the societies in which they were found. Although priesthoods were characteristic of a number of Polynesian societies (e.g., Maori, Hawaiian, Samoan, etc.), these soon collapsed under European pressure. For the remainder of the region religious institutions tended to be diffused throughout the social structure, so that an understanding of them hinged upon an understanding of their social setting. Precisely because of relative hospitality to outsiders, European impact on traditional society was strongest in Polynesia and Micronesia, whereas Melanesia was largely left alone. For these reasons Melanesia has predominated in research on traditional religions in Oceania.

A major goal of early anthropology was the creation of typological schemes to lay the basis for the reconstruction of evolutionary stages from savagery to civilization. Given the nineteenth century's intoxication with progress, human history was viewed as the intellectual movement from magic and religion to the scientific rationalism held to epitomize civilization. For this reason religion played a central role in the theoretical frameworks of writers such as E. B. Tylor and James G. Frazer, whose perspective took exotic religions as indicative of modes of thought. In the process, they identified cultural forms with cognitive capacities in the invidious comparison of savagery with civilization.

Such schemes required generalized concepts to identify characteristic features of "savage" thought, and this was the context in which some of the earliest accounts of Oceanic religions entered into scholarly discussions. Two concepts of particular importance to early theories of religion are those of *mana* and of taboo, both of which arose from ethnographic studies in the Pacific. The notion of *mana* stems from the work of R. H. Codrington, a missionary anthropologist working in eastern Melanesia in the late nineteenth century. In *The Melanesians* (1891; reprint, New Haven, 1957) Codrington identified belief in *mana* as a central tenet of Melanesian religions and defined it as a supernatural power immanent in the cosmos and capable of influencing events for good or ill. *Mana* characterized outstanding success in all enterprises as both sign and source of efficacy, was intimately tied to personal prestige, and served to mark off the singular in experience. Codrington saw all Melanesian religion as an attempt to acquire *mana* for one's own uses. Understood on analogy with electricity, *mana* gave a name to what had long been postulated as a premise of magical thought, that is, the idea that unseen and impersonal powers in the world could be tapped, accumulated, and directed toward human ends. Subsequent work in Oceania found closely analogous concepts, and the notion of *mana* was soon generalized to cover a wide range of cases. More recent ethnographers have shown Codrington's original formulation to be based on a fundamental semantic misunderstanding (see, for example, Roger M. Keesing's "Rethinking Mana," *Journal of Anthropological Research* 40, 1984, pp. 137–156). Nevertheless, the concept gained wide currency in comparative studies as a key analytic category. In a similar vein, the concept of taboo became part of the vocabulary of the anthropology of religion through early analyses of the Polynesian notion of *tapu* (see, for example, E. S. Craighill Handy's *Polynesian Religion,* Honolulu, 1927). [*See also the biography of Codrington.*]

Early treatments of Oceanic religions were attempts simply to record religious practices and beliefs in such a way that they became intelligible to European audiences, and to the extent that larger issues came into play the concern was to isolate particular features that meshed with current theories of social evolution and culture history. One consequence of this essentially typological orientation was that apparent commonalities tended to be stressed at the expense of the distinctive features of particular religious systems, fostering a spurious sense of uniformity. A second consequence was a tendency to view Oceanic religions in atomistic terms, as a series of intellectual categories divorced from the contexts of social life. A decisive shift awaited the emergence of new canons of ethnography associated with Bronislaw Malinowski's fieldwork among the Trobriand Islanders off the east coast of New Guinea.

Prior to World War I, fieldwork in Oceania was largely of two kinds. Often information was obtained by men whose familiarity with an area was grounded in missionary or administrative work. One advantage such workers had was a long-term involvement with local people, but their ethnographic work was secondary to their other duties, which were often at cross-purposes with research interests. Professional anthropologists, on the other hand, tended to pursue their researches by conducting surveys from government verandas or the decks of itinerant vessels calling in at various islands. Here systematic coverage was possible, but it came at the expense of detailed knowledge of life in any particular locale. Malinowski's contribution was the development of long-term fieldwork whose aim was to construct a comprehensive portrait of social life in immediate and concrete terms. Not surprisingly, this work produced very different results from that done by his predecessors.

Inspired by the theories of Émile Durkheim and steeped in the details of Trobriand life, Malinowski in his *Magic, Science and Religion* (New York, 1948), insisted that it was only possible to understand Trobriand religion as an aspect of Trobriand culture in general. Taking issue with those who saw religion as a thing in itself, his style of interpretation ("functionalism") stressed the social dimensions of religious beliefs and the uses to which they could be put: myths of ancestral emergence were charters for territorial claims; beliefs in ancestral spirits and reincarnation reinforced the ties of clanship fundamental to the structure of the society; garden magic coordinated the productive efforts of entire communities, while fishing magic lent the confidence necessary to perilous undertakings. For Malinowski, the interpretation of religion was less a matter of locating general categories or apprehending a particular mode of thought than discovering a pragmatic rationality in what people said and did in the context of a specific social system. [*See also the biography of Malinowski.*]

Malinowski's influence upon anthropology was enormous: his style of fieldwork became the hallmark of serious anthropology, while his version of functional analysis became basic to the anthropological tool kit. The period between the wars was marked by a number of fine-grained field studies, in which the works of Gregory Bateson, Reo F. Fortune, Maurice Leenhardt, and F. E. Williams stand out.

Fortune is best known for his *Sorcerers of Dobu* (1932; rev. ed., New York, 1963), but a far more significant work is his *Manus Religion* (Philadelphia, 1935) Enmeshed in a dense network of obligations, Manus Islanders depended on the ghosts of their fathers to punish moral breaches through illness, and when illness struck divination sought out the sufferer's lapses in confession and expiation. Fortune showed how such beliefs occasioned assessment and reparation of personal relationships while seeking to regain the sufferer's health. In the process ghost beliefs were rescued from the dead category of "ancestor worship" by examining their role in the dynamics of village life.

Bateson's *Naven* (1938; 2d ed., Stanford, Calif., 1958) was an ambitious attempt to interpret a central ritual of the Iatmul people of the Sepik River of New Guinea. In the Naven ritual, significant events in an individual's life were marked by a ceremonial inversion of sex roles, and Bateson took the problems posed by this rite as the foundation for a sophisticated development of the concept of structure in cultural analysis. In this way ritual became a lens for understanding the formal underpinnings of psychological attitudes, cosmological principles, intergroup relations, and social roles in Iatmul culture.

F. E. Williams, the Government Anthropologist for Papua until his death in World War II, conducted a number of field studies touching upon traditional religions, but his most significant contribution was his account of the so-called Vailala Madness among the peoples of the Papuan Gulf, published in his *The Vailala Madness and Other Essays* (London, 1976). An early instance of what were later to become familiar as cargo cults, the Vailala Madness was a dramatic cultural transformation in which traditional rites were abandoned wholesale as local people strove to embark on a new mode of life in the face of European contact. The movement was directed through tranced prophets, and key themes were the establishment of contact with ancestors (identified with Europeans), a transcendence of traditional divisions between the sexes, and access to European goods through ritual. Williams's reaction to the movement was ambivalent, but he drew attention to the creative dynamism latent in the interplay of skepticism and openness that marked religious belief for Papuan peoples. This observation was pregnant with implications for prevailing views postulating a relatively static integration of religion and culture.

A missionary anthropologist working in New Caledonia, Maurice Leenhardt, in his *Do Kamo: Person and Myth in the Melanesian World* (Chicago, 1979), developed a novel approach that grew out of his practical and intellectual concern with the relation between traditional religion and Christianity (see James Clifford's *Person and Myth: Maurice Leenhardt in the Melanesian World*, Berkeley, 1982). Seizing upon religious ideas (especially as embodied in myth and in linguistic categories) as a frame for experience, he analyzed New Caledonian concepts of identity in terms of time, space, and personal relationships. This phenomenological undertaking served to clarify the differences between New Caledonian and Western notions of the individual, and this analysis in turn helped to situate his understanding of the process of conversion to Christianity in terms of the transformation of the self. [*See also the biography of Leenhardt.*]

Prior to World War II, most anthropological work followed Malinowski's program with general ethnographic coverage as the goal. The war itself brought about a total halt in fieldwork and it was not until the 1950s that Pacific anthropology once again became active. When it did so there were several noteworthy differences. Most significant of these was a reorientation influenced by A. R. Radcliffe-Brown and his students. Within this perspective most aspects of culture were seen as epiphenomena to be accounted for in terms of their contribution to the maintenance of the social order as defined by systems of groups such as clans, lineages, and so on. Religious beliefs and practices were accorded a decidedly secondary role and entered into analysis only insofar as they could be shown to reinforce a system of social relations.

One result of these developments was that the study of traditional religions remained to all intents and purposes moribund as analyses of social structure dominated the field until the latter part of the 1960s. The major exception to this trend was afforded by the study of cargo cults. Though widespread throughout the Pacific, cargo cults were neglected before the publication of Kenelm Burridge's *Mambu, a Melanesian Millennium* (London, 1960), despite the availability of Williams's prewar work. Popularly associated with bizarre rites aimed at the acquisition of Western manufactured goods, cargo cults burgeoned in the wake of the massive military operations of World War II.

Burridge's work in the Madang region of New Guinea showed that the notion of "cargo" comprised not only European goods but the ensemble of moral dilemmas embodied in local relations with Europeans and the cash economy. Radically different from traditional forms of exchange, cash transactions entailed no reciprocal obligation and conferred no moral standing and thus called into question traditional measures of man. Through a dialectic of myth, dream, aspiration, and moral critique, cargo movements constituted attempts to formulate an image of a new life and a new morality, made concrete in the figure of the charismatic cargo prophet. An overall concern was to reestablish the moral equivalence basic to Melanesian societies in a Europeanized environment by transcending the limitations symbolized in the notion of cargo. Burridge's study was soon augmented by Peter Lawrence's historical account of Madang cargo movements, *Road Belong Cargo* (Manchester, England, 1964). Lawrence analyzed the career of Yali, a cargo prophet, in the context of native relations with Europeans. An important point made in both of these studies was the extent to which traditional epistemologies based upon mythology and revelatory experiences served to enable historical transformations in Madang societies. These analyses were complemented by Peter Worsley's comparative study, *The Trumpet Shall Sound* (London, 1957), which argued that cargo movements were nascent anticolonial political movements. Each of these works implied a critique of contemporary views of religion as the static appendage of social structure by underscoring the dynamic role of religion in cultural change.

In the mid-1960s, Lawrence and M. J. Meggitt edited *Gods, Ghosts, and Men in Melanesia* (Melbourne, 1965), which is a compilation of a number of detailed accounts of Melanesian religions. Yet with the noteworthy exception of Jan van Baal's *Dema* (The Hague, 1966), most other anthropological treatments of traditional religions remained fixated on social structure as the guiding interpretive frame. One innovative departure was Roy A. Rappaport's *Pigs for the Ancestors* (New Haven, 1968), which viewed the ritual cycle of pig sacrifices among the Maring as a homeostatic mechanism for maintaining ecological relationships between local populations and their environment. Even here, however, the emphasis remained upon the role of religious institutions in underwriting some form of status quo, whether sociological or ecological, portraying them as essentially parasitic upon other features of the social system.

A dramatic shift in the analysis of religious phenomena took place with the publication of Burridge's *Tangu Traditions* (Oxford, 1969) and Roy Wagner's *Habu: The Innovation of Meaning in Daribi Religion* (Chicago, 1972). In a painstaking analysis of Tangu narrative, Burridge extended the thesis adumbrated in his previous work by teasing out the ways in which, through recourse to myth, the Tangu apprehended the singular and numinous in experience. Finding more in myth than a Malinowskian charter for particular social arrangements, Burridge argued that it provided a tool for the exploration of unrealized possibilities, and he demonstrated how mythic content in turn became reformulated in the light of novel experience. In *Habu* Wagner pursued a different line of thought with similar implications. Focusing upon traditional Daribi religion, he developed a theory of innovation upon cultural ideologies that took the process of metaphorization as its key concept. Covering a range of material incuding naming, dream interpretation, the form of magical spells and the patterning of ritual, he argued for a view of cultural meaning stressing a dialectical tension between different realms of experience that afforded scope for creativity in the innovative extension of metaphors across conventional categories of signification. An essential part of Wagner's theory is that these processes be understood as normal properties of all cultural systems. Both of these works locate sources of cultural dynamism in the realm of religious phenomena and emphasize the reflective interplay of image and experience. They thus offer essentially open-ended accounts in which symbols are apprehended less as static structures than as participants in a dialectic that Williams might well have termed "culture on the move" (1976, p. 395).

Anthropology from the mid-1970s forward witnessed a growing interest in processes of symbolization, and this development, coupled with the impact of previous work, prompted a number of detailed studies placing religion once again at the heart of anthropology in the Pacific. Several provocative analyses of ritual emerged, addressing a wide range of theoretical problems.

Wagner extended the logic of his previous analysis in *Lethal Speech* (Ithaca, N.Y., 1978), a study of different genres of Daribi myth. Developing a line congenial to Wagner's work, Edward L. Schieffelin, in his *The Sorrow of the Lonely and the Burning of the Dancers* (New York, 1976), recounts the metaphorically rich *gisaro* ceremony and makes use of the concepts of opposition and reciprocity to situate an overall understanding of the Kaluli worldview. In his *Karavar: Masks and Power in Melanesian Ritual* (Ithaca, N.Y., 1974), Frederick K. Errington showed how rites involving masked dancers articulated a collective image of order against the backdrop of cultural assumptions postulating a chaotic human nature.

Male initiation rites became a focus of attention in, for example, Gilbert H. Herdt's *Guardians of the Flutes* (New York, 1981), a study of the psychological dimensions of sexual identity; Fredrik Barth's *Ritual and Knowledge among the Baktaman of New Guinea* (New Haven, 1975), an examination of the relation between ritual and knowledge; and Gilbert Lewis's *Day of Shining Red* (Cambridge, 1980), a study of hermeneutic problems. One of the most impressive contributions was Alfred Gell's *Metamorphosis of the Cassowaries* (London, 1975), in which a complex and refractory dialectic of succession and renewal became intelligible through a symbolic analysis utilizing structuralist techniques of interpretation. Structuralist principles also contributed strongly to F. Allan Hanson and Louise Hanson's *Counterpoint in Maori Culture* (London, 1983), a sophisticated analysis of complementarity and symmetry in Maori religion and culture, while Marshall D. Sahlin's account of transformations in Hawaiian culture in his *Historical Metaphors and Mythical Realities* (Ann Arbor, 1981) and *Islands of History* (Chicago, 1985) deployed similar techniques to show how metaphorical extensions of religious premises influenced the direction of historical change.

Two of the most significant recent trends in the study of Oceanic religions are the incorporation of a view that accords to symbols an active role in transforming experience and a concern to come to grips with the dynamism of religious life. These orientations grow out of general anthropological preoccupations and at the same time reflect the necessity of coming to terms with history. Pacific pagans are now few and far between, and the last century has seen the emergence of Christianity as the dominant religious form in Oceania. For examples of these trends at work, see *Mission, Church, and Sect in Oceania,* edited by James A. Boutilier et al. (Ann Arbor, 1978); Raymond Firth's *Rank and Religion in Tikopia* (London, 1970); and John Garrett's *To Live among the Stars* (Suva, Fiji Islands, 1982). If the study of Oceanic religions is to retain contemporary relevance it must take as its task an understanding of religious life harking back to Leenhardt's central problem: the retention of authenticity in the face of the christianization of the Pacific.

DAN W. JORGENSEN

OCEANS. It is natural to begin a survey of the mythology of oceans with their eponymous deity, the Greek god Okeanos (etymology unknown). All evidence testifies that Okeanos was originally conceived as a river god, rather than a god of the salt sea. This illustrates a characteristic difficulty: to treat rivers, springs, and fountains, or the symbolic and religious associations of water in general, exceeds the compass of this article, but such distinctions are not always rigorous in the mythological traditions. [*See* Water.]

In the pantheon defined by Hesiod's *Theogony*, Okeanos is the offspring of Ouranos (Sky) and Gaia (Earth), and thus of the race of Titans that included Kronos, the father of Zeus. With his sister Tethys as consort, Okeanos produced the vast brood of Okeanids, spirits of rivers and streams. Parallel to Okeanos is Pontos (Sea): born of Gaia alone, he unites with her to engender Nereus, whence the Nereids, a species of sea nymphs corresponding to the Okeanids. While Pontos remains a bare abstraction, Okeanos is imagined as dwelling with Tethys at the edge of the world, which he encircles. In descriptions of the shields of Achilles (Homer) and Herakles (attributed to Hesiod), Okeanos occupies the rim.

References in Homer (*Iliad* 14.200f., 244ff., 301f.), as well as in Plato, Vergil, Orphic texts, and elsewhere, identify Okeanos and Tethys as the source *(genesis)* of gods or of the universe. Details of this cosmogony are obscure; according to one version, the primordial waters brought forth an egg that initiated the process of creation (Orphic fragments 54, 57). Okeanos was related to underworld rivers such as the Styx, which was his daughter, according to Hesiod (*Theogony* 361; cf. Plato, *Phaedo* 112e). The Isle of the Blessed, where souls of heroes dwelled, was in Okeanos's waters (*Odyssey* 4.562–568). The relationship between the cosmogonic role of Okeanos and water as the fundamental element in Thales's philosophy is moot.

Okeanos was occasionally represented in sculptures and sarcophagus reliefs, but does not appear to have had a specific cult. The sea was worshiped and appeased in the name of Poseidon, later identified with the Roman Neptune. The primitive evolution of Poseidon is obscure (he is conspicuously associated with the horse). In the Olympian scheme, Poseidon received the waters as his province from Zeus. He was responsible for maritime calm and turbulence, and for earthquakes. As consort of the Okeanid (or Nereid) Amphitrite, he was father of the gigantic Triton, whose torso terminated in a serpent's tail. Various pre-Olympian deities abided in the sea, notably Proteus, who shared with Nereus and with the Nereid Thetis (mother of Achilles) the power to metamorphose and to foretell the future.

The idea of encompassing waters survived into medieval geography, as in the map attached to Ibn Khaldūn's *Muqaddimah* (the name *Ūqyānūs* in one manuscript renders "Okeanos"). The earth is said by Islamic writers to float on the sea like a grape or an egg.

In the cultures of the ancient Near East, oceanic waters figured largely in cosmogonic myths. According to Sumerian tradition, in the beginning was Nammu (Sea), whence arose a mountain representing heaven and earth, later separated by the air god Enlil. In the Babylonian creation story, recited at the New Year, the primordial gods are two: the masculine Apsu, representing sweet waters, and the feminine Tiamat, the saltwater ocean, from whose union come the gods. Apsu is vanquished by younger gods, but Tiamat continues the battle with the help of Kingu and other monstrous offspring; she is defeated by the storm god Marduk and divided in two, one part of her being raised to contain the upper waters. From the *Epic of Gilgamesh,* it appears that the land of the dead was reached by crossing a body of water. The same narrative incorporates the Sumerian tradition of a great flood, perhaps representing a return to the primordial state.

In Canaanite myth, the senior deity El favors Yam (Sea) against his own son, Baal (associated with fertility and rain). Yam surrenders to Baal and is spared; also vanquished is the serpent Lotan, related to the Hebrew Leviathan (cf. also the defeats of Rahab and Tannin: *Ps.* 74:13, 89:11; *Is.* 51:9; etc.). The biblical sea waters seem to retain a threatening aspect, as though not entirely submissive to creation; certain passages indicate the sea as the site of God's throne (e.g., *Ps.* 104:3; *Ez.* 28:2).

In Egyptian sources, the waters of Nun, on which the earth rests, are sometimes identified as the origin of life. At the parting of the waters appears the primal hill. Nun was also conceived as surrounding the earth (like Okeanos), so that the sun emerged each day from his waters in the east. The route to the afterworld is the river Nile, host also to aquatic deities such as the crocodile, but since the Nile was believed to have its source in the netherworld (Pyramid Texts 1551a, 1557b), the distinction between river and primal waters is not absolute.

The *Ṛgveda* (10.121) alludes to a cosmic egg (Prajāpati) that emerged from water, an idea elaborated in later commentaries (*Śatapatha Brāhmaṇa* 11.1.6) that also record a flood. The identification of Varuṇa as god of the sea is post-Vedic. The ocean is the source of *amṛta,* the liquor of immortality (analogously, the Greek ambrosia is sometimes connected with the ocean). In Hindu mythology, the cobralike sea demons called *nāgas* (feminine dragons are called *nāginis*) have their kingdom in the west or alternatively are imagined as dwelling in the underworld. In Cambodia, the first Khmer dynasty is said to have sprung from the union of the daughter of a *nāga* king with a Hindu prince.

In Chinese myth, where nature deities play a relatively unimportant part, the four seas that surround the earth are associated each with a dragon king. In one legend the king of all the dragons arose from the sea and prevented the first emperor of Ch'in from voyaging to the islands of the immortals. The antiquity of such stories is in doubt, as they appear to have been influenced by Hindu myth. Undeniably ancient (dating from the Chou dynasty) is the story of the flood, which was dammed, channeled, and drained by the god Yü with the help of a dragon. Yü then became the founder of China's first dynasty.

The Ainu (the aborigines of Japan) tell of a small bird

that dispersed the primal waters by the motion of its wings. In the *Kojiki,* the main compendium of ancient Japanese myth, the original chaos is compared to oily water, but the sea's major role appears in the tale of the sons of Ninigi, the divine ancestor of Japan's emperors. The younger son, Po-wori, a hunter, borrows and loses the fishhook of his brother Po-deri. A sea deity constructs a boat and advises Po-wori to sail to the palace of Watatsumi, god of the sea, and his daughter Tōyōtama. Po-wori marries Tōyōtama but later desires to return home. Watatsumi recovers the lost hook and gives his son-in-law two jewels to control the tides. Coming home on a crocodile, Po-wori subdues his elder brother. Tōyōtama, assuming the form of a crocodile, bears her husband a child and then returns to the sea, ashamed that he has observed her thus. Her younger sister tends and marries the son, and from this union is born the first Japanese emperor. Shrines are devoted to Watatsumi and other sea divinities.

Meander patterns on Paleolithic vessels of Europe, often in association with maternal figures, eggs, snakes, and waterfowl, suggest water as a fertility symbol. In the Finnish epic *Kalevala* (old version), which preserves Finno-Ugric traditions, the world is created out of eggs laid by an eagle on the knee that the hero Väinämöinen lifts from the sea (Väinä means "still water"). Väinämöinen subsequently sails to death's domain and escapes meshes laid to trap him by metamorphosing into various forms. The Saami (Lapp) god Cacce Olmai (Water Man), a deity of fishing, is said to assume various shapes; also reported is a mermaidlike creature called Akkruva, similar to the Inuit (Eskimo) Inue, a kind of merman.

In Celtic myths, there is a paradisiacal island called Brittia located in the ocean. This ancient account is transmitted by the Byzantine historian Procopius (cf. the Arthurian Avalon, the Irish Tir-na-nogue). Islands are the object of voyages by various heroes or demigods. Bran, a sea giant, encounters an isle of women, an isle of laughter and joy, and other fantastical places on his journey. Similarly, Brendan, in search of the Land of Promise, encounters enchanted islands and monsters; one island proves to be the back of a gigantic sea creature (cf. Sindbad's first voyage). The Roman general Sertorius is said by Plutarch to have attempted such a journey from Spain, which suggests a possible syncretism of Greek and Iberian traditions. The inspiration of Brendan's legend is evident in Dante's version of Odysseus's last voyage.

The province of the sea fell to the Celtic god or hero Ler, and more especially to his son, Manannán mac Lir, patron of sailors and merchants and the eponymous deity of the Isle of Man. Manannán rode the steed Enbarr, which could traverse water as easily as land (cf. the kelpie or sea horse in Scottish folklore).

In the Eddas, the god of the sea is Ægir (cognate with *aqua*), a member of the race of giants who is friendly to the gods. His wife is Ran, and a kenning (metaphorical phrase) speaks of the waves of Ægir's daughters. Ægir is the gods' ale-brewer and a giver of banquets. Norse myth tells of various sea monsters such as the huge fish-like creature called the kraken, as well as mermen and mermaids (see the thirteenth-century *King's Mirror*), the belief in which has persisted into modern times among fishermen of New England and elsewhere.

In the Americas, the creation myths of the Chorti, Maya Indians of Guatemala, mention four seas that are distinguished by color surrounding and beneath the world, with monstrous creatures (angels in christianized versions) beyond the waters. Among the people of Santa Elena, there is a story of a race of giants who came from across the sea. There is a hint of a primal sea in the *Popol Vuh,* the sacred book of the Quiché Maya of Guatemala.

A widespread North American variant involves the creation of land upon the primordial ocean by means of a diver, whether divine, human, or animal, who brings mud or earth up from the sea bottom. In the Salinan version (California), a dove fetches the substance after a flood produced by the Old Woman of the Sea; a turtle is the agent in Maidu (California) and Blackfeet myth. In a Huron creation account, a toad is successful; in a Mandan (North Dakota) version, it is a duck, while other stories feature the muskrat (Assiniboine, Great Plains), the water beetle (Cherokee), and the crawfish (Yuchi). There are also versions in which the waters simply recede. The Navajo emergence myth, which like the Hopi myth describes four worlds associated with four directions and four colors, has four seas as well. The Winnebago Indians (Great Plains) distinguish two classes of water powers: streams are masculine, while the subterranean waters that uphold the earth are feminine.

Altaic myth (Siberia) also exhibits versions of the diver tale, with the diver as swallow, loon, goose, or other waterfowl. Elsewhere the diver is a man or devil, often in the guise of a bird; a Christian Romanian version casts Satan as the diver. In a Samoyed flood story, a bird discovers land in a manner reminiscent of the bird in the narrative of Noah's ark. The theme of the ark occurs also in Buriat myth. Mention may also be made of a Khanty (Yenisei River) creation story, according to which the earth rests on three great fish, the sinking of which generates floods.

In a Polynesian account, Māui or another deity brings land up from the sea bottom. A Maori tale tells of a conflict between Ta-whiri-ma-tea, the god of storms or winds, and his brother Tangaroa, here the father creator of the world. Ta-whiri-ma-tea attacks Tangaroa, who takes refuge in the ocean. One of Tangaroa's two children, representing fish, retreats to the water. The other child, representing reptiles, hides in the forest, whence the antagonism between the sea and humans, who are descended from the forest deity. The Polynesian practice of burying the dead in canoe-shaped dugouts may reflect a custom of setting bodies adrift to reach the ancestral home or land of the dead. It was believed that souls were carried to Bulotu, the Tongan land of the dead, in an invisible canoe presided over by Hikuleo, the Tongan god of the dead and half-brother of Tangaroa. Near his house, in one account, were the waters of life that could confer immortality. The land of the dead, usually located to the west, was the special destination of chiefs and other notables. Legends tell of parties sailing, usually by mistake, to Bulotu.

Marine myths are not widespread in Africa, but mention may be made of a Yao (Mozambique) story in which human beings are fished out of the sea by a chameleon.

From the foregoing survey, certain broad themes may be identified. The ocean is often conceived as the primordial element, from which land and sometimes living creatures emerge. It surrounds the earth and lies under it, and beyond its waters reside the departed or the blessed, who are sometimes visited by the intrepid voyager. Now and then flood waters challenge creation. The ocean is inhabited by various monsters, often serpentine and capable of metamorphosis. Marine deities are sometimes the ancestors of imperial dynasties. Finally, in some accounts the waters of the deep are life-giving, or the source of life-giving brews.

BIBLIOGRAPHY

On the Greek Okeanos, the best study is Jean Rudhardt's *Le thème de l'eau primordiale dans la mythologie grecque* (Bern, 1971). For the Old Testament, there is a useful survey of oceanic themes in Phillipe Reymond's *L'eau, sa vie, et sa signification dans l'ancien testament* (Leiden, 1958). The ancient Near Eastern materials may be consulted in the collection edited by J. B. Pritchard, *Ancient Near Eastern Texts relating to the Old Testament*, 3d ed. (Princeton, 1969). A good sampling of creation myths, in which primordial waters play a prominent role, is Barbara C. Sproul's *Primal Myths: Creating the World* (San Francisco, 1979). The encyclopedic *Mythology of All Races*, 13 vols., edited by Louis H. Gray and George Foot Moore (Boston, 1916–1932), is uneven and often out of date in method and content, but it contains much firsthand material and is the most extensive compendium. Robert W. Williamson's *Religious and Cosmic Beliefs of Central Polynesia*, 2 vols. (1933; New York, 1977), presents the numerous variant versions. The volume *Asiatic Mythology*, edited by Joseph Hackin et al. (New York, 1932), is especially good on modern myths, as in the contribution on China by Henri Maspero.

The Japanese *Kojiki* is available in a new translation by Donald L. Philippi (Tokyo and Princeton, 1969). Sources of Celtic mythology are widely scattered, but there is a readable summary by Charles Squire, *The Mythology of the British Islands: Celtic Myth and Legend, Poetry and Romance* (1909; Fulcroft, Pa., 1975), though it is inconsistent in citing sources and not always reliable in interpretation; see also Marie-Louise Sjoestedt's *Gods and Heroes of the Celts* (London, 1949). There is some information relevant to oceans in Martin Ninck's *Die Bedeutung des Wassers im Kult und Leben der Alten: Eine symbolgeschichtliche Untersuchung* (Leipzig, 1921), along with rich if speculative interpretative suggestions. For works cited in the text, see *The King's Mirror*, translated by Laurence Marcellus Larson (New York, 1917); *The Old Kalevala* of Elias Lönnrot, translated by Francis Peabody Magoun, Jr. (Cambridge, Mass., 1969); and *Pyramid Texts*, edited by Samuel A. B. Mercer (New York, 1952), in which excursuses 14 and 15 are particularly relevant. For Ibn Khaldūn, see Franz Rosenthal's translation of the *Muquddimah*, 3 vols., 2d ed. (Princeton, 1967); the map is the frontispiece to volume 1. A readable book on modern folklore is Horace Beck's *Folklore and the Sea* (Middletown, Conn., 1973). For Maya traditions, see John G. Foughts *Chorti (Mayan) Texts* (Philadelphia, 1972).

DAVID KONSTAN

OCKHAM, WILLIAM OF. *See* William of Ockham.

ÓÐINN (Odin) is the chief god of Germanic mythology. Described as "the best [ON, *œztr*] and the oldest of all the gods" by Snorri Sturluson (*Gylfaginning* 20), Óðinn is a complex figure. He is assumed to reign with patriarchal authority over everything, but the numerous names by which he is designated (see Falk, 1924; Lorenz, 1984, pp. 91–95, 290–304) point to the great diversity of his attributes and functions.

As he appears in the Scandinavian tradition Óðinn could be described as (1) the highest god in the pantheon, (2) the lord of battles, (3) the god of the dead, (4) the patron of poets, (5) a great magician, (6) the master of the runes, (7) a perceptive one-eyed seer, or (8) an unpredictable and unreliable deity; certain of these features are also documented for his southern counterpart, Wōdan. Upon closer examination, a number of comments can be made on these various points.

Designated in the literary sources as the ruler of Ásgarðr, Óðinn is called Alfaðir ("father of all"), perhaps under Christian influence, since he is definitely not the father of all the gods. While Þórr (Thor) is often referred to as his son, the Vanir Njǫrðr, Freyr, and Freyja are certainly not related to him. As for mankind, there are two traditions. According to the *Vǫluspá* (ss. 17–18), Óðinn and his two companions, Hœnir and Lóðurr, shaped the first human couple from two logs (a creative act that Snorri Sturluson ascribes rather to Óðinn and his brothers Vili and Vé); but the *Vǫluspá* (st. 1) calls all men "Heimdallr's children," and according to the *Rígsþula* Heimdallr is the progenitor of all the classes of society (thralls, freemen, and nobles). Moreover, Óðinn often appears in triads of gods and is even called Þriði ("third"), a fact that has led some scholars to compare the divine brothers Óðinn, Vili, and Vé rather hastily with the Christian Trinity (Lorenz, 1984, p. 146). He is also the first king in the euhemeristic tales describing the legendary early history of Scandinavia (e.g., in the *Ynglingasaga*), like Wōden in the genealogy of the Anglo-Saxon kings.

As a god of battle, Óðinn provides the paradigmatic ritual for opening hostilities by hurling his spear into the enemy camp in the war between the Æsir and the Vanir, a gesture that will also consecrate the dead and captured foes to himself. As a protector of the warriors, he teaches his chosen heroes the tactics that will ensure their victory in combat, for example, when he instructs Harald Wartooth or Hadingus to deploy his forces in the field in the shape of a wedge to break the opponents' line (Turville-Petre, 1964, pp. 212, 215). He also takes certain warriors under his wing, rescuing them in the thick of battle, as when he saves Hadingus from Loker (Saxo Grammaticus, 1.23), or involves himself in a warrior initiation ritual, as when he advises Hadingus to kill a wild beast and drink its blood to absorb its strength (Saxo Grammaticus, 1.24). He is not only the lord of dead warriors (his retinue of *einherjar*) but also the patron of the turbulent and powerful *berserkir* (lit., "bear coats") or *ulfheðnir* (lit., "wolf coats"), who fought with frenzied fury (Snorri Sturluson, *Ynglingasaga* 6). [*See* Berserkers.] In the later Scandinavian tradition, recorded in Uppsala in 1070 by the secretary of the bishop of Hamburg, Adam of Bremen, "Óðinn, that is, 'frenzy,' wages war and provides man with courage against foes" ("wodan, id est furor, bella gerit hominique ministrat virtutem contra inimicos"), making him essentially a war god.

The *Ynglingasaga* (chap. 7) calls Óðinn *draugadróttinn* ("lord of ghosts"), in keeping with the southern traditions about *Wutanes her* ("Wōdan's ghostly host"), which has been traced back to the *feralis exercitus* ("spectral army") of the bellicose Harii in Tacitus (*Germania* 43.4). It has been assumed that such epithets of Óðinn as *Grímr* ("masked") might refer to the masquerading of warrior bands connected with his cult, and that his chthonic affinities were reflected by the name *Fjǫlnir* ("concealer"), but these arguments rest on disputable interpretations. *Fjǫlnir,* for example, can also mean "god of plenty" or "very wise" or perhaps "able to take many shapes." The association of the Germanic name **Wōðan*[*az*] with Mercury in the *interpretatio Romana* of the Germanic gods has also been ascribed to Wōdan/Óðinn's role as psychopomp, but other explanations seem more plausible. Moreover, it should be remembered that Óðinn gets only half of the dead on the battlefield: the other half goes to Freyja. However, Óðinn is apparently depicted as the ferryman of the dead in the *Hárbarzljóð* and in the Eddic prose narrative *Frá dauoða Sinfjǫtla*.

Óðinn's patronage of poetry is already implicit in his name: The Germanic name **Wōðan*[*az*] means indeed "master of inspiration." The Old Norse term *óðr* (from which Óðinn's name derives) denotes "inspired mental activity," not merely "intelligence," conceived as the faculty of reasoning, as it is usually translated in the *Vǫluspá* (st. 18). This is confirmed by its skaldic use in the sense of "poetry," the poet being designated as "a smith of inspired thought" (ON, *óðar smiðr*). Óðinn himself "spoke in rhymes" (Snorri Sturluson, *Ynglingasaga* 6), and one of the gifts he bestows on his protégé Starkaðr is the ability to produce poetry as fast as he talks. But Óðinn's most concrete link with poetry is the myth of the poets' mead, narrated by Snorri Sturluson in the *Skáldskaparmál* (chap. 2).

Some malicious dwarfs had killed Kvasir, an exceedingly intelligent being allegedly fashioned by the gods from their spittle after the conclusion of the truce ending the war between the Æsir and the Vanir. [*See* Spittle and Spitting.] Mixing Kvasir's blood with honey in a kettle, the dwarfs brewed it into a mead that transformed anyone who drank it into a poet or a learned man. After they had mischievously caused the drowning of a giant, they were compelled to surrender the valuable beverage to the latter's son Suttungr. This giant hid the mead in his stronghold, Hnitbjǫrg, where his daughter Gunnlǫð kept watch over it.

How did Óðinn get hold of the mead? According to the story, he tricked the serfs of Suttungr's brother into cutting their throats with their scythes while they were trying to get hold of his whetstone, after which he offered his services to their master to replace them. Calling himself Bǫlverkr, and asking only for a drink of Suttungr's mead for his wages when the harvest was over, Óðinn did the work of nine men throughout the summer. When the time came for him to receive his due reward, however, Suttungr refused to give him a single drop of the mead. Óðinn then forced the giant's brother to help him bore a hole through the rock of Suttungr's stronghold, but his former master tried to trick and even to stab him. Óðinn escaped by changing himself into a snake and crawling inside the place where Gunnlǫð was guarding the mead. The god seduced her and slept with her for three nights, after which she promised him three drinks from the precious beverage. But Óðinn swallowed all there was in the three containers in which the mead was stored and, changing himself into an eagle, flew away as fast as he could. Suttungr also took the shape of an eagle and pursued him to Ásgarðr, where, before Suttungr could catch up with him, Óðinn spewed out the mead into three crocks the Æsir had prepared. Thus, Óðrœrir (the mead of poetry) became the drink of the Æsir.

As master of the runes, using magic charms and songs (ON, *galdrar*) and resorting as well to the despicable sorcery (ON, *seiðr*) he had learned from Freyja, Óðinn is undoubtedly the great worker of magic that Snorri Sturluson describes (*Ynglingasaga* 6), the Germanic representative of the Indo-European divine "king-magician" analyzed by Georges Dumézil. It is in this function that Wōdan still appears in the Old High German second Merseburg charm at the beginning of the tenth century, where he is able to successfully work the cure for a sprain suffered by Baldr's horse, whereas other deities before him failed in their efforts.

Although he does not have an absolute monopoly on the use of runes, as made clear in the *Hávamál* (st. 143), where the elf Dáinn, the dwarf Dvalinn, and the giant Alsviþr are listed as experts in the use of runes, Óðinn unquestionably possesses the most extensive secret knowledge of their mighty magic. The runic inscriptions do not mention him as the inventor of the runes, as do the *Hávamál* (ss. 138–139) and the *Sigrdrífumál* (st. 3), where Óðinn appears under the name *Hróptr* ("conjurer"), but the Stone of Noleby (Sweden, c. 600 CE) says explicitly that the runes come from the gods. As for the spells Óðinn can cast, the *Ljóðatál* (stanzas 148–163 of the *Hávamál*) enumerates quite a few of them: curing illness, stopping a missile in midair, dispelling witches, inspiring irresistible love, and so forth.

The prose introduction to the Eddic *Lay of Grímnir* tells how Óðinn, sitting with his wife Frigg in Hliðskjálf, his high seat in Ásgarðr, is able to watch anything that happens on any of the cosmic levels of the Germanic universe—a statement that Snorri Sturluson corroborates (*Gylfaginning* 9). The special acuity of Óðinn's eyesight is explained in the myth wherein he pledges one of his eyes in exchange for a draft from Mímir's well beneath the roots of the cosmic tree Yggdrasill, for the sake of the wisdom that it provides (*Gylfaginning* 15).

Óðinn's personality shows quite a few conflicting traits: in the *Lokasenna* (st. 22), he is accused of unfairness in granting victory, but if he acknowledges that he let the less deserving win, he justifies himself elsewhere (e.g., *Eiríksmál* 7) by claiming he needed heroes to help him face the Fenrisúlfr during the ultimate combat of Ragnarǫk. However, he relishes inciting conflicts and preventing peace and deceives those who serve him. For example, when Starkaðr pronounces the ominous formula "Now I give thee to Óðinn!" after tying the noose of calf's gut round Víkarr's neck as he hits him with a reed, Óðinn changes the weak entrail into a sturdy rope and the reed into a spear, thus transforming the sham sacrifice into a regicide (*Gautrekssaga* 7; cf. Turville-Petre, 1964, p. 45). Under the identity of Bruni, Óðinn kills his devoted friend and protégé Harald Wartooth (Saxo Grammaticus, 8.220), and he does not hesitate to swear solemnly that he knows nothing about Bǫlverkr, under which name he seduced Gunnlǫð in order to swindle her father, Suttungr, out of the mead of poetry (*Hávamál* 108–109). No wonder, then, that Dagr (in *Helgakviða Hundingsbana* 2.34) declares that Óðinn is responsible for all evil, after pointing out (as in *Hárbarzljóð* 24) that the god stirred up strife among close kinsmen!

BIBLIOGRAPHY

Dillmann, François-Xavier. "Georges Dumézil et la religion germanique: L'interprétation du dieu Odhinn." In *Georges Dumézil à la découverte des Indo-Européens*, edited by Jean-Claude Rivière et al., pp. 157–186. Paris, 1979.

Dumézil, Georges. *Gods of the Ancient Northmen.* Edited and translated by Einar Haugen. Berkeley, 1973.

Falk, Hjalmar. *Odensheite.* Kristiania (Oslo), 1924.

Helm, Karl. *Wodan: Ausbreitung und Wanderung seines Kultes.* Giessen, 1946.

Polomé, Edgar C. "The Indo-European Heritage in Germanic Religion: The Sovereign Gods." In *Athlon: Satura Grammatica in honorem Francisci R. Adrados*, edited by A. Bernabé et al., vol. 1, pp. 401–411. Madrid, 1984.

Turville-Petre, E. O. G. *Myth and Religion of the North: The Religion of Ancient Scandinavia.* New York, 1964.

Vries, Jan de. *Altgermanische Religionsgeschichte*, vol. 2. 2d rev. ed. Berlin, 1957.

EDGAR C. POLOMÉ

OFFERINGS. *See* Almsgiving; Sacrifice; *and* Tithes.

OGHMA, an Irish deity associated with war and magic, can be identified in terms of mythology with the Gaulish divinity Ogmios. Lucian of Samosata, a Greek author of the second century CE, describes Ogmios with rare and remarkable precision regarding his physical appearance and theological functions:

> In their mother tongue the Celts call Herakles "Ogmios" and depict him in a most singular manner. He is a very, very old man who is almost completely bald; what little hair he has left is entirely white; his skin is wrinkled, burned and almost tanned to leather, like an old sailor's; he could be taken for a Charon or for a Japhet of the subterranean domain of Tartaros, more than for Herakles; he is dressed in lion skins and in his right hand he holds a club; the quiver is affixed to his shoulders, and in his left hand he wields a drawn bow: these are all the details of Herakles. . . . This old man Herakles draws behind him a large number of men attached by their ears by means of thin gold and amber chains resembling very beautiful neckpieces. Despite the weakness of the links, the men do not attempt to flee, although it would be easy to do so; far from resisting, holding themselves tight and falling over backwards, they all follow their leader and are gay and content, showering him with praise and all endeavoring to catch up with him. Wanting to outdistance him, they loosen the cord as if they were astonished to see themselves delivered.

In a later passage, Lucian of Samosata says that the chains tie the ears of the devoted to the tongue of the god and that in this manner the Gauls symbolize eloquence.

Among the continental Celts the name *Ogmios* also appears in several *defixiones*, or inscribed tablets, at Bregenz; these confirm his role as a binding god. But he is not cited elsewhere in the Gallo-Roman epigraphy, since the *pax Romana* caused his disappearance as a major deity. His resemblance to Herakles fits in well with the Celtic concept of war, which is one of exploit and hand-to-hand combat. (Compare the role of Cú Chulainn in the Irish epic.) The difference is that Ogmios is a god who controls war and not a hero who wages it. He is a binding god, the god of magic, and the Irish comparison complements the attribution of eloquence with that of writing.

In Ireland Oghma is the champion, brother of Daghdha, and inventor of the system of magical writing that bears his name, the *ogham* symbols. He plays a somewhat mitigated role in the mythological tale the *Second Battle of Magh Tuiredh*, but he is described in greater detail in the cycle of Édaín, where he calls himself Elcmhaire, "the great one of envy" or "the mischievous one." This war god is depicted with all the traits of a poltroon, which is not dissimilar from certain accounts of the Greek Ares. In any case the symbolism is usual: Oghma is the dark side of the sovereign divinity of which Daghdha is the bright side. The Irish epics occasionally describe a hero wielding a bloody, poisoned lance who is preceded by a caldron full of blood and venom (prototype or ancestor of the Grail of Arthurian legend) into which the lance is plunged to prevent it from killing those around it. This hero's face is bipartite: amiable and smiling on the right side, dark and menacing on the left. Under the name of Celtchar ("the crafty one"), a character from Ulster cycle, the avatar of the progenitor god finally appears: wounded above the thigh, he has lost his virility and begets neither son nor daughter. This trait still conforms to the symbolic expression.

A formidable and unnamed god, since none has dared to name him, Ogmios is designated by a name taken from the Greek and attached to his role as psychopomp: *ogmos* ("path"). The Irish theonym is not further explained by the Gaelic: this cannot be accounted for unless the same origin as the Gaulish *Ogmios* is assumed. A drawing from the *Kunstbuch* of Albrecht Durer shows the Ogmios of Lucian of Samosata; the representation strictly adheres to all the details of the ancient description.

BIBLIOGRAPHY

Guyonvarc'h, Christian-J., and Françoise Le Roux. *Textes mythologiques irlandais*, vol. 1. Rennes, 1980.

Le Roux, Françoise. "Le dieu celtique aux liens: De l'Ogmios de Lucien à l'Ogmios de Dürer." *Ogam* 12 (1960): 209–234.

Mac Cana, Proinsias. *Celtic Mythology*. Rev. ed. Feltham, England, 1983.

FRANÇOISE LE ROUX and CHRISTIAN-J. GUYONVARC'H
Translated from French by Erica Meltzer

OGYŪ SORAI (1666–1728), Japanese Confucian of the Ancient Learning school (Kogaku). Sorai was born in Edo (modern-day Tokyo), the son of Ogyū Hōan (1626–1705), personal physician to Tokugawa Tsunayoshi (1646–1709), lord of the Tatebayashi domain and later the fifth Tokugawa shogun. As a child Sorai began studying classical Chinese and at the age of seven entered the academy headed by Hayashi Gahō (1618–1680), the son of the academy's founder, Hayashi Razan (1583–1657). He progressed quickly in his studies and by the age of nine was able to write simple compositions; he even kept a diary in classical Chinese.

Sorai's otherwise conventional education and upbringing were disturbed in 1679, when he was thirteen. For reasons that are not clear, in that year Tsunayoshi banished Sorai's father to the village of Honnō in Kazusa, sixty miles from Edo. The exile was understandably difficult, as the family was denied the amenities of urban life and the company of its social equals. While these unfavorable conditions forced the adolescent Sorai to study on his own, it also gave him first-hand knowledge of rural life. In 1690 his father was pardoned and the family returned to Edo, where Hōan once again served as Tsunayoshi's physician. Sorai established an academy in Shiba, near the Zōjōji, the imposing Pure Land temple. Here he attracted the attention of the temple's abbot, Ryōya, who helped him secure a position in the house of Yanagisawa Yoshiyasu (1658–1714), the shogun's chamberlain and confidante. Sorai served Yoshiyasu for fourteen years and performed a variety of tasks: he lectured on the Confucian classics, wrote formal Chinese-style histories, punctuated and annotated Chinese texts, and taught Yoshiyasu's retainers. In 1709 he resigned his position and in 1710 opened a school called the Ken'enjuku (Miscanthus Patch Academy) in Kayabachō, not far from Nihonbashi.

Sorai's personal life was rather tragic. In 1696 he married a woman named Kyūshi who bore him five children. She died in 1705, and in time all of their offspring died as well. In 1715 Sorai married the daughter of the Mito Confucian Sasa Rikkei (1639–1698?), but she too died, sometime between 1717 and 1718, without bearing any children. The deaths of his wives and children, together with his own repeated bouts with tuberculosis, among other personal tragedies, made Sorai deeply religious. He came to believe that his survival was the work of an omniscient and omnipotent Heaven. He also attributed his scholarly successes to Heaven and believed that Heaven had chosen him to reveal to the world the long-obscured meaning of the Chinese classics. Although modern scholars have seen Sorai's belief in a sentient Heaven as a reaction to the Neo-Confucians' more rationalistic view of Heaven, there seems little doubt that his beliefs had much to do with the unhappy circumstances of his personal life.

Sorai is best known for his dictum "return to the past." The first manifestations of this neoclassicism in his work were literary. Inspired by the work of the Ming dynasty (1368–1644) literary critics Li P'an-lung (1514–1570) and Wang Shih-chen (1526–1590), he distinguished "ancient" and "modern" Chinese literary styles and urged his contemporaries to model their poetic and prose compositions on the former.

After his retirement and the opening of his school in 1710, Sorai turned from literary matters to the more conventional Confucian issues of self-cultivation and statecraft. He became a staunch critic of Neo-Confucianism: in *Bendō* (Distinguishing the Way) and *Benmei* (Distinguishing Names) Sorai recommended that his contemporaries abandon the commentaries written by Chu Hsi (1130–1200) and his followers and instead study classical literary styles, etiquette, ceremonial practices, and forms of dress.

In 1721, Sorai was asked to advise the shogun, Tokugawa Yoshimune (1684–1751), and in this capacity he proposed countless institutional reforms, most of which survive in his *Seidan* (A Discourse on Government) and *Taiheisaku* (A Proposal for a Great Peace). His most ambitious recommendation was his plan for the rustication of the warrior population of the cities and castle towns, which was designed to liberate warriors from the urban commercial economy and thus from the cycle of consumption, indebtedness, and poverty. His aim here was not to return the country to a natural economy, as is often thought, but to make warriors self-sufficient. He believed that classical Chinese institutions could solve the problems of his day, and so he recommended the adoption of the well-field, rank-in-merit, Six Office, and Six Ministry systems. He also suggested the introduction of supplementary salaries to allow talented individuals of low rank to serve in high positions, and the use of copper cash as a standard for determining the value of gold and silver.

Although Sorai's ideas and proposals seem to be the product of his profound sinophilia, they had more complex and diverse sources: first, his deep, personal belief in Heaven and its agents, the sages and early kings; second, his confidence that the culture and institutions created by the sages and early kings of Chinese antiquity were sufficiently universal to occasion their adoption in his time; third, his belief that social and cultural conditioning would eventually counteract the strangeness of Chinese culture and institutions; and finally, his belief in the value, even superiority, of classical Chinese civilization.

[*See also* Confucianism in Japan.]

BIBLIOGRAPHY

de Bary, Wm. Theodore. "Sagehood as a Secular and Spiritual Ideal in Tokugawa Neo-Confucianism." In *Principle and Practicality: Essays in Neo-Confucianism and Practical Learning*, edited by Wm. Theodore de Bary and Irene Bloom, pp. 127–188. New York, 1979. An important revision of Maruyama Masao's interpretation that considers Ogyū Sorai's thought in the larger context of Neo-Confucianism.

Lindin, Olof G. *The Life of Ogyū Sorai, a Tokugawa Confucian Philosopher*. Lund, 1973. The only biography of Sorai in English.

Maruyama Masao. *Studies in the Intellectual History of Tokugawa Japan*. Translated by Mikiso Hane. Princeton, 1974. A classic study of Tokugawa intellectual history that focuses on Sorai.

Yamashita, Samuel Hideo. "Nature and Artifice in the Writings of Ogyū Sorai, 1666–1728." In *Confucianism and Tokugawa*

Culture, edited by Peter Nosco, pp. 65–138. Princeton, 1984. This essay represents current thinking on Sorai's thought.

Yoshikawa Kōjirō. *Jinsai, Sorai, Norinaga*. Tokyo, 1975. An important and highly regarded study of Sorai and two other seminal Tokugawa thinkers by a leading Japanese Sinologist. Translated into English by Kikuchi Yūji as *Jinsai, Sorai, Norinaga: Three Classical Philosophers of Mid-Tokugawa Japan* (Tokyo, 1983).

SAMUEL HIDEO YAMASHITA

ŌHRMAZD. *See* Ahura Mazdā and Angra Mainyu.

OKINAWAN RELIGION. Okinawa is the largest and the main island of the Ryukyu Islands, an archipelago extending from Kyūshū to Taiwan and consisting of 140 islands arranged in four groups: Amami Ōshima, Okinawa, Miyako, and Yaeyama. Okinawa's influence has long been dominant, and the four island groups, despite local variations, are basically similar in language, culture, and religion. Okinawa and Japan share a common cultural and linguistic origin, but they eventually became separate polities, probably about 500 CE. Thereafter, both China and Japan exerted strong influence. Okinawa, an independent kingdom from 1429 to 1879, paid tribute to China from 1372 to 1872. Japan's influence intensified in 1609 with the conquest of Okinawa by the Satsuma clan from Kyūshū. In 1879 Okinawa was annexed by Japan, and, except for the period from 1945 to 1972, when it was occupied by the United States, it has since remained an integral part of Japan.

It is difficult to distinguish the indigenous elements of traditional Okinawan religion from those of foreign origin. From China came Confucianism for the upper classes, and the lunar calendar, divination, and ancestral rites for the lower classes. The influence of sectarian Buddhism from Japan has been minor, although Japanese folk Buddhism has influenced funerary rites and ancestral memorials. After 1879 state Shintō was introduced, but it received only formal observance. Christianity entered in 1846; after World War II it expanded as American influence increased. Since 1945 several new religious movements from Japan have attracted many followers.

Traditional Okinawan religion is best understood as a folk religion sharing many characteristics with Chinese and Japanese folk religion. The annual cycle of festivals follows the Chinese lunar calendar, and most festivals relate to farming, fishing, or ancestors. Rites of passage are observed much as in Japan. The Okinawan belief in sacred beings called *kami* is not substantially different from beliefs held in Japan. Nature *kami* are prominent, especially those related to the sea, mountains, and fields. Sacred groves are the most archaic sites for the worship of *kami*. The *kami* of wells, springs, and hearth or fire are important to households. The hearth is identified with the continuity of a household, and ashes are taken from it when a branch house separates from the main house. The *kami* of the hearth, symbolized by the three stones of the hearth, is the household's link with higher *kami*. Okinawan scholars claim that the worship of this *kami* is more ancient, universal, and central to the household than ancestral rites.

A salient feature of traditional Okinawan religion is the spiritual and ritual primacy of women. A creation myth from the *Omoro Soshi*, a collection of traditional Okinawan songs, poems, and prayers compiled in the sixteenth and seventeenth centuries, traces the creation of the world to brother and sister *kami*. At all levels of Okinawan society women take the lead in religious matters and men in secular concerns. Until 1879 the religion of the kingdom centered in a female relative (usually a sister) of the king, who acted as a priestess (*kaminchu* or "*kami*-person"; Jpn., *kannushi*). *Kaminchu* control and propitiate *kami* on behalf of their group. They also serve at regional and village levels and for each kin group. The most common type of priestess is the *nuru* (Jpn., *noro*). A village *nuru* inherits her position, lives in a shrine-house, and is responsible for protective and fertility rites. The kin-group *nuru*, of high spiritual birth, is self-recruited, serves in her natal house, and performs rituals and prays for the welfare of the family. All *nuru* serve for life. The two ritual foci of the household, the altar to the hearth *kami* in the kitchen and the ancestral altar, are both the charge of the senior female member of the household. Another female religious specialist is the shaman or *yuta*. She works alone and represents no group. She is chosen by a *kami*, and often suffers misfortune because of her calling. After an initiatory struggle she recovers, and thereafter she attracts those in need of advice and help, usually concerning health problems. Through her various supernatural techniques, she is believed to be able to discern the cause of illness and to bring about a cure. The most common supernatural cause of sickness is incorrect performance or neglect of worship. Although *yuta* are opposed by *nuru* and are proscribed by the government, they have the confidence of many followers who consult them often.

Another prominent feature of traditional Okinawan religion is ancestral rites, which reflect a high degree of Chinese and Japanese influence. Scholars have noted that ancestral rites are not basic to traditional Okinawan religion and that Buddhism exists primarily as a cult of the dead. Almost every household has an ancestral altar on which are placed the ancestral tablets. A funeral is followed by a mourning period of forty-nine days, and memorial rites are observed at specified periods over thirty-three years. A special element in Okinawan funerary and memorial observances is the use of a kin group or family tomb. The simplest and most ancient are caves sealed with stones. More recent and elaborate tombs are of two styles: the gable-roofed type and the omega-shaped tomb. In the past, following the most common form of body disposal, an encoffined body was placed in a tomb; after several years family members would remove the body and wash the bones, which were then placed in an urn and returned to the tomb. The final ritual act was to empty the urn thirty-three years later into the back of the tomb.

Following the death of many *nuru* in 1945 and changes in Okinawan social structure since the war, the ritual supremacy of women has generally declined, although the *yuta* have gained in numbers and influence over the past few decades, especially in the cities. Ancestral rites of the kin group and household seem to be maintaining their vitality, although the practice of bone-washing has disappeared and other rites are being simplified. Voluntary religious groups with male leaders are increasing. In the future, Okinawan religion will no doubt increasingly come to resemble religion in mainland Japan.

[*See also* Japanese Religions, *overview article, and* Kami.]

BIBLIOGRAPHY

For Okinawan religion two outstanding books are William P. Lebra's *Okinawan Religion: Belief, Ritual, and Social Structure* (Honolulu, 1966) and Torigoe Kenzaburō's *Ryūkyū shūkyōshi no kenkyū* (Study of the History of Ryukyuan Religion; Tokyo, 1965). The standard history of Okinawa is George H. Kerr's *Okinawa: The History of an Island People* (Rutland, Vt., 1958). Ethnological studies of three Okinawan villages can be found in Clarence J. Glacken's *The Great Loochoo: A Study in Okinawan Village Life* (Berkeley, 1955). Twelve essays on Ryukyuan prehistory, language, culture, and religion are contained in *Ryukyuan Culture and Society*, edited by Allan H. Smith (Honolulu, 1964). An interesting work based on a 1896 account of Okinawan culture is Douglas G. Haring's *Okinawan Customs: Yesterday and Today* (Rutland, Vt., 1969). The main collections of materials for the study of Okinawan religion are in the libraries of Syracuse University and the University of Hawaii. Listings of the contents of these collections can be found in Douglas G. Haring's *Catalogue of the Ryukyu Research Collection: A Special Collection of Books, Articles and Manuscripts in Relevant Languages Dealing with the Ryukyu Islands as of March, 1969* (Syracuse, N.Y., 1969); in Sakamaki Shunzō's *Ryukyu: A Bibliographical Guide to Okinawan Studies* (Honolulu, 1963); and in an update of Sakamaki's work by Matsui Masato, Kurokawa Tomoyoshi, and Minako I. Song, *Ryukyu: An Annotated Bibliography* (Honolulu, 1981).

CHARLES H. HAMBRICK

ŌKUNINUSHI NO MIKOTO, also known as Ōkuni or Ōnamuchi, is one of the major deities, or *kami,* in Japanese mythology. The earliest chronicle of Japan, the *Kojiki* (712 CE), refers to him as "the *kami* of the Great Land." According to legend, Ōkuni came to the land of Inaba with his brothers to court a Yakami beauty. Because his brothers made him carry their heavy bundle, he reached the shore of Inaba long after they did. On the beach Ōkuni found a white hare crying, and he asked the reason for the animal's distress. The hare replied that he had been bitten by a shark and that Ōkuni's brothers had advised him to bathe his wounds in salt water, but the treatment had only aggravated his pain. Ōkuni told him to use fresh water and apply sedge pollen to the wound. The hare was cured and in gratitude promised that the beautiful maiden of Yakami would marry none but Ōkuni.

Rebuffed by the Yakami maiden, Ōkuni's brothers learned of the hare's promise, and tried to kill Ōkuni. Twice he was crushed to death, first by a rolling boulder and later by a falling tree, but on both occasions his mother, Kami-musubi, came to his rescue and restored him to life.

Ōkuni then decided to leave Inaba and go to Izumo, where he met Suseri, daughter of the Sun Goddess's brother Susano-o. Suseri fell in love with Ōkuni, but to gain her hand he had to submit to many tests. After successfully passing all the ordeals, he was admitted to Susano-o's house and waited there for a chance to steal away with Susano-o's possessions. An opportunity came when Susano-o was lulled to sleep as Ōkuni picked lice from his hair. Ōkuni stole Susano-o's weapons and his koto (a zitherlike musical instrument that was sometimes used for sorcery) and carried Suseri away on his back.

Ōkuni married Suseri, but he had a roving eye and courted beautiful maidens from lands as far away as Koshi and Yamato. Although Suseri was jealous, she could do nothing about his liaison with other women, many of whom helped him to attain power and wealth.

Ōkuni allied himself with Sukunahikona, a dwarf god who had crossed the sea to Izumo in a bean pod boat. Shortly thereafter the forces of Amaterasu reached Izumo's frontiers, and a power struggle ensued. After long negotiations Ōkuni renounced his political power and retired to Kizuki Shrine (later known as Izumo Shrine). He did, however, retain spiritual power over Izumo.

Ever since these legends were incorporated into the *Kojiki*, the high priest *(kuni no miyatsuko)* of Izumo Shrine has enjoyed the privilege of presenting congratulatory prayers upon the accession of each sovereign. Legend has it that Ōkuni meets with other deities from all over Japan once a year in Izumo during the tenth lunar month, usually the season of the first crop-tasting festivals. He is revered as the guardian of good marriages and god of agricultural fertility, and is the principal deity of Izumo Taishakyō, a Shintō sect whose headquarters are located in the town of Kizuki, Shimane Prefecture.

[*See also* Japanese Religion, *article on* Mythic Themes.]

BIBLIOGRAPHY

Aoki, Michiko Yamaguchi. *Ancient Myths and Early History of Japan.* New York, 1974. A comprehensive cultural and anthropological study from the dawn of Japanese civilization (c. 300 BCE) to the rise of the civil government (700 CE). Ōkuninushi is identified here as Ashihara no Shikowo ("ugly man of the reed field").

Izumo fukoki. Translated and with an introduction by Michiko Yamaguchi Aoki. Tokyo, 1971. Ōkuninushi's role in the Izumo mythic cycle is related here.

MICHIKO YAMAGUCHI AOKI

OLAF THE HOLY (r. 1015–1030), ruler of Norway and Scandinavia's first saint. A missionary king who strove to impose religious unity on Norway, Olaf had great influence on the practice of traditional religion in Norway and Iceland. Olaf (also called Olaf the Stout and Saint Olaf) was a descendant of Harald I (known as Fairhair). He became a Viking at a young age, harrying ships in the Baltic and then off the coast of England. Later he fought for the duke of Normandy. Spurred by a prophetic dream, Olaf began his return to Norway to become king, stopping on the way to spend the winter of 1013–1014 in Rouen, where he was baptized.

In 1028 Olaf was forced to flee Norway because of conflicts with powerful Norwegian chieftains who were allied with the Danish king, Knut. While in exile he had another dream: that it was God's will that he reconquer Norway. Accordingly, he returned—with Swedish help—only to meet defeat and lose his life at the Battle of Stiklastaðir in 1030. Soon after his death Olaf was sanctified. His former enemies in Norway rapidly became disenchanted with the new Danish rulers, ousting them and declaring Olaf's son Magnus king.

The question of why Olaf expended so much effort to bring Christianity to Norway is an interesting one, especially since his mission eventually destroyed him. Monarchy was vital for Christian ideology at that time. The throne represented justice and peace. In becoming a Christian, Olaf became joined to a more enlightened world—materially richer and with higher ideals—than Scandinavia then was. He sought to create peace, and for this he needed the support of the great leaders. Approaching his goal with missionary zeal, Olaf converted his countrymen ruthlessly and confiscated the property of those who refused to convert.

The key to Olaf's success lay in his effectiveness at destroying the old religion, which he accomplished in part by exposing it to ridicule. On one occasion, reports reached the king that during the winter the farmers of Hálogaland were holding great feasts to appease the Æsir, who had become angry because the farmers had let themselves be baptized by Olaf. In this feast of propitiation cattle and horses were slaughtered and their blood spread on pedestals for the purpose of improving harvests. When Olaf summoned the farmers to account for their acts, however, they would admit only to communal drinking.

In a similar incident, the farmers of Mærin denied having included sacrifices to the Germanic gods in their Yule feasts. Olaf continued forcing the inland Norwegians to convert until Dala-Gudbrand called up a large force of farmers to oppose the king and proposed this plan of action: "If we bear Thor [Þórr] out from our temple, where he stands here in this farm and has always helped us, and if he sees Olaf and his men, they will melt away, and he and his men become as nothing" (Snorri Sturluson, *Heimskringla* 8–11). This plan was accepted. And when Olaf arrived he learned that the farmers had a god who was visibly present, everyday, made up in the image of Þórr: "He has a hammer in his hand and is of great size and hollow inside, and he stands on a pedestal. . . . He receives four loaves of bread every day and also fresh meat" (*Heimskringla* 13–16). The following morning the farmers carried out the huge statue of Þórr, and Dala-Gudbrand challenged Olaf, asking him where *his* god was. Olaf instructed a follower to strike the idol with a club if the farmers were to look away. Then he instructed the farmers to look to the east if they wanted to see the Christian god—just as the sun came over the horizon. At this moment Olaf's follower struck the idol, and as it fell to pieces, out sprang adders and other snakes and mice as big as cats. When the frightened farmers tried to flee, Olaf offered two alternatives, do battle or accept Christianity, whereupon they all accepted the new faith.

BIBLIOGRAPHY

Fully one-third of Snorri Sturluson's *Heimskringla* is taken up by the saga of Olaf the Holy. It has been ably translated by

Lee M. Hollander in *Heimskringla: History of the Kings of Norway by Snorri Sturluson,* with introduction and notes (Austin, 1964). Marlene Ciklamini has one chapter on Olaf in her *Snorri Sturluson* (Boston, 1978), and Jan de Vries's *Altnordische Literaturgeschichte,* 2 vols., 2d ed. (Berlin, 1964–1967) contains useful information on the literary traditions on Olaf. For historical details of Olaf's life and reign, see Erik Gunnes's *Rikssamling og Kristning 800–1177* (Oslo, 1976), volume 2 of the series "Norges Historie," edited by Knut Mykland.

JOHN WEINSTOCK

OLDENBERG, HERMANN (1856–1920), German Sanskritist, Buddhologist, and historian of religions. Born in Hamburg on 31 October 1854, the son of a Protestant clergyman, Hermann Oldenberg completed doctoral studies in classical and Indic philology in 1875 at the University of Berlin with a dissertation on the Arval Brothers, an ancient Roman cult fraternity. He submitted his habilitation thesis at Berlin in Sanskrit philology in 1878, going on to become professor at the University of Kiel in 1889, and then at Göttingen from 1908 until his death on 18 March 1920.

Publishing an edition and translation of the *Śāṅkhāyana Gṛhyasūtra* in 1878, the young Oldenberg then turned his attention to the Pali Buddhist texts, and it is due to him as much as to any single scholar that serious inquiry into these materials was begun. Previous decades of nineteenth-century European Buddhist research had focused on Mahāyāna Sanskrit (and Tibetan) texts, through which the historical Buddha and the early history of Buddhism were only dimly apparent. Oldenberg edited and translated into English the important Pali chronicle, the *Dīpavaṁsa,* in 1879; he also edited the Vinaya Piṭaka ("discipline basket") of the Pali Tipiṭaka (1879–1883), then published English translations of these texts (1881–1885) with T. W. Rhys Davids, founder of the Pali Text Society. The signal publication of this period of intense research on Buddhism is his *Buddha: Sein Leben, seine Lehre, seine Gemeinde* (1881), written when he was only twenty-six, and "perhaps the most famous book ever written on Buddhism" (J. W. de Jong, *Indo-Iranian Journal* 12, 1970, p. 224).

While Oldenberg's active interest in Buddhist studies never flagged, Buddhism was for him one dimension of what was to be his *Lebenswerk:* nothing less than the systematic examination of India's earliest religious history. Indeed, his achievements in Vedic studies are—if this is possible—even more consequential than his contributions to Buddhist studies. Taken together, his *Die Hymnen des Rigveda* (1888), *Die Religion des Veda* (1894), and *Ṛgveda: Textkritische und exegetische Noten* (1909–1912) constitute a triptych of enormous and continuing importance for research on the form, meters, and textual history of the *Ṛgveda Saṃhitā.* Further, his translations of several Vedic Gṛhyasūtras (*sūtra*s on domestic religious ceremonies), his book-length studies on the Brāhmaṇas and the Upaniṣads, and his numerous articles on Vedic topics complete an imposing legacy of meticulous scholarship.

Through Hermann Oldenberg's efforts, the sustained historical and literary inquiry into Vedic and Buddhist religions attained maturity. His concern to penetrate to the historical foundations of Buddhism and Vedism, which was representative of contemporary trends of German historical scholarship in the late nineteenth and early twentieth centuries, may seem somewhat naive to scholars in the late twentieth century. Oldenberg died little more than a year before the first productive season of archaeological investigations in the Indus Valley, work destined to alter decisively many then-prevailing conceptions of the earliest stages of Indian civilization and religion. One can only conjecture how he would have responded to these discoveries. It seems altogether certain, however, that he would have dealt with them in that same clear-sighted, unsentimental, and critical fashion that characterized all his scholarly work. His persisting efforts to unveil the earliest stages of India's religious thought and history, his rigorous philological method, and the degree to which he integrated insights from other disciplines, stand as important monuments that will continue to inform and guide research.

BIBLIOGRAPHY

Unhappily, the direct impact of Oldenberg's scholarship on investigations in the English-speaking world has been limited by the paucity of translations. English editions of Oldenberg's works include William Hoey's translation of *Buddha: Sein Leben, seine Lehre, seine Gemeinde* as *The Buddha: His Life, His Doctrine, His Order* (London, 1882), which should be consulted alongside the thirteenth German edition, annotated by Helmuth von Glasenapp, as well as the following books, each of which is accompanied by a valuable introduction: *The Dīpavaṁsa* (London, 1879); *Vinaya Texts* (Oxford, 1881–1885); *The Gṛhya-sūtras: Rules of Vedic Domestic Ceremonies,* 2 vols. (Oxford, 1886–1892); and part 2 ("Hymns to Agni") of *Vedic Hymns* (Oxford, 1897). Also, three of his general essays have been published together as *Ancient India* (Chicago, 1898). Of inestimable value is Klaus Janert's careful two-volume edition of Oldenberg's *Kleine Schriften* (Wiesbaden, 1967), which includes not only full texts of more than one hundred articles but also an exhaustive bibliography.

G. R. WELBON

OLD TESTAMENT. *See* Biblical Literature, *article on* Hebrew Scriptures.

OLMEC RELIGION. The Olmec occupied southern Mexico's tropical lowlands in southeastern Veracruz and western Tabasco between 1200 and 600 BCE. Like other Mesoamerican peoples of the period, they lived in villages, practiced agriculture based on maize cultivation, and produced pottery. However, they differed from their contemporaries in their more complex social and political institutions, in the construction of large centers with temples and other specialized buildings, and in their development of a distinctive style of art expressed in monumental stone sculptures and exquisite small portable objects. If they had a writing system, none of their texts have survived; everything we know about the Olmec is based upon archaeological excavations at San Lorenzo, La Venta, Laguna de los Cerros, Tres Zapotes, and other major centers. Although religion is a most difficult aspect of prehistoric life for archaelogists to reconstruct, Olmec architecture, sculpture, and artifacts provide many useful insights into their religious beliefs and practices.

Study of Olmec Religion. Archaeological, historical, and ethnographic information provides the basic data for reconstructing ancient Mesoamerican religions. Archaeological data on prehistoric cultures must be interpreted in light of information about later, better documented cultures or studies of modern groups on approximately similar levels of development. For the Olmec, the archaeological data consist of sculptures, architecture, and artifacts. We interpret these in terms of Spanish accounts of Aztec and Maya religions dating from the sixteenth century CE and of contemporary ethnographic studies of religious practices among modern Mesoamerican Indians and tropical forest groups living elsewhere in Latin America. The basic assumption underlying this approach is summarized in the assertion that ". . . there is a basic religious system common to all Mesoamerican peoples. This system took shape long before it was given monumental expression in Olmec art and survived long after the Spanish conquered the New World's major political and religious centers" (Joralemon, 1976, pp. 58–59).

Studies of Olmec religion rely heavily on iconographic analyses of the Olmec art style as expressed in over two hundred known stone monuments and hundreds of small portable objects. These studies have particularly emphasized the identification of deities while neglecting ritual and many other topics. Scholars tend to accept Joralemon's premise of continuity despite legitimate criticisms. And while this historical-ethnographic approach has been quite productive, it does have some serious weaknesses. For example, we cannot automatically assume that symbols and motifs retained the same basic meanings over several millennia and over long geographical distances. Furthermore, the much later Aztec religion, which is the primary model for comparison, may be an inappropriate model for the Olmec. The Aztec numbered in the millions whereas Olmec polities contained only a few thousand people at most. The tremendous disparity in social complexity implied by these differences may also indicate fundamental differences in their religious institutions and beliefs. Nevertheless, until archaeologists find ways to replace historical and ethnographic analogy as their primary interpretive tool, we will be forced to depend on such comparisons, and we must try to employ them as judiciously as possible.

Characteristics of Olmec Religion. The fundamental pattern of Olmec belief seems to have centered on the worship of numerous high gods or supernatural forces that controlled the universe and sanctioned the human sociopolitical structure. Human interaction with them required complex rituals in temples and other sanctified places, and could be achieved only by religious specialists whose personal qualifications or social position qualified them for the task. The belief system they served included a pantheon, a cosmology that explained and structured the universe, and a set of ritual activities that expressed the cosmology.

The pantheon. The nature of the Olmec pantheon is a topic of some controversy. Some scholars argue that Olmec supernaturals were not gods in the Western sense of recognizably distinct personalities, while others accept the existence of deities but disagree on their identifications. For example, what in this article is called the Olmec Dragon has been variously identified as a were-jaguar combining human and feline traits, a caiman, a toad, or a manatee! The reason for the confusion is that we have difficulty comprehending the subject matter of Olmec art. The beings portrayed are frequently "creatures that are biologically impossible," things that "exist in the mind of man, not in the world of nature" (Joralemon, 1976, p. 33).

The most thorough research on the Olmec pantheon has been done by Peter D. Joralemon, who originally defined ten Olmec deities (Gods I–X) but later reduced these to six, conforming to three basic dyads (Joralemon, 1971, 1976). Olmec art portrays the deities as creatures combining an endless and bewildering array of human, reptilian, avian, and feline attributes. The most commonly depicted pair are the Olmec Dragon (God I) and the Olmec Bird Monster (God III). [*See* Iconography, *article on* Mesoamerican Iconography.] The Olmec Dragon, believed to be a crocodilian with eagle, jaguar, human, and serpent attributes, appears to signify earth, water, fire, and agricultural fertility, and may have served as the patron deity of the elite. The Olmec Bird Monster is a raptorial bird, tentatively identified as a harpy eagle, with mammalian and reptilian features. Joralemon associates it with maize, agricultural fertility, the heavens, and mind-altering psychotrophic substances.

Joralemon suggests that the Olmec Dragon was a predecessor of numerous later deities, specifically the Aztec gods Cipactli, Xiuhtecuhtli, Huehueteotl, Tonacatecuhtli, and Quetzalcoatl and the Maya god Itzamná. Some authorities dispute these proposed linkages with later deities, but unfortunately we lack a coherent methodology for resolving the issues of continuity and change in deity concepts through time.

Gods II and IV form an agricultural-fertility complex. God II has maize cobs sprouting from a cleft in the top of its head, and may be an ancestor of later Aztec maize deities such as Centeotl. God IV is an infant or dwarf, probably associated with rain, whom Joralemon sees as an early form of later rain deities, such as the central Mexican *tlalocs* and Maya *chacs*.

The final Olmec dyad consists of Gods VI and VIII. God VI is a deity of springtime and renewal who symbolizes reborn vegetation, and is thought to be an analog to Xipe Totec, the Aztec god whose priests wore human skin, flayed from sacrificial victims, as a sign of rebirth. God VIII is the death god, called Mictlantecuhtli by the Aztec, and symbolized by a fleshless human jaw.

Although much remains to be learned about the Olmec pantheon, the importance of agricultural and fertility deities is evident. This is not surprising in view of the fact that farming was the most important subsistence activity among the Olmec, but it does mark the earliest clear formulation of such deity concepts in Mesoamerica and represents a major Olmec contribution to Mesoamerican culture.

Religious specialists. There is no evidence in Olmec society of an elaborate religious bureaucracy comparable to that reported for the Aztec. The small size of Olmec groups probably precluded this development. Some scholars have called Olmec society a theocracy, but there is no evidence to warrant such a conclusion, although priests were undoubtedly members of the elite. Peter T. Furst has persuasively argued that certain Olmec art objects portray the theme of a "jaguar-shaman transformation complex" in which human shamans assumed the guise of their jaguar alter egos (see Furst's article "The Olmec Were-Jaguar Motif in the Light of Ethnographic Reality," in *Dumbarton Oaks Conference on the Olmec*, edited by Elizabeth P. Benson, Washington, D.C., 1968, pp. 79–110). It is not clear whether Olmec shamans were also elite priests, but it does seem likely.

Cosmology. Although the lack of written accounts makes it difficult to reconstruct Olmec cosmology, the archaeological record contains some interesting clues. Two sculptured monuments from the San Lorenzo area form the basis of the so-called Stirling hypothesis, named after its formulator, Matthew W. Stirling. Stirling maintained that each monument shows a jaguar having sexual intercourse with a woman and that they portray the mythic origin of the were-jaguars so common in Olmec art. Unfortunately, both monuments were badly mutilated in antiquity, and their subject matter is not at all clear.

Another important insight into Olmec cosmology may be contained in depictions of caves. Sculptured scenes of people seated in caves or emerging from cavelike niches suggest an early occurrence of the pan-Mesoamerican belief that ethnic groups and deities emerged on to the surface world through caves, which served as doorways to and from the supernatural realm inside the earth. [*See* Caves.] In some cases the Olmec depictions clearly represent the mouth of the Olmec Dragon. Well-preserved Olmec-style paintings deep within caves in the states of Guerrero and Morelos far from the Olmec Gulf Coast homeland reinforce this interpretation.

Ritual. One of the least understood aspects of Olmec religion is ritual. We know something about the architectural settings in which rituals were held and about the nonperishable objects that we assume were used in ritual contexts, but Olmec dances, prayers, chants, feasts, and other behaviors are lost forever.

Pole-and-thatch temples on the summits of earth mounds are widely regarded as having been a focal point for elite rituals. These small structures most likely housed the most important cult images and served as sanctuaries where the priests and leaders gathered in seclusion to conduct the esoteric rites to which only they were privy. The open courtyards and plazas surrounding the mounds were well suited for more public celebrations attended by the general populace.

Archaeological excavations have revealed numerous unusual architectural features that were either used in ritual or had some specific sacred meaning. For example, the gigantic artificial ridges built onto the sides of the San Lorenzo plateau may represent an attempt to transform the entire community into a bird effigy similar to the much smaller effigy mounds constructed by later Indian cultures in what is now the midwestern United States. The twenty or so deep depressions in the surface of San Lorenzo probably originated as sources of soil for mound construction but were later converted into sacred water reservoirs by lining them with special materials. Flooding was prevented by elaborate drain systems constructed of hundreds of U-shaped stone troughs. These reservoirs may have provided water for domestic use, but the year-round availability of fresh water from nearby springs, the substantial labor invested in constructing the drain systems, and the water-deity symbolism on several associated monuments all suggest a ritual function. Two potential uses have been suggested: one is that they served as ritual bathing stations for priests, the other that they were holding tanks for sacred animals such as caimans or manatees.

The Olmec probably played a ritual ball game similar to those popular in later times, as evidenced by clay figurines depicting males dressed in ballplayer garb and who at times hold what appears to be a ball. A rectangular group of four mounds at San Lorenzo has been interpreted as a formal ball court; and although it lacks the rings and benches of later courts, residue of a rubber-like substance found at this site may be the remnants of a ball. Some authorities have suggested that the numerous colossal heads found at several Olmec sites depict ballplayers wearing helmets, but the most recent consensus is that these remarkable basalt human portraits represent individual Olmec rulers. The ball game played by later Mesoamericans did have secular aspects, but it is generally regarded as a primarily religious observance in which players represented supernaturals.

Evidence of a common yet perplexing aspect of Olmec ritual centered around the burial of precious objects in caches and offerings has been found at La Venta. Some caches contain only one or a few objects while others include enormous amounts of material. The small offerings include stone figurines and celts, pottery vessels, and a variety of personal ornaments, even though these are generally not associated with burials. Some offerings display ideologically significant patterns in the placement of objects, such as celts arranged in geometric patterns or stylized deity faces. One particularly interesting cache from La Venta contains jadeite human figurines placed to show a procession scene with four individuals filing past what appears to be an Olmec ruler and his retinue.

The most unusual buried features are the so-called Massive Offerings at La Venta. Huge steep-sided pits were dug into the subsoil and immediately filled with thousands of serpentine blocks laid in clay and topped with a mosaic of finely worked blocks forming a gigantic mask of the Olmec Dragon. Four Massive Offerings have been discovered at La Venta, and like many architectural features at the site they occur in bilaterally symmetrical positions vis-à-vis the site's centerline. It is possible that all the subsurface offerings at La Venta form a colossal pattern of unknown ritual significance, but we do not yet have enough pieces of the puzzle to be able to identify the pattern.

Just as Olmec constructions provide insights into the settings for ritual, their art objects and other artifacts alert us to the nature of some of the rituals. Museums and private collections contain hundreds of exotic objects to which we can reasonably assign a ritual function even though we do not know their specific uses. Anthropomorphic and zoomorphic figurines, masks, celts, "spoons," "stilettos," and a host of miscellaneous objects, frequently decorated with religious designs and symbols, indicate a well-developed set of ritual paraphernalia. The objects are often made from jadeite, serpentine, and other blue-green stones whose color obviously had some special significance. In most cases we do not know the functions of these objects but the stilettos may have served as bloodletters used in ritual autosacrifice and the "spoons" may have been used for the administration of hallucinogenic substances. Evidence for the use of mind-altering substances by the Olmecs is weak, but most scholars assume such practices were part of Olmec ritual.

Other ritual accoutrements include iron-ore mirrors, which are masterpieces of pre-Columbian lapidary work. Made from large rectangular pieces of magnetite, ilmenite, and hematite, the polished concave surfaces of these mirrors have such fine optical qualities that they can be used to ignite fires and project camera-lucida images on flat surfaces. An enigmatic grooved rectangular bar of magnetic hematite found at San Lorenzo has been shown to be a compass needle, probably used in geomantic ritual rather than as a utilitarian device.

BIBLIOGRAPHY

Anthony F. C. Wallace's *Religion: An Anthropological View* (New York, 1966) provides the framework in which this article has been written. The most recent and thorough synthesis of Olmec culture is Jacques Soustelle's *The Olmecs: The Oldest Civilization in Mexico*, translated by Helen R. Lane (Garden City, N.Y., 1984). Older but still useful books include Michael D. Coe's *America's First Civilization: Discovering the Olmec* (New York, 1968), and Ignacio Bernal's *The Olmec World*, translated by Doris Heyden and Fernando Horcasitas (Berkeley, 1969). Michael D. Coe and my *In the Land of the Olmec*, 2 vols. (Austin, 1980) is the basic source of information on San Lorenzo. The basic data on La Venta are scattered through many works; the two most important are Philip Drucker's *La Venta, Tabasco: A Study of Olmec Ceramics and Art* (Washington, D.C., 1952), and Philip Drucker, Robert F. Heizer, and Robert J. Squier's *Excavations at La Venta, Tabasco, 1955* (Washington, D.C., 1959). Karl W. Luckert's *Olmec Religion: A Key to Middle America and Beyond* (Norman, Okla., 1976) is the only book devoted exclusively to this topic, but its unorthodox methodology and assumptions lead to conclusions not supported by the data. Peter D. Joralemon's *A Study of Olmec Iconography* (Washington, D.C., 1971) contains his initial attempt to delineate the Olmec pantheon. *Origins of Religious Art and Iconography in Preclassic Mesoamerica,* edited by H. B. Nicholson (Los Angeles, 1976) contains Joralemon's definitive study of the Olmec Dragon and the Olmec Bird Monster in addition to many other useful articles. Elizabeth P. Benson's *The Olmecs and Their Neighbors: Essays in Memory of Matthew W. Stirling* (Washington, D.C., 1981) contains articles dealing with many aspects of Olmec culture, and a useful bibliography.

RICHARD A. DIEHL

ỌLỌRUN is the high god of the Yoruba people of southwestern Nigeria. He has also been referred to as Olodumare, which is believed to be an older name for this god. Ọlọrun is considered the king of the gods, and his name means literally "the owner of the sky."

As the high god, Ọlọrun stands in relation to the other Yoruba gods as a father stands to his children, and these other gods, or *oriṣa,* are in fact considered to be his children. Ọlọrun, as in many West African religions, is a remote deity without any traditional cult that worships him directly. In this respect Ọlọrun is similar to the high gods of neighboring peoples in Nigeria, such as Osanobua (or Osa) among the Edo (Benin) people.

However, he is not forgotten or ignored by the Yoruba. It is believed that all offerings and prayers ultimately find their way to Ọlọrun, but he accepts offerings and makes his wishes known through lesser gods. Eṣu, a Yoruba deity who serves as Ọlọrun's messenger, carries the wishes of Ọlọrun to the *oriṣa* and the prayers of the people from the *oriṣa* to Ọlọrun. Furthermore, Ọlọrun is remembered in most rituals, at least in the traditional conclusion, "May Ọlọrun accept it." In many proverbs and figures of speech, the name and figure of Ọlọrun are prominent, as in the morning greeting "May Ọlọrun awake us well" or the proverbs "No one but Ọlọrun may put a crown on a lion" and "Ọlọrun drives away flies from the tailless cow."

Ọlọrun is also important in the Yoruba pantheon in that he determines the fate of each person. Prior to birth, a person's ancestor guardian soul kneels before Ọlọrun and receives a destiny. This destiny is forgotten at birth, however, and can only be rediscovered through divination. Although Ọlọrun can modify individual destinies in certain ways, the amount of time given to people on earth remains fixed. Ọlọrun is also seen as a powerful moral agent insofar as he judges each soul after death. People who have lived moral lives are rewarded with a brief afterlife that is followed by reincarnation. Evildoers, on the other hand, are never reincarnated and are sent by Ọlọrun to the "place of potsherds" where they suffer in a peppery, hot, atmosphere.

The figure of Ọlọrun became more prominent during the colonial era, probably as a result of Muslim and Christian emphasis on monotheism. Although he was always believed to be the high god, Ọlọrun formerly had no specific temples or cults dedicated to him; now, however, temples dedicated to him may be found in Yorubaland. Moreover, the modern Yoruba say that Ọlọrun is the giver of law and the controller of life and death. Since 80 percent of all Yoruba claim allegiance to either Islam or Christianity, scholars have raised the possibility that these attributes or functions are accretions for Ọlọrun under the indirect influence of the monotheistic traditions. In the original form it seems that Ọlọrun may have been far more remote, removed from any interference in natural, historical (except mythic), or social events, although early tradition does associate Ọlọrun with the afterlife and the process of reincarnation. Furthermore, Ọlọrun figures initially in the creation myth—he gave the task and materials of creation to one of his sons, Ọbatala, but it was another son, Oduduwa, who was destined to finish the creation. In general, however, the *oriṣa* play a more prominent role in these areas.

Despite the sparsity of rituals attached to him in Yorubaland, Ọlọrun has diffused to the New World, particularly to northeastern Brazil. There he tends to be identified with God, the father of the Christian Trinity, and according to local theology he works primarily through his principal *orixa (oriṣa),* Jesus Christ, referred to as Oxala or Zambi. However, Ọlọrun is sometimes even identified as this principal *orixa,* so the transference is ambiguous. The day dedicated to Oxala is Friday, thought to be a possible survival from Islam. The permutations from Africa to the New World are many—Ọlọrun has been reported as a deity in the Shango cult of Recife, Brazil—so there is no simple way by which this Yoruba high god can be traced to the New World.

BIBLIOGRAPHY

Bascom, William R. *The Yoruba of Southwestern Nigeria.* New York, 1969.

Idowu, E. Bọlaji. *Olódùmarè: God in Yoruba Belief.* New York, 1963. A very competent discussion of the subject.

JAMES S. THAYER

OṂ, a contraction of the sounds /a/, /u/, and /m/, is considered in the Hindu tradition to be the most sacred of Sanskrit syllables. In a religious setting that reveres the intrinsic power of sound as a direct manifestation of the divine, a setting in which the hierarchy of scripture is headed by the *śruti* ("heard") texts and in which oral tradition has preserved the religious language unchanged over millennia, *oṃ* is the articulated syllable *par excellence,* the eternally creative divine word. Indeed, the Sanskrit word denoting "syllable" (*akṣara,* literally "the imperishable") commonly serves as an epithet for *oṃ.* Its other epithets include *ekakṣara* ("the one syllable" but also "the sole imperishable thing") and *praṇava* (from *pra-ṇu,* "to utter a droning"); the latter term refers to the practice of initiating any sacred recitation with a nasalized syllable. The syllable *oṃ* itself has been associated with the Sanskrit root *av* ("to drive, impel, animate"; *Uṇadi Sūtra* 1.141). It is represented graphically by a familiar mystical symbol combining the syllable's three components.

Articulated at the beginning and end of recitations and prayers, *oṃ* is a particle of auspicious salutation, expressing acknowledgment of the divine or solemn affirmation, in which latter sense it is compared with *amen* ("verily, this syllable is assent"; *Chandogya Upaniṣad* 1.1.8). Evidence of its use as an invocation occurs in the *Ṛgveda;* though it appears in a relatively late section (1.164.39), this note dates the practice to at least 1200 BCE.

From the sixth century BCE, the Upaniṣads make direct mention of *oṃ.* One of the oldest Upaniṣads, the *Chāndogya,* discusses the syllable at length in setting forth rules for the chanters of the *Sāmaveda* and states that "one has to know that *oṃ* is the imperishable" (1.3.4). By sounding *oṃ,* one intones the Udgītā, the essential canto of the Vedic sacrifice (1.1.5).

In the *Kaṭha Upaniṣad,* the figure Death defines *oṃ* as the goal propounded by the Vedas, and proclaims that anyone who meditates on the syllable *oṃ* can attain *brahman* (1.2.15–16). A later Upaniṣad, the *Taittirīya,* indicates that *oṃ* is both *brahman* and the cosmos (1.8.1–2): the sound symbol is identical to what it represents.

The first chapter of the *Māṇḍukya,* one of the latest of the Vedic Upaniṣads, is devoted to the elucidation of *oṃ.* The sacred syllable is divided into its four phonetic components, representing the four states of mind, or consciousness: /a/ is related to the awakened state, /u/ to the dream state, /m/ to dreamless sleep, and the syllable as a whole to the fourth state, *turīya,* which is beyond words and is itself the One, the Ultimate, the *brahman.* "One should know *oṃ* to be God seated in the hearts of all" (1.28).

The sixth chapter of the *Maitrāyaṇīya,* possibly the latest of the Vedic Upaniṣads, is devoted entirely to the discussion of the sacred syllable, referred to as the "primary sound" (6.22). The devotee is enjoined to meditate on the Self as *oṃ* (6.3). When *oṃ* is articulated, the sound "rises upward." The chapter closes with the invocation "Hail *oṃ*! Hail *brahman*!"

When the *Bhagavadgītā*—a fragment of the *Mahābhārata,* perhaps contemporary with the latest of the Vedic Upaniṣads—proclaims that "the imperishable is *brahman,*" it plays on the term *akṣara,* which may be read either as an adjective ("*brahman* is imperishable") or as a substantive ("*brahman* is the Imperishable [i.e., *oṃ*]").

Manu (*Manusmṛti* 2.74) echoes the assertion made in the *Chāndogya* regarding the articulation of *oṃ* preceding any sacred recitation, and prescribes that it be repeated not only at the beginning but also at the end of the daily recitation of the Veda, under penalty of losing the merit attached to such an exercise. He adds that Prajāpati, the creator, extracted the milk of three cows (i.e., the three primary Vedas) in order to draw the three phonetic components that make up the syllable.

Through imagery borrowed from archery, the *Muṇḍaka Upaniṣad* indicates how the articulation of *oṃ* was integrated into the practice of meditation according to Indian thought: the syllable *oṃ* is the bow, the *ātman* (the self) is the arrow, and *brahman* is the target (2.2.3–4). One must bend toward the target without diverting the mind; one must make oneself identical to the arrow. (The same image is found in the *Bhāgavata Puraṇa.*) The *Yoga Sūtra* of Patañjali mentions that the various yoga systems all insist on the importance of *oṃ* as a symbol of the devotee's attempt to unite with the Absolute, a goal that is itself the prerequisite to any practice of meditation.

In later times *oṃ* stands for the union of the three gods of the Hindu triad, Brahmā (the creative force, or /a/), Viṣṇu (the sustaining force, or /u/), and Śiva (the dissolving force, or /m/).

As the primary sound symbol for an Indian tradition maintained continuously from the age of the Vedas into modern times, the syllable *oṃ* stands charged with an unquestionable religious energy. Its use as a *mantra* for profound meditation reflects the Vedic teaching that the devotee is one with the sacred sound and all it represents. Through its constant repetition in recitations, prayers, and even recently composed sacred texts it acts as a pitch that tunes the worshiper to the heart of the prayer.

[*See also* Music, *article on* Music and Religion in India.]

BIBLIOGRAPHY

In the absence of monographical studies on the subject the reader would do well to consult André Padoux's *Recherches sur la symbolique et l'énergie de la parole dans certains textes tantriques,* "Publications de l'Institut de civilization indiennes," no. 21 (Paris, 1963).

A. M. ESNOUL

OMENS. *See* Portents and Prodigies.

OMOPHAGIA is an ancient Greek term (*ōmophagia,* "eating raw [flesh]") for a ritual in the ecstatic worship of Dionysos.

The Raw and the Cooked. All human groups, including the so-called primitives, are aware of their cultural identity by contrast to other, "uncivilized" forms of life. That the opposition of civilization to nature, of human to animal, is most drastically experienced in the dietary code, in the use of cooked food as against "raw-eating" animals, has become popular knowledge in the wake of *The Raw and the Cooked* (1969), the seminal first volume of Claude Lévi-Strauss's *Mythologiques.* This presupposes the conquest of fire, which has been decisive in the evolution of mankind and which still looms large in mythology; knowledge of fire goes together with the special importance of the hunt in early and primitive societies. A constant point of reference in human and even prehuman experience are the big carnivores, especially the leopard and the wolf, that are abhorred as well as imitated. Model hunters, at the same time dreadfully dangerous and admirably powerful, the carnivores are the paradigmatic "raw-eaters." They are man-eaters, too: when the problems of civilization and dietary codes are articulated in ritual or myth, the motif of cannibalism usually makes its appearance.

The category of "raw-eating" most generally finds two applications. In mythology, it designates various demons who naturally take the traits of predators—enemies of the gods or even certain uncanny and dangerous gods. On a more realistic level, ethnocentrism and xenophobia combine to mark certain foreign tribes as "raw-eaters," be they neighbors or faraway people known from hearsay. In Western tradition, this cliché has remained attached to Huns and Tatars. As a variant or for reinforcement, the motif of cannibalism easily comes in. It is notable that the concept of "raw-eaters" goes back to Indo-European strata, that is, to the early third millennium BCE, as shown by the correspondence of the Sanskrit *āmād* with the Greek *ōmēs-tēs;* in the same vein, a Scythian tribe was known as Amadokoi. Tribalism also admits of mythical transformations: for the Greeks, the centaurs, hybrids of man and horse, living in the woods but sometimes visiting humans to wreak havoc, were not only hunters but "raw-eaters."

In a more complex way the opposition of "raw-eating" to civilized may appear within one ethnic unity: one special group is set apart by this very characterization. The imitation of carnivores is most evident in secret societies of leopard men as attested in Africa, or the folklore of werewolves in Europe, including ancient Greece. They are expected to kill and eat in a beastlike fashion and especially to practice cannibalism. The oldest evidence for leopard men comes from wall paintings of Çatal Hüyük in Neolithic Anatolia about 6000 BCE; we cannot know details about their function or practice, except for their imitating predators through masquerade in the context of hunting.

In more modern times two groups, "raw-eaters" versus eaters of cooked meat, are attested among the Mansi, an Ugric tribe of Siberia, and Andreas Alföldi (1974) has used this attestation to illustrate a similar opposition between two groups of Luperci who performed the ancient festival of Lupercalia at Rome; in both cases it is the group of "raw-eaters" who enjoy the higher reputation as being the swifter, the more vigilant, the more powerful. It seems that in ancient civilizations the opposition of raw versus cooked has sometimes been replaced by that of roasted versus boiled meat, where roasting is more primitive, more hunterlike, more heroic. Thus in a non-Yahvistic ritual mentioned in the *First Book of Samuel* (2:11–17) the priests require raw flesh for roasting while the sacrificial community feasts on boiled meat.

A similar opposition may be enacted not through the institution of permanent groups but in the dimension of time: "raw-eating" as a transitional stage leading back to normal food, that is, to civilization reconfirmed through its opposite in the dietary code. Thus in initiations that involve a marginal status and make the initiands outcasts for a while, disuse of fire and raw-eating has a place. In Greek myth this is reflected in the figure of Achilles, who as a boy is taken from his parents to the "raw-eating" centaurs and gets his unique heroic strength by feeding on the entrails of the most savage beasts (Apollodorus, *Bibliothēkē* 3.13.6).

There are communal festivals too that bring about a temporary reversal, an atavistic return to ancient ways of life that sometimes includes the interdiction of fire and thus enforces a diet of uncooked food. In ancient Greece this is attested for a festival on the island of Lemnos and also for some forms of the Thesmophoria, the festival of Demeter. Accompanying myths tell stories about an insurrection of women against men that, however, had to give way to normality again. Of course, initiations, secret societies, and public festivals may be functionally interrelated in various ways; by themselves or in combination they keep alive the consciousness of alternatives to what is considered normal and thus in fact help to ensure continuity.

Dionysian Omophagia. Dionysos, the ancient Greek god of wine and ecstasy, is experienced by his followers most deeply and directly in a state known simply as "madness" *(mania)*. Hence his female adherents are called Maenads *(mainades)*; Bacchants *(bakchoi)* and Bacchantes *(bakchai)*, masculine and feminine, respectively, are about equivalent. High points of bacchantic activity are tearing apart a victim and eating it raw. From a pragmatic perspective, the two activities of tearing apart *(sparagmos)* and eating raw *(ōmophagia)* need not entail each other, but in the Dionysian tradition both combine to form an image of what is both subhuman and superhuman, both beastlike and godlike, at the same time.

The most influential literary text to describe Dionysian phenomena is Euripides' tragedy *The Bacchae* (405 BCE). When the Maenads, who are celebrating their dances in the wilderness, are disturbed by herdsmen, they jump at the herds and tear calves and even bulls asunder "swifter than you could shut your eyes" (ll. 735–747); later on they murder Pentheus in a similar way. Eating is not dwelt upon in this context, except as a horrible prospect (l. 1184); but in the introductory song of the play the god himself, leader of the dances, is presented as "hunting for blood by killing a he-goat, the lust of raw-eating" (ll. 137–139), and the Bacchantes are ready to identify with their leader.

In the Dionysian circle, the imagery of carnivores is ready at hand. Preference is given to the leopard, partly through an overlap with the symbolism of the Anatolian mother goddess, whose distant avatar seems to be the goddess of Çatal Hüyük. *Bassarai* (Foxes) was the title of a lost play by Aeschylus; it was a name for the Maenads who destroyed Lykurgos, another enemy of the god. Classical vase paintings (fifth to fourth century BCE) show dancing Maenads holding parts of a torn animal—a fawn, a goat—in their hands; eating, though, is hardly depicted.

Such restraint is absent from the picture drawn by Christian writers of pagan cult. "You leave behind your breast's sanity, you crown yourselves with vipers, and in order to prove that you are filled with the power of god, with bloody mouths you tear asunder the entrails of goats crying out in protest"—thus said Arnobius in *Against the Pagans* (5.19), following in part Clement of Alexandria's *Protrepticus* (chap. 12). In this view omophagia is the extreme of the pagans' folly.

A most serious problem is to decide how much of the picture evoked by Hellenic poetry on the one side and Christian polemics on the other is to be regarded as cultic reality in the context of Greek civilization of the historical period. There are many convergent testimonies, but few to convince a skeptic. A very ancient epithet of the god is Dionysos Ōmēstēs ("eating raw"), attested by the poet Alcaeus about 600 BCE. Dionysos Ōmadios, mentioned a few times in connection with human sacrifice, is often considered equivalent; linguistically, though, this epithet should rather belong to *ōmadon* ("by the shoulder"), which still refers to "tearing apart" in *sparagmos*. Firmicus Maternus, writing Christian polemics but drawing on some Hellenistic source, asserts that in a Dionysian festival "the Cretans tear apart a living bull with their teeth" (*On the Error of Pagan Religions*, chap. 6; about AD 350)—which doubtless includes elements of fantasy. In a poem entitled *Bassarika*, a certain Dionysios has a human victim, clad in a deer's skin, torn to pieces and devoured by Indians on the command of Dionysos; the remains are to be assembled in baskets before sunrise. The mystic baskets are well known from ritual, but the story with its barbarian setting is a ghastly exaggeration. A more reliable witness is Plutarch, who combines the epithet *ōmēstēs* with another, *agriōnios*, and thus refers to a well-attested festival, Agriōnia. This in turn is connected with a group of myths that tell about the women of a city growing mad, leaving the town, kidnapping their own children in order to kill and even eat them; the Pentheus myth of Euripides' *Bacchae* is in fact one exemplar of the pattern. But to bring imagination back to facts of ritual, we have nothing but the too short statement of Plutarch that there are indeed in Greek cults "unlucky and dreary days in which omophagia and tearing-apart have their place" (*On the Decline of Oracles*, 417c).

Modern scholarship has often connected Dionysian omophagia with the apocryphal Orphic myth that tells how Dionysos himself when still a child was slain, cut to pieces, and tasted by the Titans—in consequence of which, the Titans were burned by the lightning of Zeus, and from their smoke mankind arose. This seemed to place the ritual in the context of a marginal Orphic sect. But it has long been seen that this myth explicitly contradicts a strict understanding of the meaning of *ōmophagia:* the Titans use a knife, and they both cook and roast the remains of their victim. This seems to mirror more complex divisions of marginal groups, Dionysian or Orphic, with differing dietary codes and ideology, as shown especially by Marcel Detienne (1977).

A most interesting text comes from a lost tragedy of Euripides, *The Cretans* (frag. 472 in August Nauck, *Tragicorum Graecorum Fragmenta*, Leipzig, 1889), preserved by Porphyry (*On Abstinence* 4.19): the chorus of Cretans introduce themselves as "initiates of Idaean Zeus"; they have achieved this status "by performing the thunder of night-swarming Zagreus and the raw-eating dinners, and by holding up the torches for the Mother of the mountains." This is a literary elaboration; one might surmise that the poet was not too well informed about the details of Idaean mysteries and liberally added colors from the Dionysian sphere. But he succeeds in giving a meaningful setting to the rite of raw-eating, as a transient phase in initiation to be followed by strict vegetarianism, as the initiates emerge in white clothes from a temple smeared with bull's blood; this is a grim and revolting antidote through which a status of purity is achieved. *Zagreus* is an epithet of Dionysos, especially in the context of *sparagmos*.

There remains one nonliterary, realistic testimony for cult practice, a sacred law from Miletus, dated 276/275 BCE, regulating the privileges of a priestess with regard to the city as well as to private Dionysian mysteries: "It shall not be allowed to anyone to throw in an *ōmophagion* before the priestess throws in one on behalf of the city, nor to bring together the group of revelers *(thiasoi)* before the public one." This clearly is to ensure some prerogative of the city as against private organizations. Unfortunately *ōmophagion*, "something related to raw-eating," is a term that occurs only here, and no agreement has been reached among interpreters as to what exactly it should mean in this context. Is a victim (e.g., a goat) being thrown down at a crowd of ecstatic Bacchants assembled in expectation? (This is the most vivid picture, drawn by, among others, E. R. Dodds, 1951). Or is a victim being thrown down into a chasm, as attested in the Demeter festival Thesmophoria? Or is some kind of symbolic substitute (perhaps only a mere contribution in money) being "thrown into" some box? In the absence of further evidence there will be no final decision. One may still claim that in such a context ideology is more important than reality. One finds, in a major Greek city close to the classical age, the designation of "raw-eating" in a ritual that is meant to ensure the favor of Dionysos on behalf of the city and that takes precedence in the procession. There were points of reference in cult even to the more exuberant Dionysian mythology.

Comparative Evidence. A vivid description of pre-Islamic bedouin is contained in a Christian novel from the fifth century CE, *The Story of Nilus*, now finally available in a critical edition: Nilus Ancyranus, *Narratio*, edited by Fabricius Conca (Leipzig, 1983). These barbarians, the text says, delight in sacrificing boys to the morning star; sometimes "they take a camel of white color and otherwise faultless, they bend it down upon its knees, and go circling round it three times"; the leader,

> after the third circuit, before the crowd has finished the song, while the last words of the refrain are still on their lips, draws his sword and forcefully smites the neck of the camel, and he is the first to taste eagerly of its blood. And thus the rest of them run up and with their knives some cut off a small bit of the hide with its hair upon it, others hack at any chance bit of flesh and snatch it away, others go on to the entrails and inwards, and they leave no scrap of the victim unwrought that might be seen by the sun at its rising. (3.3, pp. 12f.)

The importance of the text as a description of a very primitive form of sacrifice was seen by W. Robertson Smith (1889), and explicit comparison with Dionysian phenomena was made by Jane E. Harrison (1903); there is no mention of divine possession, but the narrator seems to consider the bedouin madmen anyhow. It is not to be forgotten, however, that we are dealing with a novel, and that horror stories belong to the genre; this fact seriously impairs the authenticity of the report.

A more striking parallel has been adduced from eyewitness reports of modern Morocco, collected especially by Raoul Brunel (1926). The Aissāoūa form a kind of secret society consisting of several clans, each of which is named after an animal, and the members, in their initiation rites, are made to imitate their emblem. Clans of jackals, cats, dogs, leopards, and lions specialize in tearing apart animals and devouring them raw on the spot; in the words of an informant quoted by E. R. Dodds (1951), "after the usual beating of tom-toms, screaming of the pipes and monotonous dancing, a sheep is thrown into the middle of the square, upon which all the devotees come to life and tear the animal limb from limb and eat it raw." It is said that the flocks of those who voluntarily offer an animal to the sect will not suffer damage from real predators. Thus a marginal existence is provided with a charismatic status. This seems to be the closest analogy to Dionysian omophagia, though the social setting evidently is fundamentally different.

Interpretations. The most common interpretation of ritual "raw-eating" has been based on what James G. Frazer called "the homeopathic effects of a flesh diet": taking in life and strength from a living being in the most direct way. In Hebrew, raw flesh is called "living" flesh. The hypothesis has been added that originally the victim was identical with the god, who is thus appropriated by the worshipers in sacramental communion. A central support of this construct is seen to collapse if omophagia is not directly related to the myth of Dionysos slain. Nor does the hypothesis explain the characteristics of the abnormal usually attached to omophagia, be it a state of madness or a realm of strangers and monsters. Thus it seems preferable to see the rituals in the more general context of precarious civilization struggling with the antinomies of nature, while accepting those antinomies and trying to interpret them within the pertinent cultural systems as a breakthrough to otherness that remains bound to its opposite.

[*See also* Dionysos; Cannibalism; *and* Frenzy.]

BIBLIOGRAPHY

Alföldi, Andreas. *Die Struktur des voretruskischen Römerstaates.* Heidelberg, 1974. An attempt to trace Eurasian pastoral traditions behind Roman institutions. See pages 141–150 for a discussion of "the raw and the cooked."

Brunel, Raoul. *Essai sur la confrérie religieuse des Aissâoûa au Maroc.* Paris, 1926. An account that has played some role in interpreting Dionysian omophagia.

Burkert, Walter. *Homo Necans: The Anthropology of Ancient Greek Sacrificial Ritual and Myth.* Berkeley, 1983. An essay on patterns of myth and ritual, including the Dionysian, as formed by prehistoric hunters' traditions.

Detienne, Marcel. *Dionysus Slain.* Baltimore, 1979. A structural study on dietary codes of protest groups.

Dodds, E. R. *The Greeks and the Irrational.* Berkeley, 1951. A readable and well-documented classic. For a discussion of the Maenads, see pages 270–282.

Frazer, James G. *The Golden Bough* (1890). 12 vols. 3d ed. London, 1911–1915. An indispensable collection of materials, though criticized today for lack of theory and method.

Harrison, Jane E. *Prolegomena to the Study of Greek Religion* (1903). Atlantic Highlands, N.J., 1981. A seminal study on the primitive foundations of Greek religion. Pages 478–500 offer a discussion of omophagia.

Henrichs, Albert. "Greek Maenadism from Olympias to Messalina." *Harvard Studies in Classical Philology* 82 (1978): 121–160.

Lévi-Strauss, Claude. *The Raw and the Cooked.* New York, 1969. A basic book of French structuralism, treating Amerindian myths as a system of nature-culture antithesis.

Nilsson, Martin P. *The Dionysiac Mysteries of the Hellenistic and Roman Age* (1957). New York, 1975. A reliable account of the evidence.

Smith, W. Robertson. *Lectures on the Religion of the Semites* (1889). New York, 1969. A fundamental study on animal sacrifice from a functional perspective.

WALTER BURKERT

ŌMOTOKYŌ. Founded at Ayabe, Kyoto Prefecture, in 1892, Ōmotokyō constitutes a typical Japanese world renewal religion under the modern emperor system. Ōmotokyō absorbed vestiges of the folk religious traditions of feudal society and created a distinctive syncretic Shintō doctrine.

The founder of Ōmotokyō, Deguchi Nao (1837–1918), was the widow of a poor carpenter. On the lunar New Year, 1892, at the age of fifty-six, she was by her own account possessed by a *kami.* In this early religious experience, Nao, influenced by the teachings of the Konkōkyō sect, conceived a powerful faith in the benevolent nature of the *kami* Konjin, a belief that contrasted with established notions of that deity's malevolence. The following year, however, Nao was confined to a room as insane. It was there, under the command of the *kami,* that she began writing her *Ofudesaki* (The Tip of the Divine Writing Brush), the seminal work of Ōmotokyō. Thereafter, Nao's healing powers began to win converts to Konjin and she began actively proselytizing the Konkōkyō faith. During this period, Nao continued her work on the *Ofudesaki,* eventually leaving Konkōkyō in order to promulgate her own teachings.

Nao believed that Konjin, who resided in the northeast, was the *kami* who fashioned Paradise from this evil world; this doctrine was derived from both Konkōkyō and Tenrikyō and was intended to offer solace to the people in the face of the collapse of feudal society. She opposed capitalism and materialism, calling for a utopian age of peace and a return to an agrarian society. In *Ofudesaki* she proclaimed an eschatological viewpoint of world renewal, urging the realization of the ideal world of Miroku's (the *bodhisattva* Maitreya's) age and the salvation of the people.

Later, Nao's small following welcomed Ueda Kisaburō (later, Deguchi Onisaburō; 1871–1948), a religious practitioner, and together they created the Kimmei Reigakkai (Association of Konjin Believers and Spiritual Researchers). Onisaburō was the son of a poor farmer in the suburbs of Kameoka in Kyoto Prefecture. As a result of his many religious experiences he was able to heal the sick and had mastered syncretistic Shintō teachings and shamanistic practices. Together, Nao and Onisaburō worked to systematize their religious insights.

Ōmotokyō proposed a myth of the withdrawal of the nation's founders. This myth emphasized faith in the two *kami* Kunitokotachi no Mikoto and Susano-o no Mikoto, holding that these founding *kami,* who were the original rulers of Japan, had been expelled by evil *kami,* causing chaos in the present world. Ōmotokyō believes, however, that the time will arrive when a legitimate government of the *kami* will be realized. This notion was a challenge to the national myth that regards Amaterasu Ōmikami as the divine ancestor of the imperial line, thus clearly denying the divine status of the emperor and the legitimacy of his reign.

In its early years, however, Ōmotokyō was beset by difficulties and dissention. The proselytizing activities of Ōmotokyō's leaders increasingly suffered from police interference and suppression, and by the turn of the century the number of believers had dwindled. Internal strife broke out, and as a result of opposition to Nao and the old leaders, Onisaburō left Ayabe for Kyoto, where he became a Shintō priest.

In 1908, having broadened his viewpoint, Onisaburō returned to Ayabe with plans for the expansion of Ōmotokyō. Despite police oppression, the Kimmei Reigakkai, grew into the Dainihon Shūsaikai (the Japanese Purification Society), and then the Kōdō Ōmoto (Great Foundation of the Imperial Way). With the beginning of World War I, Ōmotokyō leadership found the time ripe for a reorganization of the world and began intensive campaigns in the streets of Tokyo, Kyōto, and Osaka. The economic and social instability of the age made Ōmotokyō, with its opposition to capitalists, landlords, and the war, an attractive ideology to intellectuals, but prominent military and business figures also became followers.

Kōdō Ōmoto, in accordance with government policy, followed a Shintō-based doctrine that emphasized patriotism. Its members held strong eschatological views and preached rites of group possession. The movement advocated a restoration of proper government by the *kami* during the Taīshō era. This "Taishō restoration" would take place, the leaders prophesied, when Ayabe became the capital of the government they had envisioned.

Onisaburō became convinced through his religious discipline that he was the Buddhist savior Miroku, and advocated a wholesale restructuring of society. Established religions were highly critical of Ōmotokyō and labeled it a heresy. With its purchase of the influential Osaka newspaper *Taishō Nichinichi Shimbun*, Ōmotokyō's apocalyptic prophesies were presented to a broader audience and the government could not but take action. In 1921, the Kyōto prefectural police raided the Ōmotokyō headquarters in Ayabe and the leaders of the movement were arrested on charges of *lèse majesté*. The central sanctuary, a Miroku hall built the previous year, was destroyed, and Nao's tomb was ordered reconstructed because it resembled that of an emperor. The charges against the religion were later dismissed in the amnesty at the time of the funeral of the Taishō emperor.

After surviving its first persecution, Ōmotokyō entered a new stage of development, expanding its activities both within and outside the country. Onisaburō dictated the large scripture *Reikai Monogatari* (Tale of the Spirit World), and while out on bail secretly traveled to Mongolia, where he unsuccessfully attempted to create a separate state by calling himself a living Buddha. Ōmotokyō, in consonance with post–World War I international humanist thought, urged the adoption of Esperanto and the use of the Latin alphabet for Japanese, and advanced the notions that all religions have the same origin and that all men are brothers. It cooperated in the Chinese charitable religious organization Tao Yüan (Dōin), developing the Federated Association of World Religions at Peking. Within Japan it formed the Jinrui Aizenkai (Association of Benevolence for Mankind). This association spread through Asia, North and South America, and Europe, cooperating with spiritual organizations in various countries.

In 1934 Ōmotokyō formed the Shōwa Shinseikai (Shōwa Sanctity Society) and under its leader, Onisaburō, it proceeded to the practical implementation of political reform. Taking right-wing politicians as advisers, they called for an end to parliamentary government and urged reconstruction of the state, giving priority to agriculture, with emphasis on the rescue of farm villages. The adoption of these positions strengthened the image of the movement as popular heretical fascism. These political views were understandably alarming to the government, which was simultaneously confronted by a series of plots by rightists and young army officers. On 8 December 1935, a 550-man unit of armed special police made a surprise attack on Ōmotokyō's headquarters at Kameoka and Ayabe, arresting 210 administrators. A nationwide search also was conducted by the commander of the Police Bureau of the Home Affairs Ministry. In the following year, 62 officials of Ōmotokyō were indicted for the crime of *lèse majesté* and for violation of the Peace Preservation Law; the Ministry of Home Affairs immediately proscribed Ōmotokyō. The indictment falsely charged that the society advocated the overthrow of the government and had plotted to seize political power. In the aftermath of this action the government ordered the destruction of Ōmotokyō facilities without waiting for a trial, demolishing the imposing sanctuary and church buildings. While in prison, the officials were tortured, but they insisted that the grounds for their indictment were false.

In 1942, after a long court battle and more than six years in jail, the officials were released on bail. Bitterly resentful of the violent oppression by the authorities and convinced of the inevitability of Japan's defeat, Onisaburō criticized the war and preached a faith based on peace and humanism to the believers who secretly visited him, revealing that his failure to participate in the war effort was a manifestation of divine will. Following the war, Ōmotokyō was reconstructed as Aizen'en and took as its historical mission the establishment of world peace. It was for the foundation of this new world, Onisaburō claimed, that the *kami* had allowed Ōmotokyō to survive the war.

[*See also* New Religions, *article on* New Religions in Japan.]

BIBLIOGRAPHY

Deguchi Nao. *Ofudesaki, the Holy Scriptures of Oomoto.* Translated by Hino Iwao. Kyoto, 1974.

Iwao, Hino, ed. *The Outline of Oomoto.* Kyoto, 1970.

Murakami Shigeyoshi. *Japanese Religion in the Modern Century.* Translated by H. Byron Earhart. Tokyo, 1980. Originally published as *Kindai nihon no shūkyō.*

Oomoto (Kyoto, 1956–). An English-language periodical, issued bimonthly; the official organ of the Oomoto and Universal Love and Brotherhood Association.

MURAKAMI SHIGEYOSHI

OMPHALOS. *See* Center of the World.

ONA RELIGION. *See* Selk'nam Religion.

ONGON. In all Mongolian languages, the term *ongon* is applied to the dwelling-place of a spirit or sacred being. In the traditional shamanistic context it refers to any spirit, together with the object in which that spirit resides. There is a great variety of such dwellings. Some are natural (e.g., lakes, trees, living animals, skinned animals), and hence certain scholars refer to the notion of *ongon* as totemism. Others are artificial (e.g., drawings on rock, wooden or felt figurines, drawings on cloth); for these the collective form *ongot* is reserved. Some are suspended and clearly visible either in or outside the yurt; others are locked away in sacks or caskets.

A ritual act, usually carried out by a shaman, is required for each of these natural or artificial mediums to become an *ongon*. For natural *ongons*, this consists of establishing a relationship with the spirit that animates and is indistinguishable from the natural being; and for artificial ones, the rite is one that introduces the desired spirit into the created receptacle. A spirit must be fastened down so that man can have contact with him and control him, for on the one hand a wandering spirit may be dangerous, and on the other an empty receptacle is in danger of being filled by an undesirable spirit.

The ritual treatment of all categories of *ongons* is essentially the act of feeding them. Food is given to living animals; meat, butter, or cream is either set down beside the figurines, placed in their mouths, or rubbed on them. Tobacco offerings accompany the food, and the practitioner smokes a ritual pipe. The sanction for failure to feed the *ongon* is sickness or death, which has led certain writers to attribute a primarily medical function to the *ongons*.

The *ongon* cult is based on the conception of a structural similarity between intrahuman relationships on the one hand and relationships that tie man to nature for sources of his subsistence on the other. Everything that happens in one domain inevitably has consequences in the other. Like humans, the animals are conceived as being organized in clans. Furthermore, relationships between humans and animals are modeled on intrahuman relationships. These relationships are both interclan (involving alliance and vengeance) and intraclan (involving filiation or descent). For humans and animals alike, being excluded from a clan creates frustration and therefore the desire to seek revenge, a cause of

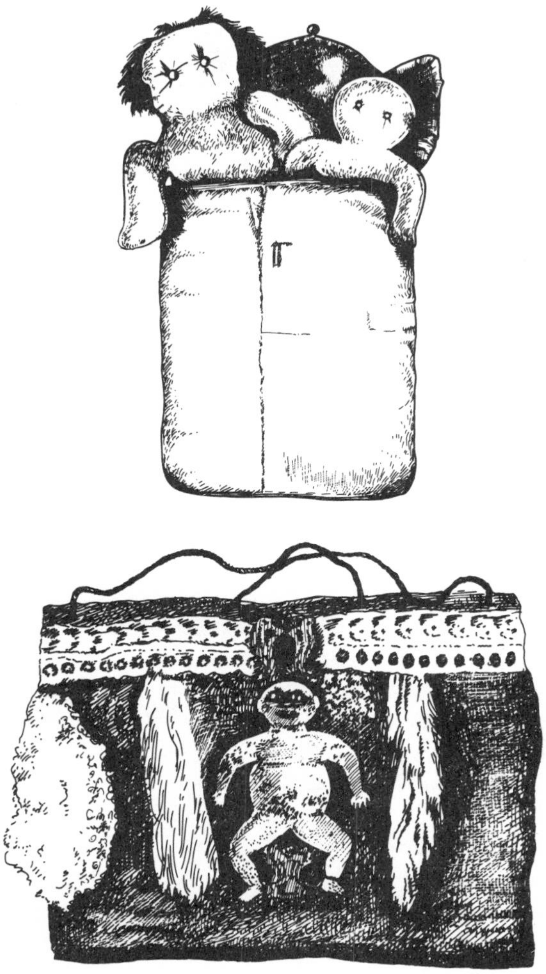

FIGURE 1. *Representative Ongons*

trouble for the whole community. Hence, in addition to clan *ongons*, there are also *ongons* representing isolated or unaffiliated spirits, which may receive the cult either from one family or from several clans.

The various modes of access to natural resources are what determine the most significant differences between *ongons*. Situated within the confines of the forest and the steppe, the Mongolian peoples have all made their living by hunting. Only subsequently did they adopt pastoralism to a certain extent. When it is hunting that provides sustenance, the relationship between man and nature is conceived of as based on the model of a marriage exchange, wherein the hunter is to the spirit dispenser of game, Bayan Khangay ("rich forest"), as a son-in-law is to his father-in-law. The hunter takes game from Bayan Khangay just as a man takes his wife from his father-in-law: he is a taker, proud of his catch, yet guilty for not having given anything in exchange. First, the ritual of the hunt aims to reduce the capture of game to a capture of food. The skeleton and the respiratory organs containing the vital breath of life are disposed of in such a way that the animal is allowed to be reborn. Next, the real compensation for the food (i.e., game taken from nature) is made by feeding *ongons* either small tamed animals (eagles, cygnets, etc.) or figurines or drawings representing animals, skins of animals, or the like. Thus this system of food exchange is similar to the exchange of women in the marriage alliance system: a man accepts his wife from one family, and in return offers his sister or daughter in marriage to another. This feeding of *ongons* is primarily intended to ensure that the hunt will not be hindered by the vengeance of decimated animal clans or the revenge of deceased unlucky hunters. In the event of an unsuccessful hunt, the *ongon* that is considered to have failed to carry out its part of the contract, although correctly fed, is reviled, beaten, destroyed, thrown out, and replaced by a new one.

Pastoralism, on the other hand, switches the nature of human-spirit relationships from one of alliance to one of filiation. The attitude of an exacting contracting party that prevails under the alliance model gives way to an attitude of veneration on the part of the filial descendent. This is because there is a patrimony (herds and grazing rights) to protect and hand down. In addition, sacrifices are made to one's ancestors in order to guarantee pastoral legitimacy. The compensation for the resources taken from the herd is the food given to the *ongon:* living consecrated animals (mature males that are raised within the herd, then slaughtered before growing old and replaced by younger males), zoomorphic representations (accompanied by a human silhouette fashioned in tin, representing a soul) or anthropomorphs (primarily representing women who died without experiencing childbirth, a check to filiation that results in the herd being stricken with epizootic diseases). As early as the thirteenth century Giovanni da Pian del Carpini noted felt dolls suspended from two sides of the yurt, made and honored by the women to protect the herds. In addition, the body of the shaman itself is a medium for spirits during the Buriat shamanic séance called *ongo oruulkha*, "introducing the spirits."

As a result of their primary function of linking the social, economic and religious worlds, the *ongons* and the shamans themselves have been subjected to severe persecution from Lamaism. This persecution dates from the time when Lamaism penetrated into central Mongolia (seventeenth century) and the Buriat Republic (nineteenth century).

[*For an overview of the larger ritual context in which the* ongon *figures, see* Shamanism, *article on* Siberian and Inner Asian Shamanism. *See also* Mongol Religions *and* Buriat Religion.]

BIBLIOGRAPHY

Harva, Uno. *Les representations religieuses des peuples altaïques* (1938). Paris, 1959. A rich and well-documented presentation that suffers from an awkward separation of fact from context.

Heissig, Walther. "Die Religionen der Mongolei." In Giuseppe Tucci and Walther Heissig, *Die Religionen Tibets und der Mongolei.* Stuttgart, 1970. Translated as *The Religions of Mongolia* by Geoffrey Samuel (Berkeley, 1980). A fine historical presentation that illustrates the struggle of the lamas to suppress shamanism and explains the emergence of a syncretic religious form.

Zelenin, D. K. *Kul't ongonov v Sibiri.* Moscow and Leningrad, 1936. Translated as *Le culte des idoles en Siberie* by G. Welter (Paris, 1952). The only comprehensive work on *ongons*, still valuable because of its abundant documentation and recognition of contractual relationships with the *ongons*. In its evolutionist perspective and insistence on the term *totemism* as a classificatory rubric, however, the work is now outdated.

Roberte Hamayon
Translated from French by Sherri L. Granka

ONMYŌDŌ is the collective Japanese name for various methods of divination, originally based on the Chinese theories of *yin* and *yang* (Jpn., *onmyō, on'yō,* or *in'yō;* the complementary forces seen in all phenomena), the "five elements" (Chin., *wu-hsing;* Jpn. *gogyō;* i.e., fire, wood, earth, metal, and water), their cyclical interactions, and the influence thereof in the natural and human spheres. The art of advising individuals and governments in the planning of all manner of activities and projects according to the movements of the sun and moon (representing *yang* and *yin*, respectively) and the stars, and the predicting of auspicious and inauspicious conditions as determined by the shifting relationships of the five elements and the sexagenary cycle (Chin. *shih-kan shih-erh chih;* Jpn., *jikkan jūnishi*) were highly developed and extensively documented in China by the beginning of the Han dynasty (206 BCE–220 CE). Some of the major texts, such as the *I ching* (Jpn., *Ekikyō*) date from much earlier.

From the time of the introduction of these texts and practices to Japan in the sixth century CE, *onmyōdō* encompassed not only *yin-yang* and five-element divination per se but also the related fields of astronomy and astrology, geomancy, meteorology, calendar making (on Chinese models), and chrononomy (chiefly with Chinese water clocks). The word *onmyōdō,* meaning the "way (practice, art) of *yin-yang,*" labels these various arts and sciences and the beliefs and practices based on them in a manner similar to the way in which the term *Butsudō* may refer to the whole range of Buddhist ideas and practices; likewise, the term *Shintō* refers broadly to the many organized forms of indigenous Japanese religious tradition (as well as its imported accretions, including some rites and festivals originally associated with *onmyōdō*). Similar nomenclature was also used for specific fields within *onmyōdō,* such as *tenmondō for astronomy and rekidō* for calendar studies. The word *uranai* ("augury") is another term used widely for the many forms of divination practiced by *onmyōdō* masters as well as by other types of seers and prognosticators. In early chronicles and works of literature, *onmyōdō* specifically identifies the divining arts as taught and performed in the official Bureau of Divination (Onmyōryō), which was established in the seventh century and which was responsible for providing the court with astronomical observations, astrological forecasts, calendars, accurate timekeeping, and the training of practitioners of these arts. However, *onmyōdō* skills were known and used by many persons outside the bureau, including scholars, physicians, and Buddhist priests, as well as by unschooled fortune-tellers and entertainers. Like many aspects of Japanese religion, *onmyōdō* has both an organized, institutional aspect and a popular, unsystematic aspect as well. Both are present in the history of *onmyōdō* from its beginnings, as is the tendency toward undifferentiated linkage with other religious traditions.

It is likely that some forms of *onmyōdō* thought and practice were known in Japan prior to what is recorded as their formal introduction. It has been observed, for instance, that the emphasis on duality in Japanese cosmogony (as narrated in the *Kojiki,* 712 CE) may reflect the influence of the *yin-yang* concept. It would appear that *yin-yang* and related elements of Chinese philosophy were fairly compatible with indigenous ideas of creation and causation, as well as with other beliefs. Although its origins were just as "alien," *onmyōdō* certainly did not meet with the kind of organized opposition that confronted the contemporaneous introduction of Buddhism.

According to the *Nihonshoki* (720), it was in 513 that Korean scholars introduced the "five texts"—a group of classic Chinese works, including the *I ching*—to the court of the (semihistorical) Emperor Keitai. In 554, Korean *I ching* professors *(Eki hakase)* and calendar masters who had been serving at the court of Emperor Kinmei were replaced by new ones. In 602, the Korean Buddhist monk Kanroku presented himself to the court of Empress Suiko, along with up-to-date almanacs and books of astrology, geography and magic. Prince Shōtoku (574–622), Suiko's nephew and regent, is said to have chosen the colors of the caps used in his civil rank system on the basis of *onmyōdō* symbolism. The "Seventeen Article Constitution" attributed to him (although perhaps a later work) has also been said to reflect *onmyōdō* concepts of social order. When the scholars Minabuchi Shōgen and Takamuko Genri returned in 640 from a long period of study in China they introduced the latest in Chinese divining texts and practices. But even at this early stage, Japanese *onmyōdō* was distinguished from its Chinese models by the extent to which it incorporated other arts of divination, natural science, and what were probably native forms of magic. Nor was *onmyōdō* thought of as a discipline entirely separate from Buddhism or the other religions, philosophies, and forms of learning imported at the same time; the *onmyōdō* teacher Kanroku, for example, was also a high-ranking Buddhist monk.

Among the Taika reforms instituted in 645 was the adoption of a system of era names (Chin., *nien-hao;* Jpn., *nengō*) consisting of two (or occasionally four) auspicious Chinese ideographs with symbolic significance based on *onmyōdō* teachings. The first era name chosen was *Taika,* literally "great change (or reform)." Eras were renamed at irregular intervals, usually when some especially good omen was reported, such as the discovery of rare metals, albino animals (particularly turtles, the color white and the creature both being deemed auspicious), or the sighting of a very favorable cloud formation. Several of the *nengō* of the late seventh and most of the eighth centuries include ideographs for metals, colors (white and red), "turtle," "cloud," and other auspicious signs. In the Heian period, *nengō* were changed more frequently, often in response to such inauspicious phenomena as solar eclipses, typhoons, droughts, and earthquakes.

Emperor Temmu (r. 672–686) is said to have been adept at the *onmyōdō* arts. An astronomical observatory was built early in his reign, and he probably used its findings in the surveying and construction of his capital at Kiyomihara, in what was believed to be a favorable location in relation to the topography and the deserted capitals of his predecessors. Generally, the north was regarded as a seat of power, while the northeast was viewed as the source of malevolence; the North Star, Polaris (Daigoku) was closely watched. As in China, Japanese capitals, including the permanent capitals Heijō (Nara) and Heian (Kyoto), were all constructed on carefully surveyed north-south axes, and official buildings and residences were placed where they might best receive favorable influences or be protected from evil ones, according to *onmyōdō* geomancy.

The Onmyōryō was organized soon after Temmu took the throne, and its structure remained unchanged for centuries. The chief of the bureau *(onmyō no kami)* was a senior master responsible for reporting the observations of his subordinates to the emperor. The bureau employed six divination masters *(onmyōji),* who performed the real work of observing and forecasting, and one professor of divination *(onmyō hakase),* who supervised ten students *(onmyōshō).* There was also one professor in each of the fields of calendar-making and astrology, each with ten students, as well as two professors of chrononomy. *Onmyōji* were also assigned to various provincial administrative centers. Famous masters of the eighth century include Kibi Makibi (693–775) and Abe Nakamaro (698–770), both of whom studied at length in China. Since divination could easily be used either in the interest of or against the government, efforts were made to limit divination activities to officially trained practitioners. The laws governing the activities of Buddhist monks and nuns (Sōniryō), enacted in 757 as part of the Yōrō Code, included specific punishments for those who falsely reported omens of disaster that might cause the people to lose confidence in the authority of the state.

The chronicles, diaries, and literary works of the Heian period (794–1185) are rich with information on the role of *onmyōdō* at court and in society. It is clear that it was at this time that *onmyōdō* reached the height of its importance. About fifty different *onmyōdō* rites are mentioned as having been observed at court. Among them were the Taizenfukunsai, honoring a Chinese deity who oversees the spirits of the dead; the Dokōsai, for Dokujin, or Tsuchi no Kami, the mischievous earth deity whose seasonal movements were closely watched; the Tensōchifusai, performed once in each reign to honor war dead and to ward off disease; and the Shikakushikyōsai, wherein the spirits that cause sickness were placated with offerings in each of the four corners of the ceremonial space and at each of the four borders of the state. The increase in the emphasis on these rites closely paralleled, and was sometimes linked to, the increase in the importance of Esoteric (Vajrayāna) ritual in Heian Buddhism. The monk Ennin (794–864), the third abbot of the Japanese Tendai school and the figure who introduced many Esoteric elements to it after his period of study in China, is also said to have introduced the worship of Taizenfukun.

Several works of the Heian period indicate that the *onmyōdō* masters stressed astronomical portents over other types of signs in their reports and forecasts. This may reflect the interest of two influential *onmyō no kami,* Shigeoka Kawahito (d. 874) and Yuge Koreo (bureau chief in the Kanpyō era, 889–898). Concern with overt astrological influences became obsessive, and plans for every type of public or private activity were first submitted to *onmyōji* for readings of the governing signs. Directional taboos *(kataimi),* dictated by the rising and falling of one's birth sign (i.e., the two signs of the sexagenary cycle that were in convergence at the time of one's birth) and their relationship to others' signs, or by the association of those signs or of certain deities with certain directions, were strictly observed. In 865, Emperor Seiwa was advised that traveling from the crown prince's residence to the palace by a northwest-to-southeast route could have fatal consequences, and he duly altered his course. Such directional changes *(katatagae)* were also made to avoid sectors favored at particular seasons by untrustworthy deities, especially Ten'ichijin, (usually called Nakagami), Dokujin, and Konjin, the "metal god." Nakagami's influences were particularly feared. He was believed to be active first in the northeast for six days, then for five days in the east, six in the southeast, five in the south and so on around the compass. The whole forty-four day period was termed a *futagari* ("obstacle"), since activity was blocked at almost every turn.

Travel to and from the dangerous northeast, called *kimon* ("demon's gateway") was also scrupulously avoided. This direction was believed to be favored by a deity called Daishōgun, an active manifestation of the deity Taihakujin, identified in turn with the planet Venus. According to Venus's position, specific days in each sexagenary cycle, and certain hours on certain days, were judged especially unlucky. If an appointment required people to travel in a prohibited direction on a given day they might veer off in a safe direction on the day prior to it; after passing the night, they could proceed toward their destination without fear of adverse effect. Sei Shōnagon, the author of *Makura no sōshi* (The Pillow Book), a journal and miscellany of court life, is among the Heian writers who describe this technique. Hikaru Genji, the hero of the great romance *Genji monogatari,* frequently cites directional taboos as a reason for absence from or neglect of one or another of his many lovers.

Within the Heian bureaucracy, the Onmyōryō became the virtually exclusive domain of the Abe and Kamo clans. For generations beginning in the mid-tenth century, *onmyōdō* practices were divided between the two clans, the Kamo being the masters of the art of the calendar and the Abe controlling astronomical studies. The twenty-fourth volume of *Konjaku monogatari shū* contains a series of stories about the exploits of illustrious members of these clans as well as those of their predecessors and of some anonymous practitioners, including Buddhist monks. The emphasis in these stories is on the use of special insights to perceive life-threatening dangers and the secret techniques used to outwit them. Abe Yasuchika, a particularly accomplished *onmyō no kami,* is said to have relied on three texts—*Konkikyō, Suikyō,* and *Jinsūryōkyō*—which he referred to as "the three *onmyōdō* classics." A Sui dynasty manual, *Wu-hsing t'ai-i* (Jpn., *Gogyō taigi*), attributed to Hsiao Chi was also used by many masters. In 1210, the *onmyō hakase* Abe Takashige was asked by Retired Emperor Gotoba to prepare a new manual based on classical texts. The result, a work known as *Onmyōdō hakase Abe Takashige kanjinki,* prescribes divination for the undertaking of construction projects and official excursions, with many examples from Heian practice.

After the twelfth century, as political power passed from the Heian court to a series of military dictators, the heyday of official *onmyōdō* came to an end. Calendar studies fell into decline, while interest shifted to numerology, *sukuyōdō,* a form of astrology strongly influenced by Esoteric Buddhism, and folk astrologies. When the Kamo line of *rekidō* masters died out in about 1400, the Abe clan reclaimed the calendar legacy and, as a reward for helpful predictions, were granted the surname Tsuchimikado and the hereditary *onmyōdō* monopoly by Emperor Gokomatsu. The Tsuchimikado name remains closely linked with the remainder of *onmyōdō* history. Tsuchimikado Shintō, also known as Abe Shintō, is a sect that combines *onmyōdō* elements with Shintō. It traces its origins to Tsuchimikado Yasutomi (1655–1717). When the shogun Tokugawa Yoshimune (1652–1751) wanted to adopt a Western calendar he was defied by Tsuchimikado Yasukuni, who asserted the right of his family—and of the Kyōto establishment over the Edo shogunate—to exercise control of the calendar. He prepared a new one, the Hōreki calendar, which was promulgated in 1754.

Meanwhile, a class of professional conjurers, the *shōmonji,* had appropriated many *onmyōdō* functions, which they combined with *sūtra* chanting, dancing and theatricals. Although licensed to perform such entertainments, the *shōmonji* were a despised class. The word *onmyōji,* which previously had denoted a learned master, came to refer to itinerant magicians who roamed the country selling charms, almanacs and advice. Eventually, in the Edo period (1603–1867), both *shōmonji* and *onmyōji* were labeled outcasts and were forced to reside in ghettos. In some of these, their descendants still practice the ancient arts of their ancestors. Many modern fortune-tellers and astrologers continue to rely on basic *onmyōdō* methods, while many Japanese still refuse to live in a house with northeastern exposure or to position their beds in a way that might invite the malignant effects that come from that quarter.

[*See also* Yin-yang Wu-hsing *and* Japanese Religion, *article on* Popular Religion.]

BIBLIOGRAPHY

The first major work of modern scholarship on *onmyōdō* was Saitō Tsutomu's *Ōchō jidai no onmyōdō* (Tokyo, 1915). More recently, Murayama Shūichi has devoted much of his career to the study of *onmyōdō*'s history, treating it most comprehensively in his *Nihon onmyōdōshi sōsetsu* (Tokyo, 1981). His work is complemented by that of Yoshino Hiroko, whose *Nihon kodai jujutsu: onmyō gogyō to Nihon genshi shinkō* (Tokyo, 1974) and *Onmyō gogyō shisō kara mita Nihon no matsuri* (Tokyo, 1978) document the role of *onmyōdō* in various early cults and rites, with many diagrams and illustrations. See also *Classical Learning and Taoist Practices in Early Japan: Engishiki,* translated by Felicia G. Bock (Tempe, Ariz., 1985). A helpful table, explaining the various applications of the sexagenary cycle, forms part of the article by Fujita Tomio, "Jikkan jūnishi" (in English), in the *Encyclopedia of Japan* (Tokyo, 1983), vol. 4, pp. 55–57. The most comprehensive history of calendar study in Japan is Satō Masatsugu's *Nihon rekigaku shi* (Tokyo, 1968). On era names, see Takigawa Masajirō's *Nengō kōshō* (Tokyo, 1974). A highly regarded study of directional taboos is Bernard Frank's *Kataimi et katatagae: Étude sur les interdits de direction à l'époque Heian* (Tokyo, 1958). Nakamura Shōhachi has transcribed and edited *Gogyō taigi* (Tokyo, 1973) and has also produced a study, *Gogyō taigi no kisoteki kenkyū* (Tokyo, 1976). A translation of the early legal codes, giving the structure of the Onmyōryō as well as a translation of the Sōniryō, may be found in Sir George Sansom's "Early Japanese Law and Administration," *Transactions of the Asiatic Society of Japan,* 2d ser., 9 (1932): 67–109 and 11 (1935): 117–149. There is extensive material on *shōmonji* and the later *onmyōji* in Hori Ichirō's *Wagakuni minkan shinkōshi no kenkyū,* 2 vols. (Tokyo, 1953–1955), some of which is incorporated in his *Folk Religion in Japan,* edited and translated by Joseph M. Kitagawa and Alan L. Miller (Chicago, 1968).

EDWARD KAMENS

ONTOLOGY. The word *ontology,* meaning "discourse about, or study of, being," was introduced into the philosophical vocabulary in the early seventeenth century. The term was originally used as an equivalent for "metaphysics," which Aristotle, in *Metaphysics* 4.1, had defined precisely as the science that treats "being insofar as it is being." Thus the enterprise of ontology had a long prehistory. [*See* Metaphysics.]

Plato had considered the question of "being" *(to on, ousia),* which for him meant the "what" of things as a stable object of certain knowledge. Hence he thought that the term *being* was properly employed only of the self-identical, changeless, and hence eternal, realm of Forms—that reality, grasped by intellect alone, which is imaged in, but at the same time contrasted with, the mutable realm of "becoming." It was Aristotle, critical of this outright identification of being with the immutable and transcendent Forms, who insisted that the verb "to be" is universally applicable and then proceeded to ask what it means to be (anything). Since, as he frequently observes, " 'being' is said in many senses," he denies in effect that the term is used univocally or that it defines an all-inclusive genus. He nevertheless thinks that its primary or focal use is to denote the *subject,* whether of discourse or of change and action: to be is to be some concrete "thing" *(ousia)*—a changing, individual composite of two correlative principles, form and matter or (in more general terms) actuality and potentiality. The former of these is the active principle of the thing's growth and development (*phusis,* "nature"), the intelligible identity of it which the mind grasps in knowledge and expresses in judgment, while the latter is the substratum of possibility that allows for change.

This analysis of what "being" means was substantively taken over in the metaphysics of Thomas Aquinas (1225–1274). Thomas, however, broadened the application of Aristotle's distinction between actuality and potentiality. It included not merely the distinction between the form and the matter that determines the "what" (*id quod,* "essence") of a thing, but also, and more fundamentally, that between what a thing is and the fact that it is (*id quo,* "existence"). Essence for Thomas is a potentiality that is brought into "act" only through existing; hence the study of being, in considering the question what it means to be this or that (thing), must focus not merely on what gives a thing ("substance") its identity but also on what accounts for its "being there," its actual existence.

In his treatise *First Philosophy or Ontology* (1729), however, Christian Wolff (1679–1754), whose work established the normal modern use of the term, understood ontology as a subdivision of metaphysics: the study of being as a genus ("general metaphysics"), to be distinguished from the subjects of "special metaphysics," that is, theology, psychology, and cosmology. *Being,* then, was for Wolff a univocal term denoting "what is" in its most universal characteristics. Aristotle's (and Thomas's) insistence on the "many senses" in which "to be" is said recedes into the background: for Wolff, the fundamental principles of being are the laws of noncontradiction and of sufficient reason. Reality is composed of imperceptible simple substances each of whose essences is exhausted by a single clear and distinct idea, and whose existence is accounted for by appeal to the principle of sufficient reason.

This science of generic being, abstract and deductive in form, was rejected by Immanuel Kant (1724–1804), for whom *ontology*—a term he used very infrequently—came in effect to be identified with his own transcendental philosophy. This enterprise was concerned not with "things in themselves" but with the subjective preconditions of human knowledge—the forms of sense-perception and the categories of the understanding—through which the "objects" of the empirical world are constituted as such. The propaedeutic study of being thus became, for Kant, an investigation of the ways in which the subject of knowing "objectifies" the content of experience and so constitutes the "beings" of the phenomenal world. Like Kant, G. W. F. Hegel (1770–1831) rejected Wolff's "dogmatic" ontology. For him, the study of being took the form of a logic, which explicated the movement—from simplicity to organic complexity, from "being" to "concept"—by which Mind *(Geist)* appropriates itself through self-objectification.

In more recent philosophy, the project of ontology, long neglected save in theological circles where traditional scholastic philosophy prevailed, reappeared in the work of Edmund Husserl (1859–1938). Husserl's search for a sure basis of human knowledge led him to elaborate a phenomenological method that sought to identify and describe "what is" as the world of the "transcendental ego" or "pure consciousness" (as distinct from the empirical self, which is a member of the object-world of scientific inquiry). It was Husserl's student and critic Martin Heidegger (1889–1976), however, who through his *Being and Time* most explicitly and influentially revived the project of ontology. For Heidegger, "being" ("to be") is radically distinguished from "beings" ("what there is"). The former is the subject of ontological, the latter of merely "ontic," discourse. The clue to the question of being is, for him, the existent human subject *(Dasein),* which *is* precisely in the act of asking what it means "to be." To grasp what it is "to be" is thus to grasp what is presupposed in the human existent's asking about its being. Ontology is thus again, as for Kant, a transcendental analysis—but not, in this case, of the preconditions of human knowing so much as of the preconditions of human "being-in-the-world."

[*See also the biographies of the philosophers and theologians mentioned herein.*]

BIBLIOGRAPHY

Gilson, Étienne. *Being and Some Philosophers.* Toronto, 1949.

Kung, Guido, *Ontology and the Logistic Analysis of Language.* New York, 1967.

Martin, Gottfried. *Kant's Metaphysics and Theory of Science.* Manchester, 1961.

RICHARD A. NORRIS

ORACLES. The word *oracle* is derived from the Latin word *oraculum,* which referred both to a divine pronouncement or response concerning the future or the unknown as well as to the place where such pronouncements were given. (The Latin verb *orare* means "to speak" or "to request.") In English, *oracle* is also used to designate the human medium through whom such prophetic declarations or oracular sayings are given.

Oracles and Prophecy. In Western civilization the connotations of the word *oracle* (variously rendered in European languages) have been largely determined by traditional perceptions of ancient Greek oracles, particularly the oracle of Apollo at Delphi. The term *prophecy,* on the other hand (from the Greek word *prophēteia,* meaning "prophecy" or "oracular response"), has been more closely associated with traditions of divine revelation through human mediums in ancient Israel and early Christianity. One major cause of this state of affairs is that in the Septuagint (the Greek translation of the Hebrew scriptures made during the third and second centuries BCE) Greek words from the *prophēt-* family were used to translate words derived from the biblical Hebrew root *nv'* ("prophet, to prophesy"). Since most oracles in the Greek world were given in response to inquiries, oracles are often regarded as verbal responses by a supernatural being, in contrast to prophecy, which is thought of as unsolicited verbal revelations given through human mediums and often directed toward instigating social change. In actuality, question-and-answer revelatory "séances" were common in ancient Israel, and it was only with the appearance in the eighth century BCE of free prophets such as Amos, Isaiah, and Hosea that unsolicited prophecy became common. Further, the preservation of the prophetic speeches of the classical Israelite prophets in the Hebrew scriptures has served to ensure the dominance of this particular image of Israelite prophets and prophecy. Therefore, modern distinctions between "oracles" and "prophecy" are largely based on the discrete conventions of classical and biblical tradition rather than upon a cross-cultural study of the subject, though the terms themselves are often used and interchanged indiscriminately in modern anthropological studies. [*See* Prophecy.]

Oracles and Divination. Oracles are but one of several types of divination, which is the art or science of interpreting symbols understood as messages from the gods. Such symbols often require the interpretive expertise of a trained specialist and are frequently based on phenomena of an unpredictable or even trivial nature. The more common types of divination in the Greco-Roman world included the casting of lots (sortilege), the flight and behavior of birds (ornithomancy), the behavior of sacrificial animals and the condition of their vital organs (e.g., hepatoscopy, or liver divination), various omens or sounds (cledonomancy), and dreams (oneiromancy). Chinese civilization made elaborate use of divination, partly as an expression of the Confucian belief in fate. Some of the more popular methods included the use of divining sticks and blocks (the latter called *yin-yang kua*), used together or separately; body divination to predict the character and future behavior of select individuals (palmistry, physiognomy); astrology; the determination of the proper location of buildings and graves in accordance with *yin* and *yang* factors and the five elements (geomancy); coin divination; planchette divination or spirit writing; and the use of the *I ching* (Book of Changes) for divination based on the symbol *pa-kua,* that is, the eight trigrams constituting the sixty-four hexagrams that provide the basis for the book. [*See* Divination.]

Oracles (or prophecies) themselves are messages from the gods in human language concerning the future or the unknown and are usually received in response to specific inquiries, often through the agency of inspired mediums. Oracles have, in other words, a basic linguistic character not found in other forms of divination. This linguistic character is evident in the sometimes elaborately articulated inquiries made of the deities in either spoken or written form. In addition, oracles themselves exhibit a linguistic character ranging from the symbolized "yes" or "no" response, or "auspicious" or "inauspicious" response, of many lot oracles, to the elaborately crafted replies spoken and/or written by mediums while experiencing possession trance or vision trance, or shortly thereafter. This linguistic character of oracles presupposes an anthropomorphic conception of the supernatural beings concerned.

In actuality, oracles are usually so closely associated with other forms of divination that it is difficult to insist on rigid distinctions. Some commentators have vainly attempted to distinguish between oracles and divination by claiming that *oracle* is used only in connection with a specific deity, one often connected with a particular place. Other forms of divination were in fact used in all the ancient Greek oracle sanctuaries, often as an alternate form of consultation. At the oracle of Delphi, for example, where Apollo was believed to be present only nine months each year, oracular consultations were held in ancient times on only one day each year, the seventh day of the seventh month (seven was Apollo's sacred number), though they became more frequent with the passing centuries. On other auspicious days it has been supposed that the god could be consulted by means of a lot oracle, the exact nature of which is disputed. Questions were formulated to receive a yes or no answer, and oracular personnel may have used some type of lot oracle to answer such inquiries. In China divination was employed in all except Confucian temples; even in temples specializing in spirit mediumship, divinatory techniques such as divining sticks and divining blocks were regularly used.

A distinction between oracles and divination was made by the Roman orator Cicero (106–43 BCE), following Plato (c. 429–347 BCE) and the philosopher Posidonius (c. 135–50 BCE). This distinction was between (1) "technical" or "inductive" divination (Lat., *artificiosa divinatio;* Gr., *technikē mantikē*), based on special training in the interpretation of signs, sacrifices, dreams, prodigies, and the like, and (2) "natural" or "intuitive" divination (Lat., *naturalis divinatio;* Gr., *atechnos* or *adidaktos mantikē*), based on the direct inspiration of the practitioner through trance or vision (Cicero, *De divinatio* 1.6.12; cf. Plato, *Ion* 534c). The Greek term for all forms of divination is *mantikē*, which, on account of its etymological relation to the term *mania* ("madness, inspired frenzy"), might appear a more appropriate designation for intuitive divination, yet even in the most archaic Greek texts it was not so used. A third category can be added, "interpretive" divination, in which a combination of inspired insight and technical skill is required.

Types of Oracles. Oracles are usually associated either with a sacred place where they are available in the setting of a public religious institution or with a specially endowed person who acts as a paid functionary or a free-lance practitioner.

Oracular places. In the ancient Mediterranean world certain places were thought to enjoy a special sanctity, particularly caves, springs, elevations, and places struck by lightning (especially oak trees). The emphasis on the oracular powers inherent in particular sites is due to the ancient Greek belief that the primal goddess Gaia ("earth") was the source of oracular inspiration. While oracle shrines were rare among the Romans (the lot oracle of Fortuna Primigenia, goddess of fertility, at Praeneste was the most popular), they were very common in the Greek world. Apollo, the primary oracular divinity among the Greeks, had oracles at Delphi, Claros, and Didyma. Zeus had oracles at Dodona, Olympia, and the Oasis of Siwa in Libya (as the Egyptian god Amun); the healing god Asklepios had them at Epidaurus and Rome; and the heroes Amphiaraos and Trophonios had oracular grottoes in Lebadea and Oropus respectively. Each of these oracle shrines required supplicants to fulfill a distinctive set of traditional procedures, and each site had a natural feature connected with its oracular potencies. Springs or pools were closely associated with the oracles of Apollo at Delphi, Claros, and Didyma and in Lycia, with the healing oracle of Demeter at Patrae, with the oracle of Glykon-Asklepios at Abonuteichos, and with the oracle of Amphilochos in Cilicia. Further, the Pythia prepared for oracular consultations by drinking water from the Kassotis spring, and the priest-prophets of Apollo at Colophon and Claros did the same (Iamblichus, *De mysteriis* 3.11; Tacitus, *Annals* 2.54). Caverns or grottoes were associated with the lot oracle of Herakles Buraikos in Achaea, with the oracles of Apollo at Delphi (where the presence of a cave—a widespread ancient opinion—has been disproved by modern archaeology) and at Claros, and with the oracle of Trophonios in Lebadea. An oak tree was a central feature of the cult of Zeus and Dione at Dodona.

In the ancient Mediterranean world three distinctive techniques were used at oracular shrines to secure three kinds of oracles: the lot oracle, the incubation (or dream) oracle, and the inspired oracle.

Lot oracles. The process of random selection that is the basis of all lot oracles is based on the supposition that the result either expresses the will of the gods or occasions insight into the course of events by providing a clue to an aspect of that interrelated chain of events that constitutes the cosmic harmony. Lot oracles used a variety of random techniques to indicate either a positive or a negative response to prepared queries, or to select one of a more elaborate set of prepared responses. Both types of response had a basic linguistic character and for that reason must be regarded as oracular. Questions to the ancient Greek oracles were typically put in such forms as "Shall I, or shall I not, do such and such?" and "Is it better and more beneficial that we do such and such?" The oracle of Zeus at Dodona was primarily a lot oracle in which questions framed by supplicants were inscribed on lead strips and rolled up. Though the exact procedure is not known, cultic personnel probably deposited the inscribed questions in a container and simultaneously drew out a question and an object from another container signifying a positive or negative answer from Zeus. The lot oracle of Herakles Buraikos used a form of divination called astragalomancy, or knucklebone divination. Knucklebones with numbers on their four flat sides were cast; the resultant numbers indicated a prepared oracle engraved on the walls of the sanctuary. One such oracular inscription, with the number of each of five knucklebones on the left and their total in the center, is the following (from G. Kaibel, *Epigrammata Graeca*, Berlin, 1878, p. 455, no. 1038; my trans.):

> 66633 24 From Pythian Apollo
> Wait and do nothing, but obey the oracles of Phoebus.
> Watch for another opportunity; for the present,
> leave quietly.
> Shortly all your concerns will find fulfillment.

For centuries the Chinese have used divining sticks and divining blocks as a lot oracle similar in basic structure to the system of astragalomancy just described. Temples commonly have bamboo tubes containing a number of sticks, each marked with a number corresponding to a slip of paper containing written advice (i.e., an oracle) in verse. The kneeling worshiper shakes a stick out of the container, and the priest then reads and explains the response in relation to the inquirer's specific problem. Divining blocks may be thrown to determine whether the correct stick has been shaken out. Like the astragalomancy inscriptions, the advice is suitably vague, but usually it suffices. A typical example is the following:

> Food and clothing are present wherever there is life, and I advise you not to worry excessively; if you will only practice filial piety, brotherliness, loyalty and fidelity, then, when wealth and happiness come to you, no more evil will harm you. (Yang, 1961, p. 262)

Such oracular responses frequently express Confucian values that are received as expressions of the will of the spirit *(shen)* whose advice is being sought.

Incubation oracles. Incubation oracles in the ancient Mediterranean world were revelatory dreams sought in temples after completion of preliminary ritual requirements. Most incubation oracles were sought in connection with healing. The most popular healing god in antiquity was Asklepios, who had more than two hundred sanctuaries by the beginning of the Christian era. Typically, preparation for a revelatory dream or vision from Asklepios included a ritual bath and a sacrificial offering; fees were paid only if the healing was successful. After the lights in the temple or, in some cases, the incubation building *(abaton)* were extinguished, Asklepios was expected to appear in either a dream or a vision and to perform a medical procedure or surgical operation, to prescribe a particular regimen, or to make some kind of oracular pronouncement, usually of a predictive nature. Another type of incubation oracle in the ancient Greco-Roman world was the oracle of the dead *(psuchomanteion)*, a shrine that facilitated consultations with the dead through dream or vision oracles. [*See* Asklepios.]

One famous ancient oracle, that of Trophonios at Lebadea in Boeotia (central Greece), was described in some detail in the early second century CE by the traveler Pausanias (9.39.5–14). While this was not technically an incubation oracle, worshipers sought and received there a visionary experience of an oracular character. Both the protocol and the mythological features of the consultations strongly suggest that the worshiper was to visit the dead in the underworld so as to receive a revelatory experience. Isolated for several days, consultants abstained from hot baths, bathed only in the river Hercyna, made numerous sacrifices, and on the night before the consultation sacrificed a ram over a pit, following the sacrificial protocol appropriate for earth or chthonic divinities. Next, two young boys called Hermais (after Hermes Psuchopompos, conductor of souls to the afterlife) led each supplicant to the river, washed him, and anointed him with oil, as in the preparation of a corpse. Priests then had the worshiper drink from the waters of forgetfulness and memory (in accordance with Greek underworld mythology), and finally they led him to the opening of a chasm, where he had to descend to meet Trophonios. Consultants emerged badly shaken and unable to laugh—a state associated by the Greeks with death. [*See* Descent into the Underworld.]

Inspired oracles. In the Greco-Roman world many of the local oracles of Apollo employed a cult functionary who acted as an intermediary of the god and responded to questions with oracular responses pronounced in the god's name. Such mediums experience the cross-cultural phenomenon of an altered state of consciousness. Bourguignon (1973) has suggested that the two primary patterns of altered conscious states be designated "possession trance" (possession by spirits) and "vision trance" (visions, hallucinations, and out-of-body experiences). Of the more than six hundred Delphic oracles collected by Parke and Wormell (1956), only sixteen are not presented as the direct pronouncements of Apollo himself. Similarly, the *tang-chi* ("divining youth") of the Chinese spirit medium cults of Singapore and mainland China south of Fukien (the mainland origin of immigrants to Singapore) speaks in the first person of the *shen* who possesses him. Though the evidence is ambiguous, it appears that forms of divination other than oracular pronouncements through mediums were preferred at oracles of gods other than Apollo.

The oracle of Apollo at Delphi was in many ways a unique religious institution that exerted a strong influence on other ancient Greek oracles. [*See* Delphi.] At Delphi, Apollo's intermediary was always a woman called the Pythia, a priestess but also a *promantis* ("diviner") and *prophētis* ("spokeswoman"), who occupied a permanent position. There is no evidence to suggest that she was selected for her clairvoyant powers. The attendants at Delphi also included five male *hosioi* ("holy ones") and two male priests called *prophētai* ("spokesmen"). Prior to the sixth century BCE, Apollo could be consulted at Delphi only on the seventh day of the seventh month; thereafter consultations were held more frequently, on the seventh day of each of the nine months when Apollo was believed to be present at Delphi. (According to Delphic legend, he spent the three winter months far to the north among the Hyperboreans.)

On a day of consultation, a goat received a ritual bath in a spring; it was then sacrificed if, by trembling appropriately, it signaled the god's presence. Next, the Pythia took her seat within the *aduton* (inmost sanctuary) of the temple upon a tripod that represented the throne of Apollo. Though ancients believed that the tripod was situated over a fissure or chasm that emitted vapors causing divine inspiration, modern archaeology has disproved this notion. But the Pythia did drink water from the Kassotis spring, and later evidence reports that she chewed laurel leaves. Inquirers were assembled in an outer room and apparently spoke directly to the Pythia, who answered them. (No evidence suggests that their questions were submitted in written form.) The priest-prophets *(prophētai)* probably wrote out responses for inquirers who were represented by envoys.

The traditional view, now discredited, held that the Pythia spoke incomprehensibly and that her utterances were interpreted and reduced to written form (often in verse) by one of the priest-prophets. Ancient and modern beliefs that the Pythia was in a state of hysterical ecstasy manifested in bizarre behavior are belied both by ancient literary evidence and by her calm demeanor in ancient vase paintings. The possession trance experienced by the Pythia appears to have been, in the categories of I. M. Lewis (1971), a state of "controlled possession," in distinction to the uncontrolled possession experienced by those not yet fully adept in managing the onset of possession. [*See* Inspiration.]

A similar phenomenon is found in Chinese spirit possession cults. The intermediaries *(tang-chi* or *chi-t'ung)* are not hereditary professionals; as a rule, they are young men or women, usually under twenty, who have an aptitude for experiencing altered states of consciousness, either involuntarily or through conscious cultivation. They are almost exclusively associated with temple worship where the *shen* who possesses the *tang-chi* is one that is customarily worshiped, and where the *tang-chi* are subordinate to the owners of the temple (the promoters of its religious ceremonies), and usually to the *sai-kung* (Taoist priests). A consultation is usually planned at a temple for a particular time when the *shen* is called down by invocation. The *tang-chi* must fast beforehand and avoid sexual intercourse, and no pregnant or menstruating woman can be present at the oracular séance. The worshipers usually number about one dozen, though larger groups are possible. Outside the temple, a flag with the eight-trigram *(pa-kua)* design indicates the presence of a *tang-chi*. The *tang-chi* both begins and ends the possession trance on a ceremonial dragon throne, which probably represents the imperial dragon throne where generations of Chinese emperors sat, representing divine ancestors.

The session begins with drums, gongs, and chants. Gradually, the *tang-chi* starts to exhibit the characteristics of possession (swaying, rolling of the head, staggering, uttering strange sounds) and often at the same time commits acts of self-injury without experiencing pain (cutting the tongue, extinguishing incense sticks with the tongue, piercing the cheeks with sticks). Consultations follow in which the *tang-chi* gives advice to worshipers, cures their illnesses, and either speaks incomprehensibly with divine wisdom (requiring the interpretation of colleagues) or addresses his colleagues in a shrill, unnatural voice representing ancient Chinese. Clothing and household items are brought to be stamped with the *tang-chi*'s blood for good luck. When no more business remains, the *tang-chi* signals that the *shen* is about to return; he then leaps into the air and is caught by assistants who lower him onto the dragon chair. Afterward, he does not remember what took place during the consultation.

Oracular persons. Professional diviners and intermediaries often have no permanent relationship to temples or shrines. They may practice their divinatory and oracular arts in their homes, in the marketplace, or in various places of employment such as army posts or governmental offices. These specialists often practice either possession trance or vision trance, but there are other possibilities as well.

Oracle diviners. During the late Shang dynasty in China (under the eight or nine kings from Wu Ting to Ti Hsin, c. 1200–1050 BCE), the *wu* (shamans) in the service of kings and nobles employed a type of oracle divination called pyroscapulimancy. More than 107,000 "oracle bones" have been excavated (47,000 inscriptions have now been published); about 80,000 were found during excavations from 1899 to 1928, and the remainder from 1928 to 1937 during excavations by the Academia Sinica. Besides being of great value for understanding Shang religion, they are of incalculable importance for Chinese linguistics. The bones themselves consist of bovid scapulae and turtle plastrons. At the moment of consultation heat was applied to a drilled hollow on the inside or back of the shell or bone, causing a crack shaped like the Chinese character *pu* (meaning "to divine, to foretell") to appear on the other side. Both question and answer were recorded on the bone or shell itself, which then became part of the royal archives. The inscriptions usually consist of several parts: (1) preface (cyclical day, name of diviner, and sometimes the place of divination), (2) injunction (usually put into a positive or negative mode), (3) crack number, (4) crack notation, (5) prognostication (e.g., "The king, reading the cracks, said: 'Auspicious'"), and rarely (6) verification. Though most of the oracle inscriptions focus on the nature and timing of sacrifices (a preoccupation of most oracle questions and responses at ancient Greek oracles), others include announcements made to spirits or concern arrivals and departures, hunting and fishing, wars and expeditions, crops, weather, and sickness and health. The oracle questions used in pyroscapulimancy were directed to the great ancestral spirit and the spirits of the deceased kings, who were expected to send down their advice and commands.

Oracular possession-trance. Two legendary figures of ancient Greece and Rome, the *sibulla* (sibyl) and the less popular *bakchis,* were paradigms of possession-trance. The number of sibyls multiplied in antiquity, and lists of them distinguished by epithets formed of place names are not uncommon (see Varro as quoted in Lactantius, *Divine Institutes* 1.6); by the end of antiquity more than forty sibyls had been distinguished. The sibyls (always female) and the *bakchides* (always male) were believed to belong to the remote past; though connected with specific regions, they were often thought of as having traveled extensively. Their oracles, which were preserved in widely circulated collections, were believed to have been uttered in hexameter without solicitation while in a state of divine inspiration or possession. The inspiring deity was invariably Apollo, with whose oracle shrines the various sibyls tended to be associated. However, the oracular utterances of the sibyls and *bakchides* were never formulated as the first-person speech of Apollo but always referred to him in the third person. The popularity of the sibyl among Jews resulted in the composition and circulation of oracles in Greek hexameter uttered in the person of Yahveh, the God of Israel.

The oracles that circulated in collections under the names of various sibyls and *bakchides* were regarded as enigmatic and in need of interpretation. One collection of sibylline oracles was kept in Rome under the supervision of the *quindecimviri sacris faciundis,* a college of fifteen priests, and was consulted only in time of national emergency, so as to obtain instructions for avoiding the peril. When this collection was accidentally destroyed by fire in 83 BCE, a new collection was made. The last consultation occurred in the fourth century CE. The fourteen books of sibylline oracles now preserved are a mixture of pagan and Jewish materials. The content of the sibylline oracles was originally dominated by matters relating to portents, prodigies, and ritual procedures, but they also came to express political and religious protest, particularly against Hellenistic Greek and then Roman hegemony in the eastern Mediterranean area. [*See also* Sibylline Oracles.]

In the Chinese tradition, female *wu* specifically called *wang-i* ("women who raise the spirits of the dead") dominate the practice of necromancy. They are frequently widows and over thirty years of age. In contrast to the *t'ung-chi,* the *wang-i* operate almost exclusively in private company and may charge fees for consultations. When consulted, a *wang-i* requires the name of the deceased and the date of death. Using incense sticks and "good luck papers," the medium invokes a particular *shen* to lead her to the kingdom of the dead. The *shen* takes possession of the medium and describes a tour of the underworld. When the correct soul is located (and it has confirmed the identification by describing, for instance, the circumstances of death), its needs are determined for later offerings and sacrifices. Often the soul (who assumes its former kinship status for the duration) speaks to family members present through the medium, in order of seniority. Rarely are more than two or three souls consulted during a séance. When the consultations are concluded, the *shen* emerges chanting from the gates of the underworld; the medium then stands up and falls back on the chair. [*See* Necromancy.]

Another type of possession trance found in Chinese tradition is *fu chi,* or spirit writing, in which the medium receives the pronouncements or responses of the possessing *shen* in writing. Consultations may be held in temples, but they occur more often in private homes. The writing stick, or planchette *(chi),* is in the shape of a Y, with the lower writing end often carved in the shape of a dragon's head. The top two handles of the stick are grasped by two bearers, one with mediumistic powers and the other a passive participant. A tray of sand is placed before the altar of the invoked *shen,* and the writing stick begins to move, often with initially violent motions, as if of its own accord. According to de

Groot (1892–1910), the *shen* often identifies himself by saying "I am Kwan so-and-so of the Great Han dynasty; I have something to announce to you, people that are now seeking for medicines" (de Groot, vol. 6, 1910, p. 1303). An interpreter with pencil and paper stands ready to interpret the incomprehensible marks in the sand. Requests may be addressed to the inspiring *shen* silently, written on paper that is then burned, or read aloud. The answers or pronouncements are discussed by those present. When the session is to be concluded, the *shen* announces his decision to return. Often automatic writing is used, not to answer specific queries but to compile sacred writings consisting of poems, myths, and histories.

Oracular vision-trance. This altered state of consciousness presupposes Ernst Arbman's widely accepted dualistic distinction between the "free soul," which is passive during consciousness but active during unconsciousness (i.e., during a trance), and the "body soul," which endows the body with life and consciousness. This shamanistic experience, however, is only very rarely connected with oracles or prophecy. The ancient Greeks had legends about those whose souls wandered away during trances—for example, Aristeas of Proconnesus, a devotee of Apollo (Herodotus, 4.13–15), and Hermotimos of Clazomenae in western Asia Minor (Apollonius, *Mirabilia* 3; Pliny, *Natural History* 7.174). Two other Greek shamanistic figures shrouded in legend were Empedocles (c. 493–433 BCE) and his teacher Parmenides of Elea (late sixth to mid-fifth century BCE). A great deal of the revelatory literature from the Greco-Roman world and the ancient Near East uses the literary motif of the vision-trance to secure divine revelation in a literary genre known as the apocalypse.

The magical diviner, a common figure in the ancient Greco-Roman world, used vision-trance to secure oracular revelation for himself and his clients. Though the oracles themselves have not survived, many magical recipe books have been preserved on Egyptian papyri dating from the third through the fifth century CE. Along with love magic, revelatory magic constitutes one of the dominant concerns of the magical papyri. In addition to the many methods of divination attested in the papyri (e.g., lamp divination, saucer divination, dream divination), several types of oracular magic are also in evidence. These include procedures for obtaining such things as visions *(autopsia)*, foreknowledge *(prognōsis)*, a supernatural assistant *(paredros daimōn)*, and oracular responses through a boy medium; there are also forms of bowl divination in which the summoned being would appear in a liquid. Several of these procedures seek to invoke the presence of a supernatural being (usually one of minor status) who will answer questions posed by the diviner regarding the future or the unknown, often on behalf of paying clients. In one example of a personal vision recipe, the diviner says "I am a prophet" and then continues with "Open my ears that you may grant oracles to me concerning the things about which I expect a response. Now, now! Quick, quick! Hurry, hurry! Tell me about those matters about which I asked you" (Karl Preisendanz and Albert Henrichs, *Papyri Graecae Magicae,* Stuttgart, 1974, vol. 2, papyrus 6, lines 323–331; my trans.).

Characteristics of Oracles. The linguistic character of oracles does not necessarily render their meaning unambiguous. While lot oracles in a positive or negative mode and oracles dealing with sacrifice and expiation are usually clearly expressed, those dealing with other matters often require the skill of an interpreter. Outside the temple of Apollo at Delphi, free-lance *exēgētai* ("expounders") would interpret the meaning of oracles for a fee. Similarly, interpreters are essential in the consultations of the *tang-chi* and in sessions involving automatic writing. In ancient Greek and Roman literature, the ambiguity of oracles that often find unexpected fulfillment became a common motif. Ambiguity also characterizes the prepared oracular responses in certain lot oracles, which must be phrased so as to apply to many situations. A similar ambiguity is found in the verses and commentaries accompanying each of the sixty-four hexagrams in the *I ching* (Book of Changes).

The inherent ambiguity of oracles was an important factor leading to the formation of oracle collections. Since their original fulfillment remained in doubt, they could be subject to new interpretations. In the Greco-Roman world, professional oracle collectors and interpreters *(chrēsmologoi)* sold their skills in the marketplace. They possessed oracle collections attributed to various sibyls and *bakchides* as well as to other legendary figures such as Orpheus and Musaeus. The archives of oracle temples often contained such collections, and in the Hellenistic period certain individuals traveled to the more famous oracles and made their own collections, which they published with commentary. Though the origin of the Confucian classic *I ching* is shrouded in legend, it too functions as an oracle book.

Function of Oracles. Oracles, like other forms of divination, are means of acquiring critical information regarding the future or the unknown that is unavailable through more conventional or rational channels. The very act of consultation requires that what may have been a vague and amorphous concern or anxiety be articulated in a specific, defined, and delimiting manner. Oracles function in a variety of ways, some of which concern the audience (i.e., the inquirer or recipient of an oracle), while others concern the mediums or specialists who obtain oracles, as well as the institutions with which these persons may be associated. In some instances divinatory techniques are consciously monopolized by the state as a means of both maintaining and legitimating political power, as for instance by the Shang dynasty of China. In other instances respected oracles beyond the control of the state are consulted in an attempt to provide religious legitimation for particular decisions or plans inherently fraught with peril or uncertainty (e.g., the utilization of Delphi by the Greek city-states). Rulers and nobles of states are necessarily concerned above all with matters of corporate interest such as war and peace, colonization, expiation and sacrifice, plagues and drought, crops and weather, coronations and succession, and ratification of laws and constitutions. Private individuals, on the other hand, tend to focus on such matters as sickness and health, travel, business ventures, marriage and childbirth, happiness and wealth, good fortune, and recovery of lost or stolen property. Seeking oracular advice on these and other vital matters helps reduce the risks inherent in human experience.

[*See also* Portents and Prodigies.]

BIBLIOGRAPHY

The only comparative study of oracles and prophecy in the ancient Mediterranean world (including Greco-Roman, Israelite, early Jewish, and early Christian oracular and prophetic traditions) is my *Prophecy in Early Christianity and the Ancient Mediterranean World* (Grand Rapids, Mich., 1983), which has a lengthy, up-to-date bibliography. Two important general cross-cultural studies of possession are Erika Bourguignon's *Religion, Altered States of Consciousness, and Social Change* (Columbus, Ohio, 1973) and I. M. Lewis's *Ecstatic Religion: An Anthropological Study of Spirit Possession and Shamanism* (Harmondsworth, 1971). Still valuable is the older study by Traugott K. Oesterreich, *Possession, Demoniacal and Other* (New York, 1930).

The best book on the oracle of Delphi is Joseph Fontenrose's *The Delphic Oracle: Its Responses and Operations* (Berkeley, 1978), with a catalog of all known Delphic oracles in English translation classified according to grades of authenticity; it includes an extensive bibliography. The earlier standard work on Delphi, with a complete catalog of oracles in Greek, is H. W. Parke and D. E. W. Wormell's *The Delphic Oracle*, 2 vols. (Oxford, 1956); the more recent book by Fontenrose, however, is far superior.

An important introduction to some non-Apollonian oracles, including a collection in English translation of written oracle questions excavated at Dodona, is H. W. Parke's *The Oracles of Zeus: Dodona, Olympia, Ammon* (Oxford, 1967). Two very readable introductions to Greek oracles are H. W. Parke's *Greek Oracles* (London, 1967) and Robert Flacelière's *Greek Oracles* (London, 1965). An important discussion of the function of orcles in ancient Greek city-states is Martin P. Nilsson's *Cults, Myths, Oracles, and Politics in Ancient Greece* (1951; New York, 1972). An older but still useful comparative study of ancient Mediterranean views of revelation is Edwyn Robert Bevan's *Sibyls and Seers: A Survey of Some Ancient Theories of Revelation and Inspiration* (London, 1928). Though now out of date, the most detailed study of Greek divination, useful for putting oracular divination in proper context, is W. R. Halliday's *Greek Divination: A Study of Its Methods and Principles* (1913; reprint, Chicago, 1967). An English translation of the Greek Magical Papyri, including many procedures for securing oracles, is now available in *The Greek Magical Papyri in Translation*, edited by Hans Dieter Betz (Chicago, 1985).

The most important recent study of the sibylline oracles is John J. Collins's *The Sibylline Oracles of Egyptian Judaism* (Missoula, Mont., 1974). A recent translation of the extant fourteen books of sibylline oracles is available in *The Old Testament Pseudepigrapha*, vol. 1, *Apocalyptic Literature and Testaments*, edited by James H. Charlesworth (Garden City, N.Y., 1983), pp. 317–472.

An older work that is still valuable for its consideration of Israelite and Arab traditions with a wide spectrum of prophetic phenomena including "divinatory prophecy," dreams and visions, ecstasy, and magic is Alfred Guillaume's *Prophecy and Divination among the Hebrews and Other Semites* (London, 1938). A book that includes many texts in English translation but that lacks critical discussion is Violet MacDermot's *The Cult of the Seer in the Ancient Middle East* (London, 1971). More recent is a book that considers Old Testament prophecy in the context of comparative studies of possession phenomena: Robert R. Wilson's *Prophecy and Society in Ancient Israel* (Philadelphia, 1980), which includes an extensive bibliography.

The most important work in English on Chinese religion continues to be the magisterial work by J. J. M. de Groot, *The Religious System of China*, 6 vols. (1892–1910; Taipei, 1967); particularly relevant is part 5 in volume 6, "The Priesthood of Animism," pp. 1187ff. A more up-to-date study is Ch'ing-k'un Yang's *Religion in Chinese Society: A Study of Contemporary Social Functions of Religion and Some of Their Historical Factors* (Berkeley, 1961), where aspects of both ancient and modern divination and oracles are considered. Also useful is David Crockett Graham's *Folk Religion in Southwest China* (Washington, D.C., 1961). An excellent anthropological study of modern trance-possession cults among the Chinese of Singapore is Alan J. A. Elliot's *Chinese Spirit-Medium Cults in Singapore* (London, 1955). The most important study of the oracle bones and shells of the Shang period, with an extensive bibliography, is David N. Keightley's *Sources of Shang History: The Oracle-Bone Inscriptions of Bronze Age China* (Berkeley, 1978). Also useful is a book written by one of the excavators, Tung Tso-pin's *Hsü chia ku nien piao* (Tokyo, 1967).

DAVID E. AUNE

ORAL TRADITION, which operates in all religious institutions, tends to be viewed by literate Western scholars as a defective mechanism for perpetuating tradition. Theologians, secular historians, and sociologists of religion, sharing a dichotomous view of oral and literate intellectual systems, have contrasted the fixity of belief in an immutable truth found in literate religious traditions with the variety and mutability of knowledge typical of oral traditions relying exclusively on memory.

However, recent research on the institutionalization of oral and written communication in different societies tends to undermine the dichotomy between "oral" and "literate" societies. It becomes increasingly clear that in both religious and secular contexts literary and oral methods of learning and teaching coexist and interact. The relative stability of knowledge in a given society depends in large part upon how these different methods are institutionalized as well as upon the educational goals and concepts of knowledge that accompany them.

In general, it seems that knowledge based on memory is not as ephemeral as previously had been thought, nor is written knowledge immutable in the actual conditions of social practice. Thus comparative research into the ways in which written and spoken words are organized and used in different societies at present tends to complicate the picture of what oral tradition is, and of how it is related to the presumed stability of written traditions. Overly simplistic models are giving way to less elegant, but perhaps richer, comparative views, which also offer a more accurate picture of the varieties of religious experience that are embodied in written and spoken words.

The two great questions underlying most of the scholarship on oral tradition in religion are those of historical continuity and communicative effectiveness. Up to the present, these two issues have tended to be addressed by different scholars using different methods. The issue of historical continuity has been prominent in the Western comparative study of religion since the late eighteenth century, when the survival of preliterate belief systems in modern European settings was first recognized.

In the twentieth century, one of the most provocative historical comparativists has been Georges Dumézil. Dumézil has gone back to the early literary sources of Indo-European mythology, history, and legend to reconstruct an ideological complex that, he contends, predates the dispersion of the ancestors of the present Indo-European linguistic groups from an original home in Central Asia into the Indian subcontinent, Asia Minor, and Europe. Dumézil argues that his ideological complex was represented in both the social organization and the cosmology of the preliterate Proto-Indo-Europeans, positing a tripartite division of both human and divine spheres of activity into priest-kings, warriors, and agriculturalist-herdsmen. For Dumézil, it is not tripartism in general (a worldwide phenomenon), but these three particular categories that characterize cultural configurations derived from a Proto-Indo-European antecedent.

Followers of Dumézil have examined more recent folk traditions in Europe, such as folk tales, legends, and sagas. In these orally derived traditions they have found evidence of the pre-Christian Indo-European tripartism, which in some cases underlies such overtly Christian subjects as the lives of the saints. Of course, the awareness of pre-Christian content in European oral tradition and its possible impact on Christian orthodoxy was noticed by the earliest Christian missionaries. Several of the nineteenth-century folklorists were clergymen who identified pre-Christian beliefs and practices among their parishioners. Dumézil and his followers, however, unlike many of their predecessors, have detected not mere isolated remnants of tradition, but a conceptual system which, Dumézil argues, informed Indo-European ideas of social and cosmic organization at diverse levels, with varying degrees of explicitness, from the explicit *varṇa* theory of the Vedic caste system in India to the cryptic reflections that Dumézil has traced in the legendary history of the Roman republic.

Dumézil's historical-reconstructive approach to the oral heritage in written traditions shares some of the weaknesses of its predecessors. A major problem is the variety of relationships between cosmology and social organization. Dumézil and his followers found the Indo-European triad in some cultures at the cosmological level, in others in the configurations of secular history, in yet others in sacred biography. In some cultures (in India, for instance), Indo-European tripartism can be traced in many contexts on a sacred-secular continuum. But as becomes apparent in the study of living religious rituals and scriptures in their social context (and as is painfully obvious to believers who take their sacred models seriously), the sacred order is often not realized in everyday social interaction, and indeed may even be systematically inverted. Anthropologists of religion such as Victor Turner and Claude Lévi-Strauss have based approaches to the study of ritual and myth on the assumption that inversions between sacred and secular discourse are systematic, and even necessary. Dumézil's style of comparison is exciting more for the possibilities it reveals for discovering the manifestations of a belief system in both sacred and secular contexts than for the particular comparative conclusions it can yield.

Although Dumézil and his followers only implicitly address the problem of oral tradition, the identification of traces of an originally oral ideology in societies where that ideology is no longer overt raises the question of the relative importance of self-consciousness in oral and literate intellectual traditions. Literacy is widely regarded by the literate as a facilitator of analytic reasoning and self-conscious intellection. It is believed to enable one to manipulate series of propositions, to reorder them, compare their implications, and identify inconsistencies that would be obscured if one could only consider them in the serial order and social contexts of their immediate presentations.

In the religious context, the writing down of tenets of belief is held to facilitate the development of orthodoxy and of internally consistent bodies of belief, which in turn may contribute to the centralization of religious institutions and religious power. There are paradoxical aspects to this set of assumptions, however, as will be seen below. In any case, Dumézil's comparative studies imply among other things that the development of complex categorical systems of sacred and secular order is possible even in preliterate societies. The continued unself-conscious operation of such conceptual systems can be traced into the literate era, in both the literate and the oral domains of different communities.

A comparative approach to the diverse manifestations of such inherited patterns leads to the question of how these patterns are transmitted and institutionalized. A second major approach to the problem of oral tradition has focused directly on the forms and processes of oral transmission. This approach was initiated by the American classicist Milman Parry, whose examination of the style and structure of Homeric verse led him and his student Albert B. Lord to the study of a European oral epic tradition that still survives in the sectarian poems of border warfare sung in contemporary Yugoslavia. Through this study, Parry and Lord sought to identify mechanisms of oral composition and remembrance that could generate and perpetuate poems of the scale of the Homeric epics.

Francis P. Magoun and other medievalists then applied the Parry-Lord theory of oral stylistics and compositional techniques to Anglo-Saxon poetry. Soon a debate developed among medievalists and biblical scholars concerning the influence on early literary style of an oral rhetoric that was believed to reflect in various ways the oral composition and transmission processes that had been described by Parry and Lord. Arguments ensued about such questions as the relative debt of the Christian poet Cædmon to either the pre-Christian oral poetics of Anglo-Saxon or to the literary tradition of Latin devotional poetry. The organization of the *Book of Psalms* and the Gospels, among other Old and New Testament writings, was examined for evidence of oral composition in both style and structure. The simultaneous existence of variants, along with the presence of formulaic language, was taken as a hallmark of oral tradition. Stylistic studies that saw in the synoptic Gospels (*Mark, Matthew,* and *Luke*), for instance, a series of variants of an original oral tradition of the life of Christ, raised once again the questions concerning the historical reliability of these texts.

In the case of Islam, by contrast, the oral substrate of the tradition was directly taken into account by the earliest Muslim theologians. The word *qur'ān* literally means "reading," and the sacred book of the Qur'ān was originally received through reading, despite the self-avowed illiteracy of the prophet Muḥammad. The first revelation came to the Prophet in the form of an angelic injunction, "Read!", to which the Prophet replied, "I cannot read." This altercation ended with the celestial voice dictating, "Read: And it is thy Lord the Most Bountiful / Who teacheth by pen, / Teacheth man that which he knew not." The Prophet, waking from a trance, remembered the words "as if inscribed upon his heart." Thus the authoritativeness of written scripture was established by explicit revelation.

The Prophet's oral recitations of subsequent revelations were transcribed by various followers. The great body of Muslim oral tradition supplementary to the Qur'ān itself, embodied in the *sunnah* ("practice, custom") and *ḥadīth* ("traditions, narration") of the Prophet, was codified by literate theologians in the century following the Prophet's death. A primary criterion for authenticity was the soundness of the chain of oral transmission by which each bit of information was preserved prior to being committed to writing. It was important to establish that the chain of oral transmitters (*isnād,* or "attribution") specified in each case was comprised of a series of individuals who were in fact contemporaries in direct communication with each other. Thus Islam, in its earliest period, confronted the issue of the reliability of oral transmission very directly. Spiritual authenticity in Islam has continued to be measured in part by the directness of verbal communication between living exponents of the faith, as for instance in the emphasis that the Ṣūfī orders place on the necessity of a sound spiritual genealogy and on direct communication with spiritual guides.

A serious limitation is imposed on our ability to understand the workings of oral transmission in biblical and other traditions by the fact that the compositional history of existing texts is often undocumented, and information about the traditions upon which they were based is scarce. Arguments for the oral origin of parts of the Bible, like similar arguments concerning devotional and secular medieval literature, proceed mainly on stylistic grounds, whereas the reconstruction of the actual process of oral composition remains inferential. In societies where literacy is the skill of a minority, verbal compositions intended for a general audience must be organized to facilitate aural comprehension, whether or not they are composed orally. Furthermore, in societies where literacy is new, the indigenous verbal aesthetic is by definition oral, and early literature might be expected to emulate it to some degree.

The ethnographic evidence we have from contemporary societies, together with the scanty indications of the compositional process gleaned from early literary documents, tends to enforce the idea that different societies distribute oral and literary processes in different ways, that there are a variety of techniques of oral composition and transmission just as there are a variety of techniques of literary composition and dissemination, and that these communicative mechanisms interact in complex ways.

Looking at religious traditions in oral and literate societies today, it becomes clear that virtually all societies develop special languages or communicative styles for religious contexts, and that these are distinguished from everyday written or spoken language. It is perhaps best to regard writing not as more authoritative or powerful per se, but as one of several possible strategies for marking off religious language as particularly powerful. Societies with prophetic traditions embodied in written scriptures may develop popular ideologies that venerate all writing, by extension from the veneration of sacred writ. In folk Islam, for instance, *ta'āwīdh* are written formulas believed to have protective power that are worn as charms on the body. Other written charms may be consumed in dissolved form or inhaled as smoke. Their texts, which are specific to the protective function desired, may be derived from holy scripture, from books of prayers compiled for the purpose of *ta'āwīdh* writing, or from a series of numbers or words arranged in geometric patterns that are considered to be powerful.

This use of written words in charms forms part of a larger continuum of protective magical practices that includes the manipulation of other physical objects (such as strings, bits of cloth, beads, foodstuffs, and fragrant herbs). Thus those who use literacy for protective magical purposes are using but one of several strategies for physically embodying sacred power and directing it to human ends. The sacred power of language is no less likely to be embodied in spoken words, even in highly literate traditions such as Islam and Christianity. The invocations, prayers, and injunctions spoken over a written *ta'āwīdh* at its creation are no less important to its efficacy than is its written text.

Much recent research by folklorists and ethnolinguists favors the view that the meaning and power of sacred language emerges from the actual enactment of words by the living, whether the "texts" that serve as the basis for such enactment are written or oral. The dynamism of such oral enactment can often triumph over the professed fixity of a scriptural tradition and become a source of diversity within the tradition. This can be seen in several examples taken from New World Christian traditions.

Some Pentecostal churches in the United States, for example, while preaching the literal truth of the Christian scriptures, seek personal experiences of possession by the Holy Spirit. One group of such churches puts particular emphasis upon the verses of *Mark* 16:17-18: "And these signs will accompany those that believe: in my name they will cast out demons; they will speak in new tongues; they will pick up serpents, and if they drink any deadly thing, it will not hurt them; they will lay their hands on the sick, and they will recover." To this end, and as part of their devotional services, they handle venomous snakes and drink strychnine in trance states induced by very intense rhythmic vocalization, clapping and dancing during sermons, personal testimony, group prayer, and song. Other Pentecostal groups take no interest in snake handling, but preserve the importance of glossolalia and other forms of vocalization in worship. Glossolalia, or speaking in "new tongues" (*Mk.* 16:17), is accepted as an outward sign of the conversion experience and is considered to be the Holy Spirit speaking through the body of the believer. Such "baptism in the Spirit," with its outward vocal forms, is believed to be necessary for salvation.

A debate arises within some fundamentalist congregations concerning the types of vocalization proper to men and women. The apostle Paul's injunctions (*1 Tm.* 2:11, 2:12; *1 Cor.* 14:34–35) that women should be silent in church are interpreted by some to mean that women should not preach but only give personal testimony, sing, and speak in tongues as the spirit moves them. Women who feel called to preach may frame their sermons more in the style of a personal testimony (or their testimonies more in the style of sermons), or they may defend their right to preach by alluding to points in scripture (e.g., *Acts* and *Joel*) where it is said that women will prophesy in the "last days," which are presumed to be at hand. Thus silence for women receives widely divergent interpretations in different communities. The literalist interpretation of scripture typical of such communities in no way inhibits the development of diversity, especially in the dimension of oral practice.

Diversity is no less apparent in Roman Catholic communities, which were until recently restricted to a uniform Latin liturgy and scripture. Within the last thirty years, among the Tarascan Indians of Tzintzuntzan, Mexico, an elaborate, nine-day communal ritual of religious processions, feasts, and dances has developed around the single verse of *Luke* 2:7: "And she brought forth her firstborn son, and laid him in a manger, because there was no room in the inn." The theme of no room in the inn has formed the basis for communal processions, called *posadas* ("lodgings"), developed with varying degrees of complexity in many Spanish-American communities. Images of the Virgin are carried through the streets during the last days of Advent, begging for lodging. Although the basis is scriptural, the design and execution of these ceremonies are a matter of emergent oral tradition. In Tzintzuntzan, the ritual has developed into a pancommunal ceremony that entails elaborate cooperation within neighborhoods, performances of songs and recitations, and a complicated cast of male and female actors who carry out the roles of holy pilgrims and inhospitable innkeepers. Stanley Brandes suggests that there are extrareligious reasons for this community's elaboration of this particular detail of sacred biography at this time. In Brandes's view, the ritual reflects changes in relations between members of the community.

A distinction introduced by Gregory Bateson can help to clarify the value of orality in many religious traditions. Bateson distinguished between communicative and "metacommunicative" functions of language. While the communicative dimensions convey information and content, the metacommunicative level conveys a relation between speaker and listener. Bateson further observed that, while the literary mode is conceived as primarily communicative, it is the oral mode that is the dimension of metacommunication. Since a primary goal of religious devotion is precisely to establish or reassert a personal relation between the worshiper and the worshiped, Bateson's distinction helps us to understand why the oral dimension is often critically important in both the embodiment and the propagation of religious belief and experience.

Even within a strictly oral tradition, however, the religious value of orality may be differently assessed, and values normally associated with literacy affirmed. In different traditions, the authenticity of religious utterance may be measured by reference to either an ideal of immutability (whether written or oral), or to an ideal of spontaneity. Wallace L. Chafe, distinguishing stylistically between oral and written English, pointed out that in Seneca, a nonwritten American Indian language, the ritual language of religion and recitations of mythic history achieve many of the same effects of depersonalization and grammatical integration that Chafe identified as markers of literary as opposed to colloquial discourse in English. In Seneca oral tradition, the ideal of ritual recitation is a fixed text, and a highly standardized vocal style and physical mannerisms accompany the recited words. According to Chafe, distinctions between oral and written style in English are thus analogous to distinctions between ritual and colloquial style in exclusively oral Seneca.

By contrast with Seneca religious language, some Christian Pentecostal groups in the American Midwest locate spiritual authenticity in religious utterances that entail possession by the Holy Spirit. A preacher in this tradition would never use any sort of written notes or outline to organize his discourse in advance. And yet this ideal of oral spontaneity in devotional practice in no way alters the conviction that the written scriptures are the verbatim word of God. Furthermore, stylistic analysis reveals a highly consistent structure and high level of formulaic language in such inspired spontaneous utterances, both in sermons and in personal testimonies. Other fundamentalist groups may tolerate or even encourage the use of written outlines by the prayer leader, as well as the use of hymnals, but the spiritual authenticity of the prayer or hymn is measured by the degree to which it is "raised up" by the group from the skeletal, written prototype into an embellished improvisational oral performance.

Similar paradoxical relations between oral and written standards of authenticity can be found in other traditions. William F. Hanks describes a shamanic prayer among Yucatec-Maya of southern Mexico, where the local religion is a complex syncretism of Christianity and pre-Columbian beliefs, largely reliant on oral tradition. In this community, the proper form of prayers is so completely dependent upon the context of oral performance that a shaman is unable to recall or reproduce the text of a prayer outside the setting of the ritual. Hanks persuasively argues that the oral text does not exist in any coherent form outside of the immediate curing rituals, for, as the shaman explains, "[It's] a thing [that] passes by you in your thought." In such an oral tradition, the role of rote learning is minimized (shamans learn how to address spirits primarily through personal dreams and visions), to say nothing of fixed texts in the form of written scripts. Nevertheless, in this same cosmology, there is a guardian spirit whose function it is to record in writing, for divine reference, the individual rituals performed by shamans.

These examples illustrate the diversity of relations between oral and literary traditions in different religious settings, and also the continuing, central importance of the spoken word as religious act. Writing has no doubt provided a mechanism to measure the mutability of ostensibly eternal oral traditions, but when scriptural traditions are examined in particular social contexts, their own mutability is equally apparent, at the level of interpretative enactment. It is in the consciousness and acts (verbal and physical) of living believers that religions manifest their meaning, and in that sense, living tradition is always oral tradition.

[*See also* Tradition; Memorization; *and* Folk Religion.]

BIBLIOGRAPHY

The departure point for a great deal of work on continuity and analytic functions in oral and literary traditions is the work of the British anthropologist Jack Goody, particularly his *Literacy in Traditional Societies* (Cambridge, 1968) and *The Domestication of the Savage Mind* (Cambridge, 1977). The best review and critique of the literature on literacy and its effect on knowledge systems is Brian V. Street's *Literacy in Theory and Practice* (Cambridge, 1984). An introduction to the work of Georges Dumézil is C. Scott Littleton's *The New Comparative Mythology*, 3d ed. (Berkeley, 1980), which includes references to Dumézil's writings, including recent translations. Victor Turner's ideas on ritual are developed in *The Forest of Symbols* (Ithaca, N.Y., 1967) and many other later articles and books. The best starting place for an understanding of Claude Lévi-Strauss's anthropological theories is his *Structural Anthropology*, 2 vols. (New York, 1963–1976). The key general formulation of the Parry-Lord oral-formulaic theory is Albert B. Lord's *The Singer of Tales* (Cambridge, Mass., 1960). John Miles Foley's *Oral-Formulaic Theory and Research* (New York, 1984), which offers a superb annotated bibliography, provides an encyclopedic review of the scholarship pertinent to the theory in both religious and secular traditions. Two excellent collections of essays on, respectively, the relations between oral and written traditions and the relations between oral and written religious language are *Spoken and Written Language*, edited by Deborah Tannen (Norwood, N.J., 1982), and *Language in Religious Practice*, edited by William J. Samarin (Rowley, Mass., 1976).

M. M. Pickthall's *The Meaning of the Glorious Qur'ān* (1930; New York, 1980) provides a reliable translation of the Qur'ān, together with a historical introduction, from which the quoted traditions about the Prophet's first revelation are taken. Annemarie Schimmel's *Mystical Dimensions of Islam* (Chapel Hill, N.C., 1975) and *As through a Veil: Mystical Poetry in Islam* (New York, 1982) contain much information on folk and orthodox Islam and vocal aspects of Ṣūfī mystical practice. Information on *ta'āwīdh* is from my own ethnographic experience in Afghanistan. There is a burgeoning literature in folklore, linguistics, and anthropology journals on language in religion, from which the short ethnographic examples at the end of this essay are a sampling. Much relevant work has appeared in the *Journal of American Folklore:* Steven M. Kane's "Ritual Possession in a Southern Appalachian Religious Sect," vol. 87 (October–December 1974), pp. 293–302; Stanley Brandes's "The *Posadas* in Tzintzuntzan: Structure and Sentiment in a Mexican Christmas Festival," vol. 96 (July–September, 1983), pp. 259–280; Elaine J. Lawless's "Shouting for the Lord: The Power of Women's Speech in Pentecostal Religious Service," vol. 96 (October–December 1983), pp. 434–459; Terry E. Miller's "Voices from the Past: The Singing at Otter Creek Church," vol. 88 (July–September 1975), pp. 266–282; and William F. Hanks's "Sanctification, Structure and Experience in a Yucatec Ritual Event," vol. 97 (April–June 1984), pp. 131–166. Other studies focusing on particular traditions include Wallace L. Chafe's "Integration and Involvement in Speaking, Writing, and Oral Literature," and Shirley Brice Heath's "Protean Shapes in Literacy Events: Ever-shifting Oral and Literate Traditions," both in Tannen's *Spoken and Written Language*, cited above. References to Gregory Bateson's ideas are further developed in Tannen's introduction to that volume.

MARGARET A. MILLS

ORDEAL is a divinatory practice that has a judiciary function. The word reached the English language from the medieval *ordalium*, the latinized form of the German word *Urteil* ("sentence, judgment"). Two kinds of judiciary ordeals may be distinguished: those prescribed by a judge or judicial body as a form of trial and those that also involve the sentencing and punishment of the accused. Ordeals of the first type are based mostly upon the drawing of lots and the identification of the guilty party among a group of suspects. Except for those that involve the simple drawing of lots, it could be said that every ordeal is designed to prove definitively the guilt or innocence of the accused. For example, a Shoshoni medicine man would take two hairs from the accused and place them in his own tent. If they had disappeared the day after, it was seen as a proof of innocence; if the hairs still remained, it indicated guilt. Ordeals of the second type are those that place the accused in mortal risk. If he escapes death, he is judged innocent; if he dies, his death is considered the due punishment of proven guilt. The most common ordeals of this sort are ordeal by poison, in which the accused is forced to ingest poisonous substances (if innocent, he will vomit them up); ordeal by water, in which the accused risks drowning; and ordeal by fire, in which the accused risks burning to death.

Types and Sources of Judiciary Ordeal. The most ancient body of laws that includes judiciary ordeals is the Code of Hammurabi (Babylonia, 1792–1750 BCE), which prescribes the so-called ordeal of the river, in evidence during the Mesopotamian era as early as the twenty-fourth century BCE. In the ordeal of the river (which belongs to the second category of ordeal because it includes sentencing and punishment), a woman accused of witchcraft or adultery was thrown into the river. If she drowned, she was considered to have been guilty, and if she survived, she was absolved. It is interesting to note that those two crimes statistically outnumber all others in the comparative documentation of ordeal and that, in the case of witchcraft, the Code of Hammurabi (stela 5, lines 33–56) seems to have imposed the ordeal (or what we would call "the burden of proof") on the accuser and not, as we would expect, on the accused.

Another application of ordeal as a judiciary instrument dates back to the high Middle Ages. Unlike the Code of Hammurabi, which records the laws of the Mesopotamian civilization, ordeal in medieval times represents an aberrant episode in European legal history that has its foundations in Roman jurisprudence. The appearance of ordeal in European culture can be directly attributed to Roman and Christian adaptation of a Germanic custom. Ordeal was adopted because it had been included in the tribal laws of the various Germanic populations (*Lex Visigothorum, Lex Burgundiorum, Lex Salica,* etc.) and because it had also come to be regarded as a manifestation of divine justice, even to the point of being called "the judgment of God."

For an example of the interaction of these two frames of reference, the one civic and the other religious, we can refer to the *Lex Frisonorum,* which prescribed the drawing of lots in the case of a crime for which more than one person was suspected. Three elements enjoined for this ordeal gave it a consecrated character: the prayer to God that he might reveal the guilty party; the request for a priest to officiate at the rite; and the obligation to execute the rite in a church or, at least, in the presence of a reliquary. The religious frame of reference was eliminated because of the negative attitude of the church, which on more than one occasion forbade the clergy to lend itself to the execution of ordeal; gradually, this led to the exclusion of ordeal by judicial institutes as well. Hence its presence in Western culture should be considered episodic and anything but characteristic.

The *Lex Salica* called for ordeals in which the accused was tested for resistance to pain and for ordeals that involved the drawing of lots. This judiciary ordeal corresponds to the practice of inflicting torture on the accused to extort confessions. The most common use of torture in trial by pain involved boiling water, but a law of 803 CE speaks of trial by sword. In the form of dueling, trial by sword appears to be the most ancient and most easily verified trial of the Germanic tradition. Recourse to a duel between accuser and accused took place when the accused could not find enough witnesses willing to swear to his innocence (the graver the crime, the more witnesses he had to produce). A refusal to duel by the accuser in itself constituted proof of the innocence of the accused, but a refusal by the accused proved his guilt. According to the *Edictus Rotharii* (643), the accused could be represented by a substitute. He could also refuse to duel, if he submitted to a different kind of trial. One trial by sword that substituted for the duel, called *ad novem vomeres,* was practiced by the Thuringians. In an ordeal that could be called trial both by sword and by pain, the accused was made to walk barefoot over nine flaming plowshares. The symbolism of the plowshares in contrast to the sword is evident: this was more appropriate for farmers than was the duel, the typical ordeal for gentlemen. As an ordeal for gentlemen, the duel endured as a standard feature of chivalric codes and has survived even in modern times as a private solution to disputes, sometimes tolerated and at other times expressly forbidden by law.

Biblical Precedents. The medieval concept of ordeal as "the judgment of God" probably found precedent in the Germanic tradition, but another of its precedents was most certainly found in the Bible. We read there that judgment came from God through lots (*Prv.* 16:33) and that the drawing of lots resolved conflicts (Prv. 18:18). In *Joshua* 7:14–22, the judiciary drawing of lots to discover the violator of a divine interdiction was elaborated: first, the tribe of the guilty party was identified, then his family, then his house, and finally the individual himself. It should be noted, however, that the same procedure, from tribe to individual, was also used for the designation of Saul as the first king (*1 Sm.* 10:17–24), and that Saul himself used it as a judiciary method to discover the violator of a civic and not a divine law (*1 Sm.* 14:40–45). In view of his royal position, which detached him from tribal regulations, Saul put to one side all the tribes of Israel and to the other himself and his son Jonathan. The lots designated him and his son, and as the choice was between them alone, the son was named guilty by the lots. In this phase of the history of Israel, the same ordeal was thus used in identifying a guilty man, whether he had broken civic or divine laws, and in the selection of the first king. This would seem to signify not only that a royal prescription is equal to a divine one but also that the acquisition of royalty is itself tantamount to a violation of divine law. In effect, the Bible describes the arrival of monarchy in Israel as a sinful usurpation of divine authority (*1 Sm.* 8), so God himself is entrusted to designate the usurper as one who has violated divine law. In substance, it was a method that freed the community from the responsibility of decision.

Ordeal and Power. It could be said that recourse to ordeal is always liberating, considering the risk of uncertainty that lies in decision making, though this understanding of ordeal depends on a typically Western concept of responsibility. Ordeal, in the biblical case, reflects a system of interdependence among the divine, the royal, and the judiciary. In abstract terms, this interdependence is seen in the formula of a king who, through divine grace, administers justice in the name of a god, or as if he were a god. But in concrete terms, the royal institution is supported by the heredity of the office, whereby a king becomes king by virtue of being the son of the preceding king. Nor can he substitute for a god as supreme judge, because he is not endowed with divine omniscience and also because he himself could become involved in a judgment as accuser or accused. As in the case of Saul, these contradictions can be resolved.

Ordeal and royalty. As one who has not inherited the throne, the first king is designated by the drawing of lots, or it is believed that he has been so designated. A well-known example of this recourse to ordeal as legendary justification of the title to the throne is that of Romulus, who became the first king of Rome because he saw twice the number of vultures as did his brother Remus. Thothmose III (1504–1450 BCE), one of the greatest of Egyptian pharaohs, prided himself on having been designated for the throne by the oracle of Amun.

If a king is involved in a judiciary procedure, he is most likely to figure as the injured party or as the object of betrayal. This crime, treason, required a "judgment from God" in the Middle Ages. It should also be noted that the only ordeal known to have existed in the Inca empire concerned betrayal: the party accused of treason was held for one day in a cell with dangerous beasts or serpents; if he came out alive, he was absolved.

However, most instances of ordeal that involved interdependence between the judicial, the divine, and the royal occurred in Egypt, where this institution had its origin. In the classical model that Egypt presents, the pharaoh takes the place of a god or is a god on earth and, as the beneficiary of divine omniscience, exercises judicial power in concurrence with the divine oracles from whom sentences were often asked. There were moments in Egyptian history—for instance, in the twenty-first dynasty (1085–950 BCE)—when the justice exacted by a divine oracle seems to have prevailed over that administered by the king or his courts; but we also know of oracular sentences being challenged, with consequent recourse to the royal tribunal.

Ordeal and divinity. The biblical precedent of the medieval "judgment of God" must be considered not only to explain the adaptation of Roman Christian ethos to Germanic custom but also for the phenomenological problem presented by the relationship between ordeal and divinity. Ordeal is an autonomous and not a cultural ritual. Thus, in some historical contexts, that relationship is considered an accessory, almost a reinforcement of the effectiveness of ordeal as a judicial method. At any rate, numerous cases of ordeals imposed for their own sake, without invocations or evocations of divinity, have been documented. The Mesopotamian river ordeal provides for no divine intervention; in fact, the Code of Hammurabi allows two alternative courses of action—ordeal or divine intervention. For one charge, adultery, the woman accused can demonstrate her innocence either by swearing "to the god" (stela 21, lines 68–76) or by submitting herself to the river ordeal (stela 21, lines 77–82; stela 22, lines 1–6). The judiciary function of swearing "by God," which persists even in the judicial halls of our own time, results from the adaptation of the concept of ordeal to the logic of a polytheistic or monotheistic religion, in which a god who punishes perjurers takes the place of the punishment implicit in the trial by ordeal. The god by whom one swears is, in substance, evoked as the judge; historically, these are usually sun gods or gods of enlightenment and, as such, omniscient. Raffaele Pettazzoni (1955) has called this judiciary role the principal function of an omniscient god. The Mesopotamian sun god Shamash, by whom one swore as proof of one's innocence, was called "lord of judgment" *(bel dini)* and was regarded as the father of Kettu (Justice) and Mesharu (Rectitude).

The Bible does not provide evidence of judiciary oaths, but biblical oaths have the quality of a pact, a vow, or a curse. The most severe Hebrew sects forbade even the taking of oaths, as did Christ, according to *Matthew* (5:33–37). Nevertheless, an ordeal was called for in cases of suspected adultery and was carried out as if it were an offering to God (*Nm.* 5:11–31). This is the so-called oblation of jealousy. The oblation to God served to evoke his presence; in front of God, the suspected woman swore to her innocence. The possibility of a lie did not require divine intervention: the punishment could be delegated to humans who administered a potion called "bitter water" that the woman had to ingest; if she was guilty, it would make her dropsical. Oaths were common, however, in Roman law, which never prescribed true ordeal as a judiciary process. The several cases in which the accused himself, outside of legal procedure, requested divine intervention to prove his innocence are considered exceptional. The most famous of such cases is that of Quinta Claudia, a Vestal Virgin accused or suspected of immorality, who submitted herself to the judgment of the Magna Mater (204 BCE).

While oaths in a judiciary action may separate divine intervention from ordeal, there are cases in which the opposite is true. Sometimes the ordeal itself is divinized. Among the Sudanese of the interior (Azaude and neighboring peoples), for example, the poison used in an ordeal is personified and assigned divine attributes. Because evidence is scanty, it is not possible to ascertain how much this description of an indigenous custom depends on European interpretation (which tends to give priority to divine figures); but it is a fact that such a process has been found even among the descendants of Africans brought to the Americas as slaves. Ordeal by poison is still common among the so-called Maroons (or "Bush Negroes") of French Guiana and Surinam, the descendants of slaves who rebelled and took refuge in the forest in the seventeenth and eighteenth centuries. This ordeal is, however, associated with an invocation to Odun, the god of justice. The name of this god goes back to the denomination *(odu)* used by the Sudanese of the western African coast (e.g., the Yorulas) to designate the signs of their geomantic prophetic system. This demonstrates the prophetic and autonomous character of ordeal more than it does its substitution for "God's judgment."

Ordeal as Prophetic Battle. We have considered ordeal as a prophetic form with a judiciary purpose. In this sense we have defined the characteristics of dueling, starting with its Germanic, medieval formulation as trial by sword. In the Germanic tradition also, Tacitus (*Germania* 10) describes a functional inversion of the duel form, not as a prophetic form with a judiciary function, but as a battle with a prophetic function. Before battle, the Germans captured an enemy soldier and forced him to fight against one of their own warriors. The outcome of the fight was taken as an omen regarding the outcome of the upcoming battle. This context seems to broaden the definition of ordeal, but in reality it extends the concept to the point of rendering it meaningless, precisely because of its functional reversal of the judiciary practice. On the other hand, this sort of weakening due to reversals of perspective conveniently brings ordeal into the field of prophecy. Ordeal becomes a judicial process, in whatever form an oracular response is sought.

The constant recourse to oath—interpretable as ordeal, as has been noted—seems to provide evidence for such a process. Nor is it necessarily true that, in the Germanic practice of the duel as an ordeal before battle, the prophetic function of the ordeal is predominant at the expense of the judiciary function. In fact, on the level of phenomenology, the battle itself can be regarded as judgment, as the solution to a dispute between two human groups (nations, tribes, clans, etc.). Battle, too, can be seen as an ordeal. The difference between reality and appearance lies not so much in facts as in interpretation. An example is the case of the battle between the Horatii and the Curiatii: it is not worthwhile to ask if it really took place or if it is only legend, because what matters for our purposes is the interpretive model it offers.

Let us begin with the disputes involved in this battle: a routine case of Roman farmers trespassing on Alba Longa territory during the reign of Tullus Hostilius and of Alban farmers encroaching upon Roman territory. The conflict was to be decided by a war. Tullus Hostilius called the gods to witness before the war, meticulously following ritual. The Roman king took great care to characterize this war as "holy" (*pium bellum* is the Latin expression used by Livy), what we would call a "judgment of God." The war, which we might call a figurative ordeal, was then replaced by a genuine ordeal: the Romans and Albans agreed to make three Roman champions (the Horatii) and three Alban champions (the Curiatii) battle each other, designating the outcome of this battle as the solution to the conflict.

The model provided by this event can be used to interpret other situations in which war figures, whether in the search for a common structure in legendary wars such as the Trojan War, or for the purpose of classifying ethnological material pertinent to war. The Trojan War, for instance, was a conflict that we could say had a judiciary nature (Menelaus against Paris) and that turned into a war between Greeks and Trojans; it even contains evidence of recourse to a duel (Achilles against Hector). To examine this from the point of view of ordeal, we could speak of a dilatory process (from duel to war) and a reductive process (from war to duel). This pattern of dilation and reduction can be applied theoretically as if the subject of disagreement allowed the two modes indifferently. A purely quantitative distinction between war and duel is possible and in fact fully justified by ethnological documentation of cultures that do not have wars of conquest in the Western sense, but in which every conflict seems to assume the aspect of ordeal.

Some of these cultures documented by ethnological research know no type of war but resolve every type of conflict by dueling, even between two groups or tribes. Among the Inuit (Eskimo), an ordeal-duel (by blows) between two champions of opposing sides took the place of war. Similarly, the Colombians resolved all hostilities between individuals, villages, and tribes with an ordeal-duel. This is also true of the natives of North America (e.g., the Tlingit), South America (the Botocudo), Africa (the Ashanti), and Australia. Even when we can speak of war, or an extended ordeal, reduction is always noticeable: it can influence the number of combatants, the arms used, the length of battle, and so forth. Among Northwest Coast Indians war between two villages ceased with the death in battle of one of the chiefs. The equivalence of war and dueling is obvious in these cases, and it is not at all exceptional that the death of the chief signals defeat almost everywhere. Although battle requires a great number of participants, only two people count as far as the ordeal is concerned. The outcome of the ordeal is always binary, since there is a choice between two eventual outcomes that are equally probable before the confrontation takes place, just as in the biblical ordeal, cited above, conducted by successive alternates. This duality is well expressed by the Latin term for war, *bellum*, which derives from *duellum*.

Fighting as ordeal, whether war or duel, reveals its ritual nature through the rules that govern it. On the other hand, ritual fighting is found in religious contexts of various kinds, but perhaps the reduction of fighting to ordeal, even though problematic, can be deduced through recourse to documentary material, as is the case with ritual fighting that precedes tribal initiation ceremonies. Initiation fighting is found in various forms and with various functions: between initiates, between initiates and initiators, between the newly initiated and the women, and so on. But to reach an interpretation that illuminates ordeal, we must view each case as proving the ability of the young to be admitted into the adult community.

Naturally, there are other ways of testing the battle skills of the young; generally, we would speak of athletics rather than of ritual battle. [*See also* Games.] All athletics, which for the most part have been connected with tribal initiations but which in ancient Greece assumed an independent development, can be looked at for their meaning as ordeal. (The custom of wagering on the winner still attests to the ordeal character of athletics.) A "judgment of God" was derived from the Greek athletic arenas, as from medieval ordeal. Athletic trials pertained to the divine; the verdict, or outcome of the competitions, lent a "divine" prestige to the victorious city.

As for the connection with battle, let us remember that every competition derives from a form of fighting; it could be said that the athletic arena figuratively substitutes for the duel, just as dueling figuratively takes the place of war. According to the logic of these figurative substitutions, athletic contests and wars were incompatible, in the sense that if the former could figuratively substitute for the latter, it became illogical to hold both athletic events and wars at the same time. As we know, every war between Greek cities was suspended during the celebration of the Olympics, as if the decision that had up to that point been delegated to the armies could be deferred to the games. This "as if" implies a theory that, although belied by the fact that real wars were only delayed and not entirely replaced by the games, permits us to glimpse a quality in Greek athletics that is not compatible with our concept of sports. They were more "war" than "sport," we could say. Angelo Brelich (1961) has brought to light the initiation-athletic elements of certain traditional Greek wars (between Cretan cities, between Eretria and Chalcis, between the Athenians and the Boeotians, between Argos and Sparta, etc.). More "ordeal" than "game," we could say, remembering that, according to one tradition, the first Olympic competition, a race, was instituted in order to establish the succession to the throne of Elis.

For its game-war-ordeal-prophecy connection, a Mexican tradition is emblematic. Moctezuma, the Aztec emperor, lost a Mexican ball game against the king of Texcoco, who had wagered his kingdom against three turkeys. The outcome of the game was to verify, with the defeat of Moctezuma, the truth of the prophecy of the arrival of the Spanish, who would conquer Mexico. On the other hand, every game, when the results are binding (as, for instance, in a game of chance), loses the quality of entertainment and assumes the dramatic aspect of ordeal. For such as interpretive orientation, consider the conclusion of Lucien Lévy-Bruhl, who notes how certain trials by ordeal—understood by him to be among the cleromantic practices—are not too far removed from the spirit of our "games of chance" (*La mentalité primitive*, Paris, 1925, p. 256).

Ordeal as Initiation Ritual. To return to the probatory, and therefore ordeal-like, function of the ritual battle in tribal initiation contexts, it can be said that, in the abstract, not only these but all the trials to which initiates are subjected are more or less comparable to the various known forms of ordeal. It is not difficult to compare initiation trials of resistance to pain with certain trials by ordeal in which such resistance serves to demonstrate the innocence of the accused. Ordeal is represented also by torture in a judiciary function; among the initiation trials inventoried by ethnologists, genuine torture does indeed appear. Along the same line of interpretation, it is not difficult to move from tribal initiation to initiations into certain cults where trial by ordeal becomes the evidence of a superhuman reality in which the initiate takes part. From another point of view, we can speak of the demonstration of exceptional powers, acquired in the circle of a given religious form. [*See* Magico-Religious Powers.] The best known of these powers is the one that allows men to walk unharmed over burning brands or red-hot stones. We could call this an ordeal by fire, very similar to the ordeal of the nine plowshares of the Thuringians. The diffusion of this trial by fire is remarkable. In ancient Latium Vetus the so-called Hirpi Sorani, cult followers of Apollo Soranus on Mount Soracte, practiced it. Walkers on burning brands or red-hot stones have been observed in ancient Cappadocia, India, China, Japan, the Fiji Islands, Tahiti, Yucatán, and elsewhere. But for edification on the religious level, Mazdaism is highly representative as a religion that simultaneously confers on ordeal, called *varah* in the Avestan tongue, the double value of the judiciary and the initiatory.

In the *Dēnkard* (7.5.4–6), a ninth-century Pahlavi text, we can see the work of Zarathushtra. The text indicates at least thirty-three ordeals to "determine who will be absolved, and who condemned." In the Avesta, there are constant allusions to the methods and functions of ordeal. From several passages (*Yashts* 12.3; *Āfrīnaqan* 3.9), it would seem necessary to extract a ritual acknowledgment (by ordeal) from the initiate whom the priest, acting as judge, submits to a trial by fire—perhaps immersion of the hand in boiling oil (more precisely, animal and vegetable fat). Elsewhere (*Vendidad* 4.46), trials of an ethical nature are found. However, for the purpose of religious edification, they are figuratively absorbed in trial by boiling liquid. There are also true judiciary ordeals: the accused "must drink water containing sulphur, water containing gold, which produce the proof of guilt, prove the lie with which he opposes the judge and deceives Mithra" (*Vendidad* 4.54). (This potion used for ordeal is spoken of in *Vendidad* 4.55 as well.) Finally, the judiciary function and initiatory function fuse in an eschatological perspective in which a supreme ordeal is the essential proof and brings about the ensuing sentence of reward or condemnation. In this regard, we read in one of the five *Gāthās* attributed to Zarathushtra that initiates will have to distinguish themselves from sinners (noninitiates) in order to have "the compensation that will be attributed to them by the ordeal of molten metal."

In conclusion, ordeal is not an accessory element of Mazdaism; rather it produces, within the boundaries of a rite or ritual, the two main characteristics of this religion: dualism and attention to *asha*, a term we can translate as both "youth" and "justice" (the "just order"). Mazdean dualism responds to the binary code with which ordeal is expressed. Attention to the *asha* corresponds to the judiciary function that, although not always in equal measure, is found in every ordeal in every context.

BIBLIOGRAPHY

In regard to divination by means of ordeal, one text is indispensable: *La divination: Études recueillies*, 2 vols., edited by André Caquot and Marcel Leibovici (Paris, 1968). On the medieval "judgment of God," see Hermann Nottarp's *Gottesurteilstudien* (Munich, 1956). Also for the Middle Ages and ordeal as war, see Kurt-Georg Cram's *Iudicium belli: Zum Rechtscharakter des Krieges im deutschen Mittelalter* (Münster, 1955). About war as ordeal, see M. R. Davie's, *La guerre dans les sociétés primitives* (Paris, 1931). On the relationship between initiations and wars in Greece, see Angelo Brelich's *Guerre, agoni, e culti nella Grecia arcaica* (Bonn, 1961). For ordeal-oath in connection with divine omniscience, see Raffaele Pettazzoni's *L'onniscienza di Dio* (Turin, 1955). For the formal connection between games of chance and ordeal, besides the Lévy-Bruhl work cited in the text, see also Johan Huizinga's *Homo Ludens*, translated by R. F. C. Hull (London, 1949).

DARIO SABBATUCCI
Translated from Italian by Miriam Friedman

ORDER OF PREACHERS. *See* Dominicans.

ORDERS, RELIGIOUS. *See* Religious Communities.

ORDINATION here refers to the practice in many religions of publicly designating and setting apart certain persons for special religious service and leadership, granting them religious authority and power to be exercised for the welfare of the community. The way each religious community practices ordination depends on that community's worldview and religious beliefs. For example, in traditions that emphasize a direct relationship with the divine being or beings, the ordained person may be thought of primarily as a mediator or priest. Communities that consider human beings to be especially troubled by evil spirits or witchcraft look to shamans or exorcists to counteract the evil influences. In religions that present a goal of inner enlightenment and purified life, the ordained person will be a monk or nun leading the way toward this goal of enlightenment. And religious communities that place much emphasis on living in accordance with the divinely given law set certain persons apart as religious scholars and judges.

Each religion sets up qualifications that candidates must meet before they can be ordained. Sometimes ordination is based on heredity. In many religions the candidate must be male, although some roles are specified for women; other traditions allow both male and female candidates to be ordained. While aptness for the religious role is always a requirement, in some traditions the person must already have demonstrated his suitability for that role before being chosen, while in others it is assumed that the office will be learned through a period of training. Every religion presupposes some kind of divine call or inner motivation on the part of the candidate.

An authority and power not possessed by the ordinary people of the community are conferred on the candidate through ordination. The source of that authority and power may be the divine powers, the consent of the community, or those who have already been ordained. Upon ordination, the person receives a new religious title. The English term *priest* can be used in many religious traditions to designate those who have been ordained or set apart, but a variety of other terms is sometimes preferred, such as *shaman, medicine man, monk* or *nun, rabbi, bishop, presbyter, deacon, minister,* or *imam.*

Ordination in Ancient and Traditional Societies. Numerous ancient or traditional societies have beliefs and practices according to which they set apart certain persons, endowing them with special authority and power for the performance of essential religious services, such as serving the gods and spirits, sacrificing, communicating with spiritual powers, warding off evil powers, healing, and the like. Among the great diversity of roles dealing with spiritual power, some basic types are priests, shamans, and medicine men.

The term *priest* generally designates a person ordained with authority to practice the cult of certain divinities or spirits. Since these spiritual powers are believed to direct and influence human existence, they must be worshiped, prayed to, consulted, influenced by sacrifices, and the like, for the continuing welfare of the human community. The priesthood may be hereditary, or priests may be called or chosen by the divinity. After selection or calling, the aspiring priest undergoes a period of purification and training. Among the Ashanti of Africa, the novice trains in private with an older priest for three years, during which time the novice's hair is left uncut. He is taught rituals, rules of priestly life and conduct, how to communicate with the various spirits, and so forth. The final act of ordination takes place at a nighttime festival, with the new priest dressed in a palm-fiber kilt and decorated with all his charms. He kneels before his instructor-priest, who shaves off his hair; any "bad matter" that is found is put in a pot, which is then taken off to the bush. The new priest dances all night to the drums and the singing of the people, and he ends the ordination ritual in the morning by sacrificing a sheep to his god.

Ancient Israelite society had a strong priesthood that served Israel's god by prayer and sacrifice, acting as intermediaries for the people. The description of the investing of Aaron and his sons (*Lv.* 8) may be an idealized account, but it presents many important symbols of ordination. All the congregation assembled for the ceremony, and Moses announced to the assembly that God had commanded this ordination. Aaron and his sons were presented, washed with water, vested with special priestly garments, and anointed with oil. Aaron and his sons laid their hands on the "ram of ordination"; after it was sacrificed, its blood was placed on the tips of their right ears, on the thumbs of their right hands, and on the great toes of their right feet. They ate the sacrificial offerings, and then they stayed in the tent for the seven "days of ordination," after which they were authorized to act as priests on behalf of the people.

While priests are holy persons who have power by virtue of their office, other religious roles in traditional societies are set apart for those who demonstrate the appropriate charisma, for example, shamans and medicine men, who are able to maintain communication with the spiritual powers and influence those powers for the benefit of humans.

Shamans (male and female) are commonly thought to be elected directly by tutelary spirits, who in a visionary experience initiate the future shaman. Among Siberian shamans, this initiatory experience involves being sick, being carried to the realm of the spirits, having the body dismembered and reconstituted, and receiving instruction in shamanizing from the god. After this visionary experience of death and resurrection, the future shaman is instructed by an elder shaman, and often there is a ceremony that confirms the initiation by the spirits. For example, the Buriat neophyte, after many years of training following his first ecstatic experiences with the spirits, is consecrated in a public ceremony. First a purification ritual is performed, in which his back is touched with a broom dipped in a goat's blood. In the ordination ceremony, the shamans consecrate the shamanic instruments that the novice will use, and the candidate is anointed with blood from a sacrificial animal on the head, eyes, and ears. The "father shaman" leads the neophyte and other shamans in the ritual of climbing birch trees that have been cut from the burial forest and set up on the sacred ground, after which all fall into ecstasy and shamanize. Finally, meat from the sacrificed animals is prepared, and everyone joins in a banquet celebrating the new shaman.

Although the Burmese are Buddhists, they still have beliefs in a variety of spirits, ghosts, and witches; in particular, the spirits called *nat*s are thought to be powerful and capable of affecting humans for good and evil, and these *nat*s are propitiated by female shamans who play the important role of "nat wives" (most are women, though a small percentage are men). Typically, through a trance or dream, a young woman is possessed or "loved" by one of the *nat*s, and any resistance is punished by the *nat* until a "marriage" is arranged. The wedding is a costly affair, performed in a *nat* "palace" where there is a ceremonial chamber. As the *nat*'s dance is performed, the bride changes into the proper costume, pays the marriage fee, and enters the bridal chamber. Two shamans perform a ceremony of putting the bride's soul to sleep, and she does a dance to the music associated with the *nat* husband. The marriage has now been consummated, and she remains secluded for seven days with her *nat* husband, after which she is known as a *nat* wife and practices as a shaman.

Among Australian Aborigines, shamans play an important role in diagnosing and curing illnesses, holding séances with the spirit world and spirits of the dead. The profession can be inherited, the person may experience a call or election, or he may seek out the role—but in any case he must be "made" through an ecstatic experience involving a ritual of initiation. Typically the initiate is taken to the bush, and the ordaining medicine man places against his breast large quartz crystals, which are thought to vanish into his body. In other symbolic rituals, he is led into a hole in the ground to a grave, and snakes are also rubbed against him to give him wisdom. The initiation is completed with a symbolic ascent to heaven to communicate with the high god. Among the Azande of Africa, the ceremony of initiation for a medicine man (or woman) includes a ritual burial following a period of purification. The elders bury the upper part of the novice's body in a hole under a mat with dirt heaped on it, on which the other medicine men dance. After about a half hour he is taken out, and medicine is put in his eyes and nostrils. After swallowing powerful phlegm expectorated by a master doctor, the aspiring novice is taken to a stream source and shown the various herbs and shrubs from which the medicine is derived. After this he is authorized to practice as a medicine man.

Zoroastrian and Hindu Ordination. Among Indo-Europeans the priesthood was an important class, as evidenced in the priesthoods of the ancient Romans, Greeks, Celts, Persians, Aryans, and others. The present-day Zoroastrians (Parsis in India) and the Hindus have continued this emphasis on a class of priests ordained to perform the important purifications, sacrifices, and other ceremonies for the maintenance of a healthy relationship between humans and the eternal divine order of the universe.

The religion of the ancient Persians, as transformed by the prophet Zarathushtra (Zoroaster) into Zoroastrianism, is practiced today in Iran and India. In Zoroastrianism, the aspirant to the priesthood must be a son of a priestly family who has gone through the childhood religious initiation (Naojot), consisting of investiture with the sacred shirt and girdle or thread. A period of training in chanting the scriptures and performing the rituals qualifies him for ordination.

There are two levels of ordination, of which the first *(nāvar)* qualifies the aspirant as a priest who can perform benedictions, investiture of children, marriages, and the like. During the first level of ordination, the candidate must perform two Bareshnūms, the highest form of purification ritual, lasting nine days each. Under the open sky a sacred liquid is applied to his whole body many times, and then the candidate makes a nine-day retreat in the fire temple. After the two rituals, the candidate bathes and puts on a new set of white clothes and a white turban. In the sacrifice chamber of the fire temple, he removes his upper garments, makes an ablution, and puts on a mouth veil. One of the priests brings him before the assembled priests and asks permission to initiate him. The silence of the assembly indicates their consent, and the candidate is taken back to the sacrificial chamber to perform the ceremony of chanting the Avestan scriptures and other liturgical rituals. These are repeated for four days, after which the candidate is declared to be qualified as a priest of the *hērbad* level.

In order to perform also the higher liturgical services, the priest must qualify himself by going through the second grade of ordination *(martab)*. In this ceremony, the priest again goes through a period of purification, then he conducts the Yasna liturgy for ten days. Now finally the priest is ordained as a *mōbad* priest, and he can fully officiate as the directing priest at all religious ceremonies.

In Hinduism, brahman priests have always played an important role. In ancient Vedic times they were thought to uphold the whole social order through their mediation, by virtue of their mastery of the sacred rituals, sacrifices, and formulas. Today, especially for people of the high castes, it is important to have a brahman household priest *(purohita)* perform the traditional rituals and chant the Vedic texts properly so that the cosmic order will continue with its health and goodness for each according to his or her place in the total order. Some brahmans prepare to be priests of temple worship, where rituals center on the ceremonial treatment of the images of the gods—although many functions of temple worship can be performed by the people without priestly help.

In Hinduism a priest must be a male from the brahman caste who has gone through the initiation ceremony (Upanayana) and received the sacred thread as a twice-born brahman. The brahman boy who aspires to become a household or temple priest studies for many years with a teacher at a Vedic training center and learns the correct way of reciting the Sanskrit Vedic scriptures.

After reaching technical proficiency in recitation of the Vedas and in performing the simpler ceremonies, the novice priest must spend a period of time as assistant to a senior priest. For those priests who are training to be domestic priests, this means accompanying the senior priest on his rounds and assisting him. The senior will formally introduce the junior priest to the assembly of professional priests, while the trainee formally announces his apprenticeship under the senior priest. In conducting the ceremonies, the junior first sits behind the senior priest, helping to recite some *mantras*; as he gains confidence, he is allowed to sit next to the teacher. Gradually the novice priest takes charge of rituals while the senior priest withdraws. In this way, eventually the new priest becomes established and recognized as a full-fledged member of the profession of domestic priesthood. One additional requirement must also be met: since tradition prohibits an unmarried priest from participating in the rituals of the *saṃskāras*, or life passages, the novice priest must take a wife.

Ordination among Jains and Buddhists. Two religions that grew up in India along with Hinduism are Jainism and Buddhism, and in these religious traditions spiritual power is understood to reside especially in the monastic communities, that is, among those monks and nuns who have left ordinary secular life to pursue spiritual perfection through ascetic practices. The monks and nuns are primarily devoted to their own spiritual perfection; yet because they possess great power they can perform religious service for the laypeople, such as chanting scripture, performing funeral rites, and teaching.

Among the Jains of India, the monks and nuns are set apart from the lay population by virtue of having embarked on the path of total renunciation. As *sādhus* (mendicants), they pursue their own goal of reaching the highest state of liberation of the soul from all traces of *karman*. For the laypeople who perform their own religious ceremonies, the *sādhus* function mainly as teachers.

Prior to ordination, the candidate will have gone through a period of training under a qualified *sādhu*. Women also are ordained into orders of women mendicants. Ordination occurs through the formal assumption of the five Great Vows *(mahāvrata)* in a public ceremony called *dīkṣā*. The five Great Vows are the vows of nonviolence, abstaining from untruthfulness, abstaining from stealing, chastity, and renouncing all love for any thing or any person. The novice casts off all lay possessions and becomes a new person. Particulars of the ceremony differ somewhat among the different sects. A Digambara monk, fulfilling that order's ideal of nudity, will stand before his teacher and renounce every possession, even his loincloth; he is given a small whisk broom, with which he is to remove insects from his sitting or sleeping place. Among Śvetāmbaras, the aspirant is given three large pieces of cloth for a new wardrobe, and also a whisk broom, a begging bowl, a blanket, a staff, and some volumes of scripture. Monks and nuns of the Sthānakavāsi sect are also given a small strip of cloth to keep tied over the mouth at all times save mealtime, to protect organisms that might be injured by an unimpeded rush of warm air. One significant part of the ritual of ordination is the act of slowly and painfully pulling hair from one's head in five handfuls, signifying the aspirant's determination to meet the severe demands of the ascetic life.

The people of the community participate in the ordination ceremony. The *dīkṣā* ceremony is accompanied by great pomp and by the performance of various religious acts by the laypeople. And on the next day, when the new monk goes out with the begging bowl to receive food for the first time, the householder who provides the food is considered to earn great merit.

Among Buddhists also, men and women ordained as monks and nuns (*bhikkhus* and *bhikkhunīs*) are set apart from the lay population by virtue of having embarked on the path toward extinguishing the sense of self and reaching nirvana. The monks and nuns contribute to the welfare of the general community, not as intermediaries between the people and the gods but as reservoirs of merit and models of spiritual perfection. Typically they perform a variety of services for the laity in chanting scripture for various occasions, performing merit-making rituals, praying for the dead, and teaching.

In Theravāda cultures like those of Burma and Thailand, it is traditional that all boys be ordained on a temporary basis and spend some time in the monastery as novice monks, as a kind of passage to adulthood. This initiation into monkhood *(pabbajjā)* is technically a monastic ordination; the young men have their heads shaved by the monks and recite the Ten Precepts of monastic life, after which they are given new Buddhist names. The Ten Precepts are the following: not to destroy life; not to steal; not to engage in sexual misconduct; not to lie; not to take alcoholic beverages; not to eat after noon; not to participate in dancing, music, and theater; not to wear garlands, perfumes, and ointments; not to use high or wide beds; and not to accept gold or silver.

Although most of the young men return to secular life after a period of time in the monastery, other men and some women take on the monastic ordination as a more permanent role and become members of the *saṅgha*

(Skt., *saṃgha*), the monastic order. The ordination ritual that marks this separation from lay life is called *upasampadā*, or higher ordination, and presupposes some twelve years' experience as a novice after the lower ordination.

The laypeople—parents and friends—play an essential role in the ordination, in terms of financial support for the ritual and the postceremonial festivities, sponsorship of the novice's application, and the like. Gifts and support of the ordination bring merit to the donor.

The monk or nun is to be essentially a homeless, celibate, ascetic mendicant. Being ordained means dying a civil death, so before the ceremony the candidate divests himself or herself of all possessions and gives up title to inheritable property. He or she brings to the ordination, as gifts from lay sponsors, the only property that a *bhikkhu* or *bhikkhunī* is to possess: the yellow robe, a begging bowl, a girdle, a small razor, a needle and some thread, a water strainer to strain insects from drinking water, and a palm-leaf fan.

The ordination ceremony takes place in an assembly of *bhikkhu*s in the special ordination chamber of the monastery, surrounded by boundary stones beyond which laypeople are not to enter. The candidate, dressed in yellow robes and with head and eyebrows shaven, kneels in front of the assembled monks and affirms in response to questions that he or she is a human being of sound body and mind, of legitimate birth, free of debts, a freeman, at least twenty years old, in possession of robes and a begging bowl, and having parental consent. The candidate formally requests admission to the *saṅgha*, and the presiding monk asks three times if any of his colleagues has any objection to the candidate. Silence is taken as consent, the candidate is pronounced a *bhikkhu* or *bhikkhunī*, and his or her new Buddhist name is conferred. The monastic rule from the Vinaya is read aloud, and the new monk promises to comply with all its rules.

Mahāyāna Buddhist communities have the same basic ordination ceremony, with some special differences. In traditional China, for example, it was customary for the aspiring monk to "leave home" by taking a senior monk as his master and receiving tonsure from him, entering into a period of training as a novice within the tonsure family headed by the "father-master."

Ordination in Chinese Buddhism traditionally involves long and complicated rites with a large number of ordinands. Monks and nuns come to the large ordaining monastery and live there for a time of strict training. After a night of repentance and purification, the ordinands kneel before the masters and witnesses, reciting the Three Refuges and accepting the Ten Vows, receiving their robes and begging bowls. Training resumes for a period of time, and at a second ordination ceremony the ordinands accept the monastic rules and go up to the ordination platform in groups of three to be examined by the ordination masters and accepted as full-fledged monks and nuns. An important ceremony in Mahāyāna ordination rituals is the scarring of the scalp with burns; cones of moxa are placed on the shaven scalp and set afire, burning down into the skin and leaving permanent scars identifying the person as a monk or nun. The ordinands finally receive ordination certificates, and they join their family and friends for a celebration in honor of their new vocation.

Ordination of Priests in Taoism and Shintō. Priests in Chinese religious Taoism function as ritual and liturgical specialists, but they also act as exorcists and healers, expelling and pacifying demons. Taoist priests *(tao-shih)* are often designated on the basis of heredity. Since the ritual of Taoism is esoteric, that is, not directly to be understood and witnessed by the laypeople, usually the aspiring priest will join the entourage of a recognized master who knows the important formulas and hidden aspects of ritual Taoism.

The aspirant's expertise is judged by several criteria. First, it is important that he have mastered the external performance of Taoist ritual: writing an artistic talisman to cure illness, exorcising evil spirits with sword and oxhorn trumpet, performing the ritual dance steps and acrobatic tumbling, climbing a blade-side-up sword ladder, and the like. But beyond the ability to perform the external rituals, what really determines the rank given to the new priest at his ordination is his knowledge and mastery of the esoteric secrets of the religion, including the meditations and breath-control techniques of internal alchemy; most important is his ability to recite the registers *(lu)* of spirits who will obey the priest's commands and enable him to communicate with the different spheres of the universe. The aspirant also learns from his master the oral explanation of the register, with the appropriate *mudrā*s, *mantra*s, and circulation of breath used in summoning and controlling the spirits.

Before the ritual of ordination, the aspirant isolates and purifies himself for a period of time in a vigil. Then he takes part in the three-day Chiao festival presided over by the master, in honor of the many gods who reside in the temple and the whole Taoist pantheon, who are summoned to participate. Local support is necessary, partly to pay the considerable expenses of the festival. Of the many rituals involved in the ordination during the Chiao festival, some take the form of tests of the candidate's ability to show power over the spirits, such as climbing the sword ladder. Finally, the candidate kneels before the master, who announces that he is qualified as a priest.

These Taoist priests who serve in temples and perform rituals for the people are called "fire-dwellers," that is, they have a hearth and home, marry, and have families. Some Taoists in traditional China pursued the path of individual realization more exclusively by taking up residence in a Taoist monastery *(tao-kuan)*. First the aspirant had to be accepted by a master at a hereditary temple as a novice. After a period of study and practice, during which the novice let his hair grow, the master performed the "rites of crown and cloth," binding the hair into a topknot and crowning the novice. Then the novice enrolled in a public, ordaining monastery for several months to prepare for ordination vows.

The main function of Japanese Shintō priests *(shinshoku)* of all ranks is to worship and serve the *kami*, the spiritual beings associated with the powerful forces of nature and the ancestors. The priests maintain good relations with the *kami* for the divine protection and welfare of the human community.

Priests often come from families with long and strong traditions of Shintō worship. In ancient times a few priestly families supplied most of the priests, although in modern times the priesthood is open to candidates from nonpriestly families also. While the numbers are small, there are also women in the Shintō priesthood. The princess as high priestess *(saishu)* at the shrine at Ise is the highest rank of all the priests, and in certain other shrines there have traditionally been women priests. Some women became priests as a result of war; when a priest was absent or killed in war, the parishioners would sometimes ask his wife to serve as priest. Priests customarily marry and raise families.

Aspiring priests study for a period of time either in the Kokugakuin (central Shintō university) or a regional seminary; occasionally taking an examination can substitute for such study. They are expected to get an academic degree, issued now by the Association of Shintō Shrines (Jinja Honchō) according to the training and merit of the individual. The ranks of priests, depending on the degree and experience, are those of chief priest *(gūji)* of a shrine, associate chief priest *(gongūji)*, priest *(negi)*, and junior priest *(gonnegi)*. The aspiring priest is appointed by the president of the Association of Shintō Shrines to a shrine responsibility appropriate to his rank.

Ordination in Judaism. The religion of Judaism after the Babylonian exile and especially after the destruction of the Temple in the Roman period moved away from a sacrificial temple cult and, consequently, the most important religious leaders became those ordained as rabbis. They functioned as judges, scholars, teachers, and expounders of the Torah and Talmud; in modern times, rabbis also function as worship leaders, officiants at marriage and burial ceremonies, and spiritual heads of local communities of Jews.

According to the Hebrew scriptures, Moses ordained Joshua by "placing his hands" *(samakh)* on him, transferring to him a part of his authority (*Nm.* 27:18–23; *Dt.* 34:9); and he also ordained seventy elders to assist him in governing the people (*Nm.* 11:16–25). Jewish tradition holds that there was an unbroken chain of ordination down to the time of the Second Temple. Traditionally the most important role of the rabbi was in giving judgments in both religious and secular matters, as covered by Jewish law. Ordination *(semikhah)* was required for membership in the Sanhedrin and the regular colleges of judges empowered to decide legal cases. The practice of laying on of hands was dropped in later times, and ordination took place simply by proclamation or with a written document. The special ordination formula included the words "Yoreh yoreh. Yadin yadin. Yattir yattir" ("May he give direction? He may give direction. May he judge? He may judge. May he permit? He may permit"). The ordinand wore a special garment, and after the ordination the new rabbi delivered a public discourse as a demonstration of his new role.

Changing times, especially the loss of religious autonomy in the Palestinian and Babylonian Jewish communities by the fourth century CE, led to the discontinuation of the original *semikhah* ordination with the early rabbinic idea of passing down divine authority for judicial powers. Eventually ordination as a rabbi became a matter of setting a person apart to function in a professional role as a rabbi, qualified by virtue of training in the Torah and the Talmud and sanctioned institutionally to render decisions for the community that engaged him. In modern times, pressure developed in Europe for rabbis to be versed in the vernacular and in secular studies, so new rabbinical seminaries were organized that put less emphasis on the Talmud and Jewish law and more emphasis on studying Jewish history and philosophy, preaching, and pastoral work as spiritual leader of a synagogue. Consequently, in contemporary Judaism there is some difference in the conception of ordination to the rabbinate. Some groups have traditional schools *(yeshivot)* that give the traditional *semikhah* ordination with its emphasis on training in the Talmud and Jewish codes. Other groups have seminaries that see preparation for the rabbinate as including not only knowledge of the Talmud and codes but also professional training to function as a synagogue rabbi within modern society.

In the state of Israel today, traditional *yeshivot* predominate, although there are branches of American Reform and Conservative seminaries. The *yeshivot* ordain males only, and the role of the rabbi is generally that of judge and scholar, not that of spiritual leader of a local congregation. In the United States, as in Europe, ordination of rabbis differs somewhat among the main Jewish groups. For example, the Orthodox seminary of Yeshiva University ordains graduates in the traditional fashion after a course of study in the Talmud and codes, and women are excluded from such ordination. Jewish Theological Seminary of America (the center for the Conservative movement) graduates its candidates as rabbis and has recently accepted its first women candidates for the Conservative rabbinate. Reform Judaism's Hebrew Union College–Jewish Institute of Religion ordains its graduates as rabbis, and for some time women have been ordained into the Reform rabbinate. Women are also ordained as rabbis in Reconstructionist Judaism. In general, rabbis of all American Jewish groups function as spiritual leaders of local congregations of Jews, although their functions differ according to the needs of the community.

Ordination in Christianity. Christians hold that Jesus Christ is the great high priest, the real mediator between God and humans, and that all Christians as members of his body participate in his priesthood. While some Christians conclude that there is no need for specially ordained leaders, most Christian groups have recognized the need for ordained priests or ministers to lead the Christian community.

Although traditionally any male Christian could aspire to become a priest or minister, in recent years many Christian denominations have begun to ordain women clergy also, while some denominations, such as the Roman Catholic church, continue to ordain male candidates only. Candidates are given a course of study and training in a theological seminary before being certified and presented to the church denominational authorities for ordination.

Those set apart for special service are given many different titles: priest, minister, pastor, presbyter, bishop, and deacon are the most common among those designating the clergy. In addition, many nonclerical roles are entered into by ceremonies of initiation or consecration: the minor orders, orders of monks and nuns, deaconesses, special church workers, and the like. The traditional clerical ministry of the church, as it developed in the first centuries, consisted primarily of bishops, presbyters, and deacons. The bishop was the "overseer" of a specific community of Christians, with the full responsibility for the ministry of preaching the word and administering the sacraments of the church. Deacons were ordained to help the bishop by serving in an administrative capacity and by working for the welfare of the people. The presbyter (elder or priest) was ordained to help the bishop as a fellow minister in performing the rites and sacraments of the church.

Ordination in the early church was a simple affair, consisting of prayer and the laying on of hands by those authorized to ordain (*Acts* 6:6, *1 Tm.* 4:14, *2 Tm.* 1:6). Texts of ordination manuals from the fourth and fifth centuries CE give sets of ordination prayers and emphasize the laying on of hands as a central ritual. The people, especially in the Greek communities, cried "Axios!" ("He is worthy!"), and the ordinand was given the kiss of peace, after which he preached and conducted the service, presiding over the Eucharist. In the medieval period other rituals were added to the ordination, such as vesting the candidate in the vestments of his order, holding a Bible over him, and giving him the implements and symbols of his new office: paten and chalice, Bible, and, in the case of a bishop, pectoral cross and pastoral staff. Bishops were anointed on the head with oil; both bishops and priests were anointed on the hands.

While ordination ceremonies differ in the various Christian communities, in recent years the liturgical renewal movement has induced many communions to restore the simple, ancient tradition of ordination. Typically this includes most of the following elements for the ordination of a priest or minister by a bishop. Ordination is done in the presence of the congregation, in the company of other priests or ministers, in the context of a divine service. The candidate is presented to the bishop by a priest or layperson, with the people declaring that he or she is worthy for the ministry. Lessons from the Bible are read, followed by a homily and the saying of the creed. The bishop examines the ordinand, who vows to be faithful to his or her calling. The bishop says the prayer of ordination, laying both his hands on the head of the candidate, while the other priests or ministers lay on their right hands. The new priest is vested and given a Bible, being greeted by the bishop and the other clergy. The newly ordained person then proceeds to function by leading the liturgy for the congregation. Afterward the people and the clergy join in a celebration.

Appointing Spiritual Leaders in Islam. In Islam, every Muslim can perform the religious rites, so there is no class or profession of ordained clergy. Yet there are religious leaders who are recognized for their learning and their ability to lead communities of Muslims in prayer, study, and living according to the teaching of the Qur'ān and Muslim law. These religious leaders belong to the learned group of orthodox Muslim scholars and jurists known as the *'ulamā'* (*'ālim* in the singular). They have studied at recognized schools of Islamic learning and have secured appointments as mosque functionaries, teachers, jurisconsults, or judges.

The religious leader who is contracted by a local community of Muslims to lead the community in public worship, preach at the Friday mosque prayer, teach, and give advice on religious matters on the local level is called the imam, belonging to the broad group of *'ulamā'*. It should be noted that the concept of the Shī'ī Muslims that an inspired religious leader is necessary for the correct guidance of the community has placed the recognized religious scholars (*mujtahid* in Iran) in a position of important power and authority, necessary for the welfare of the whole community. In certain Islamic communities, popular religious leaders possessing special divine power *(barakah),* known as Ṣūfīs or saints, provide leadership for their people in a variety of ways. Ṣūfī aspirants are trained under a master until they themselves have become recognized as masters.

Thus, despite its lack of an ordained institutional priesthood or clergy in the usual senses, Islam has produced a religious leadership that is recognizable and set apart from the ordinary people by a certain amount of religious authority.

Symbolism of Ordination Rituals. From the cross-cultural survey above, it is possible to see a general structure of meaning in the typical ordination rituals. A recurrent theme is that of death with respect to one's former status and rebirth in the new office or status of religious leader or mediator. This general structure can be analyzed in more specific detail by noting five broad types or levels of rituals associated with ordination, denoting separation, training and testing, empowerment, display of power, and support by the laity.

The rituals first of all enact various dimensions of the separation from ordinary life. Very commonly ordination involves rituals of purification. There may be a period of time during which the candidate purifies himself or herself by abstaining from sexuality, by fasting, and by performing acts of penance; rituals of washing and confessing may be part of the ordination ceremony. The fact that the candidate has been called by the divine power to leave the ordinary life will be established. The physical appearance of the candidate will demonstrate separation from ordinary lay life through special clothing, shaved head, long hair bound up in a special way, or the scalp branded with indelible scars. Symbols of death abound: initiatory sickness, symbolic death and burial, mutilation of the body, or the identification of the candidate with the blood of a priest's sacrifice. The vows taken by the candidate often emphasize separation from the former way of life, such as the vows of celibacy, homelessness, chastity, casting off all lay possessions, and nudity.

Second, the rituals of ordination certify the qualifications of the candidate by emphasizing the training he or she has received and by testing and examining the candidate. The long period of training or apprenticeship itself is often set apart by rituals as a sacred period. Rituals of ordination may include imparting secret knowledge and understanding. The candidate may be tested by questions, and the persons already ordained have to give their approval to the novice. There may be ordeals to demonstrate the candidate's mastery of sacred power, such as climbing a sword ladder, pulling hair from one's own head, or enduring the branding of the scalp.

Third, the investing of the ordinand with new authority and power is the subject of important rituals of ordination. These rituals include laying on of hands on the candidate by those already possessing the spiritual power and authority, handshakes or kisses, vesting with special garments, and handing over symbols and implements of the special office. Anointing the candidate, ritually inserting quartz into the candidate's body, or symbolically replacing his or her organs with new organs shows the rebirth or investing that takes place. Prayers call down divine power on the candidate; rituals such as climbing toward the sky or being married to a divine being fill the ordinand with new power. The masters of the office may impart final, decisive knowledge to the ordinand, such as the source of the medicinal material. The public pronouncement of ordination and the ordination certificate or diploma being handed over, together with the granting of new titles and names, may be considered rituals of empowerment. There may also be a period of seclusion after ordination during which time the new ordinand grows in spiritual power.

Fourth, the ordination rituals often include the initial display of the new power and authority of the ordinand. He or she may officiate in leading worship or celebrating sacrifices or sacraments for the people at the completion of the ordination ritual. He or she may inaugurate the new sacred life by giving a spiritual lecture, going on a first begging tour, making a round of visits to the parishioners, and the like.

Fifth, the ordination typically involves some expression of support and celebration of the new ordinand on the part of the laypeople. One of them may present the candidate, and financial support for the occasion will come from them. There may be points in the ritual of ordination when they show their support and acceptance of the ordinand. Typically the ordination will be followed by a celebration in which the people congratulate the new ordinand, give gifts, and join in a festive meal. These rituals symbolize the basic fact that, ultimately, the ordination is for the benefit of the people.

[*See also* Priesthood *and* Ministry.]

BIBLIOGRAPHY

A classic cross-cultural study of the role of priests in many religions is E. O. James's *The Nature and Function of Priesthood: A Comparative and Anthropological Study* (London, 1955), although he does not single out ordination as a special topic. For practices of setting apart religious leaders in traditional societies, Adolphus P. Elkin's *Aboriginal Men of High Degree*, 2d ed. (New York, 1977), is a thorough study of medicine men among the Aborigines of Australia; and Mircea Eliade's *Shamanism: Archaic Techniques of Ecstasy*, rev. & enl. ed. (New York, 1964), surveys the initiation of shamans in various cultures. The training and initiation of African priests and medicine men and women is discussed in Geoffrey Parrinder's *West African Religion: A Study of the Beliefs and Practices of Akan, Ewe, Yoruba, Ibo, and Kindred Peoples*, 2d ed. (London, 1961), and E. E. Evans-Pritchard's *Witchcraft, Oracles, and Magic among the Azande*, 2d ed. (Oxford, 1950). Melford E. Spiro's *Burmese Supernaturalism*, exp. ed. (Philadelphia, 1978), presents a thorough study of female shamans who become "*nat* wives" in Burmese popular religion.

Rustom Masani's *Zoroastrianism: The Religion of the Good Life* (1938; New York, 1968) includes information about initiation of Parsi priests in his discussion of the religion of the Parsis. The training and social role of household brahman priests in India today is the subject of K. Subramaniam's *Brahmin Priest of Tamil Nadu* (New York, 1974). Along with a presentation of the Jain religion, Padmanabh S. Jaini's *The Jaina Path of Purification* (Berkeley, 1979) provides a close look at the ordination and path of the Jain mendicant. Important studies of the training and role of Theravāda Buddhist monks and nuns are found in Melford E. Spiro's *Buddhism and Society: A Great Tradition and Its Burmese Vicissitudes*, 2d ed. (Berkeley, 1982), and Jane Bunnag's *Buddhist Monk, Buddhist Layman: A Study of Urban Monastic Organization in Central Thailand* (Cambridge, 1973). An important study of Mahāyāna Buddhism in modern China, including information and photographs of monastic ordinations, is Holmes Welch's *The Practice of Chinese Buddhism, 1900–1950* (Cambridge, Mass., 1967). The role of Taoist priests and their ordination rankings is discussed by Michael Saso in his *Taoism and the Rite of Cosmic Renewal* (Seattle, 1972); and much important information on Shintō priests and practices is contained in Jean Herbert's *Shintō: At the Fountainhead of Japan* (London, 1967).

A thorough study of the history of Jewish ordination is Julius Newman's *Semikhah: A Study of Its Origin, History, and Function in Rabbinic Literature* (Manchester, 1950); and several studies on the training of modern American rabbis are included in *The Rabbi and the Synagogue*, vol. 1 of *Understanding American Judaism*, edited by Jacob Neusner (New York, 1975). Of many studies of the Christian ordained ministry, *The Ministry in Historical Perspectives*, edited by Richard Niebuhr and Daniel D. Williams (New York, 1956), provides a good overview. Bernardin Goebel's *Seven Steps to the Altar: Preparation for Priesthood* (New York, 1963) presents a discussion of what the rites and ceremonies of a Roman Catholic priest's ordination mean to him; and a convenient discussion of Christian ordination together with a sample ordination service is given in *The Ordination of Bishops, Priests, and Deacons*, "Prayer Book Studies," no. 20 (New York, 1970). *Scholars, Saints, and Sufis: Muslim Religious Institutions in the Middle East since 1500*, edited by Nikki R. Keddie (Berkeley, 1972), contains many excellent studies of the religious scholars and saints who form the recognized religious leadership of Islam.

THEODORE M. LUDWIG

ORENDA. *See* Power.

ORIENTATION. Symbols of space and its order most clearly illustrate the religious act of orientation, that is, the fundamental process of situating human life in the world. Orientation is the conscious act of defining and assuming proper position in space. Fixing the human place in existence in a significant way is a religious act when it orients a human being toward the sacred. This fundamental disposition toward the sacred extends its significance from the points of orientation to all individual and social acts, as well as to all cosmic structures. In relation to the sacred, inhabited space and history become apprehensible. Various kinds of human living spaces define their order and meaning in relation to the sacred: the cosmos, the city, the village or residence space, the house, and the individual. They are described together with those manifestations of the sacred toward which they are oriented. [*See also* Sacred Space.]

Symbolic Forms. The technology of calculation and measurement used in orientation would make an interesting and controversial study in the history of science. It would include treatment of geomancy, astronomic calculation, use of the gnomon, the astrolabe, and the plumb line, canons of measure derived from human body measurements, and determinations of magnetic north, among other techniques. However, our purpose is limited to the religious meaning of the act of orientation and a description of the sacred nature of the points toward which the human situation is aligned. Since orientation involves relating an entity to a reality other than itself, it always entails a conjunction of beings and, in this sense, creates a center where all realities meet.

According to Latin historians, Romulus founded the

city of Rome by drawing a circular furrow around the Palatine hill with a plow. The trench around which the furrow was cut, and toward which it was oriented, was called the *mundus* ("world"), the same name applied to the universe. The *mundus* was a pit, an opening between the earthly world and the underworld. For the living it provided a link not only with the sphere of the dead but also with the celestial sphere, for the outline plan *(limitatio)* of the city, especially its division into four quarters, was based on a model of heavenly origin. The *mundus* itself, being a detailed image of the cosmos, was divided into quadrants. Rome was habitable because the city was built in the image of the cosmos—according to a heavenly model of the universe—around a life-giving center, a navel of the world, which permitted contact with all realms of being.

The universe itself possesses a place where communication among all cosmic realms is possible. It is to this center of the world that all other meaningful structures in the cosmos are directed and from which they derive. [*See* Center of the World.] For the religious life of Indians in the Qollahuaya region of the central Andes, Mount Kaata is the sacred center of all reality. Everything that is whole, whether it be the microcosm of the human body or the universe itself, may be identified with it. Indeed, all integrity derives from it. An individual's life cycle begins when a person's soul emerges from the highland springs; continues while it descends to its burial place at the mountain's foot; and prepares for recycling as it reascends the interior of the mountain along inner waterways, after death. This contemporary belief continues an older idea found in the Huarochiri manuscript, a sixteenth-century Quechua text which reports that Kuntur Qutu, the Mountain of the Condor, stands at the center of the world and at the center of *tahuantinsuyo,* the four quarters of the Inca world. All significant powers, both cosmic and divine, find their place and carry on their powerful processes on this mountain. The cosmic mountain, marking a center from which all creative life in the universe takes its bearings, is a widespread religious theme found throughout the histories of Europe, Asia, the Near East, Oceania, and the Americas. [*See* Mountains.]

For the Ngaju Dayak of southern Borneo the universe is centered on the tree of life, of which the inhabited world is only a small part; for the tree encompasses all existence, the totality of being, and the godhead itself. It also includes every possible period of time. As a result, all ceremonies of transition (birth, marriage, initiation, death) center on the tree of life. This allows the human being to return to the period of divine creativity, so that he or she may issue once again from the tree of life as a new creature. [*See also* Trees.]

The temple often extends the same symbolism of the sacred mountain toward which life is oriented. For instance, the Mesopotamian ziggurat was explicitly likened to the cosmic mountain. Its seven levels symbolized the number of heavens. The goddess Ningal promised the divinity Nanna that, when he had filled the rivers with waters and brought life to the fields, forests, and marshes, she would join him in his ziggurat in Ur: "In your house on high . . . in your cedar-perfumed mountain, I will come to live."

All of these images of the center toward which reality is oriented call attention, at one and the same time, to the vertical plane of the universe. In short, the world is oriented not only toward the center on a horizontal plane but to the heights of the heavens. This connecting point of heaven and earth may be envisaged as a sacred ladder, rope, liana, or bridge. In the Northern Hemisphere, the North Star becomes a crucial indicator of the center of heaven. Directly below it is oriented the sacred center of the world, where celestial and terrestrial powers join together. In the Southern Hemisphere, the Milky Way at its zenith often pinpoints the center of heaven. In Mismanay, near Cuzco in Peru, for example, the Milky Way is seen as an immense river of semen which, when it is in its zenith, runs through the center of the sky. Mismanay is sited directly below the center of the heavens. It is bisected by the Vilcanota River, the earthly counterpart of the fertilizing river of stars in the heavens. From the center one is able to determine the four points where the sun rises and sets during the solstices. Using the center of the sky marked by the Milky Way at its zenith, the people of Mismanay are able to situate themselves at the center of an organized space and ordered cycle of time. All spaces and life cycles (of humans, animals, rainbows, and supernatural beings) derive their creativity from and relate to one another through the center.

Two important ways of orienting oneself in space bear close relationship to the act of creation, as it is conceived by a culture to have taken place. In the first instance, the center has prestige as a key position for orientation because it is the first place, the place of origin of life. It is the *omphalos,* or navel, around which life takes shape. A second mode of orientation involves sacrifice to consecrate a sacred place. It draws attention to the fact that, at the beginning of time, a primordial being was sacrificed and dismembered. From its parts derives the ordered integrity of the cosmos. In this sacrificial cosmogony, orientation in the universe derives from the very structure of a primordial body, ritually positioned in space. The universe, then, has the same set of relations among its parts as does the human body when consciously shaped in the deliberate acts of ritual.

In either case, the points of orientation draw their prestige from their association with creation. [*See also* Human Body, *article on* Myths and Symbolism.]

Taking their cue from the structures of the universe as they were created, other entities are located in space and time with reference to the same manifestations of sacred power; that is, following the cosmic model. The village often becomes a small image of the ordered space of the universe, and the same is true even for a house. The Na-Khi, a Tibeto-Burman people living in the upper reaches of the Yangtze River valley of northwestern Yunnan Province in China, perform most of their important rituals at the center of the universe in their homes, which are purified and transformed into the image of Ngyu-na shi-lo ngyu, the cosmic mountain (Mount Kailāśa), by the installation of sacred ritual objects in the house (Jackson, 1979, pp. 113ff., 209). In order that the ritual objects be effective, they are empowered by means of lengthy chanting of their myths of origin.

Planners of cities aligned them to sacred forces, which filled them and made them habitable. In ancient China, at the moment when a sacred city was founded, the king was beseeched to come and "assume responsibility for the work of God on High and himself serve . . . at the center of the land . . . and from there govern as the central pivot" (Wheatley, 1971, p. 430).

The capital and the king became the points from which direction and sacrality emanated throughout the entire kingdom. The power of creation passed out through the city gates to the four quarters and the cycles of time.

Orientation is also a way in which the individual personality becomes aware of the objective in relation to the self. The Ñandeva, a Guaraní group of southern Brazil, picture the human soul as a carefully oriented spatial entity. The soul is composed of three shadows (*nane'a*, "our shadow") that are all oriented on a vertical plane toward the heavens, the source of light that brings them into existence. All the faculties of human intelligence and action are accounted for by the soul's orientation in space. *Ayvú-kué-poravé* ("the good word that we speak") is the shadow that falls directly in front of or directly behind the personality. This central shadow-soul is of divine origin and returns to its celestial source after death. The second shadow-soul is the *atsy-yguá*, the carnal essence of life, which humans share with animals. It is cast to the left of a person. To the right falls the shadow known as the *ayvú-kué* ("the word that sprouts"), which accompanies and obeys the central *ayvú-kué-poravé* (M. A. Bartolomé, 1979, pp. 111–112). The personality is oriented to the center of the celestial realm, the source of light that brings the shadow elements of the person into existence. It is this orientation to another realm of being that enables a truly human consciousness to come into proper existence.

Orientation and Human Consciousness. All of the entities in the above illustrations are oriented to and, paradoxically, derive their meaning from modes of being other than their own. The various forms of orientation to sacred reality highlight the human desire to inhabit a sacred world, a world as it was created in the beginning, new and powerful.

The kind of orientation situates human living space in meaningful relation to the beings around it. It requires a grasp of the total human situation, a sense of the whole of existence at all its levels. This fundamental stance toward being constitutes a consciousness able to distinguish and evaluate supernatural modes of being for what they are. Orientation effects what it symbolizes: the proper relation of the human situation to the very ground of being within which human life finds itself. For this reason orientation—taking one's place in the world—is conceived of in many religious traditions as the first act of fully human beings living in habitable space. By symbolically assuming one's proper position in the world, one communicates with significant powers at work in the cosmos and gains a sense of one's unique significance in relation to all else.

[*See also* Cities; Geography; Geomancy; *and* Home.]

BIBLIOGRAPHY

The constancy of the symbolic complex of the mountain is presented in Joseph W. Bastien's *Mountain of the Condor: Metaphor and Ritual in an Andean Ayllu* (Saint Paul, Minn., 1978). Other studies of orientation in the Andes may be found in R. Tom Zuidema's *The Ceque System of Cuzco: The Social Organization of the Capital of the Inca* (Leiden, 1962) and "The Inca Calendar," in *Native American Astronomy*, edited by Anthony F. Aveni (Austin, 1977), pp. 219–259, as well as in Gary Urton's *At the Crossroads of the Earth and Sky: An Andean Cosmology* (Austin, 1981), which discuss the techniques and meanings assigned to orientation in the Andes in both rural and urban settings throughout history. Anthony Jackson's *Na-khi Religion: An Analytical Appraisal of Na-khi Ritual Texts* (The Hague, 1979) illustrates clearly the way in which the house may serve as a point of cosmic orientation when ritually linked to the acts of creation. The orientation of the individual is described in Miguel Alberto Bartolomé's "Shamanism among the Avá-Chiripá," in *Spirits, Shamans, and Stars: Perspectives from South America*, edited by David L. Browman and Ronald A. Schwarz (The Hague, 1979), pp. 95–148. Paul Wheatley's *The Pivot of the Four Quarters: A Preliminary Enquiry into the Origins and Character of the Ancient Chinese City* (Chicago, 1971) is a singularly important work for understanding both the methods and meaning of orientation not only in China but around the world. Also helpful in this respect is I-fu Tuan's *Topophilia: A Study of*

Environmental Perception, Attitudes, and Values (Englewood Cliffs, N.J., 1974). Mircea Eliade addresses the question of the religious meaning of orientation in *The Sacred and the Profane: The Nature of Religion* (New York, 1959), esp. pp. 32ff. and 79ff. Heinrich Nissen's *Orientation: Studien zur Geschichte der Religion*, 3 vols. (Berlin, 1906–1910), remains a valuable resource of materials. Still stimulating is Ludwig Deubner's "Mundus," *Hermes* 68 (1933): 276–287. Further bibliography and portrayal of more recent approaches to the question may be found in Joseph Rykwert's *On Adam's House in Paradise: The Idea of the Primitive Hut in Architectural History* (New York, 1972) and *The Idea of a Town: The Anthropology of Urban Form in Rome, Italy and the Ancient World* (Princeton, 1976).

MIRCEA ELIADE and LAWRENCE E. SULLIVAN

ORIGEN (c. 185–c. 254), surnamed Adamantius (the man of steel or diamond), the greatest Christian theologian of the Antenicene period.

Life. The main source for Origen's life is the sixth book of Eusebius of Caesarea's *Church History*. His teachings are also described in a panegyric delivered by one of his students, who (despite recent doubts) is still believed to be Gregory Thaumaturgus. Much information about Origen that was contained in Eusebius's lost writings is preserved in the writings of Jerome. It is difficult to date precisely the events of Origen's life, and recent attempts to do so are not completely satisfactory.

Origen was probably born in Alexandria in 185, the first of seven children in a Christian family. His father, Leonides, taught him Greek literature and the Bible. In 202, when he was seventeen, his father was martyred (by beheading) during the persecution of Septimius Severus. To support his family, Origen opened a school of rhetoric, and at the same time Bishop Demetrius of Alexandria assigned to him the task of training catechumens. Some years afterward he left the school in order to devote himself entirely to the teaching of Christian doctrine. He divided his students into two groups; the catechumens were taught by his disciple Heraclas, while Origen instructed the more advanced students. According to Eusebius, he castrated himself (taking literally *Matthew* 19:12), and he assisted some of his students in their martyrdom. He completed his own philosophical studies at the school of Ammonius Saccas, who later was the teacher of Plotinus. To deepen his knowledge of the Bible Origen studied Hebrew, although he never became proficient in the language.

Origen began to write between 215 and 220, encouraged by a wealthy man named Ambrose. Ambrose had been led by his intellectual zeal to adopt the Valentinian heresy, but Origen converted him from that heresy and in turn was provided with stenographers and copyists—virtually a whole publishing house.

During this first Alexandrian period of his life, Origen traveled to Rome, to the Roman province of Arabia (present-day Jordan) at the invitation of the governor, and to Antioch. In Antioch he met the dowager empress Mammaea, who wished to learn about Christian doctrines. Along with all teachers of philosophy in Alexandria, Origen was forced to leave the city in 215. Origen stayed for a short period at Caesarea, in Palestine. Here, because of his great knowledge of scripture, he was permitted by Bishop Theoctistus and his colleague Alexander of Jerusalem to preach, even though he was still a layman; but Bishop Demetrius protested against this innovation and called Origen back to Alexandria. About 231 Origen was invited by the bishops of Achaia (Greece) to debate with heretics in Athens. Passing through Palestine, he was ordained a priest at Caesarea by Theoctistus and Alexander. When he returned to Alexandria, Bishop Demetrius, angry at the ordination performed without his consent, summoned a synod of Egyptian bishops and priests that ordered Origen to leave Egypt, and another synod, composed only of bishops, defrocked him. This sentence, however, was not accepted by the bishops of Palestine and neighboring provinces.

Origen was welcomed to Caesarea by Theoctistus and Alexander, and he opened a school in the city. Among his first students were Gregory Thaumaturgus and Gregory's brother Athenodorus. Ambrose followed Origen to Caesarea, bringing his stenographers and copyists, and Origen continued to compose his great works. Many homilies survive, attesting to his extensive pastoral activity. He acquired a high reputation as a theologian, and he was frequently invited by bishops to defend the faith. He traveled extensively throughout the eastern part of the Roman empire, including the provinces of Achaia, Arabia, and Cappadocia, and the towns of Ephesus and Nicomedia.

During the Decian persecution, Origen was imprisoned and several times tortured in the hope that he would apostatize, but he maintained his faith firmly. Upon the death of Decius he was freed, but his health was broken and he died, probably in 254. Up to the thirteenth century his grave could be seen in the old cathedral of Tyre.

Works. A great part of Origen's immense production is now lost, and part of what is left survives only in Latin translations by Rufinus of Aquileia, Jerome, and an unknown translator. Most of Origen's works are directly exegetical. He explained the Bible in three kinds of works: scientific commentaries; homilies preached in the church; and scholia, or short texts in which the meaning of a passage was elucidated. Today it is impossible to distinguish the scholia from the multitude of surviving fragments of Origen's lost commentaries and homilies. It has been demonstrated recently that homilies on *Psalms* once attributed to Jerome are slightly adapted translations from Origen. In all, 279 of Origen's homilies are extant. Jerome's four commentaries on Paul's letters to the Galatians, the Ephesians, Titus, and Philemon are also in great part, as the author himself acknowledges, adaptations of Origen's corresponding commentaries.

While still in Alexandria, Origen began his great bible study, the Hexapla. In this work of six parallel columns, two columns contain the Hebrew text of the Old Testament (one in Hebraic and one in Greek characters), and four columns are devoted to four Greek translations: those by Aquila, Symmachus, and Theodotion, and the Septuagint. For some books of the Old Testament, three other Greek versions are also supplied, called "Quinta," "Sexta," and "Septima." Diacritical marks are used to show what had been added or suppressed in each version. Only numerous fragments of this work have been preserved.

Among the works not directly exegetical (although Origen also discusses scripture extensively in them), the most important is the treatise *On First Principles (Peri archōn)*, the first great attempt at speculative theology by a Christian. This work was the cause of Origen's posthumous misfortunes. The entire book is preserved only in a much-discussed Latin version by Rufinus, although there are two long Greek fragments from it in the *Philokalia of Origen* by the Cappadocian fathers Basil and Gregory of Nazianzus, and many short extracts are quoted by Jerome, Justinian, and other authors. Another major book still preserved in Greek is *Against Celsus*, the main apologetic work of the Antenicene period. This work is a refutation of the *True Discourse*, an attack on Christianity by the Middle Platonist philosopher Celsus. Other nonexegetical books that survive in the original Greek are the treatise *On Prayer*, which gives one of the first explanations of the Lord's Prayer; *Exhortation to Martyrdom*, written during the persecution of Maximinus the Thracian; and *Dialogue with Heraclides*, found during World War II in Egypt and consisting of a discussion in a local synod with a bishop suspected of modalism, a form of unorthodoxy that sees Father, Son, and Holy Spirit as only one person with three names. Greek fragments survive of the lost works *Stromateis* and *On the Resurrection*. Of Origen's important correspondence, two complete letters and fragments of others have been preserved.

Three groups of sources contain all the surviving fragments of Origen's work. First are the two collections of select pieces: Pamphilus of Caesarea's *Apology for Origen*, the first book of which is preserved only in Rufinus's Latin translation, and the *Philokalia*. Second are the exegetical *Catenae*, collections of exegeses from various church fathers, including Origen, in which a given book of scripture is explained verse by verse. Third are subsequent authors' quotations from Origen.

The Exegete. Three aspects are mingled to varying degrees in Origen's entire corpus, as well as in each work: he is at once an exegete, a spiritual and mystical writer, and a speculative theologian. Exegesis and spirituality are always present in his main speculative work, *On First Principles*. Together with Jerome, Origen is one of the two main critical and literal exegetes of Christian antiquity.

For Origen, the literal sense of scripture is the foundation for the spiritual sense, and he explains scripture using philology and all the learning of his time. Spiritual exegesis, or allegorical exegesis (synonymous for Origen), begins with New Testament texts in which Old Testament images and prophesies have their fulfillment in Christ. This form of interpretation had been used by some earlier church fathers, but Origen was its first great exponent, particularly in his theory of the three senses of scriptural meaning—corporal, or literal; psychic, or moral; and spiritual, or mystical. Despite its great complexity (the result of later accretions), the heart of Origen's spiritual exegesis of the Old Testament is the manifestation of Christ as the key to the ancient scriptures. These scriptures are a prophecy of Christ, both in their entirety and in their details. In his spiritual exegesis of the New Testament, Origen applies what is said of Christ to the Christian, thus foreshadowing the things to come in the "last days." This exegesis can be understood only in the context of spiritual life, prayer, and preaching. When Origen suggests the meaning of a text whose spiritual sense is not found in the New Testament, he does not claim to give a definitive answer, but only to provide "occasions for contemplation." Often he invites his reader or hearer to follow a better interpretation if it can be found. Origen's spiritual exegesis does not have the same aim as his literal exegesis (which for modern exegetes, unlike for Origen, refers to the meaning intended by the author). Literal exegesis, for Origen, points out the materiality of an expression independently, if possible, of all interpretation. Spiritual exegesis places the passage in the history of salvation and draws spiritual food from it for the faithful. A pastoral purpose is always present in Origen's exegesis.

The Spiritual Writer. Origen is, after Clement, one of the founders of Christian spirituality and mysticism. His trichotomic conception of man derives much more from Paul and the Bible than from Platonism. The spirit *(pneuma)* is a gift of God, something analogous with the *gratia sanctificans.* The incorporeal soul *(psuchē),* the seat of free will and personality, is divided into an upper and a lower part; the upper part is the mind *(nous),* the faculty that receives the spirit, whereas the lower part, the "thought of the flesh" *(phronema tēs sarkos)* draws the soul toward the body. The body—earthly for man, ethereal for angels and the risen—is the sign of our "accidental," creaturely condition, in contrast to the "substantiality" of the Trinity, which alone exists without a body.

Man was created according to the image of God, that is, according to his Son (*Gn.* 1:26–27). This means much more than the reception of "natural" gifts; it means that a seed and a desire for divinization have been planted in man, and this seed must with God's help be developed into the perfect "likeness" of the blessedness. Such is the framework of ascetic and spiritual life, which is further explained in terms of knowledge. But the Alexandrian defines knowledge according to *Genesis* 4:1: "Adam knew Eve, his wife." For Origen's synthetic mind, knowledge is identical with love and union. Knowledge begins with the realities of this world, which, in Platonic terms, are copies of "true" realities, that is, the divine mysteries, toward which knowledge must strive. In other words, the way of knowledge begins in the Old Testament and passes through the historical Jesus—the Incarnate Word that enters the soul and leads it, just as the apostles were led on the Mount of the Transfiguration to see the Word through the man Jesus and thus to hear the words of Wisdom spoken among the perfect. The Transfiguration symbolizes for Origen the highest knowledge man can have of God upon this earth; it is the prelude to the beatific vision, in which man will contemplate, face to face, the mysteries contained in the Son of God.

Origen was one of the great creators of the mystical language and spiritual themes employed in later centuries. Before his time, the bride in the *Song of Songs* had been interpreted collectively as the church. Origen added to this interpretation an individual meaning: the bride is the soul of the Christian. The imagery of the dart and the wound of love began with him. He often used the Pauline theme of the birth and growth of Jesus in the soul, as well as the theme of the ascent of the Mount of the Transfiguration to express spiritual ascension. Different aspects of grace and knowledge were represented by light, life, spiritual foods, spiritual wine, and the five spiritual senses. He had a doctrine of the discernment of spirits, and he often spoke of Christ in a highly affective manner that was rare in Christian antiquity. His far-reaching ascetic teachings included treatments of such themes as martyrdom, virginity, marriage, spiritual struggle, virtue, and sin.

The Speculative Theologian. It is difficult to evaluate Origen's theology justly, as we know from his history. His theology "in exercise," which was sensitive to the antithetical aspects of Christianity, lacked definitions and accurate terminology. This is understandable, since Origen wrote before the great trinitarian and christological heresies that in subsequent centuries made it necessary to develop more precise terms. To make a fair assessment, the historian therefore must study all that remains of his work: no single text alone suffices to reveal Origen's thought on any point. Because he was the pioneer of theology, Origen must be examined with a strict historical method, with knowledge of the rule of faith of his time—still lacking precision—and of the heresies he fought. The historian must understand his vocabulary and the persecuted church of the third century, so unlike the triumphant church of his later accusers, who were little interested in understanding him on his own terms. Similarly, the historian must avoid projecting on Origen the heresies of later times.

The fundamental concern of Origen's work, stimulated by the search of the convert Ambrose, was to give a Christian answer to problems (derived in part from Greek philosophy) that troubled his contemporaries. He had to ensure that they did not seek the answer in gnostic doctrines, and he had to supply searching Christians with the intellectual food they needed. His efforts in this direction, for which he had prepared himself by acquiring considerable philosophical erudition, were totally misunderstood by his fourth-century and fifth-century opponents, in spite of the fact that the success of Origen's efforts had played an important part in the conversion of the Roman empire.

The philosophical foundation of Origen's theology was the Middle Platonism of his teacher Ammonius Saccas—an eclectic philosophy based mainly on Platonism and Stoicism and to a lesser degree on Aristotelianism. Origen borrowed from this philosophy both terminology and doctrines, but he used it as a theologian, not as a philosopher, to explain and develop what he found in the Bible and in the rule of faith.

It is impossible to give a detailed account of his theology in a short space. Only one of the erroneous doctrines of which he was later accused can safely be attributed to him: his favorite hypothesis of the preexistence of souls. This idea was essentially Platonic, but Origen used it to a Christian end: to refute the Marcionites, who accused the Creator of wickedness, and to answer the great difficulties raised by the two contemporary Christian solutions to the problem of the origin of souls, traducianism and creationism. According to the rule of faith of his time, Origen's hypothesis could not be described as heretical. The other controverted points—the famous *apocatastasis* (the final restoration of all things), the trinitarian subordinationism, and so on—must be examined in the context of Origen's entire work and intentions. If this is done, these opinions lose most of the scandalous character that they have acquired in his accusers' formulations.

Posthumous History. Origen has always been a contradictory figure in the history of the church. In spite of some reservations from his followers, he was the teacher of all the great Christian writers of the fourth century: in the East, of Athanasius, Basil, the two Gregories, and Didymus the Blind; in the West, of Hilary of Poitiers, Ambrose, Rufinus, and Jerome. (Jerome owed much to Origen, both early and late in his career, although in his later years he became a strong opponent of Origen.) The first attacks on Origen were launched at the turn of the fourth century by Methodius of Olympus, Peter of Alexandria, and Eustathius of Antioch; Origen was defended by Pamphilus of Caesarea.

In the second half of the fourth century enthusiastic disciples among the monks of Palestine and Egypt turned the ocean of Origen's thought into a well-dammed river, thus making of him a heretic. This "Origenism" provoked the first Origenist controversy. Origen's opponents included Epiphanius of Salamis, Theophilus of Alexandria, and Jerome; his defenders were John of Jerusalem and Rufinus. In the first half of the sixth century, Origenism—or, more properly, "Evagrianism" (named for one of Origen's enthusiasts, Evagrios of Pontus)—agitated some monasteries of Palestine, and Emperor Justinian condemned Origen in a letter in 543. He referred the question of the Palestinian Origenists, rather than that of Origen himself, to the Second Council of Constantinople (553), but the anathemas against Origenism do not appear in the council's official acts. Whereas the Byzantine church found Origen suspect, he was much read in the medieval Latin West until the thirteenth century, and he held an especially important place in the Cistercian tradition. His influence was eclipsed by the rise of Scholasticism but revived during the Renaissance, particularly through the work of Pico della Mirandola and Erasmus. Today Origen, next to Augustine, is probably the most frequently studied church father.

BIBLIOGRAPHY

A general bibliography is supplied in my *Bibliographie critique d'Origène* (The Hague, 1971), and in its first supplement (1982). Origen's works are available in *Patrologia Graeca*, edited by J.-P. Migne, vols. 11–17 (Paris, 1857), and in *Die griechischen christlichen Schriftsteller der ersten drei Jahrhunderte* (Leipzig, 1899–1953; Berlin, 1953–). English translations of his works are offered in *The Ante-Nicene Fathers*, vol. 4, edited by Alexander Roberts and James Donaldson (Grand Rapids, Mich., 1965); in *Prayer, Exhortation to Martyrdom* and *The Song of Songs, Commentary and Homilies*, nos. 19 and 26 in "Ancient Christian Writers," edited by Johannes Quasten and Joseph C. Plumbe (Westminster, Md., 1954 and 1956); and in *Homilies on Genesis and Exodus*, vol. 71 of *The Fathers of the Church*, edited by Hermigild Dressler and others (Washington, D.C., 1982). For *On Principles*, see *Origen on First Principles*, translated by G. W. Butterworth (1936; reprint, New York, 1966). For *Against Celsus*, see *Origen: Contra Celsum*, translated by Henry Chadwick (1953; reprint, Cambridge, 1980). A general presentation of Origen's life and thought is available in Jean Daniélou's *Origen* (New York, 1955).

HENRI CROUZEL, S.J.

ORPHEUS. In the sixth century BCE a religious movement that modern historians call Orphism appeared in Greece around the figure of Orpheus, the Thracian enchanter. It was long suspected that Orphism was only the very artificial product of a series of interpretations advanced by Herodotus, by Neoplatonic philosophers, and by modern historians enamored of pagan mysteries. Today, however, Orphism is better known, thanks to two discoveries that have definitely established its presence and importance in the earliest of times. In 1962, in a tomb at Derveni, near Thessaloniki, the remains of an "Orphic book," dating to approximately 330 BCE, were discovered. The book is a philosophical commentary on an Orphic theogony and cosmogony, written around 400 and consequently independent of any Platonic influence. In 1978, Soviet archaeologists announced that they had discovered three small tablets in Olbia, a Greek town on the Black Sea. The tablets attested the existence in the fifth century BCE of a group called the "Orphics" and their explicit interest in the god Dionysos.

Orphism is a complex phenomenon. It embraces a long history, from the sixth century BCE to the Neoplatonic exegeses current in Alexandria at the time of Olympiodorus (sixth century CE). Furthermore, Orphism involves three relatively autonomous types of religious phenomena. First, there are traditions concerning the birth, life, and descent of Orpheus into the underworld; his singing among the Thracians; and his tragic death (he was said to have been torn to pieces by a band of women). Next, we have a literature: writings attributed to Orpheus and several theogonic accounts. Finally, we know of certain practices and rules of conduct: proscriptions and requirements to be met by those who chose to live in an Orphic manner.

Orpheus, the citharist and enchanter, first appears around 570 BCE on a small black-figured vase. He is shown walking with a determined stride and nearly surrounded by two Sirens, great angry birds with the heads of women. A frail silhouette armed with a lyre, he clears a path for himself between these powers and their voice of death, between these hybrids whose sexual identity vacillates between the virginal, the androgynous, and the masculine. But the power of the voice and of song triumphs over the Sirens and their fatal spells. Thus before he becomes the founding hero of a new religion or even the founder of a way of life that will be named after him, Orpheus is a voice—a voice that is like no other. It begins before songs that recite and recount. It precedes the voice of the bards, the citharists who extol the great deeds of men or the privileges of the divine powers. It is a song that stands outside the closed circle of its hearers, a voice that precedes articulate speech. Around it, in abundance and joy, gather trees, rocks, birds, and fish. In this voice—before the song has become a theogony and at the same time an anthropogony—there is the great freedom to embrace all things without being lost in confusion, the freedom to accept each life and everything and to renounce a world inhabited by fragmentation and division.

When representatives of the human race first appear in the presence of Orpheus, they wear faces that are of war and savagery yet seem to be pacified, faces that seem to have turned aside from their outward fury. These humans are Thracian warriors, clad in animal skins and motley colored cloaks, and just as birds leave the sky and fish forsake the sea at the sound of Orpheus's song, so, too, do the warriors come out of the forests. In the midst of a wild audience, his head crowned with laurel, the enchanter is dressed in Greek fashion; he appears so Apollonian that only the clothing of his Thracian entourage distinguishes him from his father, Apollo the citharist. But it is in full Thracian or Oriental dress that the vases of southern Italy depict Orpheus as he descends into the underworld, searches for Eurydice, or makes a daring journey to the heart of the realm of Hades.

Orpheus's followers share in his triumph over death. A large Apulian amphora, published in 1976, pictures Orpheus in the underworld, standing and playing the lyre in the presence of a heroized corpse. That corpse is seated in a pavilion, and in its left hand it clasps a papyrus scroll, without doubt an Orphic book similar to the one unearthed near a tomb at Derveni.

The Altamura amphora presents another powerful image. Orpheus the harper stands before the Lord of the Underworld, while the daughters of Danaus, damned forever, ceaselessly pour water into a bottomless jar. Only the initiated gain victory over the death that others must suffer, and they alone enjoy the banquet and happiness of the blessed. As a result, they become heroes or even resemble the gods themselves.

In Olbia, at Derveni, and in southern Italy, writing is used to prolong Orpheus's voice: the song becomes a book. A Thracian voice, inscribed in signs on Thracian tablets, produces a great tumult of books. Some of the Orphic writings narrate the birth of the world and the origin of the gods in successive theogonies. Other books prescribe a dietary regimen and extend to their readers an invitation to attend unblemished sacrifices and sweet-smelling oblations. A book of the latter sort is the lost *Thuepolikon* (How to Make Bloodless Offerings), to which Plato alludes directly in the *Republic*.

The Orphic way of life was recorded, too. Plato summarized its strict rules in the *Laws*: do not touch beef, abstain from all meat, and offer the gods only cakes or fruit soaked in honey, for it is impious and unclean to eat flesh and to stain with blood the altars of the gods. A container for scrolls forms a part of the Orphic landscape. On an Etruscan mirror in Boston it stands at Orpheus's feet, while silent beasts encircle the song. In addition, the *teletē* ("initiation") was conspicuous among the ancient writings, that is, the account of the death of the infant Dionysos, who was ambushed by the Titans and devoured in the course of a most horrible sacrifice.

But who were these people who were interred with a papyrus scroll in their hands, who abhorred blood, who wrote cosmogonies and dreamt strange tales about the birth of the gods? What do they want with Orpheus and his silent incantations? Actually, they seek one goal and one goal only: health. They wish to heal themselves, and to do so in the only way possible: by fleeing from the world.

The Orphics are renunciants. They strive for saintliness. They devote themselves to techniques of purification in order to separate themselves from others, in order to cut themselves off from the world and from all who are subject to death and defilement. By returning to the Golden Age, to the time of the beginning, the Orphic way of life seeks to renounce, and to renounce completely, the blood on altars. It seeks to reject the eating of any flesh and in doing so to reject the values of the Greek state and that state's religious system: its discrete divine powers, its differentiated gods, and the sharp distinction that it inevitably draws between the divine and the human. The Orphic way of life implies an uncompromising renunciation that is expressed in a straightforward manner by the condemnation both of sanguinary food and of the social bond that is established within the state when an animal victim is sacrificed on the altar and its flesh shared in a common feast.

In contrast with a similar form of mysticism, the way

of life and patterns of thought associated with the followers of Pythagoras, the Orphics never felt an urge to attempt a political reform or to envisage an alternative state with an alternative political cult. For the devotees of Orpheus, who chose writing and the book as an effective symbol of their otherness, renouncing the worldliness of the state not only meant finding in vegetarianism a foretaste of life among the gods, that is, life among the gods who precede this world and its bloody altars; it also meant recasting, with a great deal of effort, the genesis of the world and rewriting the entire history of the gods. For like the sacrifice, the gods, too, constituted a single structure in which politics, society, and religion were in perfect balance. When the Orphics renounced the gods of the other Greeks, they called into question the whole fabric of social life, including polytheism, to the extent that polytheism pervaded society and played an integral role in politics.

But if Orphism could not rest content with distrusting the polytheism of others, it could also not reject it utterly. It would then have been in great danger of cutting itself off from all speech and being unable to communicate with those who were at the point of being healed. The plurality of the gods is unavoidable. Thus, the Orphics had to reconceive the divine, to transform the order of the divine forces, and to work out an alternative genealogy of powers.

It is convenient to pose this problem, in brief, primarily on the level of cosmogony and theogony. The evolution of the gods is recounted in a series of poems whose refined styles become evident as they are deciphered from new palimpsests. The Orphic gods are bizarre. To begin with, the Firstborn, the primal Generator and Generatrix, is called Phanes (Metis)—Protogonos in the Derveni book—and also Erikepaios. Descriptions of this deity offer repeated affronts to the form of the human body; it has two pairs of eyes, golden wings, the voice of a lion and of a bull, and organs of both sexes, one of which adorns the upper part of the buttocks. There is also the Zeus who rules over the fifth generation of gods and who will transfer his power to his son. Instead of being assured of ruling over the gods forever, this Zeus, on the advice of Night, sends the Firstborn straight to the pit of his belly. Thus, he becomes a womb, as it were, the shell of an egg whose dimensions are those of the All. In other tales this god cuts an even poorer figure. He marries his mother and impregnates his daughter-cum-wife, who is also his mother—a double incest. The church fathers, who assiduously observed so many couplings, turn from crimson to green.

The Orphic cosmogony/theogony contains a virtual orgy of baroque deities and polymorphic monsters, but the profusion of these multifarious gods is neither gratuitous nor insignificant. It gives meaning to their development. In the beginning was the totality, the oneness of the All, that is, the completeness of Phanes within the perfect sphere of primordial Night. In the course of five successive reigns, the ideal unity undergoes the trials of separation and division on its road to differentiation. The succession of rulers passes from Phanes—via Night, so close to Phanes—to Ouranos and Gaia, Kronos and Rhea, and finally to Zeus. Zeus, born of Rhea (Demeter), marries a second Demeter, and later he becomes the husband of yet a third, the Demeter (Kore) who will give birth to the infant Dionysos. That Dionysos, who was actually already present in the Firstborn, will institute the sixth and final generation of the gods.

What is the motivating force behind this genealogical descent? Differentiation takes place first through sexual activity, then through marriage, which works toward the separation of the divine powers. To be more specific, the first conjugal union in the world of the gods appears in the third generation: there is no *gamos* ("marriage") before that of Ouranos and Gaia. Nevertheless, Phanes takes from Night—the second Night, said to be his daughter—the flower of her virginity. This act represents the first appearance of sexuality, but there is not yet any marriage. As Proclus, a good interpreter of Orpheus, writes: "For those who are most united there is no union in marriage."

Sexuality initiates difference; marriage establishes and grounds it by bringing to completion the separation that is in full force until the reign of Zeus in the fifth generation. The Zeus of the fifth generation (in contrast to the Zeus of the fourth) displays two faces, one the face of degeneracy—his doubly incestuous marriage: the son with his mother, and the father with his daughter—the other the face of regeneration. Hearkening to Night, he engulfs the Firstborn in his entrails and ushers in the second creation of the world. This Zeus is the pregnant god who realizes within himself both the unity of all things and the distinctiveness of each. The Derveni papyrus confirms this process of differentiation, now in the origin of words and of things, for it deals with the assignation of multiple names to a single god. The vocabulary is philosophical, the vocabulary of Anaxagoras, the vocabulary of separation *(diakrisis)*. In particular, column 17 states that all things already existed in advance but that they received their names only when they were separated. Thus, naming replicates—on the level of words—the separation and distinctions brought about through sexual activity, in this case, the activity of Aphrodite and her father, Zeus. The commentary in the Derveni papyrus attempts to display the truth of Orpheus's words: the linguistic discussion appears as an additional means of conceiving the unity that subsists within the interplay of the figures of separation, a means that is available as a result of the appropriateness of the names bestowed by Orpheus.

In recasting the gods of others, Orphism gives a special meaning to the complicity of two rival powers: Dionysos and Apollo, the two gods who sum up the whole of Greek polytheism. In the various theogonic accounts—the great dramas in which Dionysos is assuredly the protagonist—Apollo plays the role of a tutelary power. He embodies genuine oracular knowledge in the Delphic landscape that he shares with Night, the daughter of Phanes. He collects and pieces together the scattered limbs of Dionysos and then lays the remains of the executed god to rest in his sanctuary at the foot of Mount Parnassus. Finally, he is metamorphosed into another great god, the Sun, who inspires Orpheus to sing his theogonic song.

But Dionysos and Apollo also meet and confront each other in the tragic biography of Orpheus and, in particular, in the indirect manner in which Orpheus is slain. In his first tetralogy based on the legends of Dionysos, Aeschylus presented an Orpheus stricken with the devout love of one god greater than all the rest. Every day, at dawn, Orpheus scales the crags of Mount Pangaeus, the highest mountain in Thrace. He wishes to be the first to salute the Sun, who is for him "the greatest of the gods" and to whom he gives the name Apollo. Dionysos, it is said, is filled with resentment at this daily ritual. He sends to Orpheus women with a barbarian name, the Bassarai. They surround him, seize him, and dismember him, tearing him to pieces immediately. In fact, Dionysos takes an interest in Orpheus's activity because Pangaeus is Dionysos's own domain, an ambiguous region where Lykurgos, the king of the Edonians, is torn apart by wild horses. Pangaeus is also where Dionysos appears as an oracular diety whose prophetess recalls the Pythia in the temple of Apollo. Thus, the Dionysos of Pangaeus has two faces, one of which is Apollonian. And the instruments of Orpheus's death are women, the fiercest and wildest representatives of the feminine gender (they appear armed with skewers, axes, stones, and hooks on Attic vases from between 480 and 430). These are women whom the voice of Orpheus is powerless to seduce, to tame, or to restrain. They would even have rejoiced in killing Orpheus—one of several details that show that they are outside the control of Dionysos, that they are not Bacchantes but ferocious beasts who cause Orpheus to be destroyed by what he most deeply despises: the feminine, which brought to humankind the disease of birth and death. In opposition to this feminine, Orpheus embodies the purely masculine, the *catharos* who is seen also in Apollo, the principle of unity, but he does so via the multiplicity of forms and by the roundabout path of Dionysian polymorphism.

BIBLIOGRAPHY

Burkert, Walter. "Craft versus Sect: The Problem of Orphics and Pythagoreans." In *Jewish and Christian Self-Definition*, vol. 3, *Self-Definition in the Greco-Roman World*, edited by Ben F. Meyer and E. P. Sanders, pp. 1–22. Philadelphia, 1982.

Detienne, Marcel. *Dionysos Slain*. Translated by Mireille Muellner and Leonard Muellner. Baltimore, 1979. See especially pages 68–94.

Guthrie, W. K. C. *Orpheus and Greek Religion*. 2d ed., rev. London, 1952.

Kern, Otto, ed. *Orphicorum fragmenta*. 2d ed. Berlin, 1963.

Linforth, Ivan M. *The Arts of Orpheus* (1941). Reprint, New York, 1973.

West, M. L. *The Orphic Poems*. Oxford, 1983.

MARCEL DETIENNE

Translated from French by David M. Weeks

ORTHODOX JUDAISM is the branch of Judaism that adheres most strictly to the tenets of the religious law *(halakhah)*. Its forebears may be identified in the eighteenth century, by which time the *qehillah*, the Jewish communal organization in each locality, had lost much of its authority in central and western Europe and its prestige in eastern Europe. This, in turn, undermined religious authority, which had heretofore relied not only on the faith of each Jew but also on communal consensus and the formal authority and prestige of communal leaders. The breakdown of the traditional community, coupled with the hope and expectation of political emancipation, encouraged new interpretations of Jewish life and new conceptions of appropriate relationships between Jews and non-Jews. These began to emerge by the end of the eighteenth century in central and western Europe and somewhat later in eastern Europe. Orthodoxy was born as the ideological and organizational response to these new conceptions.

The major tenets of Orthodoxy, like those of traditional Judaism, include the dogma that the Torah was "given from Heaven," that the *halakhah* derives directly or indirectly from an act of revelation, and that Jews are obligated to live in accordance with the *halakhah* as interpreted by rabbinic authority. But unlike traditional Judaism, Orthodoxy is conscious of the spiritual and cultural challenges of the modern world and especially of rival formulations of the meaning and consequences of being Jewish. Orthodoxy, in all its various manifestations and expressions, has never recognized any alternative conception of Judaism as legitimate. But it is aware of itself as a party, generally a minority party, within the Jewish world.

Orthodox Judaism received its earliest formulation in Hungary (then part of the Austro-Hungarian empire) in the first quarter of the nineteenth century and in Germany in the middle of the century. In both countries it constituted a response to the efforts of reformers to adapt the *halakhah* in general and the synagogue service in particular to currents in nineteenth-century culture. The reformers maintained that this was a condition for Jewish emancipation and civil equality. Orthodoxy developed in France and England at about this same time but in far less explicit and rigorous a manner. A major reason, no doubt, was that the challenge of Reform Judaism was so much weaker. The weakness of Reform Judaism in France and England may be attributable to the fact that it developed after, rather than before, the Jews had more or less obtained civil equality in those countries.

Orthodoxy arose in eastern Europe at the end of the nineteenth century, primarily in response to secular interpretations of Jewish life rather than in opposition to religious reform. The most important centers of Orthodoxy today are in Israel and the United States.

Hungarian Orthodoxy. The ideological and programmatic outlines of Hungarian Orthodoxy were formulated by Rabbi Mosheh Sofer (1762–1839), better known as the Ḥatam Sofer, the title of his seven-volume *responsa* to halakhic questions. This earliest variety of Orthodoxy is best described by the term *neotraditionalism* because it rejects any attempt at change and adaptation of the tradition. According to the Ḥatam Sofer, "all that is new is forbidden by the Torah"; the phrase is a play on the words of an injunction prohibiting consumption of "new" grain from each year's harvest until a portion is offered in the Temple in Jerusalem. Unlike some of his followers, the Ḥatam Sofer did not oppose all forms of secular education. A knowledge of some secular subjects, for example, is helpful in resolving certain halakhic problems. But in characteristically neotraditional fashion, he legitimated secular education in utilitarian terms, not as an end in itself.

The basic strategy of neotraditionalism was the sanctification of the rabbinic tradition in its entirety. Whereas traditional Judaism recognized different levels of sanctity and degrees of importance of halakhic injunctions (for example, acts prohibited by the Torah were in a more stringent category than acts prohibited by rabbinic legislation), neotraditionalists blurred the differences insofar as obligations to observe the injunctions were concerned. The tradition was self-consciously projected as woven of a single cloth, all parts of which were equally binding and sanctified. The two major instruments that the neotraditionalists fashioned to socialize the community to their ideology and values were a greatly expanded rabbinic authority and a new type of *yeshivah* (pl., *yeshivot*), or academy for intensive Talmudic study. These new and larger *yeshivot* were designed to exist in economic and ideological independence from the increasingly fragile local Jewish communities in which they were located. The *yeshivah* of the Ḥatam Sofer in Pressburg, where he served as communal rabbi from 1806 until his death, was the most important *yeshivah* in central Europe. His students, in turn, served as community leaders throughout Hungary, Galicia, and Bohemia-Moravia and in the Land of Israel (Erets Yisra'el), strengthening neotraditional influences in all these places.

The Ḥatam Sofer favored immigration to the Land of Israel. Many who favored immigration in those days were reacting to the reformers' rejection of nationalist elements in Judaism. The Ḥatam Sofer's espousal of an early form of Jewish nationalism and his projection of the importance of the Land of Israel in the Jewish tradition may also have been related to his negative attitude toward political emancipation. He feared its threat to religious authority. His followers believed they could establish a pure Jewish society, insulated from secularist modernizing influences, in the Land of Israel. They established a Hungarian subcommunity in the Land of Israel that played a major role within the old *yishuv* (the nineteenth-century settlement of religiously observant Jews, as distinct from the new *yishuv* of late-nineteenth- and twentieth-century settlers motivated by secular Jewish nationalism).

The distinctive instrument of Hungarian Orthodoxy in furthering its neotraditional objectives was the independent communal organization. In 1868 the Hungarian government convened a General Jewish Congress in order to define the basis for the autonomous organization of the Jewish community. The majority of the delegates were sympathetic to religious reform (Neologs), and most of the Orthodox delegates withdrew from the Congress. In 1870 the Hungarian parliament permitted the Orthodox to organize themselves in separate communal frameworks, which might coexist in the same locality with a Neolog community or a Status Quo community (the latter was composed of those who refused to join either the Orthodox or the Neolog community). Orthodox communities provided their members with the full gamut of religious services (kosher food, schools, religious courts, and, of course, synagogues) and represented Orthodox political interests to the government. Orthodox leaders discouraged contacts with members of the rival communities and prohibited entering their synagogues, and many Orthodox rabbis even enjoined intermarriage with them.

Hungarian Orthodoxy included both Hasidic and non-Hasidic elements. Hasidism, which originated in the eighteenth century, was bitterly opposed by the traditional religious elite, who feared that its folkishness, pietism, and ambivalence toward the central importance of Talmudic study undermined the tradition itself. Orthodoxy might have been born in opposition to Hasidism if not for leaders like the Ḥatam Sofer who sought a *modus vivendi*, recognizing that Hasidic leaders were no less antagonistic to basic changes in tradition than were the traditional religious elite. In fact, by the end of the century, the centers of Hasidic influence in the smaller Jewish communities remained least compromising in their attitude toward modernity. In the larger, more urbanized communities, one found signs of the growing attraction of German Orthodoxy with its more accommodating attitude toward modernity.

Even in an earlier period, not all Hungarian Orthodox rabbis were neotraditional in orientation. A minority were attracted by aspects of modern culture and/or believed that a more moderate approach might prove more attractive to potential deviators. Outstanding among such rabbis was German-born Esriel Hildesheimer, who served as a rabbi in Hungary until 1869. Although Hildesheimer was no less opposed to reform than his Hungarian colleagues, he aroused their particular antagonism when he established in the Austro-Hungarian community of Eisenstadt a *yeshivah* whose curriculum included secular studies. After leaving Hungary, Hildesheimer accepted the post of rabbi in an independent Orthodox congregation in Berlin. In 1873 he established a new rabbinical seminary in the more hospitable climate of German Orthodoxy.

German Orthodoxy. The year 1850 marks the emergence of German Orthodoxy, with the establishment of the Israelitische Religionsgesellschaft in Frankfurt am Main, a congregation led by Samson Raphael Hirsch from 1851 until his death. But the distinctive ideological formulation of German Orthodoxy (often known as Neo-Orthodoxy) dates, at least in embryo, from the publication of Hirsch's *Nineteen Letters on Judaism* in 1836. The publication a few years later of an Orthodox weekly by Ya'aqov Ettlinger (1798–1871) is also of significance.

Hirsch was the foremost proponent of the idea that Torah-true Judaism (to borrow a popular phrase of German Orthodoxy) was compatible with modern culture and political emancipation. Hirsch envisaged a divine order revealed in nature in which Jews could and should participate. But the divine order was also revealed in the Torah, many of whose commands were specific to Jews. The effect of Hirsch's conception, though not his intent, was the compartmentalization of life for the Orthodox Jew. Modern culture, patriotism, civil law—all became legitimate spheres for Jewish involvement since they were perceived as falling outside the realm proscribed by *halakhah*.

Hirsch and his followers directed their antagonism not at the gentile world or its culture, but rather at religious reform, and in this respect they shared the outlook of the most intransigent of the Hungarian Orthodox. Reform Judaism, as a self-conscious movement in Jewish life, began in Germany with the establishment of the Hamburg temple in 1818. In the first few decades of the century it seemed that Reform conceptions of Judaism would replace those of traditional Judaism in Germany. Indeed, the major intellectual battle lines seemed to be drawn between the moderate reformers who sought changes in Jewish practice through the reinterpretation of Jewish law and the generally younger second generation of reformers who would abrogate the authority of the law entirely. Hirsch made no distinctions between moderate and radical reformers. Although in his *Nineteen Letters on Judaism* he was critical of traditional as well as Reform Judaism and seemed to advocate a position equidistant from both, some of his early endorsement of change was mitigated with the passage of time. What Hirsch never forgot was that the attraction of reform was an outgrowth of Jewish desire for emancipation and acceptance, that traditional Judaism appeared to be an obstacle to this goal, and that unless it could be reformulated as compatible with emancipation and modern culture, it had no future in Germany.

In addition to its educational system—day schools, religious schools, and seminaries around which German Orthodoxy united—the distinctive instrument that traditional Judaism forged to socialize its adherents to its values and conceptions was the autonomous congregation, even though it was only effective in a small number of localities. The heart of the congregational activity was the synagogue service itself, where the weekly or biweekly sermons by the rabbi, in German, represented a dramatic innovation. The traditional rabbi preached only a few times a year and never in the language of the state. The German Orthodox rabbi was likely to possess a university degree, an acquisition that distinguished him from his Hungarian and, as we shall see, his eastern European and Israeli counterparts. German Orthodox Jews were most attentive to the form of the service. Many Reform innovations, influenced in turn by the Christian churches, were adopted. German Orthodox rabbis, to the dismay of their traditional colleagues in other countries, officiated in clerical gowns, encouraged the participation of choirs (all male), and paid careful attention to musical arrangements in the service. In fact, some of their innovations would have been enough to identify a synagogue in Hungary as Neolog.

In addition to the synagogue itself, the autonomous congregation might sponsor a school, assume responsibility for the supervision of kosher foods, and provide opportunity for study and semisocial activity. Only political activity and sometimes welfare services remained outside its sphere of Jewish responsibilities, remaining the prerogatives of the more inclusive *Gemeinde* (the local Jewish community).

After the passage of a Prussian law in 1876 permitting Jews to secede, Hirsch insisted, as a matter of *halakhah*, that members of his congregation resign from the Frankfurt *Gemeinde*. Most of his congregants and certainly most Orthodox Jews in Germany refused to separate themselves and establish their own *Austrittsgemeinde* (seceded community).

Hirsch's demand for secession met opposition from traditionalists such as Rabbi Seligmann Ber Bamberger of Würzburg (1807–1878), probably the greatest contemporary Talmudist of Germany. It has recently been suggested that Bamberger harbored animosity toward the "modernizing ways" of Hirsch and his followers. The secession issue may have been a convenient opportunity to rebuke him and challenge his mastery of textual sources. Hirsch himself, in his lengthy response to Bamberger's opinion against secession, noted that the latter had never accepted Hirsch's ideal of *Torah 'im derekh erets* (Torah and worldliness), which was the slogan of German Orthodoxy. Hildesheimer also favored secession and was no less antagonistic to Reform Judaism. Nevertheless, he differed from Hirsch, to whom he was personally close, on other issues. He was more favorable than Hirsch to integrating secular and sacred study. He and his followers did participate with non-Orthodox Jews in organizations dedicated to defending Jews against anti-Semitism. He was an enthusiastic supporter of the settlement of Jews and the establishment of Jewish institutions in the Land of Israel. To the chagrin of neotraditionalists, he sought means to raise the educational and vocational standards of Jews in the old *yishuv* and fought with them over this issue.

By the end of the century, Orthodoxy in both Germany and Hungary was well established, albeit with minority status within the Jewish world. Its exclusionary form of organization, its emphasis on those forms of observance that distinguished it from Reform Judaism, and its insistence that the core component of the authentic Jew's faith was the belief that God dictated the Torah to Moses suggested, in fact, that Orthodoxy was content to survive as a minority party in Jewish life, more concerned with maintaining its purity than extending its boundaries. The Orthodox camp in each country was reasonably well integrated and possessed its own organizational structure, periodicals, and schools. Its acknowledged leaders commanded deference in the general as well as the Jewish community. In fact, conservative governments, wary of radicals in general and aware of the attraction of political radicalism to so many Jews, often favored Orthodoxy, which it associated with tradition, law, and stability, over Reform. In short, by the end of the century it appeared that Orthodoxy, in one way or another, had withstood the challenge of modernity and emancipation and the blandishments of Reform. Jews in Hungary and Germany were increasingly assimilating and intermarrying. But this was a matter of greater immediate threat to Reform than to Orthodoxy.

In retrospect, Orthodoxy's strength was its ability to create small, meaningful, integrated communities that provided its adherents with a sense of identity and stability and mediated their involvement with the infinite. But Orthodoxy built upon certain assumptions. It was organized in a milieu in which one anticipated continued political and social freedom and in which the major threat to the tradition stemmed from religious reform. Its insularity from non-Orthodox Jews ill equipped it for a role in the defense of Jewish rights against a rising tide of anti-Semitism. Second, it had not yet developed ideological defenses against secular conceptions of Judaism. These, unlike Reform, argued not for religious alternatives to the tradition but for a totally new conception of the meaning of Jewishness. The most influential of these conceptions was Zionism, the notion that the Jews are a nation like other nations whose *sancta* are language, territory, and people rather than God and Torah. It was this last threat more than any other that led to the emergence of an international Orthodox organization—Agudat Yisra'el. Before such an organization could emerge, however, the level of Orthodox consciousness in eastern Europe had to undergo development.

Orthodoxy in Eastern Europe. The vast majority of eastern European Jews continued to live in accordance with the religious tradition throughout the nineteenth century, although the institutions of traditional Judaism were severely undermined. Government law had destroyed many of the traditional privileges and responsibilities of the Jewish community. The charismatic authority of the *rebeyim* (Hasidic leaders) had further undermined the status of communal leaders. At the margins of society, the small party of radical *maskilim* (adherents of Jewish enlightenment) challenged traditional patterns of Jewish life. By the middle of the nineteenth century, changing economic conditions afforded new opportunities for a few, but further impoverished the masses and shook the moral consensus within the community. They also highlighted the importance of secular education, thereby undermining the alliance of the wealthy and the religious elite. They undermined the *battei midrash* ("houses of study"), once found in virtually every Jewish locality. There, small numbers of men had spent their day in study, supported, however meagerly, by the local householders.

Traditional Judaism responded, however feebly and tentatively, to these developments, but the response cannot be labeled Orthodoxy, because it lacked one major distinguishing feature—self-awareness as one party among others in Jewish life. Traditional Jewish leaders who saw their authority questioned, Torah study abandoned, and new modes of behavior and belief increasingly legitimated differed among themselves as to how to meet the crisis. Their first concern tended to be the challenge to the primacy of textual study in the hierarchy of religious commandments. Hasidism had stressed the importance of religious experience and intention—adapting from earlier mystical Jewish conceptions the notion that in performing the commandments with true devotion and proper intent, the Jew was repairing the torn fabric of the cosmos. This stress on intention rather than behavior introduced a potential antinomianism and, no less seriously, suggested that the study of Talmud was of secondary importance in the hierarchy of religious injunctions.

The traditionalists' response was the establishment of central *yeshivot* supported by contributions solicited throughout the Jewish world. The first such *yeshivah* was established in 1802 in Volozhin (near Vilnius) by Rabbi Ḥayyim of Volozhin from his own funds. During the course of the century, *yeshivot* were founded throughout Lithuania and Belorussia (then still part of Russia). Leadership of a *yeshivah* rather than service as a communal rabbi marked one as a preeminent scholar automatically meriting deference and authority.

The *yeshivot* trained the Orthodox elite but generally failed to strengthen traditional Judaism among the masses. The Hasidic *rebeyim* filled a more important role in maintaining traditional norms, at least among their followers. But the decline of traditional patterns of observance until the last decades of the century must not be exaggerated. Rabbis such as Naftali Tsevi Yehudah Berlin (1817–1893), known as the Netsiv; Yisra'el Me'ir ha-Kohen (1838–1933), known as the Ḥafets Ḥayyim; and Yitsḥaq Elḥanan Spektor (1817–1896) retained authority and enormous prestige among the masses.

One measure of the continuing strength of the tradition was the failure of Rabbi Yitsḥaq Ya'aqov Reines (1839–1915), who later founded Mizraḥi, the Religious-Zionist movement, to establish a *yeshivah* in the 1880s. In 1881 Reines published a sharp critique of the method of study in traditional *yeshivot* and called for the reorganization of the institutions of eastern European Judaism. Jewish society, he maintained, was undergoing an ideological and institutional crisis. *Yeshivot* were crumbling, the rabbinate was weakened, and its authority was undermined because of its economic dependence on the wealthy. This, he argued, was a result of the loss of Jewish respect for the traditional leaders. His solution was the establishment of a new *yeshivah* to include secular studies in its curriculum and to produce graduates who would fill positions of Jewish leadership. Reines's view was supported by wealthy Russian Jews and Orthodox leaders from central Europe. But the opposition of the heads of the traditional *yeshivot* was enough to prevent the establishment of the new *yeshivah*.

A more successful effort at the reform of *yeshivot*, known as the Musar (ethical) movement, was initiated by Rabbi Yisra'el (Lipkin) Salanter (1810–1883). His call for ethical renewal was first addressed to the Jewish masses, businessmen and traders in particular, but failed to attract much enthusiasm. His doctrines were more influential in the *yeshivot*. While many of the heads of these academies initially resisted the introduction of the study of moral literature or discussions of moral issues at the expense of Talmudic study, the Musar movement was eventually co-opted. A limited amount of time was dedicated to the study of an ethical tract, and the custom of a weekly talk by the moral supervisor (a new position created in the *yeshivot* in response to the demands of the Musar movement) was introduced.

What traditional religious leaders did not do until the end of the century, either because they saw no need or because they did not know how to do it, was oppose the organization of rival parties with alternative conceptions of Judaism. But by the end of the nineteenth century this need was becoming apparent. In the 1870s an organization of Hasidic and non-Hasidic elements was formed to oppose the founding of a rabbinical seminary and the introduction of organizational changes in the community. In 1912 Agudat Yisra'el (Agudah for short) was established under the impetus of German Orthodox leaders, uniting the Orthodox leaders of central and eastern Europe in defense of the tradition.

Agudat Yisra'el never spoke for all religious Jews. Its greatest following was in Poland, the heartland of eastern European Jewry. Within Poland it functioned as a political party after World War I, rivaling the Zionists and the Bund (General Jewish Workers Union, a socialist Jewish party founded in 1897) for control of the Jewish street. Even within Poland it was opposed by the minority of religious Zionists and by the larger group of traditionalists, who remained indifferent to the needs that had led to its creation.

Agudah's primary strength came from the union of the Hasidic *rebe* of Ger (Avraham Mordekhai Alter, 1866–1948), whose followers numbered in the hundreds of thousands, with the leaders of the Lithuanian *yeshivot*, the most prominent of whom included Rabbi Ḥayyim 'Ozer Grodzinski of Vilnius (1863–1940). The latter carried enormous status in the world of religious Jewry. Nevertheless, in the Galician and Lithuanian regions, the masses remained aloof. The region around Warsaw and Lodz attracted Jews from the countryside. The struggle between religion and its opponents was most obvious and intense there, and Agudah prospered. In the older Jewish communities of Galicia, however, the Jewish tradition was less threatened, and religious Jews were content to leave political activity to non-Jews and secularists.

Agudah's own rabbinical authorities were, at best, tolerant of the necessity for political activity. Agudah was established to protect the traditional way of life, but political activity has an acculturating impact of its own. The Agudah press carried warnings from rabbis not to regard partisan politics as more than a temporary expedient.

Traditional religious leaders outside Agudah's ranks were impatient with the notion that some adaptation to modernity was necessary in the very defense of the tradition. Rabbi Yosef Yitsḥaq Schneersohn (1880–1950), leader of the Habad branch of Hasidism (better known as Lubavitcher Hasidism), attacked Agudah schools for including secular studies, accusing them of behaving no differently than the enemies of the tradition.

In addition to sponsoring schools whose curriculum included secular studies, Agudah established reading rooms where secular books were to be found, published a newspaper (though adherents were cautioned against reading it on the Sabbath), and organized a youth movement in which *yeshivah* students were warned not to spend too much time. Most damaging of all, Agudah's political survival required alliances with nonreligious parties, and when Agudah was the majority party in the local Jewish community, it bore at least indirect responsibility for nonreligious and even antireligious activity which the community funds supported.

Agudah, certainly in Poland, began as a neotraditionalist response to modernity. But its own efforts to defend the tradition through political instrumentalities and its own concern to control the environment within which the tradition had to function forced it into compromises that became particularly noticeable in the 1930s.

World War II brought the end to Agudah activity in eastern Europe. By the late 1930s it was apparent to many within Agudah itself that Jewish life in Poland was heading for catastrophe and that traditional responses were ineffective. Settlement in the Land of Israel became an increasingly attractive option, and Agudah muted its opposition to Zionism. Voices were increasingly heard, from within, for constructive efforts in the Land of Israel and for cooperation with the Zionists at the tactical level. Isaac Breuer (1883–1946), grandson of Samson Raphael Hirsch, a leading ideologue of German Orthodoxy, led the call for a reassessment of the Land of Israel in Agudah's program and ideology. The Balfour Declaration and the modern Zionist settlement of the land revealed, Breuer believed, the hand of providence. The Jews, he claimed, were a nation formed by Torah, but as a nation they required their own land in order to renew themselves. In 1936 Breuer settled in Jerusalem. By the time other Agudah followers were prepared to reevaluate their position, the British had closed the gates of the land to world Jewry.

Orthodoxy in Israel. Most Orthodox Jews today reside in Israel or the United States. Religiously observant Jews make up 15 to 20 percent of the Jewish population of Israel. The neotraditionalists, once quite marginal to Israeli society, play an increasingly important role. The most colorful and controversial group within their ranks is the successor to the old *yishuv*, the 'Edah Ḥaredit (Community of the Pious), consisting of a few thousand families with thousands of sympathizers located primarily in Jerusalem and Benei Beraq (on the outskirts of Tel Aviv). These are the most intransigent of the neotraditionalists. They relate to the state of Israel with varying degrees of hostility. They refuse to participate in its elections, the more extreme refuse to bear Israeli identification cards or utilize the state's services (their schools, for example, refuse government support), and the most extreme seek the imposition of Arab rule.

A more moderate neotraditionalism is found in Israeli Agudah circles. They are dominated by the heads of *yeshivot* and a number of Hasidic *rebeyim*. The most prominent continues to be the *rebe* of Ger. Agudat Yisra'el generally obtains from 3 to 4 percent of the vote in Israeli elections. Although it has been a party to the ruling coalition, it continues to condemn ideological Zionism, that is, secular Jewish nationalism. It maintains that Israel's constitution must be based upon Torah and *halakhah* as interpreted by rabbinical authority. The leading rabbinical authorities, Agudah further claims, constitute its own Mo'etset Gedolei ha-Torah (Council of Torah Sages), to whom it turns for direction on basic policy issues.

Agudat Yisra'el maintains its own network of elementary schools. Following graduation, boys continue their studies in *yeshivot qeṭannot* (minor *yeshivot*), whose curriculum consists almost exclusively of sacred text. They do not receive a high school degree. At the age of sixteen or seventeen they generally move on to advanced *yeshivot*, where study is devoted entirely to sacred writ, almost exclusively to Talmud. Girls pursue their high school studies in Beit Ya'aqov, a network of girls' schools first established in Poland. The tendency is to prepare the girls to assume housewife-mother roles.

Beneficent government subsidy, largely for political reasons, has resulted in relative prosperity among Agudah-oriented institutions. Although the party itself is seriously troubled by personal and institutional conflicts and rivalries, and while it is the object of vociferous condemnation by more extreme neotraditionalists who charge it with selling out to the Zionists, the Agudah world appears relatively secure. It sponsors or supports a number of institutions for *ba'alei teshuvah,* Jews raised in nonreligious homes who have embraced Orthodoxy and are attracted by neotraditionalism rather than religious Zionism. Its *yeshivot* attract students from all over the world. Whereas a short time ago they were considered generally inferior to their counterparts in the United States, this is no longer true. The Agudah world is an international community with centers in New York, Montreal, London, Antwerp, and Zurich, to mention the major locations, but Jerusalem plays an increasingly important role. The young seem easily socialized to the values of the community, and their large families (seven and eight children are not at all uncommon) apparently assure continued communal growth. In fact, Israeli observers are rather surprised, given the size of Agudah families, that the party has not increased its proportion of the vote in recent elections—an indication that all may not be as well as it appears on the surface. One problem is Agudah's inability to integrate Sefardic Jews (Jews originating from Muslim countries) in their leadership groups. Sefardic Jews represent an important constituency of Agudah voters (some claim almost half), and in the summer of 1984 they bolted the party because they were excluded from its leadership. Another threat is economic. Agudah's educational institutions play a major role in the socialization of the Agudah community. The extended period of study for the men, often into their mid-twenties and beyond (they are exempted from Israeli army service as long as they remain in the *yeshivot*), requires public and/or private sources of support, which may not necessarily continue in the case of economic depression or a radical change in the Israeli political climate.

The Agudah world is in, but lives apart from, Israeli society. The religious Zionists are in a different category. They make up roughly 10 percent of the Jewish population but are in some sense the symbol of contemporary Israel. Israel's political culture, particularly since the 1970s, focuses on the Jewish people, the Jewish tradition, and the Land of Israel as objects of ultimate value. Symbols of traditional religion, though not traditional theology, pervade Israeli life. Religious Zionists are viewed by many of the nonreligious as most committed to and most comfortable with these values and symbols. The political elite, in particular, has been strongly influenced by the religious Zionists and their personal example of idealism and self-sacrifice. In fact, the success of religious Zionism makes the National Religious Party (their political organization) less attractive to voters, who no longer feel they need be as defensive about threats to religion from the secular parties.

In no other society do Orthodox Jews, religious Zionists in particular, feel quite so much at home. They are separated from the non-Orthodox population by their distinctive cultural and educational institutions (in the advanced religious Zionist *yeshivot,* students are required to fulfill their military obligations but generally do so in selected units) and their own friendship groups. There are political tensions between religious and nonreligious Israelis over issues such as "Who is a Jew?," whether marriage and divorce law should be left to the rabbinate, Sabbath closing laws, and the sense of many secularists that they are subject to religious coercion. But most religious Zionists not only feel that they fully participate as equal members of the society but also sense a wholeness to their lives that they find missing outside of Israel. Nevertheless, they, too, confront the tension between tradition and modernity.

The founders of religious Zionism were influenced by modern currents of nationalism and the desire for political emancipation. Religious Zionists shared a concern for the physical as well as the spiritual welfare of Jews and an identification with nonreligious as well as religious Jews. Most of them believed that the modern settlement of the Land of Israel pointed to the beginning of divine redemption of the Jewish people. Unlike the neotraditionalists, they did not believe that Jews must patiently await the coming of the Messiah but rather that redemption was a process that Jews could initiate themselves. In other words, it was not only their espousal of Zionism that distinguished religious Zionists from the neotraditionalists, but also their acceptance of so many of the assumptions and values of modernity. Compartmentalization was an inadequate alternative.

Although compartmentalization was and always will be a temptation for religious Jews who want to participate in worldly activity without compromising their religious principles, it is an inadequate ideology for religious Zionists. The establishment of the state of Israel and its public policies are to them matters of metaphysical significance intimately related to their religiously formed conceptions of reality. The reconciliation of tradition and modernity, therefore, requires other strategies.

One such strategy is adaptationism, sometimes labeled modern Orthodoxy. It affirms that the basic values of modernity are not only compatible with Judaism but partake of its essence. Freedom, the equality of man, rationalism, science, the rule of law, and nationalism are all found to be inherent in the Jewish tradition. Secular study is affirmed as a positive religious value—an instrument whereby man learns more about the divinely created world and therefore more about God. Adaptationism includes the effort to reinterpret the tradition, including those aspects of the *halakhah* that seem to stand in opposition to modern values. Adaptationism was a popular strategy among American Orthodox Jews. There are very few Israeli halakhic authorities whose rulings are adaptationist, and they lack the ideological self-consciousness or philosophical underpinning that is found among American Orthodox.

There are limits to the extent to which Orthodoxy can affirm every aspect of modernity, and there is an apologetic as well as an adaptive side to this strategy in practice. As in other religions, family law and relations between the sexes evoke the most conservative sentiments, though even here adaptationism has proved far more accommodating of modernity than other Orthodox strategies.

An alternative strategy for religious Zionism is expansionism. Expansionism affirms modernity by reinterpreting it through the prism of the Jewish tradition. It aspires, in theory, to bring all aspects of life under the rubric of its interpretation of Judaism. The program of religious Zionism, almost by definition, is expansionist. Since religious Zionism calls for a Jewish state in accordance with Jewish law, its adherents must believe, at least in theory, that Jewish law is a suitable instrument to guide a modern state. Me'ir Berlin (1880–1949), a major political leader of religious Zionism, claimed that the religious Zionist program was "not to content itself with a corner even if the Torah was there, but to capture Judaism, Jewish life, to impose the spirit of the Torah on the market, on the public, on the State." Anyone who reflects upon this statement must wonder whether, if this is indeed the task of religious Zionists, they would not have to reinterpret major motifs in the religious tradition and introduce rather radical changes in Jewish law. In other words, expansionism of this type bears within it the seeds of adaptationism. The leadership of the religious Zionist labor movement, the religious *kibbutsim* in particular, were prepared, at least in theory and sometimes in practice, for some halakhic adaptation. But they shied away from the final step that the realization of their goal would have required—the legitimation of religious changes through their adoption by the religious public rather than the assent of rabbinical authority. The ambivalent attitude toward adaptation by the leaders may help account for the permissive interpretation that many of their followers gave to *halakhah*. It may also help to account for the failure of this branch of expansionism to develop. It made no real effort to realize in practice its theoretical pretensions to adaptation, and it never legitimated the halakhic deviations that occurred under its roof.

Expansionism today is associated with the personality and philosophy of Rav Kook (Avraham Yitsḥaq Kook). This branch of expansionism, like neotraditionalism, is halakhically uncompromising. Unlike neotraditionalism, it abjures social and cultural isolation. Its goal is to sanctify all of life. The characteristic features of expansionism that support such a worldview and make its realization feasible, in addition to its commitment to Jewish nationalism, are a redefinition of secular-religious distinctions and a belief that divine redemption is imminent.

Expansionism is necessarily nationalistic since it argues that Jews must live a natural life in all its physical manifestations in order to invest all of life with the divine spirit. In the expansionist conception, as it has worked itself out in the last few years, the state itself assumes a special sanctity, its very creation being a sign of God's favor and a harbinger of the imminent redemption.

The religious conception of the state is challenged by three facts: that Israel was established by Jewish secularists, that the avowedly nonreligious constitute a majority of the population, and that the institutions of the state are controlled by secularists. The expansionists overcome this objection by their redefinition, following Rav Kook, of secularism. They blur distinctions not only between holy and profane but also between ostensibly religious and ostensibly secular Jews. This enables the expansionists to break out of the traditional Orthodox perception, which viewed religious Jews as a beleaguered minority surrounded by hostile Jewish secularists with whom they might at best, and even then at their peril, cooperate at an instrumental level. The belief in imminent redemption that characterizes the expansionists' viewpoint reinforces their confidence in the eventual triumph of their position despite the apparent absence of support in the international arena. It also serves as a caution against any retreat or compromise that might interrupt and delay divine redemption. Finally, the belief in imminent redemption permits the evasion of troubling questions about the suitability of the *halakhah*, in its present state, to direct a modern society.

In addition to the neotraditionalists and religious Zionists, one still finds vestiges of pre-Orthodox traditionalism among some elderly Sefardic Jews of North African origin. They arrived in Israel before their own societies underwent modernization. They have no successors. Their descendants, in turn, tend to be deferential toward the tradition; they observe many of its customs and practices but are neither as punctilious or knowledgeable about the religion as are most Orthodox Jews. They categorize themselves and are categorized by others as "traditional," as distinct from the "religious" and "secular" segments of the population. They constitute a hinterland for Orthodox Jewry, though only time will tell whether they will continue to do so.

The state of Israel provides basic religious services such as religious schools, supervision over the *kashrut* of foods, religious courts, an established rabbinate with responsibility for marriage and divorce of Jews, ritual baths, and subsidies for synagogue construction and rabbis' salaries. The religious political parties act as intermediaries in the provision of welfare and educational services. Hence, the role of the synagogue is relatively minor. Though synagogues proliferate in Israel, there is probably no country in the world where they play a less important role in the life of the Orthodox Jew.

Orthodoxy in the United States. American Orthodoxy bears the mark of two waves of immigrants and a native generation that combines characteristics of each. Many of the eastern European immigrants who came to the United States during the great wave of Jewish immigration between 1881 and 1924 were traditionalists. In the confrontation with American culture and the challenge of finding a livelihood, they abandoned many traditional patterns of religious observance. The dominant Orthodox strategy that emerged in the United States was adaptationism. In fact, in the first few decades of the century it appeared as though the difference between American Orthodox and Conservative Judaism was really the degree or pace of adaptation. The institutions and ideology of American Orthodoxy were severely challenged by neotraditionalist immigrants who arrived just prior to and immediately following World War II. They established their own *yeshivot*, Hasidic *rebeyim* among them reestablished their courts of followers, and they expressed disdain for the modern Orthodox rabbi. He was likely to be a graduate of Yeshiva University, the major institution for the training of Orthodox rabbis in the United States, where rabbinical students are required to have earned a college degree. The neotraditionalists were zealous and very supportive of their own institutions. In addition, they clustered in a few neighborhoods of the largest cities. Their concentration and discipline provided their leaders with political influence, which, in the heydays of the welfare programs of the 1960s and 1970s, was translated into various forms of government assistance.

The neotraditionalist challenge to modern Orthodoxy has had a decided impact on the native generation raised in modern Orthodox homes, and the American environment has left its mark on the generation raised in neotraditionalist homes. The American-born Orthodox Jew, regardless of the home in which he was raised, tends to be punctilious in religious observance, more so than his parents, and hostile to what he considers deviant forms of Judaism (i.e., Conservative or Reform). But he is sympathetic to many aspects of contemporary culture and accepting of secular education, if only for purposes of economic advancement. With the exception of pockets of neotraditional extremists who recall the ideology and attitudes of the ʿEdah Ḥaredit in Israel, the American Orthodox Jew, even the neotraditionalist, is familiar with, if not at home in, modern culture. Finally, there is a general willingness among most American Orthodox Jews to work with the non-Orthodox on behalf of general Jewish interests, those of Israel in particular.

Among the outstanding Orthodox figures in the United States is Rabbi Menachem Mendel Schneersohn (b. 1902), the present leader of Habad Hasidism. Habad is the Hasidic group with the largest number of sympathizers in the world. It is really a *sui generis* variety of Orthodoxy because it combines a neotraditional outlook with a conversionist impulse (toward other Jews, not non-Jews) and a unique belief system centering on the charismatic figure of the *rebe*.

Rabbi Moses Feinstein (b. 1895), who came to the United States in 1937, is renowned in the Orthodox world as the outstanding *poseq* (adjudicator of religious law). Another significant Orthodox personality is Rabbi Joseph Dov Soloveitchik (b. 1903), scion of a prominent rabbinical family and considered by many the greatest living Talmudic authority in the Orthodox world. Soloveitchik, who arrived in the United States in 1932, is particularly revered in modern Orthodox circles. He has a doctorate in philosophy and can communicate in the language of the world of ideas. His thought, which only began appearing in print in the last two decades, is characterized by sensitivity to the tension between man, possessed of feelings and ideas connected to the divine within him, and the objective and demanding *halakhah* to which God also commands the Jew to subject himself.

The increasing importance of the neotraditional *yeshivot* has challenged the central role of the synagogue, but it is still the crucial mediator between most Orthodox Jews and their religious identity. Certainly, the synagogue plays a critical role in the lives of its members and recalls the importance of the autonomous congregations of German Orthodoxy. However, unlike the German congregations, the rabbi's role in the American Orthodox synagogue is more limited, though by no means negligible. The real strength of the Orthodox synagogue, which tends to be much smaller than the average Conservative or Reform synagogue, rarely exceeding 200 to 250 members, lies in the sense of community and mutual support that it offers rather than the network of services that it provides.

Orthodox Judaism Today. The dominant trend in Orthodoxy throughout the world, since the end of World War II, has been increased religious zealotry, punctiliousness in religious observance, and, with some exceptions, less explicit accommodation to modern values and contemporary culture. This is, at least in part, a result of the direction in which modern values and culture have moved. Increased permissiveness; challenges to authority, order, and tradition in general; and affirmation of self are inimical to all historical religions. But Orthodoxy has become far more skilled, after a century of experience, in developing institutions—such as schools, synagogues, political organizations, a press, and summer camps—to mute the threats of secularism and modernity. In some respects this means that Orthodoxy is more at ease with the world and tolerates certain forms of accommodation (advanced secular education is the outstanding example) that many Orthodox circles denounced in the past. But it also means an increased self-confidence and an absence of fear on the part of Orthodoxy to challenge and reject some of the basic behavioral and ideological assumptions upon which most of modern culture rests.

[*See also* Judaism, *article on* Judaism in Northern and Eastern Europe since 1500; Yeshivah; Musar Movement; Agudat Yisra'el; Zionism; *and the biographies of Sofer, Hirsch, and other influential figures mentioned herein.*]

BIBLIOGRAPHY

Hebrew items are included only where English sources are inadequate and/or the Hebrew source is of major importance.

Hayim Halevy Donin's *To Be a Jew* (New York, 1972) is a practical guide to what it means to be an Orthodox Jew.

There is very little scholarly material in any language on most aspects of the social and religious history of Orthodox Judaism. The best material has been written recently; much is available only in the form of articles or doctoral dissertations.

On the background to Orthodoxy, see the last five chapters in Jacob Katz's *Tradition and Crisis: Jewish Society at the End of the Middle Ages* (New York, 1961) and *Out of the Ghetto: The Social Background of Jewish Emancipation* (Cambridge, Mass., 1973), particularly chapter 9, "Conservatives in a Quandary."

There is no general history of Orthodox Judaism. An outline of the topic is found in two articles by Moshe Samet, "Orthodox Jewry in Modern Times," parts 1 and 2, *Mahalakhim* (in Hebrew), nos. 1 and 3 (March 1969 and March 1970). Much can be learned from the two volumes of uneven biographical chapters edited by Leo Jung entitled *Jewish Leaders, 1750–1940* (New York, 1953) and *Guardians of Our Heritage, 1724–1953* (New York, 1958).

The best history of Hungarian Jewry covering the nineteenth and twentieth centuries and devoting considerable attention to Orthodoxy is Nathaniel Katzburg's "History of Hungarian Jewry" (in Hebrew), a lengthy introduction and bibliography to *Pinqas Qehillot Hungariyah* (Jerusalem, 1975). His article "The Jewish Congress of Hungary, 1868–1869," in *Hungarian Jewish Studies*, vol. 2, edited by Randolph Braham (New York, 1969), is the most significant study of a crucial aspect of the topic. The Ḥatam Sofer is the subject of Jacob Katz's major essay, "Contributions toward a Biography of R. Moses Sofer" (in Hebrew), in *Studies in Mysticism and Religion Presented to Gershom G. Scholem on His Seventieth Birthday, by Pupils, Colleagues and Friends*, edited by E. E. Urbach et al. (Jerusalem, 1967).

The English-language material on German Orthodoxy is more plentiful. Robert Liberles's *Between Community and Separation: The Resurgence of Orthodoxy in Frankfort, 1838–1877* (Westport, Conn., 1985) treats Hirsch and his community in detail. *Judaism Eternal: Selected Essays from the Writings of Rabbi Samson Raphael Hirsch*, vol. 2, translated from the German by I. Grunfeld (London, 1956), is probably the best place to start in reading Hirsch himself. On understanding some other leaders of German Orthodoxy, see David Ellenson, "The Role of Reform in Selected German-Jewish Orthodox Responsa: A Sociological Analysis," *Hebrew Union College Annual* (Cincinnati, 1982).

For a selection from Isaac Breuer, considered the most profound thinker of twentieth-century German Orthodoxy, see his *Concepts of Judaism*, edited by Jacob S. Levinger (Jerusalem, 1974).

There is no history of eastern European Orthodoxy. Emanuel Etkes's *R. Yisra'el Salanter ve-re'shitah shel tenu'at ha-musar* (Jerusalem, 1982) is an important source for understanding the Musar movement and the world of eastern European *yeshivot*. Eliyahu E. Dessler's *Strive for Truth* (New York, 1978), edited and translated by Aryeh Carmell, is an excellent example of Musar thought. *The Teachings of Hasidism*, edited by Joseph Dan (New York, 1983), provides some flavor of Hasidic literature.

On Zionism and Orthodox Judaism, see Ben Halpern's *The*

Idea of the Jewish State, 2d ed. (Cambridge, Mass., 1969), pp. 65–95. On mainstream religious Zionism, see *Religious Zionism: An Anthology,* edited by Yosef Tirosh (Jerusalem, 1975).

The best study of the old *yishuv* and its confrontation with modern Zionism is Menachem Friedman's *Society and Religion: The Non-Zionist Orthodox in Eretz-Israel, 1918–1936* (Jerusalem, 1977; in Hebrew with English summary). An expression of the extreme neotraditionalist position is I. I. Domb's *The Transformation: The Case of the Neturei Karta* (London, 1958). On Rav Kook, see Avraham Yitsḥaq Kook's *The Lights of Penitence, The Moral Principles, Lights of Holiness, Essays, Letters, and Poems,* translated by Ben Zion Bokser (New York, 1978).

Charles S. Liebman and Eliezer Don-Yehiya's *Civil Religion in Israel: Judaism and Political Culture in the Jewish State* (Berkeley, Calif., 1983) reviews the role of traditional Judaism in Israel and devotes a chapter to the variety of Orthodox responses to Israel's political culture.

On American Orthodoxy, Charles S. Liebman's "Orthodoxy in American Jewish Life," *American Jewish Year Book* 66 (1965): 21–97, is the most extensive survey. An adaptation of Rabbi Soloveitchik's lectures is Abraham Besdin's *Reflections of the Rav* (Jerusalem, 1979), but Soloveitchik's work "The Lonely Man of Faith," *Tradition* 7 (Summer 1965): 5–67, is a better example of his speculative effort. Norman Lamm's *Faith and Doubt: Studies in Traditional Jewish Thought* (New York, 1971) illustrates the approach of a leading American Orthodox rabbi to problems of contemporary concern.

The halakhic literature remains the heart of the Orthodox enterprise. This literature is virtually closed to the nonspecialist, but the regular feature "Survey of Recent Halakhic Responses," appearing in each issue of *Tradition: A Journal of Orthodox Jewish Thought* (New York, 1958–), provides the nonspecialist with a good sense of that world. At a more academic level, see *The Jewish Law Annual* (Leiden, 1978–).

CHARLES S. LIEBMAN

ORTHODOXY AND HETERODOXY. The concepts of orthodoxy and heterodoxy are found within all the major religious traditions, expressed by a variety of terms. In relation to religious life, *orthodoxy* means correct or sound belief according to an authoritative norm; *heterodoxy* refers to belief in a doctrine differing from the norm. The two terms originated in the patristic period of Christian history, when emphasis on belief rather than practice distinguished the concerns of Christian theologians. [*See* Theology, *article on* Christian Theology.]

Each of the major religious traditions has its own modes of determining orthodoxy. The extent to which heterodoxy is considered a serious deviance varies across traditions, and also within traditions at different phases of their history. From the perspective of an overview of the history of each tradition, one can discern that differing beliefs and/or practices have been considered of vital significance over the course of time. [*See also* Orthopraxy.] Further, some traditions allow for a wide variety of different perspectives within a wider unity, whereas others tend to split up into smaller groups competing as to which shall be considered the bearer of the authentic message or teaching. [*See* Heresy.]

Every major religious tradition has had to establish criteria for the acceptance or rejection of its members. In some cases, the civil power has supported the religious authorities, whereas in other cases, it has remained neutral or disinterested. Sometimes a group has insisted on rigid criteria of purity and conformity, whereas at other times, a great diversity of opinion and practice has been acceptable. Diversity of attitudes on such matters has existed at different times within each of the major traditions.

The scriptures normally serve to delineate the characteristics of acceptable, as opposed to unacceptable, persons. [*See* Canon.] Later theological or philosophical or legal schools often take the scriptural indications as a basis for outlining systems. Elaborating the fixed systems usually involves decisions as to the canon of scriptures and the modes of authority, as well as the establishment of training institutions for those who are to impart and uphold the particular orthodoxy. The self-conscious articulation of an orthodox perspective tends to occur several generations after the establishment of a new perspective, or the successful renewal of an older tradition which has been challenged. The usual process is to project the newly proclaimed orthodox position backward onto the beginnings of the community's life.

In the twentieth century, two opposite tendencies have manifested across traditions: there is both an active fundamentalism in every tradition and a new interest in reconciling divergent streams of thought and practice. The spread of literacy has enabled lay people to evidence new forms of interest and participation in religious leadership.

Those who lean toward fundamentalism tend to think the identity for the members of the community requires one exclusive interpretation of the tradition, and that particular interpretation must be imposed. The more traditional thinkers and the modernists, however, see the traditional tolerance of diverse interpretations as a source of strength rather than weakness.

Nonliterate Peoples. Nonliterate peoples commonly affirm their group identity through myths which legitimate social relations within the group and orient the group toward the wider universe. Shamans or equivalent figures serve as mediators with sacred powers. Knowledge of the sacred mythology may be shared in diverse ways by members of the group. Changes in the mythology may come about through visions or insight. Ritual practice serves to maintain coherent identity among members.

Deviance usually involves breaking codes of behavior, particularly with respect to sexual or family matters. Deviants can sometimes be readmitted into a normal relationship with the group through rituals of purification, but sometimes they leave and join another group. Deviants are generally understood to be offending the sacred powers, and are therefore required to undergo rituals to transform them into acceptable persons.

Hinduism. Classical Hindu philosophy of religion divides religious schools of thought into two types, *āstika* (usually translated as "orthodox") and *nāstika* (usually translated as "heterodox"). Those characterized as *nāstika* are the Jains, the Buddhists, and the materialists. The word *āstika* indicates the affirmation of being, whereas *nāstika* suggests nihilism, or denial of being.

The *Maitri Upaniṣad* expresses the importance of avoiding teachers of false doctrines. The same Upaniṣad uses the term *nāstika*, translated here as "atheism," to designate one of the characteristics emanating from the dark aspects of the unenlightened self in every individual.

We do not have sources available to us from the materialist or atheist schools of thought of ancient India, therefore the views of these schools are only known from the writings of their adversaries. But in the case of the Jains and the Buddhists, the sources still exist. The classical Hindu view is that the *nāstika* schools of thought are to be condemned because of their failure to accept the authority of the Vedas—a refusal that in practice means the rejection of their hereditary function as preservers and teachers of the Vedas, as well as in their duties as the priests responsible for ritual performances.

In time a principle of interpretation of the scriptures was developed that allowed for diversity: the interpretations varied according to which affirmations were deemed central. Hence more or less emphasis might be laid on ritual or other forms of religious life. Acceptance of the scriptures was, however, a necessary precondition for acceptance within the community. In his *History of Hindu Philosophy* (Cambridge, 1963), Surendranath Dasgupta has written: "Thus an orthodox Brahmin can dispense with image-worship if he likes, but not so with his daily Vedic prayers or other obligatory ceremonies."

The coherence of Hinduism derives from the discipline of the brahmans as transmitters and preservers of Vedic ritual and wisdom. The classical view is that the ancient seers (*ṛṣis*) who received the primal wisdom set in motion the oral transmission of the Vedas which is passed on through the educational system of the brahmans. The primary revelation is thus oral, *śruti*. The secondary level of sacred literature, *smṛti*, comprises the commentaries that explain the primal wisdom and give instruction on moral conduct and related matters.

Deviance within Hindu life can take many forms. The usual procedure for readmitting offenders is purification through ritual administered by a brahman. Offense is perceived as impurity that must be removed through the restorative power of ritual.

By the tenth century CE, the Buddhists had gradually disappeared from India, although their teaching had taken root in other countries. The Jains remained as a distinctive group, sometimes supported by local rulers. When the Abbé Sean-Antoine Dubois, in his *Hindu Manners, Customs and Ceremonies* (Oxford, 1928), wrote about India as he observed it in the late eighteenth century, he formed the impression that the Jains had been on occasion dominant in certain parts of India. By the twentieth century this was no longer the case: the Jains formed a relatively small minority community. Before the Muslim conquests of India, the local rulers probably helped determine whether the people tended toward the Buddhist, Jain, or Hindu perspectives. The last-named seems to have won out and to have remained dominant during the period of Muslim rule.

Diverse processes are taking place as the Hindu tradition confronts modernity. In the early twentieth century, several effective religious personalities—not all brahmans—have attempted to articulate interpretations of Hinduism that would be acceptable to the modern age. Such writers as Vivekananda, Radhakrishnan, Tagore, Aurobindo, and Gandhi have exercised a great influence over modern Hindus.

A number of groups advocating particular interpretations of Hinduism also have come into being, such as the Brāhmo Samāj and the Ārya Samāj. These groups advocated reform of Hindu social practices. A fundamentalist interpretation of Hinduism has appealed to certain segments of the Hindu population, as evidenced most dramatically by the assassination of Mohandas Gandhi. India is a secular state; in practice, therefore, no religious group receives favored status from the government.

Buddhism. Buddhism emerged as one of the protest movements against orthodox Hinduism around the sixth century BCE. The monks and nuns who followed the teachings of the Buddha took those teachings as the only guide necessary for enlightenment. Present historians acknowledge that Buddhists held councils to resolve disputes, but since the various groups have their own versions of what occurred at those councils, there is no consensus now as to what councils were held and what issues were decided. The teachings were transmitted orally for several centuries. It is impossible to say when the oral tradition was written down. The Buddha taught that missionaries were to speak in the language of those they addressed. As a result, Buddhist teaching has moved rapidly from one language to another, and many varieties of the teaching have been handed down.

Tradition says that a council was held immediately after the Buddha's death. This council was concerned with the composition of the monastic discipline, Vinaya. A second council, held at Vaiśālī, is said to have been concerned with disputes about the severity of the monastic rules. A third council was reportedly called by the emperor Aśoka about 250 BCE. Some versions of the tradition say that this council completed the ratification of the canon of Buddhist scriptures and sent missionaries to various countries.

As source material for understanding the relationship between Buddhism and the state, and also the issues of orthodoxy and heterodoxy within Buddhism, the chronicles of Sri Lanka, whose earliest written form dates from approximately the fourth century CE, are useful. The norm for the monastic practices was the Vinaya, the code for monastic life believed to have been transmitted directly from the Buddha.

With respect to sectarianism, the Vinaya provides that, when four or more monks within a monastery differ from the others, they may leave and found their own monastery. This has made possible the development of many perspectives within Buddhism. It is the discipline of the order that maintains the unity. In Sri Lanka in the early period two large monasteries tended to dominate Buddhist life and practice: the Mahāvihāra and the Abhayagiri. In his *History of Buddhism in Ceylon* (Colombo, 1956) Walpola Rahula writes: "The Mahāvihāra . . . was faithful to the very letter of the orthodox teachings and traditions accepted by the Theravādins. The Abhayagiri monks, therefore, appeared in the eyes of the Mahāvihāra to be unorthodox and heretic" (p. 85).

At certain points in the history of Sri Lanka, one or the other of the major monasteries might be in favor, depending on the predilections of the ruler. These incidents indicate that in Buddhism, as in other traditions, the political leaders have exercised considerable control over what shall be deemed orthodox or acceptable. On the other hand, if the rulers unduly outrage the traditional values of the people, they can be in difficulty.

The sixth great Buddhist council was held in Rangoon, Burma, in 1954–1956. It reedited the Buddhist scripture and promoted movements of mutual understanding among Buddhists from different historical traditions. An ecumenical movement among Buddhists has developed, as indicated by the founding of the World Fellowship of Buddhists in 1950. Lay followers are more active in the modern period. Historically the monastic orders have dominated education and the transmission of the scriptures, but under modern conditions this is no longer the case.

Fundamentalism has been a prominent feature of the twentieth-century Sōka Gakkai. This group follows Nichiren's teaching as to the importance of one scripture only and advocates political activism as a way of imposing Buddhist virtues.

Chinese Religion. Religious life in China has been shaped since the earliest known dynasty (Shang, c. 1600 BCE) by cults of devotion to ancestors, and by a worldview that has affirmed the necessity of directing human activities toward harmony with the forces implicit in and beyond nature. Almost all schools of Chinese thought have assumed that an encompassing reality, the Tao, maintains balance and harmony among the divergent processes that constitute existence.

The emperor became a central legitimating figure, since he sanctioned the divine order and created or elevated new gods. Unlike in India, then, in China the legitimating power did not lie with priests.

The formative period of religious ferment was that of the Hundred Schools (sixth to third centuries BCE). The issues debated were generally concerned with how to develop individual character so as to overcome the divisive forces that led to social chaos. The two major schools of thought that emerged from these debates, the Confucian and the Taoist, shared the premise that the encompassing Tao existed, and that humans must learn to balance existence appropriately. They differed as to how the balance should be acquired, though neither perspective necessarily excluded the other.

The school that insisted on an exclusive orthodoxy of belief and practice was that of the Legalist, in power during the Ch'in dynasty (221–206 BCE). During this rigid regime, Confucian scholars were killed and books of traditional learning were burned. After this regime's collapse, the succeeding dynasties encouraged Confucianism as the state doctrine—a role it retained until modern times. During the Han period, Confucianism provided the government with a standard code of ritual and moral norms that regulated behavior among persons. Books were preserved, and provided a perspective from ancient days different from the immediate needs of the state. Under the emperor Wu (140–87 BCE) efforts were made to institute a national system of schools and a civil service examination system. Textual orthodoxy was established. The curriculum of the schools consisted of the Confucian classics. The aim was to produce

Confucian sages to serve the emperor and the society as civil servants and moral exemplars.

Judaism. Around the beginning of the fourth century BCE the religious leader Ezra, a priest and a scribe, returned from among the exiles in Babylon to Jerusalem, where he effected a religious reform that shaped subsequent Judaism. These events are recorded in the biblical books of Ezra and Nehemiah. The reconstitution of Judaism that occurred at this time made the scriptures available through the institution of schools and the use of public occasions as opportunities for adult education. The Bible says: "And Ezra the priest brought the law before the assembly, both men and women and all who could hear with understanding . . . and the ears of the people were attentive to the book of the law" (*Neh.* 8:2–3).

This reconstitution of Judaism gives a teaching function to the scribes (the scholars of the Law), but it also implies that the people are to appropriate the teachings by their capacity to hear with understanding. Ezra's reforms are said to have reached a climax when the people engaged in solemn covenant to enter into no more mixed marriages, to refrain from work on the Sabbath, to support the Temple, and in general to comply with the demands of the Law. The school of scribes established by Ezra, or in his name, probably instituted a framework of orthodoxy that led eventually to the canonization of the Hebrew scriptures after the destruction of the Temple in 70 CE.

Subsequently, the locus of Judaism became a rabbinic program that stressed study of the scriptures, prayer, and works of piety. Under the leading rabbi, Yehudah ha-Nasi' (135–220?), an effort was made to standardize Jewish practice. The result was the collection of rabbinic lore entitled the Mishnah, which became the primary source of reference and the basis around which the Talmud was later compiled.

Modern Hebrew uses the word *orthodox*, taken directly from the English, since no such term exists in earlier Hebrew. The word for *heterodox* is *min*, which tends to mean "individual deviant." Procedures exist for readmission of deviants. The philosopher Spinoza was excommunicated by rabbinic authorities in Holland in 1656 because of his allegedly dangerous attitudes toward biblical authority. The idea that individuals or groups might have beliefs and practices that threaten the well-being of the tradition has existed in Judaism as far back as we know. In Ezra's times, individuals and groups were excluded from the Temple for various practices considered impure, such as mixed marriages. However, the extent to which exclusion was exercised varied considerably in different historical periods. After the destruction of the Temple, the rabbis rarely excommunicated anyone. In the modern period, exclusion is not considered a significant problem.

Reform Judaism developed in Germany in the 1840s and later appeared in the United States, where it spread widely. The Reform Jewish group first used the term *Orthodox Judaism* to characterize their more traditional conservative opponents. Reform Judaism stressed the individual observance of the moral law rather than strict observance of the traditional legal codes.

Christianity. In the pastoral epistles of the New Testament, the members of the church are called upon to live "in all holy conversation and godliness, looking for and hasting unto the coming of the day of God" (*2 Pt.* 3:11–12). They are warned against "false teachers among you, who privily shall bring in damnable heresies, even denying the Lord that bought them" (*2 Pt.* 2:1).

These and similar passages indicate divisiveness within the early generations of Christians. During the first three centuries, factionalism resulted from conflicts as to purity of conduct, steadfastness under persecution, gnosis, Christology, and practical matters such as the date of Easter. When the emperor Constantine became Christian in the fourth century, he attempted to further unite his territories by promoting a unified perspective among Christians. Under his auspices the Council of Nicaea was summoned in 325, and agreement was reached on disputed matters. Dissident opinions were held to be anathema.

Eastern orthodoxy. A schism took place in 1054 between the Roman Catholic church and the churches of the Eastern Byzantine empire. The Eastern churches see themselves as a fellowship of churches governed by their own head bishops. Today there are fifteen such churches. They claim to have preserved the original apostolic faith, which they believe to have been expressed through the common Christian tradition of the first centuries. They recognize seven ecumenical councils.

Roman Catholicism. The perspective which emerged as orthodox envisaged the bishop of Rome as the primary authority. The authority of the bishops was legitimated by apostolic succession. The importance of the priesthood was linked to the centrality of the ritual of the Eucharist. The historian Eusebius, a contemporary of the emperor Constantine, wrote a history of the church which for centuries legitimated the view that the structures and doctrines of the fourth-century church were equivalent to the original practices and beliefs.

Protestantism. Reformers in the sixteenth century claimed to replace the authority of the Roman Catholic hierarchy with the authority of the Bible. They denied the doctrine of transubstantiation and held ministers to be competent to interpret the scriptures. The teachings of the church councils were to be supported only insofar as they conformed to the scriptures.

With the passage of time, the relationship between the state and the churches in Protestant countries became one of increasing separation. Therefore the differences among Christians were not linked to the need of the state for unity. If Christians differed, they had the option of leaving to establish different forms of Christianity. In the tract *A Plain Account of the People Called Methodist* (1749), John Wesley describes the early Methodists' protest against hierarchical authority legitimated by doctrine: "The points we chiefly insisted upon were four; First, that orthodoxy, or right opinion is, at best, but a very slender part of religion, if it can be allowed to be any part of it at all." The chief business of religion, according to Wesley, was to effect the transformation of consciousness, so that the believer might come to have the mind of Christ.

The Council of Trent. At the Council of Trent (1545–1563) the positions of the Roman Catholic church were reaffirmed. Many of the abuses that had preceded the Reformation were done away with, but the authority of the church hierarchy, the role of the priesthood, and the doctrine of transubstantiation were reasserted. At the same time, anathemas were pronounced against the respective Protestant opinions.

The modern period. Efforts have been made toward further mutual understanding among diverse Christian churches. At the Second Vatican Council (1962–1965), a number of studies reconsidered the roles of clergy and laity, and of biblical teaching with respect to the nature of the church. The forum for Protestant discussion of similar issues has been the World Council of Churches, which meets every six years since its establishment following World War II. It is attended by representatives of the majority of Protestant and Eastern Orthodox churches. Those who established the World Council held that mutual respect might better arise out of mutual knowledge and common action. They have envisaged a long-range process out of which a greater sense of mutuality may emerge, as a result of which historic conflicts may eventually be resolved.

Fundamentalism among Protestants usually affirms the inerrancy of the Bible and insists on one particular interpretation of scripture. Fundamentalist attitudes exist within all the major Protestant denominations.

Islam. One of the Arabic words used as an equivalent for orthodox is *mustaqīm*. It comes from the first surah of the Qur'ān in which the believers are asked to follow the straight path, *al-sirāṭ al-mustaqīm*. In this respect, the straight path is primarily a way to live. Deviance would be a matter of rejecting the divine commands. From the Qur'anic perspective, one who denies is called *kāfir* ("unbeliever," from *kufr*, "ingratitude; unbelief").

The first disputes among Muslims took place about thirty years after the death of the Prophet. These differences centered around the legitimate leadership of the community. After a brief civil war the members divided into two groups, Sunnīs and the Shīʿīs. The former acknowledged the actual leaders of the community to have been legitimate. The latter did not accept any leader apart from the caliph Ali, but rather waited for a divinely appointed leader to reappear and establish justice on the earth. A third group, the Khārijīs, attempted to enforce a strict puritanism as a criterion for membership in the community, but they failed to persuade the majority. With the passage of time, their perspective became insignificant.

Sunnī Islam and Shiism have each developed their own systems of religious law and theology, but neither explicitly excludes the other from Islam. Rather, each sees the other as misguided in its interpretations of particular aspects of Islam.

In one of the Sunnī theological statements commonly used as a basis for training scholar-jurists in the Middle Ages, and in traditional schools today—the *Commentary of al-Taftāzānī on the Creed of al-Nasafī* (trans. Edward Elder, New York, 1950)—heresy is characterized as *bāṭin* (esoteric interpretation of the Qur'ān). Such heresy is said to be equivalent to unbelief. The theologians commenting on the Qur'ān also equate unbelief with despair and with ridiculing the law. They are stating which attitudes they find unacceptable, rather than defining the characteristics that would lead to exclusion. Al-Taftāzānī deals with including great sinners in the community and affirms the Qur'anic emphasis on the forgiveness of God. The community tended to leave final judgment of sinners to God's decision on Judgment Day.

The responsibility for guidance on matters respecting membership in the community lay with jurists rather than with theologians. On occasion, if the civil power was willing to support the opinions of particular scholar-jurists, persons were condemned for their views. More often, the condemnations of scholar-jurists with respect to dissenting opinions carried little force.

Deciding which practices and opinions were considered most adequate was a slow, informal process. There were no equivalents to the Buddhist or Christian councils. Only after the fact could it be determined that a particular perspective had gained widespread support. Even so, adherents of differing opinions were not normally excluded from participation in the community.

Scholar-jurists often used abusive language about one another, but such rhetoric did not usually cause persons to be excluded from communal life.

The procedures by which the religious law, *sharī'ah*, was elaborated involved an appeal to chains of transmitters to legitimate the traditional narratives respecting the words and deeds of the prophet Muḥammad and his companions. This process of legitimation was similar to the Christian and Buddhist appeal to an unbroken line of trusted transmitters of the original teaching.

In the twentieth century Muslims have thrown off foreign domination in every major Muslim nation. The newly independent Muslim states have varied in the ways by which they have adapted the medieval religio-legal codes to modern conditions. A number of individuals have written interpretations of Islam for modern times; two of the most influential have been Syed Ameer Ali and Muhammad Iqbal.

An active form of Muslim fundamentalism has developed in the Arab world, Iran, and the Indo-Pakistan subcontinent. Such groups affirm the urgency of agreement on one interpretation of Islam, and of imposing this interpretation by means of a state controlled by morally upright persons.

[*For a discussion of the diverse ways in which orthodox belief is conceived, see* Truth. *For the consequences of disagreement within a given tradition, see* Schism *and* Expulsion.]

BIBLIOGRAPHY

Peter Berger's *The Heretical Imperative* (Garden City, N.Y., 1979) offers a recent discussion of the issues of orthodoxy in the context of modernity across all traditions. With respect to ritual processes in the conflict between orthodoxy and heterodoxy among nonliterate peoples, see Victor Turner's *The Ritual Process: Structure and Anti-Structure* (1969; Ithaca, N.Y., 1977). A comprehensive survey of Indian religious thought is contained in Surendranath Dasgupta's *History of Indian Philosophy*, 3 vols. (1922–1940; Cambridge, 1963). For modern India, see *Religion in Modern India*, edited by Robert D. Baird (New Delhi, 1981). Sukumar Dutt's *Buddhist Monks and Monasteries of India* (London, 1962) offers a survey of Indian Buddhism. For Chinese thought, Wing-tsit Chan's *A Source Book in Chinese Philosophy* (Princeton, 1963) is excellent. Robert M. Seltzer's *Jewish People, Jewish Thought: The Jewish Experience in History* (New York, 1980) is a good source for Jewish intellectual history. Three books combined together give an excellent introduction to the complex issues of early Christian development: Robert M. Grant's *Augustus to Constantine* (New York, 1970); Robert L. Wilken's *The Myth of Christian Beginnings* (Garden City, N.Y., 1971); and Elaine H. Pagels's *The Gnostic Gospels* (New York, 1979). Kenneth Scott Latourette's *A History of Christianity* (New York, 1953) gives a comprehensive survey. With respect to Islam, Fazlur Rahman's *Islamic Methodology in History* (Karachi, Pakistan, 1965) explains the processes of Islamic reasoning. W. Montgomery Watt's *Islamic Philosophy and Theology*, 2d ed., rev. & enl. (Edinburgh, 1984) describes the main schools of thought. Noel J. Coulson's *A History of Islamic Law* (Edinburgh, 1971) discusses the religio-legal structures. For the modern period, see *Change and the Muslim World*, edited by Phillip H. Stoddard, David C. Cuthell, and Margaret W. Sullivan (Syracuse, N.Y., 1981).

SHEILA MCDONOUGH

ORTHOPRAXY. Derived from the Greek *orthos* ("straight, right") and *praxis* ("doing, practice"), *orthopraxy* refers to "correctness of a practice or a body of practices accepted or recognized as correct," according to *Webster's Third International Dictionary of the English Language*. The term in English is rarely used, having been displaced by the related term *orthodoxy*, from the Greek *orthos* and *doxa* ("opinion, belief"). *Webster's Third* defines *orthodoxy* as "conformity to an official formulation or truth, esp. in religious belief or practice." Thus common English usage assumes that dogma governs practice.

The proclivity of English speakers to think in terms of orthodoxy rather than orthopraxy has historical roots. During the early centuries of the Christian church, the ecumenical councils defined and championed an orthodox creed to quell potentially divisive heresies. During the period of the Reformation, doctrinal interpretation became a battleground for orthodoxy as the various churches strove to reestablish stability in beliefs after a period of ferment and schism. In the modern world, traditional ideologies have their champions, who militantly defend orthodox views against maverick reinterpretations. As a result of this history, Westerners commonly assume that beliefs are the defining core of any religion.

Religions, however, do not begin and end with doctrine. They also entail liturgical, contemplative, or ethical practices as well as direct or mediated experiences of the sacred. If doctrines or beliefs remain the only yardstick by which a religious tradition is measured, other aspects of religious life and experience, which may in certain cases be far more important than belief, will be neglected or ignored.

Orthopraxy provides a nondoctrinal focus for analysis, an alternative model for understanding the functioning of religion in a given community. The concept of orthopraxy helps scholars to broaden their religious imaginations and enhance their religious "musicality," their sensitivity to the full scope and variety of the rhythms, patterns, and harmonies of religious life.

Orthopraxy is a particularly apt term for describing

cases in which written codes of behavior for liturgy and daily life constitute the fundamental obligations of religion. Frederick Streng has called this religious modality "harmony with cosmic law," noting that the codes delineate not only the path of individual piety but also the hierarchical and complementary roles that build a harmonious society.

Judaism, Hinduism, Confucianism, and Islam exemplify Streng's "harmony with cosmic law." The primary religious obligation in these traditions is the observance of a code of ritual and social behavior minutely stipulated in religious texts and in scholarly commentaries as interpreted by the educated religious elite. The code has sacred authority because it was established in ancient times by a god or the revered founder or founders of the tradition. These religions have no creed, no officially sanctioned statement or dogma that holds a key place in liturgy or rites of passage. In these instances religiosity is not primarily a matter of holding correct opinions but of conforming to a set of behaviors.

Orthopraxy is central to the dynamics of religious life in Judaism, Hinduism, Confucianism, and Islam. For instance, in the first three traditions observance of the religious code (orthopraxy) establishes and reinforces the cultural or ethnic identity of the community. These religions do not claim to be universal; each is associated with a specific cultural group.

Cultural and ethnic groups perpetuate their communal identity through distinctive mores based on shared symbols and values that establish behavioral boundaries between themselves and other groups (Royce, 1982). In Judaism, Hinduism, and Confucianism, the practices mandated by the sacred law define the distinctive boundaries of the culture and the identity of the group within a larger world. In these cases religion defines and reaffirms one's cultural roots rather than one's beliefs; religious and cultural identity are inseparable. Observance of the written code also ensures a semblance of unity within each group despite considerable local variations caused by linguistic or regional differences.

At first glance, Islam does not appear to use orthopraxy to maintain an ethnic identity. Islam has not been bound to one ethnic or cultural group; like Christianity and Buddhism it has become a world religion, ranging extensively across the globe among a diversity of peoples. Originally, however, Islam was strongly tied to Arab culture and identity; to become a Muslim one had to join an Arab tribe if one were not favored by Arab birth. Perhaps the original cultural boundedness of Islam, its view of itself as the religion of a distinctive and chosen people, helps to account for the centrality of orthopraxy. To be a Muslim is to accept and observe the law of Allāh. Surrender to Allāh is not a matter of belief in a doctrine; it is a matter of obedience to his commands (Smith, 1963).

Although Qur'anic law no longer maintains the original ethnic boundaries of Islam, it serves to create unity within the Islamic world, thus minimizing very real differences. Sunnī and Shī'ī interpretations of the law differ considerably, and there are local variations in the way in which the law is applied. Observance of the law, however, identifies each community as Muslim. A commitment to orthopraxy binds together all who surrender to Allāh.

In Judaism, Hinduism, Confucianism, and Islam, the sacred law also establishes a standard of religious purity that, along with knowledge of the law, defines a religious and social elite. All members of the culture traditionally were expected to observe the mores of the groups as encoded in the law, but meticulous observance was both the defining quality and the responsibility of the religious elite.

Gradations of ritual purity and observance define and perpetuate the hierarchical structure of Hindu society. Upper-caste Hindus have heavier ritual responsibilities and are expected to maintain an elevated standard of purity. Likewise, groups seeking recognition of increased social status in Hindu society must raise the level of their ritual purity. Thus in Hindu culture, the sacred law establishes a standard for both individuals and groups (Dumont, 1967).

Although Jewish, Confucian, and Islamic cultures were not characterized by the elaborately graduated ritual hierarchy of the Hindu caste system, scrupulous observance of the law and knowledge of tradition were the responsibility of the social and religious elite nonetheless. In China, the law or ritual code dealt primarily with social ethics, the standard of a humane and civilized society. However, it also prescribed ritual obligations in regard to the mourning and veneration of ancestors. The mandarin was to be the model of the civilized moral person, with a profound sense of obligation to family and community. In Judaism and Islam, the law defined a complete way of life: ritual observance, dietary code, ethics, familial and marriage practices. The rabbi in Judaism and the *'ulamā'* in Islam were scholars and teachers who embodied and interpreted the law to their congregations.

In traditions in which the observance of the law is the central religious obligation, orthopraxy establishes and maintains ethnic or religious boundaries and gradations of social and religious purity. However, orthopraxy functions in a broad range of religious traditions and circumstances. An examination of selected examples will illustrate the variety of roles orthopraxy plays in the religions of the world.

In tribal cultures, orthopraxy defines not only religious obligations; it is also the law of the tribe. Its sacred and secular functions are barely distinguishable. The tribal rulers and the ritual specialists are usually two distinct groups; yet, because they share a common tradition and sense of orthopraxy, religion and government support each other. Religion and the state can cooperate in full harmony only in a religiously homogeneous community. When religious pluralism becomes the norm, secular law must develop along autonomous principles to apply equally to all citizens, whatever their religion.

Even in large-scale and complex societies, such as pre-Mughal India or traditional China, sacred law can have an intimate connection to sovereign authority and the secular law, if one religion is overwhelmingly dominant or has established an unassailable claim as the state ideology. The Indian and Chinese rulers were not themselves the religious elite, but their sovereignty and ruling effectiveness were shaped and supported by the sacred code.

In China, Confucianism remained the official state religion and ideology until 1911, and its values were enforced by law, although Buddhism, Taoism,.Nestorianism, Islam, Judaism, and Christianity were present as well. The state accepted the existence of other religions as long as they made no claim to be the law of the land. When Taoists, Muslims, or Buddhists occasionally tried to supplant Confucian mores with their own, they were charged with rebellion and chastised by the full military power of the state.

The Chinese saw no threat in the coexistence of religions, even when two religions coexisted within the life of a single citizen. Most Chinese, in fact, combined Confucian values and practices with Buddhism, Taoism, or some other religion. Each religion, however, had its proper place in the hierarchy of the social order. As an old saying goes, "Taoism cures the body; Buddhism regulates the mind; Confucianism governs the state." Thus the Chinese found a means to reconcile religious pluralism with the maintenance of a sacred code and orthopraxy, a reconciliation that served as the basis of the Chinese social order for two millennia.

Orthodoxy and orthopraxy are also factors in the process of communal religious renewal. The history of religions offers endless variations on the theme of renewal as communities struggle to recapture the freshness and power of their tradition. Belief and practice are subject to continual reinterpretation by the religious elite, who revise their understanding of tradition according to ongoing experience, and by ordinary people, who believe and practice their religion in ways that reflect their individual, social, and historical circumstances. What makes beliefs or practices correct *(orthos)* is the consensus of the living community in a particular social and historical circumstance. In every religious drama, from everyday worship to grand ceremony, the actors negotiate the meanings and practices according to their collective and personal experiences.

Orthopraxy and orthodoxy become issues because religion and its meanings are social and shared. Private belief and experience neither mediated through the symbols of tradition nor authenticated by the living religious community isolate the individual; private belief is socially meaningless, often perceived as fantasy, or even madness. The ongoing process of religious socialization is the mediation of belief, the negotiation of significance. Collective perceptions, however, are fluid; they evolve with time and circumstances, and thus religious traditions are constantly renewed and reinterpreted.

Pluralistic cultures are torn by competing claims of orthodoxy and orthopraxy. The issue of orthopraxy dominates religious competition in sectarian groups that seek to separate themselves from a corrupt, misguided, and tainted society. Their members retreat into communities marked by a strict and demanding religious life. The Amish and the Shakers, among other groups, rejected the larger Christian culture, considering its laws and religious life fallen and depraved. They sought to live out their vision of a pure Christian life, abjuring the taint of sinful society. Members of their community who did not follow the discipline were first reproved, then shunned, and finally expelled. Correct living was the measure of the religious life.

Similar in some ways to the Amish and the Shakers, although not sectarian in intent, are the religious orders of the Roman Catholic church or the *saṃgha* of Buddhism. These communities of individuals choose the religious life in response to a special vocation; they renounce the pleasures and ties of the material world, such as sex and property, in order to live a life of purity and contemplation. Their exemplary lives of sacrifice and discipline were traditionally believed to benefit the broader community and not just themselves.

Orthopraxy can support the secular arm of the state or the rebellion of a sectarian movement. It can be a force for change or for repression of change. At times, the powerful forces for change threaten traditional values, and religious communities may hold tightly to an orthopraxy in order to maintain traditional values, as among contemporary Iranian Muslims and some Christian groups in the United States. At other times, orthopraxy evolves along with community acceptance of new realities and values, as in the loosening of regulations on drinking and card playing among American Methodists in the mid-twentieth century or the changes in Catholicism following Vatican II. An earlier example of this is the acceptance of married clergy among Pure

Land Buddhists in Japan since the thirteenth century. Orthopraxy may even serve the cause of progressive social change, as it does for many twentieth-century liberation theologians. This group sees praxis, action, and reflection on action as the core of the Christian life and they believe that correct practice (orthopraxy) is directed toward liberating the oppressed and reducing suffering in the world.

The concept of orthopraxy helps the student of religion to avoid excessive emphasis on the doctrinal model of religions, but a word of caution is in order. In most cases orthopraxy and orthodoxy are intimately connected and represent two interrelated aspects of religious life. Belief and practice at once entail and support each other.

While orthopraxy is more important than orthodoxy in tribal religions, the "ways of the gods or ancestors" are based on stories or beliefs about what the gods or ancestors did or said. These practices are not merely a random set of behaviors; they express a worldview, a coherent story of the community and its relationship to the world it knows. Likewise, there is no motivation for following a ritually correct or pure life in Judaism, Hinduism, Confucianism, or Islam without belief in and about the God or gods or sages who handed down the law. The law is rooted in and implies a particular view of the sacred, of human life, and of the world. There is no ritual behavior that is not also the expression of certain beliefs about the relationship of the human and the divine, the relationship of ordinary action and sacred command.

While belief and practice are intimately connected, it is not the case that one always dominates the other. Some religions under certain conditions stress that belief leads to practice. Other religions, such as Confucianism, stress that practice leads to and deepens belief and understanding. The student of religion must carefully observe how doctrine and practice complement and correct each other in each unique historical circumstance.

[*For a related discussion, see* Orthodoxy and Heterodoxy; *see also* Heresy.]

BIBLIOGRAPHY

In his article "Orthodoxy," in the *Encyclopaedia of Religion and Ethics,* edited by James Hastings, vol. 9 (Edinburgh, 1917), William A. Curtis noted that ". . . since religion embraces feeling and activity as well as thought, orthodoxy becomes an inadequate criterion of its worth apart from right experience and right conduct. It ought to have for its correlatives such words as 'orthopathy' and 'orthopraxy,' the inward experience and outward exercise of piety." Wilfred Cantwell Smith argues forcefully that observance of the law, and not belief, is the *sine qua non* of Islam; see Smith's *The Meaning and End of Religion: A New Approach to Religious Traditions* (New York, 1963). Frederick J. Streng has gone further to define the religious modality of "harmony with cosmic law," in which orthopraxy dominates religious life; consult his *Understanding Religious Life,* 2d ed. (Encino, Calif., 1976).

A number of anthropologists have explored the ways in which religious practices and mores serve to define the ethnic or cultural boundaries of a community. In *Ethnic Identity: Strategies of Diversity* (Bloomington, Ind., 1982), Anya P. Royce provides a review of the literature and offers an articulate analysis of strategies for maintaining ethnic identity. Barbara E. Ward demonstrates how local regions and communities within cultures unified by a standard of behavior consider their variations on the universal mores in the realm of orthopraxy; see her "Varieties of the Conscious Model: The Fishermen of South China," in *The Relevance of Models for Social Anthropology,* edited by Michael Banton (New York, 1965).

Louis Dumont explores how standards of ritual and behavioral purity establish and maintain social differences in his now-classic *Homo Hierarchicus: An Essay on the Caste System,* rev. ed. (Chicago, 1980). For a Marxist analysis of orthopraxy, see Pierre Bourdien's *Outline of a Theory of Praxis* (Cambridge, 1979).

JUDITH A. BERLING

OSIRIS, the ancient Egyptian god of the dead, whose myth was one of the best known and whose cult was one of the most widespread in pharaonic Egypt. The mythology of Osiris is not preserved completely from an early date, but allusions to it from the earliest extant religious texts indicate that the essentials of the story are as related by Plutarch in *On Isis and Osiris.*

As the oldest son of Geb ("earth"), Osiris became ruler of the land, but he was tricked and slain by his jealous brother, Seth. According to the Greek version of the story, Typhon (Seth) had a beautiful coffin made to Osiris' exact measurements and, with seventy-two conspirators at a banquet, promised it to the one who would fit it. Each guest tried it for size, and of course Osiris was the one to fit exactly. Immediately Seth and the conspirators nailed the lid shut, sealed the coffin in lead, and threw it into the Nile. The coffin was eventually borne across the sea to Byblos, where Isis, who had been continually searching for her husband, finally located it. After some adventures of her own, she returned the body to Egypt, where Seth discovered it, cut it into pieces, and scattered them throughout the country. Isis, however, found all the pieces (except the penis, which she replicated), reconstituted the body, and, before embalming it to give Osiris eternal life, revivified it, coupled with it, and thus conceived Horus. According to the principal version of the story cited by Plutarch, Isis had already given birth to her son, but according to the Egyptian *Hymn to Osiris,* she conceived him by the revivified corpse of her husband. Although Seth challenged the legitimacy of Isis' son, the gods decided in favor of Horus. The *Contendings of Horus and Seth* is preserved on a late New Kingdom papyrus, which indicates that Re, the chief god, favored Seth, but all the other great gods supported the cause of Horus. In the actual contest, Horus proved himself the more clever god. Horus avenged and succeeded his father without completely destroying Seth, toward whom Isis showed pity.

The popularity of the cult of Osiris is explained in part by the recurring cycle of kingship, with each dead king becoming Osiris and being succeeded by his son, Horus. The cult was also important because of its emphasis on the resurrection of the god and a blessed afterlife. The Coffin Texts and the *Book of Going Forth by Day* provided the knowledge necessary for any individual to share in the afterlife of Osiris. This judgment is based on the protestations of innocence by the individual and a weighing of the person's heart against the feather of truth *(maat).* The resurrection of the god is also associated with fertility, and pictures and figures of the god sprouting grain have been found among funerary furnishings. A further aspect of his fertility is his identification with the Nile River. His "effluvium," mentioned frequently in earlier religious literature, was identified by Plutarch as the flooding of the river, and New Kingdom hymns to the Nile equate it with Osiris.

There were numerous cult centers of Osiris; this is explained mythically either by the burial places of the fourteen (or sixteen) parts of his body or by Isis' attempt to conceal the real burial place from Seth. Busiris was the town of his birth, and Abydos was the necropolis generally believed to have been the place of his burial. It was at Abydos that the greatest number of shrines and stelae were set up in honor of the god and to seek blessings from him. A common scene in the funeral rites depicted on nobles' tombs in the New Kingdom commemorated a pilgrimage with the mummy by boat to Abydos.

Osiris was usually depicted as a mummified figure, but he was often represented by a column with eyes and occasionally arms (a form probably borrowed from the god Ptah). [*See* Iconography, *article on* Egyptian Religions.] Osiris had numerous epithets, including "ruler of eternity," "lord of the west," and "the weary one." The Apis bull, perhaps thought to have been an image of Osiris, was kept at Memphis. When it died, it was buried at Saqqara in the Serapeum, and a search was undertaken to find a calf replacement with the required markings. This cult of the Ạpis, known since the eighteenth dynasty, became more developed in the Late Period, and eventually a new cult of Serapis, combining some aspects of Osiris and Apis, became very popular in the Ptolemaic and Roman periods.

BIBLIOGRAPHY

Griffiths, J. Gwyn. *The Origins of Osiris and His Cult.* Rev. & enl. ed. Studies in the History of Religions, vol. 40. Leiden, 1980.

Otto, Eberhard. *Osiris und Amun: Kult und heilige Stätten.* Munich, 1966. Translated by Kate B. Griffiths as *Ancient Egyptian Art: The Cult of Osiris and Amon* (New York, 1967).

LEONARD H. LESKO

OSTIAK RELIGION. *See* Khanty and Mansi Religion; *see also* Finno-Ugric Religions *and* Southern Siberian Religions.

OSTRACISM. *See* Expulsion.

OTHERWORLD. The belief that human beings are in touch with several dimensions of reality is nearly universal. Indeed, for many cultural groups and most religious ones, the nonphysical world is far more real and important than the material one. In most cultures it is believed that those who have died move into another dimension of reality and that the living can experience the presence of the deceased as well as other aspects of the nonphysical realm. Sometimes this belief is clearly articulated; sometimes it can best be observed by witnessing the rituals that people perform. Often, what people believe is better evaluated by what they do than by what they say they believe.

The available material on the nature and quality of the otherworld has grown to voluminous proportions as anthropological studies have added to the data over the last hundred years. There are only a limited number of disparate points of view concerning its essential nature, yet there is an amazing wealth of difference in specific details. Nearly every large cultural or religious group, from archaic times to the present, has one or another of these points of view concerning the otherworld. The attitude of the religious expert differs from that of the well-informed member of the group, and the latter in turn differs from the basically unconscious attitudes of the large majority of participants in a belief system. Some of the greatest works of literature describe this otherworld in detail, among them the *Epic of Gilgamesh* of Babylon, the *Bhagavadgītā* of India, the Tibetan *Book of the Great Liberation,* several of Plato's dialogues, Vergil's *Aeneid,* Dante's *Commedia,* and Goethe's *Faust.* On the other hand, B. F. Skinner's popular *Walden Two* (New York, 1948) presents a view of a world with no otherworld as counterpart.

In order to cover this enormous wealth of material, I shall deal first of all with seven quite different understandings of the otherworld. Communion with this dimension of reality on the part of specific groups will then be examined. Recent nonreligious studies and evidence for the reality of this domain will be surveyed, along with a brief discussion of the worldviews underlying these different conceptions.

Varieties of Belief. In many cultures the otherworld is viewed as a shadowy state, gray and dull. In some groups the soul, or shade, of the person is believed to continue to live near the site of the burial. Ancient Roman and popular Chinese beliefs and rituals suggest that the ghost of the person is envious of living human beings and needs to be placated with offerings of food and other gifts. Some groups believe that the departed spirit of a person lingers near the corpse and renders it unclean. The Navajo practice of abandoning the dwelling in which a death occurs shows the fear with which many view the denizens of the otherworld. Furthermore, the modern fear of haunted places and the interest in ghosts found in nearly all cultures lingers in many of us.

In still another stratum of belief, these unhappy shades are collected together in one place, usually an underworld, to which they pass directly down from the grave. [*See* Underworld.] It is a dull, colorless place of half-existence. The Babylonians viewed the place of the dead very much as the Hebrews viewed She'ol, a place of diminished existence where there is no contact with Yahveh. The Homeric Hymns portray the same kind of place. For Dante, this place is described as limbo, where the righteous pagans must remain.

Edgar Herzog's excellent study *Psyche and Death* (New York, 1967) traces the psychological development of the understanding of afterlife from fear of the dead to a more happy view of the deceased and the otherworld. The life of the deceased from this viewpoint is seen as being much the same as a full life in this world. The otherworld contains the best of human pleasures and joys. There is also a belief that the next world will be much better than this one, with greener grass, more beautiful flowers, and a more positive relation with the divine reality. Raymond Moody's *Life After Life* (Atlanta, 1975) and Karlis Osis's *At the Hour of Death* (New York, 1977) describe dying and near-death experiences, report contacts with deceased, and give a largely optimistic picture of the otherworld. This view is found throughout the world—among some Bantu-speaking peoples and many Polynesian tribes, as well as among some American Indians; it is represented in modern times by nonreligious research into the otherworld.

The most common view of the otherworld gives a picture of several different realms: a highly desirable heaven or heavens, many varieties of fearful and horrible states, and intermediate states through which one passes to arrive at the final destination. [*See* Heaven and Hell.] The quality of the dying person determines the realm of the otherworld into which he will pass. In some cultures the status of the deceased determines the outcome: a warrior killed in battle, a king, or a chief has easy access to the realm of bliss. In later Greek religion some of the heroes were able to escape Hades and enter the realm of the gods, a blissful otherworld. This view implies a soul that is immortal or at least long-lasting; the body is seen as only the temporary carrier of the soul. Mircea Eliade has demonstrated in his monumental study of archaic techniques of ecstasy, *Shamanism* (Princeton, 1964), that this view of a permanent core of humanness and a realm into which it can pass is found all over the globe and reaches back into prehistoric times. The shaman can leave the body through ecstasy and trance and enter the otherworld. The shaman can, therefore, become the guide of the dying, who must make a perilous journey into the otherworld. The dying can also step into this other dimension to bring back souls lost there and so bring healing to those whose sickness has been caused by a disturbed relation with the otherworld.

One enters this otherworld by way of a journey, passing through difficulties and tests, often crossing a bridge that is razor-sharp. In Hinduism, Islam, some forms of Buddhism, ancient Iranian religion, and Christianity, this journey and the places visited are described using earthly symbols, but the otherworld is perceived as another dimension of reality. Less reflective thinkers in these traditions retain a geocentric point of view, picturing heaven as above and hell as below the earth. Others believe that the entrance into the otherworld is put off until the end of time, when the dead will rise and take their places in a reconstituted heavenly earth or in the abyss or will even be annihilated.

Coming to the place of bliss and avoiding the state of torment can be accomplished in numerous ways. A skilled shaman may help to effect the passage. In Islam, knowing the right formula for acknowledging God may be more significant than the quality of moral or religious practice. In Christianity, having the last rites properly performed and confessing one's sins before death are important factors. The ultimate nature of the otherworld and the powers within it determine one's place there.

In both Hinduism and Buddhism, there is another important aspect of belief in the otherworld. The nonphysical, spiritual dimension is the only reality; religious illumination consists in coming to realize this truth and then, on the basis of this realization, becoming detached from the illusion *(māyā)* of this physical world, which keeps one from fulfillment in the real world. This is achieved by spiritual and moral discipline, well exemplified in the life of Gandhi. Much the same point of view is found in gnosticism, in which the physical world is not only unreal but evil. It is irredeemable and can only be escaped by a process of knowledge *(gnōsis)* and asceticism. By the same process one enters progressively higher levels of an eternal spiritual dimension.

Belief in reincarnation or the transmigration of souls is found associated with both these points of view. Those who do not escape from the bondage of evil or the illusory material world are reborn again and again into this world. They are reborn according to their *karman,* a moral and spiritual accounting of one's life. *Karman* automatically determines the fate of the individual in the next reincarnation; rebirth can bring one into a higher or lower human state or even into an animal existence. The goal of this process is to be released from this agonizing, continuing reimmersion in the illusory material world, thus passing into heaven as a godlike being or entering *nirvāṇa*. This view has filtered down into popular thought in many Eastern cultures, and, as difficult as it is for Westerners to believe, for many of these people the otherworld is more real and important than this one.

Heaven is pictured in a welter of vivid images in the literature and in the art and sculpture characteristic of Hinduism and Buddhism. Hindu and Buddhist temples portray the real world of the gods throughout East Asia. This exciting, richly colored world is worth the moral and spiritual discipline required to become emotionally uninvolved and detached from concern with outer physical illusion. At the end of the great Hindu epic called the *Rāmāyaṇa,* the hero leaves his beloved wife so that he can come to the detachment necessary for spiritual advancement in the otherworld.

The Buddhist conception of *nirvāṇa* is unique and important; it presents a conception diametrically opposed to the richly sensuous picture of heaven presented by Hinduism and most other world religions. *Nirvāṇa* is described mainly in negatives. If, indeed, the physical world is illusion, so is the human ego, which clearly differentiates the contents of that world. According to Zen and many other schools of Buddhism, the distinction between subject and object disappears in the enlightened person. The individual becomes one with reality and merges into it. It is therefore impossible to give any significant descriptions of this ultimate state.

Many statements about *nirvāṇa* sound as if the individual was annihilated, whereas others describe *nirvāṇa* as a state of ecstatic bliss. Illumination is a taste of *nirvāṇa* for the living. Images can be another form of illusion. Thus, the path toward enlightenment leads through imageless (apophatic) prayer to an imageless fulfillment that cannot be described except in saying what the earthly condition is not. [*See* Nirvāṇa.]

The major world religions (with the exception of Buddhism) perceive inner and outer images as revealing reality rather than hiding it. Various schools in each tradition describe heaven as a place of transformation, where people are gradually or suddenly changed into the quality and likeness of the god image, becoming more and more like Allāh, Kṛṣṇa, Yahveh, or Christ. In some versions this process goes on into eternity; while in certain forms of Hinduism, after a very long time the universe returns to its divided condition, and the whole cycle repeats itself. Heaven and hell are understood by some religious thinkers as a process and by others as a static condition. Important thinkers in most traditions emphasize the inadequacy of all human descriptions of the otherworld.

The last major view about the otherworld is simply that there is none. This very important conception has dominated the Western world for several centuries and has deeply influenced Christianity. The same point of view has been held by the realistic philosophical schools in China described by Arthur Waley in *Three Ways of Thought in Ancient China* (New York, 1939). However, it is only in the cultures of Western Europe and those that derived from them that this worldview has been fully developed and has achieved wide acceptance. A few archaic cultures, including the people of Kiwai on the Fly River in New Guinea, the Fuegians, and some Bantu-speaking peoples, have little or no conception of any other world than this physical one.

The Western attitude is important because it is based on the philosophical premise that the only reality is physical or material. The only means of coming into contact with reality is through the five senses, which can be clearly differentiated, as described by Descartes in his *Discourse on the Method of Rightly Conducting the Reason* (1637). The major thrust of Western thought has been in this direction and is well exemplified in the writings of A. J. Ayer, B. F. Skinner, and Konrad Lorenz. Marxism denies the value of any world except the one created on this earth through revolution by the proleteriat. From this frame of reference, any concept of an otherworld is considered illusory, primitive (in the sense of infantile), premodern, and even dangerous. It is for this reason that the subject of otherworld is so largely ignored in modern Western culture and the recent modern evidence for the continued existence of the deceased is passed over and rejected.

If the materialistic worldview is accepted uncritically, it is quite natural to view all the data on the otherworld as of archaeological interest only. However, starting in about 1900, developments in scientific thought led to the questioning of rational materialism as a viable hypothesis. The materialist point of view is not able to account for the available data on many subjects and the evidence for otherworld in particular. In *Encounter with God* (Minneapolis, 1972) and *Afterlife* (New York, 1979), I have presented the development of this thought in detail.

Communion with the Dead. The basic worldview of a person or culture will largely determine the way the otherworld is viewed. From the point of view of Eastern religion and philosophy, the physical world is illusory and the otherworld real, and heaven or *nirvāṇa* is the goal to be sought. According to Platonism (the philosophical base for early Christianity) and the modern view of C. G. Jung, human beings participate both in a material universe and in a nonmaterial one. Thus, both the otherworld and this world are important aspects of total reality. Human wholeness depends on dealing adequately with each domain. Both moral actions (as in, for instance, learning to love) and specifically religious practices are essential to human wholeness.

In both of these points of view, the human person is more than just a physical organism operating mechanically or through conditioning. The psyche (or soul) is a complex nonphysical reality sharing the reality of a multifaceted nonphysical otherworld. The psyche can be viewed as preexistent (which leads to the idea of reincarnation) or as created at conception or birth. In both Islamic and Christian thinking, the soul is viewed as having vegetative, appetitive, intellectual, and spiritual aspects. In the views of some thinkers, only the spiritual or intellectual aspects survive in the otherworld. The Christian doctrine of the resurrection of the body maintains that most aspects of the personal nonphysical being are preserved and transformed.

In most cultures (not influenced by materialism), contact with the deceased is a part of religious practice. Eliade shows that one of the principal functions of living shamans is to pass over into the otherworld, return, and then help other people deal with both dimensions. Some shamans have mediumistic abilities and can bring back the dead, as the medium of Endor brought forth the ghost of Samuel at Saul's bidding (*1 Sm.* 28:6ff.). Once belief in an otherworld eroded in Christian cultures influenced by materialism, there was a spontaneous, popular resurgence of the practice of spiritualism, which brings the seeker into contact with the deceased through mediums and their controls.

The belief in ongoing contact with the spirits of the deceased is widespread in this and most countries. [*See* Necromancy.] Sometimes these visitations are frightening, and at other times helpful or even numinous. J. B. Phillips, the British New Testament scholar, reports in *The Ring of Truth* (New York, 1967) that C. S. Lewis appeared to him and helped him translate a difficult passage of the Bible. The Christian doctrine of the communion of saints maintains that communion between the living and the dead is possible to those who are deeply rooted within the Christian fellowship. The same idea is found in Islam and Hinduism. These experiences of meeting the deceased, inhabitants of the otherworld, can occur either spontaneously, through religious rituals (particularly highly developed in China), through the trance condition, or through dreams and visions.

Modern Evidence. With the publication of Moody's *Life after Life* in 1975, a new surge of interest arose concerning reported experiences of an otherworld and of those who existed in it. Moody's study is a careful one; this well-trained philosopher and psychiatrist is cautious not to claim more than his evidence warrants. His work was followed by that of Karlis Osis and Elendur Haraldsson's *At the Hour of Death* (New York, 1977), Michael Sabom's *Recollections of Death* (New York, 1981), and Kenneth Ring's *Life at Death* (New York, 1980). This data has been collected by medical doctors and trained psychologists; Ring's work is a careful statistical study of the data.

Many different kinds of evidence can be studied once one is no longer bound by a materialistic worldview. Some people appear to die clinically and return to life, to report a series of experiences in which they go through a process of detachment from the body, experience an otherworld, sometimes meet deceased friends, relate to a being of light, and arrive at a boundary that they cannot cross if they are to return to life.

People who are at the point of death and who then die are occasionally observed to be participating in both this world and the other one simultaneously, and give reports similar to those who have had near-death experiences. Numerous reports have been studied of encounters with people from the other side. Supporting the possibility of these reports is the development of parapsychology, which suggests that we have faculties other than the five senses for obtaining information. In

Doors of Perception (New York, 1970), Aldous Huxley suggests a theory of perception based on the thinking of Bergson, which states that we are in touch with many dimensions of reality but that the five senses block our contact with these dimensions, tying us to the physical world. Franz Riklin, a follower of C. G. Jung, has stated that the dreams of the dying usually treat the physical death of the individual as of little significance. Within the framework of Einstein's theory of relativity, physical death loses its finality, because time appears to be relative and not absolute. Some who practice meditation maintain that they are in contact with an otherworld and experience much of what has been described here. Poetic imagination also seems to give access to some other dimension.

Christianity and the Afterlife. Little of the foregoing data has been discovered by those primarily interested in Christianity. Indeed, some of this evidence has been resisted by certain theologians who state that belief in the otherworld is based on faith and acceptance of dogma, rather than on experience. In recent years, there has been very little written on the subject of heaven, hell, or the afterlife by Christian theologians. Some academic Christian thinkers maintain that profession of Christianity need not entail the belief in an afterlife or otherworld. Within the wide range of Christian belief and practice, one can find nearly all of the attitudes toward the otherworld that have been described above.

There is, first of all, an academic skepticism that either denies or ignores this aspect of reality. For some scholars, what is continuously ignored is usually of little value or concern. At the other extreme is the archaic belief in the dull, shadowy existence of the deceased and their ghostly presence at the place of death or burial. Many Christians have a view of the otherworld as a place only of bliss, which is unrelated to one's actions or beliefs. Others accept the traditional dichotomy between heaven and hell, while yet others believe in purgatory as a transitional state between the two. For some, the afterlife begins at the millennium, on a rejuvenated and transformed earth; others still imagine a heaven somewhere in the sky (although this image has become difficult to maintain, because of modern space travel). Others regard these different aspects of the otherworld as other dimensions of reality, seeing sensory images of it as purely symbolic. Still other Christians believe in reincarnation and all that it entails. Some see the otherworld as a place of continued growth and development in the presence of divine mind or divine love. This variety of beliefs is found in the other major world religions as well as Christianity.

There is almost total consensus among the religions and cultures of humankind that human beings are not totally extinguished at death and that there is continuing experience in an otherworld. Human beings are also given occasional experiences of this dimension and those continuing to exist in it. These varied views of the nature of an otherworld can be traced historically and cross-culturally; perhaps they may ultimately constitute different aspects of a reality too large for any one description.

[*See also* Supernatural, The, *and* Afterlife.]

BIBLIOGRAPHY

Dante Alighieri. *The Comedy of Dante Alighieri, the Florentine.* 3 vols. Translated by Dorothy Sayers and Barbara Reynolds. New York, 1962. The classic Christian treatment, with excellent notes and an introduction by the translators.

Eliade, Mircea. *Shamanism.* Rev. & enl. ed. New York, 1964. The authoritative study of the shaman and the technique of ecstasy by which the otherworld is mediated. Provides a cross-cultural worldview with a place for an otherworld.

Encyclopaedia of Religion and Ethics. 13 vols. Edited by James Hastings. Edinburgh, 1908–1926. Contains a wealth of detailed accounts of the otherworld in "State of the Dead" and many associated articles. Must be consulted with care because of its moralistic, Christian, and materialistic bias.

Herzog, Edgar. *Psyche and Death.* Translated by David Cox and Eugene Rolfe. New York, 1967. An excellent anthropological and psychological study of human concepts of death and the otherworld.

Jung, C. G. *Psychology and Religion: West and East.* Translated by R. F. C. Hull. New York, 1958. Provides a philosophical and psychological framework for understanding religious texts on the otherworld. Offers excellent commentary on the Tibetan *Book of the Dead* and the *Book of the Great Liberation.*

Kelsey, Morton. *Afterlife: The Other Side of Dying.* New York, 1979. The only modern Christian study providing a worldview for the otherworld and the recent nonreligious evidence for continued existence. Presents a picture of the otherworld for a critical modern reader. Contains an extensive bibliography.

Parabola (New York), vol. 2, no. 1 (1977). The entire issue deals with the subject of death and otherworld. A comprehensive cross-cultural, up-to-date overview.

Ring, Kenneth. *Life at Death.* New York, 1980. A comprehensive examination of the near-death experience with a careful statistical study.

Smith, Huston. *The Religions of Man.* New York, 1958. A short but careful and inclusive study of the major religions of humankind.

MORTON KELSEY

OTOMÍ RELIGION. The Otomí Indians of central Mexico, who speak a language of the Oto-Manguean phylum, number approximately 250,000. They occupy a vast territory located between 19° and 21° north latitude and 98° and 100° west longitude. This area, characterized by stark geographical contrasts, stretches from the steep mountain masses of the Sierra Gorda to the semiarid Mezquital plateaus, and from the Toluca Valley to the rolling hills of the Huastecan piedmont. In addition to the different sociocultural patterns that have emerged from this mosaic of environments, the blending of Indian culture with folk Catholicism from the colonial period to the present day has yielded a syncretic religion that is dominated by Christianity but includes specific forms of dualism that set the Otomí symbolic universe apart from its colonial influences.

There is little information on the origins of the Otomí, and their role in shaping the great Mesoamerican systems of thought remains unexplored. Subjects of the Aztec empire from the fifteenth century to the conquest, the Otomí came under its sway everywhere except in the outlying eastern regions (Tutotepec, Huayacoctla). Since then, Otomí religious activities have been constrained to a clandestinity favored by the dispersal of their settlements. They have come to center primarily on local patrilineal cults (agrarian fertility rites and ancestor worship), while their ceremonial and liturgical calendar continues to reflect patterns of thought similar to those of the Aztecs on the eve of conquest.

Throughout the colonial period and down to the twentieth century, their particularly fluid social organization, built on a network of patrilineagical shrines, has allowed the Otomí to resist evangelization. Yet, devotions to Roman Catholic saints coexist with native rituals and sometimes, as in the Sierra Madre, serve to camouflage them. The focal points of this dual religious life are the home, the shrines, and the sacred mountain, on the one hand, and chapels and village churches, on the other. These different ritual spaces are arranged in a hierarchy that parallels a cosmic vision of different "skins" *(ši)*, or sacred places (from the uterine cavity to the celestial vault), symbolically enclosed within each other.

At each level of the cosmic hierarchy there are correspondences based on fundamental male-female polarity. Thus, at the uppermost level of space, the sun and the moon form a complementary and antagonistic pair. The moon (Zâna), however, presents a complex and disquieting image to the Otomí. While in her syncretistic form Zâna is feminine and is associated with the Virgin of Guadalupe, in the indigenous cosmological system the moon displays a complex of complementary characteristics, including dual gender: it represents feminine characteristics (childbirth, sensuality, weaving, computing of time, death) as well as masculine ones (erection, mastery of women and their fertility). While the moon is the antagonistic counterpart to the masculine sun, it also embodies within itself the complementary forces. Further, as the heavenly counterpart to the earth goddess Hmûhoi, Zâna helps govern both creation and destruction.

The conception of a nighttime creation continues to power the Otomí imagination. One of the oldest Mesoamerican deities, the Otomí fire god known in the Aztec pantheon as Otontecuhtli ("the Otomí lord") is believed to govern, as he did in times past, the order of things. He is Šihta Sipi ("the ancestor who devours excrement"), the purifying principle whose presence marks the emergence of culture (associated with cooked food). He is also the preeminent lord of nocturnal spaces and grottoes, the realm of an imaginary world that mirrors in miniature the world of men.

To understand the logic of the oppositions that inform Otomí cosmology, it is helpful to understand the model on which they are based: the human body. As a receptacle for the field of forces animating the universe, the body reveals the difference between a diurnal, masculine, "warm" world and a feminine, nocturnal, "cold" one and the process by which energy flows between the two (in the transfer of "energy" from the man's body to the woman's).

Otomí ritual is, in essence, a manifestation of a process of fusion between polarities of which the sexual distinction is the prototype. This is seen in rituals from fertility rites *(costumbres)* to the Feast of the Dead, which is both a mourning of ancestors and a celebration of the life force contained in their bones. The interdependence of life and death is revealed most completely in Carnival. During this time the major gods are represented by an ancestral couple, such as Old Father (Šihta) and Old Mother (Pømbe), whose function is to reenact the primordial creation. From their broken bodies they kindle life and youth in a supernatural society governed by devils, demons of vegetation, and lascivious women. Paradoxically, in Mezquital, where the erosion of indigenous tradition has been most complete, Carnival remains, despite its European origins, one of the last areas of resistance to cultural hybridization. Indigenous elements are also plainly evident in a number of rituals in the Catholic liturgical cycle, such as the Feast of the Finding of the Cross (Sierra Gorda) and the Feast of the Three Magi (Rio Laja Valley).

The richest complex of rituals is found on the eastern periphery of the Otomí region, in the foothills of the Sierra Madre. A distinctive feature of the religious life here is the use of hammered bark figurines that are fashioned and given their power by shamans. These figurines, rare evidence of pre-Hispanic iconography, are a precious source for interpreting the indigenous cosmological system. They are part of the essential paraphernalia of the healing and fertility rituals organized by shamans. As adepts possessed of specialized knowledge, shamans manipulate unseen forces and are thus able to cure (by restoring the body's equilibrium) and to afflict (by casting spells at a distance).

The *cargo* system—that is, the system of ritually based obligations to participate in the functioning of the community's civil and religious life—varies significantly from one community to another. This system is a primary cohesive force binding villages *(pueblos)* and their dependent peripheries (hamlets). Such cohesion is also promoted by regional pilgrimages to sacred mountains or Catholic sanctuaries (San Agustin Mezquititlan, Chalma, Tepeaca in Mexico City).

Through their many variants, Otomí rituals reveal certain obscure aspects of Otomí cosmology that are hardly brought to light by the myths themselves. Though known in a version little changed since pre-Hispanic times, the story of the creation of the sun and moon, the foundation of the dualistic order of the universe, is not often told anymore, except in villages deeply rooted in the Indian tradition. Yet the symbolic structure of this text remains, dimly outlined, in a number of tales that pit Christ against the Devil. Similarly, the theme of the Flood, in its variations, reveals how Mesoamerican symbols combine with biblical ones according to the importance each community gives to the two traditions.

In Otomí mythology today, the Devil appears as a predominant figure everywhere. Through a process of adjustment and reinterpretation, the medieval European figure of Satan has merged with indigenous representations of evil, fertility, and impurity. The Devil now sits enthroned at the apex of the pantheon, holding sway over a band of nocturnal deities and merging with the enigmatic lunar figure of Zâna.

BIBLIOGRAPHY

Carrasco, Pedro. *Los Otomies: Cultura e historia prehispánicas de los pueblos mesoamericanos de habla otomiana.* Mexico City, 1950. A comprehensive account of the ethnohistorical sources available on the subject.

Dow, James. *Santos y supervivencias: Funciones de la religion en una comunidad otomi.* Mexico City, 1974. A very detailed analysis of the religious obligation system in Santa Monica, a Sierra Madre village.

Galinier, Jacques. *N'yuhu: Les indiens Otomis.* Mexico City, 1979. An ethnographical study of the eastern Otomí area.

Manrique, Leonardo. "The Otomí." In *Handbook of Middle American Indians.* Austin, 1969. A brief synthesis of the main cultural features of the Otomí-Pame groups.

Soustelle, Jacques. *La famille Otomi-Pame.* Paris, 1937. The first study concerning the geographical distribution and linguistic characteristics of the Otomí, Mazahua, Atzinca, Pame, and Chichimeca languages, containing also valuable ethnographical data.

Jacques Galinier
Translated from French by Robert Paolucci

OTTO, RUDOLF (1869–1937), German Christian theologian and scholar of the history and phenomenology of religions. Rudolf Otto was one of two great theological influences in Germany in the years after World War I, the other being the neoorthodox theologian Karl Barth. Otto's *Das Heilige* (The Idea of the Holy; 1917) and Barth's *Römerbrief* (Commentary on the Letter to the Romans; 1923) set the theological agenda for many years, though in different directions. While Barth rejected the liberal emphasis on Christianity as a religion, Otto centered his life work on understanding the nature of religion, its divergent expressions in the world religions, and its importance for Christian theology and practice.

Rudolf Otto was heir to the primary theological and philosophical tendencies in Germany at the end of the nineteenth century. He studied at Erlangen and Göttingen, and he taught on the theological faculties of Göttingen and Breslau until he went to the University of Marburg in 1917; there he remained the rest of his life. Among the strong influences on him we can first count Luther, the subject of Otto's 1898 dissertation, "Die Anschauung vom Heiligen Geiste bei Luther" (Luther's View of the Holy Spirit). From Luther, Otto learned the importance of religious intuition and the sense of the inward presence of God. A second major influence was Schleiermacher; Otto edited a centennial edition of Schleiermacher's *Speeches on Religion* in 1899 and later wrote that Schleiermacher had recovered the importance of "feeling" in religious experience. The dominant influence of Kant's thought is clear especially in Otto's early work, and from the philosopher Jacob Fries he took over the notion of *Ahndung* or "longing" as an aesthetic mode of perception that apprehends the meaning and purpose of existence. He discussed these two philosophers especially in his 1909 work, *The Philosophy of Religion Based on Kant and Fries.*

Unlike many other theologians of his time, Otto also interested himself in the non-Christian religions of the world. He learned Sanskrit, translated and studied important Hindu writings, and made several extensive trips to India, Burma, China, Japan, Egypt, Jerusalem, and other places in his search to understand religious experience. It was perhaps the tremendous impact of his trip to Asia in 1911 and 1912 and his early study of Sanskrit texts that led him to the analysis of religious experience first articulated in *The Idea of the Holy.*

In this widely influential book, Otto attempted to clarify the distinctively religious element in religious experience by attending especially to the nonrational factor—what is left over after the rational elements have been subtracted. This is not to say that Otto ignored the rational aspects of religion, as some have charged; indeed, his earlier work had dealt largely with religion in its rational dimensions, and this book specifically investigated the relationship of the rational to the nonrational in religious experience. Otto pointed out that the term *holy,* which should designate the special religious dimension, had lost its primary meaning and had come to designate ethical and moral self-righteousness. Its primary meaning, Otto found, eludes apprehension in conceptual terms. So Otto coined a new word, *numinous,* to stand for the holy minus its moral factor and without any "rational" aspect. The "numinous" now indicated the special religious "overplus" of meaning in the idea of the holy beyond that which is commonly thought of as rational and moral. This numinous factor, according to Otto, is *sui generis,* that is, irreducible to any other factor; it can be understood only when there has been an existential experience of it.

Otto then described the object to which the numinous consciousness is directed. This is the *mysterium tremendum,* the mystery before which one trembles, which evokes a strong sense of "creature feeling." This experience, according to Otto, includes a double dimension of response to the holy: an element of shaking fear or repulsion *(mysterium tremendum),* and an element of powerful attraction or fascination *(mysterium fascinans).* This numinous experience of the holy is basic to all religious experience, according to Otto, and is thus an *a priori* category in both its rational and nonrational elements.

Otto held that human beings have a special faculty of genuinely recognizing the holy in its appearances, a faculty that he termed "divination." This faculty of divination, which Otto drew in part from Fries's idea of *Ahndung* ("longing") and Schleiermacher's idea of "feeling," is the means by which a person senses the meaning, value, and purpose of the numinous presence. Because the numinous experience is nonrational, it evades precise formulation; the "overplus" of meaning can only be indicated by what Otto called "ideograms," that is, concepts or doctrines that cannot be understood logically but only symbolically.

After writing this seminal and incisive analysis of the nature of religious experience, Otto began to apply his category of the numinous to various facets of religion. In a series of additional essays over the next fifteen years, he analyzed many topics of religious experience in Christianity and other religions in this manner. He showed how the recovery of the numinous dimension liberates concepts like sin and guilt from their moralistic bounds and casts them in a new light, because of the sense of the mysterious Other with the accompanying feeling of creatureliness. Sin, for example, is not simply moral depreciation or transgression; it is a feeling of absolute profaneness, involving the most uncompromising judgment of depreciation of oneself as a creature, accompanied by heightened appreciation of the numen as holy mystery. The source of forgiveness thus springs directly from the numinous, from the awe of standing before the *mysterium tremendum* with a sense of one's unworthiness.

Part of Rudolf Otto's contribution to religious studies lay in his investigation of the numinous as found in the major religions of the world, especially in Hinduism. He translated some important texts into German, attempting to portray a living impression of the religious experience to which the texts testified, and interesting himself especially in the idea of salvation or the mystical experience they presented. Otto filled a gap in Western scholarship on Hinduism particularly in paying attention to Hindu devotion, not only in its ancient forms but especially in its medieval expressions, an area that had hardly been studied in Germany.

In addition to his translations, Otto provided a number of studies in the history of religions, together with some significant comparative works. In studying world religions, Otto developed a theory of the convergence of types and parallel forms. He chose examples from various traditions to show how similar religious expressions were, arising out of the common human sense of the numinous. But he was careful to show, at the same time, how parallel forms are qualified by the dynamics of the individual religion. In his view, the historian of religions must be sensitive to both similarities and differences. Otto himself presented a number of models of this comparative methodology. In his important work of 1926, *Mysticism East and West,* he provided a thorough comparison of the important Hindu philosopher of nondualism, Śaṅkara, and the medieval Christian mystic Meister Eckhardt. In this study he first showed a broad basis for common mystical outlook; then, within that framework of agreement, he was able to demonstrate the peculiar spirit of each of the two mystics in relation to their respective cultural traditions. In 1930, a second important comparative study, *India's Religion of Grace and Christianity,* appeared, in which Otto described the personalistic, theistic piety *(bhakti)* devoted to Viṣṇu and showed how this *bhakti* impulse is similar to that found in Christianity. The lost condition out of which one is delivered is conceived somewhat differently in the two religious traditions, however: deliverance out of sin and guilt in Christianity, but deliverance from the cycle of rebirth and the world of appearance in Hinduism.

As a Christian theologian Otto was interested in issues within the Christian faith, although he—more than most theologians of the time—saw the history of religions as a necessary backdrop for Christian theology. His last work, *The Kingdom of God and the Son of Man*, published in German in 1934, is a major study on Christology, one that deals with the New Testament data but does so from Otto's unique perspective on the history of religions. This work made an important contribution to the study of eschatology in the formation of New Testament thought. Otto's theory was that the ultimate source of the concept of the kingdom of God was the Iranian tradition of the kingdom of ʿĀsūrā'. Jesus' eschatology took the form of an announcement of the spiritual power of the end-time kingdom already here; Jesus' own particular role can best be defined, according to Otto, as that of charismatic evangelist and exorcist.

Rudolf Otto was also much interested in the sphere of practical religious experience. He offered many suggestions for a dignified celebration of the Christian Eucharist, and his own experimental liturgy embodied the sense of the numinous by culminating in silence. He proposed an ecumenical unity of all Christians in Germany long before the Christian ecumenical movement became popular. Through his interest in symbols and ideograms he established at Marburg a collection of religious symbols, artifacts, and apparatus of the religions of all peoples. And his broad understanding of religious similarities and differences led him to propose and participate in a "religious league of mankind," challenging the people of all religions to unite against the common problems that confront human beings.

Otto's attempts to analyze the essence of religion and to describe the religious object as the presence of the holy have been criticized by some scholars who hold that the essence of religion and of the divine object cannot be defined by phenomenological means. But his work still provides a penetrating analysis of religious experience and a model of comparative religious research, one that has stimulated much thought and that will continue to exert great influence.

[*For further discussion of Otto's work, see* Holy, Idea of the.]

BIBLIOGRAPHY

Works by Otto. Among Otto's early major works must be counted *Naturalistisch und religiöse Weltansicht* (Tübingen, 1904), translated as *Naturalism and Religion* (New York, 1907); and *Kantisch-Fries' sche Religionsphilosophie* (Tübingen, 1909), translated as *The Philosophy of Religion Based on Kant and Fries* (New York, 1931). His best known work is *Das Heilige* (Breslau, 1917), translated as *The Idea of the Holy* (1923; 2d ed., Oxford, 1950), in which he analyzed religious experience as the sense of the numinous. He followed this work with many essays devoted to the topic of numinous experience, collected in 1932 in two volumes, *Das Gefühl des Überweltlichen* and *Sünde und Urschuld* (Munich, 1932); some of these essays are in *Religious Essays: A Supplement to "The Idea of the Holy,"* (London, 1931). Two major works in which Otto presented comparative studies of Hinduism and Christianity are *West-östliche Mystik* (Gotha, 1926), translated as *Mysticism East and West* (New York, 1932); and *Die Gnadenreligion Indiens und das Christentum* (Gotha, 1930), translated as *India's Religion of Grace and Christianity* (New York, 1930). Otto's last major work was *Reich Gottes und Menschensohn* (Munich, 1934), translated as *The Kingdom of God and the Son of Man* (London, 1938). Of Otto's many textual studies and translations of Hindu writings into German, his studies on the *Bhagavadgītā* have been translated into English as *The Original Gita: The Song of the Supreme Exalted One* (London, 1939).

Works about Otto. Book-length studies of Otto in English include Robert F. Davidson's *Rudolf Otto's Interpretation of Religion* (Princeton, 1947), discussing both the background of Otto's thought and his specific proposals for understanding religious experience; and Philip C. Almond's *Rudolf Otto: An Introduction to His Philosophical Theology* (Chapel Hill, N.C., 1984), which includes a description of his life and work. Shorter general studies of Otto's thought include Joachim Wach's "Rudolf Otto and the Idea of of the Holy," in Wach's *Types of Religious Experience: Christian and Non-Christian* (Chicago, 1951), pp. 209–227; and Bernard Meland's "Rudolf Otto," in *A Handbook of Christian Theologians*, edited by Dean G. Peerman and Martin E. Marty (Cleveland, 1965), pp. 169–191. John P. Reeder has analyzed the moral implications of Otto's thought in "The Relation of the Moral and the Numinous in Otto's Notion of the Holy," in *Religion and Morality*, edited by Gene H. Outka and John P. Reeder (Garden City, N.Y., 1973), pp. 255–292; and David Bastow has studied the relation between Otto's philosophical, phenomenological, and theological positions in "Otto and Numinous Experience," *Religious Studies* 12 (1976): 159–176. Robert F. Streetman has shown the renewed relevance of Otto for current religious study in "Some Later Thoughts of Otto on the Holy," *Journal of the American Academy of Religion* 48 (1980): 365–384. Of the many studies of Otto in German, a helpful volume is *Rudolf Otto's Bedeutung für die Religionswissenschaft und die Theologie Heute*, edited by Ernst Benz (Leiden, 1971), which includes a substantial biography of Otto.

THEODORE M. LUDWIG

OTTO, WALTER F. (1874–1958), German classicist. Walter F. Otto began theological studies at the University of Tübingen in 1892, and transferred to classical studies the following year. He continued his studies at the University of Bonn, where in 1897 he was awarded the Ph.D. degree. His *Habilitationschrift* in classical studies at the University of Tübingen, under the supervision of Otto Crusius, was completed in 1905. After a period as an assistant to the *Thesaurus Linguae Latinae* (a joint project of five German universities published in Leipzig from 1900 onward) and as editor of the *Onomasticum Latinium in Munich* (in which he continued his work in the field of Roman proper names, the subject matter of his dissertation), he became a lecturer at the University of Vienna in 1911. In 1913 he was appointed professor at the University of Basel, and the next year he moved to Frankfurt am Main. A ten-year period of teaching at the University of Königsberg was followed by short teaching assignments at the universities of Munich and Göttingen. Finally, in 1946, he became professor at Tübingen.

In his most widely known work, *Homeric Gods* (1929; Eng. trans., 1954), Otto maintains that the reason that later interpreters have failed to understand and appreciate ancient Greek religion is that it lacks all those elements specific to Christianity and other religions derived from Asia; in Greek religion there is "no cordial intimacy between man and the gods," no longing for redemption, a marked hostility to magical thought, no miracles, and "no holy will before which nature trembles" (*Homeric Gods,* [1954] 1978, p. 246). "Greek thought overwhelms us by its uniqueness," says Otto. "Other religions cannot help us here, because the Greek cannot be compared with any of them" (ibid., p. 287). Greek belief "arose out of the riches and depths of life, not out of its anxieties and yearnings" (ibid.), and Greek religion is the religion of worldliness and naturalness. The Greeks saw "the eternal visage of divinity" (ibid., p. 7) everywhere throughout all the forms of life and conditions of existence. "Divinity is and remains nature" for the Greeks, Otto explains, "but as nature's form it is spiritual and as its perfection it is majesty and dignity, whose rays illumine the life of man" (ibid., p. 247). The significance of the Homeric mode of seeing and thinking can hardly be overemphasized, for it finds continual expression, "despite all temporal and individual variations, in the representative works of the Greek genius, whether in poetry, plastic art or philosophy" (ibid., p. 16). Beyond this, Otto sees in ancient Greek worship "one of humanity's greatest religious ideas," which he terms "the religious idea of the European spirit" (ibid., p. 11). For the nonprofessional readers for whom he writes, Greek religion especially comes to life in Otto's descriptions of various Olympian deities. This is particularly the case in the section (pp. 61–90) on Apollo, whom he characterizes as "specifically masculine," including qualities of spiritual freedom and distance as well as of self-doubt, and on Artemis (p. 80), who represents for Otto "freedom of another sort—the feminine," which is "free nature with its brilliance and wildness, with its guiltless purity and its uncanniness."

Another typical example of Otto's oeuvre is his short study of the Eleusinian mysteries, "Der Sinn der eleusinischer Mysterien," first published in *Eranos Jahrbuch* 7 (1939) and reprinted in the collection *Die Gestalt und das Sein* (1955). Of great significance are his observations on the unique character of the relationship between Demeter and Persephone: the relationship is so close that it is understandable, he writes, that some have seen in Persephone, the daughter, a sort of doubling *(eine Art Wesenverdoppelung)* or continuation of Demeter, the mother. (Károly Kerényi took up this suggestion and reached the conclusion that mother and daughter are basically identical.) But it is in his reflections on the meaning of the mysteries for the initiates that Otto's concerns and interests are most clearly to be seen, as, for example, in his remarks about the meaning of the ear of corn shown to the initiates. It was, he claimed, even more than a revelation of the deity; it was the manifestation of Persephone herself and the assurance of her divine presence to the initiate, a presence that remained with him in life and through death.

BIBLIOGRAPHY

Internationally, the most widely known of Otto's publications is his *Die Götter Griechenlands: Das Bild des Göttlichen im Spiegel des griechischen Geistes,* 6th ed. (Bonn, 1970), translated by Moses Hadas as *The Homeric Gods: The Spiritual Significance of Greek Religion* (1954; reprint, New York, 1978). Also available in English is *Dionysos: Myth and Cult* (Bloomington, Ind., 1965). Among Otto's other publications are the following: *Die Manen, oder, Von den Urformen des Totenglaubens: Eine Untersuchung zur Religion der Griechen, Römer und Semiten und zum Volksglauben überhaupt,* 2d ed. (Darmstadt, 1958), which challenges Erwin Rohde's notion of *psyche* by showing the distinction between *thymos,* the life-spirit, and *psyche,* that is, what remains of a person when the life-spirit leaves at the moment of death; *Der Junge Nietzsche* (Frankfurt, 1936); *Der Dichter und die alten Götter* (Frankfurt, 1942); *Die Gestalt und das Sein* (Dusseldorf, 1955), which contains a collection of twelve essays originally published between 1926 and 1951; and *Theophania: Der Geist der altgriechischen Religion* (Hamburg, 1956). Published posthumously were *Das Wort der Antike* (Stuttgart, 1962) and *Mythos und Welt* (Stuttgart, 1962), both edited by Kurt von Fritz; the latter volume also contains a critical commentary on Otto's work by the editor, as well as a bibliography of Otto's publications. Also published after Otto's death was *Die Wirklichkeit der Götter: Von der Unzerstörbarkeit griechischer Weltsicht* (Reinbeck bei Hamburg, 1963), which contains a biographical appreciation by Károly Kerényi.

Other biographical sketches of Otto include Karl Reinhardt's article "Walter F. Otto," in his *Vermächtnis der Antike* (Göttingen, 1960), and Willy Theiler's "Walter F. Otto," *Gnomon* 32 (1960): 87–90.

WILLEM A. BIJLEFELD

OUSPENSKY, P. D. (1878–1947), Petr Dem'ianovich Uspenskii; Russian author, thinker, and mystic. Ouspensky's *Tertium Organum*, written in 1911, was published in New York in 1922 and within a few years became a best-seller in America and made him a worldwide reputation. Intended to supplement the *Organon* of Aristotle and the *Novum Organum* of Francis Bacon, *Tertium Organum* is based on the author's personal experiments in changing consciousness; it proposes a new level of thought about the fundamental questions of human existence and a way to liberate man's thinking from its habitual patterns. *A New Model of the Universe,* a collection of essays published earlier in Russia, was published in London in 1930. But Ouspensky will be chiefly remembered for *In Search of the Miraculous,* published posthumously in 1949, and later in several foreign languages under the title *Fragments of an Unknown Teaching*. This work is by far the most lucid account yet available of the teaching of G. I. Gurdjieff, and it has been a principal cause of the growing influence of Gurdjieff's ideas.

Ouspensky was born in Moscow and spent his childhood there. His mother was a painter. His father, who died early, had a good position as a railroad surveyor; he was fond of music, in which Ouspensky showed no interest. Of precocious intelligence, Ouspensky left school early with a decision not to take the academic degrees for which he was qualified and began to travel and write. Through his reading and journalistic work, first in Moscow and then, from 1909 on, in Saint Petersburg, he "knew everyone." His early writings can be regarded as a final flowering of the great Russian literary tradition of the late nineteenth century. But, although influenced by such movements as the Theosophy of H. P. Blavatsky (whom he never met), he distrusted and disliked the "absurdities" of contemporary life and kept apart from the secret revolutionary politics with which almost all Russian intelligentsia of the period sympathized.

In 1915, returning to Russia from India to find that war had broken out in Europe, he gave lectures on his "search for the miraculous" and attracted large audiences in Saint Petersburg and Moscow. Among his listeners was Sof'ia Grigor'evna Maksimenko, who became his wife. They had no children.

In the same year, he was sought out by the pupils of Gurdjieff and reluctantly agreed to meet him. The meeting was a turning point in Ouspensky's life. He recognized at once the value of the ideas that Gurdjieff had discovered in the East and that he himself had looked for in vain. "I realized," he wrote, "that I had met with a completely new system of thought, surpassing all I knew before. This system threw a new light on psychology and explained what I could not understand before in esoteric ideas." He began to collect people and to arrange meetings at which Gurdjieff developed his message, and from that moment the study and practice of these new ideas constituted Ouspensky's principal aim.

In June 1917, after four months' service in the army, from which he was honorably discharged on account of poor eyesight, the impending revolution caused Ouspensky to consider leaving Russia to continue his work in London. But he delayed his departure to spend nearly a year in difficult political conditions with Gurdjieff and a few of his pupils at Essentuki in the northern Caucasus.

As early as 1918, however, Ouspensky began to feel that a break with Gurdjieff was inevitable, that "he had to go"—to seek another teacher or to work independently. The break between the two men, teacher and pupil, each of whom had received much from the other, has never been satisfactorily explained. They met for the last time in Paris in 1930.

In 1919 Ouspensky and his family remained in very harsh conditions in the hands of the Bolsheviks in Essentuki (see *Letters from Russia,* 1978). He assembled some students there but in 1920, when Essentuki was freed by the White Army, moved to Constantinople. In August 1921 he was able to leave for London, and in November, with the help of Lady Rothenmere, A. R. Orage, and other influential people, he started private meetings and lectures there. These continued until 1940, after the outbreak of World War II, when he moved his family to the United States and, with a few London pupils, began his lectures again in New York. Early in 1947 he returned to resume his work in London, where he died in October of the same year.

A characteristic of every one of Ouspensky's meetings, which he attended until a few months before his death, was their remarkable intensity. He made demands for the utmost honesty not only on himself but on his pupils as well. His method was to invite "new people" to listen to five or six written lectures read aloud by one of the men close to him. (These lectures were published in 1950 as *The Psychology of Man's Possible Evolution*.) Further understanding of the ideas had to be extracted from him directly by question and answer. Irrelevant questions were treated summarily. Simple rules, which to some appeared arbitrary, but which Ouspensky considered essential to self-training, were introduced—and explained at rare intervals. Pupils who wished further application of the training were invited to his country house in New Jersey, where practical work was organized by Madame Ouspensky. Transcripts of all the meetings are preserved in the Yale University library.

[*See also the biography of Gurdjieff.*]

BIBLIOGRAPHY

All of Ouspensky's principal works are available in English, translated and/or edited by various hands and issued by various publishers in London and New York. Among them are *Letters from Russia* ([1919] 1978), *Tertium Organum: The Third Canon of Thought; A Key to the Enigmas of the World,* 2d ed., rev. ([1922] 1981), *A New Model of the Universe: Principles of the Psychological Method in Its Application to Problems of Science, Religion, and Art* ([1930] 1971), *The Strange Life of Ivan Osokin* (1947), *In Search of the Miraculous: Fragments of an Unknown Teaching* ([1949] 1965), *The Psychology of Man's Possible Evolution* ([1950] 1973), *Talks with a Devil* (1972), and *Conscience: The Search for Truth* (1979). A selection of transcripts of Ouspensky's meetings with his pupils was published as *The Fourth Way: A Record of Talks and Answers to Questions Based on the Teachings of G. I. Gurdjieff,* edited by J. G. Bennett and translated by Katya Petroff (New York, 1957).

JOHN PENTLAND

OWLS. As a creature of two realms, the owl is a multivalent symbol admitting of both benevolent and malevolent interpretations. Like most birds, owls represent higher states of being (angels, spirits, supernatural aid, and wisdom), while their nocturnal nature and ominous hoot ally them with the instinctual world of matter, darkness, death, and blind ignorance. In a series of etchings he called *Los caprichos,* the Spanish painter Goya depicted owls as the dark forces of the irrational.

For many early peoples, owls were associated with the baleful, devouring nature of the Great Mother, and their sinister aspect as birds of ill omen prevailed over their benign connotations. In the Egyptian system of hieroglyphs, owls signify night, death, the sun that has sunk into darkness; in the Hindu tradition, they represent the soul and Yama, god of the dead; and in China, images of owls carved on funeral urns symbolize death. The owl was an attribute of the god of darkness for the Etruscans, a chthonic sign for the Celts, who called it the "corpse bird," and the taboo animal of early metallurgists. In the pagan religion of the Abyssinian Hamites, owls were sacred and were believed to embody the souls of those who had died unavenged.

Because of the owl's association with the otherworld and its mysteries, the bird was thought to be cognizant of future events and became an emblem of wisdom. Owls were regarded as auspicious in classical Greece, where they were sacred to Pallas Athena, the goddess of divine knowledge, human wisdom, and the arts; they were depicted on vases, coins, and monuments as her emblem and companion. A trace of totemism is detected in one of her epithets, Glaucopis ("owl"), which suggests that at one time the bird had been worshiped as a god and only later became an attribute of the goddess. The Romans allied the owl to Athena's counterpart Minerva, and also believed that it augured death. The funereal screech owl was anathema to the Romans, and its appearance at public auspices was deemed unpropitious. In Vergil's *Aeneid,* when Dido contemplates death upon learning that Aeneas is to abandon her, she hears the "deathly lamentations" of an owl. And Shakespeare has Lady Macbeth say "I heard the owl scream" when Duncan is murdered.

In Judaism the owl symbolizes blindness, and according to the Talmud it is an ill omen in dreams. The Hebrew scriptures classify owls among the unclean birds, and when God declares his vengeance against Zion, he condemns it to be "a habitation of dragons and a court for owls" (*Is.* 34:14). Job, in his despair, cries that he is "a companion to owls" (*Jb.* 30:29).

Throughout Christian Europe in the Middle Ages, owls were a sign of the darkness that prevailed before the advent of Christ and a symbol of those Jews who elected to dwell therein instead of in the light of the gospel. As a bird that shuns the light, the owl was equated with Satan, Prince of Darkness, who lures men into sin as the owl tricks birds into snares. A symbol of solitude when depicted with hermits at prayer, the owl denotes wisdom when it is shown at the side of Saint Jerome. Scenes of the crucifixion sometimes show the owl with Christ, whose sacrifice brought light to those in darkness.

Owls are considered the agents of magic among many peoples. Siberian and Inuit (Eskimo) shamans regard them as helping spirits, a source of powerful aid and guidance, and wear their feathers on caps and collars. Tatar shamans try to assume the bird's shape, and the Buriats keep an owl or hang up its skin to ward off evil spirits. The Ainu look on the owl as a deity. In one Samoan village the people believe that the owl incarnates their god. A malevolent pre-Columbian Aztec god is represented with a screech owl on his head.

Among certain American Indian tribes, it was believed that God's power was transmitted to the shaman through owls. The Kiowa thought that the medicine man became an owl after death, and Creek priests bore a stuffed owl as their insignia. Owl dances were performed as a magical rite, and in the Medicine Pipe

Dance of the Crow tribes, the pipe stem was decorated with owl and woodpecker feathers to symbolize night and day. For some tribes the owl represented a psychopomp: the Ojibwa called the bridge over which the dead passed the "owl bridge," and the Pima believed that owl feathers facilitated the soul's flight to the world beyond.

BIBLIOGRAPHY

Cassirer, Ernst. *The Philosophy of Symbolic Forms*, vol. 2. Translated by Ralph Manheim. New Haven, 1955. The owl as a totemic animal. Basing his concept of totemism on the mythically experienced unity and equivalence of man and animal, the author accounts for totemism as a belief that the clan was not merely descended from the animal but united with it in a magical context of the energy flowing between them.

Eliade, Mircea. *Shamanism: Archaic Techniques of Ecstasy* (1964). Rev. & enl. ed. Reprint, Princeton, 1970. Owls as powerful guardians and helping spirits, bearers of instructions to sorcerers and shamans, symbolic of their power of flight.

Ovid. *Metamorphoses*, vol. 2. Translated by Frank Justus Miller. New York, 1916. The association of owls with the dark aspects of the goddesses of the underworld and their evocation of primitive fears.

Ann Dunnigan

P

PACHOMIUS (293?–346), Christian ascetic and founder of cenobitic monasticism. Information about Pachomius has been much confused in the many legends and biographies preserved in various versions and translations. Born of pagan parents in Upper Egypt, Pachomius encountered Christianity for the first time in the city of Latopolis (Copt., Esnen; modern-day Isna) while serving in the military. There he was impressed with the seemingly virtuous life of local Christians and by the love they showed for all people. After his conscription ended, Pachomius returned to his village, Chinoboskeia (Copt., Schneset), and was baptized. Because of his great love for God, he decided to become a monk and was placed under the spiritual guidance of the ascetic Palemon. In Egypt at the time the eremitic life as established by Antony of Egypt was dominant. After receiving divine exhortation, Pachomius decided to organize a monastic community.

In an abandoned village on the east bank of the Nile, near Dendera, Pachomius established a monastery surrounded by a wall and named it Tabennis (c. 318). The small number of ascetics there soon increased greatly, creating a need for other monasteries. Under his direction, nine monasteries for men and two for women were established. In order to administer the newly established monasteries more effectively, Pachomius moved the center from Tabennis to Pebu, where he was installed as general leader, or hegumen (Gr., *hēgoumenos*). His sister Mary became the first hegumen in one of the women's monasteries. A wealthy monk, Petronius, gave financial support to Pachomius to retain control of his institutions during a general meeting of the monks in Pebu at Easter. Pachomius died on 9 May 346 in an epidemic that took the lives of about a hundred monks.

In fourth-century Egypt three basic forms of monasticism appeared: (1) the severe eremitic form, which was based on Antony's life in the desert; (2) the anchoritic monasticism of Makarios, which employed Sunday worship as one of its common elements; and (3) cenobitic monasticism as developed and practiced by Pachomius. Cenobitic monasticism centered on life inside the walls of the monastery with all the hours of the day and night strictly regulated. Monastic rule governed all the needs and activities of the monks: common prayer, common table, common work, and common use of the products of labor. According to monastic legend and tradition, an angel dictated these rules to Pachomius. Regarded as equal to scripture, obedience to them was considered a great virtue.

The hegumen was the spiritual leader of the monks, also undertaking responsibility for the financial support of the monastery in order to relieve the monks of worldly cares. Thus the monks could turn their undivided attention to spiritual exercises and toward heaven. In fact, this was the most important difference between the monasticism of Pachomius and that of Makarios: the hegumen was not only responsible for the spiritual needs of the monks but also for all material needs (e.g., housing, clothing, food, health care). On the other hand, the eremitic, anchoritic, and cenobitic lives did have common elements—removal from the world, severe asceticism, work with the hands, prayers, and obedience to the hegumen and the canons.

Pachomius wrote his famous rules for monks in Coptic, but only Jerome's translation from Greek into Latin is extant. In Coptic and Greek, only fragments are preserved, but there are also Ethiopic and Arabic translations. The long version of his rules seems to be the original. Eleven letters of Pachomius are also preserved in translations by Jerome. *Admonitions* and a small section of *Catechetical Instructions* are also available to us.

Pachomius was not a great theoretical teacher of asceticism, but he was a great organizer of its practice. His teachings were directed to the ordering of the monks' lives by strict canons. These canons were meant to insure the good operation of the cloister and to make the separation from the world pronounced, including regulating the travels of the monks and visits from the laity. The canons imposed uniformity on the monks' way of life, dress, and nourishment even when the monks were outside the monastery. Only the sick were exempt from the austere dietary rules. Pachomius's canons covered all hours of the day and night, which were strictly arranged and scheduled to cover work, prayer, and rest, as well as behavior in church and at the table.

The greatest influence Pachomius had on the history of monasticism was in the organizational thoroughness and effectiveness of his rules. He created a form of monasticism that was to extend beyond his own epoch: the development of monasticism in the East and West was largely based on his rules. He influenced such monastic leaders as Basil the Great, John Cassian, and Benedict of Nursia, either directly or indirectly, and his rules are still followed in the austere monastic life lived on Mount Athos.

BIBLIOGRAPHY

The Greek lives (i.e., biographies) of Pachomius are available in *Sancti Pachomii vitae Graecae*, edited by François Halkin, in "Subsidia Hagiographica," vol. 19 (Brussels, 1932). French and English translations of the "first Greek life" are *La première vie grecque de Saint Pachôme*, translated by A.-J. Festugière, in "Les moines d'Orient," vol. 4, no. 2 (Paris, 1965), and *The Life of Pachomius: Vita Prima Graeca*, translated by Apostolos N. Athanassakis (Missoula, Mont., 1975). A French translation of the Coptic lives is *Les vies coptes de Saint Pachôme et de ses premiers successeurs*, translated by L. T. Lefort, "Bibliothèque du Muséon," no. 16 (Louvain, 1943). See also the *Œuvres de S. Pachôme et ses disciples*, 2 vols., edited by L. T. Lefort, in "Corpus Scriptorum Christianorum Orientalium, Scriptores Coptici," vols. 23 and 24 (Louvain, 1956) for Coptic and French versions. The rule of Pachomius along with eleven letters are available in the Latin translation of Jerome in *Patrologia Latina*, edited by J.-P. Migne, vol. 23 (Paris, 1865), pp. 61–99.

Three relevant secondary works are Heinrich Bacht's "L'importance de l'idéal monastique de S. Pacôme pour l'histoire du monachisme chrétien," *Revue d'ascetique et de mystique* 26 (1950): 308–326; H. Idris Bell's *Egypt from Alexander the Great to the Arab Conquest* (Oxford, 1948), pp. 109ff.; and Karl Heussi's *Der Ursprung des Monchtums* (Tübingen, 1936).

THEODORE ZISSIS
Translated from Greek by Philip M. McGhee

PACIFISM. *See* Nonviolence.

PADMASAMBHAVA (Tib., Padma-'byuṅ-gnas; c. eighth century CE), renowned in Tibet as a great Tantric sage, exorcist, yogic practitioner, and magician. Also known as Guru Padma, U-rgyan Padma, Guru Rin-po-che, Lotus Born, and the Second Buddha, Padmasambhava is credited, along with Śāntirakṣita, with the establishment of the first Buddhist monastery (Bsam-yas) in Tibet. Tibetan sources record that he was invited to Tibet by King Khri-sroṅ-lde-btsan (755–797) in order to subdue demons that were hampering the transmission of the Dharma.

Nothing definite can be said of Padmasambhava's origins, although the historical existence of a personage bearing his name would be difficult to deny. Tibetan tradition makes him a native of Uḍḍiyāna and the discovered son of King Indrabodhi: the king is said to have discovered a boy resembling the Buddha seated at the center of a lotus blossom on Lake Dhanakośa. A large literature developed around Padmasambhava, but the *Padma thaṅ yig* (Padma Scrolls) and the *Bka' thaṅ sde lṅa* (Fivefold Set of Scrolls)—both compiled in the fourteenth century—are considered the principal works relating events of his life and times. His birth is celebrated in Tibet on the tenth day of the tenth lunar month.

Padmasambhava is said to have set out for Tibet on the fifteenth day of the eleventh lunar month of what is by Western reckoning the year 746, and to have arrived in the spring of 747; this view, however, is not without its detractors. It is not known how long Padmasambhava stayed in Tibet and how his departure came about. According to the *gter ma*, or "secret literature," he remained in Tibet for fifty years. According to Bu-ston's *Chos-'byuṅ* (History of Buddhism) he was finally sent away after performing a miraculous act that did not please the court ministers shortly after seven Tibetans had been selected and ordained as monks.

As a Tantric sage and exorcist Padmasambhava is credited with having recruited into Buddhism local deities who then became guardians of the religion. The construction of the monastery of Bsam-yas is said to have put the seal on the final submission of these local deities.

Padmasambhava transmitted the Vajrayāna (Esoteric) form of Buddhism into Tibet, wrote a commentary on the *Bar do thos grol* (Tibetan Book of the Dead), commented on the *Guhyamālāgarbha Tantra,* translated many *sūtras* and *tantras*, and lectured on the *Dākiṇyagnijihvājvala Tantra* for Dpal-gyi-seṅ-ge, one of his twenty-five disciples, who preserved his oral teachings. In that way he established the Red Hat, or Rñiṅ-ma ("old"), tradition of Buddhism in Tibet, in contrast to the Yellow Hat, or Gsar-ma ("new"), tradition organized by Tsoṅ-kha-pa (1357–1419). Padmasambhava is said to have received *tantras* through an esoteric transmission from possessors of magical knowledge *(vidyādhāra)* who were both human (e.g., Indrabodhi) and nonhuman (e.g.,Vajrapāṇi). He then hid these "treasures of scriptures" *(gter ma)* in various temples and caves and under rocks to be discovered later by such "discoverers of the treasures" *(gter ston)* as O-rgyan-gliṅ-pa (d. 1379). Padmasambhava is considered to have initiated the "quintessential instructions" *(sñin thig)* of the *atiyoga* teaching of the "inner" *tantras*. Owing to the codification of the Rñiṅ-ma *tantras* into a collection known as the *Rñiṅ-ma rgyud 'bum,* this "old tradition" of Tibetan Buddhism reached its peak in the Rdzogs-chen school represented by Kloṅ-chen-pa (1308–63) and others.

[*See also* Buddhism, *article on* Buddhism in Tibet, *and* Buddhism, Schools of, *article on* Tibetan Buddhism.]

BIBLIOGRAPHY

Evans-Wentz, W. Y., trans. and ed. *The Tibetan Book of Great Liberation.* Oxford, 1954. Prefaced with a "Psychological Commentary" by C. G. Jung. A lengthy introduction deals with Mahāyāna ideas; Tantric Buddhism; thematic problems such as time and space, self or soul; and problems of translating and editing. Included are English renderings of the biography of Padmasambhava (book 1); a translation of the section called "Knowing the Mind; the Seeing of Reality Called Self-Liberation," from Padmasambhava's *Zab chos ži khro dgoṅs pa raṅ grol* (book 2); and of the last testamentary teachings of Guru Padma Saṅs-rgyas.

Tibetan Nyingma Meditation Center. *Crystal Mirror,* vol. 4. Emeryville, Calif., 1975. See especially the section "History," by Tarthang Tulku, for a thorough treatment of the life and liberation of Padmasambhava, his twenty-five disciples, and the early chronicles of Buddhism in Tibet.

Toussaint, Gustave-Charles, trans. *Le dict de Padma.* Bibliothèque de l'Institut des Hautes Études Chinoises, vol. 3. Paris, 1933. A translation into French of the *Padma thaṅ yig* based upon a manuscript found at Lithang and compared with other renditions. This edition deals with the history of Padmasambhava in 108 songs.

LESLIE S. KAWAMURA

PALAMAS, GREGORY. *See* Gregory Palamas.

PALEOLITHIC RELIGION. The term *Paleolithic* was coined over a hundred years ago to distinguish the simple stone tools discovered in deep gravel pits or caves of the diluvial (or antediluvian) period from the polished stone tools of a later age, the Neolithic. Two incongruous criteria—geologic or climatological data and cultural or technological data—were used to distinguish the periods. Later the use of pottery became characteristic of the Neolithic age, and agriculture was seen as its chief distinguishing mark. Nowadays the term *Paleolithic* is understood in its strict sense, as the cultural equivalent of the geologic and climatological period known as the Ice Age (today usually called the Pleistocene), in which polished stones, pottery, and agriculture were still unknown. When it became clear that with few exceptions the characteristic traits of the Neolithic age appeared only some time after the end of the Pleistocene, phenomena dating from the postglacial (Holocene) period but prior to the Neolithic came to be known as Epipaleolithic or, rather unfortunately, as Mesolithic.

To be sure, the radical geologic and climatological changes that took place at this time of transition, more than ten thousand years ago, certainly affected the conditions of life and culture, but a truly epochal cultural transformation that indicates the beginning of the Upper Paleolithic period had occurred already about thirty-five thousand years ago, that is, much earlier than the environmental change. In Europe, parts of Siberia, and southwestern Asia, and perhaps in some parts of Africa, the cultural transition is marked by the emergence of tools made of thin and slender stone blades and, in some areas, by the appearance of representational art. A more meaningful classification of periods would therefore merge the Lower and Middle Paleolithic into one period and distinguish it from the combined Upper Paleolithic and the Mesolithic. (Some scholars have proposed that we use the terms *Protolithic* and *Miolithic,* but the suggestion has not won acceptance.) Outside the context of Europe, and especially with reference to America, the term *Paleolithic* is, practically speaking, not used at all.

Although the end of the Paleolithic is usually identified by the beginning of the postglacial period (c. 8000 BCE), there were no highly significant distinctions between the two periods. As far as we know today, the Paleolithic was mainly a time during which food was acquired solely by hunting (including fishing) and gathering. But such methods of subsistence were used throughout broad areas of the world during the postglacial period, too, and continue to be used in a few restricted areas today. With certain reservations, then, it is possible to show continuity between the Paleolithic period and present-day "primitive" societies that follow a similar way of life.

In theory, the Paleolithic age begins with the first appearance of human beings. In practice, both occurrences are equally difficult to pinpoint. The beginning of the Stone Age—and therefore of all prehistory—is characterized by the appearance of artificial stone tools that could be used not only for immediate tasks but also to make additional tools (Henri Bergson's "tools for making tools"). The oldest tools discovered so far are from East Africa and are between two and two and one-half million years old. Whether East Africa is therefore the real cradle of civilization or whether accidents of preservation and of research and discovery only make this seem to be the case must for the present remain an open question.

In the course of time human beings appeared in other areas of Africa and, between one and one and one-half million years ago, in parts of southern and western Europe. Finds in southeastern and eastern Asia are probably as old or even older. As early as three hundred thousand years ago humans appeared in numerous other parts of Europe and Asia. Even in Australia there is evidence of human presence more than twenty thousand years ago, and it is likely that by that time human beings had already entered broad areas of America, although their presence becomes certain only about 10,000 BCE. Thereafter even the more northerly regions of Europe became increasingly populated.

Many developments and transformations occurred during this long stretch of time; very different cultures took shape in the various regions. It is questionable, therefore, whether *Paleolithic religion* is a meaningful concept at all. Rather, our point of departure ought to be the existence of a variety of religions in the Paleolithic period. The nature and scarcity of the evidence (for the most part only fragmentary material remains) and its random character prevent us from convincingly distinguishing and defining any specific traits of these religions. The expression *Paleolithic religion* can really mean nothing more than the totality of ascertainable or inferred religious phenomena of the Paleolithic period. In addition, the term *religion* itself must be defined very broadly and be allowed to include everything that suggests dealings with a realm above and beyond natural phenomena.

Sources and Their Interpretation. Our knowledge of the Paleolithic period depends mainly on a functional interpretation of material remains, that is, a reconstruction of their use and cultural context in the life of prehistoric human beings. Such an interpretation relies, in turn, on a comparison of the available evidence with objects, facts, and processes that are directly known to us or have been transmitted in written, pictorial, or oral form from a relatively recent past. Since the situation in the prehistoric, and especially the Paleolithic, period is to be compared with that of present-day "primitive" societies rather than that of more "developed" ones, we must pay close attention to conditions and modes of behavior examined in the studies of so-called primitive peoples. These studies can help in the interpretation of archaeological finds, but not infrequently they also show that similar material objects allow divergent functional interpretations.

These remarks about interpretation apply to a high degree to religion because it is primarily a spiritual phenomenon in which the sacred or supernatural word plays an important role. It is clear that manifestations of religion cannot be determined from archaeological research since material remains are silent. Only indirectly and in special circumstances do archaeological finds yield a religious meaning. Thus the first question that students of prehistoric religion must ask is "Which objects and findings can be regarded as signs of religious intentions, experiences, and activities?" Although religion is primarily a spiritual phenomenon, it nonetheless uses a wide range of material accessories: artifacts and places that have a cultic and ceremonial significance, images and symbols, sacrificial and votive offerings. In many cases religion makes use of art; to a certain extent inferences about religious conceptions can also be drawn from burial customs.

The interpretation of such sources by analogy with present-day religious practices implies that a more or less complete correspondence or at least a great similarity is inferred from an observed partial correspondence. But not infrequently particular findings can be interpreted in different ways. For example, it is often not clear to which religious category a find belongs; sacrifices and burials, cannibalism and human sacrifices, and animal sacrifices and animal cults are not clearly distinguishable by archaeological criteria. It is not enough, therefore, to select a few religious phenomena from contemporary primitive societies and apply them to the archaeological material. Instead, it is necessary to conduct comprehensive comparative studies in order to obtain a sufficiently wide range of correlations and establish a basic correspondence of meanings. Admittedly such studies make it possible to register only general characteristics and not concrete particularities.

Even then it is still possible in many cases to give divergent interpretations, and it therefore becomes necessary to choose the one that is most likely.

The first rule, therefore, that must be observed in the interpretation of prehistoric finds is to compare them only with such recent phenomena as occur in a basically similar or corresponding context. For example, it is not possible to simply select a religious phenomenon connected with food cultivation (for example, feminine figurines of the Magna Mater type from Mediterranean and Eastern civilizations) and use it to explain one or another find connected with the culture of Paleolithic hunters and gatherers.

The vast stretch of time separating the Paleolithic period and today, the numerous opportunities for a shift in the meaning of things, and the modern dissemination and variety of phenomena all call for critical judgment in the use of ethnographic and historical analogies. One should be especially cautious in comparing prehistoric phenomena with contemporary primitive religions. On the other hand, as is clear from not a few cases, the very long interval of time that has passed does not necessarily mean that radical changes have occurred; often enough, strong tendencies toward stability are also observable. The lapse of time must be judged in relation to fundamental conditions; progressive development is accompanied by an acceleration. The first really epochal change took place only about thirty-five thousand BP, at the beginning of the Upper Paleolithic period. Thirty-five thousand years seems a short and insignificant span of time when compared with the hundreds of thousands of years' existence of the earliest human beings. It is therefore not as unimaginable as it might first appear that fundamental elements from a very early time should be preserved to our own day under comparable conditions. Furthermore, in comparison with the modern multiplicity and variety of phenomena, the number of possibilities realizable under simple conditions is limited.

A spiritual phenomenon such as religion does not develop in complete independence and isolation but depends to some degree on functional interrelations and limitations, including those of an economic and ecological kind. Careful account must be taken of duration and the interaction of tendencies toward stability or change, the multiplicity of possibilities and the limitation placed on them by general conditions, independent development, and functional interdependence. The divergent value judgments made of these criteria are the main reason for the debates among scholars about the significance and persuasiveness of the inferences they draw from comparisons.

Survey and Assessment. Our understanding of Paleolithic religion is essentially based on objects whose form and attributes themselves indicate religious or magical use or whose manner of deposition (burial, for example) or other contextual peculiarities suggests such a use, as well as on works of art whose content or situation reflects religious or magical meaning. For most of the Paleolithic (spatially as well as temporally) we have no such objects or artworks. Traces of these increase in Europe and some neighboring regions in the last part of the Paleolithic period. Previously, and outside these areas, they are scarce. Only in the immediately preceding time—the Middle Paleolithic (back to about one-hundred thousand years ago)—do we find ourselves on somewhat reliable ground.

The Middle Paleolithic. My discussion begins with finds from the Middle Paleolithic and not with the oldest finds, for we can make some useful statements about this period, especially on the basis of burials. In this context we are dealing with human beings known as the Neanderthals. Because of their external appearance, Neanderthals were initially regarded as incapable of religious ideas, unlike the more recent *Homo sapiens*. But our picture of these early human beings has since changed substantially.

Neanderthal skeletons often exhibit severe injuries, but for the most part we are not able to say with certainty whether they resulted from fights and battles. Some of the head injuries had healed; others were evidently fatal, and the hipbone of a man from a site on Mount Carmel (Israel) apparently has been pierced by some lancelike object. Not a few Neanderthals survived not only wounds but also numerous illnesses. This was apparent also from the skeleton of the original Neanderthal—the find that gave the Neanderthals their name—who despite numerous afflictions had reached the age of fifty or so, a very advanced age for his time. Evidence of illnesses is also observable in other finds, especially that of an elderly Neanderthal at Shanidar (Iraq) who was probably blind from childhood and whose right forearm had been amputated. He had survived a number of illnesses and injuries, something possible only if he enjoyed the protection and care of a community, although he was probably of little economic value to it. We have no way of knowing whether this man had other abilities and knowledge that might have made him a respected member of the group. In any case, this instance, as well as others, indicates that Neanderthals were by no means the crude savages they are sometimes made out to be but lived in a kind of community in which not only the law of the jungle and economic utility carried weight.

Burials also provide evidence of the same situation. The dead are typically found with their legs slightly flexed, usually in elongated pits; in some Near Eastern finds, however, the dead are in a tightly crouched position, as though they had been forced down into narrow holes. With some regularity they are laid on an east-west axis, usually with the head to the east and, in the majority of cases, the body lying on its right side. It is not always possible to say with certainty whether animal bones and tools found near the corpse were burial gifts.

Noteworthy, however, is the little cemetery at La Ferrassie (France) where three fine stone artifacts, suited for adults, were found in the grave of three children, including a newborn or stillborn infant. (See figure 1.) Tools of the same kind were also found with adults, and some sites have yielded pits containing animal bones and artifacts, as well as reddish fragments. For example, the head of an elderly man found at La Chapelle aux Saints (France) was covered with large plates made of bone; his body was surrounded by pieces of jasper and quartz and fragments of a red material.

There are other instances in which the dead—and especially their heads, which were often protected by stones—were partly surrounded by large bones. For example, the grave of an approximately eight-year-old boy at Teshik-Tash in the foothills of the T'ien Shan (U.S.S.R.) was surrounded by a circle of horns. The corpse of a man found in the cave of Shanidar was surrounded by blossoms of flowers that are almost all used as curatives in popular medicine today. (Although graves containing flowers may have been more numer-

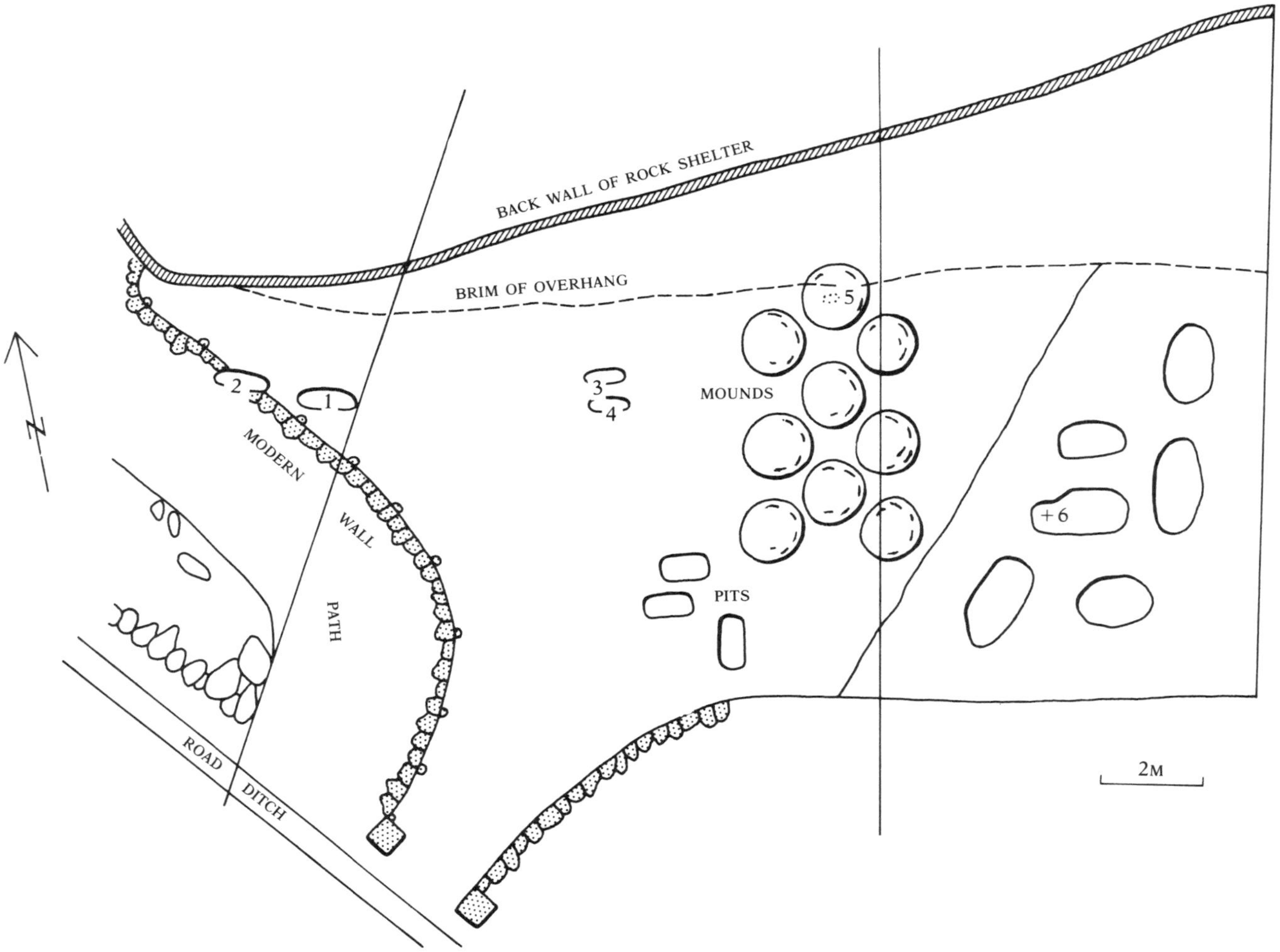

FIGURE 1. *Paleolithic Burial.* The so-called cemetery at La Ferrassie, Dordogne, France, contains burials of (1) a man, (2) a woman, (3, 4) small children, (5) a newborn infant, and (6) a child with its head detached, as well as other pits containing stone tools and the bones of small animals.

ous, only one example has been discovered, thanks to a fortunate combination of circumstances and to modern investigative techniques.)

In all these cases we find clear signs that Neanderthals took care of their fellow human beings. The burial gifts really leave no reasonable doubt that the dead were thought to continue to live in some manner. This belief explains why objects were buried along with the dead, to be used in the future; even children were provided with objects that they certainly could not have used during their lifetime. What particular shape these general ideas took we cannot say. We can at least say, however, that the Neanderthals had an understanding of death and had somehow come to grips with it.

In the cemetery at La Ferrassie, a skull of a child was found in a burial pit about a meter away from the skeleton. Isolated skulls were also found elsewhere. In a cave on Monte Circeo, about a hundred kilometers southeast of Rome (Italy), a Neanderthal skull was found on the surface of the cave floor, with the basal opening (which had evidently been widened artificially) facing upward; it was surrounded by a circle of stones, and nearby there were three heaps of auroch and deer bones. (See figure 2.) The basal openings of most of the numerous skulls found in isolation—some from an even earlier period—are believed to have been artificially enlarged, probably to facilitate removal of the brain. This practice was probably connected with the consciousness of death and may indicate a special relationship between the living and the dead; we are not in a position, however, to hypothesize about the particulars of these ideas and activities.

In the burial site at Regourdou near Montignac (France), the skull and some other bones of a brown bear were found under a large block of stone. There are also reports of finds, not associated with human burials, of individual skulls of bears, especially of the great cave bear, together with some long bones. Stone chests containing the vertebrae of the neck still attached to the skulls were reportedly found in a few caves in Switzerland, but these finds are poorly documented and uncertain. Nonetheless it would not be wise to completely doubt the validity of these finds, as many do.

The specific meaning of such finds is again unclear. Perhaps they represent simple sacrifices of the especially important parts of the prey; perhaps Neanderthal hunters, like those of a later period, buried the bones in order to ensure the survival of the animals and their species. Such a theory may explain why parts of the skull, backbone, and long bones of a bovine were placed under a great stone at the entrance of the above-mentioned cave at La Chapelle.

The Lower Paleolithic. All in all, we find clear indications that the people of the Middle Paleolithic were concerned with the phenomenon of death and with existence in another world. Some of their practices display no secular meaning but, like burial rites, show a commitment to certain binding customs.

Hominids from the Lower Paleolithic period, who date as far back as over a half million years ago, have skulls with primitive proportions and generally smaller brains than modern man. These characteristics led some researchers to doubt that these hominids were capable of achievements comparable with those of human beings from later periods. But objective findings show that the way of life of these hominids must on the whole have been the same as that of the Neanderthals. Occasionally researchers have found shelters from the Lower Paleolithic that are superior to those of the Middle Paleolithic, although they have assumed, probably with justification, that the lack of such dwellings in later times should be attributed to the unfavorable conditions of preservation.

The opposite argument has been used to explain the lack of some kinds of finds from the Lower Paleolithic, especially the absence of burials. In fact, however, even burials from the Middle Paleolithic are found only in restricted areas and in caves. Since Lower Paleolithic archaeological finds have rarely been unearthed in caves, it is not surprising that we should know of no burials in caves dating from that period. We do not know whether the hominids of the Lower Paleolithic may have buried their dead elsewhere; if they did, perhaps the evidence has simply vanished. The spiritual background and ideas that we can infer from burials may well have existed even if they have not manifested themselves in burials.

Skulls from the Lower Paleolithic, like those from the Middle Paleolithic, are often found in isolation, as with Java men, for example. Some of these as well as some

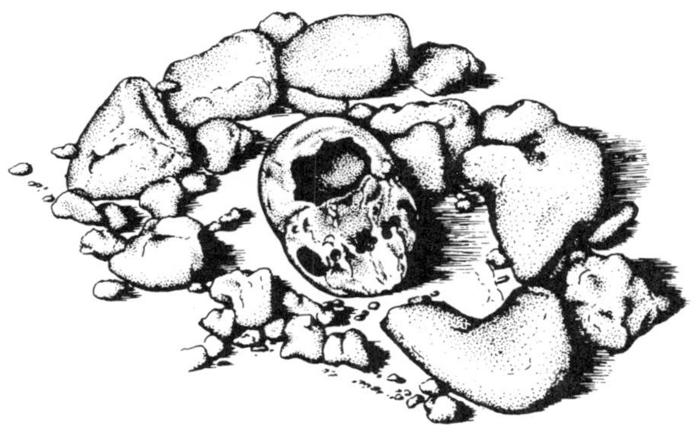

FIGURE 2. *Human Skull Surrounded by Stones.* Grotta Guattari, Monte Circeo, Lazio, Italy.

of the skulls found at the site of Peking man have a basal opening that seems to have been artificially widened. Far more skulls, and especially tops of skulls, were found than other parts of the skeleton, suggesting that the skulls were buried apart from the rest of the body. (The fact that in some strata the skulls were found in no particular order as well as mingled with animal bones has led some to hypothesize that cannibalism was practiced. If so, the cannibalism must have been carried out elsewhere and the skulls and a few other bones subsequently brought to the site. But the bones could have just as well been brought to the site without cannibalism entering the picture.) The only thing we can say is that the skulls probably received special treatment and were deposited apart. As no convincing secular explanation of the phenomenon has been offered, we should simply assume that there existed practices in which the skull played a special role that transcended the life of the individual in question.

We have no similar indications for the earliest Paleolithic, which began at least two million years ago, perhaps even earlier. Yet even sites from this time have yielded artificial stone tools that are at least as complex as those of Peking man, as well as smashed and, in various places, collected bones of animals. Some finds from this period also suggest the presence of huts or shelters from the wind. Were these finds from a later date, no one would doubt such an interpretation. But since the hominids of the earliest Paleolithic had a very small brain, some researchers think that the archaeological finds of the period are not to be interpreted as they would be if they belonged to later human beings. (Although biological factors and archaeological evidence points to the existence of communities made up of small groups of nuclear families, many scholars think they should not assume that such "human" characteristics existed during the earliest Paleolithic.) If other explanations of these early finds are sought (they are not very convincing), it is for two reasons: the finds are very old and doubtless simple, and the hominids of that period were physically "more primitive" than Peking man or the Neanderthals. Whether these are persuasive reasons may be left unanswered for the moment, but it will be important for a general assessment of these early hominids.

The Upper Paleolithic. The people of the Upper Paleolithic are equal to present-day humans in physical appearance, and they are therefore given the same name, *Homo sapiens.* People of this time were still living as hunters and gatherers. Only in the course of the later Upper Paleolithic are more definite signs of specialization, differentiation, and an accumulation of cultural possessions to be seen. As an example I mention only the pronounced presence of personal ornaments, which are also to be found in graves. This fact differentiates the people of the Upper Paleolithic from those of the Middle Paleolithic, but it does not necessarily indicate any substantial distinction between them. Only rarely do individual dead persons seem to have been given more special attention than others.

Of special interest is the grave of a powerfully built man found at Brno (Czechoslovakia) and dating from the beginning of the Upper Paleolithic. A great deal of red material was used for the burial; near the skull were over six hundred cut, tubelike fossil mollusks *(Dentalium badense).* A find of particular importance at this site, however, is the only certainly masculine figurine thus far known from the Upper Paleolithic; it is distinguished by other characteristics as well. In addition, the grave contained two stone rings of a kind previously known from only a very few examples; perhaps all of them were connected with graves. Furthermore, the grave at Brno is the only one in which a large number of round disks made of stone, bone, and ivory have been found. Thus there are a number of objects that are rarely found elsewhere or at least rarely or never appear in graves (the anthropomorphic figurine, for example). It is hard not to think that the interred man was involved in some capacity with cultic or magical things.

Our most important sources of information about religion during the Upper Paleolithic are works of art. Although the well-known paintings and drawings on the walls and roofs of caves are expressive, they do not display a great wealth of motifs. They primarily depict animals and only rarely, and then most often crudely, represent human beings. In many instances, moreover, the

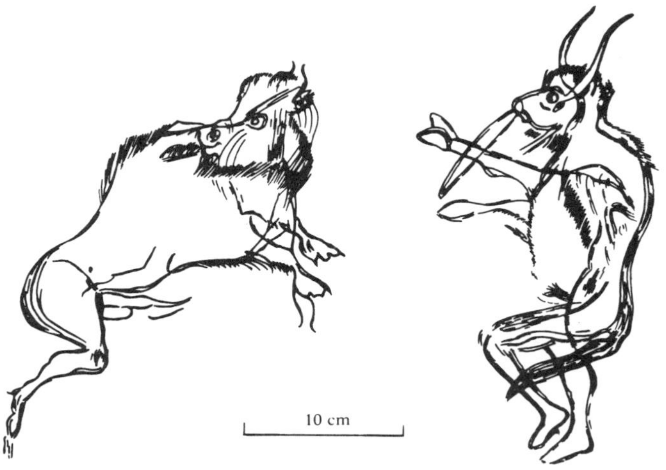

FIGURE 3. *Hybrid Human-Animal Beings.* These figures, the so-called masked dancers, appear on a wall of Les Trois Frères cave, Montesquieu-Avante, Ariège, France.

humans are not presented simply as humans but with animal attributes or as hybrid human-animal forms. Only a small number of the animals are depicted as prey, as indicated by the projectiles being thrown at them. Many anthropomorphic figures with animal attributes are regarded as masked dancers or sorcerers, but a good number are better described as composite figures. In any case, masking cannot be seen in images of animals that combine the attributes of various animals without any anthropomorphic element. (See figures 3 and 4.) There are even strange pictures for which no models could have been found in the fauna of the time. In many cases certain species predominate, but for the most part they are not the ones also found in the correlative strata of cultural relics.

A good deal of emphasis has been put on the fact that two species of animals or two groups of species frequently predominate in the pictures of a cave, but this dualism is by no means as clearly marked as is sometimes claimed. (At least there is no convincing evidence of a contrast between male and female.) At least as important is the fact that the pictures are generally unrelated to one another and that one will often cover and ruin another so that it has been possible to speak exaggeratedly of pictures being "consumed." By and large, it is the animal or, more rarely, an anthropomorphic being that is the focus of the artist's interest. The pictures are often drawn in parts of the caves that are dark and far from the entrances and, less frequently, in more accessible places. In some cases the old entrance has been blocked by a kind of stone wall. Often it is possible to view the pictures only with difficulty. Everything militates against the view that this is *l'art pour l'art,* "art for art's sake."

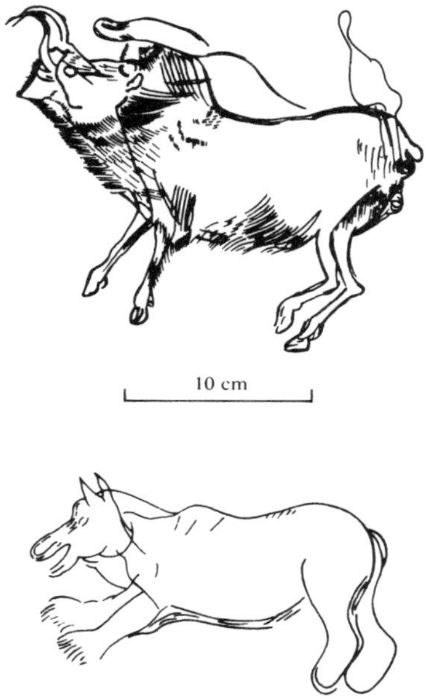

FIGURE 4. *Hybrid Animal Beings.* Also in Les Trois Frères cave, these engravings portray a deer with a bison's head (above) and a bear with a wolf's head (below).

The pictures represent, above all, the essential character of the animal, sometimes in relation to the hunt, sometimes in relation to human beings or to anthropomorphic figures, especially when the latter show a mergence of human and animal forms. Animals clearly played an extremely important part in the mental world of these hunters, insofar as this world is reflected in their art. We may probably assume that to a certain extent the artworks mirror the real role of animals; they probably point even more clearly, however, to the special evaluation of animals and of certain species in particular. Paintings in which humans and animal forms and attributes are depicted together and in which the forms and attributes of various animal species are portrayed show the close connection between the animal world and other spheres of life.

It is probable that we are dealing, at least in principle, with a manifestation similar to one that still characterizes the mental world of numerous more developed hunting cultures. Central to this "animalism" are close relations between animals and humans and a heightened importance of the animal world even outside and above the natural realms. The animalist outlook is fleshed out and developed in ways that often differ widely in their details. Thus we often find the notion of the animal as tutelary spirit and *alter ego,* the idea that human and animal forms are easily and often interchanged, and the idea of a higher being who is thought to have an animal shape or to be capable of changing and combining shapes and who is regarded as a kind of lord of animals, hunters, and the hunting grounds, as well as of the spirits of game and of the bush. Such zoomorphic higher beings are often group progenitors and culture heroes and appear also as mediators and as hypostases and personifications of a supreme god. In short, animalism is a widely found and dominant manifestation and yet, by its very nature, it should be seen as a lower or marginal sphere of religion, one that is frequently interspersed with other motifs and attitudes, including those of a magical type.

Because paintings and objects can be put in the service of both religion and magic, it is difficult and often impossible to distinguish between these two purposes. There is, however, no reason to regard rock paintings solely as instruments of magic. (This assumption arose when the study of Paleolithic art was in its infancy. The paintings were then regarded primarily as evidence of

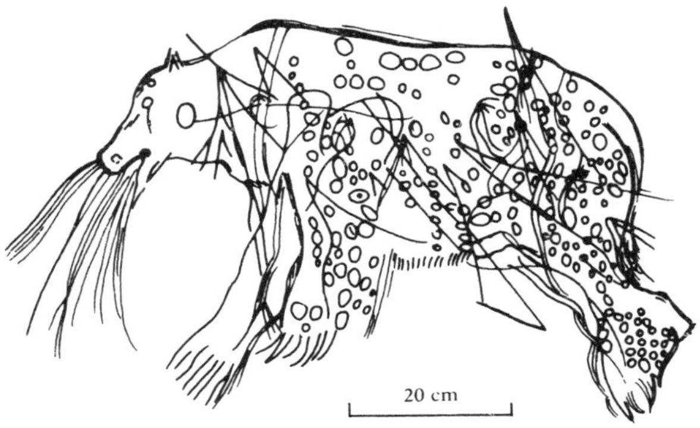

FIGURE 5. *Bear Ceremonialism.* This engraving of a wounded bear shedding blood from its mouth and nose is in Les Trois Frères cave.

totemism; totemism, in turn, was seen as a manifestation of the magical mentality.) We have no way of knowing which of the many possible uses was actually intended for Paleolithic painting.

A number of paintings of bears show peculiarities of one kind or another and occur in an unusual context. They may well have played a part in bear ceremonialism. (See figure 5.) Here the slain or to-be-slain bear is at the center of various rituals in which it is treated as a guest to whom respect is due or as an ancestor or mythical forefather. The climax of a festive meal is often the consumption of the bear's brain; the skull and long bones or even the entire skeleton are buried. Perhaps the bones and skulls of bears found at Paleolithic sites are to be interpreted along similar lines. Contemporary hunting peoples frequently bury parts of their prey to ensure a resuscitation of the animal and the preservation of its species. The deeper meaning of this ritual, however, is that it probably mystically returns the bear to the lord of the animals.

Bones of other animals are also occasionally found in circumstances indicating an intentional deposition that cannot be explained in secular terms. At some sites parts of reindeer have been discovered: head, neck, and the front part of the trunk, including the forelegs. A small scratch-drawing found at one site might depict a similar ceremony using a bovine. (See figure 6.) A deposition containing these parts of the skeleton was also found at the earlier-mentioned cave of La Chapelle. Once again, there is no way of determining whether there was a real sacrifice.

The significance of a painting of a birdlike man in the cave of Lascaux (France) has been much debated. The correct interpretation is probably that the picture depicts a man in a trance. His birdlike head and the bird shown on a pole may represent a shaman and a helping spirit. (See figure 7.) Anthropomorphic figures with the heads of birds may be interpreted similarly. The figurines of birds that have been found at sites in eastern Europe and Siberia and that were apparently nailed or hung remind us of parts of a shaman's clothing. Other pictures may likewise depictshamans—for example, the drawing of the so-called Sorcerer of Les Trois Frères—but here as in most cases other interpretations are also possible. (See figure 8.)

Whether small scratch-drawings from the early Upper Paleolithic can be interpreted as pubic triangles or vulvas is uncertain. Only later do the so-called Venus figures make their appearance. (See figure 9.) These are distinguished for the most part by their ample bodies and large breasts, which perhaps indicate pregnancy in some cases; there is no special emphasis on the primary sexual characteristics. Most of the figures do not have feet, and their arms, which are always very thin, often display decorative bracelets. Frequently, too, care has been taken to represent the style of hair or a head covering, whereas the face is not developed at all. The emphasis is clearly on the areas of the body connected with pregnancy, birth, and nursing. It is reason-

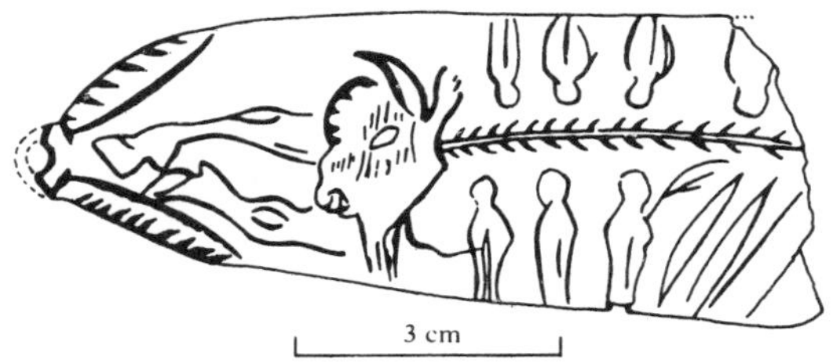

FIGURE 6. *Offering.* Presumably an offering, this shaped blade of bone (discovered at Abri Raymonden at Chancelade, Dordogne, France) bears engraved designs of men and a bison.

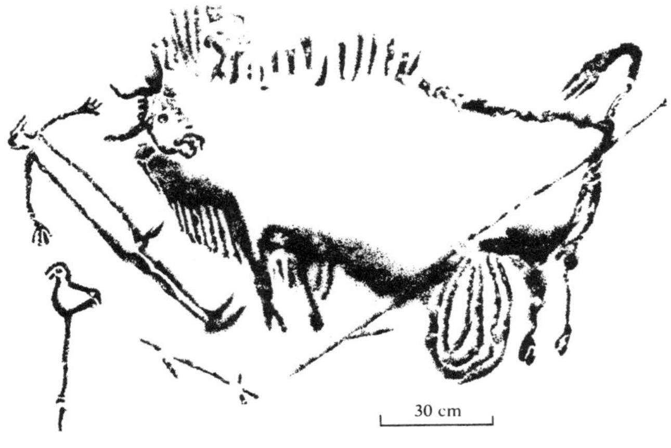

FIGURE 7. *Ritual Scene.* This painting in black outline, presumably of a ritual scene being enacted, was discovered in a cave at Lascaux, Dordogne, France.

able therefore to assume that these little figures are associated with the idea of fertility, but this need not be their only significance. The fact that the figures always appear in dwellings or camps may indicate that they were protectors of dwellings. Even today we frequently find, among peoples of the Northern Hemisphere, the idea of a higher feminine being who is, among other things, a mother or mistress of the animals, a divinity of the underworld (to which a shaman travels on his journey), a helper in the hunt and a provider of prey, a mistress of the land, of other regions, and of the powers of nature. But here again we cannot tie ourselves down to details and specific traits. In the figures and scratch-drawings of a later period it is usually possible to conclude only indirectly that women are intended. Sexual characteristics often no longer play any part in these figures, but there is a great deal of emphasis on the buttocks. Whether these figures have the same meaning as the Venus figures is an open question. But perhaps the feminine need not always be expressed in such an extreme way.

Many other questions about religion during the Paleolithic remain mysterious and unexplained. We have knowledge of only a small part of what once existed. It is clear enough, however, that we must rule out any attempt to impose a single general explanation on everything. Nonetheless, it also seems clear that animals and shapes with animal attributes, on the one hand, and a female principle, on the other, often played a part in the mental and spiritual world of the Paleolithic and fit in with the peculiar character of a world of gatherers and specialized hunters.

Theories about Paleolithic Religion. Finds from the Upper Paleolithic period, though relatively rich and potentially informative when compared with those of previous periods, surely reflect only a small part of the religious phenomena of the time. We do not even know whether the finds take us to the heart of the religion in question or simply represent marginal and secondary manifestations of it. Our observations and conclusions about the Middle Paleolithic are much scantier; they are especially important, however, because here we leave the world of human beings who are "modern" in their physical appearance and yet still find clues pointing to ideas of a world beyond this one and to precise customs connected with such concepts. If we go still farther back in time, the archaeological picture becomes more obscure. On the one hand, the conditions needed for the preservation and discovery of relics and traces of religious activities are much less favorable; on the other hand, we find no break in the continuity of material remains that can be compared with the break between the Middle and the Upper Paleolithic in Europe. Any claim of division that separates later periods from an era in which religious ideas and activities were impossible is arbitrary. In this matter we are simply groping in the dark.

We may ask whether early human beings possessed a religion, or we may even assert that a being, regardless

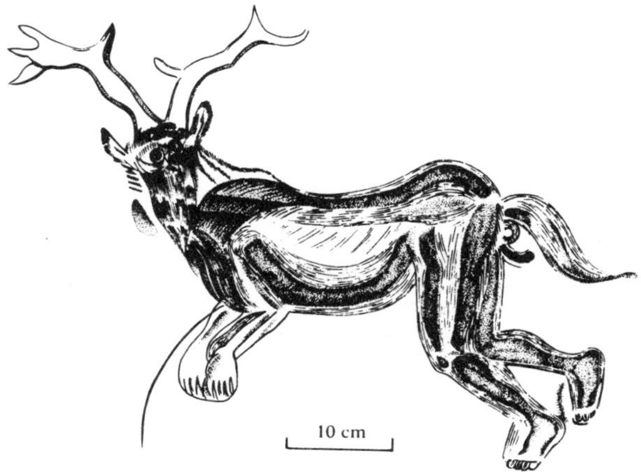

FIGURE 8. *Hunter-Wizard.* Among the hybrid beings depicted in Les Trois Frères cave is the so-called Sorcerer, shown here in the reconstructional drawing made by Henri Breuil (some details are questionable).

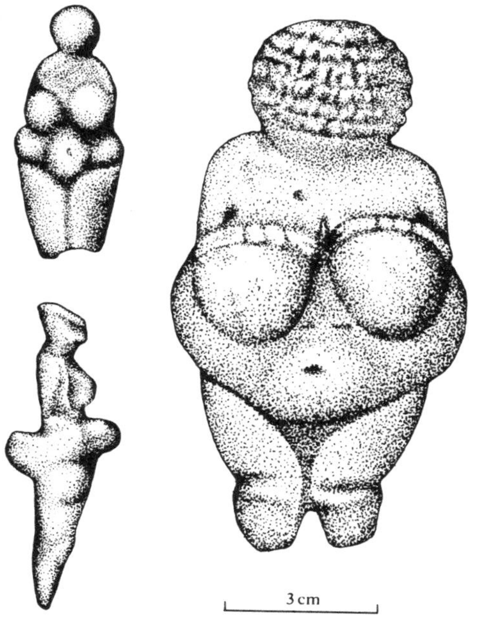

FIGURE 9. *Venus Figurines.* On the right is the so-called Venus of Willendorf, a limestone figurine from Willendorf, Wachau, Austria. On the left are two steatite figurines discovered at the Grimaldi caves at Ventimiglia, Liguria, Italy.

of his appearance, who does not possess some form of religion cannot be regarded as truly human. (Humanity could also be determined by the development of language and other indicators.) The question becomes more pragmatic if we do not make religion the sole criterion for humanity but seek to discover whether there are other material manifestations pointing to a psyche, of a kind that allows us to infer some degree of what is specifically human and justifies our speaking of human beings in the true meaning of the word. In any event, the statement that early human beings did or did not possess a religion is an eminently anthropological one. But behind it, as behind all anthropological statements, lie fundamental anthropological assumptions.

The position researchers take on the question of early religion depends not least on their picture of early human beings. Some interpreters regard the earliest stone artifacts as evidence of low intelligence and a primitive mentality; nothing else, they claim, could be expected given the small brain of the hominids of that time. Others, however, will point out that stone artifacts indicate a mediated relation to nature, such as is characteristic of human beings, and reveal that these early hominids had human insight into the nature of things. This second group of researchers is therefore inclined to regard even the early hominids as fully human in principle, although they had not yet fully evolved in every respect and would undergo further developments. In any case, the earliest archaeological finds are such that they fit without difficulty into the picture of a group of hunters and gatherers of the *Homo sapiens* type. (The main argument to the contrary, whether or not it is expressed, is that early hominid toolmakers differed physically from modern man; in particular their brain was smaller and had different proportions from the brain of *Homo sapiens*. No one, however, is in a position to say what size and form a brain must have to develop religious ideas.)

These divergent points of view then become the basis on which other matters and questions are discussed and interpreted. For example, some researchers (who, in the final analysis, belong to the evolutionist tradition of the nineteenth century) think they must deny that early humans had permanent nuclear families, the basic form of human society. Scholars differ even more on whether beliefs in psychic phenomena and other forms of religion existed among early human beings.

In this type of discussion it is all too easy to forget that in dealing with other aspects of the early period we postulate much that is not directly documented by finds. (For example, some scholars believe that at least half a million years ago human beings crossed parts of the Mediterranean where there was no land bridge and must therefore have had some kind of craft, although we have found no remains of these.) It is necessary in particular to avoid taking the simplicity of stone tools as the measure of everything else. For example, in the site at Huaca Prieta (Peru), equally primitive stone tools coexist later than 3000 BCE with cultivated plants and textiles. If we were to adopt that criterion, the presence of very simple stone tools in "more developed" cultures from later periods would almost certainly lead to erroneous judgments.

Two basic judgments on the nature of early human beings are thus possible; neither of them can be strictly demonstrated nor strictly refuted. So, too, are there two basic attitudes that can be adopted toward the question of early religion. One current view is that early human beings possessed no religion initially and only at a late date gradually moved beyond "low" conceptions of the supernatural and ascended to the level of "authentic" religion. Others, on the contrary, believe that the possession of some form of religion is a universal human trait. According to this position, if early hominids show human traits in the areas accessible to us through archaeological finds, they probably practiced some form of religion. No theory on the nature and development of the religion of early human beings can be based directly on these finds; all are hypotheses developed on the basis of later phenomena. The question in every case is whether the archaeological evidence from the Paleolithic can provide—and does provide—material grounds for these theories.

The nature and reciprocal relationship of religion and magic have played an important part in these discussions. Since the Upper Paleolithic was at one time widely regarded as a period in which belief in magic predominated, it was thought—and still is in many quarters—that researchers had a fixed point to which they could refer. To the extent that magic was considered to be an early form or a forerunner of authentic religion, the development of genuine religious forms could only have begun at a later time.

Another view, however, holds that belief in a personal god who creates and preserves the world and its order is the earliest and original form of religion; magic, according to this position, is a secondary form of religion and a product of decadence. To the extent that this view recognizes the special importance of magic in the Upper Paleolithic, it also sees authentic religion as having begun at a correspondingly earlier date. It is extremely unlikely, however, that magic occupied such a great role that it can be considered a stage in the development of religion, whether it is seen as a precursor to religion or as a degenerative form. However religion (in the strict sense) and magic are conceived and defined in detail, the two should be viewed as different types of attitudes toward the supernatural. Although these two attitudes are opposed, they are not always strictly distinguishable, with one capable of acquiring greater importance when the other regresses. When circumstances allow, both magic and religion use the same "artifacts," so that it is often impossible to distinguish between them at the archaeological level.

Even if we accept that early human beings had a religion, a further question must be posed: are there forms of religion that they could not have possibly had? We must acknowledge that there is usually a close association between certain special manifestations of religion and the general conditions in which people live; the model on which society is actually based plays a part in determining it conceptions of the supernatural. Among simple hunters and gatherers who live in small and essentially egalitarian groups, there will hardly be a place for a proper hierarchy of divinities such as is found in hierarchically ordered civilizations.

These differences are in fact only differences of expression. I do not see, however, why any of the fundamental religious categories cannot be ascribed to early man when we are trying to assess him as *homo religiosus.* In this area the criterion of early man's simplicity is sometimes invoked—but then we may ask: Is not the concrete and the personal more congenial to a simple mentality than abstractions of any kind? And if so, will not simple societies of hunters and gatherers, who are trying to achieve a basic understanding of things and processes for which they see no real explanation but on which they nonetheless depend, tend to think of personal supernatural beings (divinities) instead of more abstract powers and forces?

BIBLIOGRAPHY

General surveys of prehistory, including religion, can be found in my *Urgeschichte der Kultur* (Stuttgart, 1961) and in my *Handbuch der Urgeschichte,* vol. 1, *Ältere und mittlere Steinzeit: Jäger- und Sammlerkulturen* (Bern, 1966).

For early surveys of prehistory that assert the agnosticism of early man, see John Lubbock's *Pre-Historic Times, as Illustrated by Ancient Remains, and the Manners and Customs of Modern Savages* (London, 1865) and Gabriel de Mortillet's *Le préhistorique: Antiquité de l'homme,* 2d ed. (Paris, 1885). Contrasting views regarding the religious thought of early man can be found in Thomas Lucien Mainage's *Les religions de la préhistoire: L'âge paléolithique* (Paris, 1921); Johannes Maringer's *De Godsdienst der Praehistorie* (Roermond en Masseik, 1952), translated by Mary Ilford as *The Gods of Prehistoric Man* (New York, 1960); and my "Approaches to the Religion of Early Paleolithic Man," *History of Religions* 4 (Summer 1964): 1–22. Mainage's book is still the essential work in this area, Maringer's discussion follows the view of the Vienna school, and my essay attempts a general evaluation.

The meaning and content of Paleolithic art are discussed in the following works.

Leroi-Gourhan, André. *Art et religion au paléolithique supérieur.* 2d ed. Paris, 1963.

Leroi-Gourhan, André. *Préhistoire de l'art occidental.* Paris, 1965. Translated by Norbert Guterman as *The Art of Prehistoric Man in Western Europe* (London, 1968). A dualistic interpretation in the sexual sense.

Narr, Karl J. "Bärenzeremoniell und Schamanismus in der Älteren Steinzeit Europas." *Saeculum* 10 (1959): 233–272.

Narr, Karl J. "Weibliche Symbol-Plastik der älteren Steinzeit." *Antaios* 2 (July 1960): 132–157.

Narr, Karl J. "Sentido del arte Paleolitico." *Orbis Catholicus: Revista Iberamericana Internacional* 4 (1961): 197–210.

Narr, Karl J. "Felsbild und Weltbild: Zu Magie und Schamanismus im jungpaläolithischen Jägertum." In *Sehnsucht nach dem Ursprung,* edited by Hans P. Duerr, pp. 118–136. Frankfurt, 1983.

Reinach, Salomon. "L'art et la magie: À propos des peintures et des gravures de l'âge du renne." *L'anthropologie* 14 (1903): 257–266. Starting from totemistic interpretation and asserting magic meaning.

Ucko, Peter J., and Andrée Rosenfeld. *Palaeolithic Cave Art.* New York, 1967. A critical review, neglecting animalism.

KARL J. NARR
Translated from German by Matthew J. O'Connell

PAN is a Greek god whose name, of Indo-European derivation, means "shepherd" (cf. Latin *pastor*). In appearance, he has the hooves, tail, hair, and head of a goat and the erect posture, upper body, and hands of a man. He is frequently depicted holding either a *lagobolon,* a kind of shepherd's crook used for hunting rabbits and controlling small flocks, or a syrinx, a flutelike instrument otherwise known as a panpipe.

Pan has his origins in ancient Arcadia, a remote and mountainous area of central Peloponnesus where an Archaic dialect is still spoken. Lord of Arcadia and guardian of its sanctuaries (according to Pindar), the goat-god is very much at home in this primitive region, with its essentially pastoral economy, where the political system of Classical Greece was slow in being established. The enclosure dedicated to Pan on Mount Lycaeus (Aelianus, *De natura animalium* 11.6) functions as a sanctuary where animals pursued by the wolf seek protection. Pan thus appears as a master of animals, protecting wild and domestic creatures, while watching over the human activities of hunting and animal breeding. His actions, whether they brought sterility or fertility, were of interest primarily to shepherds and hunters, who were concerned with reproduction in the animal world.

Theocritus in his *Idylls* (7.103–114) alludes to a rite performed by the Arcadians for Pan during periods when the animals were not reproducing: young men whipped his statue in order to call the inactive god back to life. The Arcadians pictured Pan as reigning over his own flocks in the mountainous lands that constituted his domain and his sanctuaries. Thus the whole of Mount Lampeia, where the Erymanthe has its source, is a sanctuary of Pan. So is the Menale, where people believed they could hear, in the mysterious and fearful sounds of the wilderness (echoes in particular), the music of this wild shepherd.

In Arcadia Pan was considered a major god. He had a cult on Mount Lycaeus, alongside that of Zeus. We know, however, of no figurative representation of the god antedating the diffusion on his cult outside Arcadia, nor do we have any literary testimony, with the exception of some dedications that retain only the name of the god. Not until the beginning of the fifth century BCE, and after the introduction of his cult in Athens, does the image of Pan take shape. Although the god now loses some of his theological importance, as he assumes a marginal position in regard to Olympus and joins the host of minor gods, he nevertheless gains in symbolic richness, and his rites are no longer confined to the pastoral world. His cult, his mythology, and his iconography spread rapidly throughout the Greek world and were adapted to the local character of Attica, Boeotia, and especially the regions of Delphi and Macedonia.

In an account by Herodotus (6.105ff.), Pan became an official deity at Athens following his appearance in Arcadia to the messenger Philippides, whom the Athenians had sent to Sparta shortly before the Battle of Marathon (490 BCE). Pan asked Philippides why the Athenians did not dedicate a cult to him, since he had already been so benevolent toward them and would be again. Remembering this epiphany after the battle, the Athenians consecrated to Pan a small grotto on the northwest slope of the Acropolis.

The rapid spread of Pan's cult, from this time on, brought with it certain readjustments. A thorough reworking of symbolism gave this god, who was unknown to Homer and Hesiod, a complex but coherent form. In the poetry of the fifth century, numerous allusions are made to Pan. There are allusions to his natural habitat, Arcadia, which becomes a metaphor for the pastoral in contrast to the urban, the wild in contrast to the cultivated. The coexistence of the divine and the animal in Pan explains the ambiguity of a being whose power oscillates unceasingly between fear and seduction, disorder and harmony. Represented as shepherd, hunter, musician, and dancer, as an untiring and often unlucky pursuer of nymphs, Pan also appeared as the agent of "panic" fear (that collective, animal-like disorder that seizes military camps at rest, especially at night) and of a form of individual possession (panolepsy). Finally, some accounts describe the birth of Pan, whose monstrous appearance causes the gods to rejoice but sends his human nurse fleeing (Homeric *Hymn to Pan* 19). Other stories describe his unfruitful love affairs with Echo, Syrinx, or Pithys (in Alexandrine and post-Alexandrine poetry).

The philosophical destiny of the god, especially among the Stoics, is remarkable. By virtue of a Platonic play on words—the identification of Pan with *pan*, "all," in Plato's *Cratylus* (408c–d)—the goat-god becomes the personification of the All, the cosmic totality represented by the coexistence, in a single figure, of the animal (the material nature below) and the human (the spiritual nature above). Outside the Hellenic world his destiny is multiple: in Egypt he is assimilated to the god Min of the Copts, lord of the routes of the eastern desert. At Rome he becomes the Greek version of Faunus, or of Inuus, because of the influence of the legend about the Arcadian origins of the town.

From Plutarch we have the account of the death of Pan, announced by a mysterious voice to the pilot of a ship on its way from Greece to Italy under the reign of Tiberius. Pan's death upset the emperor so much that he called a committee of philologists to find out who this god was. The third-century bishop Eusebius of Caesarea believed that the death of the great Pan meant the death of all the demons of paganism, which occurred after the passion of Christ under Tiberius. Subsequently the account has been of interest to folklorists analyzing popular legends concerning "messages of death," legends that spread through northern Europe beginning with the sixteenth century, that is, at the same time that the ancient figure of Pan reappeared in literature (especially in Rabelais, in chapter 27 of his *Quart livre*).

BIBLIOGRAPHY

Cults, Myths, and Literary Destiny

Borgeaud, Philippe. *Recherches sur le dieu Pan.* Bibliotheca Helvetica Romana, no. 17. Rome, 1979.

Borgeaud, Philippe. "La mort du grand Pan: Problèmes d'interpretation." *Revue de l'histoire des religions* 200 (1983): 5–39.

Lehnus, Luigi. *L'Inno a Pan di Pindaro.* Milan, 1979.

Merivale, Patricia. *Pan the Goat-God: His Myth in Modern Times.* Cambridge, Mass., 1969.

Iconography and Archaeology

Brommer, F. "Pan im 5. und 4. Jahrhundert v. Chr." *Marburger Jahrbuch für Kunstwissenschaft* 15 (1949–1950): 5–42.

Herbig, Reinhard. *Pan der griechische Bocksgott: Versuch einer Monographie.* Frankfurt, 1949.

Walter, Hans. *Pans Wiederkehr: Der Gott der griechischen Wildniss.* Munich, 1980.

PHILIPPE BORGEAUD
Translated from French by Mary Lou Masey

PANATHENAIA. One of the great pan-Hellenic festivals of the city of Athens and its tutelary deity, Athena, the Panathenaia can be seen as a commemorative celebration of the city's foundation. The great festival was performed every four years from 570 BCE onward, though there were yearly "small" Panathenaias as well. The date was the twenty-eighth day of the month Hekatombaion (mid-July to mid-August). The ceremonial elements are the same for both forms of the cyclical feast, consisting of the following acts: first, the bringing of new fire to the temple of Athena Polias, protector of peasants and craftsmen; second, a procession *(pompē)* with a new garment *(peplos),* carried on a shiplike float, to clothe the seated olivewood statue of Athena (the *xoanon*); third, large sacrifices (of more than one hundred animals for small festivals) of sheep and cattle to be distributed among and eaten by the assembly; and fourth, an ancient form of racing *(agōn).*

During the first day, fire was kindled after sunset on the Akademos (the district outside the sacred Dipylon, or double gate), accompanied by sacrifices to Athena and Eros amid songs and dances by the youths. The fire was then carried by torch race through the Agora to the altar of Athena, where the cotton wick was lit. The mythic legitimation of this act, which was understood as the mystical significance of the rites, refers to the birth of the founding king of the city, Erichthonios: when Athena was pursued in love by Hephaistos, she preserved her virginity by having his seed spilled on her thigh, then wiping it with a cotton ball that she threw on the earth. From this seed sprang Erichthonios, a creature half human, half snake.

On the second and main day, a large procession started from the Dipylon, where the road from Eleusis entered Athens; the procession consisted of old men with olive branches, young girls with sacrificial vessels and sacred baskets, and the sacrificial animals. The focus of the procession was the large *peplos,* woven during the previous nine months by the women of Athens under the guidance of the virginal attendants of the temple of Athena (the Arrephoroi). Weaving had started at the Chalkeia festival for Athena Ergane ("Athena, patroness of crafts and craftiness"). The *peplos* was draped around the wooden statue, which had been ritually washed at an earlier celebration (the festival Plynteria in the month Thargelion, mid-April to mid-May).

While the Panathenaia can be fully appreciated only in relation to all other festivals of the agricultural year, its importance is to mark the ancient founding of the city and the start of a fertile year: it is a New Year festival. The great chariot race, during which fully clad warriors had to jump from their wagons and race on, recalls its originator, Erichthonios. Many more references are made to Athena as founder, protector, and virgin deity with strong chthonic features: central to the meaning are the multiple snake symbols. Both Erichthonios and the earlier autochthonous king Kekrops are depicted on vases as snakes winding around olive trees. Kekrops had three daughters, to whom Athena handed a closed basket in which she had secreted the snake-child Erichthonios. All three girls' names refer to fertility, containing the word for "dew," which also connotes "semen." One daughter, Pandrosos, also received sacrifices during the Panathenaia. The gist of the festival seems to be the symbolic association between fertility and autochthony, which accords well with the structural logic of the myths surrounding Athena: the goddess who was born without mother gives birth to progeny without her virginal status being violated.

[*See also* Athena.]

BIBLIOGRAPHY

Burkert, Walter. *Griechische Religion der archaischen und klassischen Epoche.* Stuttgart, 1977. Emphasizes strongly the central rite of dressing the statue of the goddess. Coherently integrates this festival into a rhythm of festivals of the city of Athens, in particular the constellation between goddess and primeval king.

Kerényi, Károly. *Athene, die Jungfrau und Mutter der griechischen Religion.* Zurich, 1952. Translated as *Athene, Virgin and Mother* (Irving, Tex., 1978). A thorough but often disorganized attempt to show the consistency of the myths around the many forms of Athena; often comes close to later structural analysis. Some daring philological derivations that nevertheless seem to capture the underlying logic of mythic narratives.

KLAUS-PETER KOEPPING

PAÑCATANTRA. The *Pañcatantra* is a collection of animal stories, in Sanskrit, compiled by an unknown author some time prior to the sixth (possibly as early as the fourth) century CE. Many of the stories were doubtless drawn from the great mass of Indian oral tradition, and part at least are of Buddhist origin, as may be seen from their close affinities to the Jātakas, or stories of the prior births of the Buddha. The *Pañcatantra* belongs in part to a class of works known as *nītiśāstra* ("science of right conduct") and partly also to the closely allied *arthaśāstra* ("science of polity"), which involves the practical and shrewd knowledge needed by an Indian king to rule his kingdom and conduct its internal and external affairs efficiently. [*See* Śāstra Literature.] Because of their practical and worldly purpose, the *Pañcatantra* fables are often amoral in tone, in contrast to the fables of the Greek storyteller Aesop, the connection with which, though much discussed, seems most unlikely on a number of grounds.

The stories of the *Pañcatantra* are set in a frame story in which a learned brahman named Viṣṇuśarman undertakes to impart political and social propriety to the ignorant and dissolute sons of King Amaraśakti of Mahilāropya. The Pañcatantra consists of five *(pañca)* books *(tantra)* of varying length. Its characters are, for the most part, animals, birds, and fish whose behavior is like that of human beings. So contrived as to lead from one to the other in a continuous series, the stories are emboxed in one another, each being introduced by a character in the foregoing story who recites a verse of general wisdom or one about a situation similar to the matter at hand. This leads to a request by one of the other characters for an explanation, which then follows in the form of an illustrative story.

Typical of the fables of the *Pañcatantra* is that of the two geese and their friend the tortoise. Because there is a scarcity of water in the lake where the three have been living happily, the geese are about to leave for another lake. The tortoise begs them to take him along. They agree to transport him if he grasps with his mouth a stick they will hold in their beaks, and warn him not to say anything if he hears people below expressing wonder at the sight. In spite of his promise, the tortoise opens his mouth to reply to the comments of the people on the ground and falls to his death. The moral of this tale is that he who fails to heed the exhortation of his friends and well-wishers comes to grief.

Because of its widespread popularity the *Pañcatantra* has been endlessly recopied and recast over the centuries, leading to many recensions. Its fables were also variously abbreviated or condensed for incorporation into other works, as for example the *Kathāsaritsāgara* of Somadeva and the *Bṛhatkathāmañjarī* of Kṣemendra, both of the eleventh century. One of the most famous abridgments is that contained in the *Hitopadeśa* (Instruction in What Is Salutary), whose author states that he drew his work "from the *Pañcatantra* and another book." Many of the fables are common parlance among Indians of all classes today, who are often unaware of a particular story's connection with the Sanskrit *Pañcatantra,* since one version or another will have been translated into almost every vernacular of India. The original *Pañcatantra* has, of course, long since perished, superseded by these countless variations and metamorphoses, whose mutual interrelations are often difficult, if not impossible, to establish with certitude.

At an early time fame of the *Pañcatantra* began to extend far beyond the borders of India, and scarcely a land can be named to which a translation of all or part of it has not come, whether centuries ago or in recent times. As figure 1 shows, the oldest translation outside India is that into Pahlavi (c. 550) made, according to the traditional account, by a physician named Burzūye, who had been sent from Persia by the Sasanid king Khusrū Anūshīrvān for the purpose of translating the *Pañcatantra* and other works of Indian wisdom. Although this translation, like the original *Pañcatantra,* has long since disappeared, two translations from it have survived. By far the more important of the two is that made into Arabic around 750 by ʿAbd Allāh ibn al-Muqaffaʿ; its title, *Kitāb Kalīlah wa-Dimnah* (The Book of Kalīlah and Dimnah), contains the arabicized names of the two jackals called Karaṭaka and Damanaka in the *Pañcatantra.* The *Kalīlah wa-Dimnah* quickly became diffused everywhere in the Arab world from Spain to India through translations into its principal languages. Of all these translations the Hebrew by Rabbi Jōʿēl has an especially significant place in the westward migration of the fables, as it was from this Hebrew version that they were finally brought into Latin and so made accessible to Europeans. The Latin translation, by a converted Jew named John of Capua, entitled *Liber Kelile et Dimne, Directorium Vite Humane,* about two centuries later became one of the earliest books printed in Europe, for its first edition appeared in 1480, barely three decades after the invention of movable types by Gutenberg. An Italian translation of the Latin *Directorium* by Antonio Francesco Doni, *La moral Filosophia del Doni,* in turn was rendered into English in 1570 as *The Morall Philosophie of Doni* by Sir Thomas North. Thus did the *Pañcatantra* fables come into English more than a thousand years after their composition, in a version standing in the seventh degree from the original!

BIBLIOGRAPHY

Complete and selective translations of the *Pañcatantra* have been made by Arthur W. Ryder under the titles *The Panchatantra, Translated from the Sanskrit* and *Gold's Gloom: Tales from the Panchatantra* (both, Chicago, 1925). An attempt was made by Franklin Edgerton in *The Panchatantra Reconstructed,* 2 vols. (New Haven, 1924), to restore the lost original *Pañcatan-*

FIGURE 1. *Genealogical Chart of the Pañcatantra Fables.* Only the older and more important derivatives of the *Pañcatantra,* both within and outside India, are given in this tabulation. For additional offshoots and some more recent translations, the genealogical chart prepared by Edgerton should be consulted. Asterisks indicate applications of the title *Fables of Bidpai* (or *Pilpay*) to various derivatives; *Bidpai* and *Pilpay* are corruptions of the name of the storyteller in the *Kalīlah wa-Dimnah.*

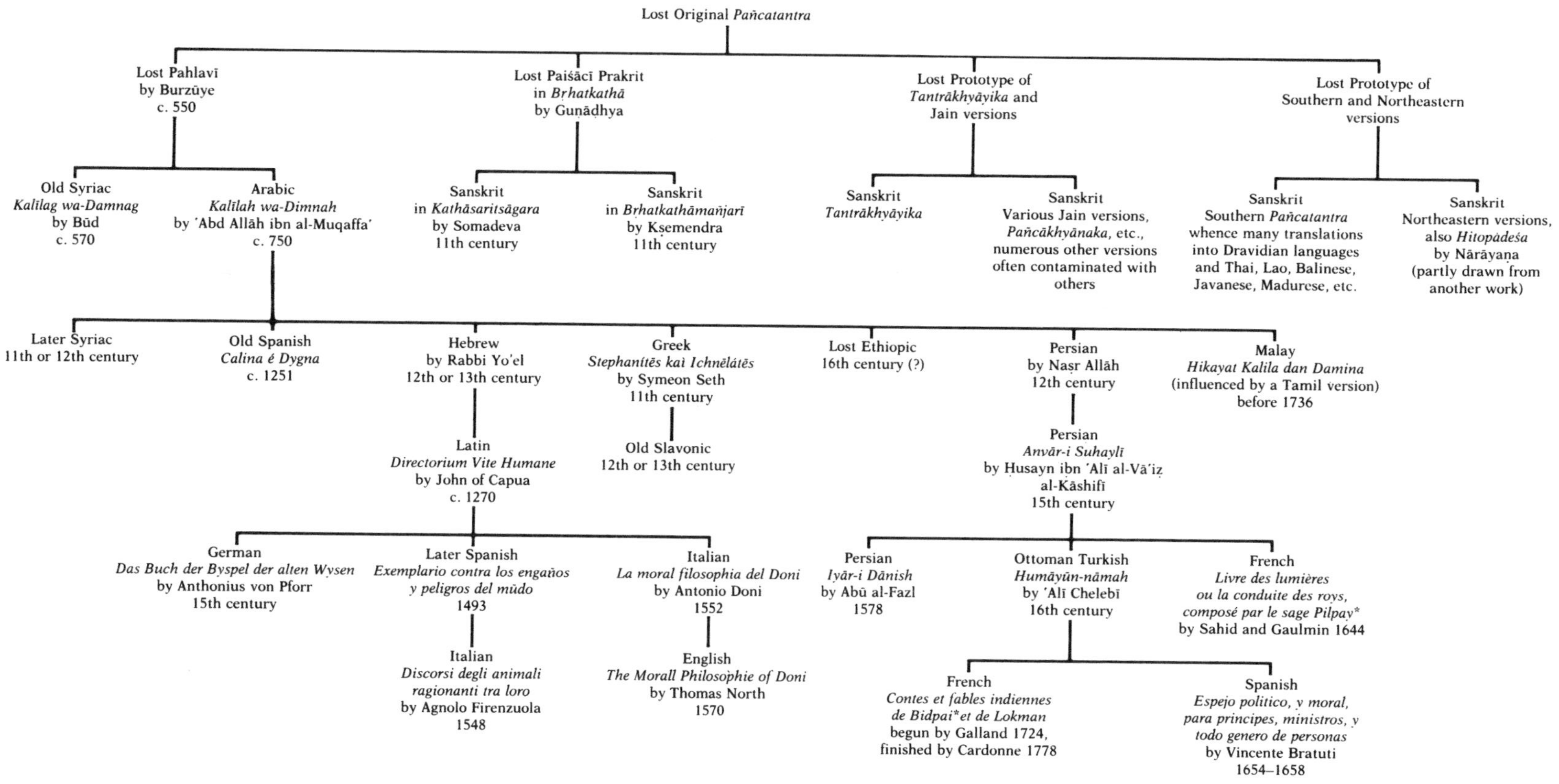

tra by a painstaking comparison of the oldest surviving derivatives. The first volume contains a detailed discussion of his method and the interrelationships of the various derivatives in addition to an English translation of the reconstructed *Pañcatantra;* the second volume has the reconstructed Sanskrit text and critical apparatus. The English translation has been separately published as *The Panchatantra, Translated from the Sanskrit* by Franklin Edgerton (London, 1965). In *Quellen des Pañcatantra* (Wiesbaden, 1978), Harry Falk compares the *Pañcatantra* fables with parallel versions in the Buddhist Jātakas and the *Mahābhārata.* This work is much influenced by Ruprecht Geib's *Zur Frage nach der Urfassung des Pañcatantra* (Wiesbaden, 1969).

A translation that is antiquated in a number of respects yet remains of great intrinsic value to the student of the *Pañcatantra* and its diffusion is Theodor Benfey's *Pantschatantra: Fünf Bücher indischer Fabeln, Märchen und Erzählungen, aus dem Sanskrit übersetzt mit Einleitung und Anmerkungen,* 2 vols. (1859; reprint, Hildesheim, 1966). A convenient and readable discussion of the fables and their progression from language to language outside India is contained in *Kalīlah and Dimnah, or the Fables of Bidpai: Being an Account of Their Literary History, with an English Translation of the Later Syriac Version of the Same, and Notes* by I. G. N. Keith-Falconer (Cambridge, 1885). Following the introduction there is a genealogical table of the principal translations that have descended from the Sanskrit original outside India. A much more detailed and accurate table, prepared by Franklin Edgerton, is to be found in *The Ocean of Story, Being C. H. Tauney's Translation of Somadeva's Kathā Sarit Sāgara,* edited by N. M. Penzer, vol. 5 (1926; reprint, Delhi, 1968), app. 2, pp. 232–242. Another general account of the migration of the fables, though much less detailed, is given by Joseph Jacobs in *The Earliest English Version of the Fables of Bidpai* (London, 1888), which reproduces Sir Thomas North's English translation, *The Morall Philosophie of Doni* (1570).

WALTER HARDING MAURER

PĀṆINI (fourth century BCE?), Sanskrit grammarian and promulgator of a complete system of grammar that standardized and codified classical Sanskrit. His importance to the history of religions in India lies primarily in the fact that grammar constitutes one of the eight sacred sciences of classical Vedic thought.

Eight grammars are known to have existed in ancient India, but all have been superseded by Pāṇini's major work, the *Aṣṭādhyāyī*. The *Aṣṭādhyāyī*—a name derived from *aṣṭa* ("eight") and *adhyāyas* ("books" or "chapters")—is also known as the *Aṣṭaka Pāṇinīya* or *Vṛtti Sūtra*. It has been called "a natural history of the Sanskrit language" (Goldstücker, 1860). The *Aṣṭādhyāyī* was composed in *sūtras* (aphorisms), a style already well in vogue by Pāṇini's time. Throughout history commentators and scholars have disagreed over the exact number of verses that can be attributed to Pāṇini and not to later interpolation. These range from 3,965 to 3,996; the latter is now the generally accepted count.

An example of Pāṇini's method can be seen in his treatment of the parts of speech. The Aindra system, thought to be the oldest Indian system of grammar, and until Pāṇini's time the most important, cites four parts of speech: *nāman* (noun), *ākhyāta* (verb), *upasarga* (preposition), and *nipāta* (particle). While retaining the *upasarga* and the *nipāta*, Pāṇini divides the *nāman* and the *ākhyāta* into subcategories and introduces a range of further classifications, thus recognizing the irregularities of many of the grammatical forms inherent in the two groups and providing a more accurate and practical framework for his grammar.

Pāṇini retains the eight cases of nouns and employs them without special definition, thereby indicating that these terms had already been established in earlier grammatical systems and were in common use. For other terms, however, he provides elaborate definitions. In some instances this indicates that Pāṇini was the first to recognize these concepts and was the inventor of the terms; in others, it indicates that he redefined and clarified a series of exact rules for their use. Among these terms are a few of the most basic concepts in classical Sanskrit grammar: *ātmanepada* and *parasmaipada* (loosely, "reflexive" and "transitive" classifications of verbs), *vibhakti* (inflection of nouns), *vṛddhi* (modification or increase of the length of vowels), and *saṃyoga* (combination of consonants).

In addition to a rearrangement, redefinition, and expansion of the principles of the Sanskrit language, the outstanding feature of the *Aṣṭādhyāyī* is its brevity of style; Pāṇini devised for his system artificial terms that function much like algebraic symbols. These code words are composed partly of "real words" and partly of linguistic elements of Pāṇini's invention. Where the Aindra system speaks, for example, of *ka-varga, ca-varga, ṭa-varga,* and so forth (i.e., the *varga*s or categories beginning with the letters *ka, ca, ṭa,* etc.), Pāṇini retains the first part of the element and suffixes the single vowel *u*. Thus *ka-varga, ca-varga,* and *ṭa-varga* are cited simply as *ku, cu,* and *ṭu*.

Pāṇini was also the author of a grammatical work, complementary to his *Aṣṭādhyāyī,* called the *Gaṇapātha*. His other contributions to Sanskrit grammar are recorded in the works of his students, who began a long line of commentators on the *Aṣṭādhyāyī*; the best known of Pāṇini's commentators is Patañjali. A tradition persists that Pāṇini was also a poet, as passages in some anthologies are attributed to him. This designation is not, however, a generally accepted one.

Like all Indian sciences, *vyākaraṇa* (the science of grammar) grew out of the study of Vedic sacrificial texts, and was considered to have had divine origins. As the promulgator of *vyākaraṇa* in its perfected form, Pāṇini himself is thus believed to have received divine assistance in the creation of his grammatical system. A legend made popular by the *Bṛhatkathāmañjari*, a collection of stories recorded by Kṣemendra (fl. eleventh century), is that Pāṇini was an intellectually deficient student so backward in his studies that he was forced to leave school. With no other recourse, he wandered to the Himalayas and practiced *tapas* (religious penance, intense meditation). This greatly pleased the god Śiva; as a reward he revealed to Pāṇini the new grammatical system.

Pāṇini must certainly have been a well-known figure to have become the subject of such legends. Stories about him also appear in two other great collections of Indian tales, the *Kathāsaritsāgara* of Somadeva (fl. eleventh century) and the *Pañcatantra* (a collection of unknown authorship dating anywhere from the fourth to the sixth century). The latter records how Pāṇini came to a violent death, attacked by a lion.

All that is known for certain about Pāṇini's life is that he was born in the small town of Śalatūra, near the confluence of the Kabul and Indus rivers. His father was either Paṇia or Paṇina (hence the derivative name Pāṇini), and his mother was known as Dakṣī, probably designating the Dakṣa *gotra* (clan) of Gandhara; Pāṇini was thus also known as Dīkṣeya or Dakṣiputra. Although it is now generally accepted that he lived in the fourth century BCE, scholars have waged lengthy debates that place Pāṇini anywhere from the seventh to the third century BCE. (Much of this debate is delineated by Goldstücker [1860], who placed the grammarian in a pre-Buddhist era.)

Regardless of when Pāṇini actually lived, we can ascertain that once his grammar became known it was put into constant use and was passed from teachers to students in a continuous progression throughout the centuries. The seventh-century Chinese pilgrim Hsüan-tsang visited Pāṇini's birthplace and in several accounts illustrates how the grammarian's principles were a central subject for the schoolchildren there. He also records a king's edict specifying that Pāṇini's grammar should be studied, with rewards offered to those who could memorize the complete text (Watters, 1961, pp. 221–224). The Kashmiri historian Kalhaṇa (eleventh century) mentions in his *Rājataraṅgiṇī* that Pāṇini's grammar "has long been studied assiduously in Kashmir" (4.635).

The *Aṣṭādhyāyī* has continued to this day to be the unsurpassed authoritative text on Sanskrit grammar. Considering the great diversity in Indian tradition and the rivalry for textual authority in almost every other Indian discipline, this is no small accomplishment.

[*See also* Vedāṅgas *and the biography of Patañjali the Grammarian.*]

BIBLIOGRAPHY

The Ashṭādhyāyī of Pāṇini, 2 vols., translated and edited by Śrīśa Chandra Vasu (1891; reprint, Delhi, 1962), is the standard English translation of Pāṇini's great work. An excellent study of the history of Sanskrit grammar that includes a detailed discussion of Pāṇini in relation to his predecessors is A. C. Burnell's *On the Aindra School of Sanskrit Grammarians* (1875; reprint, Varanasi, 1976).

The first and perhaps most thorough study by a European on Pāṇini and the commentarial tradition that developed around the *Aṣṭādhyāyī* is Theodor Goldstücker's *Pānini: His Place in Sanskrit Literature* (1860), edited by Surendra Nath Shastri (Varanasi, 1965). Other works on the same subject include Franz Kielhorn's *Kātyāyana and Patañjali: Their Relation to Each Other and to Pāṇini* (1876; 2d ed., Varanasi, 1963) and K. Madhava Krishna Sarma's *Pāṇini, Kātyāyana, and Patañjali* (Delhi, 1968).

For an interesting compilation of geographical, demographic, sociological, and religious information on ancient India based entirely on references made by Pāṇini, see Vasudeva S. Agrawala's *India as Known to Pāṇini: A Study of the Cultural Material in the Ashṭādhyāyī*, 2d ed., rev. & enl. (Varanasi, 1963).

The account of Hsüan-tsang's travels has been translated by Thomas Watters as *On Yuan Chwang's Travels in India* (1904; reprint, Delhi, 1961).

CONSTANTINA BAILLY

PANTHEISM AND PANENTHEISM. In Greek *pan* means "all," *theos* means "god," and *en* means "in." *Pantheism* means that all is God; *panentheism*, that all is in God. The two doctrines can be definitely distinguished. When considered together they may be called the pan-doctrines.

Although theism is often contrasted with pantheism and panentheism, the idea of all, or totality, is prominent in every form of theism as a doctrine of the high religions. Thus it occurs in the terms *all-knowing, all-powerful, creator of all,* and still others. Nevertheless, the most usual form of Western theology, sometimes called classical theism, holds or implies that the world of creatures is outside God. Yet it is also said by those in this tradition that in God is knowledge of all things. Can anything be outside knowledge-of-all-things? To many great minds this has seemed an unendurable paradox. To escape this apparent absurdity of a knowing that does not include the known and yet also to avoid including the world in the divine life, Aristotle denied knowledge of particular things to God, who, he held, was aware only of universal forms or ideas. Divine thought then knows only itself: it is pure thinking of thinking. Therewith Aristotle fell into other paradoxes, including that of exalting as divine a being ignorant of us and our world and hence, it seems, inferior to us. Yet classical theists accepted Aristotle's formula "unmoved mover" (meaning unchanged changer) as descriptive of God. This conception implies that there can be nothing changing in God. Was then Paul, who said, referring to God, "For in him we live and move, and have our being" (*Acts* 12:28), a pan-theologian?

When we human beings know things other than our own minds and bodies, the known things seem to be outside us. However, our knowledge of these outside things is extremely incomplete and uncertain. God must know everything at least as well and as certainly as we know our own pains and pleasures. Nothing can be so external to an all-knowing God as most things are to us. Accordingly, Plato, the first great philosophical theologian, believing in a divine Soul of the World (who knows us and whose body is the universe), made it clear that nothing was simply outside this deity: the universe as divine body is "in" the divine soul rather than the reverse. Plato was certainly a pan-theologian.

The essential difference between the two forms of pan-theology is manifest in their answers to the question "Do the creatures have genuine freedom of decision making, or does God determine everything?" Classical pantheism was a form of theological determinism: God decides or determines everything, including our supposed decisions. Both the ancient Greek Stoics and Spinoza (1632–1677) held this view. Panentheists object that, if one power determines all, there is, causally speaking, only one agent in all action. The Stoic-Spinozistic doctrine is an extreme monism rather than a genuine pluralism. Or, at best, its pluralism is unclear or ambiguous, for reality is active agency or nothing. As Plato said, "being is power"; for him every soul is "self-moved." This agrees with panentheism, which admits a plurality of active agents within the reality of the supreme agent.

The medieval tradition, following Aristotle's wisdom in this, admitted that—at least in all cases apart from God—to know something is one thing; to determine or make it is quite another. If this applies to God, there is no absurdity in holding that God knows and in that sense includes all things but does not fully determine their actions. Panentheism avoids both extreme monism and extreme pluralism, and it does this, it claims, without obvious paradox. Indeed, it sees in extremes a chief source of philosophical paradox. Also, since God does not determine all, the problem of evil is less formidable for panentheism than for either classical theism or pantheism as usually formulated. For, as one can see in Augustine, Thomas Aquinas, and many others, classical theism was always tempted by—and, in the case of the early American theologian Jonathan Edwards, frankly adopted—theological determinism.

The possible ideas of God and the created world can be classified with a precision not customary in the past by using the "modal" concepts of necessity and contingency. Classical theism contrasts the contingency of the world (meaning that it might not have existed as it actually does) with the necessary existence of God, who, it is held, could not have failed to exist. In table 1 it is assumed that both God and a world exist. Also assumed is that *God* is a religious term, in that it is appropriate to speak of worshiping, serving, and loving God with all one's mind, heart, soul, and strength.

Let N stand for necessity in God, C for contingency in God; let n and c stand for the same in creatures. Also let $>$ mean that God includes the creatures and $\not>$ mean that God does not include the creatures. In views 4 and 6 the question mark instead of the inclusion symbol means that, so far as the table goes, it is indefinite what contingent things God, as a wholly contingent being, does or does not include.

View 1 has been long and widely held; view 9 has recently become important. View 1 consists of the view that God, who is wholly necessary, does not include the creatures, who are wholly contingent. View 9 refers to the belief that God (in different respects, otherwise there would be contradiction) is necessary and also contingent and that God includes the creatures, who, in different respects, are contingent and necessary.

The reversal of the order of NC and cn (3, 6, 7, 8, 9) symbolizes the greater importance of necessity in God and of contingency in creatures. God, except according to views 4, 5, and 6, exists necessarily but may also (7, 8, 9) have some qualities that might have been otherwise. In contrast, a particular creature, according to six of the views (1, 3, 4, 6, 7, and 9), exists contingently. The n in cn (third row) is best taken to mean only that there must be some creatures or other. The C standing alone (column II) symbolizes that God might not have existed

TABLE 1. *Modal Table of Views of God and the Creatures*

I	II	III
(1) $N \not> c$	(4) $C\ ?\ c$	(7) $NC > c$
(2) $N > n$	(5) $C > n$	(8) $NC > n$
(3) $N \not> cn$	(6) $C\ ?\ cn$	(9) $NC > cn$

at all. The *c* alone (first row) means that there might have been no creatures at all, while *n* alone (second row) means that the creatures are entirely necessary.

The two definite noninclusions (1, 3) result from the law of modal logic according to which there can be nothing contingent in the wholly necessary. Three definite inclusions (2, 5, and 8) express the modal law that the necessary is in everything. The inclusions in views 7 and 9, although not required by modal logic, are permitted by it and, because of the paradox of putting the known outside the all-inclusive and infallible knowledge, are appropriate.

In column I are the three views that take God to be wholly necessary. Classical theism is expressed in view 1; classical pantheism in view 2. View 3 was held by Aristotle. The views that take God to be wholly contingent (column II) include what is usually meant by a "finite God," one entirely without any necessary, absolute, eternal, infinite, or self-sufficient aspect; this is the view held by Charles Renouvier, John Stuart Mill, William James, and others. (John Hick would be among these, except for his attempt to find a meaning for the divine preëminence that implies eternal existence and a necessary support for other existing things but is compatible with the possibility that God might not have existed.) Column III shows the modal possibilities for allowing in God a contrast between necessary and contingent qualities.

Classical pantheism, view 2, derives an advantage from the laws of modal logic, which do not allow a wholly necessary God to include the creatures if they are (even in part) contingent, but do require such a deity to include the creatures if they are wholly necessary. Thus classical pantheism has no problem on this score; but classical theism (in its usual *N*, *c* form) does, since it attributes omniscience to God. Precisely for this reason, Spinoza was scornful of classical theism. He was its first severe critic, although Aristotle would have preceded him had classical theism been known in his time.

The fact that the three views in column I were the chief forms of belief during the first two millennia after Plato may be explained in two ways. First, views 1 and 2 are the simplest of the nine views, except for 4 and 5, which reduce God to a mere accident of existence, a "fetish" according to Charles S. Peirce. Second, views 1 and 3 have an advantage over 2 and 4 in that they honor the principle of contrast (Wittgenstein), or polarity (Morris Cohen), which says that one pole of an ultimate contrast, such as necessary-contingent, has meaning only because the other does and that both must apply to reality if either does. Where all is necessary or all is contingent, both concepts lose their distinctive meanings. Hegel had a similar idea. Yet the paradox of an all-inclusive knowledge possessed by a non-all-inclusive being favors view 2, classical pantheism, as against view 1. Thus is explained the recurring opposition between first the Stoics, then Spinoza, and then the German theologian Schleiermacher on the one hand and the countless classical theists on the other. Although views 1 and 2 are perhaps the two simplest religious doctrines that can be made plausible, each has advantages and serious disadvantages when compared with the other. For several centuries, however, the determinism of early modern (Newtonian) science favored view 2.

The unpopularity of view 3 is readily accounted for. It lacks the simplicity of 1 and 2, and it either, with Aristotle and Gersonides (Levi ben Gershom, 1288–1344), denies concrete knowledge to God or shares, with view 1, the paradox of the wholly necessary God knowing something contingent—whether contingent in all or only some respects does not alter this difficulty. (Knowledge of a contingent aspect of something must itself have a contingent aspect. If proposition *p* is contingent, it could have been false, and then there would have been no such knowledge as knowledge-that-*p*.)

Aristotle, by clear implication, held view 3 but saw that he must pay the price of denying concrete worldly knowledge to God. The Scholastics and some of the Jewish and Islamic thinkers refused to pay this price yet insisted on the knowledge; but, as Spinoza saw, they failed to pay the equally obligatory logical price of *that* decision—either by admitting contingency in God as well as in the world (as the Italian Fausto Sozzini later did) or by affirming the sheer necessity of the world (as Spinoza and the Stoics did). Modal law excludes divine cognition from views 1 and 3; both the principle of modal contrast and the need to admit real freedom (therefore contingency) in God and the creatures render view 2 problematic; some would say impossible.

If we eliminate column II as dishonoring deity by making it wholly contingent, we have left column III. View 8 seems absurd—if there is any contingency at all, there must be some in the creatures. View 7 agrees with view 1, or classical theism, that God must be free not only to decide among different kinds of worlds but also to decide upon no world. Yet what good, one may ask, is this freedom to create nothing? Is not anything better than nothing? "Being as such is good" was a traditional doctrine, from Plato down. Why should one suppose it exalts divine power to think of it as capable of creating nothing as well as of creating something? This is another paradox of classical theism. So we are left with 9 as the view that retains the advantages of the others without their disadvantages. Clearly the five positive ideas of the table are all present in 9 and only in 9. Wilmon Sheldon, like Leibniz (both classical theists), held that the mistakes of philosophers were in what they denied, not in what they asserted. If so, it is view 9 that should be preferred. It symbolizes the modal structure of panentheism, or (as I call my version) neoclassical theism.

Besides the polarity of necessary-contingent, there are other ultimate contrasts that play similar roles: absolute-relative, infinite-finite, eternal-temporal, potential-actual, abstract-concrete, object-subject. Each of these yields a set of nine views subject to similar laws, except that while there are modal logics, there are no worked-out logics for the other polarities, although in my writings there are informal indications of what the logics would be like. The ninth combination, I hold, is logically favored for all pairs of universal contraries. If this is so, the American philosopher E. S. Brightman (1884–1952) did well to use the phrases "finite-infinite" and "temporal-eternal" of God.

If the *N* and the *C* in *NC*, or if infinite and finite, were to be applied to God in the same respect, column III would represent self-inconsistent views. But this is not the intention. Whitehead, for example, makes this clear by distinguishing the "primordial" and the "consequent" natures of God, describing the former as abstract, absolute, infinite, and strictly eternal and the latter as concrete, relative (dependent), finite, and "in a sense temporal." The two natures form one being by the "ontological," or "Aristotelian," principle that abstract entities are real only in the concrete. By no logical rule can view 9 be declared contradictory simply because the same being is assigned characters that would be contradictory if both were on the same level of abstractness or concreteness.

Historically, classical theism has been represented by Philo Judaeus (Jewish theologian of the first century CE), Augustine, Anselm, al-Ghazālī (Islamic theologian, 1058–1111), Thomas Aquinas, and countless other scholastics. More recently, Calvin, Luther, Descartes, Leibniz, Kant (in his *Ethics*), and the Americans Jonathan Edwards and Wilmon Sheldon—the list could be very long—have been in this tradition.

In this century classical pantheism has been losing ground. Its universal necessity is a doctrine of Brand Blanshard, but Blanshard is not a theist in any clear sense. F. H. Bradley, by one interpretation, was a pantheist (see W. L. Reese's article on Bradley in the *Dictionary of Religion and Philosophy*, 1980). Josiah Royce could also be so classified. His deity is inclusive and all-knowing, and he says that relations are universally and exclusively internal or essential to their terms, which implies universal necessity; however, the implication is never clearly admitted in so many words, as it is by Blanshard, who was influenced by Royce. Royce's favorite pupil, W. E. Hocking was a panentheist or a neoclassical theist, although he did not spell out the matter so clearly as some do.

Plato's theism has been rather poorly understood. Plato affirms self-determination ("self-motion") of those creatures that have souls and by implication also conceives the all-inclusive World Soul as self-moved. This implies some contingency in God and the world. As for necessity, Plato never suggests that not existing or not having a world was a possibility for God. In the *Timaeus* he speaks of two gods, the eternal God, the Demiurge or Creator, and "the God that was to be," the World Soul. There are hints that the Demiurge is a mythical figure, but the World Soul, with its cosmic body, seems intended more literally. The Plato scholar Francis M. Cornford suggests that the World Soul is the actual deity (Ronald Levinson says "Plato's real God") while the Demiurge is only an abstract aspect of the World Soul, its eternal envisagement of the form of the Good, according to which it acts creatively. In this interpretation, which might have somewhat surprised Plato, he can be considered the first panentheist. The Neoplatonists, however, including Plotinus, seem too unclear to be usefully classified. Their emanations from the One are apparently outside it and, as in classical theism, contribute nothing to it; and the World Soul is held less real than the One. Yet we are not told that the emanations might not have taken place or are contingent.

For two thousand years Plato's suggestion of a soul-and-body structure in God was ignored (or misunderstood), first by Aristotle and Plotinus and then by the Scholastics. More recently it was underestimated even by Whitehead. But about 1600 the heretical doctrine Socinianism, named for its founder, Socinus, proposed that God does not know or determine our decisions eternally (they are not eternally there to be known); rather, God knows them only as or after they occur. By making free decisions, we give divine knowledge new content and thus change God. Socinus may not have held that divine knowledge includes the things known, but he might as well have. At any rate his view conforms to *NC*, *cn*. A Socinian theologian defined the eternity of God in modal terms, "God is eternal in that he cannot not exist." This was a deliberate avoidance of the well-known medieval doctrine that God is immutable and impassable (meaning that no creature can influence God). This momentous event of three centuries ago—the rejection of a central doctrine of classical theism, a rejection made on behalf of the self-motion, or freedom, of souls—was passed over by historians and scholars until recently. It is still not to be found in encyclopedias and histories. Only a German book on Socinianism (by Otto Fock) tells the story.

The term *pantheism* goes back to the English writer John Toland (1670–1722), and the term *panentheism* to the German philosopher K. F. Krause (1781–1832), a student of Hegel and Fichte. Krause thought of the deity as a divine organism inclusive of all lesser organisms. He said that God is more than and includes nature and man. Consciously or not, he was to some extent returning to Plato's *Timaeus.* Toland coined the word *pantheist* and held that the universe is God. Similarly, Spinoza had spoken of "God or nature." There seems no evidence that either Toland or Krause had much influence on later doctrines, apart from funishing a label; they were minor figures in the history of thought. Oddly enough, Krause's chief influence was in Spain.

Hegel (1770–1831) must be regarded as a panentheist if he is any definite kind of theist. He holds that contraries must be united to express truth, and he uses both terms, *necessity* and *contingency.* Yet, what precisely he means by these is difficult to determine. He certainly holds that the unity of necessary and contingent, infinite and finite, universal and particular, is the truth of both. But how the unity is to be described is the problem. On this issue Hegel is, for me, unclear. F. W. H. Schelling (1775–1854), Hegel's fellow student at Tübingen, in his later writings seems a panentheist in a clearer, more definite sense than Hegel, although he is still not notably clear. He did affirm change and freedom of both God and creatures and certainly did not regard either the creator or the existence of some created order as merely contingent.

After Schelling, the German physicist, psychologist, and philosopher G. T. Fechner (1801–1887) developed a rather neat system that easily fits $CN > cn$: both God and creatures have some freedom; both face an open future; and there is no suggestion that God exists contingently or could have lacked creatures. (Here is an unusually clear case of the ninth view.) As with Socinus, most scholars gave no heed. In France, however, Jules Lequier (1814–1862), aware of the Socinians, took freedom as his "first principle," addressing God thus: "Thou hast created me creator of myself." In this he anticipated Whitehead's "self-created creature." Of course Lequier had no such idea as that the divine existence was a mere logical accident, nor did he imply divine freedom to have no creatures at all. He also clearly affirmed that our decisions make a difference to God, that they "make a spot in the absolute." That the deity includes the creatures in knowing them is not clearly stated, but it seems to be implied.

In Italy Bernardino Varisco (1850–1933) affirmed some freedom of indeterminacy for every creature (which Plato, Socinus, Lequier, and, probably, Hegel had not done) and affirmed that God includes the creatures. Varisco also held that every creature is sentient: there is no dead, mindless matter. This only Fechner, of the previous European writers in this tradition, had proposed. In America Charles S. Peirce (1839–1914) also (after about 1880) asserted that every creature has some freedom and sentience, that chance, or piecemeal contingency, is pervasive in nature, and that the future is partly indeterminate, not simply for our knowledge but in reality. He accepted the characterization of God as the "necessary being" but was not satisfied with the unqualified description of God as eternal or immutable. He did not believe that our thoughts about God could be made very precise and hence left his theological ideas somewhat indefinite and not altogether consistent. But, if he had a definite position, it could only be the ninth view.

Alfred North Whitehead (1861–1947), an English mathematician, logician, physicist, and philosopher who moved to America in 1924, soon thereafter developed a comprehensive metaphysical system, clearly theistic, and, in most respects, clearly a panentheism. The polar principle, which in application to God may be called "dual transcendence," is, as already remarked, quite clear in his writing (apart from the label, which is an invention of mine). His "category of the ultimate," creativity, implies universal freedom, with an open future even for God. Sentience, or "feeling," is taken as universal (from atoms to people), and God is characterized as "the unification of all things" (in the divine "consequent nature"). Although the divine existence is not said to be necessary, still, since God as primordial is taken as the necessary seat of the "pure potentials" without which nothing would even be possible, what "the possibility of the divine nonexistence" could mean is not apparent.

Whitehead's remarkable saying "Every creature transcends God" I take to mean that the becoming of the creature is not divinely determined and that, until the becoming is accomplished, the creature is not yet prehended by, and thus taken into, the divine consciousness, thereby enriching the latter.

I have tried to draw out, clarify, and systematize the entire development as sketched above. Whitehead was somewhat aware of the partial Platonic precedent, but he may have had little or no knowledge of some of the others. Besides using Krause's panentheism for my view, I also call it neoclassical theism. I give many arguments for this form of theism, including six theistic proofs, arguments that are convincing for those who accept the premises on which they are based.

Paul Weiss (b. 1901) seems a panentheist of some kind, since he affirms human freedom and says that, in prayer, both God and the worshiper are transformed. He implies that deity is a unity somehow inclusive of all things so far as they are good. He does not say that God is wholly necessary or that the world is wholly contingent. John Findlay (b. 1903) is similarly heretical from the classical standpoint. W. P. Montague (1873–1963) and J. E. Boodin (1869–1950) are among the recent American nonclassical theists more or less close to panentheism.

The old issues have been partly left behind. The mere contrasts—necessary versus contingent, infinite versus finite, absolute versus relative, or even eternal versus temporal—no longer serve to define deity. Divine love must be sensitive to the weal and woe of the creatures and far from a purely independent, self-sufficient, unrelative, mere absolute. Paul Tillich (1886–1965) was no classical theist, and, in the third volume of his *Systematic Theology* (3 vols., 1951–1963), he admits that the creatures contribute to the divine life. This had already been said by Nikolai Berdiaev (1874–1948), who called himself a "mystical pantheist" but spoke of a "divine time" and of creaturely freedom undetermined by God. He was essentially a panentheist, except that, like Tillich, he thought that theological truth cannot be stated literally. Schubert Ogden (b. 1928), a theologian who defends panentheism, partly agrees with Tillich and Berdiaev about the irreducibly symbolic, or nonliteral, functioning of religious language.

Among living philosophers whom I know at all well, the nearest to a classical theist is the logician Richard M. Martin, who holds that all truth is timelessly known to God. Yet since Martin (together with the influential logician W. V. O. Quine, b. 1908) thinks that modal concepts are an affair of our language rather than of the nature of things, it is hard to classify his doctrine in modal terms.

The nine views in our modal table do not exhaust possible beliefs about God or the extraordinary, supreme reality. Various forms of atheism, for example, have been omitted. An important omitted view is that the supreme reality is the only reality: what may seem to us nonsupreme, ordinary realities are only appearances of the supreme reality, appearances that we in ignorance wrongly take as realities. To the questions "To whom do the appearances appear?" and "Who wrongly takes them as more than mere appearances?" the reply of some seems to be that the questions, too, are wrong or ignorant. Really, there are no wrongly thinking realities, only the one utterly good and real absolute, or *brahman*. This is the extreme version of Hinduistic monism, called Advaita Vedānta (*advaita* means "nondual"; *Vedānta* refers to the Vedas, ancient hymns and other sacred documents of Hinduism.) Its greatest formulator was Śaṅkara (788–820).

That the doctrine makes sense is more than most Westerners can see and also more than many Hindus—Rāmānuja (eleventh century) and Aurobindo Ghose (1872–1950), for example—can or could see. But it has had countless adherents. The *Bhagavadgītā* is indefinite or ambiguous on the relationship between *advaita* (also called "acosmism," implying the unreality of the cosmos) and pantheism or panentheism. Together with Robert Whittemore, a contemporary American philosopher who went to India to inquire into the matter, I consider that the *Bhagavadgītā* can equally well be interpreted panentheistically as acosmically.

Medieval Islam was classically theistic, with an even greater tendency to deny or belittle creaturely freedom. Yet a great poet in what is now Pakistan, Muhammad Iqbal (1877–1938), a disciple of Henri Bergson, accepted the ideas of a divine becoming and of creaturely freedom.

One branch of Hinduism, the Bengali school, may, according to some of its representatives, be close to the neoclassical view. For example, it has been reported that a disciple of the school's founder, Jiva Goswami, said, "God, although perfect in love, [yet] grows without ceasing." There seems to be no sharp contradiction between this Indian view and Whiteheadian or (in many respects, at least, the same) Hartshornean theology.

Buddhism appears superficially to be entirely nontheistic. It is certainly not classically theistic, with realities outside the supreme reality. In certain forms of Māhāyana Buddhism in China, there is some movement toward classical pantheism (the Hua-yen tradition of Fa-tsang, 643–712). In Theravāda Buddhism (in Burma, Sri Lanka, and Thailand), there is nothing like theism, although the tendency to deify the Buddha seems to haunt all Buddhism. Whitehead spoke of "the diffuse God of Buddhism," but the standard theism of the medieval or Renaissance West is simply not to be found in Buddhism.

Confucianism was vaguely theistic but hardly further classifiable in Western terms. To relate Taoism to pantheism or panentheism would be even more difficult.

A sharply formulated doctrine of determinism, theological or otherwise, is a largely Western affair. (The idea of *karman* suggests it, but vaguely.) So is a sharply formulated doctrine of timeless omniscience, as in classical theism. Plato and Aristotle did not have it. Classical theism (which many scholars say is not biblical) is a largely Western (or Near Eastern) invention of the first Christian centuries. Perhaps Madhva (1197–1276) in India most nearly resembles scholastic theology.

So far, almost nothing has been said about the saying "God is love." Whitehead says that God "prehends" the creatures; since he defines prehension (so far as the prehended entity is concrete) as "feeling of feeling" and also as "empathy," which can be taken as the universal kernel of love, he is saying that God (in "perfect" or unsurpassable fashion) feels the feelings of all. What is that but to say that God (in the best possible sense) loves all? Precisely this is the final meaning of neoclassical theism. The idea of divine love is biblical for Jews and Christians, is far from unknown to Muslims and Hindus, and is, perhaps, not so alien to Buddhists as some may think.

The long reign of classical theism and the considerable appeal (for shorter periods of time and to more limited groups) of classical pantheism have, perhaps, not been adequately explained in this essay. Many arguments for one or another of these views have been omitted, partly because of space limitations and partly, no doubt, from bias, as have some objections that partisans of other views could make to neoclassical theism, or, as it is called by some, "process theism." But then, many arguments for the neoclassical and against the classical views have also been omitted. For these deficiencies, further research by the reader is the only remedy.

[*Many of the historical figures and philosophers mentioned herein are the subjects of independent entries. For further discussion of the theoretical issues outlined in this entry, see* Theism; Monism; *and* Attributes of God.]

BIBLIOGRAPHY

For historical examples of the doctrines discussed, see William L. Reese's and my *Philosophers Speak of God* (1953; reprint, Chicago, 1976). In Alfred North Whitehead's *Process and Reality* (1929; corr. ed., New York, 1978), part 5 should be consulted, as should the index references under *God.* I have presented my view in *The Divine Relativity: A Social Conception of God* (1948; reprint, New Haven, 1982) and in chapters 11–14 of *Creative Synthesis and Philosophic Method* (1970; reprint, Lanham, Md., 1983). Also recommended are *The Reality of God, and Other Essays* (New York, 1966) by Schubert Ogden, *Hartshorne and Neoclassical Metaphysics* (Lincoln, Nebr., 1970) by Eugene H. Peters, and *Process Theology: An Introductory Exposition* (Philadelphia, 1976) by John B. Cobb, Jr., and David R. Griffin. About Whitehead's theism, there are many books. For an able discussion of my reasons for believing as I do about God, see *Charles Hartshorne and the Existence of God* (Albany, N.Y., 1984) by Donald W. Viney.

See also, in *Encyclopaedia Britannica*, 15th ed. (Chicago, 1982), the article "Pantheism and Panentheism" and, in the *Dictionary of Philosophy and Religion: Eastern and Western Thought* (Atlantic Highlands, N.J., 1980), edited by William L. Reese and others, the articles on Cournot, Fechner, Iqbal, Krause, Lequier, Plato, Plotinus, and Whitehead (secs. 16–21).

CHARLES HARTSHORNE

PAPACY. The papacy is the central governing institution of the Roman Catholic church under the leadership of the pope, the bishop of Rome. The word *papacy* (Lat., *papatus*) is medieval in origin and derives from the Latin *papa*, an affectionate term for "father."

The Early Period. This era, extending from the biblical origins of Christianity to the fifth century, was marked by the ever-increasing power and prestige of the bishop of Rome within the universal church and the Roman empire.

Scriptural foundation. Traditional Roman Catholic teaching holds that Jesus Christ directly bestowed upon the apostle Peter the fullness of ruling and teaching authority. He made Peter the first holder of supreme power in the universal church, a power passed on to his successors, the bishops of Rome. (See table 1.) Two biblical texts are cited to substantiate this claim. In *Matthew* 16:18 there is the promise of Jesus: "You are Peter, and on this rock I will build my church, and the gates of Hades shall not prevail against it." In *John* 21:15–16, this promise is fulfilled in the admonition of Jesus to Peter: "Feed my lambs. . . . Look after my sheep." Modern Roman Catholic biblical scholars affirm the genuine authority of Peter among the Twelve but make the following observations: there is no New Testament evidence that Peter was ever a bishop or local administrator of any church (including Rome and Antioch); there is no direct biblical proof that Jesus established the papacy as a permanent office within the church; but there is other cogent evidence that Peter arrived in Rome late in his life and was martyred and buried there.

Catholic scholars insist, however, that even though the idea of an abiding Petrine ministry is not explicitly found in scripture, it is not contrary to the biblical tradition and indeed is implicitly rooted in it. Peter had a preeminent role in the New Testament, where he is described as the most prominent apostolic witness and missionary among the Twelve. He is the model of the shepherd-pastor, the receiver of a special revelation, and the teacher of the true faith. Gradually Christians, through the providential direction of the Holy Spirit, recognized the papacy, the office of headship in the church, to be the continuation of that ministry given by Christ to Peter and exercised through the historic Roman episcopate. Although other Christian scholars would accept many of these conclusions, they would generally deny the Roman Catholic belief that the papacy is an absolutely essential element of the church.

First three centuries. The early Christian churches were not organized internationally. Yet Rome, almost from the beginning, was accorded a unique position, and understandably so: Rome was the only apostolic see in the West; it was the place where Peter and Paul were martyred; and it was the capital of the empire. Ignatius of Antioch, in his letter to the Romans (c. 110), called the Roman church the church "presiding in love" (4.3), and Irenaeus, in his *Against Heresies* (c. 180), referred to its "more imposing foundation" (3.3.2). Although these controverted texts may not be a proof of Roman primacy, they at least indicate the lofty stature of the see of Rome.

The exact structure of the very early Roman church is not known, but it seems that by the middle of the second century monepiscopacy (the rule of one bishop) was well established. The memory of Peter was kept alive in Rome, and its bishops were often involved in the affairs of churches outside their own area. Clement I (c. 90–c. 99), for example, sent a letter from the church of Rome to the church of Corinth to settle a dispute over the removal of several church officials. Victor I (c. 189–c. 198) sought, under threat of excommunication, to impose on the churches of Asia Minor the Roman custom for the celebration of Easter. Finally, Stephen I (254–257) reinstated two Spanish bishops who had been deposed by their colleagues and also decided, contrary to the custom in Syria and North Africa, that repentant heretics did not have to be rebaptized. Although Cyprian, bishop of Carthage (d. 258), objected to Stephen's decisions, he was able to call Rome the "principal church" (letter 59, addressed to Cornelius, bishop of Rome) and to insist that for bishops to be legitimate they must be in communion with Rome.

The bishops of Rome in the third century claimed a universal primacy, even though it would be another 150 years before this idea was doctrinally formulated. Rome attracted both orthodox and heterodox teachers—some to have their views heard, others to seek confirmation. More and more, the bishop of Rome, either on his own initiative or by request, settled doctrinal and disciplinary disputes in other churches. Roman influence was felt as far away as Spain, Gaul, North Africa, and Asia Minor. The see of Peter was looked upon as the guarantor of doctrinal purity even by those who found fault with its leadership.

Fourth and fifth centuries. With the Edict of Milan (313) the empire granted toleration of all religions and allowed Christians to worship freely. This policy ended the era of persecution, increased the number of Christians, and shaped the institutional development of the papacy. Once Emperor Constantine decided to move the seat of the empire to Constantinople in 324, the papacy began to play a larger role in the West. By the time Christianity became the official religion of the empire in 381, several popes were already affirming papal primatial authority. The critical period in the doctrinal systematization of Roman primacy took place in the years between Damasus I (366–384) and Leo I (440–461). In that period, the popes explicitly claimed that the bishop of Rome was the head of the entire church and that his authority derived from Peter.

Damasus I, the first pope to call Rome the apostolic see, made Latin the principal liturgical language in Rome and commissioned Jerome to revise the old Latin version of the New Testament. At the Council of Rome (382), he declared that the primacy of the bishop of Rome is based on continuity with Peter. He deposed several Arian bishops. His successor, Siricius (384–399), whose decretal letters are the earliest extant, promoted Rome's primatial position and imposed his decisions on many bishops outside Italy.

It was Leo I, the first of three popes to be called the Great, who laid the theoretical foundation of papal primacy. Leo took the title Pontifex Maximus, which the emperors no longer used, and claimed to possess the fullness of power *(plenitudo potestatis)*. Governing the church through a tumultuous period of barbarian invasions and internal disputes, he relentlessly defended the rights of the Roman see. He rejected Canon 28 of the Council of Chalcedon (451), which gave the bishop of New Rome (Constantinople) privileges equal to those of the bishop of Old Rome and a rank second only to that of the pope. A favorite theme for Leo was the relationship between Peter and the pope. This idea had been advanced by earlier popes, but Leo elaborated it, in his sermons calling himself "Peter in Peter's see" (2.2) and his "unworthy heir" (3.4). Thus, as he noted, a particular pope may be sinful, but the papacy as such still retains its Petrine character. The Leonine distinction between person and office has proved to be of immense value and has helped the papacy survive unsuitable popes. Leo believed that Peter's successors have "the care of all the churches" (*Sermons* 3.4), and he exercised his authority over Christian churches in Italy, Africa, and Gaul. The Western Roman empire ended in 476.

TABLE 1. *The Popes.* A Roman numeral in parentheses after a pope's name indicates differences in the historical sources. The names of the antipopes and their dates are given in brackets. The first date for each pope refers to his election; the second date refers to his death, deposition, or resignation. Dates for the first two hundred years are uncertain. Abbreviations: Bl. = Blessed; St. = Saint.

NAME	DATES
St. Peter	?–64/7
St. Linus	64/7–79?
St. Anacletus (Cletus)	79?–90/2
St. Clement I	90/2–99/101
St. Evaristus	99/101–107?
St. Alexander I	107?–116?
St. Sixtus I	116?–125?
St. Telesphorus	125?–136?
St. Hyginus	136?–140/2
St. Pius I	140/2–154/5
St. Anicetus	154/5–166?
St. Soter	166?–174?
St. Eleutherius	174?–189?
St. Victor I	189?–198?
St. Zephyrinus	198?–217?
St. Callistus I	217?–222
[St. Hippolytus]	[217?–235]
St. Urban I	222–230
St. Pontian	21 Jul. 230–28 Sep. 235
St. Anterus	21 Nov. 235–3 Jan. 236
St. Fabian	10 Jan. 236–20 Jan. 250
St. Cornelius	Mar. 251–Jun. 253
[Novatian]	[251–258?]
St. Lucius I	25 Jun. 253–5 Mar. 254
St. Stephen I	12 May 254–2 Aug. 257
St. Sixtus II	30 Aug. 257–6 Aug. 258
St. Dionysius	22 Jul. 259–26 Dec. 268
St. Felix I	5 Jan. 269–30 Dec. 274
St. Eutychian	4 Jan. 275–7 Dec. 283
St. Gaius (Caius)	17 Dec. 283–22 Apr. 296
St. Marcellinus	30 Jun. 296–25 Oct. 304
St. Marcellus I	27 May 308–16 Jan. 309
St. Eusebius	18 Apr.–17 Aug. 309
St. Miltiades	2 Jul. 311–11 Jan. 314
St. Sylvester I	31 Jan. 314–31 Dec. 335
St. Mark	18 Jan.–7 Oct. 336
St. Julius I	6 Feb. 337–12 Apr. 352
Liberius	17 May 352–24 Sep. 366
[Felix II]	[355–22 Nov. 365]
St. Damasus I	1 Oct. 366–11 Dec. 384
[Ursinus]	[366–367]
St. Siricius	15 Dec. 384–26 Nov. 399
St. Anastasius I	27 Nov. 399–19 Dec. 401
St. Innocent I	22 Dec. 401–12 Mar. 417
St. Zosimus	18 Mar. 417–26 Dec. 418
St. Boniface I	28 Dec. 418–4 Sep. 422
[Eulalius]	[27 Dec. 418–419]
St. Celestine I	10 Sep. 422–27 Jul. 432
St. Sixtus III	31 Jul. 432–19 Aug. 440
St. Leo I, the Great	29 Sep. 440–10 Nov. 461
St. Hilary	19 Nov. 461–29 Feb. 468
St. Simplicius	3 Mar. 468–10 Mar. 483
St. Felix III (II)	13 Mar. 483–1 Mar. 492
St. Gelasius I	1 Mar. 492–21 Nov. 496
Anastasius II	24 Nov. 496–19 Nov. 498
St. Symmachus	22 Nov. 498–19 Jul. 514
[Lawrence]	[498; 501–505]
St. Hormisdas	20 Jul. 514–6 Aug. 523
St. John I	13 Aug. 523–18 May 526
St. Felix IV (III)	12 Jul. 526–22 Sep. 530
Boniface II	22 Sep. 530–17 Oct. 532
[Dioscorus]	[22 Sep.–14 Oct. 530]
John II	2 Jan. 533–8 May 535
St. Agapitus I	13 May 535–22 Apr. 536
St. Silverius	1 Jun. 536–11 Nov. 537
Vigilius	29 Mar. 537–7 Jun. 555
Pelagius I	16 Apr. 556–4 Mar. 561
John III	17 Jul. 561–13 Jul. 574
Benedict I	2 Jun. 575–30 Jul. 579
Pelagius II	26 Nov. 579–7 Feb. 590
St. Gregory I, the Great	3 Sep. 590–12 Mar. 604
Sabinian	13 Sep. 604–22 Feb. 606
Boniface III	19 Feb.–12 Nov. 607
St. Boniface IV	25 Aug. 608–8 May 615
St. Deusdedit (Adeodatus I)	19 Oct. 615–8 Nov. 618
Boniface V	23 Dec. 619–25 Oct. 625
Honorius I	27 Oct. 625–12 Oct. 638
Severinus	28 May–7 Aug. 640
John IV	24 Dec. 640–12 Oct. 642
Theodore I	24 Nov. 642–14 May 649
St. Martin I	July 649–16 Sep. 655
St. Eugene I	10 Aug. 654–2 Jun. 657
St. Vitalian	30 Jul. 657–27 Jan. 672
Adeodatus II	11 Apr. 672–17 Jun. 676
Donus	2 Nov. 676–11 Apr. 678
St. Agatho	27 Jun. 678–10 Jan. 681
St. Leo II	17 Aug. 682–3 Jul. 683
St. Benedict II	26 Jun. 684–8 May 685
John V	23 Jul. 685–2 Aug. 686
Conon	21 Oct. 686–21 Sep. 687
[Theodore]	[687]
[Paschal]	[687]
St. Sergius I	15 Dec. 687–8 Sep. 701
John VI	30 Oct. 701–11 Jan. 705
John VII	1 Mar. 705–18 Oct. 707
Sisinnius	15 Jan.–4 Feb. 708
Constantine	25 Mar. 708–9 Apr. 715
St. Gregory II	19 May 715–11 Feb. 731
St. Gregory III	18 Mar. 731–Nov. 741
St. Zachary	10 Dec. 741–22 Mar. 752
Stephen (II)	23–25 Mar. 752
Stephen II (III)	26 Mar. 752–26 Apr. 757
St. Paul I	29 May 757–28 Jun. 767
[Constantine II]	[28 Jun. 767–769]
[Philip]	[31 Jul. 768]
Stephen III (IV)	7 Aug. 768–24 Jan. 772
Adrian I	1 Feb. 772–25 Dec. 795
St. Leo III	26 Dec. 795–12 Jun. 816
Stephen IV (V)	22 Jun. 816–24 Jan. 817
St. Paschal I	25 Jan. 817–11 Feb. 824
Eugene II	Feb. 824–Aug. 827
Valentine	Aug.–Sep. 827
Gregory IV	827–Jan. 844
[John]	[Jan. 844]

TABLE 1. *The Popes (cont.)*

Name	Dates	Name	Dates
Sergius II	Jan. 844–27 Jan. 847	Alexander II	1 Oct. 1061–21 Apr. 1073
St. Leo IV	Jan. 847–17 Jul. 855	[Honorius II]	[28 Oct. 1061–1072]
Benedict III	Jul. 855–17 Apr. 858	St. Gregory VII	22 Apr. 1073–25 May 1085
[Anastasius]	[Aug.–Sep. 855]	[Clement III]	[26 Jun. 1080–8 Sep. 1100]
St. Nicholas I, the Great	24 Apr. 858–13 Nov. 867	Bl. Victor III	24 May 1086–16 Sep. 1087
Adrian II	14 Dec. 867–14 Dec. 872	Bl. Urban II	12 Mar. 1088–29 Jul. 1099
John VIII	14 Dec. 872–16 Dec. 882	Paschal II	13 Aug. 1099–21 Jan. 1118
Marinus I	16 Dec. 882–15 May 884	[Theodoric]	[1100]
St. Adrian III	17 May 884–Sep. 885	[Albert]	[1102]
Stephen V (VI)	Sep. 885–14 Sep. 891	[Sylvester IV]	[18 Nov. 1105–1111]
Formosus	6 Oct. 891–4 Apr. 896	Gelasius II	24 Jan. 1118–28 Jan. 1119
Boniface VI	Apr. 896	[Gregory VIII]	[8 Mar. 1118–1121]
Stephen VI (VII)	May 896–Aug. 897	Callistus II	2 Feb. 1119–13 Dec. 1124
Romanus	Aug.–Nov. 897	Honorius II	15 Dec. 1124–13 Feb. 1130
Theodore II	Dec. 897	[Celestine II]	[Dec. 1124]
John IX	Jan. 898–Jan. 900	Innocent II	14 Feb. 1130–24 Sep. 1143
Benedict IV	Jan. 900–Jul. 903	[Anacletus II]	[14 Feb. 1130–25 Jan. 1138]
Leo V	Jul.–Sep. 903	[Victor IV]	[Mar.–29 May 1138]
[Christopher]	[Jul. 903–Jan. 904]	Celestine II	26 Sep. 1143–8 Mar. 1144
Sergius III	29 Jan. 904–14 Apr. 911	Lucius II	12 Mar. 1144–15 Feb. 1145
Anastasius III	Apr. 911–Jun. 913	Bl. Eugene III	15 Feb. 1145–8 Jul. 1153
Lando	Jul. 913–Feb. 914	Anastasius IV	12 Jul. 1153–3 Dec. 1154
John X	Mar. 914–May 928	Adrian IV	4 Dec. 1154–1 Sep. 1159
Leo VI	May–Dec. 928	Alexander III	7 Sep. 1159–30 Aug. 1181
Stephen VII (VIII)	Dec. 928–Feb. 931	[Victor IV]	[7 Sep. 1159–20 Apr. 1164]
John XI	Feb. 931–Dec. 935	[Paschal III]	[26 Apr. 1164–20 Sep. 1168]
Leo VII	3 Jan. 936–13 Jul. 939	[Callistus III]	[Sep. 1168–29 Aug. 1178]
Stephen VIII (IX)	14 Jul. 939–Oct. 942	[Innocent III]	[29 Sep. 1179–1180]
Marinus II	30 Oct. 942–May 946	Lucius III	1 Sep. 1181–25 Sep. 1185
Agapetus II	10 May 946–Dec. 955	Urban III	25 Nov. 1185–20 Oct. 1187
John XII	16 Dec. 955–14 May 964	Gregory VIII	21 Oct.–17 Dec. 1187
Leo VIII	4 Dec. 963–1 Mar. 965	Clement III	19 Dec. 1187–Mar. 1191
Benedict V	22 May–23 Jun. 964	Celestine III	30 Mar. 1191–8 Jan. 1198
John XIII	1 Oct. 965–6 Sep. 972	Innocent III	8 Jan. 1198–16 Jul. 1216
Benedict VI	19 Jan. 973–Jun. 974	Honorius III	18 Jul. 1216–18 Mar. 1227
[Boniface VII]	[Jun.–Jul. 974; Aug. 984–Jul. 985]	Gregory IX	19 Mar. 1227–22 Aug. 1241
		Celestine IV	25 Oct.–10 Nov. 1241
Benedict VII	Oct. 974–10 Jul. 983	Innocent IV	25 Jun. 1243–7 Dec. 1254
John XIV	Dec. 983–20 Aug. 984	Alexander IV	12 Dec. 1254–25 May 1261
John XV	Aug. 985–Mar. 996	Urban IV	29 Aug. 1261–2 Oct. 1264
Gregory V	3 May 996–18 Feb. 999	Clement IV	5 Feb. 1265–29 Nov. 1268
[John XVI]	[Apr. 997–Feb. 998]	Bl. Gregory X	1 Sep. 1271–10 Jan. 1276
Sylvester II	2 Apr. 999–12 May 1003	Bl. Innocent V	21 Jan.–22 Jun. 1276
John XVII	Jun.–Dec. 1003	Adrian V	11 Jul.–18 Aug. 1276
John XVIII	Jan. 1004–Jul. 1009	John XXI	8 Sep. 1276–20 May 1277
Sergius IV	31 Jul. 1009–12 May 1012	Nicholas III	25 Nov. 1277–22 Aug. 1280
Benedict VIII	18 May 1012–9 Apr. 1024	Martin IV	22 Feb. 1281–28 Mar. 1285
[Gregory]	[1012]	Honorius IV	2 Apr. 1285–3 Apr. 1287
John XIX	Apr. 1024–1032	Nicholas IV	22 Feb. 1288–4 Apr. 1292
Benedict IX (first time)	1032–1044	St. Celestine V	5 Jul.–13 Dec. 1294
Sylvester III	20 Jan.–10 Feb. 1045	Boniface VIII	24 Dec. 1294–11 Oct. 1303
Benedict IX (second time)	10 Apr.–1 May 1045	Bl. Benedict XI	22 Oct. 1303–7 Jul. 1304
Gregory VI	5 May 1045–20 Dec. 1046	Clement V	5 Jun. 1305–20 Apr. 1314
Clement II	24 Dec. 1046–9 Oct. 1047	John XXII	7 Aug. 1316–4 Dec. 1334
Benedict IX (third time)	8 Nov. 1047–17 Jul. 1048	[Nicholas V]	[12 May 1328–25 Aug. 1330]
Damasus II	17 Jul.–9 Aug. 1048	Benedict XII	20 Dec. 1334–25 Apr. 1342
St. Leo IX	12 Feb. 1049–19 Apr. 1054	Clement VI	7 May 1342–6 Dec. 1352
Victor II	16 Apr. 1055–28 Jul. 1057	Innocent VI	18 Dec. 1352–12 Sep. 1362
Stephen IX (X)	3 Aug. 1057–29 Mar. 1058	Bl. Urban V	28 Sep. 1362–19 Dec. 1370
[Benedict X]	[5 Apr. 1058–24 Jan. 1059]	Gregory XI	30 Dec. 1370–26 Mar. 1378
Nicholas II	24 Jan. 1059–27 Jul. 1061	Urban VI	8 Apr. 1378–15 Oct. 1389

TABLE 1. *The Popes (cont.)*

NAME	DATES
Boniface IX	2 Nov. 1389–1 Oct. 1404
Innocent VII	17 Oct. 1404–6 Nov. 1406
Gregory XII	30 Nov. 1406–4 Jul. 1415
[Clement VII, Avignon]	[20 Sep. 1378–16 Sep. 1394]
[Benedict XIII, Avignon]	[28 Sep. 1394–23 May 1423]
[Clement VIII, Avignon]	[10 Jun. 1423–26 Jul. 1429]
[Benedict XIV, Avignon]	[12 Nov. 1425–1430]
[Alexander V, Pisa]	[26 Jun. 1409–3 May 1410]
[John XXIII, Pisa]	[17 May 1410–29 May 1415]
Martin V	11 Nov. 1417–20 Feb. 1431
Eugene IV	3 Mar. 1431–23 Feb. 1447
[Felix V]	[5 Nov. 1439–7 Apr. 1449]
Nicholas V	6 Mar. 1447–24 Mar. 1455
Callistus III	8 Apr. 1455–6 Aug. 1458
Pius II	19 Aug. 1458–15 Aug. 1464
Paul II	30 Aug. 1464–26 Jul. 1471
Sixtus IV	9 Aug. 1471–12 Aug. 1484
Innocent VIII	29 Aug. 1484–25 Jul. 1492
Alexander VI	11 Aug. 1492–18 Aug. 1503
Pius III	22 Sep.–18 Oct. 1503
Julius II	31 Oct. 1503–21 Feb. 1513
Leo X	9 Mar. 1513–1 Dec. 1521
Adrian VI	9 Jan. 1522–14 Sep. 1523
Clement VII	19 Nov. 1523–25 Sep. 1534
Paul III	13 Oct. 1534–10 Nov. 1549
Julius III	7 Feb. 1550–23 Mar. 1555
Marcellus II	9 Apr.–1 May 1555
Paul IV	23 May 1555–18 Aug. 1559
Pius IV	25 Dec. 1559–9 Dec. 1565
St. Pius V	7 Jan. 1566–1 May 1572
Gregory XIII	13 May 1572–10 Apr. 1585
Sixtus V	24 Apr. 1585–27 Aug. 1590
Urban VII	15 Sep.–27 Sep. 1590
Gregory XIV	5 Dec. 1590–16 Oct. 1591
Innocent IX	29 Oct.–30 Dec. 1591
Clement VIII	30 Jan. 1592–3 Mar. 1605
Leo XI	1 Apr.–27 Apr. 1605
Paul V	16 May 1605–28 Jan. 1621
Gregory XV	9 Feb. 1621–8 Jul. 1623
Urban VIII	6 Aug. 1623–29 Jul. 1644
Innocent X	15 Sep. 1644–7 Jan. 1655
Alexander VII	7 Apr. 1655–22 May 1667
Clement IX	20 Jun. 1667–9 Dec. 1669
Clement X	29 Apr. 1670–22 Jul. 1676
Bl. Innocent XI	21 Sep. 1676–12 Aug. 1689
Alexander VIII	6 Oct. 1689–1 Feb. 1691
Innocent XII	12 Jul. 1691–27 Sep. 1700
Clement XI	23 Nov. 1700–19 Mar. 1721
Innocent XIII	8 May 1721–7 Mar. 1724
Benedict XIII	29 May 1724–21 Feb. 1730
Clement XII	12 Jul. 1730–6 Feb. 1740
Benedict XIV	17 Aug. 1740–3 May 1758
Clement XIII	6 Jul. 1758–2 Feb. 1769
Clement XIV	19 May 1769–22 Sep. 1774
Pius VI	15 Feb. 1775–29 Aug. 1799
Pius VII	14 Mar. 1800–20 Aug. 1823
Leo XII	28 Sep. 1823–10 Feb. 1829
Pius VIII	31 Mar. 1829–30 Nov. 1830
Gregory XVI	2 Feb. 1831–1 Jun. 1846
Pius IX	16 Jun. 1846–7 Feb. 1878
Leo XIII	20 Feb. 1878–20 Jul. 1903
St. Pius X	4 Aug. 1903–20 Aug. 1914
Benedict XV	3 Sep. 1914–22 Jan. 1922
Pius XI	6 Feb. 1922–10 Feb. 1939
Pius XII	2 Mar. 1939–9 Oct. 1958
John XXIII	28 Oct. 1958–3 Jun. 1963
Paul VI	21 Jun. 1963–6 Aug. 1978
John Paul I	26 Aug.–28 Sep. 1978
John Paul II	16 Oct. 1978–

NOTE

For centuries the popes did not change their names. The first name change occurred when a Roman called Mercury, having been elected pope, chose the more suitable appellation of John II (533–535). From the time of Sergius IV (1009–1012)—his name had been Peter Buccaporca (Peter Pigmouth)—the taking of a new name has continued to the present, with two exceptions: Adrian VI (1522–1523) and Marcellus II (1555). The most popular papal names have been John, Gregory, Benedict, Clement, Innocent, Leo, and Pius. There has never been a Peter II or a John XX. John Paul I was the first pope to select a double name. The legend that a woman pope—Pope Joan—reigned between Leo IV (847–855) and Benedict III (855–858) has long been rejected by historians.

The foregoing list is based generally on the catalog of popes given in the *Annuario pontificio*, the official Vatican yearbook, with some changes dictated by recent scholarly research. It should be noted that the legitimacy of certain popes—for example, Dioscorus (530), Leo VIII (963–965), Benedict V (964), Gregory VI (1045–1046), and Clement II (1046–1047)—is still controverted. Although Stephen (752) is mentioned in the list, he died three days after his election without being consecrated a bishop.

The successors of Leo, especially Felix III (483–492) and Gelasius I (492–496), applied his principles, but the imperial government in Constantinople exerted continual pressure on the papacy.

The Medieval Papacy. The eventful period from the sixth to the fifteenth century demonstrated the unusual adaptability of the papal office. Successive popes opposed imperial control, attempted to reform the papacy and the church, and brought papal authority to its peak in the twelfth and thirteenth centuries. A severe decline followed.

The struggle for independence. The popes of the sixth and seventh centuries resisted excessive encroachments but were still subservient to the power of the emperor. The most notable pope at this time was Gregory I, the Great (590–604), a deeply spiritual man who called himself "the servant of the servants of God." A skilled negotiator, he was able to conclude a peace treaty with the Lombards, who threatened Rome; the people of Rome and the adjacent regions considered him their protector. Gregory was respectful of the rights of individual bishops, but he insisted, nevertheless, that all churches, including Constantinople, were subject to the apostolic see of Rome. He realized that direct confrontation with the emperor would be futile, and so he concentrated on developing the church in territories outside imperial jurisdiction. He established links with the Frankish monarchs which proved to be of great significance in the later Middle Ages; he also sent forty missionaries to Britain.

The break with the East began when Gregory II (715–731) condemned the iconoclastic decrees of Emperor Leo I, who had prohibited the use of images in liturgical ceremonies. The gap widened when Stephen II (752–757), the first pope to cross the Alps, met with Pépin, king of the Franks. Pépin agreed to defend the pope against the invading Lombards and apparently promised him sovereignty over large areas in central Italy. The Donation of Pépin was an epoch-making event; it marked the beginning of the Papal States, in existence until 1870. Stephen became the first of a long line of popes to claim temporal rule. Through his alliance with the Frankish kingdom, Stephen was virtually able to free the papacy from the domination of Constantinople. The last step in the division of Rome from the Eastern Empire was when Pope Leo III (795–816) crowned Charlemagne emperor of the West at Saint Peter's Basilica in 800. As a result of their new status, the popes minted their own coins, and they no longer dated papal documents according to imperial years. The primatial prominence of Rome increased when the Muslim conquests destroyed the church in North Africa and ended the strong influence of Rome's great rivals: the patriarchates of Alexandria, Antioch, and Jerusalem.

By the middle of the ninth century, Nicholas I, the Great (858–867), was able to act as the supreme judge and lawmaker for the entire church. He resisted Carolingian interference and dealt severely with recalcitrant archbishops, deposing several and overruling the decisions of others. In his relations with the Byzantine church he was less successful because he failed to resolve adequately the dispute with Photios, the patriarch of Constantinople. The assertion of primatial claims by John VIII (872–882) also met Byzantine opposition.

The tenth century was a bleak one for the papacy. After the Carolingian rulers lost power, the papacy was scandalously dominated, first by the Roman nobility and then by the German emperors Otto I and his successors. The so-called Ottonian privilege restricted the freedom of papal electors and allowed the emperor the right of ratification. There were some two dozen popes and antipopes during this period, many of low moral caliber. Depositions and impositions of popes became commonplace. Clearly, then, by the beginning of the eleventh century, the need for radical reform was urgent.

The reform movement. Advocates of reform found a dedicated leader in Leo IX (1049–1054). He traveled extensively throughout Italy, France, and Germany, presiding over synods that issued strong decrees dealing with clerical marriage, simony, and episcopal elections. Only six months of his entire pontificate were spent in Rome. Further reforms were made under Nicholas II (1059–1061), whose coronation, perhaps the first ever, was rich in monarchical symbolism. His decree on papal elections (1059), which made cardinal bishops the sole electors, had a twofold purpose: to safeguard the reformed papacy through free and peaceful elections and to eliminate coercion by the empire or the aristocracy. By not granting the emperor the right of confirmation, he directly opposed the Ottonian privilege. Nicholas also introduced feudalism into the papacy when he enfeoffed the Normans; the papacy invested them with the lands they had conquered and received the oath of fealty. This feudal contract—actually made to the apostle Peter through the pope—was the first of many. By the twelfth century, the papacy had more feudal vassals than any other European power.

The most famous of the reform popes was Gregory VII (1073–1085), surnamed Hildebrand. Endowed with great gifts, he had learned much about the papacy from his years of service under Leo IX, Nicholas II, and Alexander II (1061–1073). His ambitious program of reform focused on three areas. The first task was to restore prestige to the papacy, to resurrect it from the sorry state to which it had descended in the previous two centuries. In his letters and especially in his *Dictates of the Pope*, Gregory, like Leo I before him, identified himself with Peter; claimed universal authority over bishops, clerics, and councils; and asserted his right to make law, to render judgments that allow no appeal, and even to depose emperors. The second area of reform was directed against clerical corruption, particularly simony and incontinence. The third area concerned lay investiture—a practice whereby feudal lords, princes, and emperors bestowed spiritual office through the selection of pastors, abbots, and bishops. Gregory's determination to root out this evil brought him into direct conflict with Emperor Henry IV, whom he consequently excommunicated (and later absolved in the famous winter scene at Canossa in 1077). The Gregorian reform movement met fierce resistance and achieved only limited success, but it was an important milestone in papal history. For the first time the extensive theoretical principles of papal power were tested in practice. Henceforth, the papacy exercised a new style of leadership; the pope emerged not only as the undisputed head of the church but also as the unifying force in medieval western Europe.

The height of papal authority. The papacy reached its zenith in the twelfth and thirteenth centuries. Six general councils between 1123 and 1274 issued many doctrinal and disciplinary decrees aimed at reform and left no doubt that the popes were firmly in control of church policy. During the pontificate of Innocent III (1198–1216), one of the most brilliant of all the popes, the papacy reached the summit of its universal power and supervised the religious, social, and political life of the West. Some of the greatest popes at this time were canonists who proclaimed a pontifical world hegemony. Under Innocent III, the first official collection of canon law was published (1209), and the kingdoms of Bulgaria, Portugal, and England were made papal fiefs. Honorius III (1216–1227) further centralized papal administration and finances and approved the establishment of the Franciscan and Dominican orders. In theory, papal authority extended also to non-Christians. Innocent IV (1243–1254) believed that every creature is subject to the pope—even infidels, Christ's sheep by creation though not members of the church. This idea of a world theocracy under the popes was to be part of the theological and political justification for the Crusades.

The medieval popes took stringent action against such heretics as the Waldensians and the Cathari. Gregory IX (1227–1241) made the Inquisition a permanent tribunal to combat heresy, selecting Dominicans and Franciscans to serve as inquisitors, or judges. Heresy was considered not only a grave sin but also a crime against the state. Thus Innocent IV approved the use of torture by the state to force heretics to confess.

Two significant changes were made in the procedures for papal elections. At the Third Lateran Council (1179), Alexander III (1159–1181) decreed that all cardinals—not just cardinal bishops—could vote and that a two-thirds majority was required. The Second Council of Lyons (1274), under Gregory X (1271–1276), established the law of the conclave, whereby the cardinal electors had to assemble in the papal palace and remain in a locked room until the election was completed.

Decline of the papacy. The death of Boniface VIII (1294–1303) marked the end of the grandiose idea of a theocratic world order with all power, spiritual and temporal, emanating from the pope. Several factors contributed to the decline of the papacy: high taxation, the inappropriate conferral and control of benefices, corruption in the Roman bureaucracy, and, above all, the failure of the popes to foresee the effect of nationalism on church-state relations. The effort to construct a Christian commonwealth under papal leadership was unsuccessful, but it must be judged in context. The popes struggled to protect the independence of the church, but their temporal involvements complicated the situation. Europe at that time was a mosaic of feudal territories; nations, as we know them today, were only in the process of formation. It was a turbulent time. Yet in the Middle Ages, the papacy was the only institution in the West with the authority and stability to provide law and order. At times it went to excess, but medieval Europe owed it a considerable debt.

In 1308, Clement V (1305–1314) moved the papal residence to Avignon, which then belonged to the king of Naples, a vassal of the pope. Several factors prompted this decision: the upcoming general council of Vienne (1311–1312); the tension between the pope and the king of France; and the unsafe and chaotic political situation in Rome and Italy. The popes remained in Avignon for seventy years. During their so-called Babylonian Captivity, the popes were French, but the papacy was not a puppet of the French rulers. Centralization and administrative complexity increased, especially under John XXII (1316–1334). The cardinals assumed greater power that at times bordered on oligarchy. They introduced the practice of capitulation—an agreement made by electors of the pope to limit the authority of the person chosen to be pope—and thus tried to restrict papal primacy. The Avignon popes worked to reform the clergy and religious orders; they also promoted missionary activity in China, India, and Persia.

No sooner had Gregory XI (1370–1378) returned to Rome in 1377 than the papacy faced another crisis, the great Western schism. The election of Urban VI (1378–1389) was later disputed by some of the cardinals, who claimed coercion. Five months after Urban's election, they rejected him and elected Clement VII (1378–1394), who went back to Avignon. The two popes had their own cardinals, curial staffs, and adherents among the faithful. A council was held at Pisa in 1409 to resolve the problem, but instead still another pope was elected, Alexander V, who in less than a year was succeeded by John XXIII (1410–1415). The general council of Constance (1414–1418) confronted the scandal of three would-be popes and pledged to reform the church in head and members. Unity was restored with the election of Martin V (1417–1431). The council deposed both Benedict XIII (1394–1423) of Avignon and John XXIII of Pisa; Gregory XII (1406–1415) of the Roman line abdicated. What makes the Council of Constance important in the history of the papacy is the theological principle that dictated its actions, namely conciliarism, enunciated in the council's decree *Haec sancta*, the dogmatic validity of which is still debated. The theory of conciliarism, that a general council is the supreme organ of government in the church, was later condemned by several popes, but it did not die. It resurfaced again in the seventeenth and eighteenth centuries in the form of Gallicanism and Febronianism.

From the Renaissance to the Enlightenment. Papal authority was severely challenged between the fifteenth and eighteenth centuries. It had to face the massive religious and societal repercussions brought about by the Renaissance, the Protestant Reformation, and the Enlightenment.

The Renaissance. Martin V tried to fulfill the provisions of the decree *Frequens* (1417) that emanated from the Council of Constance, which mandated that a general council should be held in five years, another seven years later, and then one regularly every ten years. He convened a council at Siena that later moved to Pavia (1423–1424), but the plague forced its dissolution. Seven years later another council was held, meeting first at Basel and later at Ferrara and Florence (1431–1445), under Eugene IV (1431–1447). Greek and Latin prelates attended, and they were able to agree on several thorny doctrinal issues including the primacy of the pope. The decree *Laetentur caeli* (1439), the first dogmatic definition of papal primacy by a council, stated: "We define that the holy apostolic see and the Roman Pontiff have primacy over the whole world, and that the same Roman Pontiff is the successor of Saint Peter, prince of the Apostles, the true vicar of Christ, the head of the church." Unfortunately, the union between the Greeks and Rome was short-lived.

Nicholas V (1447–1455) and his successors made Rome a center of the arts and scholarship. Humanistic concerns and involvement in Italian politics dominated their pontificates. Pius II (1458–1464), one of the most notable examples of papal humanism, in the bull *Execrabilis* (1460) prohibited any appeals to future general councils, thus striking at conciliarism. The same oligarchic spirit of the earlier Avignon cardinals appeared again at the election of Paul II (1464–1471). The cardinals drew up a capitulation requiring consultation with them before any major papal appointment, but after his election Paul promptly rejected this limitation. Sixtus IV (1471–1484) concerned himself mostly with the restoration of Rome and the expansion of the Papal States; he is responsible for building the magnificent Sistine Chapel in the Vatican. The Borgian pope, Alexander VI (1492–1503), has gone down in history as one of the most notorious of the Renaissance popes although his exploits have been exaggerated. The papacy, moreover, was engaged in almost continual warfare. The most famous of the warrior popes was Julius II (1503–1513), known as Il Terribile. A capable and energetic leader, Julius became the patron of Michelangelo, Raphael, and Bramante; he commissioned the construction of the new basilica of Saint Peter's. Adrian VI (1522–1523) was an exception among the Renaissance popes; in his short pontificate he tried to introduce reform measures, but these met persistent opposition from both civil rulers and highly placed ecclesiastics. In sum, the Renaissance popes were generally more interested in politics, the arts, and the ostentatious display of wealth than in providing genuine religious leadership. Their artistic achievements were outstanding, their neglect of spiritual concerns tragic.

The Reformation and Counter-Reformation. By the beginning of the sixteenth century the papacy was severely weakened by internal decay and a loss of supernatural vision. The faithful throughout Europe were asked to contribute alms to the extravagant building projects in Rome. These factors, coupled with deep-seated religious, social, and economic unrest in Europe, set the stage for the Protestant Reformation. Martin Luther's challenge in 1517 caught the papacy unprepared. Leo X (1513–1521) and his successors badly underestimated the extent and intensity of antipapal sentiment in Europe. The popes neither adequately comprehended the religious intentions of Luther nor understood the appeal that the reformers' ideas had for many who were outraged at both the policies and the conduct of church leaders. What began in the Reformation as a movement to restore genuine apostolic integrity to the church of Rome ended with the creation of a separate church. Luther, Calvin, and Zwingli eventually repudiated all papal claims. By the time of Clement VII (1523–1534), millions of Catholics in Germany, Scandinavia, the Low Countries, Switzerland, and Britain had departed from the Roman communion. A new era in church history had dawned.

The rapid rise of Protestantism had a sobering effect on the papacy: it forced the popes to concentrate on church affairs. Paul III (1534–1549), for example, appointed competent cardinals to administrative posts, authorized the establishment of the Society of Jesus (1540), and reformed the Roman Inquisition (1542). The church's most wide-ranging answer to the Protestant Reformation was the Council of Trent (1545–1563), convoked by Paul III and concluded by Pius IV (1559–1565). In its twenty-five sessions, the council discussed the authority of scripture and of tradition, original sin and justification, the sacraments, and specific reform legislation. It did not, strangely enough, treat explicitly the theology of the church or the papacy. The council refused to accept demands for a married clergy, Communion under both species, and a vernacular liturgy. The principles of conciliarism did not affect the Council of Trent, at which the reigning popes were in control of the proceedings.

One of the effects of the Tridentine reform was a reorganization of the church's central administrative system. The Curia Romana, which had existed, at least functionally, since the first century, was plagued by nepotism, greed, and abuse of authority. Sixtus V (1585–1590), who was committed to a reform of the Curia, established fifteen congregations of cardinals to carry out church administration. The popes endeavored to consider moral character and ability in selecting cardinals, whose number was set at seventy in 1588. Under Gregory XIII (1572–1585), papal nuncios to Catholic countries proved most valuable in implementing the ideals of Trent and in supervising the activities of the local bishops. For forty years after Trent, zealous popes strengthened papal authority and prestige. They increased centralization, mandated uniformity in liturgical ritual, and renewed priestly life and seminary training. The bishops of dioceses, who now had to submit regular reports to Rome and visit it at specified intervals, became much less independent. The success of the Counter-Reformation resulted from sound papal governance and the extraordinary contributions of the Jesuits and other religious orders. Yet union with the Protestants was not accomplished; the Christian church in the West had a divided membership.

Seventeenth and eighteenth centuries. The papacy had to face new problems caused by radical shifts in the political and intellectual climate of Europe during the seventeenth and eighteenth centuries. Skepticism, rationalism, and secularism became pervasive during the Enlightenment, and many intellectuals were violently opposed to the Catholic church and the papacy. As a result, the popes were often on the defensive. In actions reminiscent of the medieval papacy, Paul V (1605–1621) in 1605, in the wake of the Gunpowder Plot, forbade Catholics to take a loyalty oath to the king of England, and in 1607 he put Venice under interdict—a penalty largely ignored. The lengthy and often acrimonious debate between Dominicans and Jesuits over grace and free will, a question not settled at Trent, was terminated during Paul's reign. In 1597 Clement VIII (1592–1605) had established a special papal commission (the Congregatio de Auxiliis) to examine the orthodoxy of the two views. Paul received the final report, and in 1607 he declared that both orders could defend their positions, that neither side should censure the opposite opinion, and that all should await the final decision of the Holy See. This decision has not yet been made.

The Thirty Years War (1618–1648), a series of religious and dynastic wars that involved most of Europe, embroiled the papacy in conflict. Paul V and Gregory XV (1621–1623) had little influence on the conduct of Catholic rulers. Innocent X (1644–1655) protested, albeit futilely, against the Peace of Westphalia (1648), because he felt that Catholics were treated unjustly. This war and its aftermath showed how ineffective the papacy had become in European politics. The spirit of patriotism contributed to the problem. Furthermore, conciliarism revived in France in the form of Gallicanism, in Germany in the form of Febronianism, and in Austria in the form of Josephism. Although each of these movements had its own particular characteristics, all had two things in common: a strong nationalistic feeling and an antipapal bias. All reflected resentment of Roman centralism, urged greater autonomy for national churches, and advocated state control of ecclesiastical matters. The Holy See had also to contend with the absolutist ambitions of Louis XIV of France. Innocent XI (1676–1689) engaged in a protracted struggle with Louis over the king's claim to the right of revenues from vacant benefices (the *régale*) and over royal support of Gallicanism. Innocent's major achievement was his diplomatic role in preventing the fall of Vienna to the Turks in 1683, thus halting Muslim expansion into Europe.

During the following decades the popes were active in many areas. Innocent XII (1691–1700) forbade nepotism and Clement XII (1730–1740) condemned Freemasonry. Benedict XIV (1740–1758) finally ended the so-called Chinese and Malabar rites controversy, which had lasted nearly two centuries. Jesuit missionaries in China and South India had adapted certain indigenous customs and rites to Christianity. Benedict XIV condemned this practice and required the missionaries to take an oath rejecting the rites. The oath remained in force until the pontificate of Pius XII (1939–1958).

In the theological area, Innocent X repudiated five propositions on the theology of grace found in the writings of the Flemish bishop Cornelius Jansen; Alexander VII (1655–1667) rejected laxism as a moral system; and Alexander VIII (1689–1691) acted similarly against rigorism. The spiritual teaching of Quietism also received papal disapproval, when Innocent XII proscribed the views of Miguel de Molinos. The most dramatic papal action of the eighteenth century occurred when Clement XIV (1769–1774), bending to pressure from the Bourbon monarchies and fearing possible schism in France and Spain, suppressed the Society of Jesus in 1773.

The Modern Period. Dramatic shifts in the prestige and authority of the papacy have occurred between the era of the French Revolution and the twentieth century.

The popes of this period, faced with the demanding challenges of a new age, have attempted to restore their spiritual authority.

Revolution and restoration. The French Revolution, which began in 1789, and the subsequent actions of Napoleon created a new political order in Europe that adversely affected the Roman Catholic church. With nationalistic fervor, France's new revolutionary government became an instrument of dechristianization, secularization, and anticlericalism. Pius VI (1775–1799), who had little sympathy with the ideals of the revolution, was unable to deal effectively with such vehement defiance of the Holy See and such massive threats to the very existence of religion. At times it seemed as if the papacy itself would be destroyed. The octogenarian and infirm Pius was taken prisoner by Napoleon and died in exile on his way to Paris. Resistance to Napoleonic aggression continued during the pontificate of Pius VII (1800–1823). The Concordat of 1801 with Napoleon, which for over a century regulated the relationship between France and the church, revealed that Pius was willing to make concessions for the sake of peace. Yet in 1809 Napoleon captured Rome, annexed the Papal States, and arrested the pope and held him prisoner until 1814. The Catholic restoration began after the defeat of Napoleon: the Congress of Vienna (1814–1815) returned most of the papal territory to the church, and in 1814 Pius restored the Society of Jesus.

The fall of the monarchy in France and its impact on the rest of Europe weakened Gallicanism, Febronianism, and Josephism. Ultramontanism—a propapal movement that began early in the nineteenth century—advocated greater centralization of church government and a vigorous exercise of papal primacy. It gained strength under Gregory XVI (1831–1846), who opposed all revolutionary movements and defended papal primacy, infallibility, and the independence of the church from the state. A great missionary pope, Gregory fully controlled Catholic mission work.

The thirty-two-year pontificate of Pius IX (1846–1878), the longest in history, was significant. Initially hailed as a liberal, he soon showed his advocacy of ultramontanism. Pius believed that rationalism and secularism eroded both the faith and human society, and he considered a constitutional government for the Papal States to be a threat to the independence of the Holy See. Although many of his ideas isolated the church from the world, he gave the Roman Catholic faithful, with whom he was immensely popular, a new sense of spiritual identity. He restored the Catholic hierarchies of England (1850) and the Netherlands (1853), began a renewal of Marian devotion by his definition of the Immaculate Conception of Mary (1854), and supported extensive missionary activity. His greatest disappointment was the loss of the Papal States in 1870, which ended a millennium of temporal sovereignty. The popes became voluntary prisoners in the Vatican for the next sixty years. Pius's greatest triumph was the First Vatican Council (1869–1870), which ended abruptly when Italian troops occupied Rome. It produced two constitutions: *Dei filius*, a reaffirmation of the centrality of revelation, and *Pastor aeternus*, a definition of papal primacy and infallibility.

Vatican I and modernity. The most formal and detailed exposition of papal prerogatives is found in *Pastor aeternus*. In regard to primacy it taught that Jesus conferred upon Peter a primacy of both honor and jurisdiction; that by divine right Peter has perpetual successors in primacy over the universal church; that the Roman pontiff is the successor of Peter and has supreme, ordinary (not delegated), and immediate power and jurisdiction over the church and its members; and that the Roman pontiff is the supreme judge who is not subject to review by anyone. In regard to infallibility, Vatican I taught that by divine assistance the pope is immune from error when he speaks *ex cathedra*—that is, when "by virtue of his supreme apostolic authority he defines a doctrine concerning faith or morals to be held by the universal church." Such definitions are "irreformable of themselves and not from the consent of the church." This last phrase is directed against Gallicanism, even though by 1870 it was no longer a major problem. The formidable conception of the papacy at Vatican I was a victory for ultramontanism. Using juridical and monarchical language, it asserted the universal spiritual authority of the pope. The council, however, did not, because of its premature termination, present the papacy within the full context of the theology of the church, and it failed to discuss the relationship between the pope and the bishops.

The popes between Vatican I and Vatican II, individuals of superior quality, had much in common. First, they were all committed to the spiritual restoration of Catholicism, using their magisterial and jurisdictional authority to that end. A profusion of encyclical letters, addresses, and disciplinary decrees helped shape Catholic thought. Second, the popes continued to centralize church administration in Rome by increasing the power of the Roman Curia and the diplomatic corps. The movement toward uniformity in theology, liturgy, and law discouraged particularism. Third, the papal office actively promoted missionary endeavors; newly converted Catholics and immigrants to North America displayed great loyalty to the Holy See. Fourth, the popes, at times reluctantly and unsuccessfully, tried to respond to the demands of a changing world. They sought amicable relations with secular governments, especially through concordats, and worked devotedly for social justice and peace.

The popes of this period continued the ultramontanist policies of the nineteenth century, but with a difference. Leo XIII (1878–1903), for example, was more open to the positive aspects of modernity. Although he denied the validity of Anglican priestly orders in 1896, he was a pioneer in ecumenism. He supported the revival of Thomism (*Aeterni patris*, 1879), encouraged Catholic biblical studies (*Providentissimus Deus*, 1893), and presented the church's position on labor (*Rerum novarum*, 1891). His successor, Pius X (1903–1914), desired to renew the interior life of the church, as is shown by his teachings on the Eucharist, the liturgy, and seminary education. The most serious crisis he faced was modernism—a complex movement supported by Catholic thinkers in France, England, Germany, and Italy who sought to adapt Catholic doctrine to contemporary intellectual trends. Calling modernism "the synthesis of all heresies," Pius condemned it in *Pascendi* (1907). During World War I, the complete impartiality of Benedict XV (1914–1922) brought criticism from all sides. In 1917 he promulgated the first Code of Canon Law. The pope of the interwar years was Pius XI (1922–1939), noted for his encyclicals on marriage (*Casti connubii*, 1930) and social thought (*Quadragesimo anno*, 1931), for his promotion of missionary work, and most importantly, for concluding the Lateran Pacts (1929). Under these pacts Italy recognized the temporal sovereignty of the pope over Vatican City. Finally, Pius XII (1939–1958), a trained diplomat with broad interests, addressed almost every aspect of church life, and in a prodigious number of pronouncements applied Catholic doctrine to contemporary problems. In *Humani generis* (1950), Pius XII gave a wide-ranging critique of the theology that followed World War II. Although he encouraged theological speculation, he reaffirmed, for example, the traditional Catholic interpretation of creation, original sin, and transubstantiation and warned against the relativizing of dogma, the neglect of the teaching authority of the church *(magisterium)*, and scriptural exegesis that ignored the tradition of the church. Under Pius, the modern papacy reached an unprecedented level of respect.

Vatican II and postconciliar developments. John XXIII (1958–1963), elected when he was nearly seventy-seven, began a new era for Roman Catholicism. His open style of papal leadership, enhanced by his appealing personality, was warmly welcomed by Catholics and non-Catholics alike. Although he is well known for his efforts in promoting ecumenism and world peace (*Pacem in terris*, 1963), the pope's greatest accomplishment was the unexpected convocation of the Second Vatican Council (1962–1965). John designed the council to foster reform and reunion, believing that a contemporary reformulation of the Christian tradition would revitalize the Catholic church and ultimately benefit all humankind. Paul VI (1963–1978) skillfully maintained the council's pastoral orientation. To implement its program, he established the Synod of Bishops, internationalized and increased the number of cardinals, reformed the Curia, and promoted liturgical reform. He made nine trips outside Italy.

Vatican II supplied what was lacking in Vatican I. Its doctrine of collegiality described the relationship between the pope and the bishops. The Constitution on the Church (*Lumen gentium*) stated: "Together with its head, the Roman Pontiff, and never without this head, the episcopal order is the subject of supreme and full power in relation to the universal church. But this power can be exercised only with the consent of the Roman Pontiff" (Article 22). The college of bishops, then, exists only under the leadership of the pope, himself a bishop. The pope is not the executor of the bishops' wishes (Gallicanism), nor are the bishops vicars of the pope (papal absolutism). Both the papacy and the episcopacy have their own legitimate authority, and the purpose of collegiality is to unite the bishops with the pope. Yet there remains the difficult theological problem of reconciling papal primacy with episcopal authority. Many theologians argue that there is only one subject of supreme authority in the church—the college of bishops—and that it can operate in two ways: through a collegial action or through a personal act of the pope as head of the college. Thus every primatial action of the pope is always collegial. The council did not establish any legal norms that would require the pope to consult with the bishops, but nevertheless it posed the moral ideal of cooperation and collaboration that should govern the relationship between the pope and the bishops.

The theory of collegiality has altered the style of papal leadership, making it far less monarchical. The closer relationship between the pope and the bishops is best exemplified by the Synod of Bishops, a consultative body that meets once every three years. Collegiality has made the papacy less objectionable to other Christians since it fosters the idea of authority as service and not domination. This aspect has been noted in the fifth dialogue of the Lutheran–Roman Catholic discussions (1974) and in the Final Report of the Anglican–Roman

Catholic International Commission (1982). Both groups recognized the value of a universal Petrine ministry of unity in the Christian church and foresaw the possibility of the bishop of Rome exercising that function for all Christians in the future.

Vatican II significantly changed the Catholic church. Along with progressive reforms, however, there were also reactions that resulted in doctrinal and disciplinary confusion. Thousands of priests and nuns left the active ministry, and some misguided experiments occurred. Dissent over Paul VI's prohibition against artificial birth control in *Humanae vitae* (1968) caused acute pastoral problems and raised serious questions about the credibility of the papal office.

In 1978 two popes died and two were elected. The pontificate of John Paul I, the successor of Paul VI, lasted only thirty-three days. Breaking a tradition that had endured for more than nine hundred years, John Paul I was not installed by a rite of coronation or enthronement. He rejected the obvious symbols of temporal and monarchical authority and was inaugurated at a solemn mass. Instead of the tiara, he was given the pallium, a white woolen stole symbolizing his spiritual and pastoral ministry. His successor, John Paul II, became the first non-Italian pope in 456 years, the first Polish pope, and the first pope from a Communist country. The most-traveled pope in history, John Paul II earned huge popular appeal with his international pastoral visits. He succeeded in personalizing the papal office to an extent never before attempted. Social justice and peace, major themes in his pontificate, were discussed in detail in *Redemptor hominis* (1979) and *Laborem exercens* (1981). It is too early to make any definitive assessment of his reign, but it appears that his main goal is the restoration of a more traditional Roman Catholicism. Uneasy with theological dissent (he has censured theologians), moral laxity, and arbitrary innovations, John Paul II has taken forceful steps to bring the Catholic church under control and to heal its divisions. In 1983 he promulgated the revised Code of Canon Law. He has survived two assassination attempts.

The papacy has had a complex but intriguing history. For nearly two millennia, showing remarkable resiliency, it has continued through times of growth and decline, glory and shame, internal and external conflicts, and radical social upheavals. In an age of widespread unbelief and unsettling technological change, the papacy can work to rekindle the spiritual aspirations of humanity.

[*For related discussions, see* Councils, *article on* Christian Councils; Schism, *article on* Christian Schism; Canon Law; Crusades, *article on* Christian Perspective; Inquisition, The; Reformation; Trent, Council of; Gallicanism; Ultramontanism; Modernism, *article on* Christian Modernism; Vatican Councils; *and biographies of popes mentioned herein. See also* Church; Church and State; *and* Ecumenical Movement.]

BIBLIOGRAPHY

Historical Works. Two standard works on papal history are Johannes Haller's *Das Papsttum: Idee und Wirklichkeit*, 5 vols. (1950–1953; reprint, Esslingen am Neckar, 1962), and Franz Xaver Seppelt's *Geschichte der Päpste von den Anfängen bis zur Mitte des zwanzigsten Jahrhunderts*, 5 vols. (Munich, 1954–1959). Dated in some respects but still very useful are two monumental studies: Horace K. Mann's *The Lives of the Popes in the Early Middle Ages*, 18 vols. in 19, 2d ed. (London, 1925–1969), which covers the period from 590 to 1304; and Ludwig von Pastor's *The History of the Popes from the Close of the Middle Ages*, 40 vols. (London, 1891–1953), which concerns the years from 1305 to 1799. Walter Ullmann's *A Short History of the Papacy in the Middle Ages* (London, 1972) and Guillaume Mollat's *The Popes at Avignon, 1305–1378*, translated from the 9th French edition by Janet Love (London, 1963), can be recommended. The papacy in the eighteenth, nineteenth, and twentieth centuries is discussed in Owen Chadwick's *The Popes and European Revolution* (Oxford, 1981); Roger Aubert's *Le pontificat de Pie IX, 1846–1878*, 2d ed. (Paris, 1964); and J. Derek Holmes's *The Papacy in the Modern World, 1914–1978* (New York, 1981). General histories of the church contain much information on the papal office. One of the most comprehensive and reliable is *Histoire de l'Église depuis les origines jusqu'à nos jours*, 21 vols. (Paris, 1934–1964), edited by Augustin Fliche et al. There is valuable material on papal documentation in Carl Mirbt's *Quellen zur Geschichte des Papsttums und des Römischen Katholizismus*, 5th ed. (1895; reprint, Tübingen, 1934), and James T. Shotwell and Louise R. Loomis's *The See of Peter* (New York, 1927).

Theological Works. An analysis of the biblical evidence is found in Raymond E. Brown et al., *Peter in the New Testament* (Minneapolis, 1973). For a detailed study of the theology of the papacy with special emphasis on collegiality see my work, *The Papacy in Transition* (Garden City, N.Y., 1980). Both books contain full bibliographies. Various theological points are discussed in *Papal Primacy in the Church, Concilium*, vol. 64 (New York, 1971), edited by Hans Küng; in Karl Rahner and Joseph Ratzinger's *The Episcopate and the Primacy* (New York, 1962); in Gustave Thils's *La primauté pontificale* (Gembloux, 1972); and in Jean-Marie R. Tillard's *The Bishop of Rome* (Wilmington, Del., 1983). For a discussion of the ecumenical dimension of the papacy, see *Das Papstamt: Dienst oder Hindernis für die Ökumene?* (Regensburg, 1985), by Vasilios von Aristi et al. Excellent articles on the same topic are contained in the following: *Papal Primacy and the Universal Church* (Minneapolis, 1974), edited by Paul C. Empie and T. Austin Murphy; *Teaching Authority and Infallibility in the Church* (Minneapolis, 1980), edited by Paul C. Empie et al.; *The Anglican–Roman Catholic International Commission: The Final Report, Windsor, Sept. 1981* (London, 1982); and John Meyendorff et al., *The Primacy of Peter* (London, 1963).

PATRICK GRANFIELD

PARACELSUS (1493?–1541), German alchemist, mystic, and physician. Philippus Aureolos Theophrastus Bombastus von Hohenheim was one of the most bizarre characters in the history of science. Commonly known as Paracelsus because in his own estimation he was greater than the great Greek physician Celsus, he was a paranoid, uncouth, abusive, and usually drunken genius, whose reputation varied widely. While his supporters dubbed him the "Luther of science," his detractors denounced him as a heretic and condemned him as the disreputable black magician who provided the model for Faust. His considerable writings offer a strange blend of medicine, religion, philosophy, cosmology, alchemy, magic, and astrology, a synthesis of natural and mystical philosophy typical of other writers before the scientific revolution separated science from religious and philosophical speculation.

Neither modest in presenting his opinions nor restrained in his language, Paracelsus launched an acrimonious attack on the medical and scientific establishment of his day. He rejected the prevailing Galenic theory that attributed disease to an imbalance of the four humors and replaced it with his own dynamic theory of diseases as specific entities attacking specific organs.

Paracelsus was an idealist and a visionary who considered chemistry the key to the universe. In his view, God was the divine alchemist who created the world by calcinating, congealing, distilling, and sublimating the elements of chaos. The alchemist had only to read the reactions in his laboratory on a grand scale to fathom the mysteries of creation. By turning alchemy away from gold-making, Paracelsus and his followers transformed it into a universal science of matter concerned with every aspect of material change.

Paracelsus's thought was shaped by both the Renaissance and the Reformation. Although he rejected the aesthetics and classicism of Renaissance humanists, he shared their anthropocentric and individualistic outlook. As Walter Pagel (1958, p. 36) has pointed out, there was a decentralizing tendency throughout Paracelsus's work. An enormous variety of noncorporeal forces (vital spirits, demons, subhumans, superhumans) work below the surface of the Paracelsian universe. Paracelsus drew his vitalist and pantheist ideas from the occult philosophies and sciences revived by Renaissance scholars—Neoplatonism, gnosticism, Qabbalah, magic, alchemy, and astrology. The analogy between the macrocosm and the microcosm characteristic of these philosophies shaped Paracelsus's theory of knowledge. He rejected scholastic rationalism in favor of a kind of psychological empiricism. Because man is the microcosm he contains within himself all the elements of the greater world, or macrocosm. Knowledge therefore consists in an intuitive act of recognition, in which the knower and the known become one.

Because Paracelsus's theory of knowledge approximates Luther's doctrine of the "inner light," the two men have been compared. Each attacked established ideologies and institutions, wrote in the vernacular, and was a master of scurrilous invective. Both enjoyed theatrics: Luther burned the papal bull excommunicating him; Paracelsus burned the works of Galen and Ibn Sīnā (Avicenna). The comparison between the two men is, however, superficial. Luther preached the bondage of the human will, while Paracelsus was an ardent advocate of free will; Luther made grace the prerequisite of salvation, while Paracelsus emphasized charitable acts; Luther sided with sovereigns, while Paracelsus's sympathies remained with the people. Although Paracelsus was in contact with many reformers, sharing their criticism of church abuses, he eventually became disillusioned and charged that the reformers were as autocratic as their Catholic counterparts. Paracelsus's religious ideas were more compatible with nondogmatic reformers such as Hans Denck (1495?–1527) and Sebastian Franck (1499?–1542?).

Religion and philosophy provided the sources for both the progressive and the obscurantist aspect of Paracelsus's thought. His repudiation of reason led him to embrace empiricism; it also made much of his writing incomprehensible. On the basis of his vitalist philosophy, he rejected mechanical explanations of biological processes in favor of an organic, holistic approach that allowed for psychological factors. The same vitalism taken to extremes, however, resulted in proliferation of the number of active, independent forces to the point that classification became impossible and causality meaningless.

With his penchant for oracular and aphoristic statements, Paracelsus was more a prophet than a scientist. His most vociferous critic, Thomas Lüber (Thomas Erastus), denounced him as a gnostic heretic. Paracelsus did believe he was divinely inspired. In this sense, he was the "spiritual man" or "knowing one" who had achieved *gnōsis*.

[*See also* Occultism *and* Rosicrucians.]

BIBLIOGRAPHY

The critical standard edition of Paracelsus's *Sämtliche Werke,* 15 vols., edited by Karl Sudoff and Wilhelm Mattiessen (Munich, 1922–1933), includes copious annotations and bibliographic references. Kurt Goldammer is in the process of editing a new and more complete edition: Theophrast von Hohenheim, *Sämtliche Werke* (forthcoming). Walter Pagel's *Paracelsus: An Introduction to Philosophical Medicine in the Era of the Renaissance* (New York, 1958) has an excellent bibliography and provides a thorough discussion of Paracelsus's sources. In his *The Chemical Philosophy: Paracelsian Science and Medicine in the Sixteenth and Seventeenth Centuries,* 2 vols. (New York, 1977), Allen G. Debus discusses Paracelsus's legacy and influence on later scientists. English translations of selected treatises can be found in Arthur Edward Waite's *The Hermetic and Alchemical Writings of Aureolus Philippus Theophrastus Bombast, called Paracelsus the Great,* 2 vols. (1894; reprint, New Hyde Park, N.Y., 1967); Henry Sigerist's *Four Treatises of Theophrastus von Hohenheim* (Baltimore, 1941); and Jolande Jacobi's *Paracelsus: Selected Writings* (New York, 1951).

ALLISON COUDERT

PARADISE. The word *paradise* originated from Old Persian *pairidaeza,* which meant "walled enclosure, pleasure park, garden." *Pairidaeza* came into Hebrew, Aramaic, and Greek retaining its original meanings. It appears three times in the Hebrew scriptures (*Neh.* 2:8, *Eccl.* 2:5, *Sg.* 4:13) and also in later rabbinic literature. In the Septuagint, the Hebrew word for "garden" was usually translated by the Greek *paradeisos.* In *Genesis* 2–3 *paradeisos* refers to the original Garden of Eden (lit., "delight").

The earliest known description of a paradisial garden appears on a cuneiform tablet from protoliterate Sumer. It begins with a eulogy of Dilmun, a place that is pure, clean, and bright, a land of the living who do not know sickness, violence, or aging. It lacks one thing only: fresh water. This, however, is soon supplied by the sun god Utu at the command of the Sumerian water god Enki. Dilmun is thereby transformed into a garden with fruit trees, edible plants, and green meadows. Dilmun is a garden of the gods, not for humans, although one learns that Ziusudra, the Sumerian Noah, was exceptionally admitted to the divine paradise.

The Garden of Eden. According to the mythical narrative in *Genesis* 2–3, God planted a garden in Eden and therein placed man to till and keep it. God also caused trees to grow in the garden. The Edenic paradise was mainly arboreal, thereby providing food for man. The original human diet seems to have been vegetarian. According to *Genesis* 9, it was only later—after the Flood—that the descendants of Adam (Noah and his family) were permitted to eat flesh. A dietary restriction remained, however, for flesh containing blood was not to be eaten (*Gn.* 9:4).

The garden was the source of the world's sweet waters. A river not only watered the garden but flowed out of it to become four rivers (Pishon, Gihon, Tigris, and Euphrates), apparently to water the four directions or quarters of the world (*Gn.* 2:10–14).

The myth recognizes a deficiency in man's life in Eden: he is alone. This solitariness is soon relieved, for God forms beasts and birds. These living creatures are brought to man to be named. The naming signifies his mastery of the animals. Still, it is said, man does not have a suitable companion. The account of the creation of woman (Eve) follows. She is said to have been created from the rib (bone) of Adam, perhaps reflecting an archaic religious identification of the essence of life with bone (rather than with blood, as in *Genesis* 9). [*See* Bones.] Adam and Eve become "one flesh."

One of the creatures of God, the serpent, approaches Eve and inquires whether God has placed any limits on the trees from which the couple may eat. Earlier in the narrative (2:9), there is reference to the Tree of Life and the Tree of the Knowledge of Good and Evil, and the warning to man that he will die if he eats of the latter (2:17). When Eve reveals the prohibition, the serpent denies that death will result and insists instead that eating the fruit will result in likeness to God in that man will then know good and evil. Both Eve and Adam eat the forbidden fruit, popularly thought to have been an apple. The knowledge they obtain is of their own nakedness; in shame they fashion simple garments.

At the sound of God walking in the garden, the couple hide among the trees. When discovered and questioned, they reveal that they have violated the divine prohibition. Sentence is passed on them as well as the serpent. Henceforth, Eve will experience pain in childbirth and subordination to her husband. Adam is condemned to till the soil under difficult conditions and ultimately to return to the soil or dust from which he originally came, that is, to die.

The concluding verses of the narrative refer to the second of the trees—the Tree of Life—which is earlier said to be in the midst (center?) of the garden. The deity appears concerned that man, if allowed to remain in the garden, will eat also of the Tree of Life and live forever. It may be that the myth intends to say that the Tree of Life was hidden among the many trees of the garden and that man, having eaten of the Tree of Knowledge, might find it. At any rate, Adam and Eve are driven from the garden, and an angel and a flaming sword are placed at the entrance to guard the way to the Tree of Life.

The first human habitat was, according to the narrative of Eden, a fertile, well-watered garden or orchard that supplied all things required by its inhabitants for nutrition and ease. The garden was a veritable oasis, perhaps to be contrasted with the desert or the wilderness, as it was in Jewish, Christian, and Islamic thought (see, e.g., Williams, 1962). The taking of life was not necessary for human sustenance. The animals and birds of Eden, while under the mastery of man, seem to have lived in more or less peaceful and harmonious relationship with him and one another. Similarly, the relationship between man and woman seems to have been harmonious. Sexual tension had not yet appeared. The original nudity of the pair and the lack of shame signified paradisial innocence. In general, the conditions of life were ideal.

The significance of the serpent is not clear. It has been suggested that the serpent hoped through Adam and Eve to discover the Tree of Life and thus secure immortality for himself. In many interpretations of the *Genesis* narrative the serpent is given a negative valuation as the tempter and deceiver of women. In some other religious traditions (e.g., Hinduism), the serpent is associated with the very things symbolized by the two special trees of paradise: wisdom and immortality.

The turning point of the narrative is the act of disobedience. It has serious consequences. That Adam and Eve should recognize their nakedness is indicative of their loss of innocence. Also, the divine-human communication possible when God walks in the garden and converses with humans becomes problematic. The consequences of disobedience are profound changes in the conditions of human life: pain, toil, and mortality are specifically mentioned (*Gn.* 3:16–19). It is the loss of paradise that gives the narrative its poignancy. However one may interpret the details, the essential meaning of the myth of the Garden of Eden is that, in the beginning, life was paradisial but something happened that changed it into what it has been since that time.

The lost paradise of Eden has sometimes been thought actually to have existed somewhere on earth. Since the Bible nowhere indicates its destruction, some people have assumed that the garden, or traces of it, could be discovered. Thus it has been imagined to exist at the headwaters of the Tigris and Euphrates rivers. It has also been "discovered" far from the Middle East. Christopher Columbus, for example, believed that the freshwater currents he detected in the Gulf of Paria between Trinidad and the South American Coast had their source in the four rivers flowing out of the biblical Eden. The luxuriant vegetation and the mild climate as well as the scents of tropical flowers seemed proof enough to confirm his speculations. Paradise has also been "found" in the most improbable places, as, for example, the Arctic Pole (see William F. Warren, *Paradise Found: The Cradle of the Human Race at the North Pole,* 1885).

The Primordiality of Paradise. The Edenic paradise was primordial. Paradise is frequently thought to have been primordial, that is, to have existed in the fabulous time of beginnings.

Hermann Baumann (1936) has called attention to African myths concerning a primordial paradise. In these myths, human beings understand the language of animals and are at peace with them. They have no need to work, and food is plentiful at hand. Disease and death are unknown. However, an event occurs that terminates these paradisial conditions and makes human life what it is today.

Myths of primordial paradise, broadly conceived, include the large number of myths in which, in the beginning, Heaven and Earth are in close proximity and, also, myths according to which Heaven is easily accessible by a concrete means such as a tree, ladder, vine, or mountain that can be climbed. As the result of the separation of Heaven and Earth or the removal of the link between them, easy communication is lost. A rupture occurs. It signifies the end of paradise and entry into the ordinary human condition.

Characteristics of the Primordial Paradise. Among the marks or characteristics of the primordial paradise are perfection, purity, plenitude, freedom, spontaneity, peace, pleasure, beatitude, and immortality. Each contrasts with the characteristics of ordinary, postparadisial human life. To this list could appropriately be added harmony and friendship with the animals, including knowledge of their language, and, as well, ease of communication with the gods and the world above.

Unlike a Darwinian view with its stress on rudimentary, imperfect beginnings, the myths of primordial paradise envision the perfection of beginnings. Moreover, the original purity of all things is preserved. Myths of primordial paradise affirm plenitude, often in terms of extraordinary abundance. Freedom and spontaneity are expressed by the absence or minimalization of constraints; there are few if any laws in paradise. As for peace, the typical scenario creates an atmosphere of ease, rest, tranquillity, the absence of tension and conflict. As noted above, human beings and animals live peaceably, sexual tension has not yet appeared, and labor is unnecessary. Indeed, things seem to be in easy equilibrium, perhaps even static. Pleasure abounds, whether described in sensual terms or as spiritual satisfactions. Beatitude, consummate bliss, is the happy lot of all the inhabitants of paradise. Paradise is outside ordinary, historical time. Hence there can be no ageing or death. Humans are immortal, for death has not yet appeared. Nor has sickness or disease or sin or injustice or any of the ills that postparadisial man is heir to.

Nostalgia for Paradise. Although the primordial paradise has been lost, it has not been forgotten. One finds expressions of the desire to recover the essential condition, the condition that would still obtain if all had gone as it should. The image of a place and time of perfect and endless peace and plenty has the power to make historical existence significant and bearable and its transitoriness acceptable. A Freudian interpretation would speak of wish fulfillment and the desire to return to the womb, but such an interpretation would be both limited and reductive. More significant than wishes, although they may be present, is the nostalgia, the haunting sense of loss and the powerful desire for recovery. The nostalgia for paradise is among the powerful nostalgias that seem to haunt human beings. It may be the most powerful and persistent of all. A certain longing for paradise is evidenced at every level of religious life.

An unusually well documented example of an actual quest for paradise is provided by the Guaraní Indians of Brazil. For more than four centuries, the Guaraní have engaged in a series of migrations in search of the "land without evil." It is thought actually to exist in this world but to be well hidden. Mircea Eliade has suggested that the paradisial images used by shamans in recounting their dreams and ecstasies have helped to keep alive the centuries-old quest (*The Quest,* 1969).

Recurring Paradises. Paradises are found in cosmically oriented as well as historically oriented religions, that is, in religions in which time is cyclical as well as in those in which it is linear and historical. In the former, paradise is not only lost but recurs, from time to time, in step with the ever-turning wheel of time.

The most impressive example in the history of religion is the Hindu doctrine of the world ages (*yugas*). It is cast in mythical terms by relating the ages of the life of the god Brahmā. Briefly, each world cycle is subdivided into four world ages. They are comparable to the four ages of Greco-Roman tradition. That tradition used the names of metals—gold, silver, bronze, and iron—to designate the successive ages. Hinduism uses the four throws of the Indian game of dice: *kṛta* (4), *tretā* (3), *dvāpara* (2), and *kali* (1). Decline and deterioration proceed as age follows age.

Kṛtayuga is the perfect age, the age of four (the winning throw in the dice game). The number four is a frequent symbol of totality, plenitude, and perfection in Hinduism. The age is known also as the *satya* ("real, true, authentic") *yuga.* During the *kṛta* age *dharma* (the fundamental universal moral order) is observed totally and spontaneously. It is the golden age, the age of truth, justice, prosperity, and human fulfillment. In other words, it is equivalent to the primordial, paradisial age of other religious traditions.

Unfortunately, the *kṛtayuga* inevitably ends and is followed by the three ages of increasing decline, culminating in the *kaliyuga,* the dark age, in which only one-quarter of *dharma* remains. In the dice game *kali* is the losing throw. In the *kali* age the nadir is reached. The world and humans are at their worst. Also unfortunately, our world is now in the *kaliyuga,* which, according to one reckoning, will last 432,000 human years. Even so, it will eventually come to an end and will be followed by the return of the *kṛtayuga,* the perfect, golden age. In other words, paradise will reappear. In the meanwhile, it exists as an image, a powerful image of perfection, plenitude, and prosperity.

Buddhism adopted essentially the Hindu cyclical view of ages, relating it to the Buddhas and *bodhisattvas*. Here, too, paradisial motifs appear, as in Mahāyāna texts describing the world at the time of the birth of the expected next Buddha, Maitreya, in this world system. In the *Maitreyavyākaraṇa* the world—more specifically, India—is described as remarkably different at the time of Maitreya's appearing. Its innumerable inhabitants will commit no crimes or evil deeds and will delight in doing good. People will be without blemishes. They will be strong, large, and joyful, and few will be the illnesses among them. The soil will be free of thorns, covered with green grass, and will produce rice without any work. Into this paradisial, or near-paradisial, world, Maitreya will come to proclaim the true Dharma.

Hesiod in the *Theogony* writes of five ages, inserting an age of heroes after the bronze age in the usual Greco-Roman sequence of gold, silver, bronze, and iron ages. He describes the golden age in paradisial terms. Men live like gods. They do not work or experience sorrow. Neither do they grow old. Though they are mortal, death comes as sleep. The fertile land is fruitful. Men are at peace and have every want supplied. They are succeeded, however, by a lesser, silver race of men.

Plato in the *Politicus* (269c ff.) speaks of cyclical return that includes times of regeneration. The time comes when ordinary processes are reversed. Thus human beings begin to grow younger rather than older, returning to infancy and finally ceasing to be. There appears then the age of Kronos in which a new race ("Sons of Earth") is born. Human beings rise out of the earth. Trees provide them with fruits in abundance. They sleep naked (in paradisial nudity) on the soil. The seasons are mild, and all animals are tame and peaceable.

Paradise as the Abode of the Righteous. The biblical conception of paradise is not limited to the primordial

Garden of Eden. With the emergence of Jewish belief in the resurrection of the dead, perhaps around 200 BCE, paradise could be taken to refer not only to the original Garden of Eden but also to the eternal abode of the righteous. That is, the righteous dead could expect to have the Garden of Eden, or paradise, as their postresurrection abode (rather than Gehenna, the fiery place of punishment of the wicked). Thus Garden and Gehenna constituted a contrasting pair. Moreover, the garden of paradise could refer as well to the intermediate abode of the righteous until their resurrection.

The location of the paradisial abode of the righteous, whether before or after the resurrection, could still be taken as earthly, as it was by some, but the tendency was to locate it above, either in heaven or in one of the multiple heavens (e.g., the third heaven).

In the New Testament, the myth of the Garden of Eden is interpreted as the account of the "fall" of humans through willful disobedience, thus emphasizing the need for and appropriateness of a savior who effects the restoration of fallen humans. In this regard, characteristically Christian interpretations of the myth of Eden have differed from Jewish interpretations. The former have emphasized estrangement from the divine and "original sin." The latter have not.

The New Testament contains three specific references to paradise (*2 Cor.* 12:3, *Lk.* 23:43, *Rv.* 2:7). These indicate experiential and eschatological conceptions of paradise. In *2 Corinthians* 12:3 a man is said to have been caught up into paradise, which in the preceding verse is identified with the third heaven. Paradise appears to be thought of as a celestial or heavenly level entered through ecstasy. Paradise may also be entered by privileged persons (for example, martyrs and the "good thief" of *Luke* 23:43). The third reference to paradise is *Revelation* 2:7, addressed to the church in Ephesus. The promise is given that one who conquers will be granted to eat of the tree of life in God's paradise. It is said in the context of a call for patient endurance and appears to link an eschatological paradise with the primordial, earthly Eden.

In the Islamic religion the Arabic word for "garden"—*janna*—is used to refer to the Garden of Eden and, as well, to the heavenly Paradise in which the God-fearing will dwell. In the Qur'ān it more commonly refers to the latter. As in the Jewish religion, there is a contrasting pair of terms: garden *(janna)* and Gehenna (Jahannam). In surah 2:25 those who believe and do works of righteousness are promised gardens with flowing rivers and abundant fruit, therein to dwell forever. Surah 47:15 promises the God-fearing a garden not only with rivers of water but rivers of milk, wine, and honey as well as every kind of fruit. The garden is a luxuriant oasis, an appealing image to any desert-dwelling people such as the first hearers of the Qur'ān. "Gardens of delight" are promised in surah 56. The inhabitants will recline on couches where they will be served from a pure spring by immortal youths. They will eat as they desire of fruit and the flesh of fowl. With them will be the *ḥūrīs*, described (56:36f.) as chastely amorous virgins.

Representations of Paradise. Paradise is susceptible to a variety of specific representations. Something that belongs to the actual world is used to refer to an ideal world.

Garden. The garden is the most common representation of paradise. This representation is not limited to religions originating in the Middle East. There is, for example, a Mahāyāna Buddhist paradise, Sukhāvatī, the "pure land" of the Buddha Amitābha. In the *Sukhāvativyūha*, the paradise of Amitābha is described as fertile, rich, comfortable, and delightful. It is filled with a great variety of flowers and fruits. Many deep, broad rivers flow through it. Birds sing pleasantly. Calm and peace pervade this garden paradise.

In Greek mythology one finds the garden, or orchard, of Hesperides, located in the far west, not far from the Isles of the Blessed. It is renowned for its golden apples. A guard stands at the entrance. There are, as well, the Elysian Fields, where, according to Homer's *Odyssey* (4.564ff.), the climate is wonderfully mild, as there is no winter. The ocean provides refreshing breezes for mortals. Their lives are said to be the easiest.

The association of garden with paradise has been persistent, as shown by Elizabeth Moynihan in *Paradise as a Garden: In Persia and Mughal India* (1979). She demonstrates the continuity of the tradition and symbolic topography of the paradise garden. She points especially to the relationship between water, the central and most essential element in the Persian garden, and trees, symbolizing regeneration or immortality and the possibility of ascension. The blissful Paradise—the reward in the afterlife—was the model for the Persian garden. The latter, with its trees reaching symbolically upward and its rippling water and fragrant flowers, never became entirely secular.

A rather different kind of example is found in the symbolization of America as a garden paradise. Charles L. Sanford has studied the depth of the search for paradise in American civilization in *The Quest for Paradise* (1961). It is well known that the early explorers and settlers of the New World spoke of it in terms of Eden. Its virgin forests, fertile soil, abundant game, aboriginal inhabitants, and freedom from the restraints of the Old World encouraged this identification. Here mankind, having left behind the Old World of Europe, could make a new beginning, as R. W. B. Lewis makes clear in *The*

American Adam (1955). Moreover, particular parts of America were identified with Eden, illustrating the possibility of a multiplicity of paradises. Thus George Alsop identified Maryland as the terrestrial paradise, saying that its trees, plants, flowers, fruits, and even its roots were signs of Adam's realm, special evidence of its innocence. John Smith believed he had discovered Eve in the Powhatan tribe and that he had chanced on a land that was as God made it, a place where heaven and earth best agreed as a land for human habitation. In a 1609 farewell sermon given for Virginia adventurers by Daniel Price, Virginia was described as the garden of the world, a land flowing with milk and honey. When the frontiersmen crossed the mountains through the Cumberland Gap into Kentucky, they saw it not only as "the dark and bloody ground" but, paradoxically, as a veritable Eden, rich in forests and game and fertile in soil. The same sort of thing was happening in Puritan New England, though often in terms of future expectations. Thus Edward Johnson considered Massachusetts a place where a new heaven and a new earth will be created by the Lord. Later, Jonathan Edwards could speak of the Great Awakening as a glorious work that would make New England a heaven on earth.

It is not difficult to understand why the garden has often provided the setting for the primordial paradise and, as well, the paradise of the dead. Whether cultivated (as it was after the discovery of agriculture) or provided by nature, a garden is a striking phenomenon. Typically, it is in evident contrast with the surrounding territory, sometimes dramatically. It seems to constitute another world, different from the ordinary one, a world in which seed, soil, and water combine in evident manifestation of fertility, vitality, and abundance. For humans it provides refreshment as well as nourishment, and signalizes an alluring mode of human existence. [*See also* Gardens.]

Island. Gardens are not the sole representations of paradise. It is also represented in other ways, frequently as an island or a mountain. These several representations are sometimes combined, as in a gardenlike island paradise. Such is the case with the Pacific Ocean island paradises of novels and the lush, vividly colored island paradises of Gauguin's paintings.

The Isles of the Blessed in Greek mythology are well known. They are an insular counterpart to Olympus, the mountain of the gods. One finds parallels in Celtic mythology, where isle as well as garden is used as an image of paradise. Moreover, the myth of the submerged world, comparable to Plato's Atlantis, is also found. Here one has the motif of a more or less paradisial world in which something went wrong, resulting in its disappearance beneath the waves.

Perhaps even more effectively than the garden, the island symbolizes a world. Its limits and contours are in sharp relief in the midst of the sea, and its microcosmic nature is evident.

An island suggests isolation. It can readily symbolize the remoteness and difficulty of access of paradise. Often a river or an ocean has to be traversed. Paradise cannot easily be found, entered, recovered. In this context the motif of journey, especially of difficult or perilous journey, appears.

Mountain. The mountain is also sometimes associated with paradise, as, for example, in connection with Jerusalem (Mount Zion) in its paradisial dimensions, or with Mount Meru of Hindu mythology. John Milton in book 4 of *Paradise Lost* describes paradise as a mountain. In fact, Milton brings together several images, for in his description the paradisial mountain is also a garden and the origin of the four rivers that course down its sides.

The distinctive characteristic of the mountain is its height. It towers above the earth and therefore can readily symbolize transcendence. Thus when paradise is thought of as a transcendental realm, the mountain is an appropriate image. [*See also* Mountains.]

Eschatological Paradises. While paradise is usually thought of as in the past, it also figures in some eschatologies. In the *Book of Revelation* there is envisioned a new heaven and a new earth and, as well, a new Jerusalem, which will come down from God (*Rv.* 21:1ff.). God will then dwell among men, and henceforth mourning, crying, pain, and death will be no more. In Jewish messianism the coming age is frequently described in terms strongly reminiscent of paradisial existence (e.g., *Is.* 11:6–8, *Ez.* 47:1–12). Norman Cohn in *The Pursuit of the Millennium* (1957) found paradisial elements in his study of revolutionary messianism in medieval and Reformation Europe.

In modern times "cargo cults" of Melanesia and Micronesia have been especially generative of paradisial motifs. Briefly, these cults are typically based on myths that prophesy that soon an ancestor-bearing ship will arrive with a wonderful cargo to be received by those who have expected and prepared for its arrival. The return of the ancestors and the arrival of cargo signal profound changes. Not only will poverty be abolished but all that belongs to the old world will be destroyed. A series of reversals will take place: servants will become masters, the old will become young, yams will grow on trees, and coconuts will grow in the ground. After all that belongs to the old world has been changed or destroyed, a new world will appear. In this world there will be freedom from laws, traditions, work, poverty, disease, ageing, and death. In other words, this radical transformation or renewal of the world signifies paradise. [*See* Cargo Cults.]

Secular Paradises. Most of the paradises referred to have been explicitly religious. However, paradisial motifs and nostalgias for paradise have appeared, especially in the modern world, in other guises. Utopias, some of which, but not all, are explicitly religious, typically have some of the characteristics of paradise, often to a lesser degree and with some concessions to actuality. It could be said that utopias are efforts to actualize the image of paradise, under the conditions of this world. [*See* Utopia.]

The strong interest in communes in recent decades, especially among the young, may be understood as a quest for a secular paradise, as may the more pervasive and continuing interest in returning to the land, evidenced first by the creation of suburbia but extending subsequently to the truly rural countryside.

[*See also* Heaven and Hell. *For discussion of the experience of lost paradise, see* Fall, The.]

BIBLIOGRAPHY

Armstrong, John H. S. *The Paradise Myth.* London, 1969. Seeks an alternative to the *Genesis* paradise myth in elements of Sumerian and Greek myths and in themes in Renaissance literature and art.

Baumann, Hermann. *Schöpfung und Urzeit des Menschen im Mythus der afrikanischer Völker.* Berlin, 1936. Myths of beginning and end in Africa.

Cohn, Norman. *The Pursuit of the Millennium.* 3d ed. New York, 1970. Revolutionary messianism in medieval and Reformation Europe and its bearing on modern totalitarian movements.

Lewis, R. W. B. *The American Adam.* Chicago, 1955. The new Adam in American literature of the nineteenth century as an expression of a native American mythology.

Lincoln, Andrew T. *Paradise Now and Not Yet.* Cambridge, 1981. Paradise in Saint Paul's eschatology.

Moynihan, Elizabeth B. *Paradise as a Garden: In Persia and Mughal India.* New York, 1979. The oldest surviving garden tradition. Richly illustrated.

Sanford, Charles L. *The Quest for Paradise.* Urbana, Ill., 1961. Origins and meaning of "the Garden of America" and its broader applications to aspects of American civilization.

Smith, Henry Nash. *Virgin Land.* Cambridge, Mass., 1950. The American West as myth and symbol.

Stevens, Henry Bailey. *The Recovery of Culture.* New York, 1949. Argues that humans once lived in a horticultural paradise before the "fall" into hunting and the subsequent sacrifice-linked agricultural period.

Sylvia Mary, Sr. *Nostalgia for Paradise.* London, 1965. A somewhat comparative study of the longing for paradise done from a Christian religious and theological perspective.

Williams, George H. *Wilderness and Paradise in Christian Thought.* New York, 1962. The ambivalent meanings of wilderness, garden, and desert in the Bible and subsequent appearances of these themes in Christian thought and literature.

Harry B. Partin

PARADOX AND RIDDLES.

Though paradoxes can seem enigmatic and riddles paradoxical, they are fundamentally different realities. Riddles are mainly instrumental and performance-oriented, whether used in sacred or secular contexts, whereas paradoxes are rooted in the heart of being and language, touching on the crux of experience and expression. Riddles are to be solved; a paradox is to be transcended, or, rather, lived.

Riddles. A riddle was called *griphos* (lit., "fishing creel," anything intricate) or *ainigma* ("dark saying") in Greek and *aenigma* ("problem") in Latin. The modern meaning of *enigma*, "that which is unknown and remains obscure," reflects this ancestry. Riddles may or may not have solutions. As the English saying "It remains a riddle" indicates, what cannot be known remains a mystery. In Greek, *mustērion* meant something beyond the comprehension of human intelligence.

Riddles have been known since high antiquity. The oldest recorded book of riddles is a Babylonian school text (Taylor, 1948, pp. 12–13). The Greek poet Pindar first called the question of the Sphinx a riddle (*ainigma*); Plato alludes to the punning riddles prevailing in his time (*Republic* 5.479). Riddles may be both playful and serious—playful as a humorous diversion or pastime, or serious as in the riddle of the Sphinx, failure to solve which would cost one's life. Such a riddle was referred to by German philologists as a *Halsrätsel* (capital riddle). By the same token, Yudhiṣṭhira restored his brothers to life by successfully solving the riddles posed by a *yakṣa* (a ghostlike being; *Mahābhārata* 3.297–298).

To the authors of the Hebrew scriptures, riddles were closely connected with wisdom, which the Lord conferred as a blessing (see Samson's riddle in *Judges* 14:13–18; on the Lord's blessing, see *Judges* 13:24). Solomon's wisdom, which "God had put in his heart" (1 *Kgs.* 10:24), was challenged by the queen of Sheba with "hard questions" (*1 Kgs.* 10:1–13; *2 Chr.* 9:1–12). The authors of medieval *midrashim* elaborated on such questions in detail, as for instance: "Who were the three that ate and drank on the earth, yet were not born of male and female?" "The three angels who revealed themselves to our father Abraham, peace be unto him," and so on (Schechter, 1891, pp. 354–356). It has been pointed out that riddles were "most characteristic of Jewish table-amusements in the middle ages" and that "all the great Hebrew poets of the middle ages composed acrostics and enigmas of considerable merit" (Abrahams, 1896, pp. 384–387, 133).

Riddles were utilized in missionary activities during the Middle Ages. It was in this context that the English bishop Boniface (680–735), for example, chose ten virtues and ten vices as a theme for riddles. Biblical passages often provided allegorical riddles (Taylor, 1948, pp. 61–65).

In Vedic India, riddles were posed as part of such rituals as the Rājasūya (coronation of a king) and the Aśvamedha (horse sacrifice). The exchange of questions and answers between the sacrificial priests was highly formalized, as in this pair: "What is it that walketh singly?" "It is yonder sun, doubtless, that walks singly, and he is spiritual luster" (*Śatapatha Brāhmaṇa* 8.2.6.9ff.). Brahmans competed in *jātavidyā* (knowledge of the origins) and *brahmodya* (theological or philosophical discussion about *brahman*). Cosmological questions were often the topics of riddles, as in the *Ṛgveda*: "I ask you about the furthest limit of earth. Where, I ask, is the center of the world? I ask you about the Stallion's prolific seed; I ask you about high heaven where abides the Word" (1.164.34). This suggests that philosophical inquiry developed in the form of riddling (see *Ṛgveda* 1.164.46; 10.129; *Atharvaveda* 9.9–10; 10.7; etc.). A verse in the *Atharvaveda* asks: "How does the wind not cease to blow? How does the mind take no repose? Why do the waters, seeking to reach truth, never at any time cease to flow?" (10.7.37; cited in Bloomfield, 1969, pp. 210–218; Huizinga, 1949, pp. 105–107).

Dealing with the mystery of existence and the universe, riddles were often considered to have a sacred quality. The possession of esoteric knowledge meant the possession of power (Huizinga, 1949, p. 108). Moreover, a magical power was associated with riddles: the idea that a spoken word has a direct influence on the world order is at the heart of the ritualistic use of riddles, such as those performed at the time of rice planting and growing (but which were strictly forbidden between harvest and the laying out of new fields), and those used on certain occasions like funerals. James G. Frazer speculates that "enigmas were originally circumlocutions adopted at times when for certain reasons the speaker was forbidden the use of direct terms. They appear to be especially employed in the neighborhood of a dead body" (Frazer, 1911–1915, vol. 9, p. 121, n. 3).

Kōan. The dialogue form of riddles—questions and answers—directly involves the listener as an active participant in the discourse. This dialogic value has been fully exploited in the Zen tradition of Mahāyāna Buddhism in the form of *kōan* (Chin., *kung an*, "public document, authoritative statute"). "Jōshū's Mu," a famous *kōan*, runs as follows: "A monk once asked Master Jōshū: 'Has the dog the Buddha-nature?' The Master replied: 'Mu!'" Even though, like this one, many *kōan*s take the form of riddles, they are not meant to be solved like riddles. "Do not mistake the 'Mu' for absolute emptiness or nothingness. Do not conceive it in terms of 'is' or 'is not,' either," warns Master Mumon (Izutsu, 1977, p. 176).

Often more than one reading of a particular *kōan* is possible. They can be interpreted and understood, but that is not why they are given to students of Zen. Rather, they are intended as themes for meditation, "the means for opening one's mind to the truth of Zen," as D. T. Suzuki puts it, adding that "*kōan* and *zazen* are the two handmaids of Zen; the first is the eye and the second is the foot." Thus without thorough training in *zazen*, or sitting meditation, says Suzuki, the Zen student will not attain spiritual truth (Suzuki, 1964, pp. 101–102). *Kōan*s are expedient means (Skt., *upāya*) that the master sets before his students; they are instrumental in bringing about *satori*, or enlightenment, but are not an end in themselves. The end is the realization of freedom and compassion.

First standardized by the Chinese master Ta-hui (Jpn., Daie Sōkō; 1089–1163), *kōan*s generally consist of questions and answers (known as *mondō*) exchanged between masters and students during the T'ang and early Sung dynasties, as well as questions put forward by teachers and anecdotes of ancient masters. Making full use of mind's ability to go beyond its discursive dimension, a *kōan* practice is designed to trigger the mind to take a "quantum leap." "To cling to words and phrases and thus try to achieve understanding" is foolish. "It is like trying to strike the moon with a stick, or scratching a shoe because there is an itchy spot on the foot" (Shibayama, 1974, p. 9).

Even though Zen may attack discursive thinking, the purpose behind it is to bring one to the primordial state of mind that is prior to the subject-object dichotomy. The following *mondō* illustrates such a state: "Once Master Yakusan [Chin., Yao-shan; 751–834] was sitting in deep meditation; a monk came up to him and asked: 'Solidly seated as a rock, what are you thinking?' Master answered: 'Thinking of the absolutely unthinkable.' The monk: 'How can one think of anything which is absolutely unthinkable?' Master: 'By not-thinking'" (Izutsu, 1977, pp. 157f.). The monk's question was based on objectifying thinking. The master's answers demonstrate objectless thinking and subjectless thinking, respectively. The not-thinking is a higher mode of the mind, and the attainment to the recognition of this state constitutes the goal of *kōan-zazen* practice.

Paradox. The original Greek meaning of *para doxa*, "contrary to received opinion or expectation," cuts through various meanings of paradox. In classical Greek, *paradoxia* meant "marvelousness" and *paradoxologeō*, "to tell marvels." Thus, paradox was more than just a contradiction; *paradoxos* meant "incredible"—contrary to one's expectation or a generally held notion *(doxa)*. This was the sense of the word retained in the New Testament passage about Jesus healing a palsied man: people were "all amazed, and they glorified God, and were filled with fear, saying, we have seen strange things [*paradoxa*] today" (*Lk.* 5:26). (In this particular context, *paradoxos* means "miraculous.")

Definitions of paradox. The word *paradox* has been understood variously as a logical contradiction, absurdity, enigma, or seeming contradiction, as when Hamlet said, "This was sometime a paradox, but now the time gives it proof" (*Hamlet* 3.1.114–115). Some define paradox as a unique form of thinking: "a dynamic, bi-polar thought which bespeaks a vital tension involving both the opposition and reciprocation of ideas" (Slaatte, 1968, p. 132). Others see paradox, "playing with human understanding," as "primarily a figure of thought, in which the various suitable figures of speech are inextricably impacted" (Colie, 1966, pp. 7, 22). Kierkegaard boldly asserts that the paradox, arising from the "relation between an existing cognitive spirit and eternal truth . . . is not a concession but a category, an ontological definition" (ed. Bretall, 1946, p. 153).

Kinds of paradox. There are logical, visual, psychological, rhetorical, and other kinds of paradoxes, such as existential. Logical paradox has preoccupied logicians and mathematicians since the time of Zeno of Elea (fifth century BCE). Some logical paradoxes are considered solvable by applying different conceptual frameworks (as for instance Zeno's paradoxes); some are considered antinomies (e.g., the paradox of Epimenides the Cretan), and still others are mind-twisters (e.g., the Barber paradox) that in the last analysis are not considered genuine paradoxes (Quine, 1962).

Visual paradoxes, such as the picture that presents a duck from one view and a rabbit from another, are now regarded more in relation to the psychology of representation (Gombrich, 1960). The rhetorical paradox as a literary genre was extremely popular during the Renaissance. *The Praise of Folly* (1509) by Erasmus set the tone; the genre was also practiced by the poet John Donne, the satirist Joseph Hall, and other English authors.

Functions of paradox. Paradox is fundamentally connected with the problem of language and being; nevertheless, it functions variously. Paradoxes in mathematics or physical science are puzzles to be solved by "putting the conceptual framework in a new perspective," so that "the limitations of the old concept are revealed" (Rapoport, 1967, p. 56). They challenge the limits of reason, stimulating activity in which scientists and mathematicians find delight. Paradoxes function as gateways to a new and more comprehensive understanding of reality. "Paradoxes have played a dramatic part in intellectual history," writes Rapoport (1967), "often foreshadowing revolutionary developments in science, mathematics and logic" (p. 50). Quine (1962) observes that in the field of logic and mathematics the confrontation with two paradoxes—one propounded by Bertrand Russell in 1901 and the other by Kurt Gödel in 1931—greatly stimulated studies of the foundations of mathematics.

It is in this sense that contradictions are regarded as a fruitful soil for the development of theories in physical science. Alfred North Whitehead noted: "In the formal logic, a contradiction is the signal of a defeat: but in the evolution of real knowledge it marks the first step in progress towards a victory" (Whitehead, 1925, p. 260). Paradoxes are regarded as a healthy challenge, the solution of which involves the acquisition of a more generalized framework of thought.

In the Christian mystical tradition of the *via negativa* (see below), as in the Zen tradition, language is regarded skeptically. Mystics claim that the ultimate cannot be known and thus cannot be adequately rendered into words. Zen masters warn that if one takes words for the ultimate reality, one will go astray; language is at best a pointer. The other side of the coin, however, is the need for fundamental affirmation of the reality beyond human thought and language. That we use words at all suggests the presence of an urge to at least intimate the ultimate reality. Paradoxical expressions are thus considered as rhetorical devices or "therapeutic paradoxes" (Ramsey and Smart, 1959, p. 220). The thirteenth-century Ch'an master Mumon (Chin., Wu-men), compiler of the *Mumonkan* (*Wu-men kuan*, 1228), demonstrates Zen teachings in a highly paradoxical language, as indicated by his anthology's title, *The Gateless Barrier*. "The Buddha Mind is the basis, and gateless is the Dharma Gate. If it is gateless, how can you pass through it?" And again: "Gateless is the Great Tao, There are thousands of ways to it. If you pass through this barrier, You may walk freely in the universe" (Shibayama, 1974, pp. 9–10).

Another view of paradox rests on the claim that it is a higher form of an expression of truth that defies a logical or linear mode of description. Metaphor or imagery functions somewhat similar to paradox; some hold that paradox involves a contradictory juxtaposition of images rather than of logical ideas (Slater, 1951, p. 115). While metaphor and images point beyond words—a symbolic operation *par excellence*—paradox points beyond a linguistic construct to some extralinguistic reality or to the domain of experience itself. Furthermore, the form of a play (like Samuel Beckett's "tragicomedy" *Waiting for Godot*) or the theme of a work itself (as in Erasmus's *Praise of Folly*) may take on a paradoxical character (States, 1978).

Whether paradox is regarded merely as a means or as a higher form of expression, its use gives credence to the supralogical level of awareness that includes religious experience, poetic intuition, artistic creativity, and much of everyday experience. A basic assumption herein is the limitation of language—or at least of certain forms of statement—and the hierarchy of intelligibility, which is not confined to logical thinking. Moreover, whether it be logical, rhetorical, or epistemological-existential, paradox always points beyond the immediate statement or utterance.

Paradox and religious discourse. Heraclitus described God as "day night, winter summer, war peace, satiety hunger" (frag. 67). Paradoxical statements are often oxymoronic in style, combining contradictions. Descriptions of the religious ultimate or religious experience are frequently dressed in contradictory language such as *plenum/nihilum, personal/impersonal, immanent/transcendent, affirmation/negation, sin/redemption.* Out of the tension between these terms emerges a horizon of meaning that is considered to intimate better the contents of religious experience. Rudolf Otto's characterization of the ultimate, or numinous, as "mysterium tremendum et fascinosum" has had a considerable impact on the study of religion. He observed: "These two qualities, the daunting and the fascinating, now combine in a strange harmony of contrasts, and the resultant dual character of the numinous consciousness, to which the entire religious development bears witness, at any rate from the level of the 'daemonic dread' onwards, is at once the strangest and most noteworthy phenomenon in the whole history of religion" (Otto, [1922] 1928, p. 31).

Ninian Smart states that "paradoxical pronouncements fulfill such a number of functions that by understanding the gist of them one can penetrate to the heart of the philosophy of religion" (Smart, 1958, p. 20). He considers paradox to be the result of a weaving together of different strands or types of experience, a worship-oriented strand and a strand of mystical experience. Citing "It is far, and It is near. It is within all this, And It is outside of all this" (*Īśā Upaniṣad* 5) as a case in point, Smart explains that the objective, transcendent, numinous, far, *brahman,* and "wholly other" belong to the strand of worship, whereas the subjective, immanent, mystical, near, *ātman,* and "within" belong to the strand of mystical experience. Moreover, these two are woven together in a way characteristic of religious experience, as shown by the exhilarating yet self-effacing experience of the mystic (Smart, 1958; see also Austin, 1967).

There is a correlation between kinds of experience and kinds of expression. "Between logical contradiction (or seeming contradiction) and certain forms of religious feeling there is a close relation," observes Arthur Lovejoy (1978, p. 279). Some consider paradox to be a more suitable, if not essential, form of expression of religious experience (Calhoun, 1955; Stace, 1960). To say God is immanent/transcendent is more than just a simple placing of these two qualities side by side; rather it describes the character of religious experience itself. [*See also* Transcendence and Immanence.]

Coincidentia oppositorum, a paradoxical logic. What is called *coincidentia oppositorum,* "coincidence of opposites," explains in part why paradoxical descriptions are applied to the ultimate. Although the idea goes back to Proclus and even Heraclitus, the terminology is generally associated with the fifteenth-century German churchman and mystic Nicholas of Cusa, who viewed this dynamism from the perspective of identity and difference. Whatever things the senses and the mind apprehend differ from one another and within themselves, he tells us in *De docta ignorantia* (On Learned Ignorance), so

> there is no precise equality among them. Therefore, Maximum Equality, which is neither other than nor different from anything, surpasses all understanding. Hence, since the absolute Maximum *is* all that which can be, it is *altogether* actual. And just as there cannot be a greater, so for the same reason there cannot be a lesser, since it is all that which can be. But the Minimum is that than which there cannot be a lesser. And since the Maximum is also such, it is evident that the Minimum coincides with the Maximum.
> (1.4; trans. Hopkins, 1981)

The logic of *coincidentia oppositorum* presupposes a unifying ground of the many, that is, equality. "Therefore, opposing features belong only to those things which can be comparatively greater or lesser" (ibid.), that is, to the relative world of plurality of things.

Mahāyāna Buddhism plows deeper into the ground of *coincidentia oppositorum* and arrives at the equation of the one and the many. Unity is multiplicity, and multiplicity is unity. Paradoxical is the character of the ultimate. The *Heart Sutra,* a gem of the Prajñāpāramitā corpus, proclaims: "Rūpaṃ śūnyatā, śūnyatā eva rūpaṃ": that is, all the phenomenal world of experience is "empty," and "emptiness" is simultaneously the whole phenomenal world of experience. In other words, zero is infinity and infinity is zero. (On the question of zero and infinity, Augustus De Morgan once wrote, "If there be in mathematics a nettle danger out of which has been plucked the flower safety, it is speculation on 0 and ∞" [Bolzano, 1950, p. v].)

D. T. Suzuki, in discussing this kind of logic of simultaneous negation/affirmation, calls it *sokuhi no ronri*, or "the logic of *prajñā*" (Suzuki, 1951, p. 18). He expounds this point, while contrasting *prajñā* ("intuition") and *vijñāna* ("reason"). "Paradoxical statements are characteristic of *prajñā*-intuition. As it transcends *vijñāna* or logic it does not mind contradicting itself; it knows that a contradiction is the outcome of differentiation, which is the work of *vijñāna*. *Prajñā* negates what it asserted before, and conversely; it has its own way of dealing with this world of dualities" (Suzuki, 1951, p. 24). Such use of paradox characterizes the Japanese school of thought known as the Kyoto school, founded by Nishida Kitarō (1870–1945).

Rosalie L. Colie has observed that "paradoxes comment on their own method and their own technique" and that "paradox deals with itself as subject and as object" (Colie, 1966, p. 7). This comes close to the Buddhist intuition described above, except that Buddhism further dissolves the distinction between subject and object.

Paradox and the knowledge of the ultimate. The Socratic tradition of *docta ignorantia* ("learned ignorance") is a paradoxical mode of knowing: I know that I do not know. "We desire to know that we do not know," writes Nicholas of Cusa in *De docta ignorantia*. "If we can fully attain unto this [knowledge of our ignorance], we will attain unto learned ignorance" (1.1). By examining the mode of inquiry and observing that it proceeds by means of a comparative relation and "hence the infinite *qua* infinite is unknown, for it escapes all comparative relation" (1.1), he concludes that "reason cannot leap beyond contradictories." Moreover, "as regards the movement of reason, plurality or multiplicity is opposed to oneness" (1.24). To recognize reason in this way is to attain "learned ignorance" or "sacred ignorance," which knows that "the precise truth shines incomprehensibly within the darkness of our ignorance" (1.26). Learned ignorance sees beyond the apprehension of plurality of things; moreover, in its self-knowledge, it sees "that there is precise truth which we cannot now comprehend" (2, prologue).

The idea of learned ignorance, a recognition of the inability of reason to comprehend the ultimate reality, has been embraced by many Western thinkers. Pascal said, "There is nothing so consistent with reason as this denial of reason" (*Pensées* 182), or, again, "Reason's last step is the recognition that there are an infinite number of things which are beyond it. It is merely feeble if it does not go as far as to realize that. If natural things are beyond it, what are we to say about supernatural things?" (*Pensées* 188). And Kierkegaard held that "it is the duty of the human understanding to understand that there are things which it cannot understand, and what those things are" (ed. Bretall, 1946, p. 153). If it is not by way of reason, then it is by way of nonknowing that one may arrive at what one knows not, held John of the Cross (*The Ascent of Mount Carmel* 1.14), and in the same spirit T. S. Eliot mused on the paradox of knowing and "ignorance" (See *East Coker*, in *Four Quartets*).

Another approach to the knowledge of the ultimate is based on the claim that, in the act of knowing, the knower and the known—that is, the subject and the object—are united. Knowledge as experience takes place in the oneness of the subject and object, as the object of knowledge is embodied by the subject. Thus, "it is not understood by those who understand it. It is understood by those who understand it not" (*Kena Upaniṣad* 9–11).

The paradox of the via negativa. Dionysius the Areopagite noted that the ultimate reality, the Deity, was beyond human thought and therefore could only be approximated by negative predication. The medieval German mystic Meister Eckhart, a faithful adherent of this method, wrote: "It is God's nature to be without a nature. To think of his goodness, or wisdom, or power is to hide the essence of him, to obscure it with thoughts about him. Even one single thought or consideration will cover it up" (frag. 30). The famous beginning of the *Tao-te ching* echoes this tradition: "The Way that can be spoken of is not an eternal way." In the Upaniṣadic tradition, *ātman* is "not this, not that [*neti, neti*]. It is unseizable, for it is not seized. It is indestructible, for it is not destroyed. It is unattached, for it does not attach itself. It is unbound. It does not tremble. It is not injured" (*Bṛhadāraṇyaka Upaniṣad* 3.9.26, 4.2.4, 4.4.22, 4.5.15).

The *via negativa*, or apophatic path, is in fact a paradoxical method of affirming the ultimate, which is considered a superlogical reality. [*See* Via Negativa.] Thomas Aquinas pointed out the contradiction inherent in this method: "The meaning of a negation always is found in an affirmation, as appears from the fact that every negative proposition is proved by an affirmative one; consequently, unless the human understanding knew something of God affirmatively, it could deny nothing of God; and such would be the case if nothing of what it says of God could be verified affirmatively" (*De potentia Dei* 7.5). The approach of mystical theology, however, has a paradoxical rather than a logical interest, as its aim is to go beyond affirmation and negation. Dionysius the Areopagite concluded his *Mystical Theology* thus: "We can neither affirm nor deny Him [the Deity], inasmuch as the all-perfect and unique Cause of all things transcends all affirmation, and the simple pre-eminence of His absolute nature is outside of every negation—free from every limitation and beyond them all." One is thus left with the *docta ignorantia*, a higher mode of knowing, which moreover remains "ignorant" of the superessential reality.

The paradox of faith. Referring to the *Book of Job*, "the paradox of the best man in the worst fortune," G. K. Chesterton (1916) wrote that "man is most comforted by paradoxes" (p. 237). A. O. Lovejoy (1948) explored the psychological need for paradoxical expression in relation to religious salvation in his essay on *felix culpa*, "the fortunate fall." He argues that Adam's sin was fortunate and as such constitutes the *conditio sine qua non* of the Christian redemptive drama. This theme "had its own emotional appeal to many religious minds—partly, no doubt, because its very paradoxicality, its transcendence of the simple logic of common thought, gave it a kind of mystical sublimity" (p. 279). His study reveals that this theme in Milton's *Paradise Lost* actually goes back to du Bartas, Francis of Sales, Gregory the Great, Leo the Great, and Ambrose, the fourth-century saint (pp. 294–295; see also Weisinger, 1953).

The paradox of sin and redemption deeply marks the thinking of religious figures. Luther held that "God conceals his eternal mercy and loving-kindness beneath eternal wrath, his righteousness beneath unrighteousness" (Althaus, 1966, p. 279). Again, "If sin is abolished, then Christ has also been done away with for there would no longer be any need for him" (ibid., p. 258). Shinran, the founder of the Japanese True Pure Land school, said: "If the good are saved, how much more the wicked" (*Tannishō* 3). The paradox of redemption is sustained by faith. The Christian doctrine of the incarnation was for Kierkegaard the paradox *par excellence*: it is, he wrote, "the 'absolute Paradox,' the paradox of God in time. If one is to believe this paradox, God himself must give him the condition for doing so by giving him 'a new organ' of apprehension—that of Faith" (ed. Bretall, 1946, p. 154). The problem of paradox and logic in religious writings can be understood as a translation of the perpetual problem of the West, namely, that of faith and reason.

Paradox, riddles, and enigma. It may be said that in the end both paradox and riddles grapple with the enigma of the universe, of human existence. If something remains a riddle to human intelligence, it remains mysterious or is understood only paradoxically.

The mystery of existence, the paradox of life, takes on a concrete formulation in the Chinese mind. Once there was an old man living with his son and a very mangy horse near a fortress in a remote border region. One day this horse, the family's only possession, disappeared. The villagers all consoled the old man for his loss, but he himself was not a bit saddened, explaining, "We never know whether this is a catastrophe or a blessing in disguise." The following spring the horse came back with a mare. The villagers now congratulated him, but his reply was the same: "We never know whether this is a blessing or a catastrophe" *(Huai-nan–tzu)*. The story continues to make this point, that to what any event may lead is inscrutable. The only thing one can be certain of is that one does not know the course of events, and that the seasons have their own rhythm.

This practical wisdom of the Taoists sees a complementary, dynamic interflow of the positive and the negative. It takes the enigma of existence and articulates it in a paradoxical way: it "conceptualizes" it in a "spherical" language. Paradox can be seen as one of the ways in which human mind rationalizes the nonrational, the inscrutable, the unknown. Paradox is a way of understanding the otherwise nonunderstandable.

Paradoxes seem baffling, striking, surprising, or nonsensical to a linear thinker. But they are also free, creative, and playful, a form of expression conducive to a "spherical thinking" that expands and contracts freely "across terminal and categorical boundaries" (Colie, 1966, p. 7). Paradox opens up the mind to a new territory, to the hitherto unknown, sometimes with a poetic effect, often with an element of surprise. Moreover, a host of thinkers have directly or indirectly recognized paradox as an integral aspect of reality. From Socrates, Plato, Yājñavalkya, and Nāgārjuna all the way down to contemporary thinkers such as Kierkegaard, Berdiaev, Nishida, and others, the list encompasses the most profound thinkers who have ever lived.

BIBLIOGRAPHY

For a comprehensive exposition of riddles, see James A. Kelso's "Riddle," in the *Encyclopaedia of Religion and Ethics*, edited by James Hastings, vol. 10 (Edinburgh, 1918). For an extensive bibliography on riddles, see Archer Taylor's *A Bibliography of Riddles* (Helsinki, 1939). Taylor's *The Literary Riddle before 1600* (Berkeley, 1948) is an invaluable cross-cultural study of riddles with an excellent bibliography on this subject. For an overview of riddles, see Mathilde Hain's *Rätsel* (Stuttgart, 1966) and Roger D. Abrahams's *Between the Living and the Dead* (Helsinki, 1980). Johan Huizinga's *Homo Ludens: A Study of the Play-Element in Culture* (London, 1949) offers a perceptive account of riddles.

For the Jewish and Arab fondness for riddles during the Middle Ages, see Israel Abrahams's *Jewish Life in the Middle Ages* (New York, 1896). Solomon Schechter's "The Riddles of Solomon in Rabbinic Literature," *Folk-lore* 1 (September 1891): 349–358, gives a full account of fifteenth-century midrash on the Solomon Riddle. Volumes 3, 7, and 9 of James G. Frazer's *The Golden Bough: A Study in Magic and Religion*, 3d ed. rev. & enl. (London, 1911–1915), contain accounts of riddles. On Vedic riddles, see Maurice Bloomfield's *The Religion of the Veda* (New York, 1969), pp. 210–218. For the *Ṛgveda* and other Hindu texts, see Raimundo Panikkar's *The Vedic Experience* (Berkeley, 1977). For *kōan*, see *Original Teachings of Ch'an Buddhism: Selected from the Transmission of the Lamp*, translated by Chung-yuan Chang (New York, 1969); *The World of Zen*, edited by Nancy W. Ross (New York, 1960); and D. T. Suzuki's *An Introduction to Zen Buddhism* (New York, 1964). On the *Mumonkan* text, see Shibayama Zenkei's *Zen Comments on the Mumonkan* (New York, 1974). Toshihiko Izutsu's *Toward a Philosophy of Zen Buddhism* (Tehran, 1977) provides a philosophical exposition of *kōan*.

On religion and paradox, see I. T. Ramsey and Ninian Smart's "Paradox in Religion," *Aristotelian Society Supplementary Volume* 33 (1959): 195–232. See also Smart's *Reasons and Faiths* (London, 1958). William H. Austin's *Waves, Particles and Paradoxes* (Houston, 1967) applies the principle of complementarity to explaining theological discourse. For the idea of the numinous, see Rudolf Otto's *The Idea of the Holy* (Oxford, 1928). W. T. Stace's *Mysticism and Philosophy* (Philadelphia, 1960) has an extensive section on religious discourse and paradox. Religious language and paradox are discussed in Robert L. Calhoun's "The Language of Religion," in *The Unity of Knowledge*, edited by Lewis Leary (Garden City, N.Y., 1955), pp. 248–262. For Heraclitus's writings, see *The Cosmic Fragments*, edited by G. S. Kirk (Cambridge, 1954). For a translation of Nicholas of Cusa's *De docta ignorantia*, see Jasper Hopkins's *On Learned Ignorance* (Minneapolis, 1981). Pascal's *Pensées* have been translated by, among others, A. J. Krailsheimer (Harmondsworth, 1966).

On Buddhism and paradox, see D. T. Suzuki's "Reason and Intuition in Buddhist Philosophy," in *Essays in East-West Philosophy*, edited by Charles A. Moore (Honolulu, 1951), pp. 17–48; see also Suzuki's "Basic Thoughts Underlying Eastern Ethical and Social Practice," in *Philosophy and Culture: East and West*, edited by Charles A. Moore (Honolulu, 1962), pp. 428–447. Robert Slater's *Paradox and Nirvana* (Chicago, 1951) studies religious ultimates with reference to Burmese Buddhism. For an exemplary work of the Kyoto School, see Nishitani Keiji's *Religion and Nothingness* (Berkeley, 1982).

The philosophy of paradox is discussed in Howard A. Slaatte's *The Pertinence of the Paradox* (New York, 1968). On paradox and faith, see *The Book of Job*, edited by G. K. Chesterton (London, 1916), an introduction to which may be found in *The Dimensions of Job*, edited by Nahum N. Glatzer (New York, 1969), pp. 228–238. For Kierkegaard's writings, see *A Kierkegaard Anthology*, edited by Robert W. Bretall (Princeton, 1946). Luther's ideas are studied in Paul Althaus's *The Theology of Martin Luther* (Philadelphia, 1966). On the idea of *felix culpa*, see Arthur O. Lovejoy's "Milton and the Paradox of the Fortunate Fall," in his *Essays in the History of Ideas* (Westport,- Conn., 1978), pp. 277–295. See also Herbert Weisinger's *Tragedy and the Paradox of the Fortunate Fall* (London, 1953).

For logical paradox, see John van Heijenoort's "Logical Paradoxes," in *The Encyclopedia of Philosophy* (New York, 1967). W. V. O. Quine gives a cogent exposition of the topic in "Paradox," *Scientific American* 206 (April 1962): 84–96. Anatol Rapoport's "Escape from Paradox," *Scientific American* 217 (July 1967): 50–56, offers another excellent view of the subject, especially in relation to decision theory. Augustus De Morgan's *A Budget of Paradoxes*, 2d ed., 2 vols. (Chicago, 1915), presents extensive materials on "paradoxers."

On science and paradox, see Alfred North Whitehead's *Science and the Modern World* (New York, 1925). Thomas S. Kuhn's *The Structure of Scientific Revolutions*, 2d ed., rev. (Chicago, 1970), deals with the shift of conceptual scheme in the sciences. Bernard Bolzano's *Paradoxes of the Infinite* (1851; London, 1950) is one of the classical studies on the topic. On the nature of knowing and paradoxes, see Elizabeth H. Wolgast's *Paradoxes of Knowledge* (Ithaca, N.Y., 1977).

One of the most thought-provoking books on paradox is Rosalie Littell Colie's *Paradoxia Epidemica* (Princeton, 1966); it deals especially with the paradoxical tradition of the Renaissance. Nicholas Falletta's *The Paradoxicon* (Garden City, N.Y., 1983) gives a concise account while presenting wide-ranging examples of paradoxes with an extensive bibliography. For an essay on *Waiting for Godot*, see Bert O. States's *The Shape of Paradox* (Berkeley, 1978). On art and paradox, see Ernst H. Gombrich's *Art and Illusion* (New York, 1960).

MICHIKO YUSA

PARAMĀRTHA, the religious name of Kulanātha (499–569), an Indian monk and translator of Sanskrit texts. Paramārtha was a central figure in the introduction of the Buddhist Yogācāra, or Vijñānavāda (idealist), doctrines to China. Born in Ujjain, India, Paramārtha traveled widely as a Buddhist missionary and was probably living in Cambodia prior to arriving in Canton, baggage full of *sūtras*, in 546. Two years later he reached the Liang capital at Chien-k'ang, present Nanking, and was summoned to audience by Emperor Wu, a great patron of Buddhism. Impressed by both the knowledge and volume of *sūtras* Paramārtha possessed, the emperor had decided to appoint him director of an ambitious translation project when the Hou Ching rebellion forced him to abandon his plan.

Fleeing to the coastal provinces, Paramārtha wandered about translating and teaching and for a year or so enjoyed the patronage of Lu Yüan-che, the governor of Fu-ch'un in the Fu-yang district of Chekiang. In 552 he was recalled to the capital by a victorious Hou Ching. After only one hundred twenty days on the throne, Hou Ching was overthrown by Hsiao I (Emperor Yüan), during whose three-year reign Paramārtha enjoyed imperial support and resided at the Chen-kuan temple in Nanking, translating the *Suvarṇaprabhāsa Sūtra (Chin-kuang-ming ching)*. After three years in Nanking, Paramārtha was forced by the unsettled political situation to resume the life of a wanderer, which, however, did not inhibit his prodigious translation activities. Yet despite such apparent energy he was depressed by his unstable circumstances, was constantly nostalgic for India, and repeatedly attempted to return home, only to be dissuaded each time by disciples and friends.

One of the more fateful of these attempts occurred in 562, when he managed to board a ship and journey the open sea for two months before a storm blew the boat into Canton. Ou-yang Wei, the governor there, and his son Ou-yang Ho, old acquaintances from Paramārtha's previous days in Canton, came to his aid and soon became his disciples. Under their patronage he translated many texts, including the *Mahāyānasaṃgraha* (Compendium of the Mahāyāna; Chin., *She-ta-sheng lun*), that were central to the development of uniquely Chinese traditions in Buddhism. The completion of these works brought him evident satisfaction, but nevertheless he lapsed into depression again, and his disciples had to thwart a suicide attempt in 568.

Hoping to brighten his outlook, his followers planned to return him to the capital, but the monks already entrenched there, fearing that Paramārtha might threaten their status, convinced the emperor of the newly founded Ch'en dynasty that his doctrines were a threat to the government. Paramārtha therefore stayed on in Canton until he succumbed to illness at the age of seventy-one.

A number of Paramārtha's translations proved influential in the development of indigenous Chinese Buddhist traditions during the Sui (581–618) and T'ang (618–907) periods. These include the *Abhidharmakośa* (*O-p'i-ta-mo-chu-she lun,* Treasury of the Abhidharma), *Madhyāntavibhāga* (*Chung-pien fen-pieh lun,* On Distinguishing the Extremes from the Middle), *Viṃśatikā,* and *Triṃśikā,* by Vasubandhu; the *Mahāyānasaṃgraha,* the *Saptadaśabhūmikaśāstra (Yu-chia shih-ti lun ch'i-shih lun)* portion of the *Yogācārabhūmi;* and Vasubandhu's treatise on Asaṅga's *Mahāyānasaṃgraha,* the *Mahāyānasaṁgraha-bhāṣya.* The last text provided the foundation for Paramārtha's own She-lun school, which came to be patronized during the Sui by Emperor Wen, and was championed and modified during the T'ang by the monk Hsüan-tsang. Paramārtha's work was the point of departure for Chih-i (538–597) and Fa-tsang (738?–838?), the principal masters of the T'ien-t'ai and Hua-yen schools, respectively. His thought was also important to the development of the Fa-hsiang and Ch'an (Zen) schools of the T'ang dynasty.

BIBLIOGRAPHY

An important source for information on the life and thought of Paramārtha is Ui Hakuju's *Shindai sanzōden no kenkyū,* volume 6 of *Indo tetsugaku kenkyū* (Tokyo, 1965). For a superb review of Paramārtha's influence on the development of Chinese Buddhism, including a complete bibliography of modern critical studies, see Diana Y. Paul's *Philosophy of Mind in Sixth Century China: Paramārtha's "Evolution of Consciousness"* (Stanford, Calif., 1984).

MIYAKAWA HISAYUKI

PĀRAMITĀS. The term *pāramitā,* Sanskrit and Pali for "perfection," refers to the virtues that must be fully developed by anyone aspiring to become a Buddha, that is, by a *bodhisattva.* The practice of the *pāramitā*s makes the career of a *bodhisattva* exceedingly long, but their fulfillment transforms the enlightenment process from one that benefits only the individual to one that is, in the words of the *Visuddhimagga,* "for the welfare and benefit of the whole world."

The idea of the *pāramitā*s as a group is not found in the oldest Buddhist literature. Such a notion developed in the general expansion of Buddhist thought and practice before the beginning of the common era, which movement gave new recognition to types of religion other than renunciation. The *pāramitā*s provided an alternative scheme of religious practice more in tune with newly developed conceptions of the Buddha and the nature of a *bodhisattva* than were the older schemes of morality, meditation, and wisdom *(śīla, samādhi, prajñā)* and the Noble Eightfold Path. [*See* Eightfold Path.]

When the *pāramitā*s appear as a group, their number varies; six and ten occur most often, but lists of five and seven are also found. It is sometimes suggested that six may have been the original number, because of an apparent progression in difficulty in such enumerations. The six are "giving" *(dāna),* "morality" *(śīla),* "patience" *(kṣānti),* "vigor" *(vīrya),* "contemplation" *(dhyāna),* and "wisdom" *(prajñā).* Such lists are found in early Mahāyāna texts (e.g., the *Saddharmapuṇḍarīka Sūtra* and the Prajñāpāramitā literature) and in the *Mahāvastu* of the Mahāsaṃghika school. The lists of ten, which include the additional virtues of "skill-in-means" *(upāya* or *upāyakauśalya),* "resolution" *(praṇidhāna),* "strength" *(bala),* and "knowledge" *(jñāna),* occur in later texts, for example, the *Daśabhūmika Sūtra* (fourth century). In such texts, the *pāramitā*s are correlated with the ten stages *(bhūmi)* of a *bodhisattva*'s career.

Other independent and relatively early enumerations of the perfections are found in the *Cariyāpiṭaka* and the *Buddhavaṃsa,* both written in Pali and considered canonical by the Theravāda school. While the *Cariyāpiṭaka* lists seven perfections, the *Buddhavaṃsa* gives ten. These have become standard in the Theravāda traditions: "giving" *(dāna),* "morality" *(sīla),* "renunciation" *(nekkhamma),* "wisdom" *(paññā),* "vigor" *(viriya),* "patience" *(khanti),* "truthfulness" *(sacca),* "determination" *(adhiṭṭhāna),* "loving kindness" *(mettā),* and "equanimity" *(upekkhā).*

The Sanskrit and Pali noun *pāramitā* is derived from the adjective *parama,* meaning "high, complete, perfect." The Thervāda has consistently understood the term in this way and has commonly used another derivative, *pāramī,* as a synonym. In contrast, the Mahāyāna tradition has analyzed the term as consisting of two words, *pāram ita,* meaning "gone to the beyond," indicating its character as a scheme of spiritual progress. The Chinese and Tibetan translations of the term *pāramitā* (*tu* and *pha rol tu phyin pa,* respectively) reflect this latter understanding of its meaning.

These interpretations may differ along sectarian lines, but the applications they suggest are found in each of the Buddhist schools. In the Theravāda, the perfections afford the practitioner one way of celebrating the significance and superiority of the Buddha, whose fulfillment of them is often said to be incomparable. Similarly, Mahāyāna devotees focus their reverence on the enormous toils of great *bodhisattvas* such as Avalokiteśvara, who are engaged in practicing the perfections. [*See* Avalokiteśvara.]

The *pāramitās* also provide a set of norms to structure the reading of the Jātakas, the collection of stories about the Buddha's previous lives. These tales, often non-Buddhist in origin and obscure in meaning, assume a Buddhist character when read with the *pāramitās* as guidelines. The *Cariyāpiṭaka,* the *Buddhavaṃsa,* and later Theravāda works (e.g., the *Nidānakathā,* the fifth-century introduction to the Jātaka collection) group and order some of the stories according to the practice and attainment of each perfection. We also see this template for reading in Mahāyāna works such as the *Mahāprajñāpāramitā Śāstra.*

The same pattern guides the illustrations of Jātakas as evidenced by such Buddhist art forms as the friezes on religious monuments of ancient India and the paintings decorating temples in modern Sri Lanka and Southeast Asia. In short, the *pāramitās* transformed the Jātakas into effective and popular sources for didactic art and literature. As Richard Gombrich observed in his study of Buddhism in modern Sri Lanka, *Precept and Practice* (Oxford, 1971), "There is a general tendency for those *Jātakas* which are canonically associated with the Bodhisattva's acquisition of a particular perfection to be more widely known" (p. 93).

The superposition of the *pāramitās* on the Jātakas, in turn, altered the perception of the perfections themselves. As gradations of the virtues became apparent, it proved practical to subdivide the ten perfections into thirty. Each *pāramitā* was divided into three degrees: an ordinary perfection *(pāramī),* an inferior perfection *(upapāramī),* and a superior perfection *(paramatthapāramī).* For example, in the Theravāda, the ordinary perfection of giving is "sacrifice of limbs," the inferior perfection is "sacrifice of external goods or property," and the superior perfection is "sacrifice of life."

The Jātakas also provide models for practicing the *pāramitās.* Through these stories about the Bodhisattva's—and thus, the Buddha's—involvement in the world, the virtues represented by the perfections are inculcated and come to be highly valued as qualities in individuals.

As the Mahāyāna analysis of the term suggests, these virtues are not merely a random assortment but are an ordered group leading to a goal. When the Mahāyāna replaced the notion of the *arhat* with the idea of the *bodhisattva* as the religious ideal to which all should aspire, the *pāramitās* provided a practical program that could be followed by new aspirants. This replacement altered some of the basic assumptions of spiritual progress. Under this new dispensation, as the *arhat* follows the Noble Eightfold Path he destroys the defilements that perpetuate rebirth but becomes enlightened only to the degree necessary to obtain release from rebirth. The *bodhisattva,* in contrast, renounces the enlightment of the *arhat* in order to pursue what is perceived as the higher and more complete enlightenment attained by Buddhas. The *bodhisattva* prepares himself for this attainment by practicing the perfections, which represent a program of positive moral development for the benefit of others. The Mahāyāna devotees negatively assess the practice of the *arhats,* claiming that it is based on restraint and removal and is without overt altruism. The perfections project the attainment of the goal into an inconceivable future and displace the sense of urgency and immediacy that motivates the *arhat's* quest. As a result, virtues such as patience, resolution, strength, and determination, which had a small place in early Buddhism, became prominent as *pāramitās.* Vigor, for instance, which had complemented the urgency felt by the disciple following the Eightfold Path, became an antidote to fatigue and despair during the *bodhisattva's* long career.

The idea of the perfections as a graduated soteriological path was developed and emphasized in the Mahāyāna, but it had a place in the Theravāda as well. This can be seen in a lengthy discussion in the *Cariyāpiṭaka* commentary by Dhammapāla, the sixth-century Pali commentator, where the perfections are treated as a spiritual path accessible to all. Some of the perfections (e.g., renunciation and equanimity) reinforce the basic assumptions of the *arhat* program, which the Theravāda never rejected.

To function as a progressive scheme leading to the final goal of enlightenment all of the perfections must be fulfilled. We can see, however, that certain perfections have assumed a greater importance. Doctrinally, wisdom *(prajñā),* the last of the six perfections, is often given pride of place in Mahāyāna writings. The *Bodhicaryāvatāra* says that "the Buddha taught that this multitude of virtues is all for the sake of wisdom"(Matics, 1970, p. 211). *Prajñā* is said to be greater than all the other virtues and to be that perfection that makes all others effective. [*See* Prajñā.] Practically, the perfection of giving *(dāna)* has great importance. Emotive stories of the practice of this perfection (e.g., the Jātaka stories of King Śibi and Prince Viśvantara) are enormously popular throughout the Buddhist world and have been favorite subjects for Buddhist art and literature. As the first and easiest of the *pāramitās*, *dāna* is accessible to the humblest Buddhist when he or she aspires to enter the path to enlightenment. Its importance as a preparation for enlightenment is amply attested by the *Viśvantara (Vessantara) Jātaka,* in which the future Buddha perfects *dāna* in his penultimate birth.

[*See also* Bodhisattva Path.]

BIBLIOGRAPHY

A survey of the *pāramitās* in Mahāyāna literature may be found in Har Dayal's *The Bodhisattva Doctrine in Buddhist Sanskrit Literature* (London, 1932; reprint, Delhi, 1975). It provides detailed interpretations of each of the perfections and relates them to other aspects of Buddhist thought. A beautiful account of the *pāramitās* and their place in the career of a *bodhisattva,* as understood by the Indian Mādhyamika tradition, is Śantideva's *Bodhicaryāvatāra,* translated by Marion Matics as *Entering the Path of Enlightenment* (New York, 1970). The *Cariyāpiṭaka* and the *Buddhavaṃsa* have been translated by both B. C. Law (Oxford, 1938) and I. B. Horner (London, 1975) in volumes 11 and 31, respectively, of the "Sacred Books of the Buddhists" series. Dhammapāla's "Treatise on the *Pāramīs,*" from the *Cariyāpiṭaka* commentary is available in translation in *The Discourse on the All-Embracing Net of Views: The Brahmajāla Sutta and Its Commentarial Exegesis,* translated by Bhikkhu Bodhi (Kandy, 1978). A *summa* of Buddhist thought on the perfections is the *Mahāprajñāpāramitā Śāstra,* attributed to Nāgārjuna and translated from the Chinese by Étienne Lamotte as *Le traité de la grande vertu de sagesse* (Louvain, 1944–1980). This is an indispensable source for the study of the *pāramitās.* Lamotte's annotations themselves are a mine of information for literacy references to the *pāramitās* and for references to the many publications that treat their iconography.

CHARLES HALLISEY

PARENTALIA. The term *Parentalia* designates the period of nine days during which Roman families would visit the tombs of the dead to honor them. This novena, private in character, began on 13 February and ended with the public feast of the Feralia on 21 February. This cycle of days received its most extended comment from the Roman poet Ovid. He interchangeably calls them the *parentales dies* (*Fasti* 2.548) or the *ferales dies* (*Fasti* 2.34). The word *Feralia* gave the ancients occasion to coin etymological puns. The word could stem either "from the action of bringing food" *(a ferendis epulis)* or "from the action of sacrificing animals" (*a feriendis pecudibus;* Paulus-Festus, ed. Lindsay, 1913, p. 75 L.). The scholar M. Terentius (Varro, *De lingua Latina* 6.13) preferred to compare the term *Feralia* to both *inferi* and *ferre,* adding, "because the ones having the right to *parentare* bring then some food to the tomb" ("quod ferunt tum epulas ad sepulcrum quibus ius ibi parentare").

Parentare, "to celebrate the Parentalia," consisted in honoring the *di parentes,* or dead, with offerings. Ovid (*Fasti* 2.537–539) was glad to list such offerings: garlands, grains of wheat, salt, bread softened with wine, a few violets. These modest offerings were appropriate for the *manes,* the shades or spirits of the dead.

One may note the variations in vocabulary used by the various authors to refer to the dead: *inferi* (Varro, *De lingua Latina* 6.13); *dis manibus* (Festus, op. cit., p. 75 L.); *manes* (Ovid, *Fasti* 2.534). *Manes* or *di manes* is very likely explained as a euphemism: "the *inferi* are called *di manes,* that is, "good ones" with whom one should be reconciled out of fear of death" (Festus, op. cit., p. 132 L.). Use of the term corresponds to a later usage (first century BCE) that substituted for the ancient expression *di parentes* or *di parentum,* as had appeared already (specifically, in the form *divis parentum;* Festus, op. cit., p. 260 L.) in a "royal" law. A deceased person was regarded as having joined the collectivity of the *di parentes* (in the funerary inscriptions, it is written in the dative or the genitive along with the collective term). The formulation of Cornelia's letter to her son Gaius Sempronius Gracchus gives evidence of the link between the verb *parentare* and the corresponding noun: "Ubi mortua ero, parentabis mihi et invocabis deum parentem" ("When I am dead, you will honor me at the Parentalia and call on the parental shade"). By this *pietas*—the expression is Ovid's (*Fasti* 2.535)—toward the dead, the Parentalia were differentiated from the Lemuria of 9, 11, and 13 May, which consisted of rites in which evil spirits were expelled (ibid., 5.429–444). On 22 February, the day after the Feralia, which commemorated a family's dead, there followed the Caristia or Cara Cognatio, which united the living members of the family in a banquet (ibid., 2.677).

BIBLIOGRAPHY

Bömer, Franz. *Ahnenkult und Ahnenglaube im alten Rom.* Bonn, 1943.

Dumézil, Georges. *Archaic Roman Religion.* 2 vols. Translated

by Philip Krapp. Chicago, 1970.
Schilling, Robert. *Rites, cults, dieux de Rome.* Paris, 1979. See pages 11–15 for a discussion of Feralia and Lemuria.
Wagenvoort, Hendrik. *Studies in Roman Literature, Culture and Religion.* Leiden, 1956. Pages 290–297 treat the *parentatio* in honor of Romulus.
Wissowa, Georg. *Religion und Kultus der Römer.* 2d ed. Munich, 1912. See pages 232–235.

ROBERT SCHILLING
Translated from French by Paul C. Duggan

PARSIS. The Parsis are a community in western India that preserves the Zoroastrian religion. As their name, meaning "Persians," indicates, they trace their ancestry to Iran, where Zoroastrianism had been the established religion of the pre-Islamic Sasanid empire (226–651 CE).

Ethnic Identity. Within India, one is a Parsi by birth, the identity being derived through the male line. The community does not accept converts; a Parsi male who marries outside the community or who has children out of wedlock, however, may raise his children as Parsis.

Resistance to intermarriage has tended to preserve biological characteristics of the Parsis' Iranian background. As a population, the Parsis are taller and fairer-skinned than the average in India and have facial characteristics, such as pronounced noses, which would mark them as Middle Easterners.

Pre-modern History. The traditional Parsi homeland in India has been Gujarat, the coastal region to the north of Bombay. Zoroastrian settlements there are documented by travelers' accounts and by inscriptional evidence as early as the tenth and eleventh centuries CE. How did the Parsis' ancestors arrive?

Clearly, the contact of Iranians with areas to the east was not a single migration at a single moment in time. Darius I ("the Great"), the Achaemenid king who ruled from 521 to 485 BCE, extended his empire to Sind, that is, to the plain of the Indus River, or present-day Pakistan. Inscriptions in Pahlavi, the language of Iran in the centuries before Islam, have been found in South Indian Christian contexts and imply religious contact of Iran with India in the early Christian centuries. During the same era there were extensive trading contacts as well.

Besides evidence of Iranian contact before Islam, we know of Zoroastrian contacts outside Gujarat. Muslim travelers in the tenth century mention various parts of India as inhabited by *gabr*s, a derogatory term for Zoroastrians. Enough of these locations are in inland North India to suggest an overland migration pattern. Persians had also gone to southern China by the eighth century; *muhapa*s (from Persian *mobed*, "priest") are mentioned there in the mid-ninth. But all the migrations to areas other than Gujarat left no discernible Zoroastrian survival into modern times, and concerning them the literary tradition preserved by the Gujarat Parsis reflects almost no awareness at all.

Parsi tradition regarding the migration to India claims a single migration, by sea rather than overland. It is found in the *Kisseh-e-Sanjan* (Story of Sanjan), a narrative composed by a priest, Bahman son of Kaikobad, in four hundred lines of Persian verse in 1600. The *Kisseh* employs a chronology characterized by round numbers and acknowledges its indebtedness to oral tradition. Its implication, therefore, that the Zoroastrians who fled persecution after the Muslim conquest of Iran (c. 642 CE) spent "a hundred years in the mountain region" and, following the advice of an astrologer, sailed together from the Persian Gulf to India, can be taken as a "rounding off" of a migration that may well have been much more gradual and complex.

In the *Kisseh*'s narrative, the Parsis, after landing, proceed to the court of a local ruler, Jadi Rana, and ask him for shelter in his city and kingdom. The king, sensing them to be an alien group, specifies five conditions for his welcome: that they explain their religion, that they switch from Persian to the local vernacular, that they adopt local dress, that they go unarmed, and that they perform marriage ceremonies in the evening rather than by day. Parsis cite a story that the king offered the new arrivals a pitcher of milk, brim full (signifying that his realm was already crowded), and that the Parsi priest responded by slipping something valuable into the milk—a pinch of sugar, his ring, or a coin, depending on the version (signifying that the Parsis would fit in and would enhance it). Many believe the *Kisseh* to contain the pitcher-of-milk account, though it does not. Nor does it mention a promise not to proselytize as one of the undertakings given to Jadi Rana. But the *Kisseh* sums up for Parsis their arrival in India and their identity there.

Once established in India, the Parsis lived in agricultural villages and coastal towns. From the fifteenth to the seventeenth centuries, documentation of contact with Iran is provided by literature known as the *revayet*s. These texts are composed of correspondence in Persian between the Zoroastrians in Iran and their Parsi co-religionists in India. The priests in Gujarat were requesting authoritative rulings from the Zoroastrian priests still living under persecution in Iran.

Modern History. The Parsis' emergence as a prosperous and influential community is closely related to the growth of Bombay as a metropolitan center under the British. From the eighteenth century onward, and especially in the nineteenth century, Parsis from Gujarat settled in Bombay, learning English as well as maintaining Gujarati, and became business entrepreneurs and educated professionals. The Parsis have had an economic and cultural influence out of all proportion to their numbers, an influence that many believe reached its peak before World War I.

On the whole, the end of British colonial rule in India affected the Parsis adversely. As early as the 1880s, Parsis such as Dadabhai Naoroji, Pherozeshah Mehta, and Dinshaw Wacha had been leaders in the emerging Indian National Congress and had seen their national identity as Indians as more fundamental than their communal identity as Parsis. To the extent that Mohandas Gandhi's leadership after the 1920s appealed to specifically Hindu values, and to the extent that national independence (1947) brought a policy of secularization that forced formerly Parsi firms to hire non-Parsis, the patriotic spirit of Parsis has been put to the test.

Another important decline in recent Parsi history has been population size. For several decades the Parsi population in India has been shrinking by 1 percent per year. Late marriage and small family size, as well as emigration, intermarriage, and conversion to other faiths, have taken their toll.

Religious Institutions. The central feature of Zoroastrian worship in India is the *agiari,* or fire temple, a normally one-story building whose inner room contains a chamber three or four meters square enclosed by grillwork and with ventilation in the roof above. There, on a bed of sand in a large metal urn, a fire is kept burning continuously, fed with wood at five times during the day by a priest who chants the traditional prayers from the Avesta, the Zoroastrian scripture. The fire is the central symbol of divine presence in Zoroastrianism, and the prayers are thought to be efficacious as *mantras*, that is, by virtue of the sounds of their words when properly pronounced. Fires are of three grades of sanctity, the holiest being the *atesh behram* fire, whose consecration requires the combination of fires from sixteen sources, each of which must be ritually purified through lengthy ceremonial re-ignitions. Only eight *atesh behram* fires exist in India: four in Bombay, two in Surat, and one each in Udvada and Navsari. Of these the fire in Udvada, on the coast 175 kilometers north of Bombay, is the most highly revered; it is said to have been kept burning continuously for over a thousand years.

While fire temples have their own endowments and boards of trustees, most other Parsi institutions are usually managed on a citywide basis by the *anjuman,* or community organization. In Bombay, Poona, and Surat, the *anjuman* council is known as the *punchayet.* A community's properties include the *dakhmas*, or "towers of silence," cylindrical walled structures open to the air, in which the corpses of the dead are placed so that their flesh may be consumed by vultures. These continue in use in Parsi settlements in western India that were founded before the late nineteenth century; settlements elsewhere in India established burial grounds, and in Iran the use of *dakhmas* was abandoned in favor of burial in the early 1970s. *Anjuman* holdings also include subsidized housing blocks for Parsis and welfare funds for the community's poor.

The priesthood is hereditary; a male may exercise the option if born into a priestly family. Normally undertaken between the ages of about seven and fifteen, training consists of the memorization and performance of the rituals, rather than historical and theological studies. In the past century, several *madressas*, or seminaries for the training of priests have replaced parental instruction, but they provide elementary rather than university-level work, largely rote. Many who receive priestly training do not support themselves as full-time practicing priests but supplement the income from their secular employment by serving at times of peak demand, particularly at the year-end *muktad* ("departed souls") days in late August, when prayers are said for the dead.

Contemporary Issues. A number of concerns have engaged the attention and the energies of Parsis in Bombay in recent years. Of these the condition of the priesthood is one. The principal priest of a parish, called a *panthaki,* is in effect the proprietor and may hire other priests at a bare subsistence wage to assist him. Not surprisingly, other lines of work tend to attract the best minds in the community.

Emotions are stirred when the traditional mode of disposal of the dead is questioned. Many Parsis continue to rationalize the use of *dakhmas* as protecting the earth, the water, and the air from the defilement other modes would entail. They also hold them egalitarian, since rich and poor alike are placed in the tower without fanfare or possessions—though the families of the rich can afford to have more prayers said for the departed. Besides burial, a proposed alternative to exposure is electric cremation, which would not involve the use of fire.

The question of who is a Parsi has been a cause of debate during the twentieth century. Priests who have been willing to perform initiation ceremonies for adopted children and children of mixed marriages have been subjected to censure by governing boards of the community's institutions in Navsari and Bombay. The pattern for twentieth-century India was decided by the civil courts in a 1909 case seeking the exclusion of a non-Parsi wife from fire temples and community institutions. In that decision, and again in 1925, the courts upheld the community's restriction of its properties to the children of Parsis and Irani Zoroastrians, plus duly initiated children of Parsi fathers by alien wives.

Migration Overseas. During the nineteenth century, Parsi traders followed the sea routes of the British empire around the Indian Ocean and Southeast Asia, settling in such ports as Cape Town, Durban, Mombasa, Aden, Karachi, Colombo, Rangoon, Singapore, Hong Kong, Shanghai, and Kobe. They were involved especially in import-export trade, marine outfitting, banking, and the professions. In many cases they maintained close ties to India, regarding their residence elsewhere as temporary and returning to India to visit their families, to perform the initiation ceremonies of their children, and to find marriage partners for them. They also went to Britain, to trade, to study, and to settle.

Following World War II and Indian independence, a new pattern of migration developed. Parsis now migrated in increasing numbers to more distant destinations: still Britain, but also Canada, the United States, and Australia. Today the largest overseas community of Parsis is in London, England, with about three thousand; the next in size is in Toronto, Canada, with about half that number.

The families in this second wave of migration were now clearly committing themselves to new environments. Their worship has consisted largely of family prayers and *jashan* (thanksgiving) ceremonies employing a fire kindled *ad hoc*. In the new Parsi diaspora, Parsis have found themselves increasingly called on to articulate their religious faith and practice intellectually in order to explain it to others. A sense of a need for the maintenance of tradition through adaptive change, including possibly the admission of non-Zoroastrian spouses to membership and certainly a sophisticated presentation of Zoroastrian faith and practice, is one of the recent contributions of the overseas Parsis. With them may lie the chapters of Parsi history still to be written.

[*See also* Zoroastrianism.]

BIBLIOGRAPHY

Desai, Sapur F. *History of the Bombay Parsi Punchayet, 1860–1960.* Bombay, n.d. (1977?).

Kulke, Eckehard, *The Parsees in India: A Minority as Agent of Social Change.* Delhi and Munich, 1974.

Menant, Delphine. *The Parsis in India.* 2 vols. Enlarged and annotated by M. M. Murzban. Bombay, 1977.

Modi, Jivanji J. *The Religious Ceremonies and Customs of the Parsees.* 2d ed. Bombay, 1937.

Paymaster, Rustom B. *Early History of the Parsees in India from Their Landing in Sanjan to 1700 A.D.* Bombay, 1954.

Seervai, Kharshedji N., and Bomanji B. Patel. "Gujarat Parsis from Their Earliest Settlement to the Present Time (A.D. 1898)." *Gazetteer of the Bombay Presidency* 9 (1899): 183–254.

WILLARD G. OXTOBY

PARTHENOGENESIS. *See* Virgin Birth.

PARTHEV, SAHAK. *See* Sahak Parthev.

PĀRVATĪ. *See* Goddess Worship, *article on* The Hindu Goddess.

PASCAL, BLAISE (1623–1662), French mathematician, religious thinker, and philosopher. Pascal was one of the greatest minds in modern intellectual history. He was educated at home by his father, Étienne, who, when living in Paris from 1631 to 1639, belonged to the society of scientists organized by Mersenne. A precocious genius, Pascal in 1639 wrote a mathematical work of which a part, *Essai sur les coniques,* has been preserved and published. From 1642 to 1644, when in Normandy with his father, he constructed a calculating machine. His mathematical and physical works include a treatise, based on experiments, disproving the theory of the impossibility of vacuum, as well as works on cycloids and on the theory of probability.

Jansenism. In Normandy Pascal was in touch with priests who were disciples of the Abbé of Saint-Cyran, and in 1646 he went through a religious conversion, but he neither abandoned his scientific work nor renounced mundane life. However, in November 1654, he experienced a second conversion, a kind of violent shock about which he wrote a short and remarkable memoir; he kept this reminder of his experience on his person to the end of his days. For some years before his conversion Pascal had been under Jansenist influence, in particular in Port-Royal. There Pascal became acquainted with the main figures of Jansenism—Antoine Arnauld, Pierre Nicole, Le Maistre de Saci—and became himself one of the leading writers and polemicists of this political as well as religious movement.

Cornelius Jansen, also called Jansenius (1585–1638), in his posthumously published *Augustinus* (1640), elaborated a theory of grace that was antagonistic to the Jesuit soteriology known as Molinism, after the Jesuit theologian Luis de Molina (1535–1600), and which contributed to the reform of the church in the spirit of moral rigorism and theocentric piety. The Molinists were attacked for making the efficacy of divine grace dependent on human free choice and thus falling into Pelagian or semi-Pelagian heresy and for encouraging moral laxity, dangerous self-confidence, and "easy devotion." Jansenius, following Augustine, emphasized the deep corruption of human nature, its inability both to know God and to help us in obeying his commandments; he praised the omnipotence of divine grace, which is presented in his writings as the condition, not only necessary but sufficient as well, of salvation. In 1643, Arnauld published his treatise on the Eucharist, *De la fréquente communion,* which became a kind of Jansenist manifesto. The battle between the two camps was carried on with ferocity in the 1650s. As a result of pressure by the Jesuits, Innocent X, in his bull *Cum occasione* (1653), condemned five of Jansenius's statements in which the Molinists detected the Calvinist heresy; Jansenius was accused of saying that some divine commandments are for humans impracticable, that Jesus Christ sacrificed himself for the elect only and not for all people, and that divine grace works irresistibly. The Jansenists argued that the condemned statements could not be found in *Augustinus* and that the pope was not infallible in the matter-of-fact question of whether or not a given book included a certain theological doctrine. In 1656, Alexander VII renewed the condemnation in a separate constitution and asserted that the heretical statements were in fact in the book; earlier Arnauld had been condemned by the Sorbonne for theological and factual errors.

Pascal intervened in the battle by publishing pseudonymously, from January 1656 until March 1657, eighteen successive writings known collectively as the *Lettres provinciales,* a literary masterpiece which, notwithstanding its listing in the Index of Forbidden Books, was to become a classic of French literature. In this pamphlet Pascal attacked the Jesuits' moral doctrine, as it was taught in the works of known writers (Le Moine, Escobar, and Bauny, among others), as well as the theory of grace on which Jesuit "laxism" and moral permissiveness were supposedly based. The letters display to some extent the influence of Cartesianism, an influence not unusual among Jansenists, insofar as they imply the separation of faith from secular reason and assert the latter's autonomy; they denounce Jesuit casuistry and educational technique, claiming that through it all kinds of sins and vices could be exculpated easily or turned into virtues; they attack the Molinist teaching that sufficient grace has been given to all, and thus, by virtue of a free decision, anyone can make it efficient and perfectly fulfill the divine law.

Pensées. In the 1650s, apart from producing a number of short theological, philosophical, and scientific texts, all of them published posthumously *(Préface d'un traité du vide, Entretien avec M. de Saci, Comparaison des chrétiens des premiers temps avec ceux d'aujourd'hui, De l'esprit géométrique, De l'art de persuader, Écrits sur la grâce, Histoire de la roulette),* Pascal worked on *Apologie de la religion chrétienne.* This major apologetical work was to be addressed to libertines, probably of the kind he knew well personally: people who were religiously indifferent, skeptical, or incredulous, rather than committed atheists; the apology was to convince them of the truth of Christianity. He did not complete this work, and the first edition (1670) of the fragments he left was incomplete and arbitrarily ordered. In a number of subsequent printings, the editors of *Pensées,* as the work came to be known, arranged the text according to its logical order as they saw it. The edition of Brunschwig (1897) was used for several decades as a standard text, yet Louis Lafuma proved that the text left by Pascal was less chaotic and better arranged than had been previously assumed; since 1952 his edition has been considered superior to all others in existence.

Pensées is beyond doubt one of the major texts in the history of philosophical and religious ideas. This extremely rich and challenging work can be read as the depiction of the ambiguity of human destiny in the face of God, who is both hidden and manifest, and in the face of our own corruption and frailty. To Pascal, nature does not lead us to God unambiguously: "Why, do not you say yourself that the sky and the birds prove God?—No—Does your religion not say so?—No. For though it is true to some souls whom God has enlightened in this way, yet it is untrue for the majority." There are no "proofs" of faith, which is God's gift. "Our religion is wise and foolish: wise because it is the most learned and most strongly based on miracles, prophecies, etc., foolish, because it is not all this which makes people belong to it. This is a good enough reason for condemning those who do not belong, but not for making those who do belong believe. What makes them believe is the Cross."

Reason is not to be condemned—our entire dignity consists in thinking—but it ought to be looked upon with suspicion, and it is crucial that it knows its limitations. Pascal was the reader of Epictetus and Montaigne; the former stressed the strength of human nature, the latter its weakness and fragility. Both are right in part, but to take only one side amounts to falling either into hubris and dogmatic self-confidence or into despair. "We have an incapacity for proving anything which no amount of dogmatism can overcome. We have an idea of truth which no amount of skepticism can overcome." It is proper that God should be hidden in part and revealed in part, and it is proper that we should know both God and our misery. Therefore to know Jesus Christ is essential, as it is in him that we find both God and our misery. Indeed, our greatness consists in being aware of our misery. The position of man as a creature located between angels and animals by no means gives us, in Pascal's eyes, a quiet abode in our natural place; being "in the middle," we are torn between incompatible desires, and our natural state is the most opposed to our higher inclinations. It is the immobility of tension, rather than of satisfaction, that distinguishes us; we are incomprehensible to ourselves, our reason and our senses deceive us, no certainty is accessible to us. Christianity, with all its "foolishness," is the only way the human condition can become intelligible and meaningful. Indeed, the mystery of original sin, the core of the Christian worldview, according to Pascal, is an outrage to reason, and yet without this mystery we cannot understand ourselves. "Acknowledge then the truth of religion in its very obscurity, in the little light we can throw on it, in our indifference regarding knowledge of it."

Although, as Pascal argues both in *Pensées* and in *De l'esprit géométrique*, human reason cannot achieve any certitude, there is a separate power, the heart, which has "reasons of its own, unknown to reason" and which is a practical, rather than intellectual, faculty whereby a choice between equally valid arguments for and against Christianity can be made. In the famous passage on the wager *(pari)*, Pascal appeals to a kind of practical reasoning in order to compel the libertine to admit that he cannot avoid the choice between religion and irreligion. It is impossible to suspend the question of immortality and of our eternal destiny: our happiness is at stake, and the search for happiness is an aspect of our nature. God being infinite and therefore inaccessible to our reason, we cannot rationally affirm or deny his existence, but neither can we suspend our judgment. We have to bet, as in a game of chance: if we bet on God having even the slightest chance of existence, we may gain an eternal life of happiness, whereas only our finite life on earth is at stake; betting against God we risk the loss of eternal life, and the possible gain is finite; it is therefore practically rational to opt for God.

It needs stressing that the wager is a way to persuade a skeptic that he ought to bet on God, however uncertain of God's existence he might be; it is neither the expression of Pascal's own uncertainty nor another "proof" of a theological truth. It is practical advice, and Pascal is aware that by itself it cannot produce genuine faith. He wants to show the libertine that he ought to behave as if God were real, and this means taming his passions and even "stultifying" himself by complying, without real faith, with external Christian rules. The new way of life eventually will make him realize that he has lost nothing in abandoning his sinful habits, and he will be converted to a true Christian faith.

By the standards of our nature, religion is uncertain, and we cannot get rid of our nature. A tension between the attraction of the world and our participation in the eternal is unavoidable. Human history and social life do not offer us any solution; history is the prey of insignificant accidents ("Cleopatra's nose: if it had been shorter the whole face of the earth would have been different"); social reality has no intrinsic value and cannot be improved. Therefore Pascal, on the one hand, sneers at all titles and ranks, reduces laws and justice to pure conventions and property to a superstition, and, on the other hand, recommends a conservative acceptance of social hierarchy and external respect for monarchy, rank, and wealth. His worldview is essentially nonhistorical.

Pascal, not surprisingly, was attacked by the eighteenth-century *philosophes* Voltaire, Diderot, and Condorcet; his skeptical view of science, to which he (unlike his critics) made very serious contributions, his belief in the naturally incurable corruption of human nature, his pessimistic assessment of the human quest for happiness, were, of course, unacceptable to the prophets of the Enlightenment. He has remained one of the main figures in the history of conflict between Christianity and modernity, and his analyses sound astonishingly fresh in our time.

BIBLIOGRAPHY

Works by Pascal

Œuvres complètes. Edited by Louis Lafuma. With a preface by Henri Gouhier. New York and Paris, 1963.

Pensées. Translated into English by A. J. Krailsheimer. Harmondsworth, 1966.

Works about Pascal

Blaise Pascal, l'homme et l'œuvre. Cahiers de Royaumont, Philosophie, no. 1. Paris, 1956.

Brunschvicg, Léon. *Le génie de Pascal.* Paris, 1924.

Brunschvicg, Léon. *Descartes et Pascal, lecteurs de Montaigne.* Paris, 1944.

Goldmann, Lucien. *Le dieu caché.* Paris, 1955. Translated by Philip Thody as *The Hidden God* (New York, 1964).

Jovy, Ernest. *Études pascaliennes.* 9 vols. Paris, 1927–1936.

Laporte, Jean. *Le cœur et la raison selon Pascal.* Paris, 1950.

Mesnard, Jean. *Pascal, l'homme et l'œuvre.* Paris, 1951. Translated by G. S. Fraser as *Pascal, His Life and Works* (London, 1952).

Russier, Jeanne. *La foi selon Pascal.* Paris, 1949.

Strowski, Fortunat. *Pascal et son temps.* 3 vols. Paris, 1907–1922.

LESZEK KOLAKOWSKI

PASSOVER is the joyous Jewish festival of freedom that celebrates the Exodus of the Jews from their bondage in Egypt. Beginning on the fifteenth day of the spring month of Nisan, the festival lasts for seven days (eight days for Jews outside Israel). The Hebrew name for Passover, Pesaḥ, refers to the paschal lamb offered as a family sacrifice in Temple times (*Ex.* 12:1–28, 12:43–49; *Dt.* 16:1–8), and the festival is so called because God "passed over" *(pasaḥ)* the houses of the Israelites when he slew the Egyptian firstborn (*Ex.* 12:23). The annual event is called Ḥag ha-Pesaḥ, the Feast of the Passover, in the Bible (*Ex.* 34:25). Another biblical name for it is Ḥag ha-Matsot or the Feast of the Unleavened Bread, after the command to eat unleavened bread and to refrain from eating leaven (*Ex.* 23:15, *Lv.* 23:6, *Dt.* 16:16). The critical view is that the two names are for two originally separate festivals, which were later combined. Ḥag ha-Pesaḥ was a pastoral festival, whereas Ḥag ha-Matsot was an agricultural festival. In any event, the paschal lamb ceased to be offered when the Temple was destroyed in 70 CE, and although the name Passover is still used, the holiday is now chiefly marked by the laws concerning leaven and, especially, by the home celebration held on the first night—the Seder ("order, arrangement").

Prohibition on Leavening. On the night before the festival the house is searched thoroughly for leavened bread. Any found is gathered together and removed from the house during the morning of 14 Nisan. This is based on the biblical injunction that not only is it forbidden to eat leaven, but no leaven may remain in the house (*Ex.* 12:15, 12:19). On Passover, observant Jews do not employ utensils used during the rest of the year for food that contains leaven. Either they have special Passover utensils or they remove the leaven in the walls of their regular utensils by firing or boiling them in hot water. Only food products completely free from even the smallest particle of leaven are eaten. In many communities, rabbis supervise the manufacture of packaged Passover foods to verify that they are completely free from leaven, after which they attach their seal of fitness to the product. There was at first considerable rabbinical opposition to machine-made *matsah* on the grounds that pieces of dough might be left in the machine and become leaven. Nowadays, with vastly improved methods of production, the majority of Jews see no objection to machine-made *matsah.*

The biblical reason given for eating unleavened bread *(matsah)* and refraining from eating leaven *(ḥamets)* is that during the Exodus the Israelites, having left Egypt in haste, were obliged to eat unleavened bread because their dough had had insufficient time to rise (*Ex.* 12:39). *Matsah* is therefore the symbol of freedom. A later idea is that leaven—bread that has risen and become fermented—represents pride and corruption, whereas unleavened bread represents humility and purity. [*See also* Leaven.]

Great care is consequently taken when baking *matsah* for Passover. The process is speeded up so that no time is allowed for the dough to rise before it is baked. The resulting *matsah* is a flat bread with small perforations (an extra precaution against the dough's rising). Some Jews prefer to eat only round *matsah,* because a circle is unbounded, representing the unlimited need to strive for freedom.

Synagogue Service. The synagogue liturgy for Passover contains additional prayers and hymns suffused with the themes of freedom and renewal. On the first day there is a prayer for dew; the rainy season now over, supplication is made for the more gentle dew to assist the growth of the produce in the fields. The scriptural readings are from passages dealing with Passover. On the seventh day, the anniversary of the parting of the sea (*Ex.* 14:17–15:26), the relevant passage is read; some Jews perform a symbolic reenactment to further dramatize the event. On the Sabbath in the middle of Passover, the Prophetic reading is Ezekiel's vision of the dry bones (*Ez.* 37:1–14). On this Sabbath, too, there is a reading of the *Song of Songs* (interpreted by the rabbis as a dialogue between God and his people), in which there is a reference to the spring (2:11–13) and to the Exodus (1:9).

The Seder and the Haggadah. The Seder, celebrated in the home on the first night of Passover (outside Israel, also on the second night), is a festive meal during which various rituals are carried out and the Haggadah is read or chanted. The Haggadah ("telling") is the traditional collection of hymns, stories, and poems recited in obedience to the command for parents to tell their children of God's mighty deeds in delivering the people from Egyptian bondage (*Ex.* 13:8). The main features of the Haggadah are already found in outline in the Mishnah (*Pes.* 10) with some of the material going back to Temple times. It assumed its present form in the Middle Ages, with a few more recent additions. The emphasis in the Haggadah is on God alone as the deliverer from bondage. It is he and no other, neither messenger nor angel, who brings his people out from Egypt. Even

Moses is mentioned by name only once in the Haggadah, and then only incidentally, at the end of a verse quoted for other purposes.

A special dish is placed on the Seder table upon which rest the symbolic foods required for the rituals. These are three *matsot*, covered with a cloth; *maror*, bitter herbs that serve as a reminder of the way the Egyptian taskmasters embittered the lives of their slaves (*Ex.* 1:14); *ḥaroset*, a paste made of almonds, apples, and wine, symbolic of the mortar the slaves used as well as of the sweetness of redemption; a bowl of salt water, symbolic of the tears of the oppressed; parsley or other vegetables for a symbolic dipping in the salt water; a roasted bone as a reminder of the paschal lamb; and a roasted egg as a reminder of the animal sacrifice, the *ḥagigah* offered in Temple times on Passover, Shavu'ot, and Sukkot. During the Seder, four cups of wine are partaken of by all the celebrants, representing the four different expressions used for redemption in the narrative of the Exodus. Since in ancient times the aristocratic custom was to eat and drink while reclining, the food and drink are partaken of in this way as a symbol of the mode of eating of free men. Some medieval authorities held that since people no longer recline at meals, there is no longer any point in the symbolic gesture, but their view was not adopted.

The Seder begins with the Qiddush, the festival benediction over the first cup of wine. The middle *matsah* is then broken in two, one piece being set aside to be eaten as the *afiqoman* ("dessert"), the last thing eaten before the Grace after Meals, so that the taste of the *matsah* of freedom might linger in the mouth. It is customary for the grown-ups to hide the *afiqoman*, rewarding the lucky child who finds it with a present. The parsley is first dipped in the salt water and then eaten. The youngest child present asks the Four Questions, a standard formula beginning with "Why is this night different from all other nights?" The differences are noted in four instances, such as, "On all other nights we eat either leaven or unleaven, whereas on this night we eat only unleaven." The head of the house and the other adults then proceed to reply to the Four Questions by reading the Haggadah, in which the answers are provided in terms of God's deliverances. When they reach the section that tells of the ten plagues, a little wine from the second cup is poured out to denote that it is inappropriate to drink a full cup of joy at the delivery, since in the process the enemy was killed. This section of the Haggadah concludes with a benediction in which God is thanked for his mercies, and the second cup of wine is drunk while reclining.

The celebrants then partake of the meal proper. Grace before Meals is recited over two of the three *matsot* and a benediction is recited: "Blessed art thou, O Lord our God, who has sanctified us with thy commandments and commanded us to eat *matsah*." The bitter herbs (horseradish is generally used) are then dipped in the *ḥaroset* and eaten. There is a tradition that in Second Temple times the famous sage Hillel would eat *matsah*, bitter herbs, and the paschal lamb together. In honor of Hillel's practice, a sandwich is made of the third *matsah* and the bitter herbs. In many places the first course is a hard-boiled egg in salt water, a further symbol of the tears of the slaves in Egypt and their hard bondage.

At the end of the meal the *afiqoman* is eaten, and the Grace after Meals is recited over the third cup of wine. The Hallel (consisting of *Psalms* 113–118) and other hymns of thanksgiving are then recited over the fourth cup of wine. Before the recital of Hallel, a cup is filled for the prophet Elijah, the herald of the Messiah, who is said to visit every Jewish home on this night. The door of the house is opened to let Elijah in, and the children watch eagerly to see if they can notice any diminution in Elijah's cup as the prophet quickly sips the wine and speeds on his way to visit all the other homes. At this stage there is a custom dating from the Middle Ages of reciting a number of imprecations against those who oppressed the Jews and laid the Temple waste. Nowadays, many Jews either do not recite these verses or substitute prayers more relevant to the contemporary situation, such as prayers for freedom to be established for all people.

The Seder concludes with the cheerful singing of table hymns, most of them jingles for the delight of the children present, such as *Ḥad Gadya'* (One Kid), constructed on the same lines as *This Is the House That Jack Built*, the cat devouring the kid, the dog devouring the cat, and so on until the Angel of Death devours the final slaughterer and then God slays the Angel of Death. Commentators to the Haggadah have read into this theme various mystical ideas about the survival of Israel and the ultimate overcoming of death itself in eternal life. All join in singing these songs, for which there are many traditional melodies. This night is said to be one of God's special protection so that the usual night prayers on retiring to bed, supplicating God for his protection, are not recited since that protection is granted in any event.

BIBLIOGRAPHY

J. B. Segal's *The Hebrew Passover: From the Earliest Times to A.D. 70* (London, 1963), with a comprehensive bibliography, deals with the history and development of the festival through the Temple period and surveys the various critical theories on the origins of the festival. For the later period the best work is

Chaim Raphael's *A Feast of History: Passover through the Ages as a Key to Jewish Experience* (New York, 1972). This book also attractively presents one of the very many editions of the Haggadah. Isaac Levy's little book *A Guide to Passover* (London, 1958) provides a useful summary of the traditional laws and customs of the festival. An anthology of teachings with a comprehensive bibliography is Philip Goodman's *The Passover Anthology* (Philadelphia, 1961). For an insightful look at the history of the printed Haggadah one may consult Yosef H. Yerushalmi's *Haggadah and History* (Philadelphia, 1975).

LOUIS JACOBS

PATAÑJALI, reputed author of the key scripture of classical Yoga, the *Yoga Sūtra,* also known as the *Pātañjala Sūtra* or *Sāṃkhyapravacana.* Nothing definite is known about Patañjali. According to Indian tradition, he is identified with the famous Sanskrit grammarian of that name who probably lived in the second century BCE. Legend knows him as the incarnation of the serpent king Ananta or Śeṣa (a manifestation of Viṣṇu), who is believed to encircle the earth. This identification is of interest for its symbolism: the serpent race that is ruled by Ananta guards the hidden treasures of the earth, that is, the esoteric lore, and Yoga is, of course, the secret tradition *par excellence.* The traditional identification of Patañjali with his namesake the grammarian, first made by Bhoja in his *Rājamārtaṇḍa* (introduction, stanza 5), is generally rejected by modern scholars.

For historical and terminological reasons, the most likely date for the *Yoga Sūtra* is the third century CE (see Woods, 1914), although the traditions from which its author draws are undoubtedly much older. This work belongs to a distinct genre of Indian philosophical writing, purporting to summarize a particular tradition—in this case, Yoga—in pithy half-sentences or aphorisms *(sūtras).* The extreme brevity of these compositions has given rise to a whole body of exegetical literature, comprising commentaries, subcommentaries, and glosses of varying length, with differing degrees of divergence from or fidelity to the original. For the *Yoga Sūtra,* over twenty such commentaries are extant.

The *Yoga Sūtra* represents an attempt to furnish succinct definitions of the important techniques and concepts of Yoga, staking a claim for the yogic tradition as an authoritative system *(darśana)* within the arena of Indian metaphysical thought. Judging from the extensive commentarial literature and from references to the text in the writings of other schools, the *Yoga Sūtra* enjoyed considerable influence and was certainly instrumental in establishing Yoga as an independent branch of Indian soteriology. The widely held opinion that Patañjali merely supplied classical Sāṃkhya with a practical framework is clearly wrong (see Feuerstein, 1980).

The text itself is composed of 195 aphorisms (in some recensions 194 or 196), distributed over four chapters as follows: (1) "Samādhipāda" (Chapter on Enstasy), 51 aphorisms; (2) "Sādhanapāda" (Chapter on Discipline), 55 aphorisms; (3) "Vibhūtipāda" (Chapter on Paranormal Powers), 55 aphorisms; (4) "Kaivalyapāda" (Chapter on Liberation), 34 aphorisms. The apparently inconsistent organization of the material has caused modern scholarship to search for an *Urtext* (see Deussen, 1920, and Hauer, 1958, both postulating five subtexts). Such attempts to reconstruct the original are generally based on the *a priori* assumption of the implicit heterogeneity ("corruption") of the text, and they tend to violate the material substantially by fragmenting it. An alternative methodological approach is that of presupposing the structural homogeneity ("innocence") of the text and delimiting this heuristic principle gradually as counter-evidence is forthcoming. On the basis of this second procedure, it is possible to demonstrate that the text can be rescued from the atomization of conventional textual criticism (see Feuerstein, 1979). According to this analysis, there appears to be only one actual break in the form of an interpolation (the whole section dealing with the "members" or constituents of Yoga, or *yoga-aṅga*). Other single aphorisms, or small groups of aphorisms, may also have been interpolated, but these are not conclusively verifiable.

The oldest extant commentary is the *Yogabhāṣya* of Vyāsa ("arranger"), probably composed in the fifth century CE. It contains the key to many, though by no means all, of the more enigmatic aphorisms, and it served as the foundation for all subsequent exegetical efforts. On the basis of a text-immanent study of the *Yoga Sūtra,* it can be shown that this scholium differs in some instances from Patañjali's interpretations, which is reflected in the terminological divergence. The next most important commentary is the *Yogabhāṣyavivaraṇa* of Śaṅkara Bhagavatpāda, who has been identified by Paul Hacker (1968/69) as Śaṅkarācarya. This is the most independent of subcommentaries and has even preserved several variant readings of the *Yoga Sūtra.* Whether or not the *Vivaraṇa* is the great *ācārya*'s work, it shows apparently no acquaintance with Vācaspati Miśra's *Tattvavaiśāradī,* composed around 850 CE. Whereas most of the post-Vācaspati commentaries are largely *bhāṣya*-dependent compositions, which holds true even of the *Rājamārtaṇḍa* by Bhoja (eleventh century), who claimed to be more self-reliant, a refreshingly original treatment of the *Yoga Sūtra* is afforded by Vijñānabhikṣu in his elaborate *Yogavārttika* (sixteenth century).

[*See also* Yoga.]

BIBLIOGRAPHY

Dasgupta, Surendranath. *The Study of Patañjali.* Calcutta, 1920. *Yoga as Philosophy and Religion* (1924). Reprint, Port Washington, N.Y., 1970. *Yoga Philosophy in Relation to Other Systems of Thought* (1930). Reprint, Delhi, 1974. Although written prior to the recent critical studies on the *Yoga Sūtra,* this trilogy contains much valuable thought on classical Yoga, showing the immense scope and subtleties of this philosophical system. Dasgupta's works are especially useful for an understanding of the exegetical Sanskrit literature.

Deussen, Paul. "Der Yoga des Patañjali." In *Allgemeine Geschichte der Philosophie,* vol. 1, pt. 3, *Die Nachvedische Philosophie der Inder,* pp. 507–578. Leipzig, 1920. Deussen's was the first (still largely intuitive) attempt to analyze the *Yoga Sūtra* into its component "subtexts." His understanding of the text inspired J. W. Hauer (1958).

Feuerstein, Georg, ed. and trans. *The Yoga-Sūtra of Patañjali: A New Translation and Commentary.* Folkestone, England, 1979. A fresh rendering of Patañjali's work, founded on my textual and semantic investigations into classical Yoga.

Feuerstein, Georg. *The Yoga-Sūtra of Patañjali: An Exercise in the Methodology of Textual Analysis.* New Delhi, 1979. The most comprehensive in-depth textual analysis of the *Yoga Sūtra* to date, reviewing all previous scholarly endeavors.

Feuerstein, Georg. *The Philosophy of Classical Yoga.* Manchester, 1980. A detailed examination of key concepts of Patañjali's philosophy, based on a "text-immanent" interpretation of the *Yoga Sūtra* that seeks to combat the exegetical monopoly of the *Yogabhāṣya.*

Hacker, Paul. "Śaṅkara der Yogin und Śaṅkara der Advaitin: Einige Beobachtungen." *Wiener Zeitschrift für die Kunde Süd- und Ostasiens* (Vienna) 12/13 (1968/69): 119–148. An important article arguing for the identity of Śaṅkara Bhagavatpāda, author of the *Vivaraṇa,* with Śaṅkarācārya, the great teacher of Advaita Vedānta.

Hauer, J. W. *Der Yoga als Heilweg: Nach den Indischen Quellen dargestellt.* 2d ed. Stuttgart, 1958. A historical and philosophical treatment of Yoga, with an original interpretation of Patañjali's work. Hauer supplied the first detailed textual analysis of the *Yoga Sūtra.*

Koelman, Gaspar M. *Pātañjala Yoga: From Related Ego to Absolute Self.* Poona, 1970. An excellent treatment of classical Yoga with particular reference to the commentarial literature in Sanskrit.

Leggett, Trevor. *Samādhi-pāda,* vol. 1 of *Śaṅkara on the Yoga-sūtra-s: The Vivaraṇa Sub-commentary to Vyāsa-bhāṣya on the Yoga-sūtra-s of Patañjali.* London, 1981. The first (and generally fine) translation of the first chapter of the *Vivaraṇa,* which shows Śaṅkara to be a highly creative thinker who was obviously informed by Yoga practice.

Rukmani, T. S., ed. and trans. *Samādhipāda* and *Sādhanapāda,* vols. 1 and 2 of *The Yogavārttika of Vijñānabhikṣu: Text with English Translation and Critical Note Along with the Text and English Translation of the Pātañjala Yogasūtras and Vyāsabhāṣya.* New Delhi, 1982–1983. The first and critical rendering of the first two chapters of Vijñānabhikṣu's masterful commentary.

Woods, James Haughton, trans. "The Yoga-sūtras of Patañjali as Illustrated by the Comment Entitled 'The Jewel's Lustre; or Maṇiprabhā.' " *Journal of the American Oriental Society* 34 (1914–1915): 1–114. A complete rendering of the *Maṇiprabhā.*

GEORG FEUERSTEIN

PATAÑJALI THE GRAMMARIAN (fl. c. 140 BCE), Sanskrit grammarian and author of the *Mahābhāṣya,* the major commentary on Pāṇini's *Aṣṭādhyāyī.* Patañjali's *bhāṣya* ("commentary") focuses on Pāṇini's work both directly and indirectly, for it evaluates both Pāṇini's verses and those of Kātyāyana's *Vārttika,* the first notable commentary on the *Aṣṭādhyāyī.* Pāṇini, Kātyāyana, and Patañjali have often been grouped together in a kind of grammatical lineage; Pāṇini and Patañjali, however, remain by far the foremost authorities on the Sanskrit language.

Scholars vary in opinion as to Patañjali's purpose in composing his *Mahābhāṣya.* Most agree, however, that the very fact that Patañjali chose to fashion his observations not in an independent grammar but in a commentary on Pāṇini's work indicates great deference to the original grammarian; it was not Patañjali's purpose to attempt to surpass him or disprove his authority. In his work Patañjali mentions directly his indebtedness to the *mahācārya* ("great teacher").

Many social changes were occurring in India during Patañjali's time. There was an influx of different peoples from bordering lands; intellectual, commercial, and political contact with regions as far as Greece was common; and class structure was undergoing substantial transitions. Social change was reflected in language: the use of classical Sanskrit (i.e., the *saṃskṛta* or "perfected" language of Pāṇini) became restricted more and more to the social and literary elite, while the rest of the population spoke one of the many Prakrits (i.e., the *prakṛta,* or "natural, unpolished" languages and dialects) that were rapidly developing.

Even spoken Sanskrit was beginning to include *apaśabda,* "vulgar, imperfect speech." For example, social stratification had reduced women to a much lower status than that which they had enjoyed during the Vedic and early Upaniṣadic periods; this was reflected in speech by a growing irregularity of feminine forms and endings that all but eliminated the feminine honorific. Patañjali observed that the grammar of Pāṇini was by now being retained almost artificially; when he observed that even some of the most respected pandits, while meticulous in religious recitation, would resort to an occasional *apaśabda* term in their ordinary speech, he realized that certain modifications were in order. Patañjali thus became the first Indian grammarian to address the difference between *laukikabhāṣya* ("empirical language") and *śāstrīyabhāṣya* ("sacred language").

Patañjali's intent was not to reflect in grammar every form of imperfect speech, but rather to incorporate some of the changes that were occurring in spoken Sanskrit so that the language could thereby be preserved in a viable form. He chose to revalidate Pāṇini's dictums and expand them where necessary. If, for example, Pāṇini allowed that three classes of nouns conformed to a certain rule, Patañjali might revise the rule to incorporate an additional class. In Pāṇini's time the Vedic *ṛ* and *ḷ* were still commonly used vocalically. Within a few centuries the two letters had shifted, with very few exceptions, to the status of consonants; this was another type of change that Patañjali accommodated.

Patañjali believed that the grammarian should stay in touch with the contemporary language and provide for reasonable changes, adhering as closely as possible to the classical rules. In this way the populace would continue to turn to the grammarians for guidance in all matters of speech.

When Pāṇini composed his grammar he was more concerned with the forms of words (*padas*) than with syntax and sentence meaning. By Patañjali's time, Mīmāṃsā and other philosophical schools had introduced a shift in emphasis whereby speech *(vākya)* and the complete thought expressed in a sentence represented the true basis of language. Patañjali's contact with these other views influenced his expansion of Pāṇini's grammar, and he thus introduced the concept of *vākyasphota,* that is, the concept that the eternal element of sounds and words, and the true vehicle of an idea, flash on the mind when a sound is uttered. This indicates an inherent *nityatva* ("infinitude") in *śabda* ("correct grammatical speech"); even *apaśabda* ("incorrect speech") can partake of this in varying degrees.

By incorporating the notion of *nityatva* into *vyākaraṇa* ("grammar"), Patañjali helped to elevate the status of the science of grammar. Pāṇini's *Aṣṭādhyāyī,* revered as it was for its insurmountable contributions to the preservation of the sacred Vedic speech and classical Sanskrit, did not belong to any particular category of Sanskrit literature before Patañjali's time. It was variously considered Dharmaśāstra, *smṛti,* Āgama, or, occasionally, Vedāṅga ("limb of the Veda"). Patañjali's observations and syntheses, in addition to his frequent reiteration that the study of *vyākaraṇa* is a religious duty, served to elevate Pāṇini's *Aṣṭādhāyī* permanently to the sacred status of Vedāṅga.

[*See also* Vedāṅgas *and the biography of Pāṇini.*]

BIBLIOGRAPHY

Patañjali's *Mahābhāṣya* is available in English translation in *Patañjali's Vyākaraṇa-mahābhāṣya,* 8 vols., translated and edited by S. D. Joshi and J. A. F. Roodbergen (Poona, 1968–1980); the edition also offers a valuable introductory section. Useful secondary works include K. Madhava Krishna Sarma's *Pāṇini, Kātyāyana, and Patañjali* (Delhi, 1968) and Franz Kielhorn's *Kātyāyana and Patañjali: Their Relation to Each Other and to Pāṇini* (1876; 2d ed., Varanasi, 1963).

CONSTANTINA BAILLY

PATRICK (c. 390–c. 460), called the "apostle of the Irish," a Christian Briton sent by his church as a missionary bishop to Ireland. During thirty years of evangelistic and pastoral work, Patrick laid foundations for the Roman church in Ireland and for the wide influence it later came to have in Europe.

Apart from numerous traditions and legends about Patrick, historians are dependent on two documents, his *Confession* and *Letter to the Soldiers of Coroticus.* Scholars agree that these are authentic but have differed as to their implications. Patrick was evidently born and raised in Roman Britain. His father, Calpornius, a Roman citizen, a well-to-do landholder, and a member of a district council, was responsible for collecting taxes in his area. From childhood Patrick spoke two languages, British (a Celtic language) and a commercial, unscholarly form of Latin. Behind him were at least two generations of Christians: his paternal grandfather was a presbyter, or priest, and his father was a deacon. Yet, during his childhood, Patrick's own faith seems to have been only nominal.

During the fourth century the invading Anglo-Saxons had pushed the Britons into the western part of England and into Wales. For generations the Irish tribes had raided the west coast of Britain for slaves. With Roman protection growing weaker toward the end of the fourth century, these raids became more frequent. About 406, when Patrick was sixteen years old, the raiders descended on the estate of Patrick's father. Along with hundreds of others, Patrick was carried off to the west coast of Ireland to work as a herdsman. For one accustomed to the culture of Roman civilization and the privileges of rural aristocracy, the hardship of enslavement by an uncouth people was a traumatic experience. Yet it kindled Patrick's faith such that it grew into a warm piety with a vivid awareness of the presence and friendship of God. He wrote, "In a single day I would say as many as a hundred prayers, and almost as many at night." After six years of captivity, when he was about twenty-two, Patrick fled his captors and made his way back to his family in Britain. The next years were probably spent in one of the monasteries of Britain. Some scholars have held that these years, or part of them, were spent in France, but from his ideas and practices and the quality of his Latin, recent scholarship has concluded that Patrick was a thoroughgoing representative of British Christianity. If he spent any time in Gaul, it was probably brief.

Sometime in the 420s Patrick dreamed that his former Irish captors were calling him back: "We ask thee, boy, come and walk among us once more" (*Confession* 23). During his slave days he had learned the Irish language (a Celtic language akin to British) and now felt drawn by God to return. His monastic years had provided him neither higher education nor fluency in Latin, but there was much evidence of his Christian dedication and ability as a leader. The British church had already sent at least one mission to a neighboring territory (led by Ninian). So they concurred with Patrick's call, appointed him bishop, and around 431 sent him and some assistants to Ireland. He was then about forty years old. He traveled to the northeast of Ireland, was welcomed by the regional king, and probably made his headquarters at Armagh, near the king's estate.

Other Christians had preceded Patrick to Ireland. The slave raids, the Irish settlers returned from Britain, and commerce with Christian tribes had brought Christian influence to the country. But the Christian presence was scattered. A year or so before Patrick's trip, Rome had sent a bishop, Palladius, to southern Ireland. His work may have overlapped that of Patrick; in any event, it was cut short by his early death. Patrick was thus the pioneer missionary in the area.

Amid the traditional religion of the druids and among the unlettered Irish, Patrick's work was typical of a fifth-century missionary bishop. He made friends, preached, baptized, confirmed, celebrated the Eucharist, encouraged the formation of monasteries, and prepared and ordained clergy. This meant that he developed a written language and taught his ordinands to read and write. He excommunicated where he felt it necessary and assumed that a bishop's authority was paramount in the church (later influence on the Celtic church shifted authority to the monasteries and the abbots). Patrick distributed relief goods supplied by the British church. He was not an academic theologian but an activist bishop.

Inevitably opposition arose from the druids and at times from within the Irish and British churches. In later years Patrick wrote his *Confession* to explain his activities. Some of his personality and message are reflected in his two writings. We find a disarming honesty and modesty, a deep pastoral concern, frequent quotations from the Bible, a sense of unworthiness, and gratitude toward a merciful and sovereign God, who cares for people and wants their responding faith and a behavior that is just and merciful. His theology was orthodox trinitarian and evangelical. He saw himself as an evangelist, a "fisher of men." He was a vigorous defender of his flock. He once wrote to "the Soldiers of Coroticus," a group of his own British people, Christians and Roman citizens, to rebuke them for raiding an Irish settlement and carrying away newly baptized youths. His ministry in Ireland seems to have lasted about thirty years, until his death, around 460. Details of Patrick's travels and work in Ireland are not available, but legends about him attest to the love and respect he must have received. Later the Irish church that he helped found contributed substantially to the evangelization of Scotland, northern England, and western Europe.

BIBLIOGRAPHY

The best of the older biographies is John B. Bury's *The Life of Saint Patrick and His Place in History* (New York, 1905). A useful translation of Patrick's writings is in Ludwig Bieler's *The Works of Saint Patrick by Saint Secundinus* (Westminster, Md., 1953). The scholarly debates, with a convincing contribution on the dates, places, and movements in the life of Patrick, are in Richard P. C. Hanson's *Saint Patrick: His Origins and Career* (Oxford, 1968). An attractive collection of maps, photographs, and drawings with a very readable text is Tom Corfe's *Saint Patrick and Irish Christianity* (Cambridge, 1973).

H. McKennie Goodpasture

PAUCK, WILHELM (1901–1981), German-American historian and theologian. Wilhelm Pauck was born in Westphalia, Germany, on 31 January 1901, and was reared in Berlin, where his father taught physics. He studied at the universities of Berlin and Göttingen, taking his licentiate in theology at Berlin in 1925 with a dissertation on Martin Bucer. The decisive influences on his intellectual development were two Berlin professors of renown, Ernst Troeltsch and Karl Holl. It was Troeltsch who first turned him to the study of theology and impressed upon him the nature of Christianity as a historical movement that must be interpreted by means of the historical method. From Holl he received magisterial instruction in Reformation history and theology, above all in studies of Martin Luther. He also heard lectures by two other giants of modern Protestant thought: Adolf von Harnack (at Berlin) and Karl Barth (at Göttingen).

Pauck came to the United States in 1925, was ordained to the ministry of the Congregational church in 1928, and became an American citizen in 1937. His teaching career, which bore remarkable fruit, spanned fifty years: at the Chicago Theological Seminary and, chiefly, at the divinity school and history department of the University of Chicago (1926–1953); at Union Theological Seminary, New York City (1953–1967); at Vanderbilt University (until 1972); and as professor emeritus at Stanford University (until 1976). He died in Palo Alto, California, on 3 September 1981.

Pauck's thought has been aptly described as an ellipse with two foci, one in the Reformation interpretation of the Christian gospel and the other in the modern historical understanding of reality. This dual commitment led him to reject two strategies that he considered equally ahistorical: either a simple "repristination" of Reformation theology (as attempted by Protestant neoorthodoxy) or a facile "accommodation" of the Christian tradition to modernity (as practiced by radical theological liberalism). His own approach to the Reformation was at once critical and conserving—the latter because Reformation religion was biblical and evangelical and thus foundational to authentic Protestantism; the former because the permanent truth of the Christian gospel cannot be identified with any of its temporary historical forms, all of which are necessarily relative to their immediate contexts and thus must be constantly refashioned in response to new historical situations. Hence Pauck maintained that the future of Protestantism lay with the historical-critical interpretation of Christianity articulated by such premier liberal theologians as Troeltsch and Harnack, rather than with the traditional "dogmatic" viewpoint espoused by the neoorthodox theologians, especially Barth.

Pauck's writings, distinguished by the vast learning and literary felicity evinced by them, moved with ease from the Reformation era through nineteenth-century liberal Protestantism to contemporary theology. Two collections of his seminal essays are of special importance: *The Heritage of the Reformation* (2d ed., rev. and enl., 1961) and *From Luther to Tillich: The Reformers and Their Heirs*, edited by Marion Pauck (1984). His preeminence as a Luther scholar is displayed in his new edition and translation of Luther's *Lectures on Romans* with a masterly general introduction (1961). Other representative publications are *Das Reich Gottes auf Erden: Utopie und Wirklichkeit* (The Kingdom of God on Earth: Utopia and Reality, 1928), a still valuable study of Bucer; *Karl Barth: Prophet of a New Christianity?* (1931); *Harnack and Troeltsch: Two Historical Theologians* (1968); and, in collaboration with his wife Marion Pauck, *Paul Tillich: His Life and Thought* (1976).

Pauck's most important achievement and enduring legacy is that he transmitted to North America the great tradition of Reformation scholarship that had emerged in his native Germany during the first half of the twentieth century. Famed as a virtuoso lecturer and a wise director of graduate students, he trained, at Chicago and New York, two generations of the leading American historical theologians and Reformation scholars. Thus, through his writings and classroom teaching, Pauck exercised an extraordinary influence on American Protestantism, enabling it to recover its Reformation roots in a form suited to its contemporary situation.

BIBLIOGRAPHY

For additional information, see Marion Pauck's "Wilhelm Pauck: A Biographical Essay" and "Bibliography of the Published Writings of Wilhelm Pauck," in *Interpreters of Luther: Essays in Honor of Wilhelm Pauck*, edited by Jaroslav Pelikan (Philadelphia, 1968), in which there appears also Pelikan's "Wilhelm Pauck: A Tribute." Other tributes to Pauck and appraisals of his career are collected in *In Memory of Wilhelm Pauck (1901–1981)*, edited by me (New York, 1982). Pauck's thought, in midcareer, was considered by David Wesley Soper in *Major Voices in American Theology*, vol. 2, *Men Who Shape Belief* (Philadelphia, 1955), pp. 980–111.

David W. Lotz

PAUL VI (Giovanni Battista Montini, 1897–1978), pope of the Roman Catholic church during most of the Second Vatican Council and the years immediately after it. Born to influential and prosperous parents in Concesio, near Brescia, Italy, the sickly young Giovanni was nurtured in an encompassing church environment and groomed for leadership beginning with his seminary career. By the time he was ordained in 1920 he had already begun making friends and adopting styles that were to be conducive to a diplomatic career in the church.

Pius XII wanted to name Montini a cardinal in 1953, but he declined this honor until 1958, when John XXIII endowed him with the title. Pius had earlier appointed the scholarly, diplomatic-minded cleric archbishop of Milan, a key post. Yet it was his years in the Vatican Secretariat of State, to which he had been related through various positions for three decades, that best prepared Montini for the papal vocation to which his colleagues in the cardinalite named him on 21 June 1963.

The first and generally disappointing session of the Second Vatican Council, called by John XXIII to effect reform and renewal in the church, had occurred in autumn of 1962. It now fell to Paul VI to authorize its continuation and to preside over it through three more sessions. Montini's previous reputation would have seen him acting far more in continuity with the conservative, cautious ways of Pius XII than with the bold and disruptive styles of John XXIII. Yet, though he always remained conservative and cautious, he did help create a climate in which the bishops undertook actions that promoted *aggiornamento*, the creative shaking up and rearrangement that John had hoped for from the council.

Through the three remaining sessions, council decrees supported ecumenism, a more open attitude toward other religions *(Nostra aetate)*, a collegiality of a sort that implied a sharing of papal power with the bishops, and many internal reforms. Paul seemed to sense more than did many of the reformers that it would not be easy to administer and lead a church in transition to the modern world. While Paul shared a passion to make the church at home in this world, he also felt distanced from secular life and warned against an easy embrace of contemporary values.

Though Paul VI was instinctively reluctant to be an iconoclast, his papacy did initiate many practices that assured continuance of conciliar styles. He worked continuously to reform the Curia, the network of Vatican congregations and offices that surrounds the pope. He changed the often repressive Congregation of the Holy Office to a somewhat more judicious Sacred Congregation for the Doctrine of Faith. He gave it more positive assignments than the old Holy Office, which had been associated chiefly with prohibiting suspicious books through the Index of Forbidden Books *(Index prohibitorum librorum)*.

More important, Paul continued renewal by establishing a Synod of Bishops, whose second meeting in 1969 was as successful as its first one in 1967 had been fumbling and inauspicious. Subsequent meetings of this synod occurred in 1971, 1974, and 1977. At each of these the pope found means to exert pressure for more change and then to counterbalance it, by example and injunction, to hold to tradition where possible.

Reform of the Curia and promotion of synods, his most important works inside the Vatican, were less visible to the church or to the public than other activities for which Paul VI is remembered and through which he left an indelible stamp on the papacy. Most visible was his personal manner. The second regularly televised pope, he was the first to be televised throughout his entire papal career, and he was the first pope to ride in an airplane. He was the subject of extensive media coverage because of the way Vatican II had projected the papacy into the center of religious and political affairs. The pope's image was that of a studious academic, a sober and often mournful figure who bore the weight of many burdens, a leader who cautioned against reckless change.

Of change there was plenty. Priests by the thousands were leaving the priesthood to go into secular work and often to marry. Their move depleted the work force and symbolized decline in the older-style clerical church. Paul took these losses personally and warned remaining priests not to have romantic notions that the church could live without faithful priests or that those who left the priesthood—or the convent, for that matter, since many members of religious orders of women were also leaving them—could accomplish as much for Christ outside their office as in them. Yet he was not able to slow the exodus from the priesthood and the orders.

Paul compensated for some of these losses by giving the church a far more positive image in the eyes of those who had once regarded it, and especially its papal leadership, as alien and self-enclosed. He became the "pilgrim pope," who in a sequence of travels deftly displayed the best his church and he as pope had to offer. In 1964 Paul broke precedent by embracing Patriarch Athenagoras during a trip to Israel, a pilgrimage rich in symbolism for both Judaism and Orthodox Christianity. The papacy had long symbolized to Jews the focus of anti-Jewish thought and action. Paul VI made efforts to enlarge upon the Vatican Council's new spirit toward Jews. Meanwhile, Roman Catholicism and Eastern Orthodoxy, having been severed from each other for nine hundred years, in symbol and in spirit came closer together through the papal and patriarchal embrace in Israel than they had at any previous time during those centuries.

Paul's early travels, during which he reached out to Judaism and, more, to Orthodoxy, showed the thrust of his papacy: for all his cautions, he is remembered as an ecumenical pioneer. First, he encouraged "secular ecumenism" by inaugurating a Vatican Secretariat for Nonbelievers and reached to other faiths in 1964 by appointing a Secretariat for Relations with Non-Christian Religions. He followed up his approach to Orthodoxy with a stop in Turkey in 1967, again to see Athenagoras. He also visited the headquarters of the Orthodox and Protestant World Council of Churches in Geneva, Switzerland, in 1969. His words and actions showed that he saw great differences between Roman Catholic and other Christians, yet he would not let these hinder his efforts to improve relations.

Second, the pilgrim pope's travels let him indicate other directions he would take the church. At the council he clearly wanted to be known as the pope of the poor and, after it, a pope of peace. To this end, in another trip without precedent, he traveled to New York to address the United Nations in 1965. Diplomats were constantly welcomed at the Vatican, always with an interest in seeing whether Paul VI's interventions might promote justice, distribution of resources, and peace. To anyone who observed, it was clear that the papacy henceforth would not be perceived as participating in world affairs only to advance its own ends. His letter *Populorum progressio* in 1967 revealed his lifelong interest in social justice and seemed to be such a departure from Vatican conservatism that in America the *Wall Street Journal* called it "warmed-over Marxism." Needless to say, Paul was radically removed from the religious or antireligious ideology of Marxism, against which he constantly cautioned.

Third, his travels allowed Paul to combine ecumenical and internationalist issues by showing his interest in church and society in developing nations. His trips were to take him to Asia in 1964, to Colombia in 1968, to Uganda in 1969, and to a number of nations (including the Philippines, where an assassin threatened him) in 1970. His efforts to deal with the poor in these nations and elsewhere were compromised in the eyes of his critics by his resistance to birth control and population planning as means of limiting hunger and misery.

Birth control was a controversial issue also within the church. In 1968 Paul went against the advice of the majority of his chosen counselors on the subject and in his letter *Humanae vitae* upheld the tradition of his predecessors, who had condemned what they called "artificial" birth control. Theologians in many nations subsequently spoke out in open revolt. Many bishops and priests had difficulties administering the church in congruence with *Humanae vitae.* Polls showed that in several nations the large majority of Roman Catholic couples did practice such birth control—a sign, to the pope, of a disobedience that became as great a burden as did the defection of priests.

Humanae vitae symbolized the efforts of Paul VI to slow change in the church. In 1967 his *Sacerdotalis caelibatus* emphatically insisted on celibacy for Latin-rite priests and dashed the hopes of those who desired some change in this concept. It was clear through these letters that the pope wanted to balance his ecumenical and diplomatic image as a flexible leader with an internal or churchly posture that would resist many kinds of compromise with the modern world. In a disciplined way, however, he also set the church on a fresh course, making it impossible for his successors to return it to its sequestered and self-defensive pre–Vatican II styles.

BIBLIOGRAPHY

The collected writings and addresses of Paul VI to the midway point in his papacy are to be found in *The Teachings of Pope Paul VI,* 11 vols. (New York, 1968–1979), but a more condensed version of these is *The Mind of Paul VI on the Church and the World,* edited by James Walsh (Milwaukee, 1964), with emphasis on Montini's religious ideas prior to his election as pontiff. The most readable of the early biographies is Corrado Pallenberg's *The Making of a Pope* (New York, 1964), which avoids hagiographical tendencies if not uncritical enthusiasms; Michael Serafian's *The Pilgrim* (New York, 1964) avoids neither but provides ample detail for an understanding of Paul's 1964 embrace of Eastern Orthodoxy and the "third world" of developing nations. Insight into the pope's character, personality, and theological thought is provided by a series of interviews entitled *The Pope Speaks: Dialogues of Paul VI with Jean Guitton,* translated by Anne Fremantle and Christopher Fremantle (London, 1968). An interesting and informative study of the administrative aspect of Paul's papacy and its link with previous administrations is Peter Nichols's *The Politics of the Vatican* (London, 1968). The best English-language source compiling contemporary evaluations of Paul's major contributions and/or missteps is *Paul VI: Critical Appraisals,* edited by James F. Andrews (New York, 1970). After the pontiff's trip to New York and the United Nations, a number of pictorial essays and journalistic accounts of the event appeared. None is outstanding, but Bill Adler's *Pope Paul in the United States: His Mission for Peace on Earth, October 4, 1965* (New York, 1965) is as good as any.

MARTIN E. MARTY

PAUL THE APOSTLE (d. AD 62), also called Paul of Tarsus, known to Jewish Christians as Saul; Christian apostle and saint. Paul was a controversial missionary who provoked intense opposition both during his career and after. His letters, which make up a substantial portion of the New Testament canon, stimulated diverse reactions and attracted problematic adherents to his beliefs. Modern research has uncovered the efforts of the post-Pauline church to soften his legacy of theological radicalism. [*See* Biblical Literature, *article on* New Testament.]

Some of Paul's letters, such as *1 Corinthians* and *2 Corinthians,* were edited a generation after Paul's death in an effort to mold them in directions suitable for the conservative consolidation of Christianity. Other letters, for example, *1 Timothy, 2 Timothy,* and *Titus,* were composed in Paul's name to serve the same purposes. In addition, several interpolations, such as *1 Corinthians* 14:33b–36 and *Romans* 16:17–20, skew Paul's message in authoritarian and sexually chauvinistic directions. *Acts of the Apostles* also presents a conservative picture of Paul.

The result is that the indisputably genuine letters *(Romans, 1 Corinthians, 2 Corinthians, Galatians, Philippians, Philemon, 1 Thessalonians,* and, with less unanimity, *2 Thessalonians)* have traditionally been interpreted in light of the later writings. This has resulted in serious confusions concerning Paul's theology, his relations with his churches and with other early Christian leaders, his outlook on major ethical issues, and the chronology of his life. Scholars have tended to be divided along ideological lines in resolving these issues, eliminating the possibility of consensus even on the most elemental facts about Paul's life.

Another problem is the tradition of theological abstraction in interpreting the Pauline letters. Because Christian theology has been shaped so largely by Pauline thought, the tendency has been to argue over every nuance, on the premise that Paul was a systematic theorist setting down doctrinal truth for all time. In fact, his letters are highly situational responses to complex congregational problems. The letters should be interpreted in light of those social realities, requiring the interpreter to reconstruct the situation largely on the basis of evidence within the letters themselves. This is rendered more difficult by traditional scholarly biases against the charismatic, sectarian, apocalyptic, and mystical experiences that animated Paul and his communities. Modern scholarship has detected the longstanding "fallacy of idealism," to use Bengt Holmberg's expression in *Paul and Power* (Philadelphia, 1978), by which Paul's theological response to problems arising from these sectarian communities has been wrongly interpreted as if it were the structuring principle of those communities.

The application of modern research techniques has allowed the apostle Paul to emerge from the mists of later orthodoxy and hagiography so that the fusion of his charismatic religious experience, his cooperative missionary activities, and his dialogical theology can be grasped. In contrast to traditional preferences that still persist among interpreters, Paul's view of salvation was cosmic rather than individualistic. His worldview was apocalyptic rather than bourgeois. He participated along with his churches in sectarian experiences of radical transformation, spiritual enthusiasm, and the expectation of future vindication. The preaching that evoked those experiences is accessible only by inferences from his letters, while his theology was the inspired but largely impromptu response to missional and congregational imperatives. The vitality and profundity of Paul's occasional remarks in the letters led to recognition of "the genius of Paul," which is the title of Samuel Sandmel's significant study (Philadelphia, 1979).

Life, Thought, and Work. In order to break from the framework of *Acts* and the later writings of the Pauline school, it is necessary to reconstruct Paul's career primarily from the authentic letters.

From Pharisee to Christian missionary. The evidence in *Philippians* 3:3–4 and *Galatians* 1:13–24 indicates that Paul came from a Hellenistic-Jewish family in the Diaspora. His zeal for the law and his persecution of early Christians in Diaspora synagogues as heretics place him close to the school of Shammai in the Pharisee party. [*See* Pharisees.] If he ever studied under Gamli'el the Elder as reported in *Acts* 22:3, he rejected his teacher's tolerance. Because he was a complete stranger to residents of Judaea (*Gal.* 1:22), it is likely that Paul was educated in Tarsus rather than Jerusalem. His Roman citizenship and his mastery of Greek, including a sophisticated grasp of Greco-Roman rhetoric, indicate he came from a prominent family that had rendered loyal service to the empire and was in a position to offer him a classical as well as a Hebrew education. Paul's trade of tent making, probably learned in the family shop, allowed him thereafter a degree of independence as a journeyman leatherworker, according to Ronald F. Hock in *The Social Context of Paul's Ministry* (Philadelphia, 1980).

In the two laconic references to his conversion in AD 34 (*1 Cor.* 15:8, *Gal.* 1:15–17), Paul alludes to a theophanic experience of encountering the risen Christ on the road to Damascus. In the context of his persecution of diaspora Christians as violators of synagogal legalism, this encounter indicated that Jesus, who had been crucified for lawlessness and blasphemy, was indeed the promised Messiah. The correctness of Jesus' message and the sin of his persecutors were proven by his resurrection and appearance to Paul. Paul's robust and confident commitment to legal obedience as the path to the messianic kingdom, characteristic of Phariseeism, was therefore shattered and replaced by a mystical identification with the Messiah (*Phil.* 3:4–8).

Krister Stendahl is correct in insisting that Paul's references to the Damascus experience preclude any interpretation in terms of resolving guilt concerning Paul's previous performance as a Pharisee. "There is no indication that psychologically Paul had some problem of conscience," producing a conversion along the lines of Augustine or Luther, Stendahl writes in *Paul among Jews and Gentiles* (Philadelphia, 1976, p. 13). Paul speaks of being "called" rather than converted, impelled by the encounter with the risen Christ to become a missionary to lawless gentiles (*Gal.* 1:15–16). Paul's zeal for the law changed into its opposite: a commitment to the inclusion of gentiles in the messianic community without imposing the burden of the law. Paul's previous intolerant exclusion of "heretics" was transformed into a lifelong commitment to messianic pluralism so offensive to zealous legalists that from that moment on Paul became the target of reprisals (*1 Thes.* 2:2, 14–16).

In the seven to eight years after his Damascus experience, Paul was aligned with the Hellenistic Christians of Arabia, Syria, and Cilicia who had been driven out of

Jerusalem after the martyrdom of Stephen (*1 Thes.* 1:15, *Acts* 8:1–4). Accepting their version of Christianity, which was critical of the Temple cult, legalistic obedience, and racial-religious zealotism, Paul became an artisan-missionary involved in creating charismatic communities of faith consisting of Jews and gentiles (*Gal.* 1:23, 2:12–16). Troubles with political authorities, which began quite early in his career (cf. *2 Cor.* 11:32–33), were probably provoked by the highly charged, sectarian apocalypticism that marked these radical communities. For a brief period of fifteen days, he visited the apostle Peter in Jerusalem (*Gal.* 1:18–20), but in Paul's letters there is no evidence of theological influence from the more conservative branch of early Christianity. By the early 40s, Paul was working in cooperation with the dynamic center of Hellenistic Christianity in Antioch. Sharing their commitment to interracial, charismatic leadership (*Acts* 13:1), to intense community life of prayer and ecstatic worship (*Acts* 13:2–4), and to the eucharistic meal as an expression of unity (*Gal.* 2:12–16), Paul became one of the leaders in the first organized mission to Cyprus and southern Galatia around the years 43–45 (*Acts* 13–14).

Judging from Paul's earliest references to his missionary preaching (*1 Thes.* 1:9–10, 2:9–13), his message centered in the apocalyptic dawn of a new age that opened salvation to gentiles. The "gospel of God" included an exposure of idolatry and a promise of escape "from the wrath to come." The resurrection of Jesus and the expectation of his return are given prominent expression. The invitation of gentiles to "faith in God" (*1 Thes.* 1:8) without the imposition of the law implies a substantial break with Pharisaic Judaism as well as with conservative Jewish Christianity in Jerusalem. Yet at this early stage there is no indication of a systematic critique of the law; in fact, a positive assessment of legal holiness is visible as late as AD 50 in *1 Thessalonians* 4:1–8, a position consistent with the negative view of "lawlessness" in *2 Thessalonians* 2:3, 7, 8. The hostile reactions of Jewish zealots to Paul's early preaching (*1 Thes.* 2:15–16; *Acts* 13:45, 13:50, 14:2–5, 14:19) can be understood on the grounds of the inclusion of despised gentiles, without assuming the abrasive rhetoric of Paul's later teaching about freedom from the law.

Beginning in approximately AD 46, Paul entered a fully independent phase of missionizing. While two earlier colleagues traveled to Cyprus, apparently with the support of the Antioch church, Paul, Silas, and Timothy struck off for the west (*1 Thes.* 1:1, *Acts* 16:6–12). Revisiting the churches of Cilicia and southern Galatia, they spent as much as a year in the northern Galatia cities of Ancyra, Pessinus, and Germa founding several churches (*Gal.* 1:2) of purely gentile members of Gallo-Grecian background (*Gal.* 3:1) despite an illness that Paul suffered at this time (*Gal.* 4:13–15). A period of shifting plans followed, in which Paul and his colleagues were dissuaded from traveling to the populous provinces of Asia and Bithynia. They ended up in Troas, where a church was founded (*Acts* 16:8–10, 20:6–12) and where they were joined by the author, traditionally identified as Luke, of the "we-source" material in the second half of *Acts*.

Sailing to Europe in the spring of AD 48, they founded the important congregation in Philippi. Predominantly gentile in background, this church entered into a formal arrangement with Paul, forming what J. Paul Sampley has called "a consensual partnership in Christ for preaching the gospel" (*Pauline Partnership in Christ*, Philadelphia, 1980, p. 51). Paul thereafter received financial support from Philippi for the extended activities of an increasing circle of missionary colleagues while continuing to work as a tent maker. Among the male and female co-workers whose names are known to us from this period are Timothy, Titus, Silas, Luke, Epaphroditus, Clement, Euodia, and Syntyche, along with local patrons and patronesses such as the Philippian jailor and Lydia. The charismatic, apocalyptic piety of this congregation contained some divisive tendencies (*Phil.* 4:2–3) and it experienced a traumatic expulsion of heretical libertinists during the founding mission (*Phil.* 3:17–20). The Philippian mission came to an end in the spring or summer of 49 with a humiliating episode of mob violence followed by judicial beating and imprisonment (*1 Thes.* 2:2, *Acts* 16:19–40).

Continuing in a westward direction after the expulsion from Philippi, Paul and his traveling companions arrived in Thessalonica, where a rapidly expanding ministry was cut short after several months by riotous opposition from the local synagogue (*Acts* 17:1–9; *1 Thes.* 2:14–17). A congregation marked by enthusiastic radicalism was formed out of Jewish and gentile converts, including a house-church patron by the name of Jason and several prominent women. Because the Thessalonian letters were composed so quickly after Paul's departure, we gain a vivid picture of a freshly established congregation. It was troubled by conflicts over sexual irregularities (*1 Thes.* 4:1–8), the status and control of ecstatic forms of worship (*1 Thes.* 5:19–22), and tensions between leaders and followers (*1 Thes.* 5:12–13). A key factor in these troubles was the misunderstanding of Pauline apocalypticism (*1 Thes.* 5:1–11, *2 Thes.* 2:1–12), which ultimately led to the incredible announcement by a Thessalonian ecstatic that "the day of the Lord has already come" (*2 Thes.* 2:2). Apparently the radicals interpreted their experience of the spirit in a way that made them believe that history had come to an end. Some of these leaders had dropped out of their daily occupations to be supported by the congregation as full-time charismatics, free from restraint (*1 Thes.* 5:14, *2 Thes.* 3:6–15). This highly inflated enthusiasm was severely shaken by the unexpected violence that had forced Paul to leave Thessalonica and thereafter resulted in the harassment and death of congregational members. Having erroneously concluded that the age of the spirit had released them from the risks of history, these shock waves led to the crisis addressed by Paul's first congregational letters composed in the spring of AD 50.

Paul's letters were written as a substitute for his personal presence, as emergency efforts to resolve congregational issues that neither he nor his traveling colleagues could deal with in person. The creativity and power of these letters are the result of his efforts to improvise responses to the unique and highly volatile situations that marked the sectarian congregations he had helped to found. In the case of *1 Thessalonians*, the innovations are immediately apparent. Building the argument into the most broadly extended thanksgiving in the annals of Greco-Roman or Hebrew letter-writing, Paul clarified the realistic potential of the charismatic faith, hope, and love that the congregation had experienced (*1 Thes.* 1:2–3:13). Rather than eliminating the "old" age of persecution and labor for daily bread, such ecstatic experiences provided the means to face life with courage and realism. But Paul's confident statements of hope and his effort to explain a traditional Judaic apocalyptic scheme to a Hellenistic audience led to the misunderstanding of the first letter, which was taken to support the view that the end of history had indeed occurred (*2 Thes.* 2:2). Paul's second letter to the Thessalonians was apparently composed shortly thereafter to summarize the message of the earlier letter and to squelch the ecstatic understanding of eschatology.

The Thessalonian crisis shows that Paul's missionary success was in part the cause of the troubles that marked his career (see *2 Cor.* 11:23–29, 6:3–10). The intense religious fervor evoked by his proclamation broke down traditional restraints to create interracial and multiclass congregations with strong but immediately divisive charismatic leadership. Sectarian congregations with this level of social innovation and a consciousness of having been redeemed from a corrupt environment naturally became the target of reprisals by synagogal and civil authorities as well as by neighbors and family members. This pattern of successful mission, provoking strong local opposition, repeated itself in the short Beroean ministry in the early fall of AD 49 (*Acts* 17:10–14). After a less successful effort to establish a congregation in Athens (*Acts* 17:33–34), Paul came in the winter to Corinth, where he began a ministry of eighteen months with the most formative and troubled congregation in his career.

The Corinthian ministry appears to have had a decisive influence on the evolution of Paul's theology. The scope of this evolution can be measured by comparing the Thessalonian letters, written at the beginning of the Corinthian ministry, with the Corinthian correspondence, which was composed five to six years later. The Corinthian correspondence deals in part with conflicts between forms of apostolic teaching. Many of Paul's most distinctive ideas appear to have arisen out of the interaction with the Corinthians: the church as the "body of Christ"; marriage as mutual submission "in the body"; respect for conscience even when it is ill-informed; the theology of the cross in dialectic with human wisdom on the one side and human weakness on the other; and the superiority of love over faith or hope.

The social context for Paul's Corinthian ministry was a series of house churches under the patronage of middle- or upper-class leaders such as Prisca and Aquila, Jason, Chloe, Stephanas, and Titius Justus. According to Gerd Theissen in *The Social Setting of Pauline Christianity* (Philadelphia, 1982), it is likely that these socially superior leaders practiced a kind of loving patriarchalism in their sponsorship of socially diverse churches. Competition between house churches came to focus on their different attachments to early Christian missionaries who functioned alongside Paul. This helps to explain the subsequent evolution of parties that boasted the superiority of their particular traditions: "'I belong to Paul' or 'I belong to Apollos' or 'I belong to Cephas' [i.e., Peter] or 'I belong to Christ'" (*1 Cor.* 1:12). The latter group, claiming to transcend human leaders, was most likely proto-gnostic in outlook, providing radical challenges to Pauline teachings and ethics. The forces dividing the Corinthians also included racial and cultural diversity, as well as the lack of space for all the house churches to meet together regularly, as shown by the archaeological evidence of Jerome M. O'Connor (*St. Paul's Corinth*, Wilmington, Del., 1983, pp. 155–158). The strategic location of Corinth as a commercial and transit center and the large crowds drawn to the biennial Isthmian Games contributed to the recruitment of co-workers and the establishment of churches in satellite cities, for example, Cenchreae under the patronage of Phoebe (see *Rom.* 16:1–2). The Corinthian ministry ended with a judicial hearing of charges raised by influential members of the local synagogue. Paul was arraigned before Gallio, the proconsul of Achaea (*Acts* 18:12–17) whose tenure in Corinth provides one of the reliable dates in the reconstruction of Pauline chronology. Because Paul was free to return to Corinth, he must have been exonerated, but he left Corinth soon after the hearing to take part in the apostolic conference at Jerusalem, one of the crucial events in the history of first-century Christianity.

The Judaizer crisis and its aftermath. The background of the apostolic conference (AD 51) was a campaign to circumcise gentile Christians and thus incorporate them into a Jewish-Christian mode of adherence to the Torah. *Acts* 15:1 provides a reliable account of the origin and content of this campaign: "But some men came down [to Antioch] from Judaea and were teaching the brethren, 'Unless you are circumcised according to the custom of Moses, you cannot be saved.'" Paul's account of the conference in *Galatians* 2:1–10 reflects the mortal threat this campaign posed against the "freedom" of gentile Christians to live without the burden of the Torah and to enjoy an inclusive fellowship with Jewish Christians despite differences in lifestyle. Some of the motivations for the sudden interest of the Judean Christians in the affairs of the Antioch church are alluded to with considerable sarcasm in *Galatians* 6:12–13. Wishing to avoid persecution "for the cross of Christ," the Judeans wanted to "make a good showing" to some unnamed third party by getting the gentiles circumcised. The most likely explanation for the Judaizer campaign was the Zealot pressure that was intensifying during the procuratorship of Ventidius Cumanus (48–52), enforcing conformity with the law and acceptance of circumcision along with noncommunication with the uncircumcised. That the Christian communities in Judaea had experienced such violent pressures is revealed in *2 Thessalonians* 1:14–16. The promotion of circumcision among gentile Christians thus promised to relieve the threat of persecution. But Paul saw that this temporary expedient would shatter the hopes of a successful gentile mission and destroy the inclusive quality of Christian fellowship between Jews and gentiles. His key doctrine of justification by faith rather than by works such as circumcision emerged out of this crisis, providing a distinctive and radical cast to all of his later theology. While claiming in *Galatians* 2:15–16 that all Christians, including Jewish Christians, "know that a man is not justified by works of the law but through faith in Jesus Christ," Paul insists on the antithesis "not by works" as the essential premise of "freedom."

In Paul's version of the apostolic conference, he was supported by Barnabas, the key leader of the Antioch church, and Titus, an uncircumcised gentile Christian, in providing an account of "the gospel which I preach among the gentiles" (*Gal.* 2:2). The leaders of the Judean churches—James, Peter, and John—acknowledged the truth of this message and the fact that its success among gentiles provided divine confirmation (*Gal.* 2:8). They agreed on a practical division of the mission along cultural lines, "that we should go to the gentiles and they to the circumcised" (*Gal.* 2:9), but that the gentile churches would undertake a financial campaign to aid the impoverished Christians in Judaea. Despite the continued opposition of a Judaizer faction, which Paul castigates as "false brethren," the integrity of the gentile mission was preserved.

The question of coexistence of Jews and gentiles in the worship life of local churches was left unresolved. Herein lay the seeds of later controversies, because Paul understood the agreement in principle on the legitimacy of his gospel to mean the acceptance of equality and solidarity between Jewish and gentile Christians. Shortly after the apostolic conference this issue came to a head when a delegation sent by James prevailed on Peter not to eat with gentile Christians at Antioch. Paul accused Peter and the other Jewish Christians at Antioch of insincerity and inconsistency in forsaking the common meal that had been a crucial element of the inclusive form of the faith at Antioch. The repercussions of this conflict are visible throughout Paul's subsequent ministry in his attempts to defend the integrity of his gospel and his apostolicity against pressures ranging from political expediency to violent opposition against the doctrine of freedom from the law.

Paul's letter to the Galatians, written in AD 53, reflects an intensification of the Judaizer crisis after the apostolic conference. A delegation of Judaizers was sent by the "false brethren" in Judaea to the exclusively gentile churches in northern Galatia, arriving there shortly after Paul had revisited these congregations on his journey from Antioch to Ephesus. As reconstructed from his highly polemical defense in *Galatians,* the emissaries proposed circumcision as a means to gain perfection and enter into the mystical promise of being "sons of Abraham" (*Gal.* 3:6–18). They advocated conformity to Jewish festivals by sanctioning their role in appeasing the astrological powers (*Gal.* 4:9–10). They insinuated that Paul himself had previously preached such conformity to the law as derived from the Jerusalem apostles, but that he had trimmed the gospel to win quick converts (*Gal.* 1:10–14, 1:18–2:2, 5:11).

Paul angrily refuted these allegations and provided a systematic defense of the freedom of the gospel. He contended that the charismatic experience of the Galatians proved that salvation comes through faith in the gospel rather than by works of the law (*Gal.* 3:1–5). Scripture itself reveals the correctness of this message, because Abraham's faith "was reckoned to him as righteousness" (*Gen.* 15:6) and the principle from *Habakkuk* 2:4 is that the just shall live by faith (*Gal.* 3:6–14). Paul went on to show that the status of being "sons of God" was conferred by faith through baptism so that a new relationship of solidarity developed among racially, economically, and sexually distinct groups (*Gal.* 3:26–29). To accept the law as binding for salvation was therefore to repudiate Christ and to again become enslaved to the principalities and powers of paganism (*Gal.* 4:1–11).

An explosive allegory concerning the two sons of Abraham was developed to show that the slave Hagar corresponds to the Jerusalem of the Judaizers, bringing a flesh-bound oppression against the children of the free woman, Sarah (*Gal.* 4:21–31). Thus the antitheses of flesh versus spirit, slavery versus freedom, and law versus promise were related to an ongoing political and ideological struggle in the church, now seen as a conflict between "the present Jerusalem" and the "Jerusalem above." The crucial issue of freedom was then used as the leitmotiv of the moral exhortation of *Galatians* 5:1–6:10. According to Hans Dieter Betz, the thrust of this argument is that "'freedom in Christ' is a gift of God, but a delicate one. It is a gift, but it is not to be taken for granted. Freedom exists only insofar as people live in freedom. . . . Those who were liberated by the Spirit can protect their freedom only by 'walking by the Spirit'. . ." (*A Commentary on Paul's Letter to the Churches in Galatia*, Philadelphia, 1979, p. 32).

Whether Paul's powerful argument was convincing to the Galatians is an open question, in light of their nonparticipation in the Jerusalem offering and the lack of evidence about their later activities. The Judaizer movement continued to be a threat to Pauline congregations, as evidenced by the polemical warning in Paul's next letter, the letter to the Philippians (3:2–6), probably written from an Ephesian prison in the winter of 54–55. A modified form of the Galatian argument also appears in Paul's last extant letter, the letter to the Romans. The political pressures from the increasingly violent Zealot movement in the diaspora communities as well as in Judaea also directly affected Paul's mission. The results were riots, charges of subversion, and plots against his life (e.g., *Acts* 20:3, 23:12–22).

The ministry in Asia. From the latter part of AD 52 through the next several years, Paul's center of missionary activities was Ephesus, the administrative and commercial hub of the province of Asia. An intensification of the collegial mission during these years involved Prisca and Aquila, who had moved from Corinth to establish their business in the new location in support of the expanding activities. Other colleagues, such as Apollos, Archippus, Aristarchus, Demas, Epaenetus, Epaphras, Erastus, Jesus Justus, Luke, Mark, Silas, Timothy, Titus, Trophimus, and Tychichus, are mentioned in the writings deriving from this period. Their activities account for the establishment of satellite churches in such cities as Laodicea, Hierapolis, and Colossae.

Perhaps for the first time in his career Paul had access in Ephesus to a larger facility, the Hall of Tyrannus (*Acts* 19:9), but he appears to have maintained his regimen as a self-supporting artisan. The availability of rapid communications between Ephesus and the cities of the Aegean Sea as well as of the hinterland brought Paul into the vortex of competing leaders, church conflicts, and societal pressures that marked the first generation of Christianity. This vivid description pertains to the Asian years:

> danger from my own people, danger from gentiles, danger in the city, danger in the wilderness, danger at sea, danger from false brethren; in toil and hardship, through many a sleepless night, in hunger and thirst, often without food, in cold and exposure. And, apart from other things, there is the daily pressure upon me of my anxiety for all the churches. Who is weak, and I am not weak? Who is made to fall, and I am not indignant? (*2 Cor.* 11:26–29)

The controversies involving the "weak" and the "falling," as well as the threats from Jews and gentiles, resulted in Paul's writing a number of letters during the Asian period, including those to the Galatians, the Philippians, the Colossians, Philemon, and the Corinthians. *Philippians* was drafted during an incarceration that apparently followed the riot described in *1 Corinthians* 15:32 and *Acts* 19:23–41. It reflects conflicts with heretical libertinists, roving Judaizers, and rival missionaries who took advantage of Paul's imprisonment by insinuating that his inflammatory gospel imperiled the future of the church. In the opening chapter, Paul gives thanks that the Philippians have shared in the suffering, conflicts, and growth of the gospel. Then on the basis of an early Christian hymn cited in *Philippians* 2:6–11, Paul develops a theology of self-emptying love and solidarity capable of resolving conflicts and enduring persecution. He requests cooperation with his emissary Epaphroditus, who is visiting Macedonia while Paul is detained.

After warning about the threat of Judaizers from outside the community (3:2–11) and from libertinists within Philippi itself (3:17–21), Paul urges local leaders Euodia and Syntyche to be reconciled. The theme of apocalyptic urgency and joy is expressed with the memorable lines "Rejoice in the Lord always; again I will say, Rejoice. Let all men know your forbearance. The Lord is at hand" (*Phil.* 4:4–5). The letter ends with thanks for the financial support the Philippians have provided for the activities of the Pauline mission. Resilient joy in the midst of tribulation is the note struck repeatedly in the letters of the Asian period.

The extensive Corinthian correspondence allows us to grasp the issues raised by that congregation as well as the evolving shape of Paul's theology. References in *1 Corinthians* 5:9 and *2 Corinthians* 2:3–9 make it likely that at least four and perhaps as many as seven separate letters are contained in the canonical *1 Corinthians* and *2 Corinthians.* Reconstructions of the interaction between Paul and the controversialists make it likely that the opening issues related to shifts in sexual roles, disturbances in the celebrations of the Lord's Supper, and the rise of sectarian divisiveness. In *1 Corinthians* 11:2–34 Paul argues the abandonment of sexual differentiation in the form of women adopting male hairstyles to express their powerful new sense of equality in the church. Paul argues that men and women should retain culturally determined indications of sexual differentiation even while leading Christian worship, but he does not question the right of women to play an equal part.

The problem of sacramental disorder was closely related to class differences that arose in connection with the common meal. In *The Social Setting of Pauline Christianity,* Gerd Theissen has related this problem to the pattern of Greco-Roman banquets in which upper-class hosts treated guests "differently depending on their social status" (p. 58). Since poorer members of the congregation would be humiliated by such practices, Paul is indignant at the violation of the unity of the church. The peculiar warning that those eating and drinking without "discerning the body" would fall under divine judgment (*1 Cor.* 11:29) makes it likely that theological issues were mixed with sociological factors in this instance. Walter Schmithals has suggested that spiritualists critical of the bodily elements in the sacramental meal aimed "to sabotage the cultic observation and to transform it into . . . a profane feast" (*Gnosticism in Corinth,* Nashville, 1971, p. 255). This is rendered more likely by Paul's assertion that the disruptions were connected with theological factions in the congregation (see *1 Cor.* 11:18–19).

The next phase of the Corinthian controversy involved resistance against traditionally Judaic sexual ethics, a rejection of the doctrine of the bodily resurrection, and an interpretation of the sacrament as a kind of spiritual medicine of immortality. Paul responds to the report of these developments brought by Stephanas, Fortunatus, and Achaicus (*1 Cor.* 16:17) by developing a concept of the body as the basis of human identity and relationship. Against the gnostic tendency to downplay the significance of bodily relations, Paul insists that "the body is for the Lord and the Lord is for the body" (*1 Cor.* 6:13), which means that casual sexual liaisons are excluded. Bodily disciplines are therefore required by faith (*1 Cor.* 9:24–27). Sacramental experiences do not relieve persons from such responsibilities (*1 Cor.* 10:1–13) because "sharing in the body of Christ" creates a unity between believers and their Lord that excludes immoral relations with pagan prostitutes and temples (*1 Cor.* 10:14–22).

Gnostic skepticism about the Christian tradition of bodily resurrection is countered by reiterating the early Christian gospel, warranted by the firsthand witnesses of the resurrection of Christ (*1 Cor.* 15:1–19). A new concept of the "spiritual body" is developed to render the doctrine of resurrection less vulnerable to the charge of mindless crudity. The gnostic teaching about the original spiritual Adam of *Genesis* 1 degenerating into the bodily Adam of *Genesis* 2–3 is repudiated by insisting that Christ is the second Adam, the spiritual redeemer from heaven (*1 Cor.* 15:35–41). The hope of Christians is that "as we have borne the image of the man of dust, we shall also bear the image of the man from heaven," that is, Christ (*1 Cor.* 15:49).

Responding to reports from "Chloe's people" (*1 Cor.* 1:12) about divisions in the congregation and to a list of controversial questions they had brought, Paul wrote the so-called answer letter from Ephesus just prior to Pentecost AD 54. The prideful wisdom that lay behind the competition among house churches in Corinth was contrasted with the word of the cross and the experience of humble hearers transformed by it. "God chose what is low and despised in the world, even things that are not, to bring to nothing things that are, so that no human being might boast in the presence of God" (*1 Cor.* 1:28–29). The gospel of grace brought and nurtured by various apostles aimed at creating a new, unified community animated by the spirit rather than by pride (*1 Cor.* 2:1–4:7). As for the gnostic leader living in arrogant incest, rather than taking pride in his capacity to transcend moral compunctions, the congregation should ban him in the hope that he would see his error (*1 Cor.* 5:1–13).

Responding to questions from the Ephesian congregation about the preferability of platonic marriages, Paul defends marriage as a permanent and mutual covenant to fulfill bodily needs (*1 Cor.* 7:1–24). Paul's own gift of celibacy is well suited to the uncertain conditions of missionizing in the end time, but he insists that each Christian should discover the path of personal responsibility in such matters (*1 Cor.* 7:25–40).

The difficult question about whether Christians should eat food offered to idols is dealt with by a new doctrine of the autonomous conscience. Paul argues that while conscience is socially conditioned, it must be followed as the guarantor of personal integrity. Those whose conscience allows them to eat such food are cautioned not to use their freedom irresponsibly so that the weak are led into destructive violations of their integrity (*1 Cor.* 8:1–13, 10:23–11:1). On the issue of whether glossolalia is the supreme gift or whether it ought to be repressed, Paul develops a doctrine that "there are varieties of gifts, but the same spirit," so that members of the congregation should exercise their various gifts in love for the sake of the common good (*1 Cor.* 12:4–14:40).

After Paul's departure from Ephesus under conditions that made it impossible for him to return, he wrote the later portions of the Corinthian correspondence. In that correspondence he dealt with the revolt stimulated by the arrival of "super-apostles" with a success-oriented theology. The humiliating circumstances of an Ephesian riot and imprisonment, the latter reflected in *Philippians,* may have rendered Paul more vulnerable to the charge that his misfortunes showed the inadequacies of his gospel. Paul admits his limitations on the principle that the treasure of the gospel resides "in earthen vessels" (*2 Cor.* 4:7), but pleads for reconciliation (*2 Cor.* 5:18–6:13, 7:2–4). He then revisited Corinth at the height of the controversy and was summarily dismissed by the congregation, thereupon writing the so-called letter of tears (*2 Cor.* 10:1–13:13), which apparently caused a softening of heart. The plans for collecting the Jerusalem offering were reactivated (*2 Cor.* 9:1–15), and the final phase of the correspondence reflects the "comfort of Christ," which Paul experienced upon meeting Titus in Macedonia the following year with news that the revolt was over (*2 Cor.* 1:3–2:13, 7:5–8:24).

In the meantime Paul had suffered the "affliction in Asia" (*2 Cor.* 1:8), probably the imprisonment reflected in the letter to Philemon, a tactful plea for the freedom of the converted slave Onesimus. During this same imprisonment, Paul apparently helped to plan the letter to the Colossians, which dealt with the threat of gnostic syncretism in churches founded by Paul's missionary colleagues not far from Ephesus.

From Corinth to Rome as diplomat and prisoner. While wintering in Corinth and its neighboring city of Cenchreae in 56–57, Paul developed the plan to deliver the offering to Jerusalem and then to begin a mission westward to Rome and Spain. Working under the patronage of Phoebe (*Rom.* 16:1–2), Paul undertook extensive preparations to become informed about the fragmented and suspicious churches in Rome so as to make possible a cooperative mission in the thoroughly gentile and nonhellenized area of Spain. The letter to the Romans was written to elicit support for this mission, proclaiming the triumphant power of God manifested in the gospel, which reveals that all humans are equal in sin but also in unmerited grace (*Rom.* 1:16–3:31). Although it proved to be Paul's most influential theological statement, the letter to the Romans served the practical purpose of finding a common basis in faith to further cooperation between conservative and liberal factions in Rome.

In contrast to the Corinthian letters, which are a jumbled composite of correspondence over a lengthy period of time, *Romans* is a well-organized and brilliantly composed essay on the theme of the righteousness of God revealed through faith (*Rom.* 1:16–17). That divine righteousness is impartial (*Rom.* 2:11) is the premise on which the status of Jew and gentile is shown to be equal, so that Abraham becomes the "father of all who have faith" (*Rom.* 4:11) rather than merely the progenitor of circumcised Jews. Since all humans are saved by faith rather than by works of self-justification, the baptism of Christians is described as the inauguration of a new life in which slavery to sin and the law has been broken (*Rom.* 6:1–23).

The problem Paul finds with the Jewish law is that it lures humans into aggressive self-righteousness that produces death in place of life (*Rom.* 7:1–25). True righteousness is the gift of God in Christ, inaugurating the new age of the spirit in which the good is accomplished not because it gains something but because it expresses the new status of belonging to "Abba, Father" (*Rom.* 8:1–16). Yet this new life occurs in the midst of a fallen world of decay, sin, and hostility, so faith is sustained by an eschatological hope in the triumph of righteousness by the ongoing experience of the love of God which death itself cannot thwart (*Rom.* 8:17–39). That the bulk of Paul's fellow Jews had not accepted this message does not negate the power of the gospel or the freedom of God over creation (*Rom.* 9:1–29). Despite the zealous resistance of legalists, the gospel will achieve its goal of converting first gentiles and then Jews, unifying the human race under grace: "For God has consigned all men to disobedience, that he may have mercy upon all" (*Rom.* 11:32).

Paul's great letter then takes up the question of ethics, arguing for the principles of responsible love and charismatic equality derived from the shared experience of the "mercies of God" (*Rom.* 12:1–13:14). The special problems of intolerance among the Roman house churches are dealt with by the admonition to pass on the same welcome to each other that they had already experienced in Christ (*Rom.* 14:1–15:7). If that occurs, the world mission that Paul had already brought as far west as Illyricum would have a chance of succeeding in uniting Jews and gentiles, Greeks and barbarians from Jerusalem to Spain, the end of the Mediterranean world (*Rom.* 15:8–33). Paul closes his letter by greeting a wide variety of Roman house churches, leaders, and missionaries, giving diplomatic expression to his lifelong commitment to messianic pluralism (*Rom.* 16:3–23).

Paul's final journey to Jerusalem, in the spring of AD 57, was undertaken against dangerous opposition in order to deliver the offering and thereby seal the unity of the church, which had been fractured by tensions between Jewish and gentile Christians of various persuasions. His plan was to sail from there to Rome. Paul construed the offering as a sign of mutual indebtedness between Jews and gentiles (*Rom.* 15:27), which explains the hostile reactions of Jewish Zealots who plotted his assassination. A substantial delegation of gentile Christians sailed with Paul (*Acts* 20:4) in this diplomatic venture, but the Jerusalem church refused to accept the offering without a legalistic subterfuge (*Acts* 21:24). The Zealot pressure against collaboration with gentiles expressed itself also in a Temple riot when Paul and his delegation arrived, and in a subsequent plot to assassinate him before he could reach the safety of the Roman garrison at Caesarea. Paul suffered an imprisonment of two years duration in Caesarea, at the end of which he appealed his case to the emperor in Rome. Thus he arrived at his desired destination in the spring of AD 60, but in chains. Two years later, when Nero restored the treason law, Paul was summarily executed.

Influence of Paul. The riotous opposition that marked the end of Paul's life was a formative element in the final decades of the first century and in the shaping of the New Testament itself. Right-wing and left-wing factions vied for the legacy of Paul in a struggle that had many counterparts in later Christian history. The splits already visible within Paul's lifetime evolved into full-scale conflicts between gnostic and orthodox congregations, both of which called on Paul as their apostle.

Written in the latter decades of the first century, *Acts* devotes about half its length to a depiction of Paul as a successful missionary who warned against heretics who would later arise (*Acts* 20:28–30). The author of *Acts* includes no references to Paul's controversial letters, his radical doctrines, or his involvement in church conflicts at Corinth, Galatia, Ephesus, Philippi, or Thessalonica. The use of Paul's letters and ideas by left-wing factions was countered by the composition of *1 Timothy, 2 Timothy,* and *Titus* by the Pauline school toward the end of the first century. The Paul of these letters is authoritarian, sober, uncharismatic, and morally conformist, teaching faith as a set of beliefs to be learned rather than as a revolutionary relationship based on unmerited grace. Other epistles, such as *Jude, James,* and *2 Peter,* were drafted to counter libertinistic and gnostic interpretations of Pauline doctrine. The fact that about half the New Testament is directly related to Paul and his story or is written in the epistolary form that he popularized makes it clear that his theology and example provided the raw materials of later controversies. Down to the time of the Christian gnostic Marcion (d. 160?) and beyond, pro- and anti-Paulinists vied for the domination of the Christian mind.

The impact of Pauline thought on later theological revolutions is well known. Augustine, Luther, Calvin, and Wesley, as well as moderns like Barth, Brunner, Bonhoeffer, and Bultmann, were decisively shaped by rediscovering Paul's doctrine of grace, his analysis of the problem of the law, and his revolutionary grasp of the righteousness of God. Their opponents in many instances cited the same materials both within and outside the authentic Pauline corpus that traditionalists in the early church had used. These conflicts leave a permanent stamp on the interpretation of Pauline materials, as shown by Krister Stendahl in *Paul among Jews and Gentiles* (Philadelphia, 1976). Although it is a mistake to view Paul as the second founder of the Christian church, it is true that he remains at the center of its most vital controversies.

[*For further discussion of issues related to Paul's religious context and teachings, see* Christianity and Judaism; Biblical Temple; Israelite Law; Messianism; Rabbinic Judaism in Late Antiquity; *and* Persecution.]

BIBLIOGRAPHY

The best nontechnical introduction to the problem of understanding Paul is Leander E. Keck's *Paul and His Letters* (Philadelphia, 1979). An excellent supplement in more technical style is available in the essays of Nils A. Dahl collected in *Studies in Paul: Theology for the Early Christian Mission* (Minneapolis, 1977). For the sequence of Paul's activities, see my *A Chronology of Paul's Life* (Philadelphia, 1979). A competent though somewhat dated introduction to the problem of interpreting epistolographic materials is William G. Doty's *Letters in Primitive Christianity* (Philadelphia, 1973). A stimulating sketch of Pauline theology is available in Robin Scroggs's *Paul for a New Day* (Philadelphia, 1977), while more detailed treatments from innovative viewpoints are available in J. Christiaan Beker's *Paul the Apostle: The Triumph of God in Life and Thought* (Philadelphia, 1980) and Daniel Patte's *Paul's Faith and the Power of the Gospel: A Structural Introduction to the Pauline Letters* (Philadelphia, 1983). For a more traditional overview, see Frederick F. Bruce's *Paul: Apostle of the Free Spirit* (Exeter, Pa., 1977). Ralph P. Martin explores a theme with broad implications in *Reconciliation: A Study of Paul's Theology* (Atlanta, 1981). Hans Hübner's *Law in Paul's Thought* (Edinburgh, 1983) is a basic study comparable to Victor P. Furnish's *Theology and Ethics in Paul* (Nashville, 1968) and my own work *Paul's Anthropological Terms* (Leiden, 1971). See also Halvor Moxnes's *Theology in Conflict: Studies in Paul's Understanding of God in*

Romans (Leiden, 1980) and my *Christian Tolerance: Paul's Message to the Modern Church* (Philadelphia, 1982).

Alongside works cited in the article above by Holmberg, Hock, O'Connor, Sampley, and Theissen, basic explorations of the social context for Paul's ministry are provided in John H. Schütz's *Paul and the Anatomy of Apostolic Authority* (New York, 1975) and Wayne A. Meeks's *The First Urban Christians: The Social World of the Apostle Paul* (New Haven, 1982). Explorations of the Hebraic setting in W. D. Davies's *Paul and Rabbinic Judaism*, 4th ed. (Philadelphia, 1981) and E. P. Sanders's *Paul and Palestinian Judaism: A Comparison of Patterns of Religion* (Philadelphia, 1977) are matched by Helmut Koester's *Introduction to the New Testament*, 2 vols. (Philadelphia, 1982), which offers the best current summary of the Pauline letters in the context of Greco-Roman culture. Technical articles dealing with the identification of Pauline opponents and the later evolution of his tradition are accessible in *Paul and Paulinism: Essays in Honour of C. K. Barrett*, edited by M. D. Hooker and Stephen G. Wilson (London, 1982). The struggle over the Pauline legacy is reflected in Elaine H. Pagels's *The Gnostic Paul: Gnostic Exegesis of the Pauline Letters* (Philadelphia, 1975) and Dennis R. MacDonald's *The Legend and the Apostle: The Battle for Paul in Story and Canon* (Philadelphia, 1983).

The most significant recent commentaries on Paul's letters are Ernst Käsemann's *Commentary on Romans* (Grand Rapids, Mich., 1980), with bibliographies mainly in German; C. K. Barrett's *A Commentary on the First Epistle to the Corinthians*, 2d ed. (London, 1971), written in nontechnical style; Victor P. Furnish's *II Corinthians* (Garden City, N.Y., 1984), a technical, comprehensive but readable study; Hans Dieter Betz's *Galatians: A Commentary on Paul's Letter to the Churches in Galatia* (Philadelphia, 1979), the definitive commentary on Galatians; and Ralph P. Martin's *Colossians and Philemon* (London, 1974) and Eduard Schweizer's *The Letter to the Colossians: A Commentary* (Minneapolis, 1981), both standard works. Ernest Best's *The First and Second Epistles to the Thessalonians* (London, 1972) and F. W. Beare's *A Commentary on the Epistle to the Philippians* (New York, 1959) are the best available on those letters.

ROBERT JEWETT

PEACE. In a negative sense religious traditions speak of peace as freedom from war and unrest. Peace can also take a positive meaning of well-being and fulfillment as goals of religious and social life. In ancient Greece the word for peace, *eirēnē*, meant primarily the opposite of war, and even when personified as a goddess, Eirēnē had no mythology and little cult. The Roman Pax was also a vague goddess, scarcely heard of before the age of Augustus and then taken as the representation of quiet at home and abroad. The Pax Romana expressed the absence of internal strife, although Seneca remarked that whole tribes and peoples had been forced to change their habitats.

In ancient Hebrew thought, peace *(shalom)* was not only the absence of war but well-being if not prosperity. A famous passage which appears twice in the Bible (*Is.* 2:2–4, *Mi.* 4:1–3) describes all nations going to Jerusalem to learn the divine law, beating their swords into plowshares and their spears into pruning hooks, abandoning their swords, and learning war no more. Micah adds that every man would sit under his vine and fig tree, an ideal picture of a small landholder in a tiny state between rival superpowers. In expectation of a better future the ideal Davidic king is called Prince of Peace, and his government is described as having boundless dominion and peace (*Is.* 9:6–7).

The Israelites used the Hebrew word *shalom* to refer to material and spiritual conditions which were joined together. Psalm 85 envisages God speaking peace to his people, righteousness and peace united, and the land yielding its increase. It is not only war that destroys peace but also covetousness, false dealing, and priests and prophets who practice abominations and say "Peace, peace, when there is no peace" (*Jer.* 6:14). To the Israelites peace was a social concept; it was visible and produced a harmonious relationship in the family, in local society, and between nations. The salutation *shalom* expressed the positive aim of encouraging friendly cooperation and living together for mutual benefit, and such a greeting, in use from the times of the judges and David, was later employed by both Jews and Christians.

The Arabic word *salām*, meaning "peace" or "health," has been in general use as a greeting or salutation since the time of the Qur'ān. One of its oldest chapters speaks of the coming down of the Qur'ān on "the Night of Power" and concludes that "it is peace until the rising of the dawn" (97:5). God calls men to the "abode of peace" *(dār al-salām)*, both in this life and in the next (10:26).

It is as a salutation that the Qur'ān has most to say about *salām*. The prophet Muḥammad said "Peace be upon you" *(al-salām ʿalaykum)* at the beginning of a message, and this was reckoned to be the greeting given to the blessed when they entered Paradise. It became the common salutation in the Islamic world, and the Qur'ān recommends its use. The *salām* formula, thought to be used by angels, is uttered after the names of previous prophets—Noah, Abraham, Moses, Jesus, and the like.

In Islamic ritual, the prayer for the blessing of God and peace on the Prophet, the worshiper, those present, and pious servants of God precedes the confession of faith. At the end of formal prayer the worshiper turns to the right and to the left, invoking the peace and mercy of God. Liturgical use helped to make the peace formula characteristic of Islam, and it is recommended to return the greeting with an additional blessing, following the Qur'anic verse "When you receive a greeting, respond with a better" (4:86–88).

Islamic eschatology, in popular tradition, has held to the hope of a future deliverer who would rule according to the example of the Prophet and give stability to Islam for a short millennium before the end of all earthly things: the Mahdi, "the guided one," would descend from heaven and fill the earth with equity and justice.

In the New Testament both the Gospels and the epistles use the Greek word *eirēnē* for "peace," although Jesus must have used the Aramaic equivalent of the Hebrew *shalom,* and *eirēnē* is given the positive sense of the Hebrew. When the apostles were sent out they were instructed to say "Peace be to this house," on entering any house, and, "If a son of peace is there, your peace shall rest upon him; but if not, it shall return to you again" (*Lk.* 10:6). The peacemaker was blessed, and the struggling early church was exhorted to "follow after things which make for peace, to edify one another" (*Rom.* 14:19).

The reconciliation of Jews and gentiles was sought through Christ: "He is our peace, who made both one" (*Eph.* 2:14). For those under external pressures, peace was a spiritual calm as well as a social benefit, as promised by Christ in his parting words, according to John, "Peace I leave with you, my peace I give you, not as the world gives it" (*Jn.* 14.27). This led on to Paul's view of the peace of God which passes human understanding, and the "fruits of the Spirit" included peace among virtues such as patience, kindness, and forbearance.

In New Testament eschatology there is little detail of the future, except in the *Apocalypse of John (Revelation).* Instead there are general statements about the ultimate triumph of good, when "God shall be all in all." Meanwhile the kingdom of God is "righteousness and peace and joy in the Holy Spirit" (*Rom.* 14:17).

In the history of the church peace has been seen on the one hand as calm for the soul and on the other as social and political reconciliation and the establishment of a just order. This has led to doctrines of a just war [*see* War and Warriors] or to judgments on social change, but more general statements speak of individual and communal well-being. Augustine of Hippo in his *City of God* (*De civitate Dei* 413–426) remarks that peace is the purpose of war between nations, for no one would seek war by peace, but as the peace of man is an orderly obedience to the eternal law of God, so the peace of God's city is "the perfect union of hearts, in the enjoyment of God and of one another in God" (19.13). Peace is our final good; eternity in peace, or peace in eternity, for the good of peace is the greatest wish of the world and the most welcome when it comes.

The salutation *Peace* is frequent in the New Testament, and it entered into the liturgy. In the traditional canon of the Latin Mass the priest said or chanted both "Dominus vobiscum" ("The Lord be with you") and "Pax Domini sit semper vobiscum" ("The Peace of the Lord be always with you"). In modern times there has been a revival of "the peace," or "giving the peace," in many churches. For example, the peace may be given throughout the congregation with the words "the peace of the Lord," and this is often accompanied by the shaking of hands or even kissing in peace.

Both social and personal ideals of peace have been important concerns of Chinese religious leaders and thinkers. The Taoist classic *Tao-te ching* comments that he who seeks to help a ruler by the Tao will oppose all conquest by force of arms. Not only will the Taoist be against war and weapons, but he will object to imposed rules and government, even to morality and wisdom, because he believes that in simplicity and fewness of desires evil would disappear.

The Taoist should adopt a peaceful or passive attitude, "actionless activity" *(wu-wei),* and by such wordless teaching he will control all creatures, and everything will be duly regulated. Colin A. Ronan (1978) has noted that Joseph Needham rejected the customary translation of *wu-wei* as "inaction" (p. 98). The Taoist, he maintained, is not idle or passive, but he is natural. He should refrain from acting against the grain, from trying to make things perform unsuitable functions, from exerting force when a perceptive man would see that force must fail. There is support for this view in *The Book of Huai-nan* (120 BCE), which criticizes those who claim that the man who acts with *wu-wei* does not speak or move or will not be driven by force. No sages, it says, gave such an interpretation, but the proper view of such quiet activity is that no personal prejudice should check the Tao, and no desires lead the proper courses of techniques astray. Nonaction does not mean doing nothing; it means allowing everything to act according to its nature.

In popular Taoism the ideals of a past golden age of peace, and of one yet to come, were expressed in the T'ai-p'ing Tao, the Way of Great Peace, which arose about 175 CE. [*See* T'ai-p'ing.] Some of its doctrines had been stated in a lost scripture decades earlier, the *T'ai-p'ing ching* (Classic of Great Peace). Its writer, Yü Chi, was a preacher and healer in Shantung province who was executed about 197, although his followers believed that he had become an immortal.

The new movement, the Way of Great Peace, was established by Chang Chüeh, who founded in 175 CE an organization of which he was the "Heavenly General." He held vast public ceremonies at which the sick confessed their sins and were healed by faith. What is just as important, Chang Chüeh sent missionaries to convert people in central and eastern China to the way of peace and healing. Crowds flocked to this movement, probably because the troubled times of warfare gave rise to the longing for a millenarian era reminiscent of the mythical golden age of peace. There was also dissatisfaction with the coldness of state Confucianism, and a yearning for a more personal religion and a more just society.

The Way of Great Peace became very popular, and eight provinces were converted by its missionaries. The central government was alarmed and prepared countermeasures. The Taoists were warned, and on the day that the governmental action began they decided to revolt. The rebels wore yellow kerchiefs on their heads, thus giving rise to the movement's other name, Yellow Turbans. Chang Chüeh and his brothers were caught and executed, but it was many years before the rebellion was finally suppressed.

In the nineteenth century the Taiping Rebellion swept across China and almost destroyed the crumbling Manchu dynasty. It raged from 1850 to 1865 and was put down only with the help of foreign powers, notably the British, and with a catastrophic loss of some twenty million lives. The leader of the rebellion, Hung Hsiu-ch'üan, sought to establish the T'ai-p'ing, the Great Peace, under a purely Chinese dynasty, but he was inspired by both Chinese and Christian ideas. The T'ai-p'ing would come in the cycle of history but would resemble the kingdom of heaven, where all people would worship the heavenly father.

Hung proclaimed his regime the Heavenly Kingdom of Great Peace and himself took the title Heavenly King. Nanking was captured in 1853 and renamed Heavenly Capital, but internal divisions and external attacks led to its collapse. By 1864 Hung had despaired of his cause; he took poison and died, and his followers were overwhelmed. Later Chinese attempts at reform and peace through strength occurred, but not all were inspired by Taoist ideals.

Indian views of peace are both personal and social, positive and negative. Many sacred Hindu texts open with the sacred syllable *oṃ*, followed for invocation and meditation by a threefold repetition of the Sanskrit word for peace: *śāntiḥ, śāntiḥ, śāntiḥ*. (These three words appear at the end of T. S. Eliot's famous poem *The Waste Land*, 1922.) The peace invoked in the Sanskrit texts is one of tranquillity, quiet, calmness of mind, absence of passion, aversion of pain, and indifference to the objects of pleasure and pain.

In the *Bhagavadgītā* the despondency of the warrior Arjuna, with which the poem opens, comes from envisaging the destruction of human beings and order *(dharma)* that war would bring. Arjuna is moved by compassion, declares that he would rather be killed than kill other beings, and lays down his weapons. His charioteer, the god Kṛṣṇa, gives several answers to Arjuna's problems, the chief one of which is that a soldier may kill the body but cannot kill the soul, or self, which is indestructible and immortal, without beginning or end. This answer ignores the question of Arjuna's compassion. The true yogin, whether he be a warrior or not, should be detached; he should act but remain unmoved by the result of his actions. Thus he can "attain the peace that culminates in *nirvāṇa* and rests in me [i.e., God]" (6.15). Kindness to all beings is occasionally suggested in the *Gītā*, but the general picture is one of peace and tranquillity unmoved by the affairs of the world.

The Jains in India have been noted for their advocacy of nonviolence, or not killing *(ahiṃsā)*, and some of their temples today bear the inscription (in English as well as in Sanskrit), "Nonviolence is the highest religion." [*See* Ahiṃsā.] They teach that *nirvāṇa* is an indescribable and passionless state beyond this world, at the ceiling of the universe. The Buddhists, contemporary with the Jains, have also taught *nirvāṇa* and have done so in negative terms. A Buddhist compendium of teachings, *The Questions of King Milinda*, agrees that *nirvāṇa* cannot be indicated in form or shape, in duration or size, by simile or argument. Yet it does exist: "there is *nirvāṇa*"; it is lofty and exalted, inaccessible to the passions and unshakable, bringing joy and shedding light.

Positive social efforts for peace were illustrated in the words and actions of the most famous Indian ruler, the Buddhist emperor Aśoka, in the third century BCE, as revealed by extant inscriptions on pillars and rocks. After thousands of people had been killed in his war against the Kalingas, Aśoka felt remorse, renounced war, sought reconciliation, and wished that "all beings should be unharmed, self-controlled, calm in mind, and gentle." Fighting was forbidden, as was all killing of animals for food or sacrifice. Medical services were provided for human beings and animals, useful herbs were planted, wells were dug, and trees were planted along roads to shelter men and beasts. Local rulers were instructed to tour among their people and teach the *dharma* of obedience to parents, generosity to priests, prohibition of killing, ownership of "the minimum of property."

In modern times Mohandas Gandhi (1869–1948) was noted for teaching *ahimsā*, but not just as a negative way to peace and justice. He coined the term *satyāgraha* (literally, "truth insistence"), defining it as "soul force" or "the force which is born of truth and love or nonviolence." Gandhi sought to follow the New Testament injunction to return good for evil as well as to follow the Jain command of nonviolence. He argued that "soul force" was the only method by which home rule could be regained for India and that it was "superior to the force of arms." Further, in a message to Hindus and Muslims on communal unity Gandhi insisted that politics should be approached in a religious spirit. He ended his speech with these words: "I ask all lovers of communal peace to pray that the God of truth and love may give us both the right spirit and the right word, and use us for the good of the dumb millions."

[*See also* Nonviolence.]

BIBLIOGRAPHY

Biblical teaching about peace can be found in many books, and useful articles are included in *A Dictionary of Christian Spirituality* (London, 1983) and *A Dictionary of Christian Ethics* (Philadelphia, 1967). Islamic texts are listed in the *Shorter Encyclopaedia of Islam* (1953; reprint, Leiden, 1974). Indian and Chinese teachings with selections from texts are easily found in *Sources of Indian Tradition* and *Sources of Chinese Tradition* (New York, 1958 and 1960), edited by Wm. Theodore de Bary and others. Taoist movements are described by Holmes Welch in *The Parting of the Way: Lao Tzu and the Taoist Movement* (London, 1957), and informative chapters on Taoism, Confucianism, and Buddhism are included in Colin A. Ronan's *Shorter Science and Civilisation in China* (New York, 1978), an abridgment of Joseph Needham's text from volumes 1 and 2 of the larger work.

GEOFFREY PARRINDER

PEARL. The making of the natural pearl commences when a grain of sand from the ocean or river floor works its way into the body of a pearl-bearing mollusk. To protect itself from this alien source of agitation, the mollusk secretes a substance (nacre, or mother-of-pearl) that slowly and cumulatively coats the foreign body until it loses its abrasive contours and becomes smooth and spherical in shape. On account of its singular origin, the pearl has been a symbol of sacred power since ancient times.

In many archaic cultures the marine shell, because of its appearance, is associated with the female genitalia, and the pearl is believed to be both the sacred product and the emblem of the feminine generative power. The pearl thus symbolizes both the life that is created and the mysterious force that begets life. One example of this reproductive symbolism is found in *Pei-ya*, a Chinese text of the eleventh century CE. The author of *Pei-ya* likens the pearl to a developing fetus and calls the oyster "the womb of the pearl." The anthropomorphic image for this sacred power is the goddess of love. In the ancient Mediterranean world, shells and pearls were often symbols for the great goddesses. In a manner analogous to the pearl's origin in an oyster, Aphrodite was born from a marine conch, and the Syrian goddess was known as the Lady of Pearls.

It is through this connection with feminine generative power that the pearl becomes a symbol for regeneration and rebirth as well. As a regenerative force, the pearl is often thought to have the power to heal or protect from harm. Throughout the Middle Ages and into the seventeenth century, a debate flourished among European physicians concerning the best way to prepare a pearl for healing purposes: should it be ground or dissolved? In either case, an elixir containing a pearl was prescribed for numerous physical ailments. An Eastern example of the belief in the power of the pearl to protect life is found in the iconography of the *bodhisattva* Kṣitigarbha, who is especially venerated in Japanese Buddhism by pregnant women and young children as the protector of all weak and suffering humanity; statues and images depict Kṣitigarbha holding a pearl, his emblem, in his left hand. Because of their connection with rebirth and resurrection, pearls have been found in the tombs of rulers in lands as far apart as Egypt and the Americas. In Laos, a pearl is inserted into each orifice of a corpse to effect safe passage into the next world.

Finding and obtaining the natural pearl is both hard work and a hazardous undertaking. Pearl fishers are known to work in pairs: one dives deep into the sea while his partner stays above to hold the other end of his lifeline and, after a predetermined time, to haul both fisherman and catch to the surface. The difficulties of locating and harvesting the natural pearl give rise to a second level of symbolism: the pearl represents the hard-won goal of spiritual striving. For example, in the parable about the merchant who found a pearl of special value and so went to sell everything he owned in order to purchase it, Jesus compares the kingdom of God to a pearl. In medieval European alchemy, one of the many names for the philosophers' stone is *margarita pretiosa*, or "precious pearl." In *The Pearl*, a Middle English tale by an anonymous author, the hero laments the disappearance of his pearl in a grassy meadow. Seeking it, he falls into another world, where he experiences spiritual renewal and regains the balance of his own inner nature. Chuang-tzu, the legendary Taoist mystic, reports how the Yellow Emperor lost his "night-pearl" during an excursion to the edge of the world. He sought for it by means of every resource at hand: by science, by analysis, by logic. But only when, in despair, the emperor turned to the "emptiness" *(hsü)* that is the ground of all things was the pearl restored to him.

The search for the pearl is also the theme of the gnostic *Hymn of the Pearl,* which relates how a prince leaves his heavenly home to recover a pearl that lies buried in Egypt in the possession of a giant serpent. The prince is sent forth by his father, mother, and brother, who watch over his journey in a way reminiscent of the second fisherman who holds the lifeline at the surface of the sea. The prince inevitably succumbs to the spell that governs all Egypt (a gnostic symbol for the illusion of cosmic existence). He loses all memory of his origins and of the pearl (i.e., he becomes spiritually ignorant or unconscious). But his watchful parents send forth a message to awaken him and to remind him of his identity and his mission to recover the pearl.

Especially in the East, from India to Japan, the pearl is often depicted in the possession of a dragon or sea monster. These mythological beings, like the serpent in the *Hymn of the Pearl,* are common symbols for chaos, that admixture of forces both cosmic and spiritual that oppose the establishment of a meaningful and inhabitable order. Thus, the search for the pearl often entails a heroic confrontation with the demonic.

Wherever the cultivation or liberation of the soul is regarded as the goal of spiritual striving, the pearl may symbolize the soul itself. This belief may have historical roots in the mythological thinking of the Hellenistic world, from which we have the formula "Ho sōma, hē sarx" ("The body is the tomb"). In this view, the subject of spiritual and eternal life is the immortal soul that exists within an alien and perishable body. According to the Mandaeans, the pearl's temporary home within the oyster provides an allegory for the temporary dwelling of the soul within the body. A variation of this imagery is found in the Coptic *Kephalaia*, a Manichaean text that relates how the soul is like a raindrop that falls into the sea and enters the body of an oyster in order to develop into a pearl. So, too, the soul acquires permanent definition and individuality by enduring life in the body. The pearl as a symbol for the actualized soul found its way into the poetry of the Ṣūfī mystic Farīd al-Dīn ʿAṭṭār:

> Out of the ocean like rain clouds come and travel—
> For without traveling, you will never become a pearl!

BIBLIOGRAPHY

Bausani, Alessandro. *Persia religiosa: Da Zaratustra a Baha'-ullah*. Milan, 1959.

Bausani, Alessandro. *Storia della letteratura persiana*. Milan, 1959.

Cirlot, J. E. *A Dictionary of Symbols*. 2d ed. New York, 1971.

Eliade, Mircea. *Images and Symbols: Studies in Religious Symbolism*. New York, 1961. Contains a comprehensive bibliography.

Jonas, Hans. *The Gnostic Religion: The Message of the Alien God and the Beginnings of Christianity*. 2d ed., rev. & enl. Boston, 1963.

BEVERLY MOON

PECHAM, JOHN (c. 1230–1292), Franciscan theologian, scientist, and educator; provincial minister of the Franciscans and archbishop of Canterbury. Pecham was born in Sussex, in the vicinity of Lewes. Educated initially at the priory of Lewes and the University of Oxford, he joined the Franciscan order about 1250 and later in the decade was sent to the University of Paris for theological studies, earning the doctorate in 1269. Pecham was regent master in theology at Paris from 1269 to 1271, lecturer in theology for the Franciscan school in Oxford from about 1272 to 1275, provincial minister of the order from 1275 to 1277, master in theology to the papal Curia from 1277 to 1279, and archbishop of Canterbury from 1279 until his death in 1292.

Pecham's theology was typically Franciscan: conservative and centered on the teachings of Augustine. Indeed, Pecham became a leader in the opposition to the new—and in his opinion heterodox—Aristotelian and Averroist ideas circulating in the universities. For example, he took strong exception to Thomas Aquinas's views on the unity of substantial form. He defended such doctrines as the divine illumination of the intellect, complete hylomorphism (the idea that everything is a composite of form and matter), and plurality of forms. Pecham also became involved in the power struggle between secular and mendicant clergy, writing a series of pamphlets in defense of the mendicants. As an educator, Pecham followed Robert Grosseteste and Roger Bacon by incorporating mathematical science into the university curriculum (including the theological curriculum). He wrote two books on optics, one of which, *Perspectiva communis*, became the standard university textbook for several centuries. An energetic, reform-minded archbishop, Pecham fought for the preservation of ecclesiastical privileges against royal encroachment and campaigned against a variety of clerical abuses, such as nonresidence and the holding of multiple benefices.

BIBLIOGRAPHY

On Pecham's ecclesiastical career, see David Knowles's "Some Aspects of the Career of Archbishop Pecham," *English Historical Review* 57 (1942): 1–18, 178–201, and Decima Douie's *Archbishop Pecham* (Oxford, 1952). For Pecham's philosophy, the most succinct and convenient source is D. E. Sharp's *Fran-*

ciscan Philosophy at Oxford in the Thirteenth Century (Oxford, 1930). On Pecham's scientific efforts see two works of my own: *John Pecham and the Science of Optics: Perspectiva communis* (Madison, Wis., 1970) and "Pecham, John," in the *Dictionary of Scientific Biography*, vol. 10 (New York, 1974), pp. 473–476. See the latter for additional bibliographic information.

DAVID C. LINDBERG

PELAGIANISM. The term *Pelagianism* designates both the teachings of Pelagius, a fourth-century Christian monk, and any teaching that minimizes the role of divine grace in salvation. Few of the ideas associated with Pelagianism in the latter sense can be directly traced to Pelagius, but because he was opposed by the great North African bishop Augustine, whose influence on Western Christian theology has been far-reaching, he has come to stand for an insufficient and erroneous doctrine of grace. [*See also the biographies of Pelagius and Augustine.*] Some have suggested that Pelagianism was the creation of Augustine and not Pelagius. But it was Pelagius's views on the Christian life, his moral rigorism, his high regard for the law, and his emphasis on discipline and the human will that laid the foundation for the controversy that gave birth to what has come to be known as Pelagianism.

Pelagius (d. 418), a monk from Britain, was living in Rome at the end of the fourth century when he came in contact with wealthy and aristocratic Romans who had lapsed into Christianity through marriage or political expedience. Adopting Christianity had done little to change their lives. Baptism, which had been thought to signify a clean break with one's past, was becoming a polite convention. Only the ascetics seemed to take seriously the radical demands of the gospel. Pelagius, however, believed that the law of the gospel should be imposed on all members of the church, not just on the monks. The word of Jesus, "Be ye perfect as your father in heaven is perfect," was addressed to all Christians; thus, according to Pelagius, "since perfection is possible for humans, it is obligatory."

As a moral reformer Pelagius met with success among a circle of supporters in Rome, but his notion of the church as a society of pure and authentic Christians had an old-fashioned ring to it at a time when the level of commitment among Christians was in decline because of a large influx into the church of merely nominal converts. He was offended when he read in Augustine's *Confessions* that humans must necessarily and inevitably sin even after baptism. Augustine's phrase "Give what you command and command what you will" seemed to him to undermine the moral law and the quest for perfection, because it placed responsibility for righteousness on God rather than on the human will.

Pelagius did not, as is often thought, deny the necessity of grace. Grace was to be understood as the revelation of God's purpose and will, the wisdom by which humans are stirred to seek a life of righteousness. It was God's way of helping humankind and was found in (1) the endowment of a rational will and the capacity to choose good or evil, (2) the law of Moses, (3) the forgiveness of sins in the redemptive death of Christ, (4) the teaching of Christ, and (5) the example of Christ. Pelagius saw no opposition between the laws of the old covenant and the gospel. He saw grace as precept and example, a view that led him to overestimate human capability and thus to invite criticism.

The controversy began in 412, at a council in Carthage, in North Africa, with the condemnation of Celestius, a supporter of Pelagius, for holding the views that (1) Adam was created mortal and would have died whether or not he was a sinner; (2) Adam's sin injured himself alone, and not the human race; (3) infants at birth are in that state in which Adam was before his sin; (4) the whole human race neither died on account of Adam nor rises on account of Christ; (5) the law as well as the gospel admits a person to the kingdom of heaven; (6) before the advent of Christ there were humans who did not sin; (7) a person can be without sin and keep the divine commands. This is not Pelagianism, but Pelagius would have agreed with some of these propositions—for example, that sinless human beings had lived before the coming of Christ. He pointed to "gospel men before the gospel" such as Noah, Melchizedek, Abraham, and Job.

As a result of the condemnation of Celestius, Pelagius, who had traveled to Palestine, was forced to defend himself in the East. His most vehement critics, however, were Westerners such as Jerome. Significantly, at two councils in Palestine in 415 he was acquitted by bishops from the East. In the meantime Augustine opened up a literary campaign against Pelagius, and this led Augustine to produce the theological works that would define Pelagianism for Western Christian theology and to formulate the objections that would lead to Pelagius's condemnation. Under Augustine's influence Pelagius was condemned by two African councils, and in 417 Pope Innocent I ratified the anathema.

After Pelagius's death in 418 (or shortly thereafter) his followers, often under much hardship, continued to defend his teachings. One of these, the gifted and articulate bishop Julian of Eclanum, a town in Apulia (southeastern Italy), though banished from his see, traveled and wrote extensively. He vigorously opposed the new ideas of Augustine, seeing in them the specter of Manichaean dualism. In a modified form Pelagius's teachings were embraced by John Cassian (360–435), a monastic writer from Marseilles (France) who is sometimes called the founder of semi-Pelagianism, though this term only came to be used in the sixteenth century. Other exponents were Vincent of Lerins (d. 450) and Faustus of Riez (408–490), both from southern France. The focus of discussion centered on the necessity of human cooperation with divine grace in salvation, and since then these questions have been central to the history of theology in the West. The dispute finally ended at the Council of Orange (429), which condemned the writings of Faustus and upheld most of the teachings of Augustine.

Only in recent years has there been a serious effort to understand the historical Pelagius and the circumstances surrounding his teaching. More often *Pelagianism* has been used as an epithet to vilify one's foes whenever there is a suggestion that human efforts displace the role of grace. In the Middle Ages Thomas Bradwardine (1290–1349), archbishop of Canterbury, wrote against the "Pelagians," meaning those of his contemporaries who subverted God's grace by stressing free will. Peter Abelard (1079–1142) has sometimes been called a Pelagian because of his view of the exemplary as distinct from the redemptive character of Christ's life and death. In the sixteenth century the Protestant reformers charged their opponents with Pelagianism because of their belief that one could prepare for grace by doing good works: Martin Luther called Erasmus a Pelagian. In Roman Catholicism Luis de Molina, a sixteenth-century Jesuit, was suspected of Pelagian convictions because he taught that God's foreknowledge of human cooperation is itself a sign of grace. The term *semi-Pelagian* arose from this controversy. Although Pelagianism has had little direct influence on Eastern Christian thought, which also never adopted Augustine's ideas, aspects of Orthodox Christian theology have been held to possess a Pelagian tinge from the perspective of Western Christian theology.

BIBLIOGRAPHY

Bonner, Gerald. *Augustine and Modern Research on Pelagianism.* Villanova, Pa., 1972.

Brown, Peter. *Religion and Society in the Age of Saint Augustine.* London, 1972.

Evans, Robert F. *Pelagius: Inquiries and Reappraisals.* New York, 1968.

ROBERT L. WILKEN

PELAGIUS (d. 418), Christian monk whose name has become synonymous with doctrines of human cooperation in salvation at the expense of divine grace. [*See also* Pelagianism.] The historical figure is more complex than the teachings associated with his name. Pelagius was born in Britain in the middle of the fourth century. Nothing is known of his background or upbringing, but he seems to have received an excellent education. He was highly regarded for his exemplary life, and even his great opponent, Augustine of Hippo, acknowledged that he was a "holy man who had made no small progress in the Christian life." He went to live in Rome sometime toward the end of the fourth century, perhaps as early as the 380s.

Pelagius was first and foremost a monk and an ascetic, a tutor to men and women seeking the life of perfection. His primary concern was moral and spiritual, not theological. He had been influenced by earlier Christian moral and ascetic literature, for example *Sentences of Sextus,* a collection of moral maxims from the second century, and the writings of Origen, the great third-century Christian teacher. From these works he learned the importance of freedom of the will, discipline, the quest for perfection, and righteousness through the doing of good deeds.

In the world of fifth-century Rome, however, moral rigorism, which had once marked the entire Christian community, was now practiced chiefly by the ascetics. Pelagius continued to believe that there should be no double standard and that the precepts of the gospel were applicable to all. For a time he was successful in urging these ideas in Rome, but as his writings became known outside of Rome, in Africa, where Augustine lived, and in Palestine, where Jerome lived, he came to be vigorously opposed.

Pelagius left Rome in 410 with his disciple Celestius to travel to Africa. Celestius was condemned by a council in Carthage in 412. In Palestine Pelagius was brought before councils in Jerusalem and Lydda in 415, but he ably defended himself and was acquitted. In the West, however, through the efforts of Augustine, he was condemned by a council in Carthage in 416 and again by Pope Innocent in 417. After being briefly vindicated by Zosimus, Innocent's successor, he was eventually condemned by a great council at Carthage in 418 and by the pope and was banished by the Roman emperors. He died in 418 or sometime thereafter.

He wrote widely, but few of his works are extant in their entirety. The most important is a commentary on the epistles of Paul, a close verse-by-verse exposition of the text of the letters with an eye to the Christian life. The influence of Origen, transmitted through Latin translations, is evident in the commentary. His major theological works, *De natura* and *De libero arbitrio,* written only after he had traveled to Palestine in 412 and come into contact with Jerome, are extant only in fragments in the writings of Augustine. Besides these works there are a number of shorter tractates and letters, some of which have only recently been shown to be genuine.

BIBLIOGRAPHY

Ferguson, John. *Pelagius.* Cambridge, 1956.

Plinval, Georges de. *Pelage: Ses écrits, sa vie et sa reforme.* Lausanne, 1943.

ROBERT L. WILKEN

PENANCE. *See* Repentance; *see also* Sacraments, *article on* Christian Sacraments.

PENATES. In the Latin world *di penates* (always in the plural) were spirits protecting a house or a city. The etymological connection with *penus* in the sense of "storing-place of the household" raises problems. The cult of the *penates* was associated with that of Vesta; both were linked to the hearth. During family meals offers of food were made to them and burned on the fireplace. Plautus speaks in *Mercator* (1.834) of the *penates* as "gods of the parents" *(di penates meum parentum)* and distinguishes them from the *lar* (singular) of the household *(familia).*

The *penates* were originally aniconic. In the late republican period images of them were put on the table. By a further development the notion of *penates* came to include all the gods worshiped in the household, beginning with Vesta and the *lar familiaris* (later also *lares* in general). In the first century CE Pompeii and even Jupiter, Venus, Vulcanus, and Fortuna were counted among the *penates.* City *penates* are known also outside Rome.

The peculiarity of Rome was that the *penates* of the city were worshiped both within the city, in a temple on the Velia not far from the Forum (on the site of the later Church of Saints Cosma and Damianus) and in the Latial city of Lavinium. According to tradition, Aeneas had brought his own *penates* from Troy to Lavinium. The *penates* had refused to move to Alba Longa when it was founded by Aeneas's son Ascanius. Toward the end of the fourth century BCE, the Greek historian Timaeus was told that the *penates* of Lavinium were aniconic objects. As soon as they were elected, Roman consuls, dictators, and praetors went to Lavinium to make sacrifices to them. Respect was still paid by Roman emperors to the Lavinium *penates.*

The aniconic *penates* worshiped on the Velia acquired human features in the late republic and were often identified with the Dioscuri (Castor and Pollux), an identification apparently repudiated by Varro (*De lingua Latina* 5.58). It is doubtful whether the *penates* preserved at Lavinium were at any time identified with the Dioscuri. According to Tacitus (*Annals* 15.41.1), *penates* of the Roman people were also preserved in the temple of Vesta on the Palatine, but this is an obscure piece of information. Equally problematic is the mention of a "priest of the *di penates*" *(sacerdos deum penatium)* in two inscriptions of Rome (*Corpus inscriptionum Latinarum*, Berlin, 1863, vol. 6, no. 7283).

BIBLIOGRAPHY

Alföldi, András. *Early Rome and the Latins.* Ann Arbor, 1965. See pages 258–271.

Latte, Kurt. *Römische Religionsgeschichte.* Munich, 1960. See pages 89 and 416.

Radke, Gerhard. *Die Götter Altitaliens.* Münster, 1965. See pages 247–252.

Radke, Gerhard. "Die *di penates* und Vesta im Rom." In *Aufstieg und Niedergang der römischen Welt,* vol. 2.17.1, pp. 343–373. Berlin and New York, 1981. Includes bibliography.

Weinstock, Stanley. "Penates." In *Real-Encyclopädia der classischen Altertumswissenschaft,* vol. 19, cols. 417–447. Stuttgart, 1937.

ARNALDO MOMIGLIANO

PENN, WILLIAM (1644–1718), Quaker religious leader and theologian, proponent of religious and political rights, and founder of Pennsylvania. Educated at Oxford, the French Protestant academy at Saumur, and, briefly, at Lincoln's Inn, Penn came under Dissenter influence and renounced a life of social prominence for Quakerism in 1667. Intent on transforming England into a more truly Christian society, he wrote many of his more than 140 books, pamphlets, and broadsides from 1668 to 1680, when he spent virtually all of his time working to organize, spread, and protect the Quaker movement, also known as the Society of Friends. Having found England resistant to change, he secured a charter for a colony he envisioned as both a haven for persecuted Friends and a model consensual society that would demonstrate to a skeptical world the fruitfulness and practicality of Quaker principles. Pennsylvania received most of his time and energy from 1680 to 1685, and Penn's duties as proprietor were his major concern the rest of his life. He remained active as a Quaker leader in England and played a central role in the successful attempt to demonstrate that Quakers were sufficiently orthodox to be acceptable under the terms for toleration established after the Glorious Revolution of 1688.

Although a source of controversy at times within the Quaker movement, Penn was at the center of the network of Quaker leaders and was probably the most effective mediator between Friends and the rest of the world. He was a close friend and collaborator of George Fox, the founder of the movement, his wife Margaret Askew Fell Fox, and Robert Barclay, the movement's major theologian. Penn traveled extensively as a preacher and organizer throughout England and in Ireland, Germany, and Holland and from 1672 was active in the London Morning Meeting, the Quakers' informal executive body. In favor of the disciplinary practices and organizational structure espoused by Fox, he was active in upholding the authority of the central leadership against the individualistic conception of authority favored by schismatics. Penn's unique contribution as a leader of Friends was his injection of a prophetic activism into the movement at a time when many first-generation leaders were settling into a more quietist, sectarian posture. He helped organize the Meeting for Sufferings in 1675 as a committee for the legal and political defense of indicted Quakers and led it into political activity in support of sympathetic candidates in parliamentary elections. His toleration treatises of the 1670s and 1680s had wide influence in the battle for religious liberty for all English Christians and effectively stated his views of mixed constitutional government and fundamental English rights.

Penn was one of the most prolific and theologically knowledgeable exponents of Quaker thought, and he distilled the visions and experiences of Fox and the "First Publishers of Truth" into the theological language of the times. His works include exhortatory letters, ethical treatises, refutations of schismatics, historical accounts of the movement, expositions of Quaker thought, and defenses against the attacks of Anglicans, Presbyterians, Independents, Baptists, and spiritualists. His distinctive approach to Quaker thought was his understanding of the "inner light" or "Christ within" as an epistemological principle making divine knowledge available in a manner that bypassed the indirect sense-knowledge emphasized in sacramental Roman Catholicism and scripture-based Protestantism. His Platonic rationalism, identification of Christ with the universal Logos, critique of scripture as a comprehensive source of revelation, and corresponding insistence on the metaphorical and symbolic nature of Christian theological formulas, such as those for the Trinity and atonement, linked him with such liberal Anglicans of his day as the Cambridge Platonists. These same ideas have many echoes in twentieth-century theology.

[*See also* Quakers.]

BIBLIOGRAPHY

Penn's correspondence, journals, religious and political papers, and business and legal records have been published in microfilm form by the Historical Society of Pennsylvania, *The Papers of William Penn*, 14 reels, 1975. The first two volumes of a projected four-volume edition of the most important of these materials have appeared, *The Papers of William Penn*, vol. 1, *1644–1679*, and vol. 2, *1680–1684*, edited by Mary Maples Dunn and Richard S. Dunn (Philadelphia, 1981–1982). A fifth volume containing a definitive annotated bibliography is also in preparation. *The Papers of William Penn* do not include the published works, which are available in a two-volume edition, *A Collection of the Works of William Penn, To Which Is Prefixed a Journal of His Life*, edited by Joseph Besse (London, 1726). Selections from this incomplete collection with many textual problems were reprinted in 1771, 1782, and 1825. No adequate biography exists; the most useful is William I. Hull's *William Penn: A Topical Biography* (New York, 1937). Penn's religious life and thought are comprehensively discussed in my *William Penn and Early Quakerism* (Princeton, 1973).

MELVIN B. ENDY, JR.

PENTATEUCH. *See* Biblical Literature, *article on* Hebrew Scriptures; *see also* Torah.

PENTECOSTAL AND CHARISMATIC CHRISTIANITY.

This form of Christianity centers on the emotional, nonrational, mystical, and supernatural: miracles, signs, wonders, and "the gifts of the Spirit" (charismata), especially "speaking in tongues" (glossolalia), faith healing, and "casting out demons" (exorcism). Supreme importance is attached to the subjective religious experience of being filled with or possessed by the Holy Spirit.

The name *Pentecostal* derives from the account of the day of Pentecost as described in chapters 1 and 2 of *Acts of the Apostles*, when the Holy Spirit descended upon the first Christians. "And they were all filled with the Holy Spirit and began to speak in other tongues, as the Spirit gave them utterance" (*Acts* 2:1–4). *Charismatic* derives from the Greek *charism*, meaning supernatural gifts of the Spirit, which are most often considered those listed in *1 Corinthians* 12–14.

Pentecostals fall into three major groupings, although in this essay I sometimes use the word *Pentecostal* as a collective term for all three groups.

1. Those who designate themselves "classical Pentecostals" trace their denominational origins directly to the Pentecostal revival in the United States at the start of the twentieth century. Only some of these denominations use the word *Pentecostal* in their official names.
2. Those who designate themselves "charismatics" trace their origins to the Pentecostal revival within the non-Pentecostal Christian communions in the United States during the 1960s. They are generally organized as prayer groups within their non-Pentecostal churches.
3. Those who hold to the essential beliefs and practices of Pentecostalism, but are not usually acknowledged as Pentecostals by "classical Pentecostals" or "charismatics" because some of their beliefs and practices are considered heretical or non-Christian. These Pentecostals are mostly nonwhite and abound in Africa, Latin America, and Asia.

The *World Christian Encyclopedia*, edited by David B. Barrett (New York, 1982), estimates the global total of Pentecostals of all types at one hundred million. Because of the great number of Pentecostal organizations, the variety of names, and the amorphous character of many groups, it is probably impossible to positively identify all Pentecostals. Nevertheless, there are certainly many millions, who collectively constitute the fastest growing segment of Christianity in the world. (All statistics herein are drawn from the *World Christian Encyclopedia*.)

Belief and Practice

Experience, not doctrine, has been the principal concern of Pentecostals. There is no unanimity on doctrine, polity, or any matter whatsoever except Spirit baptism and the practice of the charismata. The early Pentecostals were heirs to the evangelical faith of the late-nineteenth-century Holiness movement. Most American Pentecostals subscribe to the tenets of fundamentalism. Their only distinctive doctrine is that of baptism in the Spirit. Most American Pentecostal denominations believe that the "initial evidence" of Spirit baptism is always glossolalia. Other Pentecostals believe that it may be evidenced by any one of the charismata.

Speaking in tongues was originally believed to be miraculously speaking a language completely unknown to the speaker. Many Pentecostals continue to hold this view even though linguistic analysis has refuted it. Some acknowledge its nonlinguistic character but continue to assert its divine signification.

The charismatics have rejected nearly all of the Holiness and fundamentalist heritage of the Pentecostal movement. They have concentrated on integrating the experience of Spirit baptism and the practice of the charismata into the traditional beliefs and practices of their respective churches without significantly altering them. Some Protestant charismatics regard Spirit baptism as a distinct act of grace, as do all Pentecostals, but many Protestant and all Roman Catholic charismatics regard it as a renewal or actualization of the baptism in the Spirit, which all Christians receive in water baptism or on their conversion. Some Protestant charismatics hold the "initial evidence" view of glossolalia; other Protestant and all Roman Catholic charismatics reject this view.

Worship. The heart of Pentecostalism is the worship service. In the early years of the Pentecostal movement, nearly every meeting was marked by speaking in tongues, prophesying, healings, exorcisms, hand-clapping, uncoordinated praying aloud, running, jumping, falling, dancing "in the Spirit," crying, and shouting with great exuberance. Very quickly these practices were subjected to unwritten but clearly understood conventions concerning what was appropriate and when; however, Pentecostal services still appeared chaotic to the uninitiated. In the larger, white Pentecostal denominations these practices have all but disappeared. Charismatics have always maintained a high degree of decorum. The original character of Pentecostal worship, however, is still much in evidence among racial and ethnic minorities in North America and Europe and throughout sub-Saharan Africa, Latin America, and parts of Asia.

Despite differences in forms of expression, worship, for all Pentecostals, is the ritual reenactment of *Acts* 2, the recapturing of awe, wonder, and joy in the immediate experience of the Holy Spirit, and immersion in mystery and miracle. Worship provides the believer with an opportunity for individual expression, forges an emotional bond with the spiritual community, brings consolation and assurance, and lifts one into the sublime. The believer's objective is "to feel the moving of the Spirit," or in psychological terms, to experience intense arousal and discharge of emotion.

Social Character. The Pentecostal movement originated in the United States as a protest against the increasing formalism, "modernism," and middle-class character of the mainstream denominations. It was a movement of the poor, the uprooted, the socially and culturally deprived, recent immigrants, blacks, Hispanics, and other minorities in America. The movement's leaders were poor and lower-middle-class clergy and religious workers with little advanced education and from the outermost fringes of American Christendom. With few exceptions, the social character of the movement in all the countries to which it spread was analogous, and it is still overwhelmingly so in those indigenous movements that are most dynamic in Africa, Latin America, and Asia.

Pentecostalism has played a role in easing the transit of some of those who have suffered most from the transformation of preindustrial societies into modern urbanizing, industrializing ones. Pentecostalism has shown a strong ability to incorporate elements of both traditional and modern modes of thought and behavior into a subculture that has served as a bridge between the two. Its prescientific, nonrational outlook gives it an affinity with many non-Christian religions. Its emphasis on subjectivity, emotional expression, Spirit baptism, healing, exorcism, and miracles makes it highly congenial to adherents of so-called primitive religions that are characterized by animism, spirit possession, divination, shamanism, and prophetism. On the other hand, Pentecostalism has inculcated in its adherents an ethic of hard work, discipline, obedience to authority, sobriety, thrift, and self-denial—the qualities of the ideal proletarian in modernizing societies.

Mores. The early American Pentecostals were markedly ascetic, with prohibitions against tobacco, alcohol, dancing, gambling, movies, coffee, tea, Coca-Cola, cosmetics, and jewelry. Such prohibitions are no longer typical of white, middle-class American Pentecostals, but they are typical of other American Pentecostals. European Pentecostals have generally taken a more liberal position. Charismatics regard all such taboos as irrelevant. Non-white Pentecostals often tend toward extreme ascetism.

Social Ethics. The dominance of millenarianism among the early Pentecostals, and their identification of the Social Gospel with the mainstream churches, led to wholesale rejection of social activism by the Pentecostal denominations. They have always approved of individual acts of charity but have avoided corporate church involvement in social or political action. Pentecostals tend strongly toward conservative and reactionary views. They believe that society can be improved by the conversion and Spirit baptism of individuals within it; but only the Second Coming can bring the good society—and the signs of that Coming are an increase in immorality, conflict, and general social chaos. Such beliefs militate against any real social ethic.

Polity and Interchurch Relations. The early Pentecostals opposed all "man-made" organizations; they called only for spiritual unity based on Spirit baptism. Soon, however, they created a multitude of tight denominational structures of widely differing polities. But whether episcopal, presbyterian, congregational, or mixed in form, in practice all Pentecostals have tended toward the authoritarianism of the national leader(s) in denominational matters and that of the pastor in congregational matters.

American Pentecostal denominations were at first strongly separatist in their relations with one another as well as with non-Pentecostal churches. European Pentecostals, however, engaged in various regional and national cooperative efforts from an early point; they held the first All-Europe Pentecostal Conference in 1939 and the first World Pentecostal Conference in 1947.

A break in the isolationism of American Pentecostals came in 1943, when several Pentecostal denominations joined the National Association of Evangelicals. In 1948, several of the largest white Pentecostal denominations organized the Pentecostal Fellowship of North America. The general tendency of Pentecostals today is to engage in piecemeal cooperation and fellowship with other Pentecostals and evangelicals but to resist theological agreement and organizational unity. Charismatics, in contrast, are ardently ecumenical, being active in nearly all interchurch organizations at all levels. Pentecostals in Africa, Latin America, and Asia stand somewhere in between; separatism and independency are quite strong, but several denominations have joined ecumenical organizations, including the World Council of Churches.

Biblical and Historical Bases. Pentecostals trace the beginnings of their movement to the day of Pentecost described in *Acts*. [*For discussion of the Jewish observance of this festival, see* Shavu'ot.] They believe that the experience of Spirit baptism and the practice of the gifts of the Spirit that occurred on that day were meant to be normative in the life of the church and of each believer. They maintain that although the charismata ceased in the main body of the church soon after the apostolic age, one can trace an intermittent history of charismatic practices among sectarians like the Montanists, Anabaptists, Camisards, Shakers, Irvingites, Mormons, and various nineteenth-century Holiness groups. The twentieth-century Pentecostal and charismatic movements, therefore, mark the restoration of the charismata to the church.

American Pentecostalism

The Pentecostal movement developed within the radical, separatist wing of the late nineteenth-century Holiness movement in the United States. It represented an amalgam of extremist Wesleyan and Keswick views on premillennialism, dispensationalism, faith healing, and "the Baptism in the Spirit" as an enduement of miraculous powers.

The Pentecostal Revival. Charles Fox Parham, an independent Holiness preacher and former Methodist, is generally regarded as the founder of the modern Pentecostal movement. Speaking in tongues and other ecstatic behavior broke out in Parham's Bethel Bible "College" in Topeka, Kansas, in January 1901. Parham asserted that glossolalia was the evidence of "the true Baptism in the Spirit." On the basis of this teaching and faith healing, Parham's Apostolic Faith movement had some success in the lower Midwest. William Joseph Seymour, a black Holiness preacher converted by Parham, carried the movement to Los Angeles in 1906. Seymour's Azusa Street Apostolic Faith Mission became the center of a great revival, in which visitors to the Azusa mission spread the movement across the nation and around the world in only a few years.

The movement was condemned and ostracized by all other Christian churches, and at first consisted of a few small schismatic offsprings of the Holiness sects, and many independent congregations. The movement's center of strength lay in the region stretching from lower Appalachia to the Ozarks, and in the urban centers of the North and West. Adherents were drawn from vastly different religious, racial, ethnic, and cultural backgrounds. In time, these differences divided the movement into a bewildering array of small, hostile sects that were constantly splitting and resplitting. By 1916, the American Pentecostal movement had divided into three major doctrinal camps, and by the early 1930s each of these had split along racial lines.

Finished Work, or Baptistic, Pentecostals. Originally, all Pentecostals believed in three acts of grace: conversion, sanctification, and baptism in the Spirit. Beginning about 1908, William H. Durham introduced his "Finished Work of Calvary" doctrine, in which conversion and sanctification were declared a single act of grace. A majority of American Pentecostals accepted this doctrine; it was especially strong among those of Baptist and Keswick backgrounds. In 1914 a Finished Work denomination was organized: the Assemblies of God.

Second Work, or Wesleyan, Pentecostals. Those who held to the original three acts of grace were called "Second Work Pentecostals." They were predominantly from Wesleyan backgrounds and were concentrated in the South. The largest such denominations are the Church of God in Christ, the Church of God (Cleveland, Tenn.), and the Pentecostal Holiness Church.

Oneness, or "Jesus Only," Pentecostals. From 1913 to 1916, the Finished Work group was torn asunder by a controversy over the proper water baptismal formula and the nature of the godhead. Advocates of the "Oneness" position rejected traditional trinitarianism, maintaining that Father, Son, and Holy Ghost are simply different titles or offices of the one God whose name is Jesus. A number of small Oneness denominations were organized, the most important of which was Garfield T. Haywood's interracial Pentecostal Assemblies of the World. The movement consisted mostly of the very poorest Pentecostals and was strongest in the urban centers of the upper Midwest. In 1945, most white Oneness Pentecostals were brought together in the United Pentecostal Church.

"Deliverance," or Healing, Revival. The institutionalization of the American Pentecostal movement, together with generational changes and the rise of many into the middle classes, brought a decline in the fervor of Pentecostal worship, especially in the larger, white denominations. This led to a renewal movement in the late 1940s. A group of faith-healing evangelists arose to reemphasize the charismata and to deliver the faithful from formalism, sickness, and demon possession. The healers reintroduced tent revivals and attracted multitudes of non-Pentecostals.

William Branham, a Oneness Pentecostal from an impoverished Indiana family, was at first the most renowned leader of the revival. But Oral Roberts, a Pentecostal Holiness preacher from Oklahoma, soon overshadowed Branham and became the most prominent Pentecostal in the United States (he became a member of the Methodist Church in 1969).

The leaders of the Pentecostal denominations turned against the healers, who formed their own organizations. When the healing revival began to wane in the late 1950s, some of the healers turned to the new theme of prosperity. It was God's will, they said, that all believers should be wealthy. The devout believer and generous contributor to God's work would be rewarded with prosperity as well as health.

The Charismatic Revival. Many non-Pentecostals became aware of Pentecostalism through the highly publicized Deliverance revival. In the 1960s a Neo-Pentecostal, or charismatic, movement emerged in nearly all the Protestant denominations, the Roman Catholic church, and, to a much lesser extent, in Eastern Orthodox communions.

In 1951, Oral Roberts encouraged Demos Shakarian, a wealthy Pentecostal dairyman from California, to found the Full Gospel Business Men's Fellowship, International (FGBMFI) for the purpose of providing lay support for the healers. Hundreds of FGBMFI luncheon and dinner meetings were held in fashionable hotels across the nation. Many converts to the charismatic movement were first brought into contact with Pentecostalism through FGBMFI, which served as a bridge from the Deliverance revival to the charismatic revival.

Protestant charismatic revival. In 1961, Father Dennis Bennett, pastor of an Episcopal church in Van Nuys, California, announced that he had received the baptism in the Spirit and had spoken in tongues. Widespread media coverage followed, and a charismatic revival in the Protestant denominations took off, actively promoted by the FGBMFI. Fears of denominational leaders diminished when the charismatics proved to be neither schismatic nor fanatical. Their meetings were marked by restraint, and they were careful not to challenge the established doctrines and practices of their communions.

Roman Catholic charismatic revival. In 1967, charismatic practices emerged among Roman Catholic students and faculty at Duquesne, Notre Dame, and Michigan State universities. The movement grew rapidly by means of prayer groups and local, national, and international conferences. It soon surpassed its Protestant counterpart, numbering among its adherents many religious and bishops and at least one cardinal, Leon Joseph Cardinal Suenens of Belgium.

In the United States (according to Barrett, 1982) there are an estimated 6.7 million Pentecostals (including charismatics), including 1.6 million in the Church of God in Christ and another 500,000 in its schismatic offspring, the Church of God in Christ, International; 1.5 million in the Assemblies of God; 600,000 in the Church of God (Cleveland, Tenn.); and 450,000 in the United Pentecostal Church. Many thousands of small, independent congregations never appear in statistical reports.

European Pentecostalism

Thomas Ball Barratt, an English-born Methodist minister and pastor of an independent free church in Oslo, Norway (then Kristiania), was converted to Pentecostalism in New York City in 1906. His church, Kristiania Bymission, became the center of a revival in 1907 from which Pentecostalism spread throughout western Europe and the British Isles. The movement's greatest appeal was to evangelical and Holiness believers of the poorer classes.

In Scandinavia, the movement had considerable impact initially but eventually lost its momentum. There are some 300,000 Pentecostals in Sweden, most of them in the Pentecostal Revival Movement in Sweden; 73,000 in Norway, almost all in the Norwegian Pentecostal Assemblies; 30,000 in Denmark; and 65,000 in Finland.

In the United Kingdom, Anglican clergyman Alexander A. Boddy attended Thomas Barratt's meetings in 1907 and then established his All Saints Church in Sunderland, England, as a Pentecostal center from which the movement spread through the British Isles. Leadership of the movement soon passed to Welsh miners W. J. and D. P. Williams and Stephen and George Jeffreys. Overall in the United Kingdom, Pentecostalism had only modest success, until in the 1950s when many West Indian and other colonial immigrants were converted to it. There are some 250,000 British Pentecostals, and the movement is in decline. The largest denominations are the Assemblies of God in Great Britain and Ireland (70,000), Elim Pentecostal Church (45,000), and the Apostolic Church in Great Britain (40,000).

A Pentecostal revival in Germany began in Kessel-Hesse under the preaching of female evangelists from Barratt's church in 1907. Growth was limited, and the movement is now declining. There are some 2,000 Pentecostals in the German Democratic Republic, and 117,000 in the Federal Republic of Germany, including 40,000 each in the Assemblies of God and the Mulheim Association of Christian Assemblies.

Luigi Francescon and other Italian-Americans from Chicago established Pentecostalism in Italy in 1908, primarily among poor peasants in the south and in the major cities. There are about 330,000 Pentecostals in Italy, which probably does not include charismatic Roman Catholics. The largest denomination is the 30,000 strong Assemblies of God in Italy.

Pentecostal adherents number some 77,000 in the Netherlands, 10,000 in Belgium, 15,000 in Switzerland, and 3,000 in Austria. There are some 120,000 in France, including 60,000 in the Assemblies of God and 40,000 in the Gypsy Evangelical Movement. Gypsies constitute 25,000 of Spain's 30,000 Pentecostals.

Pentecostalism was brought to Bulgaria, Romania, and Russia in the early 1920s by Ivan E. Voronaev, founder in 1919 of the First Russian Pentecostal Church in New York City. In spite of fascist and communist repression, Pentecostalism survived and grew. It has remained small in Poland (20,000), Hungary (15,000), Yugoslavia (26,000), and Bulgaria (28,000) but has shown remarkable growth in Romania (200,000) and the Soviet Union (650,000).

Pentecostalism in Worldwide Perspective

There are four forms of Pentecostalism in Asia, Africa, and Latin America: (1) mission churches established by missionaries from the Pentecostal denominations of North America and Europe; (2) charismatic movements in the mainstream non-Pentecostal denominations; (3) independent schismatic offspring of the mission churches, and (4) wholly indigenous movements. Although Spirit baptism and the charismata hold a central place in the latter two forms, their Pentecostal authenticity has been questioned or denied by many Pentecostals and charismatics because of their adoption or toleration of beliefs and practices, such as polygamy and ancestor worship, from non-Christian traditional religions. The great expansion of Pentecostalism in Africa, Latin America, and Asia beginning in the 1950s coincided with the evangelizing campaigns of American healers and with the acceleration of decolonization and modernization. [*See regional surveys under* Christianity.]

Latin America. From its small beginnings in the first decade of this century, Pentecostalism has expanded greatly in Latin America since the late 1940s. In Brazil in 1910, Swedish-American steelworkers Daniel Berg and Gunnar Vingren introduced Pentecostalism in a Baptist church in Belém. Their work, the Assemblies of God of Brazil, spread widely but grew modestly in its first three decades. Since then it has grown to some four million adherents. Also in 1910, Luigi Francescon (founder of Pentecostalism in Italy) founded the Christian Congregations of Brazil in São Paulo among Italian immigrants; that denomination now numbers one million adherents. In the 1950s, several dozen independent Pentecostal bodies emerged, such as Manoel de Melo's "Brazil for Christ" movement, which has more than a million followers. Pentecostals in Brazil number about 6.5 million.

In Chile in 1907, the American Willis C. Hoover's conversion to Pentecostalism led to his eviction from the pastorate of a Methodist church in Valparaíso. Hoover then founded the Pentecostal Methodist Church, which numbers some 400,000 members. Several schisms from that church resulted in the organization of the Evangelical Pentecostal Church (400,000), the Pentecostal Church of Chile (100,000), and the Evangelical Methodist Pentecostal Church Reunited in Jesus' Name (100,000). The rapidly growing Chilean Pentecostal movement totals about 1.3 million.

Pentecostalism has shown remarkable growth in Colombia, with 200,000 believers, almost half of whom are in the United Pentecostal Church, and in Argentina, with over 300,000, of whom one-third belong to the Christian Assemblies (Italian). In the remaining South American countries there are about 300,000. One-third of Mexico's 7 million Pentecostals are Otomí Indians organized in the Union of Evangelical Independent Churches. There are some 7 million Pentecostals in Central America and the Caribbean islands.

Asia and the Middle East. Pentecostalism has had almost no success in the Muslim areas of the world. It is insignificant in the Middle East and of limited size in Asia, with the exceptions of India and Indonesia.

The Pentecostal message was brought to India in 1907 by American and European missionaries. The movement spread widely but had little impact before the 1940s, when the indigenous churches, founded in the 1920s and 1930s, began to grow rapidly. There are about 550,000 Pentecostals in India, including 120,000 in the Indian Pentecostal Church of God and 100,000 in the United Pentecostal Church in India.

In Indonesia in the early 1920s, American missionaries established the Pentecostal movement on the island of Bali, and German missionaries introduced it at Bandung, Java. Beginning in the 1950s, indigenous Pentecostalism exploded, aided by the campaigns of American healers. There are more than 2 million Pentecostals in Indonesia today, half of them in the Bethel Church in Indonesia.

The Pentecostal movement was brought to China in 1908. Success was slight, and limited mostly to the remote regions of the North and West. There are about 35,000 Pentecostals in the People's Republic of China, all in the True Jesus Church, and 75,000 on Taiwan, about two-thirds of them in the True Jesus Church in Taiwan. The movement in Japan began in 1913, but had very little growth until the 1950s and numbers around 150,000, including 62,000 in the Spirit of Jesus Church. Korea has 150,000 Pentecostals, of whom two-thirds are in the Korean Christian Pentecostal Church. The Philippines has about 550,000 Pentecostals, including 150,000 in the Assemblies of God. Most of the 40,000 Pentecostals in Australia, 15,000 in New Zealand, and 100,000 each in New Guinea and Papua New Guinea are aboriginal peoples.

Africa. In the period of its massive growth since the 1960s, Pentecostalism in sub-Saharan Africa has been a predominantly indigenous movement led by dynamic preachers and prophets. American missionaries John G. Lake and Thomas Hezmalhalch, converts to Pentecostalism from John Alexander Dowie's Christian Catholic Apostolic Church in Zion (Zion, Illinois), won most of Dowie's South African churches to the new movement following a revival in 1908 in Johannesburg. A former Dutch Reformed minister, Pieter Louis leRoux, emerged as the leader of the Apostolic Faith Mission of South Africa, which has some 200,000 followers. The segregationist policies of this and other Pentecostal mission churches led to the early loss of most of their black adherents. As a result, numerous schismatic "Zionist" churches arose—so-called because nearly all use the word *Zion* in their official names. In addition, many independent indigenous Pentecostal churches were founded by prophets who have often been regarded as demigods by their followers. There are about two million South African Pentecostals, including 600,000 in the Zion Christian Church and 430,000 in Nicholas H. B. Benghu's African Assemblies of God (Back to God).

Missionaries from South Africa, Europe, and North America had established the movement throughout most of sub-Saharan Africa by the 1920s, but it was the evangelizing efforts of native preachers that account for Pentecostalism's great success. The distribution of American Pentecostal literature in Nigeria led to the indigenous Aladura (praying people) movement beginning in the early 1920s, which spread all through western Africa in the wake of a revival in 1928. The preaching of Simon Kimbangu in the lower Congo in 1921 led to his life imprisonment, but the church founded in his name by his followers grew throughout central Africa. In the 1950s, indigenous African Pentecostalism entered a phase of explosive growth that has continued.

In 1985, there are an estimated 6 million Pentecostals in Zaire, more than half in the Church of God on Earth through the Prophet Simon Kimbangu; some 2.2 million in Nigeria, where the Apostolic Church of Nigeria, Christ Apostolic Church, and the Nigerian Christian Fellowship each have about 400,000 adherents; another million in Ghana; 750,000 in Kenya; and over 400,000 in Zimbabwe, including 260,000 in the African Apostolic Church of Johane Maranke. The total number of all Pentecostals in Africa is about 14 million and growing rapidly. [*See also* African Religions, *article on* Modern Movements.]

BIBLIOGRAPHY

The Pentecostal minister Walter J. Hollenweger, in *The Pentecostals* (Minneapolis, 1972), has compiled more information on more Pentecostal groups throughout the world than can be found in any other single book. My own *Vision of the Disinherited: The Making of American Pentecostalism* (Oxford, 1979) provides a thorough narrative, analytical, and interpretative treatment of the American movement from its origins to the 1930s. Many of the major historical, sociological, psychological, and theological issues involved in the study of Pentecostal Christianity as a whole are addressed in this work. For an eyewitness account by a leader in the Los Angeles revival, see Frank Bartleman's *Azusa Street* (Plainfield, N.J., 1980); originally published as *How "Pentecost" Came to Los Angeles* (Los Angeles, 1926). This edition has an excellent foreword by the Pentecostal historian Vinson Synan, who has also edited an important collection of essays entitled *Aspects of Pentecostal-Charismatic Origins* (Plainfield, N.J., 1975).

The origins of the Pentecostal movement in Europe may be found in Nils Bloch-Hoell's *The Pentecostal Movement* (Oslo, 1964), which is best on Scandinavia, and in Donald Gee's *Wind and Flame* (London, 1967), which is best on the United Kingdom; both treatments are theological as well as historical.

Christian Lalive d'Epinay's *Haven of the Masses* (London, 1969) lays bare the social roots of Chilean Pentecostalism; his findings have broad applicability to Pentecostalism throughout the underdeveloped world. The multiple functions of Pentecostalism are revealed in the collection of anthropological essays edited by Stephen D. Glazier, *Perspectives on Pentecostalism: Case Studies from the Caribbean and Latin America* (Lanham, Md., 1980), which examines the movement's relationship to the process of modernization.

The story of the Deliverance and charismatic revivals is told with scholarship and verve in David Edwin Harrell, Jr.'s *All Things Are Possible* (Bloomington, Ind., 1975). Also indispensable on the charismatic revival are Richard Quebedeaux's *The New Charismatics II* (New York, 1983) and the collection of essays edited by Russell P. Spittler, *Perspectives on the New Pentecostalism* (Grand Rapids, Mich., 1976). Historical and theological assessments of the Catholic charismatic movement are Edward D. O'Connor's *The Pentecostal Movement in the Catholic Church* (Notre Dame, Ind., 1971) for the American scene, and René Laurentin's *Catholic Pentecostalism* (Garden City, N.Y., 1977) for the European.

The mainstream Pentecostal position on Spirit baptism and the charismata is presented succinctly in Ralph M. Riggs's *The Spirit Himself* (Springfield, Mo., 1949). More moderate charismatic positions are laid out by the Presbyterian J. Rodman Williams in *The Gift of the Holy Spirit Today* (Plainfield, N.J., 1980), and the Roman Catholic theologian Donald L. Gelpi in *Pentecostalism* (New York, 1971).

The clinical psychologist John P. Kildahl, in his *The Psychology of Speaking in Tongues* (New York, 1972), presents a generally favorable assessment of the mental health of glossolalists. In *Speaking in Tongues* (Chicago, 1972), the anthropologist Felicitas D. Goodman concludes on the basis of her cross-cultural study that the practice involves an altered mental state. The sociolinguist William J. Samarin's *Tongues of Men and Angels* (New York, 1972) demonstrates the nonlinguistic character of the phenomenon and views it as learned behavior.

ROBERT MAPES ANDERSON

PERCUSSION AND NOISE. Numerous religious systems of beliefs and practices throughout the world involve general and specific uses and functions of percussion sounds and noises to fulfill various roles. This article explores some selected examples of the roles such elements play within specific sacred and secular ritual traditions. In addition, some attention is paid to the experience of noise and percussive sound as an integral part of ritual expression in various contexts, and a few speculative thoughts are offered on the possible psychological effects that such sound may have.

Percussive sound is here understood to represent sounds whose pitch and duration are definable, for the most part, in precise terms that are produced by conventional man-made instruments, of the membranophone and idiophone families. *Noise* refers to sounds unspecifiable as to precise pitch and duration, produced by virtually any source, from firecrackers to vocal cries and sounds imitative of nature. The major distinguishing factor between percussive sound and noise lies in the obvious fact that percussive tone belongs to a musical system per se while noise is generally produced or uttered outside a sound musical system (that is, outside vibration periodicity and a well-defined theoretical sound-musical organization). In no way does this distinction imply an aesthetic value judgment, as noise and percussive sounds can have equal, albeit quite different, expressive power.

Percussion. The use of percussion to enhance specific moments of ritual solemnity and intensity is a very widespread practice throughout the world. Whether produced by striking gongs, ringing bells, beating drums, or playing other idiophones and membranophones, percussive sounds of all sorts have probably formed an integral part of organized religious ritual since its beginnings. The specific value attached by human beings to such sounds in ritual contexts is reflected in the religious importance ascribed to musical instruments of all kinds and particularly to percussion instruments. For example, in many West African traditional religions, and in their Afro-Brazilian and Afro-Cuban counterparts, drums fulfill such central roles in the ritual life of these communities that they are sacralized through quasi-baptismal ceremonies. Such "baptisms" often involve animal sacrifices and sacred food offerings, which confer upon the instruments spiritual force, thereby allowing them to discharge their basic functions, namely to invoke and call the gods and thus to bring about spirit possession of the initiates. It is clear, however, that such ritual associations with drums are culture-specific.

The hypothesis, widespread among ethnologists, that attributes the triggering of trance or possession to an inherent power of percussion instruments, especially drums, is dubious. Laboratory experiments carried out by neurophysiologists have attempted to determine the organic and neurological effects of certain types of sound waves, unbiased by factors of cultural affect. Drumming particularly has been seen as a sound source capable of affecting the inner ear. Ethnomusicologists, however, tend to reject the various neurophysiological theories on the effects of drums on the grounds that the conditions of laboratory experiments are alien to the actual performance contexts, that the identification of certain frequencies as occasioning brain wave alterations applies equally to trance and nontrance music, and that the level of abstraction of such theories ignores the psychological conditioning inherent in the cultural system of religious beliefs and practices. Gilbert Rouget (1985), among others, has shown that the question of the relationships between spirit possession and music and musical instruments cannot be answered in universal terms because individual religious dogmas generally dictate the nature of such relationships.

Among native American (hemispheric) cultures, drums occupy a central place in ritual. For the Mapuche of Chile and southwestern Argentina, for example, the sacred drum known as *kultrún* offers an excellent example of the ritual symbolic significance assigned to an instrument. This drum accompanies the vocal performance of the *machi* (medicine woman or shaman) in fertility, initiatory, funerary, large and small therapeutic, and diagnostic rites. The *kultrún*, a single-headed wooden drum played with a mallet, is decorated with drawings symbolizing the Mapuche cosmogony. As reported by María Ester Grebe (1973), the structural dualism of Mapuche culture is represented in these drawings, which depict the supernatural world and the various divisions of the earth as well as the spatial connotations of good (east, south) and evil (west, north). The "vessel" shape of the drum and the bay tree from which it is made carry additional mythical associations. Before the head is fastened to the body of the drum, several ritual objects (coins, seeds of medicinal plants, animal hair, wheat, and corn) are deposited in the bowl. These objects symbolize fertility—the natural products of mother earth inside her belly. Moreover, the bay tree is the Mapuche cosmic tree, which, like the *kultrún* carved from its wood, has the power of "projecting its owner to the heavens" (Grebe), much like Siberian and Inner Asian shamans who in their magic trance believe themselves to be traveling in the air seated on their drums.

In addition to various functions of communication with the supernatural, the *kultrún* is believed to hold curative powers through its association with the singing of the shaman and through its efficient struggle against the spirit of illness *(wekufi)*. Without it the diagnostic, prophylactic, and healing functions of the shaman would be impossible. Such functions assigned to musical instruments are common among South American Indian cultures. Alfred Métraux (1963) indicated that the medicinal value of shamanic musical instruments lies their capacity to depict through their sound the voices of spirits. In addition, most indigenous mythologies coincide in ascribing to these instruments an origin as pristine as the world itself. Pre-Columbian high Indian cultures in Mesoamerica and South America ascribed a particularly important role to percussion instruments in sacred rituals. Archaeological exemplars of Aztec *teponaztle*s (slit drums) and *huehuetl*s (upright, cylindrical drums) reveal through extraordinarily detailed carvings on the instruments the ritual purposes that they were to fulfill. The numerous Mexican codices also provide iconographic information on the central position occupied by these instruments in specific ritual scenes. Likewise, the famous murals at the Bonampak temple (c. eighth century CE) in the state of Chiapas demonstrate the importance of drums and large rattles in Maya ritual processions. Among the Inca a small double-headed drum, known as *tinya*, carried a special ritual value of magic power, still remembered among present-day Indian communities. The *tinya* is played with a zoomorphic mallet in contemporary Peru (Ayacucho, Huancavelica) in Carnival ceremonies and in special rituals of cattle branding. The exact nature of this magic power is not verbalized by Indian percussionists but is readily acknowledged. Even in present-day Cajamarca, before the heads of the drum are firmly secured, ancient custom still requires that cloves of garlic and red peppers be inserted in the drum's body to reinforce that magic sound power. The sacredness of numerous percussion instruments in ancient Peru is confirmed through sixteenth-century Spanish chronicles that describe the type of luxurious long robes worn by the drummers on solemn occasions. Today in Puno, for special festive events drummers wear accoutrements relating to the mythical condor.

Percussion plays an important role in sacred and secular rituals in numerous other cultures as well. In India, for example, the folk drum *ḍholak* (a double-headed, barrel-shaped wooden drum) accompanies singing for birth and marriage ceremonies, and it is the sound of this drum that communicates the news to the villagers and presages good omen. The same drum joins with hand cymbals in the performance of devotional songs. In South India popular religious instruction involves enactment of the religious story known as the *Harikathā*. The reciter develops his quasi-monodrama, supported by a musician and the instrumental accompaniment of at least a *mṛdaṅga*, another barrel-shaped, double-headed drum. The North Indian devotional chanting known as *kīrtana* (used in singing the name or praise of Kṛṣṇa) was popularized by the Vaiṣṇava mystic Caitanya (1486–1533), who is considered to have invented such instruments as the *mṛdaṅga* and cymbals. In his wish to make *kīrtana* accessible to all, he is said to have introduced the *khola* (a drum made of clay) and the *karatāla* (cymbals made of brass) into this music, not only because these instruments were easily obtainable by the poor but also because they were quite appropriate to the expression of this revivalistic type of worship and the devotional mysticism implied in *kīrtana*.

Many religious traditions have obvious implications for the attributes ascribed to percussion instruments. The dogmas of such religions frequently assign to musical instruments special symbolic meaning or significance so that they are not considered mere artifacts but special reflections by association of the qualities of spirits or divinities. In Afro-Brazilian Candomblé, for example, the funeral ritual cycle known as Axêxê in the Nagô cult or Azeri in the Gege cult (both related to the Yoruba-Fon of West Africa) is performed shortly after the burial of an initiate and involves calabash drums (played with sticks) among the Nagô and a pottery jar (played by striking the opening with a fire-fan made of straw) among the Gege. The Axêxê ceremony assures the transformation of the dead initiate into the cult group's first ancestors of creation. Its practical function is to send the spirit of Iku (Death) away. All artifacts used in the ceremony are eventually broken and become parts of the *carrego* ("load of death"). Because the calabash drums and the pottery jar have been used to summon the spirit of the dead, they are broken into pieces following the ceremony and taken to a specific place revealed through divination. The *carrego* symbolizes the final severance of ties of the dead person with the cult center; since the drums become personalized in the ceremonial process, they must thus be destroyed in order to complete the severance.

The proper understanding of the experience and effect of percussion sound by and upon the members of a given cultural group can only be developed through the knowledge of the specific beliefs associated with sound and sound-producing artifacts. A good example involves the ensemble of *batá* drums (double-headed, played horizontally) of the Afro-Cuban religion of the Lucumi of Yoruba ancestry. In Yorubaland, the *batá* drums are attributed primarily to the cult of Ṣango, the god of thunder and fire. In both Africa and Cuba the ensemble comprises three drums of different sizes, and although in Africa they may fulfill separate functions, in Cuba the trio must perform together, as the three drums (known as *iyā*, *itótele*, and *okónkolo*, from the largest to the smallest) are collectively considered the organs of sound expression of the god Aña. According to the orthodox tradition, the trio of drums must be made from a single sacred tree trunk; this emphasizes the unity of the trio through which the deity speaks and manifests himself. The trio possesses a special secret, its *afóuobó*, known only by the priests dedicated to Aña. The sacred, magical power of the drums derives from this secret, physically signified by some sacred seeds, cowrie shells, and other substances placed in a small bag made of animal skin and inserted in the body of the *iyá* drum. In addition, certain sacred plants (known as *éggüe* in Cuba) are deposited in the drum cavity during construction and, in time, will crumble into a powder that confers on the drum its ultimate spiritual strength. The specific objects used are determined by the *diloggún* (the oracle as revealed by divination). In theory, a sacrificial food and animal blood offering must be performed annually in order to assure the continuity of the drums' power and effectiveness. The superhuman nature of the *batá* is also stressed by the belief among some drummers that the drums do, on occasion, sound by themselves very mysterious beats or patterns. When this occurs, the drummers inevitably consult a diviner *(babalawo),* who then consults the oracle.

Despite the great care accorded the drums during their construction and consecration, sometimes a drum simply does not deliver the expected mellow or clear-toned sound, or its sonority changes in time. In such cases, a liturgical explanation is usually offered, and the drum is retired from the trio (but never destroyed). One can only speculate regarding the basis for this aesthetic judgment; in all probability, however, drummers learn from their teachers and through their own empirical experience what should be the specific sound ideal of a drum called upon to fulfill transcendental musical and liturgical functions. Sound, in this case, is equated with the very manifestation of the supernatural.

Numerous idiophones appear as the direct attributes of the many gods of the West African pantheon. In Yorubaland, the double bell *adjá,* for example, personifies some of the qualities of Ogun, the god of iron and of war. The priests of Ogun always precede their speech to the community by shaking the *adjá,* as if the instrument symbolized the voice of the god. In Bahia, Brazil, the same *adjá,* or *xerê,* shaken by the cult leader or an assistant over the heads of the initiates, functions as a direct call to all gods *(orixás),* so that the devotees can respond (through spirit possession) to the "voice" of their god, heard through the drum. The auspiciousness of bells and rattles for spirit possession (in Bahia) is clearly indicated by the fact that several of the *ogans* (civil protectors) of the cult center are provided with such instruments during that part of the ritual in which the call to the gods takes place.

Noise. Comparatively little is known and recorded concerning the use and function of noise in religious rituals. In general, noises of various kinds are used to call the community's attention to specific moments of a ritual. Their psychological effects are probably based on both association and expectation. Solemn passages of ritual are signified in a number of cultures through the detonation of firecrackers. This is the case in the Mexican states of Puebla and Veracruz, for example, where the pre-Columbian *danza de los voladores* is performed. By the time all of the six or eight "flyers" have reached the top of the sacred post (or "tree of life") and begin to fly down (metaphorically bringing the gods' messages to the earth and, as symbolic birds, coming down to fertilize the earth), powerful firecrackers thunder in the sky. Likewise, in Bahia, Brazil, during the public ceremony known as Xirê, the impressive moment when all the gods (initiates in the state of possession) make their entrance in the main dancing room of the cult center is announced to the whole community by firecrackers, a moment of religious fulfillment that conveys a sense of happiness, frightful majesty, and awe.

Perhaps one of the oldest noisemakers associated with religious observance is the *sēmantron* or *simandron* (also known as *klepalo* in Slavic languages)—productive of a sort of holy clatter—which is either a wooden plank or metal plate suspended and struck with a stick or a mallet. Until the advent of the church bell in the West (c. seventh century), it was used widely to call people to prayer. It still serves that function today in some Orthodox and Eastern Christian churches, particularly in monasteries, such as that of Saint John on the Greek island of Patmos and that of Saint Gregorios on Mount Athos. One can only surmise what sort of psychological effects the *simandron* could have. Its clamor undoubtedly was and is still considered appropriate not only for calling prompt attention but also for imparting the sense of urgency and obligation, of mystery and fearsome solemnity, that is implied in the activity of praying.

Vocal shouts also fulfill important roles in various religious systems throughout the world. In African and Afro-American possession rites the gods have a special cry, known in Brazil and Yorubaland as *ilá,* that identifies the personality of the god at the precise moment of spirit possession. Such shouts or cries can certainly be categorized as "noise" (in contrast to singing in the usual sense). In the Jamaican Afro-Christian cults, such as the Pukkumina, or in the Afro-Cuban non-Christian religions, oral sounds of a special kind frequently accompany spiritual trance or possession. The "groaning" and "trumping" that occur in association with the Pukkumina "laboring in the spirit" consist primarily in a rhythmic and noisy inhaling and exhaling creating hyperventilation, conducive to possession states. Similarly, the Afro-Cuban Ronconeo, performed during a sacred ritual, consists in the same air inspiration and expiration accompanying the up-and-down motion of the arms by the worshipers. The rhythmic breathing is clearly audible in two alternating pitch levels, high for the inspiration and low for the expiration, sounding, according to Fernando Ortiz (1952), like an opaque bitonal drumming. Such noises are produced by the respiratory mechanism but without the intervention of the vocal cords.

The reliance on handclapping in religious rituals is also fairly widespread. Besides its frequent function of reinforcing or enhancing accompanied rhythms, handclapping in numerous cultures constitutes a highly symbolic language through which collective emotions are expressed. Some central African peoples, for example, conceive of regularly pulsating handclapping as an expression of exalting religiousness, that is, the sounds coming out of the body of humans are believed to reach the gods directly as an intimate emanation of their spirit. In West Africa and those cultural areas of Brazil and Cuba where Ifa divination is practiced, the readings of the positive Ifa signs by the *babalawo* (diviner) are accompanied by handclapping, a sign of approval and rejoicing. Functionally, sound appears in these ritual contexts as a fundamental mark of transition.

[*See also* Drums *and* Bull-Roarers.]

BIBLIOGRAPHY

Béhague, Gerard. "Patterns of *Candomblé* Music Performance: An Afro-Brazilian Religious Setting." In *Performance Practice: Ethnomusicological Perspectives*, edited by Gerard Béhague, pp. 222–254. Westport, Conn., 1984. Illustrates the functions of drums and other percussion in an African-related religion, providing detailed information on drums' sacralization and drummers' social status within the group.

Deva, F. Chaitanya. *Musical Instruments of India: Their History and Development*. Calcutta, 1978. A very comprehensive study on Indian organology relating the history of musical instruments to many other relevant sources.

Grebe, María Ester. "El Kultrún mapuche: Un microcosmo simbólico." *Revista musical chilena* 27 (July–December 1973): 3–42. This study presents an excellent model of integration of analysis of belief systems and symbolism as encapsulated in a ritual object.

Lévi-Strauss, Claude. *Introduction to a Science of Mythology*. 4 vols. New York, 1969–1981. Discusses the symbolic meaning of *din*.

Mapa de los instrumentos musicales de uso popular en el Perú. Lima, 1978. A useful general description of Peruvian folk and popular instruments by types and geographical distribution.

Métraux, Alfred. *Religion and Shamanism*. Vol. 5 of *Handbook of South American Indians*, edited by Julian H. Steward. New York, 1963. Provides excellent examples and insights.

Needham, Rodney. "Percussion and Transition." *Man* (1967): 606–614. A classic example of an attempt to relate drum sounds (i.e., percussion itself) to trance phenomena in Haitian Voodoo in strictly physiological terms.

Ortiz, Fernando. *Los instrumentos de la música afrocubana*, vols. 1 and 4. Havana, 1952–1954. The most comprehensive study on Afro-Cuban organology.

Rouget, Gilbert. *Music and Trance: A Theory of the Relations between Music and Possession*. Chicago, 1985. A thorough study, drawing on cross-cultural illustrations in the attempted formulation of a theory.

GERARD BÉHAGUE

PERFECTIBILITY. The etymology of the word *perfect* indicates the centrality of the idea of perfectibility in religion. Derived from the Latin *per facere*, the English word *perfect* implies completion or being thoroughly made. Also the Greek word *teleios* is translated as "perfect," and it lends to the concept the idea of attaining a goal or end *(telos)*. Aristotle saw human perfectibility as the capacity to achieve the goal of fulfilling or realizing one's nature. Drawing on these definitions, we can say that perfection as the goal of actualizing the highest human potential plays an important role in religion.

Anders Nygren (1960) has described the dynamic of religion as fourfold. First, religion reveals the eternal, the ultimate reality, which represents perfection in the sense of wholeness, completeness, and integrity. Second, this revelation of a perfect ultimate reality throws into sharp relief the imperfect nature of humanity. The human predicament becomes visible in its separation from the eternally perfect. Third, religion seeks to provide a means of overcoming this separation. Having judged human nature to be radically imperfect when compared with ultimate perfection, religion nevertheless declares that human beings are perfectible. Ways of purification or atonement have been made known and can be followed by the members of the religion. This affirmation of human perfectibility and the provision of means to achieve it stand at the heart of religion. As Nygren writes, "A religion which did not claim to make possible the meeting between the eternal and man, a religion which did not claim to be the bridge over an otherwise impassable gulf, would be a monstrosity" (p. 44). Religious traditions provide for the bridging of this gulf to take place in two opposite directions: either from the human side, by human initiative, or from the divine side. The final characteristic of religion results from this mediation between the human and the divine: religion makes possible the union of the soul with the eternal. Variously phrased in different religious traditions, the perfectibility of human beings is realized by identification or union with the perfection of the ultimate reality. This dynamic of religion as a means to perfection inheres in all religions but may be seen clearly in the biblical traditions of the West and in the Hindu and Buddhist traditions of the East.

Perfectibility in Biblical Religions. For the biblical traditions, God represents perfection, the embodiment of all wisdom and virtue. God possesses transcendental and metaphysical perfection. In the Middle Ages Anselm, archbishop of Canterbury (1093–1109), declared God to be "that than which nothing greater can be conceived." By contrast, human beings are separated from and judged by this divine perfection. When Isaiah saw the Lord seated upon his throne, his response was to say, "Woe is me! For I am lost; I am a man of unclean lips" (*Is.* 6:5). The Hebrew scriptures depict this understanding of God's perfection and man's imperfection in terms of the covenant. God is righteous and desires to establish his covenant with humanity. But, as the primeval history (*Gn.* 1–11) indicates, humanity, beginning with Adam and Eve, was unrighteous and violated the covenantal relationship. Eternally righteous and loving, God reestablishes his covenant with Abraham and the patriarchs. But even the chosen people continually fall short of the demands for perfection, as the Pentateuch shows. Later, the Hebrew prophets declare that only God is holy, and all human beings have turned away from God.

The New Testament and Christianity inherited and developed this understanding of human nature as fallen, sinful, or imperfect. The apostle Paul set the stage for much of later Christian theology when he described human sin as having come "into the world through one man," Adam. Whether taken literally or figuratively, the Fall depicts the human condition. And when this condition is compared with the perfection revealed in Christ, Christians perceive the imperfection that is the human predicament.

Both the Hebrew scriptures and the New Testament, however, proclaim that the human predicament can be resolved; the fallen state need not be permanent since human beings are perfectible. In the Torah, God's desire to restore the covenant with the Israelites indicates the possibility of rapprochement with the divine. This covenantal relationship is not something impossible for human beings; as *Deuteronomy* says, "This commandment is not too hard for you, neither is it far off. . . . But the word is near you, it is in your mouth and in your heart, so that you can do it" (30:11–14).

The New Testament attributes to Jesus the straightforward demand, "You, therefore, must be perfect [*teleioi*] as your heavenly father is perfect" (*Mt.* 5:48). In its context, this demand follows Jesus' reformulation of the major commandments, in which he requires inner purity, radical obedience to the spirit of the Law over and above the letter of the Law. When Jesus summarized all the commandments with the two love commandments (*Mt.* 22:37–40), he also summed up the essence of this demand for perfection. He further described perfection in the same radical fashion in his dialogue with the young man who asked what he must do to gain eternal life (*Mt.* 19:16–21). When Jesus responded that he must keep the commandments, the young man, replying that he had kept them, asked what more he lacked. Jesus answered by placing before him the radical demand of love: "If you would be perfect, go and sell what you own and give to the poor, and you will have treasure in heaven."

Although the New Testament seems clearly to demand perfection as the way out of the human predicament, the Christian tradition has debated at length the meaning of perfection and the question of human perfectibility. Augustine questioned the possibility of human perfection for two reasons. First, only God has perfection in an ontological sense; human beings are far lower in being and power. Second, because of original sin, human beings cannot now even will finite perfection. It is the human predicament that a person cannot on his own fulfill the demands stated in *Matthew* 5:48 (quoted above). The only way that progress can be made toward moral perfection and salvation is by God's grace. Without grace, people experience the situation that Paul described when he said, "I do not do the good I want, but the evil that I do not want" (*Rom.* 7:19). Thus, Augustine held that such perfectibility as humans have results from the prior action of God. God predetermines who shall receive salvation, but this predetermination does not obviate human free will. Salvation is possible for those who receive grace, but full perfection lies beyond this life even for the saints. This view, placing the initiative for perfection on God's side, has its parallel in the Hebrew scriptures and in Jewish tradition also. In his vision, Isaiah received purification from one of the seraphim who touched his mouth with a burning coal (*Is.* 6:6–7).

Pelagius, a fifth-century English lay monk, questioned Augustine's views, however, saying that God would not have commanded anything (i.e., perfection) that was impossible for man to achieve. He was much more sanguine about the human exercise of free will to achieve perfection. [*See* Pelagianism.] This commonsense approach has appealed to many Christians, and as R. N. Flew observes, the history of Christianity—and of the notion of perfectibility—can be told as the swing "between the extremes of Pelagianism and the extremes of dual predestination" (Flew, 1968, p. 99). [*See* Free Will and Predestination.]

Thomas Aquinas agreed theologically with Augustine, although he held out much more hope for human perfectibility. Absolute perfection, he said, belongs to God alone and cannot be possessed by human beings, but a lower perfection is not only possible but incumbent upon them. This "evangelical perfection" involves removing all mortal sin and cultivating the love of God. It was with regard to this kind of perfection that the Catholic church interpreted Jesus' dialogue with the young man (cited above) to imply two standards of virtuous conduct. The first consists in following the commandments, as the young man said he had done. This is the standard for ordinary virtue and salvation. Jesus' response, "If you would be perfect . . . ," sets out a higher standard, a "counsel of perfection" for those who wish to ensure salvation by works of supererogation. The church traditionally interpreted these counsels of perfection to imply the vows of poverty, chastity, and obedience.

Within Christianity, this distinction between spiritual foot soldiers and a spiritual elite provided the constitution for the anchorite and monastic movements. Mystics and ascetics of various kinds have flourished in the Christian tradition alongside mainstream Christianity. The quest of the mystics was the quest for perfection, both in the sense of freedom from sin and, even more important, in the sense of the contemplation of and union with God. Renouncing the body, they frequently employed severe asceticism to subdue the desires of the flesh. John of the Cross, for example, wore knotted ropes under his clothing in his quest for the vision of God.

The Reformation marked a swing of the Christian pendulum away from Pelagianism and back toward predestination. Martin Luther developed a radically theocentric theology in which human salvation as well as perfection depend on the grace of God. For Luther, free will could not be regarded as a means to perfection because human beings, in their fallen state, had only self-will, which was alienated from God. John Calvin also regarded humanity as totally alienated from God and unable to do anything on its own to achieve perfection. Calvin and the other reformers, however, still believed that humanity reflected the image of God and was thus perfectible by God's grace. In this world, however, even with grace, one can do no more than make progress toward perfection, for final perfection can come only in the afterlife or in the Kingdom. Modern Protestant theologians have tended to reaffirm these reformers' views of perfectibility. Reinhold Niebuhr, for example, wrote, "The ethical demands of Jesus are incapable of fulfillment in the present existence of man . . . their final fulfillment is possible only when God transmutes the present chaos of this world into its final unity" (*An Interpretation of Christian Ethics*, 1936, p. 56).

The most significant exception to the Protestant Reformation's reluctance to accept perfectibility was pronounced by John Wesley. Preaching in eighteenth-century England, Wesley placed perfection at the center of his theology. He based Methodism on the idea that all Christians should strive for perfection in this life. By perfection he seems to have meant primarily evangelical or ethical perfection, but, at times, he also described it as an absolute perfection that unites one with the love of God. Wesley was not a Pelagian, however: he believed that perfection came only by grace through faith. But he held that Christians must seek that grace and faith by following the commandments and "taking up the cross daily."

Perfectibility in Indian Religious Traditions. Turning from the West to the East, we find that the great religious traditions of Asia that began in India have affirmed human perfectibility in similiar ways. The Hindu tradition has taught that absolute perfection represents the nature of the ultimate reality. The Hindus who composed the Upaniṣads (c. 800 BCE) reflected on *brahman*, the Absolute, the source of the universe. *Brahman* transcends the world and yet is also immanent in all things in the world. The Upaniṣadic thinkers described its perfection positively by saying that it is higher than the "great" and higher than even the "unmanifest." Mainly, however, the Upaniṣadic thinkers described *brahman* by negation, "*neti neti*," saying *brahman* is "not this, not this." Because it transcends the world, it cannot be described by any terms—even positive ones—appropriate to worldly things. Later theistic Hindus, for example the author of the *Bhagavadgītā*, adapted this language to describe deities such as Kṛṣṇa as "unborn, beginningless" and generally splendid to a degree that human beings could not comprehend.

The Buddhists, although they discarded the notion of a deity, took over the idea of a transcendent absolute. This absolute can be seen as either *nirvāṇa*, the blissful state of transcendent enlightenment, or as *dharma*, the truth that both underlies and transcends all existence.

In comparison with this perfect absolute, human beings, according to the Hindu and Buddhist traditions, lack perfection in three ways. First, they lack perfection in wisdom: they do not comprehend the absolute and their relation to it. For Hinduism, especially in the Vedānta tradition, this means that individuals do not know that they too are one with *brahman*. Second, human beings lack perfection in action: because they have a wrong perception of reality, people act in ways that are contrary to the absolute truth. The term *karman* denotes for both the Hindu and Buddhist traditions this idea of action. *Karman*, or action, whether positive or negative, is based on desire and generates a causal force that must come to fruition. Finally, because of *karman* and its consequences, human beings lack perfection in their existence: they are bound up in cycles of *saṃsāra*, or reincarnation. In these cycles they are separated from the absolute reality.

Despite humanity's threefold imperfection, the Indian traditions hold that perfectibility is possible. For the Hindus, human beings are perfectible because, although they may not be aware of it, ultimately they are sparks of the divine or drops of water from the infinite ocean. The human soul (*ātman*) is one with the Absolute (*brahman*). In the Buddhist tradition, human perfectibility stands as the basic presupposition for all of the Buddha's teachings. He told people to "be refuges for themselves" and to "work out your liberation with diligence" (*Dīgha Nikāya* 2.100, 2.120). Those who did so, he proclaimed, could reach their highest human potential just as the *arhat*s, or Perfected Ones, had.

To bridge the gulf to perfection, the Hindu and Buddhist traditions set out various paths, some requiring human initiative, others requiring divine action. In the Hindu tradition, human initiative is required to follow the two paths called *karma-mārga,* the path of action, and jñāna-mārga, the path of wisdom. *Karma-mārga,* expounded and popularized by the *Bhagavadgītā,* requires that people perform their actions in life without attachment. By so doing, they will free themselves from *karman* and desire. *Jñāna-mārga* represents the classic Hindu path of meditation to achieve the wisdom that overcomes separation from the Absolute. With its counsels of asceticism and solitary meditation, this path resembles the way of the mystics in the biblical traditions. The early Buddhists' path follows this model of meditation.

Buddhism divided the path to perfection or purification into three stages: *śīla,* ethical conduct; *samādhi,* concentration; and *prajñā* (Pali, *paññā*), wisdom. These constitute a gradual path to perfection that a person can pursue over many lifetimes. At the first stage, the Buddhists said, a person must develop his ethical conduct by refraining from killing, stealing, and lying, as well as by abstaining from wrong sexual conduct and from intoxicants. Further, Buddhist ethical conduct, as spelled out in elaborate lists of precepts incumbent upon monks, nuns, and the laity, required "right livelihood": following a way of life that brings no harm to oneself or others. The highest form of ethical conduct, Buddhists taught, consists in controlling not only one's outer actions but also one's inner desires.

The second aspect of the Buddhist path is *samādhi,* trance, or, more properly, concentration. At this stage, the Buddhist, having already controlled his conduct, seeks to control and calm his mind. The mind is focused on "one point" so that it may be trained to sever its attachments to the world. The culmination of *samādhi* comes in the development of the *dhyāna*s (Pali, *jhāna*s), or higher trance states. Finally, the advanced follower reaches the stage of the development of wisdom *(prajñā)* in meditation. Here, the Buddhist achieves perfection by overcoming ignorance and seeing the truth, *dharma.* The attainment of wisdom represents the highest human potential, and Buddhists proclaim that the Buddha and countless *arahant*s have achieved this state, called *nirvāṇa.* Buddhist descriptions of these perfected individuals say that they overcame such imperfections as egocentricity, desire, sensuality, doubt, pride, and, finally, ignorance.

Despite an emphasis on individual initiative, the Buddhist and Hindu traditions also set forth ways to perfection comparable to the Christian notion of grace. Among the Hindus, the way of *bhakti,* or devotion to a deity, represents an important example of this path to perfection and salvation. In the *Bhagavadgītā,* Kṛṣṇa, the divine embodiment of perfection, declares that if a person will worship and love him, that person will be united with him. For millions of Hindus, devotion constitutes the most accessible and plausible path to perfection.

The Buddhist tradition also knows paths to perfection and liberation that depend on extrahuman grace rather than human initiative. The most striking example of this kind of path is found in the Pure Land sect of Mahāyāna Buddhism, with its worship of the Buddha Amida. Buddhist teachers such as Hōnen and Shinran in Japan proclaimed that since in this age the meditative path to purification was too difficult for most people, people must rely on the grace of Amida Buddha. They taught people the chant "Namu Amida Butsu," which invokes the mercy of Amida, as the only requirement for salvation. As in Christianity, debates have raged within Pure Land Buddhism over the relationship between divine grace and human effort in the process of salvation.

To sum up: human perfectibility represents an ideal central to Asian and Western religious traditions. Perfectibility signifies the possibility of transcending the human predicament of separation from the perfection of the ultimate reality. In religious traditions, perfectibility involves ethical purification but goes beyond that to some degree of absolute perfection in harmony with the ultimate reality. Asian and biblical traditions maintain that human beings progress gradually toward the ideal of perfection. Many Christian theologians have held that perfection can never be fully realized in this life, while Indian thinkers have viewed the process of reincarnation as the context for perfectibility.

[*For ideas about perfectibility in Christianity, see* Sainthood. *In Islam, see* Walāyah *and* ʿIṣmah. *In Buddhism, see* Tathāgata; Mahāsiddhas; *and* Arhat; *and in Taoism, see* Chen-jen.]

BIBLIOGRAPHY

Anders Nygren's *Essence of Christianity: Two Essays* (London, 1960) analyzes the structure of religion in a way that illuminates the importance of perfectibility. Two books particularly trace the notion of perfectibility in the West: John Passmore's *The Perfectibility of Man* (London, 1970) examines the history of the idea from the Greeks to modern science, while R. N. Flew's *The Idea of Perfection in Christian Theology* (New York, 1968) restricts its scope to Christian theology. The history of the idea of perfectibility in Asian religions has not been written, but two books provide a comparison of Asian and Western concepts: Shanta Ratnayaka's *Two Ways of Perfection: Christian and Buddhist* (Colombo, 1978) compares Theravāda Buddhist thought with the theology of John Wesley, and the anthology *Sainthood in World Religions*, edited by George D. Bond and Richard Kieckhefer (Berkeley, 1985), surveys notions of the perfected individual in the major religious traditions.

GEORGE D. BOND

PERFORMANCE. *See* Drama, *article on* Performance and Ritual.

PERIODICAL LITERATURE. Periodicals arise late in the history of religious publication. The first regularly published journal in any field was the *Journal des savants,* a monthly that began in Paris in 1665 and is still published today. It was followed in 1682 by the *Acta Eruditorum* (Leipzig, 1682–1731). *Altes und Neues,* the first journal devoted to religion or theology, was published from 1701 to 1719 in Leipzig. The nineteenth century was the period of rapid growth in periodical publication. The standard format was established by the journal *Theologische Studien und Kritiken,* originally published in Hamburg, Germany in 1848; it included major scholarly contributions, shorter notes on significant issues, and book reviews by established experts in the field. Specialized journals in specific fields of theology and religion proliferated throughout the nineteenth century. In the period after World War II, the advance of communications techniques and the growing global interdependence of political and economic life led to a rapid increase in periodicals devoted to the culture, literature, and religions of all parts of the world.

The best short overview of periodicals in religion and theology are the subentries under the title "Zeitschriften, wissenschaftlich-theologische" in *Die Religion in Geschichte und Gegenwart,* 3d ed. (Tübingen, 1962). K. G. Stack and Wilfred Werbeck are the authors of the section "Evangelische" (columns 1885–1888), and H. R. Schlette is the author of the section "Katholische" (columns 1888-1891). A history of journals in religion and theology is a great desideratum.

Periodicals in Religion. The listing that follows is restricted, with some exceptions, to periodicals that are accessible to the English-speaking reader. The majority of listed periodicals are published in the United States. This list generally excludes periodicals that may contain articles related to the study of religion but that are not primarily concerned with the field. In each case, after the title, the entry will give the following:

(1) Year that publication began (or years of publication, if no longer published)
(2) Country of origin
(3) Language or languages of publication
(4) Number of issues per year
(5) Any special notes as to focus, editorial scope, and so forth

Periodicals are a volatile form of publication, with frequent births, deaths, title changes, and so forth, and therefore any listing may rapidly go out of date. Editors, publishers, subscription cost, and the like, which frequently change, will not be given. Readers will find that information most easily in *Ulrich's International Periodicals Directory: A Classified Guide to Current Periodicals, Foreign and Domestic* (New York); it also names the indexing services that include each of the journals it lists.

AJS Review, (1) 1975. (2) United States. (3) English. (4) 2. (5) General Jewish interests.

American Academy of Religion: Journal. (1) 1933. (2) United States. (3) English. (4). 4. (5) World religions, Christianity, academic study of religion.

American Jewish History. (1) 1893. (2) United States. (3) English. (4) 4. (5) North and South American Jewish history. (Published under the title *American Jewish Historical Quarterly* up to 1975.)

American Jewish Yearbook. (1) 1899. (2) United States. (3) English. (4) 1. (5) Exhaustive data on World Jewry.

American Journal of Theology and Philosophy. (1) 1980. (2) United States. (3) English. (4) 3. (5) Philosophical theology.

American Scientific Affiliation: Journal. (1) 1949. (2) United States. (3) English. (4) 4. (5) Science and religion.

The Annual Review of the Social Sciences of Religion. (1) 1977. (2) Netherlands. (3) English. (4) 1. (5) Sociology of religion.

Archives de sciences sociales des religions. (1) 1956. (2) France. (3) French. (4) 4. (5) Sociology of religion.

Biblica. (1) 1920. (2) Italy. (3) English, French, German, Italian, Latin, Spanish. (4) 4. (5) Biblical exegesis, philology, theology, and history.

Biblical Archeologist. (1) 1938. (2) United States. (3) English. (4) 4. (5) Archaeology of biblical lands.

Bijdragen: Tijdschrift voor philosofie en theologie. (1) 1938. (2) Netherlands. (3) Dutch, English, French, German. (4) 4. (5) Philosophical theology.

Books and Religion. (1) 1971. (2) United States. (3) English. (4) 4. (5) News and reviews of books in the field of religion. (Published under the title *Review of Books and Religion* up to 1985.)

Cahiers de l'actualité religieuse et sociale. (1) 1947. (2) France. (3) French. (4) 6. (5) Sociology of religion.

The Catholic Biblical Quarterly. (1) 1939. (2) United States. (3) English. (4) 4. (5) Biblical and related studies.

Chaos: Dansk tidsskrift for religionshistoriske studier. (1) 1982. (2) Denmark. (3) Danish. (4) 2. (5) History of religions.

Ching Feng: Quarterly Notes on Christianity and Chinese Reli-

gions and Culture. (1) 1957. (2) Hong Kong. (3) English. (4) 4. (5) Chinese religions.

Christianity and Crisis. (1) 1941. (2) United States (3) English. (4) 26. (5) Religion and current social and political issues.

Christian-Jewish Relations. (1) 1968. (2) England. (3) English. (4) 4. (5) Documentation on Jewish-Christian relations.

Christian News from Israel. (1) 1949. (2) Israel. (3) Editions in English, French, and Spanish. (4) 2. (5) Current status of Christianity in Israel.

Church and State. (1) 1948. (2) United States. (3) English. (4) 11. (5) Religion and American government.

Church History. (1) 1932. (2) United States. (3) English. (4) 4. (5) History of Christian churches.

Church Labor Letter. (1) 1962. (2) Japan. (3) English. (4) 3. (5) Christianity and economics in Japan.

Commentary. (1) 1945. (2) United States. (3) English. (4) 12. (5) Jewish-related political, religious, and cultural articles.

Commonweal. (1) 1924. (2) United States (3) English. (4) Biweekly/monthly. (5) Public affairs, religion, literature, and the arts.

Council on the Study of Religion: Bulletin. (1) 1964. (2) United States. (3) English. (4) 5. (5) Religious studies in American higher education. (Published under the title *American Academy of Religion: Bulletin* up to 1969.)

Cross Currents. (1) 1950. (2) United States. (3) English. (4) 4. (5) Christianity and contemporary culture.

Current Dialogue. (1) 1974. (2) Switzerland. (3) English. (4) 4. (5) Christianity and other faiths and ideologies.

Ecumenical Review. (1) 1948. (2) Switzerland. (3) English. (4) 4. (5) Ecumenical relations between Christian churches and other religions.

Evangelische Kommentare: Monatschrift zum Zeitgeschehen in Kirche und Gesellschaft. (1) 1968. (2) West Germany. (3) German. (4) 12. (5) Church and society.

Faith and Freedom: A Journal of Progressive Religion. (1) 1947. (2) England. (3) English. (4) 3. (5) Liberal religious thought.

Faith and Thought: A Journal Devoted to the Study of the Interrelation of the Christian Revelation and Modern Research. (1) 1866–1951. (2) England. (3) English. (4) 3. (5) Religion and science.

Fides et Historia. (1) 1968. (2) United States. (3) English. (4) 2. (5) Religion and historical research.

Harvard Theological Review. (1) 1908. (2) United States. (3) English and other Western languages. (4) 4. (5) Religious history; history of religions.

Hebrew Union College Annual. (1) 1924. (2) United States. (3) English, French, German, Hebrew. (4) 1. (5) Jewish history.

The Hibbert Journal. (1) 1902–1968. (2) England. (3) English. (4) 4. (5) International, interreligious, theological, and philosophical studies.

History of Religions: An International Journal of Comparative Historical Studies. (1) 1961. (2) United States. (3) English. (4) 4. (5) History of religions.

International Journal of Philosophy of Religion. (1) 1970. (2) Netherlands. (3) English. (4) 4. (5) Philosophy of religion.

Interpretation. (1) 1947. (2) United States. (3) English. (4) 4. (5) Biblical studies and theology.

Japanese Journal of Religious Studies. (1) 1960. (2) Japan. (3) English. (4) 4. (5) Modern Japanese religion.

Japanese Religions. (1) 1959. (2) Japan. (3) English. (4) 2. (5) Modern Japanese religion.

Jewish Quarterly Review. (1) n.s. 1909. (2) United States. (3) English. (4) 4. (5) Biblical studies and Judaism.

Jewish Social Studies. (1) 1939. (2) United States. (3) English. (4) 4. (5) Contemporary and historical aspects of Jewish life.

Journal for the Scientific Study of Religion. (1) 1961. (2) United States. (3) English. (4) 4. (5) Sociology and philosophy of religion.

Journal of Biblical Literature. (1) 1881. (2) United States. (3) English. (4) 4. (5) Biblical and cognate studies.

Journal of Church and State. (1) 1959. (2) United States. (3) English. (4) 3. (5) Discussion of church-state relations.

Journal of Dharma: An International Quarterly of World Religions. (1) 1975. (2) India. (3) English. (4) 4. (5) Current religions.

Journal of Religion. (1) 1882. (2) United States. (3) English. (4) 4. (5) History of religions; religion.

The Journal of Religion and Psychical Research. (1) 1978. (2) United States. (3) English. (4) 4. (5) Psychology and religion.

Journal of Religion in Africa / Religion en Afrique. (1) 1967. (2) Netherlands. (3) English, French. (4) 3. (5) Religions in Africa.

Journal of Religious Ethics. (1) 1973. (2) United States. (3) English. (4) 2. (5) Ethics and religion.

Journal of Religious History. (1) 1960. (2) Australia. (3) English. (4) 2. (5) History of religions.

Journal of Religious Studies. (1) 1969. (2) India. (3) English. (4) 2. (5) Religion and religions.

Journal of Religious Studies. (1) 1972. (2) United States. (3) English. (4) 2. (5) Religion and religions. (Published under the title *Ohio Journal of Religious Studies* up to 1978.)

Journal of Theological Studies. (1) 1899. (2) England. (3) English. (4) 2. (4) History of religions; history of Christian thought.

Journal of Women and Religion. (1) 1981. (2) United States. (3) English. (4) 2. (5) Thematic issues on women and religion.

Judaism. (1) 1952. (2) United States (3) English. (4) 4. (5) Jewish life and thought.

Kairos: Zeitschrift für Religionswissenschaft und Theologie. (1) 1959. (2) Austria. (3) German. (4) 4. (5) Religions and religion.

Moment. (1) 1975. (2) United States. (3) English. (4) 10. (5) American Jewish life.

Neue Zeitschrift für Missionswissenschaft/Nouvelle revue de science missionaire. (1) 1945. (2) Switzerland. (3) English, French, German, Italian. (4) 4. (5) Missiology; religion and religions.

Neue Zeitschrift für systematische Theologie und Religionsphilosophie. (1) 1959. (2) West Germany. (3) German. (4) 3. (5) Philosophy of religion.

New Religions Newsletter. (1) 1977. (2) Canada. (3) English. (4) 12. (5) New religious movements.

New Testament Studies. (1) 1954. (2) England. (3) English, French, German. (4) 4. (5) Canonical and noncanonical New Testament studies.

Novum Testamentum. (1) 1956. (2) Netherlands. (3) English, French, German. (4) 4. (5) New Testament and related studies.

Numen: International Review for the History of Religions. (1) 1954. (2) Netherlands. (3) English, French, German, Italian. (4) 2. (5) History of religions.

One World. (1) 1974. (2) Switzerland. (3) English. (4) 10. (5) Ecumenical studies.

Parabola. (1) 1976. (2) United States. (3) English. (4) 4. (5) Thematic issues on cultural history, especially on myth and folklore.

Patristics. (1) 1972. (2) United States. (3) English. (4) 2. (5) Information and book reviews on church history.

Pokrof. (1) 1954. (2) Netherlands. (3) English. (4) 6. (5) Christianity in Soviet Russia.

Process Studies. (1) 1971. (2) United States. (3) English (4) 4. (5) Process philosophy and religion.

Radius. (1) 1956. (2) West Germany. (3) German. (4) 4. (5) Religion and society.

Recherches de science religieuse. (1) 1910. (2) France. (3) French. (4) 4. (5) Religion and religions.

Reformatio: Zeitschrift für evangelische Kultur und Politik. (1) 1952. (2) Switzerland. (3) German. (4) 10. (5) Religion and society; politics and religion.

Religion: Journal of Religion and Religions. (1) 1971. (2) England. (3) English. (4) 2. (5) Religion and religions.

Religion: The Estabished Journal of the History, Structure, and Theory of Religion and Religions. (1) 1971. (2) England. (3) English. (4) 4. (5)

Religion and Society. (1) 1954. (2) India. (3) English. (4) 4. (5) Sociology of religion; religion and society.

Religion in America (1) 1977. (2) United States. (3) English. (4) 2. (5) Religion, statistics; sociology of religion.

Religion in Communist Dominated Areas. (1) 1962. (2) United States. (3) English. (4) 4. (5) Marxism and religion.

Religion in Communist Lands. (1) 1973. (2) England. (3) English. (4) 3. (5) Marxism and religion.

Religion in Southern Africa. (1) 1980. (2) South Africa. (3) English. (4) 2. (5) African religion.

Religious Studies. (1) 1965. (2) England. (3) English. (4) 4. (5) Religion and religions.

Religious Studies Review. (1) 1975. (2) Canada. (3) English. (4) 4. (5) Sociology of religion; religion and religions.

Review of Religious Research. (1) 1959. (2) United States. (3) English. (4) 10. (5) Review of publications about religion.

Re-Vision Journal. (1) 1978. (2) United States. (3) English. (4) 4. (5) New approaches to philosophy and religion.

Revue d'histoire et de philosophie religieuses. (1) 1921. (2) France. (3) French. (4) 4. (5) History of religions; philosophy of religion.

Revue de l'histoire des religions. (1) 1880. (2) France. (3) French. (4) 4. (5) History of religions.

Semeia. (1) 1974. (2) United States. (3) English. (4) 4. (5) Thematic issues on biblical criticism.

Social Compass: International Review of Socio-Religious Studies. (1) 1953. (2) Belgium. (3) English, French. (4) 4. (5) Sociology of religion.

Sociological Analysis: A Journal in the Sociology of Religion. (1) 1967. (2) United States. (3) English. (4) 4. (5) Sociology of religion.

Sojourners. (1) 1972. (2) United States. (3) English. (4) 11. (5) Contemporary American Christian concerns.

Sophia. (1) 1962. (2) Australia. (3) English. (4) 3. (5) Philosophical theology.

Soundings. (1) 1968. (2) United States. (3) English. (4) 4. (5) Interdisciplinary studies in the humanities and religion. (Supersedes *Christian Scholar,* 1917–1967.)

Speculum (1) 1926. (2) United States (3) English. (4) 4. (5) Medieval studies.

Studies in Comparative Religion. (1) 1941 (2) England. (3) English. (4) 4. (5) Religion and religions.

Studies in Religion / Sciences religieuses. (1) 1971. (2) Canada. (3) English, French. (4) 4. (5) Religion and religions.

Tarbiz. (1) 1929. (2) Israel. (3) Hebrew with English summaries. (4) 4. (5) Jewish studies.

This World. (1) 1982. (2) United States. (3) English. (4) 4. (5) Moral and religious thinking.

Union Seminary Quarterly Review. (1) 1945. (2) United States. (3) English. (4) 4. (5) Thematic issues on religion and related areas of thought.

Update: A Quarterly Journal on New Religious Movements. (1) 1977. (2) Denmark. (3) English. (4) 4. (5) New religions.

Vestus Testamentum. (1) 1951. (2) Netherlands. (3) English, French, German. (4) 4. (5) Old Testament studies.

West African Religion. (1) 1963–1980. (2) Nigeria. (3) English. (4) 2. (5) African religion.

Worldview. (1) 1958. (2) United States. (3) English. (4) 12. (5) Religion and politics.

YIVO Annual of Jewish Social Science. (1) 1946. (2) United States. (3) English. (4) 1. (5) Social studies on European and North American Jewry.

Zeitschrift für Missionskunde und Religionswissenschaft. (1) 1886–1939. (2) Germany. (3) German. (4) 4. (5) History of religions.

Zeitschrift für Missionswissenschaft und Religionswissenschaft. (1) 1911. (2) West Germany. (3) German, English, French. (4) 4. (5) Religion and religions.

Zeitschrift für Religions und Geistesgeschichte. (1) 1948. (2) Netherlands and West Germany. (3) German. (4) 4. (5) History of religions; history of spirituality.

Zion. (1) 1935. (2) Israel. (3) Hebrew with English summaries. (4) 4. (5) Jewish history.

Zygon: Journal of Religion and Science. (1) 1966. (2) United States. (3) English. (4) 4. (5) Science and religion.

Indexing and Abstracting. Of course, researchers in religion often need to consult the periodical indexes in disciplines other than religion and theology. In the United States, these include the *Social Sciences and Humanities Index* (1907/1915–1974), the *Humanities Index* (1974–), *The Philosopher's Index* (1967–), and so on. See the *Guide to Reference Books*, 9th ed., compiled by Eugene P. Sheehy (1976), for bibliographical information.

The basic indexes and abstracting services in religion are the following:

Catholic Periodical Index. Vols. 1–3. New York, 1930–1966. Index continued in *Catholic Periodical and Literature Index.*

Catholic Periodical and Literature Index. Vols. 14ff. Haverford, Pa., 1967/1968–.

Guide to Social Science and Religion in Periodical Literature. Flint, Mich., 1964–. Cumulated every three years.

Kiryat Sepher. Jerusalem, 1924–. Bibliographical quarterly on Judaica-Hebraica of the Jewish National and University Library.

Religion Index One: Periodicals. Chicago, 1953–. Includes abstracts when authors supply them. Supplemented by *Religion Index Two.*

Religion Index Two: Multi-Author Works. Chicago, 1976. Covers publications from 1960 on.

Religious and Theological Abstracts. Meyerstown, Pa., 1958–. Quarterly. Does not cumulate.

Abbreviations. Periodical titles are usually cited in abbreviated form. *Internationales Abkürzungsverzeichnis für Theologie und Grenzgebiete: Zeitschriften, Serien, Lexika, Quellenwerke mit bibliographischen Angaben,* edited by Siegfried Schwertner (Berlin and New York, 1974), provides the most extensive listing. He includes the abbreviations for many periodicals that have ceased publication. Volume 1 of *Periodical Title Abbreviations,* 4th ed., edited by Leland G. Alkire (Detroit, 1983), provides few titles in religion but is useful for tangential disciplines.

Information Retrieval. The computerization of data banks allows for rapid recovery of bibliographic data, provided that one has access to an adequate data base. At the present time the largest data base in North America that covers religion is that based on the American Theological Library Association indexes. It includes over 250,000 bibliographic records as of June 1985, drawn from *Religion Index One* (periodicals in religion from 1949–1959 and 1974–1985) and *Religion Index Two* (works with more than one author, from 1960–1985). Access to this data base is provided through two major on-line vendors (telephone numbers are accurate as of May 1986).

BRS (Bibliographic Retrieval Services)
1200 Route 7
Latham, New York 12110
Telephone: (800) 833–4707 or (518) 783–1161
BRS makes the data base available under "key" name RELI in its standard system and also in its less expensive, menu-drive Afterdark © System.

DIALOG Information Services, Inc.
3460 Hillview Avenue
Palo Alto, California 94303
Telephone: (800) 227–1929 or (415) 858–3785
The ALTA data base is available on DIALOG 2 under File No. 190.

Scholars who do not have access to either of these online vendors can request a data-base search through the ATLA Religion Indexes Search Service, 5600 South Woodlawn Avenue, Chicago, Illinois 60637. Telephone: (312) 947–9417.

EDGAR KRENTZ

PĒRKONS. In Baltic languages, the proper noun *Pērkons* (Latv.) or *Perkūnas* (Lith.) corresponds exactly to the common noun meaning "thunder." There is no agreement among linguists about the word's original meaning. In earlier research the essence of the god who bears this name was determined purely through etymology. Consequently, three different schools of thought emerged, each claiming a different Indo-European root as the base.

The first school, using *perg- as the root, regarded Pērkons as the sky god who controlled rain and storm. Typologically he was then likened to the Vedic Parjanya ("rain cloud"). The second school, deriving the god's name from **pergu(o-),* asserted that *Pērkons* is linked with *perkuu-s,* or *ozols,* meaning "oak tree." Pērkons was then considered to be the god of trees, in particular the oak, which was his symbol of power. The third school claimed that *Pērkons* is related to the Hittite *peruaš,* from *pirua- (perua-),* meaning "cliff" or "mountain." As a result Pērkons was regarded as the god of mountains. These various hypotheses, based only on etymology, did not give a clear conception of the true nature of this god. From these hypotheses, however, emerged the definite conclusion that the name *Pērkons* is derived from Proto-Indo-European.

An examination of the Pērkons cult offers valuable insights. Peter von Dusburg, in a discussion of the history of Old Prussians in the Chronicle of 1326, notes that Pērkons was worshiped. That the Latvians also recognized him as their god is demonstrated by a reference in the statutes of the Church Synod of 1428: "a tonitruo, quod deum suum appellant" ("from the thunder, which they name their god"). These older sources, however, do not give more detailed information about the nature of the cult itself. They merely contain standard condemnations of pagan worship of natural phenomena, for which Innocent III had earlier criticized the Latvians in his papal bull of 1199. Not until the seventeenth century was a specific rite from the Pērkons cult described, by the pastor Dionysius Fabricius in his *Livonicae Historicae Series* (1611-1620):

> At times of great drought when there is no rain, neighbors gather in densely wooded hills. They slaughter a she-calf, a black goat, and a black rooster. In accordance with their sacrificial rite a great number of people gather together and hold a communal feast. They drink together and invoke Pērkons, i.e. the thunder god. After filling the first cup of beer, they ecstatically march around the bonfire three times. They then pour the beer into the fire and pray to Pērkons (Percuum) to send them rain.
>
> (Mannhardt, 1936, p. 458; my trans.)

It should be noted, as this description of the feast clearly shows, that this rite was openly performed long after these peoples had formally been christianized. The gathering of worshipers in the thick forests can be explained by the fear of reprisals from the ruling German colonial church against non-Christian traditions.

This seventeenth-century account can be supplemented with another description, written 250 years later by an eyewitness who took part in the autumn threshing celebrations:

> On beginning the threshing, a rooster was slain in a niche of the open oven and a cross was painted with the rooster's blood on the oven. The meat was cooked and eaten. On completing the threshing another rooster was slain in the same spot. A vessel containing meat, brandy, and bread was placed on the oven. . . . On Saturday evening relatives and friends were invited to a communal feast, which ended in singing and dancing.

This description shows significant differences from the seventeenth-century account in that it contains syncretistic elements; the cross, the bread, and the brandy. Nevertheless, the feast is the same, even though Pērkons is not mentioned by name in the description.

Folk songs from the same time, however, do mention the god: "What shall we give to Pērkons for last summer's thunder? A large quantity [*laste*] of rye, a large quantity [*laste*] of barley, and a large quantity [*birkava*] of hops." This text, like the previous one, refers to a sacrificial feast after the harvest. It is a feast of thanksgiving to Pērkons. His cult thus appears to have remained strong throughout the centuries.

A bloody animal sacrifice also has a central place in the cult. There is also mention of bread and the sacral drink of the Balts, beer, which is poured into the fire. Typologically the rite appears as a sacrificial feast shared by gods and men. On the one hand it is associated with a supplication, asking for assistance during hard times; on the other hand, it is a thanksgiving for a plentiful harvest. During the thanksgiving the peasant experiences ecstatic joy because he stands in a right relation with his god and because the god, in turn, provides for him. The singing and dancing associated with the feast, which lasts well into the night, even until morning, also shows this joy. The ecstatic joy may climax in the participation of the gods in the festivities, as expressed in the following folk song: "Dievs [the Baltic god of heaven] is dancing with Pērkons; I am dancing with my brother; Pērkons has the whole earth in his possession; I have nine brothers."

The function of Pērkons is clearly defined: he is a fertility god. Hence, all etymologically based guesswork is superfluous. So also are any attempts to explain his essence and character by referring to analogical divinities in other religions. It is in this connection that Pērkons has also been regarded as a war god (he has especially been likened to Jupiter Fulminans, one of the aspects of the Roman sky god) and as a guardian of justice. Such assertions lack evidence in Baltic sources. If these and similar aspects appear to be connected with his function, then this can be explained as a later modification of ancient religious tradition, or by the influence of Christianity, which may have led to the perception of Pērkons as a slayer of demons and a guardian of morality.

BIBLIOGRAPHY

Balys, Jonas. *Perkūnas lietuvių liaudes tikejimuose.* Kaunas, 1937. Complete folkloristic material with a critical introduction.

Biezais, Haralds. *Die himmlische Götterfamilie der alten Letten.* Uppsala, 1972. The only up-to-date and complete historico-phenomenological and critical study, with an extensive bibliography. See especially part 3, "Der Donner," on pages 92–179.

Mannhardt, Wilhelm. *Letto-preussische Götterlehre.* Riga, 1936. The best sourcebook on Baltic religion.

Skardžius, Pranas. "Dievas ir Perkunas." In *Aidai,* pp. 311–318. Chicago, 1953. A comparative linguistic analysis.

Zicāns, Eduards. "Der altlettische Gott Pērkons." In *In Piam memoriam A. von Bulmerincq,* pp. 189–217. Riga, 1938. A comparative analysis of the Latvian folkloristic material.

HARALDS BIEZAIS

PERSECUTION. [*The two articles that form this entry discuss the experience of persecution and martyrdom in Judaism and Christianity. For discussion of the role of martyrdom in broader perspective, see* Martyrdom.]

Jewish Experience

The related terms *martyrdom* and *religious persecution* are difficult to define rigorously. The notion of religious persecution cannot be confined simply to assaults on religious ritual and belief; the intertwining of religion with every facet of premodern existence sometimes made attacks on religious life an outlet for economic, social, and political grievances and sometimes diverted religious antipathy into economic, social, and political channels. The ambiguity of religious animosity and violence complicates the definition of martyrdom as well, forcing religious communities to examine and reexamine specific claims on behalf of those reputed to have chosen death in response to religious persecution and in testimony to the truth of their faith.

Religious Persecution in the History of Judaism. Biblical literature shows some instances of religious persecution, usually set in a political context. Thus, the Philistine capture of the Ark of the Covenant and the Babylonian razing of the Jerusalem Temple both represent in essence politically motivated attacks on religious institutions and symbols. The biblical *Book of Daniel* presents two purported incidents of more purely religious persecution. In chapter 3 King Nebuchadrezzar is alleged to have erected a golden calf and ordered all his officials to prostrate themselves before it. Three Jewish lads were reported to the king for having contravened his royal order. As punishment, they were thrown into a blazing furnace, from which they miraculously emerged alive. Impressed by both their steadfastness and their salvation, the king was supposed to have prohibited any blasphemy of the God of the three young men. In chapter 6 a similar incident is told of Daniel, with the same outcome.

During the period of Hellenistic hegemony in the Near East, there was again tension between Jews and their neighbors, and this expressed itself in both political and religious terms. Particularly striking is the story of the Seleucid king Antiochus IV and his prohibition of basic Jewish religious practices. A group powerfully devoted to the fulfillment of covenantal law rose in rebellion against the effort to limit Jewish religious practice and belief. Modern scholarship has raised serious questions concerning these alleged Antiochene injunctions, which it has found totally at variance with Hellenistic custom. As an alternative, some scholars have proposed an essentially political motive for the decrees, a parallel in effect to the earlier Philistine and Babylonian assaults on Judaism. A similarly political attack on Judaism is reflected in the Roman burning of the Second Temple in 70 CE. To be sure, by this time there was already a strong tradition of Greco-Roman animus toward Jews and Judaism. Nonetheless the policy of the Roman authorities at the close of the Great War basically reflects a desire to suppress the political rebellion that had broken out in Palestine, not to deliver a death blow to the Jewish religious faith. Similar considerations motivated the Hadrianic decrees at the close of the Bar Kokhba Revolt of 132–135. Disturbed by ongoing Jewish unrest in Palestine, the Romans decided to quell permanently the rebelliousness of these Jews by attacking its seeming wellspring, Judaism.

With the emergence of Christianity as the authoritative religion of the Roman empire in the fourth century and Islam as the ruling faith of a vast state in the seventh century, persecution of the Jews and Judaism took a decidedly new turn. Both these religions ultimately negated in theory the legitimacy of all other faiths, although each carved out a theoretical and practical status of limited tolerance for the other monotheisms, including Judaism. In many ways, the situation of the Jews in the Muslim world was somewhat better than in medieval Christendom. Critical factors accounting for this difference included the ethnic and religious heterogeneity of the Muslim world, the size and antiquity of the Jewish communities within the orbit of Islam, the absence of any unique role for the Jews in the development of Islam, and the absence of any potent anti-Jewish symbolism at the core of the religion. There was, to be sure, occasional persecution of the Jews; sometimes this occurred at the official level, as with the Almohad rulers of North Africa and Spain during the mid-twelfth century, and sometimes at the popular level, as with the uprising in Granada in 1066, triggered by popular resentment of the Ibn Nagrela family of Jewish viziers. As the Muslim world increasingly lost the impressive vitality that it had exhibited during the early centuries of the Middle Ages, the situation of its Jewish minority deteriorated, and instances of governmental persecution and popular violence multiplied.

It was in the medieval Christian world, however, that persecution of the Jews and Judaism was especially notable. Two factors in particular account for this prominence: the central place of Jews in the Christian drama of crucifixion and resurrection, and the relative newness and smallness of the Jewish communities in most—although not all—areas of medieval Christendom. At the official level, Judaism was in theory a tolerated faith, although its practice was limited in order to ensure the well-being of the ruling religion. Occasionally concern with the impact of Judaism upon the spiritual health of Christendom could lead to persecution of the Jews or could be used to justify such persecution. Thus, for example, Christian persecution of Jews arose in the early eleventh century from anxiety over the emergence of heresy in northern Europe, and at the end of the fifteenth century from dismay over the alleged backsliding of New Christians in Spain to their original Jewish faith. [*See* Marranos.] In both situations Jews were viewed as contributors to the perceived dangers and were forced into conversion or exile.

In medieval Christendom popular persecution was the more common form of anti-Jewish behavior. Widespread anti-Jewish animosities often developed within large-scale socioeconomic upheavals. During the First Crusade, spiritual exhilaration produced powerful anti-Jewish sentiment in certain fringe bands of the crusading masses. The result was a set of devastating attacks on a few of the main centers of nascent German Jewry. During the last decade of the thirteenth century and the first decade of the fourteenth, powerful social discontent in Germany unleashed wide-ranging assaults against a series of Jewish communities. The hysteria occasioned by the uncontrollable Black Death of the mid-fourteenth century once again produced massive anti-Jewish violence, as did social and religious ferment in Spain in 1391. During the mid-seventeenth century, the popular uprising of Ukrainian peasants against their Polish overlords occasioned repeated massacres in the Jewish communities of the area. In all these instances, long-nurtured stereotypes of Jewish enmity and malevolence served as the backdrop for the explosion of popular violence. The imagery of Jewish malevolence, rooted in the New Testament account of the Crucifixion, was embellished during the Middle Ages with notions of ritual murder, Jewish use of Christian blood, Host desecration, and the poisoning of wells. At points of religious exhilaration or social unrest, such imagery served alternately as the spark or the rationale for popular persecution of the Jews.

With the breakdown of the corporate premodern society and with the increasing restriction of the role of religion in modern Western civilization, the older patterns of religious persecution have generally given way. To be sure, there has been little sign of diminishing anti-Jewish hostility or anti-Jewish violence, but its religious nature is even more difficult to identify than heretofore. New definitions of Jewishness have emerged, and with them, anti-Jewish activity has taken on an enhanced political, economic, social, and ethnic cast. The late nineteenth-century racial definition of Jewishness produced the new term *anti-Semitism* for anti-Jewish attitudes and behavior. Social scientists have not yet been successful in analyzing the place of traditional religious animosities in the new complex of modern anti-Semitism.

Martyrdom in the History of Judaism. In Jewish tradition the notion of martyrdom has been expressed in the commandment of *qiddush ha-shem,* the requirement to sanctify the divine name. This commandment has very broad meaning, as seen in *Leviticus* 22:31–33: "You shall faithfully observe my commandments: I am the Lord. You shall not profane my holy name, that I might be sanctified in the midst of the Israelite people—I the Lord who sanctify you, I who brought you out of the land of Egypt to be your God, I the Lord." Sanctification of the divine name could be and has been interpreted as any noble action undertaken out of commitment to the divine will and thus reflecting glory upon the God of Israel. Not surprisingly, however, a more restricted meaning of *qiddush ha-shem* has developed as well: it has been applied in particular to those who give up their most precious possession—life itself—out of this sense of submission to God's will and who thus serve as ringing testimony to the reality and truth of their deity.

The Hebrew Bible certainly features the importance of submission to the divine will, as seen in Abraham's response to the command that he sacrifice his beloved son Isaac, in Moses' acceptance of God's call, and in the repeated prophetic acquiescence to divinely imposed missions. Generally, however, this steadfastness involves the suppression of internal psychological blocks to the divine will; only rarely does it require the overcoming of external pressures, most notably with the two incidents recounted in the *Book of Daniel.* The Antiochene persecution, whatever its motivations may have been, produced a Jewish response of martyrological resistance to the external threat and created a set of figures whose deeds would subsequently be retold as paradigms of heroic human behavior. Clearly the war of 66 to 70 CE elicited a similar sense of martyrdom, a desire to reject uncompromisingly the reimposition of Roman rule. Perhaps out of an awareness of the heavily political motivations on both sides, subsequent Jewish sources by and large overlooked this group of militant resisters and relegated the heroism of Masada to a position of relative neglect.

Entirely different was the response to the resistance against the Hadrianic persecution of the late 130s. Here the essentials of Jewish religious life were at stake, and the resisters were at the center of the Jewish community. The martyrdom of ʿAqiva' ben Yosef and his associates was accorded a major place in the Jewish liturgy and undoubtedly served to encourage succeeding generations of Jews to undertake, when required, the same commitment. Jewish law eventually codified the essentials of martyrdom by specifying key issues on which there could be no compromise.

> R[abbi] Yoḥanan said in the name of R[abbi] Shimʿon ben Yehotsadaq: "By a majority vote it was resolved in the upper chambers of the house of Nithza in Lydda that in every [other] law of the Torah, if a man is commanded: 'Transgress and suffer not death,' he may transgress and not suffer death, excepting idolatry, incest, and murder."
>
> (B.T., *San.* 74a)

This important statement limits the number of infringements upon Jewish law for which life is to be sacrificed; at the same time, it strongly reaffirms the basic principle of *qiddush ha-shem* when the infringement is major.

The persecutions cited here all reflect an assault on Judaism out of essentially political motivations. It is only with the development of Christianity and Islam and their rise to positions of political authority that the stage was set for direct confrontations between militant monotheistic faiths. In this regard the Jewish martyrdoms during the First Crusade assume special significance. The Crusader assaults of 1096 were couched in almost purely religious terms; there were no political aspects to this persecution, and socioeconomic issues were distinctly secondary. At its core, the attack on Rhineland Jewry was triggered by a radical desire to rid the world of all infidels. This was not, of course, the papal view of the crusade; it was, however, the yearning that animated the fringe bands of German Crusaders. The Jewish communities that suddenly found themselves under assault were spiritually as intense as their attackers. The result was a remarkable Jewish willingness to perish in defiance of Christian pressure and in testimony to the truth of the Jewish faith. The following utterance, imputed to the martyrs of Mainz on the verge of their death, captures the intensity of the period—the conviction of the absolute truth of Judaism; the sense that their actions represent *qiddush ha-shem,* a means of sanctifying the divine name in this world; and the resultant certainty of rich celestial reward:

> Ultimately one must not question the qualities of the Holy One, blessed be he, who gave us his Torah and commanded that we be put to death and be killed for the unity of his sacred name. Fortunate are we if we do his will and fortunate are all who are killed and slaughtered and die for the unity of his name. Not only do they merit the world to come and sit in the quarter of the righteous pillars of the world, but they exchange a world of darkness for a world of light, a world of pain for a world of joy, a transitory world for an eternal world.

The martyrs of 1096 created a compelling set of symbols to sustain themselves in the face of the terrible test imposed upon them. These included a sense of identification with the great hero figures of the Jewish past, such as Abraham, Daniel and his companions, and ʿAqiva' ben Yosef and his associates; recollection of the divinely ordained sacrificial system with the conviction that God had called upon these martyrs to offer themselves up as surrogate sacrifices on a new-style altar; introduction of rituals of purity to underscore the sanctity of the acts they were about to undertake; lavish descriptions of the celestial glories awaiting those who died on behalf of the divine name.

In subsequent instances of persecution of Jews in medieval Christendom, such purely religious motivation is rarely encountered, and thus there are rarely instances of pure martyrdom. Nonetheless the anti-Jewish violence of the Middle Ages always involved assaults on Jews *qua* Jews, and those who perished were generally seen as martyrs, no matter what the precise motivations of the attacking hordes might have been. Moreover, this medieval anti-Jewish violence always included the possibility of saving one's life by renouncing Judaism and taking on a new personal identity in the camp of the oppressor. Thus, the Jewish victims of medieval violence did in some measure choose death over repudiation of their faith and deity, although rarely with the same intensity of direct confrontation expressed by the Jewish martyrs of the First Crusade.

Just as the changing patterns of Western civilization have affected religious persecution of the Jews, so too have they altered the Jewish notion of martyrdom. One of the remarkable features of nineteenth-century racial anti-Semitism was its elimination of any element of volition in Jewish identity—choice was no longer a factor in one's Jewishness. As a result, the victims of the twentieth-century Nazi persecution—whom subsequent Jews have viewed as martyrs, since they perished essentially because of their Jewishness—no longer had any alternative available to them for leaving the Jewish fold. In this sense their martyrdom surely differs from that of former ages. Likewise, the fragmentation of Jewish life, the diminution of the place of religion within the Jewish community, and the emergence of new Jewish ideologies have combined to produce new Jewish causes and new martyr figures. The most significant of these new heroes are those viewed as martyrs to the Zionist cause. Just as it has adopted so many evocative symbols from earlier epochs of the Jewish past, this potent new movement has incorporated much of the symbolism of martyrdom from prior Jewish experience. Most of the themes of this new martyrdom parallel those already noted: deep devotion to a set of sacred ideals, resolute rejection of external threat, the sense that such willingness to perish strengthens the truth claims of the group, and the certainty of rich ultimate reward.

[*See also* Anti-Semitism *and, for an account of the Nazi persecution of Jews, see* Holocaust, The. *Related entries include* Polemics *and* Suffering.]

BIBLIOGRAPHY

The most useful general history of the Jews is that of Salo W. Baron, *A Social and Religious History of the Jews,* 2d ed., 18 vols. to date (New York, 1952–); Baron's footnotes are invaluable guides to major topics in Jewish history. The multivolume study by Léon Poliakov, *Histoire de l'antisémitisme*, 4 vols. (Paris, 1955–1977), is helpful; an English translation of volumes 1–3 is available as *The History of Anti-Semitism*, 3 vols. (New York, 1965–1978). Studies of specific persecutions include the following: for the Antiochene persecution, Victor Tcherikover's *Hellenistic Civilization and the Jews* (Philadelphia, 1959); for that of 1096, my own *The First Crusade and the Jewish Counter-Crusade* (forthcoming); for that of 1391, Yitzhak F. Baer's *A History of the Jews in Christian Spain*, 2 vols. (Philadelphia, 1961–1966); for that of 1648–1649, Bernard D. Weinryb's *The Jews of Poland* (Philadelphia, 1972). No comprehensive study of *qiddush ha-shem* is presently available. The studies of Tcherikover, Chazan, Baer, and Weinryb all analyze patterns of Jewish response to persecution along with their description of the oppression itself. Shalom Spiegel's *The Last Trial* (New York, 1967) is a brilliant study of the imagery of testing and submission to divine will throughout Jewish history. Depictions of Nazi persecution and modern Jewish martyrdom abound. See especially Lucy S. Dawidowicz's *The War against the Jews, 1933–1945* (New York, 1975); Raul Hilberg's *The Destruction of the European Jews*, rev. & enl. ed., 3 vols. (New York, 1985); Alan Mintz's *Hurban: Responses to Catastrophe in Hebrew Literature* (New York, 1984); and David G. Roskies's *Against the Apocalypse* (Cambridge, Mass., 1984).

ROBERT CHAZAN

Christian Experience

The atoning and vicarious nature of Jesus' sacrifice provides the main link between Jewish and Christian outlooks toward persecution and martyrdom. In *Mark* 10:45, a possible reminiscence from *Isaiah* 53:10–12, Jesus proclaims that he "came not to be served but to serve and to give his life as a ransom for many." It is, however, in the Johannine literature that the term *martyr* ("witness") moves quickest from its ordinary secular meaning to the Christian sense of "blood-witness." Numerous passages (e.g., *Jn.* 3:11, 5:30–33, 18:37, and *1 Jn.* 5:10) present Jesus in terms of witness to the truth or to his Father, while others associate witness to Jesus with the Paraclete (*Jn.* 15:26, cf. also 14:26) standing in opposition to the world, convincing the world of sin and judgment. Witness to the Crucifixion was revealed in "blood and water," and had in addition the missionary purpose "that you also may believe" (*Jn.* 19:34–35).

The association of the Holy Spirit with suffering and persecution because of witness to Christ was emphasized in the synoptic Gospels (*Mk.* 13:11 and parallel *Mt.* 10:19). By the end of the first century AD, these ideas had become fused into a single idea of martyrdom. Martyrs conquered (Satan) "by the blood of the Lamb and by the word of their testimony [*marturias*], for they loved not their lives even unto death" (*Rev.* 12:11). Theirs was a personal witness to the truth of Christ's claim to be Messiah and a token of the closest possible identification with their Lord. In the early years of the second century, Ignatius of Antioch in his letter to the Christians in Rome said that he would be truly a disciple of Christ when he had been found "pure bread of Christ" (chap. 4). "It is better," he urged, "to die in Christ Jesus than to be king over the ends of the earth" (6.1).

The concept of martyrdom formulated in these years proved to be long lasting. [*See* Cult of Saints.] In particular, its association with the spirit of prophecy, opposition to the world (not only to the Roman empire), and its connection with the coming of the end of this world can be seen in the *Acta martyrum* of the second and early third centuries. Thus, in 177, the anonymous writer of the *Acta* of the martyrs of Lyon understood the persecution that assailed the congregation there as "foreshadowing the coming of Antichrist" (that would precede the end of this age). (See Eusebius's *Ecclesiastical History*, hereafter cited as *H.E.*, 5.1.5 and following.) As for the martyrs, one was described in the anonymous letter as the "Paraclete of the Christians" (5.1.9). Their witness and confession placed them in direct contact with Jesus himself, and while not "perfected" until dead, they were able to "bind and loose" as partakers in Christ's sufferings. The martyrs of Lyon were not followers of Montanus, whose movement, which began in Phrygia in 172, illustrated the close connection between prophecy, eschatology, and martyrdom. Their recorded outlook, however, indicates the strong undercurrent in the same direction among orthodox communities during this period. At the end of the century, this can be illustrated from the church in North Africa. Around 197, Tertullian proclaimed in *Apologeticum* 50.16 that martyrdom, as the baptism of blood, wiped away all postbaptismal sin. A decade later (c. 207), as a Montanist, he asserted in *De fuga in persecutione*, chapter 9, that it was the only form of death worthy of a Christian, for in that event Christ, who had suffered for the Christians, might be glorified.

The idea of martyrdom developed against the background of occasional severe, if local, persecutions. Jesus had warned his followers to expect persecution (*Mt.* 10:17). Like that of the prophets of Israel, his blood would be poured out. Until the Gospels attained their final form with the Passion narrative, the suffering servant of *Isaiah* 53:1–12 was the perfect type of Christ. The earliest enemies of the Christians were the Jews, who regarded them as belonging to a dangerous, subversive movement in their midst. The martyrdom of

Stephen in about 35 was followed by the persecution under Herod Agrippa around 42. Although Agrippa died in 44, over the next fifteen years Jews did everything possible to impede the preaching of Christianity by Paul and his friends among the synagogues of the Diaspora. They portrayed Paul as "a mover of sedition among the Jews throughout the world" (*Acts* 24:5), and first in Corinth and then in Jerusalem attempted to have him executed by the Roman authorities.

Luke and *Acts* show that the authorities themselves were by no means hostile to Paul and his preaching but rather regarded Christianity as an internal Jewish matter which was not their concern. What then was the cause of the Neronian persecution in Rome in AD 64?

Persecution and Toleration in the Roman Empire. Little is known of the Christian community in Rome during Nero's reign, but three factors seem relevant. First, Nero was desperate to find a scapegoat for the conflagration which he was suspected of causing. Second, official and popular opinion in Rome reprobated any threat to the majesty of the Roman gods by foreign cults, including Judaism. Jews were also suspected of misanthropy and incendiarism. Finally, by AD 60, Jewish hostility toward Christianity had spread to Rome.

Tacitus's account of the savage repression of Christianity (*Annales* 15.44), written some sixty years later, may have been influenced by Livy's detailed account of the suppression of the Bacchanal conspiracy of 186 BC (Livy, *History of Rome* 39.8–19). The Christian movement was also regarded as a conspiracy by adherents of a foreign "false religion" *(prava religio)*, one of whose aims was to set fire to Rome. In both cases, self-confessed adherents were put to death; in particular, the Christians were executed in a cruel and theatrical way, their death designed as a human sacrifice to appease the wrath of the gods. A generation later, the writer of *1 Clement* appeared to blame this catastrophe on the "envy and jealousy" of the internal enemies of the church, namely, the Jews.

Although the Neronian persecution was not extended to Italy and the provinces, it put the Christians on the wrong side of the law. Tacitus believed that Pontius Pilate was justified in ordering Jesus' execution, and that the "deadly superstition" of Christianity deserved punishment. His contemporary, Suetonius, listed the repression of the Christians among Nero's police actions of which he approved (*Nero* 16.2). For him the Christians were guilty of practicing black magic as well as of introducing a "novel and dangerous religion." Suetonius did not, however, connect the persecution with the fire at Rome.

In the second century, Melito of Sardis and Tertullian named Domitian (81–96) as the second persecuting emperor. Domitian's repressive measures, however, in 95 aimed at discouraging forcibly members of the Roman nobility from "lapsing into Jewish ways." By this time, however, the authorities were distinguishing between Jews and non-Jews "who were living like Jews," a group which must have included Christians, and Christianity was illegal. The *Book of Revelation* indicates savage persecutions by Jews, the local populace, and the authorities in the province of Asia (western Asia Minor). In 112, the correspondence between the emperor Trajan and his special commissioner *(legatus pro praetore)* in the Black Sea province of Bithynia shows that Christians were liable to summary execution if denounced to the authorities. Pliny reports that their obstinacy in the face of questioning was an aggravating circumstance. Faced with apostasies, Pliny asked the emperor what he was to do, giving his opinion that Christianity was nothing worse than a perverse superstition and suggesting that leniency would restore the situation. Trajan replied that while Christians were not to be sought out like common criminals they were to be punished if they persisted in their refusal "to worship our gods." If they recanted, however, they were to be freed.

Instructions *(rescripta)* issued in 124/5 by Trajan's successor, Hadrian (117–138), directed the proconsul of Asia, C. Minicius Fundanus, to condemn Christians only if found guilty of criminal offenses in a court of law. They were not to be subjected to clamorous denunciations, and they had the right of turning against their accusers a charge that proved to be false. These two decisions established the policy of the imperial authorities for the remainder of the century. They had the effect of discouraging prosecutions, and Christians enjoyed relative tranquillity until the reign of Marcus Aurelius (161–180). By then, however, the official reluctance to pursue Christians had begun to yield to the force of popular suspicion of them, as reflected in charges of incest, cannibalism, and atheism. They were also held responsible for natural disasters that demonstrated, it was believed, the anger of the gods. The result was a series of severe local persecutions, such as the martyrdom of Polycarp of Smyrna in about 166 and the "pogrom" of Lyon in 177. In about 178 an informed Platonist writer, Celsus, without mentioning specific popular accusations directed against the Christians, mentions membership in an illegal organization, lack of civic sense, and subversion of traditional social structures through active proselytism as additional grounds for unpopularity and justification for oppression.

In the first decade of the third century, the increase in the number of Christians resulting from a more aggressive missionary policy resulted in persecutions in Carthage, Alexandria, Rome, Antioch, Corinth, and Cappadocia. In Carthage and Alexandria the rage of the mob seems to have been directed against converts. Eusebius associated these persecutions with the emperor Septimius Severus (193–211), and it is possible that that emperor reacted against the rising tide of mob outbreaks in some of the main cities of the empire by prohibiting conversion either to Judaism or to Christianity.

Between 212 and 235 Christians enjoyed a further period of quasi toleration under the emperors of the Severan dynasty. The revolution that removed Alexander Severus on 22 March 235 saw the beginnings of a new policy. Severus's supplanter, Maximinus Thrax (235–238), liquidated the Christian servants and officeholders at his predecessor's court and struck at the Christian leadership, sending the pope, Pontian (235–236), and the antipope, Hippolytus, into exile in Sardinia, where they both died.

In 238 Maximinus fell to a revolution inspired by landowning interests in North Africa. The next dozen years saw a period of Christian expansion and prosperity which provoked growing antipathy on the part of the pagans. In 248 there was a massive popular assault on the Christians in Alexandria, but the change of emperor that took place in the autumn of 249 resulted in the first empire-wide persecution. C. Quintus Messius Decius, who took the surname *Trajan* (249–251), was a good general and believed firmly in the traditional values of the Roman state. He was convinced that the Christians were responsible for the disasters that had befallen his predecessor. In January 250, he ordered that the yearly sacrifice made to the Roman gods on the Capitoline hill should be repeated throughout the empire, and almost simultaneously he had prominent Christians seized, whether clergy or laity. On 21 January, Pope Fabian was tried before him and executed. A similar fate befell Bishop Babylas of Antioch; Cyprian of Carthage and Dionysius of Alexandria escaped only by going into hiding. This phase was followed by the establishment of commissions in the towns of each province to supervise sacrifices to the gods of the empire and the emperor's genius. The process extended from February and March in Asia Minor and North Africa to June and July in Egypt. Some forty-three *libelli* (certificates) given to those who sacrificed have survived on Egyptian papyri. Few Christians resisted. If Decius had been able to give his undivided attention to the repression, the church might have been in serious danger. The peril, however, was already over when the emperor met his death at the hands of the Goths in June 251.

Hostility was continued under the emperors Gallus and Volusian in 252 and 253, but in 257 their successor Valerian (253–260) made a massive effort to force Christians to acknowledge and respect the Roman gods. This was the object of Valerian's first edict (summer 257), although the contributory factors may have included a desire on the part of the authorities to lay hands on the wealth that the church was believed to have accumulated. The church's leaders were arrested, interrogated, and deported. The edict also forbade Christians to hold services and to frequent their cemeteries, but otherwise left them alone. A year later, however, the emperor decided on severer measures. An imperial order reached Rome early in August 258, ordering that clergy should be executed, that Christian senators should forfeit their status and property, that a similar fate should befall highborn women, and that civil servants should be reduced to slavery. On 14 September 258, Cyprian of Carthage was summoned from his relatively comfortable place of exile to confront the proconsul of Africa. After a brief trial he was condemned as the ringleader of "an unlawful association" and as "an open enemy of the gods and the religion of Rome" *(Acta proconsularia).*

Persecution continued through 259, but ended with Valerian's capture by the Persians near Edessa in June 260. His son and successor, Gallienus, sent instructions in 260 and 261 to provincial governors to restore the property of the church and free its members from further molestation. The church, though not technically *religio licita* ("lawful religion"), had at last achieved a recognized status.

For more than forty years this situation continued. Church and empire moved closer together. In Nicomedia, the capital of the emperor Diocletian (284–305), the cathedral stood in full view of the emperor's palace. Why Diocletian decided to force the issue with the Christians nearly twenty years after he had seized power is not known; but the connection with the anti-Christian sentiments of his caesar, Galerius, and with his own policy of bringing uniformity in every aspect of the life of the peoples of the empire through the establishment of a common currency, prices, taxation, and legal framework seems clear. The great nonconformists, the Christians, could not be allowed to opt out. The Great Persecution of 303–312 (303–305 in the West) was preceded by a number of repressive acts (298–302) designed to remove Christians from public positions. On 23 February 303, the emperor posted an edict at Nicodemia, ordering the surrender of all copies of the Christian scriptures for burning and the dismantlement of all churches. No meetings for Christian worship were to be held. Christians were also disbarred from being plaintiffs in lawsuits, and lost all honors and privileges, but there was no death penalty, for Diocletian wanted no more Christian martyrs. In the summer of 303 other edicts followed, first directing that Christian clergy should be arrested and imprisoned, and then that they should be forced to sacrifice and thereafter freed.

So far only the clergy had been seriously affected, but in the winter of 303–304 Diocletian became incapacitated by illness following a visit to Rome to celebrate his twenty years' rule. Galerius took over control of the government and in the spring of 304 issued an edict ordering everyone to sacrifice to the immortal gods. This phase of the persecution saw numerous martyrs in North Africa, especially in Numidia, and a hardening of attitudes between Christians and pagans. Diocletian recovered from his illness, but was persuaded to retire from the government, which he did on 1 May 305, to live another eleven years in a magnificent military palace at Spalatum (Split) on the Adriatic coast.

The new emperors, Constantius in the West and Galerius (with Maximinus as his caesar) in the East, pursued contrasting religious policies. Persecution ceased in the West, but was restarted in the East after Easter 306. Successive edicts were accompanied by efforts by Maximinus to reorganize the pagan cult on a hierarchical basis. However, enthusiasm among the pagans was waning, and Galerius, struck down in the spring of 311 by a mysterious, deadly illness, issued an edict of toleration on 30 April, a week before he died. This "Palinode of Galerius" accepted the fact that the great majority of Christians could not be brought back to the worship of the Roman gods, considered it better for the empire that they should worship their own god than that they worship no god at all, and accorded them contemptuous toleration. "Christians may exist again, and may establish their meeting houses, provided they do nothing contrary to good order." They were also asked "to pray to their god for our good estate and their own, so that the commonwealth may endure on every side unharmed."

Meantime, in the West Constantius had died at York on 25 July 306, and his son Constantine had been acclaimed augustus by the soldiers. Though he had to be content with lesser honors for the time being, Constantine gradually increased his power, until in the spring of 312 he was ready to bid for the control of the whole of the West. He invaded Italy, defeated the usurper Maxentius at the battle of the Milvian Bridge, just north of Rome (28 October 312), and was hailed "senior augustus" by the Senate the next day. He was already strongly influenced by Christianity and, whatever the vision he saw on the day before the decisive battle, he was determined to end the era of persecution. In February 313 he met his fellow augustus at Milan, and together they published the famous Edict of Milan. [*See* Constantine.] Christians received, together with all the other subjects of the empire, complete freedom of religion, but they and the *Summus Deus* were regarded as the positive force and contrasted with "all others." Insensibly the scales had tipped toward Christianity as the official religion of the empire. By the time Constantine moved east, in 324, to challenge Licinius for control over the whole Roman world, the "immortal gods" of the Romans had been displaced as patrons and protectors of the empire. The religious revolution was complete. The church's intensive ramifications through town and countryside alike, coupled with a firm organization and a continued underlying enthusiasm for martyrdom, at least among a minority of the faithful, had proved too strong for the pagan empire.

Persecution of Heretics and Dissenters. Constantine's religious policy was founded on unity. The Christian God could not be served by two or more rival groups of ministers. Only one such group could be accepted as representing the true catholic (universal) church. At the same time, however, the strains and tensions resulting from the Great Persecution had exacerbated existing divisions in the church and caused new ones. In the West, the North African church had been divided since 311 between factions supporting or opposed to the new bishop of Carthage, Caecilian. [*See* Donatism.] In Egypt, there were divisions between the Melitians and adherents of Alexander, bishop of Alexandria. Persecution directed against opponents of the church supported by Constantine was not slow in coming. [*For further discussion, see* Heresy, *article on* Christian Concepts.]

Constantine and his sons saw themselves as the *custodes fidei* ("guardians of the faith") of the empire. This involved the suppression of paganism and dissenting views such as those of the Donatists in 346–347, and measures against individuals, like Athanasius of Alexandria, who was exiled in 356. A generation later, after the free-for-all toleration under Julian (361–363), the emperor Theodosius I in 380 published the general edict Cunctos Populos, by which the Christian religion as adhered to by Pope Damasus and Peter of Alexandria was decreed to be the sole legitimate religion of the empire.

Cunctos Populos is one of the turning points in the grim story of religious persecution. Anyone who did not accept that law forfeited his civil rights and was liable to punishment by the state. It was followed by a series of laws reiterating penalties against heretics, which reached a climax in June 392, when the emperor ordered heretical clergy to be fined ten pounds of gold and decreed that places where forbidden practices were occurring should be confiscated if the owner had connived. Pagans fared equally badly. In February 391 a law sent from Milan to Albinus, the praetorian prefect of the East, took up the legislation against paganism by the emperors Constantius II and Valens by prohibiting all sacrifices and fining people of high rank or official position who entered temples. This paved the way for a more comprehensive law late in 392 which banned every sort of pagan practice under very severe financial penalties. Informers were to be encouraged.

This framework of imperial legislation provided the means by which leaders of the catholic church were able to suppress their opponents. If, in the East, church and state formed one integrated whole under the emperor, in the West the "two swords" theory of the separate authority of church and state required the church to regard the secular power as its protector and sword against its enemies. [*See* Constantinianism.] In his long struggle against the Donatists, which lasted from 393 to 421, Augustine gradually built up a justification for the repression of religious dissent by the state. In 399 he identified the Donatists as heretics and urged that if kings could legislate against pagans and prisoners they could legislate against heretics. In 405 Augustine had imperial legislation against heretics applied to the Donatists. Denial of testamentary rights and floggings with lead whips were to be meted out to the obdurate. In 408, Augustine confessed that he was now convinced that Donatists should be coerced into the unity of Christ and quoted the Lucan text "Compel them to come in." After the proscription of the Donatists by law in 412, Augustine added to his arguments justifying persecution the statement that coercion in this world would save the heretics from eternal punishment in the next.

"No salvation outside the church," a doctrine preached by Augustine in 418 in his sermon addressed to the people of the church of Caesarea (chap. 6), implied a right to convert forcibly or otherwise the church's opponents. The precedents established in the Donatist controversy by Augustine passed into the armory of the catholic church through the Middle Ages and into Reformation times. The Albigensian crusades of 1212 and 1226–1244 witnessed terrible massacres in centers such as Béziers and Carcassonne where the heresy flourished. In 1244 the defenders of the last Abigensian stronghold, Mont Ségur, were burned alive by their victorious enemies. [*See* Cathari.] More than a century and a half later, in 1415, the same punishment was inflicted on Jan Hus at Prague.

In the Reformation, persecution of opposing churches was accepted by all parties. [*For further discussion, see* Reformation.] Henry VIII burned the Protestants Thomas Bilney and Robert Barnes; Mary Tudor sent some three hundred Protestants to the stake between 1555 and her death in November 1558; Calvin ordered the burning of Servetus in 1541. Unwillingness in the Roman Catholic church to concede that "error has any rights over truth" prolonged the period of persecution of Protestants into the eighteenth century. The bloody repression of the Calvinist Camisards in the Cévennes following the revocation of the Edict of Nantes in 1685 and the repression of Protestants in the Palatinate in 1715 and in the diocese of Salzburg in 1732 are reminders that religious persecution did not end with the formal conclusion of hostilities between Protestants and Catholics at the Peace of Westphalia in 1648. Even in World War II, the Ustasi government in Croatia unleashed what may be hoped to be the final spasm of religious persecution against the Orthodox minority in Bosnia. On the other hand, Christianity itself has been the object of persecution by the Hitlerite and Communist regimes. These persecutions have so far failed in their aims, but among Christians themselves it is to be hoped that the growth of the ecumenical movement and the decrees of Vatican II may help banish this blot from history.

BIBLIOGRAPHY

Sources

The Acts of the Christian Martyrs. Translated by Herbert A. Musurillo. Oxford, 1972. Includes useful introductions and bibliographical notes.

Lanata, Giuliana. *Gli atti dei martiri come documenti processuali.* Milan, 1973. No English translation, but contains excellent bibliographical notes and evaluation of manuscript traditions.

Lawlor, Hugh J., and John E. L. Oulton. *Eusebius, Bishop of Caesarea: The Ecclesiastical History and the Martyrs of Palestine* (1927–1928). 2 vols. Reprint, London, 1954. The best English text of Eusebius's *Martyrs of Palestine.*

Secondary Literature

Barnes, Timothy D. "Legislation against the Christians." *Journal of Roman Studies* 58 (1968): 32–50.

Barnes, Timothy D. "Pre-Decian *Acta Martyrum.*" *Journal of Theological Studies,* n.s. 19 (October 1968): 509–531.

Baynes, N. H. "The Great Persecution." In *The Imperial Crisis and Recovery, A.D. 193–324,* vol. 12 of *Cambridge Ancient History,* edited by S. A. Cook et al., pp. 646–677. Cambridge, 1939.

Brown, Peter R. *Religion and Society in the Age of Saint Augustine.* London, 1972. Contains important studies of Augustine's attitude toward religious coercion.

Emery, Richard W. *Heresy and Inquisition in Narbonne.* New York, 1941.

Frend, W. H. C. *Martyrdom and Persecution in the Early Church: A Study of a Conflict from the Maccabees to Donatus.* Oxford, 1965. Includes a bibliography of works published before 1964.

Grégoire, Henri. *Les persécutions dans l'Empire romain.* In *Mémoires de l'Académie Royale de Belgique,* vol. 46, fasc. 1. Brussels, 1951. Stimulating, like everything Grégoire wrote, though occasionally wrong-headed.

Hardy, E. G. *Christianity and the Roman Government: A Study in Imperial Administration* (1894). Reprint, London, 1925. Fine piece of work by a classical scholar.

King, Noel Q. *The Emperor Theodosius and the Establishment of Christianity.* Philadelphia, 1960.

Kitts, Eustace J. *Pope John the Twenty-third and Master John Hus of Bohemia.* London, 1910.

Knipfing, John R. "The Libelli of the Decian Persecution." *Harvard Theological Review* 16 (October 1923): 345–390.

Moreau, Jacques. *La persécution du christianisme dans l'Empire romain.* Paris, 1956. Revised and published in German as *Die Christenverfolgung im römischen Reich,* "Aus der Welt der Religion," n.s. 2 (Berlin, 1961). A perceptive and stimulating statement by one of Grégoire's pupils.

Shannon, Albert C. *The Popes and Heresy in the Thirteenth Century.* Villanova, Pa., 1949.

Sherwin-White, Adrian Nicholas. "The Early Persecutions and Roman Law Again." *Journal of Theological Studies,* n.s. 3 (October 1952): 199–213.

Ste. Croix, G. E. M. de. "Why Were the Early Christians Persecuted?" *Past and Present* 26 (November 1963): 6–38. The best short account of the persecutions and their causes.

Vogt, Joseph, and Hugh Last. "Christenverfolgung: 1, Historisch" and "Christenverfolgung: 2, Juristisch." In *Reallexikon für Antike und Christentum,* edited by Theodor Klauser, vol. 2. Stuttgart, 1954.

W. H. C. Frend

PERSEPHONE. *See* Demeter and Persephone.

PERSONIFICATION. *See* Anthropomorphism *and* Hypostasis.

PERUN was the thunder god of the heathen Slavs. A fructifier, a purifier, and an overseer of right and order, he was the adversary of the Slavic "black god" (Chernobog, Veles). His actions were perceived by the senses: he was seen in the thunderbolt, he was heard in the crackling rattle of stones or the thunderous bellow of the bull or he-goat, and he was felt in the sharp touch of an ax blade.

The cult of Perun among the Baltic Slavs is attested by the Byzantine historian Procopius in the sixth century CE. In the Russian *Primary Chronicle,* compiled circa 1111, Perun is invoked by name in the treaties of 945 and 971, and his name is first in the list of gods compiled by Vladimir I in 980. As Prone, Perun was worshiped in oak groves by West Slavs, and he is so named in Helmold's *Chronica Slavorum* of the twelfth century. Saxo Grammaticus mentions Perun's son, whom he calls Porenutius, in his *Gesta Danorum* of the early thirteenth century.

The root *per-/perk-,* meaning "to strike, to splinter," is common to Indo-European languages. Close relatives to the Slavic name *Perun* are the Lithuanian *Perkūnas,* Prussian *Perkonis,* Latvian *Pērkons,* Old Icelandic *Fjǫrgynn,* and Greek *Zeus keraunos* (from a taboo **peraunos*). Common nouns derived from the same Indo-European root—Sanskrit *parjanyah* ("cloud, thunder"), Hittite *peruna* ("mountaintop"), Gothic *fairguni* ("oak forest"), Celtic *hercynia* (from *silva,* "oak forest"), and Latin *quercus* (from **perkus,* "pine" or, earlier, "oak")—suggest prehistoric ties between Indo-European thunder gods and clouds (i.e., rain), oaks, oak forests, and mountaintops. The veneration of the Slavic **pergynja* (Russian *peregynia,* Polish *przeginia*), meaning "oak forest," is attested by Russian literary sources. West Slavic and South Slavic personal names and place-names with the root *per-* are mostly linked with "oak," "oak forest," and "hill": *Perun gora* (Serbian), *Perunowa gora* (Polish), and *Porun,* the name of a hill in Istria. The word for "Thursday" (Thor's day) in the Polabian dialect is *perǔndan,* which literally means "lightning."

In the Christian period, worship of Perun was gradually transferred to the old, white-bearded Saint Elijah (Russian, Il'ia), who traveled across the sky in a fiery chariot (as the Lithuanian thunder god, copper-bearded Perkūnas, is still believed to do). In folk beliefs, Perun's fructifying, life-stimulating, and purifying functions are still performed by his traditional instruments: ax, bull, he-goat, dove, and cuckoo. Sacrifice of a bull and a communal feast on Saint Il'ia's Day, 20 July, in honor of Perun or Il'ia were last recorded in northern Russia in 1907, when they were combined with Christian hymns and blessings. The meat was prepared entirely by men and then taken into the church and divided among the villagers (see Otto Schrader, *Die Indogermanen,* 1907).

BIBLIOGRAPHY

Darkevich, V. P. "Topor kak simvol Peruna v drevnerusskom iazychestve." *Sovetskaia arkheologiia* 4 (1961): 91–102.

Duridanov, I. "Urslav: Perun und seine Spuren in der Toponymie." *Studia Slavica Academiae Scientiarum Hungaricae* 12 (1966): 99–102.

Gimbutas, Marija. "Perkūnas/Perun: The Thunder God of the Balts and the Slavs." *Journal of Indo-European Studies* 1 (1973): 466–478.

Ivanov, J. "Kul't Peruna u iuzhnykh slavian." *Izvestiia* 8, no. 4 (1903): 140–174.

Rožniecki, Stan. "Perun und Thor: Ein Beitrag zur Quellenkritik der russischen Mythologie." *Archiv für slawische Philologie* (Berlin) 23 (1901): 462–520.

Marija Gimbutas

PETER DAMIAN. *See* Damian, Peter.

PETER LOMBARD (c. 1100–1160), also known as Peter the Lombard; Christian theologian and teacher. There is little precise knowledge of Peter Lombard's origin except that he was born in northern Italy at Lumellogno in Novarre before 1100. Peter was a student at Bologna (or perhaps Vercelli) before he went to France to study, first in Reims and then in Paris and its environs (c. 1134). While it is believed that he returned to Italy, visiting Rome in 1154, all of Peter Lombard's professional life and work is associated with a career in northern France, especially Paris, where he taught at the Cathedral School of Notre Dame. By 1143 his reputation was widespread. Sometime in 1144 or 1145 he became a canon at Notre Dame, and his teaching continued to influence students, among whom were Herbert of Bosham and Peter Comestor.

Peter Lombard participated in two significant ecclesiastical investigations concerning the orthodoxy of the teachings of Gilbert of Poitiers; the first was held in Paris on 21 April 1147, the second at the Council of Reims on 21 March 1148. By 1156 Peter was archdeacon of Paris, and on 29 June 1159 he was consecrated its bishop. He died the following year.

Today only four works attributed to Peter are considered authentic: a collection of sermons, two biblical commentaries, and the *Book of Sentences*. The thirty-three sermons were composed by Peter during the twenty years that he exercised leadership in Paris (c. 1140–1160). Until recently, many of these were attributed to Hildebert of Lavardin. Peter begins each sermon with a scriptural citation, and his homilies, although clear and precise, give little evidence of the academic interest in exegesis as a science that was developing at the time. Instead, Peter's instructions emphasize a moral and spiritual exposition.

The same approach to exegesis appears to characterize the Lombard's first biblical commentary, on *Psalms (Commentarius in psalmos Davidicos)*, completed by 1138. Peter follows the method of the teachers at Laon (northern France), glossing the biblical word with a series of patristic teachings. The prologue to the commentary, however, does include the *accessus ad auctores* formula (author, text, subject matter, intention, and *modus tractandi*) that had only recently been appropriated to scriptural exposition in some of the school works. But because this work shows no influence of the anonymous *Summa sententiarum*, which dates from circa 1137–1138, it is usually seen as an early writing of the Lombard.

Peter Lombard's *Commentary on the Pauline Epistles* (1139–1141) brings a new dynamic to his teachings. Although composed shortly after his work on the psalter these glosses reflect the doctrine and exegetical methods from the schools. For example, he includes a wider variety of patristic sources; and the contemporary teachings of both the *Summa sententiarum* and of Gilbert of Poitiers appear as well. In addition, the *Commentary* shows some influence of the discursive inquiry associated with the new theological method, which brought questions to the text in an effort to discern meaning. However, Peter Lombard remained a cautious theologian, and although this work is more didactic than its predecessor he continued to stress spiritual exegesis.

It is the Lombard's last major work, the *Book of Sentences*, that sets his teachings apart in the twelfth century. The text provided his students with a systematic and comprehensive presentation of Christian doctrine in an orderly and accessible format: book 1 examines the Trinity; book 2 discusses creation, grace, and sin; book 3 presents the doctrines of incarnation and redemption; and book 4 considers the sacraments and eschatology. Although the work is a concise synthesis, Peter's citations of authorities provided a vast range of critically selected resources on distinctions and questions that were pertinent and timely. Understandably, Augustine was favored; but accepted contemporary works were also included, such as the *Glossa ordinaria*, the *Decretum* of Gratian, and the Lombard's own scriptural commentaries. Peter also confronted the vigorous inquiry of the school theologians, such as Hugh of Saint-Victor, Peter Abelard, and Gilbert of Poitiers. Peter's responses to the issues offered a moderate, orthodox position and met the needs of the times more adequately than the numerous other collections available. The final form of the *Sentences* was completed by 1157 or 1158.

The significance of Peter Lombard for the development of theology is due to the place of the *Sentences* in the medieval curriculum. What the *Glossa ordinaria* did for scripture, and what Gratian's *Decretum* did for law, the *Sentences* did for Christian doctrine. Peter would, in fact, be remembered as the "Master of the Sentences." His student Peter of Poitiers continued to use the *Sentences* for teaching his own classes in theology, and in about 1222 Alexander of Hales officially incorporated the text into the course of studies at the University of Paris. Thenceforth all students were required to comment on the *Sentences* for a degree in theology. In this way, all medieval theologians became disciples of the Lombard, and the format, method, and distinctions of the *Sentences* continued to shape theology for more than four hundred years.

BIBLIOGRAPHY

Critical editions of the Lombard's writings can be found in volumes 191 and 192 of J.-P. Migne's *Patrologia Latina* (1879–1880; reprint, Turnhout, 1975). His sermons, attributed to Hildebert of Lavardin, are edited in volume 171 of that series (1854; reprint, Turnhout, 1978). However, the best text of the *Sentences* is *Sententiae in IV libris distinctae*, 3d ed. (Rome, 1971).

A comprehensive and critical study of Peter Lombard's writings remains to be done. One standard reference for his life and teaching is the extensive essay by Joseph de Ghellinck, "Pierre Lombard," in the *Dictionnaire de théologie catholique* (Paris, 1903–1950). Several more recent studies have brought precision to this essay. For example, Philippe Delhaye's *Pierre Lombard: Sa vie, ses œuvres, sa morale* (Montreal, 1961) summarizes the major themes of the Lombard's writings: human nature, grace, freedom, the theological and cardinal virtues, the gifts of the Holy Spirit, sin, and penance. Ignatius Brady's major essay "Pierre Lombard" in the *Dictionnaire de spiritualité* (Paris, 1985) continues these scholarly efforts. Brady's article includes an extensive, up-to-date bibliography. Another significant resource is the journal *Pier Lombardo: Revista di teologia, filosofia e varia cultura* (Novarre, 1953–1962).

John van Dyk's study of the *Sentences*, "Thirty Years since Stegmüller: A Bibliographic Guide to the Study of Medieval Sentence Commentaries since the Publication of Stegmüller's *Repertorium* (1947)," *Franciscan Studies* 39 (1979): 255–315, updates previous bibliographies and compiles the best research on this text and its influence. Van Dyk's study includes many articles in English and organizes information into significant categories: texts and editions; philosophy, theology, history; and two indexes.

EILEEN F. KEARNEY

PETER THE APOSTLE (d. AD 64?), one of the twelve apostles of Jesus and, according to Roman Catholic tradition, the first pope. The earliest sources of information about Peter are such that it is not possible to draw an altogether clear distinction between those elements in our image of Peter that are derived from his role in the church prior to his death and those that derive from the Peter of later Christian remembrance and tradition. None of our sources is primarily interested in Peter. Only a few, *Galatians* and *1 Corinthians*, were written while Peter was still alive and by someone who certainly knew him. Those sources that give a more circumstantial account of Peter were written some years, often some decades, after his death. They incorporate the story of Peter into the story of Jesus and of the early church in such a way as to raise questions about the historicity of some of the details. Are accounts of Peter's prominent role among the apostles an accurate recollection of the way things actually happened, or are they a retrojection into the time of Jesus' ministry of the role that Peter would later play in the early church? No one denies that there is a substratum of fact or event behind the New Testament descriptions of Peter, but there is considerable disagreement about what that substratum is. These problems are neither so complex nor so heavy with consequences as the problems connected with "the historical Jesus," but they are similar in type.

The Apostle. Symeon or Simon (Hebrew and Greek names, respectively) was, with his brother Andrew, a fisherman at the Sea of Galilee when they were both called to follow Jesus of Nazareth. They may have been the first called, and were to be among the closest of Jesus' followers. Simon was also called Kepha (or Kephas), which is Aramaic for "rock," the Greek form of which is *Petra* or *Petros*, whence the name *Peter*. According to both *Mark* 3:16 and *John* 4:42, it was Jesus who gave Simon this additional name, but the fact that the two accounts are quite different has led some to suggest that the name may have been given only subsequently, in view of his work in the early church, and then retrojected into the time of Jesus' ministry.

Various New Testament sources present Peter as playing a special role among the disciples during Jesus' lifetime. He is named first among the disciples (*Mk.* 3:16 and parallels, *Acts* 1:13). He is often presented as speaking on their behalf (*Mk.* 8:29, 10:28, 11:21, 16:7, and their parallels). Along with James and John, he is one of an inner circle among the disciples (*Mk.* 5:37, 9:2ff., 14:33, and their parallels).

In different ways *Matthew*, *Luke*, and *John* all tell us that Jesus entrusted to Peter some special role in the community that Jesus was to leave behind. He is the rock on which the church is to be built (*Mt.* 16:18). Jesus prays for him that, after having been tested himself, he may strengthen his brethren (*Lk.* 22:31). Jesus takes him aside and specially commissions him to feed his lambs and his sheep (*Jn.* 21:15–17). Here again there is disagreement as to whether these narratives report events that actually took place or are efforts to legitimate Peter's later role in the early church by anchoring it in the actions of Jesus. A middle position is, of course, possible: that Jesus did entrust some special responsibility to Peter, and that this was later elaborated on by the evangelists.

Peter is also the disciple whose failures are most fully described in the New Testament. When he objects to Jesus' prediction of his own suffering and death, Jesus calls him Satan (*Mt.* 16:23, *Mk.* 8:33). When Jesus' final sufferings have already begun, Peter publicly denies any association with him (*Mk.* 14:66–72 and parallels). In addition, he is described, not unsympathetically, as being impetuous (*Jn.* 21:7).

Several different strands of New Testament tradition testify that Peter was the first of the apostles to see Jesus after he was raised from the dead. Many judge *1 Corinthians* 15:5 to be part of a traditional confessional formula. If this is correct, then well before the mid-fifties of the first century it was part of Christian tradition that Jesus appeared first to Kephas. In the Lucan account it is the women who first see the risen Jesus, but then Peter is the first of the apostles to see him after the women, and his seeing is clearly more important than theirs (*Lk.* 24:1–34). In *John*, Peter is the first to enter the empty tomb. Mary Magdalene is the first to see Jesus, and only subsequently a group of the apostles (all but Thomas) are together when they first see Jesus (*Jn.* 20:1–25).

Throughout the early chapters of *Acts* (chaps. 1–12), Peter plays the leading role in the formation and expansion of the church. He is the leading preacher and wonder-worker (2:14–36; 3:1–10, 11–26; 9:32–43). He is the first to extend the Christian mission to the gentiles (10:1–11, 18).

To judge from Paul's letter to the Galatians, Peter was the most important figure in the church at Jerusalem in the late thirties (*Gal.* 1:18). According to the same source he was still one of the pillars of that church in the late forties but now is mentioned between James and John (2:9). It is in this same letter that Paul speaks of Peter as being raised up to preach to the Jews as he, Paul, had been sent to the gentiles (2:7–8). Paul gives us no detailed information about Peter's work as apostle to the Jews, but the fact that he speaks of him in this way suggests that it must have been fairly extensive, and not confined merely to his work in the church at Jerusalem. We know that Peter was in Antioch (*Gal.* 2:11–14), and it seems likely that he was in Corinth as well (*1 Cor.* 1:12). The fact that somewhat later in the first century the pseudonymous *1 Peter* is addressed to Christians in Pontus, Galatia, Asia, and Bithynia (*1 Pt.* 1:1) suggests that these regions were associated with Peter's ministry. Also, the fact that the letter is ostensibly sent from Rome (referred to in *1 Peter* 5:13 as "Babylon") suggests that a Roman activity of Peter was also a tradition at this time.

In the disputes over the obligation of gentile Christians to conform to Jewish law, Peter probably adopted a position somewhere between that of Paul and Paul's opponents. In theory he seems to have sided with Paul, but his practice apparently was not always consistent with his ideas (*Gal.* 2:11–14).

Peter's activity at Rome would later be of great importance in Christian tradition, and so has attracted considerable attention. There is no evidence linking him with Rome in the documents written during his lifetime, but the tradition that he preached at Rome is widely attested in the late first and second centuries. Because at this time the matter had not yet become important in church politics, there seems to be no good reason to question this early tradition. Equally early is the tradition of Peter's martyrdom (*Jn.* 21:18–19) and of his martyrdom in Rome (*1 Clement* 5). Archaeological investigation has not settled the question of Peter's burial place, but it has shown that by the middle of the second century Roman Christians honored a particular place as the location of Peter's burial.

Peter in Christian Tradition. Peter remained prominent in a variety of Christian traditions in the second and third centuries. Several writings were ascribed to him, either directly or indirectly, and in several others he played a leading role. Early in the second century it was asserted that the gospel according to Mark was a compendium of Peter's teaching, a view that would be generally accepted in later orthodoxy. A *Gospel of Peter*, of heretical cast according to the bishop of Antioch, was in use in Syria in the second half of the century. The *Kerygma of Peter*, a work with some similarities to the writing of the second-century Christian apologists, may have been written before midcentury. An *Apocalypse of Peter* dates from about the same time, and *The Acts of Peter* from not much later. The gnostic library from Nag Hammadi likewise contains several works in which Peter is featured: another *Apocalypse of Peter*, an *Acts of Peter and the Twelve Apostles*, and a *Letter of Peter to Philip*. These works probably date from the third century. None of these writings tells us much that is likely to be historically reliable about Peter, but taken together they indicate the importance accorded to Peter in the polymorphous Christianity of this period.

Another work, the *Kerugmata Petrou*, has been reconstructed by some scholars as among the earliest sources of the later pseudo-Clementine literature. (Some scholars deny that such a document ever existed.) This reconstructed document, of a strikingly Jewish-Christian character, describes a Peter who, along with James, takes the lead in defending Christianity against such perverters of the truth as Simon Magus and Paul of Tarsus.

It was within what would subsequently be identified as orthodox Christianity that the figure of Peter has exercised its most widespread and long-lasting influence. Within this orthodox tradition his influence has been especially important in the West. Peter has been seen as the archetypal Christian, as the prototype of episcopal church order, and as the first pope. The last has been the most influential—but also the most controverted—part of the Petrine tradition.

As early as the late first century the tradition arose that Peter (along with Paul) had made special provision for the leadership in the Roman church after their departure or death (see the authentic first letter of Clement of Rome to the Corinthians, chaps. 42 and 44). In the course of the subsequent controversy over gnosticism, the issue of the apostolic foundations of the church became very important. The same writers who stressed the apostolic authorship of the books of the New Testament also laid great stress on the apostolic foundations of particular churches. The church at Rome, because of the role allegedly played there by Peter and Paul, was singled out and came to see itself as the apostolic church *par excellence* (see Irenaeus, *Against Heresies* 3.3.1–3). Gradually this tradition of the Petrine origin of the Roman church (Paul gradually fades fromthe picture) is combined with the New Testament image of Peter as the first and even the leader of the apostles. On this basis, the Roman church is seen as the first and even the leader among the churches. At first, original succession ideas (in Irenaeus, for example) emphasized that the bishop was successor to the apostle-founder of the particular church as preacher of the apostolic gospel. By the late fourth century (some would say earlier), the claim is made that the bishop of Rome succeeds as well to Peter's apostolic primacy. It is on this basis that Rome claims authority over the entire church.

These views seem to have developed first within the Roman church itself and to have spread from there only slowly throughout the West. The Christian East had a different tradition and never fully accepted the Roman interpretation of Petrine authority. Traditionally the East too recognized a Petrine primacy within the New Testament and a kind of Roman primacy within the church universal. The nature of this latter primacy has been the subject of much dispute, and the East has fairly consistently refused to see it as involving a Roman authority over other churches, or at least over the churches of the East.

Other images of Peter have also flourished over the centuries. Peter as the keeper of the keys to the kingdom of heaven has played an important role in Christian art and folklore, taking its point of departure from the same New Testament text, *Matthew* 16:18, that has been so important in sustaining the image of Peter as the first pope. Similarly, the many images of Peter to be found in the New Testament—Peter as shepherd, as fisher of men, as confessor of true faith against false teaching, as weak and impetuous—have all been reflected at various times and places within the Christian tradition.

[*See also* Discipleship.]

BIBLIOGRAPHY

The classic modern study of Peter from a conservative Protestant perspective is Oscar Cullmann's *Peter, Disciple, Apostle, Martyr: A Historical and Theological Study*, 2d ed. (Philadelphia, 1953). Cullmann gives a generally conservative reading of the New Testament texts, but he rejects the idea of successors to Peter. Less negative on this latter point is Rudolf Pesch's *Simon-Petrus: Geschichte und geschichtliche Bedeutung des ersten Jüngers Jesu Christi* (Stuttgart, 1980). A very useful survey of the roles of Peter in the New Testament and of the methodological problems involved is given by Raymond Brown and others in *Peter in the New Testament* (Minneapolis, 1973). Eastern Christian perspectives on Peter are presented by John Meyendorff and others in *The Primacy of Peter* (London, 1963). See especially Meyendorff's contribution, "St. Peter in Byzantine Theology," pp. 7–29.

On the matter of the archaeological evidence for Peter at Rome, see Daniel W. O'Connor's *Peter in Rome: The Literary, Liturgical and Archeological Evidence* (New York, 1969) and more briefly his "Peter in Rome: A Review and Position," in *Christianity, Judaism, and Other Graeco-Roman Cults*, edited by Jacob Neusner (Leiden, 1975), pt. 2, pp. 146–160. For bibliographical information, see the section "Petrus" in the bibliography in *Archivum Historiae Pontificae* (Rome, 1968–).

James F. McCue

PETR MOGHILA (1596–1646), also known as Petr Mohyla, or Movila; Orthodox metropolitan of Kiev. As head of the Orthodox church in the Ukraine, at that time under Polish rule, Petr Moghila was chiefly responsible for the revival of Orthodoxy in southwestern Russia following the Union of Brest-Litovsk (1596), at which a large part of the Orthodox population submitted to Rome. Although willing to consider possible schemes for union with Rome, Moghila devoted his energies to strengthening the position of the Orthodox who chose to remain independent of the papacy.

Of Romanian princely descent, Moghila was born in Moldavia and educated at the Orthodox school in Lwów. He may have continued his studies in the West, possibly at the University of Paris. Widely read in classical Latin literature and scholastic theology, dynamic and authoritarian by nature, Moghila became abbot of the important Monastery of the Caves at Kiev in 1627 and was made metropolitan of Kiev in 1633, a position he held until his death.

The thirteen years of Moghila's episcopate constitute a decisive cultural turning point for Orthodoxy in southwestern Russia. In the schools that he opened for Orthodox clergy and laity, the teaching was based on Western models and was given predominantly in Latin, not in Greek or Slavonic. Western secular and religious writings were studied together with modern science. The college that Moghila established at Kiev reached a standard of excellence unequaled elsewhere in the Orthodox world of the time and continued to play a formative role throughout the seventeenth century; many of the Russians who collaborated closely with Peter the Great had been educated there. Seeking to create an "Occidental Orthodoxy," Moghila opened Little Russia to Western influences half a century before this happened in Great Russia.

Moghila's latinizing approach is evident in the wide-ranging liturgical reforms that he imposed, for example in the Sacrament of Confession, where he replaced the deprecative formula used at absolution in the Greek manuals ("May God forgive you . . .") with an indicative formula taken directly from the Roman Catholic ritual ("I absolve you . . ."). The *Orthodox Confession of Faith* that he composed in 1639–1640 was based on Latin catechisms by Peter Canisius and others. Here Moghila not only employed the term *transubstantiation* but taught explicitly that the moment of consecration in the Eucharist occurs at the Words of Institution, not at the Epiclesis of the Holy Spirit; and when discussing the state of the departed he virtually adopted the Latin doctrine of purgatory. After extensive alterations had been made in the *Orthodox Confession* by the Greek theologian Meletios Syrigos, it was approved by the Council of Jassy (1642) and by the four Eastern patriarchs (1643). Moghila himself was displeased by these changes. In his *Little Catechism* (1645) he continued to affirm consecration by Words of Institution, although he was more guarded on the question of purgatory.

The *Orthodox Confession* represents the high-water mark of Roman Catholic theological influence upon the Christian East. But the extent of Moghila's Latinisms should not be exaggerated, for on questions such as the *filioque* and the papal claims, he adheres to the traditional Orthodox viewpoint, although he expresses this viewpoint in a moderate form.

BIBLIOGRAPHY

Works by Petr Moghila. The original Latin version of the *Orthodox Confession,* as drawn up by Moghila in 1640, is now lost; an intermediate Latin version, embodying many of the changes made by Meletios Syrigos in 1642 but sometimes adhering to the 1640 text, has been edited by Antoine Malvy and Marcel Viller, *La Confession Orthodoxe de Pierre Moghila métropolite de Kiev, 1633–1646,* "Orientalia Christiana," vol. 10 (Rome, 1927). For the Greek text, as revised by Syrigos and adopted at Jassy, see part 1 of Ernest Julius Kimmel's *Monumental Fidei Ecclesiae Orientalis* (Jena, 1850), pp. 56–324; see also Ioannis N. Karmiris's *Ta dogmatika kai sumbolika mnēmeia tēs Orthodoxou Katholikēs Ekklēsias,* vol. 2 (Athens, 1953), pp. 593–686, translated into English as *The Orthodox Confession of the Catholic and Apostolic Eastern Church* (London, 1762); see also the new edition by J. J. Overbeck and James N. W. B. Robertson (London, 1898).

Works about Petr Moghila. On the cultural and educational aspects of his career, see William K. Medlin and Christos G. Patrinelis's *Renaissance Influences and Religious Reforms in Russia: Western and Post-Byzantine Impacts on Culture and Education, Sixteenth–Seventeenth Centuries* (Geneva, 1971), pp. 124–149; on his theological position, see part 1 of Georges Florovsky's *Ways of Russian Theology,* volume 5 of his *Collected Works,* edited by Richard S. Haugh (Belmont, Mass., 1979), pp. 64–78. Earlier studies include S. I. Golubev's classic work, *Kievskii Mitropolit Petr Mogila i ego spodvizhniki* (Kiev, 1883–1898); Émile Picot's "Pierre Movilă (Mogila)," in *Bibliographie hellénique, ou Description raisonnée des ouvrages publiés par des Grecs au dix-septième siècle,* vol. 4, edited by Émile Legrand (Paris, 1896), pp. 104–159; and Téofil Ionesco's *La vie et l'œuvre de Pierre Movila, métropolite de Kiev* (Paris, 1944).

KALLISTOS WARE

PETTAZZONI, RAFFAELE (1883–1959), Italian historian of religions. Pettazzoni was the principal founder (with Uberto Pestalozza) of the history of religions discipline in Italy, a discipline in which he himself enjoyed an international reputation. He participated in the foundation of the International Association for the History of Religions in 1950 and served as its second president (following Gerardus van der Leeuw) and as editor of its journal, *Numen*. Pettazzoni was professor of the history of religions at the University of Bologna from 1914 until his acceptance in 1924 of the newly created chair in the history of religions at the University of Rome, where he stayed until his retirement in 1958. In 1924, he founded the periodical *Studi e materiali di storia delle religioni*. He was a member of the Accademia Nazionale dei Lincei.

Pettazzoni's first works, *Le origini dei Kabiri nelle isole del Mar Tracio* (The Origins of the Kabiri in the Islands of the Thracian Sea; 1909) and *La religione primitiva in Sardegna* (1912), illustrate the shift of his interests from classical archaeology to the history of religions. His participation in the Fourth International Congress of the History of Religions (Leiden, 1912) was decisive in this regard. Pettazzoni's first major work, a vast monograph entitled *L'essere celeste nelle credenze dei popoli primitivi* (The Heavenly Being in the Beliefs of Primitive Peoples), was unfortunately not published until 1922, since the series that it was to inaugurate failed to appear. This initial mishap did not discourage Pettazzoni's interest in that work's subject, however. He returned to the subject of heavenly beings toward the end of his life, by which time he had overcome his earlier rather positivistic "ouranian" interpretation of these beings as "mythical apperceptions" of the sky.

There followed in 1920 *La religione di Zarathustra nella storia religiosa dell'Iran*, in which Pettazzoni interpreted the religious reform of Zarathushtra (Zoroaster) as a monotheistic reaction to a more ancient Iranian polytheism represented by the demonic *daēvas* of the Avesta. This interpretation allowed Pettazzoni to propose a rather strict definition of monotheism, which he believed to be characterized historically as a revolution against polytheism, and thus to be sharply distinct from the primitive cult of a supreme being. This distinction lay behind Pettazzoni's repeated polemic against Wilhelm Schmidt's theory of *Urmonotheismus* ("primitive monotheism").

Other works of this period include *La religione nella Grecia antica fino ad Alessandro* (Religion in Ancient Greece until Alexander's Times; 1921, reedited in 1953 with a remarkable introduction reviewing the historical formation of the religion of the Greeks), *I misteri* (Mystery Religions; 1924), and the multivolume *La confessione dei peccati* (Confession of Sins; 1929–1936), a vast inquiry that combines a systematic exploration of the subject matter with a rather positivistic hermeneutics. Confession is represented as having originated in magical attempts to expel quasi-material sins through their ritualized expression.

The production of these years was accompanied by a deeper reflection on method, which led Pettazzoni to insist on the comparative-historical method for the study of religion that he had already defended in his inaugural lecture of 1924. In the newly established journal *Studi e materiali di storia delle religioni*, he responded to the objections made to the new discipline by the Italian historicists *(storicisti)* Benedetto Croce and Adolfo Omodeo. Croce and Omodeo viewed the new discipline's comparative aims as having merely descriptive and classificatory utility, and as thus being far removed from the genuine problem of history. Pettazzoni countered by insisting that the comparative questions of origin and development were legitimate and that they were important for the study of religious and cultural identity.

In the meantime, Pettazzoni had begun to edit the series "Testi e documenti per la storia delle religioni," where he published *La mitologia giapponese secondo il primo libro del Kojiki* (Japanese Mythology according to the First Book of the Kojiki; 1929). Gradually, his attention was drawn to the phenomenology and psychology of religion. Pettazzoni resisted both psychologism and an ahistorical phenomenology, but he eventually acknowledged the essential contribution that the phenomenologist's religious sensitivity could make to the foundation of a "science of religions" *(Religionswissenschaft)*. According to his mature view, *Religionswissenschaft* should include both history of religions, focused on the processes of historical formation, and phenomenology of religion, which focuses on the essential nature and meaning of the religious facts of different cultures. Pettazzoni maintained that cultures could be properly understood only if their respective religions were taken into consideration. The Italian *storicisti* and the culture inspired by them—the laicism that had been a formative influence on Pettazzoni himself—had failed to recognize this.

Pettazzoni maintained a lasting interest in the religions of preliterate cultures. Beginning in 1948 there appeared the four volumes of *Miti e leggende*. These volumes testify to Pettazzoni's interest in the study and vulgarization of myth and mythologies stimulated by the experience of the war. In the introduction to the first volume, he speaks of a "truth of the myth" *(verità del mito)*. Myth is seen as a narrative founding of the worldview and way of life of a human group, a position that rejoins, while transcending, the functionalist intuitions of Bronislaw Malinowski.

In these same years Pettazzoni returned to his earlier interest in questions connected with the supreme beings of preliterate cultures, and more particularly with the attribute of omniscience among different kinds of deities belonging to different religious milieus, published as *L'omniscienza di Dio* (1955), aimed to contribute to a historical understanding and typology of this phenomenon. In *L'essere supremo nelle religioni primitive* (The Supreme Being in Primitive Religions; 1957), Pettazzoni entered into questions of religious stratification, probing down to the level of the archaic cultures of hunting and gathering societies. [*See* Supreme Beings.] His interest in questions concerning religion and society, the civil aspects of religion, and the religious aspects of society is documented in his *Italia religiosa* (Religious Italy; 1952) and *Letture religiose* (Lectures on Religion; 1959).

BIBLIOGRAPHY

Nineteen of Pettazzoni's previously published essays appear in English translation in a collection entitled *Essays on the History of Religions*, translated by H. J. Rose (Leiden, 1954). Among numerous biographical articles, appreciations, and bibliographies of Pettazzoni's work are the following valuable sources: Mario Gandini's *Presenza di Pettazzoni* (Bologna,

1970); and *Problems and Methods in the History of Religions*, edited by me, C. Jouco Bleeker, and Alessandro Bausani (Leiden, 1972).

UGO BIANCHI

PEUHL RELIGION. *See* Fulbe Religion.

PEYOTE CULTS. *See* Psychedelic Drugs.

PHALLUS. The phallus, like all great religious symbols, points to a mysterious divine reality that cannot otherwise be apprehended. In this case, however, mystery seems also to surround the symbol itself. We know, for example, that the phallus is important to many Greek mysteries; but the ancients—keeping cultic secrecy—did not talk about it. Even modern Śaiva Hindus, who worship openly an upright cylinder rounded at the top and called a lingam (from the Sanskrit *liṅga*, "phallus"), are not always sure they are faced with an image of a sexual organ. The traditional reticence does serve a purpose: it suggests that in the case of the phallus there is a tendency on the part of the human mind to confuse the symbolic phallus—whether human or animal, attached to the body or isolated, realistically modeled or otherwise—with the ordinary phallus that everybody knows. It is not as a flaccid member that this symbol is most important to religion but as an erect organ. This fact serves the basic meaning of phallic imagery: that the godhead, whatever it is in itself, is a great giver of life of one kind or another. This essay will not explore the more general topic of the erotic in religion, in cases where the phallus may be merely implied (as in the biblical *Song of Songs*), nor can it take up directly the association of the phallus with feminine images of generation (e.g., the complex relationship between lingam and yoni in Indian Tantrism).

The earliest appearance of the phallus as an image, probably religious, is in the arts of Paleolithic hunters. Dependent as they were upon the abundance of animals, they made images of fertility—mostly of the female breasts and vulva but also of the penis—engraved in human form on bones and antlers. The hunters seem to have been aware of a supernatural reality beyond the physical and apparent (they buried their dead with utensils, perhaps to be used after death), and it is quite possible that the phallic images were intended to evoke a divine power that lay behind the abundance of animal life. At the French cave of Les Trois Frères, a remarkable figure comes to view. Dubbed "the Sorcerer," he is a theriomorphic hybrid, with antlers on his head, the ears of a wolf, and the tail of a horse; yet he stands erect with human legs and a human phallus that is not erect but is pulled back between the thighs as if to make sure it is exposed to view. Less famous are his fellow "bison-men," or "masked dancers," depicted nearby, similarly hybrid but with human penises that are erect. One of them drives or pursues—or is merely dancing before—a strange herd of composite animals that are noticeably female. These phallic figures may be Stone Age priests in the guise of the fertile power that brings abundance, or they may be images of the supernatural power itself. [*See* Paleolithic Religion.]

With the artifacts of later agricultural societies, matters are more certain. Min, the ancient Egyptian god seen in reliefs at the chapel of Sesostris I, stands, fully anthropomorphic, with arm upraised toward a "flail," as the god behind the harvest. He is strikingly ithyphallic, with an erect penis of exaggerated length and stiffness that he is probably holding in his other hand. The unnatural character of this phallus is a sign of divine fecundity exceeding merely human powers. Preserving the early concern for animal fertility, and extending it to domestic animals, Min is called a "bull" who "rejoices in the cow, the husband impregnating with his phallus." At his rites, a bull leads a procession in which a statue of the phallic god is carried—to celebrate the current harvest and to ensure future ones by proper attention to the power responsible; to spread Min's fecundity among human households, which also require abundance; and to make it very clear to all from whom this life really comes. But Min with his long penis is also a god of roads, capable of protecting travelers, especially in the desert, and here we begin to see the complexity of phallic symbolism. [*See* Crossroads.]

Dōsojin, a deity of Japanese folk religion, can be seen today in thousands of images, typically at the edge of a rice field. There he assumes his chief role as god of harvests; but, according to inscriptions on these images, he is also the "pass-not place deity," the power who protects the field from trespassers and from other evils such as drought. Fertility, we are being told, involves the accompanying capacity to set boundaries and to defend one's territory. The erect phallus is symbolically capable of doing both—much as the obscene gesture (say, a raised middle finger) is both a sexual sign and a threat. Thus, Dōsojin may be seen as a realistically rendered, upright stone phallus, a few feet in height, or, just as likely, as a pair of phalli characterizing, presumably, his double nature. Indeed, his most frequent image is that of a "loving couple," usually holding hands but sometimes enjoying coitus in relief on a stone that may itself be phallic. Signifying the complexity of the god, this "husband and wife" point also to Dōsojin's role as a god of human fertility and of the institution of marriage, which is, of course, a kind of boundary. The god's rites, at New Year, are lively to the point of license: bands of mischievous youth are allowed to roam, good-natured insults are exchanged, and Dōsojin's own image may be beaten or urinated upon. The penis of the god is described in a bawdy song: "Too long for any female organ to receive it, he had to lay it in the fork of a tree." Trees—often a pine tree or a pair of pines—figure in the rites as symbols for the divine phallus, for what he fecundates, and for the "evergreen" harvest he makes possible.

It does seem strange that a god of boundaries should have such boundless rites; but there is in the indecency of Dōsojin's public phallus a clue to the infinite nature of the divine energy—which, nevertheless, permits itself to be contained within a field. Further, a phallus that is truly capable of defending the land may have to go "beyond the bounds of decency" to do so. Perhaps this is part of the reason—in addition to the obvious fact that fields and roads often meet—why Dōsojin, like Min, is a god of roads. Roads cross boundaries, and this Japanese god protects the traveler who has not settled down. The boundlessness of Dōsojin may even explain why ascetic Buddhism was never completely successful at suppressing his cult in favor of the *bodhisattva* Kṣitigarbha—who, like all great beings, has his "private parts withdrawn into a sheath" *(kośopagatavastiguhya,* in Śākyamitra's *Kosalālaṃkāra).* In a Buddhist temple at Nagoya, the image of Kṣitigarbha sits in contemplation; behind him is a curtain hiding a pair of phalli that are inscribed with the name *Dōsojin* (see Czaja, 1974, figs. 91, 92).

The phallic symbolism of ancient Greek religion is most extensive; the representation of Hermes offers a prime example. While late sculpture shows him fully anthropomorphic, naked and with an exposed, rather small, flaccid penis like that of other gods, his earlier images are quite otherwise. At Cyllene, Hermes was worshiped by the name of Phales—derived from *phallos*—and in the image of a phallic stone. More usually, however, his phallic image was a herm. Originally a stone heap—perhaps topped by a large upright stone—serving as a landmark in a countryside without roads, the herm developed into a quadrangular stone pillar topped by the head of Hermes and featuring at its front an erect phallus with testicles of normal human size and shape. Contrasting dramatically with the austere flat surface to which it is attached, Hermes' sexual organ is a sign, displayed originally in a pastoral setting, of the god's fertility. He is sometimes depicted as a good shepherd responsible for the abundance—and safety—of flocks; and in the Homeric Hymns, he is given care over "all the animals," domestic and wild.

This pastoral aspect of the god, however, is deemphasized in favor of Hermes' other great role as a god of boundaries—and also of roads. We find herms at the doorways and in the courtyards of houses: the divine phallus protects the property and the inhabitants. We find herms in the bedroom, at the foot of the bed: to bless a marriage, perhaps, but more usually to send the subtle blessing of a dream (the last libation of the day was poured to Hermes). These phallic pillars appear as well in gymnasiums and libraries. Beyond the apotropaic function here, we are reminded that the phallus is "physical," and that Hermes provides for the bodily well-being of athletes. The mental well-being of scholars is something else; yet Hermes is also a scholar, a *hermēneus,* or "interpreter," more generally a god of speech (see Plato, *Cratylus* 408). It is well to keep in mind that Hermes stole Apollo's cattle, much to the distress of the great god of clarity. And so it is safe to say that Hermes does not so much inspire the side of scholarship that insists upon unassailable clarity—usually assumed to be found in a mere collection of facts—but inspires instead those phallic works of "interpretation" of the facts that are rarely embraced with open arms, as if they were somehow indecent. In this connection we are reminded, too, that Stoic philosophers identified their creative *logos* ("word") with Hermes, so that the special doctrine of the *logos spermatikos* appears to take on a phallic connotation. This nuance would not have been intended, however, by the second-century Christian apologist Justin Martyr, who adopted the Stoic doctrine as the "seed of God, the Word" that impregnated the Virgin in order to become something physical or "flesh" (*First Apology* 32).

Finally, as a development of Hermes' early status as a god of landmarks, herms are placed along roads to protect and also to "guide" the traveler. But the traveler who crosses boundaries will eventually have to pass beyond the boundary of life, down into the realm of Hades. Hermes is the "guide of the soul" *(psuchopompos)* after death of the body: his phallus on the herms at graves leads the *psuchē* into the underworld, protects it from the perils of that journey, and perhaps promises some new kind of life.

The fertility of nature was left more to Hermes' son, Pan, and to Priapus, who as a minor deity is sometimes called a son of Hermes. It is Priapus who became so popular among the Romans as a god of gardens. His image can be seen within the urban garden's precinct: fully anthropomorphic, he is often depicted as an old man, holding up his robe to carry the fruits and vegetables for which he is responsible and thereby exposing to view the source of all this fruitfulness—itself almost a fruit—an unnaturally large, erect phallus. The myths consider the penis of Priapus ugly, punishment dealt out to his mother Aphrodite for her promiscuous ways. Ugly though it is, the phallus is fecund; and its ugliness is apotropaic. Horace tells us that Priapus frightens away thieves "with the crimson stick stretching from his obscene groin" (*Satires* 1.1.3–5). Against trespassers, this god threatens sexual violence, rape.

Pan remains in the countryside, where he takes on his father's role as god of shepherds watching over their flocks, and functions also as a god of hunters with the aid of his "sharp eye." He is a hybrid like the Paleolithic "Sorcerer," half animal and half human, standing upright. His lower limbs are those of a goat, as is his phallus, often shown in art as erect. In this condition, Pan chases nymphs through woods and meadow; he is a lustful god, once bragging of having had sex with all of Dionysos's Bacchantes. With his erect phallus pointing to an erotic and even lustful side of the divine life, Pan was particularly unacceptable to the ascetic Christian mind. Yet he survives in the new religion, somewhat as Dōsojin survives in Buddhism, in the iconography of the Devil—who is, however, rarely shown as ithyphallic (for an exception, see Vanggaard, 1972, fig. 22).

Pan, the Homeric Hymns say, was also unacceptable to his own mortal mother, who found the child simply ugly. Hermes loved him, however, and took him to visit the gods on Olympus, where no deity was more delighted than Dionysos. This is as it should be, for Dionysos—of whom we shall hear more below—is a god of fertility in vegetation, especially of the grapevine, and is worshiped with the image of a giant phallus. Dionysos is not a god of grains, however; their harvest is under the care of the female deity Demeter. Yet on artifacts from her secret cult, centered at Eleusis, the phallus mysteriously appears. A vase painting shows a scene from the Haloa festival: a naked woman carries horizontally a huge replica of a human penis, with testicles attached; the foreskin of this phallus is pulled back as a sign of sexual excitement—in this case, symbolic of divine generation—but so as to reveal a single eye upon the glans. The date of the Haloa is problematic since it is a "threshing" celebration that does not occur at the time of harvest; perhaps this is due to an accommodation with the wine festivals of Dionysos. But the "eye" of the Haloa phallus may indicate that the rite had freed itself from its function as fostering merely natural grain and was held for the purpose of generating a new kind of life, one that comes from greater awareness.

If the presence of the phallus in religion is a sign of the divine life, the loss of the phallus can mean the same thing. This point is made by the myth of Attis, which originated in Asia Minor and became important to Roman religion. Although versions vary, Ovid's tale describes Attis as a mortal shepherd boy devoted with "chaste love" to Cybele, "Great Mother of the Gods." She asked this beautiful youth to "be a boy forever" and guard her temple; Attis promised but failed, presumably becoming a man by falling in love with a mortal wood nymph. The Great Mother slew this other woman, and Attis—out of grief, punishment, or remorse—went mad. Crying "I have deserved it! . . . Ah, perish the parts that were my ruin," Attis cut off the "burden of his groin" *(onus inguinis)* and died *(Fasti* 4.221–246).

The youth's fellow Phrygians, and later the Romans—at least those who were not simply shocked by the insanity of it all—were deeply moved by this story of complete devotion to a goddess, of contrition and self-sacrifice, and ended the tale in various ways. Some said that Attis became the pine tree under which he castrated himself, the tree cut down by the Great Mother and carried back to her cave to sit beside her characteristic throne. Some said that purple violets sprang up from the spilled blood. Yet others reported that Attis's body would never putrefy, that his hair would continue to grow, while his "little finger" came back to life and would continue to move forever. Probably we should see in the big pine tree and in the "little finger" alternative images for the resurrection of Attis's phallus, which, when lost, came back to life in a transformed way. This would help to explain why the priests of this religion, who emasculated themselves in imitation of Attis, nevertheless called themselves Galli ("cocks"), and why it was they celebrated, after a period of ritual madness and mourning, a time of joy called Hilaria. Of course, this theme of castration lies behind the attitude toward the penis expressed in the religious phenomenon of celibacy and provides one of the meanings of circumcision.

Since what we have been examining seems to be the loss of the personal human phallus, it is important to note that the castration of a god may bring new life. Ouranos (Uranus), the Greek sky god of Hesiod's *Theogony,* was suppressing the life of his children and had to be punished. His son Kronos took the awful responsibility of cutting off his father's "members," the blood from which gave rise to the Erinyes and giants—the genitals themselves, thrown into the sea, eventually giving birth to Aphrodite, goddess of love and beauty. It is said that Indra—Vedic god of the atmosphere—seduced a mortal sage's chaste wife and merited punishment.

The husband's powerful curse caused the god's phallus and testicles—some texts say just the testicles—to fall to the ground. But other gods then gave Indra the testicles of a virile ram, and the deity eventually is called *sahasramuṣka*, "he with a thousand testicles" (*Rāmāyaṇa* 1.47.15–32; *Ṛgveda* 6.46.3).

Although the divine phallus usually functions to perpetuate or increase life within the created universe, it may be found, less commonly, in the lofty symbolism of the creation of the world itself. "In the beginning," Atum of ancient Egyptian myth was alone and weary, unable to find a place to stand in the primordial waters—and so he masturbated. "Atum was creative in that he proceeded to masturbate with himself . . . ; he put his penis in his hand that he might obtain the pleasure of emission thereby"—and create the world (Pyramid Texts, 527). The texts may say that the god ejaculated into his mouth, which "spat" forth his children, or merely that he masturbated and simultaneously spat creatively. In either case, we have here the symbolic combination of phallus and mouth that points to the *logos spermatikos* of the Stoics. Atum was able to create alone since he was actually androgynous; he is the Great He-She. So his phallus was ambiguously both penis and womb—a feature of the phallus of Dōsojin. (While the story is not the basis of a cosmogony, it is appropriate to note here that Dionysos was "born again" from Zeus's "thigh"—an ancient euphemism for the phallus—which is called a "father's womb" in Euripides' play *The Bacchae.*) Aware of the conceptual difficulties of such a rich symbol, the Egyptians eventually implied that the phallus of Atum was indeed only masculine, since his active hand was a goddess.

Among certain Aborigines of northeastern Australia, one of the mythic beings collectively named Djanggawul is said to have been present "in the beginning," when no people existed. His creative phallus was so long that it dragged along the ground digging grooves, which, the Aborigines say, may be seen yet today. Djanggawul's sisters had clitorides of similar prodigious length, and humans were created from their incestuous copulation. Wuraka, a giant being in the creation myths of the Australian Kakadu, had a penis so long he had to carry it upon his shoulder, or just sit down from the exhausting burden of it all. But he met Imberombera, whose huge stomach was full of children; somehow their meeting resulted in the birth of these children. It is an interesting comment on the potentially creative phallus that Izanagi, of the Japanese text *Nihongi* (13), found his organ "superfluous" until he met Izanami, whose female body was "incomplete." The situation suggested coitus, and together they created land.

It is when these several themes unite to form the great religious dramas of Osiris, Śiva, and Dionysos that we see the extraordinary power of phallic symbolism. Ambiguously a mortal king or a dying god of ancient Egypt, Osiris was killed by his brother Seth. According to Plutarch (*Isis and Osiris*, second century CE), the kingdom of Osiris had established a sort of golden age of civilization. But it cannot be said that all was well: Osiris had been "unwittingly" seduced into adultery by his wife's sister, was naive about the evil nature of his brother, and had been easily duped into climbing into a confining chest Seth had built for him. Isis, the wife and sister of Osiris, had recovered her husband's dead body from the chest, which had been thrown into the sea; the chest had eventually become confined itself in the trunk of a tree, which had subsequently been cut down to form the pillar of another king's house. But Seth had reappeared and this time cut up the body, scattering the many pieces, which Isis must now gather together. The story continues, but one has the impression that it is simply being retold in different ways with each episode, one of them in terms of the phallus. Plutarch says, "But of all Osiris's members, Isis could never find his private part; for it had been flung into the river Nile." So Isis made an image of this missing phallus—some say out of wood, an allusion to the tree and the pillar—and instituted a festival in honor of his symbol.

Although Plutarch's "phallic" episode is not attested by native texts, there may be a euphemistic reference in a Coffin Text's mention of the "the matter of Osiris' thigh." The reliefs at Abydos, however, speak eloquently: Osiris' body lies intact and dead; yet sticking straight up from this inert form is an erect penis of normal human size and shape. There is a "wooden" quality to this stiff organ that Osiris grasps in his hand—an act reminiscent of Min and Atum but also signifying to us that the phallus is miraculously and creatively alive. Indeed, in another relief, a falcon, identified as Isis, hovers over the erect member: it is an act of coitus, truly symbolic, in which Horus, the new king, is being conceived. If the story of Osiris is the story of his phallus, then his organ represents the civilized but naive adulterer who must be "cut off" and flung into the underworld. But there, like the phallus of Attis, it undergoes a transformation and returns to life in a new and more powerful way. On the one hand, Osiris and his phallus remain in the underworld, revaluing that place as the eternal source of creativity; on the other hand, Osiris returns to the upper world in a new form as the young Horus—who is depicted at the tomb of Ramses VI rising straight up from his father's loins, as if he himself were the resurrected phallus.

At the rites of Osiris, Plutarch states, there is present a "statue in the shape of a man with his private part erect"; this confirms Herodotus's early report (fifth century BCE) of the "use of puppets a cubit long moved by strings, which are carried about the villages by women, the male member moving and near as big as the rest of the body." These images point to a mysterious divine power capable of transforming evil and death into the joy of a fertile land (Osiris is "the Green One" and "the Bull") with a stable culture in the person of the king; they promise to all who face death the opportunity of a new life with Osiris.

Archaeologists have found in what was the Indus Valley of ancient India artifacts probably of an early religion. These include stone replicas of the human phallus, no more than about two feet in length, and an engraved seal depicting a male figure with horns and a strange face that may be multiple, sitting in a position that has come to be called yogic, with an exposed, erect penis. For all the interest they arouse, these artifacts are to date mute, since the language with which they are associated has yet to be found in a text of any length and is yet to be deciphered. The Aryan invaders who displaced the makers of these images did complain about a people "having the phallus as a god" (*śiśnādevāḥ*, in *Ṛgveda* 10.99); yet centuries later these same Aryans found themselves worshiping a Hindu god named Śiva, whose chief image, the lingam (from the Sanskrit *liṅga*, "phallus"), is usually rendered in a somewhat abstract way as a cylinder of varying length, rounded at the top and standing upright, but is sometimes more realistically modeled as an erect sexual organ attached to the body of the anthropomorphic god. [*See* Iconography, *article on* Hindu Iconography.]

With little doubt a development of the Indus Valley religion, coupled with characteristics of the fierce Vedic deity Rudra, Śiva came to represent in a personal way the impersonal ultimate reality in Hinduism, called *ātman* or *brahman*. According to the *Māṇḍūkya Upaniṣad*, this reality has to do with states of mind and is the one source of all things as well as that toward which all things tend. Śiva—with his phallus and, incidentally, with his favorite animal, Nandin, the bull—is said to be the creator of the universe but also (in his role as the third of the Hindu trinity) its destroyer.

An important story about Śiva is told in the *Brahmāṇḍa Purāṇa* (1.2.27): it is a version of the famous "pine forest" episode. The god arrives in this forest and encounters religious men who have given up the household life to live in ascetic chastity with their wives. Śiva is naked, smeared with ashes, his hair wildly disheveled: "His penis and testicles were like red chalk, the tip ornamented with black and white chalk. Sometimes he laughed horribly; sometimes he sang, smiling; sometimes he danced erotically." The ascetics' wives were utterly fascinated—and some texts say the god made love to them day and night for twelve years. The husbands, upset, said of the god, "He is mad!" and cursed his phallus: "Cause your *liṅga* to fall off. This is not the *dharma* [proper conduct] of ascetics." The *liṅga* fell with drastic consequences: "Nothing shone forth; the sun gave no heat. . . . They continued to practice *dharma*, free from egoism, free from possessiveness, but their virile powers were destroyed, and their energy was destroyed."

Horrible as it is, this situation appears to be a necessary and unavoidable phase of *ātman*. It seems also to be a sort of interpretation of Śiva's "destruction of the world" as symbolic—for the world is not actually destroyed; there is simply no heat, or light, or energy. The cure is not to return to the original situation with its wild and erotic expression of the Lord Śiva's creativity, another necessary phase of *ātman*. Instead, the men are told to make an image of the phallus they had seen, and presumably an image of the *liṅga* that had fallen. Isolated from the body and sticking up in the earth, it is a sign of the castration and even of asceticism, for the semen of a sage is said to be "drawn up," and, by symbolic association, so is the chaste phallus drawn up. It is a "pillar" *(sthāṇu)* of refusal to create. In the *Vāyu Purāṇa* (10.56f.), Śiva denies Brahmā's request to create people: "Keeping the semen drawn up, Sthāṇu stood still until the great deluge." But the image of the castrated *liṅga* is obviously also the divine erection of Lord Śiva; it is at once creator and destroyer. Should the men in the rather "phallic" pine forest worship this image as they are told, with baths, flowers, and the creative sounds of *mantras*, they will be worshiping *ātman*. What is more important, they will be "seeing" the two opposite phases of *ātman* simultaneously: to "see" *ātman* is to become free from attachment to either birth or death—and that is the goal of the Hindu religion.

Our best portrait of Dionysos—the ancient Greek god of vegetation, of the grapevine and of its spirited product, wine—is found in Euripides' play *The Bacchae*. There we find the god in mortal guise, home from traveling the roads protected by Hermes. But the long-haired, beautiful youth is not expected and not welcome in Thebes: he seems utterly foreign, with his train of ecstatic "Asian women" who dance and shout in his honor among the "silver pines" at night; they suckle animals, then wildly tear them apart, and find in their ecstasy that "earth flows with milk, flows with wine, flows with nectar of bees." The god's mortal aunts deny his divinity and conclude that he is the bastard fruit of an ordinary, mortal lust. His cousin and king, Pentheus, calls him "that effeminate foreigner, who plagues our women with this new disease, fouls the whole land with lechery." But Dionysos will not be denied. Although he brings "divine madness"—mixing light and darkness, laughter and brutality—he proclaims, "I am sane, and you are mad"; and he visits upon the city of Thebes an entirely tragic version of his possession. Pentheus becomes in the end a mere voyeur, wearing a dress and sitting in a pine tree, hoping to watch the *orgia* of the women, who now include those of his own household. They tear the tree out by its roots and tear Pentheus limb from limb; his mother carries his head away in ecstatic and deluded triumph. The wiser Cadmus, Pentheus's grandfather, cannot help but complain, "But your revenge is merciless." "And rightly," answers Dionysos; "I am a god, and you insulted me."

The phallus is not mentioned by Euripides, but it must have a great deal to do with the events depicted in *The Bacchae.* On numerous vases are painted scenes of Dionysos—usually with a beard, yet also, with androgynous ambiguity, in a dress. He is surrounded by the Bacchantes in their ecstasy and by Pan-like creatures of nature, satyrs and sileni, who are almost always ithyphallic. Dionysos may ride a bull or a mule with an erection. At the festival called the "Great Dionysia," held at Athens, the procession to the theater to witness dramas like that of Euripides included a *phallagōgia,* transport of a phallic image; colonies were required to send replicas of the phallus to this event. And in the "Rural Dionysia"—of which Aristophanes' play *The Acharnians* gives evidence—a large image of a penis, carried by specially designated *phallophoroi,* headed the procession through the village. These "phallus carriers" sang bawdy songs, insulted spectators good-naturedly, and even called the god—according to Aristophanes—"adulterer and pederast." It is Aristotle's opinion that the dramatic form of comedy "arose from the leaders of the phallic songs and processions" *(Poetics* 4*)*; but an ancient commentary on Aristophanes hastens to add that what was said was "in no irreverence but in abandonment and merriment at the phallus" (*scholia* on Aristophanes, 265). In a more sober religious mood, a mural at the Villa dei Misteri in Pompeii shows a female initiate in the Dionysos cult about to have unveiled to her view an erect object: a phallus sitting in a winnowing basket. It was in such a basket that the infant Dionysos was placed; and winnowing baskets full of fruit appear in works of art, sometimes including a fruitful erect phallus like that of Priapus.

If we return to *The Bacchae,* we can now feel the presence of a divine phallus in the lush natural setting of the rites called *orgia;* perhaps sense its loss in the destruction of the animals, but its renewed and transformed vigor in the miraculous "flow" of the earth. The phallus of Dionysos is the wine and the ecstatic state of mind with which drinking wine is associated. And it is symbolically a divine phallus that comes to Thebes so unexpectedly and works its will so autonomously: after all, it is specifically the "independent autocracy" of the penis, which opposes one's personal will, that Augustine of Hippo found so shameful (*City of God* 14.7). Of course, the phallus works perversely in Pentheus's household, but only because it has been rejected out of hand. It is interesting, then, to learn in the *scholium* to Aristophanes' play that the city of Athens, too, had once rejected Dionysos—"and a grievous disease attacked their men in their private parts" (243). A related commentary explains that the disease in this case—unlike the case in Śiva's India—was satyriasis, compulsive sexuality (*scholia* on Lucian, *Deorum concilium,* 5). The women of Pentheus's palace are certain there is nothing more to the birth of Dionysos than lust; Pentheus himself believes, with an equal lack of evidence, that the worship of this god amounts to nothing more than lechery. These people see ordinary sex and the personal penis everywhere. Had the Thebans had the opportunity to be cured, they would have done what the Athenians did—and what Isis did, and the Śaiva husbands did; they would have "made phalli to remind them of their sufferings and worshiped the god therewith" (*scholia* on Aristophanes, 243).

Since the Christian message did not incorporate this symbolism, it is no doubt significant that in the modern period the son of a Christian minister—C. G. Jung, the Swiss psychologist—found his most important dream, and the earliest of his memory, to have been a phallic dream. In that dream (recounted in his autobiography), he was faced by the symbol of a huge erect penis that he thought at first might be the trunk of a tree. Underground, like the phallus of Osiris, it sat on a magnificent throne (of Cybele?). At the top of its glans was a single eye like that one finds on the phallus of the Haloa dedicated to Demeter and Dionysos. Jung says he somehow knew, although he was not yet four years old, that this was a great secret pointing to a mysterious side of God that had been cut off—like the phallus of Śiva—by his father's ascetic religion. But he claims, too, that the vision of this phallic reality inseminated him, to create in his mature years a new and rather hermetic interpretation of religion. It is Jung's view that religious stories of the phallus are so many images for the essentially mysterious life of the psyche. They tell of the life of the creative consciousness of the ego (the death of its ignorance and pride; its transformation); and they tell especially of the source of the ego's strength, the life of the creative unconscious psyche in its divine—and phallic—depths.

[*See also* Masculine Sacrality; Circumcision; Castration; *and, in broader context,* Sexuality. *Specifically, see* Atum; Dionysos; Osiris; Pan; Priapus; *and* Śiva. *For a directly related discussion, see* Yoni.]

BIBLIOGRAPHY

Although there are some full-length treatments of the phallus theme in existence, they are not really trustworthy for scholarship; but Thorkil Vanggaard's *Phallos* (New York, 1972) is the best of them. One might consult the essay "Phallism" by E. Sidney Hartland in the *Encyclopaedia of Religion and Ethics,* edited by James Hastings, vol. 9 (New York, 1917), for materials and a point of view different from mine. But on this topic, primary sources are best; citations have been provided in the body of the essay. Also very useful are pictures: see Sigfried Giedion's *The Eternal Present: A Contribution on Constancy and Change,* vol. 1 (New York, 1962), for Stone Age figures and more; see Michael Czaja's *Gods of Myth and Stone* (New York, 1974) for excellent photographs of Dōsojin. For Egyptian and Greco-Roman phallic symbolism, the standard works should be consulted. Károly Kerényi's *Dionysos* (Princeton, 1976) is particularly informative about the Dionysian phallus. For India, the best work is Wendy Doniger O'Flaherty's *Śiva* (Oxford, 1981) along with her several compilations of myths. Phallic creation myths can be found in the useful collection by Barbara C. Sproul, *Primal Myths* (San Francisco, 1979). Marie-Louise von Franz analyzes Jung's dream in *C. G. Jung: His Myth in Our Time* (New York, 1975).

George R. Elder

PHARISEES. The Pharisees were, along with the Sadducees and the Essenes, one of the three *haereseis* ("schools of thought") that flourished among the Jews from the time of Jonathan the Hasmonean (d. 143/2 BCE) until the destruction of the Second Temple in 70 CE. According to Josephus Flavius, what distinguished them from the other two *haereseis* was their belief that the laws that had been handed down "from the fathers but which were not recorded in the laws of Moses" had to be observed, that there is a delicate interplay between fate and free will, and that every soul is imperishable, with the souls of the good ultimately passing into another body (resurrection) and the souls of the wicked condemned to suffer eternal punishment (cf. *The Jewish War* 2.162–163, 3.374; *Jewish Antiquities* 13.171–173, 18.166). These views, Josephus tells us, were so influential with the masses that "all prayers and sacred rites of divine worship were performed in accord with their exposition" (*Antiquities* 13.298, 18.14–15).

Josephus's description of the Pharisees as the authoritative teachers of the unwritten laws corresponds to Paul's holding up his being "as to the Law a Pharisee" and "as to righteousness under the Law blameless" (*Phil.* 3:4–7) and his precocious commitment as a youth to the *paradosis,* that is, the unwritten laws of the fathers, as justifying his right to speak with authority about the Law (*Gal.* 1:13–17). It also corresponds to Mark's account of the Pharisees' upbraiding Jesus for allowing his disciples to make light of the *paradosis* of the elders (*Mk.* 7:13); to Matthew's affirmation that the scribes (i.e., the Pharisees) sit in Moses' seat, and sit there legitimately (*Mt.* 23:1–3); and to the picture of the Pharisees displayed throughout the Gospels and *Acts of the Apostles* as a class of teachers enjoying an elevated and respected status by virtue of their legal expertise and their religious leadership.

Josephus's description likewise agrees with that of the tannaitic literature (the Mishnah, the Tosefta, and the *beraitot*), the repository of the oral law. Here the Pharisees are found to be identical with the *soferim* ("scribes") and the *ḥakhamim* ("sages"), who are, as in Josephus and the New Testament, the authoritative teachers of the twofold law (the written and the oral) and, again as in Josephus and the New Testament, juxtaposed to the Sadducees, who rejected the oral law and the authority of the Pharisees.

The name *Pharisees* is derived from the Greek transliteration, with a Greek plural ending, of the Hebrew *perushim,* which means "separatists, deviants, heretics." That the name may have originated as an epithet hurled at these teachers by the Sadducees, who rejected their authority, is indicated by the fact that in the tannaitic literature the term *perushim,* meaning "Pharisees," is used only juxtaposed to *tseduqim* ("Sadducees").

In contrast to the above approach and taking for granted that the Hebrew term *perushim* means "Pharisees" in most tannaitic texts, eminent scholars such as Emil Schürer (1902), Robert Travers Herford (1902), Louis Finkelstein (1962), and, most recently, Jacob Neusner (1971) have constructed a definition of the Pharisees based on a tannaitic text (*Ḥag.* 2.7) that states that the garments of *perushim* are a source of uncleanness to the *'ammei ha-arets.* According to this text, the *perushim* were pietists who were so scrupulously concerned with the laws of ritual purity that they banded together into a confraternity separating themselves from the less scrupulous masses, the *'ammei ha-arets.* These scholars also identify the *perushim* with the *ḥaverim* ("associates"), who likewise separated themselves from the masses for the same reason (cf. *Dem.* 2.3).

These two attempts to define the term *perushim* are mutually exclusive. The first definition is built on texts that only juxtapose *perushim* to *Tseduqim,* Sadducees, while the second definition is built on texts that only juxtapose *perushim* to *'ammei ha-arets.* Since the definition that juxtaposes the term *perushim* to *tseduqim* conforms not only to certain tannaitic texts but to the testimony of Josephus and the New Testament, it is to be preferred.

Essential Teachings and Institutions. The essential core of Pharisaism was its affirmation of a triad of faith that sharply distinguished it from the priestly system of Judaism that had flourished uncontested from the time of the promulgation of the Pentateuch (c. 397 BCE) until the rise of the Pharisees, probably during the Hasmonean Revolt (166–142 BCE). This triad of faith proclaimed that (1) the one God and Father so loved the individual that (2) he revealed to his people Israel a twofold law, one written down in the five books of Moses, the Pentateuch, and the other transmitted orally from Moses to Joshua to the elders to the prophets to the Pharisees (*Avot* 1.1), so that (3) each individual who internalized this twofold law could look forward to eternal life for his soul and resurrection for his body (cf. *San.* 10.1). It would seem that this highly novel triad of faith was rejected by the Sadducees, who reasserted the Aaronic, or priestly, belief that God had revealed a single, immutable written law, which made no mention of eternal life for the individual. On the basis of this triad of faith, however, the Pharisees asserted their authority over the Aaronic priesthood.

The triad of faith likewise generated novel institutions. The first of these was a body called the Beit Din ha-Gadol (Great Court), or the Great Boulē (Gr., "council meeting"). Its function was to legislate new oral laws, to transmit oral laws previously legislated, and to dissolve those oral laws no longer deemed relevant. The Beit Din ha-Gadol consisted of seventy-one authoritative teachers of the twofold law presided over by an elected *nasi'* ("prince"), who represented the majority, and an *av beit din* ("father of the court"), who represented the minority point of view (cf. *Ḥag.* 2.2). The *nasi'* and the *av beit din* were referred to as a "pair" (Heb., *zug;* pl., *zugot*). The "pairs" flourished from the time of the Hasmonean Revolt until the transformation of the office of the *nasi'* from an elective to a hereditary one, which occurred after the death of Hillel (c. 10 CE). Although during this period debate was mandatory, oral laws once passed were binding on majority and minority alike. When, however, the office of *nasi'* became hereditary, the sages were given the option of following either the oral laws of the school of Hillel or those of the school of Shammai. Following the destruction of the Temple in 70 CE, each authoritative teacher could formulate oral laws that were binding on him and his disciples. [*For another view of the Beit Din ha-Gadol, see* Sanhedrin.]

The institution launched by the Pharisees that proved to be the most durable was the synagogue. [*See* Synagogue, *article on* History and Tradition.] Although many scholars argue that the origin of the synagogue is to be traced back to the Babylonian exile, no source attests to the existence of the synagogue until after the Hasmonean Revolt. Only after the Pharisees proclaimed their triad of faith did prayer and reading from the Pentateuch and the Prophets become mandatory. The individual reaching out for an unmediated relationship with God in his quest for eternal life and resurrection needed a noncultic institution where, in the presence of other co-believers, he could proclaim the Shema' to affirm God's singularity and utter the Tefillah, eighteen blessings that include the statement that God will, with his great mercy, revive the dead. [*For further discussion of the development of the Jewish liturgy, see* Siddur and Maḥzor.]

In addition to novel institutions, the Pharisees developed new notions about God and the peoplehood of Israel. Although God was occasionally conceived of in scripture as a father, it was as the father of his people and not as the father of the individual. The Pharisees, for their part, however, spoke of the father in heaven, who so loves and cares for each individual that he revealed the road by which the individual could reach eternal life and resurrection. The Pharisees further stressed this one-to-one relationship when they coined such new names for God as *Maqom* ("all present, everyplace"), *ha-Qaddosh Barukh Hu'* ("the holy one, blessed be he"), and *Shekhinah* ("indwelling presence").

The Pharisees stressed that God had chosen Abraham to father a people to be a blessing for all the peoples of the earth, and not just for the seed of Abraham. The Pharisees therefore preached that membership in Israel was open to everyone who embraced the triad of faith (cf. *Mt.* 23:15). What defined a true Israelite was his belief that God had revealed a twofold *torah* and that God would reward with eternal life and resurrection the law-abiding individual and punish with eternal suffering those who did not live in accordance with its precepts. A pagan who ascribed to these beliefs was thus a truer member of the house of Israel than was a Sadducee, who, although born into Israel, rejected the twofold law and otherworldly rewards and punishments (cf. Josephus, *Against Apion* 2.210).

As a class, the Pharisees far more resembled peripatetic teachers, such as the Stoics, than either prophets or priests (cf. Josephus, *The Life* 12). As champions of the oral law, they made it a point to formulate their teachings in nonbiblical modes, forms, and language. Thus they wrote down none of their teachings, framed their laws *(halakhot)* and doctrines *(aggadot)* without regard for historical setting, rejected poetic modes of expression even for the prayers and blessings they formulated, cultivated logical (i.e., deductive) modes of reasoning, and introduced proof texts.

History. None of the sources, not even Josephus, was interested in the history of the Pharisees, which must, therefore, be reconstructed from indirect evidence. A likely origin for the movement is the Hasmonean Revolt, when the breakdown of traditional priestly authority as exercised by a high priest of the Aaron-Eleazar-Phinehas . . . Zadok line collapsed and the need for new leaders was desperate. Confronted by Antiochus's decrees, which threatened with death the Jews who remained true to the Law, and confronted with the question of why one should die for the Law if no reward for such martyrdom could be forthcoming in this world, a group of *soferim* responded to this crisis of survival by proclaiming that God had revealed two laws and not one, and that God would reward with eternal life those who gave up their lives. Support by the majority of the Jewish people enabled the *soferim* to overthrow the Zadokite high priesthood and convoke on their own authority a Great Synagogue, which in 142 BCE invested a non-Zadokite, Simon the Hasmonean, as high priest (cf. *1 Mc.* 14:27–35).

Beholden to the Pharisees for their high priestly office, first Simon (142–134) and then his son John Hyrcanus (134–104) gave their seal of approval to the oral law. But eventually John Hyrcanus broke with the Pharisees, abrogated their unwritten laws, and seeded the soil for the bloody civil war that broke out during the high priesthood and reign (103–76) of his son Alexander Yannai (Josephus, *Antiquities* 13.288–298, 372–383, 398–404). Alexander Yannai's successor, Salome Alexandra (76–67), made peace with the Pharisees, restored them to power, and reinstituted the oral law. In order to keep the Sadducees in line, however, the Pharisees sanctioned bloody reprisals against the Sadducean leaders (*Antiquities* 13.408–418). Recognizing that the substance of their faith required only that they be free to teach the road to eternal life and resurrection and that all public manifestations of religion, such as the liturgical calendar and worship in the Temple, would be carried out in accordance with the provisions of the oral law, the Pharisees formulated the doctrine of two realms, secular and divine, with respect to the state and a doctrine of tolerance with respect to the Sadducees and the Essenes. These doctrines were embraced by the political authorities, whether Hasmonean, Herodian, or Roman, and by the other religious groups. Thus when the first Roman procurator, Coponius (6–9 CE), ordered a census to determine the size of the tribute to be levied on the Judeans, the Pharisees urged the people to cooperate, since the Romans were not interfering in the religious sphere. And when some of their followers broke with their leaders on this issue, this difference alone was sufficient to mark them off as a fourth philosophy, a *haeresis* in their own right (*Antiquities* 18.2–10, 23–25).

This doctrine of the two realms remained firm until the outbreak of the revolt against Rome, in 65 CE, which the Pharisees sought to head off until the very last moment (*Jewish War* 2.411–414). Some of the leaders of the Pharisees reluctantly gave their support to the revolutionaries; others, however, remained adamant, and one of them, Yoḥanan ben Zakk'ai, managed to escape from the besieged city of Jerusalem and convinced the Roman general Vespasian that the Pharisees could be depended on to adhere to the doctrine of the two realms.

With the destruction of Jerusalem and the burning of the Temple, the Pharisees emerged triumphant, the unchallenged leaders of the Jewish people. The Sadducees, who consisted preeminently of priests, disappeared as a group, as did the Essenes. The name *Pharisees* fell into disuse, because it had never been used by the group itself but only by its Sadducean opponents.

The Pharisees and Jesus. As the authoritative teachers of the twofold law, the Pharisees were troubled by Jesus' refusal to bow to their authority. They therefore challenged his claim to a singular relationship to God. But this was as far as the Pharisees could go, since they were committed to the principle of religious tolerance. Jesus' teachings were, if anything, even less heretical than those of the Sadducees, whom the Pharisees challenged but did not bring to trial before either the Beit Din ha-Gadol or a lesser body called simply a *beit din* ("court") or *boulē* ("council meeting"). Since all the Gospels are in agreement that Jesus was tried before a Sanhedrin presided over by a high priest appointed by the Roman procurator, which was hence religiously illegitimate and therefore solely a political body, Jesus must have been tried on political, not religious grounds. In Jesus' day the distinction between a political Sanhedrin and the Pharisaic *boulē* was a matter of daily experience, as the Gospels testify (*Acts* 23:1–10, 26–30). Whatever role Pharisees played as members of a political Sanhedrin was strictly political and not religious.

The hostility toward the Pharisees found in the Gospels is thus to be seen as stemming from their authors' anger with these teachers for having rejected Jesus' claims and those of his followers. When put in historical perspective, it is evident that such central Christian beliefs as the Resurrection are rooted in the central beliefs of the Pharisees and that Paul's conversion is inconceivable without his extreme anxiety as to whether he had been sufficiently obedient to the twofold law to merit eternal life for his soul and resurrection for his body. Certainly the Christian triad of faith bears a formal resemblance to that of the Pharisees, with the twofold law of the Pharisees displaced by Jesus Christ. [*See* Christianity and Judaism; Jesus; *and the biography of Paul.*]

Historical Significance. The Pharisees transformed Judaism first by elevating themselves to Moses' seat and by proclaiming the twofold law, and not the written law alone, to be normative. The Pharisees' oral law gave birth to the Mishnah, the Palestinian and Babylonian Talmuds, the geonic, medieval, and modern *responsa,* and the various codes of Jewish law—all of which are, for a majority of Jews, still recognized as normative.

Second, by affirming the belief in eternal life and resurrection for every individual who internalizes the twofold law, the Pharisees established a one-to-one relationship with God the Father, strengthened the believing individual, and readied him for martyrdom when need be.

Third, by linking personal salvation to an internalized twofold law and by freeing the individual's salvation from the intermediating role of priest, prophet, or sage, the Pharisees made it possible for Judaism not only to flourish in the Diaspora but to establish centers there that exercised a higher degree of religious authority and influence than did those in the Land of Israel.

Fourth, by their success in winning over the majority of Jews to their belief in eternal life and resurrection, the Pharisees set the stage for Christianity. Had not Jesus and his disciples believed in the resurrection of the dead, it is hardly likely that Jesus' disciples would have been so certain that they had indeed seen Jesus risen from the dead. Thus the New Testament bears witness to the Pharisaic use of proof texts, the Pharisaic system of reasoning, the Pharisaic mode of oral transmission through discrete episodes, items, and dicta, Pharisaic ethical and moral teachings, and Pharisaic abandonment of poetry as a medium for law, lore, and liturgy. Although less direct, the Pharisees' teachings of eternal life and resurrection had a major impact on a central belief of Islam.

Fifth, by absorbing Greco-Roman institutional models, such as the *boulē,* Greco-Roman modes of deductive reasoning, and Greco-Roman examples of lawmakers, sages, and philosophers, the Pharisees enabled their followers to be in congruence with Greco-Roman civilization without loss of their Jewish identity.

Perhaps the most enduring of the achievements of the Pharisees was their focus on the individual and his yearnings for an eternal life for his individual soul and his individual body. By picturing God the Father as so loving every individual that his yearning for immortality might be fulfilled, the Pharisees, and the Christian and Muslim teachers who took up the refrain, enhanced the individual's sense of eternal worth.

[*For another view of this period in Jewish history, see* Rabbinic Judaism in Late Antiquity.]

BIBLIOGRAPHY

The definition of the Pharisees offered above was first articulated in Solomon Zeitlin's *History of the Second Jewish Commonwealth: Prolegomena* (Philadelphia, 1933), pp. 41–56, and spelled out in detail by him in "Ha-Tseduqim ve-ha-Perushim," *Ḥoreb* 3 (1936): 56–89, which appeared in English as "The Sadducees and the Pharisees: A Chapter in the Development of the Halakhah," in Zeitlin's *Studies in the Early History of Judaism,* vol. 2 (New York, 1974), pp. 259–291. It has been further elaborated in my own writings, especially "The Internal City," *Journal of Scientific Study of Religion* 5 (1966): 225–240; "The Pharisaic Revolution," in *Perspectives in Jewish Learning,* vol. 2 (Chicago, 1966), pp. 26–51; "Prolegomenon," in *Judaism and Christianity,* edited by W. O. E. Oesterley (1937–1938; reprint, New York, 1969); "Pharisaism and the Crisis of the Individual in the Graeco-Roman World," *Jewish Quarterly Review* 61 (July 1970): 27–52; "Defining the Pharisees: The Tannaitic Sources," *Hebrew Union College Annual* 40/41 (1969–1970): 205–249; and *A Hidden Revolution: The Pharisees' Search for the Kingdom Within* (Nashville, 1977). Although I am fundamentally in agreement with Zeitlin on the definition of the Pharisees, I diverge radically from him on reconstructing their history; compare Zeitlin's *The Rise and Fall of the Judean State,* vol. 1 (Philadelphia, 1962), pp. 178–187, with my article "Solomon Zeitlin's Contribution to the Historiography of the Inter-Testamental Period," *Judaism* 14 (Summer 1965): 354–367, and my book *A Hidden Revolution,* pp. 211–251.

For the range of scholarly opinion, see especially A. Michel and J. Moyne's comprehensive discussion and extensive bibliography in "Le Pharisiens," in *Dictionnaire de la Bible, supplément,* edited by H. Cazelles and A. Feuillet, fascs. 39–40 (Paris, 1966), and Ralph Marcus's "The Pharisees in the Light of Modern Scholarship," *Journal of Religion* 32 (July 1952): 153–164. Most influential have been the views of Emil Schürer in *A History of the Jewish People in the Time of Jesus Christ,* 2d div., vol. 2, 2d rev. ed. (New York, 1902), pp. 10–28; R. Travers Herford in *The Pharisees* (1924; reprint, Boston, 1962); George Foot Moore in *Judaism in the First Centuries of the Christian Era,* in vol. 1 (Cambridge, Mass., c. 1927), pp. 56–71; Louis Finkelstein in *The Pharisees: The Sociological Background of Their Faith,* 2 vols., 3d ed. (Philadelphia, 1962); and, more recently, Jacob Neusner in *The Rabbinic Traditions about the Pharisees before 70,* 3 vols. (Leiden, 1971), and *From Politics to Piety: The Emergence of Pharisaic Judaism* (Englewood Cliffs, N.J., 1972).

Ellis Rivkin

PHENOMENOLOGY OF RELIGION. Although the phenomenology of religion has emerged as both a major field of study and an extremely influential approach to religion during the twentieth century, formulating an essay on this subject poses serious difficulties. The term has become very popular and has been utilized by numerous scholars, who seem to share little if anything in common.

Uses of the Term

For the sake of organization, I shall initially differentiate four major groups of scholars who use the term *phenomenology of religion*. First, one notes a proliferation of works in which *phenomenology of religion* is used in the vaguest, broadest, and most uncritical of ways. Often the term seems to mean nothing more than an investigation of the phenomena of religion.

Second, from the Dutch scholar P. D. Chantepie de la Saussaye to such contemporary scholars as the Scandinavian historians of religions Geo Widengren and Åke Hultkrantz, phenomenology of religion has meant the comparative study and the classification of different types of religious phenomena. There has been little if any regard for specific phenomenological concepts, methods, or procedures of verification.

Third, numerous scholars, such as W. Brede Kristensen, Gerardus van der Leeuw, Joachim Wach, C. Jouco Bleeker, Mircea Eliade, and Jacques Waardenburg, have identified the phenomenology of religion as a specific branch, discipline, or method within *Religionswissenschaft*. [*See* History of Religions.] This is where the most significant contributions of the phenomenology of religion to the study of religion have been made.

Fourth, there have been a number of scholars whose phenomenology of religion has been influenced by philosophical phenomenology. A few scholars, such as Max Scheler and Paul Ricoeur, have explicitly identified much of their approaches with philosophical phenomenology. Others, such as Rudolf Otto, van der Leeuw, and Eliade, have used a phenomenological method and have been influenced, at least partially, by phenomenological philosophy. There have been numerous influential theological approaches, from the works of Friedrich Schleiermacher to those of Paul Tillich and many contemporary theologians (such as Edward Farley), that have utilized a phenomenology of religion as a preliminary stage in the formulation of a theology.

History of the Term. The terms *phenomenon* and *phenomenology* are derived from the Greek word *phainomenon* ("that which shows itself," or "that which appears"). As Herbert Spiegelberg establishes in the first volume of *The Phenomenological Movement: A Historical Introduction* (2d ed., 1965), the term *phenomenology* has both philosophical and nonphilosophical roots.

Nonphilosophical phenomenologies. One encounters nonphilosophical phenomenologies in the natural sciences, especially in the field of physics. With the term *phenomenology* scientists have usually wanted to emphasize the descriptive, as contrasted with the explanatory, conception of their science. (In the phenomenology of religion a similar emphasis shall be uncovered, as phenomenologists submit that their approach describes, but does not explain, the nature of religious phenomena.)

A second nonphilosophical use of phenomenology appears in the descriptive, systematic, comparative study of religions, in which scholars assemble groups of religious phenomena in order to disclose their major aspects and to formulate their typologies. This phenomenology-as-comparative-religion had roots independent of philosophical phenomenology.

Philosophical phenomenologies. The first documented philosophical use of the term *phenomenology* was by the German philosopher Johann Heinrich Lambert, in his *Neues Organon* (Leipzig, 1764). In a use unrelated to later philosophical phenomenology and to the phenomenology of religion, Lambert defined the term as "the theory of illusion."

In the late eighteenth century, the German philosopher Immanuel Kant devoted considerable analysis to "phenomena" as the data of experience, things that appear to and are constructed by our minds. Such phenomena, which Kant distinguished from "noumena," or "things-in-themselves" independent of our knowing minds, could be studied rationally, scientifically, and objectively. A similar distinction between religious phenomena as appearances and religious reality-in-itself, which is beyond phenomenology, will be found in the "descriptive phenomenologies" of many phenomenologists of religion.

Of all the uses of *phenomenology* by philosophers before the twentieth-century phenomenological movement, the term is most frequently identified with the German philosopher G. W. F. Hegel, and especially with his *The Phenomenology of Spirit* (1807). Hegel was determined to overcome Kant's phenomena-noumena bifurcation. Phenomena were actual stages of knowledge—manifestations in the development of Spirit—evolving from undeveloped consciousness of mere sense experience and culminating in forms of absolute knowledge. Phenomenology is the science by which the mind becomes aware of the development of Spirit and comes to know its essence—that is, Spirit as it is in itself—through a study of its appearances and manifestations.

During the nineteenth and early twentieth centuries, a number of philosophers used *phenomenology* to indicate a merely descriptive study of a subject matter. Thus William Hamilton, is his *Lectures on Metaphysics* (1858), used *phenomenology* to refer to a descriptive phase of empirical psychology; Eduard von Hartmann formulated several phenomenologies, including a descriptive "phenomenology of moral consciousness"; and the American philosopher Charles Sanders Peirce used *phenomenology* to refer to a descriptive study of whatever appears before the mind, whether real or illusory.

Two senses of the term. As Richard Schmitt points out in his article, "Phenomenology," in *The Encyclopedia of Philosophy* (1967), the philosophical background led to two distinct senses of *phenomenology*. There is the older, wider sense of the term as any descriptive study of a given subject matter or as a discipline describing observable phenomena. There is also a narrower twentieth-century sense of the term as a philosophical approach utilizing a phenomenological method. It is to the latter sense that I now turn.

Philosophical Phenomenology

As one of the major schools, movements, or approaches in twentieth-century philosophy, phenomenology has taken many forms. One can distinguish, for example, the "transcendental phenomenology" of Edmund Husserl, the "existential phenomenology" of Jean-Paul Sartre and Maurice Merleau-Ponty, and the "hermeneutic phenomenology" of Martin Heidegger and Paul Ricoeur. Since phenomenology has been so complex and diverse, not all that follows would be accepted by every phenomenologist.

The Phenomenological Movement. The primary aim of philosophical phenomenology is to investigate and become directly aware of phenomena that appear in immediate experience, and thereby allow the phenomenologist to describe the essential structures of these phenomena. In doing so phenomenology attempts to free itself from unexamined presuppositions, to avoid causal and other explanations, and to utilize a method that allows it to describe that which appears and to intuit or decipher essential meanings.

An early formulation of the phenomenological movement appeared as a statement in the *Jahrbuch für Philosophie und phänomenologische Forschung*, which was published from 1913 to 1930, and whose editor in chief was Edmund Husserl. Coeditors included leading phenomenologists: Moritz Geiger (1880–1937), Alexander Pfänder (1870–1941), Adolf Reinach (1883–1917), Max Scheler (1874–1928), and later Martin Heidegger (1889–1976) and Oskar Becker (1889–1964).

Husserl is usually identified as the founder and most influential philosopher of the phenomenological movement. Beginning about 1905, Husserl began to attract students, and the earliest phenomenologists were found at several German universities, especially at Göttingen and Munich. Outside of Husserl's predominant influence on phenomenology, the most significant phenomenologists were Max Scheler, an independent and creative thinker in his own right, and Martin Heidegger, who emerged as one of the major twentieth-century philosophers. [*See also the biographies of Heidegger, Husserl, and Scheler.*]

The initial flourishing of the phenomenological movement was identified with the "Göttingen Circle" and the "Munich Circle" during the period leading up to World War I, and phenomenology remained an overwhelmingly German philosophy until the 1930s, when the center of the movement began to shift to France. Through the works of Jean-Paul Sartre, Maurice Merleau-Ponty, Gabriel Marcel, Paul Ricoeur, and others, French phenomenology established itself as the leading development in phenomenological philosophy, beginning in the 1930s and continuing at least until the 1960s. Particularly noteworthy was the French attempt to integrate the concerns and insights of phenomenology with those of existentialism.

Characteristics of Philosophical Phenomenology. One may delineate five characteristics of philosophical phenomenology, which have had particular relevance for the phenomenology for religion.

1. *Descriptive nature.* Phenomenology aims to be a rigorous and descriptive science, discipline, or approach. The phenomenological slogan "Zu den Sachen!" ("To the things themselves!") expressed the determination to turn away from philosophical theories and concepts toward the direct intuition and description of the phenomena as they appear in immediate experience. Phenomenology attempts to describe the nature of phenomena, the way appearances manifest themselves, and the essential structures at the foundation of human experience. As contrasted with most schools of philosophy, which assumed that the rational alone is real and which hence had a philosophical preoccupation with the rational faculties and with conceptual analysis, phenomenology focused on accurately describing the totality of phenomenal manifestations in human experience. A descriptive phenomenology, attempting to avoid reductionism and often insisting on the phenomenological *epochē* (see below), described the diversity, complexity, and richness of experience.

2. *Opposition to reductionism.* Antireductionism has been concerned with freeing us from uncritical preconceptions that prevent us from becoming aware of the specificity and diversity of phenomena, thus allowing us to broaden and deepen immediate experience and provide more accurate descriptions of this experience. Husserl, for example, attacked various forms of reductionism, such as "psychologism," which attempted to derive the laws of logic from psychological laws and, more broadly, to reduce all phenomena to psychological phenomena. In opposing the oversimplifications of traditional empiricism and other forms of reductionism, phenomenologists aim to deal faithfully with phenomena as phenomena, and to become aware of what phenomena reveal in their full intentionality.

3. *Intentionality.* A subject always "intends" an object, and *intentionality* refers to the property of all consciousness as consciousness of something. All acts of consciousness are directed toward the experience of something, the intentional object. For Husserl, who took the term from his teacher Franz Brentano (1838–1917), intentionality is a way of describing how consciousness constitutes phenomena.

4. *"Bracketing."* For many phenomenologists, the antireductionist insistence on the irreducibility of the intentional immediate experience entails the adoption of a "phenomenological *epochē*." This Greek term literally means "abstention" or "suspension of judgment" and is often defined as a method of "bracketing." It is only by bracketing the uncritically accepted "natural world," by suspending our beliefs and judgments based on our unexamined "natural standpoint," that the phenomenologist can become aware of the phenomena of immediate experience and can gain insight into their essential structures. Sometimes the *epochē* is formulated in terms of the goal of a completely presuppositionless science or philosophy, but most phenomenologists have interpreted such bracketing as the goal of freeing the phenomenologist from unexamined presuppositions, or of rendering explicit and clarifying our presuppositions, rather than completely denying their existence. The phenomenological *epochē*, whether as the technical Husserlian "transcendental reduction" or in its other variations, is not simply "performed" by phenomenologists; it must involve some method of self-criticism and intersubjective testing allowing insight into structure and meanings.

5. *Eidetic vision.* The intuition of essences, often described as "eidetic vision" or "eidetic reduction," is related to the Greek term *eidos*, which Husserl adopted from its Platonic meaning to designate "universal essences." Such essences express the "whatness" of things, the necessary and invariant features of phenomena that allow us to recognize phenomena as phenomena of a certain kind.

Of the five characteristics of phenomenological method listed above, intentionality and the *epochē*, though central, have not been universally accepted by phenomenologists. Almost all phenomenologists, however, have upheld a descriptive phenomenology that is antireductionist and that involves insight into essential structures. The following is a brief formulation of a general phenomenological procedure for gaining insight into such essential structures and meanings, with application to the phenomena of religious experience.

In the "intuition of essences" *(Wesensschau)*, the phenomenologist attempts to disengage essential structures embodied in particular phenomena. One begins with particular data: the specific phenomena as expressions of intentional experiences. The central aim of the phenomenological method is to disclose the essential "whatness" or structure embodied in the particular data.

One gains insight into meaning by the method of "free variation." After assembling a variety of particular phenomena, the phenomenologist searches for the invariant core that constitutes the essential meaning of the phenomena. The phenomena, subjected to a process of free variation, assume certain forms that are considered to be accidental or inessential, in the sense that the phenomenologist can go beyond the limits imposed by such forms without destroying the basic character or intentionality of one's data. For example, the variation of a great variety of religious phenomena may disclose that the unique structures of monotheism do not constitute the essential core or universal structure of all religious experience.

The phenomenologist gradually sees that phenomena assume forms that are regarded as essential, in the sense that one cannot go beyond or remove such structures without destroying the basic "whatness" or intentionality of the data. For example, free variation might reveal that certain essential structures of "transcendence" constitute an invariant care of religious experience. When the universal essence is grasped, the phenomenologist has achieved the eidetic intuition, or the fulfilled *Wesensschau*.

Husserl proposed that all phenomena were constituted by consciousness and that, in the intuition of essences, we could eliminate the particular, actual given datum and move on to the plane of "pure possibility." Most phenomenologists who use a method of *Wesensschau* propose that historical phenomena have a kind of priority, that we must substitute for Husserl's imaginary variation an actual variation of historical data, and that the particular phenomena are not constituted by us but are the source of our constitution and judgment.

Though few philosophical phenomenologists have had much interest in religious phenomena, some of the vocabulary of philosophical phenomenology and, in several cases, some of its methodology have influenced the phenomenology of religion.

Phenomenology of Religion and History of Religions

The modern scholarly study of religion probably had its beginnings in the late eighteenth century, largely as a product of the rational and scientific attitude of the Enlightenment, but the first major figure in this discipline was F. Max Müller (1823–1900). Müller intended *Religionswissenschaft* to be a descriptive, objective science that was free from the normative nature of theological and philosophical studies of religion.

The German term *Religionswissenschaft* has been given no adequate English equivalent, although the International Association for the History of Religions has adopted the term *history of religions*, as synonymous with the term *general science of religions*. Thus *history of religions* is intended to designate a field of studies with many specialized disciplines utilizing different approaches.

P. D. Chantepie de la Saussaye (1848–1920) is sometimes considered the founder of phenomenology of religion as a special discipline of classification. Phenomenology of religion, which occupied an intermediary position for him between history and philosophy, was a descriptive, comparative approach involving "the collecting and grouping of various religious phenomena." One of the founders of *Religionswissenschaft*, the Dutch historian C. P. Tiele (1830–1902), considered phenomenology to be the first stage of the philosophical part of the science of religion.

C. Jouco Bleeker (1898–1983) distinguishes three types of phenomenology of religion: the descriptive phenomenology that restricts itself to the systematization of religious phenomena, the typological phenomenology that formulates the different types of religion, and the specific sense of phenomenology that investigates the essential structures and meanings of religious phenomena.

One characteristic of the phenomenology of religion about which historians of religion seem to agree is its sense of generality, with its approach invariably characterized as systematic. For Widengren, the phenomenology of religion aims at "a coherent account of all the various phenomena of religion, and is thus the systematic complement of the history of religion." The historical approach provides a historical analysis of the development of separate religions; phenomenology provides "the systematic synthesis."

The Italian historian of religions Raffaele Pettazzoni (1883–1959) attempted to formulate the diverse methodological tendencies and tensions defining *Religionswissenschaft* in terms of these two complementary aspects: the historical and the phenomenological. On the one hand, the history of religions attempts to uncover "precisely what happened and how the facts came to be," but it does not provide the deeper understanding of the meaning of what happened, nor "the sense of the religious": these come from phenomenology. On the other hand, phenomenology cannot do without ethnology, philology, and other historical disciplines. Therefore, according to Pettazzoni, phenomenology and history are two complementary aspects of the integral science of religion.

Major Phenomenologists of Religion. I shall consider the approaches and contributions of six influential phenomenologists of religion: W. Brede Kristensen, Rudolf Otto, Gerardus van der Leeuw, Friedrich Heiler, C. Jouco Bleeker, and Mircea Eliade. I shall also note several frequent criticisms of the three most influential of these phenomenologists: Otto, van der Leeuw, and Eliade. [*For more detailed treatment of Kristensen's work, as well as of the life and work of Bleeker, Eliade, Heiler, van der Leeuw, Otto, and other scholars mentioned in this article, see their biographies.*]

W. Brede Kristensen. From Chantepie de la Saussaye and Tiele, through van der Leeuw and the Norwegian expatriate Kristensen, and up to the recent writings of Bleeker and others, much of the field has been dominated by a Dutch tradition of phenomenology of religion. Sometimes this is broadened to encompass a Dutch-Scandinavian tradition in order to include phenomenologists such as Nathan Söderblom (1866–1931).

W. Brede Kristensen (1867–1953), a specialist in Egyptian and ancient historical religions, illustrates an extreme formulation of the descriptive approach within phenomenology. As a subdivision of the general science of religion, phenomenology is, according to Kristensen, a systematic and comparative approach that is descriptive and not normative. In opposing the widespread positivist and evolutionist approaches to religion, Kristensen attempted to integrate historical knowledge of the facts with phenomenological "empathy" and "feeling" for the data in order to grasp the "inner meaning" and religious values in various texts.

The phenomenologist must accept the faith of the believers as the sole "religious reality." In order to achieve phenomenological understanding, we must avoid imposing our own value judgments on the experiences of believers by assuming that the believers are completely right. In other words, the primary focus of our phenomenology is the description of how believers have understood their own faith. We must respect the absolute value that believers ascribe to their faith. Our understanding of this religious reality is always approximate or relative, since we can never experience the religion of others exactly as the believers have experienced it.

After describing the "belief of the believers," the scholar may classify the phenomena according to essential types and make comparative evaluations. But all investigations into the essence and evaluations of phenomena entail value judgments by the interpreter and are beyond the limits of a descriptive phenomenology.

Rudolf Otto. Two interdependent methodological contributions made by Rudolf Otto (1869–1937) deserve emphasis: his experiential approach, which involves the phenomenological description of the universal, essential structure of religious experience, and his antireductionism, which respects the unique, irreducible, "numinous" quality of all religious experience.

In attempting to uncover the essential structure and meaning of all religious experience, Otto describes the universal "numinous" element as a unique *a priori* category of meaning and value. By *numen* and *numinous*, Otto means the concept of "the holy" minus its moral and rational aspects. With such an emphasis on this nonmoral, nonrational aspect of religion, he attempts to isolate the "overplus of meaning," beyond the rational and conceptual, which constitutes the universal essence of the religious experience. Since such a unique nonrational experience cannot be defined or conceptualized, the symbolic and analogical descriptions are meant to evoke indirectly within the reader the experience of the holy. The religious experience of the numinous, as an *a priori* structure of consciousness, can be reawakened or recognized by means of our *sensus numinous*, that is, our capacity for this *a priori* knowledge of the holy.

In this regard, Otto formulates a universal phenomenological structure of religious experience, in which the phenomenologist can distinguish autonomous religious phenomena by their numinous aspect and can organize and analyze specific religious manifestations. He points to our "creature feeling" of absolute dependence in the experiential presence of the holy. This *sui generis* religious experience is described as the experience of the "wholly other" *(ganz Andere)*, which is qualitatively unique and transcendent.

This insistence on the unique *a priori* quality of the religious experience points to Otto's antireductionism. Otto rejected the one-sidedly intellectualistic and rationalistic bias of most interpretations and the reduction of religious phenomena to the interpretive schema of linguistic analysis, anthropology, sociology, psychology, and various historicist approaches. This emphasis on the autonomy of religion, with the need for a unique, autonomous phenomenological approach that is commensurate with interpreting the meaning of the irreducibly religious phenomena, has generally been accepted by the major phenomenologists of religion.

Various interpreters have criticized Otto's phenomenological approach for being too narrowly conceived. According to these critics, Otto's approach focuses on the nonrational aspects of certain mystical and other "extreme" experiences, but it is not sufficiently comprehensive to interpret the diversity and complexity of religious data, nor is it sufficiently concerned with the specific historical and cultural forms of religious phenomena. Critics have also objected to the *a priori* nature of Otto's project and the influences of the personal, Christian, theological, and apologetic intentions on his phenomenology. Van der Leeuw, while agreeing with Otto's antireductionism, attempted to broaden his phenomenology by investigating and systematizing a tremendous diversity of religious phenomena.

Gerardus van der Leeuw. In his *Comparative Religion*, Eric J. Sharpe has written that "between 1925 and 1950, the phenomenology of religion was associated almost exclusively with the name of the Dutch scholar Gerardus van der Leeuw (1890–1950), and with his book *Phänomenologie der Religion*." Especially notable among the many influences on his phenomenology acknowledged by van der Leeuw are the writings of the German philosopher Wilhelm Dilthey (1833–1911) on hermeneutics and the concept of "understanding" *(Verstehen)*.

In several writings, especially the epilogue of *Phänomenologie der Religion* (1933; translated as *Religion in Essence and Manifestation*, 2d ed., 1963), which contains the chapters "Phenomenon and Phenomenology" and "The Phenomenology of Religion," van der Leeuw defines the assumptions, concepts, and stages of his phenomenological approach. According to this Dutch scholar, the phenomenologist must respect the specific intentionality of religious phenomena, and simply describe the phenomenon as "what appears into view." The phenomenon is given in the mutual relations between subject and object; that is, its "entire essence" is given in its appearance to someone.

Van der Leeuw proposed a subtle and complex phenomenological method with which the phenomenologist goes far beyond a descriptive phenomenology. His method involves systematic introspection, "the interpolation of the phenomenon into our lives," as necessary for understanding religious phenomena. In the first volume of his *Classical Approaches to the Study of Religion* (1973–1974), Jacques Waardenburg describes this phenomenological-psychological method as "an 'experiential' method to guide intuition and to arrive at immediate understanding" and as the "classification of religious phenomena by means of ideal types which are constituted by a psychological technique of re-experiencing religious meanings" (p. 57).

According to van der Leeuw, phenomenology must be combined with historical research, which precedes phenomenological understanding and provides the phenomenologist with sufficient data. Phenomenology must be open to "perpetual correction by the most conscientious philological and archaeological research," and "it becomes pure art or empty fancy" (van der Leeuw, 1963, vol. 2, p. 677) when it removes itself from such historical control. Special note may be taken of van der Leeuw's emphasis on the religious aspect of "power" as at the basis of every religious form and as defining that which is religious. "Phenomenology describes how man conducts himself in his relation to Power" (van der Leeuw, 1963, vol. 1, p. 191). The terms *holy, sanctus, taboo*, and so on, taken together, describe what occurs in all religious experience: "a strange, 'Wholly Other,' Power obtrudes into life" (van der Leeuw, 1963, vol. 2, p. 681).

Influences from van der Leeuw's own Christian point of view are often central to his analysis of the phenomenological method for gaining understanding of religious structures and meanings. For example, he claims that "faith and intellectual suspense (the *epochē*) do not exclude each other," and "all understanding rests upon self-surrendering love" (van der Leeuw, 1963, vol. 2, pp. 683–684). Indeed, van der Leeuw above all considered himself a theologian and submitted that phenomenology of religion led to both anthropology and theology. Numerous scholars have concluded that much of his phenomenology of religion must be interpreted in theological terms.

Critics, while often expressing admiration of *Religion in Essence and Manifestation* as an extraordinary collection of religious data, have offered many objections to van der Leeuw's phenomenology of religion: his phenomenological approach is based on numerous theological and metaphysical assumptions and value judgments, it is often too subjective and highly speculative, or it neglects the historical and cultural context of religious phenomena and is of little value for empirically based research.

Friedrich Heiler. Born in Munich, Friedrich Heiler (1892–1967) is known for his studies on prayer, great religious personalities, ecumenism, and the unity of all religion, and a kind of global phenomenology of religion.

According to Heiler, the phenomenological method proceeds from the externals to the essence of religion. Although every approach has presuppositions, the phenomenology of religion must avoid every philosophical *a priori* and utilize only those presuppositions that are consistent with an inductive method. Heiler's phenomenology of religion, which was theologically oriented, emphasized the indispensable value of "empathy": the phenomenologist must exercise respect, tolerance, and sympathetic understanding for all religious experience and the religious truth expressed in the data. Indeed, the phenomenologist's personal religious experience is a precondition for an empathic understanding of the totality of religious phenomena.

C. Jouco Bleeker. As previously mentioned, Bleeker distinguishes three separate types or schools of phenomenology of religion: the descriptive, the typological, and the phenomenological (in the specific sense of the word). In terms of this more specific approach, phenomenology of religion has a double meaning: it is an independent science that creates monographs and handbooks, such as van der Leeuw's *Religion in Essence and Manifestation* and Eliade's *Patterns in Comparative Religion*, but it is also a scholarly method that utilizes such principles as the phenomenological *epochē* and eidetic vision. Although Bleeker frequently uses such technical terms in gaining insight into religious structures and acknowledges that these terms are borrowed from the philosophical phenomenology of Husserl and his school, he claims that they are used by the phenomenology of religion in only a figurative sense.

According to Bleeker, the phenomenology of religion combines a critical attitude and concern for accurate descriptions with a sense of empathy for the phenomena. In his conception, it is an empirical science without philosophical aspirations, and it should distinguish its activities from those of philosophical phenomenology and of anthropology. He warns that historians and phenomenologists of religion should not dabble in philosophical speculations on matters of method. Bleeker states that "phenomenology of religion is not a philosophical discipline, but a systematization of historical fact with the intent to understand their religious meaning" (Bleeker, in Bianchi, Bleeker, and Bausani, 1972).

Probably the best-known formulation in Bleeker's reflections on phenomenology is his analysis of the task of phenomenology of religion as an inquiry into three dimensions of religious phenomena: *theōria*, *logos*, and *entelecheia*.

The *theōria* of phenomena "discloses the essence and significance of the facts." It has an empirical basis and leads to an understanding of the implications of various aspects of religion. The *logos* of phenomena "penetrates into the structure of different forms of religious life."

This provides a sense of objectivity by showing that hidden structures "are built up according to strict inner laws," and that religion "always possesses a certain structure with an inner logic."

Most original is Bleeker's position that the *entelecheia* of phenomena "reveals itself in the dynamics, the development which is visible in the religious life of mankind," or in "the course of events in which the essence is realized by its manifestations." Phenomenology, it is frequently stated, abstracts from historical change and presents a rather static view of essential structures and meanings. By the *entelecheia*, Bleeker wants to stress that religion is not static but is "an invincible, creative and self-regenerating force." The phenomenologist of religion must work closely with the historian of religions in studying the dynamics of phenomena and the development of religions.

Mircea Eliade. According to this historian of religions and interpreter of religious symbols, religion "refers to the experience of the sacred." The phenomenologist works with historical documents expressing *hierophanies*, or manifestations of the sacred, and attempts to decipher the existential situation and religious meaning expressed through the data. The sacred and the profane express "two modes of being in the world," and religion always entails the attempt of *homo religiosus* to transcend the relative, historical-temporal, "profane" world by experiencing a "superhuman" world of transcendent values.

In light of Bleeker's first sense of phenomenology of religion as an independent discipline that creates monographs that describe and classify essential structures and meanings, one may note Eliade's many morphological studies of different kinds of religious symbolism; his interpretations of the structure and function of myth, with the creation, or cosmogonic, myth functioning as exemplary model; his treatment of rituals, such as those of initiation; his structural analysis of sacred space, sacred time, and sacred history; and his monumental studies of different types of religious experience, such as *yoga*, shamanism, alchemy, and other "archaic" phenomena.

Bleeker's second sense of phenomenology of religion as a specific method comes to the fore if one cites three methodological principles underlying Eliade's approach: his assumption of the "irreducibility of the sacred," his emphasis on the "dialectic of the sacred" as the universal structure of sacralization, and his uncovering of the structural systems of religious symbols that constitute the hermeneutical framework in terms of which he interprets religious meaning.

The assumption of the irreducibility of the religious is a form of phenomenological *epochē*. In attempting to understand and describe the meaning of religious phenomena, the phenomenologist must utilize an antireductionist method commensurate with the nature of the data. Only a religious frame of reference or "scale" of interpretation does not distort the specific, irreducible religious intentionality expressed in the data.

The universal structure of the dialectic of the sacred provides Eliade with essential criteria for distinguishing religious from nonreligious phenomena. For example, there is always a sacred-profane dichotomy and the separation of the hierophanic object, such as a particular mountain or tree or person, since this is the medium through which the sacred is manifested; the sacred, which is transcendent, paradoxically limits itself by incarnating itself in something ordinarily finite, temporal, historical, and profane; and the religious person evaluates and chooses the sacred as powerful, ultimate, meaningful, and normative.

The central position of symbolism or symbolic structures establishes the phenomenological grounds for Eliade's structural hermeneutics. Among the characteristics of symbols are (1) their logic, which allows various symbols to fit together to form coherent symbolic systems, (2) their multivalence, through which they express simultaneously a number of structurally coherent meanings not evident on the level of immediate experience, and (3) their "function of unification," by which they integrate heterogeneous phenomena into a whole or a system. These autonomous, universal, coherent systems of symbols usually provide the phenomenological framework for Eliade's interpretation of religious meaning. For example, he interprets the meaning of a religious phenomenon associated with the sun or moon by reintegrating it within its solar or lunar structural system of symbolic associations.

Although Eliade has his admirers, many scholars have ignored or have been hostile to his history and phenomenology of religion. The most frequent criticism is that Eliade is methodologically uncritical, or that he presents sweeping, arbitrary, subjective generalizations not based upon specific historical and empirical data. Critics have also charged that his approach is influenced by various normative judgments and an assumed ontological position, which is partial to the religious, nonhistorical mode of being and to certain Eastern and archaic phenomena.

Characteristics and Criticisms of Phenomenology of Religion. The following features, some of which have already been mentioned, are characteristic of much of the phenomenology of religion: its identification as a comparative, systematic, empirical, historical, descriptive discipline and approach; its antireductionist claims and its autonomous nature; its adoption of philosophical phenomenological notions of intentionality and *epochē*; its insistence on the value of empathy, sympathetic understanding, and religious commitment; and its claim to provide insight into essential structures and meanings. Several of these characteristics are associated primarily with the phenomenology of religion; others, while accepted by most phenomenologists of religion, are shared by other historians of religions.

Comparative and systematic approach. As I have previously noted, there is widespread agreement that the phenomenology of religion is a very general approach concerned with classifying and systematizing religious phenomena. There is also widespread agreement that this discipline uses a comparative approach. Various phenomenologists have simply defined their phenomenology of religion as equivalent to comparative religion. But even those scholars who have rejected such a simple identification have maintained that phenomenologists are able to gain insight into essential structures and meaning only after comparing a large number of documents expressing a great diversity of religious phenomena.

Empirical approach. Bleeker, Eliade, and most phenomenologists of religion insist that they are using an empirical approach, which is free from *a priori* assumptions and judgments. Such an empirical approach, which is often described as "scientific" and "objective," begins by collecting religious documents and then goes on to decipher the religious phenomena by describing just what the empirical data reveal. These phenomenologists usually maintain that their discoveries of essential typologies and universal structures are based on empirical, inductive generalizations.

One of the most frequent attacks on the phenomenology of religion is that it is not empirically based, and that it is therefore arbitrary, subjective, and unscientific. Critics charge that the universal structures and meanings are not found in the empirical data and that the phenomenological discoveries are not subject to empirical tests of verification.

Historical approach. Phenomenologists of religion usually maintain not only that their approach must cooperate with and complement historical research but also that phenomenology of religion is profoundly historical. All religious data are historical; no phenomena may be understood outside their history. The phenomenologist must be aware of the specific historical, cultural, and socioeconomic contexts within which religious phenomena appear.

Critics, however, charge that not only is the phenomenology of religion not historical, it is even antihistorical, both in terms of a phenomenological method that neglects the specific historical and cultural context and with regard to the primacy—methodologically and even ontologically—it grants to nonhistorical and nontemporal universal structures.

Descriptive approach. Unlike Müller, who intended the modern scholarly study of religion *(Religionswissenschaft)* to be a descriptive science attaining the autonomy and objectivity of the descriptive natural sciences, and Kristensen, who conceived of phenomenology of religion as "purely descriptive," the other leading phenomenologists I have considered, and perhaps all phenomenologists of religion today, do not restrict themselves to mere description of the religious phenomena. While cognizant of Kristensen's concerns about the subjective nature of much past scholarship in which interpreters filtered data through their own assumptions and value judgments, phenomenologists have gone far beyond the severe methodological restrictions of his descriptive phenomenology.

And yet these same phenomenologists invariably classify their discipline and approach as a descriptive phenomenology of religion; at the minimum, it is "essentially descriptive," and sometimes it is presented as "purely descriptive." They claim to utilize a descriptive approach and see their classifications, typologies, and structures as descriptive. Sometimes phenomenologists of religion distinguish the collection and description of religious data, which is objective and scientific, from the interpretation of meaning, which is at least partially subjective and normative.

Antireductionism. Philosophical phenomenology, in defining itself as a radically descriptive philosophy, had opposed various kinds of reductionism. It was necessary to oppose reductionism, which imposed uncritical preconceptions and unexamined judgments on phenomena, in order that phenomenologists could deal with phenomena simply as phenomena and could provide more accurate descriptions of just what the phenomena revealed.

More than any other approach within the modern study of religion, phenomenology of religion has insisted that investigators approach religious data as phenomena that are fundamentally and irreducibly religious. Otto, Eliade, and other phenomenologists of religion often defend their strong antireductionism by criticizing past reductionist approaches. Many of these past interpretations, for example, were based on "positivist" and "rationalist" norms and forced the religious data into preconceived unilinear, evolutionary explanatory frameworks. Phenomenologists have criticized the reductions of religious data to fit nonreligious perspectives, such as those of sociology, psychology, or economics. Such reductionisms, it is argued, destroy the specificity, complexity, and irreducible intentionality of religious phenomena. In attempting sympathetically to understand the experience of the other, the phenomenologist must respect the "original" religious intentionality expressed in the data.

Autonomy. Directly related to the antireductionist claim of the irreducibility of the religious is the identification of the phenomenology of religion as an autonomous discipline and approach. If there are certain irreducible modes by which religious phenomena are given, then we must utilize a specific method of understanding that is commensurate with the religious nature of our subject matter, and we must provide irreducibly religious interpretations of the religious phenomena.

The phenomenology of religion is autonomous but not self-sufficient. It depends heavily on historical research and on the data supplied by philology, ethnology, psychology, sociology, and other approaches. But it must always integrate the contributions of other approaches within its own unique phenomenological perspective.

Intentionality. Philosophical phenomenology analyzes acts of consciousness as consciousness of something, and claims that meaning is given in the intentionality of the structure. In order to perceive the religious phenomena, phenomenologists have focused on the intentionality of their data. For Otto, the *a priori* structure of religious consciousness is consciousness of its intended "numinous object." Van der Leeuw's phenomenological-psychological technique and Eliade's dialectic of the sacred are methods for capturing the intentional characteristics of religious manifestations. The major criticism made by phenomenologists of religion of reductionist approaches involves the latter's negation of the unique intentionality of religious phenomena.

Epochē, empathy, and sympathetic understanding. Many philosophical phenomenologists have emphasized the phenomenological *epochē* as a means of bracketing beliefs and preconceptions we normally impose on phenomena. It is important to clarify that Husserl and other philosophers who formulated a "phenomenological reduction" as *epochē* did not intend a narrowing of perspective and negation of the complexity and specificity of phenomena. The phenomenological reduction was intended to achieve the very opposite of reductionism: by suspending our unexamined assumptions and normal preconceptions it allowed for a critical consciousness of the phenomena previously experienced on a prereflective level, thus allowing new insight into the specific intentionality and concrete richness of experience.

The phenomenological *epochē*, with an emphasis on empathy and sympathetic understanding, is related to methodological antireductionism. If the phenomenologist is to describe the meaning of religious phenomena as they have manifested themselves in the lives of religious persons, she or he must suspend all personal preconceptions as to what is "real" and attempt to empathize with and imaginatively reenact these religious appearances. By insisting on the irreducibility of the religious, phenomenologists attempt sympathetically to place themselves within the religious "life-world" and to grasp the religious meaning of the phenomena.

There are, of course, limitations to this personal participation, since the other always remains to some extent "the other." Phenomenologists insist that empathy, a sympathetic attitude, and personal participation in no way undermine the need for a critical scholarly approach with rigorous criteria of interpretation. This phenomenological orientation may be contrasted with the ideal of detached, impersonal scientific objectivity that characterized almost all nineteenth-century approaches within the scholarly study of religion and that continues to define many approaches today.

In assuming a sympathetic attitude, the phenomenologist is not claiming that religious phenomena are not "illusory" and that the intentional object is "real." (As a matter of fact, many of the phenomenologists have made such theological and metaphysical assumptions and judgments, but these usually violate the limitations of their self-defined phenomenological perspectives.) The phenomenological *epochē* entails the suspension of all such value judgments regarding whether or not, for example, the holy or sacred is actually an experience of ultimate reality.

With a few exceptions, it seems that phenomenologists of religion, while generally upholding an *epochē* or similar values, have not subjected such concepts to a rigorous analysis. Often they give little more than vague appeals to abstain from value judgments and to exercise a personal capacity for empathetic participation, but without scholarly criteria for verifying whether such sympathetic understanding has been acheived.

Many phenomenologists have argued for the necessity of religious commitment, a personal religious faith, or at least personal religious experience in order for a scholar to be capable of empathy, participation, and sympathetic understanding. Other phenomenologists have argued that such personal religious commitments have generally produced very biased descriptions that rarely do justice to the religious experience of others. It seems that a particular faith or theological commitment is not a precondition for accurate phenomenological descriptions. Rather it is a commitment to religious phenomena, which is manifested in terms of intellectual curiosity, sensitivity, and respect, that is indispensable for participation and understanding. Such a commitment may be shared by believers and nonbelievers alike.

Insight into essential structures and meanings. As one would expect, no subject matter has been more central to philosophical phenomenology than analyses of the eidetic reduction and eidetic vision, the intuition of essences, the method of free variation, and other techniques for gaining insight into the essential structures and meanings of phenomena. By contrast, the phenomenology of religion, even in the specific sense of an approach concerned with describing essential structures and meanings, has tended to avoid such methodological formulations.

There are, of course, notable exceptions. The philosopher Max Scheler, in his analysis of "concrete phenomenology," "essential phenomenology," and other aspects of the phenomenology of religion, formulates a sophisticated phenomenological method that is greatly influenced by the Husserlian project. Another exception is the philosopher Paul Ricoeur, who in the formulation of his sophisticated hermeneutic phenomenology of religion has been profoundly influenced by Husserl and Heidegger, among others.

One generally finds, however, that most phenomenologists of religion have accepted both Bleeker's qualification that such terms as *eidetic vision* are used only in a figurative sense and his warning that phenomenology of religion should avoid philosophical speculations and not meddle in difficult philosophical questions of methodology. The result of this is that we are frequently presented with phenomenological typologies, "universal structures," and "essential meanings" of religious phenomena that lack a rigorous analysis of just how the phenomenologist arrived at or verified these discoveries. In short, in its claims concerning insight into essential structures and meanings, much of the phenomenology of religion appears to be methodologically uncritical.

Phenomenologists aim at intuiting, interpreting, and describing the essence of religious phenomena, but there is considerable disagreement as to what constitutes an essential structure. For some phenomenologists, an "essential structure" seems to be the result of an empirical inductive generalization, expressing a property that different phenomena have in common. For others, "essential structures" refer to types of religious phenomena, and there is debate concerning the relationship between historical types and phenomenological types. In the sense closest to philosophical phenomenology, "essence" refers to deep or hidden structures, which are not apparent on the level of immediate experience and must be uncovered and decoded or interpreted through the phenomenological method. Further, these structures express the necessary invariant features allowing us to distinguish religious phenomena and to grasp the religious phenomena as phenomena of a certain kind.

Controversial Issues. In my examination of the major phenomenologists of religion and the major characteristics of the phenomenology of religion, I have raised many controversial issues. In this concluding section, I shall elaborate on several of these and introduce a few others.

Descriptive claims. There are many controversial issues regarding the claim that the phenomenology of religion is a descriptive discipline with a descriptive method, especially since almost all phenomenologists go far beyond a mere description of the data, offering comparisons and evaluations of phenomena, universal structures, and essential meanings.

Many of these issues arise from the acceptance of a rather traditional descriptive-normative distinction. Consistent with the classical empiricism of such philosophers as David Hume, with the Kantian philosophical framework, and with most nineteenth- and twentieth-century approaches in the history of religions, has been the adoption by many phenomenologists of religions of a radical, at times absolute, descriptive-normative dichotomy.

Even those phenomenologists of religion who go far beyond Kristensen's descriptive restrictions frequently adopt a clear distinction between the collection and description of religious data, which is seen as objective and scientific, and the interpretation of meaning, which is at least partially subjective and normative. Despite its rejection of earlier models of positivism, it may be that the phenomenology of religion has unintentionally retained some of the positivistic assumptions regarding the investigation of uninterpreted, objective "facts."

In recent decades, however, philosophy has challenged this absolute dichotomy. What is taken as objective and scientific is historically, culturally, and socially situated, based on presuppositions, and constructed in terms of implicit and explicit value judgments. For example, how does one even begin the investigation? What facts should be collected as religious facts? One's very principles of selectivity are never completely value-free. Indeed, philosophical phenomenologists have never accepted this sharp dichotomy, since the entire phenomenological project is founded on the possibilities of describing meanings. The challenge to the phenomenology of religion is to formulate a phenomenological method and framework for interpretation that allows the description of essential structures and meanings with some sense of objectivity.

Other controversies arise from the common claim

that phenomenology aims at understanding (which involves describing meanings) and not at explaining (which involves uncovering historical and other causal relationships). "Understanding" often has the sense of *Verstehen* as formulated by Dilthey and others as the method and goal of hermeneutics. Critics challenge such methods and goals and question whether phenomenological understanding and nonphenomenological explaining can be so completely separated.

Antireductionist claims. Many critics have attacked phenomenology of religion's antireductionism, arguing that it is methodologically confused and unjustified and that it arises from the theological intention of defending religion against secular analysis. The most general criticism of this antireductionism is based on the argument that all methodological approaches are perspectival, limiting, and necessarily reductionistic. The assumption of the irreducibility of the religious is itself reductionistic, since it limits what phenomena will be investigated, what aspects of the phenomena will be described, and what meanings will be interpreted. Phenomenologists of religion cannot argue that other reductionistic approaches are necessarily false and that their approach does justice to all dimensions of religious manifestations.

The challenge faced by the phenomenology of religion is to show that its religious antireductionism should be granted a certain methodological primacy on the basis of such key notions as intentionality and insight into essential structures and meanings. It must show, in terms of a rigorous method with procedures for verification, that its particular perspective is essential in shedding light on such structures and meanings.

Empirical and historical claims. Critics often claim that the phenomenology of religion starts with *a priori* nonempirical assumptions, utilizes a method that is not empirically based, and detaches religious structures and meanings from their specific historical and cultural contexts. Such critics often assume a clear-cut dichotomy between an empirical, inductive, historical approach and a nonempirical (often rationalist), deductive, antihistorical approach. They identify their approaches with the former and the phenomenology of religion with versions of the latter. They conclude that the phenomenology of religion cannot meet minimal empirical, historical, inductive criteria for a scientific approach, such as rigorous criteria for verification and falsification. (It may be simply noted that much of recent philosophy has been directed not only at critiquing classical empiricism but also at undermining this absolute dichotomy.)

Much of philosophical phenomenology has been conceived in opposition to traditional empiricism. Husserl, for example, called for a "phenomenological reduction" in which the phenomenologist "suspended" the "natural standpoint" and its empirical world in order to intuit the deeper phenomenological essences. Although such a phenomenology has been described as a radical empiricism, it certainly employs a critique of the traditional empiricism adopted by most of the history of religions.

Controversies arise from criticisms that the phenomenology of religion is highly normative and subjective because it makes nonempirical, nonhistorical, *a priori*, theological, and other normative assumptions and because it grants an ontologically privileged status to religious phenomena and to specific kinds of religious experience. Thus critics charge that Kristensen, Otto, Van der Leeuw, Heiler, Eliade, and others have nonempirical and nonhistorical, extraphenomenological, theological, and other normative assumptions, intentions, and goals that define much of their phenomenological projects, taking them beyond the domain of a descriptive phenomenology.

The status granted to the essential religious structures and meanings is also controversial insofar as they exhibit the peculiarity of being empirical, that is, based on investigating a limited sample of historical data, and at the same time, universal. These structures are hence empirically contingent and yet also the essential necessary features of religious phenomena.

Finally, there has arisen the controversy regarding the insistence by many phenomenologists of religion that they proceed by some kind of empirical inductive inference that is not unlike the classical formulations of induction developed by John Stuart Mill and others. Critics charge that they cannot repeat this inductive inference, that the phenomenological structures do not appear in the empirical data, and that phenomenologists read into their data all sorts of essential meanings.

One response by phenomenologists, as expressed in Guilford Dudley's *Religion on Trial* (Philadelphia, 1977), is to give up their empirical and historical claims, and turn to a nonempirical, nonhistorical, rationalist, deductive approach. A different response, as expressed in my *Structure and Creativity in Religion* (1978), is to formulate a method of "phenomenological induction," different from classical empirical induction, in which the essential structures and meaning are based on, but not found fully in, the empirical data. This response involves a process of imaginative construction and idealization by phenomenologists, and the essential structures must then be rigorously tested in terms of the light that they shed on the empirical-historical data.

Questions of verification. I have repeatedly noted different criticisms of the phenomenology of religion for being methodologically uncritical. One wonders if the phenomenology of religion can continue to avoid basic methodological questions raised by philosophical phenomenology and other disciplines if it is to overcome these criticisms. Many of these criticisms, as we have seen, involve questions of verification. Intuition does not free one from the responsibility of ascertaining which interpretation of a given phenomenon is most adequate nor of substantiating why this is so. Fueling this controversy is the observation that different phenomenologists, while investigating the same phenomena and claiming to utilize the phenomenological method, have continually presented different eidetic intuitions. How does one resolve this contingency introduced into phenomenological insights? How does one verify specific interpretations and decide between different interpretations?

Such questions pose specific difficulties for a phenomenological method of *epochē* and intuition of essences. A phenomenological method often suspends the usual criteria of "objectivity" that have allowed scholars to verify interpretations and choose between alternative accounts. Does this leave the phenomenology of religion with a large number of very personal, extremely subjective, hopelessly fragmented interpretations of universal structures and meanings, each relativistic interpretation determined by the particular situation and orientation of the individual phenomenologist?

The phenomenologist of religion can argue that past criteria for verification have been inadequate and have resulted in a false sense of objectivity; but phenomenology of religion must also overcome the charges of complete subjectivity and relativism by struggling with questions of verification. It must formulate rigorous procedures for testing its discoveries of structures and meanings, and these procedures must involve criteria for intersubjective verification.

Response to controversial issues. Many writers have described the phenomenology of religion as being in a state of crisis today. They usually minimize the invaluable contributions made by phenomenology to the study of religion, such as the impressive systematization of so much religious data and the raising of fundamental questions of meaning often ignored by other approaches.

If the phenomenology of religion is to deal adequately with its controversial issues, the following are several of its future tasks. First, it must become more aware of the historical, philological, and other specialized approaches to, and these different aspects of, its religious data. Second, it must critique various approaches of its critics, thus showing that its phenomenological method is not obliged to meet such inadequate criteria for objectivity. And most importantly, it must reflect more critically on questions of methodology, so that phenomenology of religion can formulate a more rigorous method, allowing for the description of phenomena, the interpretation of their structures and meanings, and the verification of its findings.

BIBLIOGRAPHY

The most comprehensive general introduction to philosophical phenomenology remains Herbert Spiegelberg's *The Phenomenological Movement: A Historical Introduction*, 2 vols., 2d ed. (The Hague, 1965). Richard Schmitt's "Phenomenology" in *The Encyclopedia of Philosophy* (New York, 1967), vol. 5, pp. 133–151, provides another introduction, although it tends to be formulated primarily on the basis of Husserl's approach and often is more of a critical philosophical essay rather than a survey of the field. Of the many anthologies of phenomenological philosophers and their different philosophical approaches, *Phenomenology and Existentialism*, edited by Robert C. Solomon (Washington, D.C., 1972), is a commendable work.

There is no major comprehensive survey of the phenomenology of religion. The most comprehensive general introduction to scholars identified with the modern study of religion, including selections from the leading phenomenologists of religion and fairly extensive bibliographies of their works, is Jacques Waardenburg's *Classical Approaches to the Study of Religion: Aims, Methods and Theories of Research*, 2 vols. (The Hague, 1973–1974). A number of books have a chapter or section surveying the phenomenology of religion, including Eric J. Sharpe's *Comparative Religion: A History* (London, 1975) and John Macquarrie's *Twentieth-Century Religious Thought*, rev. ed. (New York, 1981).

The following are selected works by the major phenomenologists of religion considered in this article. William Brede Kristensen's *The Meaning of Religion: Lectures in the Phenomenology of Religion* (The Hague, 1960) illustrates a very restricted descriptive phenomenology. Rudolf Otto's *The Idea of the Holy*, 2d Eng. ed. (Oxford, 1950), is the best-known account of religious experience. Gerardus van der Leeuw's *Religion in Essence and Manifestation: A Study in Phenomenology*, 2 vols., 2d ed. (New York, 1963), is often considered the classic work in phenomenology of religion. Friedrich Heiler's *Erscheinungsformen und Wesen der Religion* (Stuttgart, 1961) has not been translated; his only book available in English is *Prayer: A Study in the History and Psychology of Religion* (Oxford, 1932). Of C. Jouco Bleeker's many writings on the phenomenology of religion, one may cite *Problems and Methods of the History of Religions*, edited by Ugo Bianchi, C. Jouco Bleeker, and Alessandro Bausani (Leiden, 1972), which contains Bleeker's essay, "The Contribution of the Phenomenology of Religion to the Study of the History of Religions"; and Bleeker's *The Sacred Bridge: Researches into the Nature and Structure of Religion* (Leiden, 1963), which contains an essay called "The Phenomenological Method." Of more than thirty books by Mircea Eliade available in English, *Patterns in Comparative Religion* (New York, 1958) may be noted; this systematic morphological work provides a theoretical framework of symbolic systems necessary for interpreting religious meaning. Eliade's collection of essays *The Quest: History and Meaning in Religion* (Chicago, 1969) provides some insight into his method and discipline.

Of recent books on the phenomenology of religion, the following five publications may be noted. Jacques Waardenburg's *Reflections on the Study of Religion* (The Hague, 1978) includes an essay on the work of van der Leeuw and two other essays on the phenomenology of religion. *Science of Religion: Studies in Methodology*, edited by Lauri Honko (The Hague, 1979), includes essays under the title "The Future of the Phenomenology of Religion." My *Structure and Creativity in Religion: Hermeneutics in Mircea Eliade's Phenomenology and New Directions* (The Hague, 1978), written from a perspective informed by philosophical phenomenology, surveys approaches in the phenomenology of religion and argues that Eliade has a sophisticated phenomenological method. Two works, written from perspectives often quite critical of the phenomenology of religion, are Olof Pettersson and Hans Åkerberg's *Interpreting Religious Phenomena: Studies with Reference to the Phenomenology of Religion* (Atlantic Highlands, N.J., 1981) and António Barbosa da Silva's *The Phenomenology of Religion as a Philosophical Problem* (Uppsala, 1982).

DOUGLAS ALLEN

PHILARET OF MOSCOW. *See* Filaret of Moscow.

PHILISTINE RELIGION. Although many questions about the Philistines remain unanswered, including questions about Philistine religion, a variety of sources provide a modicum of evidence on this intriguing people. Most important among these are the Old Testament (Hebrew scriptures), the Egyptian texts, and archaeological materials from Palestine.

The Philistines were a warlike people who migrated from somewhere in the Aegean basin to the southern coastal plain of Palestine; the most important and best-documented phase of this migration took place in the early part of the twelfth century BCE. The Philistine invasion of the southeastern Levant is well known from the artistic and literary accounts at Medinet Habu in Egypt, where Ramses III left a record of his military encounter (c. 1190 BCE) with two groups of "Sea Peoples," the Tjekker and the Peleset. The Egyptians repelled the invasion, and some of the Sea Peoples settled in southern Palestine. This region was called Philistia, and the Greek name for the Philistines, *Palastinoi*, later evolved into *Palestine*, the modern name for the land as a whole. The major cities of the Philistines were Gaza, Ashdod, Ashqelon, Gath, and Ekron, the so-called Philistine pentapolis. Because of their expansion into the hinterland of Canaan, the Philistines (Heb., *pelishtim*) were major rivals of the Israelites during the Israelite conquest, settlement, and early monarchy, although the Philistine threat waned after their military defeat by King David (c. 950 BCE).

There is some evidence concerning Philistine origins in the archaeological record and the nonbiblical literature (e.g., the tendency to associate the Philistine migration with the ethnic upheaval at the end of the Greek Bronze Age, around 1200 BCE). But it is the Old Testament that contains the most direct statements concerning the Philistines' ancestral homeland. Several passages linking the Philistines with Caphtor, or Crete (cf. *Dt.* 2:23, *Jer.* 47:4, *Am.* 9:7), are among the many indications pointing to an Aegean background. *Genesis* 10:14 and *1 Chronicles* 1:12 identify Egypt as the Philistines' place of origin, but this can be understood in light of the Philistine migration route.

Excavations at numerous Palestinian sites, most of which are located in the coastal plain or the Shephelah (the western foothills of the Judean mountains), have yielded significant remains of Philistine material culture; the beautiful and distinctive painted pottery of the Philistines is undoubtedly the best-known aspect of their civilization. Unfortunately—and surprisingly—there is no written text that can be attributed to the Philistines with any degree of certainty. While this dearth of Philistine literature may be eliminated as archaeological research continues, it is obvious that any attempt to describe Philistine religion is severely limited by a lack of primary Philistine texts on the subject. Nevertheless, we are not totally ignorant of the Philistine pantheon and cult, since the Old Testament and the archaeological data can be gleaned for relevant details.

In her important study *The Philistines and Their Material Culture,* Trude Dothan has provided archaeologists with a thorough analysis of the types and groups into which Philistine pottery (found at some thirty Palestinian sites) can be divided. Dothan's summary statement concerning this pottery serves as a general introduction to Philistine religion as well: "Typologically, Philistine pottery reflects the Sea Peoples' Aegean background, plus certain Cypriot, Egyptian, and local Canaanite elements" (p. 94). A careful investigation of Philistine religion reveals a similar potpourri that points to the eclectic or assimilative nature of Philistine religion. Such assimilation is evident in the Philistines' pantheon, religious practices, temples, and cult objects.

Pantheon. The members of the Philistine pantheon about whom we possess specific information—Dagon (or Dagan), Baalzebub (or Baalzebul), and Ashtoret (or Ashtaroth)—were all deities worshiped for centuries by the pre-Philistine occupants of Canaan. According to the biblical record, Dagon was the supreme god of the Philistine pantheon (*1 Sm.* 5:1–7, *1 Chr.* 10:10). Like many ancient high gods, he was probably understood as a god of war, since we read about the Philistines giving thanks to this deity after victory over two of their archenemies, Samson and Saul (*Jgs.* 16:23–24, *1 Chr.* 10:10). Dagon had temples in Gaza (*Jgs.* 16:21, 23–30), Ashdod (*1 Sm.* 5:1–7; *1 Mc.* 10:83–85, 11:4), and probably in Beth-shan (*1 Chr.* 10:10; cf. *1 Sm.* 31:10). The Ashdod temple housed a statue of Dagon. Interestingly, the biblical account points to the Philistine acknowledgment of the superiority of Yahveh over Dagon. As noted above, Dagon was an important god in the ancient Semitic pantheon (his name appears in Canaanite toponyms). He is known to have been worshiped at Ugarit, and, in fact, he was honored at ancient Ebla as early as the second half of the third millennium BCE.

Baalzebub, another member of the ancient Semitic pantheon, was closely associated with the Philistine town of Ekron (probably Tel Miqne): *2 Kings* 1:2–16 informs us that Baalzebub was consulted by an oracle and was in some way associated with healing. Baalzebul was a name used at Ugarit for Baal. Texts from the time of Ramses III indicate that the Philistines knew the god Baal when they invaded Egypt.

The well-known Semitic goddess Ashtoret probably had temples at Ashqelon (Herodotus 1.105) and at Beth-shan (*1 Sm.* 31:10). In light of the female fertility figurines discovered at a number of Philistine sites, especially the so-called Ashdoda (see below), it is not surprising that this goddess is also associated with the Philistines in the Old Testament.

In addition to these members of the Semitic pantheon, there is evidence that the Philistines worshiped Egyptian deities. The wholesale assimilation apparent in the Philistine pantheon may indicate that the Philistine settlement in Palestine was a more gradual process than has previously been imagined. It should be remembered, however, that such borrowing of divine names and/or epithets was a common practice in ancient Near Eastern religions. Indeed, the Old Testament contains frequent denunciations of the Israelites' attraction toward and participation in religious practices of their neighbors, including the Philistines (*Jgs.* 10:6).

Religious Practices and Functionaries. According to *Judges* 16:23–24, the Philistines and their leaders gathered together for sacrifices and festivals. In fact, the Old Testament records an occasion when the Philistines sent a guilt offering to the God of Israel, since they had learned to respect this other national deity (*1 Sm.* 4:6, 5:1–6:21). Apparently, the Philistines carried or wore portable idols or amulets into battle (*2 Sm.* 5:21; cf. *2 Mc.* 12:40). The advice of priests and diviners was sought (*1 Sm.* 5:5, 6:2–9; cf. *2 Kgs.* 1:2), and the art of soothsaying was developed (*Is.* 2:6). With regard to burial customs, several Philistine sites have yielded whole or fragmentary anthropoid clay coffins, use of which was probably borrowed from the Egyptians.

Clearly, the religious practices of the Philistines were similar to those of their Semitic neighbors; the absence of circumcision seems to be the one exception (*Jgs.* 14:3; *1 Sm.* 17:26, 17:36, 18:25). Indeed, the Philistines' failure to practice this ritual enabled the Israelites to refer to their archenemies as "the uncircumcised" (*Jgs.* 15:18; *1 Sm.* 14:6, 31:4).

Temples and Cult Objects. As a result of archaeological excavations at Ashdod and, more importantly, at Tell Qasile (whose ancient name is not known), we have some knowledge of Philistine religious sanctuaries. Investigations at Ashdod brought to light an open-air high place and an apsidal structure that may have had a religious function. It is the research at Tell Qasile, however, that has unearthed the first Philistine temples to be identified with certainty. At this site (on the northern fringe of Tel Aviv) the excavators, under the direction of Amihai Mazar, found a series of three superimposed temples. The first was built in the twelfth century BCE (Stratum XII) and was twice rebuilt and enlarged, in the twelfth and the eleventh century BCE (Stratum XI and Stratum X, respectively). The plans of these temples reflect Canaanite, Cypriot, and Mycenaean influences. The Stratum X temple, the largest and richest in cult objects, contained round stone column bases placed about six feet apart; upon them rested cedar columns that supported the roof (cf. *Jgs.* 16:25–30). Unfortunately, we do not know what deity was honored in any of these temples.

A large number and wide variety of cult objects have been recovered in the excavations of Philistine strata, especially at Gezer, Ashdod, and Tell Qasile. They include kernos rings and bowls, decorated bowls and vases, zoomorphic and anthropomorphic figurines, ritual stands, rhytons, and so on. Of special interest are the numerous kernos rings and bowls, especially since these Early Iron Age Philistine objects show affinities to objects from the final years of Mycenaean culture. Also important is a series of lion-headed libation cups from Philistine sites in Palestine, vessels that have similarities with rhytons from the Mycenaean-Minoan tradition.

Without a doubt, the most frequently discussed cult object associated with the Philistines is the stylized female figurine called the Ashdoda (so named after the site where it was found). The Ashdoda looks like a throne or couch into which human body parts—a head, elongated neck, armless torso, and molded breasts—have been merged; the entire figurine is elaborately painted. According to Trude Dothan, this figurine is probably "a schematic representation of a female deity and throne" (p. 234), an object with clear-cut Aegean antecedents. It is part of a group of Ashdodas, now fragmentary, found in strata at Ashdod that date from the twelfth to the eighth century BCE.

The Ashdoda, together with other artifacts and features of Philistine material culture and religion, has prompted many scholars to view Philistine religion in terms of its Aegean background. Here the term *Aegean* is used broadly and includes Crete, Cyprus, and the Greek islands and mainland. Yet it is also clear that the Philistines assimilated much—including a number of religious beliefs and practices—from their Semitic neighbors.

BIBLIOGRAPHY

A classic treatment of the Philistines is R. A. S. Macalister's *The Philistines: Their History and Civilization* (Oxford, 1913). Naturally, much of Macalister's work is dated, but his contribution to our understanding of this important people is noteworthy, especially since his volume was based largely on his own archaeological excavations at Gezer.

The most important and up-to-date source of information on the Philistines is Trude Dothan's magnificent volume, *The Philistines and Their Material Culture* (New Haven, 1982). Dothan's article "What We Know about the Philistines," *Biblical Archaeology Review* 7 (July–August 1984): 20–44, which is well illustrated and written on a more popular level, is an excellent place to begin an investigation of the Philistines. Another reliable source is K. A. Kitchen's essay "The Philistines," in *Peoples of Old Testament Times*, edited by D. J. Wiseman (Oxford, 1973), pp. 53–78. A recent and balanced study of the Philistines is John F. Brug's "A Literary and Archaeological Study of the Philistines" (Ph.D. diss., University of Minnesota, 1984).

For details on Amihai Mazar's excavation of a sequence of Philistine temples at Tell Qasile, see Mazar's two articles "A Philistine Temple at Tell Qasile" and "Additional Philistine Temples at Tell Qasile," *Biblical Archaeologist* 36 (1973): 42–48, and 40 (1977): 82–87, and his final reports, *Excavations at Tell Qasile I* (Jerusalem, 1980) and *Excavations at Tell Qasile II* (Jerusalem, 1985).

GERALD L. MATTINGLY

PHILO JUDAEUS (c. 20 BCE–50 CE), Hellenistic Jewish thinker, author of an elaborate synthesis of Jewish religious thought and Greek philosophy. Although the church fathers know him as Philo Judaeus (Jerome, *De viris illustribus* 11), modern scholars often designate him Philo of Alexandria, to distinguish him from various pagan Greek authors of the same name. Philo's work marks the climax of a long chain of Hellenistic Jewish writings. His mildly atticized Greek, which is marked by a strong Platonic coloring, is unexceptionable; his encyclopedic knowledge of Greek literature and rhetoric is impressive. Disdaining a philosophically systematic exposition of his reinterpretation of Judaism, Philo assumed instead the role of scriptural exegete. He may have believed that the success of his entire enterprise was largely dependent on his ability to convince his readers that the mystical Platonism through which his Jewish understanding was refracted was no arbitrary construct imposed on the Mosaic text, but could readily be deduced from every one of its verses.

Although fully acquainted with the Greek philosophical texts firsthand and in no way restricted to manuals or digests, Philo is clearly not to be regarded as an original philosopher. He saw his task more modestly, as that of the great reconciler who would bridge two apparently disparate traditions. Although there is still no consensus, the view is gaining ground that the apparent eclecticism of his thought is in fact representative of the Middle Platonic tradition (stretching from c. 80 BCE to c. 220 CE), a highly stoicized form of Platonism, streaked with Neo-Pythagorean concerns, which included a large dose of arithmology, or number symbolism.

Life and Works. Philo belonged to a wealthy, aristocratic Jewish family (of priestly descent, if Jerome is to be credited) that was readily attracted by the glitter of the Hellenistic world. His brother Alexander was an alabarch (usually equated with arabarch), or customs agent, for the collection of dues on all goods imported into Egypt from the East, and his wealth was such that he could grant Agrippa, the grandson of Herod the Great, a loan of two hundred thousand drachmas (equivalent to fifty-four thousand dollars); thus was established a connection that ultimately led to the betrothal of Agrippa's daughter Berenice to Alexander's son Marcus. His great wealth is further attested by his provision of silver and gold plates for nine gates of the Jerusalem Temple. His other son, Tiberius Julius Alexander, to whom Philo addressed his dialogue *On Providence* and who was described by Josephus Flavius as "not remaining true to his ancestral practices," served as procurator of the province of Judaea (46–48 CE) and as prefect of Egypt under Nero.

Of Philo himself, aside from the fact that he headed the embassy to (Gaius) Caligula in 39–40 CE and visited the Jerusalem Temple, we know very little. Though silent with regard to his Jewish education, he speaks enthusiastically of his Greek training and with engaging melancholy of his having been torn at some point from his "heavenly lookout," where he had consorted with divine principles and doctrines, to be hurled into a vast sea of civil cares. His constant use of athletic imagery, including references to specific athletic and theatrical events that he himself had attended and a triple reference to God as the "president of the games," shows him to have been an *aficionado* of the sports world. When this trait is coupled with his passionate devotion to speculative philosophy, we recognize the presence of a Diaspora Jewish intellectual of a type utterly foreign to his Palestinian counterpart.

The Philonic corpus may be divided into three groups: historical or apologetic, philosophical (comprising four treatises, two of which are in dialogue form and preserved only in Armenian and some Greek fragments), and exegetical. The last is subdivided into three Pentateuchal commentaries: the *Allegory of the Law* or those treatises which begin with a scriptural passage; the *Exposition of the Law* or those treatises whose structure is shaped by a broad theme indicated in their title; and *Questions and Answers on Genesis and Exodus*. There are also references in Philo to a number of his treatises that are no longer extant. The question of the chronology of Philo's works remains problematic but the earlier tendency to assign his philosophical works to a youthful period is no longer accepted.

Exegetical Technique. Philo's attempt to read Greek philosophy into Mosaic scripture was no innovation on his part. He was fully aware of the earlier and less ambitious attempts by Pseudo-Aristeas (c. 130 BCE) and Aristobulus (c. 175 BCE), though he was also undoubtedly heir to a rich body of scholastic tradition that has vanished but to which he frequently makes allusion. He was also fully alert to the techniques employed by many Middle Platonists in their attempt to foist post-Pythagorean doctrines, including even their own, on Pythagoras (fifth century BCE) himself. Following in their footsteps, Philo put Moses forward as the greatest authority of all, as the teacher of Pythagoras and, indeed, of all Greek philosophers and lawgivers.

The main exegetical technique for Philo's vast enterprise, however, was provided by the Greek allegorical tradition, which had been initiated by Theagenes of Rhegium (sixth century BCE) in order to defend Homer against the detractors of his theology; the gods' names were made to refer to various dispositions of the soul, and their internecine struggles to the opposition between the natural elements. The Stoics expanded the Cynics' employment of Homeric allegory in the interests of a philosophical system and made much use of the etymologizing of names (of the gods, though not of the heroes), a procedure that had much appeal for Philo. Moreover, his preoccupation with the "allegory of the soul" is very similar to the later Neoplatonic allegories clustering around Odysseus, which detect in his adventures the mystical history of the soul on its way to its homeland.

John Dillon (1977) has noted the essential unity in the tradition of commentary that Philo's exegetical works and the Neoplatonic commentaries exemplify and has concluded that their common source was the Stoic exegesis of the last two centuries BCE, especially that by Crates of Mallus and Herodicus of Babylon. Thomas H. Tobin (1983) has pointed out that Stoic and Middle Platonic allegory did not include the recognition of different levels of interpretation: the allegorical interpretations involved either a rejection of the literal or complete obliviousness to it. Philo is the earliest extant example of a writer who tries to maintain the validity of both levels; thus he involved himself in a controversy with other Jewish allegorists.

A novice in the use of Hebrew texts, Philo relied on the Septuagint, which he happily considered inspired. D. W. Gooding has demonstrated that Philo shows no awareness of the Hebrew underlying the Greek translation of the Hebrew Bible, for he uniformly cites the Septuagint, which, given its frequent inadequacy, he would surely not have done without explanation had he known the underlying Hebrew, and he occasionally offers expositions of the Greek that the Hebrew would have forbidden (see David Winston and John Dillon, *Two Treatises of Philo of Alexandria*, Chico, 1983, pp. 119–125).

Thought and Influence. Philo's understanding of biblical thought is rooted in his abiding confidence in the existence of God as a supremely transcendent being, one absolutely without quality, whose pervasive immanence rules and directs all. The first half of this seemingly paradoxical concept of transcendent immanence has its source in the Old and Middle Academies, apparently going back to Plato's successor Speusippus (d. 339/8 BCE), and was more fully elaborated by some of the Neo-Pythagoreans as well as by the Middle Platonist Eudorus of Alexandria (fl. 25 BCE), who postulated a supranoetic First Principle above a pair of opposites, the Monad and the Dyad. The second half derives from a central emphasis of Stoic teaching, which envisions the omnipresent vitality of an all-traversing Logos whose highest terrestrial manifestation is the human intellect, which is identified by both Philo and the Stoics as an inseparable portion of the divine mind. Man is thus akin to the divine and has unbroken access to it from within.

Philo defines two paths that lead to a knowledge of God's existence. In *On Rewards and Punishments* 41 he speaks of those who have apprehended God through his works as advancing on a sort of heavenly ladder and conjecturing his existence through plausible inference. The true friends of God, however, "are those who have apprehended him through himself without the cooperation of reasoned inference, as light is seen by light" (ibid.), a formula later used by Plotinus. Although there is no consensus concerning the precise significance of Philo's second way to God, it is very likely based on his notion of man's direct access to God from within and may perhaps be viewed as an early form of the ontological argument. A similar argument for God's existence seems to be found in both the works of the Stoics and in Plotinus.

Philo's theory of creation is based on Plato's *Timaeus* as interpreted by Middle Platonism. God created the universe out of a relatively nonexistent and qualityless primordial matter that contains nothing lovely and is utterly passive and lifeless. All things were created simultaneously, and the sequential account of creation in *Genesis* is only meant to indicate the logical order in God's design.

Although the human soul, as a fragment of the Logos, might be thought to have a natural claim on immortality, the latter can be forfeited if the soul is not properly assimilated into its divine source. From Philo's Platonist perspective, the body is a corpse entombing the soul, which at its death returns to its own proper life. The gradual removal of the psyche from the sensible realm and its ascent to a life of perfection is represented for Philo by two triads of biblical figures: Enoch, Enosh, and Noah; Abraham, Isaac, and Jacob. The Abraham of Philo's allegory is a mystical philosopher who, after having mastered the encyclical or general studies (symbolized by Hagar), in which stage all he could produce was sophistry (Ishmael), abandoned the realm of sense (symbolized in his parting with Lot) for the brighter regions of intelligible reality and, despite his initial flirtation with Chaldean pantheism, has attained to the highest vision of deity, resulting in his transformation into a perfect embodiment of natural law.

In *Pagan and Christian in an Age of Anxiety,* E. R. Dodds has correctly noted that the ecstatic form of prophecy as defined by Philo is not a description of mystical union but a state of temporary possession (Cambridge, 1965, p. 71f.). Philo, however, speaks also of another form of prophecy, which may be designated "hermeneutical" and is mediated not through ecstatic possession but through the divine voice. Whereas in the state of possession the prophet's sovereign mind is entirely preempted, it is clear from Philo's analysis of the giving of the Decalogue, the paradigm of hermeneutical, or divine-voice, prophecy, that in the latter the inspired mind is extraordinarily quickened. Since ecstatic possession is employed by Philo for the explanation of predictive prophecy alone, whereas the core of the Mosaic prophecy, the special laws, is delivered by him in his role of hermeneutical prophet, it is in this form of prophecy that we must locate Philo's conception of mystical union. In his allegorical interpretation of the divine voice as the projection of a special "rational soul full of clearness and distinctness" making unmediated contact with the inspired mind that "makes the first advance," it is not difficult to discern a reference to the activation of man's intuitive intellect (*On the Decalogue* 33, 35). In Philo's hermeneutical prophecy, then, we may detect the union of the human mind with the divine mind, or, in Dodd's terms, a psychic ascent rather than a supernatural descent.

Philo's mystical passages contain most of the characteristic earmarks of mystical experience: knowledge of God as man's supreme bliss and separation from him as the greatest of evils; the soul's intense yearning for the divine; its recognition of its nothingness and of its need to go out of itself; attachment to God; the realization that it is God alone who acts; a preference for contemplative prayer; a timeless union with the All and the resulting serenity; the suddenness with which the vision appears; the experience of sober intoxication; and, finally, the ebb and flow of mystical experience. Philo was thus, at the very least, an intellectual, if not a practicing, mystic.

Philo never had a major impact on Jewish thought. His name appears nowhere in rabbinic literature, and were it not for the preservation of his works by the church, they would surely have perished. In the Middle Ages Jews had access at best to an Arabic or Syriac translation of a small portion of his works. It was not until the sixteenth century that Philo was rediscovered, by ʿAzaryah dei Rossi, who read his work in a Latin translation and outlined a number of his characteristic doctrines in his *Me'or ʿeinayim* (Mantua, 1573). His attitude toward Philo, however, though appreciative, is at best ambivalent. Yosef Shelomoh Delmedigo (1591–1655) read Philo in the original Greek and made a Hebrew translation of excerpts from his writing, which unfortunately was stolen from him and never recovered. Simone Luzzato, in his Italian *Discorso* (1638) on the Jews of Venice, admired Philo, whom he cited from a Latin version, and believed that his motive for allegorizing the scriptures was to attract his pagan audience. Finally, Naḥman Krochmal (1785–1840) includes in his *Moreh nevukhei ha-zeman* (Guide for the Perplexed of the Time, 1851) a Hebrew translation of the account of Philo by J. A. W. Neander (1789–1850, née David Mendel), a baptized Jew who was a professor of church history in Berlin.

[*Philo's philosophy is also discussed in the independent entry* Logos.]

BIBLIOGRAPHY

The older literature on Philo is fully detailed in Erwin R. Goodenough's *The Politics of Philo Judaeus* (1938; reprint, Hildesheim, 1967), pp. 127–348. An excellent annotated bibliography for the years 1937–1962 is provided by Louis H. Feldman in *Scholarship on Philo and Josephus, 1937–1962* (New York,

1963). Earle Hilgert's "Bibliographia Philoniana, 1935–1975" appears in volume 2.21.1 of *Aufstieg und Niedergang der römischen Welt* (Berlin and New York, 1984) a volume completely devoted to Philo. Günter Mayer's *Index Philoneus* (Berlin, 1974) now supplements Hans Leisegang's index (vol. 7) of the *Editio maior* of Philo, 7 vols. in 4, edited by Leopold Cohn and Paul Wendland (Berlin, 1896–1930).

For German, French, and English translations of Philo, with very useful notes, see *Die Werke Philos von Alexandria*, 7 vols., edited by Leopold Cohn et al. (Breslau, 1909–1964); *Les œuvres de Philon d'Alexandrie*, 36 vols., edited by Roger Arnaldez et al. (Paris, 1961–); and *Philo*, with an English translation by F. H. Colson and G. H. Whitaker, "Loeb Classical Library" (Cambridge, Mass., 1929–1962), plus two supplementary volumes translated by Ralph Marcus (Cambridge, Mass., 1953). Fully annotated editions of Philo's works include *In flaccum*, by Herbert Box (Oxford, 1939); *Legatio ad Gaium*, by E. Mary Smallwood (Leiden, 1961); *De animalibus*, by Abraham Terian (Chico, Calif., 1981); and *De gigantibus* and *Quod Deus sit immutabilis*, by David Winston and John Dillon (Chico, Calif., 1983). A useful anthology of Philo's writings, translated by me, is *Philo of Alexandria: The Contemplative Life, Giants, and Selections* (New York, 1981).

The most balanced general book on Philo is Émile Bréhier's *Les idées philosophiques et religieuses de Philon d'Alexandrie*, 2d ed., rev. (Paris, 1925). The large monographs by Walther Völker, *Fortschritt und Vollendung bei Philo von Alexandrien* (Leipzig, 1938), and Harry A. Wolfson, *Philo: Foundations of Religious Philosophy in Judaism, Christianity and Islam*, 2 vols., rev. ed. (Cambridge, Mass., 1962), are indispensable for their very rich presentations of data but are somewhat one-sided in their interpretations. *Philon d'Alexandrie: Colloque, Centre national de la recherche scientifique, Lyon, 11–15 septembre 1966* (Paris, 1967) offers a splendid series of articles on Philo.

Valentin Nikiprowetzky's *Le commentaire de l'écriture chez Philon d'Alexandrie* (Leiden, 1977) is a rich study of Philo's exegetical approach. Excellent accounts of Philo's Platonism are John Dillon's *The Middle Platonists* (London, 1977), pp. 139–183 and David T. Runia's *Philo of Alexandria and the Timaeus of Plato* (Leiden, 1986). A very stimulating study of the exegetical sources of Philo's cosmological exegesis is Thomas H. Tobin's *The Creation of Man: Philo and the History of Interpretation*, edited by Bruce Vawter (Washington, D.C., 1983). Penetrating studies of Philo's relationship to Judaism are Isaak Heinemann's *Philons griechische und jüdische Bildung* (1929; reprint, Hildesheim, 1962) and Yehoshua Amir's *Die hellenistische Gestalt des Judentums bei Philon von Alexandrien* (Neukirchen-Vluyn, 1983). For a study of Philo's mysticism, see my book *Logos and Mystical Theology in Philo of Alexandria* (Cincinnati, 1985).

DAVID WINSTON

PHILOLOGICAL METHOD. *See* Study of Religion.

PHILOSOPHY. [*This entry explores various ways in which religion interrelates with philosophy.* An Overview *discusses fundamental questions such as what philosophy is and what it does.* Philosophy and Religion *investigates commonalities, differences, and forms of relation between religion and Western philosophy.* Philosophy of Religion *reviews the interests of Philosophy of Religion as a scholarly discipline. For discussion of particular philosophical systems and of the systematic elements of religious thought in various traditions, see* Indian Philosophies; Chinese Philosophy; Buddhist Philosophy; Jewish Thought and Philosophy; *and* Theology. *Islamic philosophy is discussed under* Falsafah; *Islamic theology, under* Kalām.]

An Overview

One of the questions most intriguing to the philosopher is the question "What is philosophy?" Perhaps no other discipline has quite so much difficulty explaining what it is about, and in no other discipline is the question of what it is so germane to the discipline itself. Some sort of answer to this question lies close at hand in the case of the natural and human sciences: biology is the study of life, anthropology the study of man, psychology the study of the psyche. Granted that these answers are not very satisfactory or edifying, they at least provide us with a point of departure; they state the specific area or realm being studied. Philosophy lacks even this point of departure, since it has no special area or realm as its subject matter.

Etymologically, *philosophy* means "the love of wisdom." Wisdom is some sort of knowledge, although it might well take some time and thought before one could say what kind of knowledge it constitutes. Perhaps we can begin by stating three things about wisdom that are quite simple and uncontroversial. (1) Wisdom does not primarily have to do with specific facts or information. (2) Wisdom is not usually to be found in a very young person; it presupposes a good deal of experience and, above all, the ability to learn from experience. (3) Wisdom must have something to do with the manner of living one's life; it must include *praxis*.

The gathering of facts or information does not automatically produce wisdom or make a person wise. Someone who reads newspapers and listens to news reports will at best be well-informed (depending on his sources), but he will not on that account be wise. At the other end of the scale, someone who studies logic and the rules of critical thinking will not automatically become wise either. He will be able to argue well; his thinking will be coherent and well-organized; he will be able to pick out flaws in the arguments of others. These are fine and necessary tools, but not wisdom. It has been pointed out that logic has no content. It is like a sausage grinder; you get out of it what you put into it, only in a better, more palatable form.

As Aristotle pointed out in his *Nicomachean Ethics*, ethics and politics are not suitable studies for the young, be they young in years or in character. Understood in Aristotle's original sense of how best to govern a city, ethics and politics require the observation of human nature and the formulation of general, flexible principles. Above all, it is necessary to recognize the fact that these sciences can never be exact in the way that the natural sciences are; to expect the kind of precision possible in natural science merely betrays false expectations and a lack of understanding of the subject matter.

Finally, one would probably expect of someone who is wise that he would lead a certain kind of life. This is meant not exclusively or, for that matter, even primarily in a moral sense, but rather in the sense of practical knowledge, of understanding. A wise person would have judgment without being judgmental. There are many great, dramatic figures in history whom one would probably not wish to call wise. In fact, Plato was most likely right: the best and wisest life is the unpretentious and undramatic life of an ordinary citizen.

One of the most illuminating statements about the nature of philosophy was made by Immanuel Kant when he said that there were three fundamental questions of concern to human beings: (1) what can I know? (2) what ought I to do? (3) what may I hope? These questions, taken together, add up to a final question: what is man? Kant attempted to answer them in his three main works: the question of knowledge in the *Critique of Pure Reason*, the question of ethics in the *Critique of Practical Reason*, and the question of what we may hope for in the *Critique of Judgment*.

Having found the question "What is philosophy?" impervious to instant answers, we might pose the question "Who is the philosopher?" In a broad sense, everybody is. Every thinking human being asks certain fundamental questions: what am I doing in the world? how did I get here? what am I supposed to be doing? what is going to happen to me? what does it all mean? Some ask themselves more abstract questions, such as whether the world has a beginning or not. The philosopher is the person who thinks and asks; he does not necessarily write books. Three of the greatest thinkers of history, Socrates, Buddha, and Jesus, wrote nothing. One could cite many more.

In a less general sense, the philosopher is the one who asks what is real. This question led the Greeks, with whom philosophy as we know it began, to inquire into the nature of change and the relation of being (what does not change) to becoming. At least three of the most philosophical questions of all were staked out by the Greeks: the relation of (1) being to becoming; (2) reality to appearance; and (3) being to thinking. This leads us to take a brief look at the history of philosophy.

History. There are some philosophers who say that philosophy is a specifically Western (Greek) phenomenon and that the East does not have "philosophy" in the strict sense of that term. This seems too biased a view; Eastern thought will be briefly discussed in this article. However, Western philosophy does have its roots in the Greeks, and we turn now to a consideration of them.

Western philosophy began with the pre-Socratics, so called because they lived before Socrates. These thinkers, often erroneously thought to be somewhat "primitive," searched for the first principle *(archē)* in things. Thales, for instance, found that principle in water, Anaximander in the boundless *(apeiron)*, Heraclitus in the *logos*, Parmenides in being. The simplicity and profundity of their vision is splendid and their influence on the two greatest of Greek thinkers, Plato and Aristotle, extensive. Thus began the tradition of the history of philosophy, of thinkers learning from each other, often disagreeing and being stimulated to formulate their own ideas. It is not the case, as has been alleged, that philosophers never come up with any definitive answers because they all disagree with one another, canceling one another out, so to speak, so that we end up with nothing at all. Each thinker learns from his predecessors; without Socrates there would never have been a Plato; without Plato, no Aristotle. Thus, the history of philosophy can be viewed as a long critical dialogue tracing shifting conceptions of reality.

Socrates was the true model of a philosopher. Contrasting himself with the Sophists, who claimed to have knowledge and the ability to teach it and who took money for their services, Socrates said that he knew that he knew nothing, and he therefore also taught nothing. In Plato's dialogue *Theatetus*, Socrates compares himself to a midwife who is herself barren but who helps others to give birth. The Sophists were the natural enemies of Socrates (and Plato). They taught a kind of empty rhetoric that enabled their pupils to sound impressive and win arguments, but the real philosophical issues and questions were lost to them.

These issues and questions eventually led Plato to formulate his famous theory of Forms, or Ideas *(idea, eidos)*. A just man becomes just by imitating or participating in the perfect, eternal, changeless reality of justice itself. Justice itself is by no means a mere mental concept; it is what is really real. This, in a nutshell, is what is generally meant by the term *Platonism.* Reality lies in the Form, or Idea, which can be known only by the mind, not the senses. Reality is not in the mind, but it is accessible only to the mind.

If we accept Whitehead's somewhat oversimplified, dramatic statement that "the whole history of philosophy is nothing but a series of footnotes on Plato," this thumbnail sketch may suffice to indicate the direction that the history of philosophy was to take. Two major periods followed the Greek one: the medieval, when philosophy came together with the Judeo-Christian tradition, and the modern, beginning with Descartes. In the medieval period, philosophy went hand in hand with theology and was employed in working out proofs of God's existence or in clarifying the status of the Platonic Forms, then known as "universals."

With his well-known dictum "Cogito, ergo sum" ("I think, therefore I am"), Descartes opened up what is called the modern period of philosophy. The term *modern,* in this case, indicates the belief that the unshakable foundation of all knowledge lies in the thinking subject. By isolating the subject as what alone is real, Descartes ushered in the era of subjectivism, with its concomitant dualisms of mind-body, mind-matter, and subject-object—dualisms that contemporary philosophers are still struggling to overcome and that permeate our everyday language and life.

Areas of Philosophy. Having stated that philosophy has no specifiable subject matter peculiar to it, we might take a look at some of the areas it prefers to deal with. These areas are articulated into what might be called different branches of philosophy. Let us preface this discussion with the remark that the phrase "philosophy of" can precede almost anything. "The philosophy of sport" and "the philosophy of fashion" impart a special perspective on an independent subject matter.

As primary branches of philosophy, we might cite ethics, epistemology, logic, aesthetics, metaphysics, and ontology; on a secondary level, philosophy of law, philosophy of politics, philosophy of science, philosophy of language, and philosophy of religion. With the exception of philosophy of religion, we shall not discuss these secondary branches.

The primary branches are as old as philosophy itself—they go back to Plato. The first four are easily delineated; the last two are more problematic. An ethic is something that every human being has; it is an idea of how he wants to live his life. Even if his ethic is what one would call highly unethical, even if his concern is solely for his own interest, this view still constitutes his ethic, his idea of the best way to go through life. The question of this "unethical" ethic is discussed in detail by Plato in his *Republic:* is the unjust man better off than the just one? Plato concludes that the height of justice is to appear unjust but to be just; the height of injustice is to appear just but to be unjust. Justice is a matter of inner balance and harmony; it has nothing to do with gain, riches, or power.

Epistemology and logic are more specialized and technical branches of philosophy. They deal with theories of how we know things and the laws of thought. Finally, although the term *aesthetics* (philosophy of art) was coined by Alexander Baumgarten only in the eighteenth century, Western inquiry into the nature of art goes back as far as Plato and Aristotle. Aesthetics and the philosophy of art reached a culmination as the meeting place of nature and spirit in the philosophy of Kant, Schiller, and the other German Idealists. The work of art, they believed, is nature transformed by spirit.

Perhaps the most intelligible way to order terms unfamiliar to the nonphilosopher such as *metaphysics* and *ontology* is initially to adopt the classification set forth by Christian Wolff (1679–1754). *Metaphysics* generally refers to that which goes beyond *(meta)* the physical, although Aristotle's book of that name is so titled simply because he wrote it after the *Physics;* the two books, the *Physics* and the *Metaphysics,* have roughly the same (metaphysical) subject matter. To put it briefly, metaphysics is supposed to deal with what is ultimate.

Wolff divided metaphysics into two branches: general metaphysics *(metaphysica generalis)* and special metaphysics *(metaphysica specialis).* General metaphysics is equivalent to ontology, the study of being, or what is (in Greek, *to on*) in its generic traits. Special metaphysics consists of three parts: rational psychology (study of the soul), rational cosmology (study of the cosmos or world), and rational theology (study of God). Immanuel Kant called these three parts the Ideas of Pure Reason. By this he meant that these were the ultimate ideas that reason arrived at in its inherent attempt to unify the manifold (synthesize).

Philosophy and Religion. Whereas in the East the relation of philosophy and religion is generally so unproblematic that there is often no clear-cut distinction between the two, the situation in the West is not so simple. The mainstream of Western philosophy was closely involved with religious questions until the late nineteenth century; there was certainly never a question of major conflict. The Greeks in general and Plato in particular pursued questions that are usually taken to be religious (e.g., the immortality of the soul, transmigration and the possibility of a future life or lives, the existence of the godlike), although there was no emphasis on man's relation to a personal deity. When philosophy joined hands with the Judeo-Christian tradition in late antiquity, it became almost indissolubly linked to theology. With that union arose the problem of reconciling philosophical thought with established dogma. For example the eternity of the world and transmigration of souls are incompatible with Christian dogma. When Descartes laid the foundation for knowledge in the thinking subject (in reason as opposed to faith), the possibility was created for the eventual parting of ways between philosophy and religion.

This parting took place in the nineteenth century with such thinkers as Feuerbach, Marx, and, especially, Nietzsche, with his pronouncement that God is dead. Since that time, philosophers may or may not have religious concerns. For example, the twentieth-century movement labeled existentialism can be divided into two camps: a theistic one (Marcel, Maritain) and an atheistic one (Sartre, Camus). Then there are those thinkers whom one could call religious but who have nothing to do with explicitly theological questions; their religious sense provides a background for their philosophizing (Heidegger, Wittgenstein). Finally, there are thinkers who believe that religious questions are not the business of philosophy, the main function of which is to develop critical argument (Russell, Moore). A twentieth-century thinker and theologian who sought to mediate between philosophy and religion, Paul Tillich, defines man in terms of his ultimate concern, which is a truly religious, but not a theological, definition. Instead of defining man as the animal with reason *(zoon logon echon)*, as Aristotle and virtually everyone after him did, Tillich defines him in terms of his link to something ultimate or divine. In a similar vein, Heidegger speaks of man in terms of his relation to being.

It was, however, chiefly theology, as distinct from religion, that joined with philosophy, by using such concepts as Plato's Good *(agathon)* and Aristotle's Unmoved Mover to interpret theological ideas. *Religion* would appear to be a broader and less sharply defined term than *theology*. The etymological root of the word *religion* is the same as that of *yoga;* the root means "to join or link," and *yoga* comes to mean "to join (man to something transcending him)."

Thus, perhaps the main question with regard to the relation of philosophy to religion is whether man is conceived as a self-contained and self-sufficient physical being whose essence coincides with his material existence or as a spiritual being whose existence points beyond himself and the "human-all-too-human." In the latter case, philosophy and religion coalesce; in the former, they diverge.

Not only is the question of belief in a divine being or some kind of transcendence at stake in the question of religion, but also the question of the nature of man. If man is conceived purely as a natural being, there seems to be no need or perhaps no room for anything godlike. One can draw a certain parallel between religion and art here. One can conceive of art, as did Freud, as a surrogate for more basic (more real) sexual drives. This conception makes a mockery of any kind of transcendence; transcendence is utterly fabricated, a futile, self-deluding, and mildly ridiculous attempt to escape the urgency of ultimately insatiable appetites. This view posits man's animality, his body, as the very basis of his being and renders his spiritual side superfluous, not to say suspect. In this view, man cannot be defined as Aristotle's rational animal; he is the botched-up animal. Animals do not suffer from doubts, despair, depression; they are totally what they are. They are "innocent." But man is "the disease of nature" (Nietzsche). "He is not what he is and is what he is not"; he is "a useless passion" (Sartre). His so-called spirituality serves only to estrange him from himself. Certainly, if man cannot achieve a certain transcendence, not just of his body, but of himself, his spirituality will only disturb the comforts of animal existence. The plays of Samuel Beckett are among the most powerful presentations of what human life utterly lacking in transcendence is like.

Diverse Philosophical Positions. Some mention must be made of the diversity of philosophical positions with regard to the nature of reality. These positions lie between the two opposite poles of idealism and empiricism, between stressing the importance of reason and of the senses. We seem to have two main accesses to the nature of the world and reality: our senses, which tell us about colors, sounds, and so forth, and reason, which tells us about things like mathematical truths and the existence of God. Those philosophers who feel that the senses are the most important access to reality tend to downplay the activity of the mind, restricting it to combining and relating sense impressions. The most influential exponent of this view was the empiricist John Locke. At the other end of the scale, we have the rationalist or idealist who mistrusts the senses because they often deceive us and who looks to reason or the mind for the foundation of knowledge. Plato was the first to articulate fully this view, which has had a long and varied history.

Many gradations exist between these two extremes of empiricism and rationalism. Some philosophers combine them in various ways; for example, Berkeley, who is both empirical and idealist (he is the philosopher who denied the existence of matter), or Kant, who insisted that we need both sense experience and the understanding in order to have knowledge. More recently, we have had such movements as pragmatism and phenomenology, which seek to overcome the duality—pragmatism by turning its attention away from such purely theoretical questions to more practical ones (if it works, it is "true"), and phenomenology by looking at the "things themselves" as they show themselves prior to any such division. In any case, these "isms" never exhaust the philosopher's thought; they are convenient labels that can help us to orient ourselves initially; more they cannot and should not be intended to do.

Eastern Perspectives. The time is approaching when Western philosophers will no longer be able to neglect Eastern thought with impunity. Hinduism and Buddhism in India, Buddhism, Taoism, and Confucianism in China, to name just two cultures, form a vast tradition from which the West can learn. But because these traditions are so vast, it will take time to get all the material translated, make it available, and assimilate it. The following brief comments are broad and sweeping.

In general, Eastern thought does not separate philosophy and religion. The main concern of its philosophy as well as its religion can be said to be soteriological, focusing on some kind of salvation of the individual. *Salvation* means literally "to make whole." In India, salvation can be conceived as union of the self *(ātman)* with the Absolute *(brahman)* in Hinduism or as the attainment of *nirvāṇa* (liberation, enlightenment) in Buddhism. In both of these religions, salvation means the cessation of rebirths and release from *saṃsāra,* the round of birth and death perpetuated by the individual's craving or ignorance. The Indian philosophical tradition is richly speculative, and many rather elaborate metaphysical systems have been developed. In particular, Indian theories of consciousness are intriguingly elaborate and subtle, far outstripping anything of this sort the West has produced. For example, certain Buddhist schools enumerate as many as one hundred elements of consciousness.

As Buddhism gradually lost ground in India, it moved on to China, where it was assimilated to the indigenous religions of Taoism and Confucianism. Chinese thought manifests a more practical and concrete temperament than the Indian, and much of the Buddhist metaphysical speculation was discarded. This tendency continued as Buddhism was later transmitted to Japan.

Thus far, Eastern influence on Western thinkers has been minimal. Leibniz (1646) was probably one of the first philosophers to show an interest in China. This is no mere coincidence; there are truly remarkable affinities between his *Monadology* and Hua-yen Buddhism. In the nineteenth century, Hegel referred to Eastern thought in his *History of Philosophy,* but his thoroughly Western bias resulted in a rather condescending treatment. Schopenhauer made use of both Hindu and Buddhist ideas, weaving them into a remarkable fabric with Platonism and Kantianism. And Nietzsche, in his attack on traditional philosophy and religion, lumped Buddhism together with Christianity, pronouncing them both "religions of exhaustion." A serious, fruitful dialogue has yet to take place.

Current Trends. In conclusion, one might well raise the timely questions of where philosophers are heading now and what sorts of issues attract their attention. The answers will, of course, vary with different countries and areas of specialization. But a few general, tentative observations can be made.

The interest in metaphysics seems to be definitely on the wane. With the great figures of German Idealism (Fichte, Hegel, Schelling) and their British counterparts, metaphysics may have exhausted its possibilities. The era of systems and of the dominance of reason and rationality would appear to lie in the past. A lingering and self-perpetuating interest in Marx and Freud is still evident in an emphasis on man as a natural being and a sexual being. If there is one trend that is dominant today, it is that philosophers are preoccupied with the question of language, though in the most diverse ways imaginable. From Wittgenstein's philosophy of ordinary language to Heidegger's poetic, noncalculative thinking to the intricacies of the French schools, philosophers are taking a hard look at the way we use and structure language or the way it structures us. These are problems that religious thinkers have long been aware of in their own province. Their particular formulation of the problem asks how we can use finite language, the language naming finite things (we have no other), to speak about something neither finite nor a thing.

It is to be hoped that the philosophers will not encapsulate themselves in technical areas of academic specialization, but will be able to face and grapple with the issues looming before us today. The gloomiest of the existentialists seem to have played themselves out without having found much solace for the predicaments they delineated, but the force of what they expressed still continues in our literature, drama, and art in a more vivid, aesthetic form.

If philosophy stays aloof from the existential concerns of the human being, as it did and does in movements so vastly different as Scholasticism and logical positivism, it loses its original (Platonic) sense of a quest for something transcending man. Aristotle said that philosophy begins in wonder. Perhaps in times of spiritual destitution such as our own, wonder could be the beginning of the end of thoughtlessness. As Heidegger, quoting his favorite German poet, Hölderlin, says: where the danger grows, there also grows the saving power. The philosopher must strive to avoid the extremes of petulant pessimism and mindless optimism.

[*The encyclopedia includes separate entries on philosophers, philosophical movements, and particular philosophical ideas mentioned herein. Philosophical aspects of religious thought are also discussed in* Aesthetics; Apologetics; Cosmology; Henotheism; Knowledge and Ignorance; Morality and Religion; Pantheism and Panentheism; Reason; Religious Experience; Revelation; Soteriology; Soul; Theism; Theodicy; Transcendence and Immanence; *and* Truth.]

BIBLIOGRAPHY

The following works, given in chronological order, represent classics in the development of Western philosophical thought.

Plato. *Collected Dialogues.* Edited by Edith Hamilton and Huntington Cairns. New York, 1963.

Aristotle. *The Basic Works of Aristotle.* Edited by Richard McKeon. New York, 1941.

Augustine. *The Confessions of St. Augustine.* Translated by Edward B. Pusey. New York, 1961.

Thomas Aquinas. *Concerning Being and Essence.* Translated by George G. Leckie. New York, 1965.

Descartes, René. *Meditations on First Philosophy.* Translated by Donald A. Cress. Indianapolis, 1979.

Spinoza, Barukh. *Ethics.* Translated by William Hale White, revised by Amelia Hutchinson Stirling. New York, 1949.

Leibniz, G. W. *Discourse on Metaphysics, Correspondence with Arnauld, and Monadology.* Translated by George R. Montgomery. Chicago, 1962.

Locke, John. *An Essay concerning Human Understanding.* Edited by Peter H. Nidditch. Corr. ed. Oxford, 1979.

Berkeley, George. *Three Dialogues between Hylas and Philonous.* Edited by Colin M. Turbayne. New York, 1954.

Hume, David. *A Treatise on Human Nature.* 3 vols. London, 1739.

Kant, Immanuel. *Critique of Pure Reason.* Translated by Norman Kemp Smith. New York, 1929.

Hegel, G. W. F. *Phenomenology of Spirit.* Translated by A. V. Miller. Oxford, 1977.

Heidegger, Martin. *Being and Time.* Translated by John Macquarrie and Edward Robinson. New York, 1962.

Wittgenstein, Ludwig. *Tractatus logico philosophicus.* Translated by C. K. Ogden. London, 1958.

JOAN STAMBAUGH

Philosophy and Religion

The two enduring forms of spiritual expression designated by the terms *religion* and *philosophy* quite obviously never confront each other as such; they enter into relations with one another only in historical and specific terms. It is in the visions of individual philosophers as they intersect with the beliefs and the practices of particular religious traditions that we find the living relations between religion and philosophy.

The Nature of Religion and Philosophy and Their Relation to Each Other. A fine example of the interaction between religion and philosophy is found in the thought of Clement (150?–215?) and Origen (c. 185–c. 254), usually known as the Christian Platonists of Alexandria because their school was located in that ancient center of Hellenistic culture. As this appellation implies, they were engaged in interpreting the basic beliefs of Christianity concerning God, Christ, man, and the world in terms of the insights of the Neoplatonic philosophy current in their time. More than a century earlier, the Jewish philosopher Philo Judaeus (d. 45–50 CE) carried out much the same enterprise for the Hebraic tradition, drawing chiefly on the thought of the Greek philosopher Plato (c. 429–347 BCE), and the Pythagorean and Stoic schools. This type of interpreting—or dialogue, if you will—involving the use of the Greco-Roman philosophical systems for formulating the ideas and elucidating the religious insights of the biblical tradition, continued throughout the Middle Ages and lasted until the end of the Renaissance.

Despite the fact that the historical interactions between religion and philosophy must always be concrete—since it is the thought of a particular philosopher or school of philosophy that is interacting with a specific religious tradition—both are themselves enduring forms to be found in every culture, and they are marked by general features that serve to distinguish one from the other. It is on this account that we not only can but must come to some theoretical understanding of how religious faith and philosophical reflection are related not only as a matter of historical fact but as one of principle. To speak of principle means to approach the task of reaching down to the roots of these two spiritual forms, universal in the experience of mankind, in an attempt to grasp what they essentially are and to determine how they should be related to each other. That the task is not easy should be obvious in view of the enormous variety of religious experiences and of philosophical outlooks recorded in human history. The task is, nevertheless, inescapable if we are to understand ourselves, and therefore we must not be dissuaded by the knowledge that no one characterization of either religion or philosophy can capture everything or satisfy everybody.

The American philosopher and psychologist William James (1842–1910), in his epoch-making study *The Varieties of Religious Experience* (1902), quite rightly described religion as concerned chiefly with a strategy for redemption calling all human beings away from the snares and illusions of natural existence and back to their true selves. That such a strategy is needed follows from the fact, not always sufficiently recognized, that every religion offers a diagnosis of the human predicament, a judgment focusing attention on some flaw or defect in natural existence that stands as an obstacle between ourselves and the ideal life envisioned by the particular religion in question. Redemption, in short, means being delivered from that flaw through a divine power capable of overcoming it. And the nature of the deliverance is determined in every religious faith by the character of the flaw envisaged. Both the diagnosis and the strategy of redemption derive from the lives and insights of the founders, sages, and prophets upon which the religious tradition rests. The articulated beliefs and practices that define a particular religious tradition are transmitted from age to age through historical communities of faith. Individuals owe their life to the tradition in which they stand, but the tradition owes its life to the continuing community sustained by the spiritual bonds existing between the members.

Philosophy, on the other hand, has as its chief concern the attainment of a comprehensive theoretical understanding of the many types and levels of being in the universe and their relations to each other, including a conception of the place to be assigned in the cosmic scheme to human beings and their experience. As far as Western philosophy is concerned, two different lines of inquiry manifested themselves in the earliest stages of development. On one side curiosity was directed toward the discovery of the most pervasive or universal traits exhibited by everything that is. Such features as unity and plurality, identity and difference, spatial and temporal location, acting and being acted upon were singled out as constituting the universal order holding sway throughout the universe. This line of inquiry can be called the quest for the categories ingredient in both the world and the structure of human thought and knowledge about it. Without pushing the identification too far, we may say that this side of philosophy is one that it shares with science. The affinity is nicely illustrated by the fact that what we call science today went by the name of "natural philosophy" in the seventeenth and eighteenth centuries, as can be seen from the full title of the famous treatise written by the English physicist Isaac Newton (1642–1727), *Principia mathematica philosophiae naturalis* (1687).

On its other side, philosophy meant a bolder and more speculative inquiry prompted by wonder about the being of things. Wonder in the face of the fact that there is anything at all and wonder about what there might be about things that sustains them and causes them to stand out against nothingness and the void. This concern for what came to be called metaphysics in one of its senses has expressed itself in the quest for a ground not only of the being of things but of human being as well; the latter concern led to the inclusion of speculative insight about the good and ideal human existence within the scope of philosophy. Understood in this sense, philosophy shows its affinity with the concerns of religion, an overlap of interest that has in the past occasioned both fruitful cooperation as well as conflict between them. The two, however, remain distinct by virtue of their different aims and approaches. This difference may be summed up in a way that is symbolic for both: the reality of the divine, however conceived, is always the initial conviction of the religious outlook, while for philosophy that reality remains the final or ultimate problem.

There is yet another difference between religion and philosophy, and its meaning becomes clear when we take into account what was said previously about the role of the religious community. Philosophical analyses and visions are the products of solitary thinkers whose doctrines have indeed formed the basis of traditions and schools of thought, witness Plato and the Greek philosopher Aristotle (384–322 BCE), but such schools do not perform the same functions as a religious community. The latter exists to bring together many individuals in a spiritual unity that transfigures life; schools of thought are primarily focal points of understanding and a place for the meeting of minds.

Much of the foregoing analysis has, of course, been based entirely on the situation in the West, where the three major faiths—Judaism, Islam, and Christianity—found themselves confronted with the autonomous philosophical systems developed in the classical world. These systems were autonomous in the sense that they were not developed under the special aegis of religious belief, even if they were sometimes influenced by religious ideas. They represent the reflections of individual minds attempting to articulate a comprehensive vision of what there truly is above and beyond appearances and mere opinions. The case of Aristotle, although in some respects unique, provides us with a clear illustration. His thought, ranging as it does over the entire spectrum of experience and existence, embraces a profound conception of God as, among other things, the Unmoved Mover. There is, as has often been pointed out, no essential connection between this conception of God and religion. In fact the thought of Aristotle on this point has often been described as the paradigm of conceptions of God without religion.

It is necessary to emphasize the autonomous nature of the classical philosophical systems for at least two reasons. One is the tension resulting from the fact that these philosophies, while useful in providing the concepts and principles through which primary religious experience and insight could be precisely expressed, stood at the same time as rival interpretations of reality to which the biblically based religions had to come to terms. To appeal to Aristotle again for an illustration, his conception of the world as eternal, or as not having come into being in time, posed a serious problem with regard to so central a doctrine of biblical religion as that of creation. Religious thinkers, therefore, could not avail themselves of his thought as a framework for theology without first reinterpreting it at crucial points. It is noteworthy that the tension thus introduced, plus the fear of distorting the religious message by expressing it in philosophical terms, led some thinkers, especially representatives of early Latin Christianity, to reject philosophy as an alien medium and to declare, with Tertullian (160?–225?), that "Jerusalem has nothing to do with Athens." This negative attitude, however, did not prevail, and the subsequent course of Western religious thought, at least until the Reformation, was marked by a continuous interaction between philosophical and religious ideas.

The second reason for dwelling on the autonomy of the philosophies that figured so largely in the religious thought of the West is that it opens to view a most important contrast with much Eastern thought. It is generally admitted that there is not to be found in the Hindu and Buddhist traditions, for example, any sharp and clear distinction between religion and philosophy. The two are closely interwoven, and there is no clear historical counterpart in the history of these traditions to the situation in the West, where more or less clearly defined religions encountered distinctive and already formed philosophies. We must, of course, bear in mind that we are speaking in very general terms; one cannot say dogmatically that no distinction whatever was drawn between religion and philosophy in the Eastern cultures, especially in view of some difficult cases such as Confucianism and Taoism. The former is often described not as a religion but as a philosophical system of ethics, and the latter seems to have had its roots primarily in philosophical reflections that in time assumed religious form. Contemporary historical scholars, moreover, in rewriting the history of Indian thought, for example, are putting more emphasis, possibly under Western influence, on the strictly philosophical theories represented by the classical systems of thought and distinguishing them from "salvation doctrines" said to be representative of religion. Be this as it may, the important point is that the problems faced by Western thinkers in relating religion and philosophy were quite different from those confronting their counterparts in the East. It is one thing to attempt to relate two forms of insight to each other starting within a historical situation in which they meet each other as quite distinct, and another to confront the problem of their interconnections in cultures where the two were never clearly separated from the outset.

Impact of Kant's Philosophy and the Empiricist Criterion of Meaning. Concentrating on Western civilization, where the interaction between religious faith and philosophical inquiry has so largely determined the history of both, we must understand the impact of two decisive developments that greatly disrupted the sort of exchange that had resulted in the monumental philosophico-religious syntheses represented by such thinkers as Augustine of Hippo (354–430); Anselm of Canterbury (1033–1109); Philo Judaeus; Moses Maimonides, the medieval Jewish philosopher (1135–1204); Bonaventure, the scholastic theologian and philosopher (1217–1274); Duns Scotus, Scottish philosopher and theologian (1265?–1308); and Thomas Aquinas, author of the monumental *Summa theologiae* (1226–1274); as well as such Muslim thinkers as Ibn Rushd (Averroës, 1126–1198) and Ibn Sīnā (Avicenna, 980–1037), who sustained for Islamic religion the same kind of dialogue with Aristotle carried on for Christianity by Albertus Magnus, the German scholastic philosopher (1200–1280) and Thomas Aquinas. The first of these developments was the attack by the German philosopher Immanuel Kant (1724–1804) on the traditional metaphysics that had so long served as a medium of expression for religious belief; the second was the claim, stemming from the philosophies of empiricism, that there is a single criterion for determining the meaning and truth value of all statements, and that this criterion is found in sense experience and the knowledge represented by science. Relations between philosophy and religion had been determined since the beginning of the nineteenth century by the response to Kant and since early in the twentieth century have been characterized by attempts on the part of religious thinkers to deal with what came to be known as the empiricist criterion of meaning.

Three strategies have been proposed for overcoming the obstacles that arose and impeded a continuation of the classical dialogue between religious insight and philosophical reflection. The first is represented by those religious thinkers who accepted the Kantian thesis that our knowledge extends no further than mathematics and what he called the general science of nature, so that metaphysics, and especially the classical proofs for the existence of God, become invalid, since they transcend the limits of what the human understanding can know. Because these thinkers were committed to upholding the validity of religion, their task was to find some new basis for it other than metaphysics and philosophy. The second strategy found expression in those who accepted the theory of one criterion of meaning and who, insofar as they were concerned with religion at all, identified it with emotion, feeling, and attitudes, all of which were said to be devoid of cognitive significance. This was the position of positivism or logical empiricism. Finally, there was the alternative associated chiefly with the name of the Austrian philosopher Ludwig Wittgenstein (1889–1951), who saw the limitations of the empiricist criterion of meaning and the difficulties involved in justifying it. Consequently, he proposed instead to focus attention not on meaning but on the use of language in different contexts of experience—aesthetic, economic, religious, moral, and so forth. These different uses of language were called "language games," and he described the language of religion as distinctive because it expresses what he called a "form of life." Just as in the preceding alternative, however, no cognitive status can be claimed for religious utterance, although it must be admitted that in shifting from meaning to use Wittgenstein intended to criticize positivism for having gone too far.

It should be evident that each of these alternatives represents a response to the Kantian philosophy, with its restriction of reason to the bounds of sense and of knowledge to science. The proponents of all three alternatives basically accepted Kant's analysis as valid, but with important differences. Those who adopted the first strategy had the strongest concern for preserving religion, and they consequently sought to find new foundations for it, while at the same time leaving Kant's position intact. The positivists, on the whole, regarded religion as outmoded and its utterances as without meaning; in this they went beyond Kant in abolishing his distinction between what can be meaningfully thought and what can be known. Kant, that is to say, held that we can validly think the idea of God, because reason demands that we do, but that knowledge of the reality meant is not possible for us. In identifying meaning with the possibility of verification in sense experience, the positivists had to deny that the idea of God is meaningful in any sense. Wittgenstein, though not alone in his criticism, had, nevertheless, the most influential voice in turning back the positivist approach. He claimed, in effect, that the use of language in theoretical science is not its only use; account must be taken as well of the functions of language in other contexts of experience, including the religious. Thus, he argued, instead of stopping inquiry before it begins by invoking the positivist criterion of meaning and declaring religious expression meaningless, the task is to understand the grammar and the logic of the language and forms of expression actually used by the members of religious communities. One very significant consequence of this approach was the discovery that "religious language" embraces a considerable variety of types of expression and that careful distinctions are necessary if each type is to be understood in terms proper to itself. The devotional language of worship, for example, differs in important respects from the conceptual language needed for theology, which in turn differs from the languages represented by myth, parable, exhortation, and prophetic insight.

Invaluable as this sort of clarification has been in fostering a better understanding of what religion is and means, it does not engage the problem of validity in religion, nor does it go very far in relating religion to other dimensions of experience. In fact the language-game approach in the hands of Wittgenstein and his followers has tended to encapsulate religion in a sphere of sheer faith—fideism—cut off from all forms of knowledge. So great a gap between reason and faith has been brought about that Wittgenstein could find no way of overcoming it. On the contrary, he even claimed that if there were a single scrap of "empirical" evidence to support what is intended to be a religious statement, it would thereby cease to be "religious." The major difficulty with such a position is that it fails to deal with the most important fact about religious belief, which is that those who adhere to it do so with the firm conviction that it is true, that reality is in accord with it, even if they are unable to give an account of what this precisely means in philosophical terms.

Enough has been said about the second and third alternatives to indicate that they are not ultimately satisfactory. I should now like to return to the first alternative and mention briefly a number of the proposals that have been made to find a new basis for religion without violating the limits imposed by Kant. I shall suggest that each of these proposals expresses something important, but that no one of them achieves a satisfactory relation between religion and philosophy. Finally, I shall propose a fourth alternative that is actually a new version of the ancient dialogue between religion and philosophy.

One of the most important religious responses to Kant was the thought of the German theologian Albrecht Ritschl (1822–1889) and his school, which made its appearance at the middle of the nineteenth century. He sought to free theology from dependence on metaphysics by stressing the essentially moral meaning of religious conceptions. Following Kant in stressing the primacy of practical reason, Ritschl envisaged Christianity as a faith aimed at the realization of a practical ideal of human life. While it is correct to say that Ritschl found the basis of theology not in metaphysics but in a value judgment expressing the practical significance of a divine reality for us, the value judgment in question is of a complex sort. Jesus, the object in human experience possessing the value of Godhead, is the occasion upon which we apprehend him as the bearer of grace, the one who reveals God as love. Insofar as we experience and evaluate the action of Jesus in revealing God, we see him as God. According to Ritschl, however, it is not through command or authority that Jesus is effective, but only through his moral teachings. In realizing God's goal, Jesus also realizes our goal, which is the fulfillment of our own purpose in life. Ritschl saw in this fundamental evaluation the justification whereby we gain admission to the kingdom of God through Jesus in the church. In making the moral dimension central, Ritschl was able to retain a theology unaffected by Kant's elimination of classical metaphysics.

This proposed solution of the relation between philosophy and religion is not, however, without difficulties. Granted that Ritschl's position involves something more than a simple reduction of the religious to the moral, the fact remains that the latter is too limited in scope to do justice to the religious concern. Morality is concerned primarily with what a person is to do, while religion aims at what a person is to be, and the problem of being presents itself at this point in the form of the need to find a basis for the unity and integrity of the person, something not to be resolved within the confines of morality and values. There is, in addition, the fact that the biblical message involves other theological concepts requiring an articulation that takes us beyond the resources of morality and valuation.

A second, and far more influential, attempt to resolve the problem was made by the brilliant Danish thinker Søren Kierkegaard (1813–1855). Using the philosophy of Absolute Spirit set forth by the German philosopher G. W. F. Hegel (1770–1831) as both a foil and the focal point of his attack, and declaring that "Kant is my philosopher," Kierkegaard insisted that Christianity is concerned primarily with the relation of faith between God and human beings and that on this account it stands over against speculative philosophy and all efforts to make Christian doctrine "rational." According to Kierkegaard, the central Christian claim that the eternal has entered time is the "absolute paradox," defying all mediation and rational explanation; God confronts man's pride and refusal to acknowledge his status as a creature, so that religion is and must always appear as an "offense." If it does not, says Kierkegaard, then it is inauthentic and conventional for having been made "palatable" or consonant with human reason. From this perspective, rooted in the primacy of *existence*—that is, the individual who finds himself "there" in a time and place confronting the problem of salvation—attempts like that of Hegel to use speculative reason to break through the mystery of the eternal entering time succeed only in distorting the essential religious message, for, Kierkegaard insisted, this message is simply "absurd" when considered from the standpoint of human reason. Although not without philosophical acumen of his own, Kierkegaard devoted himself, through his genius for irony, wit, paradox, and profound psychological insight, to the confounding of philosophy, thus opening a wide gap between reason and religion. Kierkegaard could well afford to accept the strictures on theoretical reason dictated by Kant's philosophy, since he was firmly convinced that Christianity neither can nor need be made "rational."

For all of its undoubted insights into the human condition and the meaning of God and faith, Kierkegaard's position is ultimately unstable. In the face of Hegel's massive rationalism, Kierkegaard was undoubtedly right in seeking to discover the reality of the individual and the need to appropriate Christian faith in a personal commitment, something that does not happen by understanding alone. But in equating thought with possibility, so that it necessarily abstracts from existing (the individual's being and situation), Kierkegaard not only lost the basis upon which thought can be said to penetrate and illuminate human life, but he was forced as well to turn existence into a "surd" element—"what thought cannot think." As subsequent developments proved, the step from the "surd" to the "absurd" is quite short and contains a pitfall. The withdrawal of reflective thought from existence led ultimately to the declaration that religion is illusory because human existence itself is absurd. That is to say, existence came to be thought absurd, not in the ironic and paradoxical Kierkegaardian sense, but rather in the sense established by the French philosopher Jean-Paul Sartre (1905–1980), according to which religion is abolished and no meaning attaches to human existence in itself but is found only in what we, through the heroic human will, can succeed in creating for ourselves. Kierkegaard, to be sure, is not to be held accountable for this later development, but in his insistence on the irreconcilability of religion and philosophy, he left religion open to dissolution by those who could see no rationality in it and were unpersuaded by his modern version of the ancient proclamation, "I believe because it is absurd."

Yet another alternative framework for the articulation of religious insight took the form of an appeal to "sacred history," or the history of divine redemption.

From this standpoint, theology has to do not with the classical doctrine of God expressed, as in the case of the medieval theologians, through philosophical categories, but with the activity of God, discernible through the eyes of faith, in accomplishing the redemption of the whole creation through history. This position finds strong support in the undoubtedly valid, even if sometimes exaggerated, distinction between the fundamental patterns exhibited by Hebraic and Greek thought. The latter, stressing form and the timelessness attached to being and truth, found itself, insofar as attention was focused on history at all, interpreting the course of human events in essentially cyclical terms after the fashion of the continual recurrence of forms in the natural world. Hebraic thought, by contrast, was marked not only by a powerful sense of the reality of time and a linear history, but by the belief that historical development is itself the medium through which the nature, and especially the will, of God is revealed.

Numerous attempts have been made, going back to the German theologians Wilhelm Herrmann (1846–1922) and Ernst Troeltsch (1865–1923), to establish the primacy of history as the medium for understanding and interpreting religion; no brief discussion, however, could possibly do justice to all the shades of opinion and differences of emphasis that have been expressed. If these attempts, and those represented more recently by the thought of such theologians as H. Richard Niebuhr (1894–1962), Rudolf Bultmann (1884–1976), Friedrich Gogarten (1887–1967), and John Macquarrie have anything in common, it is the belief that not philosophy but historical experience and the course of history provide both the foundation of Christian faith and the interpretative framework within which it is to be understood. It is, of course, true that this approach has deep roots in the biblical tradition; Christianity followed the faith of the Hebrew scriptures (Old Testament) in recognizing the unique conception of a linear history in and through which the will of God becomes manifest. Wolfhart Pannenberg, the contemporary German theologian, writes, "Indeed, if it is at all possible . . . to compress [the] biblical understanding of reality into a single word, that word would certainly be 'history'" (*Faith and Reality*, Philadelphia, 1977, p. 10). The strength of this position is found in what it positively accomplishes in highlighting the essential contribution of the temporal and historical—the incarnation as the disclosure of God in history—as opposed to all static conceptions of reality, wherein no provision is made either for history as a medium of revelation or for the novel and creative increment represented by the course of history itself. If, however, whether under the influence of an exaggerated contrast between the Hebraic and Greek views of the historical, or in an effort to remain within the limits of Kant's philosophy alone, proponents of the history-as-medium view hope to replace philosophy with history, serious problems arise. For, on the one hand, there is the philosophical problem of understanding the nature of historical events, the relation between interpreting and explaining them and, consequently, of having some theory about the connections between history, nature, and God. These are essentially philosophical concerns not to be resolved on the basis of the historical dimension alone. Moreover, there is no avoiding the theological issue posed by the mediating function history is to perform, for it is not only the so-called brute historical datum that is involved, but the all-important fact that this datum—especially the historicity of Jesus—must mean or point to God. This fact leads directly to the vexing problems stemming from the need to appeal to a "sacred" history that bears the religious meaning without thereby losing the historicity assumed to belong *ipso facto* to the "secular" account of the events in question. Once again, an attempt to respect what the Swiss theologian Karl Barth (1886–1968) has called the "Kantian terms for peace" in the relations between philosophy and religion, and to find a medium for religious thought other than metaphysics, turns, after the fashion of Hegel's logic, into its opposite, so that new philosophical and theological problems arise in the effort to establish this medium as the successor of metaphysics.

Other religious thinkers, sometimes called the "theologians of encounter," have maintained that religion finds its foundation neither in metaphysics, history, nor morality, but in an immediate encounter establishing a relation with a divine Thou, somewhat analogous to the situation in which two persons are related to each other through intimate bonds of love, compassion, and concern. Central to this outlook is a contrast similar to that between meeting and being acquainted with a person in direct encounter and "knowing about" that person indirectly through abstract concepts.

The small classic written by the Jewish philosopher Martin Buber (1878–1965), *I and Thou,* gave moving expression to this way of understanding the relation between man and God and exerted a powerful influence on Jewish and Christian thought alike. Buber, by no means a foe of philosophy, did, however, under the influence of Kant, draw a sharp distinction between the theoretical, conceptual knowledge of objects—what he called the "it-world"—and the experienced relations between persons who meet and acknowledge each other as such—the world of the "thou." Accordingly, Buber interpreted religion as the special relation established between the "I" and the divine "Thou." Theoretical knowing Buber saw as nullifying the "I–thou" relations precisely because it objectifies its content and leaves the world of persons out of account.

The approach to God through encounter has had its representatives among Christian theologians as well, with, of course, certain transformations necessary to accommodate that tradition. *The Divine-Human Encounter,* by the Swiss theologian Emil Brunner (1889–1966), is a paradigm of the view that man meets God in a faith that is essentially an "answering" acceptance of the divine word, something that is neither a thinking "about" God nor the communication of information. H. H. Farmer has expressed a similar idea in *The World and God,* where he declares that the experience of divine encounter "must be self-authenticating and able to shine in its own light, independently of the abstract reflections of philosophy. . . ." Barth, although his theological system is far too complex to be subsumed under the encounter thesis, nevertheless insists that God remains forever a subject, and that through the incarnation in Christ he makes himself available to be apprehended in the personal knowledge of encounter.

Some contemporary religious thinkers, influenced by the concerns of developing nations, of minorities and the disinherited, by new and more permissive attitudes in morality, and by conflicts in social relations, have turned away completely from traditional philosophical approaches to God and religion and have looked instead to the social sciences as the appropriate medium for expressing what they take to be relevant in religious belief for dealing with these concerns. A fine example of this trend of thought is found in what has come to be called "liberation theology," which focuses attention on the concerns of the oppressed. There is no doubt that this development has been playing an important role in bringing religious faith into the arena of social, economic, and political problems of the utmost urgency. In the context of the present discussion, however, it is necessary to call attention to a basic problem. A liberation theology must be, whatever else it is, a theology, which is to say that it must remain in touch with both religious and philosophical thought concerning God, since the social sciences themselves do not provide this content.

The most radical position as regards the relation between religion and philosophy finds expression in the claim that religion is exclusively a matter of revelation—the word of God—and stands in no need of mediation through secular knowledge, including philosophy. The theology of neoorthodoxy, as it was called, represented chiefly by the massive work of Barth, is based on the proposition that there is no "point of contact" between reason and revealed truth; every philosophical position is equally distant from and thus equally irrelevant to the theological articulation of religious faith. To take but one example, a secular philosopher discussing the meaning of nothingness, according to Barth, could, *ipso facto,* not be referring to the same nothing from which, in the biblical account, the creation was called forth. The rupture is complete; philosophy and religion must dwell in two separate and noncommunicating spheres.

The responses to Kant do not exhaust the interplay between religion and philosophy in the period under consideration. One must take into account as well the impact on religion of logic-analytic philosophies, as represented by Rudolf Carnap (1891–1970) and the proponents of logical empiricism, and A. J. Ayer, whose *Language, Truth and Logic* had serious repercussions not only for religious thought, but for metaphysics, ethics, and aesthetic theory as well. In fairness to Ayer, it should be noted that he no longer holds the views expressed in his epoch-making book; on the other hand, we cannot afford to ignore the sort of positivism expressed there because it was those ideas that, so to speak, did the work.

Central to the thought of both Carnap and Ayer is what has been called the empiricist criterion of meaning, or the thesis that the meaningfulness of any utterance is to be determined solely by verification (or verifiability) in sense experience, where experience is understood according to the conception of experience made classic by the Scottish philosopher David Hume (1711–1776). This view conflates meaning and truth in such a way that, in the absence of the sense datum that would verify an utterance, its constituent terms are said to be without meaning. By implication, the position includes the further thesis that with regard to any utterance it is necessary to specify what datum would count against its supposed truth, or, in short, would falsify it.

It is not difficult to envision what the consequences of applying this monolithic criterion to religious statements would be. Basic theological concepts such as God, atonement, sin, salvation, and faith, along with metaphysical concepts like being, reality, necessary existence, personality, and creativity would all be deprived of cognitive meaning, so that statements involving these and similar terms could not even be called false, since they are supposed to be, quite literally, nonsense. Those who accepted the full authority of the one-meaning criterion for all utterances, insofar as they attended to religious utterances at all, had no alternative but to identify religion wholly with emotion, feeling, or attitudes of a certain kind, with the clear understanding that these have no cognitive significance. It should be obvious that no positive or creative interaction between religion and philosophy is possible from this point of view, since it reduces religion to an emotive level at which no articulation of religious ideas is possible. The underlying assumption determining this outcome was that the only knowledge we possess derives from science. The interesting fact, however, is that subsequent discussion of the empiricist criterion of meaning led to its erosion when it became clear that positivism is itself philosophy and cannot appropriate the credentials of science.

The credit for resolving this situation in a way that allowed both for a mode of interpreting religious insight and the preservation of the linguistic approach to philosophy must go to Wittgenstein. He interpreted religion primarily in practical terms as the legitimate expression of a "form of life," but religious language carries with it no cognitive claim. For this reason religion had to become a matter of sheer faith—fideism—with the consequence that no religious utterance can be construed as making any assertion purporting to be true or false about any realities whatever. The position is a singular one indeed. Wittgenstein was, on the one hand, rightly aware of the difference between the type of significance—purpose, value, aim—embodied in religious language and the theoretical assertions and explanatory theories of science that provided the model for the empiricist criterion of meaning. Hence the shift from meaning to use. On the other hand, this shift was made with the meaning criterion still hovering in the background, so that in the end it remained the determining factor in defining the sphere of the "cognitive," and religion was excluded.

Recovery of the Dialogue between Religion and Philosophy. Nevertheless, as was noted earlier on, the linguistic analysis of religious language proposed by Wittgenstein made one important contribution to our understanding. It served to call attention to the fact that "religious language," though it purports to express a distinctive dimension of experience, is by no means to be regarded as a single, homogeneous form of discourse. The literature of the world's religions manifests a plurality of "uses," or types of expression, and great care must be exercised in distinguishing them. The language of devotion and liturgy, for example, must be distinguished from that of theology, and likewise from the languages of parable, exhortation, lamentation, myth, legend, and historical report. Each has a distinctive function, and only confusion can result from a failure to understand what each purports to express. To take but one typical example, when confronted with parabolic speech, it is a gross misunderstanding to seek the so-called literal meaning of such expressions, since their intent is of a quite different sort. A parable is a vivid and engaging story drawing on familiar experiences and things—putting a new patch on an old garment, a widow losing her last coin, tares among the wheat—for the purpose of dramatizing some religious or moral insight. Expressing the point prosaically or "literally" can never have the same effect. Important as this source of clarification may be, however, it does not take us far enough, because it does not engage those theological questions that stand at the interface of philosophy and religion, nor does a purely critical philosophy provide any basis for determining the relation between religion and cultural life. What limits all critical philosophies in this regard is the absence of any but the most implicit (and sometimes hidden) metaphysics, or general theory of reality and experience, in accordance with which the various dimensions of life can be related to each other. As we learn from history, a truly fruitful interplay between religion and philosophy takes place when philosophy is represented, not by critical methods and analytic programs, but by a substantive vision of reality such as one finds in Hegel or Whitehead.

There remains yet another alternative different from all the preceding, and it is suggested by the point just made about metaphysics. An attempt must be made to recover the classical interaction between religion and philosophy in such a way that the former will once again be intelligible despite the skepticism of the age, and the latter will find its way back to those speculative questions that human beings will never cease to raise. The rationale for such a recovery can be given by showing the adverse consequences that follow for both religion and philosophy from their separation and loss of communication. First, however, it is necessary to challenge a number of philosophical assumptions, assumptions that have been in force for a century and have served to bring about the present unsatisfactory situation. It is an error to suppose that Kant's critical philosophy must be accepted as the final word about the capacity of reason and the possibility of metaphysics while attempts are made to insert religion and theology into what Barth has called the "gaps" in Kant's thought. A more radical approach is called for, which means adopting a far more critical stance to the critical philosophy itself. As Hegel saw so well, Kant's ultimate conclusion is dogmatic in the precise sense that he simply opted for the priority of understanding over reason, and in so doing he employed mathematics and physics as the criterion of knowledge, thus judging the validity of metaphysics in accordance with an alien standard.

The underlying issue is an ancient one, going back to the difference of opinion expressed in the thought of Plato and Aristotle: is there, as Plato held, one universal method and criterion governing all thought, or, is it not the case, as Aristotle claimed, that method and standards of judgment must follow the particular subject matter in question? It is only the latter position that makes it possible to do justice to the many different spheres of meaning and dimensions of experience that actually exist, and at the same time to develop standards appropriate to a given type of thought. Speculative philosophy is not a special science, like physics or geology, and its aims and criteria of adequacy must not be thought of and judged in terms appropriate for experimental inquiries. The same is true of religion and theology; any attempt to understand either is bound to fail if no attention is paid to the special sort of meaning both purport to express. Clearly what is called for is a broader conception of reason, one that is not modeled on the most abstract patterns of thought, which, essential though they are, must exclude our most concrete and important human concerns. A reason, in short, that extends no further than the spheres of formal logic and empirical science forces beyond the bounds of rationality not only philosophy but religion and morality as well.

Earlier on, it was suggested that the rationale for seeking to recover a positive and fruitful interplay between religion and philosophy is to be found in the unfortunate consequences for both that come as the result of their separation from each other. Consider, first, the impact on religion that follows from this separation. Without the benefit of careful, conceptual articulation and the discipline of critical reflection—whether in the form of a philosophical theology or a philosophy of religion—religion is in danger of becoming obscurantist or fanatical in its basic orientation. While the central religious insights that define a tradition must be preserved and transmitted in each historical period, the culture in which the tradition finds itself and the people to whom it speaks are constantly changing. New knowledge is forthcoming, novel patterns of thought and behavior emerge, social and political conditions arise that are very different from those prevailing when the religion was first established. The world in which Augustine proclaimed the Christian message, for example, has little in common with the situation in which that same message was set forth by such thinkers as the German theologian Paul Tillich (1886–1965) or Barth in the twentieth century. A living religion must come to terms with this all-important fact and not seek to preserve itself either by refusing to confront the problems posed by the intellectual climate of the time or by retreating into an inner sanctuary untouched by secular thought and experience. It has, moreover, been persuasively argued that it is precisely through a dialogue engaging the entire spectrum of a culture that a religious tradition comes to realize previously undiscovered implications of its basic faith that further illuminate and help to transform human life. The need to relate the enduring insights of religion to new historical situations and to new generations of people who confront them presents a salutary challenge not only to obscurantism and disdain for intelligence in religion but to fanaticism as well. Having to respond seriously to the critic's question or the skeptic's doubt, as well as to the believer's plea for guidance, must engender in the religious thinker a measure of humility and circumspection not to be reconciled with the fanatic posture, which, as William James was so well aware, is the greatest evil perpetrated by religion wherever it exists. The great ages of faith in Western religion have been those in which faith and intelligence went hand in hand. That religion and philosophy should be separated must be, for religion, the greatest of disasters.

Consider now the consequences of the separation from the side of philosophy. The presence of the religious questions—the problem of God and transcendence, the place of mankind in the cosmic order and our final destiny, the issue of freedom and responsibility, the problem of evil—has repeatedly served as a goad to philosophy, orienting the thinking of philosophers in the direction of speculative themes. As we have seen, especially in the twentieth century, philosophers motivated by the desire to be scientific and to show that philosophy makes progress have worked to reduce the subject to purely critical proportions, with major emphasis falling on technical issues concerning method, knowledge, logic, and language. Speculative questions were often ignored as either without significance or beyond our intellectual capacities. Without the goad of religion (unfortunately not very powerful in the period under consideration), philosophy runs the risk of formalizing itself and of abandoning its constructive task in treating the most important human concerns. Concentration on technique alone has little value when philosophers fail to confront these concerns. A recovery of the dialogue between religion and philosophy would serve the double purpose of bringing philosophy back to the task of constructive metaphysics and of keeping religious thought within the scope of rationality, thus guarding it from the evils of dogmatism and obscurantism.

That such a recovery is a real possibility finds support in two developments of recent decades whose importance must not be overlooked or discounted. The first was the philosophical theology of Tillich, with its method of correlating philosophical questions and theological resolutions; the second was the process philosophy of the English philosopher Alfred North Whitehead (1861–1947), who emigrated to America in 1924, and the several types of theologies inspired by it. Tillich's theological method not only called for a creative exchange with metaphysical thought, but it was accompanied as well by a substantive metaphysical position in the classical mode of correlating the concepts of being and God. While Tillich's thought was marked by an undoubted originality, its appropriation was somewhat hampered because of its dependence on the philosophy of the German contemporary of Hegel, F. W. Schelling (1775–1854)—by far the least known on the American scene of the exponents of German Idealism. Despite this handicap, however, Tillich was a major force in sustaining a theologico-philosophical dialogue, and he did much to counteract the powerful antiphilosophical bias within Protestantism that had its origins in the dogmatic theology of Barth.

Like Tillich, Whitehead had a well-developed metaphysical scheme, including a network of categories for interpreting the many dimensions of experience. In Whitehead one can see how, on the one hand, religious experience and insight were brought into relation to current patterns of thought, scientific as well as philosophical, and how, on the other, these insights were incorporated into his metaphysics as part of the evidence that must be taken into account by a speculative scheme intended to be relevant for understanding everything that happens. The fruitfulness of the interplay between philosophy and religion in this particular case is all the more striking because it coincided with the recovery within the biblical tradition of an emphasis upon time, life, and history in the conception of God, features which had been eclipsed by the great stress previously placed on God as absolute, that is, unrelated to the cosmic process, and as "pure actuality," or a perfection to which the novel increment of history could make no difference.

On the basis of the foregoing analysis, we must conclude that the proper and most satisfactory relation between religion and philosophy is that of dialogical exchange, an exchange of a sort that existed for centuries until it was interrupted by the critical philosophy of Kant and the authority of the empiricist criterion of meaning. But, as we have seen, Kant's reduction of reason to the limits of understanding need not be the last word on the matter, nor should we continue to think that it is possible to accept Kant's position while at the same time attempting to find some loophole through which religion can pass. The monolithic criterion of meaning also need not be accepted, because it so clearly fails to do justice to dimensions of meaning not to be fitted into the pattern of thought exemplified by natural science. With these obstacles surmounted, the way is clear for the renewal of the mutual exchange between religion and metaphysics that has borne fruit in the past.

[*For further discussion of important currents in Western philosophy, see* Analytic Philosophy; Aristotelianism; Deism; Empiricism; Enlightenment, The; Existentialism; Humanism; Idealism; Logical Positivism; Materialism; Naturalism; Neoplatonism; Nominalism; Platonism; Positivism; Scholasticism; Skeptics and Skepticism; *and the biographies of philosophers and theologians mentioned herein.*]

BIBLIOGRAPHY

This bibliographic essay focuses on some books dealing with positions and trends noted in the foregoing article. No effort is made to include such thinkers as Kant, Kierkegaard, Hegel, James, Barth, Tillich, and Whitehead, because they are the subjects of separate entries.

James Collins's *The Emergence of Philosophy of Religion* (New Haven, 1967), both in its historical treatment and its systematic focus on underlying issues, serves to set the stage for the modern discussion concerning the intersection of philosophy and religion. Collins takes note of the important fact that prior to the eighteenth century, philosophical reflection on religious and theological topics took place for the most part within the ambit of the Judeo-Christian tradition and its fundamental doctrines. As Collins shows, however, by discussing three representative thinkers—Hume, Kant, and Hegel—in the succeeding century and a half, the situation was to change radically.

James Alfred Martin, Jr.'s *The New Dialogue between Philosophy and Theology* (New York, 1966), a clear, well-informed, and perceptive study, is the best overall account of the response by religious thinkers both in America and Britain to analytic and linguistic philosophy and to the orientation of the later Wittgenstein. Martin does not only expose the error of identifying analytic philosophy with logical positivism; he skillfully shows how the twentieth-century dialogue between analytic philosophy and theology is connected with the historical dialogue within Christendom that started with Origen and Tertullian and continued through the centuries into the discussions of Tillich, Barth, and Heidegger. In addition to critical accounts of the major writers, religious and philosophical, the book contains a useful bibliography.

Ian T. Ramsey's *Religious Language: An Empirical Placing of Theological Phrases* (London, 1957) begins with an account of what situations can legitimately be called "religious" and considers how some traditional phrases in theology—"first cause," "infinitely wise," "infinitely good"—can be given a logical structure appropriate to these religious situations. Echoing the idea that "religious language" is multiple in character, Ramsey distinguishes the language of the Bible from the language of Christian doctrine, describing each in terms of its functions and aims. In this way he hopes to avoid the many confusions resulting from lumping together under the rubric of "religious language" such diverse forms of expression as that of devotion, on the one hand, and that of theological conceptualization, on the other.

John Macquarrie's *God-Talk: An Examination of the Language and Logic of Theology* (New York, 1967), in addition to an appraisal of the impact of logical empiricism on theological discourse, includes illuminating chapters on different types of such discourse based on case-study analyses of a classical theological text—Athanasius's *On Incarnation*—and of Heidegger's philosophical theory of interpretation. The result is the delineation in theology of a plurality of meaning devices, including mythology, symbolism, analogy, indirect language, existential discourse, ontological discourse, the language of authority, appeal to direct experience, and, finally, the language of paradox.

John Hick's *Faith and Knowledge*, 2d ed. (Ithaca, N.Y., 1966), is concerned primarily with problems of religious knowledge, the distinction between belief and knowledge, and the relation of both to different conceptions of faith. It is representative of a general trend, which is the attempt to combine an analytically oriented philosophy with a neoorthodox approach to religion generally and to Christianity in particular.

E. L. Mascall's *The Secularization of Christianity* (New York, 1965) offers an extraordinarily thorough and acute analysis of J. A. T. Robinson's *Honest to God* (Philadelphia, 1963) and Paul Van Buren's *The Secular Meaning of the Gospel* (New York, 1963) in an attempt to show that, while it is essential that Christianity be presented in terms that are both intelligible and relevant to the present day, it is not necessary to jettison centuries of accumulated Christian wisdom for the purpose of communicating what in fact may prove to be merely a substitute for Christian doctrine. Whether one agrees or not with Mascall's conclusions, it is unquestionable that no better account of the topic is to be found.

Ninian Smart's *The Science of Religion and the Sociology of Knowledge* (Princeton, 1973) surveys the broad theme of the relation of religion to rationality in light of phenomenology, history, sociology, and anthropology. The author notes, quite rightly, the difference between theology as the systematic expression of the faith of a religious community and various ways of studying religion as a phenomenon involved in the total pattern of life and culture throughout the world. Although too short for an extended treatment, the discussion ranges over a very wide body of material, including references to Weber, Lévy-Bruhl, Otto, Wach, Kierkegaard, Tillich, Barth, Marx, Freud, Eliade, Berger, Jayatilleke, and Wilfred Cantwell Smith.

H. D. Lewis's *Our Experience of God* (London, 1959) decries the idea that it is the task of philosophy to construct some form of philosophical substitute for religion, or to provide proofs for religious beliefs supposedly held on inadequate grounds. The positive role of philosophy in relation to religion is to make clearer the meaning and status of religious beliefs actually held and at the same time to show their relation to the larger experiential setting in which they occur.

In *The Person God Is* (London, 1970), Peter Bertocci, a chief representative of the philosophy and theology of personalism, carries on the tradition of interpreting religious insight in philosophical terms by viewing God, the cosmic person, as the creator of "co-creators." The author considers whether the goodness of God can be empirically grounded, whether grace can be discovered in freedom, and whether religion itself can be understood in terms of the pursuit of creativity.

In the works of Charles Hartshorne, including *Man's Vision of God, and the Logic of Theism* (New York, 1941), *The Divine Relativity: A Social Conception of God* (New Haven, 1948), *The Logic of Perfection* (La Salle, Ill., 1962), *Anselm's Discovery* (La Salle, Ill., 1965), and *Omnipotence and Other Theological Mistakes* (Albany, N.Y., 1984), the critical interchange on philosophical and theological issues is sustained. Hartshorne's thought may be understood as concentrating on two distinct but closely related focal points. The first is his "neoclassical" theism based on what he calls the "principle of Dual Transcendence," according to which God contrasts with creatures not as an abstract infinite against the finite, but as a concrete "infinite-and-finite," each aspect of which contrasts with fragmentary creatures who are neither relative nor absolute in themselves. In short, Hartshorne finds that despite the great emphasis placed by the biblical tradition on time, individuality, personal responsibility, and historical development, much classical theology neglected these features by conceiving of God, not as living, but as already complete or perfect. The other focus in Hartshorne's writing is restatement and reassessment of the ontological argument as first proposed by Anselm. Here he reoriented the centuries-long discussion of this oft "refuted" argument, not by concentrating on the usual question of whether "existence is a predicate," but by directing attention to what had largely been neglected by a host of previous thinkers, namely, what is to be understood by the idea of God—the *what* of the matter—and its expression in Anselm's formula. An informative commentary on Hartshorne's work can be found in *Existence and Actuality: Conversations with Charles Hartshorne*, edited by John B. Cobb, Jr., and Franklin I. Gamwell (Chicago, 1984).

Experience, Reason and God, edited by Eugene T. Long (Washington, D.C., 1980), provides a broad spectrum of opinion by twelve authors concerning the intersection of philosophy and religion on the contemporary scene.

JOHN E. SMITH

Philosophy of Religion

The idea of a philosophy of religion is a recent one, and it assumes a differentiation between philosophy and religion that has emerged chiefly in the modern West. Much that is included under that rubric, however, dates back to ancient philosophical analysis and speculation. Philosophy of religion is the philosophical scrutiny of religion, but the meaning of those terms and the proper method and content of the field are subject to considerable dispute. Current work in the field can be divided into two types: (1) assessment of the rationality of religious beliefs, with attention to their coherence and to the cogency of arguments for their justification; and (2) descriptive analysis and elucidation of religious language, belief, and practice with particular attention to the rules by which they are governed and to their context in the religious life. The boundary between these two types is not always clear, but they can be illumined by considering their origins and some paradigmatic arguments from each.

Justification of Religious Beliefs. The first type of philosophy of religion has been concerned chiefly with theism, but analogues can be found in nontheistic traditions. Rational arguments are proposed and assessed in order to justify or to criticize religious beliefs. Because the philosophy of religion has its provenance in the West, theistic issues have dominated the discussion, but neither type should be restricted to the consideration of theism.

Most of the classical topics in the philosophy of religion are topics in philosophical theism or natural theology. Foremost among these are the existence and nature of God. Analyses of the concept of God, discussion of the divine nature and its attributes, and arguments that purport to demonstrate the existence of God constitute the principal subject matter of philosophical theism. Such attributes as unity, simplicity, omniscience, perfection, eternity, and immutability require analysis in order to clarify their meanings, to assess their compatibility, and to consider the implications of applying them outside of the contexts in which we normally ascribe knowledge, power, and goodness to persons. Many of the classical issues and arguments derive from medieval philosophy and theology.

Immanuel Kant (1724–1804) classified the arguments for the existence of God as the ontological argument, the cosmological argument, and the teleological argument, or argument from design. This classification has become canonical, though not everyone would agree with Kant's claim that these three kinds of argument exhaust the logical possibilities.

The original formulation of the ontological argument, and the one that has continued to command the attention of philosophers, was given by Anselm of Canterbury (1033–1109) in his *Proslogion* (1077–1078). Anselm argues that the existence of God can be demonstrated by a proper analysis of the concept of God. He begins by claiming that what we mean by the word *God* is "something than which nothing greater can be thought." Even one who would doubt or deny the existence of God, says Anselm, understands this concept, and thus something than which nothing greater can be thought exists in his mind. But that than which no greater can be thought cannot exist in the mind alone. Were it to exist only in the mind, it would be possible to think of it as existing outside the mind as well, and that would be even greater. Then that which existed in the mind alone would not be something than which no greater could be thought. Therefore, that than which no greater can be thought must exist both in the mind and in reality.

The monk Gaunilo, a contemporary of Anselm, criticized the argument by claiming that it could be used to demonstrate the existence of a perfect island, or of any other thing in which the requirement of existence was embedded in the idea of perfection or greatness. Anselm replied that the concept of an island is already the concept of something limited, and thus cannot contain unlimited greatness. In what has been viewed as the standard refutation, Kant argued that existence is not a property that can be added or subtracted in order to make comparisons of worth. To say that a table exists is not to add anything to the concept of table, but is to say that the concept is instantiated.

The ontological argument differs from the cosmological and teleological arguments in that it appears to depend entirely on conceptual analysis. But the argument is embedded in a prayer in which Anselm asks God for faith in order that he might understand. This context has prompted some commentators to suggest that Anselm was not offering an argument at all, but was reflecting on a faith that was derived solely from divine revelation. The *Proslogion* opens, however, with Anselm's expression of joy at having discovered a single argument that would suffice to prove that both God exists and all that we believe about the divine nature. Philosophical treatments often consider the argument in isolation from its religious context and from Anselm's claim that divine omnipotence, mercy, impassibility, simplicity, eternity, and other attributes could be derived from the same concept.

Recently there has been renewed interest in the ontological argument. In an influential article (1960), Norman Malcolm claims that Kant had refuted the argument set forth in the second chapter of the *Proslogion*, but that the following chapter and the reply to Gaunilo contain another argument that has been overlooked and that is successful. This is an argument not for God's existence but for his necessary existence. Malcolm contends that Anselm has demonstrated that the concept of God is such that God cannot fail to exist. Were he not to exist, or were his existence contingent rather than necessary, he would not satisfy our concept of God. Malcolm claims that Anselm was engaged in an elucidation of the concept that is implicit in the religious life of those in theistic traditions. He was analyzing the grammar by which that concept is governed. Alvin Plantinga (1974) has employed the very different techniques of modal logic to reformulate Anselm's argument to demonstrate the rationality of belief in the existence of God, though he holds that it cannot justify that belief.

The classical statement of the cosmological argument is found in the *Summa theologiae* (1268–1273) of Thomas Aquinas. Thomas offers five proofs of the existence of God, the first three of which are versions of the cosmological argument. Each begins with some characteristic of things in the world (e.g., change, causation, contingency) and argues that a proper explanation of this phenomenon requires that we posit a first cause or something whose existence is not dependent upon anything other than itself. Thomas begins the first way with the observation that some things in the world are changing. He then asserts that anything that is in the process of change is being changed by something else, a controversial premise that he defends and glosses by appeal to conceptions of actuality and potentiality derived from the Aristotelian tradition. But this other thing, he says, if in the process of change, is itself being changed by something else, and so on. Unless this potentially infinite series is halted, there will be no first cause of the change, thus no subsequent cause, and therefore no change. So there must be some first cause of change not itself being changed by anything, and this is what everyone understands by God.

The second of Thomas's ways begins from the relation between cause and effect, and proceeds in a manner parallel to the first. The third way takes its departure from the observation that some things in the world are contingent, and thus might not have existed. Thomas argues that it is impossible for everything to be contingent, because anything that need not be was once nonexistent. If everything were contingent, then there must have been a time at which there was nothing. If that were the case there would be nothing now, for something that does not exist can be brought into being only by something that already exists. But there is something now. So there must be something the existence of which is not contingent but necessary.

Thomas's five ways are fraught with difficulties, most deriving from their dependence upon Aristotelian physics and metaphysics. The observation that some things are changing is not a controversial one unless change is understood in Aristotelian terms. If it is understood in those terms, much metaphysical baggage is packed into what appears to be an ordinary observation, and the rest of the proof turns on unpacking that baggage. If it is not understood in those terms, the argument does not succeed. The same dilemma holds for the observation that some things are contingent. We are aware, as Thomas was not, of the controversial science and metaphysics that are assumed by the proofs.

The five ways, like Anselm's argument, are embedded in a theological context. Thomas says that Christian theology is a science that takes its principles on faith in God's revelation. Some have argued that he intended only to elucidate a faith based on revelation, but Thomas asserts that some truths about God can be known by natural reasoning and are presupposed by faith. Like Anselm, he continues, after presenting his arguments for the existence of God, to derive the manner of God's existing and certain characteristics of the divine nature.

Versions of the cosmological argument have been offered by Jewish, Christian, and Islamic philosophers, and the belief that the world cannot be accounted for without reference to the existence and activity of God seems to be a part of the religious life of any theist. Doctrines of God as creator and preserver, which are central to each of these traditions, are closely connected with the cosmological argument.

Recently, renewed attention has been given to an eighteenth-century version of the cosmological argument offered by Samuel Clarke (1675–1729). Clarke argued that Thomas incorrectly assumed that there must be a first cause to account for change, causation, or contingent being. There could be an infinite series of causes. But Clarke held that such a series would still require an explanation. In order to account for the existence of this series rather than another or none at all, we must posit a cause for the series as a whole. Clarke's argument has stimulated interest because it seems to depend neither on Thomas's assumption that there can be no infinite series of causes nor on his employment of Aristotelian science and metaphysics.

The most influential statement of the argument from design comes from a critic rather than a proponent. In *Dialogues concerning Natural Religion* (1779) by David Hume (1711–1776), the interlocutor Cleanthes sets forth a version of the argument, and much of the work is an analysis of its weaknesses and of the resulting implications for religious belief. Cleanthes argues that the order that we find in the universe, and "the curious adaptation of means to ends," can only be explained by positing some kind of mind that is analogous to human minds. The universe is one great machine. No such intricate pattern and order could be accounted for by chance. A designer must be posited, and we can infer some of his attributes from the order we observe. Like the cosmological argument, this is a formalization of an aspect of ordinary theistic belief. God is the creator, and the world shows evidence of his handiwork.

Hume raises a number of problems for Cleanthes's argument, chief among them the weakness of the analogy between the order we discover in the universe and the order or design in a machine, other explanations that are as or more plausible on the basis of evidence, and the religious inadequacy of the God that Cleanthes's argument permits him to infer. Hume is particularly persuasive in showing that naturalistic hypotheses are as well supported by the evidence as is the theistic hypothesis.

The *Dialogues* also contain a clear presentation of a classical argument against theistic belief, the argument from evil. Hume offers two forms of this argument, emphasizing logical and empirical problems. The logical form consists in the claim that theists are committed to the inconsistent conjunction of three propositions: (1) God is omnipotent; (2) God is wholly good; and (3) evil exists. As Hume puts it: "Epicurus's old questions are yet unanswered. Is he willing to prevent evil, but not able? then is he impotent. Is he able, but not willing? then he is malevolent. Is he both able and willing? whence then is evil?" The claim is that theism is incoherent. Consistency can be restored by giving up any one of the three beliefs, and examples can be found for each of these alternatives. The traditional solutions, however, have been either to deny that there really is evil when viewed from a proper perspective, or to offer what has become known as the free will defense. The first is a denial of (3) on the grounds that what seems from our parochial perspective to be evil can be seen from the divine viewpoint as contributing to the greater good. The free will defense is a clarification of the meaning and limits of (1). Free will defenders argue that it was better for God to have created a world in which some creatures have free will than one in which their actions are totally determined, that evil results from human free will, and that if God creates such a world there are certain outcomes that he cannot control, but that this fact does not compromise his omnipotence.

The second form of the argument from evil is not a matter of logical compatibility. Unlike the first form, it arises from the inference articulated in the design argument. Hume says that even though one might be able to demonstrate the consistency of theism, the evil and suffering that we find in the world blocks any inference to an all-powerful and benevolent designer. While the logical form of the problem of evil has dominated the discussion, those whose theism is grounded upon an inference from the world to a benevolent creator must consider how the evil and suffering in the world affects that inference.

Some contributors to this first type of philosophy of religion have employed the techniques of modal logic (Plantinga, 1974) and confirmation theory (Swinburne, 1977, 1979, 1981) to address classical questions of the coherence and rationality of theistic belief and the arguments for and against that belief.

Description and Analysis of Religious Language, Practice, and Belief. Those who constructed arguments for or against the existence of God did not suppose that religious faith is adopted or discarded for these reasons. Anselm wrote of his task as faith seeking understanding. These were attempts to employ reason to understand and to justify or criticize beliefs that had been received from tradition. While work on the coherence of theism and arguments for the existence of God continue, new interpretations of the classical texts have been offered that challenge the assumption that the authors of those texts were seeking to justify religious belief. Malcolm takes Anselm to be elucidating the faith of a believer rather than proposing an argument that is meant to convince the nonbeliever. Victor Preller (1967) and David Burrell (1979) argue that when restored to their theological context the five ways of Thomas Aquinas will be seen as relatively unimportant and as displaying occasions for the application of religious grammar rather than offering proofs for the existence of God. Alvin Plantinga (1974) reconstructs the ontological argument and the free will defense in order to refute challenges by critics who argue that theism is inconsistent or irrational. Despite important differences, in each of these cases the proper task of the philosophy of religion is viewed as the elucidation of religious belief rather than as the justification or refutation of that belief.

The second type of philosophy of religion consists of reflection on the distinctive character of the religious life and the placing of religious practice and belief with respect to other sets of beliefs and practices, especially those of science and of morals. This conception of the task of philosophy of religion stems from the conviction that religious doctrine and beliefs should not be subject to criteria of rationality and justification that derive from such other pursuits as science, metaphysics, or morals. Religious practices and beliefs require no justification from outside the religious life. The task of the philosopher is to understand them rather than to subject them to heteronomous criteria.

Though there are precursors, philosophical reflection on religion began in earnest in the eighteenth century. Hume distinguished two kinds of inquiry about religion, the first concerning its foundation in reason, and the second its origin in human nature. The first of these questions was addressed in the *Dialogues*, and the second in *The Natural History of Religion* (1777), in which he sketched a naturalistic account of the origin of religious belief and practice. Speculation about the origin of religion and its relation to other aspects of culture flourished in the eighteenth century.

The agenda for much subsequent philosophy of religion was set by Kant and by responses to his work. Kant held that traditional arguments purporting to demonstrate or to refute the existence of God were flawed. More important, however, he held that such arguments were bound to fail. They were illegitimate extensions beyond experience of categories and forms of judgment that are valid only within the bounds of experience. Philosophical debate about such issues is futile, leads to antinomies, and can never be resolved. The traditional topics of philosophical theism are ill-formed, and any semblance of progress is an illusion.

Kant argued that the task of the philosopher is not to contribute to the substance of science, morals, art, or religion, but to reflect critically on the kinds of judgments that are employed in each of these areas, to map the limits of their proper application, to describe the problems that result from exceeding those limits, and to offer an account of how such judgments are possible. The moral philosopher, for instance, cannot add to or detract from the sense of moral obligation that is accessible to all rational beings, but he can describe that obligation and the structure of moral judgments. The philosopher of religion ought not to argue for or against religious beliefs, but ought to restrict himself to mapping the structure of religious concepts, beliefs, and practices, and to offering an account of their origin in practical reason.

In *Religion within the Limits of Reason Alone* (1793), Kant situated religious concepts, beliefs, and practices within the moral life. He argued that people schematize or represent in imaginative terms the experience of moral obligation. The obligation to obey the moral law is viewed as if it were a duty imposed by a divine lawgiver. This kind of schematism cannot be avoided, and thus morality leads ineluctably to religion. Religious experience and practice derive from the moral life. Religious doctrines are not to be assessed for their truth or falsity. That would be to misconstrue them. They are expressions of aspects of moral experience. Kant offered an account of the concept of God and of major Christian doctrines as schemata of the moral law and of issues that arise from attempts to act in accord with it. Religious beliefs can never conflict with scientific beliefs because they serve very different functions. Religious beliefs cannot yield knowledge, but they are a necessary outgrowth of the moral life.

Friedrich Schleiermacher (1768–1834) accepted Kant's critique of metaphysics and of traditional natural theology, and he agreed that religious doctrine ought not to be viewed as making scientific or metaphysical claims, but he rejected the assimilation of religion to morality. He argued that religious doctrine and practice express an autonomous and irreducible moment in human experience that cannot be reduced to belief or action. Piety is neither science nor morals, but an affective moment in experience with its own integrity. Philosophy of religion is reflection on this moment as it is shaped by different traditions and cultures, and as it is expressed in various doctrines and practices. Schleiermacher described the religious moment as a sense of finitude or dependence. While it can be understood only by acquaintance, it is a universal moment in human experience that is accessible to all. Because religious doctrine is not a matter of belief but an expression of this affective moment as it is shaped by particular traditions, religious doctrines can never conflict with the findings of science. Religious beliefs require no justification because they are independently grounded in an autonomous moment of experience.

Following Kant and Schleiermacher, representatives of the second type have embedded the philosophy of religion within a broader philosophy of culture. The focus has shifted from the justification of religious beliefs to the identification of the distinctive character of religious experience, religious language, or religious practice. The task of the philosopher of religion is to describe that experience, language, and practice, to elucidate them, and to place them with respect to other cultural phenomena. G. W. F. Hegel (1770–1831) showed that religious concepts and beliefs are embedded in particular traditions of thought and practice and can be understood only in the light of those traditions. Søren Kierkegaard (1813–1855) continued Kant's emphasis on the will as central to the religious life but differentiated that life from a life characterized by aesthetic immediacy and one defined by Kantian morality. He explored the role of religious language both in expressing that life and in providing the occasion for an individual to confront the absolute paradox that he took to be the heart of the Christian gospel. Ludwig Feuerbach (1804–1872) and Karl Marx (1818–1883) offered accounts of religious belief and practice as idealized projections of hopes, fears, and desires that originally had more palpable objects in the material and social worlds.

Hume had located his discussion of theism within a sketch of the natural history of religion, and Hegel had traced the development of the religious consciousness through different cultural traditions. By the beginning of the twentieth century, research in the history of religions was sufficiently advanced that many philosophers of religion realized that their descriptions and analyses of religious experience, practice, and belief must, in principle at least, take account of traditions beyond Christianity and even beyond theism. Philosophy of religion could no longer be merely prolegomena to Christian theology. Most contemporary philosophers of religion would agree, but the reorientation of the discipline implied by that recognition has yet to be achieved in practice.

During the nineteenth century, work in the history of religions had been informed by Schleiermacher's claim that religion is an experiential matter that is expressed in doctrines and practices reflecting different cultures, but that is universal at the core. In the early years of the twentieth century, William James (1842–1910) and Rudolf Otto (1869–1937) both attempted to describe the distinctive characteristics of religious experience and to examine the implications for religious belief. Both drew on illustrative material from other religious traditions and viewed the object of their inquiry as religious experience considered generally, but both were chiefly influenced by Christianity.

James held that religion is principally a matter of feeling and not of belief, but that there is no distinctively religious affection. Religious fear, love, awe, and joy are ordinary fear, love, awe, and joy associated with religious objects. In *The Varieties of Religious Experience* (1902), James provided both a taxonomy of kinds of religious experience and astute philosophical analysis of such problems for the philosophy of religion as the relation between the scientific study of religion and the assessment of its meaning, significance, or value. He explored the implications of the identification of religion with a feeling or sense, and, especially in his chapter on mysticism, considered the authority of such experiences for the persons who have them and for those who do not. He argued that widespread testimony provides some evidence in support of what he took to be the common element in religious experience, a belief or sense that there is something more beyond our mundane world and that it can have a benevolent effect on the lives of individuals.

In contrast to James, and in explicit indebtedness to Schleiermacher, Otto argued that there is a distinctive moment in religious experience. That moment is not properly characterized as feeling, but it is unmistakably specific and peculiar. Otto described it as the nonrational and ineffable moment in religious experience. He coined a special term, the *numinous*, to refer to "the holy" minus its moral and rational factors. He claimed that there is a unique numinous category of value and a numinous state of mind that is *sui generis* and irreducible. The numinous moment in experience cannot be communicated but can only be known by acquaintance. Otto portrays that moment as one of creaturely feeling and a sense of finitude, of awe and fascination in response to something "wholly other." Otto later went on to study non-Western religious traditions, and particularly some strands of the religions of India, but his characterization of the numinous moment in religious experience is clearly derivative from the monotheism of the Hebrew scriptures and of Lutheran Christianity.

Philosophers of religion have drawn on material from the history of religions to investigate what appear to be common beliefs or practices. Mysticism, ritual, sacrifice, prayer, and a sense of the holy or of the sacred have been subjects of such inquiry. James held that religious thoughts and beliefs vary from culture to culture, but that feelings and conduct are invariant. Many have shared this assumption and have looked to the study of mysticism, prayer, or a sense of the sacred as a way to approach the heart of the religious life. It has become clear, however, that one cannot identify an emotion or a practice without reference to the concepts and beliefs that can be ascribed to the person who has that emotion or engages in that practice. Attempts by Schleiermacher, James, and Otto to characterize a core religious experience that is independent of those concepts, beliefs, and practices are bound to fail. James's assumption that beliefs vary while feelings and actions are invariant reflects his inability to appreciate the fact that any emotion or action must be identified under a description, and that that description must be one that can be properly attributed to the subject of the emotion or action.

In Anglo-American philosophy in the mid-twentieth century, the focus shifted from religious experience to religious language. A. J. Ayer (1936), developing his version of logical positivism, contended that religious statements, along with moral statements, were incapable of verification or falsification and therefore were not cognitively meaningful. They were to be understood as expressive utterances without cognitive content. The verifiability criterion of cognitive meaningfulness was soon abandoned because of problems that were independent of its application to religious statements, but the inquiry into the proper status of religious language continued. Some philosophers, drawing on the later philosophy of Ludwig Wittgenstein (1889–1951), argued that religious language ought not to be subject to criteria derived from such other forms of discourse as scientific or moral discourse. Rather, the task of the philosopher of religion ought to be to map the peculiar grammar governing religious uses of language. Problems arise, however, when one attempts to discriminate between distinctively religious uses and other uses of particular words and sentences.

Attempts to identify a distinctive grammar of religious language in such a way as to make that language autonomous and independent of other concepts and beliefs resemble Schleiermacher's claim that there is a distinctive and autonomous moment in religious experience. In both forms, the claim is motivated by apologetic considerations as well as by the aim for descriptive adequacy. If Schleiermacher is correct in his portrayal of religious language as expressive of a moment that is independent of concepts and beliefs, then a religious statement can never conflict with a scientific statement or a moral claim. The same words function entirely differently in a religious context from their use in a scientific or metaphysical context. "God created the world" as a doctrinal statement can never conflict with any scientific or metaphysical statement about the origin of the world. The words have different meanings in the different settings. This sharp distinction constitutes a protective strategy that precludes any conflict between religious beliefs and scientific or ordinary beliefs about the world. That strategy is continued by those who claim that religious uses of language are governed by their own peculiar grammar and are not subject to criteria from outside the sphere of religious discourse. Such strategies show that the second type of philosophy of religion, while allegedly concerned with description and elucidation in contrast to justification, may be used for apologetic purposes as well. It may serve to justify religious belief and practice by ascribing to those beliefs and practices a status that precludes any conflict with scientific knowledge or claims in other areas of culture.

Both types of philosophy of religion are represented in the contemporary literature. After a desultory period, there is renewed interest in philosophical theism. Chief among the tasks facing contemporary philosophers of religion is the need for the discipline to be sufficiently comprehensive to be accountable to other religious traditions, but to avoid the distortion that results from wrenching statements and phenomena out of their historical and cultural contexts in order to serve some comparative or apologetic purpose. This task is further complicated by the fact that the concept of religion prevalent in philosophy of religion has its provenance in the modern West. Theistic assumptions are embedded in the criteria by which we identify an experience or a phenomenon as religious. These assumptions may be masked by claims that the philosophy of religion ought to concern itself with description and analysis while remaining neutral with respect to the justification of religious beliefs and practices.

BIBLIOGRAPHY

Anselm of Canterbury. *St. Anselm's Proslogion.* Translated by M. J. Charlesworth. Oxford, 1965.

Ayer, A. J. *Language, Truth, and Logic* (1936). 2d ed. London, 1946.

Burrell, David B. *Aquinas: God and Action.* Notre Dame, Ind., 1979.

Craig, William L. *The Cosmological Argument from Plato to Leibniz.* New York, 1980.

Hume, David. *Dialogues concerning Natural Religion.* Edited by Norman Kemp Smith. Oxford, 1935.

Hume, David. *The Natural History of Religion.* Edited by H. E. Root. London, 1956.

James, William. *The Varieties of Religious Experience.* New York, 1902.

Kant, Immanuel. *Religion within the Limits of Reason Alone.* Translated by Theodore M. Greene and Hoyt H. Hudson. La Salle, Ill., 1960.

Katz, Steven T., ed. *Mysticism and Philosophical Analysis.* Oxford, 1978.

Kenny, Anthony. *The Five Ways: St. Thomas Aquinas' Proofs of God's Existence.* New York, 1969.

Mackie, J. L. *The Miracle of Theism.* Oxford, 1982.

Malcolm, Norman. "Anselm's Ontological Arguments." *Philosophical Review* 69 (January 1960): 41–62.

Otto, Rudolf. *The Idea of the Holy.* Translated by John W. Harvey. Oxford, 1928.

Plantinga, Alvin. *The Nature of Necessity.* Oxford, 1974.

Preller, Victor. *Divine Science and the Science of God: A Reformulation of Thomas Aquinas.* Princeton, N.J., 1967.

Schleiermacher, Friedrich. *The Christian Faith.* Edited by H. R. Mackintosh and J. S. Stewart. Edinburgh, 1929.

Schleiermacher, Friedrich. *On Religion.* Translated by John Oman, with an introduction by Rudolf Otto. New York, 1955.

Swinburne, Richard. *The Coherence of Theism.* Oxford, 1977.

Swinburne, Richard. *The Existence of God.* Oxford, 1979.

Swinburne, Richard. *Faith and Reason.* Oxford, 1981.

Thomas Aquinas. *Summa theologiae,* vols. 1 and 2. Translated and edited by Thomas Gilby. New York, 1964. See especially questions 1–11.

Wainwright, William J. *Philosophy of Religion: An Annotated Bibliography of Twentieth-Century Writings in English.* New York, 1978.

WAYNE PROUDFOOT

PHOENICIAN RELIGION. The names *Phoenicia* and *Phoenician* come from the Greek *phoinikē* and *phoinikias,* respectively. These terms were used by the Greeks to designate the coastal strip on the eastern shores of the Mediterranean and its hinterland, and the Semitic-speaking inhabitants of that territory. The terms may correspond etymologically to the biblical *(kena'an)* and cuneiform *(kinahhu)* names for Canaan; both the Greek and Semitic names may derive from words that refer to a reddish-purple dye for which the Phoenician dyeing industry was renowned. But there is not a precise correspondence in usage between *Phoenicia* and *Canaan.* There is, moreover, no clear evidence for what the people in question called themselves; affiliation by individual city was more likely than any pervasive national consciousness.

There is no reason to doubt the ancient claim that the Phoenicians were autochthonous, but before the late second millennium BCE there is little evidence for a distinctive Phoenician culture in the Levant. At the beginning of the Iron Age (c. 1200 BCE), though, the great political and social unrest in the Levant seems to have forced the Phoenicians into some sort of cultural coherence. This period witnessed the collapse of the Egyptian and Hittite empires and the concomitant demise of the Levantine city-states that had been their allies or vassals. At the same time, several invading groups (Philistines, Arameans, Hebrews) appeared on the scene, ultimately to establish the nation-states that would occupy the Levant throughout most of the first millennium BCE.

The Phoenicians found themselves confined to the coast, in a territory nowhere more than 60 kilometers wide, bounded by mountains to the east and the sea to the west. The northern and southern borders varied considerably, but basically the Phoenicians occupied the central portion of the coastal strip, from Tartūs (Antaradus) in the north to ʿAkko (Acre) in the south. The most important cities in the Phoenician homeland were, from north to south, Arvad (Aradus), Gebal (Byblos), Beirut (Berytus), Sidon, and Sur (Tyre).

Since they were generally cut off politically and geographically from the interior, the Phoenicians turned their attention to the sea. Even within their homeland, the Mediterranean provided them with the safest and surest path for transportation and communications. And the Phoenician mastery of navigation led them to establish a series of colonies, trading posts, and settlements across the Mediterranean to the west. These colonies, the most famous of which was Carthage (probably founded by Tyre in the late ninth century), are often called "Punic" (the Latin equivalent of Phoenician), to distinguish them from mainland Phoenicia. The colonies generally shared the two most important virtues of the mainland cities: they provided safe anchorage and they were easily defensible. Some of the Phoenician ports (e.g., Palermo and Cadiz) have remained continuously in use, but most of them (e.g., Tyre and Carthage) are too small for modern ships.

Phoenician political power was at its height in the tenth and ninth centuries BCE, with Tyre emerging as the most important city. The alliance between King Hiram of Tyre and King Solomon of Israel represents the political zenith of both nations. Close relations between Phoenicia and the Israelite kingdoms, including alliance by marriage, lasted into the ninth century. By the second quarter of the ninth century, however, all the main Phoenician cities were paying tribute to Assyrian overlords. Several uprisings, including one in alliance with Egypt in the 670s, failed to overthrow the Assyrian yoke, although Tyre itself was never actually captured. After Assyria fell to the Babylonians in 612, the Babylonians moved into the Levant; they captured Jerusalem in 587/6, and defeated Tyre thirteen years later. Nebuchadrezzar's siege of Tyre is depicted in *Ezekiel* 26:7–12.

After the fall of Tyre, Sidon emerged as the chief mainland city. When the Persians defeated the Babylonians in 539, they made Phoenicia part of their fifth satrapy, and built a royal palace in Sidon. During the period of Persian rule, the Phoenician fleets acted in Persia's interest against the Greeks. In general, however, both the Phoenician mainland and the colonies moved closer to the Greek cultural sphere. Finally, Alexander conquered Phoenicia in 332, thanks in part to a remarkable feat of military engineering (Diodorus Siculus, *Bibliotheca historica* 17.40–46). Only vestiges of Phoenician autonomy remained in the Seleucid and subsequent Roman periods.

Until the middle of the nineteenth century CE, the Phoenicians were known exclusively from non-Phoenician sources—products of the Phoenician encounters with the Greeks, Romans, and Israelites. Since that time, there has been extensive archaeological work both in Phoenicia proper and in the colonies. Material discoveries have supplied considerable data about Phoenician sacrificial and funerary practices. But native Phoenician and Punic texts (mostly funerary and dedicatory inscriptions) do not provide a sufficient context for the interpretation of those data. Any coherent account of Phoenician religion, therefore, must still rely heavily on biblical and classical sources, especially the *Phoenician History* of Philo Byblius and *The Syrian Goddess*, attributed to Lucian of Samothrace.

Two additional factors make a general description of Phoenician religion difficult, if not impossible. First, there seems never to have been a unified national religious consciousness. As a result, the major centers had their own pantheons and idiosyncratic practices. Second, Phoenician religion tended to be adaptive rather than exclusive; in particular, Egyptian, Aramean, and Greek elements are evident, as are local influences in the western colonies. It has often been claimed that there is a Phoenician "core" that can be isolated from the external influences, on the assumption that Phoenician religion substantially perpetuated second-millennium Canaanite religion. That assumption, which is mostly based on a comparison of Phoenician evidence with the second-millennium religious texts excavated at Ras Shamra (ancient Ugarit), is fraught with difficulties. Despite some important elements of continuity,

Phoenician religion seems to have been far more innovative than is generally allowed. This innovation and change continued throughout the first millennium, as the Phoenician gods, beliefs, and practices evolved in response to changing circumstances.

Deities. The Phoenicians worshiped three main types of gods under different names in different places. These gods are well characterized in the treaty drawn up in 677 BCE between the Assyrian king Esarhaddon and his newly conquered vassal, King Baal of Tyre. The fourth column of the treaty contains the traditional treaty curses, invoking the wrath of the gods against any Tyrian breach of the treaty's terms. The curses are divided into two sections. The first mentions Esarhaddon's own gods, as well as two additional gods associated with Aram or North Syria. Then the Phoenician gods are invoked: Baal-Shamem, Baal-Malage, and Baal-Safon are to raise a tempest and destroy the Phoenician ships; Melqart and Eshmun are to deprive the Phoenicians of their sustenance and clothing; and Astarte is to lead them to defeat in battle.

The epithet *Baal-Shamem* ("lord of heaven") denotes the high god of any local Phoenician pantheon. In the tenth-century inscription of King Yehimilk of Byblos, the god is summoned to bless the king for having restored the local temples. He is presumably the El ("god") of Byblos (not to be confused with the El of Ugarit) who is identified with Kronos by Philo Byblius. In the eighth-century inscription of King Azitawadda (found at Karatepe, in southern Anatolia), Baal-Shamem takes precedence over the rest of the gods. He is the Elioun/Hypsistos ("highest one") of Philo Byblius, and the Olympian Zeus venerated in Tyre, according to Dio's *History of the Phoenicians* (see Josephus Flavius, *Against Apion* 1.113). A bilingual Palmyrene inscription makes the equation of Baal-Shamem with Zeus Hypsistos absolutely certain.

In the Esarhaddon treaty, Baal-Shamem is clearly the lord of the storm, and he is appropriately identified with the old Canaanite Baal of Mount Tsafon, the weather god who was the Baal of Ugarit in the second millennium. According to Philo Byblius, the primordial inhabitants of Phoenicia considered Baal-Shamem "the sole god, the ruler of heaven," and appealed to him in times of drought. It is precisely Baal-Shamem's power to alleviate a drought that is challenged by the prophet Elijah in *1 Kings* 18. The other title of this Baal, *Baal-Malage,* probably means "lord of mariners," and refers to the god's role as patron of Phoenician seafaring. This title may be compared with the Zeus Meilichios ("gentle Zeus") of Philo Byblius; that god is identified with Chousor/Hephaistos ("first of all men to sail"), inventor of fishing equipment and the raft. Philo's Chousor, in turn, must be descended from the old Canaanite craftsman god, Kothar.

While the high god is the leading deity in the pantheon, he is not the principal object of cultic veneration. That situation is paralleled at Ugarit, where Il (El) is head of the pantheon, but he is neither the most active god in the myths nor the most popular god in the cult. The other two types of gods mentioned in the Esarhaddon treaty were evidently regarded as the protective geniuses of the individual cities, and cultic activity centered around them.

The treaty shows that Eshmun and Melqart were gods who guaranteed the fertility of the land and the fecundity of the flocks. The prophet Hosea (especially in 2:10–15) calls this type of god *ba'al* (pl., *ba'alim*), and condemns the Northern Israelites for thus identifying their own national god (cf. 2:18–19). Melqart was the city god of Tyre; his cult later spread to Egypt, Cyprus, Carthage, and elsewhere. According to Menander of Ephesus (see Josephus, *Antiquities* 8.146), the tenth-century King Hiram of Tyre (Solomon's famous ally) built a new temple for Melqart (Herakles), and innovated the celebration of the "awakening" (i.e., resurrection) of Melqart. This testimony shows that Melqart was a dying and reviving god; his life cycle evidently corresponded to the seasons of the agricultural year. Melqart's name literally means "king of the city." Since the word *city* is a widespread Semitic euphemism for the netherworld (i.e., the infernal city), the name is a further indication of Melqart's chthonic character.

Eshmun, who is linked with Melqart in the Esarhaddon treaty, was the dying and reviving god venerated at Sidon. He was later identified with the healer god Asklepios. The association of healer gods with the chthonic cycle is a common phenomenon in the ancient Near East. At Ugarit, the patron of the deified dead was Rapiu ("healer"), and his name survives in those of the late first-millennium Phoenician deities Shadrafa ("healing spirit") and Baal-Merappe ("healer Baal").

The third important dying and reviving god was Adonis, whose cult was prominent in Byblos, and especially at the spring of Aphaca, near Beirut. This god's name is attested by classical authors, and does not appear in Phoenician texts; the name is, however, clearly derived from the Canaanite *adoni* or *adonai,* which means "my lord." The well-known story of the death of Adonis (e.g., Ovid, *Metamorphoses* 10.710–739) is undoubtedly of Semitic origin.

The most prominent deity in the Phoenician and Punic cults was the goddess Astarte. In the Esarhaddon treaty she is invoked as a war goddess, but her personality was more complex; she was also a fertility goddess, a mother goddess, and a goddess of love, having assimilated her many characteristics from various older goddesses such as the Canaanite triad of Athirat, Anat, and Athtart; the Egyptian Hathor; and the Mesopotamian Ishtar. Astarte's character was so diverse, in fact, that she was identified with several Greek goddesses: Aphrodite, goddess of love and fertility; Hera, queen of heaven; and the mother goddess Cybele. In Byblos, Astarte was worshiped simply as Baalat, "lady" (feminine form of Baal), and in Carthage she was identified with Tanit (origin uncertain). She was also venerated at Tyre (as consort of Baal-Shamem), Sidon, Arvad, and Ashkelon, as well as in the colonies on Cyprus, Sicily, and Malta. She is the Ashtoret/Ashtarot so detested by the biblical authors.

In the fifth-century inscription of King Eshmunazor of Sidon, Astarte bears the epithet "name of Baal"; similarly, in Carthage, Tanit is styled "face of Baal." These epithets suggest that the Phoenicians saw Astarte as the manifestation of Baal-Shamem's numinous power. The cult of Astarte, then, was the means of access to the high god; the great mother served as a sort of mediator between the people and the heavenly Baal.

It has often been suggested that the divine triad described above—high god, great goddess, and dying and reviving god—constituted the basis of all Phoenician pantheons. Attractive as that suggestion is, it must be considered no more than tentative in light of the evidence. The cult of Beirut, for example, seems only to possess a divine couple (Poseidon and Aphrodite/Astarte), and the Tyrian Melqart seems to be both a high god and a dying and reviving god. In addition, the precise relationship between the goddess and the dying and reviving god is often uncertain.

Various other gods comprise the "assembly of the gods," the "holy ones" (so the Yehimilk inscription), or the "whole family of the children of the gods" (Azitawadda). The main feature of the different local pantheons is their diversity. In the Karatepe inscription, for example, King Azitawadda's patron god is the otherwise unknown Baal-*krntrysh* (significance uncertain). The inscription also mentions Rashap (Reshef), one of the most important West Semitic gods from the third millennium onward; but the epithet assigned to Azitawadda's Rashap is unique and problematic. In his curse against anyone who would remove the great portal he has just dedicated, Azitawadda specifically invokes Baal-Shamem, El-Creator-of-the-World, and Eternal Sun. All of these divine titles evoke numerous Near Eastern parallels, but nowhere else do they occur in this form or juxtaposition.

Another problematic deity of great importance bears the epithet *Baal-Hammon* ("lord of the brazier"). He is later identified with Saturn, but the Phoenician divine name that underlies his epithet cannot be determined, nor can anything definite be said about the god's character. He is mentioned once in the ninth- or eighth-century inscription of King Kilamuwa of Ya'adi (Zinjirli, in southern Anatolia), and later becomes enormously popular in the Punic cults of North Africa, Malta, and Sicily. In Carthage, votive stelae are regularly dedicated "To the lady, Tanit-Face-of-Baal, and to the lord, Baal-Hammon." (Elsewhere, Baal-Hammon is generally mentioned first.) In view of the close relationship between Tyre and Carthage, it is tempting to equate Tanit and Baal-Hammon with Astarte and Melqart. While some assimilation is certain, however, absolute identity is not.

Throughout the first millennium, the Phoenician divine world becomes increasingly complex. Innovations do not, however, appear to be organic developments. They stem, rather, primarily from syncretism—incorporation of external influences. Compound divine names, which appear in profusion after the middle of the first millennium, are good indications of syncretism and assimilation. For example, Eshmun-Melqart is attested in several fourth-century inscriptions from Kition (Cyprus). Milk-Astarte, whose name is probably a combination of *Melqart* and *Astarte,* is prominent in the third- and second-century texts from Umm el-Awamid (near Tyre); the significance of the combination, however, is unclear.

In addition, a number of old gods from different places appear in various cults. The old Canaanite storm god Hadad, for example, is found together with the "Syrian goddess" Atargatis in a second-century Greek inscription from Kfar Yassif, near Acre. In general, though, the old gods belong to a shadowy world of protective geniuses and malevolent demons. The proliferation of divine and semidivine guardians and healers (usually chthonic, like Shadrafa) is one of the most important developments within Phoenician religion. Early evidence comes from the two extraordinary seventh-century apotropaic plaques from Arslan Tash in north Syria, which name several of these figures. One of the plaques invokes the protection of Baal-Lord-of-the-Earth (i.e., the netherworld) and of the chthonic god Horon, who is also prominent in two second-millennium Canaanite incantation texts. And later Phoenician and Punic cults venerate the Egyptian Osiris and Bes, the Babylonian Nergal (Rashap), and the Canaanite Mekal and Anat (identified with Athena), among others.

Finally, some Phoenician gods are only attested by their Greek "equivalents," so that their Phoenician identities can only be surmised. An important case in point is the high god of Beirut, who was "Poseidon," perhaps to be identified with El-Creator-of-the-Earth.

Beliefs and Practices. Phoenician religion was certainly rooted in a rich mythological tradition. That tradition, unfortunately, does not survive in native texts. The main source is Philo Byblius's *Phoenician History*, which is supposedly a Greek translation of a Phoenician account by a priest named Sanchuniaton. Most of the extant portions of Philo's work are in book 1 of Eusebius's *Praeparatio evangelica*, and variant versions of some parts can be found in other late classical texts.

Despite the indubitable value of Philo's work, its reliability should not be overstressed. It is composed of numerous sources, and is replete with internal confusion and duplication. It conflates originally independent local traditions, and it imposes an alien euhemeristic framework on the material. Still, as Albert I. Baumgarten concludes in his important study (1981) of Philo Byblius, "behind the distortions one can see traces of a more traditional mythology and religion" (p. 268).

At the very least, Philo's work demonstrates that the Phoenicians had a cosmogonic creation myth that was combined with the generations of the gods and an account of the origin of culture. The traditions are generally comparable to such texts as the Babylonian epic *Enuma elish* and Hesiod's *Theogony* (according to Philo, Hesiod appropriated the Phoenician stories and "decked them out in every way"); they all provide etiologies and apologies for the supremacy of particular gods and cults in particular places. Thus, for example, the high god Kronos/El (Baal-Shamem?) assigns Phoenicia to Astarte and Zeus-Demarous/Adad ("Baal," that is, a dying and reviving god), constituting the divine triad (cf. *Dt.* 32:8 with Baumgarten, p. 214). Astarte herself then consecrates her shrine at Tyre. The text continues with etiologies of human sacrifice (see below) and circumcision, explaining that Kronos gave his beloved son up as a wholly burned offering during a time of "pestilence and death," and later circumcised himself.

In Phoenician religion, three kinds of cultic activity predominated: (1) rituals associated with the dying and reviving god, (2) sacrificial rites, and (3) funerary rites. There were three centers of cultic activity: (1) undeveloped natural sites, especially mountains, rivers, and groves of trees, which for one reason or another were considered sacred (cf. *Is.* 57:3–13); (2) open-air shrines, usually featuring a sacred grove, a small chapel, a sacrificial altar (the biblical "high place"), and one or more conical stone pillars, called betyls, that symbolized divine presence (to be compared with the wooden asherah poles mentioned in the Bible); and (3) fully enclosed temples with large courtyards for public ceremonies, such as Solomon's Phoenician-designed sanctuary. When the Phoenicians established a colony, they generally built a temple to serve as a center of both religious and mercantile activity. Their commercial ventures and dealings with foreigners thus came under divine protection (see the excellent discussion by Guy Bunnens, 1979, pp. 282–285).

The cult of the dying and reviving god was associated with sacred natural sites. The temple of Eshmun in Sidon was located on a hillside near the Asklepios River (modern Nahr el-Awali), and the famous shrine of Adonis at Aphaca was in the mountains outside Beirut at the source of the Adonis River (modern Nahr Ibrahim), near the sacred grove and shrine of Astarte. Lucian (*Syrian Goddess* 6–8) describes some of the rites and traditions associated with Adonis. In an annual celebration of his death, the people of Byblos would perform mourning rites and lamentations. Then they would offer sacrifices to Adonis "as if to a dead person," following which they would proclaim his revival. Celebrants were required, according to Lucian, to shave their heads; the many ritual razors found in Punic tombs may be connected with this rite, as are biblical proscriptions of such shaving. Women who refused to shave had to act as prostitutes for a day, turning the proceeds over to Aphrodite (Astarte).

Other sources confirm Lucian's general description of the feast of Adonis. It entailed a dramatic enactment of the god's funeral, a mournful procession to the temple of Astarte where sacrifices were offered, and an orgiastic banquet that celebrated the god's resurrection. It can be surmised that similar festivals took place in other Phoenician cities (see especially Édouard Lipiński's brilliant study [1970] of the festival of the burial and resurrection of Melqart).

The ultimate source of the festival is clearly the seasonal cycle; the dying and reviving god, whose demise comes with the withering summer heat, personifies that cycle. The return of the god guarantees the return of fertility to the land. To the archaic fertility cult, however, the Phoenicians appear to have added a personal soteriological dimension, which became increasingly important in the late first millennium. In this new theological context, Adonis personifies the vicarious sacrificial victim whose life is forfeit for the benefit of the individual celebrant. Noel Robertson (1982) rightly calls the god's death "a mythical paradigm of an act of personal atonement" (p. 359). The believer performs a private sacrifice (cf. *Syrian Goddess* 55) and a rite whereby he identifies himself with the victim. He then participates in the public displays of mourning for Adonis, who is the mythic projection of the sacrificial victim, and he ultimately rejoices at the god's (and, vicariously, his own) "salvation."

The concept of the vicarious victim finds its fullest expression in the Phoenician and (especially) Punic sacrificial cults. In Phoenicia proper, animal and vegetable offerings were made at the various shrines, especially in conjunction with the seasonal festivals, and in fulfillment of personal vows; human sacrifices were apparently offered in times of crisis. In the Punic cults, sacrifice was the primary (not to say only) religious act; there is no evidence for the sort of temple ceremonies and religious feasts found in the homeland.

The evidence for the Punic sacrificial cults comes primarily from Carthage, with comparable evidence from other sites in Sardinia, Sicily, and North Africa. The sacrificial precinct was known as the *tofet* (cf. the biblical sources of this term: *2 Kings* 23:10; *Isaiah* 30:33; *Jeremiah* 7:30–32, 19:6–14); the *tofet* of Carthage covered as much as 6,000 square meters. Excavations in the area have turned up thousands of urns containing the cremated remains of birds, animals, and small children. The urns have been found in three distinct archeological strata, indicating that the precinct was in continuous use from around 750 BCE until the Romans destroyed the city in 146 BCE.

Many urns were buried under stelae that were engraved either with inscriptions or designs. The designs are usually crude representations of betyls, figures of Tanit, or symbols of Tanit and Baal-Hammon: the upraised right hand, the caduceus (crescent and disk atop a staff), the disk surmounted by a crescent, and the enigmatic "Tanit sign," basically a triangle topped by a horizontal bar upon which a disk rests. The inscriptions are typically of the votive type, such as the following: "To the Lady, Tanit-Face-of-Baal, and to the Lord, Baal-Hammon, that which Matonbaal, wife of Abdmilqart son of Baalhanno son of Bodashtart vowed, because he [the god] heard his [the votary's] voice and blessed him" (Donner and Röllig, 1966–1969, no. 88).

The dedicators of these stelae evidently repaid their vows to the gods with live sacrifices, mainly of children. And while it is often suggested that child sacrifice took place only in times of duress (cf. Diodorus Siculus 20.14.4–7), the archeological evidence points toward regular, institutionalized practice. Sacrificial animals, in fact, were probably substitutes for the preferred human victims (cf. *Genesis* 22, which is, among other things, an etiology of the substitute offering).

The sacrifice was called a *mulk*-offering; the term *mulk* (biblical *Molech*) is derived from the West Semitic word for "king," and it is evidently an epithet of the god who was the recipient of the offering. This god would have been either an autonomous god of death, like the old Canaanite Mot, or, more likely, the dying and reviving god (Baal-Hammon?) in his chthonic aspect. The location of the Jerusalem *tofet* outside the city's eastern wall, at the traditional entrance to the netherworld, explicitly connects child sacrifice with the cult of death. Offering up an innocent child as a vicarious victim was a supreme act of propitiation, probably intended to guarantee the welfare of family and community alike.

Another aspect of the Phoenician attitude toward death shows up in funerary practices. The preferred mode of burial was inhumation, although there were some cremations (aside from sacrificial victims). Wealthier Phoenicians were buried in decorated coffins, in rock-cut tombs of various types. Egyptian influence is often discernible in the design of both tombs and coffins. In later times, funerary monuments were sometimes built above the tombs. The deceased were buried together with all sorts of practical and ritual objects: utensils for food, cosmetic containers, toilet articles, clothing, jewelry, coins, masks, and figurines. As Donald Harden (1980) remarks in his excellent discussion of Phoenician tombs and burial customs (pp. 96–104), "were it not for the burials, we should know little of the pottery and other things which the Phoenicians used in their day-to-day existence" (p. 104).

The funerary practices strongly imply Phoenician belief in an afterlife. That impression is confirmed by Phoenician royal tomb inscriptions, which level curses against anyone who would disturb the tombs. In the fifth-century inscriptions of both King Tabnit of Sidon and his son Eshmunazor II, part of the curse would deny the tomb violator his "rest with the Refaim." This term, meaning literally "healers," denotes the deified dead of second-millennium Ugarit (also the depotentialized shades of the Bible). As at Ugarit, presumably, dead Phoenician notables assumed a new role as chthonic healers. A first-century-CE bilingual inscription from Lybia contains a dedication "to the divine Refaim." There is insufficient evidence to permit the reconstruction of a Phoenician cult of the dead, but a first-century-BCE text from Piraeus (Greece) does mention a Sidonian *marzih* feast—the ritual banquet of the cult of the dead.

The many Phoenician religious shrines were staffed by various cultic officials, including priests, scribes, musicians, barbers (probably for the ritual shaving mentioned above), and male and female cult prostitutes. The titular head of the cult, in all likelihood, was the king (in those cities that had one). Tabnit refers both to himself and to his father as "priest of Astarte, king of the Sidonians." The word for "priest," *khn*, is common West Semitic; it occurs frequently in the inscriptions to designate the most important cultic officials, as does the feminine form *khnt*, "priestess." The priesthood was hereditary: one stela from Carthage lists seventeen generations of priests of Tanit. Since the stela is probably from the late fourth century, that line of priests might date back to the very founding of Carthage (see Harden, 1980, p. 283, n. 31, and corresponding plate 31).

Artistic representations of the priests show them bringing offerings (in one case an infant) and giving benedictions. They wear a squarish cap or a head scarf, with a stole over one shoulder and a close-fitting tunic. Something of the priests' livelihood can be determined from lists of the sacrificial tariffs of third- and second-century Carthage, of which several broken copies have survived. These tariffs detail the payments the priests received for performing various sacrifices—both in money and in portions of the sacrificial animal (cf. the opening chapters of *Leviticus*). The two main types of offering were apparently the "whole gift-offering" and the "substitute offering" (for a child?), although both terms are problematic. The priest's fee was higher for the latter; the fee also varied according to the type of animal sacrificed. Bird offerings, oblations, and meal offerings constitute separate categories in the tariff, and there is also a provision for free sacrifices for the poor.

In addition to performing their sacerdotal functions, the priests were probably the conservators and transmitters of Phoenician culture. Through their activity, the Phoenician language and traditions survived even in the most unpromising circumstances. Poignant evidence of that survival is the one extant Phoenician prayer, an improvised personal prayer recited by a merchant named Hanno, which is preserved in Latin transcription at the beginning of the fifth act of the *Poenulus* of Plautus.

BIBLIOGRAPHY

There are two excellent general works on the Phoenicians in English: Donald B. Harden's *The Phoenicians*, 2d ed. (New York, 1980), and Sabatino Moscati's *The World of the Phoenicians*, translated by Alastair Hamilton (New York, 1968). Both are well illustrated and contain extensive bibliographies of older works (which will, therefore, not be listed here). The definitive edition of the Phoenician and Punic inscriptions, still in progress, is the *Corpus Inscriptionum Semiticarum*, part 1 (Paris, 1881–). A thoroughly annotated English translation of Phoenician (but not Punic) texts is John C. L. Gibson's *Textbook of Syrian Semitic Inscriptions*, vol. 3, *Phoenician Inscriptions* (Oxford, 1982). A good selection of both Phoenician and Punic inscriptions with German translations, commentary, and glossary is *Kanaanäische und aramäische Inschriften*, 2d ed., 3 vols., edited by Herbert Donner and Wolfgang Röllig (Wiesbaden, 1966–1969). Of the utmost importance for students of the inscriptions is Javier Teixidor's "Bulletin d'épigraphie sémitique," which has appeared more or less regularly in the journal *Syria* since 1967 (vols. 44–). There is also a fine dictionary available in English: Richard S. Tomback's *A Comparative Semitic Lexicon of the Phoenician and Punic Languages* (Missoula, Mont., 1978). The standard survey of the Phoenician gods is Marvin H. Pope and Wolfgang Röllig's "Syrien: Die Mythologie der Ugariter und Phönizier," in *Wörterbuch der Mythologie*, vol. 1, edited by H. W. Haussig (Stuttgart, 1965), pp. 219–312. Phoenician and Punic personal names are collected and analyzed in Frank L. Benz's *Personal Names in the Phoenician and Punic Inscriptions* (Rome, 1972).

The student interested in the state of the art in Phoenician and Punic studies must learn Italian, the primary language of scholarly publication. The most important scholarly journal is the *Rivista di studi fenici* (Rome, 1973–). Fundamental treatments of key issues are Sabatino Moscati's *Problematica della civiltà fenicia* (Rome, 1974) and the essays of Giovanni Garbini collected in *I Fenici, storia e religione* (Naples, 1980). An excellent introduction to the present state of scholarship is the conference volume *La religione fenicia: Matrici orientali e sviluppi occidentali* (Rome, 1981). This volume includes, among a number of important studies, two seminal programmatic statements: Paolo Xella's "Aspetti e problemi dell'indagine storico-religiosa" (pp. 7–25) and Giovanni Garbini's "Continuità e innovazioni nella religione fenicia" (pp. 29–43; also in *I Fenici*, cited above, pp. 151–159).

There are many recommendable studies on special topics. Javier Teixidor's *The Pagan God* (Princeton, 1977) is a brilliant analysis of popular religion in the Greco-Roman Near East, with special attention to Phoenicia, Syria, North Arabia, and Palmyra. Two volumes of essays filled with learning and interest are Robert Du Mesnil du Buisson's *Études sur les dieux phéniciens hérités par l'empire romain* (Leiden, 1970) and *Nouvelles études sur les dieux et les mythes de Canaan* (Leiden, 1973). The two essays that reconstruct the pantheons of Byblos (*Études*, pp. 56–116) and Tyre (*Nouvelles études*, pp. 32–69) are *tours de force.* A characteristically insightful and controversial study of Phoenician religion in relation to the Bible is William F. Albright's *Yahweh and the Gods of Canaan* (London, 1968), pp. 208–264. On the dying and reviving god, two recent studies of extraordinary interest are Édouard Lipiński's "La fête de l'ensevelissement et de la résurrection de Melqart," in *Actes de la Dix-septième Rencontre Assyriologique Internationale*, edited by André Finet (Brussels, 1970), pp. 30–58 (exhaustively annotated), and Noel Robertson's "The Ritual Background of the Dying God in Cyprus and Syro-Palestine," *Harvard Theological Review* 75 (July 1982): 313–359.

A splendid account of the Phoenician colonization of the west is Guy Bunnens's *L'expansion phénicienne en Méditerranée* (Brussels, 1979). A popular account of recent excavations at Carthage that emphasizes the issue of child sacrifice is Lawrence E. Stager and Samuel R. Wolff's "Child Sacrifice at Carthage: Religious Rite or Population Control?," *Biblical Archaeology Review* 10 (January–February 1984): 31–51. The article is generally more sober than the title would suggest, and it is magnificently illustrated. For a powerful argument against the existence of institutionalized child sacrifice, see Moshe Weinfeld's "The Worship of Molech and of the Queen of Heaven and Its Background," *Ugarit-Forschungen* 4 (1972): 133–154.

On Philo Byblius's *Phoenician History*, there is a first-rate translation and commentary by Albert I. Baumgarten, *The Phoenician History of Philo of Byblos* (Leiden, 1981). No similar up-to-date study of *The Syrian Goddess* exists, although there is a readable English translation with brief introduction by Harold W. Attridge and R. A. Oden, Jr., *The Syrian Goddess (De dea Syria)* (Missoula, Mont., 1976). For a fuller commentary, *Lukians Schrift über die syrische Göttin*, edited and translated by Carl Clemen (Leipzig, 1938), is still useful.

Finally, space must be found for Gustave Flaubert's novel of Carthage, *Salammbô*, corr. ed. (Paris, 1879), inspired by his visit to the site in 1858. The chapter entitled "Moloch" includes Flaubert's gruesome account of child sacrifice.

ALAN M. COOPER

PHOTIOS (c. 820–891), patriarch of Constantinople, saint of the Orthodox church; scholar, public minister, diplomat, professor, organizer of missions, ecclesiastical writer, and hierarch. Photios was born into a noble family. His father, Sergius, was the brother of the patriarch Tarasios. Three of Photios's four brothers held high civil offices; because of his family's social position, he was able to obtain an advanced education.

In 850, when the university of Constantinople was reorganized (by Photios at the empress's request), Photios was one of the first professors called there to teach. He was sent to Baghdad in 851, together with Constantine the Philosopher, as diplomatic representative of the emperor to the caliph al-Mutawakkil. After intervention in 858 by the caesar Bardas, uncle of Michael III, the conservative patriarch Ignatius resigned. Photios as a layman was elected patriarch. Although he was eventually ordained, Nicholas I refused to recognize his election, and, under pressure from Ignatius's supporters, he officially condemned Photios in Rome (863). After the intervention of the new emperor, Basil I, in 867, Photios was deposed and Ignatius once again became patriarch.

A synod convened in 869, comprised of only a limited number of bishops, condemned Photios and definitively justified Ignatius. As Francis Dvornik has said, this synod was used exclusively by the Latins to define their attitude against Photios (Dvornik, 1948). However, ten years later, in 879, at the request of John VIII, another synod was held that canceled all decisions of the previous one and reelected Photios as patriarch. He died in the Monastery of Amoniakon, probably on 6 February 891.

Photios's most important theological views are expressed in his *Mystagogy of the Holy Spirit*, which is a detailed analysis of the doctrine of the Holy Spirit. According to Photios, the *filioque* clause, which claims that the Holy Spirit proceeds from the Father "and from the Son," was theologically unacceptable because it introduced a new principle into the Trinity. If the procession of the Holy Spirit was dependent upon procession from the Son, then this would create an unequal union among the three divine persons, destroying the balance.

Within the church, Photios thought true communion impossible without the coexistence of dogma and ethos. However, he saw the importance of accepting a diversity of institutions and ecclesiastical customs, a diversity that would be made whole by the effects of the Spirit. As a result of mission work, there were new Slavic churches demanding autonomy, which was giving impetus to changes in ecclesiastical organizations that had until that time remained uniform.

According to Photios, political authority is equal to ecclesiastical authority in the governance of a people; the functions of the emperor and patriarch are parallel. Photios's theory, known as the dual control theory, places responsibility for the subjects' material well-being in the emperor's hands; the patriarch is held accountable for their spiritual welfare. In other words, governance is equally distributed between the emperor and the patriarch, who work harmoniously for the good of the world.

Photios's theological and literary works continued to influence others long after his death. His theological work has had the most influence, especially his detailed presentation of the doctrine of the Holy Spirit, which was identical to that put forth by his successors. Photios's interest and participation in the theological and political discussions of his time directly determined the field of jurisdiction of the early Christian rulers in Slavic countries and contributed to the formation of laws and to the regulation of relations between church and state. Photios was, in fact, the first patriarch of Constantinople to initiate missionary work among the Slavs. He chose Cyril and Methodius from Thessalonica to preach Christianity in Russia, Bulgaria, Moravia, Croatia, and Slovenia. At the same time, Photios struggled to protect the rights of the ecumenical throne from the interference of the ambitious Nicholas I in southern Italy, Sicily, and on the Balkan peninsula.

Photios's corpus includes poetic and prose writings, literary works, and theological works. His most significant works are *Lexicon, Ecclesiastic History Compendium*, and *Myriobiblion* (or *Bibliotheca*), which contains the literary analyses of 280 works studied by Photios, many of which are no longer extant. Photios's *Amphilochia* is an important collection of dogmatic essays, whereas his *Mystagogy of the Holy Spirit*, an anti-*filioque* essay, presents all the arguments related to the teaching about the procession of the Holy Spirit from the Father alone. His *Against the Manichaeans* refutes the Manichaean heresy and warns about the dangers it holds for the orthodox faith. Although the *Nomocanon* and the *Epanagoge* certainly reflect Photios's opinions and were for years attributed to him, they were most likely written by his students.

BIBLIOGRAPHY

Only a few of Photios's works have been translated. See, for example, in English, *The Homilies of Photius, Patriarch of Constantinople*, translated, with commentary, by Cyril Mango (Cambridge, Mass., 1958), and, in Russian, *Patriarkha Fotiia XLV neizdannykh pisem*, edited and translated by Athanasios Papadopoulos-Kerameus (Saint Petersburg, 1896). Photios's writings are collected in *Patrologia Graeca*, edited by J.-P. Migne, with Joseph Hergenröther, vols. 101–104 (Paris, 1857–1866), and in *Epistolai*, edited by Iōannou Balettas (London, 1864). For critical discussion, see Francis Dvornik's "Photius, Father of Schism or Patron of Reunion?" in *Report of the Proceedings at the Church Unity Octave, 1942* (Oxford, 1942), pp. 19–32, and the same author's *The Photian Schism: History and Legend* (Cambridge, 1948), which includes a full bibliography and explicates the false legends about Photios. In Greek, see my *Theologia kai diaprosōpikai skheseis kata ton M. Phōtion* (Thessaloniki, 1974); in German, Joseph Hergenröther's *Photius, Patriarch von Konstantinopel*, 3 vols. (Regensburg, 1867–1869).

VASILEIOS YIOULTSIS

PHYSICS AND RELIGION. "Physics really began," said Albert Einstein, "with the invention of mass, force, and an inertial system. These concepts are all free inventions." The first modern approach toward precise definitions and use of these and other related concepts was made by Galileo Galilei (1564–1642), the father of modern physics. He initiated a distinct and new approach to the study of nature, with a characteristic integration of mathematical reasoning and experimental observation.

The Scientific Revolution. The essential philosophical basis of modern science was established during the great scientific revolution in Europe during the sixteenth and seventeenth centuries that culminated in the grand synthesis of Isaac Newton (1642–1727). All the major scientists participating in this revolution were Christians. Some of them were quite devout and some also very learned in the scriptures. Some had strong mystical tendencies; others were theologically oriented. Scientific works of several of them—for example, Copernicus, Galileo, and Descartes—were severely censured by the religious authorities; many others, including Kepler and Newton, held views out of keeping with the religious orthodoxy of their denominations. However, none of these savants, not even those who were persecuted for it, ceased being Christians or believers as a consequence of their scientific work. To be sure, given the times, any public exposure of loss of faith would have had serious consequences for them. Their religious views seem to have been much less, if at all, influenced by their scientific work than by their psychological makeup and the historical and sociological forces acting upon them. On the other hand, it is difficult to see how their scientific work was affected by their religious beliefs. It is sometimes said that the Judeo-Christian theology provided a hospitable ground for the rise of modern science, but it is also possible to say that progress in science was made in spite of, rather than because of, the distinctly biblical component of the Western mind. What the biblical stream did contribute to modern science was an ethos that facilitated the control and mastery of nature and permitted its technological exploitation. This, in turn, made possible the later Western domination of the globe.

During the revolution itself, two major attitudes toward science and religion prevailed among scientists. One was exemplified by Galileo, who, quoting a remark made originally by Cardinal Césare Baronio, said that "the Bible tells us how to go to Heaven, not how the heavens go." The concerns of the scriptures were different from those of the book of nature, and the Bible, according to this point of view, was not declaring truths of natural philosophy. The book of nature has its own principles and is written in the language of mathematics; the questions of natural philosophy should not and cannot be decided by appeal to theological authority. The second attitude was adopted by, among others, Kepler and Newton, who regarded themselves as the priests of God in the temple of nature. While they certainly endorsed the Galilean point of view regarding the distinction between the book of revelation and the book of nature, they considered their work in natural philosophy to be a hymn of praise. Their science was a celebration of the works of God, "to discourse of whom from the appearance of things," said Newton, "does certainly belong to natural philosophy." On another occasion he said, "When I wrote my treatise about our system, I had an eye upon such principles as might work with considering men for the belief of a Deity; and nothing can rejoice me more than to find it useful for that purpose. But if I have done the public any service this way, it is due to nothing but industry and patient thought."

One major change was obvious. Before the scientific revolution, and during its early phases, truths of natural philosophy were subject to theological, particularly biblical, authority. By the end of the revolution, theological and biblical pronouncements had no bearing on the propositions of natural philosophy. It has been suggested that the intellectual climate in Europe's Protestant countries was much more conducive to the growth of science than that in Roman Catholic countries. But in neither case, from the eighteenth century onward, did the church or theological authorities have any moral, philosophical, or temporal power to influence either the theory or the practice of natural philosophy.

Theology was on the retreat, trying to bolster itself by appropriating for its own purposes some theory or another in physics that might lend itself to such manipulation.

Many scientists themselves indulged in this theological service of proving the existence of God from the intricate and ingenious designs of his works. Newton provided perhaps the prime example of such activity, even though all his natural theology did not, in practice, lead him to a religious and wise life: the greatest of all scientists is said to have been a vindictive, jealous, suspicious, vain, and small-souled man. All his and other scientists' theologizing remained essentially theoretical and without influence on the actual conduct of their lives. Even as theory, theology had less and less connection with natural philosophy; within a hundred years of Newton's death, Pierre-Simon de Laplace—hailed as the Newton of France—confidently banished the hypothesis of God from the new scientific system of the world.

Assumptions of Physical Science. In general, the new science and the accompanying view of reality, of man and his place in the cosmos, and the purpose and nature of knowledge, led, as if with inexorable necessity, to a complete mechanization of the world and the accompanying despiritualization of both nature and human beings. All the other natural sciences, social sciences, and even humanities in the last three centuries have been attempting to imitate physics in its style, methods, and principles, owing largely to its precise, quantitative formulations of the laws of nature and to the remarkable success physicists have had in controlling and predicting natural phenomena. It is therefore useful for us to recall some of the fundamental assumptions of research in physics, because the age of science has been, in essential principles, the age of physics.

Essential deadness of matter. One fundamental assumption is that everything in nature is essentially dead: it has no *interiority*—no consciousness, purpose, or intention of its own. Whether one is dealing with an electron, a frog, a human being, or a culture, the assumption is that the entire existence and behavior of the object of investigation can be understood and explained in terms of its interactions with external forces, which, in turn, are themselves purposeless. An obvious aim of physical theory is taken to be the ultimate explanation of all of nature in terms of dead matter in motion. Objects do not have their own initiative; they can only react to external forces. In scientific psychology, this principle leads to behaviorism, with its emphasis on stimulus and response.

Hostility of nature. A second fundamental assumption of physics is that the universe is hostile or at least indifferent (not intentionally but mechanically) to human purposes and aspirations. Therefore, it needs to be fought and conquered. The otherness of nature is an essential presupposition of the scientific attitude; this is what allows man to exploit nature.

Body-mind duality. Closely related to these two presuppositions is another, according to which nature inside man is wholly different from nature outside. This is related to Descartes's well-known and sharp division between the *res extensa* (realm of extension) and *res cogitans* (realm of thinking). The former is the realm of the body; it is the material domain of nature. The latter is the realm of the soul, which for Descartes is the same as the mind. Nature is only material and external. What is internal is merely subjective—in the sense of being personal, private, shifting, and unreliable. Only what is external can be objective and real. Even in the external realm a further division is made between what are called *primary* and *secondary* qualities. This division is necessitated by the demand for an unambiguous intersubjective agreement about the external characteristics of an object. Only those characteristics are regarded as primary that can be quantified and measured and can thus be divorced from any consideration of the individual observer's relative quality of attention, clarity of perception, or level of being. A well-known twentieth-century statement about the importance of measurement, by the famous physicist Max Planck, is "That which cannot be measured is not real." Reality is thus, by assumption, divested of higher feelings or of sensations requiring purified perceptions; it is reduced to those characteristics that can be mechanically quantified, such as size, mass, and so on. "Just as the eye was made to see colors, and the ear to hear sounds," wrote Kepler, "so the human mind was made not to understand whatever you please, but quantity."

Reality as mathematical construct. In physics, an abstract and purely rational and mathematical construct is assumed to underlie the perceived reality. What is experienced is then called "appearance," while the mental construct is called "reality." The scientific pursuit, then, is to speculate about the imagined reality and to put these speculations to experimental tests involving only certain limited perceptions. The so-called objective reality of scientific concern is in fact a conjecture—perhaps one of the many that may be possible. However—and this is where the importance and glory of science lie—these subjective projections are confirmed (or falsified) by intersubjective experimental procedures. Nevertheless, the testing procedures are not wholly independent of the theoretical framework. Whether an experimental observation is taken to be a confirmation of a given conjecture is, as scientific experiments become more and more elaborate, increasingly a matter of interpretation.

Experiment versus experience. It is partly a consequence of what has been said above about the various presuppositions of scientific inquiry that, although the modern natural sciences are thoroughly *experimental* in character, they are in fact determinedly counter*experiential,* in the sense that scientists must not include in their data any observations that involve them personally in the immediacy of perception. It is important to distinguish clearly between *experience* and *experiment,* which have been used in quite different senses in the English language in the last three hundred years. What scientists do in their laboratories is to experiment with or on things; they make measurements based on those experiments. But it is wholly erroneous to say that they experience those things. Given enough research grants and ingenuity, good scientists can arrange their experiments, whether in physics or experimental psychology, so that they can be completely absent from their laboratories when the experimental data are being collected. Leaving out the immediacy of perception or the "minute particulars" (Blake) of reality and the secondary qualities in the collection of scientific data, one ignores most of what the arts and the spiritual disciplines have been traditionally concerned with, such as colors, sounds, tastes, feelings, sensations, purpose, and beauty. Whatever functions poetry, dance, music, or the various spiritual paths may serve, when it comes to the serious business of truth and knowledge, as understood by the modern natural philosophers, all these activities are essentially frivolous.

Herein lie the seeds of fragmentation of our sensibilities: arts and religion cannot lead to knowledge and science cannot lead to values. The resultant dichotomy between knowledge and faith, or between reason and feeling, particularly apparent in scientifically advanced Western culture, tends to be destructive of human wholeness. It is a fact of Western intellectual history that since Newton put modern natural science on a firm footing practically every major artist or poet has felt uneasy about the assumptions, procedures, or results of scientific enterprise. However, perhaps because of the separation among the domains of truth, beauty, and goodness that prevails in the mind of modern people, science has moved on, wholly indifferent to these critics, like a large iceberg unaffected by the thrashing of small fish. No matter that these small fish carried names like those of Goethe, Blake, Wordsworth, and Keats, who were all convinced that, in Blake's phrase, "Reason and Newton, they are quite two things."

The Rift between Reason and Faith. Within the Christian religious tradition the essence of religion is often identified with faith. Although religious people are not likely, unless cornered by philosophers, to equate faith with belief in a set of propositions, they themselves seem to have taken their stand in the realm of faith as distinct from the realm of knowledge. Since knowledge, which in the modern West has become more or less synonymous with science, is allied with reason, the relationship between faith and reason has become quite problematic. Faith is not always regarded as opposed to knowledge and reason, although there are some among both the opponents and the supporters of faith who think so, and who correspondingly recommend leaps of reason or leaps of faith, guarding against contamination from one or the other. More often than not, faith and knowledge are considered somewhat tangential to each other. However, if faith is regarded as having no connection with reason, because faith is radically transcendent or superrational, reasonable people tend to become indifferent to it—as in most scientific laboratories in the Western world. The sharp discontinuity introduced by Immanuel Kant between *phenomenon* and *noumenon,* the former the concern of reason and the latter of faith, is an illustration. This attempt to save faith from the onslaught of reason crystallized the separation of the two, gradually resulting in a rationality without significance and a faith without foundation. Then followed an inevitable inversion: faith that was removed from the scrutiny of philosophical analysis by Kant as superrational *noumenon* came in later for psychological analysis by Freud as subrational *neurosis.*

In the most fundamental manner, the scientific cosmology is materialistic—that is, it takes matter to be both temporally and ontologically prior to intelligence and spirit, and it therefore attempts, wherever and as far as possible, to explain all phenomena (including higher spiritual functions) in terms of dead matter in motion reacting to purposeless external forces. The fact that such explanation has not been possible does not alter the basic wish and tendency. Traditional religious cosmologies proceed in the reverse direction: from above downward, from spirit to matter. In this century, Aurobindo Ghose in India and Pierre Teilhard de Chardin in Europe have made the most outstanding philosophical efforts to reconcile the two opposed cosmological tendencies: that of the traditional religions, in which the spirit creates and descends into matter, and that of modern science, in which matter subject to accidental external forces evolves into higher intelligence and spirit. Among physicists themselves, but only among those who are concerned about the philosophical and religious underpinnings of their scientific work, the general feeling has shifted from the biblical, personal God to a philosophical intelligence, the source of truth, order, and beauty. Pascal's God, "God of Abraham, Isaac, and Jacob—not of the philosophers and scholars," was already creating trouble for Newton and his mechanical world system based on universal laws—a system that made room for God rather in the guise of a retired engineer only. Most contemporary physicists, if they describe themselves as having religious feelings at all, would accept Einstein's description of those feelings as "the rapturous amazement at the harmony of natural law, which reveals an intelligence of such superiority that, compared with it, all the systematic thinking and acting of human beings is an utterly insignificant reflection."

Religion and Twentieth-Century Physics. None of the presuppositions of modern natural philosophy or the attitudes associated with them, as mentioned above, has been in any significant manner altered by the revolutionary theories in physics introduced in the twentieth century, namely, the theories of relativity and quantum mechanics, both of which were essentially brought to their present form before the 1930s. However great the revolution in twentieth-century physics has been, it remains a revolution within science and does not compare in philosophical importance with the great revolution of the sixteenth and seventeenth centuries, which initiated an altogether new and distinct mode of inquiry into nature. That the present physics is basically of one piece with Galilean physics can easily be seen by the applicability of the heuristic principle in physics called the "correspondence principle," which states that all newer, more comprehensible theories must include, and reduce to, earlier theories under the appropriate limiting conditions. But this principle is not extended to the pre-Galilean natural philosophy. By this principle, both quantum mechanics and relativistic mechanics must, and do, yield the standard Newtonian mechanics as a limiting case.

Relativity. The special theory of relativity led to the very important formula $E = mc^2$, relating energy and matter in such a way that what was said above about the priority of matter in scientific cosmology may now need to be modified to the priority of matter-energy (sometimes labeled simply as *matter* or simply as *energy* inclusively, but in no way involving the difference in the emotional overtones in the two words, as it exists in the popular mind). According to this theory, time and space intervals do not have an operational meaning independent of each other because the simultaneity of two events depends not only on their relative position but also on their relative linear motion with respect to each other. Far from making everything relative, as is often said or implied in popular accounts, the attempt in this theory is to remove the ambiguity created by the relativity of motion by defining invariants, such as "proper time" (which includes a component of space) or "proper mass" (which includes a component of energy), that are independent of the state of motion or of rest of the observer. Einstein's general theory of relativity, which has been called "perhaps the greatest achievement in the history of thought" (J. J. Thompson), extends the results of the special theory to the case of accelerated motion and gravitation and shows how the presence of matter affects the geometry of space and time around it. These theories have often been pressed into the service of various theological, philosophical, or even political views by those seeking support from the sciences. In general, such applications are based on unwarranted extrapolations and interpretations, none of which was ever encouraged by Einstein himself. He, more than anyone else, seems to have been aware of these theories' limited domain, however marvelously exciting and revolutionary they have been in natural philosophy.

Quantum theory. The theory of quantum mechanics has created considerable theological and philosophical excitement, far more than the theory of relativity. It has revealed a deep-seated discontinuity in natural processes and entities like time and energy, so that the laws of nature yield only statistical probabilities of certain events' taking place. Individual particles are determinable only up to accuracies theoretically limited by Heisenberg's uncertainty principle as it is applicable to conjugate variables. That is, if the time is determined up to a certain accuracy, there is a calculable degree of uncertainty in the determination of energy; similarly for position and momentum and other appropriate pairs. Laws of nature still apply in a perfectly determinate and causal manner to ensembles of particles. The limitation on the precise predictability for a single particle has led many to discover a place for human free will in an otherwise completely determinate universe. This and other such attempts to find theological or mystical comfort in the latest findings of physics largely indicate a very mental, one-dimensional view of religion—concerned mainly with some propositions of belief—that is gradually being abandoned. Here and there, in some bold quarters, questions are being raised about the proper place of physics and other sciences in the light of many higher levels of consciousness—and the accompanying levels of wisdom and feeling—possible for human beings.

[*See also* Science and Religion. *For detailed treatment of the lives and works of some of the thinkers discussed herein, see the biographies of Aurobindo, Einstein, Galileo, Newton, and Teilhard de Chardin.*]

BIBLIOGRAPHY

The classic study of the philosophical revolution brought about by the great scientific revolution of the sixteenth and seventeenth centuries is Edward Arthur Burtt's *The Metaphysical Foundations of Modern Physical Science* (1925; rev. ed., New York, 1932). How this new method in natural philosophy led to the superstructure of Western domination throughout the world has been discussed by a well-known contemporary physicist, Kurt Mendelssohn, in his *Science and Western Domination* (London, 1976). Another useful book, written from a feminist perspective, is Carolyn Merchant's *The Death of Nature: Women, Ecology and the Scientific Revolution* (San Francisco, 1980). Of special importance are the following books, which also treat of the relation between science and religion: Reijer Hooykaas, *Religion and the Rise of Modern Science* (Grand Rapids, Mich., 1972); David C. Goodman, comp., *Science and Religious Belief: 1600–1900* (Bristol, 1973); and Colin Archibald Russell, comp., *Science and Religious Belief: A Selection of Recent Historical Studies* (London, 1973).

Useful supplementary material can be found in *Newton's Philosophy of Nature: Selections from His Writings*, edited and arranged by H. S. Thayer (New York, 1953), in *The Mechanization of the World Picture* (Oxford, 1961) by Edvard Jan Dijksterhuis, and in *The Religion of Isaac Newton* (Oxford, 1974) by Frank E. Manuel.

Ian G. Barbour's *Issues in Science and Religion* (Englewood Cliffs, N.J., 1966) and Stanley L. Jaki's *The Relevance of Physics* (Chicago, 1966) extend the discussion of the relation between religion and physics into the twentieth century. For a discussion of developments in physical theory, see Albert Einstein and Leopold Infeld's *The Evolution of Physics: The Growth of Ideas from Early Concepts to Relativity and Quanta* (New York, 1938). For a discussion of the philosophical problems raised by twentieth-century physics, see Henry Margenau's *The Nature of Physical Reality* (New York, 1950). The rise in the prestige and power of physicists in the United States is detailed by Daniel J. Kevles in *The Physicists: The History of a Scientific Community in Modern America* (New York, 1978). For Albert Einstein's views on science and religion and other social and cultural issues, see his *Out of My Later Years* (New York, 1950). Current discussions of the relationship between modern physics and Asian religious traditions can be found in Fritjof Capra's *The Tao of Physics* (Berkeley, 1975) and in my article "Perception in Physics and Yoga," *Re-Vision* 3 (1980): 36–42. This relationship is also the topic of two transcribed conversations: "The Physicist and the Mystic—Is a Dialogue between Them Possible?" is a conversation with David Bohm conducted by Renée Weber and edited by Emily Sellon, *Re-Vision* 4 (1981): 22–35, and "Reflections on the New-age Paradigm" is an interview with Ken Wilber, *Re-Vision* 4 (1981): 53–74. Writings on religion by the major physicists of the twentieth century have been edited and given a useful introduction by Ken Wilber in *Quantum Questions* (Boulder, 1984).

RAVI RAVINDRA

PICO DELLA MIRANDOLA, GIOVANNI

(1463–1494), philosopher of the Italian Renaissance. Pico was the youngest son of Francesco Pico, count of Mirandola and Concordia, a small feudal territory just west of Ferrara. He was named papal protonotary at the age of ten and was sent to study canon law at Bologna in 1477. Two years later he began the study of philosophy at Ferrara, and from 1480 to 1482 he studied at Padua, one of the main centers of Aristotelianism. He visited Paris, where he encountered Scholastic theology, returned to Florence, and then moved to Perugia, where he studied Hebrew and Arabic with several Jewish teachers. In Perugia, Pico developed an interest in Ibn Rushd (Averroës) and the mystical Jewish Qabbalah. In his late twenties, after a carefree youth, Pico's life took a more serious turn. He gave up his share of his patrimony and planned to give away his personal property in order to take up the life of a poor preacher. During his final years Pico came under the influence of the Dominican friar Savonarola. He died of a fever in Florence on 17 November 1494, the very day on which Charles VIII of France made his entry into Florence, after the expulsion of its ruler, Piero de' Medici.

A brilliant young philosopher, Pico is best known as the author of *Oration on the Dignity of Man*, which is considered to be the manifesto of Renaissance humanism. "I have read in Arabian books," Pico wrote, "that nothing in the world can be found that is more worthy of admiration than man." To support this humanistic assertion of the first part of the *Oration* he cites a broad array of ancient sources—the mystical writings ascribed to Hermes Trismegistos, various Persian writers, David, Moses, Plato, Pythagoras, Enoch, the qabbalists, Muḥammad, Zarathushtra, the apostle Paul, and many others. Unlike Marsilio Ficino, his friend and mentor at the Platonic academy in Florence, Pico did not give man a fixed place in the great chain of being; he described man as the object of special creation and the focal point of the world with no fixed place, outline, or task, but free to make his own choices and to seek what is heavenly and above the world, free to become a veritable angel. The *Oration* served as the rhetorical introduction to his *Conclusiones* (1486), nine hundred "theses" providing a summation of all learning, which Pico offered for public disputation. Upon publication in Rome, seven of the theses were found by a commission of Innocent VIII to be heretical and six of them dubious. Pico's apologia for them was not accepted, but Alexander VI subsequently vindicated his orthodoxy.

Pico's mature philosophical writings include the *Heptaplus* (1489), a sevenfold interpretation of *Genesis* 1:1–27; *Of Being and Unity* (1491), on the harmony of Plato and Aristotle; and a long treatise attacking astrology as demeaning to man's liberty and dignity. He allowed for sidereal influence only because of heat and light, but not because of any occult power of the stars. His thought was notable for its synthesis of Aristotelianism and Platonism, its combination of scholastic and humanist elements, and for the fascination with Qabbalah that it reflects.

BIBLIOGRAPHY

Although Pico's *Opera* (Basel, 1572) is not readily accessible, Eugenio Garin has published editions of various texts: *De hominis dignitate, Heptaplus, De ente et uno, e Scritti vari* (Florence, 1942) and the *Disputationes adversus astrologiam divinatricem*, 2 vols. (Florence, 1946–1952). For a translation of the *Oration*, see *The Renaissance Philosophy of Man*, edited by Ernst Cassirer et al., translated by Josephine L. Burroughs (Chicago, 1948), pp. 223–254. For Pico's life and thought, see Eugenio Garin's *Giovanni Pico della Mirandola* (Florence, 1937) and *La cultura filosofica del Rinascimento italiano* (Florence, 1961); Eugenio Anagnine's *Giovanni Pico della Mirandola* (Bari, 1937); and Paul O. Kristeller's *Eight Philosophers of the Italian Renaissance* (Stanford, Calif., 1964), pp. 54–71, the best brief treatment in English.

LEWIS W. SPITZ

PIETISM. [*This entry discusses pietism as a historical movement and a religious orientation within Christianity. For discussion of similar phenomena in other religions, see* Devotion.]

Pietism has been and remains an identifiable religious orientation within the churches of the Reformation. As the name indicates, it emphasizes the life of personal piety according to the model it finds in the primitive Christian community. By doing so it has hoped to complete the Reformation, which, in the judgment of many of its adherents, has never become a movement to reform the religious life of individuals. The roots of Pietism are found, on the one hand, in the mystical spirituality of an earlier day and, on the other, in the writings of Martin Luther and John Calvin, as well as other reformers like Caspar Schwenckfeld and the prominent Anabaptists.

It is difficult to fix precisely the boundaries of Pietism, either in terms of chronology or distribution. While scholars have associated Pietism largely with Lutheranism, it has been customary to date its beginning from the publication of Philipp Jakob Spener's *Pia desideria* in 1675, two years after which his followers were referred to as "Pietists." The present tendency, growing out of a great deal of recent research, is to expand the term so as to include what is now widely perceived as the same development within other communions, notably the Reformed, as well as Protestants who questioned the need for any kind of church affiliation because they found a lack of religious devotion and ethical urgency within the churches of the day. Under the circumstances, the classical phase of the Pietist movement should now be loosely regarded as a Protestant phenomenon of the seventeenth and early eighteenth centuries. It is bounded, on the one hand, by the age of post-Reformation orthodoxy, to which it reacted both negatively and positively, and, on the other, by the Enlightenment, which rejected some of its insights and incorporated others. In the sense of a prominent undercurrent within the religious self-understanding of large segments of Protestantism, Pietism as a historical entity has never ceased to exist.

The basic characteristics of the movement can be most easily isolated with reference to its classical phase. Pietists of the day believed that religiousness within the Christian tradition, if it is to be meaningful, must involve the complete religious renewal of the individual believer. The experience of such a renewal need not follow any prescribed pattern, but it must consist in a conscious change of man's relationship to God so as to bring certainty concerning divine forgiveness, acceptance, and continued concern. The fruit of such a renewal must become visible in the form of "piety," that is, a life expressive of love for God and man and built on a vivid sense of the reality of God's presence in all situations of life. Pietists believed that those in whom this religious perspective becomes actualized constitute an inclusive fellowship, namely the *koinōnia,* that was so profoundly cherished by the primitive Christian community. This fellowship was perceived to transcend every barrier of church affiliation, race, class, and nationality—even that of time. Thus Pietists characteristically addressed one another as "brother" or "sister," terms symbolic of a common experience of profound spiritual unity. This sense of religious solidarity was enhanced by an awareness of the fact that they were called upon to live in a society that chose to adhere to a value system different from their own, though it was widely supported by the major Christian communions. Hence they often assembled in conventicles of like-minded people within local parishes. Furthermore, Pietism during its classical period centered its concept of religious authority in a biblicism set originally against the formidable but lifeless theological systems of Protestant orthodoxy. Later it was opposed to the Enlightenment attempt to reduce Christian commitment to the acceptance of a few propositions held to be rationally demonstrable. In tension between these poles, Pietists strove to restore to Protestantism a theology based on a commonsense, untortured, more-or-less literal, and basically devotional interpretation of the Bible. Lastly, Pietists hoped to reform society through the efforts of renewed individuals, thus stemming the moral decay that, in their judgment, afflicted both the churches and the body politic.

Early Pietism. The rise of Pietism is best discussed with reference to five early groupings.

1. Pietism's manifestation within the Reformed territories of the Low Countries is sometimes still referred to as "Precisianism," though it may be best to drop that designation because of the difficulty of distinguishing it conceptually from Pietism as it is here understood. Pietism within Dutch Reformed churches had certain natural affinities with Puritanism, which historically comes from the same source. It is attached to such illustrious names as Willem Teellinck (1579–1629), who may be regarded as its father; William Ames, or Amesius, as he called himself (1576–1673), who, although born and educated in England, chose to teach at the University of Franeker; and Jodocus van Lodensteyn (1620–1677). Within German Reformed territories its chief theological spokesman became Friedrich Adolph Lampe (1683–1729).

2. The branch of early Pietism that has received the greatest attention is the Spener-Halle type. It was strictly a Lutheran phenomenon, profoundly indebted to Johann Arndt (1555–1621) and counting among its outstanding representatives Philipp Jakob Spener (1635–1705) and August Hermann Francke (1663–1727). Although its concern encompassed men and women in all walks of life, it addressed itself especially to the nobility.

3. Swabian Pietism, on the other hand, exhibited a somewhat different ecclesiastical, as well as social, profile. Its chief spokesman, Johann Albrecht Bengel (1687–1752), was a convinced Lutheran and partially indebted to Spener. Yet he and his followers steered the Pietist development so as to make it dominantly a movement of the people. For that reason Württemberg witnessed the eventual rise of various Pietist fellowships, made up of peasants and artisans, that often resonated to the mysticism of Jakob Boehme and hence were only loosely associated with Lutheranism. A typical fellowship was the Hahnische Gemeinschaft, named after its founder, Johann Michael Hahn (1759–1819).

4. A fourth branch of early Pietism arose within Lutheranism but followed the theological leadership of Count Nikolaus Ludwig von Zinzendorf und Pottendorf (1700–1760). This strain ultimately became the Renewed Moravian Church.

5. Not to be overlooked is the radical wing of Pietists, which was often very critical of the major communions and their close ties to the state. Especially prominent among these critics were the young Gottfried Arnold (1666–1714) and Johann Konrad Dippel (1673–1734), while the saintly Ernst Christoph Hochmann von Hochenau (1670–1721) and Gerhard Tersteegen (1697–1769) were among the radical wing's more irenical representatives.

The eighteenth century. During the second part of the eighteenth century the face of Pietism was considerably altered by the spirit of the times. In its reaction against the Enlightenment philosophy of Christian Wolff (1679–1754), who greatly influenced continental Protestantism, Pietism was forced to align itself theologically with Protestant orthodoxy, its former antagonist, while espousing at the same time the ethical sensitivity of the Enlightenment. Interacting also with the literary movement usually referred to as Sturm und Drang, which tried to legitimize man's inner experience, the freedom of the individual vis-à-vis the accepted norms of the day, and especially the place of feeling, it tended to become sentimentalized and suspicious of rational conclusions.

In one form or another Pietism eventually reached both Switzerland and Scandinavia. By various emissaries, among them Henry Melchior Muhlenberg (1711–1787), Theodor J. Frelinghuysen (1691–1748), Michael Schlatter (1718–1790), Philip W. Otterbein (1726–1813), Peter Becker (1687–1758), and Zinzendorf, it was brought to the American colonies. Its Moravian phase strongly influenced the Wesley brothers and hence the Methodist movement in America. Thus Pietism, along with Puritanism, must now be considered one of the major religious traditions that shaped American Protestantism.

Heritage of Pietism in the Protestant Tradition. The influence of Pietism on world Protestantism has been pervasive and far-reaching. With respect to the ministry, it stressed the religious and ethical qualifications of the minister above his ecclesiastical status. In the area of Protestant worship, it greatly expanded Protestant hymnody, deemphasized ritual, and tended to make the sermon central. It helped to make religious commitment the major aim of Protestant worship. Its advocacy of the devotional reading of the Bible made the latter a book of the people and produced a large corpus of edificatory literature. It was instrumental in reorienting theological education by enthroning the concept of biblical theology and by advocating the religious formation of the whole person, which inevitably resulted in the establishment of theological seminaries for prospective clergy. Its deep concern for the plight of the poor and the sick made for a massive effort to establish homes and schools that would meet their needs, and it projected the hope of a better world brought about through the involvement of concerned Christians. Its vision of a humanity in need of the gospel of Christ made for the initiation and rapid expansion of foreign and domestic missionary enterprises. Its contribution to the rise of the ecumenical ideal is clear, as is its impact on the development of modern theology, notably through the work of Friedrich Schleiermacher and his disciples. Not to be forgotten is the fact that the chief representatives of the intellectual movement known as German Idealism grew up in a Pietist environment. Its genius is discernible also in a variety of later religious movements, such as American evangelicalism.

[*See also the biographies of Spener, Francke, Zinzendorf, the Wesley brothers, and Schleiermacher.*]

BIBLIOGRAPHY

The first extensive historical study of Pietism was Albrecht Ritschl's *Geschichte des Pietismus*, 3 vols. (Bonn, 1880–1886). Although it was an unfriendly, strongly biased treatment, it brought into focus the whole Pietist movement in both the Lutheran and Reformed communions as well as among radicals. This was followed by Paul Grünberg's thorough and scholarly work, *Philipp Jakob Spener*, 3 vols. (Göttingen, 1893–1906). Subsequently there were many local histories, but only sporadic attempts to examine the general phenomenon of Pietism. There was a growing tendency to disregard Ritschl's broad concept and to limit the study to Lutheranism, specifically to Philipp Jakob Spener and August Hermann Francke, Spener's well-known successor at Halle.

After decades of neglect, Erich Beyreuther concentrated some of his prodigious energies upon the subject, notably upon Francke and Zinzendorf. His first volume in this effort was *August Hermann Francke, 1663–1727* (Marburg, 1956). A new era of Pietism study commenced when Martin Schmidt, the outstanding Pietism scholar of our day, published the first of a series of works in the field, *Das Zeitalter des Pietismus* (Bremen, 1965), edited by Wilhelm Jannasch. The present very intense interest in Pietism study was given tremendous impetus when, under the leadership of Martin Schmidt and the Francke scholar Erhard Peschke, the Kommission zur Erforschung des Pietismus was founded in Germany in 1965. On the basis of its findings the concept of Pietism was once again broadened, and under its auspices a series of volumes was published under the title "Arbeiten zur Geschichte des Pietismus" (Bielefeld, 1967–), edited by Kurt Aland, Erhard Peschke, and Martin Schmidt. In 1972, it brought out the first volume, *Abteilung 3: August Hermann Francke*, of *Texte zur Geschichte des Pietismus* (Berlin, 1972), and later the first yearbook, titled *Pietismus und Neuzeit* (Bielefeld, 1974).

During the same period I attempted to generate interest in the study of Pietism in the English-speaking world through *Rise of Evangelical Pietism* (Leiden, 1965), *German Pietism during the Eighteenth Century* (Leiden, 1973), and *Continental Pietism and Early American Christianity* (Grand Rapids, Mich., 1976). In the meantime Theodore G. Tappert had translated into English and edited Spener's *Piadesideria* (Philadelphia, 1964), based on Kurt Aland's treatment of the same work. James Tanis followed with *Dutch Calvinistic Pietism in the Middle Colonies* (The Hague, 1967); J. Steven O'Malley with *Pilgrimage of Faith: The Legacy of the Otterbeins* (Metuchen, N.J., 1973); Dale W. Brown with *Understanding Pietism* (Grand Rapids, Mich., 1978), which is limited largely to an exposition of the views of Spener and Francke; and Gary R. Stattler with *God's Glory, Neighbor's Good: A Brief Introduction to the Life and Writings of August Hermann Francke* (Chicago, 1982).

F. Ernest Stoeffler

PIGS. The pig is an animal at once unclean and sacred. Dear to demons, it is used as bait to divert them from tormenting men, but at the same time it has particular associations with sacrifices of expiation and purification. The pig is strikingly chthonic in nature, for it is usually offered to the divinities and powers of the underworld. When pigs are so bred as to grow tusks that are curved or crescent in shape, they assume the lunar symbolism of the renewal of life or of rebirth after death. Pigs are sometimes believed to be the transformations of certain divine beings.

In ancient Mesopotamia the pig was domesticated in very early times, but its use in the temple cult was extremely rare. As an Assyrian fable puts it, "The pig is not acceptable in the temples, and it is an abomination to the gods." However, it played a very important role in healing rituals and the exorcism of demons. One healing ritual prescribed the immolation of a piglet: the bed of a sick man is rubbed with its blood, the beast is dismembered, and its limbs are applied to the limbs of the sick man. In this way, the piglet substitutes for him. Pigs were especially employed against the demoness Lamashtu, the enemy of pregnant women, young mothers, and their babies. In the rite of exorcism a piglet was immolated and its heart placed at the mouth of a figure of Lamashtu. In Egypt, the pig appeared most notably in connection with the myths and rituals of Seth, the god who killed his brother Osiris and who represented the forces of evil. According to the *Book of Going Forth by Day* (chap. 112), Seth changed himself into a black pig during his fight with Horus, the son of Osiris. Whenever a pig was sacrificed to Horus and its related divinities, it symbolized the forces of evil.

Pigs were sacrificed in ancient Greece for the purification of the sacred field, the sanctuary, and the house of the priestess; they were sacrificed partly because of their association with dirt, with which evil spirits were often equated, and partly because of their association with fertility. Especially noteworthy is the use of pigs in the festivals connected with the goddess Demeter and her daughter Persephone. In the Eleusinian mysteries, for example, each initiate had to sacrifice a piglet for the specific purpose of purifying himself. Since the piglet was as symbolic of the celebration as were the torch and the *kernos* (the sacred vessel used in the Eleusinian cult), in a number of works of art it is represented in the arms of the initiates. Small pigs played a part also in the Thesmophoria, the annual fertility festival honoring Demeter and Persephone. Together with wheat cakes in the shape of serpents and human beings, pigs were thrown, probably alive, into underground chambers *(megara)*, where they were left to rot for a year, while the bones from the year before were brought up aboveground and placed upon an altar.

In the cult of Attis and Adonis as well as in the festivals of Demeter, each worshiper sacrificed a pig as an individual offering. According to mythic tradition, Attis was gored by a wild boar, and likewise Adonis was killed by a wild boar while out hunting. In commemoration of these tragic events boars were sacrificed in the Levant in the domestic rite of mourning, in which the sacrificer acted as if he had been deprived of his own life. The boar sacrifice was a vicarious offering for the life of the worshiper.

For the Jews, the pig is an unclean animal and its flesh may not be eaten nor its carcass touched (see *Lv.* 11:7, *Dt.* 14:8). In ancient times, Jews did not hesitate to risk their lives for their devotion to the Torah in this regard (e.g., *2 Mc.* 6:18–31); in the middle of the second century BCE, they stood against the Seleucid king Antiochus IV when he defiled the Temple of Jerusalem by dedicating it to Olympian Zeus, immolating pigs and other unclean animals and offering them in sacrifice. His religious policy was dictated by his concern to unify the beliefs and practices of his empire (*1 Mc.* 1:41–42), and the cult of Zeus seemed to him an appropriate focus for the religious allegiance of all his subjects. In order to break down the resistance, the king directly attacked the things that expressed Jewish faith: the Torah and its prescriptions, circumcision, the Sabbath, the ritual of sacrifices, and finally the prohibition against immolating and eating pigs.

The dietary prohibition of the Torah is pre-Israelite in origin, for abstinence from the meat of the pig was a widespread, religiously motivated custom that is well attested among the Phoenicians, the Cypriots, the Syrians, the Arabs, and in fact among all Semitic peoples with the exception of the Babylonians. Although its religious origins have sunk into oblivion, the custom has been preserved: Jews and Muslims of today abstain from eating pork in accordance with its strict prohibition by the Torah and the Qur'ān.

In the Hindu tradition, the boar appears again as an avatar of the god Viṣṇu. When a demon, Hiraṇyākṣa, cast the earth into the depths of the cosmic ocean, Viṣṇu assumed the form of an enormous boar, killed the demon, and retrieved the earth with his tusk. This mythic scenario probably developed through a primitive non-Aryan cult of the sacred pig.

The pig continues to play a highly significant role in the myths and rituals of Southeast Asia and Melanesia. Among the Ngadju of South Borneo, when cosmic order has been destroyed by violation of the divine commandments, by incest, for example, the guilty parties must slaughter a pig as a vicarious sacrifice. The entire village community in which they live (the people, houses, fields, animals, plants, and so on) is smeared with the blood of the pig, and then a "tree of life" is erected at the center of the village square before cosmic order is restored. According to the aborigines of the Melanesian island Malekula, the journey to the land of the dead starts with the offering of a pig to the female divinity who guards the cavernous entrance to the otherworld. The pig can be no ordinary one; it must have been raised by the sacrificer's own hands and ritually consecrated time and again. Especially important is the shape of its tusks: they should be curved or crescent, symbolizing the waxing and waning moon. While the pig's black body, consumed by the divinity, corresponds to the new, or "black," invisible moon, its crescent-shaped tusks symbolize the continuance of life after death, rebirth, or resurrection. The killing of pigs is understood by the Ceramese in New Guinea as a reenactment of their ancestors' murder of the maiden divinity Hainuwele, which occurred at the mythical time of beginning. Hainuwele was killed, but her dismembered body was miraculously transformed into tuberous plants (such as coconuts, bananas, and yams) and into pigs, neither of which had previously existed. Pigs are thus Hainuwele in disguise.

BIBLIOGRAPHY

The best single study of the pig in the ancient Near East is Roland de Vaux's "Les sacrifices de porcs en Palestine et dans l'ancien Orient," in *Von Ugarit nach Qumran*, 2d ed., edited by W. F. Albright et al. (Berlin, 1961), pp. 250–265, which is now translated by Damian McHugh in de Vaux's *The Bible and the Ancient Near East* (London, 1972), pp. 252–269. See also Noel Robertson's "The Ritual Background of the Dying God in Cyprus and Syro-Palestine," *Harvard Theological Review* 75 (1982): 313–359. On pigs in the myths, symbols, and rituals of Southeast Asia and Melanesia, see Hans Schärer's classic study, *Die Gottesidee der Ngadju Dajak in Süd-Borneo* (Leiden, 1946), translated by Rodney Needham as *Ngaju Religion: The Conception of God among a South Borneo People* (1946; reprint, The Hague, 1963); John Layard's *Stone Men of Malekula* (London, 1942); and Adolf E. Jensen's *Die getötete Gottheit: Weltbild einer frühen Kultur* (Stuttgart, 1966).

MANABU WAIDA

PILGRIMAGE. [*This entry consists of ten articles that examine the significance of pilgrimage in the context of religious life:*

The overview presents a review of the nature and function of pilgrimage, its structure, images, and meanings. The historical articles treat pilgrimage in various religious traditions.]

An Overview

A religious believer in any culture may sometimes look beyond the local temple, church, or shrine, feel the call of some distant holy place renowned for miracles and the revivification of faith, and resolve to journey there. The goal of the journey, the sacred site, may be Banaras, India (Hindu); Jerusalem, Israel (Jewish, Christian, Muslim); Mecca, Saudi Arabia (Muslim); Meiron, Israel (Jewish); Ise, Japan (Shintō); Saikoku, Japan (Buddhist); or one of a hundred thousand others. Whatever the site, whatever the culture, the general features of a pilgrim's journey are remarkably similar. A generalized account of one woman's pilgrimage may thus serve to illustrate the process.

> Once, in a place apart, there appeared a very holy person; miracles occurred at that place and drew multitudes of pilgrims. Later, a shrine was built by devotees.
>
> Now, in the present, those who are afflicted make a promise to the holy person in their hearts: "If you help me, I will make the journey to your shrine and perform devotions there." The journey will be arduous and inconvenient, but the goal beckons, the source out there that heals both body and soul, and worldly considerations fall away.
>
> The pilgrim sets out lightheartedly. As she travels, she joins with many others who are bound in the same direction, and bonds of friendship develop between them. During her journey the pilgrim calls at sacred way stations, each of which strengthens her faith further. When she nears her goal, and can make out the shrine from afar, she weeps for joy. When she enters the sacred domain she is conscious of actually seeing with her own eyes the place of those holy events, while her feet touch the very ground the holy one trod. At last she is in the presence of the sacred—and is in awe. She touches the shrine with her hand, then remains there a long time in bliss and prayer.
>
> Afterward, she gives offerings and makes the rounds of the lesser shrines that cluster about the main one. Before leaving she eats holy food and calls at the market for pious presents to take home. Her return journey is cheerful, for her affliction is lifted. When she arrives home, her family and neighbors feel and share in the blessings that have come to her.

The Experience of Pilgrimage. Pilgrimage has the classic three-stage form of a rite of passage: (1) separation (the start of the journey), (2) the liminal stage (the journey itself, the sojourn at the shrine, and the encounter with the sacred), and (3) reaggregation (the homecoming). It differs from initiation in that the journey is to a center "out there," not through a threshold that marks a change in the individual's social status (except in the case of the pilgrimage to Mecca). The middle stage of a pilgrimage is marked by an awareness of temporary release from social ties and by a strong sense of *communitas* ("community, fellowship"), as well as by a preference for simplicity of dress and behavior, by a sense of ordeal, and by reflection on the basic meaning of one's religion. Movement is the pilgrim's element, into which she or he is drawn by the spiritual magnetism of a pilgrimage center.

Freedom from social structure. The temporary release from social ties that characterizes a pilgrim's journey is shared by other travelers who have an affinity with pilgrims, especially tourists and mystics. Tourists may, at heart, be pilgrims, for many serious-minded ones, perhaps alienated from their own society, find an elective center in the periphery of society, in a place of power that affects them in a personal way. Like pilgrims, they switch worlds, and they may even experience transcendence in the situation of liminality, in the special state of being freed from social structure. Their outward journey, like pilgrimage, may thus be a form of exteriorized mysticism. Mystics, on the other hand, make an inward sacred journey, an interior pilgrimage. Pilgrims, tourists, and mystics are, all three, freed for a time from the nets of social structure.

Communitas. Pilgrims typically experience the sentiment of *communitas,* a special sense of bonding and of humankindness. Many pilgrims claim of their own company that "here is the only possible classless society." Yet, in each case, this *communitas* is channeled by the beliefs, values, and norms of a specific historical religion. The rules and norms that develop in pilgrimage are essential to the sense of flow that pilgrims feel when they act with total involvement. They need the frame to focus action. So pilgrimage, in its specificity, can foster exclusiveness between the religions, the sense that "ours is the only one."

Here we encounter the fact that pilgrims are usually social conservatives, while their critics are often liberals. More often than not, pilgrimage is a phenomenon of popular religion. The populations from which pilgrims are drawn tend to cling jealously to their traditional rights and customs. Thus we have the paradox that they have often rallied for national independence under pilgrimage banners such as Our Lady of Guadalupe in Mexico and the Virgin of Częstochowa in Poland.

Pilgrimage has been of concern to the orthodox hierarchies of many religions, for pilgrimage draws the faithful away from the center of organization. A devotion may arise spontaneously, not in a consecrated place, and may not keep the strictest rules of the structured religion. Once started, it is democratic, rich in symbolism of its own and in *communitas.* From the point of view of social structure such manifestations of *communitas* are potentially subversive.

Spiritual Magnetism of Pilgrimage Centers. A number of factors may be involved in the spiritual magnetism of a pilgrimage center. A sacred image of great age or divine origin may be the magnet. Such images show great variety, from a painted picture such as that of the Virgin of Częstochowa, to a lovingly clothed doll as at Tlaxcala, Mexico, to a colossal statue of the Buddha in Sri Lanka. They induce awe and devotion, for they have the power to touch the religious instinct. There is an ambivalence in such objects. Are they themselves divine or not? The ambivalence only intensifies the wonder.

Miracles of healing also endow pilgrimage centers with a powerful spiritual magnetism. Such miracles seem to occur when there are both a heightened sense of the supernatural and a profound sense of human fellowship, of shared experience. Although the study of neurological effects of religious experience is in its infancy, there appears to be a healing factor in the unitary experience that is central to religion. The repeated stories of miracles at pilgrimage centers may thus constitute more important material than has been hitherto recognized.

Many pilgrimage centers are sites of apparitions, places where supernatural beings have appeared to humans. The appearance of a supernatural being imparts magnetic power to a site whether or not it has independent beauty or significance. Pilgrims endeavor to touch objects as close as possible to the site of apparition. Through the concreteness of touch, they experience connection with the original event.

The birthplace, location of life events, or tomb of a holy person may be a pilgrimage magnet in the same way, and the land itself in certain places has power to move the spirit, so that rivers, mountains, caves, islands, and strange features of the landscape may radiate spiritual magnetism. A cave at Amarnath, India, is an example. The magically beautiful ice formation within it is worshiped as an incarnation of Śiva. Nature, at the margins of the mundane, may represent a threshold into the spiritual.

Generally, the numinosity of a pilgrimage center is palpable. After the inception of the center it takes on a long-term character, gradually unfolding throughout history.

Historical Classification of Pilgrimages. Pilgrimages have arisen in different periods of history and have taken different paths. According to one typology, based largely in a Western view of history, pilgrimages can be classified as archaic, prototypical, high-period, and modern. Although this typology is most fruitful in examining Christian pilgrimage, it can be extended to other religious traditions as well.

Archaic pilgrimage. Certain pilgrimage traditions have come down from very ancient times, and little or nothing is known of their foundation. Some of these archaic traditions, like that of the Huichol Indians of Mexico, retain a complex symbolic code. Others have been overlaid by the trappings of a later religion, although archaic customs can still be discerned; the *communitas* of past ages also carries on, providing energy for the new establishment. Such syncretism occurred at Mecca and Jerusalem in the Middle East, at Izamal and Chalma in Mexico, and at Canterbury in England. At Canterbury it was officially sanctioned; Augustine of Canterbury received a message from Pope Gregory the Great that he should "baptize" the Anglo-Saxon customs, bringing them into the fold and harnessing them for the new religion.

Prototypical pilgrimage. Pilgrimages established by the founder of a religion, by his or her first disciples, or by important evangelists of the faith may be called "prototypical." As in all new pilgrimage traditions, the foundation is marked by visions and miracles and by the advent of a swarm of fervent pilgrims. They make spontaneous acts of devotion, praying, touching objects at the site, leaving tags on trees, and so on. As the impulse for *communitas* grows, a strong feedback system develops, further increasing the popularity of the pilgrimage center. A prototypical pilgrimage tradition soon manifests charter narratives and holy books about the founder. A shrine is built and an ecclesiastical structure develops. The Jerusalem and Rome pilgrimages are prototypical for Christianity, Jerusalem for Judaism, Mecca for Islam, Banaras and Mount Kailas for Hinduism, Bodh Gayā and Sarnath, India, for Buddhism, and Ise for Shintō. Pilgrims at these sites often reenact events of the founding times.

High-period pilgrimage. In the heyday of a pilgrimage tradition an elaborate shrine, crowded with symbols, is created; side shrines, a market, a fairground, and hostels spring up near the center, and professional pilgrims make their appearance. In the Middle Ages, when the growth of Muslim power in the Mediterranean hampered Christian pilgrimage to the Holy Land, the loss was compensated by the creation of shrines all over Europe. A holy relic was commonly the focus of devotion, as, for example, at Chartres, France, where the Virgin's veil is enshrined. New World pilgrimages resembled their medieval forerunners, although New World shrines lacked relics—one of the reasons for the prevalence of images as a substitute in this region.

Meanwhile, at many European centers routinization and decline had set in. The shrines became so choked with symbolic objects that meaning was being forgotten. Thus, during the Reformation and the era of Puritanism many of them became targets of iconoclasts and were suppressed. Walsingham in England is a prime example.

Desiderius Erasmus, William Langland, John Wyclif, Hugh Latimer, and John Calvin were reformers who opposed pilgrimage and the excessive veneration of images. In recent years opposition has come from the Vatican, which denied approval to pilgrimages to Joazeiro, Bahia, in Brazil and to Necedah, Wisconsin, in the United States; miraculous or apparitional events may be ratified only after exhaustive examination by clerical officials. In Israel the rabbinate keeps watch for irregularities at the many popular pilgrimages to the tombs of *tsaddiqim* ("holy persons").

Modern pilgrimage. All over the world in the last two centuries a new type of pilgrimage, with a high devotional tone and bands of ardent adherents, has developed. Modern pilgrimage is frankly technological; pilgrims travel by automobile and airplane, and pilgrimage centers publish newspapers and pamphlets. The catchment areas of modern pilgrimage are the great industrial cities. However, the message of the shrine is still traditional, at variance with the values of today. Many Roman Catholic pilgrimages have been triggered by an apparition of the Virgin Mary to some humble visionary with a message of penance and a gift of healing, as at Lourdes, France.

Other centers have arisen from the ashes of some dead pilgrimage shrine. A devotee has a vision of the founder, which heralds new miracles and a virtually new pilgrimage, as at Aylesford, England. Both apparitional and saint-centered pilgrimages in other parts of the modern world abound, as in Japan and at the tomb of the holy rabbi Huri of Beersheva, Israel.

Concluding Remarks. Pilgrimage is a process, a fluid and changing phenomenon, spontaneous, initially unstructured and outside the bounds of religious orthodoxy. It is primarily a popular rite of passage, a venture into religious experience rather than into a transition to higher status. A particular pilgrimage has considerable resilience over time and the power of revival. Pilgrims all over the world attest to the profundity of their experience, which often surpasses the power of words.

[*See also* Relics.]

BIBLIOGRAPHY

Aradi, Zsolt. *Shrines to Our Lady around the World.* New York, 1954. A remarkably full listing of world Marian pilgrimages, illustrated, and with short descriptions.

Bhardwaj, Surinder Mohan. *Hindu Places of Pilgrimage in India: A Study in Cultural Geography.* Berkeley, 1973. A much-discussed analysis of levels or rank-order among pilgrimages in India.

Kitagawa, Joseph M. "Three Types of Pilgrimage in Japan." In *Studies in Mysticism and Religion Presented to Gershom G. Scholem,* edited by E. E. Urbach, R. J. Zwi Werblowsky, and Chaim Wirszubski, pp. 155–164. Jerusalem, 1967. Analyzes pilgrimages to sacred mountains, to temples and shrines, and to places hallowed by holy men. A pioneer article.

Kriss-Rittenbeck, Lenz, ed. *Wallfahrt kennt keine Grenzen.* Munich, forthcoming. New aspects of Christian pilgrimage, by international scholars.

Morinis, E. Alan, ed. *Sacred Journeys: The Anthropology of Pilgrimage.* Forthcoming. An essential reference covering many types and aspects of pilgrimage throughout the world, using an advanced theoretical framework.

Palestine Pilgrims Text Society (London). Volumes 1, 3, and 10 (1891–1897) are classic primary sources, constituting the texts of the earliest pilgrims to the Holy Land.

Preston, James J. "Methodological Issues in the Study of Pilgrimage." In *Sacred Journeys,* edited by E. Alan Morinis. Forthcoming. A careful and enlightened essay introducing pilgrimage in all its aspects.

Turner, Victor. "Pilgrimage as Social Process." In his *Dramas, Fields, and Metaphors,* pp. 167–230. Ithaca, N.Y., 1974. The first modern anthropological essay on pilgrimage, introducing the role of pilgrimage in the generation of *communitas,* the sentiment of humankindness; views religious pilgrimage as a moving process, not an arrangement of structures.

Turner, Victor, and Edith Turner. *Image and Pilgrimage in Christian Culture.* New York, 1978. An anthropological study of the cultural, symbolic, and theological aspects of pilgrimage, using important Mexican, Irish, medieval, and Marian examples.

EDITH TURNER

Roman Catholic Pilgrimage in Europe

During the Middle Ages the concept of Christian pilgrimage became a reality in Europe, with varied significance. Pilgrimage, making one's way to holy places, is above all an ascetic practice that lets the Christian find salvation through the difficulties and dangers of a temporary exile. It is also a means of coming in contact with that which is divine and thereby obtaining grace because of the accumulation of supernatural power in the pilgrimage site. However, there are occasions where the blessing requested has already been received, and the pilgrimage is then an act of gratitude. One can therefore distinguish two kinds of journey: the journey of the pilgrim seeking blessing and the journey of the pilgrim giving thanks. Important in both cases, however, is the interchange between God and man through the medium of the saints. It works like an exchange: a material offering (often symbolic, such as a candle) and a self-imposed mortification, the journey to the shrine, correspond to a spiritual or material favor bestowed upon the faithful, who considers it a miracle.

Principal Types of Shrine. The first type of shrine for pilgrimage evident in Europe was the sanctuary for relics, centered on a tomb or reliquary containing the remains of a saint or a fragment thereof. Usually initiated by mass devotion, such worship was validated by the bishop up to the thirteenth century and thereafter by the pope. [*See* Relics.] Among these shrines, the tomb of Peter in Rome and that attributed to James the Greater at Santiago de Compostela in Spain were by far the most frequently visited. But there were also thousands of small churches frequented mainly by local pilgrims, most of which were brought to life only once a year, on the feast day of the patron saint.

The second large category of centers of pilgrimage is that of the Marian shrines. From the twelfth century onward, the worship of Mary developed greatly in Europe, worship that continues to draw the faithful right up to the present. Two main types of Marian shrines have evolved. First are those based on the veneration of a miraculous statue, sometimes called the Black Madonna; important examples of the type are found at Chartres, Le Puy, and Rocamadour in France; Montserrat and Guadalupe in Spain; Mariazell in Austria; Einsiedeln in Switzerland; and Częstochowa in Poland. All these shrines have been frequented since the Middle Ages. A variation on this type is represented by the two locations where homage is paid in a place where the Virgin Mary was miraculously transported or resurrected: Loreto in Italy and Walsingham in England.

The second main category of Marian shrine consists of places sanctified by an apparition of the Virgin and the transmission of a message to a believer chosen by her. These apparitions are evident mainly in the nineteenth and twentieth centuries. The principal ones took place in the rue du Bac in Paris (1830), at La Salette (1846), Lourdes (1858), Pontmain (1871), and at Pellevoisin (1876) in France; at Fátima in Portugal (1917); and at Beauraing and Banneux in Belgium (1932). Of all the shrines, those dedicated to the Virgin Mary still attract the greatest number of believers.

The Evolution of Pilgrimage in Europe. There have been six main stages in the evolution of pilgrimage in Europe beginning with the Middle Ages. The period encompassing the eleventh to the fourteenth centuries saw a dramatic increase in the number of centers of pilgrimage and a corresponding rise in the number of pilgrims. During the fifteenth century and above all the sixteenth century (at the time of the Reformation), the practice of pilgrimage underwent a crisis in which its very usefulness was called into serious question (in the context of the rise of the iconoclastic movement in the churches). With the Council of Trent (1545–1563) there began a period of resurgence, the duration of which varied from country to country. The impulse was halted in France at the beginning of the eighteenth century, but it continued in the Germanic and Slavic countries right up to the time of the French Revolution. Generally speaking, the pilgrim movement became victim to the philosophy of the Enlightenment, which favoured reason above religion, and victim as well to the wish to purge the faith. (The pilgrimage is interpreted by the Roman Catholic hierarchy at this time as a form of supersition to be discouraged.) In the nineteenth century, Catholicism underwent another renewal of faith, which brought with it a renewed impulse for pilgrimage, slow in the first half of the century, then gathering momentum and reaching a peak between 1850 and 1875, probably due to the development of rail travel coinciding with a rise in the influence of the papacy. Since the end of World War I, pilgrimage has been at a notable level, while undergoing sociological change: collective pilgrimages have taken the lead over individual journeys, and more than ever before, young people are taking part in pilgrimages, previously more of an adult occupation. This contributes a notably more universal and ecumenical tone to pilgrimage. However, the modern-day pilgrimage continues, as in previous centuries, to temporarily dissolve the normal lines between social classes. It has also kept its popular nature, even if some of the folklore and customs attached to it have disappeared.

The current record for the number of visits to a shrine is held by Lourdes, to which three million pilgrims journey each year. Next comes Fátima (with two million visitors.) There are several shrines that annually receive more than one million pilgrims: the Chapel of the Miraculous Medallion at the rue du Bac in Paris, Our Lady of Rocamadour, Our Lady of Scherpenheuvel (French, Montaigu) in Belgium, Our Lady of Montserrat in Spain, the Sacré-Coeur at Montmartre in Paris and Mont-Saint-Michel in northwestern France. With regard to pilgrimages to Rome, the greatest number of believers come in the Holy Years.

Today, as during previous centuries, the pilgrimage is a manifestation of collective devotion in which are mingled the two great concerns of the faithful: the salvation of the soul and the thirst for miracles. The pilgrimage is also an opportunity for human contacts of all sorts and for economic, artistic, and religious interchanges, making it one of the most vital elements of European Catholicism.

BIBLIOGRAPHY

For a general view of the meaning of Christian pilgrimage, see Victor Turner and Edith Turner's *Image and Pilgrimage in Christian Culture: Anthropological Perspectives* (New York, 1978). A more detailed work on Roman Catholic pilgrimage in Europe, and particularly in France, is the recent and well-informed publication edited by Jean Chelini and Henry Branthome, *Les chemins de Dieu: Histoire des pèlerinages chrétiens des origines à nos jours* (Paris, 1982). With regard to the medieval period, a good study in English is Jonathan Sumption's *Pilgrimage: An Image of Mediaeval Religion* (London, 1972). More recent developments are described in the work edited by Bernard Plongeron and Robert Pannet, *Le christianisme populaire* (Paris, 1976). Finally, a good work on the greatest European contemporary pilgrimage, the pilgrimage to Lourdes, is that of Bernard Billet and Pierre Lafourcade, *Lourdes pèlerinage* (Paris, 1981).

PIERRE ANDRÉ SIGAL
Translated from French by P. J. Burbidge

Roman Catholic Pilgrimage in the New World

Roman Catholic pilgrimage shrines are found from Alaska and Canada to Tierra del Fuego. The oldest shrine in the Americas is probably Our Lady of Mercy at Santo Cerro in the Dominican Republic. Here, according to tradition, Christopher Columbus erected a cross in thanks for a victory over local Indians in the mid-1490s. The original image of the Virgin Mary is said to have been a gift from Isabella I, queen of Castile (1474–1504), and a pilgrimage chapel may have been erected as early as 1505. Thereafter, Catholic shrines spread through the Americas with Spanish, Portuguese, and French colonization. In some cases, as at Guadalupe, Amecameca, and Chalma in Mexico; Esquipulas, Guatemala; Caranqui, Ecuador; and Copacabana, Bolivia, indigenous holy places were christianized. More often, however, the establishment of shrines involved events leading to the sanctification of places not previously conceptualized as holy.

Missionaries and immigrants to the Americas from various parts of Catholic Europe introduced their own special devotions as well as regionally specific ideas about shrines and pilgrimages. Iberian and French influences were particularly important during the sixteenth through eighteenth centuries, as were ideas brought by missionaries from Habsburg Germanic regions. Diversity increased with mass migrations from other parts of Europe during the nineteenth and twentieth centuries. For example, areas of Italian settlement in Argentina, Chile, and southern Brazil have important shrines dedicated to the fifteenth-century Marian apparition at Caravaggio in northern Italy and to the Virgin of Pompei, a late-nineteenth-century cult that originated near Naples. Similarly, eight shrines of the Byzantine rite are found in the diocese of Curitiba, Brazil, where 95 percent of the population are persons of Ukrainian descent, and a shrine at Doylestown, Pennsylvania, honors the Polish Virgin of Częstochowa. As a result of multiple influences from different parts of Europe at different time periods, the pattern of pilgrimage circulation in the Americas is rich in variety.

The New World's most famous shrine is the Basilica of the Virgin of Guadalupe on the outskirts of Mexico City. Here, according to tradition, the Virgin Mary appeared in 1531 to an Indian named Juan Diego. As proof of the apparition's validity, Diego's cloak was miraculously imprinted with an image of the Virgin in the guise of an Indian maiden. The Mexican Virgin of Guadalupe has been proclaimed patroness of Mexico and of the Americas.

Other apparitional shrines of sixteenth-century origin are at San Bartolo, Naucalpan, Tlaxcala, and Zacatecas, Mexico; Cisne, Ecuador; and Chiantla, Guatemala. Later colonial-period shrines of this type are located at Chirca, Bolivia; Lima, Peru; Ambato, Ecuador; Segorbe, Colombia; San Cristóbal, Venezuela; and Higüey, Dominican Republic. One of the most recent accounts of a New World Marian apparition came from Cuapa, Nicaragua, in 1980.

Numerous American shrines commemorate European apparitions of the Virgin Mary, particularly the 1858 event at Lourdes, France. Some of the more important New World Lourdes shrines are at Mar del Plata, Argentina; Santiago, Chile; Montevideo, Uruguay; Maiquetía, Venezuela; Euclid, Ohio; Brooklyn, New York; San Antonio, Texas; and Rigaud, Canada. American shrines celebrating the 1917 apparitions at Fátima, Portugal, are found at Campo Grande and other places in Brazil as well as at Cojutepeque, El Salvador, and Youngstown, New York. A shrine at Mayo, near Buckingham, Canada, commemorates the 1879 Marian apparitions at Knock, Ireland, and several shrines in the United States and Canada are dedicated to a manifestation of the Virgin Mary at La Salette, France, in 1846.

Many New World shrines came into being when a newly acquired relic or an image of Mary, Christ, or a saint was credited with miracles. Some of these images were probably brought by early missionaries. Examples are found at Itati and Laguna de los Padres, Argentina; Monserrate, Colombia; and Zapopan and Querétaro in Mexico. Other images, such as those honored at Cedros, Honduras; Guanajuato, Mexico; Lima, Peru; La Estrella, Colombia; and Cuenca, Ecuador, were sent as gifts by Spanish royalty. Mysterious strangers are said to have left miraculous images in such places as Cuernavaca, Mexico, and Nátago, Colombia. Elsewhere, as at Baños, Ecuador, and Saltillo and Oaxaca, Mexico, the image is said to have been brought by a mule that refused to move any farther. A variation on this theme comes from Luján, Argentina. Here, at the greatest of all Argentine shrines, an ox cart carrying a statue of Mary from church to church for veneration became stuck in 1630, thus indicating the proper place for the shrine.

Shipwrecks, or the "refusal" of ships to leave harbors, resulted in the acquisition of important cult objects at Antón and Portobelo, Panama, and at Montecristi, Ecuador. The image of Christ at Bom Jesus de Lapa, Brazil, was brought in 1690 by a workman who spent years of penitence in a grotto before becoming a missionary priest, and the image of Santa Rosa of Lima venerated at Pelequén, Chile, was brought south from Lima by a soldier in 1840. Shrines of this type in the United States include those at Dickinson, Texas, where a relic of the True Cross was enshrined in 1936; San Juan del Valle, Texas, where an image of Mary was brought from Mexico by the local priest in 1949; and Miami, Florida, where a modernistic pilgrimage church has been built in honor of the "exiled" image of Our Lady of Charity that arrived from Cuba in 1961.

Many New World shrines trace their origins to the finding of relics or images, usually under mysterious circumstances, similar to events dating to early Christian times in Europe. Stories of such discoveries account for some of the most important shrines in the Americas. Among those of sixteenth-century origin was the dark image of Christ that "appeared" in a cave at Chalma, Mexico, around 1540.

Fishermen at Cobre, Cuba, found a statue of Mary floating on the waters of the bay in 1601. An image of Mary was found on a lake shore after a 1603 flood at Caacupé, Paraguay. Early in the seventeenth century, some Indians found a statue of Mary in a cave at Catamarca, Argentina. At Cartago, Costa Rica, in 1635 an Indian woman found an image of Mary in the woods. Boys found a faded painting of Mary in a hut at Táchira, Venezuela, in 1654, and the painting was miraculously restored. In 1685, just south of Bogotá, Colombia, a man looking for lost treasure found a statue of Mary.

At Yauca, Peru, in about 1700, a group of farmers found an image of Mary in some bushes. A woman on her way back from a pilgrimage to the shrine of Coromoto at San Cristóbal, Venezuela, in 1702 found an image of Mary in a tree at Acarigua. At Aparecida do Norte, Brazil, fishermen found a black image of Mary in a river in 1717. An elderly peasant man found an image of Mary buried in the ground at Suyapa, Honduras, in 1747. At Ipiales, Colombia, in 1754, a young girl saw a painting of the Virgin on a rock face. In 1780, an image of Mary was found after a rainstorm on the edge of a *solar*, a usually dry lake bed, at Copiapó, Chile.

In 1807, a flash of lightning revealed a damaged image of Mary in the corner of a convent room in Guadalajara, Mexico, and in 1868 a rustic wooden cross was found on a mountain with pagan associations near Motupe, Peru.

Other shrine-generating images are said to have been found in oak tree branches, inside trees being cut for timber or firewood, in fountains, under stones in rivers, in thorn thickets, under magueys, and in ruined churches. At least one, at Sopo, Colombia, appeared in an eroded stone.

Other important New World shrines came into being as the result of a miraculous transformation of an already existent image. For example, in 1586, the cult of the Colombian Virgin of Chiquinquirá emerged when a painting of the Madonna was mysteriously restored. Similar stories are told about once-faded copies of this image that have been venerated since the mid-eighteenth century at Aregue and Maracaibo, Venezuela. Similarly, at Talpa, Mexico, a deteriorating corn-paste image of Mary is said to have been miraculously restored in about 1644. Weeping and sweating images of the Virgin Mary have given rise to the establishment of pilgrimage shrines in several places, including Lima, Peru (1591), and Santa Fe, Argentina (1636). Pilgrimages began to the Colegio San Gabriel in Quito, Ecuador, in 1906 after students reported that a painting of Mary opened and closed its eyes several times, and a similar event in 1888 encouraged the development of pilgrimages to a Marian shrine in Cap de la Madeleine, Canada. One of the most recent examples of this type of phenomenon is a plaster image of the Virgin in the cathedral at Managua, Nicaragua, reported to be sweating copiously in 1980.

The most important devotion for northern Mexicans,

at San Juan de los Lagos in the state of Jalisco, began attracting devotees in 1623 after a traveling acrobat's daughter, thought to be dead after falling onto upright knives, came back to life when an old woman touched her with an ancient image of the Virgin. Pilgrimages generated by sudden cures have also emerged in Quinche, Ecuador (1589); Sainte Anne de Beaupré, Canada (1659); San Felipe, Guatemala (1820); and numerous other places. Shrines to which there have been a declining number of pilgrimages have often been regenerated by spectacular cures, as happened at Andacollo, Chile, in 1860 and San Juan Parangaricutiro, Mexico, in 1869.

Frequently shrines were established as community thank offerings for salvation from catastrophe. Survival of Indian attack or victory in battle has given rise to shrines in such places as Jujuy, Argentina; Recife, Brazil; Coroico, Bolivia; Villa Vieja, Uruguay; and Maipú, Chile. Riobamba, Ecuador, and San Miguel, El Salvador, are among the shrine centers that commemorate the end of earthquakes and/or volcanic eruptions. Others, like that at Yaguachi, Ecuador, emerged in the wake of epidemics, or, like that at Biblián, Ecuador, in the aftermath of threatened famine.

Votive shrines have also been created by individuals. For example, the venerated image at Guadalupe, Peru, was brought from the Spanish shrine of the same name in the mid-sixteenth century in thanks for the donor's release from prison, and a shrine at Hormigueros, Puerto Rico, is said to have been promoted by a man who was saved from a bull. The famous shrine at Chimayo, New Mexico, was established in the early nineteenth century by Don Bernardo Abeyta in thanks for health and prosperity.

Shrines also emerge in places sanctified through association with saints or exemplary, but uncanonized, persons. This type of holy place is more common in Europe than in the Americas, but there are several New World examples. These include the burial places of Santa Rosa and San Martín de Porras in Lima, Peru; the Aracanian Indian Ceferino Namuncura in Pedro Luro, Argentina; San Pedro Claver in Cartagena, Colombia; Saint John Neumann in Philadelphia, Pennsylvania; the Blessed Philippine Duchesne in Saint Charles, Missouri; and the Italian missionary nun Mother Cabrini in New York City.

Mother Cabrini is also honored at a site in the Rocky Mountain foothills near Denver, Colorado. Here, in 1912, the first citizen-saint of the United States struck a rock with her staff, whereupon a spring emerged with waters since reported to be curative. Other examples include a shrine at Midland, Canada, near the place where French Jesuit missionaries were killed by Huron Indians in the 1640s, and the Coronado Cross erected in 1976 near Dodge City, Kansas, at the place on the Arkansas River where Father Juan Padilla offered a mass for members of the Coronado expedition. Killed by Indians in 1542, this Franciscan friar was the first priest martyred in what is now the United States.

Pilgrimages have also developed at a number of places known primarily for their historical significance. Examples include the "La Leche" shrine in Saint Augustine, Florida, at the site of the first Spanish mission in America north of Mexico (established 1565); the Sacred Heart Mission church at Cataldo, Idaho; and several of the Spanish mission churches in the southwestern United States. Although not a pilgrimage center in a conventional sense, Boys Town, Nebraska, established as a home for wayward boys by Father Edward Flanagan in the early twentieth century, provides another example of a religiously significant site. It draws more than one million visitors a year and is considered an important place of inspiration.

Finally, many New World shrines, especially in North America, are of purely devotional origin. They came into being because an individual or a group believed that a pilgrimage center should be created in a particular place and set about to make it happen. Examples of such shrines include the National Shrine of the Immaculate Conception in Washington, D.C.; the Shrine of the Miraculous Medal in Perryville, Missouri; the Sanctuary of Our Sorrowful Mother at The Grotto in Portland, Oregon; and the National Shrine of the Sacred Heart at Pointe aux Trembles, Canada.

In 1983 a number of North American churches not previously conceptualized as pilgrimage shrines were scenes of pilgrimages for the 1983–1984 Holy Year of the Redemption. Given the late-twentieth-century interest in pilgrimage on the part of many American Catholics, it is possible that some of these places will become permanent centers for the devotion of pilgrims, especially if miraculous events are perceived to occur there. Certainly, shrines will continue to emerge in the hemisphere as religious significance is attached to relief from environmental stress ranging from natural disasters to political upheavals.

BIBLIOGRAPHY

No comprehensive study of Roman Catholic pilgrimages in the Americas has yet been published. Much of the information in this article comes from letters, pamphlets, booklets, photocopies of accounts in diocesan handbooks, and similar materials acquired in response to mail queries directed to Latin American bishops in 1979 and North American bishops in 1983. These materials are on file in the Department of Geography, Oregon State University, Corvallis, Oregon. Numerous descriptive works on individual New World shrines exist, but they are difficult to obtain except on site or by direct correspondence with shrine administrators. An exception is a work edited by Donald Demarest and Coley Taylor, *The Dark Virgin: The Book of Our Lady of Guadalupe; A Documentary Anthology* (Freeport, Maine, 1956).

Some of the more important shrines and those that are interesting for the folklore attached to them are mentioned in travel guidebooks and travelers' accounts. Occasional publications by national tourism agencies, such as the Mexican Government Tourism Department's *Fiestas in Mexico* (Mexico City, n.d.), provide useful information. A thorough search of the ethnographic literature in all relevant languages would undoubtedly yield a rich body of information on shrines and pilgrimages that happened to attract the attention of anthropologists, cultural geographers, and other field investigators.

Compendiums of selected shrine descriptions from a devotional point of view include Joseph L. Cassidy's *Mexico: Land of Mary's Wonders* (Paterson, N.J., 1958); Ralph Louis Woods and Henry Fitzwilliam Woods's *Pilgrim Places in North America: A Guide to Catholic Shrines* (New York, 1939); Francis Beauchesne Thornton's *Catholic Shrines in the United States and Canada* (New York, 1954); Nectario María Hermano's *Venezuela Mariana, o Sea relación histórica compendiada de las imagenes más celebradas de las Santísima Virgen en Venezuela* (Madrid, 1976); Francisco García Huidobro's *Santuarios Marianos del Ecuador* (Quayaquil, 1978); and the mammoth two-volume compilation on Marian shrines in Latin America by Rubén Vargas Ugarte, *Historia del culto de María en Iberoaméricá y de sus imagenes y santuarios más celebrados* (Madrid, 1956). Folklore-oriented descriptions of several Middle American shrines can be found in Frances Toor's *A Treasury of Mexican Folkways* (New York, 1947) and in Edith Hoyt's *The Silver Madonna: Legends of Shrines, Mexico-Guatemala* (Mexico City, 1963). Short descriptions of important Canadian churches are provided in *L'almanach populaire catholique 1984* (Sainte Anne de Beaupré, 1983), but this source does not consistently differentiate between pilgrimage churches and other notable ecclesiastical structures.

I have undertaken preliminary attempts to provide an analysis of Mexican shrines in "The Mexican Pilgrimage Tradition," *Pioneer America* 5 (1973): 13–27, as did Victor Turner in "The Center Out There: Pilgrim's Goal," *History of Religions* 12 (February 1973): 191–230. Victor Turner and Edith Turner included an overview of New World, primarily Mexican, pilgrimages in their pioneer effort to interpret Christian pilgrimage, *Image and Pilgrimage in Christian Culture: Anthropological Perspectives* (New York, 1978). Most other published works by social scientists deal with one pilgrimage center or a few regionally interrelated shrines. Examples of such studies include Daniel R. Gross's "Ritual and Conformity: A Religious Pilgrimage to Northeastern Brazil," *Ethnology* 10 (April 1971): 129–148, and N. Ross Crumrine's "Three Coastal Peruvian Pilgrimages," *El Dorado* 2 (1977): 76–86. Numerous shrine and regionally specific pilgrimage studies undertaken during the 1970s were just beginning to be published in the early 1980s. A collection of papers on Latin American pilgrimage, edited by E. Alan Morinis and N. Ross Crumrine, was in the final stages of review as of June 1985.

MARY LEE NOLAN

Eastern Christian Pilgrimage

Christian pilgrimage is rooted in the eastern domain of Christianity, primarily in Palestine, where Jesus was born and accomplished his mission, and secondarily in Egypt, the cradle of Christian monasticism. The fact that Jerusalem became the focal point of Christian pilgrimage is not surprising. For the Israelites, the Temple in Jerusalem had long served as the locus of the pilgrimage prescribed by their religious tradition.

The meaning of pilgrimage in ancient Israel and in early Christianity is similar yet differs markedly in one point: for the Israelite, a visit to the Temple was a requirement of faith to be fulfilled annually; for the Christian, that requirement had been fulfilled once and for all by Jesus Christ in his own final pilgrimage to the Temple. Therefore, the Christian pilgrimage became a journey to fulfill personal needs of piety rather than collective requirements. Understanding Christian pilgrimage and appreciating forms of Eastern Christian pilgrimage that have persisted for centuries necessitates, nevertheless, an examination of the meaning and form of pilgrimages in the Old Testament as well as in the New Testament.

Pilgrimage in the Old Testament. Ancient pilgrimage sites in the history of Israel were usually linked to a marvellous event in the life of an individual Israelite or in the collective history of the community. The site for a sanctuary was not arbitrarily chosen but was designated by God in a theophany (or divine manifestation) as, for example, Jacob's dream on his way to Haran (*Gn.* 28:10–22). The memory of the glorious event was made concrete by the erection of an altar. The journeys of Abraham, Moses, and the other patriarchs, the exile of the Israelites from Egypt and their forty-year journey through the desert were all pilgrimages, in the sense that they were the means to an end: the possession of the land where milk and honey flows and where God has made his rest (*Dt.* 12:9; *Ps.* 95:11, 132:8–14). After the building of the Temple, in which rested the Ark of the Covenant, Jerusalem became the goal for Israelite pilgrims. It was the sacred obligation of each Israelite to make an annual pilgrimage to Jerusalem, anticipating in this way the eschatological pilgrimage to God's city where all the nations of the world would gather at the end of time to inaugurate the kingdom of God.

Significance of Pilgrimage in the New Testament. The importance and meaning of pilgrimage is not explicit in the New Testament. The synoptic Gospels ascribe to Christ only one journey to Jerusalem on the occasion of the Passover feast (except for Luke's account of Jesus' pilgrimage with his parents at age twelve). John, however, assumes the regular participation of Christ in the pilgrimage feasts (*Jn.* 2:13, 6:4, 11:55, 7:2, and 10:22). The four evangelists are in accord in their messianic interpretation of Jesus Christ's final journey to Jerusalem, which culminates in the events of his crucifixion and resurrection. In this way, Christ fulfills for all time the eschatological pilgrimage into the city of God and inaugurates the kingdom of God. In this kingdom, one no longer needs to buy and sell sacrificial animals for the offering at the temple; according to the Pauline epistles, Christ has eliminated the need for sacrifice, having become himself both the sacrificed lamb and the high priest who entered behind the veil into the Holy of Holies (*Heb.* 6:9–20).

The theme of exile occurs again and again in the New Testament writings (*1 Pt.* 1:1–17, 2:11; *Heb.* 13:14; cf. *Gn.* 23:3–4; *Ps.* 39:12–13, 119:19; *Acts* 7:6–29.) For the early Christians viewed their lives as the time of pilgrims in exile, and the destination of this journey was the heavenly city of Jerusalem. So powerful was this idea that the Greek word *paroikia*, which means "sojourning in a foreign land," came to designate the fundamental unit of the Christian community, the parish.

Early Christian Pilgrimage. Imperial influence and not religious obligation became the greatest single motivating force in the growth and development of Christian pilgrimage to Jerusalem. Constantine's church-building program on the holy sites of Jerusalem (begun after the Council of Nicaea in 325) invited many Christians to go and see the sacred places where Jesus was born, lived, worked, and was crucified and raised.

As pilgrimage to the holy places of Christendom became more common, the corporate life of the church was affected as well, through liturgical development. Many of the early pilgrims came to Palestine with a desire to see the places described in biblical episodes, a desire that combined historical curiosity and pious zeal. The pattern of worship conducted at each site by the pilgrims, the central feature of which was the reading of the relevant passage from the Bible, gave rise eventually to an annually recurring cycle of liturgical festivals in commemoration of the life of Christ. In these celebrations too, the central feature remained a reading of the biblical narrative, appropriately chosen to suit not only the place but also the liturgical season.

Another significant feature of Christian pilgrimage liturgies was the practice of numerous processions. "The desire to embrace all the principal holy places in the course of the celebrations, combined with the possibility of commemorating the events of the gospel at the actual places where they were believed to have occurred, produced a form of worship distinguished by its constant movement and its arduous length" (Hunt, p. 114). These processions remind one of *ḥag*, the Hebrew word for pilgrimage feasts, the root meaning of which is "to dance" or "to move in circles."

It is noteworthy that the churches that have maintained a strong liturgical tradition, particularly all of the ancient churches of the East, have lived these pilgrimage themes symbolically through their cyclical liturgical celebrations. As pilgrims they need not fulfill either the pilgrimage to the Temple or to the holy places of Christendom; rather, a spiritual participation in the life of Christ, expressed through liturgical celebrations, is their pilgrimage. For example, Gregory of Nyssa maintains that Bethlehem, Golgotha, the Mount of Olives, and the empty tomb should always be before the eyes of the true Christian as spiritual pointers to the godly life.

The same attitude gave rise to another form of pilgrimage: visits to the holy men and women who had chosen to give themselves to a life of perpetual prayer—the monks and ascetics. Basil of Caesarea, who in 351 made the journey to Palestine and later to Egypt, Syria, and Mesopotamia, hardly mentions the holy places; he states that the object of his journey was to visit the monks and ascetics, to stay with them in order to learn the secret of their holy lives. Basil wanted to learn the method of the personal spiritual pilgrimage, the destination of which was the heavenly city of God experienced on an inner level.

The pilgrim Egeria (late fourth century) refers to another tradition, that of the pilgrimages to martyria (churches that have been built on the tomb of a saint or a martyr). She notes that the monks in Charra, a region of Mesopotamia, rarely come out of seclusion but that they do so on Easter and on the feast of the martyr to celebrate the Divine Liturgy in the martyrium.

This tradition still continues. Many pilgrims go to the monasteries of Mount Athos in Greece and to monasteries in Egypt, Syria, and other parts of the world. Among these monasteries there are many that were built near martyria or near sites that have biblical importance. In Egypt there is the monastery of Dair al-Muḥarraq, the site where the holy family rested and took refuge in their flight from Herod. Each year in Dair al-Muharraq, as at all martyria, on the feast day of the saint, pilgrims come to commemorate liturgically and later through festivities the saint in whose name the martyrium or shrine was built.

Thus, personal piety for the Eastern Christian has found expression beyond the liturgical life. Pilgrimage to Jerusalem, to martyria, and to the cells of monks has given rise to numerous customs and traditions that symbolically perpetuate the main theme of pilgrimage: the yearning of the exile to reach his destination, the promised land, the city where God rests and encounters his people.

Customs and Traditions Associated with Pilgrimage. Armenians, Copts, Greeks, Russians, Syrians, Ethiopians, and other Eastern Christians share common traditions of pilgrimage.

The pilgrimage to Jerusalem. There is no particularly appropriate time in one's life when one ought to make a pilgrimage. However, the pilgrimage *par excellence*, the journey to Jerusalem, generally becomes possible late in one's life. Once in Jerusalem, a pilgrim considers that the serious occupations of his or her life have ended. Having seen "death conquered" at the site of Christ's resurrection (the holy sepulcher), the pilgrim looks forward to his or her own death, sometimes desiring to die in Jerusalem. The Armenian term *mahdesi* ("one who has seen death") aptly describes this state. This title of honor is given to a pilgrim returning from a pilgrimage to Jerusalem. Russian pilgrims also acknowledge the overcoming of death by taking white shrouds to Jerusalem. They bathe in the Jordan river, the scene of John's baptisms, shrouded in white, in evocation of the awakened dead on Resurrection Morning. Other Eastern Christians bring their white shrouds and on Holy Friday place them on Christ's tomb, anoint them with oil from the lamps burning there, and perfume them with sweet-smelling incense. A pilgrim designated as a *mahdesi* is one who has seen the Holy Fire on Easter and who has received a tattoo on the inner right wrist, depicting most often a cross and the date of the pilgrimage.

The ceremony of the Holy Fire. Conducted jointly by all of the Eastern churches at midday on Easter Eve in the Church of the Holy Sepulcher, the ceremony of the Holy Fire is of uncertain origin, but it derives from the ritual and symbolism of the primitive church. It symbolizes the triumph of the Christian faith. The Eastern Orthodox patriarch and the Armenian patriarch (representing also the Copts, the Ethiopians, and the Syrians) enter through the door over the tomb, then emerge, each carrying a sheaf of lighted candles. This light quickly spreads among the people present, who light their own candles from it. It is said that some pilgrims take pains to carry the flame home unextinguished, preserving it in a lantern.

It is also the custom of the Armenian patriarch to distribute wafers with the resurrection imprint to all the pilgrims. This may be a symbolic vestige of a custom of hospitality that was practiced by the monks in Egypt and elsewhere in the East. Isolated in the desert, monks had to provide pilgrims with both food and lodging. As the number of pilgrims increased, the monks began to give tokens of hospitality, most often in the form of the fruit they had grown. The pilgrim Egeria called this the monks' "blessing."

Vows, offerings, and healing. Whether rich or poor, the pilgrims carry gifts of offering to the churches on the holy sites. Many bring their work or the work of skillful craftsmen; vessels and vestments to be used for the liturgical rites. Some contribute toward the building of guest rooms in the holy city where pilgrims can stay. Traditionally, pilgrims spend many months, as much as a whole year, in pilgrimage. Originally, they would come before Christmas and stay until after Easter in order to participate in the events commemorating the life of Christ. Gradually, that time has been shortened to the season of Lent and Easter.

Pilgrims come often to fulfill vows they have made. Some also bring with them the petitions of friends. If the request is for healing, they bring silver charms that represent the part of the body in need of healing. These they leave on or near the icon of the saint to whom they pray.

Returning home. The return of pilgrims to their homes has been marked ceremoniously in some Armenian communities. Usually a group of pilgrims make the journey together. Upon their return, they go to the parish church, where prayers of thanksgiving are offered on their behalf for having been able to fulfill their pilgrimage. At the conclusion of the service, the pilgrims distribute to the congregation objects of devotion that they have brought home.

They bring home oil from the lanterns that have been lighted in holy places to use for anointing and healing. Olives from two-thousand-year-old trees in the garden of Gethsemane are treasured also. Most valuable, however, are the candles that were lighted in various holy places, especially from the Holy Fire on Easter.

BIBLIOGRAPHY

L. M. Orrieux's "Le pèlerinage dans la Bible," *Lumière et vie* 15 (September–October 1966): 5–34, is a concise yet comprehensive study of the meaning of pilgrimage in the Old and New Testaments. The rise and development of Christian pilgrimage are presented in two important works: E. D. Hunt's *Holy Land Pilgrimage in the Later Roman Empire, AD 312–460* (Oxford, 1984), a thorough study that takes into account the historical, political, and liturgical aspects of Christian pilgrimage, and John Wilkinson's excellent translation of Egeria's account of her travels, with exhaustive commentary, *Egeria's Travels* (London, 1971). While the pilgrim routes and churches are discussed in Wilkinson's book, the study of the Jerusalem liturgy holds an important place and is based on the detailed information given by Egeria. L. G. A. Cust's *The Status Quo in the Holy Places* (Jerusalem, 1980) is a descriptive account of the holy places and the practices that are carried out by their principal caretakers, the Greeks, the Armenians, and the Roman Catholics. For a description of the ceremony of the Holy Fire, see pages 66–70. Concerning pilgrimage sites of the most ancient monasteries and shrines, see Otto F. A. Meinardus's *Monks and Monasteries of the Egyptian Desert* (Cairo, 1961) and Erhart Kaestner's *Mount Athos* (London, 1961).

SIRARPI FEREDJIAN AIVAZIAN

Muslim Pilgrimage

The annual pilgrimage of Muslims to Mecca, in west-central Arabia, is known by the term *ḥajj*. As a religious duty that is the fifth of the Five Pillars of Islam, the *ḥajj* is an obligation for all Muslims to perform once in their adult lives, provided they be of sound mind and health and financially able at the time. In 1982, from an estimated world Islamic population of 750 million, approximately 3 million Muslims were reported to have made the journey. The nature and size of this annual ingathering of Muslims from countless ethnic, linguistic, and political backgrounds, combined with the common sacred status that ideally makes princes indistinguishable from paupers, render the *ḥajj* experience an important expression of social and religious unity in Islamic culture.

Ḥajj in the Context of Middle Eastern Worldviews. The duty of performing the *ḥajj* rests on the authority of scripture (Qur'ān) and the recorded practice of the prophet Muḥammad *(sunnah)*, as these are interpreted by the orthodox schools of Islamic law; Shī'ī Muslims rely in addition on the teachings of the early imams, leaders descended from the family of the Prophet through the lineage of 'Alī. The *manāsik al-ḥajj*, manuals that explain the rituals and prayers required at each of the *ḥajj* stations, are adduced from these authorities. More than the symbolism found in the other religious duties of Islam, however, *ḥajj* symbolism carries overtones of ancient Arab and Judeo-Christian cosmologies, which resonate in the appointed times and places of the ritual performances.

For Muslims, the shrine in Mecca comprehends several notions: for example, that creation began at Mecca; that the father of the prophets, Ibrāhīm (Abraham), constructed the first house of worship (Ka'bah, Bayt Allāh) at Mecca; that the pagan practices of the Arabs at the Ka'bah were displayed by God's final revelation through Muḥammad, his Messenger to the Arabs and to all of humankind. Indeed, the Ka'bah determines the ritual direction, or *qiblah*, the focal point toward which canonical prayers *(ṣalāt)* and places of prayer (*masjid*, mosque) are physically oriented, the direction in which the deceased are faced in their graves, and the focus of other ritual gestures as well. The Ka'bah is regarded as the navel of the universe, and it is the place from which the prayers of the faithful are believed to be most effective. [*See also* Ka'bah.] For Muslims, Mecca has been the site of divine, angelic, prophetic, and auspicious human activity since the primordial moment of creation.

Ḥajj manuals commonly begin with the following Qur'anic epigraph: "Truly, the first House of Worship established for humankind is the one at Bakkah [Mecca], a blessing and guidance to all realms of being. In it are clear signs, such as the Place of Ibrāhīm, and whoever enters [the Meccan precincts] is safe. The *ḥajj* to the House is a duty humankind owes to God, that is, for those who are able to journey to it" (3:96–97). The significance of the prophet Ibrāhīm to the sacred origins of the *ḥajj* sites is attested widely in Islamic literature. Ibrāhīm symbolizes the pure monotheism that the ancient communities subsequently perverted or forgot. In the Muslim view, the period of Arabian history that intervened between the prophets Ibrāhīm and Muḥammad was one of religious ignorance, Jāhilīyah—a period during which monotheism was abandoned and the pilgrim stations were made to serve pagan nature deities. Yet, the pre-Islamic *ḥajj* provided important precedents of ritual sites and gestures that continued to be auspicious in Islamic times.

By the sixth century CE, the bedouin tribes of central Arabia were undergoing political and social changes, reflected especially in the growing commercial importance of settled markets and caravansaries at Mecca. Muḥammad's tribe, the Quraysh, dominated caravan trading through the use of force and lucrative arrangements with other tribes. Such trading centers were also pilgrimage sites to which Arabs journeyed annually during sacred months constituting a moratorium of tribal feuding. Although the pilgrimage remained a dangerous undertaking in the face of banditry and unpacified tribal rivalry, the special months and territories provided sanctuary for many of the shared sacred and profane activities of Arab tribal culture. The auspicious times and places of pilgrimage, along with the annual fairs and markets held at nearby locales along the pilgrims' routes, appear to have played significant roles in stabilizing the segmented polity of Arab tribalism.

The term *ḥajj* itself, like its Hebrew cognate *ḥag*, seems to reflect an ancient Semitic notion of "going around" or "standing" in the presence of a deity at a sacred mountain or shrine, or the journey to it (see *Ex.* 23:14; also *Ex.* 23:17 and 24:22, *Jgs.* 21:19, and *1 Kgs.* 8:2). The pilgrimage stations at Arafat, Muzdalifah, and Minā on the road east of Mecca appear to have been associated with solar and mountain deities prior to the rise of Islam; the "standing" at Arafat, the "hurry" to Muzdalifah, and the stoning of the pillars at Minā—the Islamic significance of which will be discussed below—were all ancient rites among the Arabs.

Islam did not destroy the pre-Islamic *ḥajj* rituals, but it infused them with new symbols and meanings. In its own conceptual terms, Islam asserted (or reasserted) monotheism over the polytheism of Jāhilīyah. The Qur'ān also declared that the sacred months of pilgrimage should be calculated according to a lunar calendar that could not be adjusted every few years—as it had been in pagan times—and the Qur'anic injunction against intercalation resulted in a lunar year of twelve months approximately every 354 days, thus distinguishing the *ḥajj* and other Muslim festivals from the fixed seasonal celebrations characteristic of pagan astral and agricultural (fertility) religions. Following the Muslim calendar, the *ḥajj* and other ceremonials rotate throughout the seasons of the year.

According to Islamic tradition, the Abrahamic origins of *ḥajj* sites and rituals had been taught by the prophet Muḥammad to the nascent Islamic community during the pilgrimage he performed just before the end of his life (632 CE). The sermon he delivered on the Mount of Mercy, at Arafat, and his removal of all pagan idols from the Ka'bah in Mecca are recollected annually during the *ḥajj* ceremonies. The imputed Abrahamic origins of the *ḥajj* ceremonies constitute a deeper, complementary layer of symbolism that serves to underpin Muḥammad's treatment of the *ḥajj* as a monotheistic ritual. Ibrāhīm's duty to sacrifice Ismā'īl (Ishmael; not Isaac as in the biblical tradition), Satan's three attempts to dissuade Ibrāhīm from following God's command, and the divine substitution of a ram for the blood sacrifice are celebrated at Minā during the festival of the Greater Sacrifice and the ritual stoning of the three pillars (see below). Mecca itself is believed to have been the wilderness sanctuary to which the banished Ḥājar (Hagar) and her infant son Ismā'īl were escorted by Ibrāhīm. The Ka'bah stands on the site of a primordial temple where Adam is said to have prayed after his expulsion from Paradise. Destroyed by the deluge, the Ka'bah was rebuilt by Ibrāhīm and Ismā'īl: during the deluge, the sacred Black Stone from the primordial Ka'bah had been sealed in a niche in Mount Qubays (east of Mecca), then brought by the angel Jibrīl (Gabriel) to Ibrāhīm for the reconstruction of the present Ka'bah, where it was set into the eastern corner. The sacred hillocks of al-Ṣafā and al-Marwah situated near the Ka'bah symbolize the points between which Ḥājar is said to have run in desperate search of water, and the gushing forth of water next to the Ka'bah is a Muslim symbol of God's providential relief to Ḥājar and Ismā'īl.

The historic seventh-century shift at Mecca from a polytheistic to a monotheistic cosmology—of which the *ḥajj* is the supreme ritual expression—is significant for the comparative study of religions and civilizations. Urban geographer Paul Wheatley (*The Pivot of the Four Corners*, 1971) argues that archaeological and textual evidence on the rise of cities throughout the ancient world point to the importance of shrines and cults that stood at the center of urban complexes. Wheatley suggests that cities such as Mecca, by focusing sacredness on cult symbols of cosmic and moral order, were able to organize the previous tribal polities into larger, more efficient economic, social, and political systems. Urban-based great traditions evolved and were perpetuated by literati who canonized the technical requirements and meanings of ritual performance at the shrines. In this way, such traditions provided for the continuity of culture over time and geographic space; they ensured that the cosmic center *(omphalos, axis mundi)* continued to be enshrined and celebrated within the sacred city. The seventh-century shift from local deities and tribal morality to a monotheistic cosmic and moral order in Islam coincided with a period of Arabian hegemony over larger neighboring civilizations. With the islamization of the Arabian *ḥajj* during this process, therefore, the pilgrimage to Mecca came to symbolize for Muslim peoples and lands across Asia, the Middle East, and North Africa the sacred origins and center of their common confessional heritage.

Requirements and Preparations for the Ḥajj. Muslim authorities generally agree on the following requirements of eligibility for the *ḥajj:* (1) one must be a confessing Muslim who (2) has reached the age of puberty, (3) is of rational and sound mind, (4) is a freed man or woman, and (5) has the physical strength and health to undertake the rigors of the journey. Islamic law also provides that a pilgrim must be in possession of sufficient and honest funds not only for the expenses of the *ḥajj* but also for the care of dependents who remain at home.

From figures available on *ḥajj* participation in relation to total Muslim population, it is clear that only a small percentage of Muslims make the pilgrimage in any given year, and that many never undertake the journey at all. In addition to the above qualifications, one is not expected to risk life, limb, or possessions if war and hostility are known to exist along the pilgrim's path. Living at great distances from Mecca has tended to make fulfillment of the duty of *ḥajj* less likely for many Muslims for obvious reasons, although in modern times some Muslim countries such as Malaysia have instituted programs to assist Muslims in saving and preparing for the journey. Children, to whom the obligation of *ḥajj* does not apply, may nonetheless accompany their parents. The schools of law generally agree that women should be accompanied by their husbands or by two male relatives who are ineligible to marry them (first-cousin marriages are common in Islam). Although legal consensus and practical considerations discourage women from making the journey without appropriate male chaperons, the law does not allow males to prevent female Muslims from fulfilling the *ḥajj* if proper arrangements can be made. The Prophet is cited as having approved of Muslims' making the *ḥajj* on behalf of deceased relatives who intended, but were unable, to do so themselves. The feeble and desperately ill may send others to Mecca on their behalf.

Thus, although *ḥajj* is a duty one owes to God, the decision as to whether and when one should undertake the "journey to the House" belongs ultimately to each individual Muslim. The authorities insist that *ḥajj* is valid at any stage of adult life. The *ḥajj*, therefore, is not a rite of passage in the sense of the ritual celebrations of birth, circumcision, marriage, and death, which have their appointed times within the human life cycle, and this aspect of the *ḥajj* duty allows Muslims, including the very pious, to delay the decision to make the *ḥajj*, in many cases indefinitely. Islam recognizes that conditions may exist that will cause postponement of the journey and charges apostasy or heresy only to those who deny that *ḥajj* is a duty to God.

A pilgrim's separation from familiar social and cultural surroundings constitutes a moment of prayerful anxiety and joyful celebration for all concerned. On the eve of departure, it is traditional for family and friends to gather for prayers, Qur'ān recitation, food, and perhaps poetry and singing about the *ḥajj*. (So, too, when the *ḥajj* rites have been completed, the pilgrim's return home will be celebrated by family and friends; in some parts of the Islamic world the homes of returning pilgrims are decorated with symbols of the *ḥajj*, reflecting local popular art forms.) Many pilgrims follow the practice of setting out from home on the right foot, a symbol of good omen and fortune. Similarly, it is auspicious to enter mosques, including the Sacred Mosque in Mecca, on the right foot and depart on the left; the right/left symbolism is associated with several ritual gestures in Islam as well as in other traditions. As on so many occasions during the *ḥajj*, the actual moment of departure calls for the recitation of a particular verse from the Qur'ān, and departing pilgrims recite the words of Noah, uttered to those escaping the deluge: "Board [the Ark]; in God's name be its course and mooring. My Lord is forgiving, merciful" (11:41). Indeed, the symbolism of separation, salvation, and safe passage is found in the pilgrimage rituals of many religious traditions. Those who complete the *ḥajj* will be entitled to the epithet *ḥājj* or *ḥajjī* (*ḥājjah* or *ḥajjīyah* if female). This honorific title indicates socially perceived status enhancement in the sense of recognition by one's peers that a sacred duty has been fulfilled, and this is a matter of universal value, if not universal achievement, in Islam.

Most pilgrims require assistance in arranging for travel, lodging, and proper guidance in the execution of rites and prayers within the Meccan precincts. During the Middle Ages, caravans of pilgrims assembled and traveled together from Egypt, South Arabia, Syria, and Iraq. Their common wayfaring experiences on the road have not produced an Islamic *Canterbury Tales*, although one Muslim writer has observed that material for such a literature abounds within the communities of pilgrims who journey each year to Mecca. During the Middle Ages hospices and hostels were established along the pilgrimage routes from religious endowments given by those in possession of both piety and wealth. In recent times, *ḥajj* travel organizations in Muslim countries have helped to arrange for chartered air, sea, and overland travel and for local accommodations in Mecca.

Of considerable importance throughout the centuries have been the *ḥajj* guides (known as *muṭawwif*s). The responsibilities of these guides and their agents include leading groups of pilgrims through the proper performance of rituals and prayers at each pilgrimage station as well as seeing to food and lodging needs. Employing a trustworthy guide is a major concern for pilgrims, as attested in *ḥajj* manuals and in conventional wisdom about preparing for the *ḥajj*. Since the rise of Islam in the seventh century CE, the Muslims of Arabia, especially the Meccans, have served a growing "*ḥajj* industry" of services for pilgrims from around the world. Recognizing that opportunities invariably arise to take advantage of those who are far from home and in a state of intense piety, in modern times the government of Saudi Arabia has sought to regulate the offering of religious, material, and health services to the millions of visitors who enter its national boundaries each year to fulfill the sacred duty.

Travel accounts by pilgrims reveal other dimensions of the *ḥajj*, such as opportunities for adventure, business, education, and even marriage. The intention to engage in business with other pilgrims is lawful, especially if it is meant to help defray the costs of the journey. *Ḥajj* manuals nonetheless caution wariness of unscrupulous sellers of goods and services, even those who may be found within the sacred precincts. Marriage among pilgrims is also permitted, and the *ḥajj* provides occasions for establishing friendships and personal relationships, although marriage and sexual contact are forbidden during the period of sacred observance at the Meccan precincts. In former times, when travel was considerably more difficult, many pilgrims followed an open itinerary and lingered at towns and cities along the way; those who thirsted for knowledge found opportunities to attend the lectures of famous teachers at mosque colleges. Biographical literature in Islam indicates that the *ḥajj* has been for many individuals an important moment or phase of life that has had numerous ramifications of lasting personal, if not social, significance.

Iḥrām, the Condition of Consecration. The *ḥajj* season lasts from the beginning of the tenth month of the Muslim calendar, Shawwāl, until the tenth day of the twelfth month, Dhū al-Ḥijjah. Although the actual *ḥajj* rites do not begin until the eighth of Dhū al-Ḥijjah, the two-and-a-half-month period known as *al-mīqāt al-zamānīyah* is reserved for travel and ritual preparations for the *ḥajj* ceremonies. The rites of preparation and consecration are comprehended by the term *iḥrām*. Pilgrims assume the condition of *iḥrām* before they pass the territorial markers, *al-mīqāt al-makānīyah*, that are situated several miles outside of Mecca along the ancient routes for caravans from Syria, Medina, Iraq, and the Yemen. Within the territory bounded by these markers lie the sacred precincts of Mecca. For the vast majority of Muslims who in modern times disembark from air and sea travel at the west Arabian port of Jidda, the rites of *iḥrām* are begun on board before arrival, or at Jidda itself. Muslims may enter Mecca and its vicinity at any time without assuming the condition of *iḥrām*, but if their intention is to perform the rites of *ḥajj* or *ʿumrah* (see below), *iḥrām* is required.

Assuming the condition of *iḥrām* before passing the territorial markers has several aspects.

1. *Iḥrām* requires a state of ritual purity, and pilgrims who enter it must perform ablutions much the same as they do for the daily canonical prayers, *ṣalāt*. The special condition of *iḥrām* also requires pilgrims to trim their fingernails and remove underarm and pubic hair, and men must shave off beards and mustaches. The further cutting of nails and hair is part of the rite of deconsecration, *taḥallul*, and is not permitted until the *ḥajj* and/or *ʿumrah* rites have been completed. A pilgrim in the state of *iḥrām* is also forbidden to use perfumes or carry symbols of personal wealth, such as silk and gold jewelry.

2. *Iḥrām* is initiated and sustained by prayers of several kinds. (a) The *nīyah* is the prayer by which each pilgrim declares his or her intention in the rites that follow. At any time of the year except during the three days of the *ḥajj* itself, Muslim visitors may enter the Meccan precincts with the intention of performing rites at the Sacred Mosque of Mecca, which enshrines the Kaʿbah. This is known as the *ʿumrah*, or "lesser pilgrimage." Pilgrims making the *ḥajj*, or "greater pilgrimage," will declare a *nīyah* also to visit Arafat, Muzdalifah, and Minā on the eighth through the tenth of Dhū al-Ḥijjah. Their prayers must stipulate whether or not they intend to interrupt the state of *iḥrām* during the interval that may lapse between the performances of *ʿumrah* and *ḥajj*. (b) A second form of prayer is the *ṣalāt*, which includes the formal prostrations in the direction *(qiblah)* of the Kaʿbah in Mecca. When pilgrims assume *iḥrām*, they perform a *ṣalāt* of two prostrations before entering the sacred territories. During the *ḥajj*, including the days of travel to and from Mecca, the five daily performances of *ṣalāt* assume the following pattern: once at dawn, the noon and afternoon prayers together at midday, and the sunset and evening prayers at dusk. (c) A third form of prayer is called *duʿā'*, "supplication." *Duʿā'* is a less formalized, more individualized expression of communication with God. A supplication is normally offered after the *ṣalāt*, especially the *ṣalāt* of *iḥrām*, and thereafter frequently at each of the pilgrimage sites. The texts of supplications recommended in the *ḥajj* manuals reveal something of the meanings these shrines and performances hold for Muslims. (d) The fourth type of prayer, the *talbiyah*, belongs to *iḥrām* alone. The *talbiyah* is uttered in a loud voice as pilgrims pass the markers of the sacred territory and frequently during the days of consecration. The brief lines of *talbiyah* begin with a phrase that means roughly "Here I am, O Lord! What is Thy command?"

3. In addition to the ablutions and prayers, *iḥrām* requires each pilgrim to exchange normal clothing for special garments. The *iḥrām* garb is simple, a visual symbol of the ideal of universal Islamic brotherhood that the *ḥajj* and *ʿumrah* rites celebrate. For males the *iḥrām* attire consists of two seamless white pieces of cloth, one attached around the waist and reaching to the knees, the other worn over the left shoulder and attached around the torso, leaving the right shoulder and arm free for ritual gesturing. Males may not wear any head covering, and their footwear is restricted to sandals that leave the backs of the heels exposed. Females wear plain dresses that extend from neckline to ankles and cover the arms. A head covering is required of females, but veiling the face is not permitted during the period of consecration. *Ḥajj* manuals are less than sanguine about the comfort of the *iḥrām* attire, especially in summer and winter seasons.

Iḥrām, then, is a state of consecration that each pilgrim must assume before he or she may enter the sacred precincts. The state of consecration exemplifies the concept of egalitarian brotherhood, or *communitas,* that many religious traditions establish ritually during pilgrimages and other rites. The *ḥaram,* or "sacred precincts," is a place in which those who enter expect to feel nearness to God, and *iḥrām* is a special moment and condition of brotherhood for all pilgrims. Within the spatial and temporal boundaries of *iḥrām,* it is forbidden to uproot plants, kill animals, or foment any social violence. Husbands and wives are enjoined to refrain from sexual intercourse, and women are counseled to conduct themselves modestly so as not to attract male attention. Familiar sociocultural identities and structures are reduced drastically, for pilgrims are now approaching the navel of creation, the primordial house where Adam and Ibrāhīm worshiped, a hallowed ground where Muḥammad recited God's final revelation to humankind.

ʿUmrah, the Lesser Pilgrimage. All accounts of the experience of the final approach to Mecca indicate that it is a moment of high emotions attending the realization of a lifelong ambition. The practical matter of securing lodging and the care of a pilgrim guide is usually the first order of business; the most valued and anticipated task, however, is a visit to the Kaʿbah for the rites of *ʿumrah.*

From ancient times, the Kaʿbah and its environs have been symbols of refuge from violence and pursuit, a sacred space in which wayfaring pilgrims could find sanctuary with the divine. The Kaʿbah is now enclosed within the roofless courtyard of the Sacred Mosque of Mecca, al-Masjid al-Ḥarām. Arriving pilgrims approach the mosque through streets teeming with the traffic of other pilgrims, vendors, and merchants, whose shops and stalls compact the urban space that surrounds the ancient shrine.

Twenty-four gates lead into the mosque courtyard (see figure 1). The four corners of the outer walls of the Sacred Mosque as well as the four corners of the Kaʿbah in the center of its grounds are oriented approximately in the cardinal directions. The Kaʿbah is surrounded by a circle of stone flooring called the *maṭāf,* the place of circumambulations. Set within the eastern corner of the Kaʿbah is the sacred Black Stone, encased by a silver rim; another auspicious stone is encased in the southern corner. The four walls of the Kaʿbah are covered with a gigantic black curtain, called the *kiswah,* which is decorated in bands of Arabic calligraphy embroidered in gold. The Gate of Peace near the northern corner of the Sacred Mosque is the traditional entrance for the performance of *ʿumrah.* Again, emotions rise at the first glimpse of the haunting specter of the Kaʿbah.

Once they have entered the Gate of Peace, pilgrims move to a position east of the Kaʿbah and face the corner with the Black Stone. The rite of *ṭawāf,* or circumambulation, begins from this point with a supplication followed by a kiss, touch, or gesture of touching the black stone. The pilgrim turns to the right and begins the seven circumambulations, moving counterclockwise around the Kaʿbah. Each circuit has a special significance with recommended prayers that the pilgrim may recite either from *ḥajj* manuals or by following the words of the *ḥajj* guide leading the group. When passing the stone in the southern corner and the sacred Black Stone in the eastern corner, it is traditional to touch or make a gesture of touching each stone with uplifted right arm and a verbal supplication. Male pilgrims are admonished to take the first three laps at a quickened pace and the remaining four more slowly.

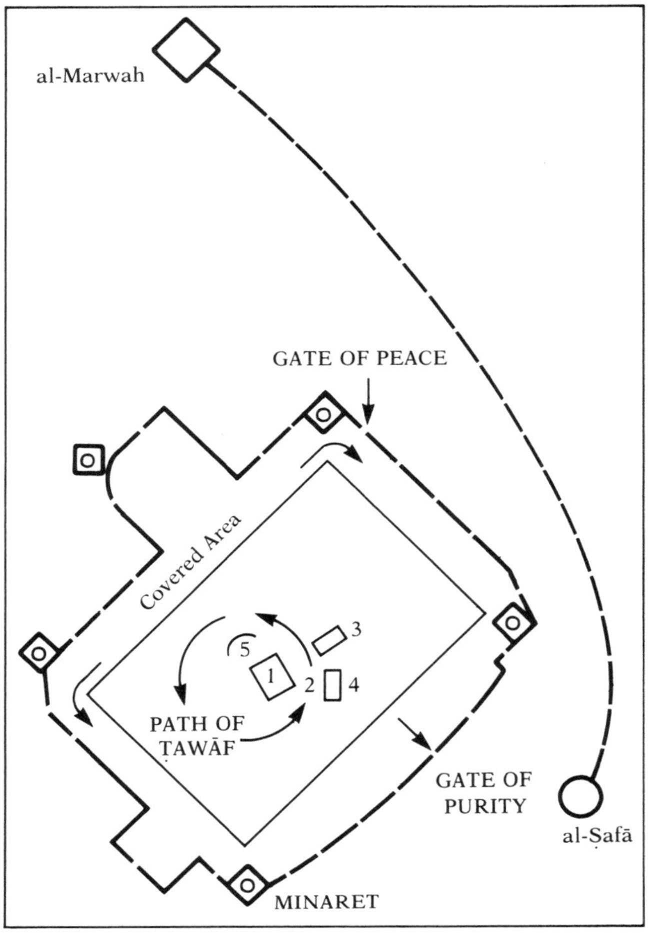

FIGURE 1. *Pilgrimage Path at Sacred Mosque.* (1) Kaʿbah. (2) Corner of the Black Stone. (3) Maqām Ibrāhīm. (4) Well of Zamzam. (5) Al-Ḥijr.

Following the *ṭawāf,* pilgrims visit shrines adjacent to the Kaʿbah. An area along the northeastern wall of the Kaʿbah between its sole door and the Black Stone is the *multazim* or "place of pressing." With uplifted arms, resting if possible on the *multazim* wall, pilgrims offer a supplication. Another place of visitation is the Maqām Ibrāhīm, which symbolizes the place from which Abraham is said to have prayed toward the Ka'bah. From within or near the covered shrine of Ibrāhīm, pilgrims perform a prayer of two prostrations. Near Maqām Ibrāhīm to the east of the Ka'bah is the well of Zamzam. A drink of its water, said to have a brackish taste, is sought by every pilgrim. On the northwestern side of the Ka'bah, a low semicircular wall encloses a space. The enclosure is known as al-Ḥijr, and it is thought to be the site of the graves of Ḥājar and Ismā'īl. Al-Ḥijr is also said to be the spot beside the Ka'bah where Muḥammad slept on the night of his miraculous journey from Mecca to Jerusalem.

After the circumambulations and visitations, pilgrims leave the Sacred Mosque (leading with the left foot) through the Gate of Purity on the southeast side. A few yards outside the Gate of Purity is the small hillock of al-Ṣafā. From al-Ṣafā begins the *sa'y*, the rite of trotting seven laps to and from the hillock of al-Marwah, which is located some four hundred and fifty yards to the northeast of the Sacred Mosque. The *sa'y* commemorates Ḥājar's desperate search for water in the Meccan wilderness and ends the rites of *'umrah*. Year-round visitors to Mecca who intend to perform *'umrah* only, or pilgrims who arrive early for the *ḥajj*, deconsecrate themselves at this time by a ritual of haircutting and by doffing the *iḥrām* garb (see below).

Ḥajj, the Greater Pilgrimage. The *ḥajj* proper begins on the eighth of Dhū al-Ḥijjah, the day of setting out for Arafat, which is located some thirteen miles east of Mecca. (For the route and pilgrimage sites, refer to figure 2.) Many pilgrims spend the first night at Minā, as the prophet Muḥammad himself is said to have done,

FIGURE 2. *Sketch Map of Major Points on the Ḥajj*

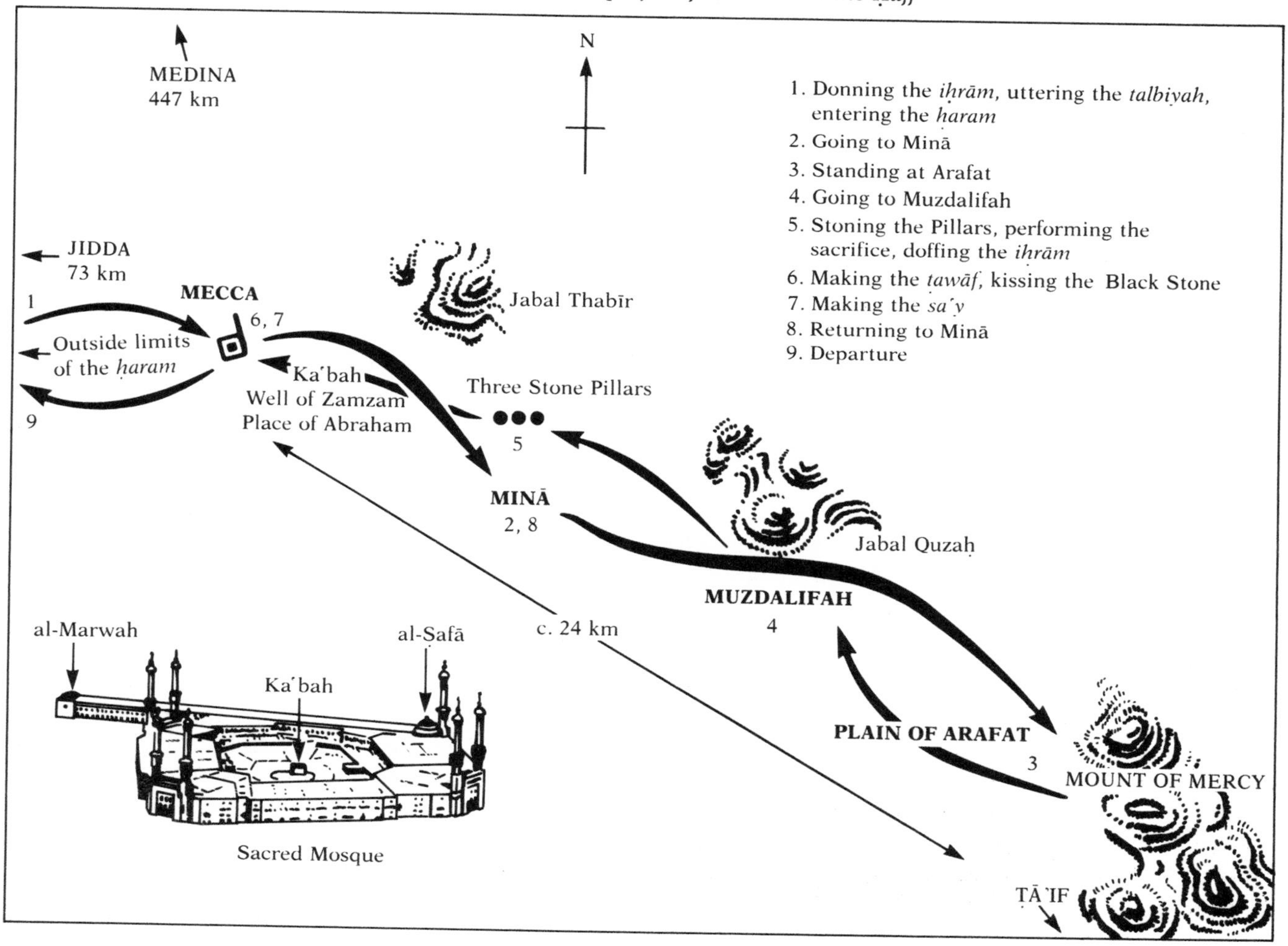

while others push on to Arafat. The goal of all pilgrims is to reach Jabal al-Raḥmah, the Mount of Mercy, located on the eastern plain of Arafat, by noon on the ninth of Dhū al-Ḥijjah.

Arafat. Muslim authorities agree that "there is no *ḥajj* without Arafat," that is, the rite of *wuqūf* or "standing" at the Mount of Mercy. According to legend, Adam and Eve first met and "knew" (*ʿarafū*) one another at Arafat after the long separation that followed their expulsion from Paradise. Tradition also teaches that Ibrāhīm went out to Arafat and performed *wuqūf.* The prophet Muḥammad addressed a multitude of followers performing *wuqūf* during his farewell pilgrimage, and the following words are attributed to him on that occasion: "O people, hear what I have to say, for I know not whether I shall again be with you here after this day. . . . Truly, all Muslims are brothers . . . and your Lord is one." Tradition also accords to this occasion the revelation of the final verse of the Qur'ān recited by Muḥammad: "This day I have perfected your religion for you and have chosen for you Islam as your religion" (5:3). On the Day of Standing at Arafat, pilgrims perform an ablution and canonical prayer at a mosque located near the western entrance to the plain. When the sun passes the noon meridian, the Mount of Mercy is covered with pilgrims. The themes of brotherhood and repentance dominate the afternoon sermons and supplications.

Muzdalifah. At sundown the somber scene of prayer changes abruptly as pilgrims scramble to break camp and begin the "hurrying" to Muzdalifah. This rite is called the *ifāḍah* ("pouring forth") or *nafrah* ("stampede") and is described in pilgrim diaries as a moment of urgent confusion. Like the preceding period of respectful standing, however, the hurry to Muzdalifah is a rite of ancient significance; it is not simply undisciplined mass behavior. At Muzdalifah, a few miles on the road back toward Mecca, pilgrims halt for a combined observance of the sunset and evening *ṣalāt* prayers. The *sunnah* of the Prophet established the tradition of staying overnight at Muzdalifah, although it is permissible after the halt in Muzdalifah to push on closer to Minā. The Qur'ān admonishes: "When you hurry from Arafat, remember God at the Sacred Grove (*al-mashʿar al-ḥarām*)," that is, at Muzdalifah (2:198). Today a mosque marks the place in Muzdalifah where pilgrims gather to perform the special *ṣalāt.* Also during the halt at Muzdalifah, pilgrims gather small stones for the ritual lapidations at Minā the next day.

Minā. The tenth of Dhū al-Ḥijjah is the final official day of the *ḥajj* season. Most of the ritual activities of this day take place in Minā and include (1) the casting of seven small stones at the pillar of Aqaba, (2) the feast of the major sacrifice (ʿĪd al-Aḍḥā), (3) the rite of deconsecration from the condition of *iḥrām,* and (4) the visit to Mecca for the *ṭawāf,* called *al-ifāḍah.*

The story of Ibrāhīm's duty to sacrifice Ismāʿīl provides the symbolic significance of the rites of lapidation and blood sacrifice. It is said that on his return from Arafat, Ibrāhīm was given the divine command to sacrifice that which was most dear to him, his son Ismāʿīl. Along the way to Minā, Satan whispered to him three times (or to Ibrāhīm, Ismāʿīl, and Ḥājar), tempting him (or them) not to obey the heavy command. The legendary response was a hurling of stones to repulse the Tempter. Three brick and mortar pillars stand in the center of Minā as symbols of Satan's temptations, and the pillar called Aqaba is the site where pilgrims gather early on the morning of the tenth of Dhū al-Ḥijjah to cast seven stones. Following the lapidations, those pilgrims who can afford it offer a blood sacrifice of a lamb or goat (sometimes a camel) to commemorate the divine substitution of a ram for Ibrāhīm's sacrifice. *Ḥajj* manuals recommend supplications that express the pilgrim's willingness to sacrifice for the sake of God that which is dear. The meat is consumed by family and friends, with unused portions given to the poor. The festival of the major sacrifice is also celebrated on this day by Muslims around the world in gatherings of family and friends.

Ṭawāf al-ifāḍah and taḥallul. After the sacrifice and feast, the process of *taḥallul,* or deconsecration, is begun with the rite of clipping the hair. Many men follow the tradition of having the head shaved, although for women, and for men if they prefer, the cutting of three hairs meets the ritual requirement. This is followed by a visit to Mecca for another rite of circumambulation known as *ṭawāf al-ifāḍah.* Pilgrims who have not yet performed the complete rites of *ʿumrah* may do so at this time.

The Kaʿbah itself undergoes purification and ritual renewal during the three days of *ḥajj.* Shortly before the *ḥajj* begins, the black *kiswah*—weathered and worn by a year of exposure to the open air—is replaced by a white one, suggestive of the *iḥrām* garb worn by pilgrims. After pilgrims go out to Arafat, Meccan authorities open the door of the Kaʿbah for the purpose of washing its interior, an act symbolic of the Prophet's cleansing of idols from the sacred house. Pilgrims returning for *ṭawāf al-ifāḍah* on the tenth of Dhū al-Ḥijjah are greeted by the sight of a lustrous new black *kiswah.* In the early Islamic period, the new *kiswah* and other presents for the shrines of Mecca and Medina were sent annually by the caliphs; these offerings were borne by camel caravan in an ornate box called a *maḥmal.* From the thirteenth century until 1927, the Egyptian *maḥmal* brought the new *kiswah* each year. Since 1927 the *kiswah* has been made at a factory in Mecca.

When the *ṭawāf al-ifāḍah* has been completed, the dissolution of the condition of consecration is made final by doffing the pilgrim garb and wearing normal clothing. All the prohibitions of *iḥrām* are now lifted, and most pilgrims return to Minā for days of social gathering on the eleventh to the thirteenth of Dhū al-Ḥijjah. On each of these days it is *sunnah* to cast seven stones at each of the three pillars in Minā. This vast amalgam of pilgrims, dwelling in a river of tents pitched along the narrow valley of Minā, eases into a more relaxed atmosphere of friendly exchanges of religious greetings and visiting with Muslims from around the world. By sundown on the thirteenth, the plain of Minā must be vacated. Though many will choose to spend additional time in Mecca, all pilgrims make a last visit to the Ka'bah for the final circumambulation, *ṭawāf al-qudūm,* which is permissible without the condition and attire of *iḥrām.* The *ḥajj* is thus complete, and each pilgrim leaves the sacred precincts with the honorific title of *ḥajjī.*

The Ziyārah, or Visitation to Holy Places. The Sacred Mosque in Mecca, the Prophet's Mosque in Medina, and the mosque of al-Aqṣā in Jerusalem are the three most sacred shrines in Islamic belief, and the three cities are especially holy to Muslims. Thus an additional pilgrimage to the Prophet's mosque and tomb in Medina is made by many Muslim visitors to Arabia each year, usually preceding or following the *ḥajj.* Although such visitations do not have the weight of religious duty in Islamic law and are not a formal part of the *ḥajj, ziyārah,* or visitation to holy places, is nonetheless an essential aspect of traditional Muslim piety. There are many monuments in both Mecca and Medina that mark the homes, graves, and events associated with the Prophet, his family, and his closest companions. Guides for *ziyārah* conduct pilgrims to these sites, where prayers and meditation are offered.

The most auspicious visitation is the one to the Mosque of the Prophet in Medina. Under the guidance of a shaykh, visitors enter the mosque through a passage called the Gate of Peace, uttering a supplication. Inside the mosque as it stands today is a brass railing that marks out the smaller boundaries of the original home and mosque of the Prophet, and within this brass railing pilgrims perform a *ṣalāt* of two prostrations followed by supplications. Nearby is the green-domed mausoleum of the Prophet, where pilgrims offer supplications and praises for the Prophet. The Prophet's mausoleum also enshrines the graves of the first two caliphs of Islam, Abū Bakr and 'Umar, for whom prayers may also be said.

The Ḥajj Interpreted. The meaning of the pilgrimage to Mecca, in general and in its many particulars, has been the subject of numerous books by Muslims throughout the centuries and by non-Muslim scholars in modern times. Although *ḥajj* is a duty that is carefully delimited by Islamic law, the great diversity of Muslims with differing degrees and kinds of piety are accommodated remarkably well within the structures of traditional interpretations. For example, the various schools of law differ in the degree of stringency each suggests for the length of time one must perform the rite of standing at Arafat. The more pious pilgrims seek to emulate what the Prophet recommended and practiced at each station within the sacred precincts, while others may choose to follow the minimal requirements of the more lenient interpretations of the schools of law. For virtually every rite, such as the blood sacrifice at Minā, physical or economic inability to meet the literal requirement can be compensated by the substitution of prayer and fasting.

The continual process of interpreting *ḥajj* meanings and requirements within the framework of Islamic symbols can be witnessed in the writings of contemporary Muslims. One problem under increasing discussion is the size of the pilgrim gathering in relation to available physical space for performance of the rites. The press of more than two million pilgrims to cast stones at the pillars of Minā, for example, has prompted Saudi *ḥajj* authorities to devise ways of organizing and regulating the social space within which the rite is performed. The mass slaughtering of hundreds of thousands of animals at Minā within a limited space and time creates a considerable health problem, particularly when the *ḥajj* occurs during the hot summer months. Some authorities have speculated on alternative ways for pilgrims to accomplish the root meaning of the sacrifice, namely, giving up that which is dear. Others, on the basis of statements drawn from the *sunnah* and the schools of law, have proposed that greater latitude should be given to the time permitted for the completion of such rites as the lapidations and the blood sacrifice.

The problem of interpretation and meaning must also be seen in relation to the political and technological changes that have affected the Islamic world. For example, the rise of nationalism has added a new dimension to the quest for ritual unity with the sacred precincts. Mass transportation has made travel to Mecca available to vastly larger numbers of pilgrims. The traditional experiences of adventure and hospitality along the *ḥajj* routes are being exchanged for the benefits of faster and safer passage by a growing majority of contemporary pilgrims. The ability to have media coverage of the *ḥajj* at home affords the Muslim community at large an audio and visual experience of the pilgrimage rites. Thus the *ḥajj* is becoming an ever more visible event to the world of Islam in modern times.

BIBLIOGRAPHY

A readable modern Muslim *ḥajj* manual is Ahmad Kamal's *The Sacred Journey* (New York, 1961). A pictorial essay with color photographs and accompanying text has been expertly prepared by Mohamed Amin, *Pilgrimage to Mecca* (Nairobi, 1978). Both the old and new editions of *The Encyclopaedia of Islam* (Leiden, 1913–1938 and 1960–) are valuable sources of information about the *ḥajj;* see especially the articles "Ḥadjdj" and "Kaʿba."

Among the works that attempt to analyze and interpret the *ḥajj* from a history-of-religions and social-science perspective, the most substantial is Maurice Gaudefroy-Demombynes's *Le pèlerinage à la Mekke* (Paris, 1923). On the *ḥajj* in relation to the study of ritual in the history of religions, see the articles by Frederick M. Denny and William R. Roff in *Islam and the History of Religions,* edited by Richard C. Martin (Berkeley, 1983). David Edwin Long's *The Hajj Today: A Survey of the Contemporary Makkah Pilgrimage* (Albany, N.Y., 1979) analyzes various social and health problems and modern attempts by the Saudi Arabian government to resolve them; it includes a useful bibliography.

Numerous accounts of the *ḥajj* by travelers and adventurers provide useful historical information about the pilgrimage at specific times in the past. The best known of this genre is Richard F. Burton's *Personal Narrative of a Pilgrimage to al-Madinah and Meccah,* 2 vols. (London, 1893). Eldon Rutter's *The Holy Cities of Arabia,* 2 vols. (London and New York, 1928), is a work written about the 1925 *ḥajj*—the period of Ibn Saud's incursion into western Arabia—and contains considerable geographical information and descriptions of the major *ḥajj* sites as well as the numerous points of visitation in and near Mecca. The role of Mecca and the Meccans in relation to the *ḥajj* was studied in Christiaan Snouck Hurgronje's *Mekka in the Latter Part of the Nineteenth Century* (Leiden, 1931).

RICHARD C. MARTIN

Contemporary Jewish Pilgrimage

Jewish pilgrimages in Israel may be classified into three main types: (1) those that originated during the biblical period, or that have as their goal historical sites from the biblical period that are located in Jerusalem and its surroundings; (2) pilgrimages to the tombs of Talmudic and qabbalistic sages, mainly located in the Galilee; and (3) emerging new centers of pilgrimage in various parts of the country dedicated to Diaspora sages and saints.

The tradition of pilgrimage, *ʿaliyyah le-regel* (literally, "going up on foot"), has been institutionalized in Jewish culture since the beginning of nationhood, with the religious prescription that committed all males to "go up" annually to the Temple in Jerusalem on three festivals (Passover; Shavuʿot, or Pentecost; and Sukkot, the Feast of Tabernacles; see *Ex.* 23:17, 34:23; *Dt.* 16:16). The essence of the pilgrimage was the entry of the pilgrims into the Temple to worship, particularly through the offering of sacrifices. After the destruction of the Temple in 70 CE, pilgrimage to the holy site in Jerusalem continued until modern times, though it lost its convivial characteristics. The Western Wall (often referred to as the Wailing Wall), which survived the destruction of the Temple, became the symbol of Jewish historical continuity, recalling the tragedy of destruction and dispersion as well as the hope of the exiles to return to Erets Yisra'el, the Land of Israel.

Other sites related to the biblical period have gradually become centers of pilgrimage. The most venerated, to this day, are the Cave of Machpelah in Hebron (the reputed burial ground of the patriarchs); the reputed tomb of Rachel, Jacob's wife (and symbol of Jewish motherhood), in Bethlehem; and the reputed tomb of King David in Jerusalem. For most of the past nineteen hundred years, however, it was usually difficult, if not impossible, for Jews to visit most of the biblical sites, because of obstructions set up by the local authorities. Thus, the Western Wall was for many centuries under Muslim Waqf administration, and Jews were not allowed to enter the Cave of Machpelah. Free entrance and worship at these sites became possible for Jews only after the Israeli army gained control of them during the 1967 war.

A second center for pilgrimages developed in the Galilee, at Safad and Tiberias, where many Talmudic sages (first to fifth centuries) and qabbalist sages (particularly during the sixteenth century) lived and were reputedly buried. The first evidence of pilgrimage to these sites dates from the thirteenth century. The most famous site is the reputed tomb of Rabbi Shimʿon bar Yoḥ'ai, since the sixteenth century the most venerated postbiblical figure in Jewish folk tradition. Bar Yoḥ'ai, who lived during the second century, was a scholar and patriot who opposed the Roman occupation and who has been accredited by popular tradition with the authorship of the *Zohar,* the classic text of Jewish mysticism. According to tradition, Bar Yoḥ'ai was buried with his son El'azar in Meron, a village on a hill near Safad. For at least four centuries, to this day, a ceremony and a popular festival have been held at Meron on the holiday of Lag ba-ʿOmer, the eighteenth of the Jewish month of

Iyyar. Usually pilgrims to Meron celebrate also at the tomb of Rabbi Me'ir Ba'al ha-Nes in Tiberias. The latter is believed by many to have been a distinguished scholar and saint, also from the second century.

Regular pilgrimages to the tombs of the sages and saints have been particularly popular in North Africa, where Muslim and Jewish beliefs have often been shared and exchanged. Among Moroccan Jewry (formerly the largest Jewish community in the Muslim world), many individuals were devoted to a particular family saint. Some of these saints' tombs acquired wide reputation throughout Morocco and became centers for large annual festivals *(hillulot*; sg., *hillulah)*. In recent years a number of these shrines have been symbolically transferred to the state of Israel, to which the majority of Moroccan Jews immigrated. Synagogues were dedicated on spots indicated by the saints themselves, as revealed to certain individuals in dreams. The new shrines, often located in poor immigrant towns, have become new centers for convivial pilgrimages.

Contemporary pilgrims often visit, at the appropriate annual dates, the biblical, the Talmudic-qabbalistic, and the new centers of pilgrimage. But they demonstrate at the various sites different patterns of devotional activity. Visits to biblical sites are shorter than visits to other sites (a few hours at most), more specifically oriented, more formally ritualized, and less convivial.

The pilgrimage and the festivities that are carried out on Lag ba-'Omer in Meron are the most elaborate. More than one hundred thousand pilgrims assemble on that day, many of them staying for several days. Boys are brought to the Meron pilgrimage for their first haircut, and the hair is burned in the fire that is kindled on the roof of the tomb to commemorate the saint's spirit. Into the same fire people also throw small personal belongings such as scarves and handkerchiefs. Money and candles are thrown onto the tomb itself; the money is later used for charity. Sheep and goats are slaughtered on the spot to provide food for the congregating people, including the poor, who are invited to take a share. A variety of ethnic groups, including Jews of Ashkenazic (eastern European), Middle Eastern, and North African extraction, meet convivially at the site, which is reputed to have miraculous powers. Structural liminality and feelings of Israeli *communitas* reach their peak here.

In contrast, the North African immigrants who participate in *hillulot* at the new shrines, though aspiring toward similar religious and moral goals, display more noticeable feelings of ethnic solidarity. Through the commemoration of North African Jewish cultural heroes, they seem to express symbolically their shared experience of emigration and their position in Israeli society.

All pilgrimages to holy sites, tombs, and shrines, during the major annual festivals or on other occasions, are deemed to carry good luck and remedy for particular misfortunes. The pilgrims pray, make offerings, and sometimes write requests on notes that they leave at the site. With the exception of the Western Wall in Jerusalem, where prayers are addressed to God, pilgrims tend to call on the ancestors and saints associated with the holy site to intercede for divine help. The belief in this practice has been expressed by a Moroccan immigrant who stated, "We travel to the saint who will ask God for mercy. When you can't get to the mayor, you approach the deputy and ask for his help."

BIBLIOGRAPHY

Ben-Ami, Issachar. *Yahadut Maroqo.* Jerusalem, 1975. See pages 110–117 and 171–197.

Ben-Ami, Issachar. "Le-ḥeqer folqlor ha-milḥamah: Moṭiv ha-qedoshim." In *Sefer Dov Sadan*, edited by S. Verssess et al., pp. 87–104. Tel Aviv, 1977.

Braslvsky, Joseph. *Studies in Our Country: Its Past and Remains.* Tel Aviv, 1954. See pages 342–358.

Deshen, Shlomo. "The Memorial Celebrations of Tunisian Immigrants." In *The Predicament of Homecoming: Cultural and Social Life of North African Immigrants in Israel*, by Shlomo Deshen and Moshe Shokeid, pp. 95–121. Ithaca, N.Y., 1974.

"Pilgrimage." In *Encyclopaedia Judaica*, vol. 13, pp. 510–514. Jerusalem, 1971.

Shokeid, Moshe. "An Anthropological Perspective on Ascetic Behavior and Religious Change." In *The Predicament of Homecoming: Cultural and Social Life of North African Immigrants in Israel*, by Shlomo Deshen and Moshe Shokeid, pp. 64–94. Ithaca, N.Y., 1974.

Vilnay, Zev. *Matsevot qodesh be-Erets Yisra'el.* Jerusalem, 1963.

MOSHE SHOKEID

Buddhist Pilgrimage in South and Southeast Asia

Victor and Edith Turner, in their book *Image and Pilgrimage in Christian Culture* (New York, 1978), have written that "if mysticism is an interior pilgrimage, pilgrimage is exteriorized mysticism." In the Buddhist tradition, one undertakes a pilgrimage in order to find the Buddha in the external world; one undertakes meditation to discover the Buddha nature within oneself. The internal pilgrimage brings one closer to the goal of *nirvāṇa* (Pali, *nibbāna*) than does the external pilgrimage, but the turning toward the Buddha who is iconically represented in the marks of his presence on earth or in relics constitutes an important preliminary step along the path to enlightenment. That the Buddha actually existed in the world, and continues to exist through traces (Skt., *caitya;* Pali, *cetiya*), must be acknowledged before one begins to follow his teachings (Skt., *dharma;* Pali, *dhamma*).

The question of the persistence of the Buddha in the world arose as he approached his physical death and his *parinirvāṇa (parinibbāna)*, or "final cessation." During his lifetime, the Buddha had attracted many followers, among whom were those who came to constitute the *saṃgha*, the order of mendicants devoted to his teachings. While the *saṃgha* could be entrusted with the responsibility of perpetuating the Dharma through practice and teaching after the Buddha's death, there remained still the problem of how people were to be attracted in the first place to the Buddhist message. This problem was resolved when the Buddha charged his disciple Ānanda to arrange for his cremated remains to be enshrined in stupas. [*See* Stupa Worship.] In the *Mahāparinibbāna Sutta* it is recorded how, after the death of the Buddha, his body was cremated, and his remains were divided into eight parts, each enshrined in a separate stupa. Two more stupas were also erected; one, built by the brahman who had divided the relics, enshrined the Master's alms bowl, and another, erected by those who had arrived too late to receive a portion of the remains, enshrined the ashes of the funerary pyre.

According to ancient legend, after the great Mauryan king Aśoka (c. 270–232 BCE) converted to Buddhism he had all but one (which was protected by *nāgas*) of the original reliquary shrines opened and the relics divided into eighty-four thousand parts, each destined for a new stupa. Although this number must be interpreted symbolically, there is historical evidence that Aśoka did, in fact, erect a number of new stupas. Moreover, the tradition that relics of the Buddha had been, as it were, placed into circulation by Aśoka served to legitimate claims that true relics of the Buddha were to be found wherever Buddhism became established.

In addition to bodily relics (Pali, *sarīradhātu*), Buddhist tradition also recognizes two other forms of relics that are taken as indicative of the Buddha's presence in the world. In Pali these are termed *paribhogikadhātu* and *uddesikadhātu*, the former referring to objects that the Buddha used (as, for example, his alms bowl) or marks (such as a footprint or shadow) that he left on earth, and the latter referring to votive reminders, such as images and stupas known not to contain actual relics.

From the edicts of Aśoka we obtain our first historical evidence of Buddhist pilgrimage, even though it is probable that the practice began before Aśokan times. In Rock Edict 8, he says that, while previously he used to go out on *vihārayātrās* ("excursions for enjoyment"), ten years after his coronation he undertook a *dharmayātrā* ("journey for truth") to the place where the Buddha attained enlightenment, that is, to Bodh Gayā. This pilgrimage appears to constitute the beginning of Aśoka's search for the true Dharma and for the significance of the Dharma in his own life as emperor.

From the time of Asóka to the present, Bodh Gayā has remained the most important Buddhist pilgrimage site in India. It is often grouped with three other sites—Lumbini in Nepal, where Siddhārtha Gautama, the future Buddha, was born; the Deer Park at Sarnath near Banares, where he "turned the Wheel of the Law," that is, preached his first sermon; and Kuśinagara in Uttar Pradesh, where he passed into the state of *nirvāṇa*. None of these other sites, nor any other in India where he was reputed to have performed miracles during his life, however, holds the significance for Buddhists that Bodh Gayā does. Bodh Gayā represents the birth of Buddhism, the place where the Tathāgata realized the fundamental truth that lies at the base of Dharma.

The quest for the Dharma appears to have been the primary motivation for perhaps the most famous of Buddhist pilgrims, the Chinese monks who journeyed from their homeland to India in the fifth century and again in the seventh century CE. Fa-hsien, the earliest of these pilgrims to have left a detailed record, departed from his home in Ch'ang-an in 399 and traveled by land through Central Asia and then across northern India. From northern India he then traveled by ship to Sri Lanka and to Java and finally returned to China in 412. While Fa-hsien's pilgrimage, like those of subsequent Chinese monks, was undertaken for the purpose of acquiring the Dharma, it reveals also another model of Buddhist pilgrimage, one much more popular with lay persons, namely a pilgrimage centered on the cult of the relics.

From his first encounter with Buddhist communities in Central Asia, Fa-hsien found not only monks but also stupas and images of the Buddha that were the foci of popular cults. He himself visited a number of places associated with incidents in the life of the Buddha, and his account serves as a brief version of the life of the Buddha. Of particular interest, given the later development of Buddhist pilgrimage in lands outside India, Fa-hsien observed "footprints" of the Buddha in areas as far removed from the region where the Buddha actually lived as the Punjab and Sri Lanka.

Shrines marking traces left by the Buddha in his supernatural visits to lands that were to become Buddhist as well as shrines enclosing relics that had been transported—naturally or supernaturally—from India to such lands often became pilgrimage centers in their own right. Indeed, for the long period between the decline of Buddhism in India in the latter part of the first millennium CE and the late nineteenth century, when cheap travel and Buddhist revival together stimulated renewed interest in the sacred Buddhist sites in India, Buddhist pilgrimage was confined mainly to Buddhist lands outside India. The emerging importance of certain sites—the so-called sixteen great places in Sri Lanka and the twelve shrines associated with the twelve-year cycle in northern Thailand—was associated primarily with the linking of political and moral communities in the world to a sacred Buddhist cosmos.

Buddhist pilgrims have long traveled to such important shrines as those housing the Buddha's footprints on Siripāda (Adam's Peak) in Sri Lanka and at Saraburi in Thailand and those housing famous Buddhist relics, such as the Temple of the Tooth in Kandy, Sri Lanka; the Shwe Dagon in Rangoon, Burma; the That Luang temple in Vientiane, Laos; and Doi Suthep near Chiang Mai, Thailand. Pilgrims visited these and other holy sites in order to acquire merit or to gain access to the presumed magical power associated with them. While some have made pilgrimages to shrines associated with traces of the Buddha as an end in itself, most have continued, as did Aśoka and Fa-hsien, to see pilgrimage as a means for orienting themselves toward the Buddha as a preliminary step along the path to enlightenment. The pilgrimage that begins by turning toward the Buddha in this world finds its culmination in an inner pilgrimage that leads to a true understanding of the Dharma.

[*See also the biographies of Aśoka, Fa-hsien, Hsüan-tsang, and I-ching.*]

BIBLIOGRAPHY

The scriptural source for Buddhist pilgrimage is to be found in the *Mahāparinibbāna Suttānta*, a text that has been translated by T. W. Rhys Davids in "Sacred Books of the East," vol. 11 (Oxford, 1881), pp. 1–136. A discussion of Aśokan pilgrimage, together with translations of the edicts of Aśoka, appears in *Aśoka* (London, 1928) by Radhakumud Mookerji. The travels of Fa-hsien have been translated by James Legge in *A Record of Buddhistic Kingdoms* (1886; reprint, New York, 1965). The *locus classicus* for an understanding of the cosmological significance of Buddhist stupas is Paul Mus's *Barabadur* (1935; reprint, New York, 1978). Marilyn Stablein has provided an overview of Buddhist pilgrimage among Tibetans in her "Textual and Contextual Patterns of Tibetan Buddhist Pilgrimage in India," *Tibet Society Bulletin* 12 (1978): 7–38. For discussions of Buddhist pilgrimage in Sri Lanka, see Gananath Obeyesekere's "The Buddhist Pantheon in Ceylon and Its Extensions, " in *Anthropological Studies in Theravada Buddhism*, edited by Manning Nash et al. (New Haven, 1966), pp. 1–26; Bryan Pfaffenberger's "The Kataragama Pilgrimage: Hindu-Buddhist Interaction and Its Significance in Sri Lanka's Polyethnic Social System," *Journal of Asian Studies* 38 (1979): 253–270; and H. L. Seneviratne's *Rituals of the Kandyan State* (Cambridge, 1978). Buddhist pilgrimage in Thailand has been examined in my article "Buddhist Pilgrimage Centers and the Twelve Year Cycle: Northern Thai Moral Orders in Space and Time," *History of Religions* 15 (1975): 71–89, and in James B. Pruess's "Merit-Seeking in Public: Buddhist Pilgrimage in Northeastern Thailand," *Journal of the Siam Society* 64 (1976): 169–206.

CHARLES F. KEYES

Buddhist Pilgrimage in East Asia

Pilgrimage, especially to sacred mountain sites, has long been a popular religious practice in both China and Japan. Since the entry of Buddhism into China in the first centuries of the common era, and since its entry into Japan through China several centuries later, pilgrimage in East Asia has become associated with Buddhist religious beliefs.

Pilgrimages in China. In mainland China there have been various pilgrimage sites, related to both Buddhism and Taoism. As for the former, there existed the following four major sites: Mount Wu-t'ai, sacred to Mañjuśrī (Skt.; known in Chinese as Wen-shu); Mount O-mei, sacred to Samantabhadra (Chin., P'u-hsien); Mount P'u-t'o, sacred to Avalokiteśvara (Kuan-yin); and Mount Chiu Hua, sacred to Kṣitigarbha (Ti-tsang). In the case of Taoist pilgrimages, one of the most famous sites is Mount T'ai. Here we shall deal with Mount Wu-t'ai and Mount T'ai. [*See* Avalokiteśvara; Mañjuśrī; *and* Kṣitigarbha.]

Mount Wu-t'ai. Located in northeastern China, Mount Wu-t'ai consists of five peaks. This sacred mountain has attracted a great number of pilgrims over the centuries, not only from every part of China but also from Manchuria, Mongolia, Central Asia, India, and Japan. It has, therefore, been referred to as the most eminent pilgrimage site in Asia. Although it was famous as the sacred site of Mañjuśrī, it is said to have been originally a sacred place related to the spiritual tradition of Taoism. It was not until the Northern Wei dynasty (386–535) that Buddhist influence became widespread in China, predominating over the indigenous Taoist tradition, and from this time Mount Wu-t'ai became a site holy to Mañjuśrī. In the T'ang dynasty (618–907), it was so popular as a pilgrimage site that many pilgrims even came to visit the mountain from foreign countries, including Tibet and India. During the same period, many books were published, collecting stories of the miracles and wonders performed by Mañjuśrī. Drawings sketching

Mount Wu-t'ai were also widely distributed. These drawings were usually put up on the walls of either Buddhist temples or individual houses all over China.

It is said to have been during the Yüan dynasty (1271–1366), when China was invaded and ruled by the Mongols, that Tibetan Buddhism, which the Mongols preferred to Chinese Buddhism, started to spread its influence at Mount Wu-t'ai. Soon Chinese Buddhism and Tibetan Buddhism came to coexist on this sacred mountain. In other words, the mountain became an important pilgrimage site for two different religious traditions simultaneously. During the Ch'ing dynasty (1644–1912), Tibetan Buddhism gradually came to predominate at Mount Wu-t'ai, partly because the Manchu Ch'ing rulers, who were not ethnically Chinese, began to take a conciliatory policy toward other non-Chinese groups such as the Mongols, who believed in Tibetan Buddhism. As a result, Mount Wu-t'ai became the most holy religious site of the Mongols. According to the reports of Japanese scholars who visited Mount Wu-t'ai in the 1930s, many fervent Mongolian pilgrims were to be witnessed there. In the case of Chinese Buddhist pilgrimage sites, it is quite common for other religious traditions, including indigenous ones like Taoism, to have been closely related to the history of the sites.

Mount T'ai. Long famous as a Taoist pilgrimage site, T'ai-shan has been continually associated with Buddhism in various ways. In Chinese history, this sacred mountain has been well known as one of the so-called Five Peaks, designated as indispensable for the protection of the whole country. The history of Mount T'ai can be separated into three phases.

In ancient times, Chinese emperors were supposed to visit T'ai-shan when they ascended the throne and were supposed to perform a special ritual for declaring their ascension, worshiping all the divinities in the sky and on the earth as well. At the same time, the emperors were said to pray for their own individual wishes, such as longevity.

It was probably toward the end of the Latter Han dynasty (25–220 CE) that T'ai-shan came to be regarded as having some connection with the world of the dead, although this was diametrically opposed to the previous belief in longevity. As time went on, therefore, Mount T'ai was thought to be related to Hell. It was believed, then, that the dead received judgment at Mount T'ai-shan as to whether they should go to Hell or not. This idea of Hell was introduced by Buddhism.

From the Sung dynasty (960–1279) up until the modern period, another new belief was associated with Mount T'ai: that of a goddess. This goddess was worshiped as one who presided over the birth and rearing of children. This special characteristic of the goddess attracted a great number of pilgrims because of its familiarity and closeness with the common people. Accordingly, miniature statues of this particular goddess were enshrined all over China in moden times.

Pilgrimage in modern China. Pilgrimages in China seemed to have disappeared after Communist China was established in 1949. Moreover, many temples and shrines belonging to various pilgrimage sites all over China were seriously damaged during the Cultural Revolution in the 1960s and 1970s. However, in recent years, pilgrimage sites have been rapidly restored and have reopened their doors to pilgrims both from China and from overseas. The majority of the foreign pilgrims are Chinese merchants living abroad. As a result of a rapid growth in the living standards of the Chinese people, there seems to be a tendency for famous pilgrimage sites to become targets of tourism.

Pilgrimages in Japan. In Japanese religious tradition, both Shintō and Buddhism have various pilgrimage sites. In Japan, pilgrimages can be divided into two general types. The first is the type exemplified by the Pilgrimage to the Thirty-three Holy Places of Kannon (Avalokiteśvara) in the Western Provinces and by the Pilgrimage to the Eighty-eight Temples of Shikoku, in which one makes a circuit of a series of temples or holy places in a set order. The individual holy places that the pilgrim visits may be separated by great distances, as in the case of the Shikoku pilgrimage, in which eighty-eight temples are scattered along a route of about 1,200 kilometers (746 miles). The order of visitation is an important feature of this type of pilgrimage. The second type is a journey to one particular holy place. Pilgrimage to the Kumano Shrines and Ise Shintō Shrine, as well as to certain holy mountains, belong to this type. In common usage, the term *junrei,* the Japanese word for "pilgrimage," usually refers to the first type only.

It is thought that pilgrimages were first undertaken in the Nara period (710–794), although the custom did not become popular until the Heian period (794–1185). With the increasing popularity of religions involving mountain worship, members of the imperial family, the nobility, and Buddhist monks made pilgrimages to remote holy mountains. Among them, Kumano in the southern part of Wakayama Prefecture is the most famous, having at that early time already developed into a large center for the adherents of mountain worship. Besides Kumano, Hasedera Temple, Shitennōji, Mount Koya, and Mount Kinpu were also popular pilgrimage sites. Early forms of the pilgrimage circuits for the western provinces and Shikoku were also established by the late Heian period. It can be surmised that many of these places were centers where Buddhist monks and ascetics engaged in austerities. [*See especially* Shugendō.] Such pilgrimages continued throughout the Kamakura period (1185–1333) and the Muromachi period (1333–1568).

In the Edo period (1600–1868) an unprecedented number of people began to visit pilgrimage centers. While the vast majority of pilgrims had previously been member of the upper classes, such as monks, aristocrats, and warriors, in the Edo period the number of pilgrims from the general populace greatly increased. This change was largely owing to the peace established by the Tokugawa feudal regime and to the improvement in the economic condition of both the farming and the merchant classes. Transportation improved, and although government policy restricted travel between provinces, an exception was made for pilgrimages. The number of pilgrims who made journeys to the western provinces, Shikoku, Kotohira Shrine, Zenkoji, Ise, and Mount Fuji increased rapidly, and many new pilgrimage centers developed in various parts of the country. During this period, pilgrims tended to travel in groups, and as more and more people participated for recreational as well as for religious purposes, temple and shrine towns sprang up with facilities for accommodating these people. One should also note an increase in the number of so-called beggar-pilgrims who wandered from one center to another. The Shikoku circuit was particularly frequented by criminals, lepers, and beggars.

Travel since the Meiji period (1868–1912) has basically preserved the Edo period pattern of pilgrimage. Even today, many travelers include visits to famous temples and shrines in their itineraries. Even pilgrimage circuits that lack any other attraction, such as the Shikoku pilgrimage, have once again become popular. Behind this phenomenon perhaps lies a nostalgia for the past, a resurging interest in religion, and a desire for temporary escape from urban life.

[*See also* Worship and Cultic Life, *article on* Buddhist Cultic Life in East Asia, *and* Mountains.]

BIBLIOGRAPHY

Adachi K. and Shioiri Ryodo, eds. *Nittō guhō junrei kōki*. 2 vols. Tokyo, 1970-1985. An annotated edition of Ennin's account of his travels in T'ang China.

Kitagawa, Joseph M. "Three Types of Pilgrimage in Japan." In *Studies in Mysticism and Religion Presented to Gershom G. Scholem on His Seventieth Birthday by Pupils, Colleagues and Friends*, edited by E. E. Urbach, R. J. Zwi Werblowsky, and Chaim Wirszubski, pp. 155-164. Jerusalem, 1967.

Maeda Takashi. *Junrei no shakaigaku*. Kyoto, 1971.

Ono Katsutoshi. *Nittō guhō junrei gyōki no kenkyū*. 4 vols. Tokyo, 1964-1969. A translation and study of Ennin's account of his travels in T'ang China.

Ono Katsutoshi and Hibino Takeo. *Godaisan*. Tokyo, 1942.

Reischauer, Edwin O., trans. *Ennin's Diary: The Record of a Pilgrimage to China in Search of the Law*. New York, 1955.

Shinjō Tsunezō. *Shaji-sankei no shakai-keizaishiteki kenkyū*. Rev. ed. Tokyo, 1982.

HOSHINO EIKI

Tibetan Pilgrimage

Pilgrimage comes naturally to the Tibetans, a people characterized by movement. The Tibetan word for a living creature, human as well as nonhuman, is *'gro-ba*, meaning "one who goes." The high mountains and sparse population of Tibet necessitate extensive travel by all sectors of the society. The all-pervasive nature of Tibetan religion automatically converts much of this travel into pilgrimage.

The characteristic feature of Tibetan pilgrimage is circumambulation, or *pradakṣiṇā*, a practice derived from Indian Buddhism, where it began as a means of paying homage to a sacred person or object. [*See* Circumambulation.] In Tibet this practice grew to encompass the whole conception of pilgrimage: the Tibetan term for pilgrimage, *gnas-skor*, means "circumambulation of sacred places." The entire circuit of a pilgrimage, from departure to return, is viewed as one great circumambulation, including within it many small circumambulations. Tibetan pilgrims characteristically circumambulate both their destinations and the numerous shrines along the way—in a clockwise direction if they are Buddhists, counterclockwise if they are followers of Bon, a religion indigenous to Tibet.

Pilgrimage and circumambulation are generally accompanied by the most prevalent practice of Tibetan religion, the recitation of *mantras*, or sacred formulas. [*See* Mantra.] The most popular *mantra* and the one most commonly recited while traveling is *oṃ maṇi padme hūṃ*, the *mantra* of Avalokiteśvara, the *bodhisattva* of compassion and the patron deity of Tibet. Pilgrims recite this *mantra* primarily to acquire the religious merit needed for a good rebirth, preferably in the Pure Land, Sukhāvatī. [*See* Merit, *article on* Buddhist Concepts.] In this way the pilgrimage becomes part of a longer journey leading beyond death.

Aside from the sanctity of the particular goal, the more difficult the pilgrimage, the more merit the pilgrim acquires. Tibetans often increase the difficulty of their pilgrimages by measuring their journeys with full-body prostrations. Ascetic practices of this sort are also meant to burn away mental defilements and purify the mind for further progress along the path to enlightenment. Merit can be further enhanced by performing a particular pilgrimage at a specified time, in certain cases once every twelve years.

In addition to acquiring merit through their own efforts, Tibetans undertake pilgrimages to receive spiritual and material blessings from the sacred objects, persons, shrines, and places they visit. Religious practitioners also go on pilgrimages to obtain teachings and initiations from spiritual masters. Such pilgrimages by Tibetans to India were crucial in the propagation of Buddhism in Tibet. Offerings left by pilgrims and the trade growing up around their travel have played an important role in Tibetan economy.

An entire literature has developed describing pilgrimage sites, locations, and routes. Short guidebooks known as *dkar chag* provide simple descriptions of particular pilgrimage places and how to reach them. Longer works such as *Mk'hyen brtse's Guide to the Holy Places of Central Tibet* (1958) describe entire pilgrimage networks. Guidebooks of a somewhat different nature give directions for journeys to such legendary places as the hidden kingdom of Shambhala. There are also numerous accounts of pilgrimages by lamas (Tib., *bla ma*), and yogins in religious biographies and histories.

The pilgrimage sites themselves can be divided into two major categories: those outside Tibet (primarily in India and Nepal) and those within it. The sites outside Tibet are primarily places hallowed by the historical Buddha, Siddhārtha Gautama, and by Padmasambhava, the Indian sage who brought Buddhism to Tibet in the eighth century. The holiest site for Tibetan Buddhists is Bodh Gayā, India, the site of the Buddha's Enlightenment. Bodh Gayā is also regarded as the "diamond seat" of enlightenment for all Buddhas and consequently as the spiritual center of the universe. Tibetans generally combine a pilgrimage to Bodh Gayā with visits to other sites commemorating important events in the Buddha's life, for example, Sārnāth, where he preached his first sermon. Another important site of Tibetan pilgrimage in India is Mandi, in the foothills of the Himalayas, where Padmasambhava is believed to have magically appeared within a lotus in the middle of a sacred lake. A number of famous Tibetan pilgrims of the past have left records of journeys to Swāt, Pakistan, where Padmasambhava is believed to have lived. The major Tibetan pilgrimage site in Nepal is the stupa of Bodnāth in the Kathmandu Valley.

Pilgrimage sites in Tibet fall into two major groups. One is composed of towns and monasteries, the other of natural sites. The three principal towns of pilgrimage are Lhasa, Bsam-yas, and Gśis-ka-rtse. The most important shrine in Lhasa, the Jo-khaṅ Temple, has an image of the Buddha believed to have been brought to Tibet by a seventh-century Chinese princess. Bsam-yas had until recently the oldest monastery in Tibet, built with the help of Padmasambhava in the eighth century. Gśis-ka-rtse is the site of Bkra-śis-lhun-po Monastery, seat of the Panchen Lama, one of the most important lamas in Tibet. Pilgrims also flock to Sku-'bum Monastery, venerated as the birthplace of Tsoṅ-kha-pa, founder of the reformed Dge-lugs-pa sect of Tibetan Buddhism.

Natural sites of pilgrimage are found mostly at caves, springs, lakes, and mountains. Pilgrims generally go to sacred caves to seek the blessings and power left in them by the meditations of sages such as Mi-la-ras-pa and Padmasambhava. Sacred mountains and lakes are generally associated with deities, usually male and female, respectively. Tibetans regard Kailāśa, the principal sacred mountain of Tibet, as the residence of the tutelary deity Cakrasaṃvara. Kailāśa (Tib., Ti-se) is also venerated as the scene of a famous religious contest in which Mi-la-ras-pa defeated a priest of the Bon religion. Like many other pilgrimage sites, Kailāśa is surrounded by three concentric circumambulation routes. Another well-known mountain of pilgrimage, Amne Machin, is regarded as the indigenous warrior god Rma-chen-spom-ra. This mountain figures prominently in the national epic of Ge-sar. [*See* Geser.] Pilgrimages to sacred sites such as Amne Machin are often combined with festivals and horse races. The circumambulation of Rtswa-ri, another important mountain, used to attract ten to fifteen thousand pilgrims once every twelve years.

From time to time groups of Tibetans also seek legendary *sbas yul*, or "hidden countries," concealed by Padmasambhava as sacred places of refuge and meditation. These journeys differ from other Tibetan pilgrimages in that the pilgrims do not expect to return from their destinations. The best-known hidden countries are 'Bras-mo-ljoṅs (Sikkim) and Padma-bkod above Assam. Millenarian migrations in search of such places have been responsible for the colonization of many Himalayan border areas of Tibet.

Finally, there is the category of mythical journeys to earthly paradises such as the hidden kingdom of Shambhala. Various texts describing these journeys make it clear that only yogins who practice meditation and undergo spiritual transformations can overcome the supernatural obstacles along the way. Shambhala itself is included in a group of five major places of Buddhist pilgrimage situated at the cardinal points of the compass. Bodh Gayā at the center, Wu-t'ai Shan in the east, the Potala (the mythical Potala, not the residence of the Dalai Lama) in the south, Uḍḍiyāna in the west, and Shambhala in the north. The mystical nature of these journeys, especially the one to Shambhala, reveals most clearly the inherent symbolism of Tibetan pilgrimage as a metaphor of the Buddhist *mārga*, or path to enlightenment.

[*See also* Worship and Cultic Life, *article on* Buddhist Cultic Life in Tibet.]

BIBLIOGRAPHY

The best overview of Tibetan pilgrimage appears in Anne-Marie Large-Blondeau's article "Les pèlerinages tibétains" in *Les pèlerinages*, "Sources orientales," no. 3 (Paris, 1960), pp. 199–245. Among primary sources available in translation, the two standard reference works on pilgrimages in Tibet are *Mk'yen brtse's Guide to the Holy Places of Central Tibet*, edited and translated by Alfonsa Ferrari and Luciano Petech (Rome, 1958), and *The Geography of Tibet according to the 'Dzam-gling rgyas-bshad*, edited and translated by Turrell V. Wylie (Rome, 1962). Robert B. Ekvall presents an extensive discussion of circumambulation and other practices associated with Tibetan pilgrimage in *Religious Observances in Tibet: Patterns and Function* (Chicago, 1964). A detailed treatment of Shambhala and hidden countries *(sbas yul)* appears in my book *The Way to Shambhala* (Garden City, N.Y., 1980). For anthropological and personal accounts of pilgrimages, the pilgrimage to Kailāśa in particular, see Corneille Jest's *Dolpo: communautés de langue tibétaine du Népal* (Paris, 1975) and Lama Anagarika Govinda's *The Way of the White Clouds: A Buddhist Pilgrim in Tibet* (Berkeley, 1970). For historical material and the religious background of Tibetan pilgrimage, see David L. Snellgrove's *Buddhist Himalaya: Travels and Studies in Quest of the Origins and Nature of Tibetan Religion* (Oxford, 1957).

Edwin Bernbaum

Hindu Pilgrimage

The seeds of Hindu pilgrimage may lie in the ceremonial bathing practices of the pre-Aryans of the Indus Valley civilization. However, explicit references to *tīrthayātrā* (journeys to sacred fords) appear in the Vedic literature. The great epic *Mahābhārata* assumes an already well established practice of Hindu pilgrimage closely conforming to the literal meaning of *tīrtha-* ("sacred ford") *yātrā* ("tour"). Reconstructed pilgrim itinerary in the *Mahābhārata* traces the outline of a grand pilgrimage of India in a general clockwise direction beginning at Puṣkara in Rajasthan and, after a traverse of different parts of India, ending at Prayāga (modern Allahabad) at the triple confluence of the Gaṅgā, the Yamunā, and the "invisible," mythical Sarasvatī.

In time the meaning of *tīrthayātrā* became generalized to encompass visits to a variety of holy sites. The *Mahābhārata* suggests that *tīrthayātrā* is a rather lonely quest for religious merit, particularly suited for those who cannot afford expensive religious sacrifices. [*See* Merit.] As a result of the development and convergence of various theistic and sectarian traditions within Hinduism, and the long syncretic pattern of its growth, the Hindu pilgrimage system became very complex. In the Puranic literature pilgrimage to holy places is often promoted as one of the means for accumulating religious merit but is not considered mandatory. Pilgrimage continues to be a very popular religious activity among Hindus, and has in fact greatly intensified with the development of transportation systems in India. Indeed, there is every indication that such "religious travel" will continue to increase in volume. Although it is extremely difficult to ascertain the annual number of pilgrims in India, twenty million would be a conservative estimate related to the nearly 150 well-known holy places.

Hindu pilgrimage sites have been classified in a variety of ways. The Puranic tradition recognizes four categories of *tīrtha*s according to the origin of their sanctity: *daiva* ("divine"), *āsura* ("demonic"), *ārṣa* ("sage"), and *mānuṣa* ("human"). Some authorities differentiate between purely sectarian and the nonsectarian sites, dividing the latter into regional and pan-Indian levels. There is a fundamental difference between *jalatīrtha*s (water-associated sites) and *mandiratīrtha*s (temple sites). At the former, self-purification by ritual bathing and the performance of rites for ancestors are the most prevalent pilgrims' activities. At the latter, devotees generally seek to establish a relational and reciprocal spatial proximity to the deity of their focus. Thus, at the *mandiratīrtha*s supplications, vows, *darśan* (holy sight), and various relational expectancies of the pilgrims tend to dominate. The *jala-* and the *mandiratīrtha*s respectively seem to reflect the complementarity of the transcendental and the existential dimensions of Hindu life.

Hindu religious literature also recognizes sacred *kṣetra*s (areas) which may include forests, groves, or even a whole mountain region such as the Himalayas but also one or more holy spots. *Kṣetra*s are cognitively demarcated areas (such as Kurukṣetra) where the manifold activities of the deities such as battles, hunts, and sports occurred, continue to unfold, or reactualize. [*See* Kurukṣetra.] Pilgrimage through *kṣetra*s is tantamount to participation in the holy experience itself. Finally, the Hindu tradition recognizes a holy man to be a *tīrtha* as well and not just a symbol thereof. Thus, Hindu pilgrimage should not be thought of as a religious journey directed exclusively toward fixed sacred spots on earth.

A totally objective basis for identifying the principal Hindu places of pilgrimage does not exist due to the many belief systems within Hinduism and many regional-cultural differences in India. Nevertheless, the *chārdhāma*s (four major abodes), Badrināth in the Himalayas, Puri on the east coast, Rāmeśvaram in the extreme south, and Dvārkā on the west coast in Gujarat are very popular with pilgrims who undertake the grand circuit pilgrimage of India. Some pilgrims consider it especially meritorious to bring *gaṅgājala* (Ganges water) from its Himalayan source and pour it on the *śivaliṅga* at Rāmeśvaram, two thousand miles to the south. Prayāga, Hardvār, Nāsik, and Ujjain form a set of four sacred places where the mammoth twelve-yearly bathing fairs are held. At Prayāg, Hardvār, and Nāsik these fairs are called Kumbha Melā (Simhastha at Ujjain). Millions of pilgrims converge to these places from all over India. Other major "transsectarian" sites of pan-Hindu importance include Gayā, Vārāṇasī, Kāñcipuram, Ayodhyā, Mathurā-Vṛndāvana, Puṣkara, and in recent times, the increasingly popular Tirupati.

Most of the principal pan-Hindu *tīrtha*s are associated with rivers. [*See also* Rivers; Ganges River; *and* Sarasvatī.] Also, the number of major *tīrtha*s with Śiva as the presiding deity is higher than those honoring Viṣṇu and his incarnations. There is only one notable place (Puṣkara) where Brahmā is the chief deity. Few, if any, pan-Hindu shrines have a goddess as the principal deity. Nevertheless, at the regional through local levels Devī (the Goddess)—known by her various appellations—assumes great importance as the chief deity, and many of her shrines are the focal points of vast numbers of pilgrims, such as the Kālī ("the black one") at Calcutta, Jvālāmukhi ("she of the flaming mouth") in Himachal Pradesh, Kanyā Kumārī ("the virgin") and Mīnākṣi ("she with fish-shaped eyes") in Tamil Nadu, and Kāmākṣi ("she with libidinous eyes") at Kāmākhyā in Assam. The Śāktas, the sectarian devotees of Śakti, recognize many specific *pīṭha*s (sites) where the Goddess is the chief deity. [*See* Goddess Worship; *article on* The Hindu Goddess.]

The Hindu pilgrim circulation system may be viewed at several spatial levels. At the highest level, represented by the more affluent and ritually higher-caste pilgrims, pilgrimage to the famous sacred places eulogized in the traditional Sanskrit literature is tantamount to reasserting the validity of a pan-Hindu belief system and religious space and thereby transcends the linguistic and regional cultural diversity of India. The motives of pilgrimage at the highest levels tend to be characterized by a quest for spirituality and purification or participation in the "reactualized" cosmic events of profound religious import. The regional and lower levels of religious circulation reflect the great variety in the Hindu social system and belief pattern. Several regional shrines of Devī are actively associated with blood sacrifice (for example, the Kālī temple in Calcutta and the Jvālāmukhi temple in Himachal Pradesh). The deities at such shrines become personalized and are propitiated by the devotees to intercede in mundane problems and crises. The devotees at these levels belong to a variety of economic groups and castes, including many scheduled castes.

The Hindu pilgrimage supersystem is an ongoing circulation mechanism that includes Hindus of various geographic regions, socio-economic strata, sects, and castes. The motives and degree of their participation may differ from one level of circulation to the other. Nevertheless, by generating an essentially continuous religious space, this circulation helps the Hindu pilgrims transcend the otherwise great linguistic and regional-cultural diversity of India.

[*See also* Kumbha Melā; Banaras; Vṛndāvana; *and* Worship and Cultic Life, *article on* Hindu Cultic Life.]

BIBLIOGRAPHY

The most comprehensive modern listing (of more than eighteen hundred places) and general description of Hindu pilgrimage places can be found in a special issue of *Kalyāṇa* 31, no. 1 (1957), titled *Tīrthāṅka*. The most detailed listing of the *Śākta Pīṭha*s to date is D. C. Sircar's "The Śākta Pīṭhas," *Journal of the Royal Asiatic Society of Bengal Letters* 14 (1948): 1–108. The epic *Mahābhārata* is the richest single source of sacred place names before the Christian era; see book 3, *The Book of the Forest*, in *The Mahābhārata*, edited and translated by J. A. B. van Buitenen, vol. 2 (Chicago, 1975).

For a cogent and authoritative source on Hindu pilgrimage in its religious and social dimension, see Agehananda Bharati's "Pilgrimage in the Indian Tradition," *History of Religions* 3 (Summer 1963): 135–167. David E. Sopher's "Pilgrim Circulation in Gujarat," *Geographical Review* 58 (July 1968): 392–425, remains a useful spatial analysis of contemporary Hindu pilgrimage. Historical and contemporary cultural dimensions of Hindu pilgrimage are discussed in my *Hindu Places of Pilgrimage in India: A Study in Cultural Geography* (Berkeley, 1973). This study also explores the normative and behavioral aspects of pilgrim circulation related to various "levels" of sacred places. The book includes several maps of Hindu holy places based on the sacred toponymies in the *Mahābhārata* and in the Puranic literature; it also offers a substantial bibliography.

A pioneering study on the economic aspects of a major Hindu temple is Burton Stein's "The Tirupati Temple: An Economic Study of a Medieval South Indian Temple" (Ph.D. diss., University of Chicago, 1958). L. P. Vidyarthi's *The Sacred Complex in Hindu Gaya* (Bombay, 1961) presents an anthropological study of a pan-Hindu pilgrimage center. German scholars of the South Asia Institute in Heidelberg and their Indian colleagues have carried out some of the most penetrating studies of Jagannath Puri. See Dietmar Rothermund and Siegfried Schwertner's *South Asia Institute: The Second Decade* (Heidelberg, 1984) for bibliography of notable contributions, including those of Hermann Kulke, Günther D. Sontheimer, and G. C. Tripathi.

SURINDER M. BHARDWAJ

PIḶḶAI LOKĀCĀRYA (1264–1369), early formulater of Teṅkalai theology for Śrī Vaiṣṇava Hindus of South India. Born in the sixth generation of disciples of Rāmānuja, and from a family learned in Sanskrit and Tamil, he lived his long life in the temple complex of Śrī Raṅgam. His father was known simply as Vaṭakku Tiruvīti Piḷḷai, "the Piḷḷai of North Street," and his mother was Śrī Raṅga Nācciyār. The couple was childless until, tradition says, Piḷḷai's guru, Nampiḷḷai, ordered him to give up his ascetic chastity. When subsequently a son was born, the couple named him Lokācārya ("teacher of the world") after one of Nampiḷḷai's own titles. Piḷḷai Lokācārya himself never married, but rather devoted himself to the service of Nārāyaṇa in his iconic forms and to teaching. In 1309, when northern Muslims raided the temple, tradition relates that he walled in the immovable icons and escaped with the movable ones to a distant village, sustaining their worship until they could be safely returned.

Teaching shaped his scholarship from an early age. Whereas his father recorded Nampiḷḷai's comments on Nammāḻvār's *Tiruvāymoḻi* in the *Bhagavat Viṣayam,* and his younger brother, the ascetic Aḻakiya Maṇavāḷa Perumāḷ Nāyaṉār, one of his own disciples, likewise composed an important commentary on Nammāḻvār's poems, the *Ācārya Hṛdayam* (The Heart of the Teacher), Piḷḷai Lokācārya produced theological textbooks such as the *Aṣṭadaśa Rahasyam* (Eighteen Secrets), a compendium of succinct treatises that systematically explain the esoteric teachings Śrī Vaiṣṇavas receive from their gurus. The work is written in the Śrī Vaiṣṇava brahman dialect, Maṇipravāḷam, and is addressed to "women and ignorant men," to free them from their painful bondage to the world and to deliver them into the joyful service of Nārāyaṇa. After the sect had divided into two schools, the Teṅkalai and the Vaṭakalai, the *Aṣṭadaśa Rahasyam* served the Teṅkalais through commentaries by the school's paramount theologian, Maṇavāḷa Māmuṉikaḷ (1370–1443).

Of the eighteen treatises, three have been highly significant for Śrī Vaiṣṇavas: *Mumukṣuppaṭi* (The Means for Those Who Desire Freedom), *Tattvatrayam* (The Three Realities), and *Śrī Vacana Bhūṣanam* (The Auspicious Ornament of Instruction). Piḷḷai Lokācārya teaches Viśiṣṭādvaita Vedānta but stresses one aspect—that of God's grace and the relative helplessness of embodied souls to emancipate themselves. As various scriptures reveal, Nārāyaṇa's consort, Śrī, or Lakṣmī, is the mediating agent between the majestic Lord and the numberless souls entangled in self-created bondage. She is compassionate toward all sentient beings and perfectly subservient to her Lord. Being totally dependent, she thus is able to influence him on behalf of those souls whom she touches with her grace. Surrender to the Goddess is all that is required for emancipation.

Piḷḷai Lokācārya thus teaches that the devotee—whether male or female of any caste whatever—who cannot fulfill the scriptural requirements of ritual, wisdom, and devotion can nevertheless attain the Lord, either through the grace that enables the devotee to give up this world out of impatient longing for God, or through such absolute trust in Nārāyaṇa and Śrī that he relinquishes the burden of his salvation to them. Furthermore, even the devotee who cannot surrender to God can still surrender to a guru. Regarding the refugee as helpless, the properly qualified guru, by virtue of his own wisdom and Śrī's activity within him, can assume his disciple's burden. Any ritual and devotional acts performed after surrender to God or guru are to derive from the refugee's desire to please God and as a witness to his neighbor, not from his desire for merit. A contemporary of Piḷḷai Lokācārya, Vedānta Deśika (1268–1369) of the rival Vaṭakalai school, took issue and taught that in addition to Śrī's activity, ritual and devotional efforts, too, are important for emancipation.

[*See also* Śrī Vaiṣṇavas.]

BIBLIOGRAPHY

A good exposition of *Śrī Vacana Bhūṣanam* by a modern Hindu guru is *Sree Srivachana Bhushanam by Sri Pillai Lokacharya: An English Glossary* by Sri Satyamurthi Swami (Gwalior, India, 1972). The differences between Piḷḷai Lokācārya and Vedānta Deśika are discussed succinctly in *Srimad Rahasyatrayasara of Sri Vedantadesika,* translated with introduction and notes by M. R. Rajagopala Aiyangar (Kumbakonam, India, 1956). John B. Carman provides an excellent discussion of the concept of surrender and its relation to Rāmānuja's thought in chapter 17 of *The Theology of Rāmānuja: An Essay in Interreligious Understanding* (New Haven, 1974). The most recent discussion of Piḷḷai Lokācārya in the history of Tamil literature is given in Tamil by M. Aruṇācalam in *Tamiḻ ilakkiya varalāṟu*, 6 vols. (Tiruciṟṟampalam, India, 1969–1972).

D. Dennis Hudson

PINARD DE LA BOULLAYE, HENRI (1874–1958), French Jesuit theologian, preacher, and writer on theology, comparative religion, and the spirituality of Ignatius Loyola. Born in Paris in 1874, Pinard entered the Society of Jesus in 1893. He was subsequently appointed professor of theology at a Jesuit institution in Enghien, Belgium, a position that he held from 1910 to 1927. During his professorship at Enghien he became interested in the study of comparative religion. He introduced a course in the history of religions that he later offered at the Gregorian University in Rome, where he lectured from 1927 to 1934.

Earlier, in 1913, Pinard had printed privately for the use of his students a manual entitled *De vera religione.* In this work he endorsed the theory of a primitive monotheism *(Urmonotheismus)* proposed by the priest-ethnologist Wilhelm Schmidt, and the theory of cultural cycles of Fritz Graebner, also an ethnologist. The manual was a detailed study of comparative problems, a foretaste of the intellectual style of his later, more important work, *L'étude comparée des religions,* the two volumes of which appeared in 1922 and 1925. Several editions were published subsequently, for Pinard continued to revise the work.

Volume 1 of *L'étude comparée des religions,* subtitled *Son histoire dans le monde occidentale,* evidenced Pinard's erudition. By means of detailed historical, biographical, and bibliographical research, he lucidly presented the periods and personages relevant to the comparative study of religion, broadly conceived, in the West. Almost an encyclopedia, the volume was followed by an extensive double index (names and topics) that appeared in 1931. The second volume, subtitled *Ses méthodes,* studied numerous methods of classification and comparison, and the associated theories of explanation and interpretation of religion, that had appeared during the past century. Pinard analyzed the philosophical positions and presuppositions of the various methods and defined precisely what each could bring to the understanding of religion on the historical plane, as well as their defects and limits. He gave considerable attention to the method of the historico-cultural school of Graebner and Schmidt, but he preferred Schmidt's rationalism to his parallel emphasis on primordial revelation. Further, Pinard emphasized the importance of the several human sciences (history, ethnology, philology, psychology, and sociology) in the comparative study of religion, calling for the convergence of these disciplines in such study. Moreover, he insisted on the unity of science and faith.

In 1937 Pinard returned to Enghien, where he devoted himself exclusively to the study of comparative religion, intending to prepare a massive dictionary; the project was interrupted, however, by the outbreak of World War II. Pinard then turned to the study of the *Spiritual Exercises* of Ignatius Loyola. Several books and articles on Ignatian spirituality appeared between 1940 and 1956. He died at Lille on 9 February 1958.

Pinard prided himself on rigorous logic and objectivity, holding irrationality, sentiment, and subjectivity in suspicion. He asserted that religion comes into existence on the basis of reason: that is, it is on the rational, deductive plane that religion first imposes itself on humans ("Dieu se conclut avant d'être vu"). Religious experience, on which he wrote several articles during his tenure at Enghien, he considered to be a complement to religion arrived at rationally.

BIBLIOGRAPHY

Pinard's major work is *L'étude comparée des religions,* 2 vols. (Paris, 1922–1925). Attention should also be directed to his early work on religious experience, *La théorie de l'expérience religieuse: Son évolution de Luther à W. James* (Louvain, 1921), and to his much later writings on Ignatian spirituality: *Exercices spirituels, selon la méthode de saint Ignace,* 4 vols. (Paris, 1944–1947), *Saint Ignace de Loyola: Directeur d'âmes* (Paris, 1947), and *La spiritualité ignatienne* (Paris, 1949).

HARRY B. PARTIN

PIUS IX (Giovanni Maria Mastai-Ferretti, 1792–1878), pope of the Roman Catholic church (1846–1878). Born on 13 May into a family belonging to the gentry of the Papal States, the future pope had his priestly formation delayed by an epilepsy-like illness. This left him with an excessively impulsive temperament for the rest of his life.

Mastai was ordained at Rome on 10 April 1815, and in an age when most young priests aimed at a successful career in the church, he stood out because of his piety and complete detachment from ecclesiastical honors. Serving as an assistant to the papal delegate to Chile (1823–1825) gave him an opportunity to see not only the difficulties that liberal governments with regalist tendencies could cause the church but also the new dimensions that missionary problems were acquiring. As bishop of Spoleto (1827), then of Imola (1832), in a region largely won over to the liberal and nationalist ideals of the Risorgimento, he won esteem not only for his pastoral zeal and sympathy for Italian patriotic aspirations, but also for his desire to improve the outmoded and repressive regime of the Papal States.

At the death of Gregory XVI, Mastai, a cardinal since 1840, became the preferred candidate of those conservatives who thought it necessary to make some concession to aspirations for a modernization of the administration of the pontifical state. He was elected pope on the second day of the conclave, 16 June 1846.

The first months of Pius IX's pontificate seemed to confirm the reputation of "liberal" that reactionary circles in Rome had pinned on this enlightened conservative. Disillusionment soon set in: first, in the area of internal reforms, because the new pope had no intention of transforming the Papal States into a modern constitutional state, and, second, when he refused to intervene in the war of independence against Austria because he thought such a step would be incompatible with his religious mission as common father of all the faithful. Economic difficulties and the pope's lack of political experience finally precipitated a crisis. The Roman uprisings of 1848–1849, crushed with the help of a French expeditionary force, left Pius IX more convinced than ever that there was an inherent connection between the principles of the French Revolution (1789) and the destruction of traditional social, moral, and religious values.

The reactionary restoration that followed upon the pope's return to Rome after his flight to Gaeta was to play into the hands of Cavour (Camillo Benso), who exploited the discontent of the middle classes and was able in 1860 to annex the greatest part of the Papal States. In 1870, the Italian army took advantage of the Franco-Prussian War to occupy Rome and its environs. Pius IX, who saw himself less as a dethroned ruler than as the owner of a property for which he was responsible to the entire Catholic world, felt he could not accept the unification of Italy and attempted, with little success, to organize Italian Catholic resistance.

Politically inexpert, Pius IX was advised mostly by men who judged affairs with the intransigence of theoreticians lacking any contact with the contemporary mind. He never understood that in the modern world the problem of the Holy See's spiritual independence could no longer be resolved by the anachronistic preservation of a papal political sovereignty. Thereafter, obsessed by what he called the "revolution," he identified himself increasingly with the conservative governments whose support seemed to provide the most effective guarantee for the maintenance and ultimate restoration of the Roman state. Moreover, seeing that the pope's temporal power had been challenged in the name of the liberal conception of the state and of the right of peoples to self-determination, he issued more and more protests against liberalism. The most spectacular of these were the encyclical *Quanta cura* (1864) and the *Syllabus of Errors* that accompanied it.

Pius IX was never able to distinguish between, on the one hand, what was of positive value in the confused aspirations of the age for a democratization of public life and was preparing in the long run for a greater spiritualization of the Catholic apostolate and, on the other hand, what represented a compromise with principles alien to the Christian spirit. He saw in liberalism only an ideology that denied the supernatural. He confused democracy with anarchy, and he could not grasp the historical impossibility of claiming for the Roman Catholic church both protection from the state and the independence from it he valued so highly.

As a result, Pius IX was unable to adapt the Roman Catholic church to the profound political and social developments of his time. Nor was he able to provide the impulse that Catholic thought needed if it was to respond effectively to the excesses of rationalism and materialistic positivism. By abandoning control of the church's intellectual life to narrow minds that could only condemn new tendencies as incompatible with traditional positions, he lost valuable time. The real roots of the modernist crisis may be traced back to his pontificate. [*See* Modernism, *article on* Christian Modernism.]

Central to the pope's zeal was a confused and clumsily expressed perception of the need to remind a society intoxicated by a scientistic conception of progress of the primacy of what theologians call the supernatural order: the biblical vision of humanity and salvation history, which is opposed to an interpretation of history as a progressive emancipation from religious values and to such a great confidence in human potentialities that there is no room for a redeemer. If we are to understand the inflexibility with which Pius IX fought his battle against liberalism, "the error of the century," as he called it, we must see this struggle as the center of his efforts to focus Christian thinking once again on the fundamental data of revelation. In his own mind, the First Vatican Council (1869–1870), which was interrupted by the entry of the Italians into Rome, was to be the crown upon these efforts. [*See* Vatican Councils, *article on* Vatican I.]

Historians have for a long time judged the pontificate of Pius IX negatively because of his failures in the realm of diplomacy and his fruitless efforts to resist the advance of liberalism. More recently, however, scholars have come to see that matters were more complex and that Pius IX's activities were a notable help in strengthening the Roman Catholic church in its religious sphere, whatever may be thought of certain debatable tendencies.

Missionary expansion advanced at an increasingly rapid pace on five continents during the thirty-two years of Pius IX's pontificate, and thriving churches were developed in Canada, Australia, and especially the United States as a result of Roman Catholic emigration from Europe, but his personal role in this expansion was secondary. On the other hand, he made an important contribution to the progress of the ultramontane movement, which caused guidance of the universal church to be concentrated increasingly in the pope's hands. This movement, given solemn approbation by Vatican I's definition of the pope's personal infallibility and his primacy of jurisdiction, did not go unresisted by those who saw the advantages of pluralism in the local churches and feared to see the episcopates come under the thumb of the Roman Curia. [*See* Ultramontanism.] But Pius IX, whose very real virtues were idealized and who benefited from a special sympathy because of his repeated misfortunes, succeeded in rousing in the Roman Catholic world a real "devotion to the pope" which remarkably facilitated the enthusiastic adhesion of the masses and the lower clergy to the new conception of the pope's role in the church. While Pius IX did all he could to encourage this trend, he did so less from personal ambition or a liking for a theocracy than for essentially pastoral reasons: the movement seemed to him to be both a condition for the restoration of Catholic life wherever government interference in the local churches threatened to smother apostolic zeal and the best means of regrouping all the vital forces of Roman Catholicism for response to the mounting wave of "secularization."

No less important were the largely successful efforts of Pius IX to promote the renewal of the religious orders and congregations, encourage the raising of the spiritual level of the clergy, and improve the quality of ordinary Catholic life. During his pontificate there developed an immense movement of eucharistic devotion, devotion to the Sacred Heart, and Marian devotion (the latter being encouraged by the definition in 1854 of the Immaculate Conception of the Virgin Mary). This movement has sometimes been faulted as superficial, but the multiplication of charitable works and pious associations and the immense development of the religious congregations give the lie to this simplistic judgment. Pius IX himself made a large contribution to these developments. First, he was an example of personal piety for the devotional movement. Second, and above all, he applied himself systematically to energizing, and at times even pushing, the development that had begun right after the great revolutionary crisis. It was precisely because he regarded an intransigent attitude as indispensable to this work of Christian restoration that he forced himself, despite his personal preference for conciliation and appeasement, to repeat unceasingly certain principles that he believed formed the basis for a Christian restoration of society.

Pius IX was handicapped by a superficial intellectual formation that often kept him from grasping the complexity of problems. In addition, the mystical confidence this deeply devout man had in Providence and the excessive importance he attached to prophecies and other manifestations of the extraordinary made him too ready to see in the political upheavals in which the church was involved only a new episode in the great conflict between God and Satan. But having said this we must not forget the very real qualities of the man—simplicity, refinement, serenity, and courage in adversity—and of the pastor, whose ruling concern was always to be first and foremost a churchman, responsible before God for the defense of threatened Christian values.

BIBLIOGRAPHY

Some of Pius IX's addresses can be found in Abbé Marcone's *La parole de Pie IX*, 2d ed. (Paris, 1868), and Pasquale de Franciscis's *Discorsi del sommo pontifice Pio IX*, 4 vols. (Rome, 1873–1882). Some letters are in Pietro Pirri's *Pio IX e Vittorio Emanuele II dal loro carteggio privato*, 5 vols. (Rome, 1944–1961).

The carefully written work of Carlo Falconi, *Il giovane Mastai* (Milan, 1981) covers only the first thirty-five years. The naively hagiographical work by Alberto Serafini, *Pio Nono* (Vatican City, 1958), stops at his election to the papacy. The excellent but thus far incomplete work by Giacomo Martina, *Pio IX*, 2 vols. to date (Rome, 1974–), is essential for a good understanding of the pope's personality but does not yet cover the final twelve years of his pontificate. On the pontificate, see Joseph Schmidlin's *Papstgeschichte der neuesten Zeit*, vol. 2 (Munich, 1934) and my *Le pontificat de Pie IX, 1846–1878*, 2d ed., "Histoire de l'Église," vol. 21 (Paris, 1962). E. E. Y. Hales's *Pio IX: A Study in European Politics and Religion in the Nineteenth Century* (London, 1954) is superficial and focuses chiefly on the political aspects.

ROGER AUBERT
Translated from French by Matthew J. O'Connell

PLANTS. *See* Vegetation.

PLATO (c. 429–347 BCE), Greek philosopher, founder of the Athenian Academy. An Athenian citizen of high birth, Plato grew up during the Peloponnesian War (431–404). One of the circle of young men who surrounded the charismatic Socrates (469–399) and shared in his critical search for the bases of communal life and individual conduct, Plato was sensitive to both the cultural and the political crisis of the Athenian city-state. With Socrates he kept his distance from the oligarchy (led by his kinsman Critias) that briefly ruled Athens at the end of the war with Sparta, and he was completely disillusioned by the succeeding democratic regime, which put Socrates to death on the allegation that he had corrupted the youth of Athens and introduced strange gods. After 399, therefore, Plato withdrew from public life. An exile for about a dozen years, he traveled widely, apparently visiting Egypt and other centers of ancient culture. He ended his travels with a sojourn among the Greek colonies of southern Italy and Sicily, where he not only began a lifelong involvement with

Dion of Syracuse (and met the tyrant Dionysius I), but also came in contact with the Pythagorean school that flourished in Italy. It was soon after his return to Athens (c. 387) that Plato began meeting with colleagues and pupils at his home near the grove of Academus outside the walls of Athens. The rest of his life—apart from two ill-starred visits to Syracuse at the behest of Dion—was devoted to teaching and inquiry in this community, where, in dialogue between teacher and pupils, the mathematical disciplines were pursued for the sake of their contribution to an understanding of the foundations of moral and political life (see *Republic* 526d–532c).

Like the other pupils of Socrates, Plato used the dialogue form in writing, not only to portray Socrates himself (in the so-called early dialogues, such as *Apology, Crito, Euthyphro,* and *Laches*) but also to present the outlines of his own growing and changing thought. In the great dialogues of the middle period—*Phaedo, Republic, Symposium, Phaedrus*—Plato develops the basic themes of his philosophical vision. In the late dialogues he pursues a variety of insights and difficulties concerning the nature of knowledge and of being *(Theaetetus, Parmenides, Sophist),* produces a treatise on the structures of the visible cosmos *(Timaeus),* and offers reconsidered accounts of the best constitution for a city-state *(Statesman, Laws).*

At the basis of Plato's philosophical vision lay a conviction that he almost certainly derived from Socrates' habit of asking after the "what," or definition, of things like justice or virtue or courage. To Plato this procedure suggested that behind, and corresponding to, the multiple instances of each such phenomenon in the world of experience, there exists an intuitable archetype or Form *(eidos).* Such Forms are not visible to the eye of the body, but only to "the eye of the understanding" (*Symposium* 219a). Each Form is, moreover, the reality of which its instances were derivative and weakened images. To these Forms in their collective character Plato assigns the epithet "being" *(to on, ousia):* an epithet that, to him, implies both stable self-identity (i.e., unchangeable eternity) and intelligibility. By way of contrast with this realm of being, he describes the visible cosmos—the world of sense experience—as the realm of "becoming" *(to gignomenon, genesis),* which, because of its instability and changeability, cannot be the object of proper knowledge, but only of opinion *(doxa).* This distinction between "being" and "becoming" (see *Timaeus* 27d) does not, however, to Plato's mind, amount to a separation. The visible cosmos not only images, but shares in, the reality of the Forms, which are its foundation and principle, and which, under Pythagorean influence, Plato apparently came to conceive as archetypal "numbers." Hence the proper governance of the natural and moral-political orders requires mental appropriation of, and assimilation to, the truth that the Forms alone fully embody; and this indeed was the aim of the education that Plato offered.

The agent, in Plato's thinking, of this mediation by which the visible cosmos images and shares in the being of the Forms is soul *(psuchē):* a category that includes not merely the souls of individual human persons, but also—and primarily—the World Soul and the souls that are the cosmic gods. The principle of life and motion as well as of intelligence (in its higher forms), soul, as Plato saw it, has an innate affinity both for the realm of being—as evidenced by its ability to intuit Form—and for the world of becoming. By virtue of the former affinity, moreover, it is, like being itself, eternal and indestructible. Soul in its various manifestations is thus the centerpiece of Plato's world; yet its nature, and the situation of the "fallen" or "forgetful" human soul, is conveyed only indirectly in his dialogues, in a series of powerful "tales" *(muthoi)* and figures, of which the creation story of the *Timaeus* is the most extended and the myth of the cave (*Republic* 514a) perhaps the most memorable.

Plato's aims in the articulation of his worldview were primarily moral and political, not religious. His philosophy is meant to provide the theoretical justification of an educational project that employs dialectic to evoke an awareness and vision of the eternal order that undergirds both the cosmos and the common life of human beings within it. It turns, nevertheless, on "the ascent of the soul to the intelligible realm" (*Republic* 517b) and on the fact that souls are "driven to busy themselves above" (517c) in a search for the Form of the Good, the ultimate reality that, itself "beyond being," is to the realm of being what the sun is to the visible cosmos. There is, then, in Plato's thought, a religious and even mystical drive toward the transcendent that was, in later generations, to make it the vehicle of a philosophical religion influential in the development not only of paganism but also of Christianity and Islam.

[*See also* Platonism.]

BIBLIOGRAPHY

Crombie. I. M. *An Examination of Plato's Doctrines.* 2 vols. New York, 1966–1967.

Findlay, John N. *Plato and Platonism: An Introduction.* New York, 1978.

Friedländer, Paul. *Plato: An Introduction.* 2d ed. Princeton, 1969.

Taylor, Alfred E. *Plato, the Man and His Work.* 6th ed. London, 1952.

RICHARD A. NORRIS

PLATONISM. Taken in its broadest sense, Platonism refers to the influence of Plato in Western philosophical, religious, and political thinking. In the Hellenistic and Roman worlds, the vehicle of this influence was the Academy, which—not without at least one lengthy break in its continuity—continued to function until 529 CE, when it was dissolved by the emperor Justinian. Conveyed not only by the writings of Plato himself, but also by the works of later disciples and interpreters belonging to the so-called Middle Platonic and Neoplatonic schools, this tradition influenced Christian and Islamic philosophy in the late classical and medieval eras, and underwent revivals not only at the time of the Renaissance but also in nineteenth-century England. In no case, however, is Platonism to be understood simply as the reproduction of Plato's original ideas. It has been an evolving, shifting, and many-sided tradition that has always involved criticism and reinterpretation of central themes in Plato's thought. [*See the biographies of Socrates and Plato.*]

The immediate successors of Plato as heads of the Academy were his nephew Speusippus (347–339 BCE) and Xenocrates of Chalcedon (339–314). To this list of the direct continuers of Plato's work the name of Aristotle might well be added, even though he founded his own school, the Lyceum, in 335 after Xenocrates had succeeded Speusippus. Aristotle was notoriously critical of Plato's way of understanding Form and of his identification of Form with being. Further, he was contemptuous of Speusippus's devotion to Pythagorean number theory, another subject of speculation that had engaged Plato and his pupils. Nevertheless Aristotle's works pursued, in their own way, the agenda of Plato's Academy, and his account of the First Principle as self-thinking Intellect *(nous)* was early adopted in the Platonist tradition.

With the succession of Arcesilaus (d. 241 BCE) as its head, the Academy took a fresh turn. The so-called New Academy—frequently labeled "skeptical"—maintained that neither Socrates nor Plato had taught any settled, dogmatic system but had pursued arguments on both sides of every question without seeking to reach definitive conclusions. [*See* Skeptics and Skepticism.] Arcesilaus maintained that the *epochē* (suspension of judgment) in which this procedure resulted represented the true philosophical position of Plato, but Arcesilaus's devotion to it was largely evoked by Stoic dogmatism, with its assertion of the existence of "indubitable perception" *(katalēptikē phantasia)*. Against this Stoic view the New Academy emphasized the doubtfulness and subjectivity of both perception and judgment. In response to the charge that such a stance left people without guidance for the conduct of life, Carneades (d. 129) developed his theory of *to pithanon* (the "persuasive" or "probable"), holding, as Cicero sums it up (*Academica* 2.10), "that there is something which is probable and, so to speak, like the truth" and that this provides a "rule both for the conduct of life and for inquiry and discussion."

It was not, however, in skepticism that Platonism was to find its future. Even in the time of Carneades and his successor Philo of Larissa (d. about 80 BCE), Platonists were beginning, though solely in defense of their own position, to employ Stoic ideas and terminology; and at the same time, in the teaching of the Stoic Posidonius of Apamea (d. about 51 BCE) there are traces of the influence of Plato. This incipient eclecticism triumphed in the person of Antiochus of Ascalon (d. about 68 BCE), and with it came a repudiation of skepticism and a new, dogmatic Platonism—so-called Middle Platonism—that eventually set the stage for the work of Plotinus and his successors.

The split between Antiochus and his teacher Philo of Larissa, a skeptic, had its basis in Antiochus's belief that the authentic tradition of Plato's teaching must be sought in the Old Academy and that this tradition embraced the contributions of Aristotle and the Stoics. Antiochus himself was in substance a Stoic, however, and thus untypical of the later Middle Platonist tradition. Nevertheless his rebellion opened the way for the growth of a school of thought that treated the Platonic corpus as an authoritative text even while it brought other points of view—Pythagorean, Aristotelian, and Stoic—to the interpretation of that corpus.

The heyday of this Middle Platonism was the first and second Christian centuries. Its most prominent representatives were Plutarch of Chaeronea (c. 50–c. 120 CE), Apuleius of Madaurus (fl. 150), Albinus (fl. 150), Atticus (c. 150–200), and the Neo-Pythagorean Numenius of Apamea (fl. 150); and to this list of pagan teachers must be added the names of the Alexandrian Jew Philo (c. 30 BCE–45 CE) and of Christian writers like Justin Martyr (d. about 165), Clement of Alexandria (d. about 215), and Origen (c. 185–c. 254), all of whom, in their different ways, represented a Middle Platonist philosophical outlook and used its resources to interpret their respective religious traditions.

These Middle Platonists did not by any means represent a uniform point of view. Some, like those of the so-called School of Gaius, with which Albinus and Apuleius are associated, incorporated significant Aristotelian elements in their presentation of Plato's thought. Others, like Atticus, fought this trend, and were more sympathetic to Stoicism. The first century before Christ saw a revival of Pythagorean ideas and practices, and the influence of these is evident in writers like Philo Judaeus and, much later, the pagan Numenius. For all their differences, however, these thinkers had much in common. In particular, they shared the corpus of Platonic dialogues, among which special attention and veneration was reserved for the *Timaeus.* There were disagreements over its interpretation. Plutarch and Atticus took the view—which commended them to Christian readers—that the story of the demiurge's "creation" of the cosmos was to be taken literally. Others, like Albinus, saw the story as a proper Platonic *muthos,* a tale intended not to explain how the cosmos came to be but to suggest how it is eternally structured.

In spite of such differences, however, all agreed, as against traditional Stoicism, that the First Principle of things was a transcendent, immaterial reality, which was equated with the Good of Plato's *Republic,* the self-thinking Intellect of Aristotle's *Metaphysics,* and the One of Pythagorean cosmology. The Platonic realm of Forms appeared in Middle Platonism as the content of divine Intellect and thus as the truth that actuated the World Soul in its work of ordering the visible cosmos. In this scheme, in which the ultimate God was sometimes distinguished from a second, "demiurgic" Intellect, the Neoplatonic hierarchy of three divine hypostases was foreshadowed. At the same time, the human ideal became the contemplative life in which the soul achieves that "likeness to God" *(homoiōsis theōi)* that Plato had commended in the *Theaetetus* (176b) and that Christians such as Clement of Alexandria and Origen recognized as the ideal implicit in the doctrine that God created Adam "in our image, after our likeness" (*Gn.* 1:26).

The task of forging a coherent synthesis out of the elements of the Middle Platonist tradition fell to Plotinus (205–270), the founder of Neoplatonism. Educated in Alexandria under Ammonius Saccas, Plotinus taught in Rome from the age of forty. The essays that he wrote for circulation among his pupils were collected by his disciple Porphyry (d. about 305) in six sets of nine known collectively as the *Enneads.* In these terse and often difficult papers Plotinus sets out a system according to which all reality, value, and awareness issue spontaneously, coordinately, and timelessly from a single transcendent and inexpressible source called the One or the Good. This process of emanation produces a graded world order in which each successive form of reality (hypostasis) images its superior at a lower level of unity. Thus Intellect—the unity of intuitive awareness with its intelligible objects (the Forms)—images the One. Soul, the third hypostasis, images Intellect, though its being and knowing are distended in time and though as "nature" it approaches division in space by giving rise to the corporeal, visible cosmos. The limit of this expansion of reality from the One is primal matter, which, Plotinus teaches, is in itself mere privation. To the emanation of reality from the One there corresponds a converse and simultaneous movement of "return" *(epistrophē),* by which each level of being seeks itself in its source and original. From this point of view, the structure of Plotinus's cosmos corresponds to the route that consciousness takes in contemplative activity as it moves from dispersion to integration. The highest normal level of consciousness is the unified awareness that belongs to Intellect; but in moments of mystical ecstasy the soul—as Plotinus records from his own experience—achieves a loss of particular selfhood in union with the One. [*See* Neoplatonism.]

Plotinus's successor was Porphyry, a commentator on Plato and Aristotle and the author of a lengthy treatise titled *Against the Christians.* In Porphyry's writings the scholastic tone and religious interests of later Neoplatonism are plainly adumbrated. He produced not only commentaries but also summary interpretations of Plotinian ontology and ethics, as in his *Sentences* and the *Letter to His Wife Marcella.* It seems also to have been Porphyry who revived the repute of a late second-century collection of revelations known as the *Chaldaean Oracles.* While skeptical of the claims that this collection made for the ritual-magical practice of theurgy, Porphyry apparently initiated the practice of interpreting the *Oracles* in the light of a Plotinian metaphysic. [*See* Theurgy.]

Porphyry's disciple Iamblichus (d. about 325 CE) wrote a commentary (now lost) on the *Oracles* and in his treatise *On the Mysteries* defended theurgy against Porphyry as necessary for the soul's union with the divine. He was also a speculative philosopher of some originality, and his articulation of the Plotinian system opened the way for the elaborate and ramified metaphysic that marked the thought of the later Academy at Athens. There, from about 400 until 529, honoring Aristotle with Plato as a founder of their tradition, a series of distinguished teachers developed both the philosophical and the religious positions that Iamblichus had defended. Most notable among these was Proclus (c. 412–485), whose *Elements of Theology* and *Commentary on the Timaeus* are monuments to the learning and dialectical skill of the Academy in its last days.

After the closing of the Academy by Justinian in 529, pagan Neoplatonism gradually ceased, and the influence of Platonism must be traced in the writing of Christian and, later, Islamic theologians and philosophers. In the Latin West, this influence was transmitted through Augustine of Hippo (354–430), whose conversion to Christianity accompanied his discovery of Neoplatonist thought as represented by writings of Plotinus and Porphyry—writings probably translated into Latin by Marius Victorinus, an eminent Roman Neoplatonist who became a Christian in his old age and contributed, after 357, to the trinitarian debate. Augustine's writings were permeated with Platonist themes, however much he reconsidered, revised, and recast them in the light of his Christian beliefs. Boethius (c. 480–c. 524), a Roman aristocrat in the service of the Ostrogothic king Theodoric and an orthodox Christian, did as much as Augustine to transmit the heritage of Hellenic philosophy to the medieval West. Aiming to provide Latin versions of the major works of Aristotle and Plato, he succeeded, before his execution at the hands of Theodoric, in rendering certain of Aristotle's logical works as well as Porphyry's *Introduction to Aristotle's Categories,* the book that originally stimulated medieval philosophical debate. His *Consolation of Philosophy,* moreover, widely read during the Middle Ages, presented a simplified Neoplatonist outlook consistent with the structures of Christian doctrine.

In the Greek-speaking East, the tradition of Christian Platonism reaches as far back as the second century. Its most distinguished early proponents, Clement of Alexandria and Origen, came into their own, however, only through the critical reconstruction of their thought at the hands of the Cappadocian fathers: Basil of Caesarea (c. 329–379), Gregory of Nazianzus (329–389), and Gregory of Nyssa (c. 335–c. 395). In the context of the later trinitarian controversy, these thinkers created a theological synthesis in which late Platonist influence is apparent both in their anthropology and in their "negative theology." A much less chastened and criticized Platonism—in this case deriving from Proclus and the Athenian School—appeared at the beginning of the sixth century in the theological works of an unknown author who wrote under the name of Dionysius the Areopagite (see *Acts* 17:34). Indebted to the Cappadocians also, Dionysius expounded a cataphatic theology *(On the Divine Names)* in which God is known as cause and source of created realities; a symbolic theology *(Ecclesiastical Hierarchy; Celestial Hierarchy)* of ascent to God; and a "negative" theology in which the soul's union with the transcendent through "unknowing" is described *(Mystical Theology).* The ideas of Dionysius were commended to the East by the commentaries of Maximos the Confessor (c. 580–662), and to the medieval West by the translations of John Scottus Eriugena (fl. 847–877), himself the author of a treatise in the spirit of late Neoplatonism titled *On the Division of Nature.*

It was largely through Dionysius and Augustine, whose influence is seen in thinkers as diverse as Anselm of Canterbury (c. 1033–1109), Hugh of Saint-Victor (c. 1096–1141), the Franciscan Bonaventure (c. 1217–1274), and the Dominicans Thomas Aquinas (c. 1225–1274) and Johannes Eckhart (c. 1260–1327?), that Platonist themes influenced medieval Latin philosophy and spirituality. Of the works of Plato, only the *Timaeus* was known, in the fourth-century Latin version of Calcidius; Plotinus and his successors were scarcely known at all, save through Boethius's translation of Porphyry's *Introduction to Aristotle's Categories.* What the Latin Middle Ages eventually harvested from the work of the late Platonists was the writings of Aristotle on natural philosophy, ethics, and metaphysics, which during and after the thirteenth century became standard texts in the liberal arts curricula of medieval universities.

Medieval Western interest in, and knowledge of, Aristotle was stimulated and in part made possible by the labors of Islamic philosophers who worked on ninth- and tenth-century Arabic versions of the works of Aristotle, Plato, and their Neoplatonist commentators. These thinkers, continuing the work of the philosophers of the late Roman empire, sought, without ultimate success, to graft the alien Greek intellectual tradition onto Islamic religious culture. Beginning with the work of al-Kindī (d. after 870 CE), this Arab philosophical enterprise was continued by al-Fārābī (d. 950), Ibn Sīnā (Avicenna, 980–1037), and the Cordovan Ibn Rushd (Averroës, 1126–1198), who was known to the Schoolmen of Europe simply as "the Commentator" (i.e., on Aristotle). The structure of their worldview was essentially that of later Neoplatonism; what the Latin West accepted of their tradition, however, was largely the corpus of Aristotle.

It was not, therefore, until the fifteenth century and the work of Nicholas of Cusa (1401–1464), Marsilio Ficino (1433–1499), and others that Plato himself, read through the eyes of his Neoplatonist interpreters, was rediscovered. Nicholas, in his *On the Learned Ignorance,* presents a view of the world that owes much to Proclus, as well as to certain Platonic dialogues; Ficino translated Plato and Plotinus's *Enneads* into Latin and made a start on Porphyry and Iamblichus. Even Aristotle, in this new age, began to be read as the ancient Neoplatonists had read him. Platonist writings and ideas, moreover, accompanied the spread of Renaissance humanism. John Colet (d. 1514), whose Cambridge lectures (1497) on Paul's *Letter to the Romans* introduced the spirit of humanist scholarship to England, was, though no speculative philosopher, a friend of Ficino and a student of Dionysius the Areopagite. [*See* Humanism.]

England, indeed, was the scene of Platonist revivals in both the seventeenth and the nineteenth centuries. The school of the "Cambridge Platonists" of the mid-seventeenth century, rebelling against Hobbesian materialism as well as against Puritan Calvinism and dogmatism, developed a view of the place of reason in religion that was largely indebted to Neoplatonism. Through Samuel Taylor Coleridge (1772–1834), Frederick Denison Maurice (1805–1872), and, later, B. F. Westcott (1825–1901), Platonic ideas influenced the development of English theology as, in the work of Alfred North Whitehead (1861–1947) and John McTaggart (1866–1925), such ideas also influenced English philosophy. Study of Plato was encouraged in Britain by the translation of his dialogues made by Benjamin Jowett (1817–1893), as it had been encouraged in Germany by the version of Friedrich Schleiermacher (1768–1834).

[*See also the biographies of philosophers and theologians mentioned herein.*]

BIBLIOGRAPHY

Armstrong, A. Hilary, ed. *The Cambridge History of Later Greek and Early Medieval Philosophy.* Cambridge, 1967.

Ivánka, Endre von. *Plato Christianus.* Einsiedeln, Switzerland, 1964.

Klibansky, Raymond. *The Continuity of the Platonic Tradition during the Middle Ages.* London, 1950; reprint, New York, 1982.

Muirhead, John H. *The Platonic Tradition in Anglo-Saxon Philosophy.* London, 1931.

Taylor, Alfred E. *Platonism and Its Influence.* Boston, 1924.

RICHARD A. NORRIS

PLAY. The idea of play may be embedded in the very metaphysics of certain cosmologies, as well as in particular ritual contexts. Although the idea of play has widespread currency in religions with differing epistemologies, the profundity of its presence corresponds to the level of premises at which it is lodged in a given religious system. The more abstract and encompassing the premises of a religion imbued with the ideation of play, the more pervasive and fateful are its systematic expressions in religious life.

Attributes of the Idea of Play. The idea of play is universal among humankind, whether or not particular cultures have terms to denote such a conception. A first attribute of play is that its assumptions are preeminently conditional, for play is a medium through which the make-believe is brought into being and acquires the status of a reality.

Especially human is the capacity to imagine and, so, to create alternative realities. In question, however, are the truth values of such realities, that is, the extent to which, and under which conditions, they are accorded validity. In the logic of modern Western culture, the imaginary is not accorded any ultimate status of validity or truth. Gregory Bateson (1972) has argued that the messages that signify the existence of play are "untrue" in a sense, and that the reality that such messages denote is nonexistent. This, of course, holds in a culture whose religious cosmology is predicated in part upon a comparatively immutable boundary between the divine and the human, with the former accorded the status of absolute truth, while the latter is perceived in no small measure as sinful and as a profanation of the former. Given its imaginary character, the idea of play in much of modern Western thought often is rendered as pretense and is relegated to the domain of the culturally "unserious," like the world of fiction and that of leisure time activities, or to the realm of the "not yet fully human," like the play of little children. Yet to equate the imaginary universally with the frivolous is to render the essential powers of play impotent and to obscure their roles in religious thought and action, especially in cosmologies where a state of existence is also a condition of untruth.

A second attribute of play is the necessity of a form of reference that can be altered in systematic ways. Play changes the known signs of form into something else by altering the reified boundaries that define and characterize the phenomenon. What is changed still retains crucial similarities to its form of foundation and so remains intimately related to it. For example, the medieval European Feast of Fools, a rite of inversion, required the form of a traditional Christian Mass that could be altered. The play-mass would have no significance for participants were it not derived from and contrasted with its everyday analogue, the traditional Mass.

A third attribute of play is that any phenomenal form can be transformed through a sense of imagination that itself remains constrained to a degree by the composition of the "original" form. This attribute may be problematic for ontologies that strongly implicate the active presence of play in the acts of creation, as in Hinduism. For since the idea of play requires the existence of forms that can be differently modeled, how can this idea be present prior to the creation of form? Nonetheless, if the Hindu cosmos comes into being as the adumbrated dream of the all-encompassing universal principle, *brahman,* then this attribute of play is not obviated, since original form itself is imaginary and illusory.

A fourth attribute of play is that it brings into being something that had not existed before by changing the shape and positioning of boundaries that categorize phenomena and so altering their meaning. One may state simply that creation, destruction, and re-creation occur and recur because those boundaries that demarcate the coherency of phenomena are altered. Therefore play is associated intimately with creativity and with creation, as Johan Huizinga (1938) and Arthur Koestler (1964) have maintained, as well as with its converse, destruction. In the most limited case of creation, that of the inversion of a phenomenally valid form, it is only the reflection of such form, still constrained by the original positioning of boundaries, that is brought into being. For example, the inversion of gender is constrained by finite permutations, as is the overturning of a clearly defined hierarchy, as long as gender and hierarchy remain the respective terms of reference of these inversions. On the other hand, cosmologies that strongly feature trickster figures also tend to be characterized by lengthier series of transformations of these types, so that it becomes difficult to state which form is the original and which the playful copy.

A fifth attribute of play is that it is an amoral medium, one that is marked by plasticity, by lability, and by flexibility in ideation—qualities closely related to those of imagination and creativity. In play, these qualities have the potential to meddle with and to disturb any form of stability and any conception of order.

A sixth attribute of play is a penchant for questioning the phenomenal stability of any form that purports to exist as a valid proposition and as a representation of "truth." The idea of play is amoral in its capacities to subvert the boundaries of any and all phenomena and so to rock the foundations of a given reality.

Whether, and to what degree, these qualities of play are integral to the metaphysics of a given religious system should illustrate how that system works. For example, whether the boundaries that divide the paranatural and human realms are quite absolute or are matters of continuous gradation and whether the character of a cosmology's population (deities, spirits, demons, tricksters, and so forth) is one of positional stability or of ongoing transformation should be illuminated by the relative presence of the attributes of play in a particular religious system.

The Idea of Play and Premises of Cosmology. The embeddedness of the idea of play does not appear to be associated, in particular, either with great religious traditions or with local ones, either with so-called tribal societies or with more complex ones. Hence the examples adduced here are of a tribal people and of Hinduism.

The Iatmul of the Sepik River area in New Guinea are a tribal people whose culture values monistic and yet dualistic conceptions of the cosmos. Both coexist, each continuously transforming into the other. For the monism of the Iatmul view of cosmic order fragments into a multitude of competing principles that explain that order. In turn, these recombine into an elementary synthesis, only to multiply once again and to flow together once more.

Thus the character of the Iatmul cosmos is one of immanent transmutability, of plays upon phenomenal form. This reverberates throughout the institutions of Iatmul society and parallels a conduciveness to paradox in Iatmul thought. This proclivity of paradox highlights ongoing disjunctions among phenomenal forms. Therefore strong tendencies toward fragmentation lurk within numerous cultural traditions that declare the validity of a coherent synthesis of differing principles in Iatmul society. Thus Iatmul men, in the heat of argument, were to display their most sacred ceremonial objects before the profaning gaze of women and uninitiated boys, thereby completely destroying for years to come the ritual efficacy of these collective representations. Superficially this behavior could appear simply as uncontrolled and destructive. Yet further consideration would reveal that such behavior was quite consistent with those premises of an Iatmul worldview that denied to boundaries a fixedness of form for lengthy durations.

In such cosmologies, as of course in others, boundaries of form are brought into being through change. Yet in such cosmologies both phenomenal form and the agencies of change are, in a sense, illusory: though they persuade that the solidity of reification is their state, this masks the more profound observation that impermanence is their condition. Here play, as illusion in action, is crucial. The ideation of play is processual: it can bring into being forms that signify the existence of the cosmos. Yet these forms themselves must be transcended through their own negation in order to reveal those deeper truths that are masked by the very force of illusion. Therefore the processuality of play, of imagination, also effaces its own creation.

Aspects of Hindu cosmology exemplify this abstract sense of play as cosmic process. The Hindu concept of *līlā* commonly is translated as the "play" of forces and energies that are continually in motion. These spontaneously create and destroy the possibility of a phenomenal world in an unending process. *Līlā*, as play, is a metaphor of flux, of movement, from which the cosmos emerges and into which it will eventually disappear. Any reification of form, implying inherent solidity and stability, denies this basic premise. Yet the premise itself cannot be realized without the creation of form, which is then the opposite of nonform, of flux. Momentarily (in cosmic terms) the premise of *līlā* must create phenomena in order to revalidate itself by then subverting and destroying them. [*See* Līlā.] The creation of phenomena is activated through the use of *māyā*, commonly translated as the force of illusion, that is, as another aspect of the idea of play as it is used here. All phenomena rest and shift on the premise of illusion. Their most abstract of purposes is to cease to exist as phenomena. [*See* Māyā.]

Among the products of *māyā* is the cosmos that gods and humans inhabit. This can be rendered as *saṃsāra,* a gloss for all phenomena that exist in the cosmos. *Saṃsāra,* too, is understood as flux, as the processual flow that shapes all forms, and not as phenomena whose reification is absolute in any sense. *Saṃsāra* is also related to the idea of play and refers to the cycle of birth and rebirth of all beings. One can attain salvation, and so escape *saṃsāra,* only by dissipating the forces of illusion that render deep flux as superficial form. For gods and humans, for renouncers and antigods, aspects of the ideation of play are both their confinement, through illusion, in the bounded phenomenal trap and their escape from it through the dissolution of fixed forms. As named beings, deities are not ultimate forms in and of themselves. Rather they are signposts on the way to salvation, just as other figures point in contrary directions. Without beginning to overcome the forces of illusion, thereby gaining insight into both creation and destruction, one is caught endlessly in the paradoxes of a world that appears stable but is in flux. Yet perceptions that are paradoxical on one level of abstraction become merely ironical on a higher one.

The logic of these ideas permeates numerous aspects of Hindu cosmology. Ideally, the creative role of the *saṃnyāsin,* the renouncer, which is dedicated to the penetration of illusion, is also built into the Hindu life cycle as the final stage of living in this reality. Therefore, in a theoretical sense, the desirability of piercing the force of illusion that makes the world possible is integral to living in that world.

Like humans, Hindu gods and antigods are not constructed culturally as unitary and homogeneous figures. Instead they are self-transforming types whose logic of composition depends on the alteration of hierarchical and lateral boundaries within and around themselves. In their transformations these figures bear witness to the ultimate impermanence of illusion and also to the necessity of this force upon which they, like humankind, depend for existence. The only final stability in the Hindu cosmos is that of motility; the only final coherence in classification is its mutation.

Such paranatural types, like other facets of Hinduism, often seem paradoxical to Western thinking, in which stability is believed to be truly real and flux is both a secondary and a deficient reality. In the South Indian Śaiva Tamil tradition, for example, Śiva is composed as a self-transforming figure. He is creator, protector, and destroyer. He is, in Wendy O'Flaherty's felicitous phrasing, the erotic ascetic. He transcends and contains the cosmos, yet also appears within it through synecdoche, the relationship of part to whole. He is trickster and tricked. He creates the antigods, the *asura*s, and, by the terms of their compact, is helpless before them as they wreak havoc. But he also transcends himself in creating his son, Murukaṉ, who destroys the antigods. There are hints that Murukaṉ at once is greater than Śiva, is Śiva, and is reabsorbed into Śiva. In this example the power of imagination, intimately associated with illusion, has the capacity to expand upon, to extend, and to transform phenomenal reality beyond those boundaries that previously had contained it in an ongoing play of generative forces. This potential is actualized since reality and the fixedness that gives it definition are illusory.

Like the permutations of malleability in Iatmul cosmology, that of Hinduism, although operating in terms of a radically different epistemology, emphasizes the fragmentation of unitary principles that flow together in synthesis only to divide once again. In both of these cosmologies the idea of play would seem to inhere in their abstract conceptualizations of phenomenal reality that, on the one hand, perch and teeter precariously on the border between cosmos and chaos and, on the other, conceive of processuality as a condition of existence.

Premises of Play in Ritual Occasions. As the focus of play shifts to the positioning of this idea in religious or quasi-religious occasions, it becomes more constricted, since its presence threatens the validity and the stability of the occasion in which it is located. Nonetheless the idea of play does accomplish certain kinds of work in particular ritual contexts.

Within ritual contexts the notion of play has perhaps the most embracing mandate in that category of occasion termed "festival." As the etymology of the English word denotes, a festival is an occasion of celebration, of joyous attitudes, and of rejoicing, marked by moods of cheer. In European tradition it has affinities with the carnivalesque and with certain liturgical periods in the Christian calendar. In the Hindu tradition it encompasses annual occasions that celebrate the powers of particular deities, and such times often are indistinguishable from pilgrimages to the deities in this culture.

Of especial significance here is that festival approximates a total collective performance, one that celebrates a holistic unity of cosmic and social order on the part of a relatively homogenized population of participants. This implies that many of the distinctions between social categories of persons—whether based on hierarchy, status, occupation, or age—may be temporarily subverted and dissolved in a playful spirit. Thus people, ordinarily separated by moral edicts and social rules, are brought together to experience the rediscovery of the significance of *sacra* that apply to all of them as a comparatively undifferentiated community of believers.

In part this may be done through inversions of social identity that reverse the relationships among everyday social distinctions, so that the high are made low and more peripheral positions become more central. This is the case in the North Indian holiday Kṛṣṇa Līlā, or Feast of Love. Or, as in the European tradition of Carnival, the spirit of festive license and the erasure of social boundaries prepare the way for the ascetic restrictions of the days of Lent. In either instance the ideation of play is crucial to establish a comparative degree of social homogeneity among participants, permitting them to receive and to experience the power of *sacra*, individually and collectively. During carnivalesque occasions the indeterminacy of play serves as a mediating prelude to the transcendence of a social collective, preparing it to be recast as a religious community.

Still, the heyday of the European Carnival was during the medieval period when the metaphysics of Christianity may have been quite different from their present-day counterparts. Then, the boundaries between the divine and the human were more mutable and interpenetrable, and the themes of the effervescent grotesque, itself a likely product of the mingling of domains, were pervasive. This more transformative cosmology was more similar in certain general respects to that of Hinduism than to its modern offsprings. And it is this kind of cosmology that encourages the genre of the religious festival. Here the playful celebration of the dissolution of boundaries creates the grounds for their reconstitution with renewed vigor.

The idea of play within ritual occasions, the boundaries of which are strongly and unequivocally reified, has a much narrower scope. Such occasions, unlike numerous festivals, tend to be organized as a clear-cut sequence of phases that follow one another in cumulative progression. Hierarchy is prominent; there are social distinctions among those who take part and between participants and others. Order is prevalent throughout, as is the measured progression to messages of the sacred. Where play is present, it rarely questions either the external boundaries that circumscribe the occasion or its internal distinctions. Instead, the mutability of play is bent to more specific purposes.

Across cultures the most characteristic of these operations is found in inversions that are featured in the commonly termed "rituals of reversal." These are not usually rituals in their own right but more often occur in a particular phase in a ritual sequence. Inversions are marked frequently by the mockery, the mimicry, and the ridiculing of one category of person or theme by another, or of a category in relation to itself. This tends to occur in a spirit of play, that is, through the subversion of one form and its substitution by another. Here the validity of existing social categories or roles is not questioned. These remain the same; only their valences change, so that access to them is temporarily altered. Moreover, the inversion of form often seems to carry connotations of an unnatural condition so that the morally correct version of form lies in the converse of what is inverted. Therefore, inversions revert to the foundation-for-form from which the inverted image was derived. Furthermore, an inverted form remains a refraction of its usual image, and this suggests that inversion maintains the very domain of discourse that is defined initially by the original form. This effectively restricts the transformative force of play and strictly limits the possible permutations of its plays-upon-form.

Nonetheless such constricted mutability may perform significant work within ritual occasions. In the Booger Dance of the Cherokee Indians of the southeastern United States, as this was practiced during the first decades of this century, an alternative reality that was experienced as threatening by the community of believers was proposed in play and destroyed through it. The Booger Dance itself was preceded and succeeded by dances associated with the dead and the defunct. The Cherokee who were disguised as Boogers inverted their everyday identities and took on those of strangers with obscene names, exaggerated features, and strange speech. They burst noisily into the dwelling where the ritual-dance series was performed. Their behavior was aggressive and boisterous, and they were perceived as malignant and menacing creatures. As each Booger danced he was mocked, mimicked, and laughed at by the onlookers. Furthermore by their moral demeanor the onlookers quieted and tamed the Boogers and eventually ejected them from the ritual space. Outside, they unmasked, and then, as Cherokee, they rejoined the others in further ritual dances.

The Boogers, familiar men inverted as fearsome strangers, represented all that was frightful and evil beyond the boundaries of the moral community. Their intrusion underlined and reinforced these boundaries rather than threatening them. By their mockery and laughter, members of the moral community queried the valid presence of these characters within the community, expelled these symbols of evil from within, and so reasserted the correctness of the moral and social orders. In this example the alternative order proposed by the Boogers does not appear to have been entertained seriously by the other participants. The reality of the Boogers was inauthentic from the outset, and therefore the make-believe of play was contrasted throughout with the verities of ritual, reaffirming them.

In other orchestrations of ritual occasions, play is used to falsify alternative realities that are proposed as authentic and that deny sacred verities. In the following example, of Sinhala Buddhist exorcisms on the southern coast of Sri Lanka, the alternative reality is adumbrated in seriousness and falsified through play. This permits the correct order to reemerge with a sense of revelation and in sharp contradistinction to the illusory character of play. In the Sinhala cosmology demons are inferior to humankind, as is humankind to deities and to the Buddha. A person possessed by a demon is understood to invert the hierarchical superiority of the human in relation to the demonic: the possessed is thought to perceive reality as one dominated by demons and not by deities. The problem of the exorcists is to destroy the superordinate demonic reality of the possessed and to reestablish the moral superiority of deities and humans. To accomplish this, exorcists first reify the validity of a superior demonic reality. The demons then appear in the human realm, confident of their superiority there. However their assertion of authentic ascendancy is subverted and destroyed through comic episodes that show this status to be illusory. The demons are proved to be laughable savages who are ignorant of the very rudiments of correct human action, etiquette, and morality. The assertions of demonic reality are dissolved through play, and the demons are ejected from the human realm to reassume their inferior cosmological position. These tests of the validity of demonic reality, through the medium of play, prepare the grounds for the revelation of the reemergence of correct cosmic order and free the possessed from the demonic grip.

This brief survey of certain of the relationships among the idea of play and aspects of the organization of religion and ritual leads to a final point that is of widespread concern to religious experience. The presence of play induces and encourages reflection on the part of believers upon the elementary premises of their religious systems. Playing with boundaries and therefore with the coherency and verity of ideation and form emphasizes that every taken-for-granted proposition also contains its own potential negation. In turn, the experience of such challenges deepens and strengthens belief in the truths of cosmology and ritual once their validity is reestablished.

[*See also* Carnival; Games; Tricksters; *and* Chaos.]

BIBLIOGRAPHY

The classic work on the role of play in the evolution of society remains that of Johan Huizinga, *Homo Ludens: Versuch einer Bestimmung des Spielelements der Kultur* (Haarlem, 1938), translated by R. F. C. Hull as *Homo Ludens: A Study of the Play-Element in Culture* (London, 1949). That play is integral to creativity is explored by, among others, Arthur Koestler in his *The Act of Creation* (London, 1964). Susanne Langer, in "The Great Dramatic Forms: The Comic Rhythm," included in her *Feeling and Form: A Theory of Art* (New York, 1953), argues for an intimate association of the spirit of comedy with that of life-renewing forces. In a contrasting vein, Henri Bergson's *Laughter: An Essay on the Meaning of the Comic* (New York, 1912), translated by Cloudesly Brereton and Fred Rothwell from three articles of Bergson's that appeared in *Revue de Paris*, persuades that the comic exposes the disjunction between the presumptions of rigidity of form and the vitality of human spirit. His work is best read in conjunction with a more semiological approach, like that of G. B. Milner, who, in "Homo Ridens: Towards a Semiotic Theory of Humour and Laughter," *Semiotica* 5 (1972): 1–30, discusses the shift to the ideation of play as a change in paradigm. The seminal essay on the paradoxical character of such a cognitive shift, at least in Western thought, is Gregory Bateson's "A Theory of Play and Fantasy," in his *Steps to an Ecology of Mind* (New York, 1972). Mary Douglas, in "The Social Control of Cognition: Some Factors in Joke Perception," *Man: The Journal of the Royal Anthropological Institute*, n.s. 3 (September 1968): 361–376, brings to the fore the plasticity of indeterminacy that the ideation of play introduces into social reality. The most comprehensive cross-cultural overview of theories of play, among both children and adults, is Helen B. Schwartzman's *Transformations: The Anthropology of Children's Play* (New York, 1978). This volume contains an excellent bibliography. *Game, Play, Literature*, Yale French Studies, no. 41 (New Haven, 1968), a special issue edited by Jacques Ehrmann, contains provocative studies on the assumptions of playful ideation. An explicit comparison of the idea of play with that of ritual is my "Play and Ritual: Complementary Frames of Meta-Communication," in *It's a Funny Thing, Humour* (Oxford, 1977), edited by Anthony J. Chapman and Hugh C. Foot. A diverse collection on the relationships between religion and playful ideation is *Holy Laughter* (New York, 1969), edited by M. Conrad Hyers. His *Zen and the Comic Spirit* (London, 1974) is an in-depth study of such relationships in one Eastern religious tradition. Useful general considerations of festival are found in Roger Caillois's *Man and the Sacred* (Glencoe, Ill., 1959), pp. 97–127, and in René Girard's *Violence and the Sacred* (Baltimore, 1977). The North Indian Kṛṣṇa Līlā is described most evocatively by McKim Marriott in "The Feast of Love," in *Krishna: Myths, Rites and Attitudes* (Honolulu, 1966), edited by Milton Singer. Medieval European worldview and the tradition of Carnival is discussed with imagination and insight, if with a modicum of exaggeration, in Mikhail Bakhtin's *Rabelais and His World* (Cambridge, Mass., 1968). Iatmul cosmology is analyzed by Gregory Bateson in *Naven*, 2d ed. (Stanford, Calif., 1958). The Booger Dance of the Cherokee is described by Frank G. Speck and Leonard Broom, with the assistance of Will West Long, in *Cherokee Dance and Drama* (Berkeley, 1951). The elements of play in Sinhala exorcism are analyzed richly by Bruce Kapferer in *A Celebration of Demons: Exorcism and the Aesthetics of Healing in Sri Lanka* (Bloomington, Ind., 1983). Among modern Christian theologians, Harvey Cox argues for the value to Christianity of a renewed interest in the spirit of play, in *The Feast of Fools: A Theological Essay on Festivity and Fantasy* (Cambridge, Mass., 1969); and Josef Pieper maintains that festivity without religious celebration is artifice, in his *In Tune with the World* (1965; Chicago, 1973).

DON HANDELMAN

PLOTINUS (205–270), founder of Neoplatonism. The life of Plotinus was written by his pupil, Porphyry, who edited his master's lectures into six groups of nine treatises written in Greek and called the *Enneads*, completed in 301. The work covers ethics, physics, the soul, the three hypostases, logical categories, and the One.

Plotinus was born possibly in Lycopolis, now Asyūt, in Upper Egypt. He studied in Alexandria under Ammonius Saccas from 232 to 243 and tried to acquaint himself with Eastern thought by joining an imperial expedition, an unsuccessful one, against the Persians. After escaping to Antioch, he arrived in Rome in 244 and established a discussion group on Platonic and Aristotelian texts and their commentators. His chief pupils were Amelius, Porphyry, and Eustochious, a physician who was with him when he died and who reported his last words: "I am trying to bring back the divine in myself to the divine in the All."

Stimulated mainly by Plato's *Parmenides* and *Timaeus* dialogues as well as the *Republic*, book 6, *Phaedo*, *Phaedrus*, and *Symposium*, Plotinus also took from Aristotle and the Stoics whatever he considered to be implied by Plato and took from the second-century philosopher Numenius certain Pythagorean doctrines. The question of Indian influence on Plotinus has been raised and disputed. Plotinus was not influenced by the *Chaldaean Oracles*, which had led some to substitute theurgy for theology and magic for thought. Plotinus's predecessors had invoked Plato to link salvation with intellectual development. Plotinus followed them and rethought the Platonic tradition.

Plotinus's aim was to understand the divinity of his soul and to restore its relationship to the divine All, and in that All, to be united with its transcendent source, the One, or the Good. The three hypostases—the One, Nous (mind, intelligence), Soul—can be considered either statically, as existing realities, or dynamically, in terms of the soul's inner life. The middle part of the human soul is discursive reason, the lower is perception, and the higher is intuitive reason (*Enn.* 5.3.3). Philosophy guides the choice of levels on which to live (*Enn.* 6.7.36).

Plotinus's views on the human body were influenced by Plato's *Phaedo* and *Timaeus*. Against the gnostics he affirms the material world's beauty and goodness (*Enn.* 2.9.8). Accepting the "cosmic religion" of his Platonic predecessors, for whom the heavenly bodies were divine, he sees sensible beauty as useful in the soul's ascent to intelligible beauty and its divine source, since beauty is the radiance of the Good; yet, along with the gnostics, he seems to blame matter for evil.

The One, beyond all limitation, is neither being nor intellect. As infinite life and positive power, it is aptly called the Good and yet can be described only negatively. Without affecting its source, Nous proceeds spontaneously from the One as an unformed potentiality and turns back to contemplate the One, becoming informed with a living community of Ideas, or living intelligences, the archetypes of all things (*Enn.* 5.8.4, 6.7.12).

Soul, proceeding from Nous and returning to Nous, remains distinct from it. The individual soul's descent into the body is a fall and yet is necessary to carry out the governance of All-Soul. Not embodiment, but imprisonment in an earthly body is evil. The soul, while still in the body, can return to the One through moral and intellectual effort. It is a rare mystical experience for some, a more continuous one for others.

Plotinus's philosophy is a religion, one without rites and sacraments or techniques of prayer and meditation, because the Good directly activates the higher soul. His mystical experiences seem to have been theistic ones (*Enn.* 1.6.9, 5.3.17, 6.7.34, 6.8.15, 6.9.11, 5.5.12).

According to A. Hilary Armstrong, in *The Cambridge History of Later Greek and Early Medieval Philosophy* (Cambridge, 1967), the doctrine of Intellect (Nous) was both the "weak point and the growing point of Plotinian Neoplatonism." The Plotinian Nous influenced the intellectual hierarchies of the later Neoplatonists, the trinitarian theology of Marius Victorinus, as well as the ideas of the Greek theologians about the divine powers and energies and angels (pp. 267–268).

Through the Cappadocian fathers in the translations of John Scottus Eriugena (fl. 847–877) and Eriugena's own work, Plotinus reached the medieval West. Augustine, freed from Manichaeism by reading treatises of Plotinus and/or Porphyry, also passed on Plotinian concepts to the philosophical theology of the West. As the founder of Neoplatonism, which was further developed by Porphyry, Iamblichus, and Proclus, Plotinus was the source of negative theology and mystical theology, which through the works of the fifth-century theologian Dionysius the Areopagite influenced Thomas Aquinas and the Rhineland mystics, Eckhart, Suese, and Tauler. Direct knowledge of the *Enneads* in the modern world came through Marsilio Ficino (1433–1499), who translated them into Latin. By its refusal to mingle myths and rituals with religious philosophy, the work of Plotinus led intellectual Christians to recognize how far reason could go in establishing divinely revealed truths, as well as how limited reason is with respect to a historically revealed and achieved salvation that calls for faith in addition to reason.

[*See also* Neoplatonism.]

BIBLIOGRAPHY

The best English translation of the *Enneads* is found in the "Loeb Classical Library," volumes 1–3 (Cambridge, Mass., 1966–); three more volumes are projected. A. Hilary Armstrong based this translation on the revised Henry-Schwyzer text and added helpful notes and a valuable introduction.

The best one-volume English translation of the *Enneads* is that of Stephan MacKenna, revised by B. S. Page, 3d ed. (New York, 1957). It contains not only Porphyry's *Life of Plotinus* but a splendid introduction by Paul Henry and a glossary of Plotinus's key terms. This translation has a certain poetic charm that the reader should not allow to obscure Plotinus's philosophical reasoning.

The most complete and scholarly introduction is Émile Bréhier's *The Philosophy of Plotinus* (Chicago, 1958). The book that best highlights the problems and tensions within Plotinus's philosophy is J. M. Rist's *Plotinus: The Road to Reality* (Cambridge, 1967). In this work will be found a bibliography of editions and translations of the *Enneads* as well as an adequate list of modern studies on Plotinus. *The Essential Plotinus*, edited and translated by Elmer O'Brien (New York, 1964), is a useful handbook containing ten extracts from the *Enneads* and readings from the sources of Plotinus's doctrines.

The extent of Plotinus's influence can be glimpsed in *The Significance of Neoplatonism*, edited by R. Baine Harris (Norfolk, Va., 1976). A collection of articles on almost every significant question raised from Plotinus's philosophy can be found in *Plotinian and Christian Studies* by A. Hilary Armstrong (London, 1979).

MARY T. CLARK, R.S.C.J.

PLURALISM, RELIGIOUS. *See* Religious Pluralism.

PNEUMA. *See* Soul, *articles on* Greek and Hellenistic Concepts *and* Christian Concept.

POBEDONOSTSEV, KONSTANTIN (1827–1907), procurator of the Holy Governing Synod of the Russian Orthodox church. Konstantin Petrovich Pobedonostsev was the last procurator effectively to control the administration of the church according to the stipulations of the Ecclesiastical Regulation of Peter the Great. Although this regulation remained on the statute books until the collapse of the tsarist regime in 1917, the upheavals of 1905–1906 in the church and the government necessitated adaptation in its application during the final decade of the old order.

Pobedonostsev served as procurator from 1880 to 1905, during which time he oversaw a major restructuring of ecclesiastical education and an impressive expansion of the parish school system. His purpose was twofold: to provide basic education to the Russian masses as they emerged from the shadow of serfdom and to ensure that that education firmly supported the tsarist political system. Within the seminaries and theological academies under his control he both raised the general level of education and tried to maintain control of its content. Unintentionally, he stimulated a major controversy over reform in the church and spent the later years of his career attempting to contain and stifle this controversy.

Among the forceful personalities Pobedonostsev dealt with in the controversy over church reform were Antonii Vadkovskii, metropolitan of Saint Petersburg (1898–1912), Sergei Witte, chairman of the Committee of Ministers (1903–1905) and prime minister (1905–1906), and Antonii Khrapovitskii, bishop and archbishop of Volhynia (1902–1914). The bishops were determined reformers, seeking to free the church from the bondage of the Ecclesiastical Regulation. During debates in the Committee of Ministers on proposed changes in legislation affecting non-Orthodox religious groups in the Russian empire, Witte was persuaded by Vadkovskii and others that termination of the Petrine regulation and restoration of autonomy of administration (possibly reviving the patriarchate of Moscow) were essential for good government of the church.

Pobedonostsev attempted to halt the momentum for reform and abolition of the Petrine system by having Tsar Nicholas II transfer deliberation of the question from the Committee of Ministers to the synod itself, where the procurator's agents would be able to control the debate. Vadkovskii, Khrapovitskii, and their allies outmaneuvered the synodal bureaucracy, however, and the synod itself declared for reform. As a result of the synod's decision, the procurator ordered the polling of all the bishops of the church in the hope that they would be opposed to a *sobor* (council) of the church and to the restoration of the patriarchate. But when the bishops had completed their replies, the overwhelming majority were found to favor a *sobor* and a sweeping reform.

During the months that the poll was being taken, Russia was wracked by violence and revolution. From the turmoil came the October Manifesto (1905), which granted a limited constitutional government. Pobedonostsev resigned as procurator, protesting against the manifesto, against Witte's having been appointed prime minister, and against the tsar's promise to summon an all-Russian *sobor*. He died within two years, convinced that his work of twenty-five years as procurator was being destroyed and that both the Russian church and the Russian state were doomed to collapse. He had been unyielding in his opposition to parliamentary forms of government, believing that they were the cause of the decadence of the West and that their introduction into Russia in any form would lead to corruption and disintegration.

Pobedonostsev's voluminous writings reflect his training as a lawyer. Among them are *Lectures on Civil Judicial Procedures* (Moscow, 1863), *History of the Orthodox Church until the Schism of the Churches* (Saint Petersburg, 1896), *Historical Juridical Acts of the Epoch of Transition of the Seventeenth and Eighteenth Centuries* (Moscow, 1887), *Course of Civil Law*, 3 vols. (Saint Petersburg, 1868–1880), *The Questions of Life* (Moscow, 1904), *Annual Report of the Over-Procurator of the Holy Synod concerning the Administration of the Orthodox Church* (Saint Petersburg, 1881–1909), and a number of articles published in journals during his public career.

BIBLIOGRAPHY

The definitive biography of Pobedonostsev in English is Robert F. Byrnes's *Pobedonostsev: His Life and Thought* (Bloomington, Ind., 1968). In German it is Gerhard Simon's *Konstantin Petrovič Pobedonoscev und die Kirchenpolitik des Heiligen Synod, 1880–1905* (Göttingen, 1969). Other useful books are John S. Curtiss's *Church and State in Russia: The Last Years of the Empire, 1900–1917* (1940; reprint, New York, 1965), Igor Smolitsch's *Geschichte der russischen Kirche, 1700–1917* (Leiden, 1964), *Russian Orthodoxy under the Old Regime*, edited by Robert Nichols and Theofanis Stavrou (Minneapolis, 1978), and my *Vanquished Hope: The Church in Russia on the Eve of the Revolution* (New York, 1981).

JAMES W. CUNNINGHAM

POETRY. [*This entry focuses on the intersection of religious motives with poetry. It consists of an introductory essay and five brief surveys:*

Other discussions of the literatures of religion, poetic or not, can be found under the names of particular religions and writings.]

Poetry and Religion

When Shelley observes in his *Defence of Poetry* (1821) that "in the youth of the world, men dance and sing and imitate natural objects, observing in these actions, as in all others, a certain rhythm or order" and that this order "marks the before unapprehended relations of things and perpetuates their apprehension," he is pointing to the origin of poetry in ritual. This observation has been confirmed by the findings of anthropologists before and since. The poetry preserved in oral traditions may represent a particularly vivid reminder of this ritual origin. [*See* Literature. *See also* Drama; Myth; Oral Tradition; *and* Quest.]

Ritual Beginnings. Ritual, as a formalization and focusing of the essential actions and movements of human life—generation, productivity, death—puts man in touch with powers he does not understand, powers that control the cycles of the earth and the cycles of his own life. Of its very nature, ritual celebrates not only the known but the unknown. Many of the earliest gods were, indeed, personifications of the unknown, mysterious powers celebrated in ritual: gods of the sun, gods of the spring, gods of the harvest.

Some say there is a healthy and inevitable passage from ritual to art, marking a movement from the practical to the contemplative. The aim of ritual is to ensure the rising of the sun or an abundant harvest, or to placate an angry sea or sky; man is concerned wholly with surviving in an often dangerous world. In this view, when ritual has passed over into art, man has, as Jane Ellen Harrison says in *Ancient Art and Ritual* (London, 1913), "come out from action, he is separate from the dancers, and has become a spectator" (pp. 72–73). To pass from ritual to art is to pass from action to contemplation. Ritual grows out of the immediate needs of life; art offers a necessary "distance" from life. What remains common to them, though, is the need to deal, whether by action or by contemplation, with the mysterious powers of the universe.

There is, however, another view of the relationship of ritual and art: that they were once integrated, and that the breakdown of that integrity has been a severe loss. In primitive society, as Gerardus van der Leeuw writes in *Sacred and Profane Beauty* (New York, 1963), "between religion and art . . . there is no actual contrast. What for us is a series of neatly separated planes, the primitive man sees as concentric circles" (p. 11). But "under the weight of our modern culture the unity of human life has been lost beyond retrieve. . . . When we dance, we do not pray; when we pray, we do not dance" (p. 34). [*For detailed discussion of religious understandings of ritual, see* Ritual *and* Ritual Studies.]

Religion and Poetry. Whether one sees the passage from ritual to art as progress or decline, it remains true that religion has continued to be seen as part of the poetic experience. While no one would claim an identity of religion and poetry, a relationship between them has often been affirmed, even as new theories of poetry have emerged. Today, views of this relationship range all the way from the dedication of poetry to the service of religious doctrine to the affirmation that a poem exists for its own sake and in a world of its own, whose values are irrelevant to religion or philosophy or even human life. Between these two extremes, however, there is room for an enormous range of other views: poetry as an expression of human aspiration and faith; poetry as an exploration of moral dilemmas posed by religious quest or commitment; poetry as a manifestation of human concern for ultimate realities; poetry as a surrogate for a religious belief that has been lost—man's refuge from the chaos around him. How we have reached this diversity of view can be appreciated by considering some of the types of poetry that have been called religious.

Some poetry is clearly and professedly religious, that is, it deals with mankind's experience of the transcendent, by whatever name it is called: the sacred, the divine, the numinous. In the Bible, the psalms are such poetry, whether they be in the form of prayers or of reflections on the psalmist's experience of God; canticles like the Song of Deborah (*Jgs.* 5) and Mary's Magnificat (*Lk.* 1:46–55) sing the praises of God for his gracious intervention on behalf of his people; much of Hebrew prophecy is in poetic form, as in the visionary experiences of Isaiah or the lamentations of Jeremiah; the *Book of Job* is a poem of epic grandeur framed by a prose narrative; and the entire *Book of Revelation* is an exalted poetic vision of the endtime and the heavenly Jerusalem.

Other clearly and specifically religious poetry includes such disparate works as the Sanskrit hymns of the ancient Indian *Ṛgveda;* the Anglo-Saxon poem *The Dream of the Rood;* medieval Latin hymns like the *Dies irae* and allegories like the *Pearl* and the *Roman de la rose;* Dante's *Commedia,* with its allegorical and symbolic exploration of religious revelation; the devotional lyrics of George Herbert in the seventeenth century and of Gerard Manley Hopkins in the nineteenth; in modern poetry, the lyric mysticism of the Hindu poet Rabindranath Tagore, the religious questing of T. S. Eliot's *Four Quartets,* and the splendid liturgical eclecticism of *The Anathemata* of David Jones.

There is a wealth of other poetry, however, that—although not expressly or professedly religious—has often been thought of as such. Such poetry may not address the deity or probe directly the human experience of God, but it does concern itself centrally—often in the form of a quest—with the human longing for certainty and for transcendence, with "ultimate realities," and with the crucial moral dilemmas of human life. Such, for example, is Keats's magnificent fragment *The Fall of Hyperion* and Shelley's *Mont Blanc*—indeed much of Romantic poetry, from the grand metaphysical visions of Goethe's *Faust* to the tortured and rebellious reflections of Baudelaire.

In earlier ages, such poetry is represented by the Homeric epics, in which the human events have their parallels and ultimate causes in the doings of the Olympians; *Beowulf,* whether it be viewed in its pagan or Christian dimensions, in its struggle with the ultimate powers of the world; and perhaps even Chaucer's *Canterbury Tales,* in which the Christian tradition serves as backdrop—moral, dramatic, and ironic—for an unparalleled gallery of human portraits. Much of modern poetry in the West may be counted "religious" in this sense: the skeptical and ironic probings of Robert Frost, the haunted meditations of Robert Lowell, the certainties and uncertainties of W. H. Auden, Wallace Stevens's metaphysical speculations, and William Butler Yeats's mystical visions.

Poetic Forms. It may perhaps be clear already that there is virtually no poetic form that has not been used for the expression of religious experience. In the Bible, for example, one finds ritual hymns (Psalm 100), elegies (David's lament in *2 Samuel* 1:19–27), epithalamia *(Song of Songs),* proverbs *(Book of Proverbs),* oracular utterances (*Isaiah* 19:1–15), prayers (*Jonah* 2:2–9), canticles (the "song of Simeon" in *Luke* 2:29–35), and symbolic visions *(Book of Revelation).* [*See* Biblical Literature.]

The longer poetic forms have been especially fruitful vehicles for religious expression: the ancient Babylonian folk-epic of Gilgamesh and the Indian epic *Rāmāyaṇa;* more "literary" epics such as Milton's *Paradise Lost;* tragedies as disparate as Corneille's *Polyeucte* and Racine's *Athalie,* Marlowe's *Dr. Faustus,* Milton's *Samson Agonistes,* and T. S. Eliot's *Murder in the Cathedral;* long idylls like the Persian poet Rūmī's *Mathnawī* (1256–1273), celebrating the search of the soul for union with God; cycles of hymns like the ancient Indian *Ṛgveda;* extended elegies like Tennyson's *In Memoriam;* and allegories of such different sorts as the medieval *Piers Plowman* and Dryden's *The Hind and the Panther.* [*See* Epics.]

Most of the shorter poetic forms have also been used to express religious feelings and aspirations, but among them—besides, of course, hymns and carols—the sonnet and the ode have been particularly favored. The ode has most commonly been used for more public utterances, as in Milton's *On the Morning of Christ's Nativity* and Dryden's *Song for Saint Cecilia's Day, 1687;* the sonnet for more personal expressions, such as the *Holy Sonnets* of John Donne and the sonnets of G. M. Hopkins.

Literary Theories. In the Western tradition, there is a critical theory that parallels the development of poetry and that affects the relationship between poetry and religion. In *The Mirror and the Lamp: Romantic Theory and the Critical Tradition* (New York, 1953), M. H. Abrams has suggested that there are four "co-ordinates" to be taken into account in any criticism of a work of art: the work itself, the artist, the subject of the work, and the audience. Each of these elements has been given primacy at one period during the history of poetic theory (pp. 6–29; see also Giles B. Gunn, ed., *Literature and Religion*, New York, 1971, pp. 5–11).

From Plato to the Renaissance is the period in the West of "mimetic" theory, which emphasizes "the reference of a work to the subject matter which it imitates" (Abrams, p. 10). Although "mimesis" (imitation) is often spoken of as Aristotelian, the notion is very commonly joined with a more Platonic conception of imitation. Although Plato rejects in the *Republic* the imitation of the temporal world, he does advocate imitation of ideal, transcendent ideas; for Aristotle, however, imitation is not of transcendent ideas but of immanent human actions. The view reflected in much of the poetry written before the Renaissance is in fact a conflation of Aristotelian imitation of immanent forms with a Platonic imitation of the transcendent. Thus the literature of this period has commonly included, at least implicitly, the essentially Platonic conception of sensible reality as in some way an imitation, reflection, or analogue of suprasensible reality—leaving open broad possibilities for religious dimensions in poetry.

The Renaissance marks a shift from a mimetic view of poetry to what Abrams calls a "pragmatic" view, of which one of the first classic expressions is Sir Philip Sidney's *Apologie for Poetrie* (1580). It is, in effect, a change of emphasis from the subject of the work to its audience. The proximate aim of poetry is to produce pleasure in its readers, but its ultimate goal is to teach, especially to teach a mode of action; thus the moral dimension of poetry becomes of primary importance. This view is continued in John Dryden's *Essay of Dramatick Poesie* (1668) and in the critical work of Samuel Johnson, especially his celebrated *Preface to Shakespeare* (1765).

Abrams's third stage is the "expressionistic" theory that emerges in the Romantic period, in which the artist himself comes to the fore. The artist's feelings, longings, and aspirations are crucial to the poetry; in their religious dimensions, therefore, the search for transcendence—whether through exploration of the inner self or through interaction of the self with nature—becomes of paramount importance. The great philosophical theorizers of the period are Rousseau, Friedrich Schlegel, and Coleridge, but works like Wordsworth's *Prelude*, the visionary prophesies of Blake, Keats's letters, and Shelley's *Defence of Poetry*, all shed light on the religious dimensions of Romantic poetry.

The final stage is that of the "objective" theory, which focuses above all on the work itself. The doctrine of "l'art pour l'art" espoused in the late nineteenth century by some of the French Symbolists and others is one expression of this view. Another, quite different approach that achieves much the same result is the neo-Aristotelianism of the so-called Chicago Critics, with their revival of the formal criticism of Aristotle. Still another, which has made lasting contributions to modern critical theory and practice, is the New Criticism of the 1930s and 1940s, led by such critics as I. A. Richards, William Empson, John Crowe Ransom, and Cleanth Brooks, who emphasized the inner structure of a poem to the exclusion of any external reference.

Although these four stages can be isolated, none of them has probably ever existed in its pure state; it is a matter of emphasis rather than of exclusive concern. Clearly, though, some stages lend themselves more than others to the expression of religious experience, notably the mimetic and expressionistic stages. The mimetic, stressing the subject of the work, is clearly open to the expression of a wide range of religious ideals, history, and experiences. The expressionistic fosters the articulation of the poet's own religious feelings, beliefs, and aspirations. One stage, the objective, has been perceived as particularly unfriendly to the articulation of religious experience. Its preoccupation with formal structure and linguistic significance, to the exclusion of allusions to sources outside the poem, clearly militates against taking seriously the poet's expression of his own religious feelings or his perception of the transcendent.

Such narrowing has usually met resistance, however. Just as the expressionistic views and methods of romanticism were eventually countered by an emphasis in criticism on the work itself, so this objective approach has in turn been balanced in modern times by other, often broader kinds of criticism of poetry: the archetypal criticism of Northrop Frye; the wide-ranging cultural approach of Edmund Wilson; the deeply historical work of Douglas Bush; the humanistic criticism of Lionel Trilling. The diversity of views in literary history has left a rich legacy of approaches for modern critics. As a result, there seems little danger of losing sight altogether of the religious dimensions of poetry.

The Language of Religion and Poetry. It is no surprise that figurative language must be used both in poetry and in the language of religion, since both deal with mystery: religion with the mysteries of transcendent reality; poetry with all the human mysteries, whether man's experience of himself and the world or his experience of the divine. Poetry, of its very nature, deals with the elements of human experience that defy rational or scientific analysis: subtleties of feeling, passionate responses, flashes of intuition. Religion has as its object what is by definition incomprehensible: the divine.

Because of the limitations of language, it is possible to speak of such things—essentially immaterial, unseen—only indirectly, by analogy with what is seen. Hence the role of such tools as imagery, as metaphor, allegory, and symbol. Thus in religious traditions: in the Old Testament God reveals himself in a burning bush (*Ex.* 3:1–6), in a pillar of cloud (*Ex.* 13:21), in a whirlwind (*Jb.* 38:1ff.); among the North American Plains Indians the image of the medicine wheel expresses their experience of the universe; and in Buddhism the image of the path is used to convey the process of spiritual enlightenment. Likewise in poetry, the author of the medieval morality play *Everyman* personifies the moral and theological virtues, Herbert uses the image of *The Pulley* to speak of man's relationship with God, and Hopkins sees in *The Windhover* an image of Christ.

Especially since the early nineteenth century, symbol has been an important vehicle for religious poetry. Allegory (and, some would add, metaphor) assumes a more or less defined set of relationships between an image and its referent; symbol, on the other hand, remains open-ended, carrying with it an undefined—and indeed undefinable—set of connotations, which grow as the symbol is used in new contexts within a poem. Thus in Coleridge's *Rime of the Ancient Mariner,* the albatross hung about the mariner's neck is a fairly well defined metaphor for his guilt, while the sun and the moon in the poem are constantly shifting symbols that grow in meaning as the poem proceeds and yet can never be fully defined. In religious poetry, the use of symbol has particular advantages: by suggesting as much as it directly says, it can articulate what is ultimately numinous and incomprehensible. Shelley's symbols of water and mountain in *Mont Blanc,* Yeats's symbol of the rose or the tower, T. S. Eliot's light and water symbols, and Paul Claudel's use of the sea as a symbol of man's varied experience of the life of divine grace, are all attempts to convey the poet's intuition of the transcendent, to articulate and communicate the incomprehensible.

Poetry and Prayer. However much poetry and religion may share—in form, in subject, in tone—they differ in the attitude one brings to each. One approaches poetry as an object not of worship but of pleasure and cognition. The religious experience, however, is by its very nature primarily an experience of worship, in which the worshiper experiences awe in the face of the transcendent. The two may, though, be interrelated, as when the poetry is of such a religious nature as to move the reader to pass beyond the poetic experience into worship, and thus arises the question of the relationship between poetry and prayer.

Abbé Henri Brémond, in *Prière et poésie* (1926), manifests a confessedly Romantic approach that sees a common genesis of poetry and prayer in inspiration: the natural gift of poetic inspiration, the supernatural gift that inspires prayer—both gifts of God, both leading toward God, but with the man of prayer going farther in his experience than the poet. Brémond has been criticized, even by his admirers, for unduly confusing the two, for there is, as Brémond himself says, one crucial difference (among others) between them: poetry, by its very nature, ends in the word; prayer, however much it may use words—public or private—along its course, ends in silence. The ultimate aim of prayer is the silence of adoration before God.

In the last analysis, though, this debate may be of less significance than the fact that poetry and prayer, and therefore poetry and religion, have mutually supported each other through the ages. Great poets—Isaiah, Aeschylus, Dante, John of the Cross, Hopkins, Tagore—have been so inspired by their experience of the transcendent God that they have been moved to utter words of incomparable beauty. And the best of this religious poetry can in turn so touch the reader as to lead him beyond poetry into prayer, beyond the experience of beauty to an experience of the ultimate Author of beauty. As Coleridge wrote, on the memorable night in 1807 when he had listened to his friend Wordsworth recite the last lines of his great *Prelude:* "And when I rose, I found myself in prayer."

[*See also* Literature.]

BIBLIOGRAPHY

Most of the work on poetry and religion is included in studies on the more general topic of literature and religion. The most useful single book is *Literature and Religion,* edited by Giles B. Gunn (New York, 1971); these essays offer an excellent range of theoretical approaches, while the editor's own introduction is a helpful survey of the history and current state of scholarship. Another distinguished collection of essays on the aesthetics of literature and religion is *The New Orpheus: Essays toward a Christian Poetic,* edited by Nathan A. Scott, Jr. (New

York, 1964), which also contains a useful bibliography. *Horizons of Criticism: An Assessment of Religious-Literary Options* (Chicago, 1975), by Vernon Ruland, S.J., is a book-length survey of the field, including a full bibliography. Sallie McFague (TeSelle) offers a methodology of literature and religion in *Literature and the Christian Life* (New Haven, 1966). Two important theological approaches are *Theology of Culture* (New York, 1959), by Paul Tillich, which breaks down the barriers between the sacred and the secular, and *Christ and Apollo: The Dimensions of the Literary Imagination* (New York, 1960), by William F. Lynch, S.J., which gives an incarnation view of the literary imagination. On the ritual origins of art, Jane Ellen Harrison's *Ancient Art and Ritual* (1913; reprint, Bradford-on-Avon, 1978) is a splendid and often moving introduction; while Gerardus van der Leeuw's *Wegen en grenzen: Studie over de verhouding van religie en kunst* (Amsterdam, 1932), translated by A. Piper as *Vom Heiligen in der Kunst* (Gütersloh, 1957) and by David E. Green as *Sacred and Profane Beauty: The Holy in Art* (New York, 1963), offers a more sustained phenomenology and theology of the arts. Part 3 is specifically on poetry and the sacred. A useful source on oral religious poetry—of such peoples as the Tatars, Polynesians, and certain African peoples—is volume 3 of *The Growth of Literature*, by H. Munro Chadwick and Nora Kershaw Chadwick (Cambridge, 1940). A classic study of prayer and poetry is Henri Brémond's *Prière et poésie* (Paris, 1926), translated by Algar Thorold as *Prayer and Poetry: A Contribution to Poetical Theory* (London, 1927). A more recent and fuller treatment is by William T. Noon, S.J., *Poetry and Prayer* (New Brunswick, N.J., 1967).

J. ROBERT BARTH, S.J.

Indian Religious Poetry

The most popular and influential devotional poetry in India is that associated with the *bhakti*, or popular devotional, movement—a wave of religious fervor that swept over India from South to North, beginning around the sixth century in the Tamil area and flourishing in the Hindi region between the fifteenth and seventeenth centuries. [*See* Bhakti.] It was a grass roots movement, protesting against formalism and priestly domination; insisting on the direct accessibility of God to everyone; attacking purely external practices and hypocrisy; and stressing the importance of inner experience, which generally meant establishing a bond of fervent personal love with the deity. *Bhakti* is also associated with the rise of vernacular literature and with a group of poet-saints whose works are in many instances the classics of their respective languages. Much of this literature was composed orally, and all of it has been transmitted largely through singing. Written versions have typically been recorded and collected after the poets' lifetimes, though some poets did write down their own works. This article focuses mainly on short verse forms (lyrics and couplets) and on Hindu vernacular poetry, though there are brief sections on Sanskrit, Buddhist, and Jain materials as well.

Hindu Poetry in Sanskrit. The most ancient texts of Indian civilization, the Ṛgvedic hymns (1200–900 BCE), can be seen as remote first ancestors of the long tradition of devotional poetry in India. These poems include paeans to various Aryan gods, many of whom assumed places in the late Hindu pantheon.

The body of Sanskrit verse most relevant to this survey is the vast assortment of Hindu *stotras*—hymns of praise, adoration, and supplication—with examples ranging over two millennia, from before the common era to the present day. These poems are found imbedded in epics, Purāṇas, *māhātmyas*, Tantras, other sacred texts, and occasionally secular texts; or as independent works attributed to various devotees and teachers. The period in which *stotras* were most abundantly produced corresponds largely to that of the *bhakti* movement. Composed in all parts of India, the hymns are addressed chiefly to forms of Śiva, Viṣṇu, and Devī (the goddess), but they are also dedicated to other deities, such as Gaṇeśa and Sūrya. Their subjects extend further to sacred cities, rivers, shrines, plants; to *gurus* and ancestors; and to the impersonal Absolute. Many *stotras* are anonymous or of dubious attribution. Among numerous named composers, a few famous examples are the philosophers Śaṅkara and Rāmānuja, the Kashmiri Śaiva devotee Utpaladeva, the Bengali Caitanyite Rūpa Gosvāmin, and the South Indian poet Nīlakaṇṭha Dīkṣita. [*See the biographies of Śaṅkara and Rāmānuja*.]

Sanskrit *stotras* are used widely in both temple and domestic worship. Their contents typically include detailed descriptions of a deity's form and accoutrements, praise of his or her attributes, references to mythological episodes, strings of names and epithets, prayers for grace and assistance, and testimonials to the devotee's grief, helplessness, love, and faith.

A. K. Ramanujan (1981, p. 109) comments on the relation between Sanskrit and vernacular *bhakti* literature. "The imperial presence of Sanskrit," he writes, "was a presence against which *bhakti* in Tamil defines itself, though not always defiantly." While vernacular *bhakti* poets often defy Sanskritic norms, there is also a continuity between the two traditions. For example, in the *Rāmcaritmānas* of Tulsīdās there are many praise poems in highly sanskritized Hindi, set apart in diction and form, obviously meant to echo the style of Sanskrit *stotras*. The *Saundaryalaharī*, a *stotra* popularly attributed to Śaṅkara, describes the experience of oneness with the divine in terms that later turn up almost identically in the Kabīr tradition. An important transitional work between North Indian Sanskrit and vernacular *bhakti* literature is Jayadeva's *Gitagovinda*, composed in Bengal around 1200. [*See the biographies of Tulsīdās and Jayadeva.*]

South Indian Vernacular Poetry. Partly in reaction to the strength of Buddhism and Jainism in the South, a great surge of faith in Viṣṇu and Śiva was touched off by poet-saints in the Tamil region between the sixth and ninth centuries. Śaiva and Vaiṣṇava saint-poets—at one level rivals, at a deeper level, collaborators in this awakening of faith—shared common themes and styles. They roamed the countryside reaching audiences of all classes and included among their number peasants, aristocrats, Untouchables, priests, women, and men. Tradition has preserved the names of sixty-three Śaiva poets, known as Nāyaṉārs, and twelve Vaiṣṇavas, or Āḻvārs. Nammāḻvār is often singled out as the greatest Āḻvār poet, Māṇikkavācakar as the greatest Nāyaṉār. Around the tenth century Nātamuṉi compiled the *Divyaprabhandam,* containing four thousand Āḻvār compositions for use in Śrī Vaiṣṇava worship. Similarly Nampi Āntār Nampi, at the request of a tenth-century king, is said to have compiled most of the *Tirumuṟai,* which includes eleven volumes of Nāyaṉār poetry (a twelfth volume, of hagiography, was added later). Śaivas often call the *Tirumuṟai,* as Vaiṣṇavas call Nammāḻvār's *Tiruvāymoḻi,* "the Tamil Veda." [*See* Śaivism, *article on* Nāyaṉārs; Āḻvārs; *and the biography of Māṇikkavācakar.*]

The *siddhas* (Tam. *cittar*) are part of an ancient pan-Indian movement characterized by its use of yogic practices and Tantric symbols. Important *siddha* poets in Tamil range from the seventh to the eighteenth centuries and include Civavākkiyar, Pattirakiyiar, and Pāmpāttic Cittar. *Siddha* poetry is both linked to and distinguishable from mainstream *bhakti* poetry. Both tend to denigrate caste, mechanical ritual, and sterile intellectuality. But while the *bhakta*s continue to adore their images of Viṣṇu and Śiva, the *siddha*s favor an interior, impersonal Lord and unequivocally attack idol worship. Stylistically, too, the *siddha*s differ from the generally more refined devotional poets. Their verse, which often utilizes folksong forms and meters, is colloquial, forceful, and simple often to the point of being crude. [*See* Mahāsiddhas.]

"Like a lit fuse, the passion of *bhakti* seems to spread from region to region, from century to century, quickening the religious impulse," says Ramanujan (1973, p. 40). In the tenth to twelfth centuries the flame burned brightly in Karnataka with the Kannada verses of the Vīraśaiva saint-poets, the four greatest of whom were Basavaṇṇa, Dēvara Dāsimayya, Mahādēviyakka, and Allama Prabhu. They composed *vacana*s, short free-verse utterances expressing intense personal experience and sometimes trenchant criticism of what the poets regarded as superstition and hypocrisy. [*See* Śaivism, *article on* Vīraśaivas.] A *vacana* by Allama Prabhu, for example, is a purely lyric outpouring:

> Looking for your light,
> I went out:
>
> it was like the sudden dawn
> of a million million suns,
>
> a ganglion of lightnings
> for my wonder.
>
> O Lord of Caves,
> if you are light,
> there can be no metaphor.
>
> (trans. Ramanujan, 1973, p. 168)

while the conclusion of a *vacana* by Basavaṇṇa has a note of biting criticism:

> Gods, gods, there are so many
> there's no place left
> for a foot.
>
> There is only
> one god. He is our Lord
> of the Meeting Rivers.
>
> (trans. Ramanujan, 1973, p. 84)

Vaiṣṇava poetry emerges in the sixteenth century with Purandaradāsa Viṭṭhala, who is remembered as the founder of the southern (Karnatak) style of classical music. The greatest composer of Karnatak music, Tyāgarāja (1767–1847), acknowledges his debt to Purandaradāsa. A devotee of Rām, Tyāgarāja composed many devotional songs in Telugu, often praising music as a pathway to God. Another well-known Telugu saint-poet is the seventeenth-century Rāmdās of Bhadrācalam, also a worshiper of Rām.

North Indian Vernacular Poetry. Four names stand out among a rich array of Maharashtrian singers between the thirteenth and seventeenth centuries: Jñāneśvar, also called Jñāndev (fl. late thirteenth century), Nāmdev (c. 1270–1350), Eknāth (1548–1600), and Tukārām (1598–1650). Jñāneśvar is best known for his long Marathi exposition of the *Bhagavadgītā,* the *Jñāneśvarī.* Nāmdev composed passionate devotional songs and consolidated the cult of the Vārkarīs ("pilgrims") to the important pilgrimage center at Pandharpur. Eknāth translated and interpreted important Sanskrit works. He also poured out his own feelings in lyric poems and in a remarkable series of dramatic monologues, putting the most profound teachings of *bhakti* into the mouths of characters generally despised by society—Untouchables, prostitutes, ropedancers, demons, the blind, and the deaf. Tukārām, perhaps the most beloved of the four, was a *śūdra* (member of the lowest of the four broad categories of caste) pressed by misfortune to reject worldly values and devote himself to God. His lyrics run from harsh contempt of self-serving religious specialists ("the wretched pandit stewed in dialectics . . . a fool among fools / wagging a sage beard") to the most tender humility ("May I be, Lord, a small pebble, a large stone, or dust / on the road to Pandharpur / to be trampled by the feet of the saints").

Nasiṃha Mehta (fifteenth or sixteenth century), the major *bhakti* poet of Gujarat, composed songs that were incorporated into the rituals of the Vallabhācārya sect. The Kashmiri Lal Ded (fourteenth century) was a woman devotee of Śiva whose poetic utterances are famous throughout Kashmir and beyond. The earliest and still most important devotional poetry associated with the Punjab, that compiled in the Sikh *Ādi Granth* (1604), is largely in an old form of Hindi. True Panjabi literature, beginning in the seventeenth century, is almost entirely by Muslims. [*See* Ādi Granth.]

The leading figures of Hindi *bhakti* poetry are Tulsīdās, Sūrdās, Kabīr, and Mīrā Bāī, followed closely by Raidās, Nānak, and Dādū. Tulsīdās (1543–1623), who wrote in the Avadhi dialect, is the author of the *Rāmcaritmānas,* a highly devotional version of the ancient *Rāmāyaṇa* epic. Popularly known as the *Tulsī Rāmāyan* it is probably the most influential single literary work in North India. Tulsīdās also wrote many lyrics. [*See the biographies of Kabīr, Mīrā Bāī, Nānak, and Sūrdās.*]

Sūrdās (sixteenth century) is the most illustrious member of the *aṣṭacāp,* or eight Kṛṣṇaite poets associated with Vallabhācārya and the sect he founded in Vṛndāvana. He is most famous for his evocations of Kṛṣṇa's idyllic childhood, but recent scholarship suggests that Sūr's often emotionally harrowing personal supplications to God and his poems of grief-stricken separation may be closer to the authentic core of his work than the popular songs of the youthful deity. According to legend Sūr was blind, and "Sūrdās" is today widely used as a title for any blind singer of religious songs. Thousands of lyrics attributed to the poet are collected in the *Sūrsāgar* (Ocean of Sur). He composed in Braj *bhāṣā,* the most important literary dialect of medieval Hindi.

Mīrā Bāī was a Rajput princess who became a wandering saint. Although she is believed to have spent the later part of her life in Dwarka, Gujarat, and a considerable body of poetry ascribed to her exists in Gujarati, she is more closely linked to her native Rajasthan and to its regional form of Hindi.

The leading poet of the Sant (or *nirguṇa,* "without qualities") school in North India is Kabīr (c. 1398–1448). Born of a Muslim family in Banaras, Kabīr was influenced more by Hindu than by Muslim traditions and is popularly believed to have been a disciple of Rāmānanda. He is known particularly for his iconoclasm and for his rough, colloquial style. Kabīr called on the name of Rām as a sound that revealed ultimate reality, but he rejected the mythology of the popular *avatāra* Rām, insisting that God was beyond form.

Gurū Nānak (1469–1539), the founder of Sikhism, composed poems revering the formless God and criticizing superstitious practices. The same is true of Dādū (1544–1603), in whose name a sect was founded in Rajasthan. Raidās, an Untouchable leatherworker and Sant poet of the fifteenth century, is respected by all classes but has a particular following among his own caste, the *camār*s.

Mention should also be made of the poetry of the North Indian yogins called Nāth Panṭhis, who belong to the same broad tradition as the Tamil *siddha*s. The most significant collection is attributed to Gorakhnāth (eleventh century?), semilegendary founder of the Nāth Panṭh, whose teachings pervaded North Indian religious thought in the medieval period. [*See the biography of Gorakhnāth.*]

The story of Bengali *bhakti* poetry begins with a Sanskrit poet, Jayadeva, whose late twelfth-century masterpiece *Gītagovinda* sets the mood for the efflorescence of Kṛṣṇaite verse in the following four hundred years. In a series of subtle and sensuous lyrics, the *Gītagovinda* unfolds the drama of love between Kṛṣṇa and Rādhā, which became the major theme of devotion in medieval Bengal. In this poetry the strand of several traditions come together: secular erotic verse in Sanskrit, Tantrism, and orthodox Vaiṣṇavism.

The name *Caṇḍidās* was used by at least two important Bengali poets whose dates can only be guessed (guesses range from the fourteenth to the sixteenth century). The enormously influential saint, Caitanya (1486–1533), though he composed very little himself, encouraged the development of Bengali song literature by establishing the widespread practice of *kīrtan,* or meeting for ardent group singing. [*See the biography of Caitanya.*] Rāmprasād Sen (1718–1785) was a powerful poet of the Śākta (Goddess-worshiping) tradition. The Bauls, unique to Bengal, are iconoclastic wanderers who hover between Hindu and Ṣūfī mysticism and worship exclusively through singing.

Vidyāpati (c. 1352–1448) was one of the earliest poets to compose religious lyrics in Maithili—a border language between Bengali and Hindi. The outstanding figure of Assamese devotional literature is Śaṅkaradeva (c.1489–1568), who introduced a devotional dance drama form still widely used today. A unique *bhakti* institution in Assam is the *satra,* a religious center with a leader, lay members, and facilities for musical and dramatic performances. Another prominent poet of the same period is Mādhavadeva (1489?–1596). The best-known medieval *bhakti* poet in Oriya was a disciple of Caitanya named Jagannāthadāsa (fifteenth century).

Buddhist Poetry. Remarkable early examples of Buddhist poetry are found in the *Therīgāthā* and *Theragāthā* (Songs of the Venerable Women and Songs of the Venerable Men) of the Pali canon, recorded around 80 BCE. The women especially describe vivid personal experiences that led to their choice of a renunciant's life.

Two great Sanskrit poets appear in the second century of the common era. Aśvaghoṣa is most famous for the *Buddhacarita,* a biography of the Buddha in the form of a *mahākāvya* (lyric narrative). Mātṛceta, perhaps an older contemporary of Aśvaghoṣa, wrote beautiful Sanskrit hymns to the Buddha. The seventh-century Chinese pilgrim I-ching reported, "Throughout India everyone who becomes a monk is taught Mātṛceta's two hymns as soon as he can recite the . . . precepts."

Over the centuries Buddhist poets, such as the seventh-century monk Śāntideva, produced many *stotras* praising the Buddha and *bodhisattvas* and expressing fervent dedication to the Buddhist path. [*See the biography of Śāntideva.*] Like Hindu *stotras,* these are found incorporated into larger texts (such as *sūtras* and Jātaka tales) as well as in independent form with attribution to particular authors. In one such hymn Śāntideva expresses his vow to save all beings:

> I am medicine for the sick and weary
> may I be their physician and their nurse
> until disease appears no more . . .
> may I be a protector for the unprotected
> a guide for wanderers
> a bridge: a boat: a causeway
> for those who desire the other shores. . . .
> (trans. Stephan Beyer)

A remarkable collection of esoteric songs known as the *caryāgīti* was produced by Tantric adepts in northeast India around the tenth to twelfth centuries. The best-known *caryāgīti* poets, Kāṇha and Saraha, also composed *dohākoṣas* ("collections of couplets").

Finally mention must be made of Tibet's powerful and original contributions to Buddhist lyric poetry. Especially noteworthy are the many songs of the twelfth-century teacher Mi-la-ras-pa (Milarepa). [*See the biography of Mi-la-ras-pa.*]

Jain Poetry. Like Hindus and Buddhists, the Jains have produced a large *stotra* literature. Their hymns, composed since at least the earliest centuries of the common era in Sanskrit and later in Prakrit, praise chiefly the twenty-four *jinas* as well as some ancient teachers of the Jain tradition. There also exists a body of vernacular Jain poetry, largely in Hindi and Gujarati. One of the most famous Jain hymns is the *Bhaktāmara Stotra* of Mānatuṅga, whose dates have been estimated to be as early as the third and as late as the ninth century. Several Jain authors composed both philosophical works and devotional poems. These include Siddhasena Divākara, Samantabhadra, Vidyānanda, and the great twelfth-century sage Hemacandra.

Many Jain *stotras* are organized around the sequential praise of all twenty-four *jinas,* the best known being the highly ornate *Śobhana Stuti* of the tenth-century poet Śobhana. As the repeated glorification of the *jinas* made for monotonously similar content, poets made great efforts to achieve originality of form, and thus the *stotras* contain the most ornate verse in Jain literature.

BIBLIOGRAPHY

A good introduction to the *bhakti* movement is Eleanor Zelliot's "The Medieval Bhakti Movement in History: An Essay on the Literature in English," in *Hinduism: New Essays in the History of Religions,* edited by Bardwell L. Smith (Leiden, 1976), pp. 143–168. Zelliot provides accounts of the regional movements and bibliographies. Missing from her lists, however, are important recent translations.

Superb translations from Tamil and Kannada are given in A. K. Ramanujan's *Hymns for the Drowning: Poems for Viṣṇu by Nammālvār* (Princeton, 1981) and *Speaking of Śiva* (Harmondsworth, 1973). Kamil Zvelebil's survey of Tamil literature, *The Smile of Murugan* (Leiden, 1973), includes chapters on both *bhakti* and *siddha* poetry. Zvelebil has also written a book on the *siddhas, The Poets of the Powers* (London, 1973), which includes a number of translations.

Charlotte Vaudeville's numerous contributions in the Hindi field include her monumental *Kabīr,* vol. 1 (Oxford, 1974), which combines a 150-page introduction with extensive translations and painstaking scholarly apparatus. *The Bījak of Kabir* (San Francisco, 1983), translated by Shukdev Singh and me, conveys a vivid sense of Kabīr's forceful style and includes essays on his style and use of symbols. Sūrdās is richly represented in Kenneth E. Bryant's *Poems to the Child-God: Structures and Strategies in the Poetry of Sūrdās* (Berkeley, 1978) and in John Stratton Hawley's *Sūr Dās: Poet, Singer, Saint* (Seattle, 1984). Tulsīdās's lyrics are available in reliable if not sparkling translations by F. R. Allchin in *Kavitāvalī* (London, 1964) and his *The Petition to Rām* (London, 1966).

An exceptionally lovely book of translations from Bengali is *In Praise of Krishna* (1967; Chicago, 1981), a collaborative effort of the scholar Edward C. Dimock, Jr., and the poet Denise Levertov. Lively translations of Rāmprasād Sen are provided in *Grace and Mercy in Her Wild Hair: Selected Poems to the Mother Goddess* (Boulder, 1982) by another poet-scholar team, Leonard Nathan and Clinton Seely. Jayadeva's *Gītāgovinda* is splendidly translated by Barbara Stoler Miller in *Love Song of the Dark Lord* (New York, 1977).

A good source for examples of Buddhist poetry is Stephan Beyer's *The Buddhist Experience: Sources and Interpretations*

(Encino, Calif., 1974). On the *caryāgīti*, see Per Kvaerne's *An Anthology of Buddhist Tantric Songs* (Oslo, 1977; Bangkok, 1985).

A multivolume, English-language *History of Indian Literature,* edited by Jan Gonda (Wiesbaden, 1973–), is in progress. Individual volumes have been published on literature in Sanskrit and the vernacular languages as well as on the literatures of particular religious traditions. Maurice Winternitz's *A History of Indian Literature,* 2 vols. (Calcutta, 1927–1933) covers ground not covered elsewhere, particularly in volume 2, *Buddhist Literature and Jaina Literature.*

LINDA HESS

Chinese Religious Poetry

To speak of religious poetry in the Chinese context is to beg several questions. First, in classical Chinese there is no exact equivalent to the word *religion:* Confucianism, Taoism, and Buddhism are traditionally known as the Three Teachings *(san-chiao).* Second, it is debatable whether Confucianism is a religion and whether ancestral worship is a kind of religious ritual. (The latter question was the subject of the so-called Rites Controversy among Catholic missionaries to China in the early eighteenth century.) Finally, although Taoist and Buddhist liturgies both contain verses, these are generally not considered worthy of description as poetry. With these reservations in mind, we may nonetheless survey what may be called religious poetry in Chinese.

The earliest anthology of Chinese poetry, the *Shih ching* (The Book of Songs), consisting of three hundred and five poems dating from about 1100 to about 600 BCE, contains some hymns to royal ancestral spirits, eulogizing their virtues and praying for their blessing. These hymns are believed to have been sung to the accompaniment of dance. In these and some other poems in the anthology, references are made to a supreme supernatural being known sometimes as Ti ("emperor") or Shang-ti ("emperor above"), and at other times as T'ien ("Heaven"). The first term, which is often translated as "God," appears to denote an earlier and more anthropomorphic concept than does T'ien. For instance, in the poem *Sheng-min* (The Birth of Our People), which recounts the myth of the miraculous birth of Hou Chi ("King Millet"), the reputed ancestor of the Chou people, Hou Chi's mother, Chiang Yüan, is said to have conceived him after treading in the print of Ti's big toe. By contrast, Heaven is generally depicted as a vague presence without specific physical attributes, sometimes wrathful but usually benevolent.

Some shamanistic songs from the kingdom of Ch'u, which flourished in the central Yangtze Valley from the seventh to the third century BCE, are preserved in the next oldest anthology of Chinese poetry, the *Ch'u-tz'u* (Songs of Ch'u), compiled in the second century CE. These songs are dedicated to various deities, such as the Lord of the East (the sun god), the Lord of Clouds, and the Lord of the Yellow River. In these songs, the relationship between the male shaman and the goddess or between the female shaman and the god is described in terms of erotic love. The sex of the speaker is not always clear: we cannot always be sure whether it is a male shaman addressing a goddess or a female shaman addressing a god. The shaman may also speak in the voice of the deity. Traditionally, these and other poems in the *Ch'u-tz'u* are attributed to Ch'ü Yüan (343?–278 BCE), said to have been a loyal courtier of Ch'u who was unjustly banished and who committed suicide by drowning himself in the Mi-lo River. He is generally believed to be the author of the longest poem in the anthology, the *Li-sao,* whose title is usually translated as "Encountering Sorrow," although the term may simply mean "complaints." In this poem the speaker sets out upon a journey through the cosmos, in a carriage drawn by dragons and heralded by phoenixes, attended by the gods of the winds and of thunder. He also courts certain goddesses without success, and finally resolves to "follow P'eng Hsien," an ancient shaman. Chinese commentators have generally taken this to mean a resolution to commit suicide but the modern scholar David Hawkes interprets it as a desire to study the occult. Although it is difficult to be sure how far the mythological figures in the poem are intended to be taken literally and how far allegorically, the poem certainly derives some of its imagery from a shamanistic cult; it has even been suggested that Ch'ü Yüan was a shaman.

During the Han dynasty (206 BCE–220 CE), the court's Bureau of Music (Yüeh-fu) composed ritual hymns to be used at the sacrifices made to imperial ancestral spirits. Similar hymns existed in later dynasties. They usually show a stilted style and have no great poetic merit. It was during the Han period that Taoism evolved from its early philosophic origins into an organized religion. At this time too, Buddhism was first introduced into China, although it did not become popular at once. Following the Han period, Chinese poets were mostly either eclectic or syncretic, and might express Confucian, Taoist, or Buddhist views in different poems or even all of them in the same poem. However, in the works of some poets, the propensity to one of the three major ideologies is fairly pronounced. The following are some of the most famous examples.

Ts'ao Chih (192–232 CE) wrote several poems about Taoist immortals, but it is difficult to say whether he really believed in them. The same may be said of Juan Chi (210–263), who in some of his poems expressed a wish for immortality but in others showed frank skepticism. Scholars disagree about the religious and philosophical beliefs of T'ao Ch'ien (365?–427), whose withdrawal from officialdom was probably motivated by both Confucian ideals of integrity and Taoist wishes for simplicity and spontaneity. Although his poetry expresses both Confucian and Taoist views, his emphasis on following nature and his acceptance of death as a part of the eternal flux are more Taoist than Confucian. The landscape poetry of Hsieh Ling-yün (385–433) evinces both Buddhist and Taoist influences. To him, natural scenery is a manifestation of spirituality, yet the self-conscious philosophizing in his poems suggests an inability to transcend worldly concerns.

During the T'ang dynasty (618–907), the golden age of Chinese poetry, Taoism and Buddhism flourished, except during the reign of Emperor Wu-tsung (846–859), who persecuted the Buddhists. Many T'ang poets were influenced by Taoism or Buddhism or both, although none openly rejected Confucianism. By coincidence, the three greatest T'ang poets, Wang Wei (699?–761), Li Po (701–762), and Tu Fu (712–770), are considered to represent Buddhism, Taoism, and Confucianism respectively in their poetry, albeit not exclusively. Wang Wei, known as the Buddha of Poetry, wrote some explicitly Buddhist poems as well as others that embody a Buddhist vision of life without specific Buddhist references. In addition, he wrote court poems and social poems. His best poetry conveys a sense of tranquillity tinged with sadness as he quietly contemplates nature; the poems explicitly preaching Buddhism are less satisfactory as poetry. Li Po, the Immortal of Poetry, received a Taoist diploma and took "elixirs of life," which may have contributed to his death. Many of his poems express a yearning for the realm of the immortals and a wish to transcend this world, although they show him also to be far from indifferent to sensual pleasures such as wine, women, and song. Whether he succeeded in attaining Taoist transcendence or not, Li Po certainly found Taoist mythology a source of poetic inspiration and a stimulus to his exuberant imagination. Tu Fu, the Sage of Poetry, wrote mainly poetry with a Confucian outlook, although some of his poems refer to Taoist elixirs of life and others evince admiration for Buddhism. Perhaps, however, these are only signs of wishful thinking or polite expressions of respect for the beliefs of others.

Among late T'ang poets, Han Yü (768–824), the self-appointed champion of Confucianism, attacked Buddhism and Taoism, yet befriended some Buddhist monks. Po Chü-i (772–846) was strongly influenced by Buddhism and also experimented with Taoist alchemy. The calm and bland tone of his typical poems may result from Buddhist influence. Li Ho (791–817) wrote much about spirits, ghosts, and shamans, but it is difficult to ascertain whether he believed in these literally or used them figuratively. Li Shang-yin (813?–858) studied Taoism in his youth and was converted to Buddhism toward the end of his life. There are many allusions to Taoist mythology in his poetry, which is, however, seldom of a religious nature.

The best-known corpus of Chinese Buddhist poetry is that attributed to Han-shan ("cold mountain"), a legendary figure of whose historical existence we have little knowledge. Indeed, some scholars believe, on the basis of internal linguistic evidence, that the poems bearing Han-shan's name were by two or more hands and that they range in date from the late seventh to the ninth centuries. The best among these poems are quietly meditative with a touch of gentle melancholy, and the worst are short sermons in doggerel. Apart from Han-shan, some Ch'an masters wrote *gāthā* (a kind of hymn) in verse. These were intended as triggers to enlightenment, to be discarded as soon as enlightenment was attained, not as poetry to be read and cherished.

During the Sung dynasty (960–1279), considered second only to the T'ang in poetic achievements, such major poets as Wang An-shih (1021–1086), Su Shih (1037–1101), and Huang T'ing-chien (1045–1105) all wrote poetry chiefly expressing Buddhist views. In subsequent periods, the literati continued to write poetry reflecting Confucian, Taoist, and Buddhist attitudes, and Buddhist and Taoist priests continued to use verses in their respective rituals and sermons, even though such verses were not regarded as poetry. As for contemporary Chinese poetry, in the People's Republic of China there is hardly any poetry that can be called religious, whereas in Taiwan a few poets show Buddhist or Christian tendencies, but they are only a small minority.

BIBLIOGRAPHY

Ch'en, Kenneth. *The Chinese Transformation of Buddhism.* Princeton, 1973. Contains a chapter on Buddhist influence on Chinese poets, especially Po Chü-i.

Hawkes, David, ed. and trans. *Ch'u Tz'u, The Songs of the South* (1959). Reprint, Boston, 1962. Complete translation of the anthology of chiefly shamanistic songs.

Karlgren, Bernhard, ed. and trans. *The Book of Odes* (1950). Reprint, Stockholm, 1974. Literal translation of the *Shih ching.* See the ritual hymns to ancestral spirits.

Waley, Arthur. *The Poetry and Career of Li Po, 701–762 A.D.*

New York, 1950. Contains discussions of Li Po's interest in Taoism.

Watson, Burton, trans. *Cold Mountain: 100 Poems by the T'ang Poet Han-shan* (1962). Reprint, New York, 1970. Selected poems attributed to the monk Han-shan.

Yu, Pauline. *The Poetry of Wang Wei*. Bloomington, Ind., 1980. Contains translations and discussions of Wang's Buddhist poems.

James J. Y. Liu

Japanese Religious Poetry

Most scholars dealing either with Japanese literature or with Japanese religion tend to agree that the interweaving of poetry with the values and modes of religious experience has been an especially significant and perduring aspect of Japanese cultural life. The term *religio-aesthetic,* while itself less than satisfactory, is often applied to this phenomenon and recognizes the tendency in Japanese culture to link the literary and religious experiences. Scholarship on this topic is rich in Japanese and growing in Western languages as well. Here the focus will be on poetry and the topic presented historically.

In the Japanese case the threshold between prose and poetry can be quite easily crossed. Since at least the middle of the seventh century this transition is usually considered to have been made when a given speaker begins to speak in relatively discrete phrases comprising sets of either five or seven syllables. Although longer forms existed, the classical *uta* or *waka* (the latter simply meaning "Japanese verse") has since then been comprised usually of a sequence of lines with a 5-7-5-7-7 syllable count; *haikai* and *haiku,* developed much later, consist of 5-7-5 syllables. This purely quantitative demarcation of poetry from prose does not, of course, differentiate finer examples from inferior types; it does, however, demonstrate why verse can be composed with relative ease and why a "rhythm" of orderly quantitative units can, when recited, be easily lent to liturgical, incantational, and apotropaic uses. The myths expressive of the archaic, Shintō worldview, although inscribed in the eighth century in Chinese characters, include whole poems in the 5-7 syllable count; an important example in the *Kojiki* is that in which Princess Nunakawa is wooed by the Eight-Thousand-Spears-Deity (Donald L. Philippi, trans., *Kojiki,* Princeton, 1968, pp. 104ff.). Similarly in early poetry the frequent affixing of simple prefixes to nouns raised their referents not only to honor but even to divine or semidivine status. The relative ease with which the technical passage from prose to poetry could be managed mirrored the freely permeable line between *kami* (divinity) and all else.

As the tradition of Japanese court poetry developed—especially in the Nara (710–784) and Heian (794–1191) periods—its diction evidenced a Shintō sensibility. Things deemed either socially or ritually "unclean" were excluded from the allowable diction and, thereby, from the world of poetry: death or bloodshed, for instance, either went unmentioned or was filtered through circumlocutions. Amorous exchanges were affirmed—but in terms of unencumbered emotional expression rather than bodily functions. Also during this period the priestly and magical uses of poetry were widely explored; Hartmut O. Rotermund's *Majinai-uta* (1973) traces these uses of poetry to early times and presents the findings of extensive Japanese scholarship on the topic. The early era's premier lyric expression is the mid-eighth-century collection, the *Man'yōshū;* it reflects an epoch when the Japanese did not yet "reflect on the meaning of meaning" because they were not yet self-conscious about the symbolization process in which they participated "naturally and fully" (Joseph M. Kitagawa, "Reality and Illusion: Some Characteristics of the Early Japanese 'World of Meaning'," *Journal of the Oriental Society of Australia* 11, 1976, p. 10).

This situation changed with the steady and strong impact of continental religions and philosophies, especially Buddhism. Buddhism was officially introduced in either 538 or 552 CE but did not greatly influence poetry until after the *Man'yōshū.* Around that time it began to gain a position of cultural and intellectual hegemony—a position retained in Japan for approximately a millennium—even though Shintō, Confucian, and Taoist elements were incorporated into the comprehensive religious synthesis of the medieval period. My *The Karma of Words* (1983) explores this development and especially the much vexed problem of the exact relationship between the practice of Buddhism and that of the poet.

Basically the vocation of the poet came to be conceived by many as a religious "way" or "path." This conception was articulated in a variety of forms. Some employed *waka* apotropaically and called it a form of *dhāraṇi* (Jpn., *darani*) so that the indigenous form, especially when recited in ritual contexts, was regarded as having the same kind of healing or protective power as the classical Buddhist formulas thought to be derived from India and Śākyamuni himself. This identification with Buddhist thought accorded immense prestige to *waka* and was indicative of the high regard in which the native language was held.

A vexatious moral and spiritual point for many Buddhists, especially tonsured monks, was the potential incompatibility between their vows as world-renouncers and the conventions of *waka*, one of which was that the truly proficient poet ought to write verse with a certain passion for beautiful things and even, at times, with a delicately rendered eroticism. This problem caused a few Buddhists at least to abandon the writing of verse; many others, however, argued their way around it. An important precedent for working out solutions to the conflict was the highly respected Chinese poet Po Chü-i (772–846) who, while referring to his verse as nothing more than "floating phrases and fictive utterances" (when compared to the *sūtras*), dedicated his poems to Buddhist temples and stated that the writing of poetry, his own "karma of words," would remain an activity throughout his life. In Japan it was primarily the monk Saigyō (1118–1190) who became for later generations the paragon of Buddhist poets. His principal passion seems to have been for the beauties of the natural world, especially the moon and Japanese cherry blossoms. An intensely religious person, he agonized over this perceived conflict but finally found a solution, one that he identified as his own *satori* or enlightenment.

omoikaesu	Today's satori:
satori ya kyō wa	Such a change of mind would
nakaramashi	Not exist without
hana ni someoku	My lifelong habit of having
iro nakariseba	My mind immersed in blossoms.

Other poets pressed the implications of the Mahāyāna logical development, which maintained that there could be no *nirvāṇa* apart from *saṃsāra*. The poet and critic Fujiwara Shunzei (1114–1204), a devout Buddhist, suggested in his *Korai Fūteishō* that, although the Japanese did not have a long line of Buddhist patriarchs comparable to those of the Indians and Chinese, their sequence of poetry anthologies was a functional and religious equivalent. These arguments seem to have won the day in Japan, but there remained some who felt the need to reject such equivalences; the eminent Zen master Dōgen (1200–1253) is portrayed as having taken that position, although he himself wrote some fine verse on Buddhist themes.

The new impact of and prestige accorded to Chinese Zen that commenced with the Kamakura period (1192–1333) led eventually to Japanese temples and monasteries becoming overseas enclaves of Chinese culture. Not only did many monks travel to China; they were also bilingual (at least in written forms) and wrote Chinese verse that was praised even by the Chinese. The classics, Taoist lore, and occasional didacticism in the Confucian style became part of this Japanese poetry in Chinese; moreover, as these Zen monks were patronized by the rich and powerful for their learning, their knowledge of Confucianism became more important than their religious vocations. Others, however, forged their Zen meditations into the basis for remarkable poetic visions; the monks Ikkyū Sōjun (1394–1481) and Ryōkan (1758–1831) are especially noteworthy examples.

One development of special importance was the intentional rejection of allegorical—including religious—significations in much verse of the medieval and modern periods, although one of the stimuli for this rejection was Mahāyāna philosophy itself. Even though by Western standards this trend might be seen as simple secularization, it was in fact a religious development. The trend moved from *waka* to *haiku*. Scholarly opinion differs about the Zen involvement of the principal *haiku* poet, Matsuo Bashō (1644–1694), who thought of himself as neither exactly a priest nor a layman ("like a bat, neither bird nor mouse"). He at least practiced the primary Buddhist principle of "right seeing" and wrote verses of extraordinary clarity about the natural world, usually without overt religious symbols or sentiments. Typical is the following, justly famous poem:

shizukasa ya	The quietness:
iwa ni shimiiru	Shrill cicada cries
semi no koe	Soaked into boulders.

Especially during the eighteenth century the Kokugaku, or school of National Learning, flourished. It was both scholarly and atavistic, although the research of its major figure, Motoori Norinaga (1730–1801), recaptured much of the spirit of the earliest period's lyrical and emotional emphasis. This movement advocated disengagement from imported Buddhist and Confucian ideas and values; during the nineteenth and first half of the twentieth centuries it was easily turned toward nationalistic sentiments and causes, although its earlier, major figures had primarily intended a reappreciation of archaic Shintō and the lyric spirit.

Two of the most self-consciously Buddhist poets of the twentieth century have been Miyazawa Kenji (1896–1933) and Takahashi Shinkichi (b. 1901), both treated by Makoto Ueda in his *Modern Japanese Poets and the Nature of Literature* (Stanford, 1983). Miyazawa Kenji was a scientist, author of engaging children's fantasies, devotee of Nichiren Buddhism and the Lotus Sutra, and writer of free verse; his fusion of scientific knowledge with the Lotus Sutra's vision of the universe is powerful, and he is already revered as something of a saint and religious visionary of the twentieth century. Takahashi Shinkichi wrote free verse informed by Zen; he arrived at this style through his earlier involvement with the European Dada movement. Christianity, although a sometimes significant influence on modern fiction, has had only a negligible impact on the writing of important verse in Japan, although narratives and symbols derived from the Bible are occasionally employed by poets.

BIBLIOGRAPHY

LaFleur, William R. *The Karma of Words: Buddhism and the Literary Arts in Medieval Japan*. Berkeley, 1983.

Plutschow, Herbert. "Is Poetry a Sin? *Honjisuijaku* and Buddhism versus Poetry." *Oriens Extremus* 25 (1979): 206–218.

Pollack, David. *Zen Poems of the Five Mountains*. New York, 1985.

Rotermund, Hartmut O. *Majinai-uta: Grundlagen, Inhalte und Formelemente japonischer magischer Gedichte des 17.–20. Jahrhunderts*. Tokyo, 1973.

Sanford, James H. *Zen-Man Ikkyū*. Chico, Calif., 1981.

WILLIAM R. LAFLEUR

Christian Poetry

Any consideration of the interplay between the predominant religion of European culture and the poetry that developed within its influence should properly begin with the textual legacy of sacred scripture. For in the Bible there is a fund of images, narrative reference, rhetorical formulas, and mythic patterns that for centuries has served as a powerful source for Western poetry, no matter whether a specific work is explicitly religious (or devotional) in nature or whether it is simply presumptive of a Christian interpretative context.

Origins: The Hymn. The earliest example of Christian poetry, the hymn, is also the most immediately expressive of doctrine and tradition. Its biblical precursors can be traced to the Hebrew psalms and the Lucan canticles (e.g., Magnificat and Nunc dimittis), in addition to fragments of apostolic hymns found both in the Pauline letters (e.g., *Eph.* 5:19, *2 Tm.* 2:15) and in the *Book of Revelation* (5:13–14). Like the Christian liturgy itself, Christian poetry was first composed in Greek. By the mid-fourteenth century, however, there existed compilations of Latin hymns by Hilary of Poitiers (d. 367) and Ambrose of Milan (d. 397), both of whom composed their texts for liturgical use. Prudentius (d. 410), best known for the allegorical poem that was to have such influence on medieval portrayals of the struggle between virtue and vice—the *Psychomachia*—also wrote many didactic hymns in a variety of meters not intended specifically for worship. The Latin hymnic tradition continued with works that were to have great influence on subsequent Christian literature: the *Vexilla regis* of Venantius Fortunatus (d. 610), the hymns of Peter Abelard (d. 1142) and Thomas Aquinas (d. 1274), and most important of all, the *Dies irae*, ascribed to Thomas of Celano (d. 1260). To the Franciscan Jacopone da Todi (d. 1306) is attributed not only the *Stabat mater dolorosa*, but also over one hundred hymns, or *laudes*, written in Italian. This tradition of vernacular poetry was nurtured in Franciscan circles and traditionally begins with Francis of Assisi (d. 1226) and his still renowned *Canticle of the Sun*.

Middle Ages. In England Christian poetry in the vernacular was inaugurated by Cædmon (d. around 680), whose Anglo-Saxon hymn to God the Creator is also the first extant poem in our language. Also attributed to him (if not to Cynewulf, a poet of the ninth century) is *The Dream of the Rood*, a visionary work in which the cross confronts the poet with an account of Christ's passion and resurrection, bidding him to follow the path of the rood thereafter in his own life. The culmination of Anglo-Saxon poetry, however, is the epic *Beowulf* (dated between 675 and 750), wherein pagan Germanic heroic traditions show signs of adaptation to the newer Christian sensibility.

The flowering of Christian medieval poetry in England occurs in the latter part of the fourteenth century. Both the *Pearl* and *Piers Plowman*, two anonymous Middle English poems, combine dream vision and allegory, a sense of spiritual crisis and the hope of victory in heaven. The most important work of this period, however, is Chaucer's *Canterbury Tales* (begun in 1386 and incomplete at the poet's death in 1400). Set within the popular medieval framework of a pilgrimage, this collection of Middle English poems represents a wide panorama of character types and narrative forms that draw heavily on French and Italian models. The work as a whole is an intriguing blend of sacred and profane, containing traditional saints' legends, as recounted by the Prioress and the Second Nun, as well as romances, as told by the Knight and the Squire, and bawdry, as employed by the Miller and the Wife of Bath. Contemporary criticism has argued over the extent to which the *Tales* should be given a Christian reading; D. W. Robertson, Jr.'s *Preface to Chaucer* (Princeton, 1962) offers the most eloquent case for doing so. Suffice it to say that whatever the case in this or that particular poem, Chaucer's work, as a whole, is unthinkable outside a Christian context.

The same might be said for the dominant form of early French vernacular poetry, the *chansons de geste*, which date from the eleventh and twelfth centuries and signal the beginning of French literature. Following the conclusions of Joseph Bédier's *Les légendes epiques* (1926–1929), most scholars consider that these narrative works, set in the ninth-century Age of Charlemagne, actually originated in churches and monasteries whose monks linked their own shrines to events, at once historical and legendary, that were associated with Charlemagne. The *Chanson de Roland,* set against the background of war with the Saracens for control of Spain and telling in particular of the battle of Roncevaux, presents characters who have become classics in Western literature: the impetuous warrior Roland (the "Orlando" of later romance-epic); the patriarchal monarch Charlemagne; the sage counselor Olivier; the priest-warrior Turpin; the traitor Ganelon. The twelfth-century Oxford manuscript of the poem, which is its earliest extant version (c. 1170), reflects a christianization of materials coming from earlier, less religious sources. It extols Christianity, chivalry, and patriotism; for even though it portrays the folly of Roland's pursuit of personal fame and glory at the expense of Christian empire and the common cause, nonetheless, when Archbishop Turpin gives the fallen Roland his blessing and commends his soul to the safekeeping of Saint Gabriel, the errant hero is sufficiently absolved to become a kind of epic saint in subsequent handling of the legend, known as the *matière de France.*

The inaugural work of Spanish literature, the *Cantar de mio Cid* (c. 1140), shares with the *Chanson de Roland* not only certain literary models but the memory of feudal Germanic custom as well as a substratum of historical event. The poem, based on the life of an eleventh-century military leader, relates the misfortunes and ultimate triumph of Rodrigo Díaz de Vivar, who, although unjustly exiled by the sovereign of Castile, remains a faithful vassal, one who continuously sends back booty from battle with the Moors; when grossly misused by perfidious noblemen, he leaves the retribution of justice to King Alfonso, the monarch who has banished him. In the course of the poem (and subsequently in Spanish mystique) Díaz, or "el Cid," becomes a paragon of justice and bravery. A pious deathbed scene, attributed by scholars to a later (and monastic) hand, attempts to bring the poem more resolutely within a Christian framework. And yet, like the *Chanson de Roland,* Spain's epic is more a celebration of battle against "the Infidel," as well as of loyalty to the anointed lord, than it is a seriously Christian poem.

A later development in narrative poetry, which turned its attention from battlefield to court, is the romance. Critics disagree over whether it arose as a sentimentalization of earlier epic materials such as the *chansons de geste* or whether, on the other hand, it represents a hearkening back to late classical models. In any event, it concerns itself with the characters and events of King Arthur's court (known as the *matière de Bretagne*) and has at its center an ideal of chivalry and a preoccupation with love, which it portrays as ennobling when sublimated in the chaste pursuit of excellence, but disastrous (both personally and socially) when acted out in adultery. Although Chrétien de Troyes (d. around 1180) was certainly not the originator of romance poetry, it is he who brought the genre to flower in French with his poems *Erec, Yvain, Lancelot,* and the unfinished *Perceval*—the story of a simple knight whose feudal service, transcending that owed to king or lady, is given to the pursuit of the Grail, a complex symbol of religious mystery associated with Christ's passion and resurrection. [*See also* Arthur *and* Grail, The.]

A fuller and far more profound working of this material is offered by Wolfram von Eschenbach (d. around 1220), whose *Parzival,* written between 1200 and 1210, introduced the Grail theme into German literature and brought both epic and romance to a new level of spiritual profundity that places Wolfram in the same lofty sphere as Dante. Building on Chrétien's tale of the "guileless fool" who through innocence and faithful commitment attains a goal that evades those who are wise in the ways of the world, *Parzival* describes a quasi-allegorical pilgrimage through error, pride, despair, and repentance, undertaken in order to attain the most distinctive of Christian virtues, humility. In its possession, Parzival is able not only to be keeper of the Grail—a paradisiacal stone representing the love of God—but also to assume the role of king among a circle of knights whose ideals are set infinitely higher than the loves and adventures that characterize the traditional Arthurian court. The poem is notable for its inauguration of the *Bildungsroman,* which, along with the Grail story itself, has had such a powerful impact on subsequent German literature. *Parzival* also shares some of the essential qualities (though none of the superficial) that distinguish the greatest medieval poem of pilgrimage and vision, Dante's *Commedia.*

Written between the time of Dante's exile from Florence in 1302 and his death in 1321, the *Commedia* is an unparalleled synthesis of theological reflection and literary form, in which hymn and allegory, epic and romance, spiritual pilgrimage and personal *Bildungsroman* are all brought together in a narrative of enduring appeal, as well as of profound religious depth. Set against a typology of Exodus and Deliverance, which is enhanced by the story's unfolding between the evening of Good Friday and the Wednesday of Easter Week in the year 1300, the poem recounts Dante's exploration of the state of the soul after death in a journey that takes him from hell through purgatory to paradise, and culminates in the beatific vision (left undescribed, of course, at the close of the final canto). In the course of this experience, which unites the journeys of Aeneas and the apostle Paul even as it surpasses them with its own totality, he is guided first by Vergil, the paragon of poetry, natural reason, and the dream of empire, and then by Beatrice, the woman who in life represented for Dante the transforming love of God in Christ and on whose behalf the poet promised earlier in the *Vita nuova* (1295) to offer such praise as no other beloved had ever received. Critics have noted Dante's debt to classical poets (whom, indeed, he draws on extensively--especially Vergil, Ovid, Lucan, and Statius—at the same time that he transforms them for his own Christian purposes), as well as his connection to medieval accounts of earthly pilgrimage and heavenly vision. Theologically, he unites Thomistic clarity with the ardor of Augustinian and Franciscan traditions. And yet what remains astonishing is the sheer originality of the work, which mixes what the fourteenth century knew about the ancient world with a very contemporary appraisal of the poet's own time—all of it filtered through the personal experience of Dante Alighieri himself (who, like Augustine in the *Confessions*, is both the wise author and the developing subject of the same work). The sixteenth century was to call the *Commedia* "divine," an adjective that later centuries have continued to find appropriate. Indeed, in the intricately constructed plan of the hundred cantos of this epic, Christian poetry attains a scope of reference and a depth of resonance that are rivaled (if at all) only by John Milton's *Paradise Lost*. [*See the biography of Dante.*]

The Renaissance. With the exception of the fourteenth-century English works noted above, the great religious movements and controversies of Europe did not after Dante produce poetry of major significance until the mid-sixteenth century. In the latter years of that century there is unmistakably evident a Christian poetic renaissance in the form of both long narrative works and meditational, or devotional, lyrics. Within the former category we find the Portuguese *Os Lusíadas* (1572), a Vergilian celebration of the voyage of Vasco da Gama to India and of his return via the Cape of Good Hope. This national epic, composed by Luis de Camões (d. 1580), tells its near-contemporary tale in mythic terms, mingling together history, Catholic religion, and the pagan Roman pantheon of the *Aeneid*. In this poem West meets East and attempts to conquer a paradise otherwise lost to Europe. Within its epic machinery, moreover, there is the working of Camões's own curious syncretism: his blending of Christianity with Neoplatonism and of pagan religion with Portuguese national (and religious) piety.

Writing at almost the same time, but closer to the censorious arm of the Counter-Reformation, Torquato Tasso (d. 1595) published his *Gerusalemme liberata* in 1581. Although he was heir to the secular romances of Boiardo and Ariosto, with their reworking of the old Arthurian material, Tasso set out instead to produce a truly Christian epic, and for this purpose he chose the subject of Godfrey of Bouillon's retaking of Jerusalem from the Saracens during the First Crusade. Although replete with the requisite battle scenes and amatory interludes of the romance-epic, he intended the poem to be read allegorically as the struggle of the soul to overcome every sort of temptation (and perhaps especially those of the flesh) in order to achieve salvation. Whatever his noble intentions, the text caused him difficulties with the Inquisition; consequently he republished it in revised form under the title *Gerusalemme conquistata* (1593), thereby achieving the requisite piety, but only at the cost of poetic interest and integrity.

The epic poem (like the Renaissance itself) came relatively late to Protestant England, but found its belated poet in Edmund Spenser (d. 1599), whose *Faerie Queene* (published in parts between 1590 and 1609), although unfinished according to its original plan, nonetheless succeeded in realizing its partial goals: the incorporation of Vergilian epic into medieval (as well as Italian) romance, a multileveled allegory, an expression of the Reformed religious sensibility, and a celebration of Elizabethan England and its Virgin Queen (the model for that Gloriana who, while never seen in the poem's Faeryland, motivates all virtuous action). Book 1, the "Legend of Holiness," is the most explicitly theological of the six books that Spenser lived to complete. Its Red Cross Knight struggles against the various avatars of wickedness in order to champion Una, the true (English) church, and in so doing to realize his identity as England's patron, Saint George. The rest of the poem is preoccupied with the vicissitudes of the moral life and the cultivation of the virtues of temperance, chastity, friendship, justice, and courtesy, each of which is championed by a representative knight and exercised in a successful combat with evil. Pervading the entire work, however, is the sense of incomplete victory and of an unfulfilled longing, the desire for a vision of peace that can never be attained in this life, whether in the Faeryland of the poem or in the sixteenth-century world to which its "dark conceit" refers. In the end, in the fragmentary "Mutabilitie Cantos," the poet places his sole faith in a heavenly city built "upon the pillours of Eternitie."

Seventeenth Century. In the first half of the seventeenth century there is evident an enormous and rich outpouring of religious verse, lyric rather than epic, which is commonly characterized, after Samuel Johnson, as "metaphysical" or, since Louis Martz (1954), as "the poetry of meditation." It is distinguished by its delight in wit, learning, and paradox, and most especially by its cultivation of farfetched metaphors or "conceits." Examples can be drawn from the poetry of Italy, Spain, France, and Germany, but it is in England that the metaphysical poem found its fullest Christian expression; its foremost exponents were John Donne (d. 1631), George Herbert (d. 1633), Richard Crashaw (d. 1649), Thomas Traherne (d. 1674), and Henry Vaughan (d. 1695). With the exception of the Welsh doctor Vaughan, all were ordained priests in the Anglican church (but Crashaw later became a Roman cleric). To a greater or lesser extent, all drew upon the techniques of religious meditation that mingle a vivid reimagining of biblical scenes, intense self-scrutiny, and an orientation of the self toward God. In this group Crashaw is in every way the anomaly, drawing as he does on the more extravagantly Baroque continental sensibility typified by the convolution and artificiality of, for example, Giambattista Marino (d. 1625). But even among the more thoroughly English Anglicans, there is a wide range of feeling: the splendid self-absorption of Donne as he worries about his own salvation; the artful self-diminution of Herbert, with his exquisitely wrought lyrics of surrender to a loving Master; the mystically esoteric Traherne; the meditations of Henry Vaughan upon nature, a preoccupation that links him in anticipatory ways to William Wordsworth and the High Romantics.

John Milton (d. 1674) tried his hand at this sort of meditational poetry in the early ode entitled *On the Morning of Christ's Nativity.* But the religious lyric was never to engage his poetic imagination. To be sure, religious controversy and theological reflection preoccupied him his entire life and filled many volumes of prose as well. But it was not until his political hopes in Cromwell's Commonwealth had been frustrated and the monarchy subsequently restored in 1660 that the "sacred muse" returned—and then with an astonishing afflatus of poetry that took its "graver subject" from moments of scriptural history: the fall of Adam and Eve, the death of Samson, Christ's temptation in the wilderness. Following the example of the Huguenot Guillaume du Bartas (d. 1590) in the composition of a biblical epic, Milton made in *Paradise Lost* (1667) a deliberate decision to turn away from classical or romance themes, at the same time, of course, as he incurred openly a vast debt to Vergil on the one hand and Spenser on the other. (His later works, *Paradise Regained* and *Samson Agonistes,* both published in 1671, draw upon Greek dramatic form.) At the center of all three poems there stands an individual "sufficient to have stood, though free to fall," and in each case Milton undertakes an exploration of exactly what this sufficiency consists of: the exercise of right reason over against the appeal of lesser appetites. As in his prose writings against monarchy and episcopacy and as in those advocating freedom of speech and of divorce, the author of the poems assumes the role of prophet. This voice is especially audible in *Paradise Lost,* where again and again he claims the inspiration of the Holy Spirit in his articulation of what scripture has chosen to say little (or nothing) about. Dante too claimed enormous authority for his poetic undertaking, but while he dared to speak prophetically to his age, he did so as a Roman Catholic, as a loyal (if contentious) son of the "universal" church; Milton, by contrast, was in the composition of his great poems a denomination of one, a solitary church.

Milton's poetic enterprise is strangely Janus-faced. Late in the seventeenth century, almost as if he were resolutely looking backward, he chose unfashionable biblical subject matter and an epic genre so played out that by the end of the century it could only be mocked in satire. On the other hand, his portraits of divinity (and perhaps especially of God the Father in *Paradise Lost*) have an Enlightenment chill, as if they had passed over into a pantheon of deities no longer believed in. But perhaps the authentically religious note in Milton's poetry is rather to be found in his magnificent evocation of the physical beauties of heaven and earth as well as in the poignancy of his presentation of humanity itself—poised between innocence and experience and between obedience and rebellion, engaged in the process of choosing a self to become. It is in such emphases as these that we can anticipate the Romantic movement that was to follow upon Milton's death by a century, arriving at a time when poetry throughout Europe seems to have cut loose from the moorings of Christian tradition in order to explore new unorthodoxies of the spirit and imagination.

[*For discussion of subsequent developments in Western literature, see* Literature, *especially the article on* Religious Dimensions of Modern Literature, *and* Drama, *articles on* European Religious Drama *and* Modern Western Theater.]

BIBLIOGRAPHY

Christianity is so interwoven into the fabric of European poetry up through the seventeenth century that any worthwhile study of Dante, Chaucer, or Milton will of necessity explore the interconnection between poetry and belief. In *The Great Code: The Bible and Literature* (New York, 1982) Northrop Frye begins with the Christian urtext and suggests the degree to which scripture informs literary culture in the West. Ernst Robert Curtius in his *European Literature in the Latin Middle Ages* (Princeton, 1953) and Erich Auerbach in his *Mimesis: The Representation of Reality in Western Literature* (Princeton, 1953) have produced classic studies of the foundations and development of European poetry, which also offer invaluable insight into the interaction of Christianity with its pagan inheritance. Helen Flanders Dunbar's *Symbolism in Medieval Thought and Its Consummation in the Divine Comedy* (New Haven, 1929) establishes a religious and cultural context not only for Dante but for medieval poetry in general. Sensitive study of the role of Christianity in the formation of European poetry is also offered in R. S. Loomis's *The Grail: From Celtic Myth to Christian Symbol* (New York, 1963), C. S. Lewis's *The Allegory of Love* (Oxford, 1936), Louis L. Martz's *The Poetry of Meditation* (New Haven, 1954), Helen Gardner's *Religion and Literature* (Oxford, 1971), and A. D. Nuttall's *Overheard by God: Fiction and Prayer in Herbert, Milton, Dante, and St. John* (New York, 1980).

PETER S. HAWKINS

Islamic Poetry

Since its founding in the early seventh century CE, Islam has become the dominant religion in various cultural and linguistic areas, all of which have produced religious poetry. This article is limited to the classical languages of Islamic literature, Arabic and Persian, and to a few of the vernaculars of lands that are parts of present-day Turkey, Afghanistan, Pakistan, and India.

Arabic. Early Islam was not entirely friendly to poetry: a well-known Qur'anic verse (26:226) sharply criticizes poets, and pre-Islamic poetry was much given to the praise of wine, sensual pleasure, and other kinds of worldliness forbidden by the new religion. But inevitably a religious poetry began to emerge, reaching its first important flowering around the ninth century as Sufism—the mystical current in Islam—turned from extreme asceticism to emphasis on a personal love relationship between the devotee and God. The emotional force loosed by this intimate and passionate relationship found natural expression in poetry. Important poets of the period include the Iraqi woman mystic Rābi'ah al-'Adawīyah (d. 801); the Egyptian Dhū al-Nūn (d. 859); and Sumnūn the Lover (d. after 900), Shiblī (d. 945), and the illustrious "martyr of love" al-Ḥallāj (d. 922), all of Baghdad. Their chief subject is the experience of love in its many aspects and phases—anguished separation, blissful union, endless striving to be worthy and faithful, and longing for death. [*See the biographies of Rābi'ah and al-Ḥallāj.*]

After the climactic life and work of al-Ḥallāj, Ṣūfī poetry declined in quality until the thirteenth century, which saw a new literary efflorescence. The greatest mystical writers of this period were Ibn al-'Arabī (d. 1240) and Ibn al-Fāriḍ (d. 1235). Although both wrote lyric poems, the former is far more famous for his prose treatises and the latter for his *Tā'īyah*, a rhetorically elaborate work of 750 lines on the mystic's journey to God. Even before this period the center of Ṣūfī poetic activity had shifted to Iran. [*See the biographies of Ibn al-'Arabī and Ibn al-Fāriḍ.*]

Persian. To delve into Persian poetry is to enter a world of literary conventions and stylistic intricacies that will not easily yield their secrets to a foreign reader. Hundreds of stock images and motifs—wine and tavern, moon and garden, idols and mosques, nightingales, goblets, attractive youths, veiled ladies, disheveled tresses, the heroes of love epics and their monumental struggles—are woven together in endless combinations, with endless nuances. Perhaps most difficult to grasp is the subtle interplay of spiritual and sensual. Is the lover drunk with wine, wild with passion for a handsome boy, or intoxicated with God? Often there is no clear answer.

The most important lyric form in Persian is the *ghazal*; arranged in loosely connected couplets with a single rhyme throughout, it lends itself well to the intricacy and allusiveness favored by Persian poets. The earliest short form used by mystics in Iran, going back to the eleventh century, is the *rubā'ī* or quatrain. Two longer forms should also be mentioned: the *qaṣīdah*, inherited from Arabic—a long praise poem with a single rhyme, introduced by an amatory poem out of which the *ghazal* probably developed; and the *mathnavī*, which combines narration, description, reflection, and emotional expression in rhyming couplets, the total number of lines ranging from the hundreds to the tens of thousands.

Though Iran produced many powerful religious poets, they all seem to revolve around the greatest luminary among them, Mawlānā Jalāl al-Dīn Rūmī (1207–1273), who took as his pen name the "Sun of Tabriz" and who originated the ecstatic dancing order, the Mevlevi (known in the West as the Whirling Dervishes). Two major poets who preceded him were Sanā'ī (d. around 1131) and 'Aṭṭār (d. 1221?), both of whom are better known for their *mathnavīs* than for shorter works. Aḥmad al-Ghazālī (d. 1126) and Rūzbihān Baqlī (d. 1209) also greatly influenced the development of Persian mystical poetry. [*See the biographies of Rūmī and 'Aṭṭār.*]

Rūmī was thirty-seven years old, a professor of mystical theology and the father of two adolescent boys, when his life was suddenly transformed by his meeting with a wandering dervish named Shams al-Dīn of Tabriz. The two mystics formed a passionate bond, forgetting the world, family, and disciples. After a year and a half, in response to the anger and jealousy of Rūmī's associates, Shams disappeared. It was then that Rūmī became a poet and a whirling dancer, pouring out his heartbreak at the loss of his beloved friend. The two were eventually reunited with the help of Rūmī's older son, then again irrevocably parted by the agency of the younger, who apparently contrived to have Shams murdered.

From 1245 until his death nearly thirty years later, Rūmī composed an abundant, rich, and profound body of poetry. His collection of lyrics amounts to some thirty-five thousand couplets, and his monumental *Mathnavī* is known as "the Qur'ān in the Persian tongue." "Rūmī's topics cover almost every aspect of life, but the center of his thoughts is Love" (Schimmel, 1982, p. 101). He writes much of the human beloved and much of love as an overwhelming force in itself, of love as God, sometimes even (though the expression must have been shocking) of the human beloved as scarcely distinguishable from God. His endlessly varied descriptions, says Schimmel, "seem to include all the symbols used by mystics in East and West" (Schimmel, 1982, p. 101).

Prominent among many religious poets who wrote in Persian after Rūmī are 'Irāqī (d. 1289), Maghribī (d. 1406), Ḥāfiẓ (d. 1390), and Jāmī (d. 1492). The last two display elaborate musical and rhetorical skills and use imagery so luxuriantly sensuous that the "mystical" component of their verses is especially ambiguous. In addition, a great quantity of Persian poetry was written in Muslim India—more even than in Persia. The Indo-Persian tradition, dating from the eleventh century, produced its first sophisticated poet in Amīr Khusraw (d. 1325—chiefly a court poet, but also the disciple of a Ṣūfī master). Even in the nineteenth century the great poet Ghālib, most important for his works in Urdu, also composed an extensive Persian *dīvān*. [*See the biographies of Ḥāfiẓ and Khusraw.*]

Turkish. Turkish mystical writing, traceable to the twelfth century, finds its first great poet in Yunus Emre (d. 1321). Yunus sometimes used classical Persian meters but preferred simpler Turkish folk forms; his strong and memorable verses still enjoy widespread popularity. He sang of all stages of the quest for God, using vivid descriptive imagery from the Anatolian countryside where he lived. Some of his most powerful poems, probably meant to be recited by dervishes who gathered to dance and chant God's name, flow again and again through a refrain that includes the name of Allāh. [*See the biography of Yunus.*]

The fifteenth-century poet Kaygusuz Abdāl composed eccentric, amusing, sometimes nonsensical verses closely related to Turkish folk traditions and comparable to a style of mystical poetry found in other parts of the world—a style that features paradox, humor, and deliberate craziness. Both Kaygusuz and Yunus were associated with the Bektāshī order of Ṣūfīs, which played an important role in Turkish religious life from the thirteenth to the early twentieth century. A third major poet of this order was Pir Sulṭān Abdāl (d. 1560). Prominent poets associated with other orders include 'Imāduddīn Nesīmī (d. 1417), Eşrefoğlu Rūmī (15th century), and Niyāzī Miṣrī (d. 1697). Though Kemal Atatürk abolished the Ṣūfī orders in Turkey in 1925, the mystical impulse has continued to express itself in poetry, a recent example being the work of İsmail Emre (d. 1973), who has been called the "new Yunus Emre."

Vernaculars of South Asia. Islamic piety has found vigorous expression in regional languages from Afghanistan to the southern tip of India. Statements by poets and teachers during the formative periods of these regional literatures reveal on one hand an anxious defensiveness about using a nonclassical language and on the other a deep pride in and love for the mother tongue. The latter had the advantages of freshness, intimacy, familiar imagery, and above all comprehensibility to the masses of ordinary people who knew neither Arabic nor Persian. Persian literary conventions were influential, but no more so than local folk traditions, including popular narratives and singing styles. Hindu symbolism mingled with Islamic as the *bhakti* movement reached its peak in North India between the fourteenth and seventeenth centuries. During this upsurge of popular devotional religion, Hindu and Muslim poets also shared a tendency to attack intellectualism, rote ritualism, and all sorts of elitism (caste, priesthood, officialdom).

Muslim political and cultural domination of India, from the earliest incursions in the eighth century until the death of the last figurehead emperor over a thousand years later, was concentrated in the northern two-thirds of the subcontinent. Pashto, Sindhi, Panjabi, Hindi, Urdu, and Bengali are some of the languages in which Muslims sang their praises and love for God and his Prophet. Much of the poetry has come down to us anonymously or with dubious attributions. An account of specific poets might begin with three disciples of the Ṣūfī saint Niẓām al-Dīn Awliyā', Amīr Khusraw (d. 1325), Ḥasan Dihlawī (d. 1328), and Abū 'Alī Qalandār Panīpatī (d. 1323), all of Delhi. From the late twelfth century, when Delhi became the seat of the Muslim empire, the local form of Hindi was being transformed by great numbers of Arabic and Persian words, resulting in a language that would eventually be written in the Persian script and called Urdu. This language began to distinguish itself literarily in a southern form known as Dakhni Urdu in the fifteenth and sixteenth centuries, gradually growing more sophisticated until it became a vehicle for the mystical verse of the Dakhni Ṣūfī Sīrāj Awrangābādī (d. 1765).

It was in the eighteenth century that Urdu truly came

into its own. Two important poets around the turn of the century were Bēdil (d. 1721) and Sirhindī (d. 1624), both associated, like Walī (d. 1695), with the Naqshbandī order of Ṣūfīs. The most towering figure among Urdu religious poets is Khwājah Mīr Dard (d. 1785), a prolific writer of both prose and verse, whose slim collection of Urdu lyrics is, in Schimmel's description, "of unsurpassable beauty."

Other great Urdu poets of the eighteenth and nineteenth centuries cannot be described primarily as "mystics"; but neither can they be seen as separate from the mystical tradition. The overriding theme of Urdu poetry (especially of its leading form, the *ghazal*) is love—love whose expression is steeped in the symbols and conventions inherited from the Persian tradition. In such poets as Mīr (d. 1810) and Ghālib (d. 1869), love of a human object, love as a transcendent principle, and love as the link to and very nature of God continue to be ambiguously juxtaposed with and superimposed on each other.

Further vernacular traditions can be only briefly mentioned. The foremost devotional poets in Sindhi and Panjabi, Shāh ʿAbdul Laṭīf and Bullhē Shāh, both died in the same year, 1752; and both, while they composed lyrics on many themes, are especially beloved for their mystical-poetic renderings of folk tales. Other important poets include Qāḍi Qādan (d. 1551) and Sachal Sarmast (d. 1826) in Sindhi; Mādhō Lāl Ḥusayn (d. 1593) and Sulṭān Bāhū (d. 1691) in Panjabi. The most renowned voice among mystical poets in Pashto is that of ʿAbdur-Raḥmān (d. 1709). During the fifteenth and sixteenth centuries a number of Ṣūfī poets writing in the Avadhi dialect of Hindi produced long allegorical narratives especially interesting for their mingling of Hindu and Muslim lore. Most important of these works is the *Padmāvatī* of Malik Muḥammad Jā'isī (d. after 1570). A body of lovely and powerful Islamic poetry also emerged in East Bengal (now Bangladesh). Each of these regional literatures has its own distinct marks, influenced by the particularities of place and local tradition.

Poetry in Honor of the Prophet. Throughout the history of Islam and in all the languages of the Islamic world, poets have expressed ardent praise and love for the prophet Muḥammad. As love of the Prophet has been called the strongest binding force in Islam, the theme may provide an appropriate summation for this survey of Islamic religious poetry.

The tradition begins during the Prophet's own lifetime, when his contemporaries Kaʿb ibn Zuhayr and Ḥassān ibn Thābit glorified him in verse. In subsequent centuries countless poets chose to dwell on the events of his life; the potency of his name; the hope of the pious in his intercession on the Day of Judgment; his identification with the symbolism of light; his beauty and noble qualities; his birth and ascension to heaven; his miraculous powers to cure and save.

Among the most famous composers of *naʿtīyah* poetry in Arabic is al-Būṣīrī (thirteenth century). The Persian tradition begins with Sanā'ī (twelfth century) and includes Rūmī, ʿAṭṭār, Jāmī, and Saʿdī, among many others. Examples abound in the Indian vernaculars as well as in Turkish and Swahili. All poetic styles and forms, from the simplest to the most sophisticated, are called into service to extol Muḥammad, the friend, the supreme exemplar, the "radiance of both worlds." The twentieth-century Urdu poet Muhammad Iqbal gives a hint of the theme's power and universality when he declares, "Love of the Prophet runs like blood in the veins of the community."

[*See the biographies of Iqbal and Saʿdī. See also* Sufism; Ginān; Nubūwah; *and* Samāʿ.]

BIBLIOGRAPHY

Brown, Edward Granville. *A Literary History of Persia* (1902–1921). Cambridge, 1957.

Bruijn, J. T. P. de. *Of Piety and Poetry.* Leiden, 1983.

Dermenghem, Émile, trans. *L'écloge du vin (al-khamriyya): Poème mystique de Omar ibn al-Faridh, et son commentaire par Abdel-ghani an-Nabolosi.* Paris, 1931.

Gibb, Elias John Wilkinson. *A History of Ottoman Poetry* (1900–1909). London, 1958–1963.

ʿIrāqī, Fakhruddīn. *ʿUshshāqnāma: The Song of the Lovers.* Edited and translated by A. J. Arberry. Islamic Research Association, no. 8. Oxford, 1939.

Pagliaro, Antonio, and Alessandro Bausani. *Storia della letteratura persiana.* Milan, 1960.

Ritter, Hellmut. *Das Meer der Seele: Gott, Welt und Mensch in den Geschichten Farīduddīn ʿAṭṭārs.* Leiden, 1955.

Schimmel, Annemarie. *As through a Veil: Mystical Poetry in Islam.* New York, 1982.

Schimmel, Annemarie. *And Muhammed Is His Messenger.* Chapel Hill, N.C., 1985.

LINDA HESS and ANNEMARIE SCHIMMEL

POLEMICS. [*This entry concerns the attempts of Jews, Christians, and Muslims to refute each others' principles while defending their own beliefs. It consists of three interrelated articles:*

Jewish-Christian Polemics
Muslim-Jewish Polemics
Christian-Muslim Polemics

For discussion of philosophical defenses of religious beliefs, see Apologetics.]

Jewish-Christian Polemics

[*This article focuses primarily on Jewish polemics against Christianity. For further discussion of the historical relation of Christianity to Judaism, see* Christianity and Judaism; Jesus; *and* Paul.]

The intensity, persistence, and significance of Jewish-Christian polemics are in large measure a function of the peculiar combination of intimacy and divergence that marks the relationship between the two faiths. It is not merely the fact that Christianity emerges out of Judaism; it is, further, the combination of the continuing centrality of the Hebrew Bible for Christians together with the profundity of the theological differences that separated Christians from Jews. In these respects, a comparison with Islam is particularly instructive. It too arose in large measure out of Judaism, but because it lacked the other crucial characteristics, polemic between Jews and Muslims, however important it may sometimes have been, never played the same role as did the Jewish-Christian debate. Muslims revered the Hebrew Bible; Muslims did not, however, elevate it to the position that it held in Christianity, and they expressed the most serious reservations about its textual accuracy. Moreover, Islamic monotheism left no room for the creative rancor that produced the philosophical dimension of Jewish-Christian discussions, which addressed such issues as trinitarianism and incarnation. Moses Maimonides (Mosheh ben Maimon, 1135/8–1204), who has sometimes been accused of inconsistency in his attitude toward the two other faiths, was accurately portraying a complex situation. On the one hand, he described Islam as a religion of "unblemished monotheism," an accolade he would not bestow upon Christianity; on the other hand, he maintained that teaching Torah to Christians can be a fruitful enterprise, while doing the same for Muslims is, from a Jewish point of view, an exercise in futility.

The dispute between Judaism and Christianity, then, revolved around both doctrine and exegesis. To Christians, Jesus was the Messiah, the ritual law was abrogated, and the church was the true Israel, not only because Christian scripture and tradition said so but because the Hebrew scriptures themselves supported such claims. Beginning with the New Testament and continuing with the earliest church fathers, Christian ingenuity was mobilized to uncover references to the full range of Christian beliefs in the Hebrew scriptures. The Jewish polemicist was required to undertake the onerous task of point-by-point, verse-by-verse refutation, and the sparse Talmudic references to debates with *minim* (a term for heretics that surely embraces many early Christians) describe precisely such conflicts in biblical interpretation.

The institutional separation of the two religions was furthered when a curse against the *minim* was inserted into the rabbinic prayer book, and doctrinal developments made it increasingly difficult even for "Jewish" as opposed to "gentile" Christians to remain a part of the Jewish people. The Jews, it was said, had been replaced by a new Israel, and their defeats at the hands of the Romans were a just punishment for their rejection of the Messiah; moreover, by the middle of the second century there were few Christians who did not believe in some form of Jesus' divinity, and this was a doctrine that remained beyond the pale of even the most flexible definition of Judaism.

In the wake of these developments, early Jewish sources record hostile perceptions not only of Christianity but of Jesus as well. In the Talmud itself, clear references to Jesus are exceedingly rare, but those that exist do include the assertion that he was a sorcerer who led his followers astray (cf. Goldstein, 1950). Outside the Talmudic corpus, there developed a more elaborate series of early Jewish folk tales that go by the name *Toledot Yeshu* and can probably best be described as a counter-Gospel. The various versions of *Toledot Yeshu* trace Jesus' life from his birth as a result of Mary's liaison with a Roman soldier through his checkered career as a sorcerer and on to his ignominious hanging between two thieves on a massive stalk of cabbage. Although such stories did not constitute binding Jewish doctrine, they colored Jewish views of Christianity and enraged Christians who became familiar with them in subsequent periods.

From the Jewish perspective, these early responses to Christianity remained episodic and peripheral. Before Christianity became the official religion of the Roman empire, there was little reason for Jews to confront its religious claims systematically; after that point, Jewish literary activity in the Christian world was on the wane, and before the high Middle Ages, Jewish arguments against Christianity were preserved primarily in Christian works. The only significant exceptions are a little book of eastern provenance called *Sefer Nestor ha-komer* (Book of Nestor the Priest), which was written by a convert to Judaism, and a handful of passages in Jewish philosophical works composed in the Muslim world.

In the second half of the twelfth century, this situation began to change. Partly because the inner dynamic of Christianity required a confrontation with Judaism, the "renaissance" of Christian literature and thought associated with the twelfth century included a renewal of anti-Jewish polemics. At this time Jewish literature too was in the midst of a vigorous revival, and Jews throughout western Europe began to engage in a literary polemic that was to remain active through the end of the Middle Ages.

Although this polemic extends to works of exegesis, philosophy, homiletics, and even liturgy and law, a list of explicitly polemical works through the fifteenth century can serve as a useful introduction to the scope and intensity of this activity.

- Twelfth century: Yosef Kimḥi, *Sefer ha-berit* (Book of the Covenant), southern France; Ya'aqov ben Reu'ven, *Milḥamot ha-Shem* (The Wars of the Lord), southern France.
- Thirteenth century: *Vikkuaḥ le-ha-Radaq* (The Disputation of Rabbi David Kimḥi), pseudonymous, provenance uncertain; Me'ir of Narbonne, *Milḥemet mitsvah* (The Obligatory War), southern France; Mordekhai of Avignon, *Maḥaziq emunah* (Upholder of Faith), southern France; Shelomoh de Rossi, *'Edut ha-Shem ne'emanah* (The Testimony of the Lord Is Perfect), Italy; *The Epistle of Rabbi Jacob of Venice*, Italy; *The Disputation of Rabbi Yeḥi'el of Paris*, northern France; Yosef Official, *Sefer Yosef ha-meqanne'* (The Book of Yosef the Zealot), northern France; *The Disputation of Nahmanides*, Spain; *Sefer nitstsaḥon yashan* (The Old Book of Polemic), Germany.
- Fourteenth century: Moses ha-Kohen of Tordesillas, *'Ezer ha-emunah* (Aid of Faith), Spain; Yitsḥaq Polgar, *'Ezer ha-dat* (Aid of Religion), Spain; Ḥasdai Crescas, *Biṭṭul 'iqqrei ha-Notsrim* (Refutation of Christian Doctrines), Spain; Shem Ṭov ibn Shaprut, *Even boḥan* (Touchstone), Spain; Profiat Duran, *Al tehi ka-avotekha* (Do Not Be Like Your Fathers) and *Kelimat ha-goyim* (The Shame of the Gentiles), Spain.
- Fifteenth century: Yom Ṭov Lippman Mühlhausen, *Sefer ha-nitstsaḥon* (The Book of Polemic), Bohemia; Shim'on Duran, *Qeshet u-magen* (Bow and Shield), Spain; the Tortosa Disputation, Spain; Shelomoh Duran, *Milḥemet mitsvah* (The Obligatory War), Spain; Ḥayyim ibn Musa, *Magen va-romaḥ* (Shield and Spear), Spain; Mattityahu ben Mosheh, *The Book of Aḥituv and Ẓalmon*, Spain; Binyamin ben Mosheh, *Teshuvot ha-Notsrim* (Answers to the Christians), Italy; Eliyyahu Ḥayyim of Genezzano, *Vikkuaḥ* (Disputation), Italy.

Polemics on Biblical and Philosophical Issues. Many of the issues addressed by the authors of the aforementioned works remained relatively unchanged from late antiquity through the end of the Middle Ages and beyond. To Jews, the fundamental Christian assertion that Jesus was the Messiah had been massively refuted by the evidence of history. Since the essential characteristic of the biblical Messiah involved the inauguration of an age of peace, virtually all Jewish polemicists pointed to the persistence of war and misery as a formidable refutation of Christianity. Moses Nahmanides (Mosheh ben Naḥman, c. 1194–1270), in fact, reports that he went so far as to tell James I of Aragon how difficult it would be for him and his knights if war were to be abolished.

Christians, of course, argued not only that scriptural evidence demonstrates that the Messiah had already come but also that it points to a first coming that would end in apparent failure. The key citations demonstrating these propositions were probably the most extensively debated biblical passages in the entire literature: *Genesis* 49:10 on the first point, and *Isaiah* 52:13–53:12 on the second.

"The scepter shall not pass away from Judah, nor shall a legislator pass away from among his descendants until Shiloh comes and to him shall the nations gather." This translation of *Genesis* 49:10, with *Shiloh* understood as *Messiah*, appeared to lend powerful support to the Christian position: since there was now no scepter in Judah, the Messiah must already have come. For this passage Jews did not have a particularly attractive alternative interpretation, but they did have a persuasive argument against the Christian position. That position, they said, cannot be valid because the scepter (understood by Christians as kingship) had passed from the Jews well before the time of Jesus; during the Babylonian exile there was no Jewish rule, and even during the second commonwealth there were no kings from the tribe of Judah. Although alternative explanations of this passage were beset by difficulties, they were nonetheless abundant: Shiloh indeed refers to the Messiah, but the verse is merely asserting that whenever there will be a Jewish king, he can legitimately come only from Judah; *scepter* and *legislator* refer not to kingship but to exilarchs and patriarchs or even to ongoing communal autonomy; Shiloh is not the Messiah but a place-name, and the verse refers to a past event, most likely the schism after Solomon's death.

With respect to *Isaiah* 53, which can be read as a description of an innocent servant of the Lord who will suffer and die for the sins of others, the situation of the Jewish polemicists was reversed: they had an excellent alternative interpretation, but some of them expressed disappointment at the absence of a crushing refutation of the christological exegesis. Despite a messianic understanding of this chapter in early rabbinic sources, medieval Jews overwhelmingly saw the servant as the exiled people of Israel, and strong arguments could be adduced for this identification. At the same time, Jews were sharply divided concerning the presence of a concept of vicarious atonement in the passage; to some exegetes and polemicists, such a concept was too Christian to be readily discerned in the Bible even if applied to Israel rather than the Messiah. Finally, specific refutations of the christological interpretation were proffered: aside from the inappropriateness of the term *servant* for a divine figure, this servant, unlike Jesus, "will see his seed and live a long life," will experience ongoing affliction and disease, and will suffer as a result of the sins of many rather than for the purpose of removing the original sin of Adam and Eve.

We have already seen that Christians considered the Jewish rejection of the Messiah to have resulted in the suppression of "carnal Israel" and its replacement by the church. Initial Jewish bewilderment at this perception gave way to a charge of Christian arbitrariness in defining biblical references to Israel, and Jews pointed to a number of citations in which favorable eschatological references that Christians took as descriptions of the church seemed inextricably linked to pejorative passages that Christians referred to the Jews. By the thirteenth century, Jews had even begun to cite their own retention of the Hebrew language as evidence that they had not been exchanged by God for people who knew the Bible only in translation.

It was not only the Jewish people, however, who were supposed to have been superseded. The same was said about Jewish law, and here the issue of allegorical interpretation of the Bible became crucial. Christians argued that, at least in the postcrucifixion era, only a nonliteral meaning is to be assigned to the legal sections of the Pentateuch, and they buttressed their position by raising questions about the rationality and consistency of biblical law. This challenge added a polemical dimension to Jewish speculations about "the reasons for the commandments." While some Jews argued against any attempt to fathom the divine intent or even denied the very existence of rational explanations, others provided both hygienic and spiritual reasons that sometimes seemed so persuasive that they became the basis for questions about the Christian failure to observe such evidently beneficial injunctions. Christian allegorization did not stop with the law; consequently, Jewish insistence on literal, contextual reading of biblical verses is a central theme of polemical literature, and some scholars have even suspected an underlying apologetic motive for the radical insistence on straightforward exegesis advocated by several significant medieval commentators like Rashbam (Rabbi Shemu'el ben Me'ir, c. 1080–1158) who were not primarily polemicists.

While Christian questions about the rationality of the law were a minor theme in medieval polemics, Jewish questions about the rationality of Christian dogma were at center stage. Many Jews were unable or unwilling to see trinitarianism as anything but tritheism. Those who did come to grips with the full complexity of the doctrine maintained that it violates logic and that multiplicity in God inevitably implies corporeality in God himself (i.e., not just in the temporary form of the historical Jesus). Most important, sophisticated Jewish polemicists maintained that any truly monotheistic understanding of trinitarianism—in which three divine persons are identified with attributes of God or understood in light of the perception of God as thought, thinker, and object of thought—fails because of the second, crucial doctrine of incarnation. If only one of three divine persons took on flesh, then true unity was irretrievably compromised.

Jewish objections to incarnation were not confined to the troubling light that it shed on the Christian concept of a divine trinity. Not only did the attribution of divinity to a human being raise the ugly specter of idolatry; it also seemed vulnerable to definitive philosophical refutation. Jewish polemicists argued that since infinity and immutability are essential characteristics of God, incarnation could not take place even miraculously. Moreover, they said, it is equally impossible to unite a human and a divine nature in a single person with each nature retaining its distinctiveness. Finally, even if all this were possible, it is hard to imagine that God could find no way to redeem humanity without subjecting himself to the filth and indignity of spending nine months in a womb and then passing through all the stages of a life that culminated in a humiliating death.

Virginal conception, although denied by Jews, was not vulnerable to the charge of philosophical impossibility. However, the specific doctrine that Mary remained a virgin during childbirth did appear to violate the principle that two bodies cannot take up the same space simultaneously. More important, the miracle of transubstantiation also seemed impossible, partly because Jesus' body would have to have been in many places at the same time.

There was, of course, also a scriptural dimension to these philosophical issues. Christians attempted to demonstrate trinitarianism by citing verses that contain plural verbs in connection with God, as, for example, "Let us make man in our image" (*Gn.* 1:26); or a threefold repetition of a key word, as, for example, "Holy, holy, holy is the Lord of Hosts" (*Is.* 6:3); or a repetition of the names of God, as, for example, "Hear O Israel, the Lord [is] our God, the Lord is one" (*Dt.* 6:4). For the incarnation, they cited the eschatological king in *Jeremiah* 23:5, whose name they translated as "the Lord our Righteousness," and, most effectively, the child in *Isaiah* 9:5–6, whose name they translated as "Wondrous Counselor, Mighty God, Eternal Father, Prince of Peace." Jews had to respond by providing alternative explanations or, in some cases, alternative translations. Thus the plural verb in *Genesis* 1:26 is either a plural of majesty or God's statement to the earth, which would provide the body into which he would place a soul. The name in *Jeremiah,* they said, should be translated "the Lord *is* our Righteousness," and the child in *Isaiah,* at least according to most medieval Jews, was named only "Prince of Peace" by God, who is himself the "Wondrous Counselor, Mighty God, [and] Eternal Father."

The scriptural evidence for virgin birth gave Jews their best opportunity to use the argument from context. The evidence, Christians said, is to be found in *Isaiah* 7:14, in which the prophet promised King Ahaz the birth of a child from an *'almah.* Jews not only argued that *'almah* does not mean "virgin" but also pointed to Isaiah's promise to Ahaz that deliverance would come before the child would know how to distinguish good from evil as decisive refutation of any identification of the child with Jesus.

Polemics on the Talmud. In its classic form, the Jewish-Christian debate centered on the Hebrew Bible. Beginning in the twelfth century, however, and especially in the thirteenth, Christians became intrigued with the possibility of utilizing the Talmud for polemical purposes, and Jews found themselves confronting two distinct but overlapping challenges from Christians quoting Talmud. Nicholas Donin, a Jewish convert to Christianity, began a campaign in the 1230s that led to a virtual trial in which Yeḥi'el ben Yosef of Paris had to defend the Talmud against charges of blasphemy. Pointing to what would otherwise have been an anachronism in a Talmudic account of Jesus, Yeḥi'el made the novel assertion that there were two Jesuses and that any pejorative Talmudic references are to the first, who had no connection whatever to Christianity. Potentially even more serious was Donin's assertion that the Talmud constituted "another law" that was entirely different from that of the Hebrew Bible. Since Jews were tolerated in part because they observed and authenticated the "Old Testament," the very existence of Jews in the Christian world could have been jeopardized by Christian acceptance of such an assertion. Yeḥi'el argued that the Talmud was, rather, an indispensable interpretation of the Bible. Ultimately, although various Dominicans and Franciscans toyed with the delegitimation of Jews on grounds related to the "other law" argument, it was the accusation of blasphemy that predominated, and this could be satisfied by the censorship of a handful of Talmudic passages.

The second approach to the Talmud is usually associated with another convert to Christianity. In the third quarter of the thirteenth century, Pablo Christiani (Cristia) began to emphasize a very minor theme in some earlier Christian polemics: that the Talmud demonstrates the truth of Christianity. Pablo and his successors did not have a positive attitude toward the Talmud, but they believed that the rabbis had preserved evidence of Christian truth. One of the earliest examples of this sort of argument is one of the best. The Talmud says that the world will last six thousand years: two thousand years of chaos, two thousand of Torah, and two thousand of the messianic age (B.T., *San.* 97a). This, said Christian polemicists, proves two crucial Christian assertions—that the Messiah has already come, and that with his arrival the age of Torah has come to an end. When Nahmanides was forced to confront Pablo in the Barcelona disputation of 1263, he insisted, of course, on the implausibility of finding Christian doctrines in a work produced by unconverted Jews, but he also made the striking assertion that *midrash* is not dogmatically binding and that Jews are therefore free to reject certain rabbinic statements. This issue became a *cause célèbre* in the next two or three centuries, largely because of the popularity of Raymund Martini's monumental *Pugio Fidei,* and the rabbis at the Tortosa disputation had to confront it under particularly trying circumstances. Generally, Jewish polemicists attempted to refute each argument individually, and they fell back on Nahmanides' position reluctantly and only as a last resort.

Jewish Polemical Use of the New Testament. At about the same time that Christians began to examine the Talmud for polemical purposes, Jews began to scrutinize the New Testament. Here too the sacred text peculiar to the other faith could simply be attacked, and here too it could be used for more sophisticated polemical purposes. Jews pointed out contradictions in the New Testament, such as the differing genealogies in *Matthew* and *Luke,* but they also argued that the Gospels themselves support the Jewish position concerning the nondivinity of Jesus and the eternality of the law. The polemical usefulness of both approaches led to a sometimes ambivalent attitude toward Jesus himself. On the one hand, he was denounced for abrogating the Torah and turning himself into a divinity; on the other, his words were cited as testimony that later Christians distorted a message that was in large measure authentically Jewish. This last approach, which was to be particularly influential in the modern period, was developed most notably in Profiat Duran's impressive and sophisticated *Kelimat ha-goyim*.

The Issues of Jewish Exile and the Role of Christianity. The effect of increased Jewish familiarity with the New Testament and growing Christian awareness of the Talmud is but one example of the way in which a largely static debate could undergo dynamic transformation under the impact of historical change. Debates about interest taking, the blood libel, heresy, icons, worship of the saints, confession, priestly celibacy, the Crusades, and more all made their way into the polemical literature. Perhaps the most fundamental effect of the historical situation lay in the Jewish need to explain exile and suffering on grounds other than God's rejection of the Jews. Since Jewish polemicists insisted on the moral superiority of Jews to Christians, the standard explanation of exile as punishment was especially uncomfortable in this context. Consequently, we find a whole array of efforts to turn the fact of suffering to polemical advantage: the Bible says that the truth would be hurled to the ground (*Dn.* 8:12); God is prolonging the exile so that the sin of the Christian oppressors should accumulate to a point where their utter destruction will be appropriate (cf. *Gn.* 15:16); God is punishing the Jews not for crucifying Jesus but for producing him. In a striking naturalistic argument, Yitsḥaq Polgar noted that Jewish suffering demonstrates that Christians and Jews stand in the same moral relationship as a bully and his victim.

Pressures ranging from the physical and economic to the moral and intellectual also led to transformations in the tone of Jewish polemics as well as to a reexamination of the role and religious standing of Christianity itself. This last development took place largely outside the context of medieval polemics, but its impact on later Jewish thought, including apologetic literature, was exceptionally significant. Medieval Jews generally regarded Christianity as an idolatrous religion. Nevertheless, in certain narrow legal contexts phrases like "the gentiles among us do not worship idolatry" were used as an *ad hoc* justification for Jewish business dealings with Christians that were pursued despite injunctions against such interactions with idolaters. Menaḥem ha-Me'iri of Perpignan (1249–1316) created a new legal category that can roughly be characterized as "civilized people" in order to distinguish Christians from ancient idolaters. Without addressing the issue of idolatry in this context, Maimonides and other authorities had assigned to Christianity and Islam the positive role of spreading knowledge of Torah and thus preparing the world for the Messiah. By the sixteenth century, some major Jewish figures had begun to misread a statement of the medieval French tosafists to mean that Noahides are not forbidden to associate another divinity with the true God; hence, although Christianity is surely idolatry for Jews, it is not so regarded for gentiles.

Later Developments. Some polemical works of the sixteenth and seventeenth centuries reflect the aforementioned and other changes, while others remain true to standard medieval views. The major works of this period include the following.

- Sixteenth century: Avraham Farissol, *Magen Avraham* (Shield of Abraham), Italy; Ya'ir ben Shabbetai of Correggio, *Ḥerev pifiyyot* (Double-Edged Sword), Italy; Meshullam ben Uri, *Zikhron sefer nitstsaḥon* (Commemoration of the Book of Polemic), provenance uncertain; *Kevod Elohim* (Glory of God), author and provenance uncertain; Yitsḥaq of Troki, *Ḥizzuq emunah* (Faith Strengthened), Poland.
- Seventeenth century: 'Azri'el Petaḥiah Alatino, *Vikkuaḥ* (Disputation), Italy; Yehudah Aryeh de Modena, *Magen va-ḥerev* (Shield and Sword), Italy; Yitsḥaq Lupis, *Kur matsref ha-emunot u-mar'eh ha-emet* (The Crucible of Beliefs and Demonstrator of the Truth), Syria.

Perhaps the most striking example of a more positive attitude toward Christianity is Avraham Farissol's remark that Jesus might well be regarded as a messiah for the gentiles. Despite Maimonides' assessment of Christianity's place in the divine scheme, this assertion, highly unusual even around 1500, was virtually unimaginable in the high Middle Ages. In the sixteenth century, Shelomoh de Modena denied the idolatrous character of Christianity by equating incarnation with anthropomorphism and noting that the latter doctrine had been declared nonheretical (although also not true) by the twelfth-century authority Avraham ben David of Posquières. There was also a shift in the Jewish attitude with respect to certain moral questions. In the Middle Ages, for example, most Jews vigorously denied that there was anything unethical about taking interest on loans; in seventeenth-century Italy, both Simone Luzzatto and Yehudah Aryeh de Modena insisted that Jewish—and not just Christian—morality frowns on this activity, but that there is no avoiding cruel economic necessity. Closer Jewish-Christian contacts in Italy also led to greater Christian familiarity with Jewish literature, including the increasingly popular qabbalistic texts, and Jews now found themselves confronted with not only Talmudic but also qabbalistic passages that were supposed to demonstrate Christian doctrines.

Initially Jewish reactions to the Reformation were positive and hopeful. Aside from messianic hopes that were briefly kindled at the prospect of division in what

Jews considered the biblical fourth kingdom (cf. *Dn.* 2:41), there was a feeling that many doctrinal points in the various forms of Protestantism seemed rather "Jewish": the rejection of papal authority, indulgences, transubstantiation, and clerical celibacy, as well as a return to the authority of the Bible. Moreover, there was the early work of Luther, *Dass Jesus ein geborener Jude Sei* (That Jesus Christ Was Born a Jew; 1523), which appeared to portend an amelioration of the Jewish condition under Protestant rule. When Luther later dashed these hopes, Jewish attitudes changed, and Jews living in Roman Catholic countries now looked to Catholic doctrines that could demonstrate the affinity of Judaism to Catholicism: the emphasis on works, the combination of scripture and tradition, the affirmation of free will and rejection of strict predestinarianism, and the retention of the traditional language of prayer. Needless to say, both Protestants and Catholics continued to affirm the central Christian beliefs that Judaism rejected, and when the Karaite Yitsḥaq of Troki wrote his *summa* of the traditional anti-Christian arguments the work became a standard reference even in the majority Rabbinite community.

The next, even more crucial turning point took place in the eighteenth century, when Jewish history moved into the modern period and Jewish-Christian relations underwent fundamental transformations. Even outside the orbit of the Jewish Enlightenment, Ya'aqov Emden of Germany maintained that Jesus and even Paul were perfectly good Jews whose purpose was to spread the seven Noahic laws to the gentiles; like Farissol's stance, this is a highly idiosyncratic position that nonetheless reflected a broader phenomenon. The central figure, however, who both foreshadows and exemplifies modern Jewish attitudes to Christianity, is Moses Mendelssohn.

A Christian theologian named Johann Caspar Lavater publicly challenged Mendelssohn to refute a defense of Christianity that Lavater had translated, or to do what Socrates would have done had he read the book and found it irrefutable. Mendelssohn, who for reasons of ideology, practicality, and temperament was not inclined to engage in polemic, responded reluctantly and cautiously. He had indeed expressed respect for Jesus in light of a conviction that the latter had made no claims to divinity. This did not mean that he was inclined to abandon Judaism, which is in perfect harmony with natural morality and religion, for a faith that contains irrational dogmas. Nevertheless, not all "prejudices" are equally harmful, and Judaism's teaching that righteous gentiles have a portion in the world to come renders missionary activity unnecessary and undesirable. This emphasis on Judaism's tolerance, rationality, morality, and respect for Christianity became the hallmark of modern Jewish discussions of Christianity, but these developments were not without ironic potential for reviving tension and polemic along new and unexpected lines.

Nineteenth-century Reform Judaism and liberal Protestantism arose out of the same environment and shared the fundamental conviction that the central message of religion is ethical. Reform Jews did away with much of the ritual component in Judaism, while liberal Protestants had grave misgivings about much of the dogmatic component of Christianity. What remained in each case was ethical monotheism. This sort of agreement, however, can lead to discord, since in the absence of a religious merger, each faith must claim that it is the quintessential bearer of the ethical message whose basic content is endorsed by both sides.

And precisely such discord developed. Christians complained about the "tasteless gibberish" spouted by Jews who claimed that theirs was the ethical religion *par excellence*, and they insisted that Jesus had introduced an advanced ethic into a Jewish society beset by dry, narrow legalism. This issue exploded into controversy after Adolf von Harnack propounded such views in his lecture series on the essence of Christianity in the winter of 1899–1900, but Jews were upset not only with Harnack but with a number of Christian historians whose scholarly work revealed the same sort of bias against Talmudic religion. The Jewish response was swift, vigorous, and international. In Germany, Leo Baeck's *Das Wesen des Judentums*, Joseph Eschelbacher's *Das Judentum und das Wesen des Christentums*, and Moritz Güdemann's *Jüdische Apologetik* denounced this Christian approach as motivated by considerations that had little to do with objective scholarship. In England, the articles of Israel Abrahams, Claude Montefiore, and Solomon Schechter pursued the same arguments. Somewhat later, Gerald Friedlander's *The Jewish Sources of the Sermon on the Mount* reflected a systematic apologetic effort to compare rabbinic morality with that of Jesus, and Joseph Bloch's *Israel und die Völker* was one of several efforts to counter Christian attacks on Talmudic morality.

This last work really addressed arguments of a more medieval sort, and it should not be assumed that such polemic simply disappeared in the modern period. Vigorous Christian missionary efforts in late eighteenth-century England inspired David Levi's rebuttals, *Letters to Dr. Priestly* and *Dissertations on the Prophecies of the Old Testament;* nineteenth-century challenges led Isaac Ber Levinsohn to write his *Aḥiyyah ha-shiloni* and other apologetic works. As recently as the 1970s, the activities of the "Jews for Jesus" and similar groups led the Jewish Community Relations Council of New York to commission *Jews and "Jewish Christianity"* by myself and Michael Wyschogrod. The tone and occasionally the content of such works can reflect modern developments in scholarship, argumentation, and civility; some of them, however, deal with arguments that are largely unchanged since the Middle Ages.

In the wake of the Holocaust, and especially since the Second Vatican Council of the early 1960s, a concerted effort has been made to replace polemics with dialogue. Even in such discussions, however, there are subtle pressures that produce the sort of advocacy that is not altogether alien to polemics. Before Vatican II, Jules Isaac and other Jewish leaders asked Christian groups to reevaluate, on moral as well as on more narrowly theological grounds, the traditional ascription of ongoing guilt to Jews for their role in the crucifixion. This time Jewish arguments fell on receptive ears, and precisely such a reevaluation took place.

With the passage of time, however, some Christian participants in dialogue have begun to inquire about the possibilities of a Jewish reevaluation of the standing of Jesus and the role of Christianity. These inquiries are rooted in the awareness that twentieth-century Jewish scholars like Joseph Klausner, Claude Montefiore, David Flusser, and Pinchas Lapide have provided—with varying degrees of enthusiasm—a positive portrait of a fundamentally Jewish Jesus. Moreover, Franz Rosenzweig spoke of Christianity as a manifestation of a divine covenant with the gentiles. Even Jewish ecumenists, however, are often wary of far-reaching revisions in their evaluation of Jesus, and it is unlikely that dialogue will produce a perception of Jesus as a quasi messiah or mitigate the historic Jewish distaste for the central dogmas of traditional Christianity.

Finally, a uniquely contemporary dimension has been injected into Jewish-Christian discussions by the establishment of the state of Israel. On the one hand, the establishment of Israel has undercut the old Christian argument based on the Jewish exile; on the other hand, it fits perfectly into some scenarios of the second coming of Jesus that are popular among Christian fundamentalists. In the context of dialogue, Jews have often attempted to explain the theological centrality of the Land of Israel in Judaism, and they have sometimes argued that Christian theology itself should lead to a recognition of the significance of the state of Israel in the divine plan. This delicate balance of politics and theology has produced both understanding and tension. It is but the most recent example of the effect of historical events on a relationship that reflects the unchanging disputes of two venerable traditions as well as the dynamic interplay of two communities acting and reacting in an ever changing world.

BIBLIOGRAPHY

There is no good survey of Jewish polemics from late antiquity to the present. A sketchy overview is provided in Hans Joachim Schoeps's *The Jewish-Christian Argument* (New York, 1963); and Morris Goldstein's *Jesus in the Jewish Tradition* (New York, 1950) surveys some Jewish discussions of Christianity through the Middle Ages. Frank Talmage's *Disputation and Dialogue: Readings in the Jewish-Christian Encounter* (New York, 1975) is a valuable collection of brief translated selections from the sources.

Judah Rosenthal provided a thorough bibliography of polemical works in his "Sifrut ha-vikkuaḥ ha-anṭi-Notsrit," *Areshet* 2 (1960): 130–179; 3 (1961): 433–439. The most comprehensive collection of such works remains J. D. Eisenstein's edited volume *Otsar vikkuḥim* (1928; reprint, New York, 1964), but the texts are unreliable and must always be checked against superior editions. For English translations of polemical texts, see Oliver S. Rankin's *Jewish Religious Polemic of Earlier and Later Centuries* (1956; reprint, New York, 1970); Hyam Maccoby's *Judaism on Trial: Jewish-Christian Disputations in the Middle Ages* (Rutherford, N.J., 1982); Yosef Kimḥi's *The Book of the Covenant*, translated by Frank Talmage (Toronto, 1972); and Yitsḥaq Troki's *Faith Strengthened*, translated by M. Mocatta (New York, 1970). See also my study, *The Jewish-Christian Debate in the High Middle Ages: A Critical Edition of the Niẓẓaḥon Vetus with an Introduction, Translation and Commentary* (Philadelphia, 1978); the introduction and commentary trace the major arguments through the thirteenth century. Other important studies of the medieval period include Daniel Lasker's *Jewish Philosophical Polemics against Christianity in the Middle Ages* (New York, 1977), Bernhard Blumenkranz's *Juifs et Chrétiens dans le monde occidental, 430–1096* (Paris, 1960), and Jacob Katz's *Exclusiveness and Tolerance* (New York, 1961). On *Toledot Yeshu*, see Samuel Krauss's *Das Leben Jesu nach jüdischen Quellen* (Berlin, 1902); on *Genesis* 49:10, Adolf Posnanski's *Schiloh: Ein Beitrag zur Geschichte der Messiaslehre* (Leipzig, 1904); on *Isaiah* 53, Adolf Neubauer and Samuel R. Driver's *The Fifty-third Chapter of Isaiah according to the Jewish Interpreters*, 2 vols. (1876–1877; reprint, New York, 1969).

Jewish reactions to the Reformation are described in H. H. Ben-Sasson's *The Reformation in Contemporary Jewish Eyes* (Jerusalem, 1970). On the modern period, see Uriel Tal's *Christians and Jews in Germany in the Second Reich: Religion, Politics and Ideology, 1870–1914* (Ithaca, N.Y., 1975), Jacob Fleischmann's *Be'ayat ha-Natsrut ba-maḥshavah ha-Yehudit mi-Mendelssohn 'ad Rosenzweig* (Jerusalem, 1964), and A. Roy Eckardt's bibliography, "Recent Literature on Christian-Jewish Relations," *Journal of the American Academy of Religion* 49 (March 1981): 99–111.

DAVID BERGER

Muslim-Jewish Polemics

Down to the eighteenth century the majority of Jews lived in countries under Muslim rule, where they shared with Christians the status of "protected" minorities, tolerated on sufferance and subject at times and in certain areas to discrimination, ill will, abuse, and assault.

Arabic literature, the classical repository of theological lore in Islam, expresses and reflects the situation over centuries. While most of this lore is of Muslim origin, Jews and Christians have contributed to it upon occasion with Arabic writings added to their literary output in Hebrew and Syriac, respectively.

The vast Arabic literature that developed in the early centuries of Islam included works on religion, sectarianism, the treatment of the minorities, and so forth. Historians and travelers seeking to sketch the development of faiths, the rise of Islam, and its victorious march through countries and continents also threw light on the non-Muslims and their beliefs. Scholarly discussion concerning non-Muslims inevitably tended to indicate the miscreants' errors. Thus polemics appeared, and, as disputations took place, polemics gave rise to defensive apologetics.

Muslim Polemics. Indeed, Muslims knew from their own scripture that Islam is a continuation of earlier dispensations, and they were familiar with the Prophet's attitude toward their carriers—the Jews and Christians. According to the Qur'ān, the Jews (identified there as Yahūd or Banū Isrā'īl, "Children of Israel") were an ancient people, descended from Abraham and later led out of Egypt by Moses. Favored by the Lord, who sent prophets to teach and guide them, they nonetheless became enmeshed in sin and disobedience, worshiping the golden calf, killing prophets, and rejecting Jesus, and were finally punished by destruction, exile, and dispersal. Further, the Qur'ān indicated that the Prophet had not only fought the pagan Arabs but also clashed with the Jews living in Arabia, especially those in Medina, and that the struggle had turned into a military clash when the Jews refused to accept the Prophet and his revelation.

These data were extended and embellished in the vast collections of traditions *(ḥadīth)* that arose in early Islam and were further enriched by an exegetical turn, as Qur'anic allusions to biblical stories gave rise to commentaries on ancient Hebrew lore. Although the Jews had been instructed about the coming of Muḥammad, the Muslim commentators explained, they ignored these allusions or sought to interpret them away or to conceal them. They also fabricated stories among the *Isrā'īlīyāt* (narratives set in the era of the Banū Isrā'īl) that were apt to mislead true believers. Jewish converts to Islam also supplied information—albeit misleading—on Hebrew lore and the Jewish past. Ka'b al-Aḥbār is the prototypical figure among them: a Jew from Yemen, he embraced Islam half a dozen years after the Prophet's death and was considered an expert on earlier scriptures. And presumably the anti-Jewish animus of the Near Eastern Christians percolated into Islamic circles following the Christians' conversion to Islam.

The earliest polemics, which can be traced to the eighth- and ninth-century disputations at the Abbasid court in Baghdad, are usually directed against both Jews and Christians. Only gradually does a polemical literature directed specifically against Jews emerge, beginning with special chapters on Jews and Judaism and with the writings of Jewish converts to Islam. Although such works are mentioned early on by Arab historians, the earliest surviving examples date only from the eleventh century.

Ibn Ḥazm. The earliest preserved substantial work of Islamic polemics against Jews and Judaism comes from the pen of Ibn Ḥazm (d. 1064), a leading figure of Islamic learning and Arabic literature in Spain. He dealt with the subject repeatedly and is the only major figure of Arabic letters to treat it.

Ibn Ḥazm apparently felt that his road to political success in the kingdom of Granada was blocked by the preeminence of the Jews, and in particular by their leader, Ibn Nagrela (known in the Jewish community as Shemu'el ha-Nagid, 993–1056), a successful administrator, diplomat, and military commander. Both Ibn Ḥazm and the Nagid wrote on theology, and both were poets, one writing in Arabic, the other in Hebrew. They met when they were in their early twenties, but the meeting was not conducive to mutual respect and appreciation.

In Ibn Ḥazm's major work, *Kitāb al-fiṣal wa-al-niḥal* (Book of Groups and Sects), a survey of theology, a section of nearly 130 pages is devoted to a critique of Jewish beliefs and texts. Passages from the Hebrew scriptures, quoted to reveal their deficiencies, are followed by counterparts from the Qur'ān, which are cited to demonstrate their excellence by comparison. Ibn Ḥazm displays a good knowledge of *Genesis,* but his knowledge of the rest of the Hebrew scriptures is weak, and he is unable to distinguish biblical data from later legends. It is possible that he used a list of suitable passages ("testimonies") culled for the purpose by others. He even cites a few items of Talmudic lore. He displays an interest in the origins of Hebrew words but here too falls prey to misinformation: quoting an informant, he explains, for example, that the name *Israel* was derived from *Asar'el* ("he detained God," *Gn.* 32:25–31, where Jacob wrestles with divine beings and prevails), thus confusing the Hebrew roots *'sr* and *srh*.

In his view, the Hebrew scriptures are replete with contradictions, absurdities, anthropomorphisms, and objectionable and irrelevant matter. The Muslims should feel no reverence toward the scriptures of the Jews and Christians, he argues, and should reject these faulty, distorted remnants of the true scripture. Reverence is due only to the inimitable truth and beauty of the Qur'ān.

Ibn Ḥazm is particularly eager to point out discrepancies in the biblical text, especially where numbers are involved, as with varying statements on the length of the bondage in Egypt or the population of the Israelites during the wilderness period. Other contradictions he claims to find in the text include the report in *Exodus* 7:20–22 that after all the water in Egypt turned into blood, the native magicians repeated the deed: where, he asks, did they get the water to prove their skill? Likewise, citing *Exodus* 12:38, he asks where the Hebrews obtained the multitude of cattle in the desert, and further, if they had such cattle, why did they complain of lack of meat? Among the anthropomorphisms he cites are passages such as "The Lord is a man of war" (*Ex.* 15:3); "And they saw the God of Israel, and there was under his feet, as if it were a pavement of sapphire stone" (*Ex.* 24:10); and the Lord's various pronouncements in *Exodus* 33 where he "spoke unto Moses face to face. . . . And he said, 'You cannot see my face. . . . And I shall take away my hand and you shall see my back, but my face shall not be seen" (vv. 11, 10, 22–23).

Unlike the Qur'ān, Ibn Ḥazm argues, the Hebrew scriptures are devoid of data on reward and punishment in the life to come. Yet the Qur'ān itself refers to biblical revelation, especially to that of Moses. How is this possible? Because, he claims, there was a true revelation of the divine word to Moses, but it was not preserved. The numerous civil strifes, wars, invasions, and defeats in ancient Israel destroyed not merely the Hebrew kingdoms but also their archives and with them, the scriptures, which went up in flames. There was no continuous tradition of learning. Indeed, there was merely one copy of the scriptures remaining in the hands of the priests, who knew only chapters, fractions of it. In Babylon, Ezra the priest concocted the Hebrew scriptures from remnants of the revelation as it was remembered by other priests and from his own additions.

Here Ezra is denounced as a master of deception lacking reason and conscience (as well as a knowledge of arithmetic). Yet, Ibn Ḥazm points out, it was Ezra who shaped the new religion during the Babylonian captivity by substituting the synagogue service for the ruined Temple of Solomon. Since the days of Moses, he says, *Deuteronomy* 32 (*Ha'azinu*, The Song of Moses) is the only chapter of the Hebrew scriptures that has been taught to the people, and even this chapter—which he quotes in full—is replete with passages that cannot be of divine origin, such as verses 20–22: "God is their father." Anyone who knows the Jews, continues our author, knows they are a filthy and witless rabble, repulsive, vile, perfidious, cowardly, despicable, mendacious. Hence Muslims should seek guidance about the children of Israel not from the Ezra-produced scripture but from the Qur'ān, which also includes data about the prophets (such as Hūd and Ṣāliḥ) who were unknown to the Jews.

Ibn Ḥazm maintains that the Jews reject abrogation of their scriptures and any suggestion of a post-Mosaic dispensation, to either Jesus or Muḥammad. For them the omniscient God's decree is immutable, and any change or caprice in divine will is not feasible. Without such a sudden change *(badā')* in divine pleasure, however, a new dispensation would not be feasible and thus, they assert, would contradict divine omniscience. But this is wrong, Ibn Ḥazm counters. Precepts are commands to perform certain acts over a limited period, beyond which time they may turn into their opposites. Circumstances in space and time are known to God, and it is his pleasure to grant life, death, and resurrection, power, decline, restoration, virtue, and evil, belief and deviation. For the Jews, work is permissible on Friday, but prohibited on Saturday, only to become permissible again on Sunday.

Indeed, the Jews recognize that the law of Jacob differs from the law of Moses. Jacob married Leah and Rachel, who were sisters, yet the law of Moses (*Lv.* 18:18) proscribes such a marriage. The people of Gibeon escaped annihilation to become hewers of wood and drawers of water for the sanctuary after they fraudulently exacted a treaty from Joshua (*Jos.* 9). God's wrath was about to consume the Israelites, but Moses' fervent appeal made the Lord repent (*Ex.* 32:10–14). Abraham offered curd and milk and meat to the angels (*Gn.* 18), but this was not a kosher diet (as set forth in *Deuteronomy* 14:3–21 and elsewhere).

Ibn Ḥazm is quick to notice irregularities attested in the lineage of biblical figures and points with gusto to the extent of bastardization among them. The lineage of the patriarchs, prophets, and kings is sullied with incest and fornication: Abraham married Sarah, his sister; Lot was seduced by his daughters; Reuben had relations with Bilhah, his father's concubine; from Judah and his daughter-in-law Tamar sprang the line of David, Solomon, and the expected Messiah.

The few samples of postbiblical lore that he knew, possibly through the Karaites, horrified him as "old wives' tales": data for example, from the ancient treatise *Shi'ur qomah* on the measurement of the divine body; the Lord's grieving about the destruction of the Temple; reference to the angel Meṭaṭron as "the lesser Lord." He also recounts that, according to the Jews, Paul was sent to the disciples of Jesus in order to mislead them into the belief in Christ's divinity. Thus Ibn Ḥazm concludes that the Jews are liars and tricksters. This trait begins with Jacob filching Esau's birthright (*Gn.* 25:29–34) and Isaac's blessing (*Gn.* 27). Though I have seen many of them, he reports, I found only two who were devoted to truth.

Although he holds that the Hebrew scriptures are forgeries and harps on the necessity of rejecting them completely and relying instead on the Qur'ān, he cannot refrain from quoting some passages that seem to fit Muslim notions. Thus he accepts *Deuteronomy* 33:2 ("The Lord came from Sinai and rose from Seir unto them; he shined forth from Mount Paran") as an "annunciation" of the advent of Jesus (via Seir, in Edom, later identified with Christendom, while Paran was taken to be a reference to Mecca). Likewise he finds in *Deuteronomy* 18:18 ("I will raise them a prophet from among their brethren like unto thee") an annunciation of Muḥammad's ministry, since the Arabs, the progeny of Ismā'īl (Ishmael), are the brethren among whom a prophet was to arise.

Ibn Ḥazm also wrote a treatise against a pamphlet alleged to have been composed by Ibn Nagrela (or his son) against the Qur'ān. Although he was unable to find a copy of this text and knew of it only from a Muslim author's refutations, he nonetheless proceeded to attack the Jewish leader and the rest of the infidels who had become so arrogant. In this treatise he also inveighs against the Muslim rulers, who enjoy their luxurious palaces and forget their duty to preserve strict Muslim domination over the infidels.

The impact of Ibn Ḥazm's polemical writings is unclear. He is not quoted by later writers, and it is possible that his adherence to the Ẓāhirī school of theology—a distinct minority within Sunnī Islam—may have limited the spread of his views. At least one brief Hebrew tract, Shelomoh ben Avraham Adret's thirteenth-century *Ma'amar 'al Yishma'e'l* (Treatise on Ishmael), reproduces and refutes passages of Ibn Ḥazm's argument on forgery, however. In any case, the full scope of the Muslim-Jewish controversy was given its first systematic exposition in Ibn Ḥazm's work: abrogation *(naskh)*, distortion or forgery in the scripture *(taḥrīf)*, anthropomorphism *(tajsīm)*, the preserved annunciation of Islam and its prophet *(a'lām)*.

Samau'al al-Maghribī. The pamphlet *Ifḥām al-Yahūd* (Silencing the Jews), written in 1163 in Marāgha (northern Iran), is the most important and influential work of Muslim polemics against Judaism. Its author was Samau'al al-Maghribī (c. 1125–1175), a Jew who converted to Islam and penned the pamphlet to mark his conversion. (It is not to be confused, however, with the Arabic pamphlet of Samuel Marrocanus, a convert to Christianity, which was translated into Latin and later into many Western languages.)

Samau'al's father was a minor Hebrew poet who had presumably fled Morocco during a wave of persecution, settled in Baghdad, and married a woman of a distinguished family. Samau'al, who studied under the eminent philosopher Abū al-Barakāt (also a Jewish convert to Islam), won fame as a mathematician and physician. His Jewish training seems to have been limited. In an autobiography added to his pamphlet in 1167, he claims that he was moved to convert by rational thinking along mathematical lines. Although he also describes visions of the prophets Samuel and Muḥammad, he still insists that purely logical arguments prevailed in his mind. A note of self-admiration is evident throughout:

> Then, after I had trained my mind on mathematical studies, especially geometry with its demonstrations, I asked myself about the differences in religious faiths and tenets. . . . I realized that reason is the supreme arbiter and that its rule should be established generally in . . . our world. . . . We realize that reason does not oblige us to accept ancestral tradition without examining it as to its soundness. . . . Mere reference to fathers and ancestry, however, is no proof. . . .
>
> I realize that the Jews had no proof . . . about . . . Moses other than the evidence of the chain of transmission, which is available for Jesus and Muḥammad just as it is for Moses . . . then all three are true prophets. . . .
>
> I have not seen Moses . . . nor have I witnessed his miracles, nor those of any other prophet. . . . A sensible person cannot believe one and disbelieve another of these prophets. . . . Rather, it is rationally incumbent either to believe all of them or to reject all of them. . . .
>
> As for disbelieving all, reason does not dictate that either. For we find that they all preached lofty morals, advocated the virtues and fought the vices, and regulated the world in a fashion beneficial to mankind.

In Samau'al's view, the record of the Jews in scientific advancement cannot compare with that of the Greeks and others; likewise, the literature of the Muslims is overwhelmingly superior.

The key issue of abrogation is demonstrated both logically and historically. Jewish legists, he says, offered discordant views on problems; how can they all be of divine origin? Indeed the law itself abounds in contradictions: in *Exodus,* for example, all the firstborn are consecrated to worship (13:2); in *Numbers,* only the Levites (8:18). As purification with the ashes of the red heifer (*Nm.* 19:11, 19:16, 19:17) is no longer available, he contends that the Jews must consider themselves impure. Prayers on exile, dispersion, and hope of restoration are clearly of late origin, yet they should not have been introduced at all in view of the injunction against adding to or diminishing from the divine word (*Dt.* 13:1).

An array of arguments is cited to prove that Jesus and Muḥammad were announced in the scriptures: *Deuteronomy* 18:15 announces a prophet from among their brethren; in *Genesis* 17:20, God promises to multiply Ishmael (here the letters of the Hebrew words for "exceedingly," *bi-m'od me'od,* numerically equal 92, which is the numerical value of the name *Muḥammad*); *Genesis* 21:21 deals with three revelations, the last in the abode of Ishmael, which is that of the Arabs.

The critique of the scripture follows. According to Samau'al, it perished long ago owing to the vicissitudes in the history of the Hebrews. King Saul (*1 Sm.* 22:16–20) massacred the line of Aaron. Centuries passed before Ezra, of the priestly Aaronids, reconstructed the scripture. As the priests begrudged authority to royalty, he added two stories derogatory to the lineage of David. One, that of the daughters of Lot (*Gn.* 19), establishes the origin of Moab and thus the illegitimacy of Ruth, the ancestor of the House of David, nay, of the expected messiah. The other story (*Gn.* 38) indicates that Boaz, husband of Ruth, was born of the union of Judah with Tamar.

Among other criticisms, Samau'al also charges that the law is oppressive and a burden *(iṣr),* as demonstrated by the dietary rules that separate Jews from non-Jews. Jews, he points out, call Muḥammad a fool and a raving madman (*meshugga',* cf. *Hos.* 9:7) and also "unfit" (Heb., *pasul,* rhyming with *rasūl,* Arab., "messenger," a name for the Prophet as Messenger of God); likewise they refer to the Qur'ān as "dishonor" *(qalon).*

No doubt there is a similarity between the arguments of Ibn Ḥazm in the eleventh century and those of Samau'al in the twelfth. Here it is probable that both were reproducing older material concerning the scriptural passages and the theory that Ezra authored the Pentateuch (the hypothesis of Ezra's role in the history of the scripture goes back to late Hellenistic texts; see Edmund Stein's *Alttestamentliche Bibelkritik in der späthellenistischen Literatur,* Lwów, 1935).

Samau'al's tract in turn proved very influential as a quarry for Muslim authors over the centuries. His arguments reappear in *Al-ajwibah al-fākhirah* (The Perfect Replies), written by the Egyptian al-Qarāfī (d. 1285), and in works by Ibn Qayyim al-Jawzīyah (d. 1350). In copying Samau'al's original pamphlet, which contained Hebrew passages in Hebrew characters followed by Arabic transliteration and translation, later scribes omitted the alien Hebrew characters. The tract was printed in Egypt in 1939 and again in the 1960s.

Al-Rāqilī. From somewhat different circumstances came Abū Zakarīyā' Yaḥyā al-Rāqilī's tract *Ta'yīd al-millah* (Support of the Faith), written in Huesca in 1360 and directed against Jews and Christians. Living in the Spanish kingdom of Aragon after the Christian reconquest, he expressed bitterness over the degradation of Islam, as Muslims fell from a position of domination to that of a tolerated minority, and especially over the treatment of Muslim peasants by Jewish officials and tax agents on behalf of the crown. Reading the biblical texts in translation, he "extracted from them passages and evidences with which to refute the Jews." God had chastised them, he observes, with permanent dispersion *(al-ghalūth al-dā'im)* and humiliation. He mentions disputations and arguments *(al-munāẓarāt wa-al-iḥtijāj)* and hopes that God "may take us out of the country of polytheism to the lands of the Muslims."

The Hebrew scriptures, he says, show that the Jews were a rebellious, unfaithful, ungrateful, accursed breed. They transgressed against every one of the Ten Commandments. According to al-Rāqilī's historical reconstruction, Hagar, the mother of Ishmael, was Abraham's wife, not his concubine. She was not a mere slave but the daughter of an Egyptian prince, and in any case, even a slave could be a prophet, as with Joseph, who was Potiphar's slave. God ordered Abraham to sacrifice his son, then prevented the patriarch from doing so. This, al-Rāqilī concludes, is an evident case of abrogation. But even though the Jewish scriptures are not reliable, he cites *Isaiah* 21:7 ("a troop of asses, a troop of camels") as an annunciation of the prophethood of Jesus and Muḥammad, respectively.

Al-Rāqilī's pamphlet belongs to a lower level of disputation conducted between two oppressed communities under Christian domination. Also within this category of less sophisticated works, appealing more to the common Muslim reader, are two pamphlets by fourteenth-century Jewish converts to Islam. One came from the pen of Sa'īd ibn Ḥasan of Alexandria, who, in 1320, while living in the Great Mosque of Damascus, wrote an account of his conversion. Dangerously ill and expecting to die, he suddenly heard a voice urging him to read a surah of the Qur'ān. He complied and was miraculously saved. He became such a fervent believer that he turned against the Jewish and Christian unbelievers and in his tracts, which quote biblical texts, demonstrates no qualms about distortions and absurdities.

Such is also the case with ʿAbd al-Ḥaqq al-Islāmī from Ceuta, who wrote toward the end of the century. In addition to relying on *gimaṭriyyah,* the argument from the numerical value of names and words, he accused the Jews of fire worship, considered Ahab the transgressor (*1 Kgs.* 16–18) a righteous king, nay, a Muslim believer, and presented the Hebrew phrase "The gentile is like a dog" as an authentic text.

Jewish Apologetics. Jewish writings, in Arabic and in Hebrew, attempted to present a defense against Islamic attacks. They were apologetic replies to Muslim arguments and to an extent constituted an effort to reinterpret the Jewish cause in the light of the new intellectual atmosphere under Islam.

Maimonides. Although Moses Maimonides (Mosheh ben Maimon, d. 1204) warned against engaging in disputations with the Muslims, because they did not accept the Hebrew Bible as a revealed text and thus shared no common ground, his *Epistle to Yemen* is virtually a polemical treatise. Its purpose was to prepare the synagogue public to counter Muslim arguments: "Some hearts have gone astray . . . faith weakened," he tells his readers. "Ours is the true and authentic divine religion revealed to us through Moses. . . . In assaults upon us some use brute force; others, controversy. Christianity and Islam combine the two methods."

The Muslim polemicists, he continues, claim to have found Muḥammad's name and country in Hebrew scriptures (*Gn.* 17:20; *Dt.* 33:2, 18:15). Jewish converts to Islam (presumably Samau'al) quoting these verses cannot really believe in them; their true purpose is to win favor in the eyes of the gentiles. Muslims, unable to indicate a single verse, accuse the Jews of having altered or concealed the text. In fact, he points out, the scriptures had been translated into Greek, Aramaic, and Latin centuries before Muḥammad appeared.

> On account of . . . our sins God has hurled us into the midst of this people, the Arabs, who have persecuted us severely and passed baneful and discriminatory legislation against us. . . . Never did a nation molest, degrade, debase, and hate us as much as they. . . . No matter how much we suffer and elect to remain at peace with them, they stir up strife and sedition, as David predicted (*Ps.* 120:7): "I am all peace, but when I speak, they are for war."

He concludes with a warning about the danger involved in reading his epistle, but he hopes that "the secret of the Lord may be entrusted to those who fear him (*Ps.* 23:14)."

Ibn Kammūnah. In a class by itself stands *Tanqīḥ al-abḥāth fī al-milal al-thalāth* (Critical Inquiry into the Three Faiths), written in Baghdad in 1280 by Saʿd ibn Manṣūr ibn Kammūnah. With the caliphate under Mongol rule, Islam could no longer be regarded as the faith of the ruler but remained the predominant faith of the masses. A review of Ibn Kammūnah's book in a sermon before a Friday mosque audience produced an angry mob assault, and the author had to be carried out of town hidden in a trunk.

The work begins with a brief discussion of religion in general, followed by chapters on the three monotheistic faiths. Two-thirds of the book is devoted to Islam and is based on Muslim texts; it is written in an unusually dispassionate spirit. Nonetheless, while Islam and its prophet receive a fair treatment, the cumulative impression is not favorable.

The chapter on Judaism contains a brief survey of biblical data and Jewish beliefs, followed by seven objections culled from Samau'al al-Maghribī. These are rebutted in turn with arguments reflecting the views of Yehudah ha-Levi and Maimonides.

Ibn Kammūnah points out that communities may live side by side for centuries and yet know each other only slightly:

> But the contact of Muslims with Jews does not necessitate a Muslim inquiry into what the Jews assert, especially since the Jews are prevented from declaring their creed, and their [canonical] books are in a tongue the Muslims do not understand. The contact of a minority with a majority affects the majority and the minority differently. Thus, when a linguistic minority is in contact with a linguistic majority, the minority learns the language of the majority while the majority does not learn the language of the minority or, at best, learns it much later. Moreover, despite numerous contacts of the bulk of the Jews with the Muslims, many Jews still do not know the basic Islamic tenets known by the rank-and-file Muslims, let alone the elite. It is even more natural that a similar situation should obtain on the Muslim side, or, at the very least, that both sides should be equal [in mutual ignorance].

Moreover, the Muslims are split into various factions anathemizing one another. He lists the Christians' internal dissensions and remarks:

> I did not find most of these retorts in discussions by Christians; I supplied these retorts on behalf of the Christians, and in supplementation of the investigation into their belief.

This evoked the admiration of a Christian opponent.

In discussing the Muslims' factions and their respective claims, he notes:

> There is room for speculation in this matter. Namely, many a person will, for worldly goals and motives, do things for which, as he most assuredly knows, the founder of his respective religion has threatened severe punishment in the

hereafter. This belief will not prevent a man from perpetrating that forbidden evil. Such is the case of the adulterer, wine-imbiber, and slanderer. In the quest for victory over opponents, human nature will urge the fabrication of reports favoring one's religion. Ignoring the prohibition against lying, a man will sometimes fabricate such a report in the [mistaken] belief that he will merit reward therefor. It may also be fabricated by one who joined a faith opportunistically—without inner conviction but rather in the quest for success, like many who nowadays join the faith of Islam in order to prevail over rivals, although they are not believers by conviction. If your assertion were true, no Muslim would ever have fabricated a false tradition; the contrary, however, is the case.

Summarizing the arguments for Muḥammad's prophethood, he contends that they remain unproven and remarks:

> That is why, to this day, we never see anyone converting to Islam unless in terror, or in quest of power, or to avoid heavy taxation, or to escape humiliation, or if taken prisoner, or because of infatuation with a Muslim woman, or for some similar reason. Nor do we see a respected, wealthy, and pious non-Muslim well versed in both his faith and that of Islam, going over to the Islamic faith without some of the aforementioned or similar motives.

Likewise, he rejects the argument that victory and power are proof of divine support:

> How, since the dominion of idol-worshipers and fire-worshipers continued for thousands of years in numberless countries throughout the world, can a multitude of followers be proof of a claim?
>
> I found they had no rebuttal to these arguments beyond the claim that the Islamic faith obviously excels over other faiths, and that it combines a maximum quantity and quality of perfection not attained by any other known faith. But he who, in rancor, makes this claim will never be able to present proof of it.

Decline of the Genre. After 1400, Muslim polemics were largely reiterations of earlier arguments presented in insignificant pamphlets. One noteworthy exception is a disputation conducted in 1796 by a Persian scholar, Sayyid Muḥammad Mahdī Ṭabāṭabā'ī; known through an account in Arabic, this event appears to have been characterized by uncommon mildness and magnanimity.

Within the Ottoman empire, probably from Christian circles, it was charged from time to time that the Jews used (Christian) blood to bake the unleavened bread for Passover. This "blood libel" emerged in Damascus in 1840 and resurfaced repeatedly thereafter.

In the nineteenth century, anti-Jewish moods and arguments began to penetrate the Muslim world from Western sources, at first especially through French anti-Semitism. In the twentieth century, the conflict in Palestine and the rise of Zionism were bound to rekindle the embers of the medieval controversy as a religious appendage to the conflict. But the literature of the religious aspect has proven extremely poor in content, confined to reiteration of arguments from the eleventh and twelfth centuries: passages from the Qur'ān and the traditions, a flood of epithets characterizing the Jews as eternally vicious fiends against the Muslims, against Muslims and Christians, and indeed, against all humanity, as enemies ever plotting against what is human and good, for the sake of world domination by Jewry and Israel.

All in all, Islamic polemics directed against Jews are an arid area of insubstantial writing, of minor interest to the Muslims themselves. For their part, the Jews kept a low profile and preferred not to retort. But many allusions to the Muslim arguments can be found in medieval prayers, as well as in exegetical and theological works.

BIBLIOGRAPHY

The classic compendium on Arabic-language polemics among Muslims, Christians, and Jews is Moritz Steinschneider's *Polemische und apologetische Literatur in arabischer Sprache, zwischen Muslimen, Christen und Juden* (1877; reprint, Hildesheim, 1965). Other early studies include several by Ignácz Goldziher in his *Gesammelte Schriften,* 3 vols. (Hildesheim, 1967–1970), and Martin Schreiner's "Zur Geschichte der Polemik zwischen Juden und Muhammedanern," *Zeitschrift der Deutschen Morgenländischen Gesellschaft* 42 (1888): 591–675.

Salo W. Baron addresses the subject, with extensive bibliography, in *A Social and Religious History of the Jews,* 2d ed., rev. & enl., vol. 5 (New York, 1957), pp. 82–108. I have also written a survey, "The Medieval Polemics between Islam and Judaism," in *Religion in a Religious Age,* edited by S. D. Goitein (Cambridge, Mass., 1974).

For specialized studies, see Jacob Mann's "An Early Theologico-Polemical Work," *Hebrew Union College Annual* 13/14 (1937–1938): 411–459; Emilio García Gomez's "Polémica religiosa entre Ibn Ḥazm e Ibn al-Nagrila," *Al-Andalus* 4 (1936): 1–28; Miguel Asín Palacios's "Un tratado morisco de polémica contra los Judios," in *Mélanges Hartwig Derenbourg* (Paris, 1909), pp. 343–366, reprinted in his *Obras escogidas,* vols. 2–3, *De historia y filogogia arabe* (Madrid, 1948); Joseph Perles's *R. Salomo ben Abraham ben Adereth: Sein Leben und seine Schriften* (Breslau, 1863); and ʿAfīf ʿAbd al-Fattāḥ Ṭabbārah's *Al-Yahūd fī al-Qur'ān* (Beirut, 1966). An Israeli view of modern developments is Yehoshafat Harkabi's *Arab Attitudes to Israel,* translated by Misha Louvish (New York, 1972).

A number of the original sources are also available in translation. Among the Muslim writers, Ibn Ḥazm's *Kitāb al-fiṣal wa-al-niḥal,* 5 vols. in 2 (1903; reprint, Baghdad, 1964), has been translated by Miguel Asín Palacios in volume 2 of his *Abenházam de Córdoba* (Madrid, 1927), and I have edited and translated Samau'al al-Maghribī's *Ifḥām al-Yahūd: Silencing the Jews* (New York, 1964). The early formulations of the debate from the Jewish perspective are reflected in the third treatise of Sa'adyah Gaon's *The Book of Beliefs and Opinions*, translated by Samuel Rosenblatt (New Haven, 1948). Other Jewish texts include Moses Maimonides's *Epistle to Yemen*, edited by Abraham S. Halkin and translated by Boaz Cohen (New York, 1952), and *Ibn Kammūna's Examination of the Three Faiths: A Thirteenth Century Essay in the Comparative Study of Religion* (Berkeley, 1971), which I have edited and translated.

MOSHE PERLMANN

Christian-Muslim Polemics

The Qur'ān itself determines the polemic area between Muslims and Christians, because it states the terms and sets the limits of Christian error. The issues it defines have been disputed ever since: God is not three; Jesus is not the Son of God; he was not crucified (cf. surah 4:157, 171), and the Bible has been falsified and misinterpreted. This "corruption" *(taḥrīf)* includes suppressing forecasts of the Prophet. Christians have similarly sought to discredit the Qur'ān, but they have been under no comparable restraint in choosing their themes, and they have often attacked the reputation of the Prophet in order to argue that his revelation was contrived and fictitious.

Muslim Polemic. Christians long remained a majority under Muslim rule, but they began to attack Islam as soon as they realized that it had come to stay; however, it is convenient here to consider first the Muslim attack on *taḥrīf*. One of the first Muslims to argue that Christians had misunderstood rather than falsified their scriptures was a Zaydi Shī'ī from the Yemen, al-Qāsim ibn Ibrāhīm (d. AH 246/860 CE). Until the severe reaction against the colonialism of the last century, most Muslim polemic was purely doctrinal. In his *Book of Religion and Empire*, 'Alī ibn Sahl al-Ṭabarī (ninth century), a former Nestorian, aims, perhaps to justify his conversion, to show that the Christian scriptures foretell Muḥammad and enjoin Islam, and his *Answer to Christians*, concerned with Christology, is again based on his knowledge of Christian sources. Supposedly earlier (c. 820) is the *Apology* of al-Hāshimī, but we know it in conjunction with its refutation by the pseudonymous 'Abd al-Masīḥ ibn Isḥāq al-Kindī, attributed to Yaḥyā ibn 'Adī (d. 974), and it is likely to be at most a revised and Christian-edited Muslim argument. Although it abuses Christianity, attacks the doctrine of the Trinity, despises the Cross, and deprecates Christian fasting, it plays into the hands of the refuter and has a contrived air. More typical is the writing of al-Jāḥiẓ (d. 869), who is aware of arguments actually used by Christians (e.g., that the Qur'ān misrepresents their beliefs), but his knowledge is superficial, and he is much put out by the existence of different Christian orthodoxies.

The Muslim critique of Christianity increased rapidly in knowledge and sophistication. The attack by Abū 'Īsā al-Warrāq on the contradictions inherent in orthodox Christology seems to have made a considerable impact and was refuted at length by Yaḥyā ibn 'Adī. Ibn Ḥazm (d. 1064) understands *taḥrīf* in the literal sense and devotes most of his *Discernment of the Confessions and Sects* to scriptural dispute and to the defects of the Gospels and other books of the Bible. Al-Ghazālī (d. 1111), in his *Excellent Refutation of the Divinity of Jesus Christ*, uses Christian scripture (known, says his Christian editor, from Muslim sources) to criticize in turn the christological positions of the Chalcedonian, non-Chalcedonian, and Nestorian churches. Muslims were now at grips with Christian apologists. Shihāb al-Dīn al-Qarāfī (d. 1285), answering the brief *Letter to a Muslim* by Paul (al-Rāhib, i.e., the Monk) of Antioch, Melkite bishop of Sidon (fl. 1160), shows a sound knowledge of Christian scripture and discusses such varied doctrines as the Eucharist and Qur'anic abrogation *(nāsikh, mansūkh)*. Ibn Taymīyah (d. 1328) also answered Paul, as a courteous address to the king of Cyprus, contrasting the Qur'ān and the Bible in authenticity and expounding long arguments against the Trinity. These disputes are quite inconclusive on both sides.

Toward the end of the European Middle Ages we begin to find Western writers converted from Christianity in the course of the Ottoman advance. 'Abd Allāh al-Turjumān (early fourteenth century), a former Franciscan, discussed the authenticity of the holy books again in his *Intelligent Man's Gift in Reply to Christians*. Murād Bay Turjumān, a Hungarian serving at the Porte, wrote a defense of Islam in Turkish and Latin (1556) and praises of the Prophet in Turkish, Latin, and Hungarian; he writes devotionally, often using the terminology of Western religious philosophy. The forged *Gospel of Barnabas*, in an unexplained sixteenth-century Italian manuscript, an *evangelium Muhammadanum* intended to accord with the Qur'anic Jesus, has been conjectured to have a Morisco or convert background.

Christian Polemic. Early polemic is at its best in the dialogue, notably that of the catholicos Timotheus I with the caliph al-Mahdī in about 781 and that of Timotheus's coreligionist Ilyās of Nisibis with the vizier Abū al-Qāsim al-Maghribī in 1026. These Nestorians naturally exploited a Christology that was at least superficially more understandable to Muslims. Such dialogue may not always have taken place as recorded, or even at all, but their conciliatory tone offers a Christian apologetic intended to be inoffensive to a Muslim audience. Timotheus's presentation of the Prophet as "in the way of the prophets" is effective, without conceding any Christian essential.

This was not the usual pattern, even in the form of dialogue. Muslim polemic was often contemptuous, but it was never as virulent as Christian abuse of Islam and the Prophet, and much matter that was largely ridiculous or irrelevant, and always offensive, cannot have been used to impress Muslims, unless imposed by force in regions reconquered by Christians. It may be assumed that polemic develops out of widespread previous discussion, and that much remains at a low level of oral culture. Even in intellectual criticism of the Qur'anic text, writers forced it to mean what they chose, including, in some Byzantine cases, the worship of Aphrodite. The Byzantine tradition includes authors writing in Greek from within Islam or from outside, among them John of Damascus (d. 749), Theodore Abū Qurrah (eighth–ninth century), George Hamartolus ("the Monk"), Nicetas of Byzantium (both ninth century), and the pseudonymous author of the *Letter to the Emir of Damascus* (c. 920–940). Nicetas is hypercritical in his treatment of the Qur'anic text; all these tend to attack the Prophet, especially his wars and his marriage to Zaynab bint Jaḥsh, the influence on him of a supposititious Arian adviser, and the doctrine of a material Paradise. The pseudo-Kindī (mentioned above), writing in Arabic, is the most consistently unscrupulous in distorting every episode of the Prophet's life as self-indulgence (mostly sexual) and aggression (banditry, assassination). He deliberately ignored the sense of the Prophet's holiness in the sources he must have used, and he supported the gratuitous notion that the Prophet expected the resurrection or ascension of his dead body.

These themes had already entered the West by the middle of the ninth century. The miniature polemic found in Pamplona by Eulogius of Cordova (d. 859), archbishop elect of Toledo, and encapsulated in his *Liber apologeticus martyrum*, contains nearly all the elements used by al-Kindī and by later Western polemicists: the Prophet is accused of aggression and libertinism; the Qur'ān is ridiculed; much is made of the disappointed resurrection; the Arabs of the Hejaz are described as brutish. Eulogius was the pupil of the abbot Spera-in-deo, who had written a short polemic, now lost, in which he attacked the Qur'anic Paradise as a brothel *(lupanar)*, but perhaps Eulogius derived from him his fairer knowledge of the Qur'anic theology of Jesus. Eulogius's friend and fellow student Alvarus attacked Islam along the same general lines in almost hysterical rhetoric based on Old Testament parallels.

Except for this use of the Old Testament, all these attacks were renewed at the Spanish Reconquest. Most medieval polemic derived from Spanish sources, supplemented, but not extensively, from the literature of the Latin states in the East. Peter of Alfonso contributed Jewish folklore to the polemic pool, but the next important step was taken when Peter the Venerable, abbot of Cluny, visited Spain from 1142 to 1143 and commissioned translations from the Arabic, including a version of the Qur'ān (little better than a paraphrase) and one of the pseudo-Kindī. This Qur'ān circulated widely in manuscript until it was printed in the sixteenth century. Al-Kindī reinforced the libels on the Prophet with circumstantial detail of which the West had no other knowledge, and his work was circulated widely in the abbreviated form that appears in Vincent de Beauvais's encyclopedic *Speculum historiale*. Generally, the main polemic heads were *luxuriosus* (voluptuous) and *bellicosus* (aggressive), but Abbot Peter's own polemic, apparently never translated into Arabic, is consciously accommodating (on the information available to him) and much concerned with the authentication of scripture. The invalidation of the Qur'ān is a main theme of the mysterious *Contrarietas elpholica*, which Mark of Toledo translated early in the thirteenth century from an unknown Arabic original. He also made a much better translation of the Qur'ān, but it was generally ignored.

The Dominican Ricoldo da Monte Croce (c. 1243–1320) traveled to Baghdad (he was there about 1291), but the discussions he claims to have had with amiable Muslim divines left no mark on his polemic, derived from the *Contrarietas* and other inherited material. He attacks the Qur'ān as confused and obscure in ways equally applicable to the prophetic books of the Old Testament. The *Quadruplex reprobatio*, perhaps by another Dominican, Ramón Martí (c. 1220–1285), shows a detailed knowledge of genuine sources, such as al-Bukhārī and Muslim ibn al-Hajjāj, which he must have combed to find instances of Islamic jurisprudence objectionable to Christians as "contrary to reason" or "contrary to the public good," while ignoring the rest. Ramón Lull (1235–1315), "proving" the Trinity by "compelling reasons" in a number of works, had little impact, however. Peter Paschasius, a Mercedarian (c. 1227–1300), used authentic knowledge from the life of the Prophet by Ibn Isḥāq (d. 767) in a forlorn attempt to justify the more absurd of the Christian libels on the Prophet then circulating. These, many of them originating in the East, enjoyed a great vogue, not only in two Latin poems and a French paraphrase but also in many fragments and in chronicles, annals, and various occasional works: an assortment of recurring legends of how a fraudulent holy book was "revealed" by a pigeon or a calf, of how Muḥammad was the dupe of a renegade Christian monk, or was even himself a frustrated cardinal. The *chansons de geste* describe a pantheon of Saracen gods, but it is doubtful if they were intended as more than a joke.

Thomas Aquinas (c. 1225–1274) advised against polemic that could not be based on shared premises. Nicolas of Cusa (1400–1464), although his polemic method shows no real advance, seems to be sincerely seeking conciliation in his *De pace fidei.* Gradually the refinement of scholarly method eliminated the worst absurdities. The greatest of the seventeenth-century Qur'anic specialists, Ludovico Maracci (1612–1700), was scrupulously exact, but rigidly critical on traditional lines; his English imitator, George Sale (c. 1697–1736), was more sympathetic, although he is regarded by Muslims today as anti-Islamic. The old polemic lines were merely reoriented toward the general critique of religion by the Enlightenment (e.g., Bayle's *Dictionnaire,* 1696–1697, s.v. *Mahomet;* Boulainvilliers's *Vie de Mahomed,* 1730; Gibbon; Voltaire).

The Modern Period. Polemic revived in the nineteenth century but was profoundly modified on both sides by the colonial experience. Orientalists and missionaries alike considered themselves the intellectual and social superiors of nations ruled by Europeans. Improved historical methods introduced a new precision without necessarily changing old prejudice. Protestant missions, from the polemicist Carl Pfander (1803–1865) to a culmination in the World Missionary Conference held in Edinburgh in 1910, never escaped intellectually from the medieval polemic, but they added some contemporary social criticism, especially of the status of women in Islam. On the Catholic side we may compare Cardinal Lavigerie (1825–1892), archbishop of Algiers, and his alliance with the *mission civilisatrice* of France. Political subordination forced Muslims to take the defensive.

A nineteenth-century *aggiornamento* led by Sayyid Ahmad Khan (1817–1898), Jamāl al-Dīn al-Afghānī (1838–1897), and Muḥammad ʿAbduh (1849–1905) was followed by a series of apologists rather than polemicists, modernists influenced in different degrees by Western Christian, and post-Christian attitudes; among these were Muhammad Iqbal (1876–1938), Ṭāhā Ḥusayn (1889–1973), Salāh al-Dīn Khudā Bakhsh (1877–1931), and Kāmal Ḥusayn (1901–1977). The use by ʿAbbās Maḥmūd al-ʿAqqād (1889–1964) of the historical techniques of the day to refute Western Orientalism has been very influential; he respected Christ as prophet, which Tawfīq Ṣidqī (1881–1920), in violent reaction against the missionaries, did not. Widely read by an English-language public, Ameer Ali (1849–1928) skillfully reversed the Christian sociohistorical attack on Islam, notably in his *Spirit of Islam* (1891) and his *Short History of the Saracens* (1899).

The English annotations to editions of the Qur'ān by Mawlānā Muḥammad ʿAlī (Aḥmadī version, 1917) and by ʿAlī Yūsuf ʿAlī (Sunnī version, 1946) put forward arguments unfamiliar to Western readers; in a general way, Muslims felt that contemporary biblical criticism supported the accusation of *taḥrīf,* though Sayyid Ahmad Khan had minimized this. The Muslim Brotherhood saw itself as simply defending Islamic civilization. Rejected by most Muslim opinion at the time, ʿAbd al-ʿAzīz Jawīsh (1876–1929) attacked Coptic Christianity as colonialist, in his paper *Al-liwā,* but the militant Islam of the later twentieth century, preoccupied with the struggle against the moderates, has yet to produce major polemic against post-Christian neocolonialists; it may be expected, when it comes, to have large social content. The *jamāʿāt* (fundamentalist groups) already hark back to Ibn Taymīyah. On the Christian side, some fanatics remain, but the tendency among Western Christians (e.g., Louis Massignon, 1883–1962, and Kenneth Cragg, b. 1913) is to shake free of inherited bias.

[*See also* Islam, *article on* Islam in Spain, *and* Modernism, *article on* Islamic Modernism.]

BIBLIOGRAPHY

For a conspectus of much of the field, Georges C. Anawati's "Polémique, apologie et dialogue islamo-chrétiens," *Euntes Docete* 22 (1969): 380–392, is invaluable, but it is short and does not cover all. For medieval Islamic polemic, see Erdmann Fritsch's *Islam und Christentum im Mittelalter* (Breslau, 1930). A short, useful account of Byzantine polemic is Alain Ducellier's *Le miroir de l'Islam: Musulmans et chrétiens d'Orient au Moyen Age, septième–onzième siècles* (Paris, 1971). For Arabic polemic, the writings of Armand Abel are crucial: *L'apologie d'al-Kindi et sa place dans la polémique islamo-chrétienne* "L'oriente christiano nella storia della civiltà," no. 62 (Rome, 1964), and many other monographs. For medieval Christian polemic, see Richard W. Southern's *Western Views of Islam in the Middle Ages* (Cambridge, Mass., 1962) and my own *Islam and the West: The Making of an Image,* 2d ed. (Edinburgh, 1980). For modern Christian polemic, Youakim Moubarac's *Recherches sur la pensée chrétienne de l'Islam: Dans les temps modernes et à l'époque contemporaine* (Beirut, 1977) spreads a fine net widely. For academic tendencies, see Jacques Waardenburg's *L'Islam dans le miroir de l'Occident,* 3d ed. (Paris, 1962), which studies five major scholars. There is no general survey of modern Muslim polemic against Christianity, but for India, see Aziz Ahmed's *Islamic Modernisation in India and Pakistan, 1857–1964* (London, 1967).

NORMAN DANIEL

POLITICAL THEOLOGY is one in a series of attempts made by Roman Catholic and Protestant theologians since the 1960s to come to grips with the foundations of Christianity in light of the twentieth-century crisis of culture. After World War I, theology had reached a kind of equilibrium wherein the Protestants were constellated about the three giants, Karl Barth (1886–1968), Rudolf Bultmann (1884–1976), and Paul Tillich (1886–1965), and the Catholics were still operating under the auspices of the scholasticism evoked by Pope Leo XIII in 1879, when he called for a renewal of Thomism. By the close of the Second Vatican Council (1962–1965), however, these liberal and neoorthodox solutions to the mediation between Christianity and modern cultures had suddenly become irretrievably passé, for it was widely felt that none of the dominant theologies, estimable as they might be, had really come to terms with the crisis of modern culture in ways that were sufficiently profound or adequately differentiated.

These deficiencies were registered within the mainly academic context of European and North American theology through the increasing influence of the nineteenth-century "masters of suspicion," Karl Marx (1818–1883) and Friedrich Nietzsche (1844–1900). Nietzsche's critique of modernity had probed the enervating effects upon life in the West caused by the invasion of other cultures and the various forms of reflection upon culture by historical consciousness in terms of nihilism and the death of God. In his unforgettable image of the "last man," Nietzsche had limned the outcome of the liberal democratic and socialist solutions to the political problem. This radical crisis of meaning and value was explored during the mid-1960s in a variety of Christian theologies: the God-is-dead theologies of Thomas Altizer, Gabriel Vahanian, and Paul van Buren; the universal-historical theology of Wolfhart Pannenberg; the post-Bultmann hermeneutical theologies of Gerhard Ebeling, Ernst Fuchs, and Heinrich Ott; and the post-Heidegger theology of Karl Rahner. Philosopher Hans-Georg Gadamer, whose *Truth and Method* became required reading for theologians in the 1960s and 1970s, resumed the meditation of Martin Heidegger (1889–1976) upon the crisis indicated by Nietzsche and formulated the issue as follows: since all normative traditions have been rendered radically questionable, hermeneutics (the auxiliary science of interpretation) has become a universal issue. However, the challenge of hermeneutics to theology is usually diffused in one of two ways. In academic theology hermeneutics is trimmed down to conventional scholarly dimensions, whereafter theology is subjected to subdisciplines that divide up the data on Christian religion for ever more minute and critical study. Alternatively, hermeneutics may be subsumed within a transcendental-metaphysical reflection (as in Rahner) or a wholly ontological reflection (as in process theology). These responses to the issue of a universal hermeneutic as formulated by Gadamer—fragmenting on the one hand, and totalizing on the other—bore the earmarks of that sort of interpretation that Marx, in his famous eleventh thesis on Feuerbach, said needed to be supplanted by practice. It became a real question whether theology was anything more than either a species of intellectual history or an academically domesticated speculation without any practical bearing or importance.

During the 1960s and 1970s this question became inescapable. At the same time a common awareness was starting to emerge of the spiritual impoverishment arising from what were cynically labeled state-controlled monopolies in the East and monopoly-controlled states in the West. In the developing nations, dissatisfaction spread at the popular, grass-roots level in opposition to the dependence engendered by colonialist and imperialist policies of advanced industrial societies. In brief, the stage was set for theology to shift from hermeneutical methods of mediating Christianity with contemporary cultures to new approaches known as political or liberation theologies.

By 1970 it was already manifest that there were two distinct originating points for political theology: from within an academic context in advanced industrial societies, and from what have come to be called "basic communities" (from the Spanish *comunidades de base*) in developing nations. It is clear that both styles of theology are seeking to come to terms with the universal hermeneutic problem as portrayed by Nietzsche, Heidegger, Gadamer, and Paul Ricoeur. But it is no less evident that they mean to follow Marx's imperative of changing, rather than merely interpreting, history.

The leading exponents of political theology in Europe, the German Catholic J.-B. Metz and the German Protestant Jürgen Moltmann, might justly be characterized as asserting that interpretation of God is a practical and political issue. There is no split between change and interpretation: human and even revolutionary change is at root interpretative; and, especially when it comes to the reality of God, interpretation is primarily a matter of practical reorientation (conversion) and concrete action (transformation of individual and collective life). Moltmann at first depended upon Ernst Bloch's philosophy of hope but later moved on, using motifs from the critical theory developed by the Frankfurt School to reinterpret Luther's theology of the cross in terms of its revolutionary social implications. Metz, ever a disciple of Rahner, was challenged by the experience of the Holocaust and by the writings of the enigmatic Jewish-Marxist satellite of the Frankfurt School, Walter Benjamin (1892–1940), to reformulate Rahner's theological anthropology in terms of less idealist and more concrete notions such as "dangerous memory," "religion as interruption," and "narrative theology." Both Metz and Moltmann have used the "dialectic of enlightenment" (that is, the secularist thesis that the progress achieved by modern science and technology and by the bourgeois and communist revolutions has been perverted by the dominance of instrumental reason and the "iron cage" of bureaucracy) as it was formulated by Max Horkheimer, Theodor W. Adorno, and Georg Lukács. Metz and Moltmann transpose that dialectic of progress and decline into the tension now being lived out between the pole of liberal democratic and Marxist "ideologies of winners" and the opposite pole of redemption with the radical evangelical challenge to solidarity with history's outcasts and victims.

Liberation theologies emanate less from the academic superstructure than from basic communities at the popular level. [*See* Christianity, *article on* Christianity in Latin America *and other articles on the regional dispersion of the Christian religion*.] They reach public discourse in the writings of teachers like Gustavo Gutiérrez (Peru), Juan Segundo (Uruguay), José Miguez-Bonino (Argentina), Jon Sobrino (El Salvador), Leonardo and Clodovis Boff and Rubem Alves (Brazil), and so on. But they are also published in documents emanating from bishops' conferences as well as in the writings and political activity typified by the Nicaraguan priest-poet-revolutionary Ernesto Cardenal. In liberation theology the experiences of political and social oppression and of massive poverty have provoked a reading of the Bible and a celebration of ecclesial sacraments that are immediately political in the sense of being directly linked to the issue of emancipation from "structural" sin. Bourgeois social, political, and economic theories do not adequately explain the institutionalized schemes of recurrence that define the Latin American experience of oppression. Thus, liberation theology debunks bourgeois notions of "development" in favor of hypotheses like "dependency" and "national security state" in which Lenin's ideas about imperialism are applied anew. This is just one instance of the theology of liberation's penchant to have recourse to Marxism (especially the humanist strands) and Leninist or Maoist strategies in order to diagnose and remedy structural sin. This approach places liberation theologians under a double constraint since, on the one hand, genuine evangelical experience of God and faith in Jesus Christ Liberator is for them the wellspring and motive for social critique and action in a way that neither Marx nor Lenin could envisage, and, on the other hand, the theoretical weaknesses in Marxist analysis and practice sometimes threaten liberation theology with collapse back into the posture of the secularist dialectic of enlightenment. Added to this, liberal democratic and orthodox Christian misunderstanding and opposition perhaps unwittingly force the practitioners of liberation theology into increasing partisanship with secularist Marxist-Leninists.

Both European political theology and Latin American liberation theology have the Marxist orientation toward overcoming specifically bourgeois biases. In other advanced industrial countries like the United States and Canada, the Marxist analysis of structural sin in terms of class yields to three other emphases: racism (black and other ethnic theologies), sexism (feminist theologies), and issues of ecology. Like the liberation theologies of Latin America, each of these orientations struggles with the ambivalence between its roots in Christian religious experience and the terms of power and legitimacy as these terms were first formulated by secularist Enlightenment thinkers. Miscomprehension and unfavorable criticism force them, too, into stances ever more indistinguishable from their secularist counterparts. But then, reactions to such extremes among their cohorts have also led to recoveries and discoveries of Christian meanings and values.

Another increasingly prominent aspect of political theology is being explored by Ernest Fortin and James V. Schall, students of political philosopher Leo Strauss (1899–1973). Strauss took up the hermeneutic challenge laid down by Heidegger only to return to premodern authors (Xenophon, Plato, Maimonides, al-Fārābī) as an alternative to the mediations of the social sciences in the mold of Marx or Max Weber (1864–1920). Straussians bring out the tension between Christianity and liberal and socialist democracies. They tend to render Christianity as utterly apolitical; as a result, whereas liberation theology tends to flatten out into Marxism, Straussian political theory is perhaps too content with Platonic or Aristotelian reasons for espousing liberal democracy at the cost of solidarity with the poor.

The work of political scientist Eric Voegelin (1901–1985), as demonstrated by his multivolume *Order and History* (1956–), makes the tension of human existence—lived out in "the in-between" ("metaxy") as expressed paradigmatically in noetic and pneumatic differentiations of consciousness—normative for practical and political thought and action. Voegelin's ideas provide an antidote to the tendency of some political theologians to collapse that tension, and his ecumenical and transcultural comprehensiveness adds scope to conventional political theology. Nevertheless, by its very power and genericness, Voegelin's enterprise has a tendency to be too global to do justice to the particular problems of political practice.

Metz's American student Matthew Lamb has recently called attention to the relevance for political theology of the work of Bernard Lonergan (1904–1984). Lonergan, by demanding that the criteria of authentic performance in science, in scholarship, and in ordinary living be reconnected with the criteria for being authentically human (thematized in his notions of religious, moral, and intellectual conversion), has given political theologians a useful framework for the mediation of saving meaning and value in history. His stance toward the future in the light of the past, along with his germinal but still little-known work in economics, Lamb suggests, provides Christians with the first genuine alternative to either Marxist or liberal democratic political and economic theory. Whatever may be the fate of political theology as we know it, its reintegration of earlier forms of theology—emphasizing retrieval of past meaning and doctrinal and systematic restatement—into foundational, practical, and political questions about the right way to live can only be salutary for the practice of faith in society both now and in the future. Many contemporary theologians believe that political theology is, in fact, the chief symptom and response to the paradigm change theology is undergoing in the late twentieth century.

[*See also the biographies of Heidegger, Lonergan, Marx, Nietzsche, and Rahner.*]

BIBLIOGRAPHY

European Political Theology

Metz, J.-B. *Faith in History and Society: Toward a Practical Fundamental Theology*. Translated by David Smith. New York, 1980. A nuanced statement of Metz's mature position, with an account of the genesis and aims of political theology, his differences with Karl Rahner, and a basic elaboration of major concepts and themes.

Moltmann, Jürgen. *The Crucified God: The Cross of Christ as the Foundation and Criticism of Christian Theology*. Translated by Robert Wilson and John Bowden. New York, 1974. Uses themes from critical social theory as transposed into the perspective of the interaction between Father and Son in the crucifixion.

Latin American Liberation Theology

Freire, Paulo. *Pedagogy of the Oppressed*. Translated by Myra B. Ramos. New York, 1970. An extended commentary on the intrinsic nexus between language and life-form as the key to initiating a reflection upon and transformation of life-practice and to our becoming subjects instead of objects of history.

Gutiérrez, Gustavo. *A Theology of Liberation: History, Politics and Salvation*. Translated and edited by Caridad Inda and John Eagleson. Maryknoll, N.Y., 1973. Probably the classic text embodying the demarche of liberation hermeneutics, it correlates biblical texts on emancipation with the contemporary social situation as brought to light through Marxist social theory.

Feminist Liberation Theology

Plaskow, Judith, and Elisabeth Schüssler-Fiorenza, eds. *Journal of Feminist Studies in Religion*. Chico, Calif., 1985; Decatur, Ga., 1985–. A semiannual journal devoted to feminist research, discussion, and dialogue in all areas of religious studies, with articles regularly by all the leading theorists as well as newcomers.

Ruether, Rosemary Radford. *New Woman, New Earth*. New York, 1975. Here one of the most solid theorists not only retrieves many feminist motifs centrally important to secular feminism but goes on to use them to show how the concerns of feminist social critique are of intrinsic value to other emphases related to racism, ecology, and so forth.

Schüssler-Fiorenza, Elisabeth. *In Memory of Her: A Feminist Theological Reconstruction of Christian Origins*. New York, 1983. A superb critical historian and a tough-minded and sane thinker, Schüssler-Fiorenza is able to document clearly how patriarchalism is not integral to Christianity, how the Christian community got derailed from its own meanings and values, and how these meanings and values can be recovered in the present to the benefit of all Christians.

Black Political Theology

West, Cornel. *Prophesy Deliverance! An Afro-American Revolutionary Christianity*. Philadelphia, 1982. A brilliant work from the second generation of black theologians that brings the emancipatory thrust of black theology into dialogue with a large number of influential "discourses," including those of Jacques Derrida and others.

Wilmore, Gayraud S., and James H. Cone, eds. *Black Theology: A Documentary History, 1966–1979*. Maryknoll, N.Y., 1979. An excellent "backgrounder" with all the most influential statements and figures, along with bibliography.

Miscellaneous Works

Fiorenza, Francis S. "Political Theology as Foundational Theology: An Inquiry into Their Fundamental Meaning." *Proceedings of the Catholic Theological Society of America* 32 (1977): 142–177. Brief, lucid, and reliable, this is the best overview of the development of the notion of political/civil theology in the West from antiquity to the present.

Lamb, Matthew L. *Solidarity with Victims: Toward a Theology of Social Transformation*. New York, 1982. A difficult yet rewarding look at the possibilities of a comprehensive, differentiated, yet committed framework (for the tasks articulated by Metz, the Latin Americans, and the critical social theorists) to be found in the thought of Bernard J. F. Lonergan.

Lonergan, Bernard J. F. *Insight: A Study of Human Understanding* (1957). Reprint, San Francisco, 1978. An invitation and phenomenological maieutic toward an appropriation of one's rational self-consciousness and an intellectual conversion of the heart of concrete practice.

Lonergan, Bernard J. F. *Method in Theology*. New York, 1972. The best elucidation to date of the foundations of theology as practical and political in a differentiated society.

Strauss, Leo. *Natural Right and History*. Chicago, 1953. The best available account of the moral and political revolution from the classic tradition of natural right and natural law to the modern horizon of natural and human rights, along with its profound ambiguities.

Strauss, Leo. *Political Philosophy: Six Essays by Leo Strauss.* Edited by Hilail Gildin. Indianapolis, 1975. An expression of the core of Strauss's orientation, of which perhaps the most beneficial statement is the essay "The Three Waves of Modernity."

Voegelin, Eric. *Order and History,* vol. 4, *The Ecumenic Age.* Baton Rouge, La., 1974. An extended expression of Voegelin's most mature position, but especially pertinent reflections on the context of political theology in what he calls "historiogenesis."

FREDERICK G. LAWRENCE

POLITICS AND RELIGION. Politics is usually understood to refer to the accumulation, organization, and utilization of power in a region, territory, or society—especially the power to govern, to decide who controls the common institutions of society and on what terms. In ordinary popular understanding, as well as in the understanding of some scholars, this power has nothing to do with religion. The modern Western privatization of religion and the idea of the "separation of church and state" have convinced many that politics and religion do have, and should have, little to do with one another. To be sure, some see a relationship in that they view religion as the transcendentalized ideology of political-economic interests. However, a broader and deeper understanding of history and civilizations reveals that politics and religion are inevitably related, and that religion influences politics at least as much as politics influences religion. They are independent variables and are often found in tension, although they may be conjoined. Indeed, the ideas that religion is and should be "private" and "nonpolitical" and that the state is "public" and "secular" derive in large measure from the enormous impact that a specific religious tradition has had upon modern Western social life and thought.

Why Politics Requires Religion

One reason for the inevitable relationship between the realms of religion and politics despite their relative independence is the fact that power is not a simple thing. Power in politics is always a compound of force, influence, and authority. On one side, power entails the mobilization of muscle, numbers, and weaponry—in short, power entails force. Still, force is seldom simply force. All the accoutrements of violence also reflect the influence of both wealth and intelligence. Moreover, force—even when understood as coercive and lethal capabilities, and even when presented in alliance with economic and intellectual influence—cannot render power in the political sense. Political power also requires meaningful purpose and vision to be accepted as authority. That is, people within or from beyond the boundaries of a political system will subvert, disobey, and resist force (and its alliances with wealth and intelligence) if they believe that a basic vision of meaning or purpose is lacking in or threatened by that political system. Indeed, history is replete with efforts to seize, dismantle, or build counterforces against regimes believed to be illegitimate, without authority. Over time, each person and group faces a choice as to what, in the final analysis, in inherently worthy of being accepted as authority. Wealthy and intelligent force will always try to claim legitimate authority; but it is a claim that rests on qualities that wealth, intelligence, and force cannot finally command or control.

What is it that ultimately confers legitimacy and allows force and influence in some instances to become authoritative for political governance? Several possible answers present themselves. In certain classical traditions of the West, a specific kind of ideal intelligence, "wisdom," was seen as a primary factor (see Strauss and Cropsey, 1972). The ideal for centuries was governance by a philosopher-king, but this dual role has always been an awkward one. When the idealism of wisdom joins with the realism of force, the accent is bound to fall lopsidedly. This unevenness is reflected in the difference between the two disciplines that focus on one side or the other of this marriage. *Political philosophy,* as generally understood, attempts to clarify the principles of wisdom that can guide leadership and institutions so that they can actualize order and enact programs to enhance virtue and achieve happiness. *Political science,* as generally practiced, attempts to identify the patterns, dynamics, techniques, and strategies necessary for the accumulation and exercise of power—most especially the kind of power that forges solidarity out of disparate "wisdoms" by gaining at least a relative monopoly over violent coercion so that the will of the sovereign may establish "law and order."

The concern for wisdom has been a major feature of political thought at least since Plato's *Republic.* The concern for the techniques of force and influence was given its classical articulation in Machiavelli's *The Prince.* Views that mix wisdom and force can be found in the works of Aristotle, Rousseau, Thomas Jefferson, and Lenin. Nevertheless, the joining of wisdom and force seldom renders enduring authority. Wisdom may guide the mind and force may affect the body, but seldom do wisdom and force—alone or together—fundamentally shape the heart or the will. Legitimacy that renders authority involves qualities of commitment beyond the powers of human mind and body. Thereby people grasp the source and norm of wisdom and learn what to live, sacrifice, and die for—indeed, what to kill for. Wisdom, in the philosophical sense, becomes decisive authority only when it is transposed from philosophy per se into religion—that is, only when it is transformed into a metaphysical-moral vision of what is "really real" beyond wisdom and force.

However much these efforts to join wisdom and sovereignty differ from one another, they have one common feature: they presume what can be called a "political theory of social life." That is, these efforts presume that the political order refers to the most comprehensive community of all human associations and is subordinate to no other. In these efforts, descriptively and normatively, political authority is assumed to be determinative for the destiny of civilization.

Historical and cross-cultural studies, however, have raised doubts about this assumption. The reason is this: the various political orders that the world has produced are deeply affected by the dynamics and values of nonpolitical communities in their midst. In the Christian scriptures, Paul observes something that non-Christians have also recognized: not many are wise according to worldly standards, not many are powerful or of noble birth. Nevertheless, the foolish and the weak have resources determinative for authority that wisdom and power do not know. Many observers agree that cultural, social, economic, and familial (clan, tribe, caste, etc.) values delimit politics as much as, if not more than, politics shapes those values. Often, these values are viewed as sacred, divine, and inviolable whether philosophers agree or not. If "wise power" should be foolish enough to threaten these values, the authority of the political order is questioned, and hence resisted and often reconstituted. In substantial measure politics is thus better understood to be a concretion of nonpolitical and nonphilosophical values expressed through or derived from what can be called "the people." The slogan "Vox populi, vox Dei" places true authority outside the domain of philosophers and kings, and presumes a social theory of political life. It is enacted in practice wherever the political leadership or political philosophy adjusts to gain or maintain the support of the lawyer or the poet, the historian or the peasant, the worker or the trader, and—especially—the prophet or the priest.

A modern and widely held secular form of this social view of politics also tends not to refer to religion as constitutive of human community or politics. Instead, it speaks of politics in terms of those activities and structures proper to the formation, preservation, reform, or transformation of the "state." (The state is understood to be a contracted artifact, one in which persons or social classes outside the regime have the capacity—some say a right, or even a duty—to construct, reconstruct, or abolish in accord with their rational interests.) Politics in such a view is not a comprehensive community but a temporal, rationally constructed, functional unit within society. It is charged with the responsibility of manifesting the interests of the people (or, more often, the leading classes), and performing those limited functions that no other entity could accomplish (e.g., defense, social welfare, road construction). This broad cluster of views, which engendered modern social contract theories of politics and displaced classical ideals of philosopher-kings, may take what have been called "liberal" or "radical" forms, as can be seen in the works of John Locke or Karl Marx. The chief problems in these views are twofold: understanding the relation of the individual to the whole, and accounting for the foundations of value and meaning. How shall authority be formed when the interests of persons and groups do not coincide? And what shall guide authority when what the people want individually or collectively is of dubious worth? (See Wolin, 1960.)

Political practice through the ages and political theory in most cultures, however, have not been able to rely on classical or on modern, secular theories of authority for long. At best these theories grasp only dimensions of political life. The reason is simple: authority in all civilizations is incomprehensible without attention to religion. That is, politics cannot be understood without recognizing that the contours of acceptable wisdom, and the definitions of which interests and which forms of rationality are to be given approval and which are to be repressed, are fundamentally shaped by a governing metaphysical-moral vision. The essence of this vision is the surpassing conviction about what is "really real," the compelling sense of what constitutes ultimate and worthy power in a transcendent sense. Wisdom, influence, interests, intelligence, and political force must serve—and must be understood to serve—powers, principles, or purposes beyond themselves. Concern for these, as well as beliefs and behaviors thought to be appropriate to such concerns, are what human beings vaguely call "religion."

That is not to say that political force and these forms of wisdom, intelligence, or interest are of minor importance, nor that they do not also shape religion. No civilization can survive without political force and leadership committed to wise and intelligent service of the interest of the regime and the people in that civilization. The threat of violence is a fact of life in every civilization. No known societal system has been able to exist without some designated authority to adjudicate disputes, to disarm and control arbitrary violence from within, and to withstand aggressive invasion from without. Further, some tasks necessary for human community can only be accomplished by political activity. The clarification of common purposes and the establishment of common rules by which to live are required. Civilization demands a power which can compel contributions of time, talent, or tax to those activities necessary for the common good.

Without at least the threat of compulsion, some sectors and members of society would gleefully ignore the common life upon which their activities depend. These functions require political leadership and institutions. That is why utopian visions—in which politics is abolished, where everyone spontaneously works for the community welfare, and where force is neither accumulated nor employed—are largely irrelevant to historical life. That is also why a religion will die out if it constitutionally cannot provide legitimacy for political order and if it cannot incorporate wisdom, intelligence, and interests through giving them normative purpose. In a quite practical sense, also, political leaders can and do influence which religions are acceptable in a region. Religions are sometimes spread by political conquest, and political leaders in a society can influence which religious leaders—and thus which religious perspectives—are to be honored (as in, e.g., the Peace of Augsburg, 1555). However, if there is not conversion as well as imposition, the glory of the conquest is brief.

In short, politics does not determine the shape and direction of civilizations or of religions. Politics is but one function in a wide spectrum of human social activities; as Max Weber pointed out, it is ever subject to religious forces beyond its capacity to control. To be sure, within the limits of its specialized tasks, and in terms of short-range objectives, political decision-makers pay little heed to nonpolitical concerns. But even what can be called "purely" political actions take place within a socioreligious framework of authority that limits the range of possibilities. In fact, politics is more fragile than its relative control through coercion makes it appear to be. The fact that power constantly gets out of hand—and, wrapping itself in sanctity, becomes temporarily uncontrollable, violent, and arbitrary—is perennially disturbing. And we know that some religions lend themselves to such uses (see Lewy, 1974). But that knowledge simply confirms the view that politics must be seen in its relationship to religion; it is never simply an autonomous human activity. If religion goes bad, perilous politics ensues (see Gunnemann, 1979).

In most cultures, through most of human history, the relationship between religion as the guarantor of legitimacy and politics as the custodian of temporal authority in a government that must meet the religious test, has been recognized. And religions have been evaluated, at least in part, according to their capacity to shape and legitimate, renew and inform societies—societies which in themselves must have political authority. Despite the fact that some observers—under the influence of certain strands of European thought—have doubted or denied the connection between religion and politics, religion has not faded in the modern age. Churches, sects, and cults abound, and, beyond these phenomena, there have emerged in the West politically active pieties of the left and the right and, in the East, the secular "civic religion" of Marxism-Leninism. Each superpower has proclaimed itself to be sacred, the other to be demonic, and each backs its claim with weapons of massive destruction whereby it can render the damnation of its opponent effective. Hindu, Buddhist, and Islamic lands are caught in the crossfire and have developed their own religious fanaticisms. The motivation of these modern ideologies can be explained less by the analysis of wise power or by clarification of rational interests than by a nuanced understanding of what human beings will live, sacrifice, die, and kill for (see Merkle and Smart, 1983). Religion, often unacknowledged as the decisive force in political life, and often unexamined as the decisive source of authority, manifests itself in strange and threatening forms.

For better or for worse, twentieth-century events—as well as modern historical and cross-cultural research—have begun to bring about a fresh recognition of what most civilizations and politicians have known all along: religion must be reckoned with in politics. What religion can crown it can dethrone; what it can legitimate it can delegitimate. What religion brings into conflict, politics cannot easily reconcile; what religion unites, politics cannot easily divide. The conflicts of the second half of the twentieth century—in Lebanon, Cyprus, Assam, Mindanao, and Northern Ireland—cannot be understood without reference to religion. Developments in Iran are incomprehensible without reference to Shīʿī Islam, as are developments in Israel without reference to Zionist Judaism. Nor can we understand the travails of Latin America or the Philippines without charting the history of Iberian Roman Catholicism in these regions and recognizing the impact of the fundamental revolution in piety taking place under the influence of liberation theology as it attempts to transform the old patterns of legitimacy, form new communities of solidarity, and thereby reconstitute regimes. Africa remains simply a puzzlement without comprehension of Sunnī Islam in the north, the confluence of tribal religions and Christianity in the middle states, and Afrikaner civil religion in the south (see Moodie, 1975). To treat Indian politics without reference to Hinduism is silly, and to speak of politics in Sri Lanka, Burma, or

Thailand without reference to Theravāda Buddhism is simply naive. Korea, Taiwan, Hong Kong, Singapore, and even the People's Republic of China continue to manifest Confucian as well as Mahāyāna Buddhist, folk religious, and Taoist influences in an amalgam called "Chinese religion"—which itself has been in fundamental tension with both the post-Maoist version of that newer, powerful secular religion, communism, and the more recent indigenization of evangelical Protestant Christianity (see Stackhouse, 1983). Those who have recognized this fact have seen the various permutations of the mutual attraction and the inevitable clashes between the pairs of primary actors in the drama of civilization's political history, whether those pairs have been the priest and the prince, the monk and the king, the minister and the magistrate, the saint and the soldier, or the abbot and the commissar (see Niebuhr, 1959). And while we have long been able to chart the main options in political life—monarchy, oligarchy, and democracy (republican, pluralistic, or "people's)—we may have been less sensitive to the ways in which the social logics of religious options have given each of these a distinctive historical shape.

How Religion Affects Politics

Several approaches to the question of how religion affects politics are possible. Many modern scholars use historical-empirical methods and focus on detailed analyses of particular religions in particular periods of cultural history. Research of this sort is invaluable and suggestive. However, it often bears within it the perilous assumptions that each religion, each social ethos, each people, and each political order is so absolutely unique that scientific cross-cultural and cross-historical generalizations are extremely precarious if not totally impossible. Attempts at overviews tend to become merely lists of particularities, each one a curiosity unto itself that has little bearing on any other time, place, religion, or political order. In contrast with that tendency, the overview presented here presumes a commonality of human religious, social, and political experience within which the particularities and peculiarities can be examined as species within genera (see Shils in Geertz, 1963).

Selected research done in the historical-empirical mode can thus be understood as case illustrations of more general patterns of the inner social logic, and hence the political logic, of religions. For example, at the level of generality, it can be said that every religion is born out of a fundamental sense that something transcendent to the world of mere appearances has been unveiled—that is, has been revealed or discovered. Insofar as the meaning of this unveiling is grasped, known, or received by human beings, it renders a metaphysical-moral vision by which ultimate reality and the whole of life are understood. Each particular unveiling, of course, has its own distinctive features and thus each metaphysical-moral vision has its own inner logic according to which the proximate world of appearances is understood, ordered, and evaluated. Each metaphysical-moral vision tends to predispose persons and groups to respond to social (including political) possibilities and crises in distinctive and somewhat predictable ways. When people become convinced that this metaphysical-moral vision does reflect what is truly transcendent, and that it can give guidance to the living of life, the result is an "ethic" that can be said to consist of four parts. I shall term these parts *piety*, *polity*, *policy*, and *political action*.

Piety. As a foundation of a religion's metaphysical-moral vision, piety may well directly influence political life when it is profoundly and personally felt by political leadership, but this influence on political leaders is highly variable. More frequently, piety influences the population that political authorities want to lead. And it is through this more diffuse influence that the general ethos of a society is shaped. That is, piety forms a subtle web of values, meanings, expectations, purposes, and obligations that constitute the operating norms of a culture and within which leadership must operate. This religiously influenced ethos is the most general—yet often barely articulate—form of religious ethic that shapes society, and thereby politics.

Polity. Piety and its web of operating norms do not survive over the generations, however, without organized means of sustaining them. Each religion tends to form a characteristic and authoritative community or company of religious leadership through which the metaphysical-moral vision is mediated. These specialized custodians of the originating vision must structure their lives in accord with one or another interpretation of that vision, which they bear for, to, and with the whole society. Piety, to put it another way, requires a *polity*, and this too affects politics. Not only may piety influence politics through the personal belief and practice of specific political leaders, as well as through the generalized formation of ethos, it also shapes the polity of the decisive religious groups in a territory, and this provides determinative models of "right order" to governments.

In Western religious and political history, for example, the polity debates between the Anglicans, the Presbyterians, and the Independents in seventeenth-century England and Scotland were decisive for the formation of modern, Western patterns of pluralistic democracy. The battle cries of the various groups, each based on a particular interpretation of what a religiously valid polity based on true piety meant for politics, are summarized in the three slogans "No bishop, No King" (said with horror), "Presbyterians for a Strong Parliament!" (said with enthusiasm), and "Independents for Freedom and Local Control" (said in protest to the other two). The gradual acknowledgment that each of these positions had truly grasped at least one aspect of the polity-implications of valid piety gave rise to a constitutional, bicameral democracy with executive leadership. The resultant democracy has taken several nuanced forms in lands influenced by Anglo-American traditions and has been widely institutionalized in law (see Stackhouse, 1984, and Woodhouse, 1938). Today, in these lands, constitutional democracy is treated as sacred, and no political force from within or without which challenges it can fail to meet with a sanctified wrath full of religious passion. This wrath can be expected even from those who have no sense of democracy's roots in religious history and who may not themselves be personally pious. (There are other, parallel examples of the influence of religious polity on politics, although in quite different forms, as will be discussed below.)

Policy. A third way in which religion shapes politics has to do with the fact that every religious community must use social and cultural means to mediate its vision. Which social and cultural means are used is dependent upon three factors: what possibilities are at hand, which ones best convey the core meanings of the originating metaphysical-moral vision to the people, and which ones meet the needs of religious leadership in preserving and extending piety and polity. The inner logic of some versions of transcendence are best conveyed by cultus, others by defined creeds; some by codes of daily behaviors, others by episodic drama, dance, or "demonstration"; some by feast, others by fast; some by female symbols, others by male symbols; and so on. The characteristic means of mediation may be called the religious *policy,* and both the cultural and the institutional means utilized have an impact upon political life. Of course, this happens most obviously if means of coercion are seen to be a religiously legitimate way to enhance the influence of religious piety and polity, or a way to enforce cultus, creed, or code.

It is in policy, in this particular meaning of the term, that most people encounter religion, for it is policy that gives shape to worship practices. In popular understanding, indeed, policy is religion. In most ways, religious policy has the least direct effect on politics, but it may also be that it has the most influential indirect effect. At least two examples of this influential indirect effect can be cited.

First, when some highly regarded form of religious policy is violated by those who would gain political leadership, the resistance is both immediate and long-lasting. (One thinks of the slaughter of cows by Muslims in Hindu areas of India, of the defacement of the figures of the saints by the iconoclasts at the time of the European Reformation, or of the defilement of the temples by successive waves of conquerers in the Mediterranean Basin or in Buddhist lands.) A political power that engages in such activity is not granted legitimate authority by the people no matter how much force it may have at its command. The seeds of opposition, often residing in religious memory for centuries, breed repeated efforts to overthrow that order and restore "proper" worship.

A second way in which religious policy may indirectly affect politics is illustrated by the observation that every successful claimant to political power must demonstrate respect for established patterns of religious policy by honoring them and participating in them. By honoring religious policies, the claimant shows, at the least, that his claim to power is not in opposition to these policies, and, at the most, that he is willing and able to defend them. A number of instances can be cited. Newly installed nobles in ancient Greece had to make their oblations to the gods. European royalty is crowned in cathedrals. Newly elected presidents of the United States have prayers at their inaugurations. A newly selected chairman of the Presidium in the Soviet Union must confess adherence to the truth of Marxism and place flowers at Lenin's tomb. And a new member of local government in Java must sponsor a traditional puppet-theater performance known as a Wayang. These gestures signal a subordination of political authority to a transcendent authority, and failure to perform them threatens to abbreviate the regime. Such behavior also mitigates the possibility that religious leadership will use piety and polity as organizing bases against the political order.

In this connection, it is important to note that the specific policies developed by religions have enormous—if quite indirect—consequences for the society as a whole, and hence for that portion of it which we define as political. For example, contemporary feminist scholars point out that the organization of religious polities is usually male-dominated, and that the symbols chosen to convey piety are more heavily masculine than feminine. This imbalance, feminist scholars argue, is maintained in Judaism, Christianity, Islam, Hinduism, Confucianism, Buddhism, and Shintō, although some of these religions are more inclusive than others and press for equality of the sexes, at least in principle. These scholars argue that such imbalance tends to legitimate male domination in all aspects of society, including politics, and they argue for a religious transformation to legitimate a new sociopolitical order (see, e.g., Ruether, 1983).

As a more direct example, a religious policy which depends upon a specific cultural institution often allies religion with sanctified aspects of culture. In this situation, specific religions become nearly identical with those social functions. Confucianism, with its accent on the learning of the great classics, reinforced the educational examination system and the sociopolitical authority of the sage. Some ancient Greek cults, some Native American religions, and some modern psychologically oriented cults tie religion to healing and therapy, and thereby sacralize the religious authority of the "medicine man." Other religious orientations see the direct connection between religion and economic success—for example, Gaṇeśa worship in Hinduism and, in quite different forms, aspects of Calvinism, Taoism, and the cargo cults. Wherever these religious policies become influential, political authorities are also expected to provide and protect the conditions for "holy" teaching, healing, or the accumulation of wealth.

Political Action. There is a fourth way in which religion affects politics, but it will not be treated extensively here. This fourth way involves specific and intentional formation of "parareligious" or "paraecclesial" political organizations. Included here are religiously identified political parties, secret or public voluntary associations centered in a religious figure or a religiously defined cause of a political sort, and religious trade or workers' unions which develop political action committees. All of these demand a base in religious piety, polity, and policy, and from that base attempt to influence political policy directly by political means. Although examples of such movements can be found in many cultures and in relationship to many religions, they are effective and influential in political life only when a high religious consensus is already present, when politics itself is sacralized, and when the social system is relatively open to such developments. These developments may occur because the social system is constituted in a pluralistic way; because it is weak and in transition to a new integration on a new religiopolitical foundation; or because its internal metaphysical-moral vision demands such efforts to make its theocracy ever more complete.

One aspect of religious political action deserves special note. Very often specific groups in a society, dissatisfied for all sorts of nonreligious reasons with the political regime, will turn to religious policies and political action—if not always to piety or polity—in order to find a "legitimate" shelter for their opposition. In Asia, some oppressed Indians have in recent years become Buddhist to oppose the caste system (see Wilkinson and Thomas, 1972); in Burma and Thailand, some tribal groups constantly harassed by Buddhist rulers have become Christian for apparently comparable reasons (see Spiro, 1970); in Latin America, "protestantized" base-communities are organizing against Roman Catholic political hegemony as it had come to be allied with feudal elites at home and transnational corporate interests from abroad; and in the industrialized nations, labor unions turn to the churches to find the metaphysical-moral, as well as the organizational, support they need to alter their political-economic status (e.g., Solidarity in Poland and the United Farm Workers in the United States). However cynically some may view this kind of movement in terms of religious sincerity, the second or third generation of those who come into a religion for these purposes often become deeply pious stalwarts of religious polity, as well as becoming politically effective through the development of indigenous policies. The particular impact, of course, will differ according to the inner logic of the originating metaphysical-moral vision. [*For further discussion of this phenomenon, see* Christian Social Movements.]

Political Significance of Religious Worldviews

The social logic of the various religions may be grasped according to four sets of variables. Each unveiling of transcendence, as it takes form in a metaphysical-moral vision and is appropriated by piety, organized in a polity, and practiced in a set of policies, can be analyzed according to (1) whether it understands transcendence to be pluralistic or unitary; (2) whether it understands transcendence to be deep within—although hidden by—the realities of existence, or beyond, over, or against existence; (3) whether the character of transcendence is personal or impersonal; and (4) whether the nature of transcendence involves constant stability or dynamic change. These variables occur in various combinations, and the implications for human spirituality, for religious philosophy or theology, and for religious faith are enormous (see Kulandran, 1981). Here my purpose is to show how selected, specific combinations of these variables influence political life.

Primal Traditions and Complex Traditions. Primal religions, on the whole, view transcendence as pluralistic, immanent, personal, and dynamic. Although many primal religions have at least an implicit notion of a transcendent high god or of a deep and impersonal ontological structure that is the source and norm of all that is, the presence of multiple spirits, manes, demons, and deities more immediately attend life and interact with humans on a daily basis. These spirits are often understood to be part of the extended kinship system—

usually a tribe or a clan—and to dwell in a special territory or in holy places within the group's domain. Geographical features, plants, and animals are also thought to have divine or superhuman powers. Religious, kinship, economic, cultural, and political boundaries coincide or overlap. Other spirits within these systems may be thought to be the ghosts of ancestors who established ritual institutions—such as men's or women's ceremonial societies, warrior castes, hunting or agricultural rites, initiation procedures, and so on—that define the identity of the society and the roles its members are to play. These religious views and practices are politically important—are, in fact, often decisive for the distribution of authority in these societies. The means for honoring, evoking, and gaining favor from this complex population of spirits (if they are good), or for repelling or avoiding them, or overcoming the damage that they do (if they are bad or disturbed), occupy much of the energy of the group and frequently require highly ritualized forms of behavior in all areas of life. Primal societies thus often involve a certain constant openness to superordinate dimensions of reality, but this openness takes paths that lead to stereotyped relationships and patterns of living (see Gluckman, 1962; Mbiti, 1969; Spiro, 1967; and Presler, 1971).

Religious piety, polity, and policy thus become the constituting fabric of political solidarity, and they are intimately interwoven with sexual, educational, therapeutic, and economic functions. The holistic character of such societies, however, means that disruption at one level brings crisis to the whole. Primal religions may be highly nuanced and variegated; indeed, many have a subtlety that seems to exceed the capacity of observers to grasp. Still, primal religions seldom are easily transported into other histories, places, or populations; nor do they survive intact when confronted with more "complex" religions, that is, those religions that lend authority to cosmopolitan civilizations. Faced with the challenge of complex civilizations and their religions, primal societies crumble or are transformed. Conversion to the newer, complex religions in order to "get power" is not infrequent, although the reception of a new religion usually involves both modification of the society and modification of the received religion. Sometimes this brings about the reconstitution of the society on a new foundation, one that generates new religious prophets and radical political movements of a syncretistic, often messianic, sort (see Lanternari, 1963). At other times, the identification of the complex religion's "high God" (or ultimate, universal power) with latent or implicit elements of the traditional culture brings about the subordination of those previously dominant traditional beliefs and practices, which are then considered magical or superstitious. It may also allow the construction of new regional or national identities that comprehend a series of primal societies and provide the metaphysical-moral vision whereby new patterns of piety, polity, and policy are worked out in indigenous terms. Some scholars see the roots of "Third World nationalism" in just such developments (see Sanneh, 1983).

Today, the continued existence of these traditional, local cultures is threatened. Primal religions that do not transform are marginalized or are swallowed whole by complex religions, to the great pain of the elders. Adherents of these religions have been converted in the course of history to Hinduism, Buddhism, Christianity, Islam, or Marxism, and, with increased cross-cultural contact, that process is increasingly rapid. In the first blush of their conversion, former adherents of traditional religions often repudiate their old ways with a vigor that is sometimes abetted by, yet also sometimes resisted by, missionaries. Nevertheless, the deep religious commitments of these traditional religions often remain among the people as folkways and preconscious loyalties or fears. Thus every complex religion bears within it deep traces of primal religions. The deep roots both of mystagogic and occult wisdom and of what Peter H. Merkl and Ninian Smart (1983) have called "tribalistic" nationalism—the attempt to locate one's own ethnic group, territory, and political power at the center of the revealed world—can be found within every complex religion even if it resists these "pagan" elements or views them as merely the vestigial customs of various ethnic subcultures.

Traces of primal elements in complex religions are of enormous consequence in political life. Every alert political leader in open societies recognizes the sanctity of these residual commitments and avoids violating the sense of religious vitality that they carry; every shrewd politician in monolithic societies knows how to resonate with the echoes of primal religions and exploits them to gain attention and totalitarian commitment (as with, e.g., the "German Christians" during the Third Reich, or, more recently, religio-political movements such as those led by Idi Amin in Uganda, Pol Pot in Cambodia, and Ayatollah Ruhollah Khomeini in Iran).

Usually, however, the complex religions tend to displace or subordinate these primal religious sensibilities. They do so by unveiling what transcends them and by legitimating patterns of culture, law, economy, and politics that challenge and transform primal societies. Generally speaking, there are two ways of subordinating primal religious sensibilities: by attending to what is "higher" or by attending to what is "deeper." Hence, although there is much overlap and parallel development, and although there has been much interchange historically, complex religions tend to group themselves in two clusters: monotheistic faiths, most of which have originated in Semitic lands, and "ontocratic" faiths, most of which have originated in Asia. By "ontocratic" is meant the view that true religion is life in accord with natural being and that the harmonious state is the supreme earthly embodiment of cosmic totality (see van Leeuwen, 1960). Both general groups seem to have arisen out of primal religious contexts, in fresh, distinctive, unveilings of transcendence.

On the whole, those religions rising from Semitic roots—Judaism, Christianity, and Islam—understand transcendence to be unitary, beyond and over existence, personal, and dynamically involved in change. This must immediately be qualified, however, in regard to Christianity, for while Christianity asserts the unity of the one true God, it also asserts that the one God is to be understood in terms of three persons (the doctrine of the Trinity), and that these persons are immanent in existence. All these traditions nevertheless assert at least a provisional dualism between God and the world with the distance overcome by the Word of God—by auditory norms that are to be heeded, obeyed, preached, taught, and repeated in rites. In all cases, the transcendent God is seen as personal, which means not only that God can relate to human persons, but that God is or has a moral will. This personal God is compassionately concerned about human events and about justice in society and world history. What happens in the world, including politics, is to be in accord with God's will. The one true God, in this cluster of faiths, abhors unjust regimes and inspires forces to rise up against them. This God calls humans to fidelity and sacrifice so that a righteous order and a just peace can be established on earth as it is in heaven. This God is believed to allow humans to see enough of the divine character and purpose through revelation (both direct and indirect—that is, as delivered through inspired prophets and scriptures, and as discernible in creation, reason, history, and the requirements of institutional life) that humans can respond to God's will. Religious piety, polity, and policy is to be shaped according to the character and purpose of this sovereign being, and those political powers which do not reflect or place themselves under these transcendent standards are not to be heeded, obeyed, or trusted. They must be changed. That is why religious wars have been possible in this cluster of traditions. The inner logic of theism in these traditions requires an ethic, philosophy, or theology of political life.

The Asian religions—although there is great divergence among them—tend to understand transcendence as a unitary reality to be found deep within the structures of existence, as impersonal in character, and as the source of constant stability amid the swirl of apparent change. It must also be recognized, in this regard, that some branches of Hinduism (e.g., the *bhakti* tradition) and of Buddhism (e.g., the Jōdo school) have elements that very nearly approximate theism in the Western sense, just as there are schools of thought (and heterodox groups) in the Semitic religious tradition that stand very close to the Eastern religions (e.g., Sufism in Islam). Generally, however, transcendence—as discovered by the ancient sages through meditative practice or ecstatic experience—is understood to be hidden deep within the cosmic order, the recesses of consciousness, the ontological nature of life, or the soul that, as "being" or "nothingness," is eternally the same. These traditions assert, generally, a metaphysical monism, even if there is an epistemological dualism between what appears to be and what really is.

The moral demand in Asian religions, above all else, is to uncover and realize this deep, harmonious unity so that the tempestuous, changing character of existence is either correctly ordered or made irrelevant. Techniques for doing this are developed in elaborate detail. What happens in the world, including politics, is to be ordered in accord with the primal ontological structure of what at the depths of existence really already is. Unjust regimes, as judged by the standards of a divine will, are less problematic than disharmonious and disorderly societies that have failed to remain in accord with their own deepest nature. Political orders which can limit disruption and provide stability are granted authority.

Obviously, Semitic and Asian religions influence political life very differently, as can be seen when the specific forms taken by particular religions within each group are compared and contrasted.

Western Religions and Politics. What Western religions share, even given all their internal divergences from one another, is an impetus toward transformation—a living in the expectation of change, an attempt to bring the entire world into agreement with their metaphysical-moral vision, and a willingness to see political power as legitimate when it honors or reflects the social logic of their piety, polity, and policy. Within this group of religions, however, differences appear that affect politics in different ways.

Judaism. The metaphysical-moral vision of the Hebraic wing of monotheism was given in the Exodus. Through the inspired leadership of Moses, God led the children of Israel out from slavery in Egypt, through a wilderness, to a mountaintop experience—where a people was constituted and a righteous law was delivered in a covenantal act—and into a promised land. This is a God who is active in political history—not on the basis of a primal religious pluralism and a spiritual immanentism (although traces of these remain), but on the basis of a unified sense of a chosen peoplehood. This is a people under the one universal God, called to be a light to the nations, and given a specific geographical place from which to do so (see Mendenhall, 1955).

Like other monotheistic religions, the Hebraic faith has had difficulty with the problem of the one and the many, both internally and externally. Internally, the people were divided into several subgroups, the "tribes" of Israel. Each tribe has its own sacred altar, ancestors, polity, and policies. Yet how they are to find unity of piety is a matter of grave debate: this is a religion with a "constitution" (the Torah), but how the people are to organize their unity under this constitution is not clear. One strong possibility is an "amphictyonic league," formed by a representative council of elders and judges when dispute or invasion threatens the fabric of faith, law, and community (see Noth, 1930). Here, the view is held that because God is Lord and King, no human can occupy those roles. Rather, the Spirit of the Lord comes among those gathered to find and do God's will as occasion requires. A second possibility for the organization of the people is the principle that because God is Lord and King, humans need to organize the structures of coercive authority on the analogy of God's kingship, especially in time of extended duress and threat to faith, law, and community. In the Hebrew scriptures (Old Testament), especially in *Samuel*, agonizing debates are found about the relative political and theological merits of centralizing religious, governmental, and military polity to form and enforce unity. This is contrasted to the more traditional pluralism, where unity is occasionally actualized by the Spirit of the Lord and celebrated in renewal of the covenant. This debate was tentatively settled by the celebration of David as the priest-king who renewed and redefined the covenant in a monarchical direction. Yet, the tradition also included the prophets, who recalled the earlier Mosaic or confederation covenants and on those bases protested the pretense of the dynastic order.

When, under the pressure of political invasions, the sense of religio-political sovereignty was lost, the importance of the law became the basis for piety as well as for judging what political (and familial, economic, and cultural) patterns had to be maintained until the sovereignty was regained. As the ongoing tradition of interpretation and worship based on this law *(torah)*, Judaism became centered in the synagogue, the organized community of faith, and the polity that preserved the piety and formed the primary policy through education and worship. For all totalitarian regimes—and all monolithic religions—these synagogues have been perceived as a threat, for they have signaled a piety, a polity, and a policy that cannot be controlled politically. Decisive for the piety that sustained and governed these developments is the expectation of a messiah who will be sent by the living God and who will restore the integrity of religion, peoplehood, and regime through righteousness.

Over the centuries, Judaism has experienced tension between unifying and pluralizing forces. In modern, pluralistic settings, Jews have often been driven by their ethical monotheism to demand justice for all peoples, a development that has sometimes led to the loss of their own sense of distinctive peoplehood. When, however, monolithic religions and totalitarian politics have joined, mobilizing populations to attempt the establishment of "tribalistic" national conformity, Jews have frequently been among the first targets. The pogroms, ghettos, and other means of the oppression of the Jews—culminating in the Holocaust—constitute one of the greatest scandals ever perpetrated against God and humanity. Religious and political history drips with blood over these questions. In response, many modern Jews have tended either to modulate their traditional orthodoxy and turn to political activism with a strongly "progressive" and communitarian bent, or to reassert traditional claims to the Land of Israel through Zionism, or both. [*See* Anti-Semitism; Holocaust, The; *and* Zionism.]

Christianity. The Christian religion is incomprehensible without this Hebraic background, yet it carried several of the motifs discussed above in a different direction from Judaism. The prophetic, priestly, and kingly roles of the Old Testament are seen by Christians as integrated and personalized in the messiah, Jesus Christ. He is the center of true piety, who has already come as the very Son of God. The transcendent is made immanent in Christ, God is personified concretely in humanity, and the decisive, dynamic change toward the eventual transformation of everything is begun. Although fundamentally monotheistic, Christianity sees in this event the unveiling of the fact that the one God is triune in nature, a claim that introduces a pluralism into the very core of its metaphysical-moral vision. Furthermore, this event called forth a movement that organized itself in congregations modeled in part on the Jewish synagogue and established an organized center of loyalty, solidarity, and community (the *ecclesia*) as the decisive polity of life, over which no political authority can be sovereign. This movement also gave rise to a policy that could preach in many tongues, incorporate the insights of various philosophies in the development of theology, and selectively adopt cultic practices from many cultures. This Christian policy broke the Hebraic sense of ethnicity and peoplehood, and made the Christian faith accessible in principle to all peoples, cultures, and nations.

These developments produced a welter of Christian orders, denominations, subcommunities, and sects, all confessing the same Lord. In a similar vein, Christianity spoke of a moral law "written on the human heart" that in principle made it universal in scope, and less dependent on specific provisions of *torah* worked out for a specific people in a specific sociocultural context. Eastern Christianity, as exemplified by Greek and Russian Orthodoxy, took these motifs in a distinct direction from Western Christianity. By arguing against certain trinitarian formulas of the West, by adopting elaborately ritualized forms of worship and iconography, and by a policy of intimate cooperation with political power, Orthodoxy became closely associated with the national identities of whole peoples and represents still that form of Christianity closest to the ontocratic traditions to be considered below (see Harakas, 1983).

In the West, as Ernst Troeltsch (1981) demonstrated, elements of Christian universalism, personalism, and dynamic expectation of pending change have been formulated in two major ways. First, Christianity sometimes moved toward compromise with the established political power (in the sense of finding the "co-promising" features of that power), then legitimated that political authority, so long as it did not disrupt the relative independence of the church. Second, Christianity sometimes doubted any promise in political life and moved in an antiestablishment direction. It did this by forming sects which either withdrew from political engagement or attempted to transform political life by aggressive action against established power.

The ways in which these two major impulses in Christianity combined and recombined chart the various periods of Western political history. The early church, for the most part, separated itself from politics. By the time of Augustine, politics was accepted but was seen as of secondary importance (see Deane, 1963). Later, the medieval church took upon itself the responsibility of fundamentally reshaping political and legal institutions in ways that many scholars view as definitive for the development of the modern West (see, for example, Berman, 1983). After the Reformation, Protestants influenced political developments in ways decisive for pluralistic, constitutional democracy: ways that limited state power and that eventually gave birth to modern ecumenical and conciliar movements. These are presently attempting to overcome the internal fragmentation of Christian polity and to influence political matters by demanding that political authorities enforce human rights, secure peace, and establish justice around the world.

In all cases, however, the idea that, through Jesus Christ, Christians know of a "kingdom" that is not *of* this world but that is a present power *in* the world, and that they must engage in the formation of churches on the basis of that knowledge, has meant that Christianity has had a distinctive, pluralizing effect on society even where the church has been authoritarian. It also meant that political authority was considered secular and temporal. For Christians, all those ancient and obscure battles between popes and emperors, bishops and kings, ministers and magistrates have meant that an eternal and sacred *nonpolitical* zone of freedom from temporal and secular political regimes has become established in societies influenced by Christianity (see Figgis, 1956; Nichols, 1951). From that basis, Christianity built cathedrals, hospitals, schools, and universities, as well as new definitions of family life, guilds, and corporations distinct from the state. To be sure, Christianity seemed identified with domination by a specific regime during the Crusades, in moments of Calvinist theocracy, and in times of Spanish colonial expansion. Nevertheless, such efforts were and are repudiated by Christianity, and it is presumed everywhere these temporary distortions did not hold sway that Christianity meant liberation from the "principalities and powers." In its political implications, "Christian freedom" means that people have a God-given right to form an association—that is, an ecclesial polity—outside any regime and from that basis influence the regime by policies based on piety and not determined by realities of political power. Catholic Christianity tends to carry out its policies by sacramental monopoly and authoritative teaching; Protestant Christianity by personal conversion and public preaching. In spite of these differences, modern, Western, pluralist, constitutional democracy—guided by a concern for human rights that no political force can challenge in Christian-influenced lands—is largely rooted in this heritage (see Stackhouse, 1984). And it is within this framework that literally hundreds of Christian political parties, action groups, legal associations, and unions have been formed to transform one or another aspect of political life. Further, wherever Christian missions have penetrated, piety, polity, and policies are developed that pluralize traditional views of religio-political solidarity. The militant zeal with which some Westerners assail "godless totalitarian regimes," even if they tolerate authoritarian ones so long as such regimes allow the preaching of the gospel and the relative independence of the church (see Thielicke, 1968), is rooted in this religious metaphysical-moral vision. This seeming paradox results in great perplexity and consternation for those who do not know or understand the continuing religious influences in political life.

When Christians lose their metaphysical-moral vision, they tend toward a humanism of either the classical sort, fascinated by aristocratic wisdom, or toward a rationalistic, contractarian liberalism, or toward some attempt to combine the two. Yet, even under modern conditions of secularization and the extensive influence of nonreligious liberal political theory, the direct and indirect authority of the Christian heritage continues to shape political life.

Islam. Born at a time and place at which neither Judaism nor Christianity was effectively meeting the challenge posed by the breakdown of the primal religions of the Semitic world to the east, but sharing many of their root visions, Islam most radically accented the sense of the unity and truth of one transcendent God. In what Muslims view as the greatest unveiling of all, God revealed his will through the prophet Muḥammad. The result is the Qur'ān, the final, "uncreated" word of God. All life is to be ordered in accord with what is now revealed in the Qur'ān, and piety begins in simple submission. To be sure, however, neither that wondrous book nor the submitted heart could reveal all the details that have to be known for daily living. Hence, Islam too developed a polity and a policy to carry out its piety. The polity was formed by the integration of tribal senses of brotherly bonding with a supra-tribal sense of "national" peoplehood among all who submitted to this revelation of this one God. The "Brotherhood of Islam" became identical with the "Nation of Islam" and produced the most consistent and all-comprehending solidarity structure of any of the Semitically derived religions. In the Islamic view, the true dynamic of history was to be manifested through the extension of these principles throughout the world. From the time of Muḥammad, this polity was identical with and constantly taken as the decisive guide to political authority, and it served as the determinant as to what force could be granted legitimate authority. Islam rejected the ideas of an ethnically defined chosen people, the formation of synagogues or ecclesia, and the idea of a secular political order. Instead, wherever it has penetrated and gained a majority, it has attempted to institute an Islamic state as a matter of both piety and polity. The state was also to become the chief instrument of religious policy (see Gibb, 1928).

This effort is enhanced by the particular policy Islam has worked out. Piety and polity are communicated and extended through its system of holy law and jurisprudence (the *sharī'ah*) by which the rules for the conduct of all aspects of life are implemented—in family life, commerce, social activities, and governance. In what appears to be an intentional rejection of Christian developments of the separation of church and state, divergent cultic practices, and trinitarian theology, Islam is closer to orthodox Judaism (with its reliance on *torah*) in that it accents a system of universalistic law to guide its expansion and the behavior of its adherents. It differs from Judaism, however, in that its sense of peoplehood is neither ethnically, spatially, nor culturally limited. Islam imposes the universalistic content of its law wherever it goes, with enormous consequences for political life (see Watt, 1968). Under the imprint of Islam, cultures as divergent as those of Egypt, Jordan, Iraq, Bangladesh, and Malaysia have recognizably similar tendencies in political life. Even Iran, as governed by the Islamic Shī'ah sect, in contrast to the Sunnī groups that comprise the majority elsewhere, has comparable impulses. By the social logic of its metaphysical-moral vision, Islam must continue to expand its "universalistic" influence by extending its political sway and by intensifying its enforcement of *sharī'ah* in all aspects of life (see W. C. Smith, 1957). Islam thus finds the pluralistic models of constitutional secular government as present in the West, and as partially represented in modern Israel, to be inherently contrary to its piety. Islam finds the nearer opponent the more scandalous. The consequences of the Islamic position toward the West are explosive, both for internal and for international politics. It is an explosiveness matched only by a pending struggle between Islam and "godless Communism," a situation likely to shake the world and already anticipated in the Soviet occupation of Afghanistan. For Islam, a fully secularized society and state is unthinkable.

Judaism, Christianity, and Islam are religions that want to bring politics to the service of higher truth—more universal in principle and in practical reach. All of these religions, in their impact upon politics, are peppered with distortion, scandal, and terror; they are also salted by moments in their histories when they were able to call upon their deepest presuppositions to provide rich resources of wisdom and rational calculation of interests for the common good. But the force that drives these religions, and that will be of incalculable import for political life so long as they continue to exist, is that they will constantly try to transform the world in the name of God. In the process, they are likely not only to clash with each other, but—more dramatically—with primal religions, with the ontocratic religions of the East, and with the humanistic religions of modern secularism. Politics can only work with, and sometimes around, these realities—but not against them. And only those traditions that provide for religious pluralism and that separate religious piety, polity, and policy from the direct exercise of political force can prevent what the Hebrew scriptures call "holy war," Christians "crusade," and Muslims *jihād* from becoming the form of the clash.

The "Ontocratic" Traditions. Within the second group of religions, those of a more ontocratic character, I first consider those of Chinese, and then those of Indic, origin.

Chinese religion. As deeply as can be traced in Chinese history, clan-centered primal religions were practiced that entailed the worship of ancestors, spirits, and the powers of nature (see Heine-Geldern, 1956). As the more complex religions rose in that part of the world, these primal patterns were less displaced by a vision of a transcendent God than subordinated by a deepening of a metaphysical-moral vision. This deepening vision saw a transcendent ordering principle within and behind these powers—an ultimate principle of harmonious interdependence between the cosmos, its spirits and forces, and the world of humans, a world that through its actions governed the relations of parts to whole. Humanity is understood to be constituted of and constantly influenced by principles and forces that emanate from the heavens, the earth, and the winds. If persons and groups live in accord with these powers, "wealth, peace, long life, and many children" are the results. Above all, the state must be organized with natural groupings of clans and clan ancestors, as the historical replication of the deepest harmonies of the universe, to keep social order from disruptions. Thus, human beings—especially those involved in governance—must participate in the cosmic pattern, ordering all life by enacting appropriate behaviors and ceremonies that symbolically put everything in its proper, naturally hierarchic order (see Creel, 1970). There is little emphasis here on auditory disclosure of a transcendent, ethical, and personal will. Instead, there is the visual and kinesthetic disclosure of the transcendent "order of being," an order which is manifested in and through all when each part of the whole exemplifies what, at its deepest level, it truly is.

The polity of Chinese religion was the empire, throughout its many dynasties. But the ideal of the empire seldom involved direct totalitarian rule, for it was always qualified by religious policy. That is, although there were no institutional checks on the hereditary monarch, the range of actions available to him were circumscribed by ceremonial requirements initially governed by the priests and, eventually, controlled by the Confucian literati. The Confucian sages developed a highly complex and sophisticated system of education and examination in the ancient classical texts, in which the "right knowledge" of how to preserve the harmony between the cosmos, regime, family, and self was decisive. The policy of reliance on learned, aesthetic, administrative experts to consolidate and propagate legitimate authority differs strikingly from the policies of primal religions' magic, Jewish synagogue, Orthodox liturgy, Catholic teaching, Protestant preaching, and Islamic political jurisprudence. Traditional Taoist and Mahāyāna Buddhist priests were radically subordinated in influence by the Confucians, and became the custodians of primal folk-religious impulses among the peasantry. The Confucian scholars became the nonordained custodians of an ethical religion focusing its authority on the ideal of a well-run state, wherein all fulfilled the duty of refined harmony by raising a family, obeying the elders, honoring the ancestors, and deferring to officials, thereby supporting the empire. The governing classes were to learn the classics, take office, and implement the ontic-ethical principles in aesthetic behavior and administrative authority. Indeed, in following those principles the literati were to advise the emperor how to behave, and to replace him when he did not or could not follow their advice. Such a religion produced an extremely high and complex civilization—one characterized by stability and continuity despite enormous struggles between warlords, regions, and clans, as well as invasions from abroad. Such a religion, however, has had great difficulty in coping with change. The dynamic theistic religions from the West have threatened it periodically, and the secular religion of communism seems, at least temporarily, to have broken its back. (Some scholars argue, however, that the post-Maoist communism of modern China is simply a repristination of an ethical nationalism, led by a new order of literati who study modern, scientific texts, rather than ancient, classical ones.)

One cannot deny that patterns of piety, polity, and policy as deep and complex as China's seem to continue to affect even the People's Republic of China, as well as traditions in Korea and Japan where exported versions of this tradition mixed with, and reshaped, indigenous religions. Throughout countries in Southeast Asia, also, Chinese minorities hold these traditions dear.

Hinduism. India mothered two of the world's greatest religions—Hinduism and Buddhism, the latter born out of the former. The fundamental metaphysical-moral vision of Hinduism entails a belief that behind all that is, is a divine, suprapersonal oversoul (Brahmā), a spiritual reality which is the source and norm of all that exists. The variations of this theme are enormous in Hinduism, in part because of the vast resources of the sacred writings (the Vedas, the Upaniṣads, the epics, etc.) from which Hindus draw inspiration, and in part because in practice Hinduism has absorbed and become modified by an enormous number of motifs from primal religions, heterodox movements, and foreign influences. For all the difficulties of presenting a coherent picture of this rich family of beliefs and customs, it is possible to trace the main outlines of Hinduism as it bears on politics. This can be accomplished by identifying certain characteristic and dominant, although by no means exhaustive, motifs in religious piety, polity, and policy (see Basham, 1963).

One aspect of piety that is decisive is the notion that each person—some Hindus contend, each living thing—contains a "soul" *(ātman)* that is, in fact, a part of *brahman,* temporarily alienated from its "ground." This soul is governed by a fundamental law of metaphysical rectitude *(dharma)* that not only must be discovered, but also must be obeyed so that *ātman* can find its way back to reunion with *brahman* through a long series of reincarnations *(saṃsāra).* In the course of this pilgrimage, the soul must have somewhere to reside in the apparent, material world, and it resides in persons. In fact, each person is a part of a group in a great chain of groups of persons, each group having its own appropriate form of behavior according to the relative level of self-realization in the soul's *dharma,* which is also a relative indicator of the reintegration with *brahman.* The metaphysical-moral vision, thus, is of a universe whose nature is essentially spiritual and only secondarily material, hierarchically arranged according to the scale of realization and fulfillment of the process of the soul's reabsorption *(mokṣa).* Piety stamped by this vision is focused on the discernment and cultivation of the deep powers within the self (see Organ, 1970).

This Hindu understanding of piety has deep implications for religious polity, since the decisive and holy groupings are those endogamous groups of persons—practicing strict commensalism and connubium, and formed locally into extended joint families—which occupy the higher rungs of the ontic social hierarchy (see Dumont, 1970). These "castes" (*varṇas*) and subcastes (*jātis*) are, as it were, the eternal, living vessels present in the material-social world to receive the souls on their pilgrimage to reabsorption. The highest of these groups is the *brāhmaṇa,* or priestly, caste, and the second is the *kṣatriya,* the hereditary, dynastic ruler-warrior caste. Political undertakings and institutions that are deemed legitimate by Hinduism must honor the religious authorities above them, obey their instructions in *dharma,* and see that all the *jāti*s are kept intact and in order, lest the whole fabric of civilization obscure what is really real and the souls, on their way to the oversoul over eons of reincarnation, lose their way. The implications of this system are worked out in highly sophisticated detail in such authoritative writings as the *Laws of Manu* and other Dharmaśastras, which are interpreted by the Brahmanic pandits and enforced by rulers.

The policies by which this piety and polity are forwarded are rich and complex, and are centered in forms of cultural expression, such as the institution of the guru (the teacher-instructor), the building of *āśrama*s and temples, and the rendering of homage to images of the gods (those visual representations of the ineffable spiritual reality that ultimately cannot be represented). There are literally hundreds of ways of communicating the spiritual forces that point to *dharma,* from astrology, sacred dance, asceticism, numerology, and color-coded symbolism, to discourses, devotional poetry, lyrics, and hymnology (to name but a few). In this way the fundamental metaphysical-moral vision of Hinduism has penetrated every aspect of Indian cultural life. Only Islam, from an entirely different perspective, has determined the whole of existence as thoroughly as Hinduism: the former has accomplished this by pressing all of life's variety into a unified mold; the latter by infusing the immense variety of life with a spiritual substratum to sustain and sanctify it.

Hindu politics, formed by this tradition over at least three thousand years, has gone through considerable travail in modern history. Islamic invaders replaced the *kṣatriya* rulers with their own maharajas, although much of Hinduism in the villages and outside the courts was left intact, thus preserving a representative, inter-*jāti* body for local governance *(panchiat).* Subsequently, the British rode to power on the backs of commercial interests and introduced Western patterns of law and political order. These, in turn, have only recently been replaced by the Indian constitutional government. This government itself is a result of the impact of the Hindu renaissance at the turn of the century culminating in Gandhi's invocation of certain, selected Hindu sensibilities—also influenced by Christianity—in a mass movement toward independent nationalism (see Ghose, 1973). The vast pluralism of independent India allowed it to form the world's largest operating democracy with a secular, constitutional government, but it is a democracy in which ontocratic and caste considerations govern much of political existence. Hereditary and dynastic rule in a hierocracy of being is viewed as inevitable. Indeed, today India is troubled by pressures from minority groups—Muslims, Buddhists, Sikhs, Christians, and tribalists—who are convinced that the ostensibly secular and democratic Indian politics is designed to hinduize them, while militant Hindu organizations such as the Rashtriya Swayan Sevak are active in many parts of India to restore what they perceive as a truly Hindu order against foreign elements. However much philosophers may study and honor the wisdom of India, however much Westerners (as well as liberal, socialist, Christian or westernized Indians) fret about the economic state of the people, and however much these deserve attention, it is religious considerations embodied in caste-related communalism that continue to determine the political situation of India and to limit its contributions to the world.

Buddhism. Hinduism had been challenged long before the modern age: Buddhism was born out of a spiritual attempt to redefine Hinduism's metaphysical-moral vision, and consequently it has overtones of efforts to overthrow the authority of the Brahmanic priests, an act which would, or could, transform the caste system and alter the place and role of politics.

Buddhism, of course, was born out of the great unveiling of transcendence by Gautama, who through meditation reached the enlightened insight that the metaphysical-moral vision of his Hindu predecessors was mistaken. Suffering in this world was neither a necessary part of the soul's pilgrimage to its home in the acosmic oversoul, nor caused by disruption of the cosmic or caste order. These, in fact, are illusions; for the source of ill is attachment to these, and other, "things." At the deepest level, things (including, ultimately, *ātman* and *brahman*) are not real. What is real, and of transcendent worth, in the Buddhist view, is the knowledge of how enlightened release from these and other things may be found: by detachment. The sophisticated epistemological and acosmic ontology of Buddhism cannot be conveyed here, but some principal ways in which it has been grasped in piety, polity, and several policies as they bear on politics can be identified.

At first, Buddhism led to an intense piety of self-help: it is held that each person must find out the truth alone, by withdrawal from the world. This idea led to the formation of monastic orders of those who left the world behind, and to the most sustained and consistent form of asceticism the world has seen. Yet the transcendence which each person discovers is unique, and hence the idea of transcendence in Buddhism is quite variegated. At least in theory, this has meant that Buddhism is the least political religion yet encountered in terms of its own inherent vision. The orders of monks (*saṃghas*) are not primarily concerned about a normative group polity. Monasteries have, of course, a certain discipline, but the true monk is beyond all that and in no way is concerned about political life, including the political life of the order. Certainly questions of how political life relates to power, interest, force, and even worldly wisdom are, in principle, incidental.

However, these aspects of Buddhism had enormous indirect influences, for they destroyed in principle—and in actuality for a period of time in India—the authority of the Brahmanic castes. Functionally, that left the *kṣatriya* class, the class of Buddha himself, a relatively free hand. Buddhism has, consequently, everywhere been spread and supported by kingly rulers—from the days of Aśoka through the Chinese warlords in the north to Korean and Japanese courts, and through the nobility of Sri Lanka, Burma, and Indochina in the south to the king of Thailand today (see Swearer, 1981, and de Bary, 1960).

Ironically, in its expansion Buddhism carried precisely those ideas against which it argued (see Spiro, 1970, and B. L. Smith, 1978a and 1978b). Thus, almost inadvertently, it has carried with it categories of ontocratic caste structures (the part of Hindu political theory that is most hierarchically ordered) and rich cultural forms—arts, music, astrology, numerology, poetry, and so forth—throughout Asia as far as Japan and Indonesia. In each context, it altered and was altered at the popular levels by the absorption of primal religious sensibilities—as well as by Confucian and Taoist motifs in the north—as it gave a more universalistic piety to the cultures it encountered. Thus, Buddhism's basic policy has taken on nearly as many cultural forms as Hinduism. Yet, wherever it is present it has a special affinity with royal hegemony and has been viewed as the most magnificent jewel in the crown of the rulers. Protected by them until displacement by colonial rule, modern Buddhism is often closely associated with militant nationalist identity (see D. E. Smith, 1966).

Concluding Remarks

Some scholars have argued that the acosmic ontology of Buddhism, and its close association with centralized political-military rule (somewhat like Eastern Orthodox Christianity, and the Roman Catholicism of Iberian colonialism in other traditions), has conditioned some cultures to be especially susceptible to the new secular religion of communism (see, e.g., Sarkisyanz, 1965). Whether that is a fully warranted argument or not, it is impossible to conclude this overview without reference to the fact that all of the religions here treated presently feel pressure from communism. They are not sure whether to view it as a political-economic system that is opposed to all religion; as a social science that they can wed with their own religion; or as a new "secular religion" that combines the dynamic elements of the Semitic religions' sense of historical change with an interest-based rationalism. As a secular religion, communism produces a fully immanental, antimoral, antimetaphysical, and often nationalistic ideology (piety) organized by the party (polity) and spread by military revolution and industrial development (policy).

The full answer to the question of the relationship between religions and communism is beyond the scope of this entry. We know, however, that the world's religions—including even communism, if it is a religion—must even now assess how they are to live in a world where the absolute triumph in unmodified form of any of them is unlikely in the near future, and at the same time recognize that ecumenical perspectives to prevent mutual destruction are not obvious. That is a task which requires testing these religions' metaphysical-moral foundations to see whether any of them can guide a cosmopolitan, pluralistic world. The question is: Can any of them shape piety, polity, and policies in a global context, that is, in a context where political power has a new capacity to destroy us all and has, thus, lost much of its legitimate authority?

[*General themes discussed in the foregoing article receive further treatment in* Bureaucracy; Civil Religion; Community; Economics and Religion; Kingship; Law and Religion; Messianism; Morality and Religion; Revolution; Secularization; Society and Religion; Theocracy; *and* Wealth. *The encounter of Marxist theory and the political practice of state communism with religious traditions is treated in* Marxism. *For detailed treatment of the impact of Western civilization and Christianity upon primal religious traditions, see* African Religions, *article on* Modern Movements; Australian Religions, *article on* Modern Movements; Cargo Cults; Ghost Dance; North American Religions, *article on* Modern Movements; *and* Oceanic Religions, *article on* Missionary Movements.

For further discussion of topics bearing on politics and religion within specific religious traditions, see the following articles. South Asian traditions: Cakravartin; Saṃgha, *article on* Saṃgha and Society; *and* Varṇa and Jāti. *China:* Confucian Thought, *article on* The State Cult; Millenarianism, *article on* Chinese Millenarian Movements; *and* T'ai-p'ing. *Japan:* Japanese Religion, *article on* Religious Documents. *Judaism:* Jewish People; Persecution, *article on* Jewish Experience; *and* Zealots. *Christianity:* Christian Social Movements; Church, *article on* Church Polity; Church and State; *and* Political Theology. *Islam:* Caliphate; Imamate; Modernism, *article on* Islamic Modernism; *and* Ummah.]

BIBLIOGRAPHY

For basic theories of political life, as influenced by religious and philosophical developments in the West, see Sheldon S. Wolin's *Politics and Vision* (Boston, 1960); *History of Political Philosophy*, 2d ed., edited by Leo Strauss and Joseph Cropsey (Chicago, 1972); Karl W. Deutsch's *The Nerves of Government* (New York, 1966); *Authority*, edited by Carl J. Friedrich (Cambridge, Mass., 1958); the third volume of Max Weber's *Economy and Society*, 3 vols. (Berkeley, 1978); and Ernst Troeltsch's still-unsurpassed *The Social Teaching of the Christian Churches* (1931; Chicago, 1981). *Religion and Politics in the Modern World*, edited by Peter H. Merkl and Ninian Smart (New York, 1983), is perhaps the most useful symposium on contemporary developments.

The most important comparative overview of religions as they bear on social and political life remains Max Weber's *Gesammelte Aufsätze zur Religionssoziologie*, 3 vols. (Tübingen, 1920–1921), all parts of which are now translated under various titles. Significant comparative modifications of Weber's views can be found in *Old Societies and New States*, edited by Clifford Geertz (New York, 1963); *The Protestant Ethic and Modernization*, edited by Schmuel N. Eisenstadt (New York, 1968); Guenter Lewy's *Religion and Revolution* (Oxford, 1974); Reinhard Bendix's *Kings or People: Power and the Mandate to Rule* (Berkeley, 1978); Carroll J. Bourg's "Politics and Religion," *Sociological Analysis* 41 (1980): 297–315; and my *Creeds, Society and Human Rights* (Grand Rapids, Mich., 1984).

Studies of special importance in regard to the monotheistic religions include George E. Mendenhall's *Law and Covenant in Israel and the Ancient Near East* (Pittsburgh, 1955); Martin Noth's *Das System der zwölf Stämme Israels* (Stuttgart, 1930); George E. Wright and R. H. Fuller's *The Book of the Acts of God*, rev. ed. (London, 1960); H. A. Deane's *The Political and Social Ideas of St. Augustine* (New York, 1963); C. N. Cochrane's *Christianity and Classical Culture* (Oxford, 1957); Harold J. Berman's *Law and Revolution: The Formation of the Western Legal Tradition* (Cambridge, Mass., 1983); John Neville Figgis's *Political Theory from Gerson to Grotius, 1414–1625* (1916; Cambridge, 1956); *Puritanism and Liberty*, edited by A. S. P. Woodhouse (London, 1938); James Hastings Nichols's *Democracy and the Churches* (Philadelphia, 1951); E. Digby Baltzell's *Puritan Boston and Quaker Philadelphia* (New York, 1980); Reinhold Niebuhr's *The Structure of Nations and Empires* (New York, 1959); Helmut Theilicke's *Theological Ethics*, vol. 2, *Politics* (Philadelphia, 1968); Stanley S. Harakas's *Toward Transfigured Life* (Minneapolis, 1983); Arend Theodoor van Leeuwen's *Christianity and World History* (New York, 1960); Harry J. Benda's *The Crescent and the Rising Sun* (The Hague and Bandung, Indonesia, 1958); W. Montgomery Watt's *Islamic Political Thought* (Edinburgh, 1968); Wilfred Cantwell Smith's *Islam in Modern History* (Princeton, 1957); H. A. R. Gibb's *Islam*, 2d ed. (Oxford, 1978), formerly *Mohammedanism* (1969); John O. Voll's *Islam: Continuity and Change in the Modern World* (Boulder, 1982); T. Dunbar Moodie's *The Rise of Afrikanerdom* (Berkeley, 1975); Jan P. Gunnemann's *The Moral Meaning of Revolution* (New Haven, 1979); and Rosemary Radford Ruether's *Sexism and God-Talk* (Boston, 1983).

Those titles of greatest importance in regard to the "ontocratic" religious traditions and their encounter with monotheistic traditions or communism include the following: Thomas A. Metzger's *Escape from Predicament: Neo-Confucianism and China's Evolving Political Future* (New York, 1977); Peter Weber-Schäfer's *Oikumene und Imperium: Studien zur Ziviltheologie des chinesischen Kaiserreichs* (Munich, 1968); H. G. Creel's *The Origins of Statecraft in China* (Chicago, 1970); Robert von

Heine-Geldern's *Conceptions of State and Kingship in Southeast Asia* (Ithaca, N.Y., 1956); Ch'ing-k'un Yang's *Religion in Chinese Society* (Berkeley, 1961); Robert N. Bellah's *Tokugawa Religion* (New York, 1957); *Sources of Chinese Tradition*, compiled by Wm. Theodore de Bary and others (New York, 1960); A. L. Basham's *The Wonder That Was India*, rev. ed. (New York, 1963); *The Sources of Indian Tradition*, compiled by Wm. Theodore de Bary and others (New York, 1958); Troy W. Organ's *The Hindu Quest for the Perfection of Man* (Athens, Ohio, 1970); Sabapathy Kulandran's *The Concept of Transcendence* (Madras, 1981); Louis Dumont's *Homo Hierarchicus* (Chicago, 1970); Sankar Ghose's *Nationalism, Democracy and Socialism in India* (Bombay, 1973); Gunner Myrdal's *Asian Drama* (New York, 1971); Melford E. Spiro's *Buddhism and Society* (New York, 1970); *South Asian Politics and Religion*, edited by Donald Eugene Smith (Princeton, 1966); Francis L. K. Hsu's *Clan, Caste and Club* (Princeton, 1963); Donald K. Swearer's *Buddhism and Society in Southeast Asia* (Chambersburg, Pa., 1981); *Ambedkhar and the Neo-Buddhist Movement*, edited by T. S. Wilkinson and M. M. Thomas (Madras, 1972); *Religion and Legitimation of Power in Thailand, Laos, and Burma* (Chambersburg, Pa., 1978) and *Religion and Legitimation of Power in Sri Lanka* (Chambersburg, Pa., 1978), both edited by Bardwell L. Smith; and Emanuel Sarkisyanz's *Buddhist Backgrounds of the Burmese Revolution* (The Hague, 1965). Clifford Geertz's *Negara* (Princeton, 1980) is one of the most fascinating recent studies of the alliance between religion and "sanctified" aspects of culture, as it traces the "holy" religious theater that dominated politics in nineteenth-century Bali. Finally, there are my own essays on the topic, "The World Religions and Political Democracy," *Religion and Society* 29 (Fall, 1982): 19–49 and "Faith and Politics in South East Asia," *This World* 4 (1983): 20–48.

Among useful treatments of the religions of primal societies are John S. Mbiti's *African Religions and Philosophy* (New York, 1969); Lamin O. Sanneh's *West African Christianity* (London, 1983); Henry H. Presler's *Primitive Religions in India* (Madras, 1971); Irving Goldman's *Ancient Polynesian Society* (Chicago, 1970); *Essays on the Ritual of Social Relations*, edited by Max Gluckman (Manchester, 1962); Vittorio Lanternari's *The Religions of the Oppressed* (New York, 1963); Victor Turner's *The Ritual Process* (1969; Ithaca, N.Y., 1977); Jomo Kenyatta's *Facing Mount Kenya: The Tribal Life of the Gikuyu* (1938; New York, 1962); and Melford E. Spiro's *Burmese Supernaturalism* (Englewood Cliffs, N.J., 1967).

MAX L. STACKHOUSE

POLLUTION. *See* Purification *and* Taboo.

POLYNESIAN RELIGIONS. [*This entry consists of two articles. The first provides an overview of the general features of Polynesian religious belief and practice. The second examines mythic themes common throughout the lore of Polynesian religious traditions. For detailed treatment of the religious systems of particular Polynesian cultures, see* Hawaiian Religion; Maori Religion; *and* Tikopia Religion.]

An Overview

Polynesia consists of several thousand islands contained within an immense triangle in the central Pacific with its corners at Hawaii, New Zealand, and Easter Island. Polynesian peoples also inhabit a few "outliers" to the west of the triangle, such as Tikopia and Ontong Java in the Solomon Islands. Polynesian islands range from the huge, continental North and South Islands of New Zealand through the high, volcanic islands found in the Hawaiian, Samoan, and Society (Tahitian) chains, to the tiny, low atolls of the Tuamotu archipelago. Although a good deal of cultural diversity does exist within Polynesia, even more noteworthy—given the vast distances between island groups and the striking ecological differences between the continental, volcanic, and coral islands—are the cultural consistencies that hold throughout the region. These include closely linked languages, related forms of social and political organization, and similar religious beliefs and ceremonies.

While numerous isolated beliefs and practices from the pre-European period survive on many islands, the native Polynesian religion described in this essay no longer exists in a pure state. Conversion to Christianity began in Tahiti at the beginning of the nineteenth century. The process was essentially completed on most major islands by the middle of the century, although some remote islands, such as Tikopia, were not fully Christian until a hundred years later.

A Case Study: Kapingamarangi. Discussion begins with a description of some religious practices on one island—as it happens, an island of little significance by most measures. But it will serve as an introduction to Polynesian religion generally, because it is possible to detect in the religious practices of that island patterns that are basic to religion throughout Polynesia.

Kapingamarangi is a tiny, isolated atoll located to the south of the Caroline Islands in the western Pacific. It consists of an oval coral reef surrounding a lagoon six to eight miles in diameter, along the eastern edge of which are about thirty islets. The total land area more than five feet above sea level is less than one-half of a square mile; this is the living space for about five hundred inhabitants. Although it is an outlier, located well outside the Polynesian triangle, the culture and people of Kapingamarangi are distinctly Polynesian.

Every day, according to traditional beliefs, the gods would visit Kapingamarangi. They came from the sea, emerging in mid afternoon off the southeastern portion of the atoll and making their way northward along the outer reef toward an islet called Touhou. Shortly before sunset a priest would call out an invitation to the gods. They would come ashore at Touhou and proceed to a special cult house. They entered the seaward end of the house, which a pair of priestesses had just opened for them by taking down the wall screens. The high priest stood outside the opposite (lagoon) end of the cult house and delivered evening prayers, after which the priestesses replaced the wall screens. The following morning, just before sunrise, the high priest came again to the house. This time he went to the seaward end, took down the wall screens, delivered morning prayers, and then replaced the screens. The gods, who had spent the night in the house, departed after the prayers had been addressed to them, retraced their path along the outer reef to the southeastern part of the atoll, and, about midmorning, returned to the sea. Several hours later they appeared again, and the entire process was repeated.

These daily events on Kapingamarangi encapsulate, in microcosm, many of the basic elements of religion throughout Polynesia. Although numerous variations may be found in different islands, Polynesians are unanimous in these beliefs: that the gods inhabit a realm distinct from the physical world populated by human beings; that they are frequent visitors to the physical world; that the gods are responsible for a great deal of what happens in the physical world, including events both beneficial and detrimental to human beings; that humans may exercise, through properly executed ritual, some control over the visits of the gods to the physical world and what they do here; and (what is one of the most distinctive features of Polynesian religion) that the gods may be ritually induced to withdraw from the physical world in circumstances where their influence is not, or is no longer, desirable. At bottom, Polynesian religion is a story of gods who are immensely active in this world and of people who attempt to control the activities of the gods by directing their influence into places where it is desired and expelling it from places where it is not. The essence of Kapingamarangi's daily cycle—the entrance of the gods into the human world, ushering them into a place of human choosing, requesting their assistance in matters of human needs, and then dismissing them to their own spiritual realm—was enacted in a thousand ways throughout Polynesia.

Cosmos. The universe, with its spiritual and physical realms, its myriads of gods, human beings, plants, and animals, was established by a series of creative acts. Myths from Samoa and the Society Islands tell of an uncreated creator god—Tangaloa or Ta'aroa (elsewhere Tangaroa, Kanaloa, etc.)—who was stirred to create the beginnings of a world. In other myths the first spark of creation is a series of abstract mental qualities and urges, existing and evolving in themselves: thought, remembrance, consciousness, and desire. In most Polynesian accounts of creation, existence was soon differentiated into a male sky and a female earth. These were joined together in copulation. The earth gave birth to a number of sons, the major gods of the Polynesian pantheon. Their numbers and identities differ among the various islands, but frequently the names Tane, Tu, and Rongo appear in one linguistic form or another among them. Tangaroa, the creator already mentioned for certain myths from Samoa and Tahiti, often appears in other myths as another of the sons of the earth and sky.

With the sky pressed so closely to his terrestrial mate, the living space between them was dark and cramped, and their sons could scarcely stand upright. They resolved to separate their parents. After numerous fruitless efforts, one of the sons succeeded in wrenching the lovers apart and raising the sky to the position it now occupies. Perhaps this is a mythological source for the notion that existence is divided into a spiritual and a physical realm, because on many islands the gods were thought to dwell in the heavens. (The spiritual realm normally includes more than just the heavens, however. As described already, the gods of Kapingamarangi came from the open sea. The underworld, as the home of the dead, was also widely considered to be part of the spiritual realm.)

Further stages of creation are usually expressed in genealogical terms. In a Samoan myth, various sorts of rocks and plant and animal species are born and mate to produce still other furnishings of the earth through many generations following the initial union of celestial and terrestrial rocks. In the ninth generation, Pili, a lizard, mates with a tropical bird, and their three sons and daughter are the first human beings. In the mythology of the Maori of New Zealand, the progenitor is the god Tane. Unable to create alone, he sought an *uha,* or female partner. He found a great many of them, and from his unions with them were born water and the various species of insects, birds, and trees and other plants. Through all this, however, Tane was frustrated in his abiding desire to create humankind. Finally he and his brothers, the sons of the sky and the earth, shaped a woman from the earth. Tane breathed life into her nostrils, mouth and ears. Unsure of himself, he then copulated with the various orifices and crevices of her body. This was the origin of the bodily excretions, for the places fertilized by Tane gave birth to saliva, mucus, earwax, excrement, and perspiration. Finally Tane tried her genitalia, and she bore a daughter, whom they named Hine-titama. Later Tane incestuously took his daughter as his mate, and she gave birth to the first human beings.

It fell to a number of heroes, of whom the most famous throughout Polynesia was named Māui, to put the finishing touches on creation. In those earliest days the sun moved rapidly across the sky, making night much longer than day. People found it difficult to accomplish their work in the brief span of daylight. Māui (or, on some islands, a hero of another name) journeyed to the place where the sun emerges from the underworld at dawn, and there he laid a snare. When the sun appeared Māui caught it and gave it a drubbing with his club (made, in some versions of the story, from the jawbone of one of his female ancestors). Thenceforth it could move only slowly and painfully across the heavens, and thus was the day lengthened to equal the span of the night. Mythic heroes are also credited with fishing up many islands from the depths of the sea. The North Island of New Zealand is known as Te-Ika-a-Māui, or Māui's fish, because he caught it with a fishhook (also made from the same jawbone), which he baited by smearing it with his own blood.

Gods. The spiritual realm was thought to be populated by an indefinitely large number of beings, known in most islands by some variant of the term *atua*. The term may be translated as "god," although it should be borne in mind that in Polynesia this is a remarkably broad category. Some gods have never lived as humans (for example, the sons of the earth and sky), while others are spirits of deceased ancestors or of quasi-human entities such as stillborn babies and menstrual clots. Some gods are benevolent, others are mischievous or downright malicious, and still others have no particular moral qualities at all. The gods have a diverse range of occupations and interests. Their number includes creator gods; gods responsible for various "departments" of existence (such as the sea, the forests, cultivated plants, and so on); gods that concern themselves with particular places, particular tribes, or particular families; gods of warfare, fishing, carpentry, and various other occupations; even gods that specialize in bringing on certain diseases or ravishing people whose hair was a certain color. All in all, they are an extremely numerous and varied lot.

While the gods properly belong to the spiritual realm, it was thought throughout Polynesia that (as with the daily visits of the gods to Kapingamarangi) they would frequently enter the human world. Indeed, so extensive was their influence deemed to be that Polynesians tended to attribute any condition or event for which a physical cause was not immediately apparent to the work of the gods. Among a great many other things, this included thunder and lightning, shifts in the wind, and the growth of plants, animals, and people. The gods were authors of dreams and human artistic accomplishments; they underwrote the rank and power of chiefs and success in love or war; and they generated courage and cowardice, illness and accidents, and even involuntary twitches in the muscles.

An indication of the variety of events that Polynesians would attribute to the gods is recorded by the traveler and artist Augustus Earle. When he sailed from New Zealand to Australia in 1828, several Maoris also made the trip. Earle writes in his *Narrative of a Residence in New Zealand* (Oxford, 1966):

> The second day after we were at sea, I saw a group of savages lying round the binnacle, all intently occupied in observing the phenomenon of the magnetic attraction; they seemed at once to comprehend the purpose to which it was applied, and I listened with eager curiosity to their remarks upon it.
>
> "This," said they, "is the white man's God, who directs them safely to different countries, and then can guide them home again. . . ."
>
> Nothing could exceed the delight manifested by our New Zealanders as we sailed into Port Jackson [Sydney] harbour; but above all, the windmills most astonished them. After dancing and screaming with joy at beholding them, they came running and asking me "if they were not gods."
>
> (pp. 196–197)

Polynesians took great stock in omens. Belief in godly instigation of events of all sorts, and that the gods had knowledge superior to that of humans—knowledge of what was happening far away, or would happen in the future, for example—led Polynesians to think that many events could be read as messages from the gods about matters of importance to humans. Dreams were a particularly rich source of information from the world of the gods. One's own spirit or soul could leave the body in sleep, traveling great distances as the gods do, and gathering all sorts of intelligence while out of the body. Sometimes the message of dreams was straightforward, as when a Maori woman's dream that raiders were gathering in the hills to attack her village was confirmed when scouts found that raiders were indeed in the hills. Other dreams needed expert interpretation to reveal their meanings. If a Maori man dreamed of skulls lying on the ground, and decorated with feathers, it was a sign that his wife was pregnant; moreover, the color of the feathers foretold the sex of the baby.

Diviner priests in Hawaii and Tahiti would read the outcome of a proposed battle in the entrails of sacrificial animals. The configurations of rainbows, clouds, and other heavenly phenomena were everywhere understood as omens. Should a Maori war party see the moon situated above the evening star, for example, they would abandon plans to attack a fortified village because the battle would go against them. The moon situated below the evening star, on the other hand, was a sign that their attack would be crowned with success.

An important way in which Polynesian gods were thought to make their influence felt in the physical world was literally to enter and possess human beings. Often this was an unwelcome situation, for the intruding god might be malicious and proceed to bite, twist, or pinch the individual's internal organs—a common explanation for disease. On the other hand, certain persons were particularly prone to spirit possession by which a deceased chief, ancestor, or some other god would communicate with human beings. The medium would go into a trance, during which his or her tone of voice might change drastically. That was thought to be the voice of the possessing god, conveying information about the cause of some disease, the identity of a thief, the outcome of a military expedition, or some other matter of importance to the human community.

The gods also frequented animals of various species: sharks, herons, lizards, owls, and so on. Since the indwelling gods were often malicious, and in any event had power enough to make them dangerous to ordinary people, such animals were regarded with fear, or, at least, with a great deal of circumspection. Lizards were thought in many islands to be favorite earthly vehicles for particularly malevolent gods, rendering these animals objects of terror to people. In his *Journal of a Ten Months Residence in New Zealand* (London, 1823), the early visitor Richard Cruise reported that when a visiting ship's officer in the early nineteenth century brought a lizard to a Maori women in order to ascertain the local word for it, "She shrunk from him in a state of terror that exceeded description, and conjured him not to approach her, as it was in the shape of the animal he held in his hand, that the Atua [god] was wont to take possession of the dying, and to devour their bowels" (p. 320).

Mana and Tapu. Persons, places, and things that were possessed by or were otherwise under the influence of the gods were often referred to by one or the other of the two most well-known concepts in Polynesian religion: *mana* and *tapu.* While these terms have usually been understood by Western observers to function as nouns—so that one might have a certain amount of *mana,* infringe a *tapu,* or put *tapu* on or remove it from something—some scholars think that they properly describe states of being rather than things. From this perspective, *mana* or *tapu* are similar to fame: one may "have" fame, but that is not like having a concrete thing such as a computer.

Mana (a form used in many Polynesian languages) refers to the state of being that is enjoyed by those objects, places, or persons that benefit permanently (or at least for an extended period) from the strengthening influence of the gods. A primary mark of *mana* is outstanding effectiveness in action. Hence the term was applied to certain weapons (many of which had proper names and unique qualities, as did the swords Excalibur and Nothung in European lore) that were thought to be invincible in and of themselves.

Individuals who had distinguished themselves by outstanding accomplishments as warriors, navigators, priests, or artists were thought to have *mana.* At least as important, *mana* characterized certain families and descent lines. Polynesian society on many islands (particularly on Tahiti and the other Society Islands, and on Samoa, Tonga, and Hawaii) was highly stratified, with great gulfs of rank separating the chiefs and other nobles from the commoners. The rank of the nobility passed from generation to generation, reaching its culmination in the line of firstborn children. These lines traced their descent back to the high gods and existed under their special protection. Their rank and position was validated precisely by this relationship to the gods, which was the source of their intense *mana.* In many respects the relationship was so close that those of exalted rank were considered to be very like gods themselves. In Tahiti high chiefs were carried on the backs of servants whenever they ventured out, because if their feet had touched the ground, that spot would have been made so sacred that it could no longer be used for ordinary purposes. All persons along the chief's path had to bare their bodies to the waist as a sign of deference. In Hawaii the concern that nobles not marry spouses of standing lower than their own resulted in the approval of brother-sister marriage for chiefs of the highest rank. The offspring of such unions were considered to be divine, and all persons were required to prostrate themselves in their presence.

Tapu, a form used in the Maori and Tahitian languages, is a term taken into English as "taboo," and is close in meaning to *mana.* It too is concerned primarily with the influence that the gods exercise over people, places, and things of the physical world. *Tapu* is often defined with reference to restrictions or prohibitions, it being *tapu* to enter a certain place, eat certain food, touch certain objects, or undertake various other activities. The word, however, refers not so much to the sheer fact of restriction as to the reason for it: that the place, person, or object in question was possessed by or under the influence of the gods and therefore had to be treated with extreme care.

It is tempting to translate *tapu* as "sacred," but that term has a consistently positive connotation that is by no means always the case with the Polynesian concept. As has been noted already, to be under the influence of a Polynesian god is not necessarily a desirable condition, for it may entail physical or mental illness, loss of courage, or any number of other unwelcome states. All of these may be described in terms of *tapu*. This points up one distinction between *tapu* and *mana*. While both terms refer to states brought on by the influence of gods, *mana* was limited to conditions characterized by outstanding effectiveness of action or elevated rank. *Tapu* might also be used in those circumstances, but it describes detrimental or debilitating states as well.

Again, both *mana* and *tapu* may refer to states of long duration, but these were perhaps more commonly described in terms of *mana*. On the other hand, only *tapu* was used to describe conditions in which the influence of the gods was experienced for relatively brief or defined periods—such as during festivals or religious ceremonies, seasons for growing crops, expeditions for hunting, fishing, or raiding, or times of tattooing or building a canoe or house. Since Polynesian rituals dealt primarily with such temporary influence of the gods, channeling it into areas of life where it was desired at the moment and away from areas where it was not, they were much more concerned with *tapu* than *mana*.

One reason that the *tapu* state tended to be of relatively short duration was because it was easily transmitted. *Mana* could be diminished or lost by defilement of some sort, but it was not easily communicated from one person or thing to another, except from parent to child by descent. To the contrary, *tapu* was considered to be a highly volatile state that was readily transmitted. This, indeed, is the primary reason why the term is so often translated as "forbidden" or as having to do with prohibitions: because it was necessary to hedge someone or something in the state of *tapu* with all sorts of restrictions in order to prevent its unintentional communication to other persons or things to which it might be detrimental. At this point it is well to recall that *tapu* refers not to a thing but to a state of being under the influence of gods. Should that influence pass from one person or thing to another, as Polynesians thought it commonly did, then the person or thing newly brought under godly influence would enter a state of *tapu*. If the godly influence should completely leave the "donor" in this situation, then that person or thing would be released from the *tapu* state.

Transmission of *tapu* was normally by direct or indirect contact. In many parts of Polynesia menstrual blood was thought to be dangerously *tapu*, and great precautions were taken to avoid contact with it. The Marquesan belief was that such contact produced leprosy. Throughout Polynesia food was considered to be an excellent conductor of *tapu*. Today women of Rapa, in the Austral chain, avoid preparing anyone's food but their own while they are menstruating. In ancient Tahiti and Hawaii men and women ate separately on a regular basis in order to insulate the male from the dangerous influences connected with the female.

An intriguing example of how *tapu* may spread involves an unfortunate dog at Ruatoki, New Zealand. The dog contracted the extremely dangerous *tapu* associated with the dead because it rooted in a grave and began to chew on the corpse of a recently deceased person. The situation deteriorated when the dog, chased by numerous enraged Maoris, tried to escape by swimming across the Whakatane River. It was caught and killed in midstream, but by then the entire river had become *tapu* because the dog had been swimming in it. After that its water could not be used for any purpose until a priest had performed a special ceremony to release the river from *tapu*.

Ritual. Polynesian ritual covered an extensive field of activity. It could be destructive, as in witchcraft rites that directed gods to injure or kill their victims. Maori legend, for example, tells how a sorcerer bewitched a New Zealand tribe called Maruiwi by calling upon the god Ira-kewa to confuse their minds so that they began to wander about in the night, walked over a high cliff, and fell to their deaths. Other rites were performed for the more constructive purposes of securing fertility of crops or success in voyaging, hunting, or fishing. Some rites consisted of no more than conventional incantations that an individual might mutter to secure the gods' approval or avoid their wrath when crossing a forest or a stream; others were elaborate festivals demanding immense preparations and lasting for days, or even, as in the case of the Hawaiian festival called Makahiki, for months. In all cases, however, Polynesian ritual had the same purpose as the daily rites on Kapingamarangi, that is, to move and focus godly influence in accordance with human wishes.

Understood in this way, it is possible to distinguish three phases in Polynesian ritual. The first is an invitation to the gods to come to the place where the ritual is taking place. The second is an attempt to induce the gods to lend their influence or support to whatever goal (fertility of crops, victory in battle, success in an inter-island voyage, and so on) the rite is designed to promote. While these two phases are found in the ritual process of many religions, a third phase receives particular elaboration in Polynesia. In this phase, after the purpose of the rite has been achieved, the gods are dismissed and their influence is terminated.

Invitations. Polynesian gods were conceptualized as behaving very much like human beings, so ritual invitations to them were similar in kind to the way one might invite human guests. In Tahiti this included preparing an attactive place for them. Tahitian rituals normally took place in rectangular enclosures called *marae.* Between rituals very little attention was paid to the *marae.* The gods were not present, so there was no danger, no particular *tapu* associated with the *marae* at such times. When a ceremony was about to take place, however, a necessary prelude was to clear weeds and sweep the courtyard, to repair and scrape moss from the stone altar, to set up perches upon which the gods might settle, and in general to make the *marae* as attractive as possible for the gods who were to be summoned to it. Before lineage gods were invoked in Tonga, special mats would be spread out as places for them to sit.

Rituals normally began with an invitation to the gods to attend. In Tahiti lesser gods might be dispatched as messengers to invite the greater gods, and priests would intone long chants that described how each emissary had located the god it had been sent to fetch and was leading it to the *marae.* Other Tahitian chants inaugurating rituals were designed to awaken the gods from sleep. Hawaiians would sometimes appeal to the gods' sexuality, attracting them to a ritual with an erotic hula dance.

New Zealand Maori invited the gods to certain places by setting out material objects in which they could take up residence. Rudely carved stone images, called "resting places for the gods," would be placed in fields after sweet potatoes had been planted. The intention was for gods to enter the images, whence they would establish a state of *tapu* over the crop by lending their growth-stimulating power to it. Other special objects, either natural or man-made, were placed in forests, near the sea, or in fortified villages. These constituted domiciles for the gods who ensured an abundance of birds and rats in the forest, fish of various species in the sea, or protection for the village. It was important to conceal these objects carefully, lest they fall into the hands of some malefactor who would perform certain spells causing the god to depart and bringing disaster on the forest or village.

Priests in certain parts of New Zealand carried "god-sticks": small, carved wooden pegs that, when wrapped in a certain way and stuck in the ground, would be entered by gods. Idols or images were thought to provide housing for the gods in many parts of Polynesia. In the early nineteenth century the several chiefs who were competing to become king of a centralized Tahiti went to great lengths to secure the image of the war god Oro. Where the image was, so the belief went, there Oro himself would come, bringing with him success in war and politics.

New Zealand Maori were particularly conscious of boundaries between the human and the spiritual worlds. Frequently their rituals would be held at such places, where the gods could readily pass from the spiritual realm into this one. One of the most intriguing of these boundaries had to do with the village latrine. This was commonly built on the outskirts of a village, often on the brow of a cliff or steep hill, over which excreta would fall. The latrine consisted of a pair of carved posts that supported a low horizontal beam where the feet would be placed while squatting. Handgrips to assist in preserving one's balance were planted in the ground in front of the beam. The beam was thought to be a boundary between the realms of existence: the physical world was on the village side of the beam, with all its human hustle and bustle, while the region behind the beam, where excrement fell and where people never went, was the spiritual world. Of the numerous rituals the Maori performed at the latrine, none presents a clearer view of it as a point of emergence of the gods into the physical world than the consecration of the Takitumu canoe. According to Maori lore, this was one of the canoes that brought their ancestors to New Zealand. The tradition relates how Takitumu was placed in a state of *tapu,* so as to enjoy the gods' protection during the long and dangerous voyage, by literally hauling the canoe up to the latrine and inviting the gods to embark.

Propitiations. Once the gods had arrived at the site of the ritual, the next phase was to carry out the purpose for which they had been invited. This might be to convince them to do something for the human community, or to thank them for services already rendered. A common means of accomplishing either of these ends was to give the gods gifts. In many places in Polynesia the gods were thanked for their assistance by offering them the first crops harvested, the first birds snared, or the first fish caught. War gods might be given the first enemy killed; often a hook would be placed in his mouth and he would be announced as the first fish. Human sacrifices were offered in many parts of Polynesia including Hawaii, Tahiti, Tonga, the Marquesas, Mangaia (in the Cook Islands), and New Zealand. Human lives were sacrificed for a variety of purposes, including the commemoration of significant events in the lives of high chiefs, the launching of important new canoes, or the opening of major houses. People in Tonga would strike off joints of their little fingers as sacrificial supplications to the gods to restore relatives to health.

Another common means of influencing the gods on ritual occasions was by incantations. After a Maori priest had induced a god to enter his godstick by wrapping it in the proper way and sticking it in the ground, he would step back a few paces and intone his requests. Often the priest held a bit of string that was tied to the stick and that he would jerk occasionally to prevent the god's attention from wandering.

The efficacy of an incantation, and, indeed, of a ritual observance in its entirety, was thought to depend on the perfection with which it was accomplished. This mispronunciation of a word, a breath drawn in the wrong place, or any disturbance of the general atmosphere surrounding the rite, was thought to abort the whole ceremony. On many islands, during a religious ceremony the people who were not participating in the rite were constrained to remain in their houses, lighting no fires and making no noise. Cocks must not crow, nor dogs bark; absolutely nothing was allowed to disrupt the highly *tapu* atmosphere of the rite. In the Society Islands, should a woman or child wander near the place where a ritual was occurring, the intruder would be killed immediately (perhaps by the husband or father) and offered to the gods as a sacrifice to amend for the disturbance. Perhaps such rules and practices, although far more severe, were not different in intent from a Maori priest tugging at the string tied to his godstick in order to prevent the attention of the gods from being distracted by matters other than those addressed in the ceremony.

The emphasis on perfection of delivery of incantations and performance of ceremonies indicates that Polynesians believed their gods to be concerned with the outer form of worship. Inner feelings and convictions were not relevant issues in Polynesian religion. New Zealand provides the most striking bit of evidence for this proposition. An imaginative chief there arranged for the necessary incantations that accompanied the planting of crops to be delivered by a talking bird!

Dismissals. The final phase of Polynesian ritual was the departure of the gods and, with them, the termination of the state of *tapu*. Occasionally this constituted not a phase but the rite in its entirety. This would apply to rituals designed to cure illness or to counteract witchcraft, where the god involved was malevolently inclined and the sole purpose of the rite was to exorcise it. In other cases, as in the departure of the gods from Kapingamarangi's cult house each day at dawn, the gods were excused in the final stage of ritual, after prayers or thanks had been addressed to them or when the beneficial results for which they had been summoned had been realized. Many Polynesians believed, for example, that crops could grow, battles be won, or houses and canoes be successfully built only with the assistance of the gods. Only, that is, when the field, warriors, weapons, builders, tools, and raw materials were in a state of *tapu*. But that very *tapu*, together with the numerous restrictions designed to control its unintended spread, rendered it impossible for the crops to be eaten once they were harvested, for warriors to take up normal activities after battle, for people to live in the house or to travel in the canoe when built. Therefore it was necessary to excuse the gods once their contribution had been achieved—to release the crop, the warriors, the house, or the canoe from the state of *tapu*.

A person, place, or thing that had been released from *tapu* entered a state of being known on many Polynesian islands as *noa*. Often translated as "common" or "profane" (in contrast to views of *tapu* as "sacred"), *noa* may be understood simply as the opposite of *tapu*—as the state of not being under the influence of the gods. Rituals or segments of rituals designed to provide a release from *tapu* were often designated by words such as *fa'anoa* (in the Society Islands) or *whakanoa* (in New Zealand), meaning "to make *noa*."

Normally the dismissal of the gods was, as in Kapingamarangi, a temporary situation. They would be invited back the next time their assistance was needed. Occasionally, however, the lifting of the *tapu* state was intended to be permanent. This of course applied to disease-dealing or otherwise malicious gods. People wanted to escape their influence forever. But it might also be the case with a god from whom assistance had been expected, if it became clear that the god was not performing satisfactorily. Tahitians had a special ceremony for casting off a god. If a family found that it was receiving few benefits from the god it venerated, the family priest would address a special incantation to the god. He would berate it roundly for its feeble support, and inform it that the family would have nothing more to do with it. Then they would select another god that promised to be more helpful.

A variety of means were available to terminate the state of *tapu*. One was simply to get away from the god. Many gods were restricted in their spheres of influence, so if a person were suffering from a disorder known to be caused by a certain god, the healer's prescription might be for the patient to leave the area frequented by that god.

The more common tactic, however, was to send the

gods or their influence away. One of the most common ritual agents used for this purpose throughout Polynesia was water. By sprinkling or immersion in salt or fresh water, Polynesians of Samoa, the Marquesas, New Zealand, the Society Islands, and Hawaii would return to the *noa* state after participating in war, rituals, funeral observances, and other activities. The rationale was doubtless that the water washed away the godly influence responsible for the *tapu*.

Fire was another agent for releasing persons and things from *tapu*, because of its capacity to consume or drive out indwelling gods. In the Society Islands sickness or insanity might be caused by a malicious spirit that dwelt in a stone buried by a witch near the victim's residence. Should a diviner ascertain where the stone was concealed, he would unearth it and throw it into the fire to destroy or expel the infecting spirit.

Probably the *tapu*-eradicating properties of fire account for the fact that, in New Zealand, cooked food (that is, food that has been exposed to high heat or fire) was one of the most common agents used in rituals concerned with the expulsion or transfer of godly influence. Some scholars claim the Maori view to have been that cooked food repelled the gods, others that it attracted them. In any event, it was very commonly a part of *whakanoa* rituals, such as that in which the hands of someone who had been cultivating a garden, curing an illness, or cutting the hair of a chief were released from *tapu* by passing a bit of cooked sweet potato or fernroot over them.

The Maori were extremely careful in their direct or indirect association with cooked food when they were in a state of *tapu* that they wished to preserve. They were most reluctant to enter European hospitals, where water to wash patients might be heated in pots previously used for cooking. The same reasoning explains why some Maoris who had embraced Christianity and wished to purge themselves of the influence of the pagan gods would purposely wash their heads in water heated in cooking pots. One European trader engendered the wrath of a Maori chief when he joked that a cooking pot that he had for sale would make a fine helmet for the chief, and made as if to put it on his head.

The Maori concern with thresholds between the spiritual and physical realms, discussed above in connection with ritual means of bringing the gods into this world, is also important in rituals designed to send them out of it. One cure for illness was to bite the latrine beam, presumably with the intention of repatriating the affecting god to the spirit realm by sending it over the threshold between the worlds. After a session of training in sacred lore, which required that students be in a state of *tapu* if the learning process were to take place successfully, the students would bite the latrine beam in order to return to the *noa* state. Finally, a warrior who was afraid before battle might fortify himself by biting the beam, although it is not entirely clear in this case whether the purpose was to be rid of a fear-producing god, or to take on the influence of a courage-producing one.

Unquestionably one of the most intriguing agents for the ritual release from *tapu* was the female. In New Zealand and the Marquesas Islands new houses would be made free of *tapu* by having a woman enter them. Women participated in the *tapu*-dispelling phase of the war ritual known as Luakini in Hawaii. In New Zealand women would eat the first tubers and thereby render a newly-harvested crop of sweet potatoes *noa*. Maoris would rid themselves of the malicious spirit that might be lurking in a lizard by killing the animal and then having a woman step over it. Marquesans would exorcise the demon afflicting a sick person by having a naked woman leap over or sit on the affected part of the patient's body. Women were not permitted to assist at major rites in the Society Islands, for fear that their presence would expel the gods. For the same reason women were not allowed to go near sites of canoe or house construction in New Zealand or, in the Marquesas, to have any contact with men who had been made *tapu* prior to turtle fishing or battle.

The usual interpretation is that the gods found women to be repugnant, particularly because of their connection with menstrual blood (a substance thought, on this interpretation, to be more polluting than any other). Hence the gods would withdraw upon the appearance of a woman, taking their *tapu* with them. An alternative view is that the gods were attracted to women rather than repelled by them, and that women therefore terminated *tapu* by absorbing the godly influence into themselves. On this interpretation the female is understood, as is the Maori latrine, to represent a passageway between the godly and human realms of existence. The rites in which women acted to dispel *tapu* would of course be examples of the movement of godly influence through the female from the human to the spiritual world. Certain practices in New Zealand can be interpreted as the movement of godly influence in the opposite direction, as when students about to be instructed in sacred lore would enter the state of *tapu* by eating a piece of cooked food that had first been passed under the thigh of a woman.

The view of the female as a passage between the two realms leads to some possible insights into the Polynesian view of birth and death. In New Zealand and the

Society Islands incantations addressed to newborn infants of rank welcomed them into the physical world from the world of the gods. An infant, that is, was apparently viewed as an embodied spirit that had passed from the spiritual realm to the human realm. And, of course, the infant accomplished the transit by being born of a woman.

Polynesians understood death as the passage of the soul from the physical world to the spiritual realm, where it continued to exist as a god or spirit of some sort. Most interesting is that, in New Zealand at least, this passage too was thought to be made through the female. This is evident in the intriguing story of the death of the culture hero Māui. Having fished up islands and slowed the sun, Māui resolved to bestow upon humankind the ultimate gift of eternal life. He intended to accomplish this by killing Hine-nui-te-po, the female personification of death. Accompanied by his friends, the birds, Māui came upon her while she was asleep. His plan was to kill her by entering her vagina, passing through her body, and emerging at the mouth. He cautioned his friends not to laugh if they found the sight amusing, for fear of waking her. Then he stripped naked and, binding the thong of his club tightly about his wrist, he proceeded to enter the sleeping woman. But predictably the birds found the sight hilarious and they burst out in raucous laughter. That awakened Hine-nui-te-po who, discovering Māui attempting to enter her, clenched her thighs tightly together and crushed him to death. And such, opined a Maori commentator, is the fate of all humans: to be drawn at death into the genitals of Hine-nui-te-po.

Hence the female seems to constitute a two-way passage between the spiritual and physical realms of existence, for humans as well as for the gods. Moreover, the very distinction between human beings and the gods now begins to collapse. Humans, arriving at birth from the supernatural realm, apparently were thought to have a spiritual existence before birth, and they definitely were thought to return to the spiritual realm as ghosts and ancestral gods after death.

For a final bit of evidence of a Polynesian belief that human beings exist as spirits in the godly realm prior to birth, we may return to where we began—the tiny atoll of Kapingamarangi. After a woman had given birth, she and her infant would go for a set of birth ceremonies to the islet of Touhou. That is the place, it will be recalled, where the gods would come ashore every day. Therefore, while it might actually have been born on another islet, the infant was ritually introduced into Kapingamarangi on the islet of Touhou, just as the gods were. After a period of ceremonies on Touhou, mother and child participated in a ritual that took place on Werua islet, located just to the north of Touhou. After that, they would return to their home islet and to normal life.

Interpreting this, we see that the child, like the gods, has come from the spiritual realm of Touhou. But whereas the gods remain gods by leaving Touhou and traveling south, the same direction from which they came, the child becomes human by leaving Touhou to the north. From that point forward the child becomes a full member of human society. In essence this is not unlike ceremonies that release one from *tapu* in other parts of Polynesia, rites in which the removal of godly influence enables a person to participate without restriction in normal human existence.

BIBLIOGRAPHY

Two general books are E. S. Craighill Handy's *Polynesian Religion* (Honolulu, 1927) and *Anthropology and Religion* (1959; reprint, Hamden, Conn., 1970) by Peter H. Buck (Te Rangi Hiroa). Both are written by acknowledged experts in the field, although, as their dates imply, neither benefits from contemporary methods of anthropological analysis. The same may be said for the larger but less influential compendia by Robert W. Williamson, *Religious and Cosmic Beliefs of Central Polynesia*, 2 vols. (1933; reprint, New York, 1977), and *Religion and Social Organization in Central Polynesia* (Cambridge, 1937). Katharine Luomala's *Māui-of-a-Thousand-Tricks* (Honolulu, 1949) is an interesting study of myths, dealing with a single culture hero, drawn from all parts of Polynesia. The most thoroughly documented of traditional Polynesian cultures is New Zealand's. George Grey's *Polynesian Mythology* (London, 1922) is a widely read collection of Maori myths. Despite its forbidding title, J. Prytz Johansen's *The Maori and His Religion in Its Non-Ritualistic Aspects* (Copenhagen, 1954) is a rich and fascinating analysis, as is his companion book, *Studies in Maori Rites and Myths* (Copenhagen, 1958). More recent Maori studies are Jean Smith's *Tapu Removal in Maori Religion* (Wellington, 1974), and F. Allan Hanson and Louise Hanson's *Counterpoint in Maori Culture* (London, 1983). For the Society Islands, the most useful works are Teuira Henry's *Ancient Tahiti* (Honolulu, 1928) and, by Douglas L. Oliver, a three-volume compilation of information from the sources plus analysis of his own, *Ancient Tahitian Society* (Honolulu, 1974). A good deal on religion may be found in E. S. Craighill Handy's *The Native Culture in the Marquesas* (1923; reprint, New York, 1971); William Mariner's *An Account of the Natives of the Tonga Islands*, 3d ed., 2 vols. (Edinburgh, 1827); Edward Winslow Gifford's *Tongan Society* (Honolulu, 1929); and John B. Stair's *Old Samoa* (1897; reprint, Papakura, New Zealand, 1983). Books with useful information on Hawaiian religion are Martha Warren Beckwith's *Hawaiian Mythology* (1940; reprint, Honolulu, 1970) and David Malo's *Hawaiian Antiquities*, 2d ed. (Honolulu, 1951). Religion of the Polynesian outliers has been well analyzed in Torben Monberg's *The Religion of Bellona Island* (Copenhagen, 1966); Raymond Firth's *The Work of the Gods in Tikopia*, 2d ed., and *Tikopia Ritual and Belief* (both, London, 1967); and finally, the source from which the information on Kapingamarangi in this essay is taken, Kenneth P. Emory's *Kapingamarangi: Social and Religious Life of a Polynesian Atoll* (Honolulu, 1965).

F. ALLAN HANSON

Mythic Themes

Although one might argue whether the gods created the Polynesians in godlike form or the Polynesians created the gods in their own image, it is a truism that in Polynesia gods and people are aspects of the same reality and form a continuum of the sacred and the profane. Even as, in relative terms, the gods are sacred and the people profane, so also are the chiefs sacred and the commoners profane. This axiom underlay the sociocultural organization of the Polynesians and gave religious justification to ranked social and kinship structures. The mythological threads of Polynesian religions developed an intimate association among gods, chiefs, priests, and people. High gods, demigods, ancestral gods, culture heroes, spirits, elves, and people were intertwined in different ways in each island group to create separate religions that were particularized and parochial while at the same time part of a homogenous religious fabric that was spread over a vast expanse of ocean containing hundreds of large and small Polynesian islands.

Polynesia can be conveniently divided into western Polynesia (including Tonga, Samoa, Tuvalu, the Tokelau Islands, Niue, the Futuna Islands, and Uvéa) and eastern Polynesia (Hawaii, the Society Islands including Tahiti, the Marquesas, the Cooks, the Australs, Mangareva, the Tuamotus, Easter Island, and New Zealand). A number of small islands lie outside the Oceanic region commonly designated as Polynesia [*see map accompanying* Oceanic Religions, *overview article*], but they have Polynesian religious and cultural traditions (Rennell, Bellona, Tikopia, Anuta, Ontong Java, Kapingamarangi, Takuu, Sikiana, and others). These "outliers" are closely related to western Polynesia. Fiji, Lau, and Rotuma, on the western fringe of Polynesia, are in some ways closely related to western Polynesia, although religiously Fiji is probably more closely related to the Melanesian islands to the west. The religion of each of these groups and its mythological basis formed a coherent whole with the social organization. The connections between gods, ancestors, and humans were often made visually apparent and ritually maintained through religious architecture and works of art including songs, dances, sculptured images, and, most fundamental of all, oral literature. Although it is difficult to separate sacred and secular in Polynesia, the emphasis in this article will be on the mythological themes that help to explain the religious element of the society with its emphasis on *mana* and *tapu*, rather than on the mythological basis of secular storytelling. From a Polynesian point of view, the terms *mythic* and *mythological* are not entirely appropriate because these sacred traditions are considered historical and unquestionable in much the same sense as is *Genesis* by many Christians.

Cosmogony. One of the most important and widespread mythic themes in Polynesia deals with the origins of the universe, the gods, and various aspects of nature. From the primary void or chaos came heaven and earth, which lay close together. The Sky Father (variously, Langi, Rangi, or Atea) and the Earth Mother (Papa or Fakahotu) clung together in a warm embrace and, in the cosmogonic myths of many of the islands, were the progenitors of the gods, the land and sea, the elements, and of plants, animals, and people. Rangi and Papa were usually forcefully separated by gods or demigods.

In western Polynesia the most important agent in this separation was usually some form of the high god Tangaroa (Tangaloa) or the demigod trickster, Māui. In Tonga, for example, Māui-motua (the senior Māui) pushed up the sky; this let in the light and permitted humans, who had previously crawled as crabs, to stand.

> Our land was created
> Shrouded from above
> And we crawled as crabs.
> The first and second skies
> Tell to Māui-motua
> To push them high
> So the breeze can come in, for it is hot
> And bring light to the land
> And then we stood up
> And walked about proudly.

In Rotuma, Lagi and Otfiti ("heaven" and "earth") were joined together. The male and female principles of heaven and earth, Lagatea and Papatea, were the progenitors of the high god Tangaloa. When Tangaloa was born he rose to a kneeling position and pushed Heaven and Earth apart; he did not rise to his full height, however, because of the distress of his parents who did not want to be completely separated.

In eastern Polynesia, especially among the Maori of New Zealand, cosmogonic origins were more detailed. While Rangi and Papa clung together, they produced offspring: the four great gods Tane, Tangaroa, Tu, and Rongo, known throughout Polynesia, as well as two specialized gods Haumia and Tawhiri. These offspring felt cramped in their dark close quarters and debated if and how they should separate their father and mother. Except for Tawhiri, who disagreed, each son attempted to separate the parents. Rongo, god of cultivated foods, tried; Tangaroa, god of fish and reptiles, tried; Haumia, god of uncultivated plants, tried; and Tu, god of destruction, tried. Tane, god of the forests, found that he was strong enough but that his arms were too short; so he placed his head against his mother and pushed his father up with his feet. Tawhiri, god of the winds, rose with his father. Upset by Tane's success, Tawhiri sent his own offspring—the four great winds, smaller but more violent winds, clouds of various kinds, and hurricanes—against him. Tawhiri's brothers and their offspring were terrified. Tangaroa's fish offspring plunged deep into the sea, but the reptiles sought safety in the forests of Tane, even though many of Tane's trees were snapped and destroyed. Rongo and Haumia hid themselves in Mother Earth. Only Tu withstood Tawhiri's wrath and finally defeated him. During the long storm Tawhiri's progeny multiplied to include rains of various kinds, mist, and dew. Finally, light increased and the progeny of the other brothers increased. Rangi and Papa have never been reconciled to their separation; and, to this day, Papa's sighs rise to Rangi as mist, and Rangi's tears fall to Papa as dewdrops.

This cosmogonic story explains not only Tawhiri's periodic outbursts, but also the reasons for disagreements among the other brothers. Tangaroa was upset that some of his progeny deserted him for the forests of Tane, and Tu took revenge on his brothers for deserting him in battle against Tawhiri. Tane gives wood for canoes, spears, and fishhooks to the children of Tu in order to destroy the offspring of Tangaroa. The latter, however, overwhelms canoes, land, and trees with his relentless waves. Tu also traps the birds of Tane's forest, enmeshes the children of Tangaroa in fishnets, uproots the children of Haumia and Rongo, consumes all his brothers' offspring as food and controls his brothers with incantations.

Variations of this theme, especially the belief in a primal pair and their existence in a void or darkness (often called *pō*), exist in other eastern Polynesian areas. In some locales, Tangaroa was thought to be the originator of all things in the universe; in others his place was taken by Tane; while in others Tangaroa and Tane together serve this function. In the Society Islands, for example, a great octopus held the sky and earth together in his great arms. Ta'aroa (Tangaroa) existed in the darkness of contemplation, and from this darkness he called the other gods into being. When Ta'aroa shook himself, feathers fell and turned into trees, plantains, and other green plants. Ta'aroa then called the artisans to fashion him into something beautiful—a carved wooden image in most versions. Rua (the Abyss) killed the octopus by conjuring, but it did not release its hold, and, still in darkness, the demigods Ru, Hina, and Māui were born. Ru raised the sky as high as the coral tree, but ruptured himself so that his intestines floated away to become the clouds that usually hang over the island of Bora-Bora. Māui, the trickster, then used wedges to support the sky and went to enlist the help of Tane, who lived in highest heaven. Tane drilled into the sky with a shell until light came through. The arms of the octopus fell away and became the island of Tubuai. Tane then decorated the sky with stars and set the sun and moon on their courses. The fish and sea creatures were given places and duties, and the god Tohu was given the job of painting the beautiful color on the fish and shells of the deep. In Tahiti, Tane was symbolized by a piece of finely braided coconut-fiber sennit, while in the Cook Islands, Tane the artisan was symbolized by beautifully made basalt adzes lashed to carved handles with braided coconut fiber.

In Hawaii, Kāne (Tane) and Kanaloa (Tangaroa) were not usually represented in tangible form. Kāne, the ultimate ancestor of the other gods, was usually associated with the upper atmosphere, while Kanaloa, in paired opposition, was associated with the sea and its creatures. Lono (Rongo) and Kū (Tu) were less distant and abstract and were concerned with agriculture, plants, rain, pigs, peace and war, forests, canoes, houses, and crafts. Many attributes of Lono and Kū were interrelated; they depended on each other both as necessary opposites and as aspects of each other. Various attributes of Lono, Kū, Kāne, and Kanaloa might be considered as separate gods. There were hundreds of these gods, each known by a compound name that coupled the god's name with a specific attribute, such as Kāne-hekili (Kāne of the thunder) or Kūkā'ilimoku (Kū the snatcher of land, that is, the war god).

In addition to the four major gods of eastern Polynesia, other gods were often associated with specific aspects of nature. Sometimes separate gods, such as Haumia and Tawhiri in New Zealand, were given the care of particular natural phenomena, such as uncultivated food and the winds, that were elsewhere part of the domains of the four great gods. Special gods appeared to meet special requirements of different natural environments, as did Pele the goddess of volcanos and Poli'ahu the snow goddess in Hawaii. In short, the four great gods, especially in eastern Polynesia, were usually concerned with the creation of the universe, of most of the elements of nature, of the rest of the gods, and, ultimately, of human beings. Most of these cosmogonic stories begin in the *pō*, or primal darkness, and tell how one of the gods alone (often Tangaroa) or the Sky Father and Earth Mother together created the other gods and, eventually, all their progeny, each of which was a personification of a selected aspect of nature. Each island or island group had a slightly different cast of characters and emphasized different plants, animals, and natural phenomena. Whereas in the Cook Islands the creation of the universe was involved with a coconut shell which was organized in layers with Vari or chaotic mud at the bottom, in Hawaii a gourd and its association with Lono was more important. To maintain a connection with Lono, an *ipu o Lono* ("gourd of Lono") was kept in a sacred area of each household to receive offerings and prayers, which were usually concerned with fertility and protection against sorcery. In other areas a local deity sometimes replaced or elaborated one or more of the four great gods. Thus, in New Zealand the existence of two gods of food, Haumia and Rongo, indicates the importance of uncultivated food to the Maori, which was not the case in other Polynesian areas; and in Hawaii the existence of Pele and Kū, both gods of destruction, suggests a philosophical distinction between destruction by nature and destruction by man.

Origin of the Islands and People. In western Polynesian creation myths more emphasis was given to the creation, genealogies, and interrelationships of human beings than to the creation, genealogies, and interrelationships of the gods from whom human beings descended. In Tonga, for example, the god Tangaloa 'Eitumatupu'a climbed down from the sky on a great casuarina tree and cohabited with a woman of the earlier Tongan population, which had descended from a worm. The child of this union was 'Aho'eitu. When 'Aho'eitu was old enough he went to the sky to visit his father and returned with several celestial inhabitants who became his ceremonial attendants. Half man and half god, 'Aho'eitu became the first Tu'i Tonga ("paramount chief"). The succeeding Tu'i Tonga descended from 'Aho'eitu and were born of the daughters of the highest chiefs in the land. Several Tu'i Tonga were assassinated, and in about the fifteenth century (CE) the incumbent twenty-fourth Tu'i Tonga appointed his younger brother as a subsidiary ruler, the Tu'i Ha'a Takalaua. The Tu'i Ha'a Takalaua was given only temporal power, while the Tu'i Tonga retained for himself high rank and spiritual status. The sixth Tu'i Ha'a Takalaua created a similar split in authority, reserving for himself high rank and giving to one of his sons the title of Tu'i Kanokupolu and the tasks of ruling and collecting tribute. All three lines descended from 'Aho'eitu and were further linked by marriage. The origins of Tangaloa, the sky, the island of Tonga, or the other elements of nature, however, are often not detailed. The gods were less important than was the way that the chiefs traced their genealogies to them.

Tangaloa (Tangaroa) and Māui were the important male gods in western Polynesia, while the female god Hikule'o was in charge of Pulotu, the underworld (a concept undeveloped in eastern Polynesia). Tangaloa was often considered the sole creator god, whose universe was the sky and a vast expanse of ocean. According to a Samoan story, Tangaloa threw a rock into the ocean, and it became Manu'a, one of the Samoan group of islands. Tonga was said to have been created when the gods threw down chips of wood from their workshops. In Tonga, the first occupants were worms, a female of which cohabited with Tangaloa to start the first ruling dynasty. Samoans believed Samoa had been created when Tangaloa threw down a rock as a place for his bird-daughter to live. He also sent vines to the island; the vines developed maggots, which in turn generated humans. Rather than being thrown down from the sky, or sometimes in addition to this type of creation, a widespread mythic theme of island origin recounts that the islands were fished up from the sea bottom by Māui or, occasionally, by Tangaloa or Tiki.

In some areas of eastern Polynesia humans originated when the god Tane, or a separate character in the creation story, Tiki (Ti'i), impregnated a female form that had been shaped by the god from sand and that held the essence of the female principle, Mother Earth. In other areas Tangaloa created Ti'i, the first man, for Hina, who was thought of as a goddess in some locales and as the first woman in others. In Tahiti the chiefs traced their genealogies to Ti'i and Hina. Along with the creation of human life came the creation of death. According to the Maori, Hina-titama, an offspring of Tane and Hina the Earth-Formed, mated with her father and had several children. Her realization that this union was incestuous drove her to the underworld; from there she snared their children one by one. This was the origin of death. The origin of human life is usually associated with the Sky Father and the male principle, while the origin of death is usually associated with the female principle.

In some areas there are quite different accounts of the origins of mankind. On Easter Island the most important god was the local deity Makemake, who was not only the patron of the rituals of the bird cult but was also the creator of humans. In Tuvalu the male parent was the sun, the female parent a stone, altering the more generalized sky and earth into more specific aspects of the upper and lower atmospheres.

Although the origin of individual plants or animals may not be specified, items of local importance are often given stories of their own. For example, in Tahiti one of the lovers of the demigoddess Hina was an eel named Tuna from whom the coconut plant originated after he was buried. Hina, who embodies the essence of femininity, is also credited with the origin of the banyan tree, which grew on earth after she dropped a branch of such a tree from her abode in the moon. Similarly, in Tonga kava and sugarcane originated from the head and body of a dead child who was killed as food for a visiting high chief. This child was not eaten but buried, and the two plants grew from her grave. A rat that had eaten from the *kava* plant staggered but regained its balance after eating from the sugarcane plant. This was the origin of the ritual drinking of *kava* and of the ritual eating of sugarcane that accompanies *kava*-drinking.

In Hawaii an extremely complicated mythology reveals the intimate relationships among gods, humans, and elements of the natural environment. The order of the islands' origins is given in great detail—starting in the east with the island of Hawaii, moving west through the major islands of the Hawaiian chain, and ending at Niihau (an afterbirth), Lehua, Kaula, and finally the low reef islands. The parents of the islands were primarily Wākea (Sky Father) with Papa (Earth Mother). Wākea's secondary mates were Kaula and Hina while Papa's secondary mate was Lua. In addition, the Kumulipo chant sets out the origin and order of all plants and animals in the universe as well as the origin of gods and men. Kāne and Kanaloa were the first gods to be born, La'ila'i was the first woman and Ki'i the first man. Some generations later the goddess Haumea bore children to Kanaloa and then took a husband among men and became the goddess of childbirth. In many forms, nature, gods, and people interacted—not only to create, but also to change and destroy.

Māui. The demigod Māui was the trickster who upset the status quo. Māui has been immortalized by Katharine Luomala in her study, *Māui-of-a-Thousand-Tricks* (Honolulu, 1949). Māui's most important deeds included fishing up islands on his magic fishhook (taking the place of Tangaloa in other areas), snaring the sun, and stealing fire from the gods. He also had specialties in the traditions of some areas, such as pushing up the sky in Tonga and Uvéa (taking the place of Tane, who often performed this feat in eastern Polynesia), trying to overcome death in New Zealand, and in Tokelau taking the place of the original male parent. Māui was often considered a magician, but his most admired characteristic was trickery against authority. In classic tales Māui usually does not create, for this was the domain of the gods. Instead, as half man and half god, he transformed what had already been created into something useful to man. Thus, he slowed down the sun, which previously had raced across the sky, so that days would be long enough to beat out and dry bark cloth, grow and prepare food, and build temples to the gods. Māui stole conveniences of the gods (such as fire to cook food) for the comfort of men. Māui was the archetypal culture hero who could deal with both gods and humans. [*See also* Māui.]

The mythic themes of Polynesian religion are complex social metaphors that helped to justify rank and social stratification to a people concerned with genealogy, respect and disrespect, and aspects of nature that needed to be explained and appeased. The gods and mythical heros were blamed for, and became part of, human vanity. Polynesian religion was an outgrowth of Polynesian social structure which focused on genealogical connections and the integration of the gods with nature and the human condition.

BIBLIOGRAPHY

Bibliographies on Polynesian mythology are very extensive, but they usually focus on specific islands or island groups. The best bibliography, of more than three hundred entries, can be found in Katharine Luomala's *Māui-of-a-Thousand-Tricks: His Oceanic and European Biographers* (Honolulu, 1949). As sources of first resort, the following works are recommended.

Beckwith, Martha Warren. *Hawaiian Mythology* (1940). Reprint, Honolulu, 1970.

Best, Elsdon. *Maori Religion and Mythology.* Wellington, New Zealand, 1924.

Burrows, Edwin G. *Western Polynesia: A Study in Cultural Differentiation.* Göteberg, 1938.

Dixon, Roland B. *The Mythology of All Races,* vol. 9, *Oceanic* (1916). Reprint, New York, 1964.

Emory, Kenneth P. "Tuamotuan Concepts of Creation." *Journal of the Polynesian Society* 49 (1940): 69–136.

Firth, Raymond. *Rank and Religion in Tikopia: A Study of Polynesian Paganism and Conversion to Christianity.* London, 1970.

Fornander, Abraham. *Fornander Collection of Hawaiian Antiquities and Folklore.* 3 vols. Bishop Museum Memoirs, vols. 4–6. Honolulu, 1916–1920.

Gifford, Edward W., comp. *Tongan Myths and Tales.* Honolulu, 1924.

Grey, George. *Polynesian Mythology and Ancient Traditional History of the New Zealanders.* London, 1922.

Luomala, Katharine. "Polynesian Mythology." In *Encyclopedia of Literature,* edited by Joseph T. Shipley. New York, 1946.

Luomala, Katharine. *Voices on the Wind: Polynesian Myths and Chants.* Honolulu, 1955.

Poignant, Roslyn. *Oceanic Mythology: The Myths of Polynesia, Micronesia, Melanesia, Australia.* London, 1967.

Adrienne L. Kaeppler

POLYTHEISM.

[*This entry surveys the views concerning the development of polytheism and discusses its nature and character. For descriptive accounts of the known forms and historical occurrences of polytheism, see individual entries on the religions and civilizations concerned.*]

The term *polytheism,* derived from the Greek *polus* ("many") and *theos* ("god") and hence denoting "recognition and worship of many gods," is used mainly in contrast with *monotheism,* denoting "belief in one god." The latter concept is considered by theological apologists and nineteenth-century cultural evolutionists alike as a "higher" form of belief, to be superseded (at best) by modern, scientific atheism. To understand polytheism, we must look at the base component *theism,* meaning the belief in "gods" as distinct from other types of powerful or supernatural beings (ghosts, ancestor spirits, etc.). Unfortunately, no discussion of polytheism can ignore the connotations implied by the Greek word *theos,* especially as it is the Greek term that has influenced most Western discourse on the subject. Clearly Japanese *kami* (whose number according to Shintō tradition is 800,000) and Greek *theos* are not quite the same; nevertheless I shall, at the risk of oversimplification, stay with traditional Western usage.

Historical (or rather, pseudo-historical) theories concerning the origin of polytheism were closely related to the evolutionist views that characterized early *Religionswissenschaft.* Primitive humanity was aware of its dependence on a variety of powers that were often conceived as individual nonmaterial ("spiritual") beings—for instance, the spirits of departed humans, especially ancestors—or as supernatural entities. One of the many modes of contact with this world of spirits was shamanism, a level of primitive beliefs and ritual behavior that has also been referred to as "polydaemonism." Sometimes more important figures emerge in these systems, especially in connection with accounts of the origins and beginnings of all things (first ancestors, culture heroes, originator gods), but such figures are not always central in the actual cultic life of the community. Even originator gods often remove themselves subsequently to the highest heavens and remain inactive. [*See* Deus Otiosus.] Although no longer generally accepted, this account of things has been reproduced here because for some time scholars have viewed it as a kind of initial stage in religious development, the last and final stage being monotheism. In this view, animism and polydaemonism become polytheism, and the latter evolves (how and why, nobody seems to know) into monotheism.

An opposing view known as the "Ur-monotheism school" (associated with Wilhelm Schmidt and the so-called Vienna School that defended also the *Kulturkreiselehre*) asserted that monotheism was the original creed of mankind and that polydaemonism and polytheism developed as mankind degenerated from a more innocent state. The element of theological apologetic in this theory is evident (though by itself that fact constitutes no argument either for or against its validity). In fact, it is an anthropological refurbishing of the traditional theological doctrine that Adam and his descendants were obviously monotheists, but that at some time between Adam and Noah, and then again after Noah, a process of corruption set in. The medieval Jewish version of this process is spelled out in detail by Moses Maimonides (Mosheh ben Maimon). Polytheistic humanity was then reintroduced to monotheism by divine revelation or by more mature philosophical reflection. There is an element of truth in the latter assertion, for although there is no evidence whatsoever of an evolution from polytheism to monotheism, it seems true to say that monotheism appears either as a sudden, revolutionary development (for example, no really polytheistic stage can be demonstrated in ancient Israelite religion) or else as a monistic tendency (as in late Roman antiquity or in certain forms of Indian religion), as a result of which the multiplicity of gods (divine powers or manifestations) are subsumed under one superior, all-embracing principle ("the One," "the All," *brahman,* etc.).

The Nature of Polytheism. Turning from speculative historical guesswork to the phenomenology or morphology of polytheism, one is struck by the curious fact that polytheism, while it is one of the major and most widespread phenomena in the history of religions, has attracted less than the attention it deserves. It seems to have fallen, as it were, between the two stools of "primitive religions" and monotheism. Or perhaps we should say three stools, if we also take into account nontheistic religions such as Buddhism. Like all phenomenological ideal types (to borrow Max Weber's term), polytheism does not exist as a pure type. The historical variety is not easily reducible to a common denominator. Greek polytheism is different from Japanese Shintō, and the latter is different again from Maya religion. Nevertheless some basic and characteristic features are discernible, even though not all of them may be present in each and every case.

Perhaps the most striking fact about polytheism is its appearance in more advanced cultures only. (This may, incidentally, be one of the reasons why the evolutionists saw it as a post-primitive phenomenon.) In most cases, at least for our purposes, the phrase "advanced cultures" means literate cultures (e.g., China, India, the ancient Near East, Greece, and Rome), though polytheism is occasionally also found in nonliterate cultures (e.g., in Mesoamerican and South American pre-Conquest religions, among the Yoruba people of West Africa, or in Polynesia). Usually such cultures also practice a more sophisticated type of agriculture (for example, one in which the plow supersedes the hoe), although, once again, this is not necessarily the case everywhere. In the case of Polynesia it could be argued that the bountiful earth itself produced the surplus that rendered possible the social and cultural background of polytheism (social stratification, division of labor, authority structures, and so forth), which elsewhere depended on more advanced types of food production. "More advanced" cultures are those whose economy in some way provides sufficient surplus to create a certain distance between man and nature. Society no longer lives with its nose to the grindstone, as it were. The result is increased division of labor (including bureaucracies and a priesthood), social stratification (including warrior castes, chieftains, royalty), and political structures (cities, city-states, temple establishments, empires). Greek polytheism flourished in city-states; Mesopotamia (Sumer, Assyria, Babylonia) and Egypt were kingdoms and at times empires, and the same holds true of pre-Conquest Mesoamerica and Peru. The Indo-Aryan and pre-Zoroastrian Iranian religions certainly were not primitive. Similarly, the Yoruba kingdoms of Ọyọ and Ifẹ (present-day Nigeria), for example, clearly represent a high though nonliterate culture, as does early Japan with its *kami* worship, practiced long before the infiltration of Chinese culture and literacy.

The above considerations are not meant to explain or otherwise account for the appearance of polytheism. They merely suggest the cultural and spiritual background against which the emergence of polytheism becomes intelligible. In every religion, society attempts to articulate its understanding of the cosmos and of the powers that govern it, and to structure its relationship with these powers in appropriate symbolic systems. In the societies under discussion here, man already faces the cosmos: he is closely linked to it but no longer inextricably interwoven in it. There is a sense of (at least minimal) distance from nature and even more distance from the powers above that now are "gods," that is, beings that are superhuman, different, powerful (though not omnipotent) and hence beneficent or dangerous—at any rate their goodwill should be secured—and to be worshiped by cultic actions such as sacrifices. These divine beings are personal but not material (although they can assume bodily shape temporarily and for specific reasons); above all, their behavior and motivations are similar to those of humans. Their relevance to human life is due to the fact that, unlike the primitive high gods (originator gods of the *deus otiosus* type), they intervene in human affairs, either on their own initiative or because called upon to do so in prayer, sacrifice, or ritual.

One of the most distinctive characteristics of gods, as compared to human beings, is their immortality. Though not eternal in the abstract, philosophical sense, the gods, as the worshiper knows them, are the "immortals." Herein lies the main distinction, not (as in monotheistic religions) in a fundamental difference of essence that then, on the philosophical level, becomes transcendence. Even when the difference is emphasized, it is not a contrast between creator and creature, but one of levels of power and permanence. The relation is one of bipolarity; man and the gods, though different, are related. Hesiod (*Works and Days* 108) tells us "how the gods and mortal men sprang from one source." Even so, "one is the race of men, one is the race of gods, and [i.e., although] from one mother [i.e., Gaia] do we both derive our breath. Yet a power that is wholly separated parteth us: in the one there is nought, while for the other the brazen heaven endureth as an abode unshaken forever" (Pindar, *Nemean Odes* 6.1–5).

Yet although the gods to whom man is related are durable and permanent, this does not mean that they do not have origins or a history. Unlike the biblical God who makes history but himself has no history, let alone a family history, their history is the subject of mythological tales, including accounts of their family relations, love affairs, offspring, and so on. Hence the mythological genealogies, stories of the gods that preceded the ones ruling at present (e.g., Greek Ouranos-Gaia; followed by Kronos, followed by Zeus; or, in later Indian religion, the replacement of originally principal gods like Indra, Varuṇa, and Mitra by Śiva, Viṣṇu, and other deities). These gods are personal (in fact, this personal character is also one of the main features and constitutes one of the main philosophical problems of monotheism), and herein resides their religious significance: they are accessible.

Such a generalization must, of course, be somewhat qualified in view of the phenomenon of "dying and rising" gods such as Adonis, Attis, Osiris, Dumuzi, also in polytheistic myths and rituals. [*See* Dying and Rising Gods.]

Most polytheistic religions possess, as has been indicated in the preceding paragraph, a highly developed mythology that is not restricted to theogony and cosmogony though it is often used, or deliberately manipulated, to account for things as they are and to legitimate the cosmic, social, political, and ritual order. But such is not always or necessarily the case. Perhaps the best example of a highly developed polytheism with an elaborate ritual system but almost totally lacking a mythology is ancient Rome. In this respect the contrast with ancient Greece is striking. Yet even when we have a rich body of mythology, its imagery reaches us in comparatively late literary elaborations. Thus the mythology of ancient (pre-Buddhist) Japan is accessible to us only in literary works composed after the absorption of Chinese (i.e., also Buddhist) influences.

Without implying commitment to any simplistic theory about the divine order always and necessarily being a mirror of the human and social order, one cannot deny that the two are correlated. The polytheistic divine world is more differentiated, more structured, and often extremely hierarchized, because the human view of the cosmos is similarly differentiated, structured, and hierarchized. There are many gods because man experiences the world in its variety and manifoldness. Hence there is also specialization among the gods, of a nature that is either local and tribal-ethnic (gods of specific localities, cities, countries, families) or functional (gods of specific arts, gods of illness, cure, fertility, rains, hunting, fishing, etc.). The highly developed Roman sense of order could take things to extremes, and the early Christian fathers in their antipagan polemics made fun of the Roman *indigitamenta*, or invocations of highly specialized gods. Each householder had his *genius;* women had their Junos; children were protected when going in, going out, or performing their natural functions by Educa, Abeone, Potin. In fact, there was a goddess responsible for the toilet and sewage system: Cloacina. (The Roman example illustrates another important principle. Deities can be mythological beings of symbolic immediacy, to be subsequently "interpreted" or rationally allegorized; they can also be the personifications of abstract concepts.)

To cite another example of parallel hierarchy, few divine worlds were as hierarchical as the Chinese; in fact, these realms seem to be exact replicas of the administrative bureaucracy of imperial China. Just as the illustrious departed could be deified by imperial decree, so gods too could be promoted to higher rank. (Japan subsequently adopted this Chinese model, as it did so many others.) As late as the nineteenth century, these imperial promotions were announced in the *Peking Gazette*.

The possibility of elevation to divine rank of living or departed humans (in the Western world such was the case with Hellenistic kings and Roman emperors) calls for a qualification of an earlier statement that polytheism displays an unbridgeable difference (though not quite as radical as that of monotheism) between men and gods. For, much as humans can occasionally attain to divinity, the gods can assume human shape (as in the example of the Hindu *avatāras*) or exist in human manifestation (as in the Japanese concept of *ikigami*). [*See* Apotheosis *and* Incarnation.]

An important corollary of polytheism is that, though the major deities can be very powerful, no god can be omnipotent. Only a monotheistic god, being *monos*, can also be all-powerful. With growing moral differentiation, originally ambivalent gods split into positive (good) and negative (bad, evil, or demonic) divinities. Thus the original Indo-Aryan *asuras* (deities) became, in Vedic and post-Vedic India, demonic antigods, in opposition to the *devas*. The multiplicity of gods of necessity produced a hierarchy of major and minor gods and a pantheon, or overall framework in which they were all combined. The more important gods have names and a distinct personality; others form the *plebs deorum*, a body often indistinguishable from the nameless spirits of animism. Many gods are experienced as real though unidentified, and hence a Roman might invoke the deity *si deus si dea* or distinguish between *dei certi* and *dei incerti* (rather like addressing a prayer "to whom it may concern"). There even is a reference to *aius locutus* "[the god] who has spoken [on a certain occasion, whoever he may be]."

When polytheism is superseded by monotheism, the host of deities is either abolished (theoretically), or bedeviled (i.e., turned into demons), or downgraded to the rank of angels and ministering spirits. This means that an officially monotheistic system can harbor a functional *de facto* polytheism. No doubt for the urban masses in fourth-century Rome, the cult of the Christian martyrs was merely a kind of transformation of the earlier polytheistic cults, and the same is probably still true of much Roman Catholic Christianity, especially in rural areas.

Some scholars consider henotheism (the exclusive worship of one god only without denying the existence of other gods) as an intermediary stage between polytheism and monotheism, the latter being defined as the theoretical recognition of the existence of one god only, all the others being (in the language of the Old Testament) sheer "vanity and nothingness." The terminology seems somewhat artificial (both *hen* and *monos* signify "one" in Greek), but it attempts to express a real distinction. Thus it has been claimed that henotheistic vestiges can still be detected even in the monotheistic Old Testament (e.g., *Exodus* 15:11, "Who is like unto thee among the gods, O Yahveh," or *Micah* 4:5, "For all nations will walk each in the name of its god" while Israel walks in the name of Yahveh, their god for evermore). The fact that the most frequent Old Testament name for God, *Elohim*, is an originally plural form is often mentioned in this connection, but the arguments are doubtful and perhaps influenced by lingering evolutionist patterns of thought. Henotheist tendencies are also evident in Vedic religion and, to a lesser degree, in the *bhakti* ("devotion") directed toward a variety of later Hindu deities. [*See* Henotheism.]

One problem that cannot be ignored is the disappearance (with a few exceptions) of polytheism as a result of either monotheistic "revolutions" (e.g., ancient Israel, Islam) or unifying tendencies. Indeed, too little scholarly attention has been paid to the strange fact that polytheism has gradually disappeared except in some East Asian religions. In most contemporary philosophical discussions the alternatives considered as available to society seem to be monotheism or atheism; polytheism is treated as an important phenomenon or stage in the history of religions but hardly ever, philosophically or theologically, as a live option.

The quest of an overarching unity (one universe in spite of the multiplicity of forms of existence; one natural law under which all other laws can be subsumed) is clearly one factor that led to a view of the divine as one. By using impersonal language, it is relatively easy to speak of "the divine" in the singular. A personal god is a more difficult matter. But at any rate unifying tendencies are discernible everywhere, even in antiquity. The Greek dramatist Aeschylus speaks of "the one with many names," and the *Ṛgveda* says of the evidently one god that "men call him Indra, Mitra, Varuṇa, Agni." The polytheistic paganism of the late Roman empire was syncretistic in the sense of evincing a tendency to identify the individual gods of the various (Greek, Roman, Oriental, Germanic) cultures. Hence it becomes possible to speak of a "pseudo-polytheism," a religious system that preserves the traditional polytheistic terminology but considers the many gods mere manifestations of what is ultimately one divine principle. This tendency is especially noticeable in many modern types of Neo-Hinduism. For some Hellenistic writers (e.g., Marcus Aurelius) the grammatical distinction between *theos* (singular) and *theoi* (plural) has become practically meaningless.

All monistic—even nontheistic—views on the higher and more sophisticated doctrinal levels notwithstanding, a *de facto* functional polytheism can continue to exist among the masses of devout believers. This is not the place for a psychological and sociological analysis of the role of the cult of saints among many Roman Catholics. In India, no matter what monist or nondualist doctrines are theoretically held, the religious life of the mass of believers is a *de facto* polytheistic one. The case of Mahāyāna Buddhism is even more striking. On the doctrinal and scholastic level, as well as on the level of higher mystical experience, there may be no god or divine being, and the key terms are *emptiness, nothingness,* and the like. Yet the ordinary Buddhist (and even the Buddhist monk) relates to the many Buddhas and *boddhisattvas* that in fact constitute the Buddhist pantheon like a polytheist to his gods.

[*For further discussion of this topic, see* Gods and Goddesses. *See also* Anthropomorphism.]

BIBLIOGRAPHY

There is little, if any, systematic literature on the subject. Discussions of polytheism can be found in articles on monotheism in the older, standard encyclopedias (the *Encyclopaedia of Religion and Ethics,* edited by James Hastings, *Die Religion in Geschichte und Gegenwart,* and so on) as well as in accounts of specific polytheistic religions (for example, Germanic and Celtic; ancient Near Eastern; Greek and Roman; Indian, Chinese, and Japanese; Mesoamerican and South American). Perhaps the first modern discussion of polytheism, in the Western sense, is David Hume's *The Natural History of Religion* (1757), though Hume's account is obviously shaped by eighteenth-century European Enlightenment attitudes. Systematic considerations can be found in Gerardus van der Leeuw's *Religion in Essence and Manifestation,* 2 vols. (1938; Gloucester, Mass., 1967); E. O. James's *The Concept of Deity* (New York, 1950); and Angelo Brelich's "Der Polytheismus," *Numen* 7 (December 1960): 123–136. On the relationship of polytheism to more highly developed political organization (e.g., the Greek polis), see Walter Burkert's "Polis and Polytheism," in his *Greek Religion* (Cambridge, Mass., 1985), pp. 216–275.

R. J. ZWI WERBLOWSKY

PONTIFEX. The Latin noun *pontifex,* designating certain Roman high priests, is thought of as deriving from *pons* ("bridge") and *facere* ("to make"). This etymology, held by Varro (*De lingua Latina* 5.83), is accepted by the majority of modern scholars. Yet the discrepancy between this definition of "bridge maker" and the broad extent of the pontifical function has aroused some resistance among scholars both ancient and modern. At the beginning of the first century BCE the *pontifex maximus* Q. Mucius Scaevola (cited by Varro, ibid.) preferred to see in the word *pontifices* a corruption of the word *potifices* (from *posse,* "to be able," and *facere,* "to do," undoubtedly in the sense of "to sacrifice"). Today, there are those who think that *pons* originally meant "path," even "obstacle path," by reason of its likeness to the Vedic *pānthāh.*

Commentators since antiquity have been struck by the contrast between the apparent specialization of the titleholder (Varro referred to the construction and restorations of the bridge of Sublicius by the pontiffs) and the importance of the role. The contrast is transparent in Festus: in one and the same paragraph he points out the attribution to the *pontifex maximus* of the fifth and last rank in the hierarchy of priests, even while defining him as the "judge and arbiter of things divine and human" (Festus, ed. Lindsay, 1913, p. 198 L.). Indeed, the *pontifex maximus* (aided by the pontifical college, which successively numbered three, nine, fifteen, and sixteen members) had become, from simple adviser to the king, the true head of Roman religion. Under the republic, it was he who sat in the Regia, which had become the *domus publica* of the pontifical college. He was the one who named—more precisely, it was said that he "seizes" *(capit;* Gallius, 1.12.15)—the *rex sacrorum* ("king of the sacrifices"), the *flamines*, and the Vestals whenever a vacancy occurred, and he had the right of supervision over all of them. He convoked and presided over the Comitia Calata, the assembly that witnessed the inauguration of the *rex sacrorum* and the *flamines maiores* ("greater priests"). During that same assembly there also took place each month on the nones the proclamation by the *rex* of the month's holidays *(feriae primae menstruae;* Varro, *De lingua Latina* 5.83).

For a long time the pontiffs were the true regulators of time, in that the calendar was not published until 304 BCE, when this was finally done at the instigation of the *aedilis curulis*, G. Flavius (Cicero, *Pro Murena* 25). In their archives the high priests kept all documents concerning the *sacra publica*, the public religion: lists of divinities to invoke *(indigitamenta);* prayer formulas *(carmina)* for the fulfillment of vows, dedications, and consecrations; cultic rules *(leges templorum);* and prescriptions for expiatory sacrifices *(piacula)*.

Fundamentally, pontifical activity was carried out on two levels. On the liturgical level the high priests participated actively in public ceremonies, as for instance the anniversaries of temples. (The sacrificial utensils, the knife, *secespita*, and the ax, *sacena*, are among the pontifical symbols; Festus, op. cit., p. 422 L.) On the theological level the high priests provided decisions and responses *(decreta* and *responsa)*, which came to constitute the *ius pontificium* ("pontifical law"). The authority acquired by the *pontifex maximus* explains why, following the example of Julius Caesar, Augustus chose to add this dignity to his set of titles in 12 BCE. Thereafter it remained attached to the imperial function.

BIBLIOGRAPHY

Bleicken, Jochen. "Oberpontifex und Pontifikalkollegium." *Hermes* 85 (November 1957): 345–366.

Bouché-Leclercq, Auguste. *Les pontifes de l'ancienne Rome.* Paris, 1871.

Dumézil, Georges. *La religion romaine archaïque.* 2d ed. Paris, 1974. See pages 573–576. This work has been translated from the first edition by Philip Krapp as *Archaic Roman Religion*, 2 vols. (Chicago, 1970).

Hallett, Judith P. "Over Troubled Waters: The Meaning of the Title *Pontifex." Translations and Proceedings of the American Philological Association* 101 (1970): 219–227. A reconciliation of *pons* with the Vedic *pānthāh*.

Rhode, Georg. *Die Kultsatzungen der römischen Pontifices.* Berlin, 1936.

Szemler, G. J. "Pontifex." In *Real-encyclopädie die Altertumwissenschaft*, vol. 15. Munich, 1978.

Wissowa, Georg. *Religion und kultus der Römer.* 2d ed. Munich, 1912. See pages 501–521.

ROBERT SCHILLING
Translated from French by Paul C. Duggan

POOR CLARES. *See* Franciscans.

POPULAR CHRISTIAN RELIGIOSITY. Popular religiosity in Christianity is usually described as the religious expressions, practices, forms, and attitudes belonging to vast sectors of Christians who (1) have minimal formal religious education; (2) have achieved a deep symbiosis between their religious and cultural behaviors; (3) emphasize the role of religion with regard to their temporal, material needs. These factors are usually combined in different proportions according to places, times, and social situations. Although always necessary to take into account in any interpretation of popular religiosity, they are not exclusive factors; for example, the historical ways by which Christianity came about in particular peoples and areas may be important also.

Most scholars agree on the special relevance of cultural factors. The fact that Christian forms and practices are assimilated and even reinterpreted in reference to indigenous cultural expression is paramount in the elaboration of divergent expressions of Christianity. This is particularly true with regard to the so-called popular cultures, or cultures of poor and simple peoples.

There have been expressions of popular religiosity in all times and places throughout Christian history. Therefore, popular religiosity is not something accidental or provisional. Rather it is essential to Christianity as a universal religion. Popular Christianity, however, is more apparent in Roman Catholicism and in the Christian Orthodox churches, because of their emphasis on sacramental symbols, than in Protestantism. [*See* Worship, *article on* Christian Worship.] However, this statement is becoming more and more relative to the extent that Protestant denominations implant themselves in non-European cultures.

Popular Christianity is also often referred to in opposition to "elite Christianity." In this sense "elite Christianity" is the prevailing form of Christianity of educated, Western, and Western-oriented peoples, influenced in the last centuries by Enlightenment rationalism and secularization. This form of Christianity emphasizes the moral and functional values of Christian faith, deemphasizing its mystic, symbolic, and festive dimensions. From this standpoint, popular religiosity often would be considered a "low form" of Christianity.

This derogative outlook on popular religiosity, often attendant on the outlook of cultural superiority on the part of Western elites, prevailed in the nineteenth and early twentieth centuries. It is undergoing a global reassessment in the late twentieth century, as the drawbacks of a secularized and rationalistic Christianity become increasingly evident, as the elites become more aware of their own cultural limitations and their unidimensional interpretations of life and religion, and more important, as there is a growing appreciation of the cultural and religious values and wisdom of popular cultures.

Historical Orientation. Popular Christianity is widespread in Africa, Latin America, and parts of Asia, especially the Philippines. It is also found in Europe, though there secularization and rationalism have undermined its force during the last centuries. Yet old Christian Europe is the cradle of current popular religiosity, whose roots can be traced back to medieval Christianity.

It is beyond the scope here to discuss popular religiosity during the European Middle Ages. Its origins lie in the encounter of Christianity with the non-Christian religions and cultures that constituted the ground of medieval Europe: Celts, Iberians, Germans, Slavics, and so on. The Byzantine Christian influence was also important in nurturing popular religion. [*See* Icons *and* Iconoclasm.]

Perhaps the best synthesis of medieval popular religiosity is found in the Cluny spiritual movement, brought about throughout Europe by the Benedictine monks of the Cluny foundations. Cluny popular spirituality built up devotionalism associated with saints, the names of Jesus and Mary, the Eucharist, and on behalf of the dead. Franciscanism, a movement of popular spiritual renewal, added some devotions that became part of popular Christianity. These include the passion of Christ, the crib, and the stations of the cross. European and American popular religiosity subsequently were fostered by Roman Catholic restoration movements in the seventeenth and nineteenth centuries.

In the epoch of America's evangelization, the people of the Iberian Peninsula enjoyed many forms of popular devotions. The missionaries, as they came to America, were able to select the most valuable. This Iberian popular religiosity blended with (and somewhat reinterpreted) elements of indigenous religions, and later with the traditions of African slaves. The blending of Christianity with other religions has also brought about various forms of syncretism. This is the case particularly in the Andes highlands, in Brazil, and in the Caribbean. [*See* Christianity, *articles on Latin America and the Caribbean region*.]

Characteristics of Popular Religion. Several tendencies or characteristics of popular religion may be noted. First, there is the tendency toward autonomy. On the one hand, popular religiosity remains Christian and uses the religious channels of Christianity to express itself. On the other hand, it emphasizes values and practices that do not always coincide with official Christianity; for example, the feasts of saints may be more important than the liturgical commemorations of Christ, or Sunday mass may be replaced by masses in veneration of the dead.

Second, popular religiosity emphasizes devotions and religious symbols as mediations to God. It emphasizes the presence of God in nature, in images, in places, and in material things related to religion, such as candles and holy water. Because heart, sentiment, and poetical discourse are so important in popular cultures, relationship to God is expressed through mediations (symbols) that speak to the heart: narratives, images, places, things, persons. In many cases, this blend of religious and cultural practices can overemphasize the cultural dimension so much that in the long run religious practices are devoid of conscious religious signification. For example, in the case of traditional processions that become merely a part of cultural or even touristic events, popular religiosity has been unduly acculturated, and its various expressions are referred to as "folklore religion."

Third, popular religiosity manifests a strong sense of God's presence in everyday life. God intervenes continuously in favor of his children, and this intervention can be prompted by promises of the faithful and by certain devotions. For these purposes, mediations to reach God, such as saints, certain feasts, particular places, and prayer, have great importance.

Fourth, popular religiosity is collective; it is often expressed in multitudinous events such as processions, pilgrimages, and mass celebrations of Good Friday and Christmas. During significant religious events, the convocation power of popular religiosity can be enormous. [*See* Carnival.]

Fifth, popular religiosity is sensitive to commuting experiences. Processions and pilgrimages to shrines and holy places embody a special grace of God that for many people may be the climax of their yearly religious experience.

Sixth, popular Christianity emphasizes the religious meaning of life and death. The crucial stages of human life are opened to God and find their sense in God: the beginning of life (birth), the transmission of life (matrimony), the end of life. Here, death is the paramount religious experience and is surrounded by many rituals. This sense of the presence of God in the crucial moments of life also explains the fact that Christian sacraments related to those moments draw extensive participation. Popular religiosity is well aware of the new dimension that Christ gave to human suffering. It readily accepts suffering as the will of God and as a mystery, yet this attitude is not devoid of an element of fatalism as well.

Seventh, the image of Jesus Christ is of major importance in popular religion. This image is complex and paradoxical. On the one hand, Jesus is looked upon as a powerful God who performs miracles and is somewhat distant. The value of Christ's humanity is overshadowed. It is more important to resort to Jesus' power than to imitate him and follow his teachings. On the other hand, there is deep devotion to the cross and to the passion of Jesus. The crucified Christ is close to the people, always nearby to hear prayers and to be the source of love.

Finally, popular Christianity upholds the religious value of the weak. The very poor, the sick, the elderly, and children are the locus of God's presence. Popular religion is aware that our attitude toward the needy has to do with God and with goodness and evil. In this sense, popular Christian religiosity is based not only in ritual expressions but also in solidarity and mercy among the poor.

Prospects of Popular Christianity. To the extent that popular religion is deeply rooted in religious and cultural traditions alike and remains a component of the cultural identity of the people, it is basically conservative. Popular Christianity has survived the pressures of the culture of the Enlightenment, of rationalism, and of diverse forms of secularism. It has turned out to be an important factor in the persistence of Christian faith in the masses. The last century of the second millennium has seen one major change in the evolution of popular Christianity—from a rural to an increasingly urban phenomenon. Popular religion, traditionally rural, is becoming the popular form of Christianity in the poor areas of the cities and is therefore undergoing significant changes. Because urban popular religion becomes much less multitudinous and collective and tends to confine itself to the family and even to private practices, it becomes less conspicuous and less expressive. Its cultural heritage is not so strong as it was in rural settings. Some practices and symbols are dropped altogether, but others, more in affinity with new work and life systems, take their place.

Popular Christian religiosity is a privileged area in which Christianity meets other religions in terms of religious experiences and expressions common to a wide social context. It is, therefore, particularly relevant with regard to religious ecumenism.

[*See also* Cult of Saints *and* Pilgrimage, *articles on Roman Catholic and Eastern Christian pilgrimage.*]

BIBLIOGRAPHY

Studies of popular Christian religiosity are relatively new, at least on a systematic basis. So far, most of the material has come from Latin America and thus has Roman Catholicism as its usual focus. Catholic bishops have issued two official church documents on the subject that sum up the current consensus and provide a good synthesis. The proceedings of the Second General Conference of Latin American Bishops, held at Medellín, Colombia, in 1968, have been published in English as *The Church in the Present-day Transformation of Latin America in the Light of the Council*, 2 vols. (Bogotá, 1970–1973); see, in volume 2, "Popular Pastoral." Proceedings of the Third General Conference, held at Puebla, Mexico, in 1979, have been issued as *Evangelization at Present and in the Future of Latin America* (Washington, D.C., 1979); see chapter 3, "Evangelization and People's Religiosity." Both these works were issued under the auspices of the U.S. Conference of Bishops.

A synthetic and comprehensive presentation from the pastoral standpoint can be found in my book *The Challenge of Popular Religiosity* (Manila, 1983). Also relevant is a larger work edited by the Consejo Episcopal Latinamericano (CELAM), *Iglesia y religiosidad popular en América Latina* (Bogotá, 1977), including articles dealing with different aspects of popular Christianity (historical, anthropological, theological, pastoral) as well as several case studies.

For further bibliographical information, consult *Boletín bibliográphico latinoamericano* (Madrid, 1976) and *Revista eclesiástica brasileira* 36 (Petropolis, Brazil, 1976).

SEGUNDO GALILEA

POPULAR RELIGION. Every society exhibits divisions and segmentations based upon the classification of its members and their activities, functions, and relationships (e.g., sex, work, knowledge, etc.). However, it was long a universally common assumption that the meaning of any institution within the society, or the meaning of the society as a whole, was the privileged province of the upper, or elite, levels of the society. Indeed, the idea that social meaning could be gained from any other level, especially the lower levels of the social structure, is a relatively new notion. The setting forth of the notion that a positive and necessary knowledge of society could be gained from its lower levels defined this strata as a locus of interpretation, meaning, and value.

The idea that the positive meaning of a society is represented by the "common people," "the folk," or the peasants may be seen as an expression of "cultural primitivism," the dissatisfaction of the civilized with the quality and style of civilization and the expression of a desire to return for orientation to the archaic roots of the culture. This "discovery of the people," to use Peter Burke's apt phrase, began in the late eighteenth and early nineteenth centuries in Europe. The philosophical justification for this orientation can be seen in the writings of Giovanni Battista Vico (1668–1744) and Johann Gottfried Herder (1744-1803). Probably more than any others, these two thinkers represented new theoretical approaches to the nature of history, religion, and society. They distinguished the notions of the *"populari"* and "the *volk*" as the basis for an alternate and new meaning of humanism apart from the rationalizing and civilizing processes set in motion by the European Enlightenment.

The discovery of two new and different forms of societal orders—one outside Europe (the so-called "primitives"), the other internal to European cultures (the peasants and the folk)—was prompted, in fact, by a search for origins. The search was in some senses antithetical, and in other senses supplementary, to the meaning of the origins of the West in the biblical and Greek cultures. The discovery that the archaic levels of human culture and society had an empirical locus in existing Western cultures became the philosophical, theological, and ideological basis for the legitimation of these new structures of order in modern and contemporary societies.

The notion of popular religion has to do with the discovery of archaic forms, whether within or outside Western cultures. It is at this level that the meaning of popular religion forms a continuum with both primitive religions and peasant and folk cultures in all parts of the world. This continuum is based upon structural similarities defined by the organic nature of all of these types of societies rather than upon historical or genetic causation.

Primitive and peasant-folk societies are, relatively speaking, demographically small. The relationships among people in these societies were thought to be personal in nature. Underlying all modes of communication is an intuitive or empathetic understanding of the ultimate nature and purpose of life.

This is what Herder meant by "the organic mode of life," an idea given methodological precision by the social philosopher Ferdinand Tönnies, who made a typological distinction between communities ordered in terms of *Gemeinschaft* and those expressing a *Gesellschaft* orientation to life and the world. *Gemeinschaft* represents community as organic form; *Gesellschaft* is society as a mechanical aggregate and artifact. A similar distinction is made by the anthropologist Robert Redfield when he describes preurban cultures as those in which the moral order predominates over the technical order. The moral order, in this interpretation, is the common understanding of the ultimate nature and purpose of life within the community. The notions of the organic nature of community *(Gemeinschaft)* and the primacy of the moral order lead to different meanings of the religious life in primitive and folk or peasant cultures as compared to societies in urban *Gesellschaft* orientations. Futhermore, the relationship or the distinction between the religious and the cognitive within the two kinds of societies differ.

While it can be said that religion is present when a distinction is made between the sacred and the profane, the locus of this distinction in primitive and folk-peasant cultures is a commonly shared one. There is a unified sense of those objects, actions, and sentiments that are sacred, and those that are profane. The religious and the moral orders tend to be synonymous; thus, the expression of religious faith on the ordinary and extraordinary levels of these cultures form a continuum. The extraordinary expressions are those that commemorate important punctuations of the temporal and social cycles (e.g., a new year, the harvest and first fruits, birth, marriage, and death). The ordinary modes are expressed in the customs, traditions, and mundane activities that maintain and sustain the culture on a daily basis.

One of the goals of the early studies of folk, peasant, and popular cultures was to come to an understanding of the qualitative meaning of religion in human cultures of this kind. Attention was focused on the meaning of custom and tradition, on the one hand, and upon the qualitative meaning and mode of transmission of the traditional values in cultures that were not predominantly literate.

The two early innovators, Herder and, especially, Vico, had already emphasized the modes and genres of language of the nonliterate. Vico based his entire philosophical corpus on the origin and development of language, or, to be more exact, of rhetoric. By the term *rhetoric* Vico made reference to the manner in which language is produced as a mode of constituting bonds between human beings, the world, and other beings outside the community. Closely related to Herder's philosophy of culture and history is the work of the Grimm brothers in their philological studies of the Germanic languages. Their collection of fairy tales, *Märchen*, and folk tales represents the beginning of serious scholarly study of oral traditions. In the work of the Grimms, the first articulation of the relationship between genres of oral literature and modes of transmission are raised. This relationship is important, for, given the presupposed organic form of nonliterate societies, the genres of transmission of ultimate meaning, whether ordinary or extraordinary, defined a locus of the religious. The romantic notion (present in Herder and in the theologians Friedrich Schleiermacher and Paul Tillich), namely, that religion is the ultimate ground and substance of culture, underlies the importance given to transmission, manifestation, and expression of this form of culture as religion. Religion is thus understood to be pervasive in society and culture, finding its expression not only in religious institutions, but in all the dimensions of cultural life.

The genres of the folk tale, folk song, art, and myth became the expressive forms of popular religion. The investigation of poetic meaning and wisdom, and of metaphorical, symbolic expressions, emerged as sources of the religious sentiment in the traditions of popular religion. The initial "discovery of the people" as a approach to the interpretation of culture and society and as a new form of human value was made under the aegis of intuitive methods within literary studies and from the perspective of a speculative philosophy of history. Once serious scholarly attention was given to the data of the popular, certain ambiguities were noted. The original discovery of the people was based, by and large, on a contrast between the popular and the urban, or the artificiality of the urban mode as a form of civilization. In this sense, the popular represented the archaic and original forms of culture; it was its roots. However, the meaning of the popular could not be limited to the conservative, value-retaining, residual, self-contained unit of a society or culture. One of the basic elements in the meaning of a popular cultural tradition was the mode of its transmission, and it was precisely this element that allowed the meaning of such a tradition to be extended beyond that of the nonliterate strata of society—the rural peasants and the folk.

Varieties and Dimensions. Critical investigations of the meaning of popular culture and religion from the disciplinary orientations of the anthropology and history of religion, and from the sociology of knowledge, revealed a wide variety of the forms of popular religion. From the anthropological and historical perspectives, one is able to delineate and describe the characteristic modes of experience and expression of religion at the various levels of the cultural strata, and to show the dynamics of the interrelationships of the popular forms with other cultural strata. The sociology of knowledge provides an understanding of the genesis, contents, and mode of thought and imagination present in popular religion, and demonstrates how various strata within a social order participate in the values, meanings, and structures of popular religion.

Though scholarly, disciplinary approaches led to a more precise definition of the popular and to a critique of the original meaning of the popular and popular religion, such studies also brought about a proliferation of different meanings and interpretations of popular religion. Of these, the following seven are the most significant.

1. *Popular religion is identical with the organic (usually rural and peasant) form of a society. The religious and moral orders are also identical; in this sense, popular religion is closely related to the meanings of primitive and folk religion.* This is the original meaning of popular religion as the religion of folk and peasant culture. Though the distinction between the folk and peasant religion and the religion of the urban areas is clear-cut in the industrial periods of all cultures, such a distinction does not rest simply on this basis. In the feudal periods of various cultures, this distinction is more pronounced in relationship to certain practices and in the hierarchical structures of the society. Within feudal structures, the upper classes participated in and controlled a form of literacy that was confined within this group. In various cultures, this meant access to an orientation of religious meaning revolving around sacred texts. In China, for example, there appeared Confucian classics; in India, the Sanskritic literary tradition; in Christianity, the Bible, and so on.

The limitation of the modes of literacy suggest that though there are authoritative sacred texts, they are situated in a context that is often dominated by illiteracy and oral traditions. The line of demarcation between the culture of literacy and that of the oral traditions is seldom clear-cut. In many cases, the traditions of literacy embody a great deal of the content, form, and style of the oral traditions of the peasants and the folk. Prior to the universalization of the modes of literacy in many cultures, the prestige of literacy was to be found in the belief in, and regard for, the sacred text, which itself was believed to have a magical, authoritative meaning in addition to the content of its the particular writings. The written words of the god or gods (the authoritative text) resided with, and was under the control of, elites within the culture.

Another characteristic of folk-peasant societies is that they define the lives of their members within the context of a certain ecological niche (agricultural, pastoral, etc.), and the modes and genres of their existence are attached to this context by ties of tradition and sentiment. The group and the ecological structure thus define a continuity of relationships. The sentiment and the moral order of communities of this kind are synonymous with the meaning of their religion. In agricultural peasant and folk cultures, the rhythms of the agricultural seasons are woven into the patterns of human relationships and sociability. The symbols and archetypes of religion are expressions of the alternation and integration of the human community, the techniques of production, and the reality of the natural world. In most cultures this type of popular religion carries the connotation of religion as *ab origine* and archaic. Robert Redfield has suggested that the folk-peasant mode of life is an enduring structure of human community found in every part of the world. As such it is not only an empirical datum of a type of human community, but may also represent an enduring source of religious and moral values.

2. *Popular religion as the religion of the laity in a religious community in contrast to that of the clergy. The clergy is the bearer of a learned tradition usually based upon the prestige of literacy.* Another type of popular religion is notable in religious communities where literacy is by and large limited to the clergy. The clergy carries out the authority of the tradition through the use of religious texts. The laity may memorize and repeat certain of these texts in worship and rituals, but they are not in possession of the instruments and institutional authority of sacred literacy. Both clergy and laity may participate in and honor other traditions that arise from the life of the laity. Such traditions are those related to the sacralization of agricultural seasons and worship centered around the cults of relics and saints, holy persons, pilgrimages, and so on.

Another meaning of this kind of popular religion stems from a society in which literacy is not confined to the clergy or elite. The laity may have access to certain authoritative or quasi-authoritative texts without being in possession of the power of normative interpretation and sanction of these texts. They therefore interpret these texts in their own manner, according to their own needs and sensibilities. A notable case of this kind of popular religion is the account given in *The Cheese and the Worms* (1980) by Carlo Ginzburg of the Italian miller Domenico Sandella (nicknamed Menochhio), a literate peasant who created and thought through an entire cosmology radically different from that of the church authorities. In other cases the clergy may create for the laity popular religious literature of a devotional or catechismal nature that takes on the forms of a more pervasive popular culture of the laity. This can be seen in the adaptation of archetypes from the authoritative tradition to a popular structure: for example, the popularization of Kuan-yin in Buddhist literatures, and the local and popular traditions concerning Kṛṣṇa among Hindus. In another example, Christmas (the celebration of the birth of Jesus Christ), which developed from older, popular (pagan) traditions, has been adapted to the popular cultures and economies of modern societies.

3. *Popular religion as the pervasive beliefs, rituals, and values of a society. Popular religion of this type is a kind of civil religion or religion of the public. It forms the general and wide context for the discussion of anything of a religious nature within the society.* Two studies of Greek religion may be used to illustrate this point. Martin P. Nilsson, in his *Greek Folk Religion,* described the religion of the countryside, the folk-peasant religion of ancient Greece. Jon D. Mikalson, in his *Athenian Popular Religion,* treats Greek religion not in terms of class structures, nor through a distinction between the rural and the urban, but rather concentrates on the views and beliefs that were a part of the common cultural experience of the majority of Athenians during the late fourth and fifth centuries CE. Mikalson goes on to point out that one of the most important sources for this type of popular religion was the orations presented in law courts, where the orators addressed juries that numbered from five hundred to twenty-five hundred or more Athenian male citizens.

Similar forms of popular religion are found in all cultures where the religious substratum of the culture radiates into, and finds explicit expression—or vague nuances and derivations—in the formation and processes of public institutions other than those dedicated to specific religious ceremonials. As such, this form of popular religion provides a generalized rhetoric and norm for the meaning and discussion of religion within the context of the culture in which it is found. In most cases the meaning of this kind of popular religion is expressed in terms of a dominant religious tradition that has had a profound and pervasive influence upon the culture. For example, in the Western world, one could speak of Christendom or biblical orientations; in India, of the Sanskritic language and cultural traditions; in China and other parts of the Far East, of the Confucian and Buddhist traditions; and, in Islamic countries, of the Islamic tradition. In each case a specific religious orientation has so informed the cultural life that it has become the "natural" and normative language of religion in general, and the secular forms of cultural life as well give expression to their origins in that religious tradition.

Of particular interest in this regard is the discussion surrounding the issue of "civil religion" in the United States since the end of World War II. This discussion has come to the fore in many democratic societies due to the growing democratization and secularization of the processes and institutions within societies of this kind. The case of the American republic is an extreme example of this problem because, as a nation-state, it is not philosophically based upon an explicit or implicit meaning derived from either an archaic or aboriginal religion, nor upon any meaning of a named, empirical religion. Neither did the nation's founders find it necessary to come to terms with the religion of the original inhabitants of the land as the Spanish did in Mesoamerica and South America. The notion of "God" or "Nature's God" is used as an analogue for an archaic principle of founding, but its connotations remain vague; thus, specific religious groups interpret this principle in their own manner in accord with the principle of religious freedom in the United States. However, this same meaning is not limited to its interpretation by specific religious groups; it is also evoked and given extensive interpretation in the speeches of prominent political, judicial, and public figures, and in documents of the nation's history. Sidney M. Mead (1963) and Robert N. Bellah (1968) have shown how the symbolic interpretations of the meaning of the "God of the Republic" in the rhetoric of American presidents have attempted to define—and persuade the citizenry of the United States of—the public religious and moral meanings and implications of the American Republic.

4. *Popular religion as an amalgam of esoteric beliefs and practices differing from the common or civil religion, but usually located in the lower strata of a society.* Popular religion in this form more often than not exists alongside other forms of religion in a society. Reference is made here to the religious valuation of esoteric forms of healing, predictions of events not based on logical reasoning, and therapeutic practices that have an esoteric origin and may imply a different cosmology than the one prevalent within the society as a whole. In most cases the practitioners and clients have not eschewed the ordinary modes of healing and therapy; the esoteric beliefs and practices are supplementary, representing a mild critique of the normative forms of this kind of knowledge and practice in the society at large. This form of popular religion is present in industrial societies in practices such as phrenology, palm reading, astrology, and in the accompanying esoteric, "metaphysical" beliefs. The pervasive nature of this kind of popular religion may be noted by the fact that in almost all of the larger cities of industrialized countries, every major newspaper and magazine finds it necessary to carry astrological forecasts or some other symbolic mode that appeals to an alternate interpretation of the world.

5. *Popular religion as the religion of a subclass or minority group in a culture.* Particular classes defined by their ethnicity or by an ideology or mythology associated with their work (e.g., miners, blacksmiths, butchers, soldiers, etc.), form another mode of popular religion. In most cases such groups do not represent foreign communities residing in another culture, but pose the problem of "otherness" or strangeness for people outside their communities due to their racial type or occupation. These groups are, nevertheless, integrated into the social structure as a necessary ingredient of a common cultural ideology and its functioning; they constitute "a part of the society by not being a part of it." In most traditional cultures of the world, certain occupations, such as mining or blacksmithing, represent this meaning. They are restricted to certain places of residence within the villages and they in turn have their own rituals and alternate understandings of the nature of the cosmos. While the role and function of such occupations is understood by the rest of society, and is felt to have a place in its general cosmology, they nevertheless form the basis for an alternate understanding of the nature of society. Examples of the ethnic and racial meaning of this form of popular religion may be seen in the history of the Jews within Christendom or the religions of Afro-Americans in the New World.

6. *Popular religion as the religion of the masses in opposition to the religion of the sophisticated, discriminating, and learned within a society.* This is a variation on the difference between the laity and the clergy in hierarchical and traditional societies. Reference is made in this form of popular religion to a meaning of the masses that is the product of democratic polities and industrialism. Whereas in the older, traditional, hierarchical societies, the clergy and the laity both possessed traditions, the modern definition of "the masses" implies the loss of tradition and canons of value and taste, which are now defined in terms of a privileged class order of the elite who have had the benefit of special education. Alexis de Tocqueville's comments on the meaning of democracy in America imply that democracy and mass culture are synonymous. The form of popular religion will tend to express the existential and ephemeral concerns of the mass population at any moment of its history.

7. *Popular religion as the creation of an ideology of religion by the elite levels of a society.* From the very beginning of the study of popular culture and religion, the discovery, meaning, and valuation of "the popular" was undertaken by elites within the society. Especially with the coming of industrialization and the rise of the nation-state, the provincial traditions of the peasant and rural folk within a culture had to fall under the political and ideological meanings of larger generalizing and centralizing orders of the state and its bureaucracy. To the extent that the ideological meaning of the rural and peasant cultures served the aims of the state, it was promoted as the older, traditional meaning of the state deriving from its archaic forms. Popular culture and religion in this mode was invented and promoted by the state through folklore societies, museums, and by the promotion of historical research into the past of the society. On the basis of a genuine and authentic folk and peasant tradition of culture and religion, a new meaning of the popular forms is now embraced and supported by the state.

Given this variety of forms and meanings of popular religion, it is appropriate to ask what is the common element in all of them. There are two common elements. First of all, "the popular" in any of its varieties is concerned with a mode of transmission of culture. Whether the group be large or small, or whether the content of the religion be sustaining or ephemeral, "the popular" designates the universalization of its mode of transmission. In peasant and folk situations, this mode of transmission is traditionally embodied in symbols and archetypes tht tend to be long-lasting and integrative. In modern industrial societies, the modes of transmission are several, including literacy, electronic media, newspapers, chapbooks, and so on. Such modes of communication bring into being a popular culture that is different from, but may overlap with, other social strata within the culture. Due to the intensity of these forms of communication, the content of the forms of popular culture is able to change quickly. It is not, however, the content that is at the fore here, but the type of cognition afforded by the modes of transmission. Given the intensification of transmission and the ephemerality of content, this form of popular religion and culture is semiotic—it is embedded in a system of signs rather than in symbols and archetypes.

The Nature of Culture. The meaning of popular religion presupposes an understanding of the nature of culture that is capable of making sense of differences and divisions within the totality of any culture. Furthermore, the notion of culture must allow room for the meaning of religion as one of the primary modes of transmission of the cultural tradition.

Clifford Geertz's description (1965) of religion as a cultural system is one of the most adequate understandings of culture as a mode of transmission. His definition is as follows: religion is (1) a system of symbols that acts to (2) establish powerful, pervasive, and long-lasting moods and motivations in people by (3) formulating conceptions of a general order of existence and (4) clothing these conceptions with an aura of factuality so that (5) the moods and motivations seem uniquely realistic. This notion of religion as a cultural system enables one to understand how religion is the expression and transmission of a conception of the reality of the world, and it is clear that such a powerful and pervasive notion must of necessity imply a mode of transmission.

If this notion of religion as a cultural system is seen in relationship to Robert Redfield's analysis of the divisions and distinctions within a cultural system, a basis for the meaning of popular religion within a cultural milieu is established (Redfield, 1955). Redfield makes a broad distinction within a culture between what he calls the "great tradition" and the "little tradition." The "great tradition" is that of the learned elite and often the ruling class, while the "little tradition" is that of the large classes and groups of the lower classes. His combination of these two theories allows us to understand the meaning of popular religion from the point of view of culture as a whole. However, in all parts of the world, due to industrialization and modernization, it is becoming increasingly difficult to define the meaning of culture in these terms. Whereas political power may continue to reside in an elite ruling class that has hegemony over many forms of cultural expression, the modes of transmission, through literacy and electronic media are so intense that the distinction between the elite and the lower class as well as between the urban and rural milieus fail to mark a line of demarcation that is true to social reality. From this point of view, the modes of communication and transmission have as much or more to do with the integration and wholeness of the culture as the content of symbolic clusters or ideological meaning.

Considerations of this sort raise issues regarding the locus and meaning of religion in contemporary industrialized societies. Because of the intensity of transmission, the content of what is transmitted tends to be ephemeral; thus, the notion of religion as establishing powerful, pervasive, and long-lasting moods and motivations is shifted away from content and substance to modes of experience. Popular religion is thus no longer defined in terms of sustaining traditions, but in the qualitative meaning of the nature of experience. Thus, in attempting to describe popular religion in modern societies, the investigator may undertake research in a wide variety of media where members of the culture express their experiences, such as television, radio, and newspapers; and in occurrences such as sports and recreational events, political activities, and so on. Seen from this point of view, the popular approximates some aspects of the older and original notion of "popular" as the peasant-folk and organic meaning in a society. In the peasant-folk, organic society, the mode of transmission were relatively slow, and thus the content of the transmission predominated, allowing for the comprehension of the symbolic content to consciously and unconsciously inform the life of society. In modern industrial societies, transmission is almost universal throughout the society, but the content is no longer the bearer of organic and integrative form.

Social Change. The notion of an organic social order, whether defined as a primitive, peasant, or folk culture, often implies complete equilibrium, integration, and stasis in a society. This is hardly ever true: all societies exhibit divisions and segmentations of various kinds, and these are often expressed in religious terms. They may be seen in the religious meanings defined by gender as well as in the gradations of the types of religious knowledge wherein certain types of esoteric or secret knowledge is held by an elite, and a more public and general religious meaning is present in the society at large. A good example of this is given in Marcel Griaule's account of the knowledge of Ogotemmêli, the old Dogon sage. The knowledge held by Ogotemmêli has a correspondence to the public meaning and symbols of Dogon religion, but his knowledge is more profound and possesses a metaphysical dimension. This type of knowledge and these types of human beings are found in many traditional societies.

A similar situation is present in societies where shamans possess a different and superior knowledge to that of ordinary persons. Where differences of thought and social structure exist, there is always the possibility for a tension among and between social divisions and/or modes of thought; these tensions at any moment may lead to the expression of novelty, thus causing changes in the society as a whole.

In addition to internally induced changes in organic societies based on differences of thought or social divisions, change may also arise from certain pervasive rituals. The rite of initiation is especially conducive to the influx of new religious orientations and changes in the social order. Initiation is that ritual concerned with the creation of new human beings. It introduces the initiand into the human community through the religious experience of the world of sacred beings in mythic times. Often in initiation rituals, the candidate is made to experience a regression to a time before creation and then to ritually imitate the archetypal stages of the first creation. The ability to imitate, recreate, or renew the cosmos is a possibility present in every initiation ritual, and this experience may become the basis for social change within the society. The notion that there can be a new mode of being is the basis for radical change in this religious ritual.

There is hardly any knowledge available on the expression of initiation leading to broad societal change in non-European societies prior to the coming of the Europeans; however, initiation cults of this kind in pre-Christian European cultures attest to their implications for changes in the societal order. The Greco-Oriental mystery religions posed an extreme tension between the public religious cults of the Hellenistic period in their expression of a deeper and more personal experience of sacred realities.

The preponderance of the data regarding the relationship between popular religion and social change has come primarily from religious traditions defined by their geographical extension in time and space, where the religious tradition has become synonymous with a cultural tradition (e.g., Hinduism, Islam, Christianity, etc.). These traditions cover a wide variety of forms of social divisions and thought. As such, the tensions among and between them are many, and are much more intense. It is in such traditions that the distinctions between the organic structure of society and the elite ruling class is most pronounced. Exchanges of thought and experience between these two major structures of society may occur in ritualized forms such as the festival, carnival, and pilgrimage. These ritual forms allow for a lessening of the social divisions, and for the communication and integration of modes and styles of life that are not governed by the everyday power defined by the political and social differences between the two groups. Not only do such rituals permit the relaxation of social differences, they allow for the interchange of vital knowledge between the two groups. M. Bahktin shows how these particular ritual forms have led to the creation of specific literary genres among the elite and literate members of the culture, especially as this is related to the carnival and the festival. Literary critics have long attested to the effect of the ritual pilgrimage on the literary imagination. E. Le Roy Ladurie, in his work *Carnival in Romans* (1979), has shown how the carnival provided the setting for revolutionary activities of the peasants and townspeople. Daniel L. Overmyer has described a similar situation in the White Lotus sect and the school of Lo Ch'ing (1443–1527) in China in the sixteenth century (Overmyer, 1976).

Movements and actions of this kind from the popular strata of the society have been called "pre-political" by Eric J. Hobsbawm (1959). By this he means that the people have not found a specific form of political ideology in which to express their aspirations about the world. While this may be true in most cases, such aspirations expressed in religious terms, and it is on this level of expression that unique dimensions of the meaning of popular religion emerge. In a manner reminiscent of the initiation structure of primitive societies, peasant and folk societies express a new self-consciousness of their solidarity through archaic symbols drawn from the genres of their lives and from a reinterpretation of the traditional religion. In many cases, symbols and teachings of the traditional religion are understood in a more literal manner, expecially as these symbols and teachings express renewal and change, the end of one order and the beginning of a new one. Banditry, outlawry, and other actions that violate the social order are permitted in the revolutionary milieu, for they are sanctioned by what Victor Turner has called the liminal state, which forms the context of the revolutionary activity. This state is a regression to chaos on the level of society.

Two major types of religious personages appear in popular religious movements of this kind: the prophetic figure and the outlaw. The prophet as a religious personage is not unique to the situation of popular religion. In most cases, figures of this sort are a part of the traditional teaching of the culture. From the stratum of popular religion, the meaning and role of the prophet is enhanced as the critical and condemnatory voice of the people against the abuses and injustices of the ruling and elite class. It is the prophet who relates the existential situation of the people to primordial religious depths forged from the life of the people and a new interpretation of the religious tradition.

The outlaw is the heroic religious figure in popular revolutionary religious movements. The archetypal outlaw is the one whose banditry establishes justice within the society; the outlaw takes from the rich to give to the poor. Myths and legends of the outlaw, such as Robin Hood in England, Janosik in Poland, Corrientes in Andalusia, or Finn in Irish and Scottish tales, abound.

The religious meaning of renewal of the world is a prominent theme of popular revolutionary movements. Within Western religious traditions, this theme is derivative of the religious symbol of the Messiah, whose coming announces the destruction of the old world or the radical renewal of the world. The world will be reversed—turned upside down—thus therewill be a redress of all wrongs. These millennial expectations are not only goals of a movement; they pervade all the activities of its followers, allowing for a reordering of psychic structures as well as opening up the possibility of a new social religious order on the level of popular religion.

Global Structures. With increasing rapidity and intensity since the late fifteenth century, the Western world—through exploration, conquest, and military and economic exploitation—brought the non-European world under its modes of communication through the structures of the modern industrial system. The Western systems of economics and communications were the bearer of Western forms of religious mythology and ideology, often characterized by millennial hopes. From this point of view, the West became the center of the world; the other areas, the peripheries. In other words, the West took over the role and function of the ruling elite, with other parts of the world playing the role of the older peasant or folk societies.

There has been a religious response to this hegemony of the West in almost all parts of the world. In many cases, a new elite comes into being in the colonized countries, imitating the structures and forms of the Western center. This, in turn, creates a new form of the popular—the traditional religion of the indigenous culture becomes a popular religion and must reorder itself in relationship to the power and authority of the new, indigenous elite. The situation does not simply create a tension of opposition. The religious and ideological meaning of the West will inform, in varying degrees, the whole of the society, and the reordering of the indigenous tradition will represent an amalgam of the older indigenous forms and a reinterpreted Western religious tradition. New meanings of popular religion will emerge in this context. Making use of the communication systems of the Western colonizers, many of these movements will move beyond the provincial confines of their local culture in one of their modes. A notable example is the universal influence and acceptance of Afro-American music in almost all parts of the world. Walter J. Hollenweger has argued in his work *The Pentecostals* (1972) that this form and style of religion represents a global phenomenon, an alternate and critical response binding together religious communities in all parts of the world.

[*See also* Folklore. *For essays on folk religion in various traditions, see the composite entry* Folk Religion *and the comparable piece on* Popular Christian Religiosity.]

BIBLIOGRAPHY

While religious institutions exist on the popular, folk, and peasant levels of culture, the meaning of religion is not centered in the segmented religious institution. Because of the nature of these kinds of societies, religion is more often diffused throughout the forms of societal life. Given the various forms and modes of popular, folk, and peasant societies and communities, it is too much to say that religion is identical with the totality of the community. However, almost all aspects of the communal life are capable of expressing the religious life. This bibliography thus covers those works dealing specifically with popular religion as well as the wider range of the forms of popular, folk, and peasant communities.

History of the Study of Popular Religion. For interpretations of the philosophical impact of Giambattista Vico and J. G. Herder, Isaiah Berlin's *Vico and Herder* (London, 1976) is the best introduction. See also *The New Science of Giambattista Vico*, translated by Thomas Goddard Bergin and Max Harold Fisch (Ithaca, N.Y., 1948). Commentaries on the writings of Vico are found in Donald Phillip Verene's *Vico's Science of Imagination* (Ithaca, N.Y., 1981) and in *Vico: Selected Writings*, translated and edited by Leon Pompa (Cambridge, 1982). For Herder, see Frank E. Manuel's abridged edition of his *Reflections on the Philosophy of the History of Mankind* (Chicago, 1968). Interpretive studies of Herder are H. B. Nisbet's *Herder and the Philosophy and History of Science* (Cambridge, 1970), G. A. Wells's

Herder and After (The Hague, 1959), and Frederick M. Barnard's *Herder on Social and Political Culture* (1969). For a short and illuminating essay on the impact of the Grimm brothers on the study of modern literature, see William Paton Ker's *Jacob Grimm,* "Publications of the Philological Society," vol. 7 (Oxford, 1915). A highly critical study of the Grimm brothers' method and scholarship is found in John M. Ellis's *One Fairy Story Too Many* (Chicago, 1983).

The best history of the study of folklore in Europe is Giuseppe Cocchiara's *The History of Folklore in Europe,* translated by John N. McDaniel (Philadelphia, 1981). Peter Burke's *Popular Culture in Early Modern Europe* (New York, 1978) is historically oriented but is more systematic than historical. Older works such as Stith Thompson's *The Folktale* (1946; reprint, New York, 1979) and Alexander H. Krappe's *The Science of Folk-lore* (1930; New York, 1962) are still valuable. They should be supplemented by Alan Dundes's *The Study of Folklore* (Englewood Cliffs, N.J., 1965) and Richard Dorson's *Folklore and Folklife* (Chicago, 1972).

Some of Max Weber's works bear on certain problems of popular religion; see especially *The Protestant Ethic and the Spirit of Capitalism,* translated by Talcott Parsons (London, 1930); *The Sociology of Religion,* translated by Ephraim Fischoff (Boston, 1963); *The City,* translated and edited by Don Martindale and Gertrud Neuwirth (Glencoe, Ill., 1958); and *From Max Weber: Essays in Sociology,* translated and edited by Hans H. Gerth and C. Wright Mills (Oxford, 1946). From an earlier sociological school there are the works of Ferdinand Tönnies, *Community and Association,* translated and edited by Charles P. Loomis (London, 1955), and William Graham Sumner's *Folkways* (Boston, 1907). Much can still be learned from Ernst Troeltsch's *The Social Teaching of the Christian Church,* 2 vols., translated by Olive Wyon (1931; Chicago, 1981), as well as from Joachim Wach's *Sociology of Religion* (Chicago, 1944). Wach's work remains the only sociology of religion written by a historian of religions and is thus valuable for that reason. Clifford Geertz's informative essay "Religion as a Cultural System" can be found in *Anthropological Approaches to the Study of Religion,* edited by Michael Banton (New York, 1966), and in *Reader in Comparative Religion,* edited by William A. Lessa and Evon Z. Vogt (New York, 1965).

Regional Studies of Popular Religion. Numerous publications have been devoted to popular, folk, and peasant religions around the world. Without attempting to cover all areas of the globe, I offer here a sampling of works that are valuable for their contribution to theory as well as for their descriptive detail.

Africa. *African Folklore,* edited by Richard M. Dorson (New York, 1972), covers most of the genres of folklore in Africa. Two sections, "Traditional Narrative" and "Traditional Ritual," are especially relevant to the notion of popular religion. Ruth Finnegan's *Oral Literature in Africa* (London, 1970) is a highly controversial work. She makes a strong argument for the literary nature of oral literature and finds many interpretations by anthropologists and folklorists wanting because they fail to appreciate the literary character of this form of literature. She devotes a chapter to religious poetry, but she confines the meaning of *religion* to a very conventional usage. Jan Vansina's *Oral Tradition,* translated by H. M. Wright (Chicago, 1965), is a thorough working out of the problems and methods involved in using oral testimony as historical data. The data for his work are the traditions of the Kuba. This work has bearing on the relationship between the modes of transmission and the nature and meaning of the knowledge that is transmitted.

Japan. Cornelis Ouwehand's *Namazu-e and Their Themes* (Leiden, 1964) is important for the light it sheds on the reception and alternate interpretations of events on the folkloric levels of Japanese society. Especially in the case of catastrophic event, on the folkloric levels there is the appearance of a kind of savior figure as a motif of the understanding of these events. Ichori Hori's *Folk Religion in Japan,* edited by Joseph M. Kitagawa and Alan L. Miller (Chicago, 1968), is the best general study of the forms and structures of folk religion in Japan. *Studies in Japanese Folklore,* edited by Richard M. Dorson (Port Washington, N.Y., 1963), covers the folk traditions of various classes of workers and is one of the best studies of the traditions of workers. Michael Czaja's *Gods of Myth and Stone* (New York, 1974) is a thorough study of the mythic and religious significance of certain forms of fertility symbols and rituals in Japan; it is informed by sophisticated methodology.

Ancient Greece. Of the many works in Greek religion, I mention only three, the classic study of N. D. Fustel de Coulanges, *The Ancient City,* new ed. (Baltimore, 1980), Martin P. Nilsson's *Greek Folk Religion* (New York, 1961), and Jon D. Mikalson's *Athenian Popular Religion* (Chapel Hill, N.C., 1983).

Europe. Most studies of popular religion in Europe are to be valued as much for their detailed content as for their theoretical approach and methodological contributions. Marc Bloch's *Feudal Society,* 2 vols., translated by L. A. Manyon (Chicago, 1961), is a pioneer work in focusing on the entire range of the cultural reality of the feudal period. Two representative works dealing with the amalgam of religious traditions in Europe are Albert B. Lord's *The Singer of Tales* (Cambridge, Mass., 1960) and Gail Kligman's *Căluş: Symbolic Transformation in Romanian Ritual* (Chicago, 1981).

Norbert Elias's *The Civilizing Process* (New York, 1978), *Power and Civility* (New York, 1982), and *The Court Society* (New York, 1983), all translated by Edmund Jephcott, demonstrate the social behavior patterns and psychological attitudes that define the processes that create the class and value orientation of the ideology of civilization. Similar processes, but directed from a centralized governmental center, are described in Eugen Weber's *Peasants into Frenchmen* (Stanford, Calif., 1976). A detailed account of popular culture in France is found in Robert Muchembled's *Popular Culture and Elite Culture in France, 1400-1750,* translated by Lydia Cochrane (Baton Rouge, 1985). One of the most prolific and brilliant scholars of popular religion and culture in France is the *Annales* historian Emmanuel Le Roy Ladurie. His works include *Montaillou: The Promised Land of Error,* translated by Barbara Bray (New York, 1978); *Carnival in Romans,* translated by Mary Feeney (New York, 1979); and *The Peasants of Languedoc,* translated by John Day (Urbana, 1974).

Religion and the People, 800–1700, edited by James Obelkevich (Chapel Hill, N.C., 1979) is a good survey of some important themes in the study of popular European religion. One of the essays in this volume, Lionel Rothkrug's "Popular Religion and Holy Shrines," has been followed up in Rothkrug's *Religious Practices and Collective Perceptions: Hidden Homologies in the Renaissance and Reformation* (Waterloo, Ont., 1980). The importance of this work lies not only in the detailed description of such phenomena as the cult of Mary on the popular level but equally in the way it raises the issue of the forms of perception and knowledge that stem from certain modes of religious apprehension. Concrete historical detail is given to issues of the sociology of religious knowledge that are discussed more abstractly by Georges Gurvitch in *The Social Frameworks of Knowledge*, translated by Margaret A. Thompson and Kenneth A. Thompson (Oxford, 1971).

Carlo Ginzburg's *The Cheese and the Worms*, translated by John Tedeschi and Anne Tedeschi (Baltimore, 1980), an account of the cosmology of a sixteenth-century Italian miller, is fast becoming a classic of popular religion. Miriam Usher Chrisman's *Lay Culture, Learned Culture: Books and Social Change in Strasbourg, 1480–1599* (New Haven, 1982), shows the impact of printing and literacy on the various cultural layers of this period. William A Christian's *Local Religion in Sixteenth Century Spain* (Princeton, 1981), examines the spirituality of several towns in New Castile. A. N. Galpern's *The Religions of the People in Sixteenth-Century Champagne* (Cambridge, Mass., 1976), undertakes a similar investigation of this area. *The Pursuit of Holiness in Late Medieval and Renaissance Religion*, edited by Charles Trinkaus and Heiko A. Oberman (Leiden, 1974), contains essays covering almost all aspects of late medieval and Renaissance religion. Of particular interest is part 2, "Lay Piety and the Cult of Youth." James Obelkevich's *Religion and Rural Society: South Lindsey, 1825–1875* (Oxford, 1976), deals with the churching of agrarian laborers by the Methodist church. It goes far in showing the interaction of the lower classes and the middle and upper classes as this is related to the form and structure of the religious institution.

There is, finally, a beautifully written book by the folklorist Henry Glassie, *Passing the Time in Ballymenone* (Philadelphia, 1982). In this study of a rural community in Ireland, the author demonstrates in his research the moral meaning of this kind of community. While there is no one chapter or section devoted to religion, the entire work reflects the religious orientation of a small Irish village. The closest one comes to an explicit meaning of religion is in part 8, "A Place on the Holy Land."

Modern America. There are few general and systematic studies of American popular religion. For orientation to the issues of the meaning of "the people," "culture," "religion," and the national state in the American democracy, Alexis de Tocqueville's classic *Democracy in America*, 2 vols. in 1, translated by George Lawrence and edited by J. P. Mayer (Garden City, N.Y., 1969), is still a very good orientation. H. Richard Niebuhr's *The Social Sources of Denominationalism* (1929; New York, 1957) is one of the few works that raises the issue of the relationship of popular lower-class-strata religion to the founding of religious institutions in the United States. W. Lloyd Warner's *The Living and the Dead* (New Haven, 1959) is an anthropological interpretation of the major sacred and secular symbols in American society. The methodological point of view lends itself to the meaning of American religion from the perspective of popular religion. Sidney E. Mead's *The Lively Experiment* (New York, 1963) is a group of essays that touch upon the broader religious symbolic values of American cultural reality as the context for religious understanding.

Catherine L. Albanese's *America: Religions and Religion* (Belmont, Calif., 1981) is the first systematic attempt to deal with all the religious traditions in the United States in an integrated manner. As such it eschews the normativity of the mainline traditions as the basis for American religion, thus allowing for the meaning of popular religion to become an empirical and methodological ingredient in the study of American religion. See also Albanese's *Sons of the Fathers* (Philadelphia, 1976) for a discussion of the manner in which popular religion instituted and responded to the apotheosis of George Washington as the founding father of the nation.

Will Herberg's *Protestant, Catholic, Jew* (Garden City, N.Y., 1955) shows how denominational designations were used to define cultural modes of popular American religiosity. For a discussion of civil religion in the United States, see Robert N. Bellah's "Civil Religion in America," *Daedalus* 96 (Winter 1967): 1–21. Peter W. Williams's *Popular Religion in America* (Englewood Cliffs, N.J., 1980) is excellent for data but lacks methodological sophistication. The later two works contain the best bibliographical sources for the many forms of popular religion in the United States.

China. Daniel L. Overmyer's *Folk Buddhist Religion* (Cambridge, Mass., 1976) is one of the few thoroughgoing discussions of folk Buddhism in China and is distinguished by its methodological astuteness. *Popular Culture in Late Imperial China*, edited by David Johnson, Andrew J. Nathan, and Evelyn S. Rawski (Berkeley, 1985), brings together several essays on popular culture of this period. Of special note are "Religion and Popular Culture: The Management of Moral Capital in the Romance of the Three Teachings" by Judith Berling, "Values in Chinese Sectarian Literature: Ming and Ch'ing Pao-chuan" by Daniel L. Overmyer, and "Language and Ideology in the Written Popularizations of the Sacred Edict" by Victor H. Mair.

Theoretical Studies. Almost all of the works cited above discuss theoretical issues, but there are, in addition, a number of valuable works written from a purely theoretical orientation. Among them are three books by anthropologist Robert Redfield that have had great influence on the study of popular culture and religion: *The Primitive World and Its Transformations* (Ithaca, N.Y., 1953), *The Little Community* (Chicago, 1955), and *Peasant Society and Culture* (Chicago, 1956). Two works by Milton Singer are also recommended; although devoted to the Hindu tradition, they have much broader implications for many of the issues of popular religion and its relationship to urbanism and the great traditions: *Traditional India: Structure and Change* (Philadelphia, 1959) and *When a Great Tradition Modernizes* (New York, 1972).

Approaches to Popular Culture, edited by C. W. E. Bigsby (Bowling Green, Ohio, 1976), is an illuminating group of essays that demonstrate the ambiguity and difficulty of clear definition of the meaning of popular culture. Of particular interest are "Popular Culture: A Sociological Approach" by Zev Barbu, "Oblique Approaches to the History of Popular Culture" by Peter Burke, and "The Politics of Popular Culture" by C. W. E. Bigsby. The political and ideological meaning of popular culture is also explored in Herbert J. Gans's *Popular Culture and High Culture* (New York, 1974).

Finally, for a group of essays discussing the meaning of social history in various historical contexts, see *Reliving the Past*, edited by Olivier Zunz (Chapel Hill, N.C., 1985).

CHARLES H. LONG

PORTALS. A portal is any gateway or doorway, insofar as it elicits ritual actions or becomes a locus of concentrated architectural symbolism. It is a space framed to call attention to spatial transition; thus it has characteristics of both a path and a place. Since a portal often separates a sacred precinct from a profane one, or a regulated from an unregulated zone, it is both a termination and a beginning. As a structure that is both inside and outside the same zone, and one that attracts dangerous as well as beneficent forces, it is a site of considerable ambivalence.

The most rudimentary forms of a portal are the cave entrance, the stone heap, the upright post, and two uprights supporting a lintel. More elaborate ones add not only familiar features such as a threshold, doors, knobs, and hinges, but also figures, inscriptions, porches, domical towers, cupolas, niches for statues, and crowning arcades. In some eras portals have been so emphasized as to become freestanding monuments separated from buildings, bridges, or city walls. No longer only markers of paths, they become places in their own right. Three famous examples are the Great Gateway (1630–1653 CE) at the Taj Mahal in India, the *pai-lou* ("entrance") leading to the Temple of the Sleeping Buddha (eighteenth century) near Peking, and the Gates of Paradise (1403–1424 CE), designed by Lorenzo Ghiberti for the Florence Baptistry (c. eleventh century CE). In cases where a road originates or terminates at a gate—for instance, the Ishtar Gate of Babylon (c. 575 BCE) and its grand procession way, or the Lion's Gate (rebuilt by Sultan Suleyman in 1538-1539 CE) leading to the Via Dolorosa in Jerusalem—it seems that the portal usually sanctifies the path rather than vice versa. It is not uncommon for a pilgrim to have to pass through several preliminary gateways on a road leading to a major portal. [*See* Pilgrimage.]

Functions. The widespread, cross-cultural separation, elaboration, and multiplication of portals suggests that their importance far exceeds their two most obvious functions, namely regulating traffic and providing military defense. Other functions are to commemorate noteworthy events, memorialize cultural heroes and royalty, instruct the faithful, propagandize strangers and outsiders, advertise the nature or use of a building, and dramatize the status of inhabitants.

The bronze doors (1015 CE) of the cathedral at Hildesheim in Germany, for example, teach Christian believers to consider Jesus' crucifixion and resurrection as both a parallel and a reversal of the disobedience of Adam and Eve by presenting the two stories on opposing door leaves as a visual *concordantia* of the Old and New Testaments. The best-known examples of Roman triumphal arches, such as the arches of Titus (82 CE), Trajan (114 CE), and Constantine (312 CE), commemorate the victories and accomplishments of generals and emperors. Portals such as the Stonehenge monuments in Wiltshire, England, and the Gates of the Sun (c. 1000–1200 CE) at Tiahuanaco, Peru, probably had astrological and initiatory uses.

In both East and West, portals have been the object of intense syncretism. Consequently, historians of art and religion are able to trace a remarkable continuity of style and consistency of symbolism connecting Indian *toraṇa* with Chinese *pai-lou* and Japanese *torii* (of which there are twenty different styles). Egyptian pylons and *heb-sed* tents (under which a pharaoh appeared as the god Horus or Re during a jubilee festival) are historically linked with Greek *propulaia*, Roman triumphal arches, the entrances of synagogues, and the cupolas of mosques and churches.

Symbolism. In most cases portal symbolism is distinctly celestial. Besides decorative stars, rosettes, and solar discs, birds and wings appear over portals with considerable frequency; the Japanese characters for *torii* mean "bird" and "to be." Among ancient Hittites and Egyptians a winged solar disc formed the lintel, which was supported by two pillars often personified as guardian spirits. The identification of a lintel with a deity or royalty, and of columns with protector spirits or intermediaries, is widespread.

In theocratic societies royal dwellings, like the divine kings who inhabited them, were sacred. Portals, since they were one of the architectural features most obvious to commoners, stood for the entire palace, which itself stood for the king, who in turn incarnated the divine. The Ottoman court in Istanbul, for example, was referred to as "the divine portal." As a result of this tendency, a single pillar or the imprint of a facade on a coin could stand (especially in sixth-century Thrace) for the entirety of royal/divine power. The ability of an image of a portal to evoke such authority was probably enhanced by the practice of administering justice at city gates. Only the throne rivals the gateway in embodying the convergence of heavenly and imperial authority. Jesus' claim to be the "door of the sheep" (*Jn.* 10:7) reaches back to a Mesopotamian sensibility typified by a hymn to King Ur-Nammu (2113–2096 BCE) addressing him as "Thy gate, thy God." The name "Babylon" itself means "the gate of the gods." The guardianlike pillars of fire and cloud (*Ex.* 13:21) that lead the Israelites in the desert could be interpreted in relation to the personified door posts, Boaz and Jachin (1 *Kgs.* 7:21), that flanked Solomon's Temple. Pillars in both freestanding and supporting forms frequently undergo stylization as trees or mountains, thus serving as symbolic links between heaven and earth.

Rites. Evidence testifying to the importance and meaning of portals is not only architectural but also ritualistic. Large-scale portal rites in the West have been intensely royal. Examples include the Babylonian New Year processions, the Hellenistic epiphany (a cultic action in the mysteries at Eleusis), the Roman Adventus, and the Great Entrance (of the Byzantine rite)—all ceremonies for greeting royalty or divinity. The intentions of participants seem to have been to purify and protect as well as celebrate and elevate. Also, testing and humiliation at gateways is a ritual practice, one with evidence extending from Ishtar's tests at each of the seven portals of the underworld to modern border crossings.

Small-scale ritual practices at portals are still an active part of folklore. Making offerings, smearing blood on doorposts, burying the dead beneath thresholds, removing shoes, touching pillars, and either jumping, crawling, or being carried over thresholds are common. Lustrations and baths are widespread preparatory rites for passing through portals. Jews touch *mezuzot* on the doorposts of their houses; Catholics dip their fingers in holy water and make the sign of the cross upon entering churches. From the tradition of carrying brides across thresholds to the shrinking doors of *Alice in Wonderland*, and from popular old idioms like "gates of hell" to recent ones like "gates of the dream," popular religion, folklore, and fairy tales are replete with threshold customs and with dangerous doors that miraculously open or that one must not (but surely will) enter.

Motifs. Not only do portals become freestanding structures and objects of veneration, but the portal as a motif becomes metaphorically extended beyond its monumental form. Tombstones are carved in the shape of a doorway, and ossuaries have doorways etched on them, thus associating the dead with the divine. Altars incorporate architectural features of portals; by analogy, both the tabletop and the lintel are cathedras (Gk., *kathedrae*, "divine seats"). Virtually any vessel of transition, such as a mother's body, becomes a doorway. The church itself in the Carolingian era (eighth to tenth centuries CE) was regarded as a *porta coeli* ("heavenly portal"). And in modern times the threshold *(limen)* has provided the key metaphor for the widely utilized theory of ritual developed by Arnold van Gennep in *The Rites of Passage* (Chicago, 1960).

Finally, there is suggestive evidence that the shaman's experience of a difficult passage across a bridge or through a narrow pass may be a variation on the theme of smiting doors and clashing rocks (for example, the Symplegades through which Jason and his argonauts had to pass). The image of the *vagina dentata* ("toothed vagina") may be another variant. But the portal, unlike the bridge and symbolic vagina, emphasizes royally authorized security rather than shamanistically induced risk.

[*See also* Caves; Tombs; Towers; *and* Procession.]

BIBLIOGRAPHY

Bernard Goldman's *The Sacred Portal: A Primary Symbol in Ancient Judaic Art* (Detroit, 1966) is a careful art-historical analysis of the portal symbolism of the fifth-century synagogue at Beth Alpha. Because he sets his study so fully in its context, the book is probably the best single volume on the gateways and door symbolism of the ancient Near East. An excellent companion to it is E. Baldwin Smith's *Architectural Symbolism of Imperial Rome and the Middle Ages* (1956; reprint, New York, 1978), a tightly argued study of the imperial city-gate concept and its appropriation by Christianity and Islam. John Summerson's chapter on "An Interpretation of Gothic" in his *Heavenly Mansions* (New York, 1963) traces the development of the *aedicula* ("little house") from its ceremonial function as a miniature shrine within a shrine to its role in inspiring the shape of Gothic arches and finally to its demise as mere decoration on Georgian door castings.

J. A. MacCullough's article, "Door," in the *Encyclopaedia of Religion and Ethics*, edited by James Hastings, vol. 4 (Edinburgh, 1911), is dated but remarkably useful. The classic work on which both this article and Van Gennep's theory depend is H. Clay Trumbull's *The Threshold Covenant: Or the Beginning of Religious Rites*, 2d ed. (New York, 1906). Gertrude R. Levy's *The Gate of Horn: A Study of the Religious Conceptions of the Stone Age* (London, 1948) is a valuable source of information on primitive gates, especially those bearing horns, at megalithic sites in Malta and Paleolithic caves in southwestern France. *Romanesque Bronzes: Church Portals in Medieval Europe* (London, 1958), by Hermann Leisinger, shows the richness of myth and art to be found on church doors.

A reliable compendium of pictures and line drawings, as well as a general source of comparative materials on gates, is Banister Fletcher's *A History of Architecture*, 18th ed., revised by J. C. Palmes (New York, 1975). On the relation of portals to the shaman's narrow pass and the *vagina dentata*, see Mircea Eliade's *Myths, Rites, Symbols*, 2 vols., edited by Wendell C. Beane and William G. Doty (New York, 1975); Stephen Larsen's *The Shaman's Doorway* (New York, 1976); and Jill Raitt's "The *Vagina Dentata* and the *Immaculatus Uterus Divini Fontis*," *Journal of the American Academy of Religion* 48 (1980): 415–431.

RONALD L. GRIMES

PORTENTS AND PRODIGIES are signs that, if understood or interpreted correctly, can reveal personal destinies and the will of the gods. They may be observed and interpreted either by the person who witnessed them or, more usually, by a priest specializing in the science required.

Portents and prodigies are one of the sources of the art of divination (*divinatio* in Latin, *mantikē technē* in Greek). The diviner, who is capable of predicting the future, could have recourse either to the exegesis of observed signs or to prophetic inspiration, a kind of delirium *(mania)* deriving from his possession by some divinity who comes into contact with diviners, sibyls, or Pythian priestesses.

Some of the words designating portent or prodigy in the languages of classical antiquity (Greek, Latin, and also Etruscan, which remains largely obscure to us) have a clear origin and significance; others have an original meaning that eludes us.

Sēmeion in Greek and *signum* in Latin correspond closely to the word *sign.* The ancients lived in a world where signs were ever present and were to be found in the most diverse parts of the universe: heaven, earth, and underworld. Portents and prodigies often appeared in everyday observation. Even today, popular belief often attributes favorable or unfavorable meanings to apparitions, no matter how natural: to animals of certain breeds, aspects, or colors, or to certain ecclesial phenomena like a flash of lightning or a thunderclap in a peaceful sky.

Omens. The most universal portent is the word or phrase heard by chance. Although it is not intended for the listener, it is perceived to have some bearing on one's daily life. In antiquity, as today, people imagined that utterances spoken or heard fortuitously could foretell a dark future or a bright and happy one. The listener, of course, might fail to recognize the omen for what it was, and remain deaf to its warning.

The Roman had the right to accept a portent—an *omen*—by declaring it in a loud and clear voice. This was the meaning of the expression *omen accipere* ("to accept the omen"). But the Roman could just as easily strip the omen of its value and efficacy by declaring in a loud and clear voice that he or she refused to take it into account: *omen exsecrari, abominari* ("omen execrated, abominated"). The ancients also knew how to transform the omen's value and meaning by adroit wording that modified or transformed its scope. Celebrated narratives from Latin writers illustrate the efficacy of human speech in this regard, as in Ovid's *Fasti* (3.330ff.), in which he legendary king of Rome, the pious Numa Pompilius, avoided by clever replies Jupiter's cruel demand for human lives to expiate the stain left on the soil by a bolt of lightning.

Auspices. As with all peoples of Indo-European origin, the most important and frequent portents for the Greeks and Romans were furnished by the flights, cries, and behavior of birds. The importance of birds as portents is clear in Aristophanes' comedy *The Birds,* which was performed at the festival of the Great Dionysia in Athens in 414 BCE. In this play, in which distant memories are muted by the satiric medium, the birds proudly bestow upon themselves leading roles as true guides, not mere advisers of human beings. Although this might simply be poetic fancy, it must reflect the memory of a very ancient reality whose origins are lost in the mists of protohistory.

In the vast domain of portents conveyed by birds, ancient Italy deserves attention. From its origins, Rome had a very important priestly college, the augurs, whose responsibility was to preserve scrupulously and apply methodically the religious regulations pertaining to signs given by birds, that is, auspices. By their presence, advice, and collaboration, the augurs could ensure the propriety of the actions of the magistrates. They possessed the compilations of sacred precepts, the *Libri augurales,* which preserved in full detail the rules of auspication and the precise record of controversies over procedure.

Numerous Greek and Latin texts describe minutely the ritual capture of the auspices, a ceremony dating from the beginnings of Rome. The fratricidal rivalry of the twins Romulus and Remus was adjudicated and the founder of the city selected through precise augural interrogation of the divine will. Romulus's *lituus,* a curved stick, which he used to take the portents, became the characteristic emblem of the augural *sacerdotia.*

The object of augury was to obtain signs testifying to the agreement of the gods with the city in any political, religious, or military actions it wanted to undertake. The juridical and pragmatic Roman mind knew how to organize the ritual needed to obtain this assent in the most efficacious way possible. A sacred formula, which served as a veritable pact between humans and gods, was read in a loud and clear voice by the priest who was to perform the augury. The formula specified both the time and place in which the signs were to be observed. The augurs thus received certified, enabling signs that had legal force and value in themselves. But the ceremony could be marked also by accidental, unforeseen phenomena that had to be taken into account.

The Romans were not, to be sure, the only people in Italy who possessed such an augural law. The longest religious inscription that classical antiquity has left us, the Eugubine tablets, attest to the existence of augural law among other Italic peoples, especially the Umbrians. According to this well-known text, a sacerdotal college called the Attiedii Brotherhood practiced a system of explication very similar to that used by the Roman augers. In both cases, the observation and interpretation of portents was carried out with the same formalism and attention to minute detail in the ritual procedures. The question put to the gods was the same among both peoples: were they in agreement with the proposed enterprise or not?

Haruspices. Among the series of portents that lent themselves to observation, those furnished by a sacrificial victim consecrated on the altar of a divinity held a major importance in classical antiquity and in other civilizations. The reason is clear. By virtue of its consecration, the sacrificial animal passes from the domain of the human to that of the god. The gods express their disposition by means of the victim itself in the moments preceding, accompanying, and following the sacrifice. It was important, then, to observe everything in the victim's behavior with the greatest attention: when it was led to the altar and when it received the mortal blow, the crackling of flesh on the brazier, the colors of the flame, and the speed of the smoke's ascent into the sky.

But the clearest and most decisive indications were provided by the examination of the entrails of the sacrificial animal by experienced specialists: in Greece, the Iamides, diviners at Olympia; in Etruria and Rome, the haruspices. The haruspices, according to the ancients, enjoyed an immense reputation and seemed to practice a science that was infallible. They can be compared only with the *baru,* Babylonian priests who in the second millennium BCE had a veritable library of clay tablets at their disposal. These tablets detailed a complex doctrine based on minute observation of the organs of victims that was transmitted from one generation to the next.

For the haruspex, as for the *baru,* each fact noted at the sacrifice—i.e., form, color, presence or absence of specific parts of the viscera—unfailingly foretold the approach of specific events, favorable or foreboding, in human society. Rome received its haruspicinal science primarily from Etruria, which, long before it was conquered, had entrusted its best diviners to Rome. But did Etruria develop this discipline independently, or did it borrow elements from the Greek world or even from regions of the Near East? The latter is more likely, although the paths such influences followed are difficult to determine.

In various lands of the Near East, numerous terracotta models have been discovered. These models represent organs of sacrificed sheep and bear inscriptions clearly indicating the portents foretold by anomalies in the organs. Etruria is the source of the famous bronze liver found in the Po plain in 1877 near the city of Piacenza. The convex surface of the Piacenza Liver is divided into two lobes bearing the names of the sun (Usil) and the moon (Tiur). The concave surface, admirably sculptured and engraved, is divided into a large number of compartments, on which can be read forty-two inscriptions and twenty-seven names of divinities. This is a graphic illustration of the haruspex's fundamental belief: that the gods actually occupy different parts of the sacrificed animal, and their places there correspond to those they occupy in the sky.

Other Portents. The sky, in antiquity, was the home of reigning gods and the place from which they launched comets, falling stars, lightning, and thunder (sources of joy or, more often, terror), considered in some places portents, in other places prodigies. [*See* Sky.] Lightning and thunder were major phenomena, intended to warn humans, who noted with the keenest attention the path of meteorites and deep claps of thunder, foretelling, according to Cicero, the most serious perils for the city and state.

The Etruscans developed most fully the so-called science of interpretation of major celestial portents. [*See* Etruscan Religion.] Indeed, the master of thunder and lightning, the Etruscan Tinia, was the homologue of the Hellenic Zeus, undisputed master of meteorological phenomena, and of the Roman Jupiter, who hurled thunderbolts during the day (Summanus was master during the night). The Etruscans developed a complete methodology for the interpretation of thunderbolts, including directions for expiation if the portents were unfavorable.

The Greek historian Diodorus was not exaggerating when he wrote, "Etruscan keraunoscopia [*keraunos* was the Greek word for thunder and lightning] was renowned throughout nearly the whole earth" (5.40.2). Seneca, in *Natural Questions* (2.32ff.), discourses knowingly on the differences between Roman and Etruscan approaches to portents, and on the importance the Etruscans placed on thunder portents. He wrote, "Since the Etruscans relate everything to divinity, they are persuaded not that thunderclaps foretell the future because they have been formed, but that they take form because they must foretell the future."

If portents are taken to include inanimate objects and the earth itself, they are even more numerous in the Greek, Roman, and Etruscan traditions. The importance of portents furnished by waters, especially the waters of springs, is attested by texts and archaeological data. These portents depended on the way the water spurted out from the depths of the earth, and also on the way that objects thrown into them were carried along or sank. They were attributed to nymphs reigning over these streams and to various female divinities who were objects of popular devotions in different parts of the ancient world.

Like the surface of water, the mirror was thought to present future events in its reflected images. Drawing lots by choosing among similar objects also appeared to translate either the will of the gods or the will of destiny. Thus, as a response to a question, the white bean drawn by the Greek diviner represented a positive answer, the black bean a negative answer. At Delphi, the center of divination in the ancient world, Apollo spoke through the mouth of his priestess, the Pythia, but she, too, in certain cases, had recourse to drawing lots.

In inspired divination, the priest or prophetess, after attaining the necessary precondition, entered into direct contact with the deity. The god then spoke through their voices and permitted them to prophesy the future, albeit in obscure terms that required professional exegesis.

The premonitory dream is the object of one of the most widespread human beliefs, and in antiquity it was connected with rituals of incubation. The believer, after carrying out certain rituals before induced sleep, sees in a dream what the priests interpret upon awakening.

The World of Prodigies. To move from portents to the world of prodigies is not really to change domains, because the prodigy, like the portent, is a sign, a warning the gods transmit to humans. Nevertheless, there is a serious difference between the two, which lies in the importance and gravity of the sign. The prodigy, wherever it appears, is a truly exceptional phenomenon that disrupts the normal course of things for a time.

The Greeks could call the prodigy *sēmeion,* but the proper term is *teras,* whose semantic field is the same as that of the archaic term *pelōr.* Both words lack an Indo-European etymology and undoubtedly represent loan words derived perhaps from one of the Near Eastern civilizations. Despite their importance in Etruscan divination, we do not know the Etruscan word or words designating prodigies. Although the word *teras* is found in one of two Etruscan inscriptions, the exact meaning of the word in this context cannot be confirmed.

In Latin, the numerous names for the prodigy reveal the importance the notion possessed in the Roman mind. It is called *prodigium, monstrum, miraculum, ostentum,* and *portentum.* It is not easy to distinguish among the usages of these different words. *Prodigium* is the most often used; its etymology is unclear. *Monstrum* and *miraculum* are applied to something unexplainable in a living creature, human or animal. *Ostentum* and *portentum,* properly speaking, designate what the gods present to humans. None of these terms implied, however, the idea of portent, in the sense of warning about the future. We should note finally that the Roman term *miraculum* became specialized in modern languages to designate all events that ignored natural laws, particularly those associated with Christ. In the shift from paganism to Christianity, the word remained very much alive.

In Etruria, as well as in Rome and the rest of the Italic world, prodigies appeared in various forms. In Greece, as in many other countries, the prodigy could occur in any aspect of nature: earth, sea, sky, underground, in the realms of humans, animals, vegetables, and inanimate objects. The prodigy was attributed to one or another of the gods. The most diverse chthonian phenomena—subterranean rumbles, volcanic displays, earthquakes, and tidal waves—terribly feared in themselves, were also considered forewarnings of the most dire events. Sources of terror for the ancients, these phenomena required expiatory ceremonies intended to pacify the gods.

Prodigies in Etruscan Life. Etruria devoted a part of its sacred books to *ostentaria,* collections of rules for observing, explicating, and expiating prodigies. For this function, Rome called on the knowledge of the haruspices. For these priests, as for the Greeks, a prodigy could have a favorable or an evil and disastrous meaning. Presumably it was different in Rome, at least at the beginning of its history. We know the world of Etruscan prodigies rather well because Roman writings accord them considerable importance and familiarize us with the haruspices' behavior vis-à-vis the most extraordinary phenomena. The exegeses were often subtle, but usually based on a rather clear symbolism. A comet, a meteor, or a ringing that seemed to burst out of a serene sky could mark the end of a *saeculum,* one of those centuries that formed the history of Etruria. As in Greece, seismic activity on Tuscan soil foretold the most serious events. Conversely, however, certain prodigies could foretell the high destiny of humans, often divining in certain individuals the charisma necessary for kingship. Before the first two Etruscan kings of Rome, Tarquinius Priscus and Servius Tullius, acceded to the throne, they had been marked by prodigies announcing their elevated destiny. The former, upon arriving in Rome had his hat removed by an eagle, which then replaced it, uttering loud cries. Divine favor distinguished Servius Tullius during his childhood, for flames would surround his head for long periods, frightening those around him, and then flicker out.

It is clear that haruspices did not need uncommon wisdom to interpret correctly miraculous phenomena by means of transparent symbolism. But the priests were also masters of ritual as well as of the propitiatory expiations rendered necessary by any prodigy that they thought defiled the land or the city. The priests purified places that had been struck by lightning by interring all objects that it had touched. Compelled by a deep sense of cosmic order, they pitilessly eliminated abnormal creatures as products of the cruelty of nature. The appearance of monsters in the animal or human realm was a tangible sign of divine wrath, representing a disturbance of the rhythm and laws of the universe. Thus, the haruspices made monsters disappear from the face of the earth by fire or drowning, but without laying hands on them, lest they suffer contagion from the contamination.

Prodigies in Roman Life. In Rome, the prodigy went through a perceptible evolution; its characteristics were modified during the course of history. In the beginning, according to Greek and Roman historians, the prodigy was not a divinatory sign, not a simple presaging of an important event. An unforeseen event that appeared in some form of nature broke the course of natural laws and indicated the wrath of the gods, a rupture of the peace the gods maintained with Rome. A sudden disruption of the *pax deum* represented a terrible threat. Such a situation most often came about through the failure of either citizens or the state to fulfill religious duties. To obtain the reestablishment of the crucial *pax deum,* high authorities had at their disposal an arsenal of expiatory measures. They addressed the keepers of whatever religious traditions were indicated—the pontiffs, the guardians of the Sibylline Books, or even the haruspices—to act without delay in restoring calm to a world momentarily threatened. This was known as *procuratio prodigiorum* ("prodigy management"), and it influenced greatly the evolution of Roman religion. [*See* Prodigia.]

In the crises that characterized Roman religious history from the time of the Second Punic War, an anxious public felt new divinatory needs. Portents and prodigies became nearly indistinguishable, except for the force of the meaning they signified. To be sure, the expiation of contamination continued, but the search for divinatory meaning now intervened. At the end of the republic and the beginning of the empire, Hellenic mystery religions and religions of the Near East increased in popularity, and Christian monotheism made gradual inroads. The person of the emperor, now the center of religious life, was surrounded by an entire series of charismatic signs, portents, or prodigies. The belief in traditional prodigies, however, gave way gradually to other more complex and increasingly widespread beliefs that came from Greece and the East. Astrology and magic became more important, and it was only in great crises that the haruspices, the most ancient priests in Italy, dared to show their strength by calling attention to the prodigies whose secrets they had jealously guarded.

[*See also* Oracles *and* Divination.]

BIBLIOGRAPHY

Works on Portents

Bouché-Leclercq, Auguste. *L'astrologie grecque.* Paris, 1899.

Catalano, Pierangelo. *Contributi allo studio del diritto augurale,* vol. 1. Turin, 1960.

Nougayrol, Jean. "Les rapports des haruspicines étrusque et assyro-babylonienne, et le foie d'argile de *Falerii veteres.*" In *Comptes rendus, Académie des Inscriptions et Belles Lettres,* pp. 509–519. Paris, 1955.

Thulin, Carl O. *Die etruskische Disciplin* (1906–1909). 3 vols. Reprint, Darmstadt, 1968.

Works on Prodigies

Aumüller, Ernst. "Das Prodigium bei Tacitus." Ph.D. diss., University of Frankfurt, 1948.

Bloch, Raymond. *Les prodiges dans l'Antiquité classique: Grèce, Etrurie et Rome.* Paris, 1963.

Brassmann-Fischer, Brigitte. *Die Prodigien in Vergils Aeneis.* Munich, 1966.

Macbain, Bruce. *Prodigy and Expiation: A Study in Religion and Politics in Republican Rome.* Brussels, 1982.

Weinstock, Stefan. "Libri Fulgurales." *Papers of the British School at Rome* 19 (1951): 122–153.

RAYMOND BLOCH

Translated from French by Marilyn Gaddis Rose

POSEIDON is the ancient Greek god who embodies primitive power—the power of the untamed, the brutal, the wild. His name, which has not yet been convincingly explained, occurs on clay tablets from Pylos dating from the period preceding the destruction of Mycenaean civilization (1200 BCE). The god thus belongs to the older strata of Greek religion. His exact place in the Mycenaean pantheon is unknown, but he seems to have been more important that Zeus, who was the most prominent Greek god in the Classical period. The tablets of Pylos also mention the Posidaion (a sanctuary most probably located within the city of Pylos) and a goddess Posidaeja (possibly Poseidon's wife, though she is not heard of in later times).

In the Classical period, Poseidon was mainly connected with the sea, earthquakes, the horse, and men's associations. In Homer's *Iliad,* most commonly dated from the eighth century BCE, Poseidon is pictured as the ruler of the sea. When he drives over the waves, his chariot remains dry and the monsters of the deep play beneath him: "They know their lord" (*Iliad* 12.28). In the post-Homeric period, he was not so much the god of the sailors as of the fisherman, whose tool, the trident, became his symbol.

Besides the sea, Poseidon was also connected with the earth. His anger was considered the cause of the earthquakes that hit Greece regularly (Homer refers to him as *gaiēochos*, "earthshaking"), but the god was also invoked to end them; in many cities (especially on the western coast of Asia Minor) Poseidon was worshiped with the epithet *asphaleios* ("the immovable one"). When volcanic activity in 198 BCE caused the emergence of a new, small island, the inhabitants of neighboring Thera, as was typical, dedicated a temple to Poseidon Asphaleios on it.

Poseidon was also widely associated with horse breeding and racing; Greek myth even made him the father of the first horse, and the father or grandfather of the famous horses Pegasus and Areion. Whereas the goddess Athena was considered to be responsible for the technique of horse racing, Poseidon was connected with the wild, nervous, and powerful nature of the horse. Consequently, Athena was invoked during the race, but Poseidon before or after.

Finally, Poseidon was connected with men's associations. His temples were the meeting places of the pan-Ionic league and of the early amphictyony that comprised Athens and its neighbors. Various epithets of the god connect him with specific clans and tribes. Elsewhere Poseidon was worshiped with the epithet *phutalmios* ("the fostering one"), which points to an association with rites of initiation. Indeed, myth relates that the god's love turned the girl Kaineus into an adult man; her sex change is a mythical reflection of the ritual transvestism of the initiands. At a festival for Poseidon in Ephesus, boys acting as wine pourers were called "bulls," just as the god himself was sometimes called "Bull." All this evidence seems to point to a onetime connection of the god with Archaic men's associations (*Männerbünde*) and their ecstatic bull-warriors, which also could be found among the early Germanic peoples. [*See* Berserkers.]

The Greeks experienced the power of Poseidon as both numinous and untamed. His sanctuaries were usually located outside city walls. Although his power was inescapable, the god was given no place within the ordered society of the Greek city-state.

BIBLIOGRAPHY

The best collection of sources for Poseidon's cult is still the reliable discussion in Lewis R. Farnell's *The Cults of the Greek States*, vol. 4, *Poseidon, Apollo* (Oxford, 1907), pp. 1–97. The epigraphical material presented by Farnell on a number of epithets is now supplemented by Fritz Graf's *Nordionische Kulte* (Rome, 1985), pp. 171f., 175, and 207f. Marcel Detienne and Jean-Pierre Vernant subtly discuss Poseidon's relationship with the horse in *Cunning Intelligence in Greek Culture and Society*, translated by J. Lloyd (Atlantic Highlands, N.J., 1978), pp. 187–213. Fritz Schachermeyr's *Poseidon und die Entstehung des griechischen Götterglaubens* (Bern, 1950), the only book-length study of Poseidon, is too speculative. The best modern introduction to the god is in Walter Burkert's *Greek Religion* (Oxford, 1985), pp. 136–139.

JAN BREMMER

POSITIVISM. The terms *positivisme* and *positiviste* were coined by Auguste Comte (1798–1857), who first employed them in his *Discours sur l'ensemble du positivisme* (1848) and his *Catéchisme positiviste* (1852). [*See the biography of Comte.*] Comte's neologisms were accepted by the Academie Française in 1878. Equivalent English terms were employed by John Stuart Mill in his *Auguste Comte and Positivism* (1865).

For Comte, "positive philosophy" means real, certain, organic, relational philosophy, and positivism is a philosophical system founded on positive facts and observable phenomena. Because positive facts are not isolated but comprehended by the positive sciences, positivism is a philosophy drawn from the whole of those sciences, and the scientific method determines positivist doctrine. But positivism, as developed by Comte, is both a philosophical system and a religious system that develops from that philosophy.

Positivism and the Three-State Law. In his *Cours de philosophie positive* (1830–1842), Comte explains the relation of positive philosophy to the positive sciences: "The proper study of generalities of the several sciences conceived as submitted to a single method and as forming the several parts of a general research plan." He compares positive philosophy to what is called in English "natural philosophy." However, this latter does not include social phenomena, as does positive philosophy.

Comte contrasted positive philosophy to theological philosophy and metaphysical philosophy. These three philosophies are distinguished according to a three-state law of human knowledge, first presented in *Plan des travaux scientifiques nécessaires pour réorganiser la société* (Plan of the Scientific Tasks Necessary for the Reorganization of Society, 1822) and developed in the *Cours de philosophie positive*. The first lesson of the course sketches the progressive march of the human mind and the whole development of human understanding through three methods, or states, of philosophizing: theological, or fictitious; metaphysical, or abstract; and scientific, or positive.

Before the positive method was developed, philosophers, using the metaphysical method, had recourse to abstract forces to explain all natural phenomena; before the metaphysical method, they had recourse to theological modes of explanation—to supernatural entities, to first and final causes—in the search for absolute truth. Though the positive way of philosophizing is, according to Comte, the highest accomplishment of the human mind, the most fundamental of the three methods remains the theological, which is itself divided into three substates: the fetishistic, the polytheistic, and the monotheistic. Comte appreciates the role of each of these substates in the development of the human mind and in the "intellectual history of all our societies"; they ground the possibility of three logics within positive logic: a feeling logic, a picture logic, and a sign logic. The "fetishistic thinker" is the founder of human language and of the fine arts; he is nearer to reality and to scientific truth than is the "dreamy theologist." Theologism, identified with polytheism, is thus opposed to both fetishism and positivism. Monotheism, the third of the theological substates, is "basically metaphysical theology, which reduces fiction by means of reasoning." The metaphysical state is always presented by Comte as a transitional state between theology and positive science, but it also operates as a principle of transformation in the movement from fetishism to polytheism, and from polytheism to monotheism. Beyond this, the metaphysical continues its mediation in the "anthropological revolution" that begins with Comte's own synthesis.

Time, Progress, History. Comte did not create the idea of positivism; it was created by the scientific progress of his century. Emphasis on the relation between the concept of positivism and the concept of progress helps to avoid misconstruing positivism as a nondialectical position based on the mere assertion that scientific data exist. The three-state law introduced to the system of the sciences the notion of time as threefold, dialectical, and progressive.

The predecessors of positivism can be identified among the founders of positive science. Comte often invoked the names of Francis Bacon (1561–1626), Galileo Galilei (1564–1642), and René Descartes (1596–1650); nor did he forget Roger Bacon (1220–1292), pioneer of the experimental method and among the finest medieval thinkers engaged in natural philosophy.

Roger Bacon's *scientia experimentalis* ("experimental science") was the first form of positive science and as such was conceived in correlation with the idea of progress. The idea of progress arises from the dialogue between man and nature—between the questions of man and the answers of nature. Along with experience, experiment is the foundation of the man-nature dialogue, which has been expressed in mathematical formulas; an example is Galileo's *De motu* (On Motion).

From the thirteenth to the seventeenth century, a developing critical attitude effected a transition from the common religious beliefs of the theological period. During this transition, authority was rejected in favor of evidence and observation. Roger Bacon, in his *Opus maius* (Great Work), and Francis Bacon, in his *Novum organum* (New Instrument), discuss authority as a cause of error. By circumventing such error, progress in the sciences and the advancement of learning became possible: the concept of progress emerges with the birth of positive science.

Giordano Bruno (1548–1600), in *La cena de le ceneri* (The Ash Wednesday Supper), writes that truth is in progress: "Time is the father of truth, its mother is our mind." A concept of time was thus introduced into the scientific method. It was further developed by subsequent philosophers. Galileo's *Discorso del flusso e riflusso del mare* (Discourse on Flood and Ebb) demonstrates that nature does not concern itself with the human capacity to understand natural laws: man must create a method to understand nature. In *Discours de la méthode* (Discourse on Method), Descartes introduces a method of reasoning that requires time, as opposed to evidence (which reveals itself in the present). Bernard Le Bovier de Fontenelle (1657–1757) emphasizes the history of scientific progress in his *Entretiens sur la pluralité des mondes* (Talks on the Plurality of Worlds).

The notion of history, implied by the concept of progress, was further developed by Anne-Robert-Jacques Turgot (1727–1781) in *Les progrès successifs de l'esprit humain* (The Successive Developments of the Human Spirit) and by Condorcet (1743–1794) in *Esquisse d'un tableau historique des progrès de l'esprit humain* (Sketch of a Historical Picture of the Successive Developments of the Human Spirit). The progress of enlightenment becomes the motor of history, a movement beyond the progress of virtue emphasized by the three monotheistic religions: Judaism, Islam, and Christianity. A manifold time is therefore necessary to Comte's conception of science: the time for discovering the truth, or method; the time of scientific progress, or the history of discoveries; the time for the awakening of consciousness from simple sensation.

Science and Sociology. The three-state law reiterates and condenses observations of Turgot and Condorcet on the human mind in a formula that belongs to a new science of the system of sciences: sociology or anthropology. The law must be understood in correlation with the system of the sciences presented in the course on positive philosophy, in which Comte demonstrates the three-state law in each of the several sciences, from mathematics to biology to sociology. The aim of the course is realized with the coordination of all scientific conceptions and the birth of a new science: social science. Here, the social scientific discovery of social history reveals the intimate interrelation of scientific and social development. Moreover, mind and history play upon one another. Thus, Comte's philosophy of mind is also a philosophy of history and, hence, positivistic.

The paradigm of the three-state law organizes the classification of the sciences, and the relation between law and classification may be expressed in the definition of positivism as *scientia scientiarum*, or science of sciences. Robert Flint (1838–1910), in *Philosophy as Scientia Scientiarum and a History or Classifications of the Sciences* (Edinburgh, 1904), writes:

> Philosophy as *scientia scientiarum* may have more functions than one, but it has at least one. It has to show how science is related to science, where one science is in contact with another; in what way each fits into each, so that all may compose the symmetrical and glorious edifice of human knowledge, which has been built up by the labours of all past generations, and which all future generations must contribute to perfect and adorn. (p. 4)

For Comte, historical practice itself implies the social theory of the three-state law, which implies the logical and historical necessity of social science, which implies positivism, positive philosophy, or the system of positive knowledge. In its turn, positivism implies a practice of social reorganization, advocated by Comte both at the beginning and at the end of his own intellectual history.

Religion and Positivism. That the question raised by positivism with regard to religion was the most important problem for believers at the end of the nineteenth century can be observed in such studies as *Science et religion dans la philosophie contemporaine* (Science and Religion in Contemporary Philosophy) by Émile Boutroux (1845–1921) and *The Varieties of Religious Experience* by William James (1842–1910). Boutroux gives a positivist account of the relation of science to religion and recognizes their common components of solidarity, continuity, love, and altruism, but he does not see a relation of these components to the positivist starting point in the observation of concrete things. Thus, Boutroux is unable to admit the principles of religion as he conceived them: God and immortality of the soul. The positivist philosophers Richard Avenarius (1843–1896) and Ernst Mach (1838–1916), on the other hand, rejected all absolute entities. In a letter dated 14 July 1845, Comte himself wrote to John Stuart Mill:

> Actually, the qualification of *atheists* suits me, going strictly by etymology, which is almost always a wrong way to explain frequently used terms, because we have in common with those who are so called nothing but disbelief in God, without sharing in any way with them their vain metaphysical dreams about the origin of the world or man, still less their narrow and dangerous attempts to systematize morals.

Nevertheless, in another letter to Mill, Comte did not reject praying. "For a real positivist, to pray is to love and to think, first to think by praying, then to pray by thinking, in order to develop subjective life toward those whose objective life is accomplished" (28 October 1850). To the claim of Emil Du Bois-Reymond (1818–1896)—"Ignorabimus" ("We shall ignore [nonnatural events]"), such positivists as Alfred Fouillée (1820–1912) replied "Sperabimus" ("We shall hope"). Fouillée assented in some spiritualist claims; like Herbert Spencer (1820–1903), he admitted an unknowable.

The Impulse of Positivism. Positivism is characterized by the will to realize a synthesis that takes into account all human concerns. Some positivists, like Émile Littré (1801–1881) and Abel Rey (1873–1940), reduce philosophy to a mere history of scientific thought. Nevertheless, Littré concluded that beyond the positivist object of thought there is a reality unattainable yet within our range of clear vision. Instead of God or the unknowable, Comte proposed humanity as the focus of his synthesis, and his "religion of humanity" attracted many followers in France and abroad, especially in Brazil.

BIBLIOGRAPHY

For discussion of the birth and development of positivism, see Henri Gouhier's *La jeunesse d'Auguste Comte et la formation du positivisme*, 3 vols. (Paris, 1933–1941). Exegesis of the entire philosophical and scientific enterprise of Comte and the positivists can be found in my *Entre le signe et l'histoire: L'anthropologie positiviste d'Auguste Comte* (Paris, 1982), *Le positivisme* (Paris, 1982), and *Le concept de science positive: Ses tenant et ses aboutissants dans structures anthropologiques du positivisme* (Paris, 1983). For a study of religious positivism, see Walter Dussauze's *Essai sur la religion d'après Auguste Comte* (Paris, 1901) and Paul Arbousse-Bastide's "Le positivisme politique et religieux au Brésil" (Ph.D. diss., Sorbonne, 1953). Paul Arbousse-Bastide treats Comte's philosophy of education in *La doctrine de l'éducation universelle dans la philosophie d'Auguste Comte*, 2 vols. (Paris, 1957). Pierre Arnaud's *Le "Nouveau Dieu"* (Paris, 1973) examines positive politics.

ANGÈLE KREMER-MARIETTI

POSSESSION, SPIRIT. *See* Spirit Possession.

POSTURES AND GESTURES are primal aspects of religious belief and behavior and as such have emerged, with other elements of culturally symbolic expression and communication, at the threshold of human existence. Their use is not, of course, restricted to the human species; nonhuman animals display a wide variety of postures and gestures that serve to demarcate species from each other and to signify territorial dominance, propagation procedures, and social hierarchy. However, culturally generated and transmitted postures and gestures, which may retain elements of phylogenetically evolved ones, nevertheless transcend these in their specific configurations of learned and intentional patterns, significations, and symbolizations.

Every religious tradition recognizes an intimate relationship between inward dispositions and external postures and gestures of the human body, which is capable of expressing and celebrating a great range of attitudes, moods, motivations, and intentions, whether sacred or profane. The study of postures and gestures has not progressed as far as the study of other aspects of religion or as far as the study of social science as a whole; but such study—especially the emerging disciplines of kinesics, ethology, and semiotics—deserves close attention.

Islam: A Case for Preliminary Observation and Analysis. Among the Abrahamic religions, Islam contains in its ritual observances a rich and varied repertory of postures and gestures that are mastered by every adherent. Christianity also has many body movements and gestures of deep significance, but they are neither universally performed within the tradition nor permitted across all classes of believers. All Muslims perform the *rak'ahs* (bowing cycles) of each *ṣalāt*, or prayer service, with a combination of standing, bowing, prostration, and sitting postures accompanied by coordinated head, hand, arm, and foot gestures. By contrast, the postures and gestures of Christian worship, for example in the Roman Catholic tradition, are assigned to laity or clergy in a carefully regulated manner; although certain basic forms, such as kneeling and making the sign of the cross, are shared, the laity nevertheless do not raise the sacramental elements, nor serve them, nor bless—these are gestures reserved for ordained priests.

A Muslim, or a knowledgeable outside observer, can tell at a glance and from a distance when a Muslim is at formal prayer *(ṣalāt)*, and moreover at what point in the ritual, just from observing postures and gestures. If the worshiper is standing, with the hands placed slightly in front and to the sides of the head, with the thumbs aligned with the earlobes, then the observer knows that the prayer has just begun with the utterance "Allāhu akbar" ("God is most great!"). But the worshiper seated with knees on the floor and buttocks resting on the ankles is either at the midpoint of the cycle or near the end, depending on the precise placement of feet and hands. If the right hand is resting on the right thigh, and gathered into a fist, with the index finger waving slowly back and forth, and if the left foot has been placed beneath the right ankle, under the buttocks, then the cycle is nearly finished. If it is the final cycle in the series—and each daily *ṣalāt* has a set number of required *rak'ahs*—then the observer will know that the prayer is nearly over by the worshiper's turning of the head to the right and the left, uttering a blessing in each direction. This is the only point in any *ṣalāt* service at which the worshiper turns aside in any manner from the *qiblah,* or direction of Mecca. Other important parts of the *rak'ah,* which itself means "bowing," are actual bowing and, most important, a full prostration with the forehead touching the floor or ground; this gesture, called in Arabic *sajda,* is the climax of Islamic worship, when the slave of God symbolizes his total submission and obedience. If the worshiper is seen in the sitting posture, but with hands extended in front, palms upward, he or she is not engaged in the formal *ṣalāt,* probably, but is performing *du'ā',* the voluntary prayer of personal petition frequently uttered after formal worship and at other auspicious times, such as at the close of a Qur'ān recitation, especially of the entire text. Or a prostration may be enacted in conjunction with the recitation of a special Qur'ān verse—whose hearing renders meritorious an immediate *sajda*—but omitting the other postures and gestures of the full *rak'ah.* [*See* Ṣalāt.]

Social Functions of Religious Postures and Gestures. Religious postures and gestures serve not only to symbolize and regulate devotion; they also demarcate religious communities and subcommunities. If one sees, for example, in a Middle Eastern or Southeast Asian context, where the vast majority of people are Muslim, a person kneeling in an attitude of devotion, with hands folded or palms pressed together, with head bowed and eyes closed, one is seeing a member of the Christian tradition or possibly a Buddhist. Muslims do not kneel at prayer, fold their hands, or bow their heads with closed eyes like the Christians. Moreover, within Christianity itself there are significant variations that identify specific churches, denominations, and sects and, in some cases—as evident from art and iconography—distinct historical periods. Kneeling, for example, is a biblically warranted posture of piety that has been adopted at some time or other by most Christian communities. But in formal worship, Christians from different traditions do not necessarily all kneel at the same point, or for the same reason. Some Christians kneel in adoration, whereas others reserve that posture for penitence, which is often done in private. Some Christians stand while receiving Communion, whereas others kneel.

Likewise, there are varying ways of making the sign of the cross, two of which distinguish Roman Catholics from Eastern Orthodox: the former move the hand from the left to the right shoulder, whereas the latter move the hand from right to left. Both gestures are unambiguously Christian, yet the slight difference symbolizes also a great historical and communal separation. Similarly, particular Islamic subcommunities may exhibit variations of gesture: for example, in the standing position of formal worship some allow the hands to hang loosely at the sides, whereas others fold them gently in front of the body. By contrast, as already noted, the Islamic cultus of posture and gesture is remarkably uniform throughout the world and has been so since its early formalization. A Baptist of narrow experience who visits a high church Episcopal service would be at sea about what to do next in the liturgy: stand, kneel, or sit? But every Muslim with minimal religious upbringing would be at home in Islamic worship anywhere in the world. Even a Muslim who does not understand a word of Arabic—though most do know a few religious phrases—probably knows the postures and gestures of worship in every detail.

Symbolic Range of Religious Postures and Gestures. Religious postures and gestures are cultural products and are transmitted in various ways and with different understandings. Consequently, the question of whether there is an intrinsic relationship between inward dispositions and outward manifestations is difficult to resolve. It would seem that in most cases these manifestations are intentional signs that serve to reinforce as well as express doctrines and attitudes. Nevertheless, they are similar in many cultures; there is a high correlation between certain postures and gestures and a wide range of emotions and purposes that are usually if not exclusively religious or magical. Among these are adoration, affirmation, blessing, consecration, curse, gratitude, greeting, humility, invocation, meditation, mourning, oath taking, penitence, pleading, praise, prayer, protection, remorse, reverence, sorrow, and submission.

Kneeling is often associated with adoration, blessing, confession, humility, penitence, pleading, petition, remorse, and submission, especially in Christianity. [*See* Knees.]

Prostration is a dramatic posture expressing submission, penitence, consecration, and humiliation. It is especially closely associated with Islamic worship, but known also in the Bible and other religious contexts.

The sitting posture sometimes symbolizes religious attitudes, particularly in the Buddhist attitude of concentration wherein the legs are crossed, right over left, with soles facing upward, hands resting on the thighs, with thumbs touching. This "Lotus Position" is basic to Buddhist meditation as well as to Hindu yoga. [*See* Haṭhayoga.] Muslims commonly sit in a posture similar to the Lotus Position when in a mosque or adopt it as a normal posture anywhere. Egyptian Muslims like to rock back and forth in this position when listening to Qur'ān recitation, which can be highly rhythmic. A similar practice is found among Jews. Sitting is also understood as a royal and a divine posture, as evidenced by thrones and mounts, from whence commands and judgments descend.

Standing is a posture that in religious tradition signifies respect, as evidenced when Christians stand for the reading aloud of the gospel lesson. Early Christians stood for congregational prayer, and standing throughout the service is still practiced in Eastern Orthodoxy. Muslims stand at the beginning of the *ṣalāt* when making their *nīyah,* or "intention," and uttering the first *takbīr,* "God is most great!" The Islamic funeral service may be performed only in a standing position, and it is recommended that Muslims stand in respect when a funeral procession passes, because a soul is being transported to its place of repose until the Resurrection. The most profound point of the Islamic pilgrimage to Mecca *(ḥajj)* is the *wuqūf,* or "standing" ceremony, when the pilgrims stand for hours in repentance and hope for mercy from God. So important is this ritual standing to the Muslim that its omission for any reason invalidates the individual's pilgrimage; unlike certain other elements of the pilgrimage, the *wuqūf* must be performed beginning on a set day and at noon.

Dance as practiced in religious contexts combines many postures and gestures in complex configurations. The American Indians, for example, developed dance for religious and magical purposes in pursuit of healing, hunting success, rain, good crops, and victory over enemies, as well as for critical and calendrical rites having to do with matters such as puberty, initiation, seasons, harvests, and natural calamities. Dance has been of central importance in the religious life of peoples in all regions, and it extends far back into prehistory. The Mevlevīs, members of the Ṣūfī order of "dancing" or "whirling" dervishes founded by Jalāl al-Dīn Rūmī (d. 1273), spin around their leader like heavenly bodies rotating about the sun. The twentieth century has seen a renewed interest in both Roman Catholic and Protestant worship in sacred dance, in the conviction that the body and its movements are repositories of holiness and a fundamental means for communing with God and celebrating the mysteries of salvation. Likewise, celebration of the whole person, soul and body, was a basic dimension in the worship of the Jews of biblical times, who danced and clapped their hands in joy in the presence of God. [*See* Dance.]

Hands, which express the broadest range of religious and magical meanings and are major instruments of gesture in all traditions, are used in such motions and configurations as are necessary for blessing, praying, consecrating, healing, anointing, protecting, welcoming, ordaining, and other purposes. [*See* Hands.]

Mudrā, a Sanskrit word meaning "sign, gesture," denotes a highly ramified and conceptually sophisticated symbolic hand language developed by the closely related Indian religions Hinduism and Buddhism; it interpenetrates and connects various levels of their belief, behavior, aesthetic sensitivity, and communal life. *Mudrā*s take many forms, each of which symbolizes a doctrine or truth or realization or experience. In Buddhism, for example, a fundamental event in the founder's career may be symbolized by means of *mudrā*. *Mudrā*s are used extensively in ritual, iconography, dance, drama, and teaching in Hindu and Buddhist regions. Without an understanding of *mudrā*, one could not interpret and thus fully appreciate the hundreds of stone reliefs concerning the Buddha's cosmic evolution that adorn the magnificent stupa of Borobudur in Central Java. [*See* Mudrā.].

Not only the hands, but also the arms have been important in religious gesture. Extending the arms out to the sides has been practiced as a gesture of solar adoration. Coptic Christians spread out their arms in the form of a cross at baptism. Ancient Egyptian, Sumerian, Babylonian, and Etruscan worshipers spread their arms in prayer. Ancient Egyptians, Buddhists, and Romans prayed with arms crossed on the chest. Present-day extending of the arms by Armenian Christians is symbolic of the Trinity; in this position the neophyte turns toward the west and spits at the Devil, then turns east with spread arms and faces heaven in acknowledgment of Father, Son, and Holy Spirit.

Mouth and lips, too, have been prominent in sacred gesture among very diverse peoples. Magical practices have included spitting three times into the folds of one's garment to avoid the evil eye (ancient Greece), spitting on children for the same reason (ancient Rome), spitting into the eye of a close relative to prove the absence of evil-eye intentions (ancient and modern Greece), and other spitting gestures, such as the Shintō and Buddhist practice in Japan of spitting at healing deities. The Qur'ān instructs one to take refuge from the "evil of the women who blow on knots," meaning the witches who cast harmful spells by ritual spitting on knots tied in a cord (113:5). [*See* Spittle and Spitting.]

Kissing particularly is often used in ritual gesture. Women kissed Christ's feet (*Lk.* 7:38). The thresholds of churches have traditionally been kissed, as have been relics, burial sites, and other powerful repositories of the holy. Muslim folk practices include the kissing of saint shrine enclosures for *barakah* ("blessing"). Christians have been known to kiss the Bible when taking an oath. Shīʿī Muslims sometimes kiss copies of the Qur'ān. Jews kiss the *mezuzah* when leaving or entering the home. Mecca pilgrims try to kiss the holy Black Stone embedded in the Kaʿbah, in imitation of Muḥammad's custom. Ancient Greeks kissed the sacred oak of Zeus at Aegina. Catholics kiss the crucifix. Many ancient Near Eastern peoples kissed the hands, feet, and clothing of sacred images. Pope John Paul II kisses the ground of the countries he visits. Muslim youth kiss the hand of their Qur'ān teacher as a gesture of deep respect not only for the teacher as a person but for the treasure that he carries and imparts. [*See* Touching.]

In addition to postures adopted by the living are those imposed upon the deceased by others acting on their behalf. Burial in a fetal position, for example, has been known for prehistoric archaeology and ethnography. This unusual practice may have come about to prevent the spirit of the deceased from wandering about after death, especially in cases wherein the body has been tightly bound. An alternative interpretation is that the position imitates the state in the womb, with burial representing a sort of return. Most peoples lay the body on the back for burial, sometimes with particular orientations. Muslims sometimes bury their dead lying on the right side, with the face pointing toward Mecca; even if the body is supine, the face is oriented in that direction. Al-Ghazālī, the great Muslim theologian (d. 1111), advised the pious to go to bed at night lying on the right side, facing Mecca, because sleep in the Islamic view is a "little death," from which an individual might not wake. Again, Christian baptism by immersion imitates a posthumous position, in which the initiate submits passively as the officiant symbolically buries the old person who is presently to be cleansed and resurrected in the new life in Christ.

Social, Magical, Avoidance, and Self-destructive Gestures. Perhaps the most extensively studied, if not the most richly developed, social gestures among civilized peoples are those found in Mediterranean societies, such as Italy, France, Spain, Greece, Egypt, Lebanon, Turkey, Syria, and the Maghreb. Most of the postures and gestures cannot be interpreted as religious; in fact, many are utterly profane, even obscene, and have been so since antiquity. An example is the sign of the fig, made with the thumb protruding from between the index and middle fingers. This is a sexual insult, usually, and in the Middle Ages was declared illegal if directed at religious images and symbols. The sign of the horns, made by extending the index and little fingers from a closed fist, and directing it toward the eyes of a threatening person, has long been an apotropaic gesture. Among Muslims, for example in North Africa, a gesture called the Hand of Fāṭimah is made by extending the fingers toward a supposed enemy in order to neutralize the evil eye. If uncertain whether harm is actually intended, the gesturer may make the gesture under a cloak or other covering, particularly when the danger is not perceived to be grave. The "horns" are also sometimes thus covered.

Social postures and gestures sometimes involve ritual avoidances. Among Muslims, especially in the Middle East and Southeast Asia, a strong distinction is made between the right and left sides of the body. Only the right hand is considered clean and fit for gesturing, giving, receiving, blessing, greeting, eating, and touching. The left hand is considered as unclean because it is used for humble tasks only, such as the toilet. It is a great breach of propriety to use the left hand for what is properly a right-hand function. The right foot leads when entering a mosque, but one leaves a holy place left foot first. The toilet room is entered left foot first and exited with the right foot leading. The soles of the feet are considered, by Muslims and other Eastern peoples, to be unclean, and so it is essential to avoid directing them toward anyone (as an American may inadvertently do when resting the feet on a desk top). In Java it is considered arrogant and disrespectful for a boy or man to cross his legs or ankles in the presence of a superior, especially while sitting in a chair. Although that is a cultural taboo, the observance of it is especially noticeable in pious Muslim contexts, where proper physical deportment is a mark of the religious person. Social postures and gestures in highly stratified traditional societies, like Java, provide valuable clues about religious worldview.

In religious practice certain self-destructive gestures exist that express powerful emotion. One is the ritual flagellation practiced by Christian ascetics, especially during Passion Week. A structurally similar practice is the self-flagellation, often with chains, of Shīʿī men in processions associated with the Tenth of Muḥarram, the anniversary of the martyrdom of Imam Ḥusayn ibn ʿAlī at Karbala, Iraq, in 680. The ancient Israelites mourned by putting ashes on their heads (*2 Sm.* 13:19) or tearing their hair and beards (*Ezr.* 9:3). Modern Palestinian women beat their breasts, tear their hair, scratch their cheeks, and throw soot on their heads in mourning, gestures that can be traced back to ancient times.

[*See also* Human Body.]

BIBLIOGRAPHY

For an excellent collection of sources and an extensive bibliography, see Betty J. Bäuml and Franz H. Bäuml's *A Dictionary of Gestures* (Metuchen, N.J., 1975). Religious postures and gestures have yet to be given much attention by students of religion, at least as a comprehensive subfield. However, a comprehensive literature on ritual and devotional practices, including detailed analysis and interpretation of postures and gestures, exists within numerous religious traditions. In addition to ritual, liturgical, and scriptural sources, a variety of other sources, for example, works on law, ethnography, and art history, provide information on the subject.

The relatively new sciences of ethology, kinesics, and semiotics give great promise of increasing our understanding of posture and gesture. Konrad Lorenz's studies, for example, offer some provocative ideas concerning the relationship between phylogenetically transmitted and culturally transmitted gestures in animals and humans; see his *Behind the Mirror: A Search for a Natural History of Human Knowledge* (New York, 1977).

FREDERICK MATHEWSON DENNY

POTLATCH is any of a disparate variety of complex ceremonies among the Indians of the Pacific Northwest Coast of North America, associated with the legitimization of the transfer or inheritance of hereditary aristocratic titles and their associated rights, privileges, and obligations. Potlatches are characterized by the reenactment of the sacred family histories that document the legitimacy of the claimant to the rank, by ritual feasting, and by the formal distribution of gifts by the host group to its guests, each according to his rank. Though the wealth distributed at a potlatch may be quite substantial, the amount distributed is much less important than the requirement that it be distributed according to the correct social protocols and moral prescriptions.

Potlatches have traditionally occurred at points of social stress accompanying any part of the process of ascension or succession to rank: investiture into a new name; the building of a house; erecting of a totem pole or other emblem of hereditary prerogative, such as a marriage or a child's coming of age; or alternatively as a mortuary feast for a previous rankholder, as a means of acquiring prestige; and sometimes even as a means of discrediting rival claimants. The legitimacy of the rankholder's claims is proven by his dual ability to command the allegiance of his family group in putting together such a complicated ceremony and to perform correctly the formal display of his family's origin myths and ceremonial objects. The acceptance of gifts by the guests signals their acceptance of the validity of his claim.

Anthropologists have focused on the secular, social aspects and functions of the potlatch—on the way in which potlatches maintain social equilibrium, consolidate chiefly power over commoners, provide for the orderly transfer of wealth and power, provide a measure of group identity and solidarity, redistribute surplus wealth and level economic imbalances, provide outlets for competition without recourse to violence, and provide an occasion for aesthetic expression and dramatic entertainment. Irving Goldman has suggested in his *The Mouth of Heaven* (1975) that, since in Northwest Coast philosophy all status, power, and wealth are considered to be a gift from the beneficent supernatural beings who provide the materials that humans need to survive, the potlatch is inherently a religious institution, fundamentally endowed with a sacramental quality. Each of the family origin myths, whose retelling is such an important part of the potlatch, tells of how one of a particular family's ancestors was able to make a covenant with a supernatural being. In return for the right to collect food of a specific type at a specific location, to possess an aristocratic name, to impersonate (and thus become) the supernatural being in ceremonies, and to invoke the aid of that being in times of distress, the ancestor accepted the responsibility of performing the rituals that would ensure the reincarnation of that supernatural being. This covenant expresses the mutual dependency of human and supernatural, and the potlatch is the ceremony through which the aristocrat fulfills his responsibilities to the supernatural being.

The chief is the representative of his house to the spirits and in his person are brought together all the historical, social, and spiritual aspects of his group's identity. He is the being who links the spiritual world to the social world, and his costume and behavior at potlatches clearly state the duality of his role as spirit in human form. Indeed, since chiefs are the representatives of particular supernatural beings, the distribution of wealth to other chiefs at potlatches can be seen as a metaphorical distribution by one supernatural being to others, and as such it represents the flow of substance throughout the entire universe.

The potlatch, obviously a rite of passage for human beings, a death of an old identity and a rebirth into a new one, is also a rite of passage for the supernaturals. The supernatural beings sustain human beings not only by giving them power and knowledge, but by being their food—when supernatural beings come to the human world, they put on costumes that transform them into animals. The objects displayed, transferred, or distributed in potlatches are manifestations of the bodies of supernatural beings: the flesh and skins of animals (which, since they are thought to be the animals' ceremonial costumes, imply that humans survive by ingesting the ceremonial, spiritual essence of their prey); the coppers (large, ceremonial plaques that represent repositories of captured souls awaiting reincarnation); and the feast dishes (which are the coffins for the animal substance before the humans who partake of that substance begin the process of its reincarnation). Potlatches, in a sense, are funerals for the supernaturals and inherently involve the reaffirmation of the eternal moral covenants between mankind and the other inhabitants of the universe. As animals sacrifice their flesh that humans may eat it and live, so humans must sacrifice themselves or their wealth, which is a symbol of themselves, that the dead may be reborn.

In Northwest Coast thought, moral order and spiritual purity are achieved through acts of self-sacrifice, and the giving away of possessions places humans in harmony with the moral order of the universe. The universe is imagined to have been originally a place of self-interest and possessiveness, that is, until culture heroes started the process of distribution. Northwest Coast peoples believe that the universe will collapse back into the primordial chaos of selfishness unless humans continually reaffirm their willingness to disburse their possessions, to pass out wealth to their fellow men, and to pass on rank to their children. The potlatch provides the ceremonial realization of that commitment to the cosmic moral order and is a reaffirmation by all its participants—hosts, guests, ancestors, the unborn, and supernatural beings—of the system of moral covenants and mutual dependencies that lie at the basis of Northwest Coast society. The potlatch reenacts myth, and then, through redistribution, recreates its processual nature, thereby becoming a graphic representation of the continuing reality and salience of those myths, linking the past to the present, the dead to the living, the sacred to the mundane, the human to the supernatural, the local to the cosmic, and the momentary to the eternal.

It should be noted that the potlatch underwent substantial change during the nineteenth century. Heavy governmental and missionary pressures contributed to the abandonment or secularization of many Northwest Coast Indian rituals. Potlatches and all other native ceremonies were illegal in Canada between 1876 and 1951, and though some ceremonies were carried out in secret, Northwest Coast religion was irreparably altered. The potlatch and other ceremonies have played an important role in the native renaissance of the 1960s, 1970s, and 1980s, but few studies of the potlatch in contemporary Indian life have been conducted, and very little can be said of the particulars of its role in Indian society today.

BIBLIOGRAPHY

Philip Drucker and Robert F. Heizer provide a lucid review of the literature and a discussion of the potlatch as a social institution in *To Make My Name Good* (Berkeley, 1967); Helen Codere's *Fighting with Property: A Study of Kwakiutl Potlatching and Warfare, 1792–1930* (New York, 1950) deals with the issue of historical changes in the potlatches of the Kwakiutl; Irving Goldman's *The Mouth of Heaven* (New York, 1975) reexamines many of the Kwakiutl materials collected by Franz Boas and argues for a new religio-philosophical interpretation of Northwest Coast culture.

STANLEY WALENS

POVERTY as a principle of voluntary deprivation or limitation of material possessions is incorporated into a number of the world's major religious traditions. What each culture sees as necessary for the fulfillment of human aspirations determines the way in which poverty is viewed. In many cultures, almsgiving is associated with poverty and religious obligation; the sharing of one's excess or even of the necessities of life with the deprived is often seen as the moral responsibility of the materially fortunate. Frequently, it also denotes a sense of detachment from worldly goods in the quest of a higher good. Historically, religious and philosophical figures have tended to regard voluntary poverty as a spiritual good in that its fosters the principle of self-sufficiency, a reduction of dependency upon the surrounding world. The notion that one could easily become possessed by possessions was, for such groups as the Stoics, Cynics, and Pythagoreans, a reason for incorporating some degree of poverty in their codes of personal discipline.

Hinduism views poverty as one of several ascetic practices that promote liberation for the individual from *saṃsāra* (the cosmic process of ceaseless becoming) and union with *brahman* (the ultimate principle of life). Poverty thus provides a welcome release from worldly cares, responsibilities, and social restrictions, but it is always to be undertaken with the intent of release for a greater good. Pious men (*sādhus*) and women (*sādhvīs*) often vow to relinquish all worldly attachments and values for a life of renunciation and austerity. According to some proponents, the ascetic life renders its adherent casteless inasmuch as societal classification, like every other institution of the worldly life, has been renounced. Poverty, however, is seen not as an end in itself but as a means to attain union with *brahman* or supernatural powers. By surrendering wealth, possessions, and all the things of the world that keep humans in mental bondage, the ascetic *(saṃnyāsin)* is enabled to dwell undistractedly in meditation on *brahman.*

Judaism has generally insisted upon care and consideration of the poor. While not denying the need for some mortification, it has accorded little value to poverty as a positive principle; asceticism, especially in extreme forms, is antithetical to Judaism's basic belief that the provisions of the world are to be enjoyed and that sacrifice of the necessities of life is only rarely justified. Hence, for Jews, poverty is generally viewed as a misfortune; the blessings bestowed by God upon his people include material prosperity and other earthly pleasures. Nonetheless, the Talmud does present some positive reflections on poverty. There, for example, the verse "I have tried you in the furnace of affliction" (*Is.* 48:10) is explained as one that "teaches that the Holy One, Blessed be He, went through all the virtues in order to bestow them upon Israel, and found none more becoming than poverty" (B.T., *Ḥag.* 9b). Many more passages in Judaic literature, however, point to a middle way between extreme wealth and destitution, reminding Jews that the ideal is to provide for oneself, one's family, and those less fortunate, and always to have trust in God as the provider. Although there have been several dissident groups that subscribed to simple living and ascetic practices (e.g., the Therapeutae and the Qumran community), the community at large has tried to eliminate poverty from its midst and has rejoiced in material prosperity as a blessing from God.

Within Buddhism, poverty was early on adopted as a discipline characteristic of its monastic communities *(saṃgha).* In these communities, membership is open to all persons without distinction of race, caste, or birth, and monks and nuns are formally bound by a vow of poverty, that is, the relinquishment of all personal possessions. Renunciants are usually provided with an alms bowl and three vestments, which are supposed to constitute their only belongings. Dependent upon the generosity of others, they are not allowed to request donations; they must present themselves at households to receive whatever food might be placed in their bowls. If they receive no food, they are to show no resentment but are to move on to another house. Upon returning to community quarters, they share a simple meal.

Historically, the rule of individual poverty has not been extended to monasteries as corporate entities. In the beginnings of Buddhist monasticism, the "mendicants" (*bhikṣus* and *bhikṣuṇīs*) were instructed to follow the wandering life of ascetics, depending for their livelihood upon gifts from the laity. [*See also* Mendicancy.] Their only home or shelter was to be the trees of the forest, small huts constructed of leaves and branches, or natural or artificially constructed caves. Later, wealthy lay people donated more elaborate and permanent dwellings to monastic communities and, as with many Christian monastic groups, some Buddhist monasteries came to be richly endowed, their resources allowing their residents to wield considerable influence in their neighborhood.

From its earliest history, Christianity has ascribed great value to voluntary poverty, viewing it as one of the more effective means to personal holiness. Built upon the belief that Christ, as Son of God, modeled a poverty of spirit in choosing to come to earth to redeem a fallen humanity, poverty emerged as one of the three basic vows of monastics endeavoring to emulate him. Along with chastity and obedience, it acquired the status of an evangelical precept based upon the words of Christ, in this case his advice to a wealthy youth: "If you would be perfect, go sell what you have, give it to the poor, and come follow me" (*Mt.* 19:21). By denying themselves material possessions and sometimes even their use, monastics are considered co-workers with Christ in restoring the world to a lost primordial state of innocence and bliss. This principle of poverty was later established by the church as one of the official vows to be accepted by monastics at the time of ordination.

Throughout Christian history, the spirit and observance of poverty within a given religious order has varied according to the impetus of its founder and the economic standards of the time. Over the centuries, circumstances have continually demanded adaptations to new conditions and changing fortunes. Monastic poverty, which became prevalent during the fourth and fifth centuries, bears the marks of the rural poverty that predominated during those centuries and even into the feudal period, while the poverty of the later mendicant orders (e.g., the Franciscans and Dominicans) reflects the influence of the development of urban society. Often, as religious communities flourished and large landholdings were donated to them, corporate wealth replaced poverty altogether and, in some instances, new foundations were established in protest against luxuries that were perceived, at least by some members (e.g., the Cistercians and Carthusians), as inimical to the spirit and practice of the original vows. In practice, observance of the vow of poverty was intimately related to the vow of obedience, in that overseers of the communities could and did determine which possessions might be retained by individual members. After the Protestant Reformation in the sixteenth century, many religious communities were abolished and, within Protestant groups, formal vows of poverty were replaced by emphasis on almsgiving and the support of needy members of the congregation. [*See also* Almsgiving.]

In Islam, poverty of spirit as an aspect of *zuhd* (self-denial) developed gradually from the idea of abstinence from sin to that of abstinence from material goods and sensual pleasures. Poverty's inclusion in the ascetic life is usually attributed to an utterance of Muḥammad: "Poverty is my glory." Muḥammad himself exercised voluntary poverty and instructed his followers to be moderate in acquiring possessions. Communities of ascetics arose during the first centuries of Islamic history, but asceticism as a way of life became more prevalent among later groups of mystics, such as the Ṣūfīs, for whom poverty was adopted as one of the six "chief stations" of spirituality. There has been some disagreement among Ṣūfīs themselves, and between various other Muslim groups, about whether it is more meritorious to practice poverty as an expression of love for and trust in God or whether it is better to be wealthy and grateful to God for his beneficence. Most Ṣūfīs, however, hold that a person who desires union with God will recognize in poverty an efficacious means of achieving liberation from all that distracts from God. To the commonly used word *faqīr* ("poor one"), Ṣūfī ascetics have given a spiritual sense indicative of a "poverty of spirit" that acknowledges one's need of God.

In modern times, there is evidence of a growing movement at the grass-roots level of many religious traditions, both Eastern and Western, to organize communities dedicated to fostering simpler lives based on sufficiency rather than luxury. As new cultural conditions create new needs and options, both the spirit and the practice of poverty continue to be reexamined.

BIBLIOGRAPHY

Brandon, S. G. F., ed. *A Dictionary of Comparative Religion.* London, 1970.

Clasen, Sophronius. "Poverty." In *New Catholic Encyclopedia,* edited by William J. McDonald, vol. 11. New York, 1967.

Knoop, Douglas. "Poverty." In *Encyclopaedia of Religion and Ethics,* edited by James Hastings, vol. 10. Edinburgh, 1918.

Parrinder, Geoffrey. *Dictionary of Non-Christian Religions.* Philadelphia, 1971.

Spiro, Melford E. *Buddhism and Society.* 2d. enl. ed. Berkeley, 1982.

Stutley, Margaret, and James Stutley. *A Dictionary of Hinduism.* London, 1977.

ROSEMARY RADER

POWER. The term *kratophany* literally rendered is "the appearance of power." Mircea Eliade, however, who made this a technical term in English, used it to indicate an appearance of the sacred in which the experience of power dominates. Thus, that every kratophany must be, at the same time, a hierophany ("appearance of the sacred") is certain by definition, while the converse is less clear; indeed, assent to it will hinge upon the degree to which one regards the concept or experience of power to be an irreducible part of the concept or experience of the sacred. [*See* Hierophany.]

That the idea of power is central to much religious experience can be seen by means of a simple mental exercise: try to imagine hierophany without the elements of awesomeness, authority, or effectiveness. Most will agree that it is possible to imagine intellectual constructs such as truth or value without power, but hierophany seems to require more. Here is one difference between philosophy and religion, between the intellectual grasp of an idea and the experience of a sacred reality: the religious experience involves the whole personality and not merely the intellect. It includes the emotions as well as less obvious aspects of human awareness such as the kinesthetic sense and deep instinctual and symbolic structures. Finally, it may be that the sense of reality and the sensing of power are inextricably combined into what is experienced as a unity that might be labeled "real presence." As a category of modern physics, power can be described as a potentiality, or a potential ability to do "work," which in turn implies the expenditure of energy to change the distribution of energy in a given system, just as water piled up behind a hydroelectric dam has great potential for generating electricity because of its advantageous location with respect to the direction of gravitational forces. Unlike water, however, the sacred always remains potential even after awesome power has been expended, and it is this mysterious characteristic of being an inexhaustible source of power that in part gives to hierophany its paradoxical tendency both to attract and to repulse.

The normal reactions to sacred power within a given culture can conveniently be classified under the rubrics of *mana* and *taboo. Mana* implies a positive attitude toward power within an object or symbol or person—power that can be appropriated for useful purposes. *Taboo* implies the opposite, namely, power in an object or symbol or person that must be avoided for safety's sake or at least hedged about with special "insulating" rites before it can be made useful. Examples are amulets and charms, holy books, saints' relics, and living sacred persons. Infraction of such governing rules constitutes sacrilege and usually brings down cultural or cultic sanctions upon the guilty, or even the direct intervention of sacred power itself.

Perhaps the most important, because clearest, example of the role played by power in religion can be seen by examination of the meaning of cosmogonic myths and of what appears to be the psychological reality that informs them, namely, the universal experience of the prestige of origins. Here, above all, is demonstrated the positive side of sacred power in its intrinsic creativity. Here is the power to bring a world into being, to shape reality, and thereby to found human cults and cultures. It is literally true that within cosmogonic myths everything that happens is a unique demonstration of creative power, since everything that happens does so for the first time. Examples abound, but consider only the Dreaming adventures of many sacred beings in Australian tribal religions, where the seemingly trivial acts performed while traveling around the countryside actually create the landscape and populate it with sacred places gravid with meaning. Or consider the Shintō myths in which with nearly every gesture of the gods—whether by sexual contact, by breaking or cutting something, or by uttering special words—new deities came into existence, deities whose intimate relationship with nature and culture made them constitutive of the world.

More dramatic examples may be found in the Hebrew scriptures, in the *Book of Job,* for example, where frequent references are made to God's creative power in ordering the world and controlling the awesome forces of the cosmic ocean. As the text comes down to us, Job's response is one of terror and repentance without understanding. The Hindu classic *Bhagavadgītā* provides another forceful revelation of the sacred as power in Arjuna's trembling witness to Lord Kṛṣṇa's true nature: nothing less than the world process is portrayed in the deity's simultaneous destructive function as death and his creative function as the womb of all beings.

Power and Theories of the Origins of Religion. Although scattered speculations can be found in the classical civilizations of China, India, and Greece, theoretical reconstructions of the possible origins of religion stem in their modern forms from the European encounter with those cultures that, from about the time of the Enlightenment until a few decades ago, were known collectively as "the savages." Knowledge of these so-called primitive (or archaic, or nonliterate) peoples made a strong impression on the Western imagination. Among other things, it played an important role in the foundation during the nineteenth century of such academic disciplines as psychology, sociology, and anthropology. Perhaps because many of the more detailed accounts of such cultures came from religious professionals and perhaps also because it was an age in the West of great religious ferment, the discovery of primitive cultures was both a discovery of exotic social customs and of strange and disquieting systems of belief and ritual. The most significant systematic attempt of this period to reconstruct a "natural history" of religion was E. B. Tylor's *Primitive Culture* (1871). There the theory of animism was first propounded.

Tylor defined *animism* as belief, or a tendency toward belief, that all nature was endowed with a spiritual, animating essence, or soul. Thus, by anthropomorphizing analogy, every natural power or object was directed by a personality possessing intellect and will. According to this theory, all things were supposed by our primitive ancestors to be humanlike—if not in outward appearance, then in their inner being. Power was implied in this view in that the power of being of every thing, its uniqueness and its efficacy, was assumed to be potentially greater than what we would call its mere physical possibilities. Yet the experiences that lay behind this animistic worldview were not, in Tylor's view, fundamentally of power, with its exciting, often daunting emotional concomitants, but were instead of a different and more coolly logical kind. He reasoned that primitives must have been perplexed by their own dreams and thoughts, in which they themselves as well as other people, both living and dead, and not present in the usual sense, appeared. Adding this to their own natural experience of themselves as thinking, willing, self-moving beings, primitives must have concluded that a soul, or animating principle, must inhere in all things and that it could sometimes be separated from the body. In this way, Tylor sought not only to explain primitive beliefs but also to define a proto-religious stage of cultural evolution. Religion, or more strictly the prerequisite for religion, he went on to define as "a belief in spiritual beings." Animism, then, is but one type of religion, namely, the belief that all things have souls, or, as it were, both a material and a spiritual "body" or aspect.

Tylor's theory of animism, and indeed his view of religion as a phenomenon that properly encompasses both primitive and so-called higher forms in a unified theory, provided the *locus classicus* of most anthropological work, including the formation of new theories, until well past the turn of the century. The main thrust of theorizing in this period was to reconstruct the origins of religious behavior itself, that is, to isolate the most elementary impulse, feeling, or experience that constituted the *sine qua non* of religion, and to place all forms of religious behavior on an evolutionary scale of development from this point of origin. It should be noted here that a shift in emphasis in anthropological studies occurred in an early reaction to what was deemed by many to be Tylor's excessively intellectualist view of human nature, at least as it was displayed regarding primitives. Increasingly anthropologists viewed human beings primarily as active creatures whose thought processes are subordinated to action: thought "rationalizes" action to the degree that ideas are formed only in reaction to deeds and to provide a more or less emotionally satisfying intellectual justification for them. It is here that the idea of power, in a variety of forms, began to play its part in the great quest for origins.

Animatism is the name given to a theory, formulated by R. R. Marett, that sought to build upon the work of Tylor. Although he accepted animism as a higher stage in religious development, Marett rejected the "intellectualist fallacy" inherent in the theory of animism insofar as it claimed to represent the first stage of religion. He suggested instead that primitives experience the world as fundamentally divided into the familiar and the unfamiliar. The unfamiliar object is so because it exhibits some sort of strangeness suggestive of hidden power. This he called variously "occult power" and "the sacred." To the compound of unusual and hidden power he added the notion of life in much the same sense that Tylor had used *animus,* that is, life or soul, except that he believed that, at the stage of animatism, the primitive mind had not yet made the leap from life or life force to separable soul. This meant that animatism could also properly be understood as "preanimism." [*See* Animism and Animatism.]

The full articulation of this theory was published in 1909 in Marett's *The Threshold of Religion,* but as early as 1900, he had made the first steps toward it in his establishment of the Oceanic word *mana* as a general category of religious experience. He based his usage primarily upon the work of R. H. Codrington (see *The Melanesians,* 1891), who reported that for many South Pacific island cultures, the religious system was based upon a single concept, which they called *mana.* Among the Melanesians, *mana,* the power that inhered in all things, had special significance for their religious and social system, because it could be concentrated in some objects and because it inhered in a concentrated form in some people. Indeed, the hierarchical structure of their society was justified upon the basis of the aristocrats' inborn great *mana.* Everything possessed some *mana,* and, in this respect, the term might be translated "the power of being." Since so much was made of its concentratability, however, in many cases the term is better rendered as "sacred." But for many scholars, particularly in the nineteenth century, this usage permitted an unacceptable broadening of the meaning of *sacred,* since *mana* could be transferred from one object or person to another. Many tended to classify this notion not as religious but as pertaining to magic. The fluidity of *mana* made it a kind of physical energy, or at least analogous to such an energy: the transfer could be affected by touching one *mana*-charged object with another with less *mana;* in particular, a person of high *mana* could infuse an object with some of his or her *mana* by handling it.

It was not long after the publication of Codrington's findings that similar discoveries began to be made in other parts of the world. American anthropologists were especially active at this time, and the Huron *orenda,* the Lakota *wakan,* and the Algonquin *manitou* were soon added to the list of *mana*-like concepts. Later the Arabic *barakah* and East Asian terms such as the Chinese *ling-pao* and the Japanese *kami* were suggested as counterparts to the Melanesian idea of *mana.* From such evidence, Marett then posited a general psychological tendency of human beings to experience the world as well as themselves under the guise of a controlling religious concept: sacred or occult power. This view has had great influence among scholars. However, contemporary anthropology does not generally accept Marett's insistence that even the most elementary religious experience engrafts to the notion of power the assumption of personality—or, to put it another way, that *mana* and animatism are necessarily combined. It may, of course, be true in certain cultures, as he argued, that because *mana* most powerfully manifested itself in certain types of persons, it was treated as if it were the willpower of a human being, but it is not true in all cultures. And the value of the term *mana* is just in its use as a general descriptive category denoting a sacred power that is not in itself personal. Thus, in fact, the modern usage implies a psychological, if not necessarily chronological, priority to the idea of *mana* over even Marett's animatism.

Power and the Nature of Religion. In 1909, with the publication of *Les rites de passage,* Arnold van Gennep applied the label *dynamistic* to the theories of the origin of religion put forth by Marett (1900) and by J. N. B. Hewitt (1902), based upon the experience of the sacred as power. But van Gennep drew a sharp line between what he called dynamism, or the conceptual framework that assumed impersonal sacred power, and animism, which assumed that sacred power was personal. Since his goal was to classify rituals, and to a large extent to understand by means of classification, he did not enter into the theoretical debate concerning the origins of religion. Yet, because of the obvious value of his way of discussing ritual activities, his work did influence the theoretical debate, if only by showing that it was possible to make significant contributions to the study of religion without choosing a position concerning the question of origins.

No less implicit in van Gennep's work was the assumption of the centrality of the idea of power in religion, not so much in its own theorizing or attempts at self-understanding, but in its actual behavior. Thus he coined the term *magico-religious* to emphasize the practical side of human interaction with sacred power. All ritual activity he labeled as magical because it was in the realm of technique; that is, it sought to implement a practical goal, namely, to influence or even to manipulate the sacred power for useful purposes. It was, therefore, the efficacy of the sacred, its potentiality to effect change or to prevent change—in short, its power—that van Gennep emphasized in his basic insight that ritual, or, at any rate, many rituals, seek to effect transitions from one state or situation to another.

At about the same time that Marett and van Gennep were formulating their views of religion, other theories about the nature and, to some extent, the origin of religion were being formulated outside the conceptual circle of the new discipline of anthropology. Influenced by anthropological and ethnological studies, but operating in a very different intellectual framework, was Rudolf Otto, a theologian who took as his spiritual mentor Friedrich Schleiermacher. In *Das Heilige* (1917), Otto presented what might be called a phenomenological psychology of religion, in that he sought to describe the structure of human reaction to what is experienced as "the holy." Otto's work as a religious theorist, because of his attitude toward human nature and in his introspective approach to religion, may be considered a late flowering of the Romantic movement. He exhibits a qualified anti-intellectualist stance toward religious psychology: religion is an ineradicable part of human nature, present from the beginning, but, while religion itself admits of historical development, the psychological makeup of human beings, which makes religion possible, does not. Therefore, any religious experience, however far removed in time and space, can be understood by the modern student, because it shares a fundamental unity with all religion. Further, Otto appeals in a famous passage to the reader's own experience, rather than to his rational faculties, as the guarantor of the accuracy and usefulness of his descriptions:

> The reader is invited to direct his mind to a moment of deeply-felt religious experience, as little as possible qualified by other forms of consciousness. Whoever cannot do this, whoever knows no such moments in his experience, is requested to read no farther; for it is not easy to discuss questions of religious psychology with one who can recollect the emotions of his adolescence, the discomforts of indigestion, or, say, social feelings, but cannot recall any intrinsically religious feelings. (Otto, [1917] 1923, p. 8)

The fundamental religious experience Otto termed as the feeling of the presence of "the numinous." In this, his theory closely approximates that of Marett's "occult power" (or mysterious power or the sacred). But Otto sought in a systematic way to show that this feeling existed psychologically prior to any conceptualization of a god or spirit or soul and, at the same time, was the religious *sine qua non* behind these concepts. As he put it, the "ideogram" of the numinous must be present in the "concept" of god, since the former is the nonrational, feeling component of the rational concept. The mental process by which ideograms become concepts he called "schematization."

Implicit in his argument is a tension between experience or feeling, on the one hand, and *a priori* ideas, on the other, since he wished to affirm both the priority of religious experience and the truth of certain religious concepts. Indeed, it is his strong allegiance to a belief in the superiority of Christian theological formulations that has been largely responsible for Otto's lack of influence in anthropology and in related disciplines concerned with the study of religion. Added to this was his insistence upon the *sui generis* character of religious experience, which tended to isolate religion from other psychological realms, such as the experience of beauty, sexual pleasure, or terror.

The heart of Otto's system is his description of the feelings that, to a greater or lesser extent and in varying mixtures, all religious experiences evoke. These are *mysterium tremendum* and *mysterium fascinans.* The ambivalence in the human response to the object of religion we have already encountered in the dichotomy of *mana* and taboo, the positive and negative aspects of sacred power. In Otto's schema, van Gennep's work focused primarily upon the *fascinans* aspect, since the efficacy of sacred power is necessary for ritual goals to be realized, although of course van Gennep also discussed rituals of avoidance. It is particularly in the analysis of the negative side of the dichotomy that Otto's unique contribution to the understanding of religious experience can be seen. Choosing as his illustrative data primarily the canonical literature of Christianity, but supplementing it with references to such famous Christian virtuosi as Martin Luther as well as to Islamic and Hindu mystics, he documents minutely the daunting presence of the numinous in the more complex or "higher" religions. For purposes of exposition, he divides his first category into two. The first is *mysterium,* which he explains as having its closest analogy in the feeling of uncanniness that irrationally can seize us when, for example, we are listening to ghost stories or passing graveyards. This feeling emphasizes the radical otherness *(das ganz Andere)* of the numinous and results in a uniquely religious dread. If, according to Otto, this feeling is allowed to predominate in the religious experience, aberrations such as demon worship can result. To this is inextricably joined the element of *tremendum,* the overpoweringness of the numinous, whose ideogram in Christianity is God's wrath. Moving from experience *(der Moment)* to ideogram to developed theological concept, *tremendum* becomes divine omnipotence.

Tremendum, therefore, is the place in Otto's schema where the experience of sacred power has its proper location. He further elaborates its effects by the ideogram of "creature consciousness," the elementary feeling articulated by the thought of having been created, assembled, as it were, as a kind of contingent and therefore somewhat arbitrary and temporary configuration with no intrinsic merit or value or power. To sense this is to feel that one is nothing over against the infinite power and presence of the Other. Out of it come the relatively sophisticated ideas of creation and of sin. Notice that sin is now partly derived not only from the memory of having contravened a law or broken a taboo; it is also intrinsic to the religious encounter itself, particularly from the encounter with power in its overwhelming immensity. Of course we refer here to the joining or schematization of *tremendum* and the doctrine of sin, especially of original sin, which Otto argues finally makes the Christian concept of sin credible and intellectually satisfying.

It could be argued that the element of *fascinans,* or attraction, in the numinous experience also implies a tacit recognition of kratophany, but in Otto's own handling of it, *fascinans* is expressed in such terms as love, duty, and the motivation to pursue the religious life. It is an elementary recognition or experience of value rather than a perception of utility or status, which seem to predominate in the idea of *mana.*

Mircea Eliade and the History of Religions. Mircea Eliade linked his own work in the phenomenology of religion with that of Otto when in *The Sacred and the Profane* (1957) he expressed admiration for Otto's descriptions of religious experience. Yet he sought to establish, at the same time, a different perspective, one that took as its starting point the categories of the sacred/profane dichotomy first given prominence by the French sociologist Émile Durkheim. Eliade was concerned with what might be called collective psychology, rather than a psychology of individual, particular experiences. His work has sought to catalog and explain (as in *Patterns in Comparative Religion,* 1958) the great collective representations, that is, symbols, by which religious meaning is mediated in a variety of cultural contexts. In accepting Otto's description of the "irrational" aspect of encounters with the sacred, Eliade infuses his use of the term *sacred* with specific meaning that includes power as a central element. Thus the encounter with sacred power is seen in the structure of the symbols of the sacred, while power is one of the necessary attributes of the sacred.

Eliade is perhaps most like Otto when he discusses archaic techniques of ecstasy, as he does at length in his *Shamanism* (1951). Here he shows that the shaman often unwillingly encounters, and is possessed by, sacred power in an unequal test of strength that leaves the human personality transformed. The result is the ability ritually to achieve *ecstasis,* or a projection of self out of self, in order to tap the power of sacred realities as a religious specialist serving the community. But the interpretation of shamanism is not restricted to psychological aspects: the symbols, for example, of drum and "flying costume," by which shamanic rituals are accomplished, are also presented, as well as myths that both buttress and explain the worldview of shamanism.

Throughout his works dealing with archaic religion, Eliade has emphasized the creative power of myth and of the sacred beings whose stories myths are (see *Myth and Reality,* 1963). Of course, this power is understood by those for whom myths still live as the power of the sacred itself, made knowable and thus usable through myth. For Eliade, cosmogonic myth is perforce the most important type, since it taps into the ubiquitous psychological tendency that he has termed the assumption of the "prestige of origins." Here, knowledge of the origin of a thing is equivalent to having power over that thing. Thus knowledge of the origin of the world as contained in the cosmogonic myth gives human beings power over their entire environment. Rituals that celebrate this knowledge by reiterating the myth, or, more dramatically, by reenacting it, are at least very useful to the scholar in attempting to grasp the meaning of a religious worldview. Eliade has also noted that the prestige of origins and the supposed power of origins continue to function psychologically, often unconsciously, in modern secular contexts.

The sacred has power, in Eliade's view, both to make the world meaningful by providing a religious worldview and to provide a means of escape from a desacralized and therefore meaningless world (*Cosmos and History,* 1949). His work on yoga (*Yoga: Immortality and Freedom,* 1954) details this latter function of sacred power in Hinduism and Buddhism. In *samādhi,* the yogin achieves the final stage in the personal journey by which the true self realizes its identity with the sacred. This state brings with it not only the bliss of a superconsciousness but also a number of sacred powers: knowledge and sensitivity beyond the ordinary as well as psychophysical powers (*siddhi*s) that mark the accomplished practitioner of yoga.

In his discussion of yoga, Eliade also touches upon an especially revealing concept of Hinduism, namely, *tapas.* This idea, which is very old in the Indian subcontinent, can be rendered as "the power of asceticism," or "the sacred power by which the world was created." Sometimes, indeed, in later popular folk tales and myths, *tapas* becomes the power of desire and of sexual potency, which both creates all beings and threatens all with dissolution. Yoga as an ascetic discipline is thought to tap the power of *tapas,* for it is sometimes understood that *tapas* is the power by which the extraordinary accomplishment of final liberation is won. Among the devotional cults of modern Hinduism, the Śaivas honor Śiva, the phallic creator god who is also the prototype of all yogins.

Belief in the power of sacred models to raise individuals to new states of being (see *Rites and Symbols of Initiation,* 1958), especially as this power is brought to bear in rituals, is documented in Eliade's work on "initiation scenarios," which are so widespread even in secular literature and fantasy. These survivals of living symbol systems continue to haunt modern people's dreams and imaginative creations. In archaic societies, these symbols of death and rebirth—of being swallowed by a monster, for example—are especially significant ways by which the power of the sacred can bring about the transition from childhood to adulthood, from ordinary living human being to powerful ancestor, from ordinary human to powerful shaman. In salvation religions, these same techniques and symbols are employed in the crucial transition from a state of damnation to that of salvation and beatitude.

The amazing ability of symbols to endure through the ages and despite profound cultural changes, as Eliade has documented in the historical portions of his work, testifies to the power that symbols wield in human life. These powerful symbols appear to possess almost a life of their own, inasmuch as they are constitutive of the human personality. To possess sacred power is at the same time to be possessed by it, a view that Rudolf Otto would heartily support and one that the psychologist C. G. Jung emphasized with his theory of archetypes. [*See* Archetypes.]

Phenomenologically, it is impossible to determine the source of symbols either within or without the self that experiences them. Indeed, Jung regarded religion as a traditional response to especially powerful symbols that arose from the hidden energy- and meaning-centers of the psyche, that is, the archetypes. What a symbol in a dream of myth masked or partially revealed of an archetype could be determined from the human reaction to it. Archetypal symbols engender great fear, awe, and longing: they are the mainsprings of our deepest and strongest emotions, and are experienced as numinous centers of power:

> When an archetype appears in a dream, in a fantasy, or in life, it always brings with it a certain influence or power by virtue of which it either exercises a numinous or fascinating effect, or impels to action. . . . Owing to their specific energy—for they behave like highly charged autonomous centres of power—they exert a fascinating and possessive influence upon the conscious mind and can thus produce extensive alterations in the subject. (Jung, 1953, p. 80)

The very process of maturation, both culturally and individually, which Jung believed to be the main focus of religious behavior, is a process of the ever deepening experience of archetypal images and of the progressive transformation of archetypally generated symbols.

Thus, in Jung's thought the ideas of power and of religious experience were strongly associated. Religion was one way of dealing with these internal structures although by no means the only way. On the other hand, religious behavior was derived from these structures as the driving force of both thought and action.

Van der Leeuw and the Phenomenology of Religion. One major work on the nature of religion requires special mention, because it uses the idea of power as its central organizing principle. This is Gerardus van der Leeuw's *Phänomenologie der Religion* (1933), translated into English as *Religion in Essence and Manifestation* (1938). Van der Leeuw begins his ambitious work with a discussion of the experience of power as the founding impetus of religion:

> The religious man perceives that with which his religion deals as primal, as originative or causal; and only to reflective thought does this become the Object of the experience that is contemplated. . . . Theory, and even the slightest degree of generalization, are still far remote; man remains quite content with the purely practical recognition that this Object is a departure from all that is usual and familiar; and this again is the consequence of the *Power* it generates. (van der Leeuw, 1938, p. 23)

He thus describes a pretheoretical mode of perception in which the experience of power and otherness are combined, and in which the notion of efficacy dominates. This power originates and causes events; it is thus fundamentally creative.

Van der Leeuw quickly finds the traditional language of scholarship to be misleading, since it improperly distinguishes religion and magic at this elemental level:

> It is precisely a characteristic of the earliest thinking that it does not exactly distinguish the magical, and all that borders on the supernatural, from the powerful; to the primitive mind, in fact, all marked "efficiency" is *per se* magical, and "sorcery" *eo ipso* mighty. . . . Magic is certainly manifested by power; to employ power, however, is not in itself to act magically, although every extraordinary action of primitive man possesses a tinge of the magical. (ibid., pp. 24–25)

Although he often calls this elemental level of religiosity "primitive," he rejects the hypothesis that it exists as a stage in religious evolution. For him, the term designates a level of thought and experience that is found, to a degree, in all religions at all times. Further, van der Leeuw considers the notion of an ordering power, or sacred order, as in the Sanskrit *ṛta* or the Chinese *tao,* to be theories about power as advanced as the notion of an individual soul as a personal center of power.

Van der Leeuw interprets taboo as perhaps the most elemental reaction to the experience of sacred power: one is characteristically fearful in the face of the disparity of power, and taboo is an attempt to mount some defense against it. Indeed, he derives the Roman *religio* from an experience of dread. Thus religion for the Romans was a system of taboos set up in response to the awesome appearance of sacred power. "Observance," he writes, "is just benumbed awe which, at any moment, can be revived" (ibid., p. 50).

The entire first part of *Religion in Essence and Manifestation* is a long essay demonstrating that the notion of power is the key to understanding a wide variety of religious phenomena. For example, celestial symbols are an important part of many religions because they manifest cosmic power in such a way that humans can model their behavior upon the orderly motions of heavenly bodies, thus tapping their great power. Again, animal cults and totemism van der Leeuw explains as an attempt by humans to obtain for themselves the powers that animals control by virtue of their superior strength and skills, such as the ability to fly. The totem animal is especially significant in this regard because it "is a sort of reservoir for the potency of the tribe or clan" (ibid., p. 79). Angels represent a projection or emanation (they are "messengers") of specific powers of gods; sacred kingship is a recognition that the power of the most powerful man is, in part, sacred power, while belief in salvation implies faith in an extraordinary power of transformation.

Part 2 of this work takes up the reaction to sacred power as apprehended within: that is, the effect of the experience of power on human lives. Here religious functionaries, such as priest or shaman, are discussed, as well as the transformed life of the saint. Finally, religious organization, the social reaction to power, is sketched out.

Further description of van der Leeuw's work must founder because of his own interpretation of the phenomenological task: he eschewed any conscious hermeneutic or theory of religion as false to the data. Thus his work cannot be neatly summed up by reference to a relatively simple theoretical model. But in much of his work, the basic experience of power functions as much as a heuristic device as a basic insight into the nature of religion.

Another scholar who has influenced the notion of religious power held by students of religion in recent years is Georges Dumézil, who sought to develop some structural tools for dealing not with all religions but with that large class of religions known to have been derived from Indo-European cultures. His fundamental thesis is that the gods of Indo-European peoples reflect, and in turn are reflected in, the social structure of a given culture. This structure, in three main divisions, can be described in terms of the functions, or typical activities, performed by the gods or social classes in question. Although this thesis has far-reaching implications, most important for present purposes is the fact that in many cultures, most clearly in ancient India in the Vedic literature, these functions, in turn, seem to be based upon different concepts of power. Thus, because the concerns of the third-function gods are fecundity and productivity in the terrestrial sphere, they possess a special power or energy that controls and thus either promotes or inhibits the growth of herds or the abundance of harvests. This power was often thought of as sexual in nature.

But it is in the second and first functions, as Dumézil defined them, that differences in the basic nature of power become most apparent. Here he distinguishes sharply between the mysterious, hidden, even magical, power of the first-function gods and the merely physical power wielded by the gods of the second function. The second function belongs to the warrior, in India especially to Indra, who slew the cosmic demon Vṛtra, and who was the protector of the Aryan tribes and the leader of the human warriors. Indeed, so important did this physical power become that there is evidence in the *Ṛgveda* that Indra to some extent replaced Varuṇa, the primary first-function god. Varuṇa and Mitra together are the representative of the function of sovereignty, whose position at the apex of the hierarchy of gods and humans was, originally at least, assured by the power they wielded. The first function Dumézil characterizes in general as celestial, priestly, and concerned with the exercise of magical and juridical sovereignty. Varuṇa especially is "a great sorcerer, disposed more than any other on the level of sovereignty to *māyā*, magic which creates forms either temporary or permanent, disposed also to the knots in which he binds the guilty, a capture both immediate and irresistible" (Dumézil, 1968–1973, vol. 1, p. 148).

Coupled both to the characteristic celestial symbolism and to the idea of mysterious power is the association of Varuṇa and Mitra with the cosmic order, *ṛta*. Increasingly subservient to this impersonal order, the first-function gods nonetheless reflect and to a degree wield the very power by which the cosmos moves. This dynamism was especially impressive because the means of its motion was unseen: just as the stars or the sun followed their preordained courses; just as the seasons followed their patterns and other events such as disease occurred as punishments whose agents or mechanism, so to speak, could not be discovered by means of the ordinary senses; just so did the sovereign gods control the very power by which the world was ordered and by which its order was maintained. Physical power, the power of Indra and of war, could be understood, if not always defended against. Even the enormous physical power of a god was still physical and palpable, and therefore of a fundamentally different nature than was *māyā*, the unseen and all the more frightening power of Varuṇa.

In the human realm, according to Dumézil's thesis, the social structure also reflected these different types of power. Of course it is the brahman caste, the hereditary priests, who wield Varuṇa's power, to some degree, because of their knowledge of the rites of sacrifice. In the cult, the priests function as mediators of sovereign sacred power: the words and actions of the rituals place in the priestly hands this same mysterious power, which is the power to influence cosmic forces for the benefit of humans.

Although Dumézil's point of departure is the Vedic texts of India, he applies this schema also to later Indian epics as well as to Persian, Greek, and other European religious literature. Beyond this, other scholars have sought to extend the three function theory to non-Indo-European cultures as well. Most notable of these, perhaps, is Atsuhiko Yoshida, whose "La mythologie japonaise: Essai d'interpretation structurale" (1961–1963) is the most thorough attempt to apply these categories not so much in order to show Indo-European influences upon Japanese mythology but as a useful interpretive tool.

Power, Magic, and Charisma. The use of the term *magic* has had a checkered career, both within Christian theological circles and within the realm of comparative religion or history of religions *(Religionswissenschaft)*. On the one hand, it has shared the pejorative connotations of such terms as *superstition* and *idolatry* in its emic or confessional evaluation; on the other hand, as evidenced by such compounds as *magico-religious*, from the etic viewpoint the term has been used in a purely descriptive way, as, for example, in the work of Arnold van Gennep, noted above. From this latter perspective, magic denotes simply sacred power experienced as impersonal and, to a degree, manipulatable: it is power in its most useful mode, since it can be turned to one's advantage with what we might call a minimum of harmful side effects. Providing only that the formulae and rituals are properly followed, results are predictable, even automatic. For many theologically inclined thinkers, this notion, and even more the attitude toward the sacred that it implies, must necessarily be a "lower" form of religion, or degenerate religion—or perhaps not religion at all. This is because it is felt to be incompatible with the proper sense of reverence and dependence due to a personal god as in Christianity or Judaism. From this perspective, to treat God as an object of magic is to blaspheme since this tends to reduce the majesty and freedom of the deity.

The lack of consensus among scholars as to the proper definition and use of the term *magic* reflects not so much differences in perception as differences in the purposes to which the data are put. From the purely descriptive point of view, a distinction between magic and religion, or between magical religion and pure religion, has proved practically impossible to make. But from the normative, theological point of view, the term *magic* has proved too useful a term to be easily given up, since it delineates what is felt to be a theologically unacceptable attitude toward the power of God. Thus, even when a pejorative sense is not intended in descriptive works, it is often improperly assumed by many readers.

Examples of the difficulties that lie in wait for those who would distinguish between a manipulative approach to the sacred and a properly humble and propitiatory approach are easily produced. Subtle psychological distinctions must be made, since the existential concern of all religious people for their own welfare makes a totally unself-serving approach to sacred power improbable, if not impossible, for ordinary human beings. Put another way, we may ask how often Christians pray for forgiveness of sins out of nothing more than a pure and unselfish love of their god? Or again, rites of passage, which are ubiquitous, seek always a more or less definite personal or communal gain—but who can assess with complete certainty the motivation of the participants? Discounting "manipulativeness" can lead to a restriction of the term *religion* to such an extent that it is lost as a useful descriptive term.

Another conceptual tool relating to religious power is *charisma*, a term made popular by the sociologist of religion Max Weber (in *Religionssoziologie*, 1922), who defined it as the authority by which individuals were accorded status and power over others or, related to that, by which the functions or offices themselves—regardless of the officeholder—were felt to be worthy of respect. Indeed, Weber expressly linked charisma both to *mana* and to the Iranian *maga* (Skt., *māyā*), from which our word *magic* is derived. Looked at closely, it may be seen that the notion of charisma, at least from the limited horizon of sociology, is rather mysterious. That is to say, the reason or means whereby one person is accorded this respect, or is seen as having a special inner power of attraction, is not explained or well understood. Certainly such things as character, unusual skills, great stature or strength, or force of mien or manner all seem to contribute, but, finally, *charisma* remains a relational term that classifies the reaction of others to the person whom scholars then label as charismatic.

The Chinese religious tradition offers a concrete example of belief in charisma, and even of theorizing about it within two ancient systems of thought, namely, Confucianism and Taoism. These two religions, although often antagonistic, nonetheless share a common origin and a number of common ideas. Two are especially relevant here: *tao*, or cosmic order, and *te*, variously translated as "virtue," "character," "power," or "charisma." It is possible to view these two concepts not only as closely associated in Chinese thought but as two aspects of a single reality: sacred power. *Tao* is in many ways similar to the Sanskrit *ṛta*, in that it is not only order but also the power that drives a dynamic universe. All things ultimately derive from *tao* (Lao-tzu appropriately calls it "the mother of all things"), and all things move and change according to its "laws." To be sure, it is not entirely knowable, although Confucianism is more optimistic on this point, with its emphasis on study of the way of the ancients and its belief that *tao* is perfectly embodied in *li* (ritual or decorum).

When *tao* is perfectly embodied in a person, then he is called a sage. Such a one is as perfect an exemplar of the universal *tao* as a human being can be. To be a sage is to be perfectly in harmony with *tao*. But taken from the point of view of the individual, such a one has great *te* or personal power. This power, like *tao*, although it may be embodied in a person, is not in itself personal: it is without consciousness, or will, or emotion; it has no purpose. The intrinsic power of a sage is expressed, both in Confucianism and in Taoism, in the image of the sage-king Shun, who "acted without action"—yet all things were accomplished, and the empire was at peace.

Shun is also likened to the pole star, which merely sits facing south, while all things revolve around it in a kind of cosmic ballet.

This *te* or charisma is brought down to earth, as it were, in the Confucian ideal of the *chün-tzu*, the "superior man" or "true gentleman," who also brings about by example, by ritual, and by the power of his presence the longed-for proper ordering of human society. It is not, of course, that he does nothing; rather, he is so well attuned to *tao* (or to "heaven," *t'ien*) that whatever he chooses to do will be the correct thing in the circumstances. When such a person is a ruler, or, one might say after Weber, when charisma of person is combined with charisma of office, one has an especially powerful force for harmony. Interestingly, however, even here, at least in the more mystical Taoist writings, a sage does not will the right, does not arrive by careful thought or logical deduction at the right course of action; rather, because he is a sage, such action will spontaneously occur, sometimes with the sage as direct agent, but sometimes at the hands of others mysteriously influenced by him.

This mysteriously acting power, action at a distance and without conscious will, sounds in many ways like the Vedic *māyā*. It is sacred power, at work in the human world, that reflects and ultimately is one with the sacred power that underlies all activity in the world of nature.

Is such a belief crude magic, or perhaps mere superstition? Some would answer in the affirmative. Certainly it insists upon the impersonal nature of the sacred and of the workings of sacred power. And the will to manipulate this power to benefit self, or the society as a whole, is strong, especially in Confucianism. Yet there is also awe and reverence for the power: it is difficult to gain, and it has its own ways. Others would claim that this example shows the impossibility of separating magic and religion, that they are inextricably merged into the idea of sacred power and into the active responses of human beings as they have perceived that power over the millennia of religious history.

[*See also* Sacred and the Profane, The; Magic; *and the biographies of the principal scholars mentioned herein.*]

BIBLIOGRAPHY

Codrington, R. H. *The Melanesians: Studies in Their Anthropology and Folklore* (1891). New Haven, 1957.

Dumézil, Georges. *L'ideologie tripartie des Indo-Européens.* Brussels, 1958.

Dumézil, Georges. *Mythe et epopée.* 3 vols. Paris, 1968–1973.

Eliade, Mircea. *Cosmos and History: The Myth of the Eternal Return* (1949). New York, 1959.

Eliade, Mircea. *Shamanism: Archaic Techniques of Ecstasy* (1951). Rev. & enl. ed. New York, 1964.

Eliade, Mircea. *Yoga: Immortality and Freedom* (1954). 2d ed., rev. & enl. Princeton, 1969.

Eliade, Mircea. *The Sacred and the Profane* (1957). New York, 1959.

Eliade, Mircea. *Patterns in Comparative Religion.* New York, 1958.

Eliade, Mircea. *Rites and Symbols of Initiation: The Mysteries of Birth and Rebirth* (1958). New York, 1975.

Gennep, Arnold van. *The Rites of Passage* (1909). Chicago, 1960.

Hewitt, J. N. B. "Orenda and a Definition of Religion." *American Anthropologist* 4 (1902): 33–46.

Jensen, Adolf E. *Myth and Cult among Primitive Peoples* (1951). Chicago, 1963.

Jung, C. G. "The Psychology of the Unconscious" (1943). In *The Collected Works of C. G. Jung,* vol. 7. Princeton, 1953.

Leeuw, Gerardus van der. *Phänomenologie der Religion.* Tübingen, 1933. Translated by J. E. Turner as *Religion in Essence and Manifestation,* 2 vols. (1938; reprint, Gloucester, Mass., 1967).

Marett, R. R. "Pre-animistic Religion." *Folklore* 11 (1900): 162–182.

Marett, R. R. *The Threshold of Religion.* London, 1909.

Otto, Rudolf. *Das Heilige.* Breslau, 1917. Translated by John W. Harvey as *The Idea of the Holy* (1923; 2d ed., London, 1960).

Tylor, E. B. *Primitive Culture* (1871). 2 vols. New York, 1970.

Vries, Jan de. *The Study of Religion.* New York, 1967.

Wach, Joachim. *Sociology of Religion* (1944). Chicago, 1962.

Weber, Max. *Religionssoziologie.* Tübingen, 1922. Translated by Ephraim Fischoff as *The Sociology of Religion* (Boston, 1963).

Yoshida, Atsuhiko. "La mythologie japonaise: Essai d'interpretation structural." *Revue de l'histoire des religions* 160 (1961): 47–66; 161 (1962): 25–44; and 163 (1963): 225–248.

Yoshido, Atsuhiko. "Nihon shinwa to In-o shinwa." In *Nihon shinwa no hikaku kenkyu,* edited by Obayashi Taryo. Tokyo, 1974.

ALAN L. MILLER

PRAJĀPATI belongs to the powerful ritual center of Vedic traditions and their discourses known as the Brāhmaṇas, where he is the supreme being and father of the gods. He is the link between the ancient Puruṣa mythology that instituted sacrifice, on the one hand, and the late Vedic bifurcation into a metaphysics of the impersonal Absolute *(brahman)* and the personal god Brahmā, on the other. In the religious history of South Asia, cosmogony, sacrifice, the soma cult, asceticism and self-mortification, the concept of salvation, the ritualization of procreation, and the advisory role of the grandfather of the gods are all dependent to a significant degree on the various guises of Prajāpati.

As lord *(pati)* of creatures *(prajā),* Prajāpati is best known in the tenth book of the *Ṛgveda* through speculations about the creation of the world. Identified there with several cosmogonic motifs, he is later associated in the Brāhmaṇas more precisely with Puruṣa, thereby assuring his preeminence in the sacrificial drama of creative transformations through self-sacrifice. Like Puruṣa projecting himself sacrificially into world being (*Ṛgveda* 10.90), Prajāpati is said in the Brāhmaṇas to have sacrificed himself in the exhausting fervor of ascetic and erotic heat *(tapas)*, the cosmic result being, first, *brahman*, the sacred verbal power, and then the various components of creation, including gods and humans (see, e.g., *Śatapatha Brāhmaṇa* 6.1.1.8ff.). Elsewhere, he himself is regarded as the result of *tapas*. A constant theme in these discourses is the human necessity of repeating the exemplary primordial event by reintegrating all the space, time, and being that the Puruṣa-Prajāpati sacrificial victim, dispersed into manifestation, represents. The Vedic *śrauta* ritual known as the Agnicayana became one of the major expressions of this Brahmanic doctrine of sacrifice: by identifying Agni as Prajāpati, the ceremonial installation of fire *(agni)* was advanced to a soteriology. A yearlong procedure systematically reconstituted the world as a five-layered altar, its fire-center-heart being the recovered *ātman* ("self") not only of Prajāpati but also of his human correspondent, the sacrificer *(yajamāna)*. Another great *śrauta* ritual was the Vājapeya, the "drink of strength," a *soma* ceremony in which the mystical totality of Prajāpati and the power of the number seventeen were realized. By entering such ritually produced correspondences as these, the sacrificer was able to avoid repeated death *(punarmṛtyu)*. This ideology prefigured the later Upaniṣadic notion of *ātman-brahman* equivalence and of spiritual liberation obtained not by ritual but by intuitive knowledge.

Prajāpati's control over human and animal reproductive energies assured him the same prominence in the domestic ritual, mythology, and folklore that he gained in the texts for the great cosmic ceremonies. *Ṛgveda* 10.121, a hymn of creation addressed to the "golden germ" *(hiraṇyagarbha)*, identified Prajāpati as the "fiery seed" within the cosmic waters. The images of seed, egg, embryo, and parturition continued into the *Atharvaveda* and the Gṛhyasūtras that became manuals for such life-cycle rites (*saṃskāras*) as marriage, impregnation, production of a male, safe delivery, first feeding, and first tonsure. Prajāpati was also included as one of certain male figures surrounded by four feminine powers in gestation symbolism.

Prajāpati has numerous zoomorphic expressions, some of them evidently archaic. The boar, Emūṣa, is identified with him in the mythology of the cosmic earth diver, the creature that descends to procure a fragment or prototype of earth-world, as are two creatures prominent in the Agnicayana, the bird and the tortoise (all three perpetuated in later Hindu Vaiṣṇava myths). The goat, bull, cow, horse, stag, ant, and other animals are also drawn into Prajāpati's orbit of symbols. Vedic deities linked with Prajāpati include Vāyu, Varuṇa, Dakṣa, Vāc, and, in an incestuous theme, his daughter Uṣas. In the post-Vedic texts, Brahmā absorbs his character as Hiraṇyagarbha, and the Prajāpatis are, variously, the ten or seven spiritual sons of Brahmā.

[*See also* Agni.]

BIBLIOGRAPHY

The clearest, most concise explication of Prajāpati in the myth-ritual speculation of the Brāhmaṇas is Mircea Eliade's *A History of Religious Ideas*, vol. 1 (Chicago, 1978), pp. 223–235. On Prajāpati in the Agnicayana ritual and theology, see Frits Staal's *Agni: The Vedic Ritual of the Fire Altar*, vol. 1 (Berkeley, 1983), chapters 4 and 5, especially pages 65ff. (on Śāṇḍilya's teaching in the *Śatapatha Brāhmaṇa*), 115ff., and 159ff. The popular (i.e., nonpriestly) traditions of Prajāpati outside the sacrificial cult are illuminated in Jan Gonda's "The Popular Prajāpati," *History of Religions* 22 (1982): 129–149. All three authors point to the archaic rather than the late Ṛgvedic character of Prajāpati; only Staal suggests an indigenous Indian origin.

David M. Knipe

PRAJÑĀ. The Sanskrit term *prajñā* (Pali, *paññā;* Tib., *shes rab*), variously translated as "wisdom, gnosis, insight," or "intuitive knowledge," is central to all Buddhist traditions, imparting unity to them as well as serving to distinguish them from other philosophical and religious systems. *Prajñā* is primarily understood as a complete comprehension of the nature and aspects of phenomenal existence *(saṃsāra)*, the forces that govern it, the method of becoming free from it, and the reality that stands beyond it. Although the notion has been expounded in a variety of ways by Buddhist thinkers, it serves for them all as an intellectual and spiritual faculty that imparts a correct grasp of Buddhist teachings, guides and perfects the spiritual life, imbues it with a sense of direction, and brings it to maturation.

Early Buddhist scriptures record that Śākyamuni Buddha frequently explained to his followers how, during his striving toward enlightenment, he mastered the four consecutive stages of mental concentration *(dhyāna)* and gained knowledge of his previous lives, knowledge of the past and future lives of other people, and knowledge of the destruction of the depravities *(āsrava)*. Awakening to this threefold knowledge was considered by early Buddhist thinkers as the factor fundamental to the transformation of the practitioner into an *arhat*. One becomes an *arhat* by mastering these three kinds of knowledge, but it is the knowledge of the destruction and elimination of the depravities that possesses the decisive and essential power to bring final deliverance. [*See* Arhat.]

The standard code of religious training for the early disciples (*śrāvakas*) comprised a trilogy of morality *(śīla)*, meditation *(samādhi)*, and wisdom *(prajñā)*. Through the practice of morality, it was held, one becomes purified, perceptive, and mindful, and thus prepares and develops the ground for meditation. Being mindful, one is able to control the senses, thus conducing to the practice of meditation, through which the mind becomes purged of the five "hindrances" *(nīvaraṇa)*. In the course of well-developed meditational techniques one becomes able to pursue the four consecutive stages of mental concentration *(dhyāna)*. Skill in practicing these concentrations leads to gaining and perfecting the threefold knowledge. That is, one first applies one's thought to the knowledge of one's own former lives; second, one directs the mind to the knowledge of the demise and rebirth of other people; and third, one gains the knowledge of the destruction of the depravities. The third knowledge is the most important, for it contains the penetrating and comprehensive insight into phenomenal existence and thus brings final deliverance. Once this knowledge is acquired, an intrinsic understanding of the sorrow and impermanence of *saṃsāra*, its cause, the means of pacifying it, and the path that leads to its elimination is intuitively gained. Being endowed with such knowledge, one's mind becomes free from the four depravities—sensual desire, attachment to life, wrong views and opinions, and ignorance. One understands perfectly that birth is destroyed, that religious aspirations are accomplished, and that there remains nothing more to be strived for or achieved. One has thus reached the state of *prajñā*, which endows *arhat* status on the practitioner.

The threefold knowledge comprised within *prajñā* is often grouped together with three other kinds of knowledge, that of magical feats, intuitive hearing, and clairvoyance. Within this set of six knowledges, jointly known as the six "superknowings" *(ṣaḍabhijñā)*, the first five are regarded as spiritual and psychic endowments and the sixth, the knowledge of the destruction of the depravities, as an inherent function of the mind in its purified state. *Prajñā* stands both at the beginning of the path of spiritual purification and at its final stage. The practice of morality and meditation alone, although indispensable, cannot bring about the realization of the final goal. It is *prajñā* that imparts unity, perfects virtues, and provides the guidance toward the goal, thus bringing its realization. Its presence at the initial stages of religious striving is not fully apparent or understood, but in spite of its being obscured by impurities and imperfections, *prajñā* is active as the controlling factor throughout the religious career of the practitioner. It grows and unfolds with the gradual purification and perfection of human personality. In Buddhaghosa's *Visuddhimagga* we have an excellent exposition of the gradual stages in which *prajñā* unfolds itself: the roots of *prajñā* are purity of morality and purity of the mind. Purity of morality is achieved through the observance of monastic rules, through correct living, and through control of the senses; purity of the mind is attained through meditational practices. The foundation of *prajñā* lies in correct comprehension of, and acquaintance with, the aggregates (*skandhas*), the elements of existence (*dharmas*), the twenty-two faculties (*indriyas*), the causal nexus of dependent origination *(pratītya-samutpāda)*, and the Four Noble Truths *(āryasatya)*. The inherent quality of *prajñā* consists of a perfect and thorough comprehension of the various categories and aspects of phenomenal existence and the comprehension of the correct path of liberation.

In Vasubandhu's *Abhidharmakośa* the attainment of the immaculate and perfect *prajñā* is said to be a process of gradual purification of impure *prajñā*s that are inborn and natural to the human personality. The accumulation of *prajñā* can be achieved in three ways: through listening to Buddhist teachings, through mental reflection, and through contemplation. The elements (*dharmas*) of existence are here divided into two groups, conditioned *(saṃskṛta)* and unconditioned *(asaṃskṛta)*; the unconditioned elements are further divided into space *(ākāśa)*, emancipation through discerning knowledge *(pratisaṃkhyānirodha)*, and emancipation through nondiscerning knowledge *(apratisaṃkhyānirodha)*. These three elements are considered to be unchanging, pure, and timeless. Discerning knowledge *(pratisaṃkhyā)* refers to a pure *prajñā* of transcendental order that brings the destruction of all desire and imperfection and that is thus viewed as synonymous with *nirvāṇa*. Within the division of the elements into the twenty-two faculties (*indriyas*), *prajñā* is listed among the five moral faculties, along with faith, vigor, mindfulness, and meditation. These five faculties, together with the last three faculties of the group as a whole—namely, the knowledge of the unknown *(ajñātam ājñāsyāmi)*, the faculty of perfect knowledge *(ājñā)*, and the faculty of the "one who knows" *(ājñātāvī)*—are considered the predominant factors in the purification from worldly entanglements. These three faculties are unified by the common factor of *ājñā*, or perfect knowledge, which leads to the realization of the truths which are unrealized, uncomprehended, unknown, and unattainable.

One section of the *Abhidharmakośa* deals with an exposition of the ten kinds of correct knowledge *(jñāna)*. Within this group of ten, four relate to the Four Noble Truths (the knowledge of suffering, the knowledge of its origin, the knowledge of its cessation, and the knowledge of the Eightfold Path), further analyzed into sixteen characteristics as enumerated here: The truth of suffering is the knowledge of impermanence, pain, sorrow, and nonexistence of self *(anātmya)*. The second truth is the knowledge that understands the cause, origin, successive evolvements, and terminal effects of the causal nexus that is the empirical person. The third truth is the knowledge of the abolition of the impure *skandhas*, of calming the three poisons (ignorance, hatred, and desire), of the absence of pain, and of the presence of freedom. The fourth truth is the knowledge characterized by the correct path, the requisite resources, the potential attainment of *nirvāṇa*, and the departure into it. The notion of *prajñā* comprehends all these sixteen characteristics of the Four Knowledges. [*See also* Four Noble Truths *and* Dharma, *article on* Buddhist Dharma and Dharmas.]

Many Mahāyāna Buddhist texts, in particular the Prajñāpāramitā Sūtras and the important commentaries on them, deal in great detail with the exposition of *prajñā*. *Prajñāpāramitā*, or "perfection of wisdom," is seen as the essence of all wisdom and knowledge. It is explained from various angles and approaches, often through the use of figurative descriptions, dialogues, and similes. Perfection of wisdom, expounded and praised as the highest value and goal of human aspirations, is proclaimed as the mother of all the Buddhas and becomes personified as the goddess Prajñāpāramitā. Within the newly construed concepts of cosmic Buddhahood, the theory of the three Buddha bodies *(trikāya)*, and the philosophical exposition of "emptiness" *(śūnyatā)* as an identity or nonduality of conditioned existence *(saṃsāra)* and unconditioned reality *(nirvāṇa)*, *prajñā* receives a much broader and deeper interpretation than it did in the early stages of Buddhist thought. There, its role and function, although fully recognized, were somewhat overshadowed, insofar as *prajñā* was viewed almost exclusively as a tool for gaining individual deliverance, as exemplified in the idea of arhatship.

In the Mahāyāna one strives for supreme wisdom and perfect enlightenment in order to share these gifts with all living beings by guiding them on the path toward this state. Acquisition of, and abode within, perfect wisdom becomes the primary goal. The focus of the Prajñāpāramitā teachings is on the penetration into the true sense of things by metaphysical discernment and by appropriate moral conduct, as advocated by the *bodhisattva* ideal. A *bodhisattva*, out of compassion *(karuṇā)* for all living beings, pursues the path of the *pāramitās* ("perfections") in order to gain the supreme enlightenment, which he wishes to impart to others. The philosophical tenets of the Prajñāpāramitā teachings are a further development of the earlier teachings. First, one must acquire the wisdom of understanding the nonexistence, or emptiness, of self and of the elements of existence. By making the distinction between the conditioned and unconditioned elements—and through the comprehension of the conditioned elements as empty, impermanent, and as repositories of unhappiness—one acquires the wisdom of knowing that they are not worth pursuing, adhering to, or striving for. The next step leads to considering the unconditioned elements characteristic of *nirvāṇa* as also being empty insofar as they are devoid of any identification with the conditioned elements of existence and with anything that concerns one's life. Having reached this stage of wisdom, the perception of the emptiness of both the conditioned and unconditioned elements, one advances to the next stage of perfect wisdom, through which one is able to identify the conditioned *(saṃsāra)* and the unconditioned *(nirvāṇa)* with the aim of transcending both their common identity, characterized by emptiness, and their inherent differences. Once one considers them as being without any real distinction one reaches a state of transcendent nonduality in which all opposites—negation and affirmation, *saṃsāra* and *nirvāṇa*—are identified and comprised within the notion of emptiness.

This speculative process, realized through meditation and moral purification, brings about the realization of supreme and perfect wisdom. The path toward that realization is demonstrated by the *bodhisattva*'s career. A *bodhisattva*'s striving for supreme enlightenment follows the unique course of practicing six or ten "perfections." He also practices the thirty-seven principles conducive to enlightenment *(bodhipakṣā dharma)* practiced by an *arhat*, but it is the practice of the perfections that dominates all his activities and occupies the central position in his spiritual journey. By means of perfect wisdom he gains the correct understanding of the true nature of reality and of the very means *(upāya)* that he can employ for the benefit of others; concurrently, he surpasses and transcends the categories of *saṃsāra* through his wisdom. Thus, through his compassion he remains in *saṃsāra* and pursues the cause of living beings; through his perfect wisdom he abides in the sphere of *nirvāṇa*. [*See also* Bodhisattva Path; Upāya; *and* Karuṇā.]

There is an inherent relationship between perfect wisdom and all the other perfections. The other perfections bring spiritual purification and progress and provide the ground for perfect wisdom to grow and to reach its fullness. Without them, perfect wisdom can neither be fully developed nor attained. On the other hand, perfect wisdom accompanies, guides, and elevates the other perfections to the status of being truly perfections. On their own the other perfections can bring positive results within the world of *saṃsāra,* but they cannot lead beyond it. Thus, their elevation from the sphere of *saṃsāra,* within which they are practiced, is facilitated by perfect wisdom. The harmonious growth and development of all the perfections leads to spiritual maturation and to the acquisition of perfect wisdom, which coincides with enlightenment. [*See also* Pāramitās.]

Using his dialectical method, Nāgārjuna (c. 150–250), the chief exponent of the Mādhyamika philosophy, demonstrated that through conceptual constructions *(vikalpa)* we perceive reality as phenomenal existence. By stripping away all thought constructions we arrive at the perception of absolute reality, which Nāgārjuna defined in a negative way as "emptiness" *(śūnyatā).* According to him, conceptual constructions are motivated by ignorance *(avidyā),* and the process of unveiling the true reality is activated by *prajñā* and compassion. He applied the term *emptiness* to both phenomenal existence and absolute reality. Phenomenal existence is emptiness as it does not possess a true nature of its own *(niḥsvabhāva);* absolute reality is also emptiness in that it is devoid of all conceptual distinctions, since the comprehension and realization of absolute reality escapes and transcends all intellectual categories. Its realization can only be achieved through the intellectual and spiritual intuition represented by *prajñā. Prajñā* as free of all concepts and speculations coincides with the absolute reality as defined by emptiness. As an intuition of the absolute reality, where all knowledge and the absolute coincide, *prajñā* penetrates into the absolute and views it without making distinctions or differentiations that conceptual thinking entails. It simply views the absolute just as it is. *Prajñā* is not the same as an intuition resulting from empirical perception or from discursive thinking; it is an intuitive insight into total reality and thus is described as infinite, inexpressible, universal, and unfathomable. [*See also* Śūnyam and Śūnyatā.]

In the Vijñānavāda school, *prajñā* coincides with supreme truth *(paramārtha);* as unobstructed and lucid knowledge it comprises everything that can be known *(sarvajñeyānāvaraṇajñāna).* It implies the correct comprehension of Buddhist teachings, the correct vision of the path, and the knowledge of all intellectual categories and appropriate conduct. It is neither thought nor lack of thought; it does not think but springs naturally from thought. Its object is the inexpressible and indescribable nature of things. It is free of any characteristics, as it is inherent and manifest in its object of cognition. As an unconstrued knowledge *(nirvikalpajñāna),* it stands beyond all mental categories and constructions. It does not make up the description of reality or the destruction of consciousness. It is nonconceptual and free of reflection. It is intuitive, born spontaneously, and surpasses all kinds of ordinary and mundane knowledge. *Prajñā* as the perfect wisdom in all its aspects is the knowledge of the absolute reality *(tathatā).* [*See* Tathatā.]

The Tantras, following the philosophical assumptions of the Mādhyamika school, assert the basic unity of *nirvāṇa* and *saṃsāra.* The purpose of different kinds of Tantric practices is to eliminate the apparent duality of these two entities, which are wrongly conceived as dual because of defilements and lack of knowledge. The sphere of knowledge and understanding of nonduality between these two is perceived in *nirvāṇa,* the chief force and attribute of which is constituted by wisdom *(prajñā).* In Tantric meditation and ritual performances wisdom is explicitly identified with *nirvāṇa* and means *(upāya)* with *saṃsāra.* The highest truth as mystical experience is described in the Tantras as the union or mingling of wisdom and means. In ritual and meditational practices, wisdom is symbolized by a bell, a lotus, or a sun, as well as by the vowels. In yogic practices involving a female partner, wisdom is identified with a *yoginī.* In the union of wisdom and means, it is wisdom that plays a dominant role, for although it is unattainable without means, it embraces the highest truth of emptiness. In Tantric texts wisdom is frequently named Nairātmyā ("absence of selfhood"), and it is with her that a Tantric practitioner, as means, attempts to become united. Wisdom is mostly characterized as having a female aspect, but it also appears under a masculine aspect, symbolized by a *vajra,* an epitome of the perfect and indestructible truth. Buddha Vairocana and any other Buddha of the Tantras comprehend within them the whole truth and wisdom just as much as does the goddess Prajñāpāramitā or Nairātmyā. In such cases, the Tantric goddess is made to transmute into the male deity. In yogic practices with a female partner, it is the *yogin* who is absorbed into wisdom. [*See also* Buddhism, Schools of, *article on* Esoteric Buddhism.]

Comparing *prajñā* with *jñāna,* one can make the following observations. *Prajñā* is a religious term that at once encompasses both knowledge and deliverance. Within the context of worldly existence permeated by ignorance, *prajñā* comprehends false notions and leads away from everything that binds one to this world. *Prajñā* is a spiritual realization gained through correct knowledge and moral purification. Buddhist thinkers of all times refrained from categorizing *prajñā* in the same way as they did *jñāna*. *Prajñā* was always seen as being beyond the categories of knowledge and as being born naturally within a fully perfected practitioner; *jñāna*, on the other hand, was categorized and graded from that of ordinary empirical knowledge to the level of the highest and transcendent knowledge. From the scholarly approach it is possible to make clear distinctions between the highest levels of knowledge, often described as being intuitive, and *prajñā;* doing so is difficult, though, because these notions very often overlap and coincide. The correct assessment of their relationship should be sought, perhaps, in seeing the acquisition of knowledge as an important and necessary factor that, along with meditation, induces the presence of *prajñā*. [*See also* Jñāna.]

In the early phases of the Mahāyāna, compassion and wisdom are given equal status. However, at some stage in the Buddhist writings wisdom assumed a dominant role. Mañjuśrī, as a manifestation of wisdom, became frequently invoked and praised. The glorification of wisdom reached its climax in the Prajñāpāramitā and Mādhyamika literature, in which *prajñā* is constantly praised and extolled while *karuṇa* is seldom mentioned. During the later phase of the Mahāyāna a reverse process occurred. Compassion became more emphasized, and Avalokiteśvara, as its manifestation, assumed a predominant position, overshadowing other *bodhisattvas* and even the Buddhas. Despite extreme tendencies in literary works, in iconography, and in practice, the tradition has always recognized that proper balance between compassion and wisdom must be retained, for it is the practice of both that brings enlightenment. Compassion as the basis for enlightenment is not a simple feeling of pity but an application of appropriate practical means *(upāya)* that lead toward the realization of the final goal. The employment of different means (such as the practice of the Perfections—giving, morality, etc.) and *prajñā* always go together. *Prajñā* cannot be fully realized without *upāya;* in turn, *upāya* cannot ascend beyond the worldly existence without *prajñā*.

[*See also* Nirvāṇa; Indian Philosophies; *and* Buddhist Philosophy. *For a cross-cultural perspective, see* Wisdom.]

BIBLIOGRAPHY

In the early Buddhist scriptures *prajñā* is dealt with in many passages in the four Nikāyas, but the most comprehensive and condensed expositions are found in later writings, namely in Buddhaghosa's *Visuddhimagga*, translated by Pe Maung Tin under the title *The Path of Purity* (London, 1971), and in Vasubandhu's *Abhidharmakośa*, translated by Louis de La Vallée Poussin under the title *L'Abhidharmakośa de Vasubandhu*, 6 vols. (1923–1931; reprint, Brussels, 1971). Much reliable information and many references to the original sources can be found in I. B. Horner's *The Early Buddhist Theory of Man Perfected* (1936; reprint, London, 1975) and also in K. N. Jayatilleke's *Early Buddhist Theory of Knowledge* (London, 1963).

All the necessary information relevant to the Prajñāpāramitā literature is contained in Edward Conze's *The Prajñāpāramitā Literature* (The Hague, 1960; reprint, Tokyo, 1978). The most succinct exposition of *prajñāpāramitā* is contained in the shorter *sūtras*, and a translation of nineteen of them, including the *Vajracchedikā*, can be found in Conze's *The Short Prajñāpāramitā Texts* (London, 1973).

The *Mahāprajñāpāramitā Śāstra*, which contains a detailed exposition of *prajñā*, was translated into French from the Chinese translation of Kumārajīva by Étienne Lamotte as *Le traité de la grande vertu de sagesse*, 5 vols. (Louvain, 1944–1980). Asaṅga's *Mahāyānasaṃgraha*, which expounds the Yogācāra position, was also translated by Lamotte as *La somme du Grand Véhicule d'Asaṅga*, 2 vols. (Louvain, 1938–1939).

Other recommended works include T. R. V. Murti's *The Central Philosophy of Buddhism*, 2d ed. (London, 1955; reprint, London, 1970); Étienne Lamotte's *The Teaching of Vimalakīrti*, translated by Sara Boin (London, 1976), a translation of the *Vimalakīrtinirdeśa Sūtra;* Marion L. Matics's *Entering the Path of Enlightenment: The Bodhicaryāvatāra of the Buddhist Poet Śāntideva* (New York, 1970); Har Dayal's *The Bodhisattva Doctrine in Buddhist Sanskrit Literature* (London, 1932; reprint, Delhi, 1975); and David L. Snellgrove's *The Hevajra Tantra*, 2 vols. (London, 1959).

TADEUSZ SKORUPSKI

PRAKṚTI is a Sanskrit word meaning "nature, origin, progress." As a philosophical concept it refers to one of the two basic principles of the Sāṃkhya school, material nature, or materiality. Materiality, according to the Sāṃkhya school, is manifest and unmanifest. There are other specific terms for the designation of unmanifest materiality, such as *mūlaprakṛti* ("original materiality") or *pradhāna* ("main principle"). *Prakṛti*, however, is a term designating materiality in both its manifest and its unmanifest forms. The usage of this term dates back to the middle group of Upaniṣads, composed in the few centuries before the common era.

The concept of materiality is first seen in the Vedic creation myths. Although these myths vary, they all take as their starting point the existence of an original being, such as the "first man" (see, e.g., *Ṛgveda* 10.90). The subsequent development of the concept of *prakṛti* can be divided into two periods, a creative-formative period and a classical period.

The creative-formative period is well reflected in the Upaniṣads (from c. 900 BCE to the first centuries CE) and the *Mahābhārata* (composed between the fourth century

BCE and the fourth century CE). "The first being was alone, and it desired to be many." Such descriptions are numerous in the Upaniṣads. The being that wishes to multiply itself is known by several names: *puruṣa,* Prajāpati, *ātman,* and—a term of particular note—*mahān ātman.* This "large self" is unborn and yet it exists, as described in, for example, the *Bṛhadāraṇyaka Upaniṣad* 4.4.22. The *mahān ātman* next embodies itself in creation. This creation is an expansion of the self, and in its embodiment as creation the self is complete.

The self is aware of itself, as expressed in the phrases "I am!" or "I myself am this creation." This awareness initiates such processes as cognizing, perceiving, and so forth. The self cognizes as if it had different sense faculties. For example, it hears, although it does not have ears. The various processes that the awareness initiates gave ground to the distinction of the different principles (*tattvas*) as a result of an analysis that required a single function for a single principle.

The *Mokṣadharma,* the twelfth book of the *Mahābhārata,* calls the first-born the "large one." The "large one" is born on account of its knowledge. But the "large one" is not the only one to whom this function is ascribed. Similarly, here the *buddhi* (usually translated as "intellect") is considered the creator of the universe. The "large one" and the *buddhi* are two concepts that overlap from this time.

Such overlapping is prominent in the theory of the evolution of the universe as described in the *Mokṣadharma.* Here two cosmogonic patterns are presented. In one pattern, as typified by *Mokṣadharma* 187, the intellect *(buddhi)* exists in three *bhāvas,* later usually known as *guṇas* (constituents of materiality). In this pattern of evolution the sequence runs: intellect, then mind, then senses, and so on. The other pattern adds ego and places it between the intellect and the mind, whereby the sequence of evolution becomes intellect, then ego, then mind, and so forth. There is also a difference in how the three *bhāvas* relate to the intellect. In the first pattern, the three *bhāvas* are not inherent in the intellect; in the second pattern, the three *bhāvas* are "psychological" qualities of the individual beings.

The second period in the development of the concept of *prakṛti* is the classical period. The classical period found its expression in the Sāṃkhya classic, the *Sāṃkhyakārikā* of Īśvarakṛṣṇa (c. 350–550 CE). Both patterns of evolution are recorded in the *Sāṃkhyakārikā* (vv. 24–25). The first pattern is based on the ramification of ego. This ramification forms three distinct qualifications of ego which are also ascribed to the *guṇas.* In the early descriptions of the evolution theory, they are the three *bhāvas.*

A version of the second pattern, on the other hand, became the established pattern for the theory of evolution in the Sāṃkhya school (cf. *Sāṃkhyakārikā* 3 and 22). In this pattern, all principles (intellect, ego, etc.) emerge from the original unmanifest materiality. Evolution starts when intellect emerges from the original unmanifest materiality; this intellect produces ego. From ego several principles emerge: mind, the ten faculties (the five sense faculties and the five action faculties), and the subtle elements. From these subtle elements, the material elements emerge. Hence there are twenty-four principles of materiality. According to the Sāṃkhya school, materiality together with consciousness form the twenty-five principles that comprise the universe.

In both patterns of production, the transformation of the original materiality into twenty-three developed principles is explained by a relation of cause and effect. Since the various principles, which are simply different forms of the original unmanifest materiality, emerge from materiality, the original unmanifest materiality is understood as the cause of the produced principles that become its effects. Since the original materiality is unmanifest, it can be known only through its effects. This theory of causality relies on an effect that is already preexistent in the cause *(satkāryavāda),* just as yogurt is latent in milk.

Materiality is distinctly described in two ways, the original unmanifest and the manifest. The Sāṃkhya school postulates a pulsating universe, which means that creation and reabsorption follow one another; at the time of reabsorption, materiality is in a dormant and unmanifest state. During this time, the three *guṇas* are in a state of equilibrium. Upon the disturbance of the equilibrium, materiality starts to emerge in varying combinations of the three constituents.

The manifest materiality is characterized as being the opposite of consciousness in the *Sāṃkhyakārikā* 11. For example, materiality is caused, finite, spatial, active, composite, dependent, undifferentiated, productive, has a substratum, and is formed of three constituents. Although multiple in its transformations, it is only one. Since materiality is nonconscious, it is dependent on consciousness to make the experience of materiality conscious.

Prakṛti, in short, is one of the dual principles of the Sāṃkhya school that finds its origin in Vedic creation myths. Originally, however, the creation began with the first being, which eventually gave up its procreative function, bequeathing it to *prakṛti.* Thus *prakṛti* is always connected with the theory of the evolution of the universe.

[*The role of* prakṛti *within the specific context of classical Indian philosophy is discussed in* Sāṃkhya. For *dis-*

cussion of the ontological complement of prakṛti, *see* Puruṣa. *See also* Guṇas.]

BIBLIOGRAPHY

A detailed exploration of the origins of the concept *prakṛti* can be found in J. A. B. van Buitenen's three-part article "Studies in Sāṃkhya," *Journal of the American Oriental Society* 76 (July-September 1956): 153–157, 77 (January-March 1957): 15–25, and 77 (April–June 1957): 88–107. For a succinct study of the development of the concept *prakṛti* see J. A. B. van Buitenen's "The Large *Ātman*," *History of Religions* 4 (1964): 103–114. The most updated detailed study of the Sāṃkhya school is the forthcoming *Sāṃkhya: A Dualist Tradition in Indian Philosophy* by Gerald James Larson and Ram Shankar Bhattacharya, the third volume of the *Encyclopedia of Indian Philosophies*, edited by Karl H. Potter (Princeton and Delhi).

EDELTRAUD HARZER

PRALAYA, or doomsday in the Hindu eschatological scheme, comes at the end of the fourth and worst of the four ages, or *yuga*s, at the end of each *kalpa*, or day of Brahmā. The Purāṇas, which describe this process in great detail, differ as to the precise length of time that this process requires, but the scale is always astronomical, involving hundreds of thousands of years. At the end of the *kalpa*, the heat of the sun becomes so intense that it dries up the whole earth and sets the three worlds (heaven, earth, and the underworld) on fire; when they have been entirely consumed, enormous clouds appear and rain falls for hundreds of years, deluging the whole world until the waters inundate heaven and all is reduced to the primeval ocean of chaos. In anthropomorphic terms, this is the moment when Brahmā, whose waking moments or whose dream has been the source of the "emission" of the universe from his mind, falls into a deep, dreamless sleep inside the cosmic waters. And at the end of that sleep, at the end of the period of quiescence, the universe, or the consciousness of the god, is reborn once more out of the waters of chaos.

This circular pattern contains within it an infinite number of linear segments. For India, like Greece, developed a theory of four ages of declining goodness. Whereas the Greeks named these ages after metals, the Indians called them after throws of the dice, the first and best being the *kṛtayuga*, which is followed by the *tretā*, the *dvāpara*, and finally the present age, or the *kaliyuga*. The importance of the metaphor of dice is also manifest in the fact that the royal ceremony of consecration included a ritual dice game; in the second book of the *Mahābhārata*, King Yudhiṣṭhira loses his entire kingdom in a game of dice against an opponent whom he knows to be a cheat, thus inaugurating a period of exile that is also a part of the ritual of consecration. Moreover, as Madeleine Biardeau has convincingly argued, the catastrophic battle that ends the *Mahābhārata*, an Armageddon in which all the heroes as well as all the villains are killed, is a reenactment on the human level of the cosmic doomsday that is constantly alluded to in the epic. This human doomsday, like the big dice game in the sky, begins with Yudhiṣṭhira's unlucky loss and ends, inevitably, with the losing throw for mankind.

Yet the "end" that comes after the *kaliyuga* is not the end at all, but a new beginning; a new *kṛtayuga* will follow after the fallow interval. Moreover, there is a "seed" of mankind that survives doomsday to form the stock of the new race of men. Sometimes this seminal group is said to be the Seven Sages, whom Viṣṇu in the form of a fish saves from the cosmic flood; sometimes it is Manu, the ancestor of all mankind, and his family; sometimes it is an unspecified group of "good men" who resist the corruption that overtakes everyone else at the end of the *kaliyuga*, a group that retires to the forest to live in innocence while the cities of the plain drown in their own depravity. This "seed" functions on the macrocosmic level as a metaphor for the transmigrating soul on the microcosmic level, the *ātman* that leaps across the barrier between individual human death and rebirth, just as the good "seed" leaps across the barrier between one *pralaya* and the next cosmic emission, or *prasarga*. In the Vedantic mythology of the late Purāṇas, and in Indian literature in general, recurrent images of doomsday serve to emphasize the insubstantiality of the world; the things that we think of as permanent are constantly destroyed and recreated.

BIBLIOGRAPHY

A good introduction in English is provided by Hermann Jacobi's article on the "Ages of the World," in the *Encyclopaedia of Religion and Ethics*, edited by James Hastings, vol. 1 (Edinburgh, 1908). Details of the Sanskrit texts are cited in Willibald Kirfel's *Das Purāṇa Pañcalakṣaṇa* (Bonn, 1927), though without any useful interpretation. The classic discussion remains Mircea Eliade's "Time and Eternity in Indian Thought," in *Papers from the Eranos Yearbooks*, vol. 3, *Man and Time*, edited by Joseph Campbell (New York, 1957), pp. 173–200. A thoughtful and complex interpretation of the *pralaya* may be found in Madeleine Biardeau's *Études de mythologie hindoue* published in the *Bulletin de l'École Française d'Extrême Orient* (Paris, 1968, 1969, 1971, and 1976).

WENDY DONIGER O'FLAHERTY

PRĀṆA. The Sanskrit term *prāṇa* (from the conjunction of *pra* and *ana*, "breathing forth") can signify

(1) the Absolute *(brahman)* as the transcendental source of all life, (2) life in general, (3) the life force or "breath" of life in particular, (4) respiration, (5) air (in secular contexts only), and (6) the life organs (i.e., the five cognitive senses, the five conative senses, and the sense-related mind, or *manas*).

The third connotation is of special interest to the historian of religion, since it conveys a vibrant psychophysical reality (visible to the *yogin*) similar to the Greek *pneuma* and the Melanesian *mana*. In this sense, *prāṇa* is a creative force, defined in the *Yogavāsiṣṭha* (3.13.31 et passim) as the "vibratory energy" *(spanda-śakti)* that is responsible for all manifestation. Most metaphysical schools of India—one of the exceptions being Hīnayāna Buddhism—subscribe to this notion, although the details of interpretations differ.

In archaic Vedic thought, *prāṇa* is considered to be the "breath" of the macranthropos, the cosmic Puruṣa (e.g., *Ṛgveda* 10.90.13; *Atharvaveda* 11.4.15), and the breath or life force of the human body is regarded as a form of that all-pervading *prāṇa*. Later writers make a terminological distinction between the life force that interpenetrates the entire universe as a sort of subtle energy—called *mukhyaprāṇa* or "principal breath"—and the life force that sustains and animates the individual body-minds. *Prāṇa* in this latter sense has from earliest times been classified into five individualized breaths. These speculations, dating back to the *Atharvaveda* (see esp. chap. 15), betray a culture of intense introspection and acute sensitivity to bodily processes.

The five individualized breaths, sometimes known collectively as *vāyu* ("wind"), are the following:

1. *prāṇa:* the ascending breath issuing from the navel or the heart and including both inhalation and exhalation
2. *apāna:* the breath associated with the lower half of the trunk
3. *vyāna:* the diffuse breath circulating in all the limbs
4. *udāna:* the "up-breath" held responsible for belching, speech, and the spontaneous focusing of attention in the esoteric "centers" (*cakras*) of the brain, as realized in or associated with higher states of consciousness
5. *samāna:* the breath localized in the abdominal region, where it is chiefly associated with the digestive process

The soteriological literature of the post-Śaṅkara period often adds to this classical pentad a further set of five secondary breaths *(upaprāṇa)*, about whose locations and functions, however, there is no unanimity. These are the following:

1. *nāga* ("serpent"): generally held responsible for belching and vomiting
2. *kūrma* ("tortoise"): associated with the opening and closing of the eyelids
3. *kṛkara* ("*kṛ*-maker"): thought to cause hunger, hiccups, or blinking
4. *devadatta* ("God-given"): associated with the processes of sleep, especially yawning
5. *dhanaṃjaya* ("conquest of wealth"): responsible for the decomposition of the corpse; also sometimes said to be connected with the production of phlegm

These ten types of breaths are generally conceived of as circulating in a complex lattice of bioenergetic pathways called *nāḍīs* ("ducts"). They are widely thought to constitute an experiential field or bodily "sheath," the *prāṇāmaya-kośa* (*Taittirīya Upaniṣad* 2). In the *Chāndogya Upaniṣad* (2.13.6), the five principal breaths are styled "the gatekeepers to the heavenly world," which hints at an esoteric understanding of the close relationship between breathing and consciousness. This connection was later explored in the various soteriological schools, notably in *haṭhayoga*.

Sometimes *prāṇa* and *apāna* simply represent inhalation and exhalation, but in yogic contexts both terms are used in the technical sense noted above. Particularly in *haṭhayoga*, both breaths play an important role in the technique of breath control *(prāṇāyāma)* as a means of curbing, through sensory inhibition, the rise and fall of attention.

[*See also* Yoga; Cakras; *and* Haṭhayoga. *For a discussion of* prāṇa *in a cross-cultural perspective, see* Breath and Breathing.]

BIBLIOGRAPHY

Brown, George William. "Prāṇa and Apāna." *Journal of the American Oriental Society* 39 (1919): 104–112.

Ewing, Arthur H. "The Hindu Conception of the Functions of Breath." *Journal of the American Oriental Society* 22 (1901): 249–308.

Wikander, Stig. *Vāyu: Texte und Untersuchungen zur indo-iranischen Religionsgeschichte.* Uppsala, 1941.

GEORG FEUERSTEIN

PRATĪTYA-SAMUTPĀDA. The term *pratītya-samutpāda* (Pali, *paṭicca-samuppāda*), "dependent origination" or "dependent arising," was first used by the Buddha to characterize the understanding of the nature of human existence that he had attained at his enlightenment. Essentially a doctrine of causality, this notion is so central to Buddhist thought that a proper understanding of *pratītya-samutpāda* is often declared tatamount to enlightenment itself. In it, an entire complex of notions about moral responsibility, human freedom, the process of rebirth, and the path to liberation coalesce.

Pratītya-samutpāda was promulgated against a background of four contemporary theories of causality. These were (1) self-causation *(svayaṃ kṛta)*, advocated by the traditional Brahmanic philosophers; (2) external causation *(parakṛta)*, upheld by the materialist thinkers; (3) a combination of self-causation and external causation, advocated by the Jains; and (4) a denial of both self and external causation, probably championed by certain skeptical thinkers who refused to recognize any form of causation. While all four of these theories were explicitly rejected by the Buddha, the brunt of his analysis was directed against the former two.

According to the Buddha, a theory of self-causation leads to the belief in permanence *(śāśvata)*, that is, the recognition of a permanent and eternal "self" *(ātman)*, which the Buddha found to be an unverifiable entity. External causation, on the other hand, implies the existence of an inexorable physical law of nature *(svabhāva)* that would render the human being a mere automaton with no power to determine the nature of his own existence. Ultimately, such a position divests beings of all bases for personal continuity and hence, moral responsibility. This he referred to as the theory of annihilation *(uccheda)*. *Pratītya-samutpāda*, on the other hand, is presented as the "middle *(madhyama)* position" between these two extremes. This middle position is explained in great detail in the *Discourse to Kātyāyana*, which serves as the *locus classicus* of all subsequent interpretations of the Buddha's "middle path." Following is the text of the discourse available to us in the Pali version:

> Thus have I heard. The Blessed One was once living in Savatthi. . . . At that time the venerable Kaccāyana of that clan came to visit him, and saluting him, sat down at one side. So seated, he questioned the Exalted One: "Sir, [people] speak of 'right view, right view.' To what extent is there right view?"
>
> "This world, Kaccāyana, is generally inclined toward two [views]: existence and nonexistence.
>
> "For him who perceives, with right knowledge, the uprising of the world as it has come to be, whatever view there is in the world about nonexistence will not be acceptable. Kaccāyana, for him who perceives, with right knowledge, the ceasing of the world as it has come to be, whatever view there is in the world about existence will not be acceptable.
>
> "The world, for the most part, Kaccāyana, is bound by approach, grasping and inclination. Yet, a person who does not follow that approach and grasping, that determination of mind, the inclination and disposition, who does not cling to or adhere to a view: 'This is my self,' who thinks [instead]: 'suffering that is subject to arising arises; suffering that is subject to ceasing ceases,' such a person does not doubt, is not perplexed. Herein, his knowledge is not other-dependent. Thus far, Kaccāyana, there is 'right view.'
>
> "'Everything exists'—this, Kaccāyana, is one extreme.
>
> "'Everything does not exist'—this, Kaccāyana, is the second extreme.
>
> "Kaccāyana, without approaching either extreme, the Tathāgata teaches you a doctrine in the middle.
>
> "Dependent upon ignorance [*avidyā*] arise dispositions [*saṃskāra*]; dependent upon dispositions arises consciousness [*vijñāna*]; dependent upon consciousness arises the psychophysical personality [*nāma-rūpa*]; dependent upon the psychophysical personality arise the six senses [*ṣaḍāyatana*]; dependent upon the six senses arises contact [*sparśa*]; dependent upon contact arises feeling [*vedanā*]; dependent upon feeling arises craving [*tṛṣṇā*]; dependent upon craving arises grasping [*upādāna*]; dependent upon grasping arises becoming [*bhava*]; dependent upon becoming arises birth [*jāti*]; dependent upon birth arises old age and death, grief, lamentation, suffering, dejection and despair. Thus arises this entire mass of suffering. However, from the utter fading away and ceasing of ignorance, there is cessation of dispositions . . . from the ceasing of birth, there is ceasing of old age and death, grief, lamentation, suffering, dejection and despair."
>
> (*Saṃyutta Nikāya* 2.16–17)

Existence *(atthitā;* Skt., *astitva)* and nonexistence *(n'atthitā;* Skt., *nāstitva)* referred to here are not simple notions of empirical existence or nonexistence. In the Indian context, existence implies permanence; hence the Buddha's appeal to the empirical fact of cessation of phenomena to reject the notion of existence. Nonexistence refers to complete annihilation without any form of continuity, hence the Buddha's appeal to the empirical fact of arising of phenomena. Thus, the fundamental philosophical problem involved here is how to account for continuity in human experience without either having to posit permanence of some sort or accept absolute discontinuity.

Linguistic conventions of his day did not provide the Buddha with a term to express his ideas, hence it was necessary to coin an entirely different compound term: *pratītya-samutpāda*. *Samutpāda* literally means "arising in combination," or "co-arising." But when compounded with the term *pratītya* (a gerund from the root *i*, "to move," with prefix *prati* meaning "toward"), implying "moving" or "leaning toward," the term means "dependence." *Pratītya-samutpāda* may, therefore, be translated as "dependent arising." Formulating his experience in this way, the Buddha was able to avoid several metaphysical issues that have plagued most discussions of the principle of causation in the East as well as in the West.

Attempts to understand how a cause produces an effect have led philosophers to adopt a reductionist perspective and look for an "essence," or "substance" in the cause that gives rise to the effect. Such a perspective is also motivated by a desire to predict with absolute certainty the manner of the emergence of the effect from the cause. By speaking of the *dependence* of the effect on the cause, which is what the term *pratītya-samutpāda* is intended to express, both the reductionist or essentialist perspective and the impossible task of predicting an event with absolute certainty are avoided.

Thus, the Buddha spoke not of self-sufficient things or substances but of "dependently arisen phenomena" *(pratītyasamutpanna-dharma)*. These refer to phenomena that have already occurred. There is no implication here that individual and discrete phenomena *(dharma)* are experienced and that their "dependence" upon one another is imagined (as was understood by the Humeans) or is the result of transcendental categories of understanding (as the Kantians believed). On the contrary, both phenomena and the manner of their dependence are part of human experience. However, this "dependence" is then stretched out, by means of an inductive inference, to explain the events of the dim past as well as of the future. This is the manner in which the Buddha arrived at the uniformity of the principle of dependence. When he claimed that this "dependent arising" has remained as such despite either the arising of the Tathāgatas or the nonarising of the Tathāgatas he was hinting at the universality of that experience. The uniform and universal principle of dependence is expressed in a most abstract way in the oft-recurring statement: "When that exists, this comes to be; on the arising of that, this arises. When that does not exist, this does not come to be; on the cessation of that, this ceases" (*Majjhima Nikāya* 1.262–264).

In the *Discourse to Kātyāyana* this principle of dependence is utilized to explain the processes of human bondage as well as of freedom. The positive statement of the twelvefold formula, beginning with the statement "Depending upon ignorance arise dispositions," explains the human personality in bondage, avoiding both eternalistic and nihilistic views. The human person is here referred to as *nāma-rūpa* (the psychophysical personality). The nature of that person is conditioned mostly by his or her consciousness *(vijñāna)* which, in its turn, is determined by his understanding (and in the case of the person in bondage, by his lack of understanding—*avidyā*) and the dispositions *(saṃskāra)* formed on the basis of that understanding. Conditioned by such understanding and dispositions, a person comes to experience *(sparśa, vedanā)* the world around him through the six sense faculties *(ṣaḍāyatana)* and to respond by being attracted to it *(tṛṣṇā)*. Thus, his behavior *(karman)* comes to be dominated not only by the world he experiences but also by the way in which he experiences it. If he is attracted by that world he tends to cling to it *(upādāna)*. His whole personality, what he wants to be or achieve, will be determined by that craving and grasping. Such would be his becoming *(bhava)*, not only in this life, but also in a future life *(jāti)*. Involved in such a process of becoming *(bhava)*, he will be pleased and satisfied when he obtains what he craves and unhappy and frustrated when he does not. Yet even his satisfactions, which are temporary at best, turn out to be dissatisfactions as his craving and grasping continue to increase. Such is the mass of suffering he will experience through successive stages of life and in subsequent births.

A proper understanding of phenomena as impermanent *(anitya)* and nonsubstantial *(anātman)* would enable a person to pacify his dispositional tendencies *(saṃskāropasama)*. Pacification of dispositions leads to a better understanding of one's own personality as well as the world of experience. Perceiving phenomena as being nonsubstantial, one will neither assume the existence of an inexorable law nor believe in complete lawlessness. When he responds to that world of experience with his understanding of conditionality his responses will not be rigidly predetermined *(asaṃskṛta)*. Abandoning passion or craving *(tṛṣṇā)*, his actions will be dominated by dispassion *(vairāgya)*, and more positively, by compassion *(karuṇā)* for himself as well as others. Thirsting for nothing, with few wants, he will be freed from most of the "constraints" and lead a happy and contented life until death. With no grasping, there will be no more becoming *(bhava)* and hence the cessation of any possible future births *(jātikṣaya)*. The recognition of the possibility of replacing ignorance *(avidyā)* with wisdom *(jñāna, vidyā)* and craving and grasping with dispassion and compassion leaves the individual with the capacity to attain freedom. Thus, the principle of dependent arising avoids both strict determinism and absolute indeterminism; it is neither an absolutely inviolable law nor a chaotic lawlessness.

The explanation of the human personality, both in bondage and in freedom, was of paramount importance for the Buddha. Hence the discussion of the principle of dependence is confined to these two aspects in the *Discourse to Kātyāyana*. Elsewhere, however, he applies this principle to explain most other aspects of human existence. For example, without positing a first cause or any primordial substance he applied the principle of dependence to explain the evolution and dissolution of the world process. This principle is also utilized in the explanation of the process by which one comes to have knowledge of the world through sensory as well as extrasensory means. Moral behavior, social life, and religious and spiritual phenomena are given causal explanations as well. For this reason, the Buddha did not hesitate to declare, "He who sees dependent arising sees the doctrine *(dharma)*" (*Majjhima Nikāya* 1.190–191).

The Abhidharma period was the most active and highly vibrant epoch of scholastic activity in Buddhist history. During this period the contents of the discourses were carefully analyzed and presented in nondiscursive form. In the process, the "dependently arisen phenomena" referred to by the Buddha came to be listed and classified, together with an analysis of the various types of causal relations *(pratyaya)* that obtain among them. However, a few centuries later, metaphysical speculations began to emerge in the Buddhist tradition. Two schools of Buddhism, the Sarvāstivāda and Sautrāntika, speculating on the concepts of time and space, produced theories of momentariness and atomism, thereby engendering insoluble problems such as the metaphysical notions of absolute identity and absolute difference. Contradicting the Buddha's notion of nonsubstantiality, the Sarvāstivādins accepted an underlying "substance" *(svabhāva)* in phenomena, while the Sautrāntikas surreptitiously introduced a metaphysical notion of a transmigrating personality *(pudgala)*. [*See* Sarvāstivāda *and* Sautrāntika.]

The Pali Abhidharma work *Kathāvatthu* criticized and rejected these views. In spite of this criticism, these views continued to survive. The early Mahāyāna *sūtras* represent another attempt to get rid of the substantialist metaphysics of these two schools by emphasizing a negative approach to the problem of reality, one based upon the notion of "emptiness" *(śūnyatā)*. [*See* Śūnyam and Śūnyatā.] For example, one of the early Mahāyāna *sūtras*—the *Kāśyapaparivarta*—continued to describe the "middle path" in negative terms, while at the same time retaining the positive version discussed in the *Discourse to Kātyāyana*.

Nāgārjuna's famous treatise, the *Mūlamadhyamakakārikā*, considered by many as the most sophisticated philosophical justification of Mahāyāna, is a determined attempt to return to the original message of the Buddha by criticizing the substantialist views of the Sarvāstivādins and the Sautrāntikas. Restatement of the principle of "dependent arising" without having to posit a substantial connection *(svabhāva)* between a cause and an effect (as the Sarvāstivādins did), or to emphasize their difference (as the Sautrāntikas did), seems to be the foremost concern of Nāgārjuna. "Emptiness" here becomes a synonym for "nonsubstantiality" *(anātman)*. [*See* Mādhyamika *and the biography of Nāgārjuna.*]

The Buddha's conception of karmic continuity and moral responsibility also had to be rescued from the substantialist interpretations of the Buddhist metaphysicians. Nāgārjuna seems to have been aware of a statement popular among the Buddhists relating to the doctrine of *karman* that read: "*Karma*s do not perish *(na praṇaśyanti)* even after a hundred myriads of aeons. Having attained the harmony of conditions *(sāmagrī)* and the proper time *(kāla)*, they bear fruit for the human beings" (La Vallée Poussin, 1903, p. 324). Inspired probably by this verse, Nāgārjuna (*Mūlamadhyamakakārikā* 17.14) upheld the notion of a nonperishable *(avipraṇāśa) karman*, comparing it with the unacceptable interpretations offered by the substantialists. After denying a "self" *(ātman)*, he proceeded to compile chapters on the "harmony of conditions" *(sāmagrī)* and on time *(kāla)*, giving a nonsubstantialist interpretation of these.

Having devoted twenty-five chapters to recasting the full range of Buddhist ideas in terms of the doctrine of "emptiness," Nāgārjuna returns to the conclusion of the *Discourse to Kātyāyana* in chapter 26, where he analyzes the twelvefold factors describing the human personality in bondage as well as freedom. Thus, Nāgārjuna's treatise should more appropriately be considered a grand commentary on the *Discourse to Kātyāyana*, this being the only discourse referred to by name in the text.

Nāgārjuna's exposition of the twelvefold formula in chapter 26 (which incidentally consists of twelve verses) focuses on the positive statement of the Buddha regarding the human life process, that is, how a human being conditioned by ignorance suffers in bondage. The negative statement of the Buddha explaining freedom is briefly outlined in the last two verses of this chapter.

Nāgārjuna begins the chapter explaining how the destiny *(gati)* of a human being, as he continues with his life-process, is determined by ignorance and dispositions. Taking a cue from the *Mahānidāna Suttanta*, where the Buddha speaks about consciousness *(viññāṇa*; Skt., *vijñāna)* entering the mother's womb in order to influence the psychophysical personality formed therein, Nāgārjuna explains the psychophysical personality *(nāma-rūpa)* as being infused *(niṣicyate)* by consciousness that is dispositionally conditioned. [*See* Vijñāna.] The most interesting addition to the formula appears in the explanation of the three links: the psychophysical personality *(nāma-rūpa)*, the six spheres of sense *(ṣaḍāyatana)* and contact *(sparśa)*. At this point Nāgārjuna introduces the contents of a passage explaining the process of sense experience occurring in the *Mahāhat-*

thipadopama Sutta that, though implied, is not specifically stated in the twelvefold formula. This passage refers to the various conditions needed for sense experience, namely, the existence of the unimpaired sense organ, the object that has come into focus, and the availability of attention arising in such a context. The rest of the formula is then briefly presented without explanations. Verse 10 introduces the idea of the perception of truth *(tattva-darśana)* in place of the cessation of ignorance *(avidyā-nirodha)*. Nāgārjuna did not have to specify what this conception of truth is, for he has already compiled twenty-five chapters in its explanation. It is the perception that all (experienced) phenomena are empty *(sarvam idaṃ śūnyaṃ)* of substance *(svabhāvato)*.

[*See also* Buddhist Philosophy; Soteriology, *article on* Buddhist Soteriology; Soul, *article on* Buddhist Concepts; *and* Nirvāṇa.]

BIBLIOGRAPHY

For a detailed study of *pratītya-samutpāda*, see my *Causality: The Central Philosophy of Buddhism* (Honolulu, 1975). My translation and annotation of the *Mūlamadhyamakakārikā* of Nāgārjuna, *Nāgārjuna, The Philosophy of the Middle Way* (Albany, N.Y., 1986) gives further elaboration to the view that Nāgārjuna's *Mūlamadhyamakakārikā* is in essence a commentary on the *Discourse to Kātyāyana*. See also Alex Wayman's detailed treatment, "Buddhist Dependent Origination," *History of Religions* 10 (1971): 185–203. The passage on the imperishability of *karmas* quoted above can be found in Louis de La Vallée Poussin's *Mūlamadhyamakakārikās de Nāgārjuna avec la Prasannapadā commentaire de Candrakirti* (Saint Petersburg, 1903), p. 324. This same passage was the occasion for an entire treatise, Vasubandhu's *Karmasiddhiprakaraṇa*, translated by Étienne Lamotte as "Le traité de l'acte de Vasubandhu: Karmasiddhiprakaraṇa," *Mélanges chinois et bouddhiques* 4 (1935–1936): 151–263.

DAVID J. KALUPAHANA

PRATT, JAMES B. (1875–1944), American philosopher. Born in Elmira, New York, James Bissett Pratt graduated from Williams College in 1898 and received an M.A. from Harvard in 1899. He spent the next year at Columbia Law School, following which he traveled in Europe and studied with Otto Pfleiderer in Berlin. In 1903 Pratt returned to Harvard and in 1905 was awarded the Ph.D. degree, with special commendation from both William James and Josiah Royce. James became one of his closest friends, but Pratt never accepted pragmatism. In fact, Pratt's *What Is Pragmatism?* (1909) contains some of the most trenchant criticism of pragmatic theory in all the controversial literature on the subject.

In 1905 Pratt returned to Williams as instructor in philosophy and remained there until his retirement in 1943. He was made assistant professor in 1906, professor in 1913, and, on the death of Professor John E. Russell, was assigned the Mark Hopkins Chair of Intellectual and Moral Philosophy in 1917. He received honorary degrees from Amherst (1930), Wesleyan (1935), and Williams (1943). In 1934 he was president of the American Theological Society (eastern branch) and, the year following, of the eastern division of the American Philosophical Association.

Pratt was the author of thirteen books and well over a hundred articles in technical and popular journals. In 1913–1914, travel and study with his wife in India produced *India and Its Faiths* (1915), a scholarly study of Asian religions written in such a compelling style that it reached a wide popular audience. Later travels in China and Japan led to *The Pilgrimage of Buddhism* (1928), which was widely acclaimed. In 1931–1932, he lectured at Rabindranath Tagore's school at Santiniketan in Bengal.

In 1920 Pratt joined with six other philosophers to bring out *Essays in Critical Realism*. This work challenged the points of view of the American "critical realists" and the "new realists" of Great Britain. Critical realism, Pratt was wont to say, should have been called "dualistic realism"; he believed that the efficacy of the self was lost both in idealism and in naturalism. In *Matter and Spirit* (1922), also in *Naturalism* (1939), and most comprehensively in *Personal Realism* (1937), he advocated an epistemological dualism, asserting that mental states are terminal entities that point beyond themselves in an intentional way. He was also a dualist in metaphysics, arguing for a "dualism of process" by which the ability of the self to interact with the body and break into the mechanistic causal chain could be maintained. Toward religion he took a positive attitude. In *The Religious Consciousness* (1920) and *Can We Keep the Faith?* (1941), he defended a liberal, reasonable form of belief. "I do not see," he wrote, "how [philosophy] can avoid the conviction that insight and love are at the very heart of Being."

BIBLIOGRAPHY

Besides the works mentioned above, Pratt also wrote the following: *The Psychology of Religious Belief* (New York, 1907), *Democracy and Peace* (Boston, 1916), *Adventures in Philosophy and Religion* (New York, 1931), *Reason in the Art of Living* (New York, 1949), and *Eternal Values in Religion* (New York, 1950). Pratt's important articles are too numerous to mention; he was a frequent contributor to the *Harvard Theological Review* and the *Journal of Philosophy*, as well as other journals. A memorial volume, *Self, Religion, and Metaphysics: Essays in Memory of James Bissett Pratt,* edited by Gerald E. Myers (New York, 1961), is suggested for further reading.

J. S. Bixler

PRAYER, understood as the human communication with divine and spiritual entities, has been present in most of the religions in human history. Viewed from most religious perspectives, prayer is a necessity of the human condition. When the human material world is accounted for in an act of creation resulting in a cleavage or separation from the divine or spiritual world, prayer is one means by which this gap of createdness is overcome, if but momentarily.

Abundant texts of such communications exist as well as extensive literatures about them. Still, the general study of prayer is undeveloped and naive. The question of the universality of prayer has yet to be seriously addressed to the relevant materials. A careful comparative and etymological study of just the terminology that designates acts of human-spiritual communication has yet to be done among even the widespread and best-known religious traditions. Studies of prayer in terms of modern communications theories and semiotics are limited and rare. The theories, as well as the intuitive understandings, of prayer have been heavily influenced by Western religious traditions.

A general schema will be used in the following consideration of the typologies, theories, and interpretive issues of prayer phenomena. First, prayer will be considered as *text,* that is, as a collection of words that cohere as a human communication directed toward a spiritual entity. Second, prayer will be considered as *act,* that is, as the human act of communicating with deities including not only or exclusively language but especially the elements of performance that constitute the act. Finally, prayer will be considered as *subject,* that is, as a dimension or aspect of religion, the articulation of whose nature constitutes a statement of belief, doctrine, instruction, philosophy, or theology.

Prayer as Text. Prayer is thought of most commonly as the specific words of the human-spiritual communication, that is, as the text of this communication, such as the Lord's Prayer (Christian), the Qaddish (Jewish), and the prayers of *ṣalāt* (Muslim). Scores of prayers appear in books of prayer, books of worship, descriptions of rituals and liturgies, ethnographies of exclusively oral peoples, and biographies of religious persons. [*See* Lord's Prayer; Siddur and Maḥzor; *and* Ṣalāt.]

A common basic typology of prayer has been formulated by discerning what distinguishes the character and intent expressed by the words of prayer texts. This kind of typology includes a number of classes, all easily distinguished by their descriptive designations. It includes petition, invocation, thanksgiving (praise or adoration), dedication, supplication, intercession, confession, penitence, and benediction. Such types may constitute whole prayers or they may be strung together to form a structurally more complex prayer.

This kind of typology serves to demonstrate the extent of prayer phenomena. It may be used as a device for the comparative study of religion. It suggests that prayer is widespread and has a commonality as well as diversity. The most extensive use of this kind of typology was made in studies, done mostly in the nineteenth and early twentieth centuries, of the development of religion over time. Petitionary prayers were thought to be most widespread and thus the oldest form of prayer. The presence of ethical, moral, and spiritual concerns in petitionary prayers was believed to have come later as a development beyond purely personal and material needs. While these developmental aspects are no longer considered valid nor are they of much interest in the study of religion, this content typology has continued to provide the basic descriptive language of prayer.

In his classic early anthropological study *Primitive Culture* (1873), E. B. Tylor attributed a psychological and spiritual character to prayer. He called prayer "the soul's sincere desire, uttered or unexpressed" and "the address of personal spirit to personal spirit." In perhaps the most extensive comparative study of prayer, *Prayer: A Study in the History and Psychology of Religion* (1932), Friedrich Heiler understood prayer in much the same terms, describing it, using Hebrew scriptural imagery, as a pouring out of the heart before God. Thus, in both of these classic descriptions, prayer is characterized as free and spontaneous, that is, heartfelt. Such characterization is still broadly held and is, for most, so obvious that critical discussion is unnecessary. However, when the understanding of prayer as a free and spontaneous "living communion of man with God" (Heiler) is conjoined with the general restriction of prayer to the text form, incongruency, confusion, and dilemma arise. Prayer texts, almost without exception and to a degree as part of their nature, are formulaic, repetitive, and static in character, much in contrast with the expected free and spontaneous character of prayer. In the case of Tylor, whose study of culture and religion was directed to the documentation of the evolution of culture, this was particularly confounding. His theory called for religion to follow magic and thus for prayer to follow magical spells and formulas. Yet the abundance of liturgical and meditational prayer forms in the cultures he considered the most fully developed confounded his thesis. Tylor could resolve this dilemma only by holding that prayer "from being at first utterances as free and flexible as requests to a living patriarch or chief, stiffened into traditional formulas whose repetition required verbal accuracy, and whose nature practically assimilated more or less to that of charms" (Tylor, vol. 2, p. 371). Thus, the structural characteristics of prayer that contradicted the expectations of prayer were held to be a product of civilization and evolution.

Heiler was also confounded by this incongruity. He held that prayer texts were, in fact, not true prayers, but were rather artificially composed for the purpose of edifying, instructing, and influencing people in the matters of dogma, belief, and tradition. Heiler's study of prayer, therefore, was a failed effort from the outset in the respect that he denigrated his primary source of data for his study of prayer, leaving him wistfully awaiting the rare occasion to eavesdrop on one pouring out his or her heart to God. Heiler's predisposition for the psychological nature of prayer, conjoined with his failure to make any clear or useful distinction between prayer as text and prayer as act, placed his consideration of prayer in a nonproductive position, one that has generally discouraged the academic study of prayer, especially beyond particular prayer traditions.

Due to the nature of the materials available, prayers must often be considered primarily, if not solely, as texts, whose study is limited to the semantic, informational, and literary aspects of the language that constitutes them. Despite such limitations, the texts of prayers reflect theological, doctrinal, cultural, historical, aesthetic, and creedal dimensions of a religious culture.

Prayer as Act. Intuitively prayer is an act of communication. In its most common performance, prayer is an act of speech. [*See also* Language.] Prayer has been considered as act, including not only the words uttered but some of the performance elements of the speech act, in order to classify and describe prayers in terms of the identities of those praying, the occasions of prayer, the motivations for praying, and such physically descriptive matters as body and hand attitudes. These classifications have been primarily descriptive with institutional and psychological aspects in the foreground.

The distinction between personal and ritual prayer has often been made when viewing prayer as act. Personal prayer, regarded as the act of persons pouring forth their hearts to God, has been considered by many as the truest form, even the only true form, of prayer. Yet, the data available for the study of personal prayer are scant. Still, the record of personal prayers found in letters, biographies, and diaries suggests a strong correlation and interdependence of personal prayer with ritual and liturgical prayer in language, form, style, and physical attitude. A person praying privately is invariably a person who is part of a religious and cultural tradition in which ritual or public prayer is practiced.

Ritual prayer, by not conforming to the naive notions of the spontaneity and free form of prayer, has often been set aside. It was not incorrect of Heiler to understand ritual prayer as being composed for the purpose of edifying, instructing, and influencing people in the matters of dogma, belief, and tradition, although this is but a partial understanding. But Heiler radically truncated his, and consequently many others', understanding of prayer by denigrating these important functions. Such aspects of prayer must be recognized as important and often essential to the continuity and communication of tradition and culture. In its capacity of performing these important functions, the formulaic, repetitive, and standardized characteristics of prayer are effective pedagogically and to enculturate.

Furthermore, and importantly, it can be shown that prayer when formulaic, repetitive, and redundant in message can be a true act of communication, even heartfelt. In recent years a range of studies has developed showing the performative power of language and speech acts. Simply put, these studies show that language and other forms of human action not only say things, that is, impart information, they also do things. Ordinary language acts may persuade, name, commit, promise, declare, affirm, and so on; and these functions are often more primary than that of transmitting information.

The study of prayer has yet to be extensively influenced by this understanding of the performative power of language, but it is clearly relevant. From this perspective, the many dimensions of the act of prayer apart from the heartfelt communication with God can be appreciated more fully. For example, a prayer of invocation, through its form as well as its content, when uttered in the appropriate ritual context, serves to transform the mood of the worshipers. It sets the tone and attitude of worship. It effects the presence of the spiritual in the minds of worshipers. Likewise, a prayer of benediction releases worshipers from a ritual domain. It serves to extend the reorientation achieved in ritual to the world beyond while releasing people from the restrictions imposed by ritual. Prayers of praise direct the attention of those praying to positive divine attributes, they effect and reflect a doctrine of God, while prayers of confession and penitence direct the attention of those praying to negative human elements, they effect and reflect a doctrine of sin and humankind. Even when formulaic and without a motivation arising directly from individual felt needs, the emotive experience and affective qualities of these prayers differs markedly according to their type. Prayers of praise or thanksgiving are joyous, uplifting, and outgoing, while prayers of confession and penitence are introspective and somber. The formulaic character of liturgical prayers invites participation by establishing a frame of expectation, a pattern that becomes familiar.

Studies of the performative power of language suggest that such enactment capabilities of speech are conventionalized, formalized, and ordinarily involve physical action as well as the utterance of words in order to be felicitious. In other words, a prayer act, to have effect, to be true and empowered includes not only the utterance of words, but the active engagement of elements of the historical, cultural, and personal setting in which it is offered. It may include certain body postures and orientations, ritual actions and objects, designated architectural structures or physical environments, particular times of the day or calendar dates, specified moods, attitudes, or intentions. For example, a Muslim does not enact *ṣalāt* (daily ritual prayer) by simply uttering the words "Allāhu akbar." Rather, *ṣalāt* is a performance that requires proper timing, dress, directional orientation, a sequence of bodily actions that includes standing, prostration, proper attitudes—all of these, as well as the proper recitation of a sequence of words.

When prayer is considered as act, the unresponsive and noncreative dimensions that seem inseparable from the rigidity of words tend to dissolve, for a prayer act always involves one praying in a historical, cultural, social, and psychological setting. These ever-changing contextual elements are necessarily a part of the act. In some prayer traditions, the Navajo of North America for example, it has been shown that highly formulaic constituents of prayer are ordered in patterns and conjoined with familiar ritual elements in combinations that express very specifically the heartfelt needs and motivations of a single person for whom the prayer is uttered. Analogous to ordinary language where familiar words can be ordered according to a single set of grammatical principles in infinite ways to be creative and expressive, prayer passages may be ordered in conjunction with ritual elements to achieve the same communicative capabilities.

The importance of the performative power of prayer acts is attested within many religious traditions by the expressed view that the most important prayers are those spoken in a special language, those mumbled, or those uttered silently, even those that are accomplished without words. Other nonspeech forms are also commonly recognized as essentially prayer, such as song, dance, sacrifice, and food offerings. These nonspeech forms may be understood as heartfelt and spontaneous human acts directed toward the spiritual world, but they may also be understood as religious forms whose enactment strengthens emotion, sustains courage, and excites hope.

When prayer is considered as act, a whole range of powerful characteristics and religious functions may be discerned. Here the issue is not primarily to show that prayer is communication with the spiritual or divine, or even necessarily to discern what is communicated, but rather to direct attention to the comprehension and appreciation of the power and effectiveness of communication acts that are human-divine communications. Likewise, when seen as act, the distinction between prayer and other religious speech acts—chant, spell, and formula—is less significant than it often is when distinguished and evaluated within particular religious traditions or theories of religion.

Various traditions of Buddhism present a test case in the consideration of prayer as they do many categories and dimensions of religion. For those traditions that are not theistic, like Theravāda Buddhism, prayer understood as human-divine communication is not possible. [*See* Meditation.] However, a number of kinds of Buddhist speech acts, such as meditational recitations, scriptural recitations, *mantras*, and *bodhisattva* vows, have certain resemblances to prayer, especially in terms of many of its functions. [*See especially* Mantra.] Commonly the distinction between prayer and these Buddhist speech forms has simply been ignored and they are considered as forms of Buddhist prayer. It would be more valuable to comprehend specifically the similarities and differences of the various forms and functions of these Buddhist speech acts compared with prayer acts of theistic traditions. In their similarities lies the nature of religion, in their differences lies the distinctiveness of Buddhism among religious traditions.

Prayer as Subject. In religious traditions, prayer is not only words recited, prayer is not only an action enacted, prayer is also a subject that is much written and talked about. It is the subject of theory, of theology, of sermons, of doctrine, of devotional guides, of prescribed ways of worship and ways of life, and of descriptions of methods of prayer. In the style and interest of a number of academic fields that consider human communication processes and the language forms that take these communications as their subject, we propose to term this dimension of prayer "metaprayer," signifying thereby the communications in religious traditions about prayer. The extent of literature in religious traditions about prayer is massive and ranges from personal meditations on the "way of prayer" to formal theologies and philosophies of prayer. In these writings, prayer becomes the subject by which to articulate the principles and character of a religious tradition or a strain within a tradition.

There are countless memorable and distinctive meta-prayers. The following examples illustrate the range and character of these statements. In Plato's *Timaeus* (27b–c), Socrates and Timaeus discuss the necessity of prayer:

> *Socrates:* And now, Timaeus, you, I suppose, should speak next, after duly calling upon the gods.
> *Timaeus:* All men, Socrates, who have any degree of right feeling, at the beginning of every enterprise, whether small or great, always call upon God. And we, too, who are going to discourse of the nature of the universe, how created or how existing without creation, if we be not altogether out of our wits, must invoke the aid of gods and goddesses and pray that our words may be above all acceptable to them and in consequence to ourselves.

On the Lord's Prayer, Immanuel Kant in 1793 wrote in *Religion within the Limits of Reason Alone* that "one finds in it nothing but the resolution to good life—conduct which, taken with the consciousness of our frailty, carries with it the persistent desire to be a worthy member in the kingdom of God. Hence it contains no actual request for something which God in His wisdom might well refuse us" (trans. Greene and Hudson, New York, 1960, p. 183).

Friederich Schleiermacher, in a sermon entitled "The Power of Prayer" (*Selected Sermons*, London, 1890, p. 38), describes prayer in familiar, sweeping terms: "To be a religious man and to pray are really one and the same thing."

Powerful and provocative are the many statements on prayer of Abraham Joshua Heschel. In *Man's Quest for God* (New York, 1954) he wrote, "The issue of prayer is not prayer; the issue of prayer is God" (p. 87). In an essay entitled "On Prayer" he wrote, "We pray in order to pray. . . . I pray because I am unable to pray. . . . . We utter the words of the *Kaddish: Magnified and sanctified by His great name in the world which He has created according to His will.* Our hope is to enact, to make real the sanctification of this name here and now" (*Conservative Judaism*, Fall 1970, pp. 3–4). And finally, in *The Insecurity of Freedom* (New York, 1966) Heschel wrote, "Different are the languages of prayer, but the tears are the same. We have a vision in common of Him in whose compassion all men's prayers meet" (p. 180).

In Western religious traditions, prayer has raised classic issues, the resolution of which corresponds to interpretive traditions. One notable issue is whether or not prayer, particularly petitionary prayer, is necessary or useful, since God is understood as all-knowing and all-caring. The explanation of this issue is an articulation of a theology and an anthropology, and it constitutes a statement of faith. Another classic issue has been whether prayer is monologue, dialogue, or neither. If one holds that prayer is monologue, one must explain how prayer is prayer at all rather than meditation or personal reflection. If one holds that prayer is dialogue, one must describe how God participates in the communication act. Theologies and philosophies of Western traditions no longer give much attention to prayer, but it has nonetheless been a significant topic in many of the classic theological and philosophical systems.

In *Varieties of Religious Experience* (New York, 1902), William James, upon considering a number of statements about prayer, concluded that "the fundamental religious point is that in prayer, spiritual energy, which otherwise would slumber, does become active, and spiritual work of some kind is effected really."

In *Young India*, on 24 September 1925, Mohandas K. Gandhi wrote:

> Prayers are a confession of our unworthiness, or our weakness. God has a thousand, which means countless, names, or say rather that He has no name. We may sing hymns to Him or pray to Him, using any name we prefer. Some know Him by the name Rama, some know Him as Krishna, others call Him Rahim, and yet others call Him God. All these worship the same spiritual being. However, just as everyone does not like the same food so all these names do not find acceptance with everyone. . . . This is to say that one can pray, sing devotional songs not with the lips but with the heart. That is why even the dumb, the stammerer and the brainless can pray.

And on 10 June 1926, he wrote in *Young India:* "It seems to me that it [prayer] is a yearning of the heart to be one with the Maker, an invocation for his blessing. It is in this case the attitude that matters, not words uttered or muttered."

A final example taken from American fiction not only illustrates that metaprayer appears in a variety of forms of literature, but that metaprayer may even be used to disavow the use and efficacy of prayer. In the following passage from Mark Twain's *Adventures of Huckleberry Finn*, Huck distinguishes his own religiousness from that of old Miss Watson:

> Miss Watson she took me in the closet and prayed, but nothing come of it. She told me to pray every day, and whatever I asked for I would get it. But it warn't so. I tried it. Once I got a fish-line, but no hooks. It warn't any good to me without hooks. I tried for the hooks three or four times, but somehow I couldn't make it work. By and by, one day, I asked Miss Watson to try for me, but she said I was a fool. She never told me why, and I couldn't make it out no way.

Conclusion. In the general study of prayer, the term *prayer* has been used loosely to designate a variety of human acts, principally speech acts associated with the practice of religion, especially those that are communications with a divine or spiritual entity. There can be no precise definition given the word when used in this way, for it serves as but a general focusing device for more precise comparative and historical study. The term gains definitional precision when seen as any of dozens of terms used in specific religious traditions as articulated in practice or in doctrine.

What can be articulated to facilitate the general study of prayer is the significance of the tripartite distinctions of prayer as text, as act, and as subject.

BIBLIOGRAPHY

Prayer as a general religious phenomenon has received scant attention by students of religion. There are no recent global or extensive studies. The discussions of prayer that continue to be the standard, while obviously inadequate, are E. B. Tylor's *Primitive Culture: Researches into the Development of Mythology, Philosophy, Religion, Language, Art, and Custom,* 2 vols., 4th ed. (London, 1903), and Friedrich Heiler's *Prayer: A Study in the History and Psychology of Religion,* edited and translated by Samuel McComb (Oxford, 1932). Most of the general studies of prayer are strongly psychological in character. Prayer was a topic of extensive consideration by William James in *The Varieties of Religious Experience: A Study in Human Nature* (1902; New York, 1961), pp. 359–371. Prayer and related religious speech acts are of interest in phenomenologies of religion; see, for example, Gerardus van der Leeuw's *Religion in Essence and Manifestation,* 2 vols., translated by J. E. Turner (London, 1938), pp. 403–446.

Statements of a comparative nature are found scattered throughout the literature, especially comparing specific prayers among Western religious traditions. However, broader and detailed comparative studies of prayer do not exist. Extensive studies of prayer that have attempted to see prayer in more general and universal terms may still be of interest, even though they have a dominantly Christian perspective. Such studies include Alexander J. Hodge's *Prayer and Its Psychology* (New York, 1931) and R. H. Coats's *The Realm of Prayer* (London, 1920).

An exemplary study of prayer that makes a clear distinction between prayer as a text, act, and subject is Tzvee Zahavy's "A New Approach to Early Jewish Prayer," in *History of Judaism: The Next Ten Years,* edited by Baruch M. Bokser (Chico, Calif., 1980), pp. 45–60.

Sources for prayer within specific religious traditions can be found under the heading "Prayer" in the *Encyclopaedia of Religion and Ethics,* edited by James Hastings, vol. 10 (Edinburgh, 1918), which includes a number of articles, some now outdated, on various religious traditions. See also *The Oxford Book of Prayer,* edited by George Appleton and others (New York, 1985).

There are numerous studies that demonstrate the importance of considering prayer as act. Harold A. Carter's *The Prayer Tradition of Black People* (Valley Forge, Pa., 1976) is a fine study of the American black prayer tradition; it traces the African heritage, describes the theological influences, discerns the major functions, and demonstrates the remarkable power of this prayer tradition in the context of black movements in American history. Gary Goosen's "Language as a Ritual Substance," in *Language in Religious Practice,* edited by William J. Samarin (Rowley, Mass., 1976), pp. 40–62, considers Chamul prayers as encoding messages interpreted in terms of Victor Turner's method of considering symbols.

On the performative power of Navajo prayer, see my "Prayer as Person: The Performative Force in Navajo Prayer Acts," *History of Religions* 17 (November 1979): 143–157. On the centrality of prayer to the whole system of Navajo religion, see my *Sacred Words: A Study of Navajo Religion and Prayer* (Westport, Conn., 1981). A notable study of prayer as a tradition of creative acts of oratory, focusing on the inhabitants of sea islands along the Atlantic Coast of the southern United States, is Patricia Jones-Jackson's "Oral Traditions in Gullah," *Journal of Religious Thought* 39 (Spring–Summer 1982): 21–33.

An examplary study of nonspeech acts considered as communication acts similar to prayer is Gabriella Eichinger Ferro-Luzzi's "Ritual as Language: The Case of South Indian Food Offerings," *Current Anthropology* 18 (September 1977): 507–514.

The performative power of speech acts, relevant to the study of prayer as act, has been shown in many essays. See, for example, Benjamin C. Ray's " 'Performative Utterances' in African Rituals," *History of Religions* 13 (August 1973): 16–35; Stanley J. Tambiah's "The Magical Power of Words," *Man,* n.s. 3 (June 1968): 175–208; and Tambiah's *Buddhism and the Spirit Cults in North-East Thailand* (Cambridge, 1970).

While folklore studies have become interested in the performance of many speech forms, especially among exclusively oral peoples, prayer is a form that has received little attention despite its abundant resources and importance within the traditions studied.

On the consideration of second-order language acts (metalanguages), see Alan Dundes's "Metafolklore and Oral Literary Criticism," *The Monist* 50 (October 1966): 505–516, and Barbara A. Babcock's "The Story in the Story: Metanarration in Folk Narrative," in her and Richard Bauman's *Verbal Art as Performance* (Rowley, Mass., 1977). Sources for prayer as subject are coincident with the second-order interpretative and critical literary traditions of all religions. In the contemporary religions and popular literature of the Western traditions, prayer is a constant topic. It has also been a consideration of major theologies and philosophies, as shown for modern Western thought in a summary treatment by Perry Le Fevre, *Understandings of Prayer* (Philadelphia, 1981). In *Prayer: An Analysis of Theological Terminology* (Helsinki, 1973), Antti Alhonsaari considers the theological issue of whether prayer is monologue or dialogue, discerning systematically the forms of prayer that correspond to the combinations of the variable on which this metaprayer discussion turns. While the rubric "Prayer" is not so dominant among non-Western religious traditions, there are nonetheless abundant comparable statements about prayer and prayerlike phenomena found among the writings of the interpreters and believers in these many traditions.

SAM D. GILL

PREACHING. Views of preaching will vary widely, even within the Christian religion, in whose faith and practice the preacher, by and large, plays a more central role than in the other great religions. But common to all is the dialectic of tradition and experience: human communities, in their attempt to articulate religious experience and to order social life by that shared experience, preach. These communities will inevitably authorize persons to ritualize and storify their integrating myths; to preserve, interpret, and teach the current relevance of their sacred writings; to connect the past with the present and the future; and, in most cases, to win converts to the faith. The preacher, whether the *khaṭīb* of Islam, the enlightened master of Buddhism, or the Puritan divine, moves between the tradition, usually as held in a canon of sacred writings, and the changing contours of individual and social life.

The community must dance out its sacred story, be reminded of its forebears, tell itself again where it has come from and who it is, speak about the unspeakable, chart its course in a sea of change, hand over what it has experienced to the inexperienced young, control the powers, envision the future in the light of the past, make sense out of history, confront the terrors, move through the seasons of individual and social life. More often than not alongside the rituals by which a religious community accomplishes this will appear a person speaking, giving language to ritual and connecting the history of a particular group with an overarching, venerable story. This storyteller, interpreter, teacher, and guide will be the preacher.

This man or woman—it has most often been a man—will move between the reality of religious experience and the relativity of its expression. The American Episcopalian Phillips Brooks, in a classic definition (*Lectures on Preaching,* 1877), called preaching "the communication of truth through personality." By *truth* Brooks meant that which stands at the center of the life of faith; by *personality* he meant the specific biographies and social realities in which that truth once again dawns. Or, as the Lutheran Joseph Sittler put it, all preaching is organic to a time, a place, and particular personalities. At the same time, this speech for here and now, among this congregated community, has its origin in that which transcends time, space, and language.

This realization, that the preacher attempts to speak of the transcendent, however that might be conceived, in relative, limited human language, led the Swiss theologian Karl Barth to write his vast *Church Dogmatics,* which begins with the doctrine of the word of God. How, asked Barth, can a human being speak of the divine? Barth's answer was straightforward, if unsatisfying to some: God chooses to speak in our language, just as God chose to speak in Jesus of Nazareth and in the holy scriptures. Barth set forth his well-known schema of the threefold form of the word of God: the word made flesh, manifest in a person; the written word, the canon; and the word spoken and ritualized in preaching and sacrament. Within the Christian tradition most definitions of preaching would at least take account of Barth's formulation.

Similarly, the Zen master confronting his students with a *kōan,* a short question designed to communicate by puzzling, indeed by confusing, the disciple, recognizes, as Barth did, both the limitation and the power of language in religious experience. Jesus, especially in his parables—and here we are as close to Jesus the preacher as we are ever likely to get—spoke always obliquely of "the Kingdom." This was the all-encompassing reality of his life and teaching, but he stopped short of saying in so many words what it was. Rather, in the parables' earthy concreteness Jesus communicates in terms of the relativities of mundane life his own apprehension of God. In all cultures, the preacher stands between actual religious experience and the parochial human expression of that experience. The protestation of unworthiness that one hears from Isaiah (chap. 6) and the demurrer of Jeremiah (chap. 1) attest to this problematic situation that preachers everywhere know.

History of Preaching in Christianity. In the Christian tradition the first preachers understood their vocation in the light of Jewish practice and the developing Christian liturgy. Apart from the New Testament, one of the earliest pictures we have of Christian worship is that of Justin Martyr (c. 155). The community meets for worship around the Eucharist, and the one who presides at the table reads and comments upon the prophets and the "memoirs of the apostles." Here are combined the ordinary usage of the synagogue, as depicted in the accounts of Jesus preaching in his home district (*Lk.* 4:16–30), and the new elements of the Eucharist and the developing Christian canon. From that time until this, Christian preaching has taken place alongside the liturgy and in connection with the scriptures. Even in those times and places when word and sacrament have been split apart, particularly since the Reformation, there has been at least tacit understanding that preaching is a function of the communing church and responsible to its canon. The importance given to preaching and the way in which it is defined will vary according to the particular group's view of scripture and the church.

Preaching in the New Testament church is evangelical, that is, the speech of a growing community and an expanding missionary movement. The preacher sets forth the kerygma, the essential story of the life, death, resurrection, and expected coming of Jesus Christ. In the *Acts of the Apostles* and the letters of Paul, preaching is primarily a rehearsal of the great events, the mighty deeds of salvation, at the center of which is Jesus Christ, no longer simply the one who himself teaches and preaches but the one preached about. Preaching is placarding, the faithful recounting of the story of redemption, handed down by word of mouth through the first generation of the church and eventually written into the early history, in narrative and epistle, of the community.

Alongside the kerygma the earliest preachers taught the people the rudiments of the faith and the social and ethical implications of the gospel. Although preaching in its essence was understood as the recital of saving actions, the early church would not have separated preaching from teaching, *kērugma* from *didachē*. From the beginning the church saw an organic relationship between gospel and law, in the sense of the application to the socioeconomic realm of the kerygma, and struggled constantly to keep the two differentiated and in their proper relationship. At every stage in the history of preaching this has been a vexing problem.

During the first few centuries of the church's life, the preacher was teacher, spiritual leader, and apologist. The sermons of the fathers reveal conceptions of the church as the ark of salvation, the Christian life as a spiritual journey needing pastoral guidance, and the world as hostile to the true faith. The preacher, then, is one who calls people to the church, builds them up in faith, and wards off enemies of the truth. The church, accordingly, becomes a primary hermeneutic (the context and overarching concern that provides principles of interpretation) for exposition and application of the canon and for setting the agenda of preaching. In time the church would wax so strong, in the coalescence of religion and culture that we call Christendom, that the institution and its refined ritual would eclipse preaching.

The Reformation's critique of the church led to a new estimate of preaching. Luther raised the pulpit above the altar and, though he did not intend the separation of Eucharist from preaching, set the preacher at the center of the church's life. Preaching was, once again, to be evangelical *and* didactic: the great theme of the Reformation, justification by grace through faith, called for the first, and the obvious need for instructing the people in the faith called for the second. Luther's sermons have continued as models of this pastoral understanding of preaching, for their warmhearted evangelical fervor and their pertinence to the practical matters of everyday life.

In other times and places, theologians and preachers have not been so adept at keeping together gospel and what homileticians call the application of the gospel. Luther's theology gave him a perspective from which to view each text of scripture, but this theology stood in the wings, as it were, to coach the preacher in exegesis and exposition. Lesser lights than Luther tended to harden the doctrines of the Reformation and to preach them as gospel. And the ethical implications of the gospel, coming more and more to the fore, usurped so large a place in preaching as actually to redefine the word in the direction of a moralistic discourse. Where these tendencies, toward academic theology and preoccupation with morality apart from the graciousness that the reformers knew, combined, churchgoers heard increasingly dogmatic and moralistic sermons.

But the experience of Wesley's "warmed heart," Spener's piety, or the Calvinist's soul-searching was never completely submerged; what was explosive in the Reformation was always at least latent in Christian experience. This persistent strain combined, in the American scene, with an urgent need to christianize a potentially pagan frontier, to produce revivalism. The sermon in the United States can hardly be understood apart from this phenomenon of the individual with a Bible bent on saving souls. Preaching in this context becomes, variously, social control, hucksterism, moral and social reform, entertainment, the church's reassertion of its place over against culture, the gathering and renewing of the congregation, the act of making religious experience accessible to the uninitiated.

In every case, from the earliest days of the church through the Reformation to the present, preaching is defined in the light of one's understanding of the religious community and its relationship to the environing culture. For example, where the church stands over against the culture, preaching will have both an evangelical and an apologetic function. When the church identifies itself with a social class, as in the recent history of Latin America, preaching may become highly prophetic, even confrontational. Where the church identifies closely with its environment, as it does in a homogeneous Protestant America, among the Calvinist Afrikaners of South Africa, or in nationalistic Germany, preaching may become a conserving amalgam of religious and cultural affirmations. It was to this latter situation that Karl Barth spoke: the major thrust of the neoorthodox movement in theology has been to call preaching back to a renewed understanding of the church and the distinctive character of its language. Barth's definition of proclamation, preaching plus sacrament, was an effort to hold the preacher close to the kerygmatic center of the New Testament and so to the church's distinctive message.

But even neoorthodoxy, in its insistence that preaching is the word of God, would not deny what is clearly a presupposition of the Hebrew prophets and the Christian preachers and of all the world's religions: truth is discernible within the realm of history. Truth invades the human sphere: this is self-evident in the person of the religious teacher who speaks the truth in the local idiom within the limits of culture. At the same time, the religious communicator, even while recognizing cultural and linguistic limitation, will have a sense of the transcendence of truth to the merely provincial. This may well be the common ground upon which the Hindu holy man, the Taoist sage, the Buddhist teacher, the Jesuit, and the Protestant preacher stand: that each speaks the truth for his or her time and place, truth transcendent to all, connecting all. [*See* Truth.]

Function of the Preacher. Preaching, as broadly defined here, has educative, social, ethical, and political functions. The teacher-preacher passes on a body of knowledge, a way of devotion, and a social and ethical code around which a given community coheres. These quite practical considerations should not obscure the fact that mythmaking as a primary form of symbolizing is virtually universal in human societies. The preacher-teacher is one who apprehends and lives in the community's mythology in a special way, acts that out in his or her person, and in ritual and speech perpetuates the myths and their power among the group. This is no less true in the Judeo-Christian tradition than it is in primitive shamanism or among the Maori of contemporary New Zealand. The enlightened guru or master, the leader of the prayers who preaches, the ethical teacher, the poetic sage—all participate in and perpetuate the community's integrating myth by telling the stories again and again and by showing their pertinence to the group's present needs.

The religions of humankind, while by no means all centered upon the spoken word to the extent that distinguishes the Judeo-Christian tradition, include in their religious practice persons whose role and function could be described as preaching. Most religious communities provide for a figure who serves in one or more of the roles that preaching comprises: authoritative leader-spokesperson, interpreter of the sacred writings, prophetic voice, priestly celebrant of the tradition, pious or moral exemplar, creative deviant. The emphasis given to one or the other of these functions will vary as widely as the forms this speech may take, but the phenomenon is nonetheless apparent among the world's religions.

Islam. Even in Islam, which is quintessentially a religion of the people, the imam is the authoritative leader and teacher of the local mosque. His first duty is as leader of the *ṣalāt*, the ritual worship. He intones the necessary words, and the assembled faithful follow precisely the various postures he assumes, bowing and prostrating themselves. Closely tied to this ritual is the reading of the Qur'ān and the Friday sermon, at noon or sunset, in which the imam expounds upon Muslim doctrine. Because Islam comprises all the faithful, irrespective of national boundaries, and because the Qur'ān offers guidance for the whole of human intercourse, the imam's sermon may be highly political and socially prescriptive. Complex as it is, Islam accommodates, among its various denominations, leaders who are political reformers, traveling revivalists (Aḥmadīyah), learned scholars, and the local village imam, who functions as priest, community leader, and teacher. The historical and theological ties of Islam to the Judeo-Christian tradition manifest themselves in the liturgical, political, and homiletic functions of the imam. [*See* Imamate.]

Confucianism. The sage perpetuates Confucianism, teaching and modeling a way of appropriating the tradition to the community's life. Confucius himself saw his role not so much as an originator as a transmitter. Though he was primarily a teacher of ethics and a conservator of inherited customs and values, Confucius believed that his teaching was grounded in the will of Heaven. In the most commonplace courtesies and rituals of respect the moral structure of the universe was manifest. If one takes as homiletic (the word suggests moral discourse) the application of universal truth to the present necessities of a community's life, then Confucius was a preacher. In his relationship with the rulers this sense that his teaching had its origin in the moral order led him to prophetic speech. And, again, in his case the teaching of wisdom was in tandem with careful ritual observance.

The compilers of the *Tao-te ching* share Confucius's interest in common life and mundane matters, but there is a love of the natural and an attentiveness to the earthy and human that one does not find in Confucius. Chuang-tzu (fourth century BCE) saw the Tao in the most down-to-earth matters, and he taught with wit and imagination, resorting constantly to analogy. His critique of Confucianism—that it was unduly moralistic and did not allow people to live simply and naturally—finds its form in his particular style, which relies upon the human, the natural, and the earthy to communicate the Tao. The apprehension and expression of the Tao, and of the implications of that for ethical living, are for Chuang-tzu a matter of imagination. Religion, like its expression in speech, is for the Taoist at once practical and aesthetic.

Buddhism and Hinduism. Both Buddhism and Hinduism have a place for the enlightened teacher; at the same time, both traditions reserve an exalted place for the withdrawn holy man whose spirituality is above communication in words. The Buddha himself overcame the temptation to live in the Dharma, above the annoyance and labor of teaching that doctrine, so difficult to comprehend and communicate; he condescends to teach others the saving truth. The very form that the teaching takes—for example, the riddles of the Zen master—stems from the difficulty of telling in words what the enlightened one knows. In Hinduism the guru teaches; he is highly honored for his efforts in religious education. Like all religious teachers and preachers, he attempts to apply the tenets of religion to everyday domestic and political life. At the same time, a place is reserved for the holy man who does not teach or preach but lives in a detached state of spirituality. He has reached the last stage of the spiritual journey, a communion with the infinite beyond ordinary human language.

Christianity. Among Christians, the role and function of preacher and preaching is understood in many ways. The changing social circumstances of a given group will often alter their understanding of the place of the preacher among them. The divisions of Christianity into three major streams, Roman Catholicism, Eastern Orthodoxy, and Protestantism, and into many diverse denominations within those categories, are due in large measure to historical and sociological factors. The way in which the authoritative leader is perceived by the differentiated group will be no less dependent on the community's social, economic, and political situation. The function of preaching may be understood variously as evangelistic, dogmatic, prophetic, aesthetic, priestly, cultural, propagandizing, or promotional, depending upon the group's perception of its immediate and long-term needs. One cannot account for the present perception and practice of preaching within the Christian churches by reference to a merely theological rationale, though theologies of preaching are not to be discounted.

Roman Catholicism. The Roman Catholic church has shown throughout its history a distinctly homiletic bent, in the sense that the church has been willing through innovation and adaptation to communicate its tradition in the local idiom of those whom it has evangelized. This is not to say that the Roman Catholic church has consistently given priority to preaching as such. In fact, for a thousand years or more the elaboration of the Mass replaced the spoken word. At the same time, the rich drama of the Mass and encrustations of culture it attracted are, in one sense, evangelical: the church attempted to bring its tradition to people where they were and in an idiom they could understand. It is one of the ironies of ecclesiastical history that this impulse displaced the preacher from the Catholic rite.

It was, however, this same impulse—the drive to meet various peoples on their own terms—that led to some of the strongest movements in the history of preaching. The preaching orders, the Dominicans in particular, launched a movement to take the gospel to the masses; they preached outside the churches, popularized Christian teaching, and used the exempla that appealed to untutored peasants. Ironically, even the abuses to which the Protestant reformers objected came from this impulse to make available to the people in the simplest terms the resources of grace that resided in the Catholic tradition. Given the assumption that the church was the ark of salvation, whatever would bring people into the fold and keep them tied to holy mother church could be deemed evangelical.

More recently, following this same impulse toward the vernacular, the Roman Catholic church has been giving a larger place to preaching in the context of the Mass. The priest's homily is very likely to be an exegesis of scripture coupled with down-to-earth pastoral application to the life of parish and community. Preaching is increasingly understood to be a means of grace, not merely moral instruction, and pastoral guidance on ethical and moral issues to stem from the prior proclamation of the saving gospel. In those countries of the world where the Roman Catholic church finds itself aligned with the poor and the disfranchised, particularly in Central and South America, the sermon becomes a rallying cry for social change and even political resistance. In some places, both the Mass and the sermon have become highly radicalized, as *la iglesia que nace del pueblo* ("the church that is born from the people") finds its center in the Eucharist around a common table and in the vernacular sermon that takes account of present exigencies and shared aspirations.

Eastern Orthodoxy. Eastern Orthodoxy, emphasizing as it does the transcendent mystery of God, the value of silence, and the power of symbolism to communicate what can hardly be spoken, does not give so large a place to preaching. John Chrysostom (347–407), the "goldenmouthed" preacher of Antioch and Constantinople, distinguished himself, as did his great contemporary in the Western church, Augustine (354–430), for sermons that were biblical, practical, and straightforward. For a thousand years—in fact, until the coming of the Reformation—preaching did not again achieve the biblical integrity and direct pastoral style of Chrysostom and Augustine. In the Eastern church, the place and power that Chrysostom accorded the pulpit has not been duplicated.

Protestantism. Protestantism, diverse as it has been from its beginnings, has consistently emphasized preaching. The reformers of continental Europe all gave a large place to the sermon, and even in the Anglican tradition the homily at morning prayer was of considerable importance. The sermon was always for instruction in the true way of salvation, reformed doctrine, and right living. William Farel's view of the preacher's task is representative of the Calvinists' position:

> He does not depart from Holy Scripture lest the pure Word of God be obscured by the filth of men, but bears the Word faithfully and speaks only the Word of God. And having expounded his text as simply as possible and without deviating from Scripture, as God gives grace he exhorts and admonishes the hearers, in keeping with the text, to depart from all sin and error, superstition and vanity, and return wholly to God. (*Liturgies of the Western Church,* ed. Bard Thompson, 1962, p. 216)

The functions of the Protestant sermon are evangelical, dogmatic, pastoral, moral-ethical, and prophetic. In some communions, particularly in the more liturgical churches, the sermon has an aesthetic function, and when the media come into play, especially television, the sermon combines the functions of recruitment, pastoral care, and promotion. Whatever function the sermon assumes, the Protestant preacher will include an appeal to a biblical pericope, however tangential the text in its context may be to the subject at hand.

The inclination of the Protestant preacher is toward practical application of the gospel to everyday life. Luther, for example, followed his sermons with pointed, often lengthy "admonitions" to faithful religious practice and right social behavior. He, more than many, saw the difference between gospel and law, and he was at pains to keep the two in proper relationship:

> As often as the Word of God is preached, it makes [our] consciences before God happy, broad, and certain, because it is a word of grace and forgiveness, a good and beneficial word. As often as the word of man is preached, it makes [our] consciences in themselves sad, narrow and anxious, because it is a word of law, wrath, and sin pointing to what we have not done and all that we ought to do.
> (quoted in Dietrich Ritschl, *A Theology of Proclamation,* 1960, frontispiece)

The minister—it is assumed that it is the minister who preaches, certain revivalist itinerants and the sinecures of the mass media notwithstanding—negotiates between the free and gracious declaration of the gospel and the imperatives of that proclamation. Since it is in the nature of Protestantism to be constantly reforming and, at its best, self-critical, this is a continuing tension in preaching. Luther kept to his central doctrine of justification by faith, whatever text might lie before him, and to the hermeneutical principle that every part of scripture, especially those tending toward legalism, should be judged by Christ. Luther's words could be the benchmark of preaching that follows the Reformation's lead:

> The church is the pupil of Christ, sitting at his feet and hearing his word so that she may know how to pass judgement on everything, how to serve in one's calling, how to administer public offices, aya, also how to eat, drink, and sleep, that there may be no doubt about the proper conduct in any walk of life but surrounded on all sides by the Word of God, one may constantly walk in joy and in the light.
> (quoted in Roland Bainton and Ḥerbert Brokering, *A Pilgrimage to Luther's Germany,* 1983, p. 81)

At the same time, the preacher presents the gospel as prior to all human action, the sermon itself an event of this saving grace. The reformers moved in this dialectic, which continues to prove problematic for their successors, between what Herbert H. Farmer (1942) in his classic work on preaching called "ultimate demand and final succour."

Identity and Authority of the Preacher. The reformers would say that it is, finally, Christ who preaches. Such diverse apologists for preaching as the Quaker George Fox, the Presbyterian John Knox, and the churchly Luther held to this notion: it is Christ who is present in the spoken word, clothed in language as he was once in human flesh. Luther was insistent on this:

> A preacher should neither pray the Lord's Prayer nor ask for forgiveness of sins when he has preached (if he is a true preacher), but should say and boast with Jeremiah, "Lord thou knowest that which came out of my lips is true and pleasing to thee" (Jer. 17:16); indeed, with St. Paul and all the apostles and prophets, he should say firmly, *Haec dixit dominus,* God himself has said this (I Cor. 1:1–10). And again, "In this sermon I have been an apostle and prophet of Jesus Christ" (I Thess. 4:15). Here it is unnecessary, even bad, to pray for forgiveness of sins, as if one had not taught truly, for it is God's word and not my word, and God ought not and cannot forgive it, but only confirm, praise and crown it, saying "You have taught truly, for I have spoken through you and the word is mine."
> ("Against Hanswurst," in *Luther's Works,* ed. Hans J. Hillerbrand, 1974, vol. 41, p. 216)

The one who may rightly preach is Christ, the word made flesh and present to the church by the spirit. Most rationales for the authority of the Christian preacher begin here.

A similar idea would not be uncommon among some other religions. In both primitive and more highly developed religions, the spokesperson is often the one possessed by the deity: the god speaks through the orator. The preacher's authority derives from a special relationship to the deity and in connection with the ritual practice that effects and communicates that relationship. One does not have to look far for examples in shamanism, among the Greek oracles and contemporary charismatics, or in almost any ritual of ordination to ministry, wherever it is believed that a potent, life-giving and life-directing spirit comes upon men and women, causing them to speak and authenticating their words. Or the spokesperson may be an ascetic, whose authoritative words come from meeting the deity in lonely and self-denying contemplation and mystical experience. Even in those religions that emphasize the transcendent distance between the human and the divine—Islam, for example—the preacher-prophet is popularly understood to stand in a special relationship to God, and the words of the Prophet are accordingly authoritative. This relationship is often understood in terms of a "calling": the preacher-prophet has been called directly by the deity to speak the authoritative words. [*See* Vocation.]

All preachers are enlightened, in one way or another. The Eastern master-teacher, the studious rabbi, the backwoods preacher, the witch doctor, the theologically schooled and duly ordained minister—each holds special knowledge important to the religious community. One has come to this esoteric knowledge by way of formal education, another by experience, another by the coming of the spirit or pious insight into the sacred canon: in each case the community recognizes its stake in this knowledge and the preacher's possession of it. Even in those communions that seem indifferent to education as such, no one would be allowed to preach without demonstrating access to this saving body of knowledge. That is the wider meaning of what is commonly accepted in Christendom—that ordination to preach and administer the sacraments is inseparable from some kind of education.

The preacher's authority will usually depend not only upon the relationship to the deity and to special knowledge but to a specific canon. The recognized texts, whether the Bible, the Qur'ān, the Vedas, or the well-honed oral traditions of less-developed communities, provide the matrix out of which authoritative pronouncement comes. What may have originated as history, lore, epistle, poetry, legend, or parable, once canonized, becomes increasingly solidified and used to buttress the community's values. On the other hand, sacred canon may stand over against a community, when the canon is interpreted for its own sake, and the result will be an authoritative, self-critical prophetic voice. The tendency, however, will be to require the spokesperson both to adhere to the text and to reinforce in connection with that the accepted practices and mores of the group. In some cases (for example, in the use of the lectionary in Christian liturgical practice) the preacher's speech will be directed, to one degree or another, by a calendar of readings from holy writ.

The community expects, then, that the spokesperson will be faithful to its inherited scriptures. This will entail a pious, personal appropriation of the sacred writings to the life of the preacher and a responsible interpretation of the writings in the service of the community. What is desired in most cases is exegesis of the texts. That is, the community assumes that the texts have integrity, that they are crucial to its life, and that they deserve to be heard in their own right. The preacher, even if she or he does not follow a lectionary, must attempt exegesis, the leading out of the meaning of the texts themselves, and to avoid eisegesis, a too pragmatic, parochial, or shortsighted willingness to use the text for one purpose or another. At the same time, the community's interest in bringing the texts to the service of its felt needs will lead, inevitably, to a measure of eisegesis, that is, to allow the texts to take on new meaning in new situations. This is sometimes referred to as the polyvalence of the texts—language takes on its own life with use and communities allow this because of their changing needs—and makes certain that the authoritative spokesperson will be both exegete *and* eisegete.

Authority is granted to this special, functional person; it is imputed merely by virtue of occupying the office. At the same time, authority is won and reinforced by the spokesperson's continuing relationship to the community, its values, and its significant rituals. The community may vest authority in the person as such; that is, the group may require that its values and mores be exemplified in the individual's personality or behavior. In this case, role and identity are closely identified, and the credibility of public speech depends to a considerable extent upon the preacher's private views and personal behavior. In another community, however, the basis for authority will be not so much the person's identity as the functional role. Luther, in a Christmas sermon, anticipated the later strong statement of the Second Helvetic Confession (1566) on the person and office of the minister:

> Whoever believes the word pays no attention to the one who proclaims it. He does not honor the word because of him who preaches it, but, on the contrary, he honors him who

> preaches because of the word; he never elevates the preacher above the word, and even if the preacher should perish or, as a renegade, preach a different message, he rather gives up the person preaching than the word. He abides with what he has heard—no matter who the preacher might be, no matter whether he is coming or going, no matter what happens.
>
> ("The Gospel for the Early Christmas Service," in *Luther's Works*, 1974, vol. 52, p. 32)

Authority, in this view, rests with the community, its sacred writings and the truth to whose service it has called the person ordained to serve the tradition. Preaching, no less than the sacraments, has authority and authenticity quite apart from the identity and conduct of the preacher. For another group, however, the spokesperson's authority may issue largely from personal graces and charismatic gifts.

In any case, the one who may preach is perceived to be an authoritative figure to the degree that he or she serves the community's needs for connection with its past, integration of its present experience, and projection of its life into a believable future. Preaching is by its very nature conservative, in the sense that it perpetuates the community's inherited values. The preacher is very likely to assess the present, to guide the community's decisions, and to project the future on the basis of what has been. Even the prophetic voice, the calling of the community to accounts, is likely to rise from the group's memories; its remembered story leads to an envisioned future. In a given sermon, the preacher will more often than not point to a text, remind the people of their history, tell a well-known story, and then proceed to prescribe action or to paint a picture of the desired future. This follows from the root meaning of *tradition*, "handing over" or "handing down"; the word is dynamic and suggests the dialectic of all preaching, between the inherited story and the changing stories of individuals and groups. [*See* Tradition.]

Contemporary Issues. Homiletic thought in this century, among European and American theologians and preachers, has been influenced by the ecumenical movement; liberal, neoorthodox, evangelical, and liberation theologies; the media; and the increasingly pluralistic, heterogeneous environment created by electronic communications in what Marshall McLuhan called "the global village." Liturgical renewal is having its impact on preaching, particularly the reforms that Vatican II brought to the Roman Catholic church. The social issues of the times, especially civil rights, the distribution and husbanding of the world's resources, war and nuclear power, have commanded the attention of many pulpits, particularly in the 1960s and 1970s. The question whether Christian churches should, in their preaching, move beyond personal piety and strictly religious practice into the political and social arena was first raised by the Social Gospel movement in the late nineteenth century and remains, for many, unresolved.

Beginning in the 1960s and stemming from the preaching and teaching of figures such as Edmund Steimle, for twenty years preacher on *The Protestant Hour* and professor of homiletics at Union Theological Seminary in New York City, homileticians have focused on narrative, storytelling, and metaphor as paradigms for the sermon. Paul Tillich's analysis of religion and culture and Amos Wilder's studies of the New Testament's genres have opened the way for an increasing interest among homileticians in the arts. Biblical and theological studies have followed, making an ever larger place for the imagination in the interpretation of scripture and in theological reflection. The result is to be seen in many quarters in preaching that is at once more biblical, personal, creative, and contextual, as, for example, in the sermons of the Presbyterian minister and writer Frederick Buechner.

Though women have actively been at work in the leadership of the Christian churches from the beginning, the woman in the pulpit is a relatively new phenomenon. The major seminaries in the United States and Canada now have large proportions of women among their students, some as high as 50 percent. These women bring to the pulpit new styles, a new tone, and insistent questions about theological and liturgical language, until now largely masculine in its pronouns and references. The presence of women in the pulpit raises questions about the authority of preaching and the succession of those ordained to this task, and it intensifies the question of the relationship between ministry—one's standing and function in the community—and public speech.

Time magazine included in its list of America's seven outstanding preachers in the 1980s two blacks, and the preeminent chair in homiletics in the United States was then held by a black. The black pulpit, always at the center of that community's religious life, gained prominence with Martin Luther King, Jr., and has become ever more visible. Black preaching, to which homileticians have given close attention, is distinguished by its pervasive hermeneutic—involving a people who have suffered, survived, remained hopeful—the fervor and color of its style, the preacher's imagination, and the communality of its content and delivery. Henry Mitchell, a black theologian and preacher, who gave the Lyman Beecher Lectures on Preaching at Yale in 1974, said that black preaching is folk communication. The preacher speaks as much out of the community's experience as to it, and in the preparation and delivery of sermons is dependent upon the group for communication organic to their situation. This is not to say that such a notion is exclusive to the black church: Harry Emerson Fosdick, perhaps the most influential American preacher of the twentieth century, defined preaching as "pastoral counseling writ large": preaching always springs from the real life and felt needs of the people. The community as the matrix of preaching is, however, a distinctive characteristic and strong contribution of the black church to religious life.

Continuing issues in preaching will reflect changing notions of ministry, persistent issues of justice, the struggle of minority groups and developing nations for recognition by the world's powerful nations and religions, evolving patterns of human sexuality and social organization, the tensions within religions between the catholic and the provincial, local religious practice in the face of growing internationalism and instantaneous global communication, the use of nuclear energy and the indispensable ecosphere, and the adequacy of inherited religious traditions for the present human situation. Those who preach—who by definition attempt to bring to bear in the experience of a specific community at a given time and place the traditions of the past—will confront these mammoth problems in such immediate questions as these: Are creativity and authority compatible? How does identity relate to role, being human to functioning in a religious community? What is the connection between the prophetic and the pastoral, between standing over against the group and belonging to the community? Does religion entail ethics? Can helpful language come from ancient ritual?

The one who interprets the sacred writings for the present hands over what has been life-giving to the community in the past and is needed again if it is newly understood. As a key figure in such a role the Christian would point to Jesus, whose preaching from the scriptures and in the commonplace language of his people appropriated the tradition to his times. The Muslim might point to Muḥammad in the same way, just as the Jew values the teachers of Israel. In each example language makes the difference, that is, language as speech, unique in its immediacy and contemporaneity. Thus one unifying image among the religions is the person who, out of the tradition of a community, and in the context of its significant rituals, speaks freshly to the needs of a people.

BIBLIOGRAPHY

For the history of preaching, the best sources are the thirteen-volume *Twenty Centuries of Great Preaching,* compiled by Clyde E. Fant and William M. Pinson (Waco, Texas, 1971), and, for a more concise account, Yngve Torgny Brilioth's *A Brief History of Preaching* (Philadelphia, 1965). Any theology of preaching must consider the first volume of Karl Barth's *Church Dogmatics: The Doctrine of the Word of God,* published in two parts (Edinburgh, 1936–1956). Richard Lischer discusses the place and use of theology in preaching in his *A Theology of Preaching: The Dynamics of the Gospel* (Nashville, Tenn., 1981). An older, now classic book on the nature and practice of preaching is Herbert H. Farmer's *The Servant of the Word* (1942; Philadelphia, 1964). The most widely used textbooks in preaching, on theology, theory, and method, are Henry Grady Davis's *Design for Preaching* (Philadelphia, 1958) and Edmund A. Steimle, Morris J. Niedenthal, and Charles L. Rice's *Preaching the Story* (Philadelphia, 1980).

For specific treatment of exegesis and preaching, see Elizabeth Achtemeier's *Creative Preaching: Finding the Words* (Nashville, Tenn., 1980). On preaching as a function of the community, Henry H. Mitchell's Lyman Beecher Lectures, *The Recovery of Preaching* (New York, 1977), and John R. Fry's *Fire and Blackstone* (Philadelphia, 1969) show how interpretation of the canon and homiletic form and style respond to the needs of the group. The most important book for the biblical and theological background to the implications of storytelling and the arts for preaching is Amos N. Wilder's *The Language of the Gospel: Early Christian Rhetoric* (New York, 1964). Good companions to that are several books that demonstrate the affinity of preaching and the poetic: Sallie McFague TeSelle's *Speaking in Parables: A Study in Metaphor and Theology* (Philadelphia, 1975); Frederick Buechner's *Telling the Truth: The Gospel as Tragedy, Comedy and Fairy Tale* (New York, 1977); R. E. C. Browne's *The Ministry of the Word* (London, 1958); and Charles L. Rice's *Interpretation and Imagination* (Philadelphia, 1970). Walter Brueggemann's *The Prophetic Imagination* (Philadelphia, 1978) is the best work on the nature of the prophetic. Herman G. Stuempfle, Jr.'s, *Preaching Law and Gospel* (Philadelphia, 1973) is the best work on law and gospel in preaching. On the form of the sermon, Fred B. Craddock's book *As One without Authority* (1971; Enid, Okla., 1979) is the best work. A discussion of the preaching of Jesus is found in John Dominic Crossan's *In Parables: The Challenge of the Historical Jesus* (New York, 1973). Recommended examples of contemporary American sermons are Frederick Buechner's *The Magnificent Defeat* (New York, 1966) and *The Riverside Preachers,* edited by Paul H. Sherry (New York, 1978).

CHARLES L. RICE

PREANIMISM. In the years around 1900, the scholarly debate about the origins and evolution of religion was still in large measure dominated by the theories put forward by E. B. Tylor thirty years previously, notably in his *Primitive Culture* (London, 1871). The key concept was *animism,* which denoted both a primitive belief in spiritual beings and a belief in the "animation" of nonhuman beings—from the higher mammals down to trees, plants, and stones—by spirits or spirit forces. [*See* Animism and Animatism.] By 1900, however, Tylor's theory had been challenged by two of his Oxford disciples, both of whom were and remained his personal friends. In his *Cock Lane and Common Sense* (London, 1894) and definitively in his celebrated *The Making of Religion* (London, 1898), Andrew Lang had questioned the animistic hypothesis from one direction, suggesting that "perhaps there is no savage race so lowly endowed, that it does not possess, in addition to a world of 'spirits,' something that answers to the conception of God" (*Cock Lane and Common Sense,* p. 334). At a meeting of the British Association in 1899, the animistic theory was questioned from another direction, this time by the philosopher-anthropologist R. R. Marett. Whereas Lang was saying that adherents of the animistic theory had been prevented by their presuppositions from even noticing the evidence in favor of what he called "high gods" among peoples on a low level of material development, Marett claimed that the term *animism* was ambiguous and that the mental processes it assumed were too sophisticated to have been present at the lowest level of human evolution [*See the biography of Marett.*]

Marett's paper "Pre-Animistic Religion" was first published in the journal *Folk-Lore* (June 1900, pp. 162–182); it subsequently formed the first chapter of his book *The Threshold of Religion* (London, 1909; 2d exp. ed., London, 1914). Although brief, its argument was revolutionary. On the one hand, it suggested that in view of the double meaning of the word *animism* in Tylor's *Primitive Culture,* a distinction might be drawn between animism proper, as a belief in spiritual beings, and the belief in the "animation" of animals, plants, and natural objects, which he proposed to call "animatism." This of course had nothing to do with any theory of the origin of religion as such, but was merely a plea for greater terminological precision. On the other hand—and this appeared to be an outright challenge to the Tylorian hypothesis—Marett also ventured the opinion that animism was simply not "primitive" enough to represent the earliest form of religion. Beneath (though not necessarily chronologically prior to) the belief in spirits, he argued, there is a more amorphous sense of the world as being filled with the manifestations of supernatural power. [*See* Power.] This notion was unlikely to have been reasoned out in the first instance; rather it involved a "basic feeling of awe, which drives a man, ere he can think or theorize upon it, into personal relations with the supernatural" (Marett, 1914, p. 15). In search of a word to characterize this power, Marett settled finally upon the Melanesian word *mana,* as described by the missionary R. H. Codrington in his book *The Melanesians* (Oxford, 1891). Mentioned only in passing in his 1899 paper, alongside other "power-words," over the next few years *mana* came to eclipse the others as a *terminus technicus* to describe what lay at the root of preanimism.

Mana, however, was by no means an exclusively Melanesian concept. It was common to the whole of the Pacific, to Polynesia as well as Melanesia. It had been first noted by Captain James Cook in 1777 and long before Codrington's time had been fairly fully discussed in relation to the Maori of New Zealand. F. E. Maning in his book *Old New Zealand* (Auckland, 1863) had stressed, for instance, that *mana* had no single meaning but was associated with such diverse ideas as "virtue, prestige, authority, good fortune, influence, sanctity, luck" (Maning, [1863] 1927, pp. 239–240). However, the early preanimists remained generally unaware of the New Zealand material and were content to rely for the most part on Codrington's evidence as transmitted first by Marett and subsequently by the German and French sociologists.

Marett himself was most unwilling to "dogmatize" about religious origins and always expressed himself with great caution. Thus although in his 1899 paper he went so far as to suggest that what he there called "supernaturalism" might be "not only logically but also in some sense chronologically prior to animism" (Marett, 1914, p. 11), he did not say in what sense. Again—and this is important in view of the direction subsequently taken by the debate—he did not categorize *mana* as unambiguously impersonal. In a later paper, in fact, he stated explicitly that *mana* "leaves in solution the distinction between personal and impersonal" (1915, p. 119) and noted that although it may in some circumstances be used in a somewhat impersonal way, it is always necessary to take account of "the ambiguity that lies sleeping in *mana*" (p. 121). Other writers on the subject found this degree of ambiguity unmanageable and unwelcome.

In the wake of Marett's work, the first decade of the twentieth century saw the appearance of a great deal of writing on the subject of preanimism and on *mana* and its various equivalents. In Germany, Wilhelm Wundt of Leipzig wrote extensively in his *Völkerpsychologie* (1900) about "die präanimistische Hypothese," followed by K. T. Preuss in a series of articles in the journal *Globus* (1904–1905). Both, however, seem to have assumed Marett's theory to have been conceived in direct and complete opposition to Tylor—a charge that Marett, who admired Tylor greatly, strenuously denied. In France, the *Année sociologique* school (which included Durkheim, Hubert, and Mauss) produced a theory very similar to Marett's, perhaps independently, though Hubert and Mauss's article "Esquisse d'une théorie générale de la Magie" appeared in *Année sociologique* only in 1904, and Durkheim's *magnum opus* did not appear until 1912.

By this time, however, *mana* had been coupled with a bewildering variety of terms drawn from primal cultures in various parts of the world, all of which, it was claimed, conveyed the same basic sense of that supernatural power that had inspired an initial human response of awe. A proportion of these words had been culled from the vocabularies of various Amerindian peoples: from the Iroquois came *orenda* (as in Hewitt's "*Orenda* and a Definition of Religion," *American Anthropologist*, n.s. 4, 1902), from the Algonquin *manitou* and from the Lakota *wakan* and *wakanda.* The Australian Aranda (Arunta) term *arungquiltha/arúnkulta*, the Malagasy *andriamanitra*, the Fijian *kalou*, and even the Old Norse *hamingja* and the Hindu *brahman* were added to the list, which by 1914 had assumed considerable proportions. *Mana*, however, continued to serve as the flagship of the preanimistic fleet.

It is important to remember that Marett had stated (not in his original article but at the Oxford Congress of the Science of Religion in 1908) that it was by now his express intention to endow *mana* with "classificatory authority to some extent at the expense of the older notion [i.e., animism]" (Marett, 1915, p. 102). Every new science had to create its own specialist terminology; this being so, Marett was proposing the use of *mana* whenever and wherever circumstances appeared to warrant it as a technical term expressive of preanimistic religions and virtually independent of the etymological meaning of the word in its original Pacific context. In the light of Marett's express intention, it is slightly embarrassing to note the solemnity with which some scholars have subsequently believed themselves to be demolishing Marett's argument by pointing out that the etymology of *mana* is not altogether what he supposed it to be.

Another critical point concerns the supposed impersonality of the power of *mana*. As we have seen, Marett was initially insistent that *mana* is an ambiguous concept, even as he knew perfectly well that his chief informant Codrington had stated that it was always associated with and derived from persons, spirits, or ghosts. On at least one later occasion, however, in his article "Mana" in Hastings's *Encyclopaedia of Religion and Ethics* (vol. 8, Edinburgh, 1915), he was prepared to state that *mana* was "in itself impersonal" while always associated with personal beings. (Often in such contexts he used the analogy of electricity, which remains latent until tapped and channeled.) The ambiguity between personal and impersonal remained in force nonetheless. But just as Marett read *mana* through the prism of Codrington, one feels that almost all later debaters have read Marett through the prism of the greater international celebrity Émile Durkheim.

To Durkheim, writing in *The Elementary Forms of the Religious Life*, first published in French in 1912 and in English in 1915, there were no ambiguities. Caution was replaced by assertion. According to Durkheim, Marett had shown "the existence of a religious phase which he called *preanimistic*, in which the rites are addressed to impersonal forces like the Melanesian mana and the wakan of the Omaha and Dakota" (1968 edition, p. 201). Durkheim categorically stated that *mana* was "an impersonal religious force" (pp. 192, 198), "an anonymous and diffused force" (p. 194); because it was not, according to Codrington, a supreme being, Durkheim concludes that it must possess "impersonality" (p. 194). We need look no further for the later impression that preanimism must of necessity involve belief in impersonal forces; it comes not from Marett but from Durkheim.

The preanimistic theory of the origin of religion (as it had developed between 1900 and 1914) first began to be called in question in the years following World War I. In 1914 Nathan Söderblom (who had been a professor in Leipzig from 1912 to 1914) published in the *Archiv für Religionswissenschaft* an article, "Über den Zusammenhang höherer Gottesideen mit primitiven Vorstellungen," in which the customary preanimistic points were discussed (see also Söderblom, *Gudstrons uppkomst*, Stockholm, 1914, pp. 30–108). One of his students, F. R. Lehmann, was inspired by this article to take up the question of *mana* and in 1915 presented his dissertation on the subject, in which he penetrated beyond Durkheim and Marett to Codrington, and beyond Codrington to the etymology and implications of the common Polynesian/Melanesian word *mana* itself.

Lehmann's researches had the effect of discrediting altogether the notion that the term *mana* had ever been used in the Pacific region to denote an impersonal force. Even when trees, stones, or other inanimate objects were declared to possess *mana*, this was because spirits had associated themselves with those objects, and not by virtue of their having an impersonal force of their own. Paul Radin had made substantially the same point in 1914, when he asked, "What warrant have we for thinking of the god as a deity plus power, and not merely as a powerful deity? Are we not committing the old error of confusing an adjective with a noun?" (*Journal of American Folklore* 27, 1914, p. 347). Following Lehmann, and in the increasingly antievolutionary atmosphere of the interwar years and beyond, more and more frequent criticisms were leveled against the preanimistic hypothesis, the interpretation of *mana* that had supported it, and against those who had written in these terms. A powerful broadside against the theory was produced by the Germanist Walter Baetke, in his book *Das Heilige im Germanischen* (Tübingen, 1942), and another by Geo Widengren, in a polemical article, "Evolutionism and the Problem of the Origin of Religion" (*Ethnos* 10, 1945, pp. 57–96). Widengren, incidentally, admired Baetke's work; and it was in the Baetke festschrift that Lehmann described the course of his research in the area of *mana,* in an article called "Versuche, die Bedeutung des Wortes 'Mana' . . . festzustellen" (pp. 215–240). Widengren summed up: "The best experts in the field of Melanesian religion have explicitly stated that *mana* is actually never an impersonal power"; it is "in reality a quality. It goes without saying that not *mana* in itself but persons and things possessing *mana* are the objects of worship" (p. 84). One last critic may be quoted. In his 1958 *Patterns in Comparative Religion* and in virtually identical terms in his 1968 *Myths, Dreams and Mysteries,* Mircea Eliade denies the existence of any such "impersonal and universal force" as *mana* was once thought to represent, not least because "impersonality" is "without meaning within the archaic spiritual horizon" (Eliade, 1968, p. 129). All these critics, however, have tended to attribute to Marett extreme opinions that were actually those of Durkheim.

It remains to be noted that Rudolf Otto, in his celebrated book *Das Heilige,* produced a theory of the origin of religion in an ineffable *sensus numinis,* in the course of which he praised Marett for coming "within a hair's breadth" of his own views. Otto, too, was criticized by Baetke and Widengren, who used arguments very similar to those they had used against Marett and the preanimists. Otto's *numen* could hardly be called "impersonal," however.

Preanimism and the debate about preanimistic religion belong less to the world of religion as such (and hardly, it would seem, to the area of primal religion at all) than to the intellectual history of the early twentieth century in the West. Possibly the popularity of the concept was not unrelated to the West's growing estrangement from fixed forms of religious belief and doctrine and its simultaneous maintenance of a sense that there might be "something" (rather than "someone") in charge of the world's destiny. It involved the evolutionists' conviction that religion had emerged out of something other than, and simpler than, religion. It also made assumptions about personality and (at least after Durkheim) impersonality that later critics found it all too easy to demolish. The critics, however, may have gone too far in the opposite direction. In their desire to disassociate themselves from the evolutionists, they have frequently misrepresented and misinterpreted them, without realizing that the evolutionists themselves were quite capable of raising objections—often the same objections—to their own work. Preanimism as such can be neither proved nor disproved as a rudimentary stage in the evolution of religion. There may, however, remain an area of religion within which supernatural (or at least uncontrollable) power is sensed, while remaining inchoate and unconnected with any firm notion of deity. This need not be a stage out of which more precise notions emerge. It is just as likely to be found at the end of a long process of decline, and thus to be as much posttheist as preanimist. We have no word that can be used as a technical term to describe this. *Preanimism* clearly will not do, because of the implicit sequence involved. Some use might however still be found for the term *mana* in this connection. In 1907 Marett wrote that "the last word about *mana* has not been said" (p. 219). By 1965, *mana* had almost been dismissed from the technical vocabulary of the study of religion. It may be high time for its reexamination.

[*See also* Evolutionism.]

BIBLIOGRAPHY

References to the "preanimistic hypothesis" will be found scattered throughout the anthropological literature of the first half of the twentieth century. The seminal articles are gathered in R. R. Marett's *The Threshold of Religion,* 3d ed. (London, 1915), and Émile Durkheim's application of the theory is found in *The Elementary Forms of the Religious Life,* translated by Joseph Ward Swain (1915; reprint, New York, 1965), in which see especially pages 191–204. For the subsequent attempted demolition of the theory, reference must be made to the German works of F. R. Lehmann, beginning with *Mana: Der begriff des "ausserordentlich wirkungsvollen" bei Südseevölkern* (Leipzig, 1922) and ending with his essay "Versuche, die Bedeutung des Wortes 'Mana' . . . festzustellen," in *Festschrift Walter Baetke,* edited by Kurt Rudolph et al. (Weimar, 1966), pp. 215–240; and Walter Baetke's *Des Heilige im Germanischen* (Tübingen, 1942). See also Geo Widengren's "Evolutionism and the Problem of the Origin of Religion," *Ethnos* 10 (1945): 57–96, which follows substantially the same line.

ERIC J. SHARPE

PRE-COLUMBIAN RELIGIONS. *For discussions of the indigenous religious traditions of the Americas, see* Caribbean Religions; Mesoamerican Religions; North American Religions; *and* South American Religions.

PREDESTINATION. *See* Free Will and Predestination.

PREHISTORIC RELIGIONS. [*This entry consists of three articles on the religious expressions of prehistoric peoples:*

An Overview
Old Europe
The Eurasian Steppes and Inner Asia

The first considers the notion of prehistory and its applicability in the study of religion. The companion pieces focus on two areas where study of prehistoric cultures has been particularly fruitful.]

An Overview

The term *prehistory* refers to the vast period of time between the appearance of humanity's early hominid ancestors and the beginning of the historical period. Since the invention of writing is used to mark the transition between prehistory and history, the date of this boundary varies greatly from region to region. The study of prehistoric religion, therefore, can refer to religious beliefs and practices from as early as 60,000 BCE to almost the present day. Generally, however, the term *prehistory* is defined by its European application and hence refers to the period from the Paleolithic period, which occurred during the Pleistocene epoch, to the protohistoric Neolithic period and the Bronze and Iron ages.

The biases of a literate culture are apparent in the term. Clearly, a people's literacy bespeaks their accessibility by a literate culture, but it is not, as has often been assumed, an adequate criterion for determining intellectual or cultural depth and complexity. To divide human cultures by the single invention of writing suggests that literacy somehow marks a specific stage of mental development or a radical turning point within the development of human culture conceived of according to an evolutionary scheme. Neither such a radical break nor such an inevitable evolutionary development can, however, be demonstrated.

This division notwithstanding, it should be noted that prehistory is understood to be singularly human. In his *Philosophical Investigations*, Wittgenstein quips, "If a lion could talk, we could not understand him." Wittgenstein is suggesting that language would not enable us to understand a "world," or perspective, that was so radically distinct in kind from our own. In contrast to Wittgenstein's lion, prehistoric humanity is regarded as understandable: a psychic unity between prehistorical and historical humanity is assumed. We believe that with sufficient evidence the prehistoric "world" can be grasped. The problem is accessibility, not difference in kind.

Access to a prehistoric culture, however, is highly problematic. And when one attempts to understand a phenomenon such as religion, the problem becomes acute. We understand religion primarily in terms of "language," that is, its principal characteristics are its interpretive meanings and valuations. The wordless archaeological remains of prehistoric religion—cultic or ceremonial artifacts and sites, pictures and symbols, sacrifices—have provided limited access to the religious "language" of prehistoric cultures. For example, knowledge of how corpses were disposed during the Neolithic period does not reveal why they were so disposed. Consequently, even when there is clear evidence of a prehistoric religious practice, interpretation of the nature of prehistoric religions remains highly speculative and disproportionately dependent upon analogies to contemporary "primitive" cultures.

Our knowledge of prehistoric religion is therefore the product of reconstructing a "language" from its silent material accessories. Among the oldest material forms of cultic practice are burial sites, dating from the Middle Paleolithic. [*See* Funeral Rites.] One can trace, from the Upper Paleolithic on, a growing richness and diversity of grave goods that reach extravagant proportions during the Iron Age. The practices of second burials, the burning of bodies, and the ritual disposition of skulls are also common. Megalithic graves date back to the Neolithic period. Despite the cultic implications of these massive stone constructions (e.g., ancestor cults), a uniform religious meaning remains undemonstrated.

Evidences of sacrifices from the Middle Paleolithic period in the form of varied quantities of animal bones near burial sites suggest offerings to the dead. Sacrificial traditions that were associated with game (e.g., bear ceremonialism) date back to the Upper Paleolithic. There is no evidence of human sacrifice prior to the Neolithic period, and hence this practice is associated with the transition from a hunter-gatherer culture to an agrarian culture and, consequently, with the domestication of plants and animals. [*See* Sacrifice.]

Prehistoric works of art dating back to the Paleolithic period—paintings, drawings, engravings, and sculpture—are the richest form of access to prehistoric religion. The primary subjects of these earliest examples of graphic art were animals; humans, rarely depicted, were often drawn with animal attributes. The intimate and unique role of animals in the physical and mental lives of these early hunter-gatherers is clearly demonstrated. (This role is also evidenced in the sacrificial traditions.) Though some form of animalism is suggested, the religious significance of these animal figures is difficult to interpret. [*See* Animals.]

Shamanistic practices are also reflected in this art, especially in the paintings of birds and of animals that have projectiles drawn through their bodies. Common in prehistoric sculpture is the female statuette. Although frequently related to fertility, these figurines are open to numerous interpretations of equal plausibility (e.g., spirit abodes, ancestor representations, house gods, as well as spirit rulers over animals, lands and other physical or spiritual regions, hunting practices, and natural forces). [*See also* Lord of the Animals.]

It is unlikely that we shall ever be able adequately to interpret the "language" of prehistoric religion. The material evidence is too scarce and the nature of religious phenomena too complex. There is, however, a meaning in these wordless fragments that is itself significant for any study of religion. The power and depth of these silent archaeological remains cause one to recognize the limitation of written language as a purveyor of religious meaning. The connections one is able, however tenuously, to draw between the evidences of religious life among prehistoric peoples and the beliefs and practices of their descendants address the conditions that have inspired human beings, from our beginnings, to express our deepest selves in art and ritual.

[*See also* Paleolithic Religion *and* Neolithic Religion.]

BIBLIOGRAPHY

Breuil, Henri, and Raymond Lantier. *The Men of the Old Stone Age: Palaeolithic and Mesolithic* (1965). Translated by B. B. Rafter. Reprint, Westport, Conn., 1980.

James, E. O. *The Beginnings of Religions: An Introductory and Scientific Study* (1948). Reprint, Westport, Conn., 1973.

Jensen, Adolf E. *Myth and Cult among Primitive Peoples*. Translated by Marianna T. Choldin and Wolfgang Weissleder. Chicago, 1963.

Levy, Gertrude R. *The Gate of Horn: A Study of the Religious Conceptions of the Old Stone Age* (1948). Reprint, New York, 1963.

Maringer, Johannes. *The Gods of Prehistoric Man*. Translated and edited by Mary Ilford. New York, 1960.

Ucko, Peter J. *Anthropomorphic Figurines of Predynastic Egypt and Neolithic Crete*. London, 1968.

MARY EDWARDSEN and JAMES WALLER

Old Europe

The term *Old Europe* is used here to describe Europe during the Neolithic and Copper ages, before it was infiltrated by Indo-European speakers from the Eurasian steppes (c. 4500–2500 BCE). The Indo-Europeans superimposed their patriarchal social structure, pastoral economy, and male-dominated pantheon of gods upon the gynecocentric Old Europeans, whose millennial traditions were officially disintegrated. Nonetheless, these traditions formed a powerful substratum that profoundly affected the religious life of European cultures that arose during the Bronze Age. Western Europe remained untouched by the Indo-Europeans for one millennium longer; Crete, Thera, and other Aegean and Mediterranean islands maintained Old European patterns of life until about 1500 BCE.

The agricultural revolution spread gradually to southeastern Europe about 7000 to 6500 BCE. A full-fledged Neolithic culture was flourishing in the Aegean and Adriatic regions by 6500 BCE. The Danubian basin and central Europe were converted to a food-producing economy circa 6000 to 5500 BCE. Around 5500, copper artifacts first appeared, leading to the creation of a fully developed copper culture in the fifth millennium BCE. The rise of agrarian cultures in western and northern Europe occurred about two millennia later.

The Old European religion of southeastern Europe and the Danubian basin persisted through three millennia, 6500–3500 BCE; the Neolithic period extended from 6500 to 5500 BCE, the Copper Age from 5500 to 3500 BCE. In northern Europe, the Neolithic period continued to about 2000 BCE. (Dates given here are calibrated radiocarbon dates.)

Old European beliefs and practices have been reconstructed primarily through analysis of the archaeological record. The evidence examined includes temples, temple models, altars, frescoes, rock carvings and paintings, caves and tombs, figurines, masks, and cult vessels, as well as the symbols and signs engraved or painted on all of these.

Cult objects, particularly figurines, provide some clues to the types of rituals performed by Old Europeans and the deities they worshiped. The richest finds have been unearthed in southeastern and Danubian Europe, as far north as the Carpathian Mountains. This region encompasses present-day Greece, Italy, Yugoslavia, Bulgaria, Romania, the western Ukraine, Hungary, and Czechoslovakia, as well as the Aegean and Mediterranean islands. The second region yielding cult relics is western Europe (present-day Spain, Portugal, France, and the British Isles). The best-preserved monuments are megalithic tomb walls engraved with symbols and images of deities, stone stelae, and figurines associated with burials.

Despite the multitude of culture groups in Old Europe and the diverse styles of their artworks, the pantheon of deities was the same throughout the vast landmass. Old European religious beliefs stemmed from the gynecocentric Paleolithic and early agricultural world, created by a birth giver, mother, root gatherer, and seed planter and concerned with feminine cycles, lunar phases, and seasonal changes. Skylight and stars, prominent in Indo-European mythology, hardly figure in Old European symbolism.

The images of Old Europe are those of the earth's vitality and richness. The transformative processes of nature are symbolically manifested in sprouting seeds, eggs, caterpillars and butterflies, and in such "life columns" (symbols of rising and spontaneous life) as trees, springs, and serpents, which seem to emerge from the earth's womb. Sacred images represent both the miracle of birth—human, animal, and plant—and the awe and mystery surrounding the cyclic destruction and regeneration of life.

Most Old European sacred images symbolize the ever-changing nature of life on earth: the constant and rhythmic interplay between creation and destruction, birth and death. For example, the moon's three phases—new, waxing, and old—are repeated in trinities of deities: maiden, nymph, and crone; life-giving, death-giving, and transformational deities; rising, dying, and self-renewing deities. Similarly, life-giving deities are also death wielders. Male vegetation spirits also express life's transitional nature: they are born, come to maturity, and die, as do plants.

Goddesses and Gods. The Old European evidence reveals clear-cut stereotypes of divinities that appear repeatedly throughout time and geography in sculptural art. The stereotypes include anthropomorphic deities and innumerable epiphanies in the form of birds, animals, insects, amphibians, stones, and hills.

Goddesses. The principal goddesses are composite images, encompassing an accumulation of traits from the preagricultural era.

The water-bird goddess appears with a beak or a pinched nose, a long neck, a beautiful head of hair or crown, breasts, wings or winglike projections, and protruding female buttocks outlined in the shape of a duck, goose, or swan. Her epiphany is a water bird, most frequently a duck. (See figure 1.) There is an association between this divinity and divine moisture from the oceans, rivers, lakes, bogs, and the skies. Meanders, streams, V's, and chevrons are her principal symbols. (The V sign, duplicated or triplicated in the chevron, probably derives from the shape of the pubic triangle.) They can be found on objects that are associated with her and also as decorations on her images. She is associated with the number three (triple source, totality) and with the ram, her sacred animal. The symbols give a clue to her function as a giver of life, wealth, and nourishment. She is of Paleolithic origin. Since the early Neolithic she also was a weaver and spinner of human fate and giver of crafts and was worshiped in house shrines and temples.

A related image of the life-giving goddess appears in the shape of a water container (large pithos), decorated with M's, nets, brushes, meanders, and running spirals (see figure 2). She also appears in figurines marked with net-patterned pubic triangles and squares, symbolic of life-giving water.

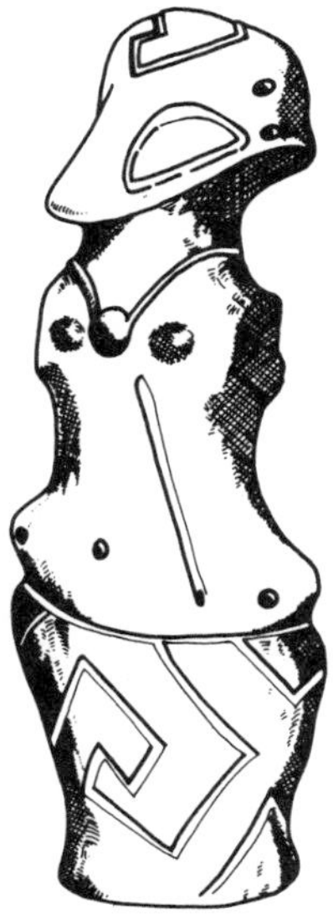

FIGURE 1. *The Water-Bird Goddess.* Terra-cotta duck-masked deity. Her skirt and crown bear white encrusted meanders and V's. Vinča culture, Vinča, Yugoslavia (near Belgrade); 4500–4000 BCE.

The snake goddess has snakelike hands and feet and a long mouth and wears a crown. The snake spirals and snake coil are her emblems. She is life energy incarnate. As a symbol of fertility and well-being of the family she is worshiped in house shrines. Her crown very likely was a symbol of wisdom as it still is in European folklore. The horns of a snake, resembling a crescent moon, link this deity with lunar cycles. In megalithic tomb-shrines of western Europe, the winding snake figures as a symbol of regeneration. In symbolism, the snake coil

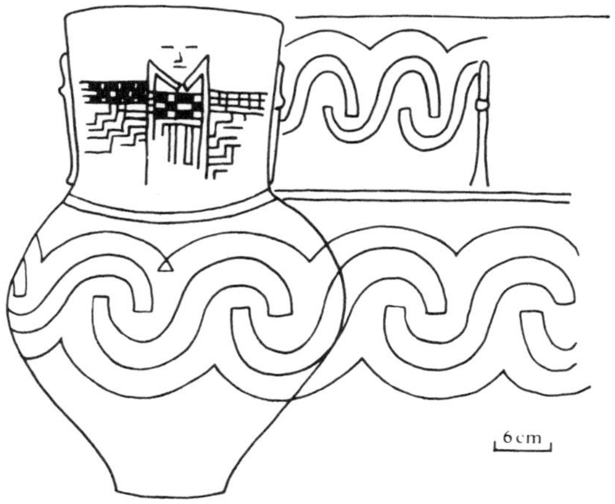

FIGURE 2. *The Life-giving Goddess as a Water Container.* Her face appears above an M-shaped sign. The large bands of running spirals, the parallel lines, and the checkerboard pattern are all symbols of water. Early Vinča culture, 5200–5000 BCE.

is a source of energy comparable to the sun; and both are metaphors of the regenerating eyes of the goddess.

The birth-giving goddess is portrayed in a naturalistic pose of giving birth. She is well evidenced in Paleolithic art in France (Tursac, c. 21,000 BCE) and in all periods of Old Europe (from the seventh millennium onward). The vulva, depicted alone (known from the Aurignacian period, circa 30,000 BCE, and throughout the Upper Paleolithic and Old Europe), may have served as *pars pro toto* of this goddess. Her epiphanies were the doe (both deer and elk) and the bear, stemming from an early belief in a zoomorphic birth-giver, the primeval mother.

The nurse or mother holding or carrying a child is portrayed in hunchbacked figurines or, in more articulate examples, as a bear-masked madonna carrying a pouch for a baby and as a bird, snake, and bear-masked mother holding a child. Images of her date from the early Neolithic and appeared throughout the Copper Age and into historical times.

The vulture or owl goddess, a maleficent twin of the birth-giving goddess, appears as Death in the guise of a vulture, owl, or other predatory bird or carrion eater, yet has qualities of regeneration. [*See also* Birds.] A vulva, umbilical cord, or labyrinth is painted or engraved on her images. Hooks and axes—symbols of energy and life stimulation—are engraved on western European stone stelae and on passage-grave slabs representing the owl goddess. In one of the Çatal Hüyük shrines of central Anatolia (seventh millennium BCE), the beaks of griffins emerge from the open nipples of female breasts. The owl goddess's breasts, depicted in relief on slabs of megalithic gallery graves in Brittany, also suggest that regeneration is in her power.

The snowy owl appears in a number of engravings on the Upper Paleolithic (Magdalenian) cave walls of France, probably already as an epiphany of Death. There is rich evidence of the owl goddess throughout the Neolithic, Copper, and Early Bronze ages. During the last period, the owl form became the usual shape of urns. Burials of birds of prey as sacrifices to this goddess are known from the Paleolithic (Ksar Akil, Lebanon, mid-Paleolithic; Malta, c. 15,000 BCE), earliest Neolithic (Zawi Chemi Shanidar, northern Iraq, more than 10,000 years before our time), the Neolithic, and the Bronze Age (Isbister, Scotland). It is clear that large wings had enormous symbolic importance for millennia. (See figure 3.)

The White Lady, or Death, is portrayed with folded arms tightly pressed to her bosom and with closed or tapering legs. She is masked and sometimes has a polos on her head. Her abnormally large pubic triangle is the center of attention. A reduced image of her is a bone. Her images are made of bone or of such bone-colored materials as marble, alabaster, and light-colored stone. She dates back to the Upper Paleolithic, has been found throughout Old Europe, and appears in the Aegean Bronze Age as the Cycladic marble figurines. Most of the

FIGURE 3. *The Vulture Goddess.* With tremendous, broomlike wings she swoops down on headless humans. Fresco from Çatal Hüyük (shrine in Level VII, 8), central Anatolia; early seventh millennium BCE.

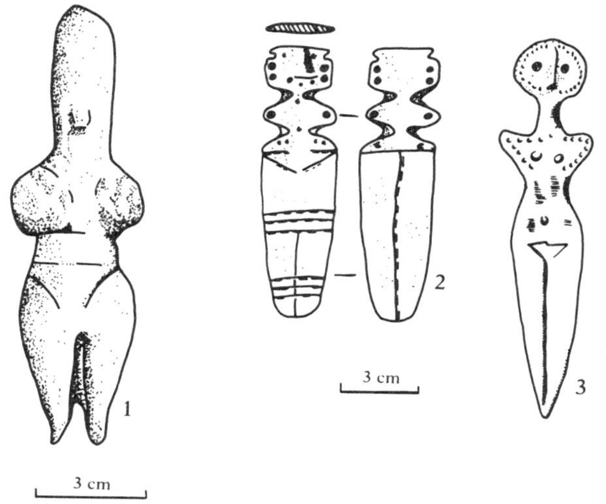

FIGURE 4. *The Stiff Nude, or the White Lady (Death).* These figurines come from Neolithic and Copper Age graves. (1) White marble figurine with a phallus-shaped head from a Neolithic Aegean culture, Cyclades; c. 6000 BCE. (2) Front and and back views of a bone figurine with a mask and bound legs; Karanovo culture, Ruse, northern Bulgaria; c. 4500 BCE. (3) Clay figurine from a young girl's grave; late Cucuteni culture, Vykhvatintsi cemetery, Moldavian S.S.R.; c. 3500 BCE.

White Ladies were recovered from graves and found singly, in threes, or in groups of six or nine. (See figure 4.)

The goddess of regeneration appears in myriad forms, the most prominent of which are fish, toad, frog, hedgehog, triangle, hourglass, bee, and butterfly. All these appear in art as amphibians, animals, insects, and hybrids: fish-woman, frog-woman, hedgehog-woman, hourglass with bird's feet or claws, bee and butterfly with a human head. (See figure 5.)

The peculiar relationship, even equation, of the fish, frog, and toad with the uterus of the regenerating goddess accounts for their prominent role in European symbolism. The importance of the hedgehog probably derives from its equation with a wart-covered animal uterus. As life and funerary symbols, hedgehogs continued to appear throughout later prehistory and history. When manifested as a bee, butterfly, or moth, the goddess is thought to symbolize reborn life. Frequently, these images emerge from a bucranium, also the symbol of the female uterus as evidenced from the earliest Neolithic. (See figure 6.) The key to understanding the equation of the female uterus with the bucranium lies in the extraordinary likeness of the female uterus and fallopian tubes to the head and horns of a bull (Cameron, 1981, pp. 4f.).

The pregnant goddess (Mother Earth) is portrayed naturalistically as a nude with hands placed on her enlarged belly. The abdominal part of her body is always emphasized. She is also depicted as a bulging mound and oven. In the infancy of agriculture, her pregnant belly was apparently likened to the fertility of the fields. Her image was associated with lozenges, triangles, snakes, and two or four lines. (See figure 7.) Her sacred animal is the sow. She is the Mother of the Dead: her uterus or entire body is the grave (hypogea of Malta and Sardinia, passage graves of western Europe, and court tombs of Ireland) or temple (Malta).

Although evidence of her exists from the Upper Paleolithic, it was probably not until the Neolithic that she became the earth mother and bread giver, appearing enthroned and crowned. She is the dominant figure in the early phases of the Neolithic. Her figurines are

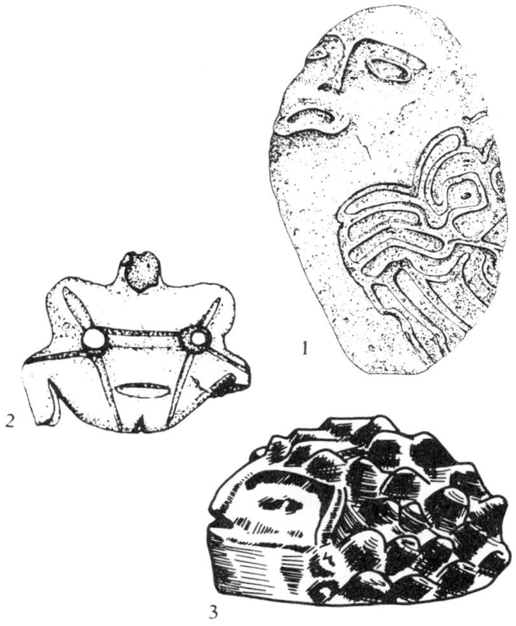

FIGURE 5. *The Goddess in Her Regenerative and Transformative Aspects.* (1) Fish Goddess (Fish Woman). A considerable number of the fish-faced sculptures from Lepenski Vir in northern Yugoslavia are engraved with labyrinths, which suggests that the goddess represents a generative womb. Lepenski Vir I c, shrine no. 28, c. 6000–5800 BCE. (2) Frog Goddess. A major Old European and Anatolian archetype is the frog goddess. The perforations on this black-stone amulet suggest that it was meant to be attached to something else. Early Sesklo culture, Achilleion, Thessaly; c. 6400 BCE. (3) Hedgehog Goddess. The goddess appears here in the form of a sculpted lid. Karanovo VI culture, Căscioarele on the Danube, southern Romania; c. 4500 BCE.

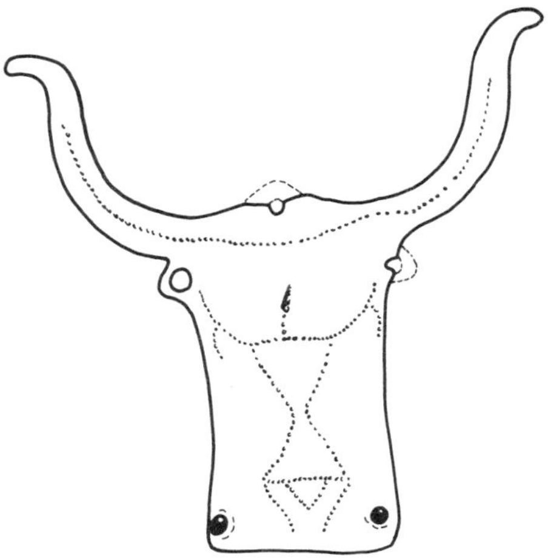

FIGURE 6. *The Bee Goddess.* The new life arising from a sacrificed bull is often portrayed as the goddess in her epiphany as a bee. Such portrayal may be related to a belief in the spontaneous generation of insects from a bull's carcass. Here a punctate silhouette of the bee goddess is rendered on a bull's head carved from bone plate. Cucuteni B culture, Bilcze Zlote, upper Seret River Valley, western Ukraine; c. 3700–3500 BCE.

FIGURE 7. *Pregnant Earth Goddess in an Open Shrine Model.* The goddess is depicted with her hands placed on her enlarged belly. In front of her is a round hole used for libations, and she is flanked by two schematic male figurines, which may represent attendants performing a ritual. Undulating lines, such as those decorating the exterior of this model, are often associated with the Pregnant Goddess. Ghelaeşti-Nedeia, county of Piatra Neamţ, northeastern Romania; Cucuteni culture, c. 3900–3800 BCE.

found on oven platforms (as at Achilleion, Thessaly, c. 6000 BCE; author's excavation, 1973), never on altars in house shrines, which were used exclusively for bird and snake goddesses.

Pairs of larger and smaller figurines known from all periods of Old Europe represent both the major and minor aspects of the goddess, sometimes as a mother-daughter pair (an analogy to Demeter and Persephone). Furthermore, the major temples of Malta consist of two constructions, one larger and the other slightly smaller, both in the anthropomorphic shape. This suggests again the dual or cyclical nature of the goddess as both summer and winter, old and young.

Gods. There are only two certain stereotypes of male gods: (1) the Sorrowful Ancient and (2) the mature male holding a crosier.

The Sorrowful Ancient is portrayed as a peaceful man sitting on a stool, hands resting on knees or supporting his face. Since the Sorrowful Ancient appears together with seated pregnant figurines that probably represent harvest goddesses, it can be assumed that he represents a dying vegetation god.

The bull with a human mask and the goat-masked male sculptures of the Vinča culture (fifth millennium BCE) may portray an early form of Dionysos in the guise of a bull or a he-goat—the god of annual renewal in full strength. However, lack of documentation from other culture groups warrants his preclusion as a stereotype.

The mature male holding a crosier and seated on a throne, from Szegvár-Tüzköves (Tisza culture, Hungary), may be a relation to Silvanus, Faunus, and Pan, historical-era forest spirits and protectors of forest animals and hunters who also are depicted with a crosier. This image, as well as representations of bearded men, is probably of Upper Paleolithic origin (cf. bison men and other half-man, half-animal figures from the French caves of Les Trois Frères, Le Gabillou, and others). The type is poorly documented; only single examples of sculptures are known. The majestic posture of the Szegvár-Tüzköves god, however, suggests its importance in the pantheon.

Other images of the masculine principle, such as nude men with bird masks in leaping or dancing posture, were probably portrayals of participants in rituals, worshipers of the goddess. Male images are rare among the Old European figurines; usually they constitute only 2 to 3 percent of the total number recovered in settlements.

Summary. The concept of a divine feminine principle is manifested in human, animal, and abstract symbolic form: woman, water bird, bird of prey, doe, bear, snake, bee, butterfly, fish, toad, hedgehog, triangle, and hourglass form. Her manifestations are everywhere; her worship is attuned to the infinite round of life, death, and renewal.

Judging by the stereotypes that recur in figurines over the millennia, the religion of Old Europe was polytheistic and dominated by female deities. The primary goddess inherited from the Paleolithic was the Great Goddess, whose functions included the gift of life and increase of material goods, death-wielding and decrease, and regeneration. She was the absolute ruler of human, animal, and plant life and the controller of lunar cycles and seasons. As giver of all, death wielder, and regeneratrix, she is one and the same goddess in spite of the multiplicity of forms in which she manifests herself.

The prehistoric Great Goddess survives still in folklore. She appears as Fate (or sometimes as the three Fates), who attends the birth of a child and foretells the length of its life. She appears as White Lady (Death) with her white dog. Sometimes she is recognized in the toad or frog that brings death and regeneration, in the water birds and snakes that bring well-being and fertility, or in the crowned snake, whose crown grants the power of seeing all things and understanding the language of animals.

Although degraded to the status of a witch, the Old European vulture (or owl) goddess lives on in fairy tales as an old hag with a hooked nose who flies through the air on a broom. She can slice the moon in half, cause cows to go dry, tie blossoms into knots, destroy human happiness, and inflict illness.

In European folklore as well as in prehistory, witches and fairies most often appear in groups with one the most important, the queen or "lady." This pattern reflects an ancient gynecocentric and matrilinear social structure.

As a consequence of the new agrarian economy, the pregnant goddess of the Paleolithic was transformed into an earth fertility deity in the Neolithic. The fecundity of humans and animals, the fertility of crops and thriving of plants, and the processes of growing and fattening became of enormous concern during this period. The drama of seasonal changes intensified, which is manifested in the emergence of a mother-daughter image and of a male god as spirit of rising and dying vegetation.

Let us note here that fertility is only one of the goddess's many functions. It is inaccurate to call Paleolithic and Neolithic goddesses fertility goddesses, as the fertility of the earth became a prominent concern only during the food-producing era. Hence, fertility is not a primary function of the goddess and has nothing to do with sexuality. The goddesses were primarily creatresses of life; they were not Venus figures or beauties and most definitely not wives of male gods. It is also inaccurate to call these prehistoric goddesses mother goddesses, a misconception found often in the archaeological literature. It is true that there are mother images and protectresses of young life, as well as a Mother Earth and Mother of the Dead, but the other female images cannot be categorized as mother goddesses. The bird goddess and the snake goddess, for example, are not mothers, nor are many other images of regeneration and transformation, such as the frog, fish, and hedgehog. They personify life, death, and regeneration; they represent more than fertility and motherhood.

Shrines and Sanctuaries. Much of the corpus of information about the Old European religion comes from shrines, which have been found as models, within homes, or standing free. They demonstrate the close connections between secular and sacred life, especially in relation to functions performed by women.

Temples. The fifty or more clay models of temples discovered so far allow us to see the workings of Old Europe's shrines in striking detail. Usually found in front of or near the site of a former altar, these miniature shrines, generally small enough to be held in a person's hand, were probably gifts to the goddess of the temple. They are doubly revealing: in addition to reproducing the temple's configuration, the models are often elaborately decorated with symbolic designs and inscribed with religious symbols. Frequently a divine image in relief adorns the gables, rooftops, or roof corners of the temple.

Among the earliest models discovered are several from the Neolithic Sesklo culture of Thessaly in Greece. Dating from about 6000 BCE, they portray rectangular buildings that have pitched or saddle roofs, painted checkerboards or striated rectangles on their walls, and decorated gables. Noteworthy openings in their roofs and sometimes in their sides make them look, perhaps not coincidentally, like tiny birdhouses. A group of clay models from a slightly later date was found in a mound of the Porodin settlement near Bitola in Macedonia, southwestern Yugoslavia. Produced by the Starčevo culture of the central Balkans, dating from about 5800 to 5600 BCE, these models are capped with unusual features. Cylindrical "chimneys," located in the center of their roofs, bear the mask of a goddess; a necklace spreads down over the roof. The temple building below seems to have been constructed as the literal "body" of the deity; the structure, with the cylinder head on top, seems to be essentially a deified portrait bust. Perhaps for a mythologically related reason, a number of these

FIGURE 8. *Temple Model.* Reconstructed terra-cotta temple model from Porodin, Macedonia, with wide, inverted T-shaped entrances on all sides and a goddess mask on a cylinder on the roof. Apparently, such models were gifts to the goddess worshiped in the temple.

shrine models have mysteriously shaped entrances, either inverted T's or triangulars. (See figure 8.)

Other temple models from the Vinča culture of the central Balkans (late sixth millennium BCE) and from the Tisza culture (around 5000 BCE) in present-day eastern Hungary are often distinctly bird-shaped and have numerous incisions on their sides to indicate plumage. Their entrances have a round hole on their top half—again, like those found in birdhouses. Motifs of a bird goddess are found throughout the Vinča culture and Old Europe in general, and it seems likely that these openings were fashioned as symbolic entrances for the visiting goddess in the epiphany of a bird.

An exquisite, unusually large model of a temple with numerous large, round openings was discovered in the settlement on the island of Căscioarele on the Danube River in southern Romania. Dating from about 4500, this model has dramatically enhanced knowledge of Copper Age architectural and cult practices. The shrine model itself consists of a large substructure supporting four individual temples, each of which has a wide, arched portal crowned with horns. The facade is pierced by ten round apertures and is decorated with irregular, horizontally incised lines. This detailing suggests wood construction. The top surface of the substructure probably constituted a terrace that could hold a large congregation. Presumably—if this was, as it seems to be, a model of an actual structure—the whole temple complex was at least ten meters tall, with the individual roof temples measuring about three meters in height. The structure is clearly of European tradition, and no close parallels to this configuration exist.

Other models of two-story temples have been found at Old European settlements at Ruse on the lower Danube River in Bulgaria, Izvoarele in Romania, and Azmak in central Bulgaria. Still another model, this time from the Ros River Valley at Rozsokhuvatka in the western Ukraine, depicts a two-story sanctuary standing on four legs, with the second floor constituting a two-room temple. This model is from the Cucuteni culture, dating from about 4300 to 4000, the farthest outpost of Old European civilization in the northeast. This culture has been made famous through systematic excavations of entire villages, whose spacious, two- to four-room houses include altars and platforms, as well as by its magnificent ceramic art. The model has wide entrances on both floors and a platform, adorned with bull horns and perhaps used for worship, in front of the large portal on the second floor. A round window appears in the rear, and horizontal beams that support the roof are indicated in relief.

The walls of many models of temples were painted and decorated with incisions, excisions, and encrustations in symbolic motifs. Often these were arranged into panels in the same manner as on cult vases. The parallels between these forms are often particularly revealing. One dominant Old European motif, for example, found repeatedly on the models, cult vases, and other votive objects, is the meander, or the figurative representation of a snake; sometimes an abstract derivative of this image, in the form of single or pairs of spiraling lines, will appear.

A model of a Vinča temple unearthed in Gradešnica in northwestern Bulgaria, dating from about 5000 BCE, is a good example of the use of these symbolic decorations. (See figure 9.) Each wall and roof of this model constitutes a separate panel, each marked with a different design of meanders or sinuous lines, chevrons, and dotted bands. The vertical panels on either side of the entrance are inscribed with signs in a configuration that

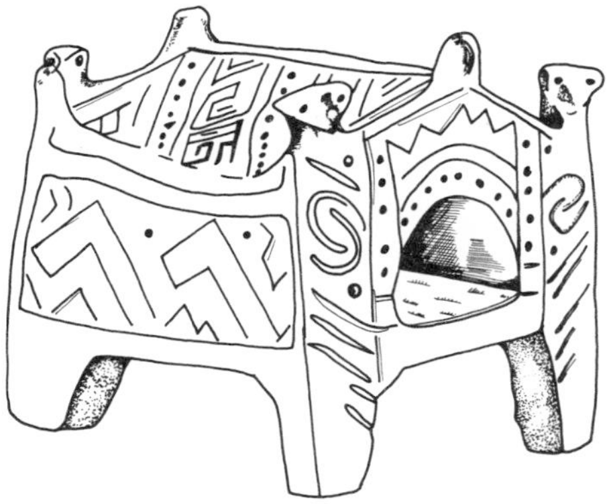

FIGURE 9. *Temple Model.* A terra-cotta model marked with sacred signs and symbols. The gable and the corners of the roof are topped with masked heads. Vinča culture, Gradešnica, northwestern Bulgaria; c. 5000–4500 BCE.

may comprise some sort of formula associated with the temple's goddess. Above the entrance to the temple are bands of dots and zigzags—snakeskin designs—further suggesting that the shrine belongs to a deity, perhaps the snake goddess. Above the facade, a schematic head in the center probably represents the actual goddess, and the masked heads on the corners may symbolize her divine associates.

Still other models, although otherwise complete, are roofless, so it is possible to peer into the scene of the cult activities. Such open models have a dais along the back wall and a bread oven on the side wall. A model of a roofless temple from Popudnia, a late Cucuteni settlement north of Uman in the western Ukraine, sits on four cylindrical legs and consists of a main room and vestibule; between them is a rectangular entrance with a threshold. On the right side of the large central chamber are benches and a large rectangular oven on a raised platform. To the right of the oven sits a female figurine with her hands on her breasts; near the outer wall another female figurine is grinding grain, and close by is a depression for storing flour. Almost in the center of the shrine stands a raised platform in the shape of a cross.

Among the actual temples is a two-story temple uncovered in Radingrad, near Razgrad in northeastern Bulgaria, by Totju Ivanov of the Archaeological Museum, Razgrad, from 1974 to 1978. Probably similar to the four-legged Rozsokhuvatka model from the Ukraine, this Karanovo culture temple dates from about 5000. Its first floor had a ceramic workshop with a large oven to one side; on the other side was a clay platform with tools for making, polishing, and decorating pots. Flat stone containers for crushing ocher stood nearby. Exquisite finished vases and unbaked ones were also found in the room. The second floor, like that of the Rozsokhuvatka model, comprised the temple proper. Inside was a large rectangular clay altar seventy-five centimeters high, and to its left stood a vertical loom and many figurines and temple models. A number of the vases near the altar were filled with clay beads.

One important discovery was that of a pillar temple, unearthed in the village of Căscioarele. Excavated by Hortensia and Vladimir Dumitrescu of the Institute of Archaeology, Bucharest, from 1962 to 1969, this Karanovo culture sanctuary, found just below the model of the edifice, dates from the early part of the fifth millennium BCE. Rectangular in plan, the sixteen- by ten-meter temple was divided into two rooms by six rows of posts. The interior walls of one room are painted red with bands of cream-colored curvilinear designs; above the entrance is a striking terra-cotta medallion with a red snake-coil outlined by a thin line of cream. This room contains also two hollow pillars, both measuring about two meters in height, that were originally modeled around two tree trunks. The thicker one was encircled by posts and, like the walls, had been painted three times with different designs. Near it lay an adult skeleton in a crouched position. The thinner pillar, measuring about ten centimeters in diameter, stood close to the interior wall and was painted with cream ribbons on a reddish brown background. Next to it was a terracotta bench or dais about forty centimeters high with painted curvilinear ribbons of cream color. Nearby lay numerous fragments of painted vases and of large vessels decorated with excised motifs. Rituals or mysteries performed here were probably connected with the idea of regeneration and the invocation of the vital source of life. The pillars, decorated with the running angularized spiral or snake motif, can be interpreted as life columns. The tradition of the life column motif can be traced as far back as the seventh millennium BCE, when it appeared in Çatal Hüyük frescoes, and in the Sesklo temples of Thessaly around 6000 BCE. In representations on Old European vases, life columns are usually shown flanked with horns, whirls, spirals, male animals, and uterus symbols.

The remains of an early Cucuteni shrine in Sabatinivka in the southern Bug River Valley of the Ukraine present an even more dramatic picture. (See figure 10.) A rectangular building of about seventy square meters, this temple has a clay-plastered floor and an entrance area paved with flat stones. The center of the room contains a large oven with a female figurine at its base. Nearby stood an incense burner and a group of vessels; these included a dish containing the burned bones of an ox and a channel-decorated pot with a small cup inside, once used for libations. Also nearby was a group of five concave grinding stones and five seated terra-cotta figurines with their bodies leaning backward. Along the rear wall, sixteen other female figurines were seated in low, horned-back chairs on a six-meter-long altar. In the corner adjacent to the altar stood a clay throne with a horned back and a meter-wide seat that had originally been covered with split planks. Altogether, thirty-two of these nearly identical, armless figurines with massive thighs and snake-shaped heads were found in this sanctuary. Oddly, several of them had been perforated through the shoulders, and one held a baby snake.

The Sabatinivka sanctuary demonstrates that bread ovens, grinding stones, and storage vessels played a fundamental role in the cult rites performed at Old European shrines. The seated figurines strongly suggest that temple worshipers participated in a ritual grinding of grain and baking of sacred bread and that these ceremonies were supervised from a throne, at least at Sa-

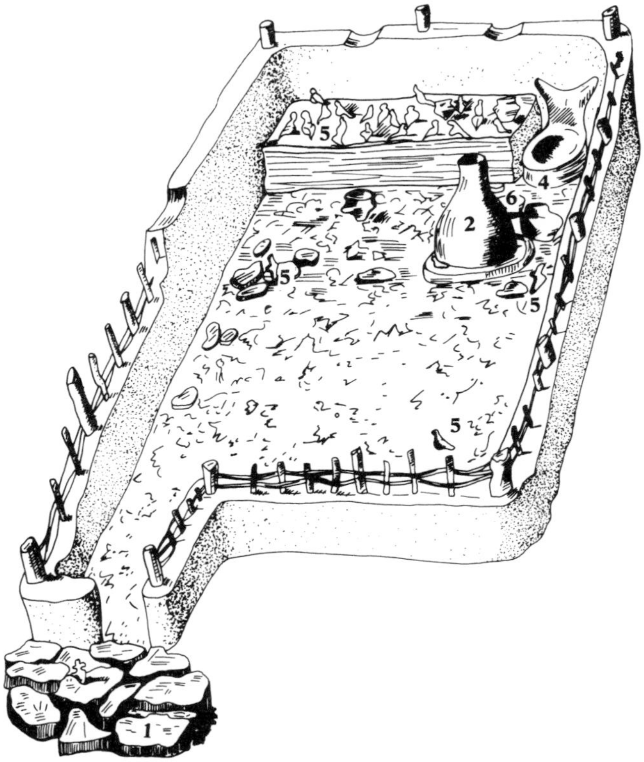

FIGURE 10. *Shrine.* An actual shrine from Sabatinivka, Moldavian S.S.R.; dating from c. 4700–4500 BCE. Occupying seventy square meters, the building contained (1) a stone slab floor, (2) an oven, (3) a dais, (4) a clay chair, (5) figurines, and (6) a group of vases near the oven. Shrines like this, which resemble the miniature models of temple shrines often found inside them, were the scene of religious rituals in Old Europe.

batinivka, by an overseer, probably a priestess. It seems likely that sacred cakes were dedicated to the goddess at the conclusion of the rites. Also the clay figurines on the altar may have been presented as votive offerings to the goddess or used as effigies to celebrate her presence.

These images of cult practices are further illuminated by a site near Trgovište in northeastern Bulgaria, excavated in Henrieta Todorova of the Institute of Archaeology, Sofia, in 1971. This house shrine site at Ovčarovo, a product of the Karanovo culture, dates from about 4500–4200 BCE. The site yielded remains of twenty-six miniature cult objects, including four figurines with upraised arms, three temple facades or possible altar screens, decorated with chevrons, triple lines, and spirals around a central motif of concentric circles—nine chairs, three miniature tables, three vessels with lids, several large dishes, and three drums. It seems possible that this large collection of objects may have been used in different groupings at various times according to the required tableau of each particular ceremony.

The four figurines were painted with meanders and parallel lines. But most interesting was the presence of drums, which suggests the ritual use of music and dance in Old Europe. Other cult objects include miniature vessels with lids, found on small tables where they may have been used as sacrificial containers. Slightly larger than the figurines, these dishes or basins may have been used in some form of lustration or spiritual cleansing during the ceremony. The nine chairs, finally, may have been used to seat three of the figurines—the fourth is larger than the others—alternatively at the three altars, three tables, or the three drums. These miniature replicas are particularly important because life-size Old European altars and tables holding sacrificial equipment have rarely been preserved.

A very interesting cache of twenty-one figurines, probably used for the reenactment of earth fertility rites, came to light in an early Cucuteni shrine at Poduri-Dealul Ghindaru, Moldavia, northeastern Romania. The figurines were stored in a large vase. In addition, there were fifteen chairs or thrones on which larger figurines could sit. The figurines are from six to twelve centimeters in height. The different proportions, workmanship, and symbols painted on the figurines suggest a clear hierarchy in this tableau. The three largest ones are painted in red ocher with symbols that are typical of Mother Earth: antithetic snakes coiling over the abdomen, lozenges on the back, and dotted triangles and lozenges over the ample thighs and legs. The medium-sized figurines have a striated band across the abdomen and stripes across their thighs and legs. The small figurines were rather carelessly produced and are not painted with symbols. Such differences may reflect different cult roles ranging from dominant personages (goddesses or priestesses) to assistants and attendants.

Although merely a selection in themselves, these Old European temple sites demonstrate that a long and varied list of cult paraphernalia—sacrificial containers, lamps, altar tables and plaques, libation vases, ladles, incense burners, and figurines—could have been employed in worship rituals. While the sacred rite of breadmaking appears to have been among the most consecrated and pervasive practices, there may well have been many additional distinct categories of religious ceremonies.

Caves. In the tradition of their Upper Paleolithic ancestors, the people of Old Europe used caves as sanctuaries. [*See also* Caves.] An excellent example of an Old European sanctuary is the cave of Scaloria in southeastern Italy, which dates from the mid-sixth millennium BCE. It consists of a large cave that is connected by a narrow tunnel to a lower-level cave containing a pool of water. The upper cave, which shows signs of seasonal occupation, contains a mass grave of 137 skeletons. The cave yielded stalagmites, stalactites, and pottery decorated with crescents, snakes, plant motifs, and egg or uterus shapes. These decorative symbols indicate that the cave was a sanctuary where funerary and/or initiation rites of mysteries took place, associated with the idea of regeneration and renewal. Many as yet unexplored cave sanctuaries have been discovered along the Adriatic coast and Greece's Peloponnese Peninsula.

Tomb-shrines. In central Europe, a sacred place of tombs and shrines has been discovered at Lepenski Vir in the Iron Gate region, northern Yugoslavia, during the excavation of 1965–1968 (Srejović, 1972). The trapeze-shaped (i.e., triangular with the narrow end cut off) structures with red lime plaster floors of Lepenski Vir, dating from the late seventh to the early sixth millennium BCE, are dug into an amphitheater-like recess in the bank of the Danube. The essential feature of the shrine is the rectangular altar built of stones, which has an entrance in the shape of the open legs of a goddess, similar to that found in Irish court tombs. At the end of the altar stood one or two sculptures representing the fish goddess and a round, or egg-shaped, stone engraved with a labyrinthine design.

Fifty-four red sandstone sculptures were found. The dead were buried in similar triangular structures; they were placed on the red floor with their heads in the narrow end and positioned so that their navels were in the very center of the structure.

The main activities at Lepenski Vir were ritual sacrifice and the carving and engraving of sacred sculptures and cult objects. Paleozoologists were astonished to find a very high proportion of dog bones in the early phases of the site, when there were yet no herds to be watched by dogs. The bones were not broken up, indicating that dogs were not used for meat, and the often intact skeletons lay in anatomical order. Large fish bones (carp, catfish, sturgeon, pike) were identified in almost all structures; one exceptionally large catfish may have weighed from 140 to 180 kilograms! Twenty shrines contained a red deer skull or shoulder blade, which often was associated with the bones of dogs and boars. In three cases human bones were found in hearths. It can be seen from the above that the sacrificial animals at Lepenski Vir were fish, deer, dogs, and boars—the animals known from prehistory and early history to be associated with the life-giving aspect of the goddess (deer, fish) and with her death aspect (dog and boar).

Summary. That the preponderance of figurines found in Old European shrines are female suggests that religious activities during this period were largely, if not exclusively, in the hands of women. Although men participated in religious ceremonies—for instance, as bird- or animal-masked dancers—it is women who are portrayed in the overwhelming majority of figurines as engaged in cult activities or as supervising these events from thrones. Furthermore, the rituals mirror daily secular tasks associated with women, most importantly, preparation of bread from grains, manufacture of ceramics, and weaving.

In the process of sacralizing their creative lives, women in Old Europe developed many religious practices whose occurence in later periods is taken for granted. For instance, the four elements so central to ritual historically—air (incense), earth (bread and clay objects), fire (lamps and ovens), and water (liquid contents of vessels)—were represented in Old Europe. Also integrated into rites were music and dance, the use of masks, sacrificial offerings, lustration, and rites involving bread and drink.

[*See also* Goddess Worship *and* Megalithic Religion, *article on* Prehistoric Evidence.]

BIBLIOGRAPHY

d'Anna, A. *Les statues-menhirs et stèles anthropomorphes du midi méditerranéen.* Paris, 1977.

Atzeni, Enrico. *La Dea Madre: Nelle culture prenuragiche.* Sassari, 1978.

Cameron, D. O. *Symbols of Birth and of Death in the Neolithic Era.* London, 1981.

Delporte, Henri. *L'image de femme dans l'art préhistorique.* Paris, 1979.

Dumitrescu, Vladimir. *Arta preistorică in România.* Bucharest, 1974.

Gimbutas, Marija. "The Temples of Old Europe." *Archaeology* 33 (November–December 1980): 41–50.

Gimbutas, Marija. "The 'Monstrous Venus' of Prehistory or Goddess Creatrix." *Comparative Civilizations Review* 7 (Fall 1981): 1–26.

Gimbutas, Marija. *The Goddesses and Gods of Old Europe, 6500–3500 B.C.: Myths and Cult Images.* Berkeley, 1982.

Kalicz, Nándor. *Clay Gods: The Neolithic Period and Copper Age in Hungary.* Translated by Barna Balogh. Budapest, 1970.

Marshack, Alexander. *The Roots of Civilization: The cognitive Beginnings of Man's First Art, Symbol, and Notation.* New York, 1972.

Mellaart, James. "Earliest of Neolithic Cities: Delving Deep into the Neolithic Religion of Anatolian Chatal Huyuk," pt. 2, "Shrines of the Vultures and the Veiled Goddess." *Illustrated London News* 244 (1964): 194–197.

Mellaart, James. *Çatal Hüyük: A Neolithic Town in Anatolia.* New York, 1967.

Srejović, Dragoslav. *Europe's First Monumental Sculpture: New Discoveries at Lepenski Vir.* London, 1972.

Thimme, Jürgen, ed. *Art and Culture of the Cyclades.* Translated and edited by Pat Getz-Preziosi. Chicago, 1977.

Twohig, Elizabeth Shee. *The Megalithic Art of Western Europe.* Oxford, 1981.

MARIJA GIMBUTAS

The Eurasian Steppes and Inner Asia

During the Aeneolithic epoch of the fifth to the third millennium BCE two types of cultures developed in the steppe zone of Eurasia. One was a sedentary culture of primitive agriculturists and livestock breeders. They lived in clay-walled dwellings that were grouped in fortified settlements. To this type belong the Anau (Jeytun) culture of southern Turkmenia, whose scientific study was inaugurated with the excavations made by Raphael Pumpelly's American expedition to the Anau mounds near Ashkhabad, and the Tripolye-Cucuteni culture between the Dnieper River and the eastern Carpathian Mountains. (The Tripolye-type remains were identified by the prerevolutionary Russian scholar V. V. Khvoiko.) These cultures are known in detail today primarily through the work of Soviet scholars.

The Aeneolithic cultures were closely connected with the oldest centers of agricultural civilization in the Near East—the Anau culture directly so, and the Tripolye-Cucuteni through the medium of the archaeological cultures of the Balkans. Adjoining the Aeneolithic cultures were those of livestock-breeding steppe tribes. In the steppe areas around the Caspian and Black seas, from the Urals to the Crimea, was the Pit-Grave cultural community; in the south of Siberia, in the Minusinsk Basin, was the Afanas'evo culture. The tribes of these two groups of cultures were closely related.

Tripolye-Cucuteni Religion. The religious concepts of the Tripolye-Cucuteni tribes are revealed by analysis of amulets, paintings on pottery, anthropomorphic and zoomorphic statuettes, models of dwellings and utensils, altars, and so on. The clay models of dwellings are in the form of two-storied houses with an accentuated rounded or quadrangular upper story. Inside is a representation of a bread-baking oven, with an anthropomorphic idol next to it. Excavations of the settlements have revealed that some houses contained clay altars in the form of a female figure, sometimes with a bird's head or a head in the shape of a chalice or cylinder. There were also ritual clay dippers. Sanctuaries adjoined the dwellings and were entirely separate from them, and the cult they housed was evidently a fertility cult. In the sanctuaries were distinctive clay "horned thrones" whose backs imitated bulls' horns.

The most abundant source for understanding the Tripolye ideology are the pottery with its paintings and moldings, and the statuettes. The paintings on Tripolye vessels are divided into three vertical zones that evidently represent a tripartite concept of the universe. In mythological depictions the sun is associated with the bull, and also, at times, with the female principle (the female breast). This apparently symbolizes a cosmogonic configuration of the world that combined the male and female principles. The snake as well occupied a high position in the mythological hierarchy. The world was thought to have the form of a square or a circle, and a female deity may have taken part in the process of creation, as suggested by a vessel with a female figure in relief embracing it, as it were, with both arms. A parallel is the Sumerian goddess Ninhursaga, who gives form as "mistress creator" or "mistress potter." Religious customs included ritual dances; dancing female figures are depicted on several vessels. The dances may be Dadolaic ceremonies for bringing rain, or magic fertility rites.

Anthropomorphic plastic art, especially statuettes, is combined with ornamental designs and portrayals. There are several types of female statuettes, some with signs of pregnancy. One group of statuettes has designs with a diamond shape—a sexual symbol. In this way, the female principle and the idea of fertility were emphasized, as also seen in depictions of a snake on the stomachs of clay female statuettes that were clearly pregnant. The snake is a frequent motif in the oldest European art, and this motif often has a cosmogonic meaning. But on these statuettes the snake, as in Crete, appears as an attribute of a female deity; everywhere in the ancient East the snake symbolized fertility. [*See also* Snakes.] Direct evidence of this is given by a group of statuettes in which the clay is mixed with flour or grains, and by another group with depictions of plants or animals. Thus, the cult of fertility and the deity (deities?) of fertility were prominent in the religion of the Tripolye-Cucuteni tribes.

Anau Religion. A complex system of religious beliefs existed among the Anau tribes. Both dwellings and cultic structures expressed spatial concepts, with squarish and rectangular buildings predominating. Structures at the center of a group of buildings had a special type of hearth, in which a fire was lit for cultic ceremonies. At Karadepe two sanctuaries, side by side, have squarish hearths. Adjoining are auxiliary structures. This cult center may be regarded as a proto-temple, although it also served as a granary. Together with large sanctuaries there were domestic ones, with traces of large fires inside, raising the hypothesis that they were deliberately burned down.

Vessel paintings show clear-cut spatial and geometric concepts and relationships. Goat and tree (vegetation) motifs testify to a fertility cult; sometimes the goat is next to the tree. Unquestionably, there was a cycle of beliefs associated with the reproductive power of the goat, which in general serves as a symbol of the fructifying powers of nature and which may function as an attribute or embodiment of a corresponding deity. The goat motif is one of the most widespread in ancient Eastern glyptics; association of the goat with vegetation (the tree) also signifies a connection with the earth. [*See also* Sheep and Goats.] Another mythologem reflected in the designs is a bird with the sun disk.

Equally important for revealing religious concepts are the earthenware statuettes. Most are of sitting women with arms schematically raised at the sides, with well-defined facial features, and with markedly emphasized breasts, pelvis, and buttocks. The sitting pose itself was evidently evoked by fertility concepts and an association with the chthonic principle. It symbolized birth and, more generally, the birth and organization of the cosmos. The marks and depictions on the statuettes confirm and develop this symbolism. Some of the statuettes are holding a child and perhaps a goat. The back and bosom of one statuette are covered with numerous female breasts; other statuettes are covered with schematic depictions of trees, and sometimes of snakes. It is not possible to formulate concretely the religio-mythological cycles reflected by these statuettes, but one may surmise that they were connected with communal cults. The feminine protectors of earthly births and the ancestors of communal groups were worshiped. These female deities had created an orderly world out of chaos and had established cosmic and terrestrial law and order. On them, then, depended the continuation of humankind, the reproduction of wild and domestic animals, and the fertility of fields.

Cult Centers. In the Late Bronze Age (end of the third through the second millennium BCE), large cult centers with monumental edifices appeared in the agricultural and livestock-breeding communities of southern Central Asia. One such center, at Altyn-tepe in southern Turkmenia, consisted of a stepped towerlike edifice, a burial complex, dwellings ("the house of the priest"?), and household buildings. Most grandiose was a four-stepped towerlike edifice with a facade 26 meters in length and an estimated height of 12 meters. In configuration it resembled a Mesopotamian ziggurat. In one of the buildings of the burial complex was an altar, together with a gold bull's head, a wolf's head, and a plaque with astral symbols. The bull's head is akin to analogous but earlier Mesopotamian depictions, although it is more schematic. Characteristically, the Altyn-tepe bull has on its forehead a moon-shaped lapis lazuli laid-plate. The cult and image of the bull were widespread among early agricultural cultures (such as Çatal Hüyük), especially in Mesopotamia. A "heavenly bull" or a moon deity may have been worshiped at Altyn-tepe. Much later, in Zoroastrianism, the moon was called *gao čithra* ("having bull semen"). It was from this semen that all animals had been born, whereas from the semen falling on the ground domesticated plants had arisen. The mythic First Man had stood on one side of the Mythic River, and on the other side was the First Bull (*Greater Bundahishn* 1a.12–13, 6e.1–3; *Yashts* 7.3–6).

Another, later, cult center, Dashly 3 (second half of the second millennium BCE), has an entirely different structure. In the center of a square enclosure (roughly 150 meters on each side) is a round edifice in the form of a circumambulatory gallery, its interior divided into compartments and its exterior having nine salient towers. Three passageways lead into this gallery, whose interior includes chambers with fire-bearing altars. Parallel to the central edifice and outside it are two concentric walls that divide the space into three circles. All the enclosing walls are very thin and were clearly not used as fortifications.

This cultic ceremonial center mirrors in its structure a cosmogram of a ritual universe (Indic *maṇḍala*), as well as a sociocosmic model of society with its tripartite division. The central part is the spiritual center of the universe, and the three outer rings must correlate with a tripartite universe. The tripartite division of Indo-European (in this case, proto-Indo-Iranian) communities was clearly reflected in this plan. In the center—the focus of the entire composition—are reflected again the sacred triads (three gates, nine small towers). During rituals the sacred altars were lit and animals were sacrificed. This group of tribes evidently combined the idea of a tripartite world with a concept of the four sides of the world joined in a square. There is a certain correspondence with the ancient Iranian concept of *vara* and the divine fortress of the Kafirs.

Burial Grounds and Rites. A significant migration of tribes took place in the Eurasian steppes during the second millennium BCE. Indo-Iranian tribes left the area of the Timber-Grave culture (the steppes between the Urals, the Volga, and the northern Black Sea region) and the western area of settlement of the Andronovo tribes (western Kazakhstan). They migrated south to Central Asia, spreading through that region in several waves and bringing in Indo-Iranian language, social institutions, and beliefs.

The rites performed at the Sintashta burial ground (in the southern Ural region, northeast of Magnitogorsk) had a pronounced Indo-Iranian character. The tribes that used this and related burial grounds from the eighteenth to the sixteenth century BCE carried out both individual and group interments. The wooden burial cover was held up by wooden posts; the most ancient of Indian scriptures, the *Ṛgveda*, makes reference to a similar practice. In the graves are massive finds of the bones of sacrificial animals. For example, in Pit I five horse skulls were in a row along a wall; along the opposite wall were four skulls of hornless oxen and a horse skull. In another grave were seventeen skulls of cows, rams, and horses. There were also dog bones. In a number of graves horse skulls and leg bones were laid at one end of the burial chamber, and a chariot, complete with wheels and spokes, stood at the other end. Horse skeletons were generally laid either behind each other or with skulls and legs facing each other. Many of the buried were warriors. On the earth-covered tombs, long-burning fires had been built. The chariots and steeds reflect the beliefs that the soul departs for the world beyond on a chariot and that the steed is the fire deity's companion. The same may be said of the dog. The sacrifice of animals is reminiscent of another ancient Indian sacrificial custom, the Agnicayana. [*See also* Vedism and Brahmanism.]

The Sintashta burial ground reflects a stage of ancient Indian beliefs earlier than that found in the *Ṛgveda*. Moreover, elements of the funeral rites have parallels to those in a wider area. For example, many steppe tribes of western Europe used burial covers on posts and cremated the deceased. In the Bronze Age, cremation and the corresponding cycle of beliefs existed in a vast area of the Eurasian steppes, particularly among the Fedorovo tribes of Kazakhstan and the Timber-Grave tribes of the Volga and northern Black Sea areas.

These Bronze Age beliefs were also widespread in Central Asia. In the Tigrovaia Balka burial ground, one central *kurgan* (burial mound) was surrounded by a ring of twenty, and another by forty-one, small mounds under which hearths were found. During the burial ritual, a ring of fire was lit around the entombed persons. This fiery barrier bore witness simultaneously to a belief in a circular universe (isomorphic with the ancient Indian belief) and to its fiery essence. This group of beliefs was further developed in the religion of the Saka peoples of the Eurasian steppes.

Saka Religion. The vast area of the steppe and mountain-steppe zones, from the Aral Sea in the west to the Minusinsk Basin in the east and including Mongolia, Sinkiang, and Central Asia, was inhabited by tribes related culturally, and probably ethnically, to the East Iranians—the Saka group, mentioned in Old Persian and Greek sources. They spoke an East Iranian language. The tribes of Central Asia and of southern, western, and central Kazakhstan are termed Saka; those farther to the east are called Saka-Siberian.

In the Greco-Roman sources, references to the Saka beliefs are very scant. They may be supplemented by material from the ancient sacred works of the Indo-Iranians, especially the Avesta and the Vedas; from Middle Persian Zoroastrian works; and from the religious concepts of contemporary East Iranian and Indo-Aryan peoples. On the other hand, the archaeological materials of the Saka tribes, dating from the seventh century BCE to the beginning of the common era, are unusually abundant, especially the burial grounds and works of art. They are the main source for our assessment of the Saka religion, which had an overall similarity to that of the Scythians, although the two were by no means identical.

Divine gifts. An important mythological isogloss uniting the religious beliefs of the European Scythians and the Asian Saka is the motif of divine gifts. According to the account of Quintus Cortius Rufus, a Latin biographer of Alexander the Great, the Saka received from the gods the yoke, plow, spear, arrow, and chalice (7.8.17–18). The first two are associated with obtaining the fruits of the earth; the spear and arrow, with the defeat of enemies; and the chalice, with libations to the gods. The three-layered social condition emerges here with absolute clarity.

Sun cult. In the *Histories* of Herodotus, Queen Tomyris of the Massagetae pronounces the formula "I swear by the sun, the lord of the Massagetae" (1.212). Oaths by the sun and by fire were widespread among Iranians in antiquity and in medieval times. But even until recently the inhabitants of the Pamir, who formerly called the sun "great," swore by the "sun's head" as their strongest oath. They perceived the sun as an anthropomorphic being. The ancient Iranians had the same anthropomorphic concept of the great luminary. To them the sun was the visible form of the supreme deity, Ahura Mazdā—his child or his eye. The fact that these concepts were those of the Saka as well is made evident by the word for "sun" in the medieval language of Khotan, which is, as in the Pamir dialects, *urmaysde* (cf. Old Iranian *Ahura Mazdāh*). [*See also* Ahura Mazdā and Angra Mainyu.]

Concerning the beliefs of the Massagetae, Herodotus wrote: "The only god they worship is the sun, to whom they sacrifice horses. The idea behind this is to offer the swiftest animal to the swiftest of the gods" (1.216). According to the Avesta, the ancient Iranians repeated: "We worship the shining sun, the immortal, the rich, [who owns] swift steeds *(aurvaṭ-aspem)*." They conceived of the sun's movement across the sky as that of a gleaming carriage to which heavenly steeds were harnessed. In the *Ṛgveda* as well, that is, among the ancient Hindus, the theme of white heavenly steeds in connection with the sun god (Sūrya) is elaborated in great detail. Thus, in the *Ṛgveda* the sun repeatedly appears in the form of a horse, Dadhikrā (Dadhikrāvan).

After the beginning of the common era, the solar cult in India greatly increased in importance because of the arrival there of the Central Asian Saka and the related Yüeh-chih. By the first millennium CE there were temples honoring the sun in various places in Central Asia, particularly Merv and Ferghana. Nothing is known about their structure. Some edifices in the south of Siberia give us an idea of the cult places associated with the sun and with steeds, the sun's attribute.

The Arzhan *kurgan* (in Tuva), a very ancient monument of Scytho-Siberian culture (eighth and seventh centuries BCE), had a round stone platform mound about 110 meters in diameter and 3 to 4 meters high. Under the mound was an enormous wood edifice, in whose center was a square (8 by 8 meters) wooden frame. In the middle of this structure was a smaller one with a king and a queen interred in coffins, surrounded by six wooden coffins and two small enclosures in which the king's courtiers were interred. Here too were the king's personal horses. Lines of logs, like spokes of a gigantic wheel, came radially out of the central structure. The entire surface was divided into seventy trapezoidal compartments by cross-pieces forming concentric lines. Some of these compartments had additional divisions. In nine of the compartments there were mass burials of horses; burials of humans and horses were found in a number of other compartments. The king was dressed in a rich garment of wool and one of sable; both he and his female companion had numerous gold ornaments. The ground in the royal compartment was covered with horse tails and manes. The courtiers too were clothed in costly garments and had gold ornaments. The mass horse-burials included groups of fifteen or thirty old stallions, evidently gifts to the king from tribal units subordinate to him.

The Arzhan *kurgan* clearly testifies to a developed cult of the sun. The king is at the center of a gigantic wheel, which symbolized the solar chariot or, rather, the sun itself. The concept of the "solar wheel" is widespread in Indo-European thought. Not only is the king equated with the sun, at the center, but the steeds accompanying the sun are placed, both individually and as a body, in strictly defined groups within the construction. This clearly indicates that they are immediate participants of the myth depicted by the Arzhan *kurgan.* The horses of the *kurgan* enter, as it were, the inner essence of the sun on the one hand, and on the other they indicate the way by which souls may reach this luminary.

Such sepulchral "temples of the sun" were not isolated instances. Another, simpler, variant is the Ulug-Khorum *kurgan* (also in Tuva), in whose center is a semispherical stone mound 22 meters in diameter. Thirty-three meters from the mound's center is a stone wall. The ring between the foundation of the mound and the wall is divided into sections by thirty-two radial spokes made of stone. On the stone are incised depictions of horses. [*See also* Sun.]

Cult of the horse. Throughout the entire Scythian, Saka, and Saka-Siberian areas there are burials of horses, both individual and collective, and either with or without human burials. In Central Asia and Kazakhstan there were until recent times a number of variants of the custom of dedicating a horse to the deceased. The Kafir of Nuristan retained the practice of setting up on the grave a wooden statue of a horseman, and in Central Asia, dolls on a wooden horse were set up. All this reflects a perception of the chthonic nature of the horse and, on the other hand, of its functions as an intermediary between worlds—an animal hastening to the upper worlds and conveying the soul of the deceased there.

The cult of the horse was associated with its otherwordly nature, and this cult was reflected in numerous depictions of horses. Very frequently these were made on cliffs and mountains, as the Oglakhta pictograph in the Yenisei region, and the pictograph on the Aravan cliff in Ferghana. In Chinese sources, Central Asian, and especially Ferghana, horses are termed "heavenly," evidently reflecting local concepts. A "heavenly steed" was said to live in a mountain cave in Tokharistan. Wherever there were many horse depictions in mountainous areas, as at Oglakhta, there were sanctuaries dedicated to the heavenly steed.

In ancient Central Asian legends, sacred horses dwell in a lake, a motif that may be traced back to ancient Iranian beliefs. In the Avesta, the deity of water and river streams, Aredvī, was drawn by four horses, whereas the rain deity, Tištrya, appeared in the form of a white horse with golden ears and muscles who received rainwater from the celestial lake, Vourukaša. It is possible, however, that the concept of the horse as a water steed has an even older, Indo-Iranian, foundation. [*See also* Horses.]

Thus, the Saka tribes had a cult of a supreme deity with pronounced solar coloration. Originating in the ancient Iranian pantheon, which is known from Zoroastrian works, this deity may have been Ahura Mazdā, Mithra, or perhaps Mithra Ahura; moreover, different hypostases of this deity may have had primary significance among different Saka tribes. The cult of the horse and the cult of fire in its various manifestations (see below) were associated with the worship of this deity.

Cult of fire. The cult of fire played a large role in funerary ritual. In the Uigarak and Tagisken burial grounds (Aral Sea region); in those of Besshatyr (the Semirech'e region of Kazakhstan), Kokuibel (the Pamirs), and Tashkurgan (Sinkiang); and in the Sauromatian burial grounds of the North Caucasus the funerary structure was sometimes burned, either with total or partial cremation of the deceased, or without such cremation. Funerary pyres were sometimes burned over the deceased or around the funerary platform, and sometimes the deceased was covered with coals from a pyre that had been lit to one side of him.

In the Pamirs, the Aral Sea area, and among the Sauromatians the deceased was colored red or red paint was placed in the grave. The color red functions as a symbol and substitute for fire. Perhaps this was based on a deeper stratum of beliefs with a universal cosmological dichotomy, in which red denoted the world of the beyond, and painting the deceased red led him from the world of the living and joined him to the world of the dead. All these customs are echoes of Indo-European beliefs in the necessity of cremation. A number of Saka tribes believed that burning the deceased and his property was a sacrifice to the gods. For the deceased himself it was a "blessing," since the tongues of the flames, like horses, would perforce carry him off to heaven.

The Saka world had other manifestations of the cult of fire, differing among the groupings of the Saka tribes. The tribes of the Semirech'e and adjoining regions of Sinkiang had censers and sacrificial altars with depictions of animals, processions of beasts, and scenes of battle between beasts. The censers reflected the mytheme of the "tree of the world" and the tripartite division of the universe. They constituted a sacred cosmogram whose functions, realized in the ritual of the fire cult, were denoted by animals and their groupings. [*See also* Fire.]

Myths. The available data confirm that the Saka had a well-developed (although less complex than among the ancient Hindus) system of myths. It united deities and their animal incarnations with the cosmological concept of the triadic nature of the universe (and of all that existed) and that of the "tree of the world." These deities and concepts were united with the sacred act isomorphic to the Hindu *yajña* (lit., "worship of the god"; later, any sacred act). In these beliefs, in complex oblique ways, the earthly and the divine, the profane and the sacred, were interwoven. Through sacrifices associated with fire and animals, a socially defined human being became a participant in a series of transformations. When the small sacred area of the sacrificial altar extended to the limits of the entire universe, the person making the sacrifice was embodied in the altar itself (an emanation of the deity), in the sacred fire, and in the animals associated with the deity or deities. In this way he merged with the infinite.

On a felt rug from Pazyryk *kurgan* V (Altai), there is a frequently repeated scene: a goddess with the appearance of a man sits on a throne, wearing a long-sleeved garment covering her to the feet. On her head is a spiked crown. Her left hand is raised to her mouth, and in her extended right hand is a flowering sacred tree. Before her is a mounted archer with a quiver. This is one of the feminine deities of the Saka pantheon. If she originates in the Scythian pantheon, she is most likely Tabiti or, perhaps, Api. The scene is a divine wedding, with the king acquiring divine status.

Cult of gold. According to Ctesias (see Diodorus 2.34.1), the Saka built a sepulcher above the grave of their queen, Zarina, in the form of a huge pyramid. On top of it "they set up a colossal gold statue, to which they rendered heroic homage." Archaeological excavations have not unearthed the gold statue, but "golden burials" have been found. At the Issyk *kurgan*, not far from Alma-Ata, a princely burial dating from the fourth or third century BCE has been discovered. The deceased wore a headdress richly decorated with gold clasps and plaques; his clothing and footgear were almost solidly covered with gold plaques. More than four thousand gold objects, as well as two silver vessels, were found at this burial. In northern Afghanistan, at the Tillya-tepe mound, princely graves of the first century BCE to the first century CE were found. The deceased wore gold-embroidered clothing decorated with small gold plaques. Each grave contained from twenty-five hundred to four thousand of these plaques. The deceased were indeed clad in gold; they also wore gold crowns, and under their heads gold or silver chalices had been placed.

In ancient Iran, in Parthia, only the king could sleep on a golden couch. The Achaemenid kings, including Cyrus II, were buried in gold sarcophagi. Gold symbolized royal power in ancient India (*Śatapatha Brāhmaṇa* 13.2.2.17). In Kazakhstan and Afghan "golden" burials the idea that gold is the symbol of the king—of his power, his fate, and his good fortune *(farn)*—was the dominant one in decorating royal corpses with an enormous quantity of gold, a literal "wrapping" in gold.

These concepts are underlain by deeper ones, according to which gold is the inner content and the outer environment of divinities, for example, Agni and other gods of ancient Indian mythology. In the Hindu epics there are "golden-eyed" and "golden-skinned" gods. The newly born Buddha Śākyamuni's body was radiant like the sun and shone with gold (Aśvaghoṣa, *Buddhacarita* 1.1.14, 1.1.45). The ancient Iranian god Vainu wore red clothing decorated in gold, and in medieval Iran a person whose skin had a golden hue was thought to be divine. The wrapping of a corpse in clothing covered with gold distinguished it from ordinary corpses, making it a divine being from another world, for the deceased ruler was like the setting sun. The same beliefs gave rise to the custom of setting up gold statues on the graves of the Saka kings or covering their corpses with gold.

The Issyk royal headdress. Our knowledge of the religious beliefs of the Saka tribes facilitates analysis of the complex spiked headdress of the Issyk prince. Above the diadem are two horse's heads turned in different directions but with a single body. In back are two more horse heads, as well as vertical arrow shafts and bent plates that imitate birds' wings. The decorations on the sides have a distinct zonal character, with mountains, trees with small birds on them, mountains with snow leopards, and medallions with depictions of goats and snow leopards. On top of the headdress is a figurine of a snow leopard. This cosmogram is the Saka variant of the sacred macrocosm and also a depiction of the "tree of the world." It is undoubtedly associated with the texts of rituals, invocations, and myths, and was an iconographic embodiment of some of these.

The Saka king undoubtedly functioned also as a priest. He was believed to know and to personify the cosmological structure of the world; it was he who correlated it with the social structure of the tribe or tribes. The *axis mundi* went through the king, as embodied in his head and crown. This was the most sacred point in space, corresponding with the sacred space and axis of the sacrificial altar.

Still more concrete conclusions may be made. Double horse heads with a single body may reflect beliefs in divine twins that are akin to beliefs widespread among different Indo-European traditions. Their contrast with depictions of ordinary earthly horses laid out side by side sets off and emphasizes the former's unearthly power. The facial part of the headdress is associated with symbols of royal power in the form of birds' wings with feathers. This may stand for the ancient Iranian god of victory, Verethragna, who was symbolized by the bird of prey *vāregna.* An amulet made of feathers from this bird gave *khvarenah,* in this case "royal good fortune." For the ancient Hindus, the eagle was the personification of Indra, and Agni the "eagle of the heavens." The symbolism of royal power is reinforced by the vertical arrows and by the figurine, atop the headdress, of a ram—the symbol of Farn, the Iranian deity of royal destiny and good fortune.

The depictions on the sides of the headdress are in three tiers, which reflect the concept of a tripartite model of the world. The bottom layer, in turn, is in three parts, recalling the ancient Indian belief that there are three worlds, this one and two beyond. The idea of triplicity permeated the Saka cosmogony and was its essence; however, each of the component elements was not homogeneous. The concept of a tripartite universe corresponded to the tripartite structure of Saka society.

Thus, the depictions on the Issyk royal headdress linked together the king's earthly and sacred power (as portrayed on the frontal part) and his cosmic essence (as portrayed on the sides). All this is united with the diadem below and the figurine of the ram above—the pole toward which everything strives and which embodies the divine attribution of the king.

Burial customs. Mircea Eliade has established that after a mythic, cosmic catastrophe only devout people, shamans, and so on may ascend to the heavens, with the help of a "sacred cord" (tree, cliff, etc.). To facilitate their ascent, at the interment of these persons wooden stakes are set up in the burial pits, or stone columns are placed on the burial mounds (as in the Pamir).

Burial rituals and customs varied considerably among the different Saka tribes. Among the large *kurgans* of the Pazyryk group, a chamber made of logs was sometimes set on top of the stone foundation of the burial pit, which was about 4 meters deep. On top of the chamber, the pit was packed with logs and stones. Its surface was covered with rounded earth, topped with a stone mound that had a diameter of 36 to 46 meters. The burial pit was quadrangular, oriented to the cardinal directions. The largest *kurgans* had a double log chamber, protected from pressure by a wooden covering resting on posts. In the northern third of the burial pit, horses (up to ten) were buried and carts were placed. In the largest *kurgans,* human burials were in log coffins with covers. One such sarcophagus was decorated with roosters cut out of leather, another with reindeer cutouts. The chamber walls were draped with felt rugs. The burial chambers and rites of the Bashadyr and Tuekta *kurgans,* also in the Altai, were similar. Although the *kurgans* were robbed in antiquity, the objects were so diverse and their remains so amazingly well preserved, owing to permafrost, that they give a clear impression of the ancient inhabitants' appearance, their material culture, and, in part, their beliefs.

In Scythian times in the Altai region, deceased persons of outstanding importance were embalmed, by rather complex methods. Evidently, these deceased were believed to play a special role in the world beyond. The Scythians, for example, embalmed the corpses of their kings (Herodotus 4.71).

Some of the Altai princely burials have preserved traces of the removal of muscle tissue. Hecataeus of Miletus (fl. 500 BCE) wrote of the Massagetae: "They consider it the best kind of death, when they are old, to be chopped up with the flesh of cattle and eaten mixed up with that flesh" (Strabo, *Geography* 11.8.6). Similar evidence is found in Herodotus (1.216). Classical sources and the Avesta hint at the ritual killing, among a number of Iranian-speaking peoples, of aged men. In the Altai, small pieces of the deceased's flesh were apparently eaten; in this way his spiritual and physical qualities and his social rank were acquired. If a woman consumed one of these pieces of flesh, her subsequent children would inherit the outstanding qualities of the deceased. A deeper stratum of these animistic beliefs is the totemic one. Also associated with animistic beliefs was the custom of placing in the grave nail parings from the deceased and small sacks containing his hair. The burial was accompanied by purifying and ecstatic rites, particularly the smoking of hemp.

The religious worldview of the Saka was reflected in the artworks of the animal style. Analysis of these works and of the materials associated with funerary rituals confirms the existence of shamanistic beliefs and practices, especially in Siberia. The origins of the heroic epos of the Inner Asian and Siberian peoples date to Saka times. The greatest Iranian epic hero, Rōtastahm (Rustam), had the epithet *Sagčīk,* "from among the Saka." His name is a symbol of the hero.

[*See also* Indo-European Religions, *overview article;* Iranian Religion; Indus Valley Religion; Scythian Religion; *and* Sarmatian Religion.]

BIBLIOGRAPHY

Books covering the overall subject of this article do not exist. A general review of the Aeneolithic sites of the Eurasian steppes is *Arkheologiia SSSR: Eneolit SSSR,* edited by V. M. Masson and N. Ia. Merpert (Moscow, 1982). The first work on the Aeneolithic and Bronze ages of Central Asia to contain information on religious beliefs was *Explorations in Turkestan: Expedition of 1904; Prehistoric Civilizations of Anau,* 2 vols., edited by Raphael Pumpelly (Washington, D.C., 1908). The most recent review and analysis is Philip L. Kohl's *Central Asia: Palaeolithic Beginnings to the Iron Age* (Paris, 1984), which has an outstanding bibliography and only a few serious omissions.

Two excellent monographs by Elena V. Antonova are devoted to the religion of the Aeneolithic and Bronze Age tribes: *Antropomorfnaia skul'ptura drevnikh zemledel'tsev Perednei i Srednei Azii* (Moscow, 1977) and *Ocherki kul'tury drevnikh zemledel'tsev Perednei i Srednei Azii: Opyt rekonstruktsii i mirovospriiatiia* (Moscow, 1984). The latter is a fundamental work that investigates in depth the religions of the ancient agriculturist tribes of the entire East, from Anatolia to Central Asia.

For extensive material on the beliefs of the Tripolye tribes, see S. M. Bibikov's *Rannetripol'skoe poselenie Luka-Vrublevetskaia na Dnestre* (Moscow, 1953). See also Aina P. Pogozheva's *Antropomorfnaia plastika Tripol'ia* (Novosibirsk, 1983). The beliefs of the Tripolye-Cucuteni tribes are examined in the context of other European beliefs in Marija Gimbutas's *The Goddesses and Gods of Old Europe, 6500–3500 B.C.* (Berkeley, 1982); her interpretations, however, are sometimes unjustifiably bold.

For the religion of the proto-Iranians, Iranians, and, in particular, the Saka, see Mary Boyce's *A History of Zoroastrianism,* 2 vols. (Leiden, 1975–1982). It is an excellent investigation of the origins and early history of Iranian religions. An outstanding overall review of these religions, especially that of the Saka, is Geo Widengren's *Die Religionen Irans* (Stuttgart, 1965), based on nonarchaeological materials. On the Saka, see also Julius Junge's *Saka-studien: Der Ferne Nordosten in Weltbild der Antike* (Leipzig, 1939) and my own archaeologically based study *Kangiuisko-sarmatskii farn* (Dushanbe, 1968), translated as "Das K'ang-chü-sarmatische Farnah," *Central Asiatic Journal* 16 (1972): 241–289 and 20 (1976): 47–74.

Comprehensive descriptions and valuable analyses of the materials from the Saka archaeological complexes can be found in M. I. Artamonov's *Sokrovishcha sakov* (Moscow, 1973) and in Karl Jettmar's *Die frühen Steppenvolker* (Baden-Baden, 1964), translated as *The Art of the Steppes* (New York, 1967). For a general survey of all the Saka materials in Central Asia, see my book *Eisenzeitliche Kurgane zwischen Pamir und Aral-See* (Munich, 1984).

Monographs devoted to recent discoveries at individual complexes usually include a chapter on religious beliefs. Among them are K. A. Akishev's *Kurgan Issyk: Iskusstvo sakov Kazakhstana* (Moscow, 1978), K. A. Akishev and G. A. Kushaev's *Drevniaia kul'tura sakov i usunei reki Ili* (Alma-Ata, 1963), O. A. Vishnevskaia's *Kul'tura sakskikh plemen nizov'ev Syrdar'a v VII–V vv. do n.e.: Po materialam Uĭgaraka* (Moscow, 1973), M. P. Griaznov's *Arzhan: Tsarskii kurgan ranneskifskogo vremeni* (Leningrad, 1980), S. I. Rudenko's *Kul'tura naseleniia Gornogo Altaia v skifskoe vremia* (Moscow, 1953) and *Kul'tura nasaleniia Tsentral'nogo Altaia v skifskoe vremia* (Moscow, 1960), V. I. Sarianidi's *Bactrian Gold: From the Excavations of the Tillya-Tepe Necropolis in Northern Afghanistan* (Leningrad, 1984), and my *Drevnie kochevniki "Kryshi mira"* (Moscow, 1972). Considerable attention is devoted to the Saka religion in two outstanding works by D. S. Raevskii: *Ocherki ideologii skifo-sakskikh plemen: Opyt rekonstruktsii skifskoi mifologii* (Moscow, 1977) and *Model' mira skifskoi kul'tury* (Moscow, 1985).

B. A. Litvinskii

Translated from Russian by Demitri B. Shimkin

PRESBYTERIANISM, REFORMED. The word *presbyterian* refers both to a particular form of church government and, more generally, to churches that are governed by presbyters but have many other characteristics. The word *reformed* defines a theological perspective. The two words usually but not always belong together. Most Reformed churches are presbyterian, but they may also be congregational and occasionally episcopal in governance. [*See* Church, *article on* Church Polity.]

Historical Origins of Presbyterianism. Presbyterians are catholic in their affirmation of the triune God and of the creeds of the ancient catholic church: the Apostles' Creed, the Nicene Creed, and the Chalcedonian definition. They are Protestant in the sense of Martin Luther's treatises of 1520. Their Reformed roots are in the Reformation at Zurich, under the leadership of Ulrich Zwingli (1484–1531) and Heinrich Bullinger (1504–1575); at Strasbourg, under Martin Bucer (1491–1551); and at Geneva, with the work of John Calvin (1509–1564).

Reformed theology at the time of the Reformation. Reformed theology was a type of Protestantism—as distinct from Lutheranism, Anglicanism, and the theology of the radical Reformation—that originated in Switzerland, the upper Rhineland, and France. Most of the early Reformed theologians had a background in Christian humanism. [*See* Humanism.] They were more energetic and radical in their reform of medieval Catholicism than were the Lutherans. The Lutherans' practice was guided by the principle that everything in church life contrary to the word of God should be eliminated. The Reformed church insisted upon positive scriptural warrant for all church practice.

Reformed theology was characterized by its emphasis upon the doctrine of God, who was conceived not so much as beauty or truth but as energy, activity, power, intentionality, and moral purpose. Reformed theologians believed that all of life and history is rooted in the decrees or purposes of God. They emphasized the lordship of God in history and in the salvation of the Christian as emphasized in the doctrine of predestination. They shared the Lutheran doctrine that no one ever merits salvation and that salvation is always grace, always forgiveness. Yet they understood the Christian life as obedience to the law of God and as the embodiment of the purposes of God. As far as the relation of Christian faith to society was concerned, they neither withdrew from society nor identified Christian faith with culture. They were converters of culture and transformers of history, at least in intention.

A central theme of Reformed theology was the glory of God. The salvation of souls and concern for one's own condition was subordinate to giving God the praise, acknowledging his grace, and fulfilling his purpose in personal life and history. The Reformed churches were also characterized by an emphasis on the life of the mind as proper service of God. John Calvin, the most influential of Reformed theologians, was not a speculative thinker. While rejecting curiosity as destructive of faith, Calvin insisted that Christians should know what they believed; the way a person thinks determines action. Calvin also placed high value upon verbal expressions of faith. The sermon became the focus of Reformed worship. Through its example of disciplined, logical thinking, the sermon became a factor in influencing culture in Reformed communities. [*See the biography of Calvin.*]

The major theological works that shaped Reformed theology in Presbyterian churches were Calvin's *The Institutes of the Christian Religion* (1536), *Institutio Theologiae Elencticae* (1688) of Francis Turretin, and *Systematic Theology* (1871–1873) of Charles Hodge. The most influential creeds have been the Scots Confession of 1560 and the Westminster Confession and Catechisms.

Reformed liturgy. In liturgy the Reformed churches placed a premium upon intelligibility and edification. As with life generally, Calvin insisted that worship should be simple, free from theatrical trifles. The sacraments were limited to the Lord's Supper and baptism, which were believed to have been instituted by Jesus Christ. Within the Reformed tradition some emphasized a preaching service, intending only an occasional celebration of the Lord's Supper. Others believed that the normative service united preaching and the Lord's Supper. Among the more prominent documents of the liturgical tradition are Ulrich Zwingli's *Liturgy of the Word,* Guillaume Farel's *The Order Observed in Preaching,* Calvin's *The Form of Church Prayers,* John Knox's *The Form of Prayers, The Westminster Directory of Worship,* the *Book of Common Order* (Church of Scotland), and the *Book of Common Worship* (Presbyterian Church in the USA). [*See the biographies of Zwingli, Farel, and Knox.*]

Presbyterian polity. The word *presbyterian* has its primary reference not to theology or liturgy but to church government. The prominence of the word in the names of churches has two sources. First, the Reformed churches all believed that the way a church is ordered is important. This was especially the case with Calvin, who devoted long sections of the *Institutes* as well as a major part of his active life to questions of church governance and order. He believed that order is determined by theology and, in its turn, shapes life. Second, English-speaking Presbyterians were involved in lengthy and at times bitter struggles over the order of the church, sometimes with those who shared their theology. This was true in the sixteenth- and seventeenth-century Church of England, which included in its membership Congregationalists and Presbyterians as well as Episcopalians and in which many Episcopalians were also Reformed in theology. The Congregationalists and Presbyterians formed dissenting churches in England. Presbyterians in Britain and Northern Ireland never forgot these controversies, especially the attempts to impose episcopacy by governmental authority in Scotland and Ulster. The word *presbyterian* first began to be used in Scotland in the first half of the seventeenth century. Since then it has been the designation of English-speaking, Reformed Christians who maintain a presbyterian polity. Reformed churches on the European continent with presbyterian polities are called Reformed after their theology.

Presbyterianism is not a fixed pattern of church life but a developing pattern that has both continuity and diversity. Many features of the system vary from time to time and from place to place. In the United States, for example, Presbyterianism developed from the congregation to the presbytery, to the synod, to the General Assembly. In Scotland, Presbyterianism grew out of a gradually evolving notion of how the church should be governed, out of conflict with episcopacy, and from the General Assembly down to the congregation.

Presbyterians find the roots of their polity in the reforming activity of Calvin. With the reform of doctrine, the city council in Geneva had also driven out the bishop and the whole clerical establishment. This gave the reformers greater freedom in shaping the order of the church than in places where so much of the traditional structure remained intact. Calvin gave special attention to the organized life of the church partly because of his personal inclinations as a trained lawyer and also out of the theological conviction that proper order was necessary for both the piety and the purity of the church.

In his doctrine of the church, Calvin's primary emphasis was on the action of the Holy Spirit, who created the church through word and sacrament. Jesus Christ is the only head of the church, and under him all are equal. In addition, Calvin struggled all his life for a church that was independent of state control. He held to the notion of a Christian society with a magistrate whose work in the civil order is a vocation from God, but ideally Calvin wanted church and state to work together under God yet in independence of each other organizationally. Calvin placed great emphasis on the minister, who interprets and applies the word of God. On occasion Calvin refers to the preacher as the "mouth of God." The importance of the minister in leading worship, in preaching, in teaching, and in pastoral care is one of function not of status. Calvin insisted that the government of the church should be in the hands of a consistory (council) composed of ministers and elders chosen from the congregation. (In Geneva the choice was limited to members of the city council.) He was opposed on theological grounds to government by individuals who were neither good nor wise enough for such responsibility, and he was likewise opposed to rule by the masses, who were not sufficiently qualified to govern. In both church and state, Calvin advocated government by an aristocracy, in the Aristotelian sense of the qualified, tempered by democracy. In representative government the will of God was more likely to be done. With few exceptions (Hungary, for example), Reformed churches that looked to Geneva for leadership were governed by a council.

Calvin also worked for a disciplined church. Discipline was the primary responsibility of the consistory. Calvin located the exercise of discipline at admission to the Lord's Table. The consistory examined communicants on knowledge based on catechetical instruction and on manner of life. Another of Calvin's achievements was the restoration of the office of deacon as exercising the church's ministry of compassion to the sick and needy.

Calvin developed a polity only for Geneva and the surrounding countryside; hence, in his own work he left the full development of church structure open-ended. Some have argued that Calvin's polity is compatible with episcopacy, but the most that can be established is that Calvin did not oppose existing administrative and judicial episcopal structures.

Although some Calvinists became Congregationalists, Calvin's successor in Geneva, Theodore Beza, was an ardent Presbyterian. Beza guided the Reformed church in France as it worked out the first presbyterian church government on a national scale, with local, district, provincial, and national assemblies composed of ministers and elders. [*See the biography of Beza.*] Presbyterianism also became the form of church government in the Netherlands and other Reformed churches on the continent. It received its great emphasis, however, in Scotland, where the controversy about the structure of the church, whether it should be congregational, presbyterian, or episcopal, was vigorously contested and received an importance not given to questions of polity elsewhere.

There are four basic principles of presbyterian polity. The first is the authority of scripture. Some Presbyterians, such as Thomas Cartwright in Puritan England and James Henley Thornwell in American Presbyterianism, contended that presbyterianism was the biblical form of church government. Most Presbyterians have argued that presbyterianism is agreeable to scripture. Traditionally, Presbyterians have wanted to test government as well as doctrine by scripture. They have always subordinated church government to the gospel and have never made the form of government a test of the reality of the church.

The other three principles of presbyterian polity relate to form of governance and relations among clergy and between clergy and laity. Presbyterians have emphasized the unity of the church governed by a graded series of church courts. These assemblies are composed of ministers and elders elected by the people. The word *church* applies both to the local congregation and to the whole body of believers. There is no local congregation without its participation in the whole body of believers, and no church without local congregations. It is in the governance of the church through assemblies that presbyterianism most clearly differs from episcopacy and congregationalism. A third principle is the parity of ministers, who have the same and equal authority under the one head of the church, Jesus Christ. Finally, the fourth principle is the right of the people to call their pastors and to elect those who govern them. Sometimes this right has been limited by circumstance to approval or consent, but the demand to exercise the right of the people has continually reasserted itself.

Among the primary documents of Presbyterian polity are book 4 of the *Institutes; Ecclesiastical Ordinances of Geneva; the First Book of Discipline* and the *Second Book of Discipline* of the Church of Scotland; the *Book of Discipline of the Elizabethan Presbyterians.* Also primary are the Westminster Assembly's *Form of Presbyterian Government* and *The Form of Government* of American Presbyterian churches.

The Presbyterian Churches. The Church of Scotland continues the tradition in which English-speaking Presbyterianism was first established. The Congregational church in England and Wales and the Presbyterian Church of England became the United Reformed Church in 1972. By 1982, the United Reformed Church, the Church of Scotland, and the Presbyterian churches of Ireland and Wales had approximately 3.4 million members.

The Presbyterian churches in the United States have their origin in emigration from Scotland and Northern Ireland. Puritan influences were also strong. The Presbyterian Church at Hempstead and later Jamaica, Long Island, was composed largely of Puritans and is probably the oldest continuing Presbyterian Church in the United States, dating from 1644. The first presbytery was organized under the leadership of Francis Makemie, who had come from Ulster, at Philadelphia in 1706. The organization of a synod followed in 1717, and the adoption of the Westminster Confession and Catechisms as theological standards occurred in 1729. The General Assembly held its first meeting in 1789. American Presbyterians have divided on three occasions. The Old Side–New Side division (1741–1768) had to do with the accommodation of the church to the American frontier; the New School–Old School division (1837–1864 and 1869) was concerned with doctrinal and ecclesiastical issues; the Presbyterian Church in the U.S.A. and the Presbyterian Church in the Confederate States (later the Presbyterian Church in the U.S.) split in 1861 and reunited in 1983. The Presbyterian Church in the U.S.A. had a uniting membership of approximately 3.2 million in 1983.

The Cumberland Presbyterian Church originated in a split from the main body of Presbyterians during the revivals in the first decades of the nineteenth century. A major portion of the Cumberland Church reunited with the Presbyterian Church in the U.S.A. in 1903. The Second Cumberland Church, with a predominantly black membership of 10,000 in 1978, exists independently but in close cooperation with the main body of Cumberland Presbyterians.

The Associate and the Reformed Presbyterians, who originated in secessions from the Church of Scotland, continued their existence in the immigration to the United States. The major body of Associate and Reformed Presbyterians, having become the United Presbyterian Church (1858), merged with the mainstream of Presbyterians in 1958, becoming the United Presbyterian Church in the U.S.A. The Associate Reformed Presbyterian Church, located largely in the South, and the Reformed Presbyterian Church of North America continue the traditions of the Scottish secession Presbyterians.

Other Presbyterian churches originated out of the controversies generated by the conservative and liberal theologies of the twentieth century. The Orthodox Presbyterian Church, a withdrawal from the Presbyterian Church in the U.S.A. in 1936, the Bible Presbyterian Church, a split from the Orthodox in 1938, and the Presbyterian Church of America, organized in 1973 in a pullout from the Presbyterian Church in the U.S., have their origins in these controversies.

Presbyterianism came to Canada chiefly through emigration from Scotland and represented all the divisions of Presbyterianism there. In 1875 they united in one church. The majority combined in 1925 with Congregationalists and Methodists to form the United Church of Canada. The Presbyterian Church in Canada reported a membership of 186,584 in 1970.

Presbyterian churches in Australia and New Zealand were also established by Scottish immigrants. In the 1961 census, 9.3 percent of Australians declared themselves to be Presbyterian. In 1977 the Presbyterians, Methodists, and Congregational churches formed the Uniting Church in Australia (1,194,088 members in 1982). The Presbyterian Church of Australia Continuing in 1982 had 150,000 members. Scottish immigration and the Church of Scotland's support of immigrants are the basis of the Presbyterian Church of New Zealand (500,000 members in 1982).

Presbyterian churches have been established throughout the world by the missionary movement of the nineteenth and twentieth centuries. Strong Presbyterian churches exist especially in Korea and also in Brazil, Mexico, and Africa. The World Alliance of Reformed Churches, which is now organized on the basis of theology rather than polity, reports a worldwide membership of 40 million in 1985. This includes younger churches in Africa, South America, and Asia with Reformed theologies but not necessarily presbyterian polities.

BIBLIOGRAPHY

Bolam, C. Gordon, et al. *The English Presbyterians: From Elizabethan Puritanism to Modern Unitarianism.* London, 1968.

Henderson, George D. *Presbyterianism.* Aberdeen, 1955. A comprehensive introduction to the origin and development of presbyterian polity.

Leith, John H. *Introduction to the Reformed Tradition: A Way of Being the Christian Community.* Rev. ed. Atlanta, 1981. Chapters on the ethos, theology, polity, worship, and the cultural expression of the Reformed community.

Loetscher, Lefferts A. *A Brief History of the Presbyterians.* 4th ed. Philadelphia, 1984. Brief but reliable.

McNeil, John T. *The History and Character of Calvinism.* Oxford, 1954. Comprehensive, reliable, judicious. The work of a distinguished historian who cherished the tradition.

JOHN H. LEITH

PREUSS, KONRAD T. (1869–1938), German ethnologist and historian of religions. Konrad Theodor Preuss was born on 2 June 1869 in the Prussian city of Eylau (present-day Bagrationovsk, U.S.S.R.). Shortly after completing school in Königsberg in 1887, he began studying history and geography at the university there and in 1894 received his doctorate from these departments. In 1895 he took a position at the Berlin Ethnological Museum; during his career there he first became head of the North and Middle America department and, eventually (in 1920), director of the museum. He received a professorship from the University of Berlin in 1912, and from that time on he conducted lectures and seminars in North and South American ethnology and archaeology. He also conducted an interdisciplinary colloquium in religious history. In accordance with regulations, Preuss retired from his positions in 1934; his retirement did not, however, hinder his scientific work. Preuss's publications, which appeared on a regular basis throughout his career, concentrated on American ethnology and linguistics.

Within the anthropological study of primal religious traditions, Preuss became known as the foremost German exponent of the "preanimist" theory of magic. Preuss, along with those who followed his theoretical course, held that there had been a stage in human religious development prior to the stage named "animism" by evolutionist anthropologists. During this "preanimist" stage, human beings had construed causality in nature in accordance with belief in the efficacy of magical practices in influencing the environment. [*See* Preanimism.] In this connection, Preuss spoke of the "primal ignorance" of mankind.

The preanimist hypothesis was quickly disputed and has since been thoroughly rejected (see, e.g., Adolf E. Jensen's *Myth and Cult among Primitive People,* 2d ed., 1969). Deities of later religious eras, even after the existence of an impersonal power came to be accepted, were attended with the same magical methods that Preuss had indicated had been employed by people of an earlier age. But Preuss had already recorded his theoretical construct in a series of articles entitled "Der Ursprung der Religion und Kunst" (*Globus* 86 and 87, 1904–1905), and he retained these principles throughout his life.

The experience Preuss gained on two field-research expeditions furnished additional information. The first of these expeditions (1905–1907) brought him into contact with the Cora, Huichol, and Mexicanos tribes of the Sierra Madre of Mexico's Pacific coast. The second journey (1913–1915) was devoted to the study of the Witóto in the lowlands and the Cágaba in the highlands of Colombia. In the religion and mythology of the Witóto, especially, Preuss was able not only to recognize correspondences between various myths and the particular cults that enact them but also to see the roots of these correspondences in an ancient period (see *Religion und Mythologie der Uitoto,* 2 vols., 1921–1923; cf. *Der religiöse Gehalt der Mythen,* 1933). The cultic religions that followed the preanimistic stage were the direct result of these deep-rooted sentiments; they were later superseded by religions in which prayers, not magical practices, were employed.

These later religions were built around a central supreme deity. The form taken by this deity became a major concern for Preuss in his work *Glauben und Mystik im Schatten des Höchsten Wesens* (1926). In contrast with Wilhelm Schmidt's view that there had been a universal *Urmonotheismus* ("primitive monotheism") at the earliest stage of human religious evolution, Preuss did not believe that the supreme being was a predominant element during the initial stage of religious development.

According to Preuss's view, religion is more than the "expressive repetition of prayers of thanksgiving and humble obedience to a supreme deity" (see "Fortschritt und Rückschritt in der Religion," *Zeitschrift für Missionskunde und Religionswissenschaft* 47, 1932, p. 241).

Like that of other gods, the supreme deity's origin can ultimately be traced, Preuss thought, to perceptual impressions of nature. Beside the theoretical problems surrounding the question of the origin of the idea of God, Preuss devoted the remainder of his career to the study of ancient Mexican religion and history.

BIBLIOGRAPHY

For further information, see F. R. Lehmann's article, "K. Th. Preusz," in *Zeitschrift für Ethnologie* 71 (1939): 145–150.

Otto Zerries
Translated from German by John Maressa

PRIAPUS was an ithyphallic deity of ancient Greece and Rome. He is known mainly as the god of Roman gardens, where images of him, usually holding up his fruit-laden garment to exhibit his outsize sexual organ, were often placed. However, from the time of his appearance at the dawn of the Hellenistic age well into the Christian Middle Ages, Priapus (Gr., Priapos) may have a basis in some very different realities. From Ptolemy II Philadelphus (Athenaeus, 5.201c), for whom Priapus occupies a mythico-political position, to the epigrams in the *Greek Anthology* or to the kitchen gardens of Priapea in the *Corpus Priapeorum*, this god—whom Horace makes into an obscene scarecrow (*Satires* 1.8)—finds no place among the theological definitions proposed by the ancients. Neither do they seem to have assigned him his own place in their pantheon, even though he was traditionally considered to be the son of Dionysos and Aphrodite and could have been part of the Dionysian *thiaseii* ("revels"). There is, however, one notorious exception: in the system of Justin the Gnostic, the ithyphallic Priapus becomes central to cosmogony; indeed, he is the supreme being, "the one who made creation, even though nothing existed before" (*Elenchos* 5.26.33).

The fate that history has dealt this *divus minor* ("minor god"; *Corpus Priapeorum* 53) is therefore surprising, for both ancient and modern authors have ceaselessly confused him with other figures of sexuality: Pan, the satyrs, and Hermaphroditus, as well as his own father, Dionysos. This confusion is perhaps due to the fact the Priapus's congenital feature is his oversize and perpetually erect penis, so that authors have often tended to identify everything hypersexual with him. It is as if his excessive sexuality has confused the erudite mythographers. Also, when Diodorus Siculus (4.64) and Strabo (13.1.12) try to describe Priapus, they can do so only by mentioning his "resemblance" to the Attic gods Ithyphallos, Orthnes, Konisalos, and Tychon, all ithyphallic powers about whom almost nothing is known except the priapic resemblance that defines them.

However, in spite of these frequent confusions, the ancient sources give this divinity a specific character. Unlike his phallic colleagues, Pan and the satyrs, who are hybrids, Priapus is fully anthropomorphic. He has neither horns nor hoofs nor a tail. His sole anomaly and unique pathology is the immense sexual organ that defines him from birth. Fragments of myths tell how the newborn Priapus was rejected by his mother, the beautiful Aphrodite, for no other reason than his deformed ugliness *(amorphos)* and his disproportionate virile member. It is this oversize organ, described by the Latin texts as "terribilis" (Columella, *De re rustica* 10.33), that allows Priapus to be recognized in images and that identifies him in writings by giving him the form necessary to one of his major functions, that of protecting small-scale cultivations against the evil eye or against thieves by threatening sexual violence to all who pass near the domain he guards (*Planudean Anthology* 241; *Corpus Priapeorum* 11, 28, 44, 59, 71).

In both Greek and Latin epigrams, it is the ithyphallic effigy of the god, often carved from the mediocre wood of a fig tree and daubed with red, who is the speaker pronouncing obscene threats. But Priapus is all talk and no action. In guarding his little gardens, as well as in his amorous adventures, he is often ineffectual. Ovid (*Fasti* 1.391–440, 6.319–348) relates how Priapus failed in his courtship of the beautiful Lotis (or Vesta in another version) and found himself empty-handed every time, his sex up in the air, derided by an assembly laughing at the obscene spectacle of the god frustrated and obliged to flee, his heart and his member heavy.

But it is perhaps the ancient physicians who, in their nosology, best illustrate certain aspects of this impotent phallocrat. *Priapism* is the term they use to name an incurable disease in which the male organ persistently remains painfully erect. The medical texts of Galen (8.439, 19.426) and Caelius Aurelianus (3.18.175) also insist on an important point: priapism must not be confused with satyriasis, a comparable disease in which the pathological erection does not exclude either seminal emission or erotic pleasure, which is not the case in priapism.

This difference between the ithyphallism of Priapus and that of the satyrs may indicate still another division: Priapus, the citizen of Lampsacus, whose representations are always anthropomorphic, can be classified close to humans, whereas the satyrs, who are hybrids between men and beasts, belong with demons and the wild. It is as if immeasurable sexuality, which is impossible for a human, is viable for beasts and half-humans.

Aristotle specifies in his biological writings that nature has endowed the virile member with the capacity to be or not to be erect, and he wryly notes that "if this organ were always in the same state, it would be an annoyance" (*De partibus animalium* 689a). This, however, is precisely the case of Priapus, who, always ithyphallic, never knows the slightest sexual relief. The ancients considered such phallic excess to be a kind of deformity. The same kind of ugliness characterizes the functional aspects of apotropaic objects that, like Priapus, evoke laughter (Aristotle, *Poetics* 5.1449a) in order to distance evil. This also holds for those amulets that, as Plutarch reminds us, "draw the bewitcher's gaze" with their strange aspect *(atopia)*.

Given his laughable ugliness, which turns people away, and the Dionysian milieu he belonged to, Priapus remained for a long time a vulgarized figure of ancient fertility. Yet, the appeal of this little god of gardens has endured across the centuries. In the late Middle Ages he was known even to the Cistercians (*Chronique de Lanercost*, 1268); he was rediscovered by the artists and craftsmen of the European Renaissance; and his image has continued in use as guardian of gardens down to the present day.

BIBLIOGRAPHY

Herter, Hans. *De Priapo*. Giessen, 1932.

Morel Philippe. "Priape à la Renaissance: Les guirlandes de Giovanni da Udine à la Farnésine." *Revue de l'art* 69 (1985): 13–28.

Olender, Maurice. "Éléments pour une analyze de Priape chez Justin le Gnostique." In *Hommages à Maarten J. Vermaseren*, edited by Margreet B. de Boer and T. A. Eldridge, vol. 2. Leiden, 1978.

Olender, Maurice. "L'enfant Priape et son phallus." In *Souffrance, plaisir et pensé*, edited by Alain de Mijolla. Paris, 1983.

Richlin, Amy. *The Garden of Priapus: Sexuality and Aggression in Roman Humor*. New Haven, 1983.

MAURICE OLENDER

Translated from French by Claude Conyers

PRIESTHOOD. [*To explore the religious significance of priesthood, this entry consists of seven articles:*

An Overview
Jewish Priesthood
Christian Priesthood
Hindu Priesthood
Buddhist Priesthood
Shintō Priesthood
Taoist Priesthood

The first article presents a cross-cultural overview of the types, roles, and religious functions of priests and priestesses, with examples drawn from various religious traditions. The companion pieces deal with six traditions in which the priesthood is a central feature of cultic life.]

An Overview

Cross-cultural use of the terms *priest* and *priesthood* is an example of a familiar pattern in modern description of religion. Frequently, terms with European meanings and linguistic derivations are pressed into service for the description of a range of phenomena worldwide. If we pay attention to this fact, we can often enhance our appreciation not only of the terminology itself but of the material to which it is applied.

Usage in the West. In the case of *priest*, we can discern a "core" meaning in the Western use of the term. At this core, one may argue, are two identifying factors. The priest, first, performs a sacrificial ritual, usually at a fixed location such as an altar. Second, the priest does so as a specialist on behalf of a community or congregation. When both of these factors are present, we have priesthood in a strict or narrow sense.

In fact, the strict sense of the meaning of *priest* prevailed prior to modern times, while looser and more inclusive applications of the term have come into use more recently. This development has to do with religious and conceptual horizons of the Christian West, in which the vocabulary of Latin and its derivatives has been dominant. In the traditions of the Judeo-Christian West, our point will become clear when we consider circumstances in which the term *priest* has not been used. The two principal cases are the Jewish and the Protestant.

For Judaism, priesthood is a well-defined and central role in the biblical tradition. The performance of sacrifices was one of its essential characteristics. The priests carried out the sacrificial ritual at altars, and from the seventh century BCE onward such ceremony was centralized at the temple in Jerusalem. When, however, the Jerusalem temple was destroyed, the sacrificial practices lapsed, and there were no longer active priests, even if there were hereditary priestly families. Religious leadership in the synagogue, which replaced the temple, passed to the rabbis in their role as teachers. The only continuation of ancient Israel's animal sacrifice is among the small community of the Samaritans, whose officiants to this day are referred to as priests. As far as the Hebraic context is concerned, the terms we translate by *priest* regularly imply the performance of sacrifice, and in the absence of the sacrifice the concept has been considered inapplicable.

Protestants do not generally refer to their clergy as "priests" either. (In this context, the Anglican communion's usage is closer to a Roman Catholic than to a Protestant understanding of things.) But Protestants do have a conception of priesthood, referred to as "the priesthood of all believers." Each member of the community, in this view, is his or her own priest, with direct access to God. The salient feature of priesthood which this Protestant understanding illustrates, then, has not so much to do with sacrifice as such but with the priest's role as an officiating intermediary. In avoiding the term *priest* as a designation of their own clergy, most Protestants have implied a repudiation of the notion that priestly ordination should elevate any man above his fellow human beings or confer on him any access to the divine that is denied others. Protestants did differ from Rome on the senses in which the Lord's Supper, the eucharistic meal of the Mass, might be considered in itself a sacrifice, for they held that Jesus' self-sacrifice was commemorated rather than repeated. But the truly sore point was the privileged, controlling status enjoyed by the officiating Roman clergy. In the Reformation context, then, an essential characteristic of priesthood was its privileged role of mediating benefits and requests between the divine and the human community.

Before we leave the historical meanings of priesthood we may take note of the derivation of the term *priest* itself. Etymologically, the word in English comes from the French *prêtre* and ultimately from the Greek *presbutēs*. In Greek, however, that term means "elder"; hence in the course of Christian usage the semantics of the term shifted from the ordained person's place in ecclesiastical polity to his role as a cultic celebrant. Semantically, on the other hand, the chief words whose meaning corresponds to "priest" are *hiereus* in Greek, *sacerdos* in Latin, and *kohen* in Hebrew.

Description of Priesthood in Non-Western Religion. A great many other activities and attributes of priests in the European Christian tradition have built up a range of connotations of the term and role extending far beyond the two critical factors we have reviewed so far. Priests in the West generally wear ceremonial robes while officiating and have distinctive details of street clothing; hence, Western visitors to Japan, for instance, termed the robed personnel of temples "priests," whether Shintō or Buddhist. Priests in the Latin Christian tradition are unmarried; hence the disposition of visitors to Sri Lanka, Burma, or Thailand sometimes to refer to Buddhist monks as "priests," even if the status of their ritual as a sacrifice is debatable. Priests are inducted into their office through ordination; hence the tendency to view tribal societies' ritually initiated specialists in divination, exorcism, healing, and the like as priests. Priests deliver sermons and moral injuctions; hence, presumably, occasional references to the *'ulamā'*, or religious scholars of traditional Islamic lands, as priests, despite the fact that they are neither ordained nor do they perform ritual sacrifice.

In the extended, cross-cultural uses of the term *priest*, then, a priest is any religious specialist acting ritually for or on behalf of a community. With a term used in so broad and flexible a general sense, one excludes little from the category. Ritual activities as such, however, do not make the laypeople who perform them priests; a priest, in any useful sense of the term, is characteristically an intermediary set apart by a recognized induction into office and functioning on behalf of others. Nor does religious specialization or professionalism on behalf of a lay clientele necessarily constitute someone as a priest; there are healers, teachers, and the like who function as professionals but whose activity is not tied to the ritual of a sanctuary.

Eligibility for Priesthood. The world's priests in various traditions can be divided into what one might term *hereditary* priesthoods and *vocational* priesthoods. In the first case, the priestly prerogatives and duties are the special heritage of particular family or tribal lineages. The ancient Hebrew priesthood, for example, was reserved to the Levites, or descendants of Levi. Levi does not figure in the list of Israelite tribes in *Numbers* 1 (where Ephraim and Manasseh as sons of Joseph each have a place on the list of twelve), but the Levites appear to have gained tribal status in the tradition of *Genesis* 49 (also a list of twelve, including Levi and Joseph but not Ephraim or Manasseh).

Similarly, hereditary is the priesthood in Zoroastrianism, the national religion of pre-Islamic Iran, which today still claims a hundred thousand Iranian and Indian adherents. Traditionally, fathers who were practicing priests trained their sons in the proper recitation of the prayers. More recently, *madrasah*s (schools) for the training of priests have been established. A priest's son may exercise the option to become a priest, and even if he does not do so, the grandson may; but after two or three generations of inactivity the eligibility of the line lapses.

The brahman class of India constitutes another important example of priests whose eligibility is hereditary. The traditional Indian social scale known as the caste system places the priests in the highest rank in terms of prestige and respect, ahead of the warrior-rulers. Not surprisingly, the warrior class had already gained greater practical power by the time documented by extant historical records. The other strata continued nonetheless to behave in the apparent confidence that their own positions might be legitimated, confirmed, or blessed by the brahmans, however impoverished the brahmans might become.

It is generally expected that the clergy in hereditary priesthoods will marry, so that the line may be perpetuated. Indeed, the genealogical awareness of hereditary priesthoods is often as carefully documented as is that of royalty, and for similar reasons. Families claiming the right to officiate in a particular location are known to record their descent back a number of centuries in order to substantiate their legitimacy. Hereditary control of certain temples, whether in Japan or India or elsewhere, can imply some financial advantage, such as access to housing on the premises or to the temple's revenues as income.

Many professions and lines of work are reflected in people's surnames, and a family association with priesthood is no exception. The Jewish surname *Cohen* is an example, as is also *Katz* (an acronym for "righteous priest"), even though the temple sacrifice has not been performed for nineteen centuries. Among Lebanese and other Arabic-speaking Christians a common surname is *Khoury*, an Arabic word for "priest," and another is *Kissis*. Common among the Parsis, the Zoroastrian community of India, is the family name *Dastur*, meaning "high priest."

What one may call a vocational priesthood, on the other hand, recruits its members from the pool of promising young people in the community. [*See* Vocation.] It has the potential advantage of selectivity for devotional, intellectual, or moral qualities. All branches of Christianity recruit their personnel on a vocational basis, often promising challenge rather than comfort as the reward of the priestly life. Celibacy is something that a tradition of vocational priesthood can require, as does the Roman Catholic Church, but many vocational priesthoods still permit marriage, such as those of the Greek Orthodox, Russian Orthodox, and other Eastern Christian churches.

Even in the case of vocational priesthoods, the notion of lineage is not absent, but it is expressed in terms of the transmission of legitimacy from teacher to pupil or from ordaining authority to ordained, as, for example, in Tibetan Buddhist lineages or the Christian notion of apostolic succession.

In the vast majority of the world's religious traditions, eligibility for priesthood has been restricted to males. The Hindu, Buddhist, Taoist, Zoroastrian, and Christian traditions have had exclusively male clergy until modern times. Judaism likewise restricted the rabbinate (its equivalent to the more inclusive current sense of the term *priest*) to males. In today's world various branches of both Christianity and Judaism have begun to ordain women to serve as the ritual and spiritual leaders of congregations. To the extent that Islam has leadership analogous to priests, it too has been exclusively male. Only in some "primitive" tribal traditions such as in Africa and some "archaic" traditions such as Shintō and the religions of ancient Greece, Rome, and pagan northern Europe do we find much evidence of priestesses. In most of the world religions there are analogous but supporting roles for women as nuns, deacons, or other assistants. Contemporary initiatives calling for equality for women have raised serious questions concerning the subordination that these roles imply.

Another feature of eligibility for priesthood is a sound physical and mental condition. Apart from practical considerations of community leadership, this requirement is frequently supported by a notion of perfection as appropriate to the sacrificial ritual. Just as a sacrificial animal is expected to be whole and without blemish, so should the sacrificer himself be. Traditional Roman Catholic custom has required in particular that the hands of a priest, which perform the sacrament, be without deformity.

Training and Ordination. A wide variety of instruction, training, and initiation for work as a priest exists among the world's religious traditions. [*See* Ordination.] The content of the training is generally a blend of three components that one could term the practical, the theoretical, and the disciplinary.

The practical side of a priest's training includes most saliently the skills the community expects for correct performance of ritual. In a great many traditional settings the efficacy of a prayer or incantation has been held to depend on the acoustic correctness of its utterance. To tap divine power, the formula may need to be invoked in the right language, in the right words, with the right pronunciation, and even with a precise musical intonation. The Hindu concept of *mantra* as a verbal formula entails such training on the part of those who will pronounce *mantra*s, and in the view of many Zoroastrians the exactness of the priests' pronunciation of the liturgical prayers in the Avestan language is what makes the prayers effective.

Consequently the appropriate priestly training amounts to rote memorization of the text of the Vedas in the Hindu case and of the Avesta in the Zoroastrian. This may be begun at a quite early age, and the course is sometimes completed before the candidate reaches puberty. It is knowledge of the text, rather than understanding, that is cultivated. Achievements of memorization in premodern societies can be quite impressive;

the Hindu surname *Trivedi,* for example, etymologically means "one who has committed to memory three of the Vedas."

Besides the formulas of the ritual text itself there is much else for a priest to learn: where the ceremonial objects and the officiant should be placed; how the right time for an observance is to be determined; and so on. Where the celebration of a ritual has depended for its timing on direct observation of the sun, moon, or stars, the training of a priest has necessitated mastering a certain amount of practical astronomy. Where the means of divination have included the bones or entrails of animals, the priest has of necessity had to be a practical veterinary surgeon. Indeed, it is instructive to observe in the history of cultures that many professions that became independent specializations have had their origin as branches of priestly learning. But this should not distract us from the fact that priestly training that is merely rote in nature, and oriented only toward ritual performance, may not be sufficient for the demands of the modern world.

What can be termed theoretical training stands at the other end of the spectrum. The world's major religious traditions have all at one time or another undergone challenges of critical inquiry, often philosophical in character. Their scholars have wrestled with the epistemological and metaphysical implications of religious cosmologies, and the ethical and psychological assumptions entailed by religious views of human nature and personality. Some of these traditions have come to expect of their officiating clergy that they not only perform rituals but also minister to the intellectual life of their congregations. Training for priesthood thus may contain a substantial component of historical and philosophical study, in which the prospective congregational leader is given at least a rudimentary exposure to the results of scriptural and doctrinal scholarship.

The perceived need for competence in theoretical matters has generally led religious communities to develop courses of formal academic instruction for their priests (or comparable personnel) in theological studies. Throughout the Islamic world, religious scholarship flourished in a type of school known as a *madrasah* meaning etymologically "place of study." In small towns these institutions might be modest, but many of the *madrasah*s in the chief cities of medieval Islam were substantially endowed, and to this day certain of their buildings are numbered among the finest monuments of traditional Islamic architecture. In medieval Europe, the origin of universities as institutions was frequently closely tied to the need to educate the Christian clergy, and in a number of northern European countries since the Protestant Reformation both Protestant and Roman Catholic theological faculties have continued to be integral parts of the older universities.

In eighteenth- and nineteenth-century America, the founding of many of the older colleges and universities was based on a similar desire to insure that there would be an educated clergy. The American principle of separation of church and state, however, contributed to the emergence, in the state universities, of curricula in which Christian theology played no part. Religious denominations trained their clergy in separate seminaries, but mainline Protestant bodies by the late nineteenth century were presuming a university bachelor's degree as a prerequisite for entry into them. The normal ordination course emerged as three years following the B.A., roughly from the age of twenty-one to twenty-four. The development of comparable three-year post-B.A. rabbinical curricula from the late nineteenth century onward is one of the marks of Jewish acculturation to the American environment. And the entry of Roman Catholic institutions into close ecumenical cooperation from the 1960s onward made the three-year post-B.A. theology degree standard for Catholic priests as well. The creation of cluster arrangements among Protestant and Catholic theological seminaries has resulted in a significant sharing of resources and experiences in the educational preparation of Christian clergy.

Under the heading of "discipline" can be considered a third kind of preparation for priesthood. [*See* Spiritual Discipline.] In various cultures, from tribal to modern, the priest-to-be is expected to undertake regimes of physical or spiritual self-cultivation—the better to be worthy of, or effective in, the practice of his role.

The concept of purity seems to be associated with a great number of these disciplinary practices and is expressed in a variety of forms. Bodily cleanliness is a frequent requirement, so that the candidate before ordination, or the celebrant before a ritual, may need to undergo a bath in water, or the ablution of some parts of the body, to remove any polluting substances of a physical nature. Or the washing of the body may be a symbolic act, in which magical, mental, or spiritual pollutants are contained or eliminated. Among some peoples, semen, as a product of sexual desire or activity, is held to be polluting. For instance, a certain preparation of a Zoroastrian priest for the conduct of cermonies involves a ritual extending over several days, which is invalidated and must be started over if the candidate shows signs of sexual excitement.

Celibacy for priests is a discipline for which a number of rationales have been offered. There is, of course, the just-mentioned notion of sexual activity as a physical pollution. Beyond this may lie a cosmological or metaphysical view most characteristic of gnostic and Manichaean thinking, that the very perpetuation of physical existence in this world hinders the eventual release of pure spirit from its imprisonment in inherently evil matter. The early Christian rejection of gnostic teachings made procreation a positive good and an obligation—but for the laity. Other rationales for priestly celibacy have had to do with eliminating contenders for one's allegiance: the celibate priest, it is held, can give all his time to his ecclesiastical duties, can move whenever and wherever the need arises, and can take personal risks in the cause of his community which a husband or parent might feel constrained to avoid. Finally there is the justification of discipline for discipline's sake: the very confronting of a challenge, even if that challenge itself be arbitrary, makes one a stronger or more worthy individual who can hope to be found worthy and acceptable by God.

The most nearly universal discipline among the world's priesthoods is probably the discipline of meditation. To speak of this, we must deal with the question of whether a common "core" or set of identifiable characteristics of meditation exists such that we can speak of it cross-culturally. Leading candidates for such characteristics are three: some formal physical posture (such as sitting or kneeling), a suspension of conversation with other individuals (though one may be expected to chant or pray aloud), and a concentration of the awareness on divine or transcendent power (sometimes aided by facing an image or symbol). The priest in his exercise of his role may be expected to lead others in meditation; in his training, he is prepared by its practice. A general feeling of well-being or decisiveness can be a personal benefit of meditation to those who practice it; but as a spiritual discipline, meditation needs to serve an unselfish goal, the control of the self and dedication of the priest's personal identity to a power or cause beyond himself.

Upon completion of his training, the priest is ceremonially inducted into the exercise of his role, a process to which Westerners often apply the Christian term *ordination*. Essential here is an ordaining authority such as a senior priest or a religious council. What results over time is a succession of priests, transmitting the role from generation to generation and basing its authority on the legitimacy of the founder of the line. Thus, among Christians, the notion of "apostolic succession" implies that each priest has a pedigree of ordination going back to the apostles, the first generation of Jesus' followers. Buddhist lineages are similar in that monks or pupils trace their ordination back for centuries to earlier teachers.

The process of ordination generally involves some sort of examination or ritual test to ascertain that the candidate is properly prepared. Where formal schools and curricula exist, it is seldom the diploma of the school as such that certifies the candidate, for the school may be distant or its curriculum or methods the subject of dispute. Rather, the local religious jurisdiction conducts its own examination, satisfying itself as to the candidate's dedication and competency.

The actual ceremony of ordination may involve the first wearing of clothing or an ornament or emblem which sets priests apart from others in the society. It generally includes some symbolization of the transfer of power; notable in Christian ordination is "the laying on of hands," in which clergy place their hands on the head of the new ordinand. Another common feature of the ordination process is the ordinand's first performance of a ritual act reserved to priests, such as celebrating a sacrifice or invoking divine pardon or blessing on the worshipers.

Priesthood and the State. Any consideration of the relationship of priesthood to the political governance of society must encompass a diversity of cultures. In this context, variation from one time and place to another is so great that the distinctiveness of individual cases probably outweighs in importance the generalizations that can be ventured. Nonetheless, certain types of patterns can be observed that are reflected in more than one historical and social context. For schematic purposes, we shall designate them as follows: the priest as chaplain, the king as priest, the priest as king, and the priest as critic.

By "the priest as chaplain" we mean the many cases in which the priest is a functionary attached to the ruling circles. In tribal societies this may take the form of the frequent presence or attendance of the sacrificer, dancer, diviner, or healer at the hut of the tribal chieftain. In such situations, the priest is on call in supporting roles in the conduct of the affairs of the tribe, and he receives contributions in return from the chieftain or from the tribe as a whole. Essentially the same professionalization is manifested in many of the great ancient empires. Priests were kept as part of the palace retinue, serving both to maintain the ritual worship attended by the court personnel and to deliver omens or otherwise to pronounce auspicious the acts of the royal house. Royal patronage could establish one religious tradition in preference to another, as in the case of Iran in the third century CE, when an ambitious Zoroastrian high priest, Karter, eliminated rivals such as the Manichaeans. Established religion implies a subsidized priesthood, as is evident in the chapels of European palaces and castles dating from medieval to modern times.

It suggests a divine sanctioning of a nation's institutions, even in relatively secularized contexts. Although the Christian tradition maintains a theoretical distinction between what one is to render to God and what to Caesar, Christian priests have frequently asked God to bless the Caesar of the day. An instructive contemporary example is found in the prayers of invocation offered by clergy on behalf of religiously diverse public constituencies—state functions such as the opening of a legislative session or the graduation ceremonies of a tax-supported university.

Under the heading "the king as priest" may be grouped those situations in which the chief ruler himself performs ceremonial acts of a religious nature. Some of these may be directed toward his own benefit as an individual, but in far more cases the purpose of the ritual is the welfare of the community as a whole. When this is so, the king's priestly role is demonstrably that of a cultic intermediary between the divine and the community. The New Year observances in ancient Babylonia are an example. In them, the king participated in an annual reenactment of the divine creation of the world, recalling the narrative in which the chief god slays the primordial watery chaos-monster and, by splitting its carcass, structures the world into water-surrounded heavens above and water-surrounded earth below. The drama served as a charter of rights and responsibilities for the king as the god's representative or intermediary, maintaining an order in society consonant with the divinely established order of the physical universe. Not very different in its function was the ritual practiced in ancient China, at the sanctuary in Beijing known as the Temple of Heaven. In this, the king performed the annual sacrifices on an open-air altar, symbolically mediating the unity of the cosmic order with that of society.

There are few instances of "the priest as king" that are not in some way debatable. In some cases, leaders have come to political power through having gained a spiritual following first. Muḥammad's career as a prophet is one example; but his leadership as an intertribal negotiator or as a military commander can hardly be called priestly. The American black civil rights movement of the 1960s and the Iranian revolution of 1979 offer two cases in which the professional religious leaders were the principal leadership possessed by people who were excluded from the ruling establishment; but once having gained power, each of these movements relied on other bases than the cultus for its maintenance and extension. Among the Jews in the Hellenistic era, the Hasmoneans were kings from a priestly lineage; but as a dynasty, they behaved as kings rather than as priests. On the whole, indeed, priests in the exercise of their cultic role seem to have become chaplains more often than kings, losing real political power and economic status rather than gaining it, as in the case of the brahmans of India. Perhaps the notion that priests might gain power to become kings is an elusive dream of priestly writers in much the way that the ideal of the philosopher-king is the philosopher's wishful thinking.

To speak of "the priest as critic" is to locate situations in which the priest's voice is one calling for penance or reform. To consider reform part of the vocation of a priest is in keeping with much current Christian discussion. It does, however, raise a semantic issue that calls for a historical answer. For were not the ancient Hebrew reformist critics characteristically referred to as prophets, while the priests were more the cultic chaplains of the establishment? This is indeed true for the period of Israel's religion before the sixth-century BCE Babylonian exile. Thereafter, however, prophecy tended to lapse as an institution, and it consequently became the mandate of others, particularly the clergy, to be "prophetic" in the moral sense. However much prophets and priests may have had clearly differentiated functions in antiquity, the role of the prophet as the voice of conscience in the community has become part of the portfolio of the priest in the centuries since. Struggles for justice and protests for peace throughout the Christian world today bring us constant reports of priests who summon up the courage to defy the current regime, as part of their calling as priests. Activist priests in other communities, such as the Buddhist, have sometimes made a similar contribution.

The Future of Priesthood. The challenge of maintaining an ancient ritual tradition in a modern secular and technological age is a major one. In most of the modern world's religious communities, recruitment of priests is a pressing problem. The celibate life, for instance, surely deters many Roman Catholic males from opting for a priestly vocation, and the desire to marry is clearly a major impetus in the case of many who leave the priesthood. Economic considerations are also a factor: the offerings of the faithful sometimes no longer support a priest in the comfort, compared with other lines of work, that they once afforded. Priests have been reduced to mendicant roles even in those communities which have not characteristically expected priests to be poor. Among the Zoroastrian Parsis of India, most priests are paid on a piecework basis for prayers said, as opposed to being salaried; this fact has contributed to a certain distaste for priests as peddlers of their ritual services, though the community has left them little alternative.

Even more serious than this is a widespread decline

in intellectual respect for priests throughout the contemporary world. The factors operative here are probably both philosophical and sociological. Philosophically, modern secularist criticism of traditional religous affirmations has to a certain extent called the content of the priest's affirmations into question, and the response from the pulpit has unfortunately sometimes been pietistic obscurantism. But at least as important has been the sociological fact of the growth of other skills and professions around the world. Formerly, priests often enjoyed status as the only educated, or the most educated, persons in small communities. Formerly, as we have suggested, skills and institutions associated with priesthood were the basis from which other professions and institutions were launched. Today, however, it is not unusual for the spiritual leader of a congregation to count among his flock scientists, engineers, or other professionals whose training is much more highly focused than his own. Some commentators suggest that priesthood as a vocation is in a vicious circle of decline in status, in that the caliber of personnel now being attracted is hardly such as to serve as models for recruiting the best minds of the next generation to a priestly vocation. The challenge of life's ultimate questions, however, persists. Priesthood will probably attract able personnel in significant and perhaps sufficient numbers for many generations to come.

[*See also* Ministry.]

BIBLIOGRAPHY

General studies of priesthood are relatively few. Two that can be recommended are E. O. James's *The Nature and Function of Priesthood* (London, 1955) and Leopold Sabourin's *Priesthood: A Comparative Study* (Leiden, 1973).

WILLARD G. OXTOBY

Jewish Priesthood

[*This article discusses the nature of ancient Israelite priesthood. For discussion of the subsequent and contemporary religious leadership of the Jewish people, see* Rabbinate.]

The most common biblical term for "priest" is the Hebrew word *kohen* (pl., *kohanim*). It is a West Semitic term known in other ancient societies, and although it is a primitive noun, not derived from any verbal root, its meaning can be established from context. The term *levi* (pl., *leviyyim*), on the other hand, often used to designate certain types of priests, has eluded precise definition, but is translated as "Levite." It seems to be a North Israelite term for "priest" in its earliest biblical occurrences.

The problem that has faced historians in reconstructing the history of Israelite priesthood is the character of the biblical literary evidence, itself, which confronts us with two alternative traditions of Israelite history. In the first, that of the Torah in general, and the Priestly tradition in particular, priests are the tribe of Levi, one of the twelve tribes of Israel, descended from and named after one of Jacob's twelve sons, though usually represented as being different from the other tribes in certain respects. The Levites had no territory of their own, were counted separately in the census, and relied on cultic emoluments, most notably the tithe, for their support. According to some biblical traditions, the Levites became collectively consecrated, or were collectively chosen for sacred tasks because of their loyalty to the God of Israel when others were wayward. In this set of traditions, the Levites were at one point demoted, relegated to maintenance functions and the like. Only one family of priests—the Zadokites according to *Ezekiel* 44, and the Aaronites according to *Leviticus* 8–10 and other priestly texts—were retained as proper priests, fit to officiate in the cult. Another set of biblical traditions, less systematically presented but apparently authentic, portrays priestly groups as professional associations in their initial stages, which became consolidated along family and clan lines through the usual tendency of families to inhabit the same towns and locales and to transmit esoteric skills within the family or clan. Clans, however, were not exclusively ancestral; they admitted outsiders to the study of their skills and eventually to full membership. These processes eventually led to the emergence of identifiable priestly, or Levitical, families, inhabiting towns throughout the land. Biblical writers could thus speak of "Levites" as a tribe, albeit a tribe different from other tribes.

Throughout the period of the northern Israelite and southern Judahite monarchies and even prior to that time, priests were appointed by heads of families, military commanders, kings, and other leaders, and served in their employ. During the period of the Second Temple, when Judaea and Jerusalem were under the domination of foreign empires, the priesthood of Jerusalem played an important political role, the priests serving also as leaders of the Jewish communities.

This is one dimension of priestly status. In religious terms, priests were consecrated persons, subject to laws of purity and restricted in all matters, including marriage and the performance of funerary functions. Priests also wore distinctive vestments.

Common to both dimensions is the factor of skilled training. Priests were taught from *torot* (sg., *torah*), "instruction" manuals for cultic officiation, instruction of the people, adjudication, and oracular and therapeutic functions. Priests also administered temple business and maintained temple facilities. In the postexilic period of the Second Temple of Jerusalem, after the status of the city had changed from a national capital ruled by native kings to a temple city under foreign imperial domination, the priests of Jerusalem assumed quasi-political functions as well. They managed community affairs, while leading priests represented the Judean community to the imperial authorities, first Persian, then Ptolemaic and Seleucid.

Preexilic biblical sources refer to chief priests (sg., *kohen ha-ro'sh, Jer.* 52:24) and their deputies (sg., *kohen ha-mishneh, 2 Kgs.* 23:4), whereas the Priestly tradition provides the title "the high priest" (*ha-kohen ha-gadol, Lv.* 21:10) which was more widely used in the postexilic period. We learn about the internal organization of the priesthood from later biblical literature and from the writings of Josephus Flavius (fl. first century CE), as well as from the Mishnah (second–third centuries CE). Priests were assigned to tours of duty called *mishmarot,* "watches," usually of one week's duration, during which they lived in the Temple complex. The Mishnah mentions priestly officials, such as *ha-segan* ("the director") and *ha-memunneh* ("the priest designate"), who were in charge of specific temple functions in offices of the day.

Priests were supported by levies and donations to the Temple (or temples, in the earlier period) and were required to partake of sacred meals within the Temple precincts. There are indications that, especially in the postexilic period, but perhaps earlier as well, priestly families amassed independent wealth and owned large estates.

Priestly functions may be summarized in the following five categories: (1) cultic functions, (2) oracular functions, (3) therapeutic functions, (4) instructional and juridical functions, and (5) administrative and political functions.

1. *Cultic functions.* The indispensable role of the priest was to officiate in the public sacrificial cult, a role for which only priests were fit. In addition to officiating, priests were involved in the preparation of sacrificial materials and the examination of sacrificial animals and their assignment to specific rites.

2. *Oracular functions.* Both early sources on priestly activity and the subsequent Priestly codification of priestly functions lend prominence to oracular inquiry. The only permitted type of divination was by means of casting lots to secure a binary, or yes or no, response. Often mentioned in this connection is the *efod,* a finely embroidered vestment with a pouch in which the two stones called Urim and Tummim were most likely kept (*Ex.* 28:6, *Lv.* 8:7). Although it is the general view that such oracular inquiry was more characteristic of the earlier periods, their inclusion in the Priestly codes of law, and in certain postexilic references to priestly activity suggests that their utilization persisted (*Ezr.* 2:63). The Urim and Tummim could determine innocence or guilt, and lots are recorded in the Priestly tradition as the means for assigning territories to the tribes.

3. *Therapeutic functions. Leviticus* 13–15 prescribes a quasi-medical role for the Israelite priest relevant to the treatment of certain skin diseases, which also appeared as blight on leather and cloth and on plaster-covered building stones. The purificatory priest combined medical procedures such as symptomatic diagnosis, quarantine, and observation, with magical and sacrificial rites dealing with the threat of these afflictions. Although nothing is said of this role elsewhere in the Bible, comparative evidence of similar functions in Mesopotamia and Egypt suggests that this was a realistic function of priests.

4. *Instructional and juridical functions.* The priest was brought into contact with the people through his role as one who taught the people the *torah* ("instruction"), the correct procedures in religious and legal matters. Priests usually served as judges, and the high courts were traditionally located in the Temple complex of Jerusalem at certain periods. This was true of the Sanhedrin of Hellenistic and Roman times. The key verb often used in characterizing this priestly activity is the Hebrew *horah* ("to teach").

5. *Administrative and political functions.* Priests managed the business of the Temple, which involved accounting, assessing the value of donations in various forms, maintaining the Temple plant, and carrying out periodic inspections and purifications. At times, especially in the postexilic period, but perhaps earlier as well, priests did double duty as tax collectors in royal outposts and later as traveling collectors.

In the postexilic period Levites, as distinct from priests, performed nonsacral tasks in maintaining the Temple, and the later biblical books speak of them as gatekeepers and temple singers or musicians (e.g., *Neh.* 7:1). This latter role is also suggested by the captions attached to many psalms, attributing them to Levitical clans.

The various biblical traditions, including the Priestly traditions themselves, agree on the view that not ritual but rather obedience to God's command in all things, especially in relations "between man and man," is the ultimate goal of religious life. And yet it was the priesthood that made it possible for the individual Israelite and the community as a whole to experience the nearness and presence of God.

[*For further discussion of* kohanim *and* leviyyim, *see* Levites.]

BIBLIOGRAPHY

Cody, Aelred. *A History of Old Testament Priesthood.* Rome, 1969.

Gray, G. B. *Sacrifice in the Old Testament.* Reissued with an introduction by Baruch A. Levine. New York, 1971. See pages 179–270.

Kaufman, Yeḥezkel. *The Religion of Israel.* Translated and abridged by Moshe Greenberg. Chicago, 1956.

McCross, Frank, Jr. "A Reconstruction of the Judean Restoration." *Journal of Biblical Literature* 94 (1975): 4–18.

Milgrom, Jacob. *Studies in Levitical Terminology I.* Los Angeles, 1970.

Milgrom, Jacob. *Studies in Levitical Terminology II.* Berkeley, 1974.

BARUCH A. LEVINE

Christian Priesthood

Christian priesthood is rooted in the priesthood of Jesus Christ. Like the doctrines of the Trinity and the papacy and the christological definitions of the early church councils, the doctrine of Christian priesthood is a later development of teaching and evidence found only in germ in the New Testament.

The Gospels show that Jesus during his earthly ministry gave some of his followers a share in his mission of proclaiming God's kingdom in word and deed (*Mk.* 3:13–15, 6:7–13, and parallels). [*See* Apostles *and* Discipleship.] They were to be his representatives by reproducing in their own lives the central characteristics of Jesus himself: poverty, obedience to the Father's will, and total commitment to the service of God and neighbor.

The post-Resurrection understanding that those so commissioned continued the mission of Jesus himself (*Jn.* 20:21), and that they could pronounce forgiveness and judgment with divine authority (*Jn.* 20:23, *Mt.* 18:18), is a development of the authority given by Jesus to the disciples during his public ministry: to proclaim in word and deed the imminent coming of God's kingdom. After Jesus' resurrection the apostles continued to exercise this commission by proclaiming that in Jesus' life, death, and resurrection God's long-awaited kingdom had already come.

The letters of Paul, who was considered by the ancient church to be "the apostle" par excellence, contain the earliest reflection on ministry in the Christian community. Consistent with Mark's report that Jesus "called to him those whom he desired" (*Mk.* 3:13), Paul often emphasizes his own divine call (*1 Cor.* 1:1, *2 Cor.* 1:1, *Gal.* 1:1). In *2 Corinthians* Paul counters criticisms from within the Corinthian community by saying that he has a "dispensation of the Spirit" (3:8) to which he has been constrained by "the love of Christ" (5:14) revealed to us in his death and resurrection, the redemptive event in which "the old has passed away, behold, the new has come" (5:17). This is the work of God who "through Christ reconciled us to himself and gave us the ministry of reconciliation" (5:18). In this single sentence Paul speaks both of the central event of God's redemptive work and of his own role in this "ministry of reconciliation." Paul clearly sees his ministry not as the result of human initiative, but as something instituted by God in the saving event of Christ's death and resurrection. Thus Paul feels justified in calling those who have received the ministerial commission "ambassadors for Christ, God making his appeal through us. We beseech you on behalf of Christ, be reconciled to God" (5:20). God alone is the one who accomplishes reconciliation. He does so, however, through Christ and through the ministry of those who have received Paul's commission as "working together with him [God]" (6:1).

These "ambassadors" do not represent an absent Christ, however, for he is present in the Christian community (*Mt.* 18:20). Rather, they are commissioned to make Christ's presence a tangible reality through the preached word, through the sacraments (which are means of personal encounter with Christ), and through their example of Christian living. Their representative function resembles that of Christ himself. Christ's words do not substitute for an absent Father, but make the Father present (*Jn.* 14:9f.). Similarly, Christ's ministers mediate his word and work, not by standing between the community and Christ, but by making his saving message and action present in, and available to, the community.

Such an understanding of ministry makes it possible for Paul to treat his own human weaknesses as unimportant (*2 Cor.* 3:5–6, 12:9–10), while criticizing those who claimed personal qualifications for ministry but lacked the divine call (*2 Cor.* 2:17). Conscious of his human inadequacy, Paul exercised his ministry in the power of the Spirit (*1 Cor.* 2:3–5) while asserting divine authority to judge those who claimed special charismata (*1 Cor.* 12–14), and to compel obedience (*1 Cor.* 14:37, *2 Cor.* 13:10, *Phlm.* 8), since "Christ is speaking in me" (*2 Cor.* 13:3).

Despite this divine authority, Paul remains totally dependent upon Christ's saving work (*1 Cor.* 4:13, 15:9), and upon the community's prayers (*Phil.* 1:19, *Col.* 4:3). His commission is to serve both Christ and the community by speaking only what Christ has commanded (*Rom.* 15:18), conscious that he must give an account of his stewardship (*1 Cor.* 4:4f.), and by building up the community's faith, not lording it over them but working "with you for your joy" (*2 Cor.* 1:24).

Priestly terminology is never applied in the New Testament to ministers of the Christian community. They are described in functional terms taken over from Greek profane usage: *episkopos* (overseer, superintendent), *apostolos* (messenger, ambassador), *presbuteros* (elder, chairman), *diakonos* (servant). The New Testament uses the cultic term *hiereus* (priest) for Jewish and pagan priests, for all the baptized collectively (*1 Pt.* 2:5, 2:9; *Rev.* 1:6, 5:10, 20:6), and for Jesus Christ (e.g., *Heb.* 4:14, 7:24, 7:26).

Hebrews, alone of the New Testament books, offers a developed doctrine of Jesus as the one Christian priest, whose priesthood has replaced the Levitical priesthood of the Jerusalem Temple. Originally the Jewish priest had more than the cultic, "godward" function emphasized in *Hebrews*, however. He interpreted God's will to the people (a function later taken over by the prophets). The priest taught the Torah (a function that by New Testament times was assigned to the scribe). His cultic function was to place on the altar the blood and parts of the animals that were killed by the worshipers. A balanced theology of Christ's priesthood, and of ministerial priesthood in the Christian community, must reflect the two-way interchange between God and man present in the original, Old Testament notion of priesthood, and not merely the narrower, cultic, and purely "godward" function prevalent in the time of Christ.

The earliest Christians, being Jews or Jewish proselytes, thought of themselves as the renewed (and not as the new) Israel. They continued to worship in the Temple and to regard its priesthood as valid (see, e.g., *Acts* 3:1). The idea of a new Christian priesthood that replaced the Levitical priesthood emerged only after the destruction of the Temple in AD 70, when gentiles became numerically dominant in the Christian community. In a parallel development the synagogue became less tolerant of doctrinal diversity in the decade from 80 to 90 and excommunicated sectarians, including Christians. The writing of *Hebrews* is generally assigned to this period.

Even *Hebrews* does not associate Christ's priesthood with the Last Supper or the Eucharist, however. This required a further development: the emergence, at the end of the first century, of the explicit teaching that the Eucharist was a sacrifice, presided over by a Christian priest (see, e.g., *Didache* 14.1–3). From the beginning of the second century, Christian writers increasingly applied cultic, sacerdotal terminology to the church's ministers. Two factors encouraged this development: the desire to present the church as the new Israel, in which God's promises to the old Israel were fulfilled; and the desire to show the pagan world that Christians possessed a priestly system and worship superior to all others.

An enormous literature has attempted, with small success, to trace back into the first century the distinction clearly visible in the second century between bishops and presbyters. While the apostles lived, their personal authority, and the expectation of Christ's imminent second coming tended to render questions of church governance moot. These questions became acute as the apostles died and Christians increasingly realized that the church would continue in history, perhaps for a long time.

The classic thesis that Jewish-Christian churches were governed by presbyters, and gentile churches by a bishop or deacons, is a simplification of slender and often conflicting evidence. All that can be said with confidence is that the presbyteral and episcopal systems merged in the decades following the death of the apostles, and that by the mid-second century the threefold ministry of a "monarchical" bishop, assisted by presbyters and deacons, was established practically everywhere.

Several factors favored the acceptance of this system of monarchical episcopacy. Local churches wanted a senior presbyter to represent Christ at the Eucharist, to ordain others, and to represent the community in correspondence with other churches, in general church gatherings, and in disputes with gnostics and other dissidents.

This second-century bishop was the chief pastor not of a diocese, however, but of an urban congregation, exercising what would today be regarded as the normal pastoral and sacramental functions of a priest. Close contact with his presbyters (who were more like modern curates), and with his flock, softened the unlimited authority ascribed to the bishop by Ignatius of Antioch at the beginning of the second century.

The celebrant of the Eucharist is nowhere in the New Testament designated with certainty. The claim that originally any Christian could preside at the Eucharist is as unproven, however, as the older hypothesis that members of the Twelve always presided when present, until they began to pass on this power to others by ordination. The silence of the New Testament on this point proves only the absence of any dispute about the celebrant significant enough to have left its trace.

In the year 96, the author of *1 Clement* seems to have referred to bishops as eucharistic celebrants (44.4). Ignatius of Antioch, writing about 110, clearly assumes that the celebrant is a bishop or a presbyter whom he delegates (*Smyrnaeans* 8.1). By the end of the second century the full-blown concept of the Christian priest is clearly evident, though for some time thereafter reflections about ministry, as well as the cultic term *sacerdos* (from Latin *sacer,* "holy," and *do,* a variant of *dare,* "to give"; thus, "one who offers sacrifices"), refer to the bishop and not to presbyters.

Cyprian (d. 258), the first of the Fathers to apply on any large scale texts about the Old Testament priesthood to Christian priests, is also the first to extend the term *sacerdos* to presbyters (*Epistles* 61.3, 72.2). Yet as late as the mid-fifth century we still find traces of the older usage (for example, in Leo's *Sermons* 59.7), which limited this term to bishops. Presbyters became the normal, rather than merely delegated, celebrants of the Eucharist from the third century on, with the establishment of churches in the countryside and the erection of several churches in major cities.

Rapid clericalization of the priesthood followed the proclamation of Christianity as the official religion of the Roman empire by Constantine in 313. Civic privileges granted to the clergy encouraged the development of a clerical caste system and obscured the servant role that is prominent in the Gospels (see, for example, *Mk.* 10:42–43 and parallels). Bishops began to become prelates, more remote from their clergy and flocks than their predecessors had been in the days of persecution. The multiplication of church buildings, served by presbyters, and the decline in missionary activity favored the development of a more cultic image of the priest. The Middle Ages saw the climax of this development. With the known world already evangelized (except for Jews and Muslims, who were assumed to have heard the gospel and rejected it), the priest became above all a cultic functionary who offered the sacrifice of the Mass and (in the case of some priests, but by no means all) administered other sacraments as well.

From the twelfth century on an unconscious but fateful reversal of the terms *corpus Christi (verum)* and *corpus Christi mysticum* led to the further sacerdotalization of priesthood. According to long-standing consensus, the priest was ordained for the *corpus Christi,* or "body of Christ" (Paul's term for the church). In reaction to the spiritualizing eucharistic doctrine of Berengar of Tours (d. 1088), theologians began to emphasize that *corpus Christi,* now usually amplified with the suffix *verum* ("true" or "real"), designated Christ's eucharistic body. This previously was called the *corpus Christi mysticum* (Latin *mysticum* from Greek *musterion,* signifying the sacrament). Once the *corpus Christi* for which the priest was ordained was understood to be the Eucharist, his transition from the minister of the gospel to the cultic servant of the altar was complete.

The Reformation criticism of priesthood focused on the priest's cultic role. Luther, followed by the other reformers, violently attacked the doctrine of eucharistic sacrifice, claiming this view contradicted the teaching in *Hebrews* that Christ's sacrifice on Calvary was unique, unrepeatable, and all-sufficient. The priest's function, according to the reformers, was to proclaim Christ's sacrifice and in the Mass to offer the memorial of it that Christ had commanded at the Last Supper. The Catholic apologists, fatally handicapped by centuries of concentration in eucharistic theology on questions regarding the real presence and transubstantiation, were (with rare exceptions) unable to counter this attack with the notion of sacramental memorial found in Thomas Aquinas. They merely reiterated that the Mass was a sacrifice and the principal work for which the priest was ordained. [*For further discussion, see* Reformation *and* Eucharist.]

The Roman Catholic response in the Council of Trent to the Protestant reformers' positions on priesthood was brief, stating only as much of "the true and Catholic doctrine" as was necessary "to condemn the errors of our time" (twenty-third session, 15 July 1563). In its dogmatic decrees the council emphasized the priest's cultic role, rejected the proposition that priests who did not preach were no longer priests, but still managed to speak of them, in Luther's words, as "ministers of the word and sacraments." The council's reforming decrees, on the other hand, had much to say about the priest's pastoral role and made the ability to preach one of the conditions normally required for priestly ordination. [*See* Trent, Council of.]

The deliberately limited scope of Trent's dogmatic decrees on priesthood was quickly forgotten, however. During the four subsequent centuries of mutual polemic, Catholics and Protestants alike assumed that Trent had stated the whole of Roman Catholic belief about ministerial priesthood, rather than only those articles of belief that had been disputed by the reformers. In consequence the Catholic priest was understood to be primarily the cultic dispenser of sacraments, even if he also preached. The Protestant pastor on the other hand, even when called "priest" as in Anglicanism, was understood to be above all the preacher of the word, even if he also administered sacraments. The waning of polemic, a consequence of better historical knowledge about the positive concerns both of the sixteenth-century reformers and their Catholic opponents, and of the decision of the Catholic church at the Second Vatican Council (1962-1965) to participate in the modern ecumenical movement, has made it possible to discover the considerable measure of consensus in Catholic and Protestant views of Christian priesthood.

Forsaking a tradition dominant in Catholic theology since the thirteenth century, which defined priesthood in terms of the presbyterate, Vatican II returned to the older view, never lost by Eastern Christianity, that the "fullness of the sacrament of orders is conferred by episcopal consecration" (*Constitution on the Church* 21). No less important was the council's rediscovery of the ancient idea of collegiality. Instead of viewing ordination as merely the conferral of cultic "powers," the council saw it as incorporation into a collegial body of ministers with a special role in building up Christ's body, the church.

While insisting strongly on the priest's presiding role at the Eucharist and as minister of other sacraments, the council gave special emphasis to the ministry of the word, saying that presbyters and bishops alike have "the primary duty of proclaiming the gospel" (*Decree on Priests* 4; cf. *Constitution on the Church* 25). The contrast with the anti-Protestant polemic of the previous four centuries could hardly be more striking.

Growing convergence from the Protestant side has been aided by rediscovery of the biblical notion of remembrance *(anamnēsis)* as the making present and effective in the present, through liturgical celebration, of an unrepeatable past event. This has helped to resolve the Reformation impasse over eucharistic sacrifice and to promote a view of the priest's cultic-sacerdotal function that respects the uniqueness of Christ's sacrifice. [*See* Anamnesis.]

Eastern Orthodoxy has avoided the clericalism prevalent for centuries in the West by viewing ordination not as the conferral of cultic powers but as incorporation into one of the church's constitutive orders (laity, diaconate, presbyterate, episcopate). The East views the priest in his relationship to the congregation he is ordained to serve and has never known the Western system of "private masses" or the theology they produced.

Consensus statements of official ecumenical bodies since Vatican II representing besides Catholics, Anglicans, Lutherans, those of the Reformed-Calvinist tradition, and the World Council of Churches, include agreement that the church's ordained ministry is different in kind and not merely in degree from the common priesthood of all the baptized; that the priestly ministry of the word and sacraments reaches a special intensity when the ordained minister presides at the celebration of the Eucharist; and that although ordained ministers represent the church before God in worship, they are not the church's representatives in a modern democratic sense, but represent Christ to the church and to the world.

[*See also* Ministry.]

BIBLIOGRAPHY

The best modern summary, from the New Testament to Vatican II, is David N. Power's *Ministers of Christ and His Church: The Theology of the Priesthood* (London, 1969). The biblical evidence is well surveyed by André Feuillet in *The Priesthood of Christ and His Ministers* (Garden City, N.Y., 1975). Raymond E. Brown's *Priest and Bishop: Biblical Reflections* (London, 1971) offers stimulating reflections about the biblical and immediately postbiblical evidence. A judicious survey by a German Protestant is Hans von Campenhausen's *Ecclesiastical Authority and Spiritual Power in the Church of the First Three Centuries* (Stanford, Calif., 1969). The collective work by B. Botte and others, *The Sacrament of Holy Orders* (London, 1962), contains valuable articles on the biblical and patristic evidence, medieval developments, and priesthood in the Orthodox East. Henri de Lubac's *Corpus Mysticum: L'eucharistie et l'église au moyen âge* (Paris, 1949) documents the medieval change of terminology and its consequences. *Modern Ecumenical Documents on the Ministry*, edited by Alan C. Clark and H. R. McAdoo (London, 1975), is useful for those unable to use Harding Meyer's "Wer ist sich mit wem worüber einig? Überblick über die Konsensustexte der letzten Jahre," in *Theologischer Konsens und Kirchenspaltung*, edited by Peter Lengsfeld and Heinz-Günther Stobbe (Stuttgart, 1981). Eastern Orthodox, Lutheran, Calvinist, Anglican, English Free Church, and Old Catholic views of priesthood are presented by representatives of those traditions in *Amt und Ordination in ökumenischer Sicht*, volume 5 of *Der priesterliche Dienst* (Freiburg, 1973), edited by Herbert Vorgrimler as number 50 in the series "Quaestiones Disputatae."

Bernard Cooke's *Ministry to Word and Sacraments: History and Theology* (Philadelphia, 1976) surveys twenty centuries of development, emphasizes the tension between church office and charism, and argues for new forms of ministry in today's changed cultural situation. A much briefer but more radical statement in this sense is Edward Schillebeeckx's *Ministry: Leadership in the Community of Jesus Christ* (New York, 1981), which has been criticized for erecting on slender historical foundations postulates too weighty for them to bear. An enlightened conservative work containing this criticism, and many fresh positive reflections as well, is Gisbert Greshake's *Priestersein: Zur Theologie und Spiritualität des priesterlichen Amtes* (Freiburg, 1982).

JOHN JAY HUGHES

Hindu Priesthood

Hindu priesthood has its origins primarily in the Vedic religion, in which the primary focus was the ritual tradition. The Indo-Aryan–speaking invaders of northwestern India in the middle and late second millennium BCE were apparently divided into a threefold hierarchy of social classes with religious as well as economic functions, the priestly class being uppermost and distinct from the warrior, and both of these relatively small echelons ranking above the masses, the pastoral, artisan, and agricultural producers. Kings and chieftains were evidently drawn from the warrior tradition, but the function of sovereignty itself involved divine-human relationships perceived as sacrificial exchanges and therefore the sacred work *(karman)* of an elite priesthood, whose members came from the priestly social class *(brāhmaṇa)*. That this sacerdotal elite was diversified according to long tradition, being responsible not only for a wide range of cultic functions but also for the composition and preservation of the sacred traditions of oral poetry, is documented from comparative study of the *Ṛgveda*, the oldest of the Vedic texts, composed c. 1200 BCE, and the Avesta of ancient Iran. Similarities in the functions not only of Vedic brahmans and Iranian magi but also of Celtic druids and Roman flamens have led some scholars to discuss a proto-Indo-European priestly tradition. In the absence of interpretable literary records from the Indus Valley, it remains undetermined what contribution a hypothetical Harappan priesthood may have made to subsequent South Asian religions.

Vedic Priesthood. The expansion of the priesthood during the period of composition of Ṛgvedic hymns and subsequent texts has a complicated history. The initial verse of the *Ṛgveda* identifies Agni, god of fire, as divine priest and *hotṛ*, or invoking priest, originally the "pourer" of libations (his Avestan counterpart in name and function being the *zaotar*). The *Ṛgveda* itself came to serve as the handbook of this essential priest, who called the gods to the sacrifices. *Ṛgveda* 2.1.2 honors Agni not only with the *hotṛ*'s office but also with those of the *adhvaryu*, or administrative priest, and the *brahmán* (possibly indicating *brāhmaṇācchaṃsin*), *potṛ*, *neṣṭṛ*, *agnīdh*, and *praśāstṛ*, with the householder, *gṛhapati*, as eighth priest. In several respects this staff corresponds to ancient Iranian sets of seven or eight priests. But the fully developed Vedic staff for the great *soma* rituals consisted of four major officiants, or *ṛtvij* (a number including the *udgātṛ* with the *hotṛ*, *adhvaryu*, and *brahmán* from the above group), and allowed each to employ three assistants for a total of sixteen, occasionally seventeen if an additional priest was required. Just as the *Ṛgveda* was the manual from which the *hotṛ* recited, so the three subsidiary Saṃhitās eventually came to be specific texts for the other principal *ṛtvij* and their assistants, the *adhvaryu* instructing and proclaiming from the *Yajurveda*, the *udgātṛ* and his acolytes singing as a quartet from the *Sāmaveda*, and the *brahmán* serving as proctor or monitor for the rituals, silently observing and listening for errors in need of expiation, his relationship to the *Atharvaveda* being only nominal since his training necessarily included coverage of all three primary Vedas. *Ṛgveda* 10.71.11 alludes to the tasks of the four major priests, that of the *brahmán* being the relating of knowledge *(vidyā)*, a significant clue to the nature of this important figure who, as transcendent fourth, represents the totality of priesthood. As *brahmán* (masculine) he is one who knows *bráhman* (neuter), the cosmic word in poetic formula. He "knows" and applies to the human world this *vidyā* of cosmic correspondences, his efforts being simultaneously ritual, speculative, intuitive, even magical. The *bráhman* as cosmic revelation is thus the sacred responsibility of the *brahmán* priest, and by extension, of the entire social class *(varṇa)* of *brāhmaṇas*.

In the early centuries of the first millennium BCE, Vedic civilization expanded across North India, and sacerdotal literature explored new genres beyond the four Vedic Saṃhitās, including Brāhmaṇas, or theological and ritual discourses, and *sūtras*, treatises for both levels of rituals, the great public *(śrauta)* ceremonies requiring three fires and a staff of priests, and the domestic *(gṛhya)* ceremonies dependent upon a single fire and priest. There developed an interactive system of schools (*śākhās*) to safeguard and transmit oral traditions, each linked to one of the Vedas just as priests claimed descent from one of the traditional seven *ṛṣis*. Partly competitive but largely cooperative, these schools produced a specialized, highly skilled priesthood that was eventually to be found throughout the Indian subcontinent, and fragments of which exist in marginal areas, particularly in South India, still today. *Prayogas* and *paddhatis* developed as combinative handbooks for specific rituals, as, for example, in detailing the procedures for the morning and evening milk-offering known as the Agnihotra, or for funerary and ancestral rites.

In ancient and classical India the sacrificer *(yajamāna)*, belonging to any one of the three high *varṇas*, engaged one or more priests for the performance of his rites. His family priest was the *purohita*, an office known already in the *Ṛgveda*. The *purohita*'s spiritual guidance as *guru* or *ācārya* came to be regarded as highly as his textual skill as *śrotriya* or his ritual expertise for life-cycle rites (*saṃskāras*). The *purohita* linked to a king could become a powerful state figure, as illustrated by Kauṭilya, court chaplain to the emperor Candragupta Maurya (late fourth century BCE) and author of the influential political treatise known as the *Arthaśāstra*.

Hindu Priesthood from the Classical to the Modern Period. From the middle of the first millennium BCE, the Vedic sacrificial structure and its priestly custodians had faced competition from renunciant movements (including the Jains and Buddhists), Upaniṣadic speculation, and yogic techniques, all dispensing with or "interiorizing" the sacrifice. Then emergent Hindu theistic movements promoted devotion *(bhakti)* and worship *(pūjā)* above *yajña*, the Vedic sacrifice. The great *śrauta* system enjoyed a revival in the classical Gupta period, but began to disappear as an institution after the fifth century CE, while the Vedic domestic ritual system was absorbed into Hindu faith and practice, as indeed was its priesthood; the brahmans were now divided into temple officiants in villages, towns, and cities, or linked as *purohita*s in traditional hereditary exchanges of services with twice-born classes, known as the *jajmāni* relationship (in the vernacular, from Vedic *yajamāna*, "sacrificer-patron"). Increasingly, brahman priests found themselves to be one category among specialists of the sacred as "Hinduism" slowly broadened its base to accommodate virtually every religious expression of the multicultural subcontinent. Still the most versatile of priests by virtue of their paramount social position and range of linkages across classes and caste groups (*jāti*s), brahmans nevertheless gave significantly more space to nonbrahman religious specialists, who doubtless had long been part and parcel of religious life but had been accorded neither prominence nor legitimation in Vedic and Sanskrit Brahmanic literatures.

By the early medieval period the "priesthood" of Hinduism could be said to have included at least three distinct groups, each with its own interior hierarchy: a remnant of Vedic brahmans (Vaidikas) whose textual and ritual locus remained one or another Vedic school; a larger segment of brahmans whose textual and ritual base was not the Vedas but largely the Sanskrit epics, Purāṇas, and Āgamas, and whose recourse was increasingly toward regional vernacular renditions of these in Tamil, Konkani, Bengali, Hindi, and so forth; and a far larger representation of nontextual priests, unlettered but not unlearned, drawn largely but not exclusively from the lower castes and marginally Hindu tribal peoples, connected with an inexhaustible variety of localized shrines and cult phenomena, and more likely than their brahman counterparts to be concerned with village boundary, hero and goddess cults, spirit possession, exorcism, divination, healing, sorcery, astrology, and shamanic calls to office. Villages afforded priestly roles within virtually every caste or even subcaste. Temples in urban areas displayed wide latitude in the range of priests, including (to cite one eleventh-century example) some fifty priests among a staff of hundreds, all ranked in office and salary from the brahman *paṇḍita* down through lesser priests appointed to serve acolyte deities in the temple or perform animal sacrifices, and even listing as part-time priests specialists in the *Ṛgveda*, *Sāmaveda*, and *Yajurveda*.

Hindu priesthood in the twentieth century retains many features of the past, including the hereditary *jajmāni* relationship, the location of brahman priestly subcastes near the top of the *jāti* hierarchy (although, interestingly, not as high as most nonpriestly brahman subcastes), a strong emphasis on purity and consecrated ritual status, a hierarchical organization as well as a sectarian one, and a bewildering range of specialization from every caste group, from the incongruously high-caste but low-ranking brahman funeral priest of North India (the *mahāpātra*) to the low-caste barber who performs the same function in parts of South India, to the priests from a wide range of brahman and nonbrahman castes who frequent the great holy centers and engage as patrons the incoming pilgrims. The village or urban brahman *purohita* and his nonbrahman counterpart may find themselves jacks-of-all-trades, called upon to recite *mantra*s, perform or advise on life-cycle rites, inaugurate a new house, provide horoscopes, sanction marital arrangements, advise on illnesses, counteract the evil eye, arbitrate disputes, perform accounting, or administer the age-old ritual attentions to the images in the household shrine. The urban brahman priest of a famous Vaiṣṇava or Śaiva temple, like the nonbrahman *pūjāri* of the crudest roadside rock shrine, will find his role more circumscribed than that of the domestic priest, yet still fixed in the same office of mediation between the human and divine worlds.

[*Priesthood in other Indo-European traditions is discussed independently in* Druids; Flamen; Godi; *and* Magi. *For the etymology and various usages of the term* brāhmaṇa, *see* Brahman; *see also* Vedism and Brahmanism.]

BIBLIOGRAPHY

There is no detailed study of the Vedic priesthood and its history. *Agni: The Vedic Ritual of the Fire Altar*, 2 vols., edited by Frits Staal (Berkeley, 1983), presents the *śrauta* staff of priests in the context of the Agnicayana ritual (vol. 1, pp. 40–54); numerous color plates from the 1975 Kerala Agnicayana and an excellent bibliography make this an indispensable work. Volume 2 contains a catalog of living and recently deceased Vedic sacrificers with brief regional histories, "Śrauta Traditions of Recent Times," compiled by C. G. Kashikar and Asko Parpola (pp. 199–251). The Indo-Iranian background to Vedic priesthood is summarized by Bruce Lincoln in his *Priests, Warriors and Cattle* (Berkeley, 1981); see especially pages 60–63, with references. Henk W. Bodewitz's "The Fourth Priest (the *Brahmán*) in Vedic Ritual," in *Selected Studies on Ritual in Indian Religions: Essays to D. J. Hoens*, edited by Ria Kloppenborg (Leiden, 1983), has summarized and contributed to interpretations of the fourth *śrauta* priest. An innovative and influential discussion of the relationship among Vedic priests, their sacrificer patrons, and renunciation is Jan C. Heesterman's "Brahmin, Ritual and Renouncer," *Wiener Zeitschrift für die Kunde Süd- und Ostasiens* 8 (1964): 1–31. Still useful for both Vedic and later Hindu priesthood is the overview by Arthur Berriedale Keith, "Priest, Priesthood (Hindu)," in the *Encyclopaedia of Religion and Ethics*, edited by James Hastings, vol. 10 (Edinburgh, 1918).

The best single book on Hindu temple priests is the field study by C. J. Fuller, *Servants of the Goddess: The Priests of a South Indian Temple* (New York, 1984), with details on the hierarchy of priests in the Mīnākṣī temple of Madurai, Tamil Nadu. L. P. Vidyarthi, B. N. Saraswati, and Makhan Jha's *The Sacred Complex of Kashi* (Delhi, 1979) includes a dozen types of sacred specialists active in Banaras. Among the best anthropological field studies to include sustained and informed discussion of priestly activities in villages are Lawrence A. Babb's *The Divine Hierarchy: Popular Hinduism in Central India* (New York, 1975), especially chapter 6, a comparative study of brahman priests and the *baiga* (nonbrahman priest-exorcist) of Chhattisgarh, Madhya Pradesh; and David F. Pocock's *Mind, Body and Wealth* (Totowa, N.J., 1973), especially chapter 3 on goddess cults in central Gujarat, in which the *bhuvo* (nonbrahman priest) is possessed by a particular *mātā*, or goddess.

David M. Knipe

Buddhist Priesthood

The English word *priest* is frequently used by both Buddhists and non-Buddhists alike to refer to the Buddhist holy men of various Asian cultures. The use of the term is due more to the concomitant presence of Roman Catholic priests in Asia during the early periods of colonial history than to Buddhistic understandings of the religious vocation per se. Normatively, Buddhist holy men are fundamentally more concerned with cultivating wisdom *(prājñā)*, mental concentration *(samādhi)*, and ethical virtue *(śīla)* in pursuit of personal spiritual attainment than with the performance of mediating ritual actions for the religious or material benefit of the laity. Moreover, it is clear from studies of the early Buddhist scriptures that early Buddhism was originally antagonistic to the performance of rites as a means for spiritual advancement. In one *sūtra (Saṃyutta Nikāya* 4.218–220), for example, the Buddha ridicules ritualistic practices of brahman priests who, by the recitation of *mantras* (magical incantations), believe that they are assisting the dead by empowering their progress through a heavenly afterlife sojourn. In contrast to this practice, the Buddha specifically identifies the power of performing moral actions in this lifetime to determine the quality of life in the next. Furthermore, clear distinctions between Buddhist holy men and priestly ritual specialists are found in the religious vocabularies of most Buddhist peoples. In Tibet, Buddhist holy men are known as *bla-mas*, while local priests involved in the manipulation of occult powers are known as Bon-pos, or adherents of the indigenous Bon religion. In Sri Lanka, *kapurālas* officiate at *dēvālayas* (shrines to gods) where they chant their *yātika* (entreaties) to the *devas* (gods) on behalf of lay petitioners. This practice is in contrast to that of Buddhist *bhikkhus* (monks), who formally do not become involved with the supernatural powers attributed to deities. In virtually every Buddhist culture, Buddhist holy men have been more clearly associated with the cultivation of spiritual qualities within than with the orchestration of divine powers operative at various levels of the external cosmos. Indeed, the Sanskrit and Pali terms used for Buddhist clerics are, respectively, *bhikṣu* and *bhikkhu;* these terms literally mean "beggar" or "mendicant," and do not connote a priestly role as such.

In the canons of early Buddhist literature, however, it is also clear that the Buddha was a compassionate teacher who foresaw the need for a priestly or ministerial dimension of Buddhist mendicancy. While this priestly dimension was not expressed through the clerical performance of rites, it is nevertheless evident in the Buddha's injunctions to "wander for the benefit of the many," to become a "field of merit" *(punyakṣetra)* for the laity, and to preach *dharma* (truth, doctrine, teaching) to those seeking understanding. When these injunctions are understood in relation to the altruistic ethic of *dāna* (the perfection of giving) and the metaphysical centrality of *anātman* (non-self, self-lessness), the basis for a mediating priestly role of service within the context of the Buddhist religious vocation becomes evident.

The priestly dimension of the Buddhist religious vocation assumed greater degrees of importance and specificity as the tradition spread beyond India to East and Southeast Asia. In the process of acculturation, Buddhist holy men actually assumed many of the responsibilities and functions of ritual specialists indigenous to those areas. Today, it is not uncommon to find Buddhist holy men in Tibet who are experts in exorcism, or monks in Sri Lanka who are highly proficient in astrology, or, until recently, Buddhists in China who played roles similar to Taoist priests in performing funeral rites for the dead. In both Theravāda and Mahāyāna traditions Buddhist holy men have become ritual specialists who serve the laity through popular ritual practices whenever specific needs have arisen. They have also ministered to the needs of the laity in nonritualized ways. Specific examples of sacerdotal functions clarify the manner in which we may regard the vocation of the Buddhist holy man as priestly.

Chinese religion has been characterized from ancient times to the present by an exceedingly deep reverence for ancestors. It is the duty of the living to remember and venerate their deceased kin. In light of the fact that renunciation of social and family ties is incumbent upon Buddhist holy men, Buddhism came under severe criticism, especially from Confucian quarters, during its early history in China. To mollify critical Chinese, Buddhists quite consciously popularized the legend of Mu-lien (Maudgalyāyana), one of the Buddha's closest disciples, who, according to tradition, dramatically and heroically attempted to save his deceased mother, who had been reborn in hell due to her inadvertent consumption of meat. Buddhist apologists stressed that Mu-lien endured many forms of torture and in the process suffered vicariously for his mother in a variety of miserable hells. At the moment of his greatest need, however, he was succored by the Buddha, who announced the happy news that his mother could be saved if a body of monks would come together and perform a mass for her soul. This legend became the basis for the widespread practice of Buddhist monks offering masses for the dead of their lay supporters. These masses were also popularized by disseminating the mythologies of the *bodhisattva*s Kṣitigarbha (Chin., Ti-tsang; Jpn., Jizō), who vowed to delay his own entry into *nirvāṇa* until he saved all suffering souls dwelling in the many hells, and Avalokiteśvara (Chin., Kuan-yin; Jpn., Kannon), who wandered through the hells of the damned preaching *dharma* for their eternal benefit. Masses for the dead were held to transfer to Ti-tsang the positive karmic power derived from sacrificial and moral actions in order to assist him in his salvific endeavors, and/or to call upon Kuan-yin to bring the suffering of the damned to an end.

In modern Japan, the chanting of scriptures on behalf of the dead remains one of the preeminent responsibilities of the Buddhist holy man. In this manner, Buddhist clerics share priestly duties regarding primary rites of passage with Shintō priests, who are generally called upon to officiate at birth or naming ceremonies and weddings. When priestly duties are seen in this fashion, it is apparent that Buddhist clerics share a complementary role with priests of other religious traditions. In Japan, the ritual responsibility of caring for the dead has fallen to Buddhist clerics, while their Shintō counterparts ritually assist the living during occasions of social transition.

The ritual care of the dead also forms an important part of the priestly role of Buddhist monks in the Theravāda countries of Burma, Thailand and Sri Lanka. Following the death of kin, families assemble for commemoration rites on the seventh day, after three months, and after one year. At these times monks are invited by the family to receive alms *(dāna)*, to preach *(bana)*, or to chant sacred scriptures (Pali, *paritta;* Sinh., *pirith*). Karmic merit derived from these religious acts is then transferred to the departed. The subsequent anniversary dates of family deaths are annually commemorated in this manner, and it is not unusual for a given family to undertake a *dāna* (almsgiving) on the behalf of various departed family members several times a year. Accordingly, all departed family members of the preceding generation are continuously "assisted."

The basic religious reason for the continued care of the departed is rooted in the fundamental concept of karmic retribution and rebirth. In traditional Buddhist cultures the ultimate path to *nirvāṇa* is one that spans many lifetimes; it is incumbent upon family members to assist their departed kin in progressing to this ultimate goal. The specific role of the Buddhist monk in these rites is pivotal: on the one hand, his presence constitutes a worthy object for the performance of meritorious actions, inasmuch as he symbolizes the virtues of the Buddha, the Dharma, and the Sangha (the Buddhist order); on the other, his sermons invariably focus on the central reality for Buddhists that all conditioned life in *saṃsāra* is temporary, subject to change, and compounded. Whatever is subject to uprising is also subject to decay. Whatever is subject to birth is also subject to death. It is the monk's calling to make known this message.

Aside from rites pertaining to the dead, the most evident priestly role in the lives of Theravāda Buddhist monks involves the performance of *paritta*, the chanting of specially selected Buddhist *sūtra*s in Pali, which when recited are believed to be infused with protective sacral power. The chanting of these *sūtra*s usually lasts for the duration of a night but in some cases may last for as long as a week or a month, depending upon the specific purpose. The chanting is performed by a number of monks seated under a *maṇḍapa*, a specially constructed canopy. During the chants each monk holds a sacred thread that has been placed in a water vessel. The specific texts are believed to be *buddhavācana* ("words of the Buddha"), and chanting them therefore charges the sacred thread with power that protects and sanctifies one, and that cultivates prosperity and peace. At the conclusion of the chanting the thread is tied around the wrists of all who are present, monks and laity alike, an action symbolizing the distribution of sacral power.

Paritta ceremonies may be held on any occasion that signifies a new beginning or that needs to be considered auspicious. In Sri Lanka, the chanting of *pirith* precedes the opening of Parliament, the building of personal residences, campaigns for an end to political strife, or before the Kaṭhina ceremony, in which new robes are given to members of the *sangha* at the end of the *vassa*, the rain-retreat season. Studies of *paritta* indicate that its chief purpose is to establish conditions under which the individual, family, village, or state can carry out required duties favorably. Of all the priestly roles performed by Buddhist monks, the chanting of *paritta* best epitomizes sacerdotal responsibilities, for it is within this ritual context that the monk most dramatically performs the task of mediating sacred power. By articulating the words of the Buddha through chant, he magically diffuses sacred power for the benefit of the faithful.

Buddhist monks have also traditionally filled the roles of spiritual advisers and teachers of the laity. In ancient times eminent monks in traditional Asian cultures were selected by the royalty to educate the elite youth. In medieval Southeast Asia virtually all adolescent males donned the yellow robes of the *bhikkhu* for at least one rain-retreat season to be taught the essentials of Buddhist life; this practice still continues in Thailand and Burma. In modern Sri Lanka, monks spend most of their *poya* ("full moon") days educating the laity about Buddhist precepts and meditation. It is also not uncommon for monks and "nuns" (strictly speaking, the *bhikkhunī sangha* is now defunct) to counsel laity regarding personal or family problems. This is increasingly true in urban areas where belief in the power of the gods to intercede on one's behalf appears to be waning.

The *sangha*, however, is a refuge not only for the laity but for its own members as well. An especially poignant petition made by aspiring monks during the process of their ordination rite *(upasaṃpadā)* illustrates how Buddhist monks serve as priests for one another: "I ask the *sangha*, reverend sirs, for the *upasaṃpadā* ordination: Might the *sangha*, reverend sirs, draw me out of compassion for me" (Vinaya Piṭaka 4.122). The life of the Buddhist holy man has normatively been characterized by compassion, and it is out of compassion that he offers his own services to the wider community of faithful adherents.

It is precisely this ethic of compassion that serves as the motivating force for new forms of priestly expression now emerging in Buddhist societies. In more traditional societies, the Buddhist holy man performed a variety of ritual tasks for the benefit of the laity in addition to cultivating the spirituality necessary for advancing along the path to eventual *nirvāṇa*. However, modernization and the influence of other religious traditions, especially Christianity, have affected the Buddhist clergy in significant ways. It is now not uncommon to find *sangha* social services in Theravāda countries like Thailand and Sri Lanka. In Japan, weekend meditation retreats take place in the center of bustling commercial metropolises and are advertised in local papers as therapeutically worthwhile within the high-intensity pace of the Japanese lifestyle. In virtually all Buddhist countries, temples and monasteries organize pilgrimages to famous historical shrines and sacred places. While these new forms of Buddhist priesthood have yet to endure the test of tradition, they bear witness to the vitality of Buddhist clerics endeavoring to work for the welfare of the many.

BIBLIOGRAPHY

Bareau, André. *Les sectes bouddhiques du petit véhicule.* Saigon, 1955.

Dutt, Sukumar. *Buddhist Monks and Monasteries of India.* London, 1962.

Holt, John C. *Discipline: The Canonical Buddhism of the Vinayapitaka.* Delhi, 1981.

Joseph, Marietta B. "The Vihāras of the Kathmandu Valley." *Oriental Art* 17 (1971): 121–143.

Kariyawasam, A. G. S. "Bhikkhu." In *Encyclopedia of Buddhism,* edited by G. P. Malalasekera, vol. 3, pp. 36–43. Colombo, 1971.

Kitagawa, Joseph M. *Religion in Japanese History.* New York, 1966.

Leclère, Adhémard. *Le bouddhisme au Cambodge.* Paris, 1899.

Mendelson, E. Michael. *Sangha and State in Burma.* Edited by John P. Ferguson. Ithaca, N.Y., 1975.

Miller, Robert J. *Monasteries and Culture Change in Inner Mongolia.* Wiesbaden, 1959.

Pathoumxad, Krough. "Organization of the Sangha." In *Kingdom of Laos,* edited by René de Berval. Saigon, 1959.

Prip-Møller, Johannes. *Chinese Buddhist Monasteries.* Copenhagen, 1937.

Rahula, Walpola. *History of Buddhism in Ceylon: The Anuradhapura Period.* Colombo, 1956.

Rahula, Walpola. *The Heritage of the Bhikkhu.* New York, 1974.

Saha, Ksanika. *Buddhism and Buddhist Literature in Central Asia.* Calcutta, 1970.

Sok, Do-ryun. "Son Buddhism in Korea." *Korea Journal* 4 (1964) and 5 (1965).

Suzuki, D. T. *The Training of the Zen Buddhist Monk* (1934). New York, 1966.

Tambiah, Stanley J. *Buddhism and the Spirit Cults in North-East Thailand.* Cambridge, 1970.

Tucci, Giuseppe. *Tibet: Land of Snows.* Translated by J. E. Stapleton Driver. New York, 1967.

Visser, Marinus W. de. *Ancient Buddhism in Japan.* 2 vols. Leiden, 1928–1935.
Waddell, L. Austune. *The Buddhism of Tibet* (1895). Reprint, Cambridge, 1958.
Welch, Holmes. "Dharma Scrolls and the Succession of Abbots in Chinese Monasteries." *T'oung pao* 50 (1963): 93–149.
Welch, Holmes. *The Practice of Chinese Buddhism, 1900–1950.* Cambridge, Mass., 1967.

JOHN C. HOLT

Shintō Priesthood

The term *shinshoku* ("Shintō priesthood") is used in modern Japan to refer to those persons serving at shrines in the performance of various religious duties. Prior to the Meiji period (1868–1912) no uniform organization existed within the Shintō priesthood, with the result that clerical titles and functions varied widely depending on the period and shrine involved.

Clerical Titles. Religious titles in use since premodern times include the following:

1. *Saishu* (supreme priest/priestess). The *saishu* is highest-ranking priest at the Grand Shrine of Ise, in charge of all ceremonials and administration relating to the shrine. In the early historical period, the post was filled by a member of the Nakatomi family from the central government's Bureau of Kami *(jingikan),* but after the mid-sixteenth century, the post became a hereditary office of the Fujinami branch of the Nakatomi family. From the Meiji Restoration (1868) to the end of World War II, the post was held by a male member of the imperial family, and by a female member thereafter.

2. *Kuni no miyatsuko* (provincial governor). Originally holding joint political and religious office, these persons were restricted primarily to ritual functions following the Taika Reforms (645).

3. *Gūji* (chief priest). Originally, the *gūji* was an administrative official with a status superior to other clerical ranks who held responsibility for construction and finance at the largest of shrines. Depending on the status of the shrine, a supreme chief priest *(daigūji)* might have placed under him a junior chief priest *(shōgūji)* or associate chief priest *(gongūji).* At present, the *gūji* holds joint responsibility for all administrative and ceremonial functions within a shrine.

4. *Kannushi* (master of divinities). This title refers to the priest holding chief responsibility for a shrine and the role of central officiant in divine ritual. In later times, the term came to be used as an overall synonym for members of the Shintō priesthood.

5. *Negi* (senior priest). Deriving from the old Japanese word for "entreat" *(negai),* the title *negi* referred to priests primarily engaged in addressing prayers and general worship to the deities. The term later came to indicate a post directly subordinate in rank to the *kannushi* of a shrine, and was also used as a general synonym for members of the priesthood. At present, it refers to a clerical rank subordinate to *gūji.*

6. *Hafuri* or *hafuribe* (liturgist). One of the oldest titles within the Shintō priesthood, this term was used variously to refer to a specific priestly office next in rank to *kannushi* and *negi,* or as a general appellation for members of the priesthood, a usage it retains today among the common people.

7. *Tayū.* Formerly an honorific title given to middle-grade government officials, this term later came to be used as a general title for Shintō priests, in particular those *religiosi* serving the Grand Shrine of Ise. It is still used among the common people as a general name for Shintō clerics.

8. *Jinin* (divine attendant). Formerly, *jinin* were low-ranking functionaries of shrines, entrusted with miscellaneous duties.

9. *Tōya.* A lay member of a local parish organization *(miyaza),* selected from qualified parish members to serve for a specific period as ritualist for the parish shrine. Still widely seen in villages around the Kyoto-Osaka area, the custom of selecting a shrine *tōya* from the lay community on a rotating yearly basis was apparently a general practice for shrine organizations in premodern periods. With the development of a specialized priesthood, the post has changed in many areas into that of a lower-ranking, part-time priest, or a lay role requiring its incumbent to serve only on certain ceremonial occasions.

10. *Shasō.* The *shasō* were Buddhist clerics serving at shrines as part of the historical phenomenon known as the harmonization of Shintō and Buddhism *(shinbutsu shūgō).* Depending on the shrine, such priests were given a wide variety of titles, but the practice ceased after 1868 with the governmental policy enforcing the separation of Shintō and Buddhism.

Women held high ceremonial positions within early Shintō, but they were gradually relegated to roles assisting the male members of the priesthood. The following are representative of roles for females serving at shrines in the premodern period:

1. *Saigū* or *saiō* (supreme priestess). A *saigu* was an unmarried imperial princess sent as the emperor's representative to the Grand Shrine of Ise. The practice continued until the early fourteenth century.

2. *Saiin* (high priestess). A *saiin* was an unmarried imperial princess sent to serve at the Kamo Shrine in

Kyoto, following the custom practiced at Ise. The practice continued until the twelfth century.

3. *Mikannagi* (priestess). This was a general term for young girls aged seven to eight, selected from the daughters of *kuni no miyatsuko* to attend the deities served by priests from the government Bureau of Kami.

4. *Monoimi* (abstainer). *Monoimi* were young girls selected from among daughters of the shrine clergy to lead lives of exceptional ritual purity. Incumbents could be found at many of the great shrines under various titles.

5. *Miko*. The term *miko* is a general title designating female attendants serving at shrines. Formerly ranking below *kannushi, negi,* and *hafuri* as regular members of the priesthood, *miko* at present serve exclusively in supplementary roles, often as sacred dancers.

In addition to the foregoing, numerous other terms have been used as general referents for the Shintō clergy, including *shake, shanin, shashi,* and *shikan*. Individual shrines might also make use of a variety of special titles to refer to specific clerical ranks, such as *uchibito, tone, tanamori, gyōji, azukari,* and *oshi*. In the ancient period, political administrators simultaneously served as ceremonial officiants; there was no independent, professional clergy. For example, the leader of a clan *(uji no kami)* would lead his kinship group in ritual worship of the clan deity. With time, these two roles became specialized, and as professional clerics became more numerous the tendency was strong for such individuals to pass their religious profession on to their descendants.

The Shintō Priesthood from 1868 to 1945. Following the collapse of the Tokugawa regime in 1868, the authorities of the new Meiji government revived the ancient concept of *saisei-itchi* (unity of worship and rule), thus placing all shrines and members of the Shintō priesthood under direct government control. Since shrines and priests were thus considered to belong within the public domain, a comprehensive national ordering of shrines and priests was instituted to replace the non-unified ranks, duties, numbers of staff, statuses, and remuneration that had previously existed independently from shrine to shrine.

Under this system, priests of the Grand Shrine of Ise were given the outright status of national officials, with the special title *shinkan* (divine official); the titles and complement of clergy at Ise included one *saishu*, one *daigūji*, one *shōgūji*, eleven *negi*, twenty *gonnegi* (associate *negi*), forty *kujō* (lower-ranking priests), and others. Since the *saishu* was to offer worship in place of the emperor, a member of the imperial family was appointed to the post. The *daigūji* was under the direction and supervision of the Minister of Home Affairs, assisting the *saishu* in matters of ceremonial, and exercising overall control and management of other priests. The *shōgūji* allotted administrative duties and acted as a ceremonial assistant to the *daigūji*. Together, these three priests directed the activities of *negi* and other lower-ranking priests in the various ceremonies and administrative responsibilities of the shrine.

Imperial shrines *(kanpeisha)*, and national shrines *(kokuheisha)* were divided respectively into three classifications based on size, and the priests of these shrines were treated as quasi-government employees *(junkanri)* appointed under the jurisdiction of the Minister of Home Affairs and local magistrates. (The only exception was the Yasukuni Shrine in Tokyo; the ministers of the army and navy had the power of appointment for the priests of this shrine.)

These shrines were allotted one *gūji*, one *gongūji* (limited to six major shrines including the Atsuta Jingū), in addition to one *negi*, one or two *shuten* (lower-ranking priests), and (at Atsuta only) up to thirteen *kujō;* these priests were responsible for all ceremonial and administrative functions at their respective shrines.

Smaller shrines at the level of *fu* (urban prefecture), *ken* (prefecture) and *gō* (district) were allotted one *shashi* and several *shashō*, while village shrines *(sonsha)* and unranked shrines *(mukakusha)* were staffed by several *shashō*, who were responsible for all ceremonial and administrative functions. *Shashi* and *shashō* were priests of low rank, selected by local magistrates from among candidates recommended by lay leaders of the parish. These priests were also treated as quasi officials of the national government.

Individuals selected for these various priestly ranks were required to be males over the age of twenty who had either passed a qualifying examination or had received an education preparing them for the priesthood at an approved educational institution. No provisions were made for female members of the clergy.

The Priesthood since 1945. Following Japan's defeat in World War II, the Occupation authorities abolished the system of national shrine control and disestablished priests from their previous status as public officials. Shrines were given the same treatment as other religious bodies; their chief priests were allowed to exist as religious judicial persons. In February 1946 the Jinja Honchō (Association of Shintō Shrines) was established in Tokyo as an administrative organ to oversee the activities of shrines; with the exception of a few choosing independent status, the majority of Shintō shrines in Japan became members of the association. As a result, the majority of priests at present are appointed in accordance with the regulations of the Jinja Honchō. As of 31 December 1983, the number of priests included within the association was 19,810, including 1,306 (6.6 percent) women.

Depending on the size and status of the shrine, the complement of priests may include a *gūji, gongūji* (generally one only), a *negi* (usually one), and several *gonnegi.* With a status equivalent to chief director for a religious judicial person, the *gūji* must be above twenty years of age and is appointed by the president of the Jinja Honchō on the basis of recommendations from lay representatives of the organization. While the *gūji* has authority to set the number of *negi* at his shrine, the approval of the president of the association is required for the appointment of a shrine's *gongūji.*

Requirements for individuals appointed as priests include a specialized education, general learning, and training at shrines. Qualifications are divided into five levels and are acquired by passing a qualifying examination or by graduating from an accredited Shintō institution with training for the priesthood. Once appointed, priests are ranked in six grades, based on their qualifications, performance, and years of service, and these grades are reflected in the formal costume worn on ceremonial occasions. With a uniquely revered position among Shintō shrines, the Grand Shrine of Ise maintains an independent system of clergy, based on the tradition followed previous to World War II.

Members of the Shintō priesthood not only serve in the performance of formal shrine rituals but also bear responsibility for such administrative tasks as the upkeep and management of shrine facilities and finances. While Shintō ceremonial places heavy emphasis on ritual purification *(saikai),* priests are also expected to display a personal culture and character in their everyday lives consonant with their traditional role as protectors of the faith and leaders in community worship. Since the end of World War II, a strong need has been felt for the active involvement of priests in proselytizing activities among the parish and community of believers, and great expectations are placed on them as well for activities in the areas of social welfare and education.

[*See also* Shintō.]

BIBLIOGRAPHY

Few references specifically relating to the Shintō priesthood are available in English, although some information may be gleaned from the articles included within *Basic Terms of Shintō* (Tokyo, 1958), compiled by the Shintō Committee for the Ninth International Congress for the History of Religions. Among works in the Japanese language, the *Shintō daijiten,* 3 vols. (Tokyo, 1937–1940), represents the most comprehensive dictionary of Shintō yet printed and includes several articles relating to the Shintō priesthood. Quotations from historical sources regarding the titles, functions, and qualifications of Shintō priests can be found listed topically in the section "Shinshoku" ("Jingi-bu": 45–46) of the *Koji ruien* (1898; reprint, Tokyo, 1967). Basic issues relating to the Shintō priesthood are treated by Ono Motonori (Sokyō) in his *Shintō no kiso chishiki to kiso mondai* (Tokyo, 1964), pp. 472–553, while the historical development of the priesthood is particularly emphasized by Umeda Yoshihiko and Okada Yoneo in their article "Shinshoku," in *Shintō yōgoshū, saishi-hen,* vol. 2 (Tokyo, 1976), compiled by the Institute for Japanese Culture and Classics at Kokugakuin University.

Toki Masanori
Translated from Japanese by Norman Havens

Taoist Priesthood

The three traditional components of Chinese religious life are the ancestor cult, Buddhism, and communal religion. The Taoist priest *(tao-shih)* is one of three ritual specialists in the service of the communal religion. The other two are called "divining lads" *(chi-t'ung)* and "masters of method" *(fa-shih);* the first is a medium, the second an exorcist. The function of all three is identical, namely, to bring the power of the gods to bear on local problems. What distinguishes them is basically the number of gods whose power they can bring to bear: the medium is the mouthpiece—or the amanuensis—of a single local god; the exorcist is familiar with all the local gods; and the Taoist knows how to invite the gods of the entire universe.

The medium is someone who simply "lends his body to the gods." The exorcist is the medium's master, because his technical knowledge of the system of forces that ordinary people refer to as "gods" and "ghosts" enables him to direct the medium's trance to a useful end. The Taoist is completely self-possessed: the forces he uses in the war against evil are not those of a medium but his own. His chief function, in fact, is not that of an exorcist, a warrior, but that of a civil official in the court of the Tao. He has risen beyond mastery of methods to mastery of the "system" as a whole. According to that system, the Tao is a vast womb containing within it three pure energies that, over time, give birth to all things. The Taoist's real contribution to the war against evil results from his capacity, by means of his ritual, to transform his own body into the body of the Tao and then to conduct all things back to their origin in purity. His rituals, based on texts written in literary Chinese, are complex scenarios for the symbolization of this process. Combining virtually all the arts—painting, music, song, dance, gesture, recitation, and visualization—they make of the Taoist a truly universal man.

Such universal mastery requires long training, and

this the hereditary character of the position makes possible: not only does the Taoist grow up surrounded by all the arts of Taoist ritual; he also inherits a veritable family treasure of texts and traditions. In addition, he usually completes what he has learned from his father by studying with one of his father's colleagues, often a close relative. Taoists traditionally run temples of the City God and of the Eastern Peak. Illness and bad luck, present or anticipated, are the two principal reasons that bring people to a Taoist in the temple of the City God. When the right day and hour to make intercession for a given individual have been determined, the priest performs a brief ritual to "avert calamity and pray for good fortune." It consists essentially in the presentation of a written memorial giving the names and birthdates of the faithful and calling on the "old man of the walls and moats," in exchange for a "pure offering of fruit, rice, and sweets," to "cause the nefarious stars to retreat and the lucky constellations to advance." This memorial is first read and then transmitted to heaven by burning.

Mediums, exorcists, and Taoists all work side by side in the temple of the Eastern Peak. Mediums, operating in tandem with exorcists, offer consultations with the dead. Exorcists, sometimes with the help of mediums, attack hell and deliver souls that are imprisoned there. Taoists perform brief versions of *kung-te* ("merit" ceremonies), whose purpose is at once to deliver souls from hell and to set them on the road to heaven.

More elaborate versions of these merit ceremonies are performed in specially constructed tents near the house of the bereaved family. The minimum sequence of rituals includes the Summons of the Soul, the Opening of a Road in the Underworld, and the Reimbursement of the Treasury. In this last ritual a huge mound of mock paper money is burned for the soul's use in the afterlife, as well as to pay for its sins and other debts so that it may be liberated from hell and allowed to "ascend to the hall of Heaven." In the Opening of the Road, the Taoist, himself an "immortal official," transmits an ordination certificate to the soul of the deceased and so, by making it a posthumous Taoist, enables it to enter Heaven.

Very simple ritual acts the Taoist priest normally performs in the altar room *(t'an)* of his own house. A simple ritual of healing, for example, consists in passing lit sticks of incense along the patient's body while uttering an appropriate formula, or in writing and consecrating a symbolic character—the secret name, not of a god or the pantheon but of an energy configuration in the priest's own body—which the client will then carry on his person to protect himself from harm.

On many other occasions the Taoist works in the client's house, whether to pacify earth spirits disturbed by the construction of a new building or to drive out evil spirits that have caused "soul loss," illness, or a difficult pregnancy. His basic method is always the same, consisting on the one hand of appeasement offerings for the spirits causing the trouble and on the other of the deployment of his own spiritual armies to drive the forces of evil into a corner—the "demon gate" in the northeast—or out of the house and area altogether. This is often supplemented by scattering purifying agents such as salt or rice around a room or house, pasting up symbolic characters to guard entranceways, and sweeping out evil with a broom or swatting it out with a rolled-up mat. Normally, when the ritual has proven successful, for example, when healing has occurred, the priest will return to "gather in his armies," "remove the symbol," and "reimburse the gods" with an offering.

All ritual acts referred to thus far are performed for individuals or for families, and parallel forms of most of them are performed by other specialists. The one ritual domain that is purely Taoist both in origin and in execution is the Chiao ("offering"). Originally, offerings were performed on specially constructed altars under the open sky. The altar was composed of three "steps" of pounded earth representing the three layers of the physical universe. The three-stage entry rite represented an ascension to Heaven, and the ritual itself then took place "in Heaven."

Nowadays, offerings are usually performed inside temples of sponsoring communities. The priests convert the temple into a Taoist "land of the way" *(tao-ch'ang)* by hanging scroll paintings along the left, right, and front walls. On the left and right are represented the spiritual forces of the Four Spaces, that is, Heaven, earth, water, and man, as well as various "marshals." Some of these marshals guard the entry to the altar; others represent the forces within the body of the high priest by means of which he communicates with the Tao.

The forces of the Four Spaces are painted as officers in the court of the Tao, holding their court tablets and standing in an attitude of reverence facing the front. Along the front, which is the honorable north side normally occupied by the temple divinities, are strung five portraits: in the center is the Heavenly Worthy of the Primordial Beginning (Yüan-shih T'ien-tsun); to the right, from the observer's point of view, is the Heavenly Worthy of the Potent Treasure (Ling-pao T'ien-tsun); and to the left is the Heavenly Worthy of the Way and Its Power (Tao-te T'ien-tsun; i.e., Lord Lao, or Lao-tzu). They are the Three Pure Ones (San Ch'ing), the so-called Taoist triad.

Collectively, they represent the Tao, that is, the real

order of the universe as it comes into being and returns into nonbeing without disruption or disharmony. Temporally, they represent the three successive stages of the cosmogony described in chapter 42 of the *Lao-tzu:* "The Tao gives birth to the one, the one to the two, the two to the three, and the three to the ten thousand things." Spatially, they represent the universe inhabited by man, that is, Heaven, earth, and man, as opposed to Heaven, earth, and water. Religiously, they represent the Three Treasures, defined as the Tao, the revealed scriptures, and the masters who transmit these scriptures.

The north wall is completed by the hanging, on the far right, of the scroll of the Jade Emperor (Yü-huang), who is the head of the popular pantheon (and the guarantor of the exorcist's alliance with the gods), and on the far left, that of the Emperor of the Purple Empyrean (Tzu-wei), the chief stellar divinity.

The spiritual forces of the Four Spaces along the side walls are thus being depicted as paying homage to the order of the universe represented by the five scrolls along the northern wall. But their gaze is directed in successive stages from the five to the three to the One, the Heavenly Worthy of the Primordial Beginning, the "treasure of the Tao," that is, the Tao insofar as it manifests itself and can be represented: they are going in "audience before the Origin" *(ch'ao-yüan).* This is even clearer when the five scrolls are staggered in height and/or distance from the central table in the altar area. Hung in this manner, the five scrolls are also seen to represent the three "steps" of a sacred mountain. Access to this sacred world is through a curtain attached to the back of the central table: it represents the "golden gate" *(chin-ch'üeh),* and it is opened only when the Taoists themselves are ready to "go in audience before the Origin," that is, communicate with the Tao.

The central table, around which the Taoist priests—occasionally one, but usually three or five in number—stand, is called the "cave table" *(tung-an).* As the standard gloss of the word *tung,* "cave," in Taoist texts is *t'ung,* "to communicate," it is clear that the Land of the Way is a mountain containing a cave inside which occurs communication. Across from the cave table, on the inferior south side, is the table of the Three Realms, that is, Heaven, earth, and water. On it are placed the offerings for the spiritual forces of this world. Among them are the divinities normally worshiped in the temple itself, and in some areas this is demonstrated by removing their statues from their normal place of honor to bleachers set up behind the table of the Three Realms. They become, thus, spectators of the ritual performed by the officers of the Tao, and what they witness is a representation of the true order of the universe.

On one level, then, Taoist ritual is a portrayal of how the world works, a reminder to the gods of their place in the universal order. On another level, it is the community's communication with the Tao through the intermediary of its high priest. This communication takes the form of a written memorial *(shu),* which is read during nearly every ritual in the Offering. It gives the name, date, purpose, and program of the Offering, together with the name and religious title of the chief officiant, the address of the temple, and the names of the community chiefs. At the very beginning of this document, the temple community is described as desiring, by means of the Offering, to "worship the Tao."

Just as the modern altar is focused on the central painting, so is the Offering concentrated in the Audience, a ritual that occurs midway through the program. This ritual, in turn, depends entirely on the body of the high priest, whose forces first carry the community's message to the Three Pure Ones and then return with the response of community merit. This esoteric Audience, addressed to the Three Pure Ones and performed inside the body of the high priest, is the indispensable prelude to the ritual for the Statement of Merit that is addressed to the head of the popular—exoteric—pantheon and is performed on a stage outside the temple. The name of this central officiant, in the early texts as well as in modern times, is *kao-kung,* "high merit." He is also called the Central Worthy *(chung-tsun)* because he finds himself, like the Heavenly Worthy of the Primordial Beginning, in the middle of two, four, or even six assistants.

The highest ranked of these acolytes is the chief cantor *(tu-chiang).* His role is to perform the external ritual, composed of its visible and audible elements, whereas the Central Worthy performs the internal ritual, that is, the exteriorization and reintegration of the forces of his own body that constitute the real communication with the Tao. These practices belong to the esoteric tradition transmitted from master to disciple, beginning with the revelation of the first master, Lord Lao, to the first disciple, Chang Tao-ling. The Central Worthy is thus a link—by virtue of his ordination, when he becomes an "immortal" certified by the "chancellery of the Three Heavens" of which Chang Tao-ling is the chancellor—in an unbroken chain going back to Lord Lao, the third of the Three Pure Ones who rule the Three Heavens. When he communicates with the Tao he is recapitulating what his master taught him, namely, how to use the second treasure, the sacred scriptures, to "go in audience before the Origin." [*See also* Chiao.]

It is in this very precise sense that the modern *kao-kung* is the spiritual heir of Lao-tzu's "saint": he knows how to "embrace the One" (*Lao-tzu* 22); he knows how to imitate the Way, "whose movement is one of return" (*Lao-tzu* 40). In his ritual he acts out, and so enacts—brings into play—the forces of the Way. The Audience ritual is therefore described as "walking the Way," a term that may also be translated "enacting the Way." In the same vein, Taoists traditionally define their function as "carrying out transformation in Heaven's stead."

Insofar as the Taoist priest's ritual action, when broken down into its component parts, may be shown to involve a variety of techniques, he is also the descendant of the "masters of recipes" *(fang-shih)* first singled out as a group in the dynastic history of the Latter Han (25–220 CE). Among these masters were calendrical experts, healers, astrologers, magicians, alchemists, and adepts of the art of long life. All of their techniques, to lesser or greater degrees, inform Taoist ritual. [*See* Fang-shih.] More important, some of these early masters are described as being capable, like the *Huai-nan-tzu*'s "real man," of "making ghosts and gods to do his bidding." According to a commentary on this phrase from the early third century, "it means he is capable of transformation: when someone, rather than sharing his body with ghosts, learns how to put them to work, that is [or, he is] the Tao."

[*See also* Worship and Cultic Life, *article on* Taoist Cultic Life; Taoism; *and* Chen-jen.]

BIBLIOGRAPHY

The best general survey of Chinese communal religion is J. J. M. de Groot's *The Religious System of China*, vol. 6 (1892; reprint, Taipei, 1967). Alan J. A. Elliott's *Chinese Spirit-Medium Cults in Singapore* (London, 1955) is a thorough study of mediumism in a single Chinese community. A good synthesis of anthropological observation and the Taoist textual tradition is Kristofer Schipper's *Le corps taoïste* (Paris, 1982); see especially chapters 3–5: "Divinity," "Masters of the Gods," and "The Ritual." See also his "The Written Memorial in Taoist Ceremonies," in *Religion and Ritual in Chinese Society*, edited by Arthur P. Wolf (Stanford, Calif., 1974). The only Western work on the Offering, *Taoism and the Rite of Cosmic Renewal* (Seattle, 1972) by Michael Saso, is of very uneven quality, but may be consulted for its descriptions of individual rituals. Ngo Van Xuyet's *Divination, magie et politique dans la Chine ancienne* (Paris, 1976) is a complete translation and study of the chapter on the "masters of recipes" in the *Hou Han shu* (Latter Han History). See my book *Wu-shang pi-yao: Somme taoïste du sixième siècle* (Paris, 1981) for a study of *The Essence of the Supreme Secrets*.

JOHN LAGERWEY

PRIMITIVE MONOTHEISM. *See* Supreme Beings *and the biography of Schmidt.*

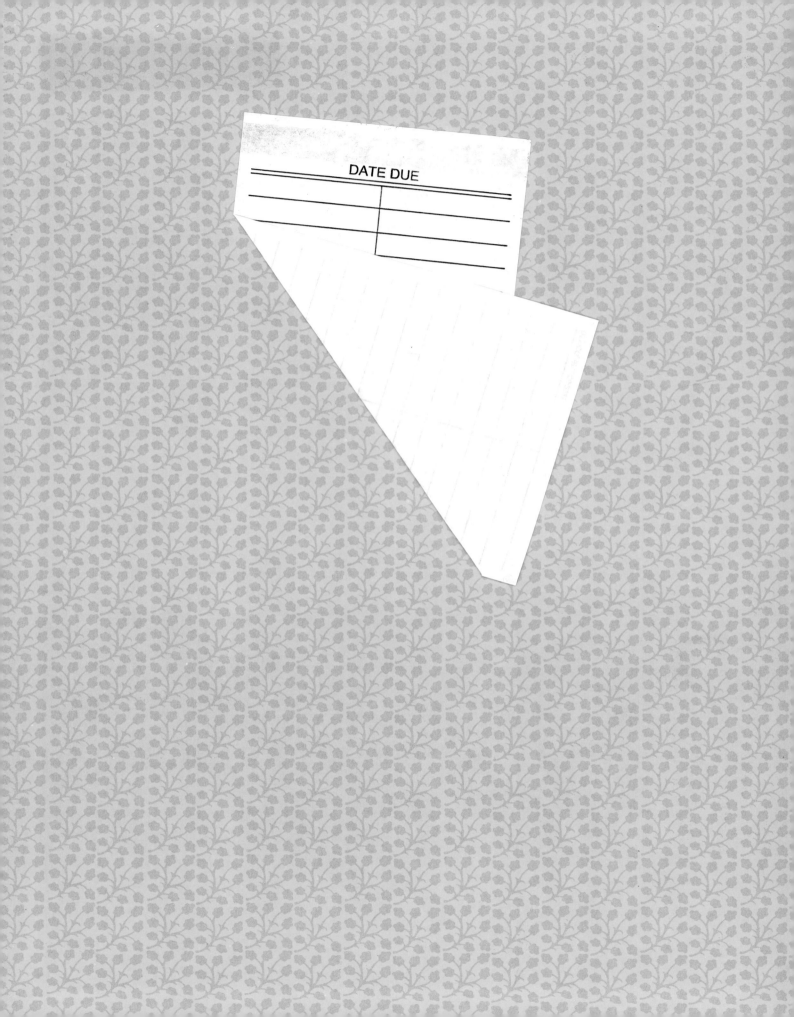